IRANICA

Herausgegeben von Alberto Cantera
und Maria Macuch

Band 34

2025

Harrassowitz Verlag · Wiesbaden

Maria Macuch

Sasanian Law in its Social Context

2025

Harrassowitz Verlag · Wiesbaden

Bibliografische Information der Deutschen Nationalbibliothek
Die Deutsche Nationalbibliothek verzeichnet diese Publikation in der Deutschen Nationalbibliografie; detaillierte bibliografische Daten sind im Internet über https://dnb.de abrufbar.

Bibliographic information published by the Deutsche Nationalbibliothek
The Deutsche Nationalbibliothek lists this publication in the Deutsche Nationalbibliografie; detailed bibliographic data are available in the Internet at https://dnb.de

For further information about our publishing program consult our website https://www.harrassowitz-verlag.de

Printed on permanent/durable paper.
Typesetting and Layout: Tatsiana Harting and Claudius Naumann
Printing and binding: Memminger MedienCentrum AG
Printed in Germany

ISSN 0944-1271 ISBN 978-3-447-12385-3
e ISSN 2750-4751 eISBN 978-3-447-39681-3

*This book is dedicated to the memory of three persons dear to my heart. To my father, Rudolf Macuch, whose lifelong commitment to scholarly work has shaped my life from the very first recalled moments, sitting as an infant in the midst of his handwritten manuscripts and opened books in that mysterious world into which his warm presence and unconditional love pulled me.** *To my mother, Irandokht, a true daughter Irans, who loved the sufi poets and Jesus of Nazareth, a Christian at heart long before she was baptized as an adult. She was the one to choose the name Maria for me and from her love of animals I learned that every single living being is unique and precious, that respect for life in its different manifestations is the most important lesson to learn. Only later did I realize how unique she was herself as an emancipated woman born in a patriarchal society, who defied all rules, chose her own calling and her own partner. And to the one true love of my life, Günter Gobrecht. His outstanding intellect and deep emotional intelligence were only two aspects of a complex and charismatic personality, a truly sovereign spirit with a wounded soul. From him I learned the importance of being a real person, independent in thought and act, and the meaning of solitude and contemplation in a world of ever increasing sound and fury. I owe them far more than I can ever know.*

* On my father, the man and the scholar, see MACUCH 2008c, 2014d, 2014e and *Wikipedia* (English); the scholarly correspondence between LADY DROWER and my father has been partly published in BUCKLEY 2012, pp. 135–187.

Contents

Preface XV

Introduction . . . 1

1 Preliminary remarks . . . 1

2 The terminology of law and justice . . . 4

3 Law and justice in Zoroastrian doctrine . . . 6

4 Law as a social construct . . . 10

CHAPTER I. Legal Sources and Instruments of Law . . . 13

Introductory: reconstructing Sasanian law . . . 13

A) Legal sources . . . 15

1 Original records: inscriptions, seals and Pahlavi documents in the cursive script. . . . 16

1.1 Inscriptions and seals . . . 16

1.2 Pahlavi papyri and other documents from Egypt . . . 17

1.3 The 'Pahlavi Archive' . . . 17

1.4 Legal documents from Tabarestān . . . 18

1.5 Documents from Tang-e Bolāghī . . . 20

2 Pahlavi legal sources: the Sasanian Law-book and the marriage contract . . . 20

2.1 *Hazār dādestān* 'One Thousand Judgements' . . . 20

2.2 *Paymānag ī kadag-xwadāyīh* 'Marriage Contract' . . . 22

3 Pahlavi texts relating explicitly to the Avesta . . . 23

3.1 *Dēnkard* 'Acts of the Religion' . . . 24

3.2 *Hērbedestān* 'Book of Priestly Studies' . . . 27

3.3 *Nērangestān* 'Book of Ritual Directions' . . . 27

3.4 *Wīdēwdād* 'Law Repelling the Demons' . . . 28

3.5 Pahlavi exegesis of the *Wīdēwdād* (*Juddēwdād*) . . . 29

3.6 *Xorde Avesta* 'Small Avesta' . . . 30

3.7 *Frahang ī ōīm-ēk* 'Glossary (Beginning) with the Word "One"' . . . 30

4 Pahlavi 'traditions' (*Riwāyat*-literature) of the post-Sasanian period 31
4.1 *Šāyist nē šāyist* 'Valid and not Valid' and its supplementary texts 32
4.2 *Dādestān ī dēnīg* 'Religious Judgements' 33
4.3 Pahlavi *Riwāyat* accompanying the *Dādestān ī dēnīg* . . . 34
4.4 Pahlavi *Riwāyat* of *Ādurfarrbay and Farrbay-srōš* 34
4.5 *Riwāyat ī Ēmēd ī Ašawahištān* 'Tradition of Ēmēd, Son of Ašawahišt' 36
4.6 *Wizīrkard ī dēnīg* 'Religious Decisions' 36
5 New Persian Zoroastrian 'traditions' (*Riwāyats*) 38
6 Early Judaeo-Persian legal texts 39
7 Sogdian and Bactrian legal documents 41
7.1 Sogdian documents 41
7.2 Bactrian documents 43
8 Khwarezmian legal texts 45
9 Legal sources in Syriac 46
9.1 'Marriage Law' and 'Vita' of the Patriarch Mār Abā 47
9.2 'Corpus Iuris' of the archbishop Īšōʿbōxt 48
9.3 'Law of Succession' of the archbishop Simeon 49
9.4 Acts of the martyrs 49
10 The Babylonian Talmud 49
11 Sources in Persian and Arabic 51
11.1 The 'Letter of Tansar' 52
11.2 The 'Testament of Ardašīr' 53
11.3 The 'Code (of Ardašīr)' 53
11.4 The 'Book of Deeds of Anūširwān' 54
11.5 Historiographical sources 54
12 Armenian sources 55
12.1 The *History* of Łazar Pʿarpetsʿi 55
12.2 The *History* of Ałuankʿ 56
12.3 The *History* of the Province of Siwnikʿ 56
13 Classical sources 57

B) Instruments of law 59
1 Development and categorizations of Zoroastrian law 59
2 Theology and jurisprudence 64
3 Legal theory and practice 66
4 Technical terms and legal language 72
5 The concept of legal rights 85
6 Animal rights 90

CHAPTER II. Legal Identity and Kinship Ties 93

Introductory: Sasanian elites and kinship as a central unit. 93

1 Social organisation and hierarchy 95

2 The law of persons and legal status 101
2.1 Slaves and freedmen 104
2.2 Nobles and commoners 110
2.3 Citizens and 'non-Iranians' (foreigners) 113
2.4 Zoroastrians and infidels. 118
2.5 Men and women 120
2.6 Conclusions: social stratification and legal rights 124

3 Kinship, family and descent groups 126

4 Matrimony and succession 133
4.1 Marriage types 134
4.1.1 *Pādixšāy* marriage 134
4.1.2 *Čagar*-marriage. 142
4.1.3 *Xwasrāyēn/gādār*-marriage 145
4.2 Exogamy (*bayăspān*), endogamy and marriage within the nuclear family (*xwēdōdah*) 148
4.3 Temporary marriage 157
4.4 Intermediary succession (*ayōgēnīh*) and substitute succession (*stūrīh*) 163

5 Categorization of children 175

6 Guardianship (*sālārīh*) 177

7 Family law: a refined network of institutions. 183

CHAPTER III. Property and Inheritance. 187

Introductory: Descent groups and property law 187

1 Fundamental concepts 188
1.1 Terminology and types of property (*xwāstag*; *xīr*). 189
1.2 Possession (*dārišn*) and ownership (*xwēšīh*) 193
1.3 Substance (*hun*) and fruit (*bar*). 197

2 Basic components of a family's total patrimonial estate (*abarmānd*) 202
2.1 Hereditary possession (*xwāstagdārīh*) 206
2.2 Property 'in ownership' (*pad xwēšīh*) 210
2.3 Property 'in trust; for substitute succession' (*pad stūrīh*). . . . 213
2.4 Property 'for the soul' (*pad ruwān*). 220
2.5 Conclusions 229

3 Inheritance 230
3.1 Intestacy 231
3.2 Testament 235

4 Joint property (*hamxwāstagīh*) and partnership (*hambāyīh*) 245

5 Social consequences of property law and the Mazdakite upheaval . . 253

CHAPTER IV. Contracts and Obligations 260

Introductory: the significance of the contract in Zoroastrianism 260

1 Technical terms for contracts and other documents 263
1.1 *pašn, pašt.* 264
1.2 *paymān, paymān-nāmag.* 266
1.3 *wizīr* 268
1.4 *dib, nibēg, nāmag* 270
1.5 *abarmad* 273
1.6 *nāmag/gitt(ag)* ⟨GT(k); gt(k)⟩; *pādixšīr, mādayān* 275
1.7 *čak, pădirāy, ayādgār* 279

2 The function of seals 286
2.1 Seals of private individuals 287
2.2 Personal seals of officials 290
2.3 Administrative seals 293
2.4 Evaluation of seals 296

3 Transfer and acquisition of property 301

4 Transactions and obligations 306
4.1 Loans and credit law (*abām/abāmdān*) 310
4.1.1 The loan contract without security 319
4.1.2 Real and personal security 323
4.1.2.1 The pledge or pawn (*graw*) 326
4.1.2.2 *Hypotheca* or mortgage of the substance (*āgraw*) . . 336
4.1.2.3 *Antichresis* or mortgage of the fruits (*grawagān*) . . 343
4.1.2.4 Suretyship (*pāyandānīh*) 349
4.1.3 Liabilities and claims of the family 360
4.1.4 Debt cancellation 364
4.2 Lease (*tāg*) 367
4.3 Sale (*frōxš*) and barter (*guharēn*) 372
4.3.1 The sale contract 374
4.3.2 Earnest money 377
4.3.3 Sales in public and private 380
4.3.4 Prohibited sales 382
4.3.5 Lawsuits 385

4.3.6 Barter 388
4.3.7 Gifts and donations (*dād*) 389

CHAPTER V. Sins and Offences 400

Introductory: The religious dimension of penal law 400

1 Historical development: from the private feud to legal proceedings . 404

2 Constitutive elements of a crime 411

3 Criminal offences 422
3.1 Assault, physical injury and homicide 423
3.2 Theft and robbery 434

4 Other transgressions 451
4.1 Sexual offences 452
4.2 Offences against family law 460
4.3 Violation of legal responsibilities 462

5 Degrees (*pāyag*) of sins in Zoroastrian law 468

CHAPTER VI. Civil and Criminal Proceedings 487

Introductory: religious norms and the jurisdiction of the State 487

1 Criminal offences prosecuted by the State 489

2 The judiciary 494
2.1 Judicial and public officials 496
2.1.1 The judge (*dādwar*) 496
2.1.2 Religious authorities in the judiciary 503
2.1.3 Public officials with judicial power 510
2.1.4 Lower officials and members of the court 518
2.2 Instances and appellate courts 522
2.3 The jurisdiction of religious minorities 526

3 The law of procedure 533
3.1 Civil proceedings 533
3.1.1 Filing action 534
3.1.2 The preliminary hearing 536
3.1.3 The trial 537
3.1.4 Evidence 542
3.1.4.1 The legal predecessor (*dastwar*) 542
3.1.4.2 Witnesses (*gugāy*) 545
3.1.4.3 Documentary evidence 550
3.1.4.4 The oath (*war*) 551

3.1.5 Offences against the judiciary and obstruction of justice 561
3.1.6 The verdict 569
3.2. Criminal proceedings 572
3.2.1 The accusation 573
3.2.2 The preliminary hearing(s) 576
3.2.3 The trial 578
3.2.4 The verdict and punishments 580
3.3 Litigation costs 585

CHAPTER VII. Sasanian Law and other Legal Systems 588

Introductory: the impact of Sasanian law 588

1 Rabbinic law in the Babylonian Talmud 590
1.1 Iranian legal terms in the Bavli 591
1.2 Allusions to Sasanian institutions and concepts 603

2 East Christian (Nestorian) law 609
2.1 Iranian legal terms in the *Corpus Iuris* of Īšōʿbōxt 609
2.2 Iranian concepts in East Christian law 615

3 Islamic law 621
3.1 The pious foundation (*waqf*) 622
3.2 Temporary marriage (*mutʿa/ṣīġe*) 628
3.3 The Twelver Shīʿite law of inheritance 632

4 Roman (Byzantine) law 638

APPENDIX I. *Dādestān ī dēnīg*: On Inheritance and Family Law (*Pursišn* 53–61) 641

APPENDIX II. *Dādestān ī dēnīg*: On Sale (*Pursišn* 49, 51, 52) 657

APPENDIX III. *Dēnkard* 3: Excerpts on Law and Justice 664

APPENDIX IV. *Dēnkard* 3 and 7: Excerpts on the Mazdakite Movement . 669

APPENDIX V. *Dēnkard* 8: On Judicial Dispute (*pahikār-radestān*) 674

APPENDIX VI. *Dēnkard* 8: On Assault, Wounding and Bodily Harm (*zaxmestān/rēšestān*) 679

APPENDIX VII. *Dēnkard* 8: On the Thief (and his) Accomplice (*abar duz abāg*) 685

APPENDIX VIII. *Hērbedestān* 6.6–7: On Illicit Sexual Intercourse 690

APPENDIX IX. *Riwāyat ī Ādurfarrbay ud Farrbay-Srōš*: On the Oath (*Pursišn* 66, 72, 74). 696

APPENDIX X. *Tabarestān* 17, 18 and 24: Loan Contracts 700

APPENDIX XI. *Tabarestān* 13 and 23: Documents on Leasehold 711

APPENDIX XII. *Tabarestān* 1–8; 10: Records of Civil Proceedings 715

Case 1 715

Case 2 721

Case 3 722

APPENDIX XIII. *Tabarestān* 22 and 22bis: A Criminal Act 723

APPENDIX XIV. *Tabarestān* 11 and 28: Two Cases of *stŭrīh*. 728

APPENDIX XV. *Tabarestān* 20 and 26: Payment Entitlements (*čak*) 735

APPENDIX XVI. Overview: Capital Crimes (*margarzān*) 738

APPENDIX XVII. Sources Cited by the Compiler of the Law-book. . . . 741

Glossary of Legal Terms and Phrases. 749

Abbreviations 799

General abbreviations 799

Texts 799

Journals and editions 800

Bibliography 803

List of Figures and Tables 835

Index. 837

Preface

The present volume is an attempt to reconstruct systematically all branches of Sasanian law as far as they can be recognized in the fragmentary sources at our disposal and to delineate the specific functions of characteristic legal institutions within the framework of the social system in which they took form. My main aim is to contextualize the dispersed information on these unique legal constructions, not just to describe them, but to expose the concealed basic ideas on which they were built. Due to the sparseness of our sources, this is neither a history of Zoroastrian law, nor a comparative study of Sasanian law, although both areas will be touched on. After a lifetime of intense study of the dispersed, often bewildering and enigmatic legal material, my goal was to understand the fundamental concepts on which Sasanian law was constructed, to explain first to myself, then to a larger interested public, why and to which purpose it developed its characteristic legal institutions, how they interacted and complemented each other within the parameters of a multifaceted legal system. Although I have already addressed in several previous contributions some of the topics that will be discussed in the following chapters, a coherent, systematic portrayal of the many fascinating aspects of Sasanian law was still missing. This volume will hopefully be a useful guide through the manifold structures of the legal system, show the interdependency of many individual features of the law and unveil the intricacies of its technical language, the main clue to understanding many short and elliptical entries in the bulk of the legal sources.

Needless to say, it is almost impossible to satisfy to the same degree both experts in the field of Iranian Studies and a general scholarly public interested in Sasanian law and legal history. The former would need less standard explanations and presumably prefer a more extensive discussion of the numerous philological and contextual problems of the cited material, whereas the latter, on the contrary, would favour a broader account of the fundamental assumptions and characteristic institutions of the law, gladly dispensing with the linguistic details. I have tried to find a compromise between these two extremes, adding for the general public explanations an Iranist might find superfluous and extending discussions of problematic passages, crucial for our understanding of an important issue, for the specialist. Throughout the work I have made use of the technical terms employed by Sasanian jurisconsults, adding translations and longer explanations when necessary. It was essential to use the original terms, as they often encompass a mass of legal information in a single word or phrase, which cannot be rendered adequately in another language with the same precision.

It is my pleasant task to thank those friends and colleagues who have made the publication of this volume possible. I am most grateful to my successor to the chair of Iranian Studies at the Freie Universität Berlin and co-editor of the series *Iranica*, ALBERTO CANTERA, for his steadfast encouragement of this endeavour and for his generous contribution to the publication costs. My sincere thanks are also due to my two longstanding colleagues responsible for formatting the volumes of this series, TATSIANA HARTING and CLAUDIUS NAUMANN, for their patience with the unavoidable inconsistences in a work which took form across several years, for their valuable suggestions and their competent typesetting.

Berlin, July 2024 MARIA MACUCH

Introduction

1 Preliminary remarks

During the five centuries of Sasanian dominion (224–651 CE) the inhabitants of the Iranian Empire, Ērānšahr (Realm of the Iranians), were subject to an astonishingly sophisticated and efficient legal system. In combination with a vast administrative bureaucracy and well-organized judiciary, Sasanian law was in force in all the provinces of the huge empire during this dynasty's rule and remained effective for a long time after the Muslim conquest of Iran in the 7th century as customary law in many regions, particularly in the provinces south of the Caspian sea and in the Zoroastrian communities of the southern provinces, Fārs and Kermān. In recent years research on Sasanian law has revealed its wide-reaching impact on those contemporary legal systems, which were formed or further developed in the large Christian and Jewish communities of Ērānšahr, notably the canon law of the East Christians (Nestorians) and rabbinic law in the most important Jewish legal compilation, the monumental Babylonian Talmud. Sasanian legal concepts also contributed substantially to the development of Islamic institutions that were created in the formative period of Islamic law in the ninth century CE, especially within the framework of Shīʿite (Jaʿfarite) law, and are still effective up to this day.

The law of the Sasanian Empire is itself a complex amalgam of various strata, encompassing ancient Zoroastrian precepts, customs and rules conserved in the Avestan texts and applied as they were understood in the Sasanian period (reflected in the *zand*, the Pahlavi translation-cum-commentary of the Avesta) besides a large range of other age-old laws and procedures that might have been partly adapted or formed in earlier centuries under the influence of neighbouring legal systems, particularly Ancient Mesopotamian and Egyptian law. The history and development of Iranian law is largely obscure, but it stands to reason that the Sasanian kings did not form a completely new legal system, but rather adapted the laws of their predecessors to a large extent, probably conceding greater influence to Zoroastrian religious authorities in the process. We can reasonably infer that an effective Iranian legal system emerged as a combination of religious norms and customary law long before the establishment of Sasanian rule, but was subject to many changes across the centuries. The Achaemenid king Darius I (522–486 BCE) famously praises himself in the Behistūn inscription for establishing 'my law' (*manā dātā*), presumably already a mixture of Zoroastrian precepts, customary law and Mesopotamian legal traditions.[1] According to Plato, who uses the Greek *nomos* (law) for *dāta-*, Darius 'set an example of what a good lawgiver and king should be, for he established laws that have kept the Persian Empire to this day'.[2] Unfortunately almost nothing has survived of this renowned law apart from a few very general principles listed by Darius in his inscriptions, which correspond well with Mazdean precepts.[3]

Zoroastrian norms and beliefs, transmitted in the sacred texts of the Avesta, formed not only the basis of Mazdean theology, but to a large extent also the *theoretical* foundation of Sasanian law, as we may conclude from the numerous glosses and commentaries in the *zand* of the Avestan texts referring to legal matters. A large part of the Avesta seems to have been in fact dedicated to legal issues, but most of these texts (called *dādīg* 'pertaining to law') have been lost and would indeed remain unknown to us if they had not been summarized in *Dēnkard* Book 8, a late Pahlavi synopsis of religious material from the 9th century.[4] The few surviving Avestan texts containing legal matters demonstrate how the Pahlavi exegetes proceeded: besides translating the (by then largely incomprehensible) Old Iranian texts into the language of their own times, Middle Persian, one of their main tasks was to relate the Avestan legal entries to the altered circumstances of their own age and show the continuing relevance of the sacred material. In the shorter Pahlavi glosses individual Avestan words and phrases, which were translated literally into Middle Persian, were often elucidated by a corresponding Sasanian technical term or phrase well known to legal experts, without further explanation. The texts also contain longer commentaries with detailed legal discussions and sometimes also case studies, which were appended directly to the translated passages.[5] Legal matters were also scrutinized in separate treatises, called *čāštag* ('teaching, doctrine') containing individual interpretations of a theologian-cum-jurisconsult or the doctrine of a specific legal school. As the sacred corpus was regarded as omniscient and eternally valid, these late commentaries deliberately ignore (or deny) any historical changes, but there can be no doubt that significant alterations had taken place in all fields of law by the Sasanian period. The rather elementary rules construed for a pastoral community in the Avestan texts could no longer cover the concrete needs of a multi-stratified hierarchical society in a multi-ethnic empire and, as in other legal systems based on religion, the meaning of the sacred texts was determined, interpreted and extended by the hermeneutic authority of religious sages.

1 On the use of the Old Persian term in the inscriptions of Darius I (*manā dātā*, DB 1.23; *dātam taya manā*, DSe 20f., DNa 21f.) and Xerxes (*dātam taya manā*, XPh 18f.) see König 2018, pp. 126–140, with further references.

2 Plato, Laws III.695c, *apud* Miller 2007 (2015), p. 5.

3 On these see König 2018, pp. 135–138. On legal sources of the Achaemenid and Parthian periods see below Chapter I, p. 15, fn. 1.

4 See Chapter I, pp. 24–26.

5 For an example of a longer commentary (from the *Hērbedestān*) see Appendix VIII.

The process of detangling the two fields of theology and jurisprudence seems to have set in at an early stage of Zoroastrian law, at a time when mainly priests were engaged in solving conflicts and passing judgement, besides performing the necessary rituals and supervising moral behaviour in the Mazdean communities. The need to distinguish between religious affairs and legal matters, both originally central areas of priestly work, seems to have led to a distinction between these two sectors already in the Avestan material and very clearly in Pahlavi religious literature. One of these two categories, called *wināh ī ruwānīg* 'sins pertaining to the soul', deals with moral and ritual issues (such as violating purity rules, failing to observe the ritual, harming beneficent animals, etc.), the other, *wināh ī hamēmālān* 'offences regarding opponents' handles all types of transgressions directed against other members of the Zoroastrian community that can be subject to jurisdiction, encompassing both civil disputes and criminal acts.[6] It is important to note that these two categories did not exclude each other: all actionable illegal acts belonging to the second group were at the same time damaging to the soul of the delinquent and, vice versa, specific sins pertaining to the soul could also be harmful to another individual (such as adultery, harming a beneficent animal under the guardianship of another person, etc.). But a significant distinction lay in the consequences: 'sins pertaining to the soul' were atoned for by paying a fine (*tōzišn*) to religious authorities and following the rules set by them for the atonement of sins (repenting, confessing, performing deeds appropriate for the expiation of sins), whereas 'offences regarding opponents' could only be atoned for by compensating the damaged or injured person (or his next-of-kin) directly by paying a fine or smart money or satisfying him by some other means. Although the two areas remained intertwined from a religious point of view, the separation of sins against one's own soul from offences against other persons seems to mark the beginning of Zoroastrian law as an individual discipline.

By the Sasanian age jurisprudence had evolved into an advanced and complex field, firmly based on Zoroastrian tenets, but in practice detached from theology, although many of the jurisconsults named in the texts were at the same time theologians.[7] This detachment, particularly in those specific fields of law that could not be derived from the Avestan material, seems to have facilitated the adaption of ideas and legal institutions in a re-contextualized and adjusted form into the juristic material of the neighbouring religious legal systems mentioned above. It is deplorable that we are so badly informed on the historical development of Iranian law—apart from very general descriptions[8]—but the

6 On this classification of offences see Chapter I, pp. 62–63; Chapter V, pp. 400–401; Chapter VI, pp. 487–489. A similar distinction may be found in Jewish law which divides transgressions into '(1) sins against one's fellow man and (2) sins against God' (Herzog 1936, p. xxvi).

7 On theology and jurisprudence see Chapter I, pp. 64–66.

8 On one of these see Chapter V, pp. 404–411.

sources at our disposal demonstrate impressively how differentiated the legal system had become by the end of the Sasanian period.

The available material does not convey any direct information on legal theory. The fundamental legal concepts discussed in the following chapters of this study are hence all reconstructed on the basis of the meticulously precise use of legal terminology (which is, however, only seldom explained, and has to be interpreted in the context of the texts) and a large range of complex case studies, illustrating how specific legal norms were applied.

2 The terminology of law and justice

The general term for 'law, legal order', *dād* (from Old Persian *dāta-* 'law'),[9] is not used as frequently in Pahlavi legal texts as its derivative *dādestān.* In our most important legal source, the Sasanian Law-book,[10] *dād* in the sense of 'law, legislation' occurs only once.[11] It might be relevant that it is attested solely in a context referring to the 'law of the State' (*dād ī šahr*),[12] presumably a synonym for the more frequently attested *ēwēn* (< **abi-dayanā-*)[13] 'custom, norm, law', which appears in a similar context together with *šahr* (< Av. *xšaϑra-;* OP *xšaça-*) 'empire, realm, kingdom, state', as *ēwēn ī šahr* 'law of the State'.[14] The passages in which these two terms occur are very short and do not contain any explanations, but we can reasonably infer that both *dād ī šahr* and *ēwēn ī šahr* refer to some kind of official legislation of the Sasanian State, a set of laws in which also specific corporal penalties (*xwar* < Av. *x^{v}ara-* lit. 'wound, sore')[15] for offences were noted, a kind of criminal code or penal code, designated as *xwar ud dād ī šahr* 'penalty and law of the State'.

9 See fn. 1 and 3 above.

10 See Chapter I, pp. 20–22.

11 The lemma *dād* in the index of Macuch 1993, p. 698, is a homonym meaning 'age' in all references.

12 MHDA 35.5–6: *ud an ī guft kū drustīh ī xwar ud dād ī šahr rāy wināhišn-iz pādifrāh ōgārišn ē kunišn* 'And that which says: because of holding upright the penalty and the law of the State (*xwar ud dād ī šahr*) and also because of the (caused) damage (*wināhišn*) he (= the perpetrator) has to be punished and expelled.' (Macuch 1981, p. 61, with a slightly different translation p. 218).

13 Already attested in the Šābuhr inscription on the Kaʿba-i Zardušt (ŠKZ § 35.1), MP ⟨'dwyn⟩ *ēwēn* (mpI 24); Parth. ⟨'bdyn⟩ *aβδēn* (paI 19), see Huyse 1999, vol. I, p. 48; vol. II, p. 111 (with further references); for the Bactrian equivalent αβδδινο 'custom' see Sims-Williams 2000, p. 173; MMP ⟨'ywyn⟩ *ēwēn* 'custom, sort' Durkin-Meisterernst 2004, p. 82.

14 MHDA 35.8: *ud ka pas ka-š gīrēnd ēwēn ī šahr rāy be drōšišn* 'And when he (= the person considered as a thief) is later caught, because of the law of the State (*ēwēn ī šahr*) he has to be branded (= punishment for theft).' (Macuch 1981, pp. 61, 218). On *dād ī šahr* and *ēwēn ī šahr* see Colditz 2023.

15 Originally a degree of sin, see Chapter V, pp. 474–475.

In contrast, its derivative *dādestān* (< **dāta-stāna-* lit. 'place of law') is a frequently employed expression, not only in the concrete literal sense of 'law court', but also with a large range of other meanings. In the context of litigation *dādestān* designates the 'lawsuit, case, process, proceedings' (as in *dādestān rāyēnīdan* 'to conduct legal proceedings' and *tā dādestān sar bawēd* 'until the lawsuit comes to an end'), also 'judgement, verdict, sentence, judicial decision' (as in *dādestān az rāyēnišn mānēd* 'the verdict from [on-going] proceedings has yet to be passed' and in the compound *dādestān-nāmag* 'recordings/book of judicial decisions, Law-book').[16] In the Tabarestān documents it is attested in the sense of 'jurisdiction', 'judiciary' and 'justice' (*abar Taburestān dādestān* 'in charge of jurisdiction in Tabarestān'; *pad rāh ī dādestān* 'by means of the judiciary'; *dādestān kardan* 'to administer justice').[17] In compounds such as *dādestān-pus* 'son according to the law, legitimate son' and *dādestān-duxt* 'legal daughter, legitimate daughter' and in other derivatives the term has the meaning of 'law, legal, legitimate' (also in the adverb *dādestānōmandīhā* 'according to law' and the adjective *dādestānīg* 'pertaining to law, legal').[18]

So far we may surmise that the semantic range of *dādestān* in the context of the judiciary encompasses the manifold meanings 'law court, lawsuit, legal proceedings, jurisdiction, judiciary, judgement, verdict, judicial decision, law, justice', all referring primarily to the *practical application* of law, whereas *dād* and *ēwēn* are the general terms for 'law' in the sense of a *body of normative rules* constituting the legal order of the community or the state (based in the Sasanian period at least *theoretically* on the corpus of Zoroastrian tenets in the legal divisions of the Avesta, called *dādīg* 'pertaining to law, legal'). In contrast to the (equally ambiguous) Roman *ius* the term *dādestān* is not directly attested with the meaning of 'a right', but the notion is inherent in the compounds denoting the 'legitimate' members of a lineage in family law (*dādestān-pus*, *dādestān-duxt*, *dādestān-brād*, *dādestān-xwāh* 'legitimate son, daughter, brother, sister' respectively).[19] These terms designate family members who have specific 'rights' (in the sense of 'privileges'), which do not extend to other sons, daughters, brothers and sisters in the family of a *paterfamilias* (*kadag-xwadāy*). The idea of 'justice' is inherent in the abstract *weh-dādestānīh* (lit. 'good justice; good decision, judgement', and the comparative form *weh-dādestāntar* 'better justice') and, in later texts, *meh-dādestānīh* 'great(er) justice'. The compound designates an approach to jurisdiction that is far more than a mechanical application of norms and laws and involves a sincere search for the best solution

16 For all attestations see Macuch 1993, index, p. 698.

17 Tab. 24.2 (Macuch 2019, p. 132); Tab. 28.2 (Macuch 2020, p. 199); Tab. 22.24 (Macuch 2019, p. 126); Tab. 11.25–26 (Macuch 2020, p. 192) respectively.

18 For attestations see Macuch 1993, index, p. 699, and DkM 693.12; 700.20; 714.7 and DkM 693.8; 731.17 respectively.

19 On these legal terms see Chapter II, pp. 130, 163, 175–176; on the concept of a legal right see Chapter I, pp. 85–90.

to a legal problem by doing more than formally required by the law. It entails a commitment to truthfulness that is more than a commitment to legal tradition and authority alone and is, in short, a search for the true 'spirit of the law'. This approach can involve decisions, which do not conform to the 'letter of the law', at times even explicitly contradicting legal doctrine (*čāštag*), in order to reach 'better justice'.[20]

Given the significant impact of religious beliefs in this context it will be useful to ask, how law and justice were positioned in Mazdean doctrine and, furthermore, whether Zoroastrian law developed a concept of legal rights comparable to that of other advanced legal systems (a question which we will discuss more extensively in Chapter I, pp. 85–90).

3 Law and justice in Zoroastrian doctrine

The third book of the *Dēnkard* addresses the significance of law and justice in several passages from the perspective of religious doctrine. Although this is a late source of the 9th century containing a mixture of traditional Zoroastrian material and many references to Greek and late Hellenistic philosophy, several of these sections on law (*dād*) and justice (*dādestān*) fit in well with the Mazdean conviction that both have a divine origin. They seem to reflect genuine traditional Zoroastrian beliefs (even if the theological constructions might be late).[21] Dk. 3.78[22] on the 'beneficent truth (*xwābar rāstagīh*) of the law (*dād*) of the Mazdean religion' elucidates how law was perceived in Zoroastrian doctrine, following a structure that corresponds to the 'three utterances' (*se wāzag*), *i.e.*, the famous Zoroastrian triad *hūxt*, *humat*, *huwaršt* (good thoughts, good speech, good acts). In analogy to this triad the law (*dād*) of the Mazdean religion also encompasses three dimensions:

1) the law of the corporal world (*gētīy*) which is in force as long as a person is 'in a corporal state' (*pad tanōmandīh*);
2) the law of the spiritual world (*mēnōy*) that prevails after the soul has left the body;
3) the law which is finally fulfilled by the Restoration (*frašgird*) of the world at the end of time after the final defeat of the Evil Spirit.

The first dimension of law in the *gētīy* state consists of the rules and regulations Mazdeans have to follow during their corporal existence. These are: abstaining

20 See Chapter I, pp. 70–72; Chapter VII, pp. 610–611; also Macuch 2019a; for examples of the application of this method of arguing see Macuch 2022c and 2024a.

21 On the mixture of Zoroastrian traditional material and Greek and late Hellenistic philosophy in *Dēnkard* III see especially Josephson 2012 and 2019; also König 2018, p. 147.

22 The whole text is in Appendix III, pp. 665–667.

from harming and killing another person (*pahrēz ī [az] margīh ud bēš ī kas*); but also refraining from wounding and harming oneself (*rēš ud bēš ī xwēš tan*); recompensing (*āsānīh ud šnāyišn*) a person who is entitled to compensation, including adherents of an 'evil religion' (*ag-dēnīh*); keeping contracts with the righteous (*ahlaw*) and the unrighteous (*druwandīh*); not breaking (*nē druxtan*) a contract (*mihr*) with anyone.

After leaving the corporal state (*pas az tanōmandīh*) the law of the *mēnōy* dimension prescribes that the souls (*ruwān*) should give account (*āmār*) of their intent (*kām*),[23] knowledge (*dānišn*) and power (*tuwān*) during their *gētīy* existence. This law determines the measure (*sāmān*) according to which virtuous deeds (*kirbag*) can be used as a remedy (*biziškīh*) to neutralize (*darrēnīdan*, lit. 'split') sins and offences (*wināh*) committed during one's lifetime. That is, the law of the *mēnōy* dimension measures precisely the degree of guilt and merit of the individual soul by balancing virtuous behaviour and sins against each other. This is an important aspect of religious law, which in fact reaches far beyond the fictive *mēnōy* state into concrete legal practice in the *gētīy* and is effectively used by religious instances to evaluate and punish especially *ruwānīg* offences (see below).

Finally, the law of the Restoration (*frašgird*) is the infallible law of the Creator, Ohrmazd, who will restore by his good wisdom (*hu-frazānagīh*) his creation by eliminating the Adversary (*ēbgat*), clearing out hell by purifying sinful souls and restoring all righteous souls to a corporal form to exist eternally without death (*jāwēdān a-marg*) in eternal bliss (*purr šēdā*).

The *gētīy* and *mēnōy* dimensions of law are again taken up in Dk. 3.302[24] in a discussion of the divergent abilities and competences of judges operating in these two areas of existence. According to this passage the *mēnōy* judge (*dādwar*) is infallible, since he passes judgement regarding acquittal (*bōzišn*) or conviction (*ērang*) on the basis of his inner vision (*wēnišn*). His judgement is 'binding' (*ēwar*): he knows precisely to whom a thing belongs in ownership (*kē xwēš čiš*), he can detect the intention of a robber (*appar-kām*) and the intention of a thief (⁺*duzagān-menišn*) and due to his infallible inner vision he knows who is truthful and who is deceiving (*kē rāst kē drōzan*).[25]

In contrast, the *gētīy* judge (*dādwar*) can only pass judgement leading either to an acquittal (*bōzišn*) or to a conviction (*ērang*) on the basis of statements (*pad saxwan*), which he considers as reliable (*pad ēwar dārišn*). Whereas the *mēnōy* judge has complete clarity (*rōšn*) due to his *mēnōy*-vision (*pad menoy-wenišnih*), not every *gētīy* judge has an alert (*a-xuftag*, lit. 'unsleeping') vision. Hence he can only reach judgement (*wizīr kardan*) by relying on those statements of the

23 On the importance of determining a person's intent (*kām*, *menišn*) in judging offences see Chapter V, pp. 411–422.

24 The whole text is in Appendix III, pp. 667–668.

25 On the intent of the thief and the robber see also Chapter V, p. 414.

plaintiff, the defendant and witnesses (*az pēšēmāl ud pasēmāl ud gugāyīhān saxwan*), which he considers as reliable, and by following legal and ritual norms (*dādīg ud hādīg … ēwēn*).

Dk 3.292.2[26] on the 'different substances or origins (*ǰud-bunīh*) of law and violence' juxtapositions law (*dād*) and violence (*must*): the substance (or origin, *bun*) of law is knowledge (*dānāgīh*) that in turn stems from innate wisdom (*āsn-xrad*), which is inherent in the whole creation of Ohrmazd. In contrast, violence (*must*) stems from ignorance (*duš-āgāhīh*), which is based on lust (*waran*), both of which were *not* created by Ohrmazd. Another passage[27] attributes the substance or origin (*bun*) of the 'goodness of law' (*dād nēkīh*) to knowledge (*dānāgīh*), the 'evil of lawlessness' (*a-dād anāgīh*) to ignorance (*duš-āgāhīh*).

The topic of 'innate wisdom' (*āsn-xrad*) as the original foundation of law and justice is also addressed in a somewhat confusing passage (Dk 3.52)[28] on 'taking legal action with religion' (*abar rāyēnišn [ī] dādestān abāg dēn*). Justice (*dādestān*) is explained as an offspring (*pad zahagīh*) of innate wisdom (*āsn-xrad*) and the Good Religion (*weh-dēn*), existing with the latter in one rank and brotherhood (*ēk radagīg brādarīh-iz*). Due to justice (*dādestān*) all people (*mardōm ī hamāg*) partake of innate wisdom and have a share in its inheritance (*padiš wāspuhragānagīh*). Justice (*dādestān*) is from the same offspring (*ham-zahag*) as the innate wisdom of Ohrmazd. Infidels (*ag-dēnān*) cause harm by disseminating their evil religion, but the injury (*āzāristagīh*) caused by adherence to an evil religion (*ag-dēnīh*) will be vanquished 'on the scales' (*pad-iz tarāzūg*) of the same judgement (*ham-dādestān*) by which injury is assessed in the Good Religion.

If I have understood these sections correctly (particularly the twisted syntax of the last passage), they state that the knowledge (*dānāgīh*) necessary to construe law and justice, the opposite of violence and ignorance, is based on the innate wisdom (*āsn-xrad*), conveyed by Ohrmazd to the whole of his creation. All people have a sense of justice (*dādestān*) due to being created by Ohrmazd. Hence, not only adherents of the Good Religion will be judged on the scales (*tarāzūg*) of justice, but also those who believe in an evil religion (*ag-dēn*), whose sense of law and justice has been contaminated.

Although specific theological constructions might be late, on the whole these passages corroborate the information to be gained from other Zoroastrian sources, implying that law and justice have a divine origin in Mazdaism and are central religious categories. They were obviously perceived as being effective not only in the worldly existence, but *beyond the grave* in the spiritual state and in the world to come after the Restoration. Unsurprisingly, this concept,

26 For the whole passage see Appendix III, p. 667; also König 2018, p. 147.

27 Dk 3.393.2 (de Menasce 1973, p. 351) DkD 289.14–15 (DkM 373. 15–16): *dād nēkīh bun dānāgīh ud a-dād anāgīh bun duš-āgāhīh* 'The substance/origin of the goodness of law (lies) in knowledge and the evil of lawlessness (lies) in lack of knowledge.'

28 The whole text is in Appendix III, pp. 664–665.

which reaches beyond the boundaries of law and justice in the corporal world, bestows immense power on those members of the Zoroastrian priesthood, who were engaged in the application of the law. As we have noted above, religious authorities were active as judges in both categories of law, the *wināh ī hamēmālān* (offences regarding opponents) and *wināh ī ruwānīg* (offences pertaining to the soul). Disputes between litigants in the first category were conducted according to the law of the corporal world (*gētīy*) by both State judges and religious authorities,[29] whereas only the latter judged 'sins pertaining to the soul' following Zoroastrian tenets.[30] After a person's death, it was held that a triad of three divinities (presumably identical with the *mēnōy* judges mentioned in Dk 3.78) pass judgement over the soul: Mihr (Av. Mithra), Srōš (Av. Sraoša) and Rašn (Av. Rašnu), who holds the scales (*tarāzūg*) of justice upon which the sins and virtues of the deceased are weighed.[31] One of the most significant tasks of Zoroastrian religious and legal authorities was to minimize the amount of sins and offences that would accumulate during the lifetime of an individual and determine this person's destiny on Rašn's scales in the hereafter. The accumulation of both sins and merits forming the soul of the individual is expressed by the phrase *ō bun* (*būdan*) '(to accrue) to (one's) stock/account',[32] containing one of the central legal terms of property law: *bun* 'substance, capital, principal, stock, core assets', the more or less permanent part of every corporal 'thing' (*xwāstag*), vis-à-vis *bar* 'fruits, income', the impermanent part.[33] In legal usage the 'substance' of the property of high-ranking aristocratic families and affluent members of the Zoroastrian priesthood consisted of various assets accumulated across several generations, forming the wealth of noble lineages.[34] In a religious context the parallel use of the term seems to imply that sins and merits accrue in the course of a person's life, forming the 'capital' or 'stock' (*bun*) of the individual's soul. The basic idea corresponds well with religious doctrine: every Zoroastrian shapes the essence of his or her own soul in the corporal world (*gētīy*). It is up to the individual to increase his/her assets by performing meritorious deeds (*kirbag*) and to reduce (or remove completely) liabilities (*i. e.* sins) by following the prescriptions of religious authorities for the atonement of sins. This was achieved by paying a fine (*tōzišn*) to the authority in charge and following the rules set for atonement by repenting, confessing and performing deeds appropriate for the expiation of sins. The sum of all good or evil thoughts, words and deeds forms the 'substance' of the soul of the deceased, which is then evaluated on the threshold to the hereafter by Rašn on his scales (*tarazug*) of justice on the three nights following the person's death and determines the soul's

29 On the hierarchy of the Sasanian judiciary see Chapter VI, pp. 494–526.
30 See Chapter V, pp. 399–401.
31 See Chapter V pp. 401-402.
32 See Chapter V, pp. 402-403.
33 See Chapter III, pp. 197–202, and Macuch 2015d, pp. 245–259.
34 See Chapter III, pp. 202–229.

destiny. Interestingly, according to Dk. 3.53, not only adherents of the Good Religion are assessed in the afterlife in this manner, but also infidels (*ag-dēnān*) who cause harm in the corporal world by disseminating their beliefs. They too will be assessed 'on the scales' (*pad-iz tarāzūg*) of the same judgement (*ham-dādestān*) by which Mazdean souls are judged (with the major difference, as we may add, that infidels would not have had the chance to minimize their sins in the *gētīy* state due to the lack of guidance by Zoroastrian religious authorities).

This doctrine is the closest one gets to a theory of equal justice and normative rights extending to all adherents of the Good Religion and (if our interpretation of Dk. 3.53 is correct) even infidels, including men, women and all classes and strata of society. Although this is not explicitly said, the whole *ruwānīg*-system is based on the idea that every Zoroastrian, regardless of gender, wealth, power or position in the social hierarchy, has the same 'right' qua affiliation to the Mazdean religion to be assessed by the Divine Judge Rašn in the spiritual state according to his or her own individual merits.[35] Salvation is *not* a question of divine grace, but the result of a precise evaluation of the individual's personal spiritual assets, a divine 'duty' the infallible Rašn has to perform, correlating to the 'right' of the deceased to just judgement. This seems to be the ideal model according to which religious authorities assessed 'sins pertaining to the soul', a category that presupposes the equality of all Zoroastrians before the law with corresponding consequences both for judgement in the 'corporal' (*gētīy*) world and judgement by the Divine Judge in the spiritual (*mēnōy*) state. This religious background must have been a significant factor in encouraging Mazdeans to keep the rules and confess their sins, besides providing the clergy with a perpetual source of income, hereby consolidating their power and significance in Sasanian society. But despite the equalitarian dimension of Sasanian Mazdaism, encompassing all Zoroastrians, this is an idea far removed from the concrete social and juristic realities of Ērānšahr, a State with a judicial system clearly based on a hierarchical concept of society, as will be seen in the following chapters.

4 Law as a social construct

The texts we have scrutinized above suggest that law was in Zoroastrianism, as in Judaism and later in Islam, a central religious category. The significance of legal norms is not only apparent in the assessment of transgressions by the priesthood (in both *ruwānīg* and *hamēmālān* categories) during the *gētīy* state of existence, but in the idea that leading a life according to Zoroastrian precepts is decisive for the verdict given by the Divine Judge and the future of the soul in the *mēnōy* state. It seems that, at least from this perspective, religious

35 On the concept of legal rights according to Sasanian legal terminology see Chapter I, pp. 85–90.

law retained an egalitarian dimension, conceding to all Zoroastrians, regardless of status, the equal right to be judged impartially according to their sins and merits in this world and the next. As we will see in Chapter V (section 5), the priesthood retained an ancient system of assessing transgressions and imposing penalties, in which the punishments for offences are not based on the social standing, gender or wealth of the wrongdoer. By its mechanical character in assessing the degree of a transgression this system might in fact reflect the ideal of impartiality and an original notion of the equality of all Mazdeans before the law.

In the Sasanian period, however, there can be no doubt that the legal system of the State was conceived for a hierarchical society that did not recognize juridical equality of its citizens, but conceded numerous privileges to its noble lineages and its wealthy elite, placing the aristocracy and the Zoroastrian priesthood on the highest level of the social system. As in other societies, Sasanian law was an integral part of the whole social system and initiated strategies that can be only understood in this specific context. Our legal sources reveal unequivocally that various fields of jurisprudence were developed to promote the economic and political interests of the most prominent echelons of society. In this respect Sasanian law does not differ substantially from other ancient legal systems, which favoured the wealthy and privileged and explicitly called for a differential treatment of citizens according to their social standing.[36] It comes as no surprise that jurisprudence in general has supported the interests of the ruling classes across history, but the Sasanian system seems to stand out in this respect by its construction of numerous elaborate legal devices, designed to enhance and preserve the privileges of affluent lineages and approved of by Zoroastrian authorities. Some of these are not only unique, but important building blocks of Sasanian rule, one part supporting the other in a complex web of intertwined mutual dependencies. The Mazdakite upheaval in the 6th century demonstrates indirectly how the Sasanian State was upheld by its legal system. By questioning, rejecting and finally removing all the legal institutions that kept social hierarchy intact the Mazdakites brought about the complete collapse of the social system, which could only be saved by re-installing the former laws. The stability of the late Sasanian Empire was highly dependant on this well functioning, coherent legal system, based on a network of institutions, not to be found in this specific combination in any other legal culture.

The following overview is a preliminary attempt based on my previous work on legal sources to comprehend the motivating forces behind the creation of the unique institutions of the Sasanian legal system and to reconstruct its most important features following the limited material at our disposal. The vast network

36 The law of the Roman Empire, for instance, openly rejected juridical equality and the legal code of Hammurabi based penalties for transgressions on the social standing of both wrongdoers and victims (*apud* Baumgartner 1996, p. 415).

of intertwined legal institutions, especially in the areas of family and property law, could hardly have emerged coincidentally, even if these complex legal constructions were not consciously created and may have developed gradually over a long period of time. The following chapters will focus on the most important fields of jurisprudence with the aim of reconstructing underlying structures as far as possible and revealing how they served the specific interests of powerful groups, thus forming society in a way that could not be easily changed from within. By the late Sasanian period the legal system in all its branches had become a crucial tool for stabilizing social hierarchies, for upholding the unequal distribution of property and for consolidating the status of those elites who held power in Ērānšahr over five centuries.

Chapter I

Legal Sources and Instruments of Law

Introductory: reconstructing Sasanian law

Although it has been long assumed that Iranian law of the Sasanian period had a significant impact on the development of many neighbouring legal systems of late antiquity, including Rabbinic, East Christian (Nestorian) and later Islamic law, Zoroastrian jurisprudence has remained largely an unknown entity outside the specific field of Iranian Studies. The main reason is *not*—as has been maintained in several publications—a lack of relevant sources, but rather the discouraging fact that the available texts do not yield their information easily. In the period we are dealing with Zoroastrian law had already developed from its simple beginnings in a pastoral society (in the first millennium BCE) across many centuries to its most sophisticated known form in the legal system of the Sasanian State (224–651 CE). Jurisprudence had become an advanced discipline, but Iranian legal sources from the Sasanian period offer no explanations of fundamental juridical principles and institutions, nor definitions of the technical terms employed by jurisconsults in their often short, but precise commentaries. Fortunately there are far more texts at our disposal, both Iranian sources from earlier and later periods as well as foreign material, allowing us deeper insight into numerous peculiarities of Zoroastrian law and its long development, although reconstructing a coherent history of Iranian jurisprudence still seems to be an insurmountable endeavour. Legal passages and terms may be found scattered in a variety of Iranian texts, covering a time span of more than one-thousand years, reaching from Old Iranian (Avestan) material to Sogdian, Bactrian, Khwarezmian, Middle Persian (Pahlavi) and New Persian sources of the Islamic era, besides the texts produced by the Jewish and Christian communities of the Sasanian empire. The most significant legal material at our disposal stems from the late Sasanian period (7th century), in which law had already evolved into an individual discipline, based on Zoroastrianism, but distinguished from theology, with a large scope of complex intertwined institutions and a precise language of its own, allowing legal authorities to communicate accurately and concisely in their own specific jargon.

Due to the diversity of the extant material, reconstructing Sasanian law of this late period presents several difficulties. The first problem lies in the nature of the available sources: no legal codex, digest, basic commentary or systematic work on jurisprudence has survived, which could help us understand fundamental tenets of the law and the legal system of Sasanian Iran as a whole. The only extensive Pahlavi legal compilation dedicated exclusively to juridical matters, the so-called Sasanian Law-book of 'One Thousand Decisions' (see 'Sources', pp. 20–22 below), does not offer a systematic overview, but is a loose collection of complicated cases and decisions, including exceptions to the norm, with no explanations of terms or institutions whatsoever. Diverse legal fields of this complex system can, however, be reconstructed by taking all the specific details transmitted in these casuistic discussions into consideration and comparing them with earlier and later Iranian texts as well as the various reports on Iranian law in foreign sources.

The second problem has already been mentioned: legal material is dispersed in a large variety of Iranian texts and foreign sources from different periods, each of which presents its own individual philological, contextual and historical difficulties. Despite the fact that many of these sources have not yet been edited adequately, ideally all the material has to be taken into consideration in order to understand juristic developments and to achieve a coherent reconstruction of the late Sasanian legal system. This is in fact a task requiring a team of scholars from different disciplines rather than a single individual, but only very few researchers to date have dedicated their research to this field.

The third problem derives from the first: technical terminology is used with meticulous precision in the legal texts of the Sasanian period, but neither the terms nor the specifics of legal language are explained in the oldest, most relevant written records. The decipherment of legal language presents a veritable challenge, not only because there is often too little information to work with, but also because of the gradual changes that took place across the centuries, particularly the gradual vulgarization of Zoroastrian law after the downfall of the Sasanian empire and its later replacement by Islamic law. Although a few definitions, notably in the fields of family law and inheritance, are recorded in late Pahlavi and New Persian Zoroastrian texts of the Islamic period, they only seldom correspond exactly to the information we have been able to gain from the legal material of the Sasanian age, even though the same terminology is used in many cases. Due to numerous fundamental changes after the Muslim conquest of Iran, gradual alterations in the use and meanings of legal terms took place, which must be taken into consideration whilst comparing these late treatises with the Sasanian material. There is, however, an important exception: Sasanian law continued to be practiced after the downfall of the Empire in certain Iranian territories well into the reign of the Umayyad Caliphate, leaving original records of invaluable worth for our topic. The newly discovered legal documents in the Pahlavi cursive script from eighth century Ṭabarestān (see below pp. 18–20) not only correspond in their precise employment of legal language and in many other details exactly to Sasanian jurisprudence (with, as it seems, possibly a few minor administrative changes), but indisputably prove that the legal system was still very much intact in this area south of the Caspian sea in the early Muslim period. The continuing relevance of Sasanian law in the formative period of Islamic law could explain the striking similarity of several important regulations in certain fields of Islamic, particularly Shīʿite law. The emergence of many parallel institutions in Islamic jurisprudence can hardly be explained on its own without taking customary Iranian law (besides other older legal systems) into consideration (see Chapter VII, pp. 621–638).

The fourth difficulty lies in the impossibility of dating most Zoroastrian sources exactly: late compilations of the Islamic period may contain material from the very beginnings of Zoroastrian jurisprudence, whereas earlier written records of the Sasanian period could represent a more recent phase in the evolution of law. Moreover, large gaps in the transmission of the sources make it almost impossible to reconstruct an exact history of Iranian law in its different stages from its simple beginnings to its most advanced known form under the Sasanians and its gradual decline after the Arab conquest of Iran in the Zoroastrian communities of the Islamic period, but it is possible to rebuild a few developments in certain fields.[1]

A) Legal sources

Material on Zoroastrian and Sasanian law has survived in historical, religious and legal sources, text passages and commentaries, inscriptions and original documents in a large variety of different text genres. Since it is impossible to categorize many of these written records according to an exact chronology due to the reasons I have mentioned above, this short overview of the most important sources follows different criteria, grouping the texts according to language, subject matter and genres.

1 There is too little material on the legal systems of the Iranian empires before the advent of the Sasanians. The bulk of juridical sources from the Achaemenid period consists of cuneiform tablets written in the Neo-Babylonian dialect of Akkadian, reflecting age-old legal structures of the area rather than specifically Iranian law. A few legal details from the Achaemenid period are transmitted in the 5th century BCE Aramaic documents from the Jewish colony in Elephantine, Egypt (Cowley 1923; Greenfield 1977; Porten 1980), as well as in the letters of the Egyptian governor Aršama (Driver 1957; Tuplin/Ma 2020), and in other Aramaic texts (Kraeling 1953), using Iranian titles and terms (on the papyri from Egypt see also Keenan/Yiftach-Firanko/Manning 2014). To these long-known texts we can now add 30 Aramaic leather documents (and 18 inscribed wooden sticks) from ancient Bactria, near the city of Balkh, from the 4th century BCE (the final years of the Achaemenid Empire up to the year 7 of Alexander the Great) in the Khalili collection, consisting of letters and accounts connected with the court of the Achaemenid satrap of Bactria, Akhvamazda, and his governor, Bagavant (see the *editio princeps* by Naveh/Shaked 2012). Only very few texts have survived from the Parthian age, among these three parchments documenting the sale of a vineyard from Awrōmān, two in Greek, dating from 88 BCE and 22/21 BCE, one in Parthian (ca. 53 CE? See Henning 1958, pp. 28–30; Skjærvø 1995; Weber 2010, pp. 566–567; for an overview see Huyse 2009, pp. 89–90). There is far more material on ancient Iranian law in the Avestan texts, but it is unclear, whether Zoroastrian norms and regulations were adapted in some form to the legal systems of the Achaemenid and Parthian empires.

1 Original records: inscriptions, seals and Pahlavi documents in the cursive script

1.1 Inscriptions and seals

Among the inscriptions left by the Sasanian monarchs only very few supply information relevant to our topic. The great trilingual inscription of Šābuhr I on the *Kaʿba-ye Zardušt* in *Naqš-e Rostam* (ŠKZ)[2] from the third century (written between 260 and 262 CE)[3] and the Pahlavi inscription of the prime minister Mihr-Narseh in *Fīrūzābād*[4] from the fifth century are supplementary sources on legal foundations, conveying several data on pious and charitable endowments not to be found in other texts. Several technical terms, albeit without explanations, are also utilized in the four inscriptions of the famous third century High Priest Kirdīr in *Naqš-e Rağab* (KNRb), *Sar Mašhad* (KSM), *Naqš-e Rostam* (KNRm) and on the *Kaʿba-ye Zardušt* (KKZ).[5] The two inscriptions of Šābuhr I at *Hājjiābād* (ŠH) and *Tang-e Borāq* (ŠTBq)[6] and of Narseh at *Paikūlī* (NPi)[7] provide details on the structure of the aristocracy, for whom—as we may assume—many laws, particularly in the fields of family and property law, were specifically created. Seals and bullae, notably those of the administrative type, transmit titles of officials who were engaged in the administration of the Empire and in the legal system, providing information on the structure of the provinces and confirming many specifics of Sasanian rule described in other sources.[8] Although the knowledge to be gained from the inscriptions and seals is limited, they are nevertheless important both as original records from the Sasanian period as well as supplementary sources, complementing other texts which contain more detailed accounts.[9]

2 See the most recent edition of the inscription by Huyse 1999 with references to previous research.

3 On the date of the inscription see Huyse 1998, pp. 111–112, and 2009, p. 91; for an overview see Huyse 2009, pp. 91–94.

4 The short inscription, mentioning the endowment of a bridge, has been edited by Henning 1954a.

5 For a parallel overview of the inscriptions with a partly similar content see Back 1978, pp. 384–487.

6 These two parallel inscriptions of Šābuhr I transmit a hierarchy of the Sasanian aristocracy in the third century; see overview in Huyse 2009, p. 95, with further references. For a parallel reading of the two inscriptions see Back 1978, pp. 372–378.

7 Humbach/Skjærvø 1978–1983 with a detailed survey of previous research; see also overview in Huyse 2009, pp. 96–98.

8 On the administrative geography of the Sasanian Empire according to epigraphical evidence see especially Gyselen 1989, 2001, 2002a, 2019a and particularly her latest monograph 2019b, see also recently Gyselen 2024a, 2024b and 2024c.

9 On the use of seals in Sasanian administration and jurisdiction see Macuch 1997 and Chapter IV, pp. 286–301 below. For a convincing interpretation of specific titles on seals and bullae see Purwins 2019.

1.2 Pahlavi papyri and other documents from Egypt

Far more significant for our topic are original Middle Persian documents written in the ambiguous Pahlavi cursive script. An astonishing number of economic texts, administrative records, legal documents and letters written mainly on papyrus (with a few texts on parchment, linen and leather) has survived from the short period of the Sasanian occupation of Egypt (619 to 629 CE) under Husraw II (called Parwēz 'The Victorious'). The large amount of documents, produced in a relatively short period of ten years, reveals the importance attached to written records and archives in Sasanian administration, besides allowing insight into various dealings of daily life and transmitting legal technical terms and titles. Although most of the ca. 1000 items, many of them surviving only in fragments, have been already known for a long time since their discovery in the last twenty years of the 19th century, the bulk of the documents has still not been deciphered.[10] This unfortunate state of affairs is due not only to the uncertainties involved in reading the ambiguous Pahlavi cursive script and the fragmentary state of the texts, but to the sudden disappearance of a large part of the huge collection of papyri in Vienna, comprising ca. 604 items of the Austrian National Library (Österreichische Nationalbibliothek) after the Second World War. In the 1990s, after the downfall of the Soviet Union, it became known that these papyri had been transported from Berlin, where OLAF HANSEN[11] had been working on their decipherment, to the Hermitage in St. Petersburg. Apart from the Vienna collection and the second largest collection of papyri in the Egyptian Museum in Berlin (ca. 219 items), the documents from Egypt are today dispersed in various museums and libraries, mainly in Europe and the USA.[12]

1.3 The 'Pahlavi Archive'

The texts of the so-called 'Pahlavi Archive' consist of an exciting new find of documents from Iran on leather, parchment and linen from an archive near the

10 One of the oldest collections of the *Papyrussammlung* of the Austrian National Library in Vienna consisted of Pahlavi papyri brought to Vienna by TH. GRAF in 1882 from excavations in Fayyūm. The collection was continuously enlarged between 1883 and 1936, encompassing finally 604 items, see WEBER 2007, p. 729.

11 HANSEN had already published his pioneer edition of the papyri which are today in the Egyptian Museum in Berlin (HANSEN 1938) and was at that time one of the very few experts of the Pahlavi cursive script capable of deciphering the Vienna documents. His primary edition of the Berlin papyri is by now outdated and has been replaced by the new edition of DIETER WEBER (2003), who is today, besides PHILIPPE GIGNOUX, the foremost specialist on texts written in the Pahlavi cursive script. On the documents from Egypt see also WEBER's 1992 edition of ostraca and papyri and his further contributions of 1991, 2002, 2008a, 2009, 2013a.

12 For an exact list of the museums and libraries and their collections of papyri and other Pahlavi documents from Egypt see WEBER 2013a, p. 222; on the Vienna collection see WEBER 2007.

city of Qom, south of today's capital Teheran. The documents were smuggled to Europe and America in the nineteen-eighties of the 20th century and are now dispersed in two main collections: (1) the so-called 'Pahlavi Archive' of the *Bancroft Library* in Berkeley, California (USA), consisting of 260 items, and (2) the smaller collection of the Institute of Iranian Studies of the *Freie Universität Berlin* (Germany) with 30 items. A few documents are in the Los Angeles Museum of Art and dispersed in private collections in Europe and Iran.[13] As Dieter Weber has elucidated, the texts can be dated to three periods: (1) the Sasanian age, between Husraw II (590–628 CE) and the beginning of the reign of Yazdegird III (633–651 CE); (2) the early Islamic era in the second half of the 7th century, encompassing most of the economic texts and the letters; (3) a later period (after 715 CE), corresponding to the erection of the first mosques in the region of Qom. By investigating the geographical environment of the names of the villages and places mentioned in the documents he has also been able to locate them exactly in a region around Qom (*Kom*) and south of the city, which is also explicitly named in two texts.[14] Most of these documents are receipts and letters, alluding to economic matters, lists of goods and records of transfer in kind. Although the bulk of the material does not consist of legal texts (with a few interesting exceptions), the documents nevertheless enhance our knowledge of law by their use of technical terms and legal formulae in a large range of different economic records, reaching from the Sasanian period in the first half of the 7th century to the transition period immediately after the Arab conquest of Iran up to the 8th century.[15]

1.4 Legal documents from Tabarestān

Recently original legal documents written in the Pahlavi cursive script have surfaced which are most significant for reconstructing Iranian law as it was practised in the first century after the Muslim conquest of Iran. To date the collection comprises thirty-four documents of varying length from the region of Tabarestān (corresponding roughly to Māzandarān today), south of the Caspian Sea, where the Iranian legal system remained in force many decades after the downfall of the Sasanians before the formation and dissemination of Islamic law. They are dated to the 8th century, between the years 71 and 107 of the so-called post-Yazdegird era (PYE; commencing with the death of Yazdegird III

13 The documents housed in Berkeley have been edited in a series of articles by Philippe Gignoux (see particularly Gignoux 2009 and 2010 with further references). These have been partly re-edited in Weber 2014a, who is also working on the texts in Berkeley (see also Weber 2007, 2011, 2013b, 2014b, 2015, 2017b, 2019a, 2019c, 2022b). The Pahlavi documents in Berlin have been edited by Weber 2008b. For an overview of Weber's studies on documents in the Pahlavi cursive script and an extensive bibliography see the laudatio in his *Festschrift* (Macuch 2024b).

14 On dating and locating the documents see Weber 2012 and 2014a.

15 On the legal terminology in the documents in Berlin see Macuch 2008b.

in 651 CE), correlating to 722/723–758/759 CE.[16] The documents record diverse legal cases, employing the same precise legal terminology of Sasanian jurisprudence, corresponding both in content and jargon to our most important source, the Law-book of 'One-Thousand Decisions' (see pp. 20–22). The texts were first introduced to the scholarly public by PHILIPPE GIGNOUX in 2012, who, following the instructions of the proprietor, betrayed no details whatsoever on the circumstances surrounding this truly spectacular find.[17] We are fortunately now in a position to say more on the provenance of the documents. An Iranian colleague has recently informed me that the documents were found in two hand-constructed and sealed troglodytic caves, called Dīv-tāgh ('demon-arc') and Tāgh-kheneh ('arc-house'), on Mount Serkhel, located in Do-āb in the region of Savādkūh in the province of Māzandarān. The sites were excavated illegally and the documents sold by smugglers, but since only part of the caves had been explored, more texts may still be found. The circumstances of this find, among many other details, will be described in his forthcoming book (in Persian) on the Tabarestān documents.[18]

Although credit is due to GIGNOUX for detecting and being the first to tackle these difficult documents in his *editio princeps* as well as for deciphering many words and passages correctly, his edition is not the final word.[19] In the meantime all the hitherto known documents have been re-read by DIETER WEBER in collaboration with the present author and provided with a legal commentary resulting in new editions of the documents which differ considerably from GIGNOUX's preliminary work.[20] The texts consist of court records, transcripts of legal proceedings, administrative letters, contracts, records on leasehold, loan, compensation, inheritance and many other legal and administrative issues, employing

16 GIGNOUX (2012, p. 35) dates the documents between 86 and 107 of the post-Yazdegird era (PYE), corresponding to 737–758 CE, but he has erroneously read the numbers in Tab. 12 as 91 PYE (*ibid.*, p. 66) and in Tab. 13 as 93 PYE (GIGNOUX 2014, p. 38), whereas the correct readings are definitely 71 PYE (WEBER 2016b, p. 187) and 73 PYE (WEBER 2017a, p. 133) corresponding to 722/723 and 724/725 CE respectively.

17 He later adds that the proprietor excluded two of the documents (numbers 9 and 29) from publication, see GIGNOUX 2014, p. 33.

18 I am most grateful to AHMAD BAVAND SAVADKOUHI from the Foundation of Savadkouh Researches, Center of Speleology in Savadkouh, for this invaluable information (per emails of Feb. 17 and 22, 2022) and for allowing me to pass it on to the scholarly community.

19 Preliminary edition of all the available documents by GIGNOUX 2012, 2014 and 2016; on the seals attached to the documents see GYSELEN 2012a, 2012b, 2019c and especially her most recent study 2023.

20 The texts are all re-edited and commented in the series Res Orientales: WEBER 2016a and MACUCH 2016a (Tab. 1–8 and 10); WEBER 2017a and MACUCH 2017c (Tab. 13, 14, 15, 17, 18, 23); WEBER 2019b and MACUCH 2019b (Tab. 21, 22 and 24); WEBER 2020a and MACUCH 2020b (Tab. 11, 28, 27); WEBER 2022a and MACUCH 2022a (Tab. 16, 19, 20, 22bis, 25); WEBER 2016b and MACUCH 2022b (Tab. 12, 26). On the Tabarestān documents see also MACUCH 2024c.

the same legal terminology known from Sasanian law. They moreover refer to diverse matters in a manner which corresponds with the details we are able to reconstruct on various branches of law from other Pahlavi legal texts. As important primary sources they are used extensively in the following chapters.

1.5 Documents from Tang-e Bolāghī

Recently in 2019 during excavations in the province of Fārs four documents bearing clay sealings were found in a wooden box covered by a wooden plank and secured by iron bands. According to Weber 2023 (pp. 178–180) the box was found in a canyon called Tang-e Borāq, south of Isfahān, northwest of Shīrāz, but Gyselen 2024c (pp. 105–107) writing on the sealings, maintains that the box was found in another site called Tang-e Bolāghī, northeast of Shīrāz. The only document edited to date by Weber 2023 (TB 1) stems from the year 20 of King Husraw II (= 610 CE) and is a letter to a certain Zurwāndād containing specifics on the sale of grain in a contract retaining the specific form and terminology of a sale contract. The other three documents have not yet been deciphered, but convey, according to Weber, further conditions on the delivery or sale of grain in a contractual form.

2 Pahlavi legal sources: the Sasanian Law-book and the marriage contract

2.1 *Hazār dādestān* 'One Thousand Judgements'

Although we have a large scope of miscellaneous Middle Persian texts at our disposal discussing legal issues, only one Pahlavi source has survived, in which jurisprudence is dealt with as a separate, individual discipline, completely detached from theology and religious law. To judge by the material used by the compiler of this work, a great number of treatises of this kind, called *dādestān-nāmag* 'Law-books' or *čāštag* '(Legal) Commentaries', must have existed in the Sasanian period, but only this one extensive collection of legal statements and case studies has come to us in a unique manuscript, dubbed *Mādayān ī hazār dādestān* 'Book of One Thousand Judgements' by the first editor of the facsimile, but actually titled *Hazār dādestān* 'One Thousand Judgements'.[21] The work is a lengthy compilation of actual and hypothetical case-histories, collected by a certain Farroxmard ī Wahrāmān from court records, testaments and other documents kept in archives, various works on jurisprudence, legal commentaries (*čāštag*) and discussions (*Pursišn*) of jurisconsults and other long lost texts

21 The manuscript has been published in two parts in the facsimile editions by Modi 1901 and Anklesaria 1912, who called it *Mādayān ī hazār dādestān* ('The Book of One Thousand Judgements'). However, to judge by the syntax of the sentence in which the title appears, it must have originally been known as *Hazār dādestān* 'One Thousand Judgements'. On the title see Macuch 1993, p. 10f.

(these are listed in an overview in Appendix XVII, pp. 741–748 below). Why this collection of legal cases has survived, whereas presumably many others have been lost, is a mystery. We are not informed, when the compilation was undertaken, and have no further knowledge of the compiler of this important work, who may have lived in the first half of the seventh century (the last Sasanian monarch mentioned in the text is Husraw II, 590–628 CE) or maybe in later times after the Muslim conquest of Iran.[22] But no matter in which year he undertook the task of collecting this material, the sources he used are definitely from the Sasanian period, as we may conclude from several observations. Farroxmard not only cites testaments, founding documents, contracts and other legal records, often giving the names of well-known Sasanian dignitaries, but presents an extensive scope of complex case studies taken from the daily work of the courts besides noting controversies on some of the most complicated legal problems. The cited cases are taken from all three main fields of civil, criminal and court law and impart invaluable information not only on Sasanian jurisprudence, but on various aspects of everyday life as well as unique details on kinship groups and the social structure of society. It should be noted, however, that this is by no means a coherent work, but rather an eclectic mixture of statements and (at times puzzling) decisions with no attempt at systematizing the material. This could point to a rather late collection of miscellaneous texts. On the other hand, this source differs basically from late Pahlavi texts of the next two categories (see sections 3 and 4 below) in two important respects: (a) it does not mix theological, ritual and legal matters, but focuses entirely on juristic issues; (b) it employs a well-developed, precision orientated technical language without offering any

22 GIGNOUX (2012, p. 31) dates the Law-book to the 9th or 10th century, whereas ANKLESARIA 1969, p. 23, suggests that the compiler, Farroxmard ī Wahrāmān, may have been a brother of the Great Mobed (*mowbedān mowbed*) Farrbay-srōš ī Wahrāmān, of whom a *Riwāyat* from the year 377 (era of Yazdegird = 1008 CE, reckoned from the coronation of the last Sasanian monarch in 631 CE) has survived (see below). This late date has been recently taken up by KÖNIG 2019, p. 264, in his important overview of the genesis of Pahlavi literature and manuscripts (dating Farrbay-srōš's *Riwāyat* to the year 1028 CE of the post-Yazdegird era, beginning in 651 CE with the downfall of the last king of this dynasty). Despite his meticulous reconstruction of the genealogy of priestly families involved in producing Pahlavi texts (see diagram on p. 267) we have in fact no irrefutable proof that Farroxmard was indeed related to Farrbay-srōš, apart from the common patronymic Wahrāmān, which was definitely not an uncommon name. KÖNIG's overview does, however, make it rather likely that Farroxmard's work was produced within the same timespan as the rest of the Pahlavi texts. But even if we assume that the compilation emerged in the early eleventh century, there can be no doubt that the content of the work was copied or adapted from far older material, consisting of the documents and texts listed in Appendix XVII from the archives of the Sasanian era which were still available at this late period (possibly in private priestly collections) to the compiler. Besides these sources, which Farroxmard names himself in his work, the unique legal style and the precise terminology and language of the compilation, which differ considerably from that of the later *Riwāyat*s, have to be taken into consideration, as will be demonstrated in section B below (pp. 72–85).

explanations. The text sources and documents Farroxmard used were written specifically for legal experts, who were well trained in jurisprudence and had no need of definitions. These became necessary only *after* the downfall of the Sasanian State and the decline of its jurisdiction. Moreover, the complex casuistic of the Law-book points to a period, in which Iranian law was still practiced on a daily basis and judgments could be implemented by the State.[23]

2.2 *Paymānag ī kadag-xwadāyīh* 'Marriage Contract'

Another important purely legal source is the specimen of a marriage-contract (lit. 'contract on [rights and duties of] the master of the house'), included in the edition of *Pahlavi Texts* collected by JAMASP-ASANA (1897–1913). Although the date given in this specific contract points to the 13th century CE, the contents of the clauses are definitely from a far earlier age, presumably Sasanian, as we may conclude from the legal language of the contract, which corresponds precisely with that of the Law-book, showing full knowledge of all its complex implications.[24] The Sasanian provenance of this marriage-contract becomes quite obvious when compared with later Zoroastrian marriage-contracts from the Islamic period, transmitted both in Pahlavi (Pāzand) and Persian, which have no similarity to the model marriage contract in JAMASP-ASANA's collection. The ancient contract is a meticulously conceived legal document, using the precise technical terminology known to us from Sasanian jurisprudence with a mass of legal connotations and implications, whereas the later Zoroastrian marriage-contracts are very simple products of a community in which Sasanian law was obviously no longer practised or even known, even though a few random formulae and legal expressions have been conserved.[25]

23 After the important pioneer work of the German scholar CHRISTIAN BARTHOLOMAE at the beginning of the 20th century (BARTHOLOMAE 1910 and 1918–1923), who discussed several passages of the Law-book, without attempting to edit the whole text, mainly two scholars have dedicated their work to deciphering this important legal source, the Russian scholar ANAHIT PERIKHANIAN (see editions PERIKHANIAN 1973 in Russian and its English translation 1997) and the present author (editions MACUCH 1981 and 1993). Due to many different readings and interpretations of the material the editions by PERIKHANIAN and MACUCH differ in numerous respects. Whereas BARTHOLOMAE's work is by now outdated in many parts (specifically family law and succession), the edition of the whole text published by BULSARA 1937 does not comply with scholarly standards and is completely unreliable.

24 For the Pahlavi text of the marriage-contract see JAMASP-ASANA 1897–1913, pp. 141–143. The well-known edition by MACKENZIE and PERIKHANIAN 1969 is by now completely outdated. See the new edition by MACUCH 2007b with a new interpretation and discussion of the legal terminology as well as the content of the clauses.

25 The text of a New Persian Zoroastrian marriage-contract has been transmitted in UNVALA 1922, I, pp. 423,13–425,1; the Pāzand text in UNVALA, *ibid.*, pp. 418–423, and ANTIA 1909, pp. 170–174. The Pahlavi version of this late marriage-contract, which is probably a re-transcription into Pahlavi from Persian, is contained in a manuscript belonging to the collection of JAMASPASA.

Without these valuable Pahlavi sources a reconstruction of the judicial system of the Sasanian Empire would be completely impossible. They differ fundamentally from the next two groups of Pahlavi texts in that they deal with jurisprudence and legal topics as a completely separate discipline with its own precise technical language due to the separation of theology and jurisprudence (particularly in legal practice) by the late Sasanian period. Legal issues are neither mixed with theological problems nor are they discussed in the context of any other religious or ritual matters.

3 Pahlavi texts relating explicitly to the Avesta

The *theoretical* basis of Sasanian law were the sacred Old-Iranian (Avestan) Zoroastrian texts, known according to their Pahlavi designation (*abestāg/abastāg* 'praise')[26] as the Avesta, which were put to writing and translated into Middle Persian sometime in the late Sasanian period, between the 4th and 6th centuries CE.[27] Although Avestan, the language of the ritual and the sacred texts, was still in use for ritual recitations, by the time of the Sasanians both language and content of the texts had become obscure and difficult to understand even by the majority of priests who were engaged in reciting the Avestan liturgies they had learned by heart. We may assume that a large number of professional theologians and exegetes were engaged from the very beginnings of Sasanian rule in interpreting the material, but at some point it had also become necessary to translate the Avestan texts into the language of the times, Middle Persian or Pahlavi.[28] Since the content of the texts also had to be elucidated, the translations of the

26 For an overview of the various interpretations of the word *abestāg* with references to previous research see SUNDERMANN 2001. SUNDERMANN's own suggestion for translating the expression as 'testament', which has been accepted by some scholars, cannot be upheld due to several reasons, see Chapter III, fn. 227.

27 On the Avestan texts see overview by HINTZE 2009a; on the Pahlavi translation of the Avesta see CANTERA 2004 with references to previous research and an in-depth discussion of the date of the Pahlavi version and its value for studying the Avesta.

28 The question, whether Pahlavi commentaries on the Avesta existed before the sacred texts themselves were put to writing in the precise Avestan script, invented specifically for this purpose, has been discussed controversially (on problems dealing with the transmission of the Avesta see the collection of articles in CANTERA 2012). There is evidence that Avestan terms used in Sasanian jurisprudence were not only written in the unequivocal Avestan script, but also in the ambiguous Pahlavi script, *e. g.*, the Avestan term *yōhē pasčaēta*, lit. 'who (succeeds) him afterwards', designating the '(legal) successor', written ⟨'ywkh ps'cyt'⟩ (MHD 21.5; MACUCH 1993, p. 170), or ⟨w's'sy''n'⟩ Av. **vasasə.yāna-* 'who grants favours at will' (MHD 62.14; MACUCH 1993, pp. 411, 417), both only transmitted in Pahlavi script. For an extensive discussion of the latter term see MACUCH 2022c, pp. 315–317, and Appendix II, fn. 69. This could point to a long tradition of theological and legal discussions on difficult Avestan words and passages, including quotations from the original text in the Pahlavi script, which were put to writing in commentaries even before the invention of the Avestan script.

Avesta were accompanied by clarifying Pahlavi glosses and longer commentaries, containing numerous allusions to Sasanian law, which have not yet received the full attention they deserve in the context of our topic.[29] The Avestan texts together with their Pahlavi versions were known as *abestāg ud zand* 'the Avesta and its Exegesis' (that is, its Pahlavi translation-cum-commentary), a term designating the Zoroastrian religious tradition (*dēn*) in its entirety.[30]

3.1 *Dēnkard* 'Acts of the Religion'

The *Dēnkard* is a huge compendium of the 9th century, encompassing altogether nine books (the first two Books and the beginning of the third one are missing), in which a vast blend of material from different ages and origins has been assembled, creating one of the most impressive sources for the study of the Zoroastrian religious tradition (*dēn*) in its various facets.[31] Particularly Books 8 and 9 of this extensive work are dedicated to a summary of the contents of the Sasanian canon of religious texts according to their Pahlavi exegesis (*zand*).[32] This synopsis was previously believed to be a description of the canonized corpus of the Avesta of which only a small fraction of an originally huge corpus (dubbed the 'Great Avesta') has survived. The existence of a large Avestan corpus has been, however, rightly questioned and explained as a late scholastic construct. As Michael Stausberg has perceptively argued, the 21 *nasks* ('sections', see below) described in *Dēnkard* 8 are an attempt to categorize the entire Zoroastrian religious tradition (*dēn*), not alone the Avestan corpus.[33] The synopsis in *Dēnkard* 8 supports his interpretation, being based explicitly on the considerably more extensive Pahlavi exegetical literature (*zand*) rather than specifically on the Avestan original texts. This work is our main source of information on the religious tradition of the late Sasanian and early Islamic period, and—more importantly for our topic—on the legal material embedded in the sacred texts from the point of view of Sasanian (and possibly later) theologians, exegetes and jurists. Moreover, the legal sections of the Avesta summarized in Book 8

29 For an example of the work involved in using these Pahlavi commentaries as legal sources see Macuch 2012b.

30 On *abestāg ud zand* see Cantera 2004, pp. 1–13, with an extensive discussion of previous translations and explanations of the terms; *zand* might be derived from Av. *āzaiṇti-*, for which Benkato 2017 suggests an etymology from the root √*zan* 'to know', with *ā-* prefix and *ti*-suffix, meaning 'explanation, interpretation (of a sacred text)', a meaning still present in Manichaean *āzand*, a technical term for the literary genre of the 'parable'. On the etymology of the word see the overview in Hintze 2017b, pp. 51–52.

31 On the *Dēnkard* see now Rezania 2017, who maintains that it was designed entirely as an apologetic work, not intended as a Mazdean encyclopaedia, as de Menasce 1973 had assumed (p. 339). For references to editions and further research see Macuch 2009a, pp. 130–137.

32 On Book 8 see now the (Persian) edition by Fārsānī 1397/2018; on Book 9 Vevaina 2023 and 2024.

33 Stausberg 1998.

are—apart from a few chapters and passages in several extant Avestan texts—the only preserved sources on Zoroastrian law that reflect a stage in the history of Iranian jurisprudence *prior* to the legal system of the Sasanian period, albeit in a form strongly influenced by later interpretations and changes.[34] Innumerable problems have stood in the way of interpreting and translating the legal material in this important, but demanding source due to the shortness of the entries, the difficult style of the *Dēnkard*, its ambiguous phrasing, the partly unknown legal and theological terminology and the synoptical character of the text.[35]

According to the summary in Book 8, the sacred corpus of the *dēn* was divided into 21 *nask*s ('sections', lit. 'bundles') corresponding exactly to the number of words (twenty-one) in the *ahuna vairiia* (MP *ahunwar*), the holiest prayer of the Zoroastrians.[36] These were in turn categorized according to the number of verses (three) in the prayer into three groups (*bazišn*) of seven sections (*nask*) each: (1) *gāhān* 'gathic (texts)', (2) *dādīg* 'legal (texts)' and (3) *hādamāns*^{a}*rīg* '(texts) pertaining to the ritual'. Although this division into three groups of seven sections, following the holy prayer, is artificial and not all the texts of the 'legal' (*dādīg*) group actually belong in this category, their inclusion in the corpus of sacred texts reveals the importance attached to legal matters in Zoroastrianism.[37] According to one sequence in the *Dēnkard* the titles of the seven legal *nask*s are given as the following: (1) *nīgādom* < *nīkātama-* 'the lowest'[38]; (2) *duzd-sar-nizad/ōzad* ('the head of the thief struck down/severed'?); reading variants: *duzd ī druz* ⁺*tan* ('the *druz*-embodied thief'?) or *duzd ī* ⁺*drōzan* ('the lying/false thief'?)[39]; (3) *huspārom*;

34 At least three strata must be kept in mind and distinguished in using Book 8 as a legal source: the Avestan period; the Sasanian age and Muslim Iran up to the 9th century (see also Macuch 2007a, pp. 156–157).

35 The earlier attempts to offer an entire translation of Book 8 of the *Dēnkard* by West 1892 and Sanjana 1916 are by now completely outdated and unreliable. A new Persian edition of the whole text of Book 8 has been recently published by Fārsānī 1397/2018. A few sections relevant for our study are transcribed and translated in Appendices V–VII.

36 On the important implications of this division into 21 *nask*s see Vevaina 2010; see now also König 2022b, pp. 184–188. For a concise overview of the surviving parts of all the *nask*s and their content see Kellens 1989, p. 37.

37 On the legal *nask*s of the *Dēnkard* see Cantera 2004, p. 15, and Macuch 2007a.

38 According to Klingenschmitt 2000, pp. 228–229.

39 The readings suggested for the last element of ⟨GNB'-sl-n/wct'⟩ *duzd-sar-nizad/ōzad*, written ⟨n/wct'⟩, read *nigad* by West (1892, p. 74, no. 2: 'the thief's head downstricken') and *ōzad* by Cantera (2004, p. 15, no. 61) are both problematic, since the form *nizad* is not attested in extant Pahlavi texts and for *ōzad* we would expect the spelling ⟨'wct⟩ or ⟨'wzt⟩ (not ⟨wct⟩); as far as I can see *ōzad* is always written as a heterogram ⟨YKTLWN-t'⟩ in the Pahlavi texts. The title is not taken from the Avesta, but is a Pahlavi construction (see also Cantera, *ibid.*). Fārsānī 1397/2018, p. 104, has an interesting and completely different suggestion: *duzz druz tan* 'the druz-embodied thief' (my English translation; *duzz ī druz* ⁺*tan* would be a reading closer to the ambiguous script). With a slight emendation of the last word one could also reconstruct: ⟨GNB' Y ⁺dlwcn⟩ *duz(d) ī* ⁺*drōzan* 'the lying/false thief'. Since the expression does not reoccur in this section or, as far as I can see, anywhere else, it is impossible to decide, which one—if any—of these readings is correct.

(4) *sagādom* (< **uskātama-* 'the uppermost')[40]; (5) *wīdēwdād* (< **vī-daēuua-dāta-* 'law repelling the demons')[41]; (6) *čihrdād* (< **ciϑrō-dāta-* 'races created'); (7) *bayān* *⁺yašt/yasn* (< **bayanąm yašti-/yasna-* 'hymn to/worship of the divinities')[42]. Following the summary of these texts in the *Dēnkard*, we may surmise that the last two texts (*čihrdād* and *bayān ⁺yašt/yasn*) dealt predominantly with the mythical history of Iran and hymns dedicated to the divinities respectively, and hence did not contain legal material, but were included in the legal group in order to keep the neat pattern of three times seven in the formal division of the *nasks*.[43] There also seems to be another division of legal texts inherent in the sequence given here, to which we will return below.

Although the bulk of the legal material described in Book 8 is lost, a few Avestan texts with Pahlavi *zand* (translation-cum-commentary) mentioned in the *Dēnkard* have survived, revealing how juridical matters were discussed and incorporated into the religious material. Zoroastrian exegetical literature (*zand*) is a rich source of information not only on theological aspects of Mazdaism in the late Sasanian era, but on many legal institutions and norms, due to a particularly legalistic approach to religious matters.[44] In most cases the commentators of the Avesta were not only theologians but also jurisconsults, who aimed to relate the content of the sacred texts to the changed social and legal conditions of their own time, thus touching upon many details of the legal system not transmitted in other sources. It seems that the exegetes strove to accomplish two main tasks: (1) to *explain the archaic material* composed in a language no longer spoken or understood to their contemporaries, (2) to show the *continuing relevance* of the Avestan text in their own age. The Pahlavi commentaries are, however, often enigmatic, offering no explanations of technical terms and institutions, and are often only useful if the legal context is already well known from other sources. Dispersed legal material in short glosses and longer comments may be found particularly in the following three works, which are also summarized in the synopsis of the legal *nasks* in the *Dēnkard*.

40 See KLINGENSCHMITT 2000, pp. 228–229.

41 On the title see fn. 51 below.

42 The word is written ⟨yst'⟩, which could be a misspelling (?) for both *yasn* and *yašt*. On the correction to *⁺yasn* see CANTERA 2004, p. 15, no. 64. On the *bayān⁺yašt/yasn* see KÖNIG 2012.

43 According to the *Dēnkard* itself these two latter lost *nasks* were introduced by a different propitiation, indicating that they originally probably did not belong to the legal texts at all (DkD 304.6f./DkM 678.9): *ān ī ō dād pad jud šnūmanīh kard ēstēd čihrdād* (*ud*) *bayān* *⁺yašt/yasn* 'those which were added to the legal (*nasks*) with a different propitiation (are) the *čihrdād* (and) the *bayān ⁺yašt/yasn*'. There is a second list of legal *nasks* in the *Dēnkard* (with the same titles), placing these two *nasks* at the beginning of the sequence, which is strange, but confirms the assumption that their addition to the legal group was an artificial device aiming to keep the division of three times seven (MACUCH 2007a, pp. 153–154; KÖNIG 2012, pp. 361–363, has painstakingly reconstructed the content of the lost *bayān* *⁺yašt/yasn nask*). On the division of the *nasks* see now also KÖNIG 2022b, pp. 184–188.

44 See also KOTWAL/KREYENBROEK 1992, p. 20, who have rightly stressed this important aspect of *zand*-literature with respect to the *Hērbedestān*.

3.2 *Hērbedestān* 'Book of Priestly Studies'[45]

According to the Zoroastrian tradition transmitted in the *Dēnkard* the *Hērbedestān* was part of the *huspārom nask*, dedicated predominantly to ritual matters, which in turn belonged to the group of legal (*dādīg*) *nask*s of the Avesta. The text deals with the proper procedure in matters relating to religious education—obviously one of the important tasks of the Zoroastrian *hērbed* according to our text. It discusses various questions regarding the proper conduct of teachers and students in a large range of different situations, the consequences of improper behaviour as well as the legal problems that ensue when women seek religious instruction and when non-believers convert to Zoroastrianism. The Pahlavi commentary repeatedly alludes to several well-known institutions of Sasanian jurisprudence by making use of technical terms and employing the short formulae of legal language without any further explanations. Interestingly, not only the longer comments, but also many of the short glosses elucidating Avestan expressions and their Pahlavi renderings reveal by their precise use of legal terms that the exegetes made an explicit connection between the content of the Avestan text and Sasanian legislation.[46] Although it is a separate text with a different subject matter, the *Hērbedestān* is transmitted in the manuscripts together with the next work, presumably since both texts are part of the same larger division of the *huspārom nask* and clearly belong to the non-liturgical, hermeneutical or scholarly-theological tradition of Zoroastrianism.

3.3 *Nērangestān* 'Book of Ritual Directions'[47]

This long text, like the *Hērbedestān*, belonging to the non-liturgical Zoroastrian tradition, is classified in the sequence of juridical divisions as part of the *huspārom nask* in the group of legal *nask*s. It is divided into three segments (*fragard*) of varying length, concerned mainly with the Zoroastrian ritual in its various forms, consisting of two basic categories, (a) short services (the *Drōn* ceremony with a liturgy that could include the *Yašt* to the divinity of the day); (b) high rituals (always including the recitation of the *Gāthās*).[48] The text elucidates a vast blend of questions relating to ritual practice, such as the manner of

45 The title has been translated differently, see references in Kotwal/Kreyenbroek 1992, p. 15. Editions by Humbach/Elfenbein 1990 and Kotwal/Kreyenbroek 1992; see also review by Macuch 1994b and editions of chapter 5 by Hintze 2009b (Avestan text) and Macuch 2009c (Pahlavi version) and part of the long commentary to chapter 12 by Macuch 2009f.

46 On the use of technical terms and allusions to Sasanian law in the glosses and commentaries see examples in Macuch 2009c and 2009f; a longer commentary on illicit sexual intercourse from this source is in Appendix VIII, pp. 690–695 below.

47 The whole text including the Avestan and Pahlavi versions in three lengthy segments (*fragard*) has been edited by Kotwal/Kreyenbroek 1995, 2003 and 2009.

48 According to Kotwal/Kreyenbroek 2003, p. 22; on the long liturgy see Cantera 2021; on animal sacrifice Cantera 2022.

reciting individual rituals correctly, the consequences of technical mistakes, the problem of evaluating these within the framework of the Zoroastrian system of sins and offences (on these see Chapter V below), problems relating to the sacrifice of animals, the remuneration of priests for their services, and many others. Although the material to be gained on jurisprudence is not quite as evident here as in the preceding work, legal technical terms are used in the commentaries and a similarly meticulous approach to ritual matters may be observed. This is hardly surprising, given that the text of the longest segment, the second *fragard*, is based on the teaching of the commentator Sōšāns, who was also one of the most influential and renowned jurisconsults of the Sasanian period.[49] The Pahlavi commentary repeatedly goes beyond the topic of the Avestan version, expanding the discussion to include concrete legal problems Zoroastrian priests were confronted with, such as apostasy,[50] and refers in many cases *en passant* to jurisprudence by the use of legal formulae. To date still no attempt has been made to use the information on Zoroastrian law in these passages or to contextualize them within the framework of Sasanian jurisprudence.

3.4 *Wīdēwdād* 'Law Repelling the Demons'[51]

The only *nask* of the legal group (see section 3.1 above) that has been completely preserved in the Avestan original is the *wīdēwdād*, probably due to its recitation in the Zoroastrian liturgy. Although the text comprises the longest of all Zoroastrian liturgies, it not only has a liturgical function, but is one of the most important sources on Zoroastrian law of the Avestan period due to a large number of passages on legal matters. The text has come to us in two types of manuscripts, the *sāde* ('plain') type, consisting only of the Avestan text, and those with Pahlavi translation and commentary, divided into 22 sections or chapters (*fragard* 'division'). The bulk of the regulations consist of purity laws, elucidating the means of protecting Ahura Mazdā's good creation from contamination caused by the creatures or demons of the Evil Spirit, specifically by contact with dead matter (Av. *nasu-*; MP *nasā*) of any kind. Numerous other sections deal with diverse Zoroastrian norms, which in the Pahlavi *Wīdēwdād* manuscripts are translated and explained in commentaries relating to the legal system of the Sasanian period. Technical terms are scattered throughout the Pahlavi version, alluding in most sections on purity to so-called *ruwānīg* sins (predominantly chapters 3, 5–12, 16, 17, 18), offences against one's own soul, which constituted

49 See Kotwal/Kreyenbroek 2003, p. 17.
50 Kotwal/Kreyenbroek 2003, ch. 23, pp. 30–35.
51 The title of this lengthy work (< Av. **vī-daēuua-dāta-*, long misread as *Vendidad*) has been previously translated as 'Law against the Demons' or, following Benveniste 1970, 'Loi d'abjuration des Dieux'. The present rendering follows Cantera 2006, 'das Gesetz, das die *daēuua* fernhält' [lit. 'law keeping away the demons'] based on his explanation of *daēuua-* (MP *dēw*) as evil entities causing impurity (p. 62).

an important individual category of Zoroastrian law (see below pp. 62–63). The most significant passages and chapters for our purpose are those dealing with legal topics from the fields of civil and criminal law, which were connected in the Pahlavi exegesis to norms of the Sasanian period either explicitly or by employing well-known technical terms. These include—among others—sins and penalties and their categorization according to religious law (section 4), criminal offences and sins deserving death (section 15), different types of contracts and the consequences of the breach of contract (section 4) as well as a large scope of regulations on the proper treatment of converts to Zoroastrianism (section 4), persons under guardianship and beneficent animals (sections 13, 14, 15). Use is also made of legal language throughout the Pahlavi glosses and commentaries in other chapters apart from the ones cited.[52]

3.5 Pahlavi exegesis of the *Wīdēwdād* (*Juddēwdād*)

The Pahlavi version of the *Wīdēwdād* (MP *ǰuddēwdād*) transmitted in the manuscripts together with the Avestan original, is not the only surviving Middle Persian commentary to this text. It seems that in the Sasanian period there was not only one commentary—the one that has reached us in the extant Avesta-cum-Pahlavi *Wīdēwdād* manuscripts—but that several separate elucidations of this text existed, written or compiled by different authors. We know of at least two such exegetical works, one composed by the sage Mēdōmāh, who was a prominent jurisconsult of the Sasanian age with his own school of law, the most frequently cited one besides the legal school of Abarag (to which we will come back later). His exegesis is called *Juddēwdād ī Mēdōmāh* '"Law Repelling the Demons" by Mēdōmāh' and is cited several times in another Pahlavi text (the *Šāyist nē šāyist*, see 4.1 below), but has not survived as a separate text.[53] Another commentary has, however, come to us as an individual compilation

52 For an overview see Kellens 1989, pp. 39–40, and Hintze 2009a, pp. 38–46. The pioneer translations of Darmesteter 1880 and Wolff 1910, pp. 317–439, are by now completely outdated. Work on the *Wīdēwdād* has been predominantly undertaken in recent years by Alberto Cantera (Berlin) and his team, see Cantera's website Avestan Digital Archive (https://ada.geschkult.fu-berlin.de/). The Pahlavi version of the text has been translated by B.T. Anklesaria 1949 (based on the edition by Jamasp 1907) and recently by Moazami 2014 (based on the editions of Anklesaria and Jamasp). Cantera's own dissertation of 1998 (Salamanca), encompassing the first four chapters of the *Wīdēwdād*, has unfortunately not been published, but will be referred to in the following chapters. An edition and translation of both the Avestan and the Pahlavi versions of chapters 10–15 has been published by Andrés-Toledo 2016, based on the largest collation of Pahlavi *Wīdēwdād* manuscripts to date. For an extensive list of *Wīdēwdād* manuscripts, many of which have been discovered only recently see Andrés-Toledo/Cantera 2012, and the additions to this long list in Andrés-Toledo 2016, pp. 11–18.

53 Šnš 2.1: *pad sidīgar fragard ī ǰuddēwdād ī Mēdōmāh paydāg* … 'In the third section of the *Juddēwdād* of Mēdōmāh it is revealed …' (Tavadia 1930, p. 30). On the *Juddēwdād ī Mēdōmāh* see König 2010b, pp. 115–118, with quotations from the text.

with the title *Zand ī fragard ī juddēwdād* 'Exegesis of the Chapters of the "Law Repelling the Demons"', an anonymous work with a far more extensive commentary on the *Wīdēwdād* than the one transmitted together with the Avestan manuscripts.[54] This work, which has been recently edited by MOAZAMI 2021, is mainly concerned with questions of pollution, contamination and impurity, citing the opinions of about seventeen commentators and paraphrasing numerous passages from 16 chapters (*fragard*) of the Pahlavi *Wīdēwdād*.[55] Whether the text contains useful material on legal matters will have to be seen, but it does employ technical terms, which are also used in jurisprudence.

3.6 *Xorde Avesta* 'Small Avesta'

Material on Zoroastrian and Sasanian law can also be found in another collection of shorter miscellaneous works, known by the collective title *Xorde Avesta*, consisting of various types of texts in Avestan, Pahlavi (Pāzand) and Persian, which are grouped differently in the manuscripts.[56] According to KÖNIG the name given to this compilation is not derived from the Avesta, nor is it a Middle Persian designation (a collective title **Xwurdag abestāg* does not seem to have been in use in Pahlavi literature).[57] The title is a rather recent invention, not even employed in the Persian *Riwāyats* of the 15th–18th centuries (see section 5 below), for a collection of devotional texts, consisting of prayers (*niyāyišn*), blessings (*āfrīngān*), recitations for the five watches of the day (*gāh*), invocations of the divinities for the days of the month (*sīrōze*), penitential texts (*patit*) and hymns to the divinities (*yašt*), for use in daily acts of worship of both lay people and priests.[58] Allusions to legal matters and technical terms are attested in many of the short glosses and the penitential sections are particularly important for reconstructing the Zoroastrian system of criminal offences and penal law.[59]

3.7 *Frahang ī ōīm-ēk* 'Glossary (Beginning) with the Word "One"'

Short, but invaluable explanations of legal terms—besides other expressions and phrases—are transmitted in a late Avestan-Pahlavi work, not quite correctly

54 This long forgotten text was re-discovered and described by KÖNIG 2010b.

55 According to WEST, *apud* KÖNIG 2010b, p. 118. For a discussion of certain aspects of pollution in this work in comparison with Talmudic law see SKJÆRVØ/ELMAN 2014.

56 For a concise description of the *Xorde Avesta* see KÖNIG 2012.

57 KÖNIG 2012, pp. 372–373.

58 The Pahlavi texts have been edited and translated by DHABHAR 1927 (edition) and 1963 (translation); the prayers (*niyāyišn*) by TARAF 1981; the *Sīrōze* by RAFFAELLI 2014; the penitential sections (*patit*) by BUYANER 2016. On the *gāh*s see HINTZE 2007.

59 See BUYANER 2016, who discusses in his extensive commentary numerous aspects of these hitherto largely neglected texts, including technical terms and Zoroastrian penal law. On Zoroastrian penal law see also Chapter V below.

designated as a 'glossary', traditionally known as the *Frahang ī ōīm-ēk* 'Glossary (Beginning) with the Word "One"' (Av. *ōīm* 'one', explained by MP *ēk* 'one').[60] It is in fact a kind of primer elucidating Avestan words and technical terms not only by giving their Pahlavi equivalents (referring explicitly to the *zand*)[61], but also by citing Avestan phrases and including a few grammatical observations and explanations. The entries are in part extremely difficult to understand due to their shortness and the fragmentary use of Avestan phrases taken from unknown texts, torn out of context, which are in turn explained by elliptical Pahlavi sentences, by no means easier to interpret. Although the date of its compilation is not known, the text was presumably written after the invention of the Avestan script and the canonization of the Pahlavi translation and commentary of the Avesta, presumably in the 6th century under Husraw I (531–579).

***

Although Pahlavi exegetical literature (*zand*) and the other Pahlavi works described above were definitely composed in different periods (extending from the canonization of the *zand* in the late Sasanian age to the 'renaissance' of Pahlavi writings in the 9th century) to the various purposes described above, they share three common features: (a) they are based on or relate explicitly to Avestan texts and passages; (b) matters relating to religion, ritual and law are mingled and treated as an inseparable unity; (c) the approach to religious matters is decidedly ritualistic and legalistic.

4 Pahlavi 'traditions' (*Riwāyat*-literature) of the post-Sasanian period

Religious and legal treatises called *riwāyat*s or 'traditions', a term adapted for this specific genre of literature from the Arabic designation (from the base *rawiya* 'to report, narrate, transmit'), originally given to a later type of Zoroastrian texts written in New Persian in the Arabic-Persian script (see section 5 below), form the last group of relevant Middle Persian sources. The Pahlavi *riwāyat*s were mostly compiled or composed in the post-Sasanian period (with the possible exception of the first compilation, see section 4.1 below) with the main aim of preserving ancient Zoroastrian traditions and explaining complex institutions in order to keep them from disappearing altogether in the wake of

60 Editions Reichelt 1900–1901 and Klingenschmitt 1968, who has unfortunately only published a transliteration, not his excellent in-depth study in his dissertation, which has still not been replaced by a new edition.

61 The content is described as follows: *abar be šnāxtan ī wāz ud mārīgān ī abestāg kū-š zand čē ud čiyōn* 'on the recognition of Avestan words and terms, that is (on) the essence and nature of its *zand*', see Klingenschmitt 1968, p. 5f.

the fundamental changes after the Muslim conquest of Iran. Most of the texts have reached us in late redactions of the 9th–13th centuries, transmitting a large spectrum of inquiries regarding religious and legal matters put to one or several religious authorities, often also citing the interpretations of older sages or legal schools of the Sasanian period. The comments relate to doctrinal matters, purity rules, correct ritual practices, proper moral behaviour, besides legal problems, notably from the fields of family law, succession, property law and transactions with non-believers. Although the *riwāyats* strive to conserve age-old traditions, the texts themselves bear testimony to the gradual changes that took place in both legal and religious fields across the centuries when compared with older material. The most important treatises for the purpose of our topic are:

4.1 *Šāyist nē šāyist* 'Valid and not Valid'[62] and its supplementary texts[63]

This is probably the oldest extant treatise of the *riwāyat* type, an anonymous compilation known traditionally under this heading, although it does not bear a title in the manuscripts.[64] The text, which could already have been compiled in the late Sasanian or the early Islamic period, is transmitted together with a supplement, published separately by Kotwal 1969. We may assume that the anonymous author or compiler had knowledge of the Avesta or at least of its Pahlavi Exegesis, since a large number of different *nask*s are cited and he repeatedly refers to divergent opinions represented in different theological and legal schools of the Sasanian period, such as that of Mēdōmāh and Abarag. Even more importantly, his main sources were the 'teachings' or 'doctrinal works' (called *čāštag*) of theologians and jurists, whose interpretative writings are also explicitly cited in the Sasanian Law-book (see section 2.1 above), revealing a vivid tradition of scholarly debate in these fields in the pre-Islamic period. Although the *Šāyist nē šāyist* deals mainly with religious practice, particularly the ritual, grades of pollution and purification rites, it also contains material on the classification of Zoroastrian offences, the various grades of sins and their atonement (based on the *Wīdēwdād nask*) as well as scattered statements on important matters of family law and inheritance, specifically in chapters[65] 1.1–1.3 (degrees of sins and penalties); 1.3–1.4 (legal schools); 6.1 (status of disabled persons); 8.1–8.13, 8.20–23; 10.17 (sins and atonements); 8.14–8.15 ('offences against adversaries', *wināh ī hamēmālān*); 8.16 ('sins relating to the soul', *wināh ī rūwānīg*); 8.18 (significance of next-of-kin marriage, *xwēdōdah*); 10.8–10.9 (unlawful slaughter of animals); 10.18 (appointment of a false judge); 10.19 (obligation of a woman to marry); 10.21 (adoption of *čagar*-children); 10.35 (status of

62 Edited by Tavadia 1930. For a concise overview see Macuch 2009a, pp. 146–147.

63 Edited by Kotwal 1969.

64 See Tavadia 1930, p. 1.

65 Following the division in Tavadia 1930.

women as priests). More legal material is to be found in the supplementary texts, specifically chapters[66] XI (grades of sin and their atonement); XII.14 (on *čagar*-children); XVI (petty sins and their atonement); XVIII (merit of *xwēdōdah*).

4.2 *Dādestān ī dēnīg* 'Religious Judgements'[67]

Both the author of this lengthy treatise and the date of its composition are well known: Manuščihr, son of Juwān-ǰam (or according to another possible reading Gušn-ǰam[68]) lived in the second half of the 9th century, as we know from dated letters he wrote to his brother Zādspram and the latter's congregation in Sīrgān (near Kirman) in the year 880 CE. As high-priest or 'leader' (*pēšōbāy*) of the Mazdeans[69] from a family of priests, he was both 'spiritual master' (*rad*) and 'head of the guild (of priests)' (*pēšag-framādār*) of two important bulwarks of Zoroastrianism in the post-Sasanian age, Pars and Kirman.[70] As we may conclude from a dispute on a matter of purification with his brother Zādspram, who was also a priest (*hērbed*) in the subordinate ranks of the priestly hierarchy, Manuščihr was one of the extremely conservative Zoroastrian authorities of this period. We may safely assume that he was a strict traditionalist, keen on conserving established rites as exactly as possible despite the changed conditions in the Zoroastrian communities of Muslim Iran, and that he had profound knowledge of controversial positions with regard to correct purification practices and other regulations (particularly of the theological and legal schools of Mēdōmāh and Abarag, who are both cited repeatedly in his letters[71]). His work on 'Religious Judgements' is written in the traditional form of questions put to an authority (himself), followed by corresponding answers, 92 altogether, written in a difficult, tedious, lengthy and dry style, employing many religious and legal technical terms. Contrary to the argumentative style in his letters, the *Dādestān ī dēnīg* usually does not present different theological approaches, but offers authoritative judgements, which reflect the author's orthodox views on various religious subjects, from descriptions of heaven and hell and eschatological issues to matters of the ritual. Interestingly, he is *far more flexible* in his discussion of legal problems relating to those fields of

66 Following the division in KOTWAL 1969.

67 Editions by T.D. ANKLESARIA 1911 (part one, Questions 1–40) and P.K. ANKLESARIA 1958 (part two, Questions 41–92; unpublished thesis); WEST 1882 (antiquated) and JAAFARI-DEHAGHI 1998 (the first part of the text, up to question 40). Several of the legal chapters have been translated by DE MENASCE 1964a. For an overview see MACUCH 2009a, pp. 142–144; the present author has edited and discussed several legal sections from the unedited part of the Dd, see Appendices I and II; also MACUCH 2022c and 2021 a.

68 See GIGNOUX/TAFFAZOLI 1993, p. 21.

69 On the title *hudēnān-pēšōbāy* 'leader of the adherents of the Good Religion' see fn. 76 below.

70 See WEST 1882, p. xiii.

71 The *Nāmagīhā ī Manuščihr* 'Letters of Manuščihr', see overview in MACUCH 2009a, pp. 141–142, with further references.

law which were still within the jurisdiction of the Zoroastrian community in the 9th century, notably transactions with non-Zoroastrians, family law and inheritance: particularly questions 40 (on the penalty for conversion to another faith); 49, 52 (transactions with foreigners and infidels); 51 (commercial law); 53, 61 (inheritance and succession); 54 (obligations of a *pādixšāy* husband); 55–60 (family law, 'substitute succession', *stūrīh*, and guardianship, *sālārīh*); 62 (legal status of infidels); 64 (the origin of next-of-kin marriage, *xwēdōdah*); 65, 81–88 (remuneration of priests); 71–76 (sodomy, *kunmarz*); 77 (adultery).[72]

4.3 Pahlavi *Riwāyat* accompanying the *Dādestān ī dēnīg*[73]

The *Dādestān ī dēnīg* is usually transmitted in the manuscripts together with this anonymous work, which has no title and differs by its generally comprehensive style from Manuščihr's tedious work. It is best described as an anthology of Zoroastrianism, dealing with a large blend of heterogeneous topics such as cosmology, eschatology, excerpts from wisdom literature and the epic history of Iran besides questions of religious practice. It was probably written or compiled in the first half of the 10th century by a priest or maybe two redactors, who had knowledge of the Avesta, at least in its Pahlavi Exegesis.[74] Being a rather late work, it presents generally a more extensive treatment of certain topics, which were well known and hence often only mentioned *en passant* in older Pahlavi texts, such as, for example, the unique religious significance attached to the practice of next-of-kin marriage (*xwēdōdah*) and its legal consequences (chapter 8). Other sections of interest for our topic are chapters 6, 12 (on covenant-breaking); 7, 11, 15, 41 (offences and penalties); 14 (slaughtering animals); 30 (transactions with non-Zoroastrians); 34, 43 (marriage, obedience and divorce); 39 (obligations of wife and husband); 42 (acquisition of wealth and trading).

4.4 Pahlavi *Riwāyat* of *Ādurfarrbay and Farrbay-srōš*[75]

These two treatises, from the 9th and 11th centuries, written in the typical *Riwāyat*-style of inquiry and answer, are transmitted together in the manuscripts, the longer one consisting of a total of 147 questions put to the high-priest Ādurfarrbay ī Farroxzādān, followed directly by 4 questions put to the Chief Mobed (*mowbedān mowbed*) Farrbay-srōš ī Wahrāmān and—in a second sequence—another 30 questions asked of the same Farrbay-srōš with corresponding replies. The first authority, Ādurfarrbay, son of Farroxzād, is not only

72 New editions: Macuch 2022c (*Pursišn* 51) and Macuch 2024a (*Pursišn* 49 and 52); see also below Appendix II, pp. 657–663; for *Pursišn* 53–61 see Appendix I, pp. 641–656.

73 For the Pahlavi text see Dhabhar 1913. Edition by Williams 1990. For an overview see Macuch 2009a, pp. 143–145.

74 See Williams 1990, I, pp. 10ff.

75 Edition of the Pahlavi text with English translation in two volumes by B. T. Anklesaria 1969.

known as one of the two compilers of the monumental *Dēnkard*, he also held the important title of 'leader of the adherents of the Good Religion' (*hudēnān-pēšōbāy*)[76] in Pars in the first half of the 9th century, at the time of the Caliph al-Ma'mun (815–833 CE), and is one of the chief actors in the small Pahlavi treatise *Mādayān ī gizastag Abālīš* ('Book of the accursed Abālīš'), in which he answers seven theological questions asked by an apostate called Abālīš in a contest in the presence of the said Caliph.[77] The work of the second authority, the Chief Mobed Farrbay-srōš, son of Wahrām, is dated to the era Yazdegird 377, corresponding to 1008 CE (or, if it refers to the post-Yazdegird era, 1028 CE). In his *Riwāyat* Ādurfarrbay discusses a large number of legal problems relating particularly to Zoroastrian family law, but also to matters of property and credit law, areas, which obviously remained within the jurisdiction of the Zoroastrian communities after the Muslim conquest of Iran, specifically questions 1–17, 19, 73–78 (on guardianship, *sālārīh*, and different forms of marriage); 18, 21–22, 24–28, 70–71, 142 (on 'substitute succession', *stŭrīh*, and 'intermediary succession', *ayōgēnīh*); 29–30 (status of non-Iranians, *an-ēr*); 74–75, 131 (property 'for the soul', *pad ruwān*, and for 'name ceremonies', *nāmagānīh*); 13–14, 62 (contracts and agreements); 66–69 (credit law); 58–61, 72, 74, 132–139 (law of procedure). The most interesting questions in Farrbay-srōš's treatise are (in the first row of four inquiries) numbers 3 and 4 (on 'substitute succession', *stŭrīh*, and 'intermediary succession', *ayōgēnīh*). The treatise of Ādurfarrbay is particularly interesting because of passages reflecting various historical strata, from the complex legal system of the Sasanian period to the simplified jurisdiction of the Zoroastrian communities in the Islamic age. In these he refers not only to decisions of his own period, but mentions the different interpretations of authorities well known from both *zand*-literature and the Sasanian Law-book, who can be dated with a large degree of certainty to the Sasanian period. He not only uses legal terms with perfect understanding of the complex legal institutions involved and their implications, but reveals how quotations from the Avesta were used to underline rulings and how these were discussed in learned circles.[78] His work, moreover, reflects discrepancies between legal theory and practice and shows how these differences of opinion were received in the post-Sasanian period.[79]

76 On the title see B. T. ANKLESARIA 1969, II, p. 3, and BOYCE 1979, p. 147. This was a new epithet which came into being in the Abbasid period possibly in correspondence with the Muslim title *amīr al-muʿminīn* 'Commander of the faithful'.

77 According to ANKLESARIA 1969, II, pp. 1–2; 4. On this text see overview in MACUCH 2009b, p. 136, with further references.

78 On the Avestan quotations in this work see KLINGENSCHMITT 1971.

79 Unfortunately none of all this is visible in ANKLESARIA's 1969 translation, who obviously had no knowledge of legal terminology or of the Sasanian legal system. His English rendering of these parts of the Pahlavi text is mostly misleading; for examples see *Pursišn* 68 (MACUCH 2017b) and *Pursišn* 73 (MACUCH 2017a). *Pursišn* 66, 72 and 74 are edited below in Appendix IX, pp. 696–699.

4.5 *Riwāyat ī Ēmēd ī Ašawahištān* 'Tradition of Ēmēd, Son of Ašawahišt'[80]

Life in the Zoroastrian communities of the late tenth century is reflected in another important treatise known by the name of the high-priest or Chief Mobed (*mowbedān mowbed*) in 955 CE, Ēmēd, son of Ašawahišt. The text has the typical *riwāyat* structure, consisting of altogether 44 questions (put to the said high-priest by a certain Ādurgušāsp ī Mihrātaxš ī Ādurgušnasp) and the corresponding answers, dealing essentially with practical matters of the cult and the ritual, but also including legal topics from the fields of family law, property and succession, especially questions 1–4, 7–8, 18, 22–24, 31 (marriage, inheritance, 'substitute succession', *stūrīh* and 'intermediary succession', *ayōgēnīh*); 5–6 (guardianship, *sālārīh*); 25–26 (legal consequences of conversion); 27–30 (next-of-kin marriage, *xwēdōdah*). These sections on legal matters are eminently valuable not only because of the comprehensible descriptions of complex institutions known from the Sasanian period, but because Ēmēd links them to acute cases of his own age, hereby revealing how these institutions were adapted to the changed conditions of the 10th century. Moreover, his explanations have been—apart from the corresponding sections of the *Dādestān ī dēnīg* and the *Pahlavi Riwāyat of Ādurfarrbay and Farrbay-srōš*—the key to deciphering many passages of the Sasanian Law-book on marriage and inheritance, since they offer explanations and definitions of technical terms lacking in the earlier material. One must, however, bear in mind that these elucidations are both late and simplified, hence do not correspond in usage exactly to the highly complex fields of law reflected in the Sasanian sources.

4.6 *Wizīrkard ī dēnīg* 'Religious Decisions'[81]

Although this work composed in the *riwāyat* style was the first complete Pahlavi text to be printed in the Pahlavi script by SANJANA 1848, there is still no complete edition or translation, as the authenticity of the text was questioned immediately after its publication by a rival of the SANJANA family in Bombay and most of the copies were destroyed.[82] An edition is being presently prepared by DANIEL SHEFFIELD. The compilation, consisting of 121 sections, claims to have been written by Mēdōmāh, the cousin of Zoroaster, one of the prophet's first disciples, who narrates the story of Zoroaster's life in the first person in chapter 21.[83] As several priests are known by this name—among them the famous

80 The Pahlavi text has been edited by B.T. ANKLESARIA 1962 and rendered into English by SAFA-ISFEHANI 1980, whose translation is unfortunately completely unreliable. On this text see also DE MENASCE 1962.

81 SANJANA 1848.

82 See SHEFFIELD 2009, who refers to the account of these events by Madan and Katrak.

83 SHEFFIELD 2009, p. 182; for attestations of the name in the Avesta see MAYRHOFER 1979, no. 218.

commentator and founder of a theological and legal school in the Sasanian period already mentioned several times—the author of the text might have been confused with Zoroaster's disciple with the same name, but the narration in the first person can also be explained as an (unusual) literary device. It is impossible to date the work exactly, but the unusual style and repetitions from other well-known texts point to a rather late date (10th or 11th century?). The contents consist of the typical blend of religious and legal subjects already described in other works of the *riwāyat* type with quotations from the Avesta: questions pertaining to the ritual and to ceremonies of different kinds, marriage and inheritance, on Ahriman and his noxious creation, punishments, sacred fires, a genealogy of the prophet Zoroaster and an account of his life. The most important sections for our purpose are: chapters 16, 20 (inheritance); 18 (property, inheritance and divorce); 27 (status of children from a non-Zoroastrian wife); 50 (penalties for thieves, robbers and slanderers); 52 (the proper time to conclude a marriage contract); 109 (amount of property a woman may hold).

***

These treatises in the *riwāyat* style have four features in common: (a) theological, ritual and legal problems are again treated as an inseparable unity; (b) explanations of legal terms and complicated institutions are included, which are completely lacking in the material of the first group (original documents) and the second group (Pahlavi legal sources); (c) legal terminology and institutions are simplified; (d) legal controversies reflecting different schools and individual interpretations of jurisconsults are absent or reduced to an absolute minimum. The main purpose of these late works seems to have been the conservation of age-old Zoroastrian laws and customs, hence the wish to include definitions of legal terms and institutions. Being late, these explanations often do not correspond exactly to Sasanian usage due to gradual simplifications in the centuries following the downfall of the Empire, but Zoroastrian authorities were still well acquainted with the main features of Sasanian law and many specific traits of family law and succession (including the rules of 'intermediary' and 'substitute succession' as well as next-of-kin marriage within the nuclear family) were still known in the 9th to 11th centuries. Although these descriptions are significant for understanding a large number of legal institutions of the Sasanian period (and we are lucky to have them because of the deplorable lack of explanations in earlier texts), the changes they inadvertently reflect also make it crucial that they be contrasted with earlier sources of the first, second and third categories above before being called on for a reconstruction of the legal system of the late Sasanian Empire.

5 New Persian Zoroastrian 'traditions' (*Riwāyats*)

There is a huge gap of four to five centuries between the last Pahlavi treatises of the *riwāyat* type (the last known one is that of Farrbay-srōš from 1028 CE, see section 4.4 above), and the emergence of the first Zoroastrian 'traditions' in New Persian, written in the Arabic-Persian script in the 15th century. These *New Persian Riwāyats*[84] were recorded in Iran, beginning in 1478 CE (= 847 YE, beginning with the coronation of the last Sasanian monarch in 631 CE), when the Pārsīs (or 'Persians', as the Zoroastrians who emigrated to India after the Muslim conquest of Iran were called) sent a certain Nariman Hoshang with a number of questions to the religious authorities of the Zoroastrian communities in Iran asking for authoritative answers to problems relating to religious and legal matters by their co-religionists.[85] These inquiries continued for about 300 years, up to the year 1773 CE (= 1142 YE, when the last of the *riwāyats* was composed. Although these Persian texts of the 15th to 18th centuries are important sources for our knowledge of Zoroastrianism in the Muslim period, they must be used with utmost caution for our topic. Besides many particulars of religious practice they also contain simple definitions of legal terms and institutions, using the same technical terms known from Pahlavi texts in their New Persian forms in the Arabic-Persian script. Significant as they are for reconstructing the history of Zoroastrian law *after* the Muslim conquest, they also bear testimony to the dramatic changes, which took place in those legal fields that still fell under the jurisdiction of Zoroastrian communities, especially marriage, family law and inheritance, in the centuries after the Pahlavi script was abandoned. Although the texts continue to use Sasanian legal terminology, the connotations and implications of the terms no longer correspond in most cases to the earlier stages of Zoroastrian law, neither to the institutions of the Sasanian period, nor to those described in the Pahlavi *riwāyats* of the 9th and 10th centuries. This is particularly true of Zoroastrian family law and marriage, which had obviously altered considerably by the 15th century, when the first Persian *Riwāyats* were composed, undergoing changes typical for a legal system which is no longer carried by a state and has definitely become the law of a religious minority. The whole structure of succession and inheritance, conceived to serve affluent aristocratic lineage groups in the Sasanian period, had become superfluous by this time and complex technical terms in this field were not only further simplified, but even explained differently.[86] Despite the huge discrepancies, the Persian

84 The Persian text of one of the longest compilations of *riwāyats* has been published by UNVALA 1922 in two volumes and partly translated into English by DHABHAR 1932.

85 UNVALA 1922, I, Introduction, p. 2.

86 For example, the Pahlavi terms *ayōgēn* ('intermediary successor') and *stūr* ('proxy; substitute successor') belong to the field of succession (see Chapter II, pp. 163–174) and designate persons acting as proxies within the framework of complex institutions with the obligation to generate a son for a sonless man. In contrast, the corresponding forms in

Riwāyats cannot be discarded as a source altogether, since they also show, on the other hand, in several respects an astonishing continuity of ancient customs, traditions and legal prescriptions, many of which can be traced back to the Sasanian period (for example, the general scheme of succession, which includes females[87], and the amount of shares due to the heirs, among other customs). Following sections are of interest for comparison with Sasanian law: on breaking contracts (*mehr-drūǰ*)[88]; giving the oath (*sōgand nāmeh*)[89] and evidence[90]; loans and interest[91]; transactions with infidels, unlawful trading and acquisition of wealth[92]; ten segments on family law, marriage, divorce and inheritance[93]; adultery[94]; 'sin of the opponents' (*hamēmāl*)[95]; next-of-kin marriage (*xwēdōdah*)[96] and marriage ceremonies and contracts.[97]

6 Early Judaeo-Persian legal texts

Early Jewish-Persian or Judaeo-Persian is the designation for the New Persian language, spoken by the Jews in Iranian territories and their environment between the 8th and 12th centuries CE and written in Hebrew characters. Most of the texts of the small corpus of early Judaeo-Persian texts were found in the late 19th century in the storage-room of the synagogue in Cairo (the 'Cairo Geniza') and are now dispersed in various libraries and museums. Another sensational discovery was made quite recently in 2011, when villagers found a cache of fragmented Jewish-Persian manuscripts (among others) in a cave used by the *Ṭālibān* in Afghanistan (dubbed the 'Afghan Geniza'). The texts consist of a large range

the New Persian *Riwāyats* (*ayūk/ayūkān* and *stor/star/satar* respectively) are re-defined as two types of wives in different forms of marriage (see the Persian text in Unvala 1922, I, pp. 180–182; translation by Dhabhar 1932, pp. 195–196). Although I have already mentioned the obvious discrepancy between the use of these terms in Sasanian law and in the Persian texts more than forty years ago (Macuch 1981, p. 8), there are still anachronistic attempts to reconstruct Sasanian marriage law on the basis of the definitions given in the New Persian *Riwāyats*!

87 On the similarities to Shīʿite law, which contrasts sharply with the Sunnite law of succession, but corresponds in this respect perfectly with Sasanian and later Zoroastrian law see Macuch 2017d and Chapter VII, pp. 632–638.

88 Unvala 1922, I, pp. 42–44; Dhabhar 1932, p. 37.

89 Unvala 1922, I, pp. 45–54; Dhabhar 1932, pp. 39–51.

90 Unvala 1922, I, pp. 55–56; Dhabhar 1932, pp. 51–53.

91 Unvala 1922, I, pp. 54–55; Dhabhar 1932, pp. 51.

92 Unvala 1922, I, pp. 57–59; Dhabhar 1932, pp. 54.

93 Unvala 1922, I, pp. 173–189; Dhabhar 1932, pp. 179–204.

94 Unvala 1922, I, pp. 196–202; Dhabhar 1932, pp. 208–210.

95 Unvala 1922, I, pp. 202–204; Dhabhar 1932, pp. 210–211.

96 Unvala 1922, I, pp. 307–309; Dhabhar 1932, pp. 292–294.

97 Unvala 1922, I, pp. 418–425. Dhabhar 1932 has not translated this part of the text. On the New Persian *Riwāyats* see also Vitalone 1987 and (in Persian) Dālvand 1391/2015 with a detailed description of the manuscripts.

of various topics and genres, including religious commentaries, medical topics, magical invocations, letters and legal documents. Although the legal material prior to the find in Afghanistan has already been edited and known for some time, it has still not been examined in the context of Iranian law. Being the only available sources for studying the development of New Persian in the transition period between Middle and New Persian, the early Jewish-Persian records are of particular linguistic interest and have been mainly analysed in this context. The legal sections of this material, however, also show astonishing similarity in the use of juridical terms and formulae to the newly found Tabarestān documents (see section 1.4 above), on the one hand, and to Sasanian usage, on the other, and could testify to the continuity of customary juridical practice, based on the legal system of the Sasanian Empire, in the transition period after the Muslim conquest.[98] This is hardly surprising if we take into consideration that the large Jewish communities in Iran and specifically in Mesopotamia were subject to the law of the Empire during Parthian and Sasanian dominion over Babylonia and that the main corpus of Rabbinic law, the Babylonian Talmud, was produced in this period, absorbing several tenets of the Iranian legal system and adapting technical terms (see section 10 below and Chapter VII, pp. 590–608). The most significant published Jewish-Persian sources for our topic are: (a) The 'Jewish-Persian fragment from Dandān-Uiliq' (in the northeast of the Khotan oasis), a fragment of a business letter from the second half of the 8th century, dealing with the trading of sheep (and possibly also clothing and slaves), in which a few legal terms are attested.[99] (b) The 'Law Report from Ahwāz', dated to 1020 CE, documenting a quarrel on the illicit sale of purloined property.[100] (c) The 'Jewish-Persian argument', an early text, not dated, but written definitely before the 12th century, expounding—as the title indicates—an argument in favour of the prophethood of Moses, with archaic vocabulary, including a large number of terms and formulae also attested in Pahlavi legal literature.[101] The letters and legal documents found recently in Afghanistan have still not been published, but promise to further enhance our knowledge of customary Iranian law as it was practised in the Jewish communities between the 8th and 12th centuries.

98 For a comparison of a recurring formula in the Tabarestān court records and in the text of the so-called 'Jewish-Persian argument' see MACUCH 2016a, p. 149.

99 Edition of the fragment by UTAS 1968 with further references.

100 See ASMUSSEN 1965–1966 with references to previous research and an annotated glossary of words contained in the 'Law Report', but no translation, and MACKENZIE 1966 with a translation of the text.

101 The text has been edited by MACKENZIE 1968, who, based on the linguistic evidence, correctly assumes that it should be dated earlier than the 12th century (p. 249).

7 Sogdian and Bactrian legal documents

Legal documents and letters, containing economic and juridical material, have also been found in two other Middle Iranian languages, Sogdian and Bactrian, which have—apart from a few isolated attempts—not yet been compared to Sasanian law or been taken into consideration as sources for a reconstruction of the legal conditions at the time of their composition in the eastern territories of Sogdiana (corresponding roughly to Tajikistan and Uzbekistan today) and Bactria (in northern Afghanistan today). Although both regions were for a long time independent, they became part of the Sasanian Empire sometime in the 3rd century and were ruled for roughly one-hundred years by Sasanian officials between the 3rd and 4th centuries.[102] Despite divergences (which become obvious when we compare the surviving marriage contracts), there seem to be, on the other hand, several very similar features, including certain formulae and terms known from Pahlavi juridical texts, in both the Sogdian and Bactrian documents. This could point either to a common historical legal ancestor or to a parallel development or to adaptions from Sasanian law or to the mutual interaction of neighbouring legal systems in the Middle Iranian period (or to all four of these possibilities). Be it as it may, an in-depth comparative study of the legal sources is still lacking due to immense philological and contextual problems, many of which still remain to be solved despite the admirable efforts of some of the foremost scholars of Iranian Studies.

7.1 Sogdian documents

Sogdian merchants and traders used the excellent strategic location of Sogdiana between the two main rivers of Central Asia, the Oxus (*Amū-daryā*) and Jaxartes (*Sīr-daryā*), with its ancient capital Marakanda (Samarkand) on the so-called Silk Roads for their trade interests and founded numerous colonies along the famous trading routes between China, India and Iran.[103] Sogdian became a kind of *lingua franca*[104], used not only for correspondence in mercantile matters with the home land, but as a vehicle for transporting cultural achievements, ideas and religions between the countries. Besides many Manichaean, Christian and Buddhist manuscripts in the Sogdian language, bearing witness to the religious

102 The exact dates depend on how the starting point of the Bactrian era is calculated (see section 7.2 below on the Bactrian documents). Šābuhr I in his *Kaʿba-ye Zardušt* inscription already puts claim to territories in Bactria and Sogdiana (ŠKZ 3; Huyse 1999, I, §3, p. 24) and certain territories of the Kushan Empire were annexed after the campaigns of Šābuhr II in 356 CE.

103 Sogdiana is already mentioned in Avestan literature and in the Old Persian inscriptions, see attestations in Szemerényi 1980, p. 26f.

104 Sogdian as the *lingua franca* of the Silk Road(s) was later replaced in the Islamic period by Persian, revealing the continued importance of Iranian traders along these routes connecting East and West, see Fragner 1999.

activities of the Sogdians in these regions, inscriptions and other original documents have also been found, all of immense importance for reconstructing the history of the territories and communities along the Silk Roads. The oldest historical documents relevant for our topic, known as the 'Ancient Letters', are a group of five letters and a few fragments of three further letters, written on paper, which were discovered by Sir AUREL STEIN 1907 among the ruins of a barracks in a watchtower of the Chinese Wall between Dunhuang and Loulan, and have been dated between 313 and 314 CE.[105] Besides containing unique information on the settlements and the Sogdian network of caravans along the Silk Road, the letters convey bits and pieces of information on financial and legal matters, referring, for example, to monetary and testamentary dispositions (letter II) and to a loan (letter V).[106] Admittedly, these legal allusions are short and to the point, but they do convey the impression that the Sogdian traders and merchants on the Silk Roads relied on a well functioning legal system, possibly based theoretically on Iranian (Zoroastrian) law and linked in some manner to the Sasanian legal system, to support and promote their business transactions.

More fruitful for comparison with Sasanian legal texts is a group of documents from the 8th century, discovered by Russian archaeologists in 1933 and the following years in the ruins of a fortress located on Mount Mugh in northwestern Tajikestān, east of Samarkand. Some 75 documents in Sogdian were found in the course of the excavations, known as the 'Mugh (or Mug) Documents', consisting of financial records, legal texts (contracts) and letters in the archives of the Sogdian prince Dēwāstīč, the last ruler of Penjikend, and other Sogdian nobles, who were killed by the Arab conquerors of Sogdiana after the siege of the fortress in 722 CE.[107] The legal documents—which are not the only

105 The dating of the letters has been discussed controversially for a long time, after the date proposed by HENNING 1948, placing them in the 4th century, between 312–313 CE, had been questioned (for a detailed overview of the discussion with references to previous research see GRENET/SIMS-WILLIAMS 1987). In the meantime convincing arguments have been brought forward by GRENET/SIMS-WILLIAMS/DE LA VASSIÈRE 2001, pp. 101–102, for assuming that HENNING's fourth century proposal was correct and the letters should be dated, only with a slight change, to the years between 313 and 314 CE. On the date of the letters see now GRENET 2023, pp. 63–69.

106 For an overview of the 'Ancient Letters' see SIMS-WILLIAMS 1985. A preliminary edition of the letters was prepared by REICHELT 1928–1931; new editions of the letters were published mainly by SIMS-WILLIAMS 2001a (letter II), 2001b (letter V), 2005a (letter I), 2017 (letter IV) and GRENET/SIMS-WILLIAMS/DE LA VASSIÈRE 2001 (letter V). SIMS-WILLIAMS' most recent edition of 2023 is now intended to supersede all his previous editions and translations of the Ancient Letters I–V (p. 25). On the historical background of the letters see GRENET 2023, pp. 63–69.

107 The scholar who succeeded in making the decisive breakthrough in deciphering these difficult documents is VLADIMIR ARONOVICH LIVSHITS, who based his research on the later form of Sogdian, Yagnobi, and published a preliminary edition in Russian (LIVSHITS 1962). The documents themselves were published in the *Corpus Inscriptionum Iranicarum* Series as facsimile by BOGOLYUBOV/LIVSHITS/SMIRNOVA 1963. Taking

interesting ones for our topic, since the letters and the financial records also contain administrative titles and legal terms—include the longest surviving legal text in the Sogdian language, a marriage contract (Nov. 3) with an accompanying guarantee letter (Nov. 4)[108]; an agreement for the sale of a cemetery building (B-8)[109] and an agreement for the sale of three mills (B-4)[110]. To these legal texts we may add another new find, the contract for the sale of a female slave in Sogdian, discovered in the Turfan area.[111]

7.2 Bactrian documents

Greek reign in Bactria was terminated in the second half of the 2nd century BCE by the Kushans of the nomadic tribe of the *Yüeh-čih* (according to Chinese sources) from North Central Asia, who invaded this region and established their rule. The ethnical provenance and original language of the Kushans is unknown, but by the time of King Kanishka I (2nd century CE) at the latest they used both the Iranian language of Bactria and the Greek script for their written records. For a long time only a few inscriptions in Bactrian were known,[112] but since the 1990s a series of sensational finds have come to light, which have not only revolutionized our hitherto fragmentary knowledge of the Bactrian language, but promise far more insight into the legal and economic history of Bactria in late antiquity than was hitherto possible. Besides the *Rabāṭak* inscription, important for dating the Kushan kings,[113] more than 150 legal and financial documents in the Bactrian cursive script, derived from the Greek script, have come to light, written on leather, linen and wood, which were offered for sale in the bazaar of Peshawar and in the antique market. Most of the texts are from the environment of Rōb (Rūī today) in the northern Hindukush, a smaller

the research of more than three decades after the publication of his standard edition into consideration, LIVSHITS later prepared a new, revised Russian edition of the Mugh documents (LIVSHITS 2008), which was translated by TOM STABLEFORD into English and edited by SIMS-WILLIAMS with additional notes and his own suggestions (LIVSHITS 2015). The first Mugh document and the marriage contract were also re-edited by YAKUBOVICH 2002 and 2006.

108 LIVSHITS 2015, pp. 17–36; on the marriage contract see also YAKUBOVICH 2006 with references to previous research.

109 LIVSHITS 2015, pp. 37–43.

110 *Ibid.*, pp. 44–52.

111 According to YAKUBOVICH 2006, p. 308 (referring to an article in Japanese by YOSHIDA/MORIYASU 1988).

112 A few fragmentary inscriptions in Surkh Kotal in North Afghanistan were found in 1954; the longest inscription in Bactrian, the *Kanishka* or *Nokonzok/Nukunzak* inscription, in 1957

113 On the importance of the *Nokonzok/Nukunzak* inscription together with the *Rabāṭak* inscription (discovered 1993 in the Afghan province of Baghlan) for the chronology of the Kushans see SIMS-WILLIAMS/DE BLOIS 1998. The decipherment of the *Rabāṭak* inscription was not only crucial for dating the Kushan kings, but also for deciphering the legal documents, see SIMS-WILLIAMS/CRIBB 1996.

group from Gūzgān/Jūzǰān, somewhat more to the north-west. The documents stretch across several centuries and are dated in an unknown era, beginning with the year 110 up to the year 549. NICHOLAS SIMS-WILLIAMS, to whom we owe the main work of decipherment, initially fixed the beginning of this era (named the 'Kushano- Sasanian era') at 233 CE, the assumed date of the conquest of the Kushan Empire by the Sasanians (which would mean that the Sasanians ruled over Bactria between 233 and 380 CE), dating the documents between 342 and 781 CE correspondingly.[114] Together with DE BLOIS he later revised this assumption and suggested the year 223 as the starting point of the Bactrian era, based on the establishment of the Sasanian Empire under Ardašīr I (dubbed 'the Sasanian era').[115] The records include legal texts, contracts and receipts, endowment documents, a deed of manumission, a marriage contract as well as financial records, lists, accounts and letters; two Buddhist texts have also survived.[116] The most important documents for our purpose are (following SIMS-WILLIAMS' categorization): A (marriage contract)[117]; C, T, Tt (deeds of gifts)[118]; D (statement of produce due from an estate)[119]; F (deed of manumission)[120]; I, Ii, J, L, m, U, V, W, aa, ab, Nn (contracts for purchase or lease of estates)[121]; P (contract for the purchase of a slave)[122]; K, Q, Ss, ac (loan contracts)[123]; Aa, B, E, G, H, M, an (receipts)[124]; N, O, R, S, Uu, X (undertakings to keep the peace)[125]; Y (judicial

114 SIMS-WILLIAMS 2002, p. 231.

115 See DE BLOIS 2006; SIMS-WILLIAMS/DE BLOIS 2005 and REZAKHANI 2010, pp. 194–195 (who objects to this dating).

116 For an overview see SIMS-WILLIAMS 1997 and his important editions of the documents 2000 (legal and economic texts), 2007 (letters and Buddhist texts), 2012a (a revised edition of the legal and economic documents) and 2012b (plates of all the Bactrian documents). Three of the documents from Jūzjān (O, R and S) are included in the editions of 2000 and 2012a; all of the Jūzǰān documents have been edited in SIMS-WILLIAMS 2005b. For a list of his numerous contributions to the decipherment of the Bactrian documents (up to 2009) see his Festschrift, edited by SUNDERMANN/HINTZE/DE BLOIS 2009, p. XXXIIff.

117 SIMS-WILLIAMS 2000, pp. 32–35; 2012a, pp. 26–29.

118 SIMS-WILLIAMS 2000 (C) 38–41, (T) 98–105; 2012a (C) 32–35, (T) 98–103, (Tt) 104–105; 2005b (Tt) 18–19.

119 SIMS-WILLIAMS 2000, pp. 42–43; 2012a, pp. 36–37.

120 SIMS-WILLIAMS 2000, pp. 44–47; 2012a, pp. 38–41.

121 SIMS-WILLIAMS 2000 (I) 50–51, (Ii) 52–53, (J) 54–61, (L) 64–71, (U) 110–113, (V) 114–125, (W) 126–135, (aa) 148–150, (ab) 150–151; SIMS-WILLIAMS 2012a, (I) 44–45, (Ii) 46–47, (J) 48–55, (L) 58–65, (Nn) 74–79, (U) 106–111, (V) 116–125, (W) 126–135, (aa) 146–149, (ab) 148–149; SIMS-WILLIAMS 2005b, (Nn) 12–13.

122 SIMS-WILLIAMS 2000, pp. 82–87; 2012a, pp. 84–87.

123 SIMS-WILLIAMS 2000, (K) 62–63, (Q) 88–91, (ac) 152–153; SIMS-WILLIAMS 2012a, (K) 56–57, (Q) 88–91, (Ss) 96–97, (ac) 150–151; SIMS-WILLIAMS 2005b, (Ss) 18–19.

124 SIMS-WILLIAMS 2000, (B) 36–37, (G) 48–49, (H) 48–49, (M) 72–73; SIMS-WILLIAMS 2012a, (Aa) 30–31, (B) 30–31, (E) 36–37, (G) 42–43, (H) 42–43, (M) 66–67, (an) 152–153.

125 SIMS-WILLIAMS 2000, (N) 74–79, (O) 80–81, (R) 92–93, (S) 94–97, (X) 136–143; SIMS-WILLIAMS 2012a, (N) 68–73, (O) 80–83, (R) 92–93, (S) 94–97, (Uu) 112–115, (X) 136–141; SIMS-WILLIAMS 2005b, (O) 14–15, (R) 14–15, (S) 16–17, (Uu) 20–21.

declaration in the form of an open letter)[126]; af–al (lists and accounts)[127]. After the impressive philological work of decipherment by SIMS-WILLIAMS several studies have appeared on the content of the documents as well as legal terms and formulae including comparisons with Sasanian law.[128]

8 Khwarezmian legal texts

The ancient Iranian language of Khwarezmia (or Choresmia, north-west of Sogdiana) was still in use up to the 14th century before it was definitely replaced by Turkish. Besides coins, inscriptions, documents on leather and wood (from the 3rd century) and funerary inscriptions from the 7th and 8th centuries (in Middle Khwarezmian), the main body of surviving material (in late Khwarezmian) consists of some 400 legal sentences, phrases and glosses, written in the Arabic script and incorporated into several Arabic works, mainly the 12th century *Muqaddimat al-ʾadab* 'Prologue on Good-breeding', of az-Zamaḫšarī (1075–1144 CE) and two treatises on jurisprudence, by al-Ḫwārezmī (*Yatīmat ad-dahr fī fatāwā ʾahl al-ʿaṣr* 'The Unicum of the Age Concerning the Legal Decisions of the People of the Period') and by az-Zāhidī (*Qunyat al-Munya* 'The Acquisition of the Object of Desire'), both from the 13th century. This unique material not only reflects traditional local legal practise in Khwarezmia, but uses a number of Iranian technical terms, which are known from Pahlavi legal literature and could indicate a similar juridical background or even some kind of historical connection to the law of the Sasanian Empire. The Khwarezmian material was rediscovered by the Turkish scholar AHMED ZEKI VELIDI TOGAN (1890–1970), who extracted the Iranian passages from a series of Arabic *fiqh*-texts, mainly those named above, and was studied predominantly by HENNING and MACKENZIE, who both focused their work on the linguistic phenomena.[129] The legal connotations will still have to be studied.

126 SIMS-WILLIAMS 2000, pp. 144–145; 2012a, pp. 142–143.

127 SIMS-WILLIAMS 2000, pp. 156–163; 2012a, pp. 156–165.

128 See especially SHEIKH 2023 on the Bactrian legal documents. YAKUBOVICH 2006 has compared the Sogdian, Pahlavi and Bactrian marriage contracts, but he still used the now completely outdated edition of MACKENZIE/PERIKHANIAN 1969 (see the new edition of the marriage contract MACUCH 2007b). On the economic documents see REZAKHANI 2010. For a preliminary attempt to understand the use of legal terminology in comparison with Sasanian law see MACUCH 2008b. On the Bactrian texts of the Islamic period see also AZAD 2016.

129 For an overview of the Khwarezmian material see MACKENZIE 1983. The history of the rediscovery of the legal passages is recounted in MACKENZIE 1989 and 1990, pp. 1–3, with references to previous research. An edition of the Khwarezmian material in the Arabic text of the *Qunyat al-Munya* has been published by MACKENZIE 1990.

9 Legal sources in Syriac

The Christians of the Sasanian Empire, known as East Syrian (or Nestorian) Christians, constituted the most prominent religious minority apart from the Jews. Although they were persecuted in certain phases of Sasanian history, specifically after 340 CE during the reign of King Šābuhr II (309–379), and sporadically up to the middle of the 5th century, in 410 CE the sovereign Yazdegird I (399–421) acknowledged the Church of the East and seems to have even sanctioned the construction of churches, martyr's shrines and monasteries, obviously accepting Christians as non-Mazdean members of the large Empire with a status similar to that of the Jews.[130] By the 6th century under Husraw I (531–579), Christians had definitely found their place in the political hierarchy of the Empire by cooperating with the Zoroastrian ruling elite and participating in Sasanian institutions, although individual Christians and their leaders could be and still were prosecuted for criminal offences by the State. Syriac literature, composed by Christians in the Sasanian period, is not only singularly important for reconstructing the life of this religious minority in late antiquity, but presents a rich treasury of contemporary information on the political and social history of the Sasanians, including many administrative details not to be found in other sources. A large number of works on the martyrdom of Christians with drastic descriptions of their sufferings also transmit details on the trials held against them during these waves of persecution (which seem to have had a political and economic background rather than being the result of religious intolerance alone).[131] Apart from these texts with information on criminal proceedings initiated by the State, several legal works have also reached us, designed to regulate issues of civil law in the Christian communities of the Empire. These were based almost completely on Sasanian law with the sole exception of those juridical fields incompatible with Christian standards. Interestingly, despite the fact that Mazdean tenets were refuted in certain areas, particularly in the field of family law and inheritance, the impact of Sasanian law still remains visible, since even the divergent regulations were formulated with reference to and in direct rejection of Zoroastrian norms (see sections 9.1. and 9.2. below and Chapter VII, pp. 620–621).

130 On the Christians of the Sasanian Empire and their status within the political hierarchy see Payne 2015b.

131 See Payne 2015b, pp. 38–48, who convincingly argues that the 'great persecution' of Christians under Šābuhr II was more a matter of internal politics rather than religious intolerance, the main cause being the refusal of the Christian Bishop to cooperate in the levying of taxes, which constituted an act of contumacy against the State liable to punishment.

9.1 'Marriage Law' and 'Vita' of the Patriarch Mār Abā

Mār Abā, the author of the first Christian 'Marriage Law', was Catholicos of the church of the East from 540 to 552 during the reign of the Sasanian King Husraw I (531–579).[132] He is one of the remarkable personalities of the 6th century, whose life and reforms are exceptionally well documented both in his own canonical writings and in an account of his life, which not only conveys interesting details on Sasanian criminal proceedings, but allows insight into the political intrigues and conflicts at King Husraw's court. One of the intriguing aspects of his life is—according to his 'Vita'—the astonishing fact that Mār Abā was prior to his conversion to Christianity a Zoroastrian, probably of noble descent, who worked as an official of the State in the service of the King.[133] After his conversion and election as head of the church he gained fame for being the first to establish Christian marriage laws in explicit refutation of the Zoroastrian law of matrimony. Being well acquainted with both Zoroastrian religious norms and Sasanian family law, he shows the exceptional zeal of a convert in refusing any compromise with the Mazdean clergy, but betrays, on the other hand, his Zoroastrian origin by demonstrating a legalistic approach to religious matters and initiating an individual set of precise rules for Christians. Because of his steadfast propagation of Christianity and his strict handling of legal issues he was prosecuted by the Mazdean clergy with a series of very serious accusations, which are recounted with remarkable details on Sasanian criminal proceedings in his 'Vita'.[134] His 'Marriage Law' includes a long list of conjugal alliances forbidden to Christians, inadvertently giving insight into the most important Zoroastrian marital relationships and indirectly confirming for the 6th century the information on Sasanian family law transmitted in Pahlavi sources. He not only attacks Zoroastrian customs, but important legal institutions of Sasanian jurisprudence by forbidding almost all the significant endogamous matrimonial bonds, which played a crucial part in the law of succession, with far-reaching social and political consequences. Unsurprisingly, one of the main accusations of the Mazdean clergy against the Catholicos refers to his strict marriage laws, which also must have had an enormous impact on the organization of Zoroastrian kinship and lineages, when individuals, like Mār Abā himself, converted from Zoroastrianism to Christianity.[135]

132 See Sachau 1914, pp. 255–285, for both the Syriac text and German translation of Mār Abā's 'Marriage Law'.

133 The Syriac text of his 'Vita' has been edited by Bedjan 1895, pp. 206–274, and translated by Braun 1915, pp. 188–220. For studies of his life see Peeters 1951, Pigulevskaya 1963, Hutter 2003.

134 On the trial against Mār Abā in the light of Sasanian law see Macuch 2014c.

135 On the legal and political significance of Mār Abā's 'Marriage Law' see Macuch 2014c, pp. 52–53, and below Chapter II, pp. 155–157.

9.2 'Corpus Iuris' of the archbishop Īšōʿbōxt

The Law-book of Īšōʿbōxt (Jesubōxt; lit. 'saved by Jesus'), archbishop of the Christians of the province of Pars in the 8th century, is not only the most extensive surviving legal text, encompassing all fields of jurisprudence (of which only a few are lost[136]), but one of the most significant Syriac sources for reconstructing especially those branches of Sasanian law, which are largely missing in Pahlavi literature.[137] Īšōʿbōxt composed his Law-book for the use of the Christian community of Pars, basing it almost entirely on legal practice and the age-old Sasanian judicial system, which was still largely in force in eighth century Iran. Nothing further is known of the author of this work, apart from the few details transmitted in the Corpus Iuris itself. From these the editor, Eduard Sachau, has deduced that he wrote originally in Middle-Persian, using either the Syriac or the Pahlavi script.[138] The original Pahlavi version of the text is unfortunately lost and only the anonymous Syriac translation has survived, which was undertaken at the instigation of the Nestorian patriarch Timotheos, living from 780 to 823 in Baghdad, at a time when Īšōʿbōxt was not longer alive.[139] Although Īšōʿbōxt's work employs the precise legal terminology of Sasanian jurisprudence, incorporating invaluable explanations of technical terms, most of them have been rendered into Syriac. Despite this drawback, it must be said that the translator did his very best to choose the exact Syriac equivalents of complex terms and coped in a masterly manner with elaborate legal trains of thought. If a technical term was too multi-layered to be rendered by a single word and the translation would not have conveyed the exact meaning of the original, he refrains from translating it altogether and retains the original Iranian expression.[140] To judge by the legal terminology, both in translation and in the Iranian original, the only branch of jurisprudence diverging from Mazdean customary law seems—unsurprisingly—to have been marriage and inheritance, both refuted vehemently by Īšōʿbōxt, specifically in his section on the law of succession (chapter IV), in which he describes Zoroastrian mores in detail. But even in this field hidden adaptations from Iranian law may be detected (see Chapter VII, 2.2, pp. 615–620). Despite the evident Sasanian provenance of most other regulations, this work has still not been studied intensively as a complementary source to Pahlavi legal literature.

136 On the missing branches of law in Īšōʿbōxt's Corpus Iuris see Sachau 1914, Intr., p. XIV.

137 See Sachau 1914, pp. 1–201; on Īšōʿbōxt's date in the second half of the 8th century (around 775–779 CE) see *ibid.*, Intr., p. IX.

138 *Ibid.*, Intr., pp. VIII–XVII.

139 *Ibid.*, pp. XV and 289.

140 A few of these expressions have been discussed by de Menasce 1969. On the Iranian technical terms in Īšōʿbōxt's work see also Macuch 1989 (on *abēsaxwan*, a term that also occurs in the Bactrian legal documents) and Macuch 2019a (on *wehdādestānīh*). See also below Chapter VII, pp. 609–614.

9.3 ‘Law of Succession’ of the archbishop Simeon

The third legal tractate produced in Iran is another Syriac translation of a Middle-Persian original, written by Mār Simeon, archbishop of Rēw-Ardašīr, probably in the 8th century, shortly after Īšōʿbōxt.[141] His ‘Law of Succession’ seems to be based to some extent on Īšōʿbōxt’s work, but without the refutation of Zoroastrian law, which is so predominant in the latter’s description of this branch of jurisprudence. Whether his treatise could be relevant for our study of Sasanian law, will have to be seen, when the text has been studied more intensively.

9.4 Acts of the martyrs

More than 40 texts have been transmitted describing the martyrdom of Christians in the Sasanian period, specifically during the so-called ‘great persecution’ under Šābuhr II (309 379), but also in subsequent centuries up to the late Sasanian period.[142] Many of these texts were mainly written in order to describe the steadfastness of the Christians in their faith despite the torments afflicted upon them by Zoroastrian authorities, but several reports also contain important material on the judicial administration of the State, transmitting titles of officials as well as other specifics on the trials conducted against these martyrs. Since the data on criminal cases are sparse in the Sasanian Law-book and very rudimentary in other Pahlavi sources, the acts of the martyrs offer supplementary information enabling us to reconstruct criminal proceedings to a limited extent and to note punishments in a far more detailed manner than would be possible without these contemporary sources.[143]

10 The Babylonian Talmud

Besides the Christians, Jews were another dominant minority in the Sasanian Empire, living in close proximity with Zoroastrians for over a millennium in the largest Jewish community of Mesopotamia (Babylonia in Jewish sources, corresponding roughly to the province of Āsōristān under the Sasanians, Iraq today). In this cultural environment, with the main academic centres of rabbinic scholarship situated between the rivers Tigris and Euphrates (in Nehardea, Sura, Pumbedita and Mahoza) in the vicinity of the Sasanian capital Seleucia/

141 According to Sachau 1914, Intr., pp. XIX–XXI; Syriac text and edition in *ibid.*, pp. 203–253.

142 See Payne 2015b, pp. 38–58, with detailed references to previous research, see also fn. 131 above. On the two preliminary text editions of Assemani 1748 and Bedjan 1891 see Wiessner 1967, pp. 7–11. Hoffmann 1880 and Braun 1915 have translated several acts of the martyrs.

143 This is notably the case with regard to the so-called ‘Acts of the Simon circle’ (for a reconstruction of the legal proceedings see Wiessner 1967) and the details transmitted in Mār Abā’s ‘Vita’ (see above 9.1. and Macuch 2014c).

Ctesiphon, the Babylonian Talmud (also called Talmud Bavli), the foremost source for Jewish law and theology, was produced and completed during Sasanian rule sometime in the fifth or sixth century. The Talmud (lit. 'instruction'), is a huge compilation on practically all normative aspects of Jewish life, divided into 63 long tractates, in which the legal, theological and ritual opinions, interpretations and debates of numerous generations of rabbis have been recorded. It is made up of two main components, both consisting of written redactions of oral traditions known as the 'Oral Torah' (lit. 'teaching'), that is, regulations, laws, statutes and interpretations of many generations of rabbis, which are not in the 'Written Torah', that is, the Pentateuch (or Five Books of Moses). These two elements are (a) the *Mishna*, a collection of statements, discussions and Biblical interpretations of rabbinic sages (the *Tannaim*) from ca. 10–220 CE, edited by R. Judah the Patriarch around 200 CE, and (b) the *Gemara*, a series of extensive commentaries, interpretations and discussions of the *Mishna* by later generations of rabbis (the *Amoraim*) from 220 until the end of the 5th century. Besides the Babylonian Talmud, another important work of Jewish law was produced during the period of the *Amoraim*, the Jerusalem Talmud in Palestine, which is, however, neither as extensive nor as authoritative as the Bavli. Moreover, the two Talmuds differ considerably in many parts, which could be due not only to diverse traditions, but also to a large extent to the impact of the cultural environment, in which these compilations came into being.[144]

Although many generations of talmudic scholars have engaged themselves in understanding the text, the Bavli still presents enormous interpretative problems in almost all fields due to its often shortened, elliptical style (which is also typical for Zoroastrian exegetic literature, the *zand*), its lack of explanations and the multi-layered debates of the rabbinic sages, including confusing re-interpretations of passages, no longer understood unequivocally by themselves. Moreover, as the product of a heterogeneous cultural environment, there is hardly a single difficult passage of the Talmud, whose provenance has not been discussed controversially in recent research, particularly with regard to the impact of Iranian mores and law on rabbinic debates and decisions in the Bavli. This is hardly surprising, given that most passages referring to Zoroastrian customs and norms or using Iranian technical terms—be it in the original or in translation—often remain completely enigmatic as long as the social, religious and legal background is not painstakingly reconstructed. Although in the past two decades the Zoroastrian environment of the Bavli has been subject to scrutiny in a number of studies revealing the impact of Iranian culture on many passages of the Talmud, a consensus among talmudists in this matter does not seem to be in sight.[145] The methodological difficulties

144 For an excellent introduction to the history and composition of the Talmud see ELON 1994; on Jewish law see HERZOG 1936.

145 Especially YAAKOV ELMAN and his student SHAI SECUNDA have contributed to understanding the Iranian background of the Bavli; see ELMAN's numerous articles listed in the Festschrift in his honour edited by SECUNDA/FINE 2012, pp. xv–xxii; see also SECUNDA

involved in deciding, whether congruent ideas in the two religions emerged independently or originated in one culture and were adapted by the other, seem to be in certain cases insurmountable. From the standpoint of an Iranist, there can be no doubt that Zoroastrian mores and Sasanian law played an important part in several rabbinic debates. We are on solid ground particularly in those cases using Iranian technical terms, taken directly from Sasanian legal language, or in discussions referring explicitly to Iranian law. In these instances there can be at least no doubt that Sasanian jurisprudence was known and included in rabbinic reasoning and controversial debates, even though this may have been restricted to those areas of law with no direct religious connotation.[146]

Despite the described difficulties, the Babylonian Talmud is a most significant work for scrutinizing the extent of interaction between two of the most influential legal systems of late antiquity due to two main reasons: (a) it is a contemporary source that explicitly acknowledges the validity of Iranian law as the law of the State also for Jews (at least in certain areas, such as taxation, and in criminal cases); (b) it employs Iranian technical terms in several instances (in the original and in translation) and alludes to Iranian law, revealing that Babylonian rabbis and Jewish authorities not only had exact knowledge of the Sasanian legal system, but seem to have adapted diverse regulations in fields which were not directly related to religious matters. (On Iranian elements in the Talmud see Chapter VII, section 1.)

11 Sources in Persian and Arabic

Supplementary information on social, administrative and legal institutions, may be gained from a few texts originally written in Pahlavi and later translated into Arabic or Persian. Although some scholars have questioned the authenticity of these texts, they contain so many accurate descriptions and characteristic details that they could only have been either forgeries from the Sasanian period itself or, more probably, late redactions of authentic texts in the late Sasanian or, less probably, early Islamic period, in which many specifics of pre-Islamic culture were still well known. The most significant for our topic are:

2014 (on the Iranian background of the Bavli) and the collection of contributions on the same subject in the volumes edited by Bakhos/Shayegan 2010 and Gabbay/Secunda 2014. Brody 2016 has criticised this approach, maintaining that the impact of Iranian culture (and particularly Sasanian law) on the Jewish community of Babylonia was far less than assumed in the bulk of the studies dedicated to this subject.

146 I have commented on the juridical background of Iranian legal loanwords and allusions to Sasanian law in the Babylonian Talmud in several articles, see Macuch 1999 (on the technical terms *pursišn-nāmag* and *muhr ī wāwarīgān*); 2002b (on the expression 'servant of the fire'); 2008a (on the term *dastwar*); 2010b (on various allusions to Sasanian law), 2014b (on the status of Jewish jurisdiction according to Sasanian law); 2015d (on substance and fruit in Sasanian and Talmudic law) and Macuch 2016b (on the Iranian law of suretyship explicitly called upon in the Talmud). See also Chapter VII, pp. 590–608 below.

11.1 The 'Letter of Tansar'

The 'Letter' attributed to Tansar (or Tōsar), the chief *hērbed* of Ardašīr (223/ 224–241/242), founder of the Sasanian Empire, has only survived in a Persian translation of an Arabic version of the Pahlavi original.[147] One of the diligent translators of Pahlavi works into Arabic, the well-known eighth century Muslim convert Ibn al-Muqaffaʿ from Fars (who died around 760 CE), translated the 'Letter' into Arabic. Most of his works, including the 'Letter', have not survived, but in the 13th century the historian Ibn Isfandiyār from Tabarestān discovered the Arabic translation and re-translated it into Persian, his native tongue, incorporating it into his 'History of Tabarestān' (*Tārīḫ-i Ṭabarestān*). Allegedly the 'Letter' is a reply to a (lost) letter of Gušnasp, the king of Parišwār and Ṭabarestān, in which Tansar tries to persuade the reluctant Gušnasp to declare allegiance with Ardašīr. Although Ibn Isfandiyār's Persian re-rendering of the Arabic translation is the only complete text that has reached us, there are also a few Arabic citations from the 'Letter' in the works of Masʿūdī and al-Bīrūnī. These seem to have had another source than Ibn al-Muqaffaʿ's translation, probably based on another Arabic rendering of the 'Letter', since in some of them the name of the prime minister is read Tōsar, whereas Ibn al-Muqaffāʿ reads Tansar. These two divergent versions reflect the ambiguity of the Pahlavi script, which allows both readings, suggesting that the citations in Masʿūdī and al-Bīrūnī were based on another translation of the original Pahlavi letter.[148] Although the name of Ardašīr's chief *hērbed* is known from the *Dēnkard* (Books 3 and 7)[149], the authenticity of the 'Letter' has been questioned because of certain historical inaccuracies and it has been designated as a literary forgery composed for political reasons in the period of the Sasanian King Husraw I, dating it to the 6th century. Boyce, on the other hand, questions this interpretation, stressing the important fact that in a predominantly oral culture texts were reworked in transmission and adapted to the needs of later generations, concluding that the 'Letter' could well have been a 3rd century original, which was later extended and elaborated in the 6th century to suit political purposes.[150] After comparing the 'Letter' to the 'Testament of Ardašīr' (see section 11.2 below) Grignaschi concludes that it should be dated, like the 'Testament', to the first years of the reign of Yazdegird III (633–651) before the Arab conquest.[151] Be it as it may, to judge by its content there can be absolutely no doubt that the 'Letter' is an

147 The letter of Tansar has been edited and translated by Darmesteter 1894; re-edited by Minovi 1932 and re-translated by Boyce 1968a.

148 For details on the transmission of the letter with references to previous research see Boyce 1968a, pp. 2–3.

149 *Ibid.*, pp. 5–6.

150 *Ibid.*, pp. 11–21.

151 Grignaschi 1966, pp. 8–9.

authentic text from the Sasanian period in a late redaction, containing significant information on the structure of the State, particularly the division of society into four estates, on the social status of nobles and commoners, on their different rights and duties, on succession, as well as significant supplementary information on criminal law.

11.2 The 'Testament of Ardašīr'

The 'Testament' ascribed to the founder of the Sasanian Empire has been preserved in Arabic translation in two copies: (a) under the title *ʿAhd Ardašīr b. Bābak ʾilā man yaḫlifuhu bi-ʿuqbihi min mulūk Fārs* ('Testament of Ardašīr, son of Bābak, to those who will succeed him among the kings of Persia,') in a manuscript in Istanbul[152], and (b) in Ibn Miskawayh's *Taǧārib al-ʾumam* ('Experiences of the Nations').[153] The interesting parallels between the 'Testament' and the 'Letter of Tansar' (see section 11.1) led Grignaschi to the conclusion that both texts were definitely of Sasanian origin, but products of the early years of Yazdegird III in the 7th century before the Arab conquest.[154] The 'Testament' contains a similar blend of information on the structure of the State, the division into four estates, and a section on succession, but being shorter, does not supply as many interesting details on legal issues as the 'Letter of Tansar'.

11.3 The 'Code (of Ardašīr)'

This short treatise, included in the manuscript of Arabic translations of Pahlavi original texts found by Grignaschi in Istanbul[155], has no title, but belongs to the genre of *āyīn* texts. It is ascribed to Ardašīr by its discoverer due to the similarities he found to a Pahlavi text mentioned by Ibn an-Nadīm in his *Fihrist* (called *Kitāb mā ʾamara Ardašīr bi-stiḫrāǧihi min ḫazāʾin al-kutub allatī waḍaʿahā al-ḥukāma fī-t-tadbīr* 'The book which Ardašīr ordered to be excerpted from the treasury of books, which the sages had composed on the problem of how to manage affairs'). It contains a set of rules of conduct directed to the aristocracy of the provinces, providing supplementary information on the structure of Sasanian society and its division into estates, but the Arabic translation unfortunately only offers a summary of the second part.[156]

152 This text was discovered among other Arabic translations of Pahlavi originals in the archives of the Başvekâlet in Istanbul (all in the ms. Köprülü 1608) and published by Grignaschi 1966.

153 See Boyce 1968a, p. 14, and Grignaschi 1966, p. 6, with references to previous research.

154 Grignaschi 1966, pp. 2f., 8f. Text, translation and commentary pp. 46–90.

155 See fn. 152.

156 Grignaschi 1966, pp. 3–4. Text, translation and commentary pp. 91–128.

11.4 The 'Book of Deeds of Anūšīrwān'

The *Kārnāmaǧ* ('Book of deeds') of Husraw I (531–579); with the epitome *anušīrwān* 'of the eternal soul') is an excerpt from the biography of the Sasanian king (*Sīrat Anūšīrwān*), of which several sections have been transmitted in Arabic translation by Ibn Miskawayh in his *Taǧārib al-ʾumam* (see section 11.2). The text, which GRIGNASCHI dates to the beginning of the 7th century, provides information on Husraw's procedural dealings with heretics, on the position of the chief *mobed*, on the measures the king undertook to protect peasants from extortion and other affairs of the State.[157]

11.5 Historiographical sources

Material on different customs and legal institutions as well as the political and social organization of Sasanian society can also be found scattered in several later Persian and Arabic historiographical treatises and other texts, notably the well-known chronicles of aṭ-Ṭabarī (839–923 CE), *Taʾrīḫ ar-rusul wa'l-mulūk* 'History of the Prophets and Kings'[158] and the extended Persian version of Ṭabarī's History by Balʿamī (completed ca. 964 CE), *Tārīḫ-i Balʿamī* 'History of Balʿamī'[159]; Ibn Qutaiba's (d. 889 CE) *ʿUyūn al-aḫbār* 'Choice Reports' (possibly based on works of Ibn al-Muqaffaʿ); Dīnawarī's (828–889/896 CE) *Kitāb al-aḫbār aṭ-ṭiwāl* 'Book of the Long Historical Narratives'[160]; two works of Masʿūdī (d. ca. 957 CE), *Murūǧ aḏ-ḏahab* 'Prairies of Gold'[161] and *Kitāb at-tanbīh wa'l-išrāf* 'Book of Admonition and Supervision'[162];Yaʿqūbī's (d. 900 CE) *Taʾrīḫ* 'History'[163]; Ḥamza al-Iṣfahānī's (written 961 CE) *Taʾrīḫ sanī mulūk al-arḍ wa-ʾl-anbiyāʾ* 'History of the Noble Kings of the Earth and the Prophets'[164] ; Ṯaʿālibī's (961–1038 CE) *Ġurar aḫbār mulūk al-furs wa siyarihim* 'Prime Reports on Kings of Persia and their Biographies'[165]; Ḫwārezmī's (composed 976 CE) *Mafātīhu'l-ʿulūm* 'Keys to the Sciences'[166]; and Ibn Balḫī's (12th century CE) *Fārsnāmeh* 'Book of Fārs'[167] among others. Legal and administrative issues have also been incorporated in Firdausi's famous National Epic, the *Šāhnāma* 'Book of Kings',[168] a supplementary source which still has not been scrutinized in this regard.

157 GRIGNASCHI 1966, translation and commentary pp. 16–45.
158 DE GOEJE 1879–1901; translation of the part on Sasanian history: NÖLDEKE 1879..
159 BAHĀR/GONĀBĀDĪ 1962.
160 GUIRGASS 1888 and AŠ-ŠAYYAL 1960.
161 DE MEYNARD/DE COURTEILLE 1861–1877, corrected by PELLAT 1962–1997; DE GOEJE 1894, translation CARRA DE VAUX 1896.
162 DE GOEJE 1894, translation CARRA DE VAUX 1896.
163 HOUTSMA 1883, translation GORDON *et al.* 2018.
164 GOTTWALDT 1844.
165 ZOTENBERG 1900.
166 VAN VLOTEN 1895.
167 LE STRANGE/NICHOLSON 1921.
168 KHALEGHI-MOTLAGH 1988–2008.

12 Armenian sources

In Late Antiquity Armenia was partitioned between the two great political powers of the age, Rome and Iran. By the fifth and sixth centuries the greater part of historic Armenia fell under the control of the Iranian Empire, with the capital in Dvin, the seat of the Sasanian administration and the state archives.[169] The districts under Persian rule, known as Persarmenia to the Romans, were governed by a Sasanian *marzbān* (lit. 'protector of the border'), who exercised authority in administrative, judicial and also religious matters. The magians in the province of Armenia fell under the jurisdiction of a Zoroastrian legal authority, a *mowbed*, who resided in the capital and passed judgement according to Iranian law. A large number of Iranian administrative and legal terms from almost all fields of law entered as loan-words into Armenian, bearing witness to the extent in which Iranian administration and jurisprudence were implemented in Persarmenia under Sasanian hegemony. Although the provenance of these technical terms has been known for a long time[170] and several studies have been carried out on Armenian provincial structures and the role of the elites,[171] there is hardly any research on the impact of Sasanian law on Armenian legal culture. As far as I can see, we owe the only substantial contribution in this field to Timothy Greenwood, who, after scrutinizing legal passages and allusions to Iranian law in Armenian literature, concludes that numerous references attest a legal culture very near to, if not even adapted directly from the Sasanian system.[172] In this important preliminary study he analyzes several relevant passages in the following works:

12.1 The *History* of Łazar P'arpets'i

This famous *History of the Armenians* was written at the end of the fifth or the beginning of the sixth century CE by an author from the village of P'arpi, who received part of his education in Byzantium and became a Christian cleric. Łazar P'arpets'i's work comprises three books, beginning with information on the division of Armenia between the Byzantine and Sasanian empires in the fourth century in book I, followed by descriptions of Armenian uprisings against Iranian dominion in the next two books. Although as a Christian cleric Łazar P'arpets'i was clearly opposed to Iranian policies and Zoroastrian beliefs,

169 On Armenia under Byzantine and Iranian rule see the extensive study by Garsoïan 1985; on the division of Armenia between the Romans and the Persians see Blockley 1987; on Sasanian history in Armenian sources see Gignoux 1995–1998; on Zoroastrianism in Armenia see Russell 1987.

170 The Iranian loan-words in Armenian have been studied by Hübschmann 1897, among these a very large number of legal terms, pp. 91–259.

171 See Garsoïan 1985, 1999 and 2009.

172 Greenwood 2017.

his *History* is a major source on fifth century Iran, providing a mass of information on the judicial and administrative work of Iranian officials. Greenwood (2017) calls our attention to several passages referring to inheritance, property law and pious foundations, which correspond significantly with certain well-known features of Sasanian jurisprudence.

12.2 The *History* of Ałuankʻ

This classical tenth century historiographical work on Caucasian Albania and the eastern territories of Armenia attributed to Movsēs Kałankatuatsʻi is rather a composite work, written in three books by at least two different authors or compilers. As Greenwood (2017) has elucidated, the *History* preserves a collection of documents, which record the decisions of the council of the church of Ałuankʻ held at Partav in 705, revealing an advanced legal culture in this area at the beginning of the eighth century. He is able to show remarkable correspondences with Sasanian law in the field of pious endowments, notably in the final document of the series, which summarizes a dispute over church property.

12.3 The *History* of the Province of Siwnikʻ

In this compilation on the history of Siwnikʻ, an eastern territory of historic Armenia, written in the year 1299 CE, the metropolitan bishop of this region, Stepʻanos Orbelan, takes recourse to a mass of important sources reaching back several centuries, encompassing ecclesiastical correspondence, theological treatises and documents on property transactions in favour of the bishops of Siwnikʻ and the monastery and churches where they were based. According to Greenwood (2017), the bishop exploited the episcopal archives, quoting altogether fifty-two deeds as well as summaries or extracts from another twelve documents, the earliest from the year 288 of the Armenian era (30 April 839–29 April 840 CE) and another twenty-four dating between 839 and 945 CE. The earliest cluster of documents consists of four charters, which record the transfer of villages as pious endowments to the see, preserving both Middle Persian loan-words and transliterations of technical terms as well as legal formulae. These records not only retain features of Sasanian legal practice, but bear witness—alongside the eighth century Pahlavi documents from Tabarestān (see section 1.4 above)—to the longevity and persistence of Iranian legal culture in territories belonging to the Sasanian Empire long after its downfall. After Greenwood's conclusion that 'Armenians living under Sasanian rule acknowledged and used Sasanian law', an exact scrutiny of the Armenian documents cited in this work would definitely be a significant contribution to our knowledge of Iranian jurisprudence in the Sasanian period and after the Muslim conquest of Iran.

13 Classical sources

The well-known classical legal sources and other historiographical texts on the Sasanian period do not contribute directly to our knowledge of Iranian law, but the former provide comparative material and the latter complementary information on Iranian customs, institutions and diplomatic relations between Rome/Byzantium and Sasanian Iran. Particularly the well-known Byzantine historians Procopius, Agathias, Menander the Guardsman, Johannes Malalas and Theophylact Simocatta have been consulted as sources for the history of Sasanian Iran to a large degree, but have still not been scrutinized sufficiently with regard to the details they transmit on Sasanian administration, titles of officials and the organization of the empire. Although the texts are often biased and contain misunderstandings and mistakes, they also offer valuable information not to be found in any other sources on the late Sasanian period.[173]

Another important future task would be a detailed comparison between Sasanian and Roman/Byzantine law, taking into account both the historical development of legal institutions in the two systems and the social context in which they emerged. Needless to say, the material on Roman law is not only far more extensive, but has been subject to intensive scholarly scrutiny, whereas studies on Iranian law are only in their primeval stage. Several features of Roman law in various branches of jurisprudence have been extremely helpful in understanding the Iranian texts and there are many remarkable parallels, which should be further examined (for example, the use of the Iranian term *xwāstag* almost exactly in the sense of the Roman *res* in a legal context[174]; the corresponding institutions of the *dastwar* in Sasanian procedural law and *auctor* in ancient Roman law, among other similarities).[175] The well-known sources on Roman/Byzantine law include the great legal collections in the Theodosian Code of 438 CE, containing the imperial edicts since the reign of Constantine, and the famous *Corpus Iuris Civilis*, compiled in the sixth century for the emperor Justinian I, consisting of an introduction to private law for the purpose of instruction (*Iustiniani Institutiones*), passages and quotations from the work of renowned classical jurisconsults (*Digesta* or *Pandectae*), a collection of imperial laws (*Codex Iustinianus*) and new laws from the years 535 to 575 CE (*Leges Novellae*).[176] Other presumably relevant sources have survived besides this huge

173 On the importance of the Byzantine sources for Iranian Studies in general and specifically for the late Sasanian period see Schmitt 2004 and Huyse 2015 with further references and a bibliography of editions and secondary literature.

174 On *xwāstag* in comparison to *res* see Macuch 2015d, p. 247, 2016a, p. 157, and Chapter III, pp. 189–190 below.

175 On *dastwar* see Macuch 1988b and 2016a, pp. 150–151. On these terms and institutions see also Chapter III, pp. 195–196, on property law see Chapter VI, pp. 542–544, on procedural law, Chapter VII, pp. 639–640.

176 For a concise description of Justinian's *Corpus Iuris Civilis* see Wieacker 1961, pp. 242–287; Wesel 1997, pp. 156–157; Manthe 2000, pp. 111–115 with further references.

compilation of normative law, allowing insight into legal practice in diverse territories of the Byzantine Empire, such as the Syro-Roman Law Book, an eastern source of the late fifth century, known through a number of Syriac, Arabic and Armenian manuscripts,[177] and more importantly, tens of thousands of papyri from Egypt, including wills, petitions, official records and court proceedings among other documents. Although the papyri are fragmentary, difficult to interpret and in most cases restricted to Egypt, making it difficult to generalize the evidence they supply, they are important records of legal activity within the Byzantine Empire and provide, moreover, exactly the kind of information needed to contrast normative statements with legal practice.[178] To date no in-depth study has been undertaken to compare this vast material with the Iranian legal texts. It would not be too far-fetched to assume that Rome/Byzantium and the Iranian empires of the Parthians and Sasanians were not only rivals and competitors, but also inspired each other in certain areas, including legal matters.[179]

***

The Iranian legal texts and documents of the first and second groups described above are the most detailed and trustworthy sources for reconstructing the jurisprudence of the Sasanian era, whereas scattered passages in the material of the third and fourth groups offer fragmentary, but valuable supplementary information. Although these texts were composed in different periods and reflect various phases of jurisprudence, including changes across the centuries, Sasanian law can only be reconstructed by taking *all* the available evidence into consideration. The material of the third group relating to the Avesta, particularly the Pahlavi *zand*, offers insight into contemporary religious, ritual and legal practice, conveying details not only on the use of technical terms but also on controversies and discussions of theologians of the Sasanian period, who were at the same time well-known jurisconsults. But since these texts were written for experts perfectly acquainted with both religious and legal matters, there was no need to add any explanations of institutions and technical terms. Definitions were only included later in Zoroastrian texts of the post-Sasanian period, written in order to conserve age-old religious norms and to save ancient traditions. The evidence of these late sources can only be used with caution. Numerous historical changes took place across the centuries due to the impact of other legal

177 The origin of these manuscripts must have been a Greek source of the late fifth century, see the edition of Bruns 1880, pp. 153ff.; new edition with introduction and commentary Selb/Kaufhold 2002.

178 On the Egyptian legal papyri see Taubenschlag 1955; Thomas 1987, pp. 59–110, and Wesel 1997, pp. 241–250. See also the website of the Oxford Centre for the Study of Ancient Documents (https://www.csad.ox.ac.uk/).

179 Preliminary attempts to compare the two systems can be found in Corcoran 2011, Forest 2020 and Macuch 2004 (on pious foundations).

systems of the Near and Middle East and every age (probably even every legal school) added its own individual interpretation to the transmitted texts, relating them to their own time, thereby altering or modifying the exact meanings of legal terms and institutions. Moreover, as the law of a religious minority, Zoroastrian jurisprudence deteriorated visibly after the fall of the Sasanian empire in the seventh century. By the 10th century the once refined and complex Sasanian legal system had been reduced to a few areas of law, which still remained under the jurisdiction of the Zoroastrian communities, notably matters dealing with marriage, family law, succession, obligations and simple legal transactions. Even in these remaining fields certain characteristic features of the Sasanian legal system were later no longer understood correctly and many institutions were gradually adapted to the changed conditions under Muslim rule. By the time of the New Persian *Riwāyats* (fifth group of sources, written between the 15th and 18th centuries) so many changes had taken place that these Zoroastrian texts no longer reflect Sasanian legal institutions, although the same terminology is employed in the fields of marriage and inheritance. Hence the Zoroastrian tradition is in itself problematic and fundamental alterations have to be taken into account whilst using the late Pahlavi and Persian sources to reconstruct the legal system of the Sasanian period. In the past years large steps have been taken towards this goal, but although the main institutions of Sasanian law and its diverse legal branches are by now well known, a huge mass of material still remains to be studied, notably in the foreign sources described above and documents only recently found.

B) Instruments of law

1 Development and categorizations of Zoroastrian law

The sources bear testimony to a well-organized and sophisticated legal system in the late Sasanian period, capable of dealing with the multi-layered problems of a complex society, using all the important instruments of an advanced discipline, but we have hardly any information on the development of Zoroastrian law and the emergence of the Sasanian system. As all other legal systems Iranian law has of course a history, even though there is a persistent tendency to ignore or deny historical changes in the Zoroastrian sources. The main reason seems to lie in the close relation between religion and law, in the theoretical ideal that law should be an exact reflection of the unchangeable ethical norms, moral precepts and traditions of the Mazdean Religion as revealed to the founder Zarathustra and established in the Avesta.[180] Although there must have been some awareness

180 Although the historical existence and impact of Zarathustra is a matter of debate among Iranists today, in the Sasanian period (and later) he was definitely regarded as the founder

that changes and modifications took place across the centuries, the orthodox position propagated in Pahlavi religious texts is that of the 'Early Masters' or 'First Teachers' of the faith, the *pōryōtkēšān*, whose teaching alone is relevant and clearly distinguished from other interpretations of the sacred texts, which were often regarded as heresies.[181] Religious norms established in this early (not datable) period constituted the first laws and remained—despite all changes—an important ingredient of Zoroastrian jurisprudence in every age, similar to other religious legal systems of the Near and Middle East, notably Talmudic, Christian and Islamic law.

With the growth of the Zoroastrian communities and the establishment of state structures, however, the need emerged to differentiate between various fields, between the work of the priest, the theologian and the jurist, which led to a distinction of at least two or, according to another source, three legal branches of Zoroastrian jurisprudence at an early, presumably pre-Sasanian stage of law. In the description of the legal (*dādīg*) sections or *nasks* of the Avesta, summarized in the *Dēnkard* (see above pp. 24–26), the sequence of *nasks* actually seems to reflect this ancient division of juridical material into two main groups.[182] If we exclude two *nasks* (*čihrdād* and *bayān⁺yašt/yasn*) in the sequence of seven from the category of 'legal' texts because of their non-juridical content, four legal divisions remain besides the *wīdēwdād*. These are placed within their own individual framework, beginning with the section called *nīgādom*, or 'lowest', and ending with the section called *sagādom*, or 'uppermost'. The *wīdēwdād* is not included into this framework, but is placed after this group, indicating a division of the legal *nasks* into two categories, which we may define as follows:

1. Sections dealing with jurisprudence proper, *i. e.*, civil and criminal law. These are the four divisions, beginning with the *nīgādom* 'the first' (< *nīkātama-*), followed by two sections (*duzd-sar-nizad/ōzad* [or *duzd ī druz ⁺tan*; *duzd ī ⁺drōzan*][183] and *huspārom*) and ending with the *sagādom* 'the last' (<**uskātama-*).[184] In this sequence the names of the first and last divisions are constructed in a similar manner, signalizing the beginning and the end of the specific group of legal *nasks* dealing specifically with juristic issues.
2. Regulations treating mainly religious issues, Zoroastrian purity rules, offences against the ritual and ethical norms in the *wīdēwdād* (<**vīdaēuua-dāta-* 'law keeping the demons away')[185].

---

and prophet of Mazdaism. For an overview of the various approaches to the question of Zarathustra's historicity see the contributions in Stausberg/Vevaina 2015.

181 See Molé 1961, p. 11; on heresies also Macuch 2021 with further references.

182 On the sequence of legal *nasks* in two different passages of Dk 8 see Macuch 2007a, pp. 152–155.

183 On the reading of the title of this division see p. 25 and fn. 39 above.

184 On the terms *nīgādom* and *sagādom* see Klingenschmitt 2000, pp. 228–229; also p. 25 and fn. 38 and 40 above.

185 See Cantera 2006, pp. 61–62.

Although the description in the *Dēnkard* is late, this attempt to categorize legal texts must be far older than the Sasanian (or post-Sasanian) period, since the two groups correspond roughly to the designations repeated several times in the *Yasna* as *dāta- zaraϑuštri-* 'the law of Zoroaster' and *dāta- vīdaēuua-* 'law keeping the demons away',[186] both parts together constituting Zoroaster's law, the *dāta- vīdaēuua- zaraϑuštri.*[187] The terms are not explained in the Avesta, but they were later understood in Pahlavi literature to refer to the two groups of legal texts or *nask*s mentioned above. The idea behind the Avestan division is repeated and explained in the late (9th century) *Wizīdagīhā ī Zādspram* using a terminology that corresponds exactly to Av. *dāta- vīdaēuua-* and *dāta-zaraϑuštri-*: the legal *nask*s consist of two parts, (1) the 'law keeping the demons away' (*dād ī ǰud-dēw, i. e.*, the *wīdēwdād*), and (2) the 'law of Zarathustra' (*dād ī Zardušt*) consisting of the 'other laws' (*abārīg dād*).[188] Both terms are used together in the *Wīdēwdād* in the Avestan phrase *dātəm yim vīdōiiūm zaraϑuštri* 'this law of Zoroaster keeping the demons away', rendered into Pahlavi by *dād ī ǰud-dēw ī Zardušt* ('Zoroaster's law keeping the demons away'). The latter phrase denotes the legal material as a whole, encompassing ritual, moral and juristic elements, explained in the commentary to the Pahlavi translation as consisting of three elements. The commentator (writing presumably in the late Sasanian period) distinguishes clearly between different legal categories, separating the *wīdēwdād* dealing with purification laws and rites, from the legal texts concerned with reaching verdicts and passing judgement (*wizīr ud dādwarīh*) in the *nīgādom* and those pertaining to the ritual (*yazišn*) in the *huspārom.*[189]

These three branches of law originally reflect central areas of priestly duties which consisted of preserving creation and averting the onslaught of the demons by carrying out three main tasks: (1) performing the ritual correctly and impeccably, (2) observing purity rules and propagating proper moral behaviour, (3) settling disputes and acts of violence among fellow Mazda-worshippers according to Zoroastrian norms.

These different work areas of Zoroastrian priests are reflected not only in the sequence of 'legal' *nask*s in the *Dēnkard* and the elucidations in the two passages quoted above, but also in a parallel division of sins and offences into

186 Y 1.13; 2.13; 3.15; 4.18 etc.; see attestations in Bartholomae 1904, col. 726.

187 See Cantera 2006, p. 62, and Macuch 2007a, p. 154.

188 WīZ 28.2: *dād-iz ō dō ēk dād ī ǰud-dēw ī ast ⁺wīdēwdād ud ēk dād ī Zardušt ī ast abārīg dād.* 'The legal (*nask*s are) also (divided) into two (types): one (is) the law keeping the demons away (*dād ī ǰud-dēw*), that is, the *wīdēwdād*, and one (is) the law of Zoroaster (*dād ī Zardušt*), that is, the other laws' (Macuch 2007a, p. 155).

189 Vd 5.25: *ast kē ēn pad nasuš ud ān pad nīgādom pad wizīr ud dādwarīh ud ān ī pad huspārom nērang ī yazišn gōwēd* 'There is (a commentator) who says: This (law, that is, the *wīdēwdād*) is about the Nasuš (= the female demon of the corpse and decay) and that (law) in the *nīgādom(-nask)* is about (legal) decisions and judgement, and that (one) in the *huspārom(-nask)* is about the power of the religious service (*yazišn*)' (Macuch 2007a, p. 154).

two main groups in Pahlavi religious literature. Two types of transgressions are named with different implications:[190]

1. 'Offences regarding opponents' (*wināh ī hamēmālān*) comprising *all* types of offences by which another member of the Zoroastrian community is damaged or injured. The examples given in Pahlavi literature encompass controversies in civil cases (such as disputes on proprietary rights and the payment of loans and debts), as well as complaints relating to criminal acts (such as theft, robbery, assault, manslaughter, homicide). The term denotes all acts liable to jurisdiction involving damage or harm caused to another person in both areas, which are today separated into civil and criminal law.
2. 'Sins pertaining to the soul' (*wināh ī ruwānīg*). These are acts endangering the delinquent's own soul, committed against religious norms (such as violating purity regulations or failing to observe the ritual correctly) and other transgressions against Zoroastrian ethical norms (sexual sins, immoral behaviour, harming beneficent animals etc.). The term designates particularly offences against ritual and moral laws, but also includes criminal acts endangering the soul.

This theoretical (therefore simplified) classification of Zoroastrian sins and offences does *not* imply that all illegal acts belonged to either one or the other category. Transgressions could belong to both categories with different consequences. Offences of the first group against other members of the community (*wināh ī hamēmālān*) were also sinful acts against Zoroastrian precepts and norms. They were hence at the same time sins committed against the delinquent's own soul. On the other hand, certain sins 'pertaining to the soul' (*wināh ī ruwānīg*), such as adultery with another man's wife or injuring a beneficent animal belonging to another person, were—besides endangering the delinquent's own soul—at the same time offences damaging another member of the community, hence liable to atonement and punishment according to both categories.[191] The distinction between the two types of offences is not the result of divergent definitions of offences, but rather reflects the two main means of atoning for sins. The different implications are explicitly stated in the *Šāyist nē šāyist*:

Šnš 8.1
wināh ī hamēmālān andar hamēmālān wizārišn ud ān (ī) ruwānīg andar radān wizārišn ud ka čē dēn radān framāyēnd kunēnd wināh be šawēd ud kirbag (ī) az ān frāz kunēnd uspurrīg rasēd.

'The "offence regarding opponents" (*wināh ī hamēmālān*) should be atoned/paid for (*wizārišn*) towards the opponents; the "(sin pertaining) to the soul" (*ān [ī] ruwānīg*) should be atoned/paid for (*wizārišn*) towards the spiritual masters

190 See also Macuch 2003a, pp. 172–174, and 2009e, pp. 181–182. On the concrete implications of this division in legal practice see Chapters V, pp. 400–403, and VI, pp. 487–489.
191 See also Buyaner 2016, pp. 354–357.

> (*radān*). And if they (= the sinners) do what the spiritual masters (*radān*) command, then the sin goes away, and the good deed which they perform afterwards reaches them completely.'[192]

The terminology in this passage is ambiguous, since the verb *wizārdan* 'to atone for' also has the specific meaning of 'to pay, recompense, reimburse' in a legal context. Hence in our sentence the gerundive (participium necessitates) *wizārišn* has both meanings: 'should be atoned for' as well as 'should be paid for'. The passage—among other attestations[193]—suggests that the main difference between the two types of offences lay in the manner of compensation: (1) in the case of 'offences regarding opponents' by compensating the damaged or injured person directly (by paying a fine to that person, fulfilling a contract, or by some other means); (2) in cases of 'sins pertaining to the soul' by paying a fine to religious authorities (the *radān*) and following the rules set by them for the atonement of sins (confessing, repenting, doing deeds appropriate for repentance).

The classification of offences into these two categories is only mentioned in Pahlavi religious texts, not in the legal sources at our disposal, but it indicates that at some period the need was felt to separate the different fields of religion and law to a certain degree, when not completely. In the Sasanian period, or maybe even earlier, two areas of law had already developed—possibly from this initial differentiation of sins—which we would designate today as 'civil and criminal law', on the one hand, and 'religious norms', on the other. We may further conclude that the Sasanian judicial system established by the State with its clear judicial hierarchies was exclusively concerned with the first category of offences involving 'opponents' (*wināh ī hamēmālān*), whereas Zoroastrian religious authorities dealt with *both* areas according to their competences (they were also engaged as judges in the Sasanian system, see Chapter VI, pp. 503–509), with the *exclusive* right to pass judgment in cases involving the second group of sins directed against one's own soul (*wināh ī ruwānīg*).

Apart from this presumably early theoretical division of Zoroastrian law into at least two main areas, we are not informed in the legal texts of any other kind of systematization. Although the Sasanian Law-book deals with various legal fields divided into chapters (family law, marriage, inheritance, property law, the law of obligations, civil and criminal proceedings, among others), it is not a systematic treatment, as we have already mentioned, but a collection of disparate case studies with no discernable structure (see pp. 20–22). Given the advanced stage of jurisprudence by the late Sasanian period, the lack of a systematic treatment is strange and could be rather due to the type of sources which have survived and to the huge gaps in the transmission of legal material. The *Law-book of Īšōʿbōxt* (p. 48) with its exact categorization of legal fields was based on Sasanian law, suggesting that there must have been other similar

192 See Tavadia 1930, p. 104, and Macuch 2003a, p. 176.
193 See attestations Macuch 2003a, pp. 174–177.

systematic treatises on legal topics in Pahlavi, which might have served as a model for Īšōʿbōxt's work. Unfortunately none of these—if they existed—have survived. We are not even informed, whether there was a theoretical distinction between civil and criminal law (the ancient division mentioned above does not separate the two categories), but there must have been some kind of distinction, since we know exactly that Sasanian law differentiated in practice precisely between civil and criminal proceedings (see Chapter VI).

2 Theology and jurisprudence

Despite the separation of ritual and moral matters from legal issues according to the categories mentioned above, the connection between theology and jurisprudence continued to remain very close in the Sasanian period. The religious importance of jurisprudence was emphasized in late Pahlavi literature by depicting the prophet Zoroaster himself as the foremost lawgiver, who instructs his followers to proceed against adversaries under all circumstances according to the law and the rules of legal procedure.[194] Moreover, several unique features of the legal system leave no doubt that Sasanian law was based *theoretically* on Zoroastrian norms. But interestingly neither the practical work of jurists involved in the daily tasks of the State courts, nor the decisions of the judges were derived directly from the Avesta. This would rather point to a legal system that had become to a large extent independent of theology in its daily practice, despite being ideologically based on Zoroastrian precepts.

The continuing impact of religion on law may be deduced from several observations. In the first place, the names of famous theologians, who were commentators of the Avesta, such as Sōšāns, Mēdōmāh, Abarag, Dādfarrox, Pēšagsīr (among others), are also given in legal literature as the foremost juristic authorities.[195] They not only developed various schools and discussed divergent interpretations

194 As in WīZ 26.1–2: *abar sē dād ī Zardušt pad pahlomīh čāšīd* (1) *fradom ēn a-pahikār-radīhā be (ō) kasān ma šawēd.* (2) *dudīgar ka-tān a-dādestānīhā abar rawēnd* *⁺dādestānōmandīhā pēš abganēd.* 'On the three laws (*dād*) that Zoroaster taught as the foremost. (1) The first (law is) this: do not proceed against other persons in the manner of a non-judicial dispute (= private feud; *a-pahikār-radīhā*). (2) The second (is) this: if (others) go forward against you in an unlawful manner (*a-dādestānīhā*), proceed (against them) according to the law!' (Gignoux/Tafazzoli 1993, pp. 87–89) (the third law prescribes next-of-kin marriage, *xwēdōdah*); on the terms *pahikār-radīh* 'judicial dispute' and *a-pahikār-radīh* 'non-judicial dispute' see Macuch 2002a and Chapter V, pp. 404–411.

195 The most frequent names have been collected by Gignoux 1995 in a preliminary study on religious controversies in Pahlavi texts. A tentative chronology of the commentators of the *zand* was attempted by Cantera 2004, pp. 207–220, Secunda 2012, and Macuch 2017a, pp. 265–269. Due to the meagre information in the sources it would be futile to attempt a new chronology of commentators or legal schools. Names of the jurisconsults cited in the Law-book are listed in Appendix XVII.

of religious and legal matters, but their commentaries, called *čāštag* 'teaching, doctrine', became important guidelines to jurisprudence and are mentioned repeatedly in legal literature. Second, Zoroastrian priests trained in both theology and jurisprudence, the *rad* and *mowbed*, were engaged as judges in the Sasanian legal system besides other State officials who were not religious dignitaries. In the hierarchy of the legal system these religious authorities were placed higher than the State judges called *dādwar* (of which there were at least two types, the 'lower judge', *dādwar ī keh*, and the 'higher judge', *dādwar ī meh*). The latter were engaged in lower instances, whereas the *rad* and *mowbed* presided in the courts of appeal. The head of the Zoroastrian Church, the *mowbedān mowbed* or Chief Mobed was at the same time the highest legal official (besides the King himself), whose judgement could not be questioned.[196] Third, the same specific vocabulary and jargon of Pahlavi legal sources is also used in many glosses and commentaries (*zand*) to the Avesta with implications similar to those described in legal literature, attesting to the continuing engagement of theologians in both fields. Fourth—and most important for our assessment of Sasanian law—some of the most significant legal institutions in the field of family law and inheritance would have been impossible in a society confessing any other religion except Zoroastrianism in the form it had reached by the Sasanian period. Almost none of the complex institutions defining the structure of kinship in Sasanian Iran could have developed in a society following another creed (for example, Manichaeism or Christianity, both dangerous challenges to Zoroastrianism). As will be seen in the field of family law, one of the most important underlying features of the whole system is the Zoroastrian acceptance and promotion of next-of-kin alliances of an incestuous kind, also fictive ones, in combination with the obligation to be fertile and to procreate as many children as possible to join the cosmic battle against the Evil Spirit. Zoroastrian ideas also shine through in other branches of law, such as the rules regarding the correct behaviour of Mazdeans towards beneficent animals, the establishment of pious and charitable foundations, the appropriate distribution of food among co-religionists and the obligation to take care of the needy.[197] A passage in the late *Dēnkard* seems to have conserved an early ideal of Zoroastrian jurisdiction: the decision of the judge (*dādwar*) should be based on three major sources of law, the Avesta (*awistāg*), its Pahlavi translation and commentaries (*zand*) and the consensus of the Righteous (*ham-dādestānīh ī wehān*).[198] However, if we follow the testimony of the Law-book (and other later sources)[199] there was far more to be taken into consideration in the Sasanian courts of justice than these three important elements constituting Zoroastrian law.

196 Macuch 1981, pp. 188–208; for a survey of the judicial system see also Macuch 2009e, pp. 193–194, and Chapter VI below.
197 See Macuch 2003a on animals; 1994a, 2004 and 2009d on pious foundations; 2012a on food distribution and the obligation of taking care of the needy.
198 DkM 712.20f.; quoted in Macuch 1993, p. 12, no. 34.
199 For an example from a late source see Macuch 2017a.

Although the Avesta and its Pahlavi translation and commentaries (*zand*) remained the *theoretical* basis of the legal system, *in practice* by the late Sasanian period jurisprudence had become an individual discipline, only loosely connected to theology. Society had changed considerably since the legal *nask*s of the Avesta had been composed and neither the sacred texts nor their theological interpretations sufficed to cover the concrete needs of a complex society in a huge Empire with large communities of religious minorities (notably Jews and Christians). This development may be deduced from three crucial observations. First: the Sasanian Law-book of 'One-Thousand Decisions' has conserved a large range of particularly difficult juristic cases from diverse legal fields, revealing how extremely complex the legal system of the Sasanian State had become. There are only two allusions to the Avesta in the whole text, which, moreover, both refer clearly to the Pahlavi legal commentary in the *zand*, not to the Old Iranian original texts.[200] Second: Legal theory and practice began to drift apart due mainly to the daily work of the courts, which had to solve numerous unexpected, concrete problems that had not (yet) been taken into consideration in the theoretical treatises of religious authorities and theologians. Discrepancies between legal doctrine (*čāštag*) and practice (*kardag*) emerged, which were noted and even accepted as an inevitable part of legal work. Moreover, devices were developed by which the strict rules laid down in legal doctrine could be circumvented in order to achieve 'better justice'. Third (and most importantly): law developed a precise language of its own, clearly distinguishable from both the theological argot and the daily vernacular. It is this exact use of technical language that characterizes the legal texts of the Sasanian period, revealing not only the intricacies of a complex system, but also the importance attached to the exact administration of justice as one of the most important pillars of the State.

3 Legal theory and practice

These two last features of Sasanian law—discrepancies between legal theory and practice and the development of a precise technical language—were not only important instruments of jurisdiction, but also of change. We may assume that the work of daily courts took up a central position in the Sasanian State from the very beginning and that difficulties inevitably emerged when disputes were brought to court, which could not be adjudicated on the basis of the theoretical work of religious and legal authorities. Although the commentators of the Avesta did their best to relate the ancient texts to the changed conditions of their own time (as we may conclude from many legal commentaries in the *zand*) and to find juristic solutions, there can be no doubt that this theoretical work could never cover all possible variations and many unpredictable conflicts emerging in real life. Unforeseen problematic cases called for a far more flexible handling of

200 MHD 15.1; 48.15 (Macuch 1993, pp. 129, 132, and pp. 308, 324 respectively).

legal matters than prescribed in legal theory. The problem was solved by various means. One of these was to distinguish between proceedings complying strictly with the 'doctrine' (*čāštag*) of canonical law and those that were adjudicated on the basis of other criteria, called *kardag* or legal 'practice'. The latter term is employed in this specific context with two major meanings: *kardag* designates both (1) a *judicial procedure* conducted at the free discretion of the court, diverging from the prescriptions of canonical law; (2) the *guideline or norm* resulting from decisions reached in these instances for other similar cases.[201]

Judgments based on *kardag* diverged explicitly from solutions one would expect in cases conducted according to legal doctrine. Court transcripts recorded whether a decision had been reached by applying canonical law or by following the *kardag* procedure. For both cases there were specific formulae: *ō kardag kard ēstēd*, lit. '(the case) is put to *kardag*', reveals a procedure diverging from canonical law, whereas *ō kardag nē kard ēstēd*, lit. '(the case) is not put to *kardag*' or *az kardag hišt ēstēd* '(the case) is withdrawn from *kardag*'[202] explicitly states that the court has *not* taken this course of action (but has kept to the prescriptions of canonical law, as we may infer). These formulae were used with regard to a permanent rule of procedure in the described cases. See the following example referring to the offence of 'stealing *openly*' (*apparīh*, lit. 'robbery', which was distinguished exactly from the crime of 'stealing *secretly*', *duzīh*, lit. 'theft').

> MHD 102.12–13
> *apparīh ī nē pad čīš ī keh ō kardag nē kard ēstēd.*
>
> '(The offence of) "stealing openly" (*apparīh*) which does not regard a petty case (*čīš ī keh*), is not put to *kardag* (procedure).'[203]

The sentence is somewhat garbled by the double negation, but the sense is clear: a judicial procedure involving an act of robbery (= 'stealing openly', *apparīh*) that does *not* relate to a negligible or trivial matter (*čīš ī keh*) cannot be adjudicated at the free discretion of the court, but has to follow the prescriptions of canonical law. In other words: in the case of a publicly visible offence, only trivial cases were adjudicated according to *kardag* procedure. The short passage

201 On these two terms with examples from the Law-book see Macuch 1981, pp. 146–162; see now also Colditz 2015, pp. 230–237.

202 The 3.sg. *ēstēd* of the auxiliary verb *ēstādan* (denoting the perfect) + perfect participle *kard* is used here in the sense of a perfect present or 'static perfect' in which the concluded act results in a permanent condition, or, as in our case, in a permanent rule of procedure: *ō kardag kard ēstēd*, lit. 'it has been put to *kardag*' = 'it is (always) put to *kardag*'; *ō kardag nē kard ēstēd*, lit. 'it has not been put to *kardag*' = 'it is not (ever) put to *kardag*'; *az kardag hišt ēstēd*, lit. 'it has been withdrawn from *kardag*' = 'it is (always) withdrawn from *kardag*'. See the conclusive example MHDA 13.8–9 below. On the construction see Henning 1933, p. 246, and Durkin-Meisterernst 2014, p. 384f. (albeit with no examples from legal texts).

203 Macuch 1993, pp. 616 (transliteration), 624 (translation), 635, no. 19 (commentary). On stealing openly and secretly see Chapters IV, pp. 380–382, and V, pp. 434–437.

has vast legal implications that can only be understood correctly by taking the full scope of the technical terms into consideration: _apparīh_ was not only used in its literal sense of 'robbery', but contrasted with _duz(d)īh_ 'theft' and transferred figuratively to other offences. For example, in the context of the 'breach of contract' (_mihrōdrujīh_) the delinquent was punished according to the penalty for 'robbery' (that is 'stealing openly') if the contract had been concluded in the presence of witnesses. But if the contract had been drawn up _without_ witnesses, the convicted delinquent was punished according to the penalty for 'theft' ('stealing secretly'). These two expressions had become technical terms by which both the procedure and the penalty were established in parallel cases that did not have to do with theft or robbery in a concrete sense at all, but were connoted with committing an offence openly or secretly in correspondence with the original distinction between these two types of criminal acts (see also Chapters IV, pp. 380–382, and V, pp. 434–437).

Another example for _ō kardag kard ēstēd_ and _(az kardag) hišt ēstēd_ with respect to the common procedure in 'petty cases' confirms our interpretation of the passage and seems to refer to adherents of another creed or religion, if my hypothetical reading and interpretation of the Avestan (?) _hapax legomenon_ _*yō x^{v}a-daēnā-_, written in the Pahlavi script ⟨ywk hw'dyn'⟩, in this sentence is correct:

> MHDA 13.2–3
> _*yō x^{v}a-daēnā_ (ywk hw'dyn') _pad keh ō kardag kard ēstēd ud pad abārīg hišt ēstēd._
>
> '(The offence of one) "who (follows) his own creed" (_*yō xva-daēnā?_) is put to _kardag_ (procedure) in a petty case (_pad keh_) and in other (cases it is) withdrawn from (_kardag_ procedure).'

This is only _one_ possible interpretation of the concise passage and does not claim to offer a final solution.[204] The sentence is far too short to allow reliable conclusions and we can only speculate on its exact meaning, but if the reading _*yō x^{v}a-daēnā-_, lit. 'who (follows his) own creed' is correct, one could assume that it is a quotation from a lost Avestan context, denoting a Zoroastrian who follows an unorthodox creed (diverging from the one propagated in religious

204 Other interpretations and readings are possible, particularly since there is a short lacuna at the beginning of the sentence in the manuscript, which could point to a few missing signs (perhaps the first word should be read ⟨'ywk'⟩ _ēk_?). In Macuch 1981 (transliteration p. 35; translation p. 141; commentary p. 150, no. 11) I had emended the first word of the sentence ⟨ywk'⟩ to ⟨dwc⟩ _duz_ 'thief' (assuming that this was a parallel passage to the sentence with _apparīh_ 'robbery' cited above, MHD 102.12–13) and read the next letters as ⟨HN' DYN'⟩ _ēd dādestān_ 'this judgement'. Although the reading _*yō xva-daēnā-_ suggested above is not certain (particularly since the word is not attested in the Avestan script, but only in the Pahlavi script), I prefer it today to emending any part of the manuscript, which—as I have been able to ascertain time and again—has been transmitted with very little, if any, mistakes; _*xva-daēnā-_ '(following) one's own creed/vision' may be compared to _xva-δāta-_ '(following) one's own law', see Bartholomae 1904, col. 1862.

orthodoxy).[205] As an Avestan term it would convey additional authority to the decision recorded here, which would also explain, why it is used instead of the corresponding Pahlavi term *xwaddōšag* '(person) following his own creed',[206] (or, if it refers to an adherent of another religion altogether, *ǰuddēn* or *ag-dēn* 'infidel'). Perikhanian, reading **yō hvā daēna-* 'Zoroastrian', has a diametrically opposed understanding of the term and—also in other respects—a completely different translation of the sentence.[207] She does not comment her version, but if the term is a general designation for the Zoroastrian, the question arises: would it be necessary to transmit a self-evident fact, namely that the laws, regulations and proceedings described in the Law-book apply to Zoroastrians? Given the scope of this source, one would, on the contrary, expect to learn how these regulations were handled with respect to *non-orthodox* Zoroastrians (or *non*-Zoroastrians). The content can be compared with another passage of the Law-book, in which we are informed that adherents of another religion (*ag-dēn*) were subject to the same laws as Zoroastrians, albeit with the exception of important regulations concerning succession and inheritance.[208] Be it as it may, the statement can be understood along the same lines as in the previous example: legal disputes involving adherents of a different creed, as I surmise, (or: Zoroastrians, if we follow Perikhanian's reading) were adjudicated in 'petty cases' (*pad keh*) in a judicial procedure conducted at the free discretion of the court (*kardag*). In 'other (cases)' (*abārīg*), that is, cases *not* relating to a trivial matter, the prescriptions of canonical law had to be kept.

Despite this flexible handling of problematic cases, judgements based on *kardag* were *not* considered as 'final' or (lit.) 'reliable, binding' (*ēwar*), but were more or less temporary solutions, which had to be revised if a 'reliable/binding' procedure (*pad ēwarīh*) based on canonical law (*čāštag*) was required by one of the litigants immediately or in a court of appeal. See for example the following ruling:

MHDA 13.8–9
ʾnwʾn[209] *ka pad rāyēnišn xwāhēd ō kardag kard ēstēd ka pad ēwarīh xwāhēd az kardag hišt ēstēd.*

'If he (= the litigant) demands a compensation by trial, (then the case) is put to *kardag* (procedure). If he demands it (= the compensation) by a "reliable" procedure (*pad ēwarīh*), (then it) is withdrawn from *kardag* (procedure).'[210]

205 On diverging interpretations of the Avesta and the problem of defining heresy see Macuch 2021.
206 On the meaning of this term see Cantera 2003.
207 Perikhanian 1997, p. 268 (see also p. 414).
208 MHD 60.16–61.1 (Macuch 1993, pp. 409; 415; 425–426). On the implications of this ruling see Macuch 2014b, pp. 148–150. Examples in the Babylonian Talmud and in Syriac sources also reveal that non-Zoroastrians could file suits and were even exclusively judged in Sasanian courts in criminal cases.
209 The legal term ⟨ʾnwʾn⟩ (reading?) means 'compensation, remuneration', see Bartholomae 1918, vol. I, p. 8, and Macuch 1993, p. 481, no. 1, with further references.
210 Macuch 1981, pp. 35; 142; 151, no. 17 (commentary).

The formulae discussed up till now (*ō kardag kard ēstēd* and *az kardag hišt ēstēd*) were used to designate permanent rules of legal practice. It seems that the court could conduct a procedure at its free discretion on a regular basis only in instances involving trivial offences, whereas other transgressions of a graver nature and cases demanding a 'reliable, binding' (*ēwar*) verdict were adjudicated according to the formalities and rules prescribed by canonical law (*čāštag*).

Nevertheless it was obviously still possible to bypass legal doctrine in both civil disputes and criminal cases, if these were not necessarily 'trivial'. Another formula was employed when a matter was decided according to *kardag* procedure in an individual case, which did not fit into the 'regular' scheme: *pad kardag mad*[211] or *pad kardag mad ēstēd*[212] '*kardag* (procedure) was applied' (lit. 'it came to *kardag* procedure') refers to individual decisions of the court deviating from legal doctrine. For example, in a dispute involving two claims to an inheritance based on a testamentary disposition, on the one hand, and on a donation *mortis causa*, on the other, the court decides on the basis of *kardag* procedure to proceed in accordance with the donation, instead of complying with the testament (which would have been required according to legal doctrine).[213] In other instances using this formula the accused in a criminal offence is convicted according to *kardag* procedure.[214] Proceedings and decisions that differed (at times considerably) from theoretical requirements were labeled *pad kardag*[215] ('according to legal practice; *via administrationis*') and distinguished from those which kept to canonical law, called *pad čāštag* ('according to legal doctrine; *ex lege*').[216]

Another method of circumventing the strict regulations of canonical law in legal practice is mentioned both in Pahlavi texts and in Īšōʿbōxt's *Corpus Iuris* (see p. 48 above). The legal expressions employed in this context are *passand* (lit. 'pleasure, liking') and *wehdādestānīh* (lit. 'good justice, law; good decision, judgement') and the comparative form *wehdādestāntar* 'better justice' (besides the exact opposite *wattar-dādestāntar* 'worst justice'). The specific technical meaning of *passand* (which is rendered in Īšōʿbōxt's Syriac version by *ḥasīrūt dīnā* 'decrease of justice')[217] is 'reduction of justice to the minimum required by law', as we may conclude from the example given by Īšōʿbōxt in a case of debt: If a man owns both money and interest to another man and the debtor cannot pay back both the sum he has borrowed and the interest because of poverty, illness or the like, and asks the creditor to rest content with only the capital, this

211 MHD 31.7 (Macuch 1993, pp. 222, 226).
212 MHDA 13.10f., 12 (Macuch 1981, pp. 35, 142).
213 MHD 31.6–8 (Macuch 1993, pp. 222; 226; 233, no. 17, commentary).
214 MHDA 13.9–11 and 13.11–13 (Macuch 1981, pp. 35; 142; 152, no. 18, commentary).
215 A few illuminating examples are: MHDA 13.7 (Macuch 1981, pp. 35; 142); MHD 8.12 (Macuch 1993, pp. 90, 95); MHD 30.9 (*ibid*., pp. 221, 225).
216 See attestations in Macuch 1993, p. 697.
217 Sachau 1914, pp. 13–14 and 289–290.

Table 1. Overview of terminology: legal theory and practice

Pahlavi term	Definition/Translation
čāštag	legal doctrine, teaching, theory; canonical law
pad čāštag	according to legal doctrine; *ex lege*
kardag	legal practice; specifically: 1) a *judicial procedure* conducted at the free discretion of the court 2) the *guideline or norm* resulting from legal practice
pad kardag	according to legal practice; *via administrationis*
ō kardag kard ēstēd	'(the case) is put to *kardag* (procedure)'
ō kardag nē kard ēstēd	'(the case) is not put to *kardag* (procedure)'
az kardag hišt ēstēd	'(the case) is withdrawn from *kardag* (procedure)'
pad kardag mad (ēstēd)	'*kardag* (procedure) was applied'

is called *passand* or 'leniency (in justice)'. It denotes a legal procedure by which one of the involved parties *renounces a certain legal right* given to him by contract or agreement, because the other party is not able to fulfil the conditions both parties had originally agreed upon. Legal authorities are called upon to support *passand* in specific cases, as in our example, by admonishing the claimant to renounce a claim his opponent cannot fulfil due to his personal situation in the interest of higher justice.[218] The term does not appear in this sense in the Sasanian Law-book, but, as DE MENASCE has perceptively noticed, it is attested in the *Mēnōy ī xrad* (2.52) in exactly this sense of 'leniency (in justice)' in the following entry: *abāg dušmenān pad dādestān kōxš abāg dost pad passand ī dōstān raw* 'Strive against enemies according to (strict) legal procedure (*dādestān*); proceed with friends according to the leniency (*passand*) due to friends.'[219]

The principle denoted by the term *wehdādestānīh* (lit. 'good justice'; rendered into Syriac as *yatīrūt dīnā* 'extension of justice')[220] is exemplified by Īšōʿbōxt in his definition of *behdādestānīh* (the later Persian form of MP *wehdādestānīh*) as follows: If a person gives his daughter the same portion of inheritance as that of a son, *i. e.*, twice the share she is entitled to by law, so that she might not remain unmarried, this is called 'extension of justice'.[221] In other words,

218 Īšōʿbōxt, Book I, Chapter VI (SACHAU 1914, p. 15).

219 DE MENASCE 1964c [= 1985], p. 121 (with a divergent translation). The passage he quotes (p. 120) from the *Hazār dādestān* containing the verbal form *passandē* has nothing to do with the technical term we are concerned with here; on this formula see below Chapter IV, pp. 303, 305. On *passand* in the sense described here see also NYBERG 1974, pp. 152–153. The transcription *mēnōy* (instead of *mēnōg*) follows SKJÆRVØ 2009, p. 481, fn. 12.

220 SACHAU 1914, pp. 13–14 and 289–290.

221 *Ibid.*, p. 13.

wehdādestānīh designates a legal procedure by which a person is willing to go beyond the boundaries of formal prescriptions by *extending a certain legal right* given to another person, with the technical meaning of 'going beyond the minimum prescribed by law, doing more than legally required'. The comparative form *wehdādestāntar*, lit. 'better justice', is used in the Sasanian Law-book in the context of the 'oath' or 'ordeal' (*war*) with relation to a person who is best suited to take the oath in a judicial procedure based on the evidence of the ordeal. The person to be chosen should 'fulfil justice better', that is, his oath should be better suited to induce a judgement *exceeding the minimum requirements* of law. The exact literal opposite of the comparative *wehdādestāntar* is *wattar-dādestāntar*, lit. 'worst justice', with the technical meaning of 'remaining behind legal prescriptions; *ignoring even minimum legal requirements*'. In the late Pahlavi texts *mehdādestānīh*, lit. 'great justice' (and the adverbial form *mehdādestānīhā* with the comparative ending, *mehdādestānīhātar* 'greater justice', exceeding the minimum requirements of law') seem to have replaced *wehdādestānīh* and *wehdādestāntar*, but were employed—at least in a legal context—with the same technical meaning.[222]

To conclude, there were different means of modifying juristic norms and altering the strict rules of legal doctrine: (1) by detaching judicial procedure in 'trivial cases' (*čīš ī keh*) and in other individual instances from the prescriptions of canonical law (*čāštag*) and delivering judgements which diverged from the precepts of legal theory; (2) by applying the opposite principles of *passand* and *wehdādestānīh*, the possibility of *renouncing* and *extending* a legal right in order to achieve 'better justice'. Discrepancies between the theoretical work in the commentaries (*čāštag*) of theologians and jurists on one hand, and legal practice (*kardag*) following a divergent procedure, on the other, were also the main motors of change, leading to gradual alterations over the years and the development of an individual, complex judicial system, which no longer had to rely completely on ancient prescriptions in order to solve concrete problems.

4 Technical terms and legal language

One of the most important instruments of law is a precise professional language, without which no sophisticated legal system, whether ancient or modern, could function properly. Pahlavi legal sources are amazingly consistent in their use of a specific juristic jargon (a few examples have been already cited above) and terms of art, enabling short and precise communication between all experts engaged in legal activities. Although theoretical considerations are not transmitted—as they seldom are in the Iranian texts—it is this precise use of legal language combined with the meticulous interpretation of formulations in stipulations and wills, agreements and contracts, that reveals the high level

222 On these terms see Macuch 2019a with further references.

Table 2. Overview of terminology: leniency in justice and extension of justice

Pahlavi term	Translation	Definition
passand	leniency (in justice); (Syriac translation:) *ḥasīrūt dīnā* 'decrease of justice'	reduction of justice to the minimum required by law; doing less than legally required; renouncing a legal right
wehdādestānīh	extension of justice; (Syriac translation:) *yatīrūt dīnā* 'extension of justice'	going beyond the minimum prescribed by law; doing more than legally required; extending a legal right
mehdādestānīh	extension of justice	(= *wehdādestānīh*)
wehdādestāntar	(person) who fulfils justice best	(in the context of the oath:) Person whose oath leads to a judgement exceeding the minimum requirements of law
wattar-dādestāntar	(person) who fulfils justice worst	person who does not fulfil even minimum legal requirements

Iranian jurisprudence had reached by the late Sasanian period.[223] The advantages of professional language have been described elsewhere and may be summarized as follows: (1) legal terms convey a *clear meaning* to jurists (with the disadvantage that they are usually incomprehensible to a layperson, despite the fact that many expressions are taken from the common vernacular); (2) legal jargon can be used to avoid lengthy explanations and to enable *effective and efficient communication* between experts (with the disadvantage that this can lead to elliptical and shortened phrases incomprehensible to non-jurists, who are not acquainted with the exact legal background); (3) professional language contributes to *minimizing misunderstandings* and reducing the well-known ambiguities and inaccuracies of language (even if these cannot be removed completely). In all advanced systems legal language is used with meticulous precision, enabling jurists to communicate with each other shortly and precisely, without the need to repeat explanations of well-known institutions and legal precepts.

Sasanian law is no exception to this rule. The legal texts employ a precise legal language that can be traced back to various sources, conveying a mass of information to the expert in a single word or phrase with implications invisible to a layperson. This economy of language is in fact one of the reasons why so many of the short glosses in legal passages of the *zand* (Pahlavi version of the Avesta) remain difficult to fathom and are still to a large extent incomprehensible to

223 On Sasanian legal language and technical terminology see also Macuch 2005a, 2005b and 2015c.

us, although Sasanian theologians and jurists obviously had no problem understanding these concise entries due to their knowledge of the *argot* in which they communicated with each other.[224] Unfortunately only very few editions of the Pahlavi sources named above are conscious of the impact of this precise language, which often only seems sparse and elliptical because we are still ignorant of the exact meanings and connotations of many expressions despite huge progress in this field in the past years. Middle Persian legal *termini technici* may be traced back to three major sources:

- words and phrases taken from the Avesta, or its Pahlavi translation and commentary, the *zand* (such as *adwadād* '[offence of] withholding nourishment', from Av. *aδβadāitī-* 'act of placing on the way, leaving on the road', or *yōhē pasčaēta* 'who [succeeds] him afterwards'; see below);
- expressions from the daily vernacular, defined by jurists in a specific manner and regularly used in a legal context in this restricted sense (such as in property law the precise distinction between *xwēšīh* 'ownership' and *dārišn* 'possession' or the phrase *mad ud rasēd*, lit. 'that which has come and will be attained', for *bona adventitia*, the surplus income of family property, which is not originally part of the *patrimonium*);
- technical terms derived from the practice of the courts and the administration (such as *nibištag* 'bill of indictment' or the distinction between different types of transcripts, *saxwan-nāmag* 'record of statements', in a civil case and *pursišn-nāmag* 'record of interrogation', in a criminal trial).[225]

Iranian legal terms from the two latter categories can be found as loan-words in various other legal systems of the Near and Middle East, notably the Canon law of the East Christians (Nestorians), Armenian and Jewish (Talmudic) law. Sasanian technical terms are also found in the Sogdian, Bactrian, Khwarezmian and Early Jewish-Persian legal material.

Terms of the first category taken from the Avesta were not used in the daily colloquial, but were part of the technical terminology of both Sasanian theology and jurisprudence, known exclusively to those schooled in these disciplines and at times reflecting an older stage of Zoroastrian law. An example is the Avestan phrase *yō hē pasčaēta* 'who (succeeds) him afterwards', derived from an Old Iranian context lost to us from a (presumably legal?) text which has not survived. The phrase is attested in the field of succession and inheritance as a technical term designating the 'legal successor' of a *paterfamilias*, regardless of the question, whether succession took place directly (as in the case of a male) or indirectly (as in the case of a female). Since this differentiation between direct (male) and indirect (female) succession was particularly important in Sasanian law, the use of the Avestan phrase as a technical term for *both* types probably

224 For an example from the *Hērbedestān* see Macuch 2009c.
225 The sources of legal terminology are discussed in Macuch 2005a.

reflects an older level of jurisprudence. The use of a single expression for 'legal successor' could date from a period in which the complex rules of succession and inheritance, as we know them from late Sasanian law, had not yet been fixed in the manner we are able to reconstruct from Pahlavi legal material (for more details see Chapter II, section 4).

Another example of a technical term taken from the Avesta reveals that expressions from the sacred texts were subject to gradual alterations corresponding to the changes that had become necessary in jurisprudence across the centuries. The Avestan expression *aδβadāitī-* 'act of placing on the way, leaving on the road' , derived from < *aδβan-* 'way, road' and √*dā* 'to set, place'[226] (or from a possible variant **aδβadāta-* 'placed in the road, left on the way') designates 'abandonment', the offence of a parent or guardian leaving a person (a child or another dependant person under custody) to his/her fate. The literal meaning of the word gives us a clue as to the original offence: *aδβadāitī-* probably expressed the act of deserting a minor or any other person for whom one has legal responsibility in the literal sense of 'leaving him/her on the road'. The Pahlavi form of the word, *adwadād*, designates not only an offence in the original sense of abandoning a person under one's custody by deserting him/her, but in the *far wider sense* of failing to heed the rules of proper guardianship by withdrawing sustenance. It expressly denotes the offence of 'depriving a person, a sheepdog or a fire of nourishment; not providing a person or animal under guardianship with food or a sacred fire with fuel; failing to maintain persons under custody'. Another interesting aspect of the technical term is that it refers not only to a tort liable to punishment (that of 'withholding nourishment'), but also to a state of emergency caused by a shortage of supplies, for which no specific individual could possibly be held responsible: *adwadād* also means 'inability to maintain because of a lack of food or shortage of supplies'. This ambiguity of meaning seems to reflect an early stage of law in which the intention of an individual was not yet one of the crucial factors determining that person's responsibility for the resulting harm. Following the rule of 'strict liability', the guardian was held legally accountable for not providing for persons and animals under his guardianship, even if this was due to a state of emergency. Interestingly, the term also acquired an extended meaning with regard to the obligation of transmitting Zoroastrian values and knowledge to the next generation. In the context of teaching students, *adwadād* denotes the offence of a teacher not willing to convey his knowledge with the meaning of 'withdrawing *spiritual* nourishment', not giving a pupil religious sustenance in the sense of refusing to teach a disciple willing to learn. In this expression both features of Zoroastrian law become visible, the material aspect in the offence of disregarding one's duties as guardian by depriving a person, animal or fire of sustenance (or, following the rule of 'strict liability', not being able to provide for them in an appropriate manner due

226 Bartholomae 1904, col. 62; Kellens 1995, p. 29.

to a lack of supplies), and the spiritual side in the grave sin of refusing to give religious education to a person longing for it.[227]

Phrases taken from the Avesta could also be used as technical terms. The expression *srēnag/sēnag masāy ud bāzā masāy*, lit. 'the size of a buttock and size of a forefoot' designates the daily ration of a mature man and is derived from Av. *sraoni.masah-* 'the size of a buttock' and **bāzu.masah-* 'the size of a forefoot'[228] (*sēnag* 'breast', the alternative form attested in in several manuscripts, is a variant of the original *srēnag* 'forefoot'). This interesting phrase illustrates perfectly the original custom of paying in kind by allocating meat rations from the front and hind part of a slaughtered animal, which was one of the main tasks of the priest.[229] Beneficent animals were killed within the framework of the ritual as a sacrifice to the divine beings. After sacrificing the animal the priests apportioned the roasted meat among persons entitled to sustenance in the Zoroastrian community according to exact rules.[230] In jurisprudence the phrase is used as a technical term to denote the remuneration of persons engaged in serving the family as guardian (*sālār*) or 'proxy' (*stūr*). These persons were entitled to a portion of the family income corresponding to the ration they would receive daily in terms of pieces of meat ('the size of a buttock and size of a forefoot'), but the phrase is not to be taken literally. It was rather a basis for assessing the payment due to guardian and 'proxy' for fulfilling their tasks in the family.

227 I have discussed the diverse meanings and implications of the term extensively in Macuch 2012a and 2012b. See also below Chapter V, pp. 463–468.

228 For attestations of the Avestan terms see Bartholomae 1904, cols. 1633 and 956, respectively.

229 This is explained exactly in the Pahlavi commentary to the Avestan phrase *paṇcadasa pasuuō sraoni.masā̊* 'fifteen (pieces) of a sheep the size of a buttock' (FīO XXVb; Reichelt 1900–1901, pp. 209.12–210.3; Klingenschmitt 1968, no. 720) as follows: *pad ⁺ham-wēnāgīhā bāzā masāy 15 ⁺pah sēnag masāy 15 bāzā masāy čiyōn nēmag ī pēš bāzā masāy ud ān ī pas sēnag masāy čiyōn gōspand-ē(w) arz 12 drahm ī purr 30 kardag har rōz-ē(w) 2 kardag ayāb hāwand xwarišn-iz ī 2 kardag arzēd rōzīg ī mard ī purnāy ī bōxtag rāy gōwēd mādag ī wastarag hāwand ī arz ī xwarišn handāxt.* 'In accordance with "the size of a forefoot" (*bāzā masāy*): 15 (pieces) of a sheep "the size of a buttock" (*sēnag masāy*); 15 (pieces) of "the size of a forefoot" (*bāzā masāy*); that is, the front half (is) *bāzā masāy* and the hind (part is) *sēnag masāy*; this corresponds to 30 pieces of a sheep worth 12 full drachms. Two pieces or the equivalent in food worth 2 pieces are said to be the daily ration of a mature, respectable ("blameless") man. The money for clothing is measured according to the value of the food.' A similar phrase (albeit in another context) is attested Vd 6.20: *bāzu stauuaŋhəm vā sraoni.masaŋhəm* 'of the strength of an arm or the size of a buttock', translated by *bāzā zahā ayāb srēnag/sēnag dra(h)nāy* 'of the strength of an arm/forefoot or the length of a buttock/breast'. For different attestations of the two terms and a discussion of their development see Macuch 1990.

230 On animal sacrifice in the Zoroastrian ritual see Cantera 2022; on the regulations regarding the allotment of food in Zoroastrianism see Macuch 2012a with further references. On the rejection of this priestly right of food allocation by the Mazdakites see Macuch 2015b.

As we may conclude from post-Sasanian Pahlavi sources, their remuneration was calculated according to the monetary value of the meat rations and did not necessarily have to be paid in kind. In the Sasanian Law-book the phrase is used with reference to the family guardian (*dūdag-sālār*), who receives no share in the inheritance of a *paterfamilias*, therefore is entitled to receive separate payment in this form for his services to the family.

Although a relatively large amount of Avestan expressions continued to be used in legal language (also in their Pahlavi forms)[231], the bulk of technical terms in the fields of family law, property, obligations and procedural law consisted of words taken from the daily vernacular. These were defined exactly in a legal context and used in this specific sense. As a social construct law is subject to change and modification in continuing interaction with the moral and social norms of society, even if its point of departure is an ancient religion. Although the precepts of the Avesta continued to be observed, they no longer sufficed to satisfy the multiple needs of a complex, heterogeneous society. With the development of diverse fields of law it became necessary to expand legal language and to construct new terms based on the language spoken by jurists and used in the courts.

The legal sense of a word could be determined by giving a precise meaning to an expression used otherwise in an ambiguous and imprecise sense in the daily vernacular. An example—known in every advanced legal system—is the precise differentiation between two important terms of property law: 'ownership' and 'possession'. These two terms are usually used in a vague sense in spoken language, but defined and distinguished from each other exactly in legal argot, even though the definitions can vary in detail from system to system. In Sasanian law *xwēšīh* 'ownership' denotes the full title or right of dominion over property, the power to enjoy, use, possess and dispose of it at one's discretion, a concept similar to *dominium* (or *proprietas*) in Roman classical law, albeit with one important exception: in Sasanian law *xwēšīh* is *not* an 'absolute right' (as in *classical* Roman legal theory, on which our own concept of ownership is based), but a 'relative right', which could be contested by claimants who were able to offer better proof of ownership. 'Possession', or *dārišn* in Sasanian law, on the other hand, is distinguished exactly from 'ownership'. It corresponds roughly to *possessio* in Roman law and designates the *de facto* possession of a property which can, but does not necessarily include ownership (as in cases of leasehold, tenancy, goods in pledge, etc.) and might even be unlawful (as in the case of a stolen object). As in other advanced legal systems, the distinction between *dārišn* 'possession' and *xwēšīh* 'ownership' is crucial in Sasanian property law and the foundation upon which some of the most important legal institutions (such as *ruwānagān* and *stūrīh*) were built.

231 Many of these are attested in the *Frahang ī ōīm*, see Reichelt 1900–1901, Klingenschmitt 1968 and above, pp. 30–31, and will be referred to in the following chapters.

The two terms are used with meticulous precision in all legal texts and never confused.[232]

There are numerous examples of technical terms derived from some of the most common words of the spoken language. It is hardly possible to understand a legal text using these expressions correctly without exact knowledge of the juridical background and the precise legal implications of the terminology involved, as another example may illustrate. Two terms derived from the frequently attested verbs *madan* 'to come' and *rasīdan* 'to arrive', the perfect participle *mad* 'came' and the present/future 3.sg. *rasēd* 'arrives, will arrive', have specific legal meanings, when they are used in the context of property law. Sasanian law distinguished between two main types of possessions: (1) property inherited from the forefathers (*abarmānd ī pidarān*) and (2) property acquired by different means, such as gifts and donations (*dād*), earnings and revenue (*handōzišn ud windišn*), interest (*waxt, waxš*) etc. The latter category of property that a family acquired *after* inheriting the 'total estate' (*abarmānd*) of a lineage was called collectively *mad ud rasēd*, lit. '(property that) has come and shall arrive', a technical term comparable to *bona adventitia* in classical Roman law, designating every kind of surplus income, which did not belong initially to the former category of property inherited from the forefathers. The terms could also be used separately in this context, with *mad* (lit. 'came, has come') designating the surplus to family property which had already been attained up to a certain period, and *rasēd* (lit. 'arrives, shall arrive') the surplus anticipated for the future (for example, the interest to a loan).[233]

Another example is the use of the term *gādār* (lit. 'fornicator, lover, husband'), an agent noun of the verb *gādan* 'to fornicate, copulate with', in the context of Sasanian marriage and family law: *gādār kardan* ('to take a *gādār*') is *not* simply another form of the verb *gādan*, nor does it literally mean 'to take a lover'. The form is built in analogy to *zan/šōy kardan* 'to take a wife/husband' respectively and is linked to a specific type of marriage, called *xwasrāyēn/ūn*, lit. '(having) one's own *manus* (or: guardianship)'[234]. The *xwasrāyēn/ūn* marriage was a specific type of matrimony with implications that differed significantly from both those of the common 'arranged' or 'privileged' marriage (called *pādixšāy*) as well as those of the 'auxiliary' marriage (called *čagar*). It was a type of 'consensus' marriage, based on the desire of a man and woman to enter matrimony on their own. In contrast to the 'privileged' (*pādixšāy*) type, which was arranged by a woman's guardian (usually a male in her native lineage, her father, brother or uncle), *xwasrāyēn/ūn* marriage was concluded by the bride's own choice. None of the rights and duties of wife and husband

232 On 'ownership' and 'possession' in Sasanian law see Macuch 2015d and Chapter III, pp. 193–197.

233 On the use of these terms in the Sasanian Law-book see Macuch 1993, pp. 157–169, and in the Pahlavi marriage contract, Macuch 2007b, p. 199. See also Chapter III, pp. 192–193.

234 On the etymology of the word see Chapter II, fn. 165.

in *pādixšāy*-wedlock were in force in the 'consensus' marriage, which seems to have been a rather rare and unusual type of matrimony. Religious authorities nevertheless supported it as a last resort if a young girl's guardian failed to marry her in good time after she had reached puberty and it also seems to have been a possible form of marriage for a widow, who had no further obligations towards her deceased husband or her natal lineage (see Chapter II, pp. 145–147). The act of entering this type of matrimony is expressed by *gādār kardan* with the technical meaning 'to take a husband in a marriage of the *xwasrāyēn/ūn*-type'. As this example illustrates, it is occasionally difficult to find appropriate translations for technical terms due to the mass of information contained in a single word or phrase. Without knowledge of the legal background the expression remains incomprehensible. This is also true of many other terms employed in the context of family law and inheritance (*ayōgēn*, *stūr*, among others) which we will discuss in Chapter II, pp. 163–174.

A third group of legal expressions emerged in the courts of Sasanian Iran, many of which were also derived from the daily vernacular. We may assume that from the very beginning of Sasanian reign the work of jurisconsults and State courts was crucial for keeping public order and providing justice. The difficulties involved in adapting ancient regulations conceived for another type of community in the ancient Zoroastrian legal texts to the necessities of a large State must have been evident to theologians and clearly noticed in the daily practice of the courts. The dilemma was solved to a certain extent by distinguishing between proceedings complying strictly with 'legal doctrine' (*čāštag*) and those following another judicial procedure at the free discretion of the court (*kardag*), as we have already noted above. Moreover, in the field of procedural law it became necessary to distinguish between proceedings in civil and criminal cases, which in turn led to the development of various terms denoting different kinds of court transcripts, *e.g.*, *saxwan-nāmag* 'record of statements' in a civil dispute; *pursišn-nāmag* 'record of questioning (or investigation)' in criminal cases, and *yazišn-nāmag* 'record of recitation', documenting the procedure of taking an oath (*war*). The general expression *nibištag* (lit. 'written document') designated in the context of criminal procedure specifically the 'bill of indictment'. These terms were used exclusively within the framework for which they were conceived, hereby conveying exact information on the type of trial or procedure they were documenting. The term *pursišn-nāmag* is also attested as a loanword—among other Iranian technical terms—in the Babylonian Talmud in the context of criminal law, indicating that the Jewish rabbis were well acquainted with Sasanian court procedure (see Chapter VII, pp. 594–595).

Other technical terms derived from the daily colloquial were employed with a specific meaning in procedural law. The well-known term *dastwar*, used in the sense of 'authority' in Pahlavi texts (later in the sense of 'priest, minister'), has a specific meaning in the context of the civil lawsuit, which has now been confirmed by the testimony of the original legal documents from

Tabarestān.[235] In a dispute over proprietary rights *dastwar* denotes a litigant's 'legal predecessor', the person, who has sold (or transferred in any other manner) to the litigant the object that has now become the cause for legal action. As the original proprietor, the 'legal predecessor' has the duty to defend the purchaser in court, if a third party claims possession or ownership of the transferred object and to verify that the transaction was legitimate. This method of proving a person's proprietary rights by testifying for the purchaser (or transferee) corresponds exactly to the obligation of the *auctor* in ancient Roman law (see Chapters IV, pp. 385–387, and VI, pp. 542–544).[236]

The court records from Tabarestān (see pp. 18–20) not only use *dastwar* in exactly this sense, but also convey other technical terms and phrases hitherto unknown. One example is the hendyadis *čim ud bōzišn* 'evidence and proof', in the formula *az čim ud bōzišn hammis* 'together with evidence and proof'. Although both terms are attested separately in Pahlavi legal literature, the words do not occur in this combination as a specific formula. In the Tabarestān documents they are the formulaic words spoken by the defendant in court as a pledge that he will provide evidence to exonerate himself in a civil dispute: he commits himself to appear in court, when summoned, 'together with evidence and proof'. A similar formula, partly retaining Sasanian legal terminology, is attested in two early Judaeo-Persian texts as *bwzyšn wḥwct* (*bōzišn u ḥuǰǰat*) 'evidence and proof' with the Arabic *ḥuǰǰat* 'proof' in the place of *čim* in the Pahlavi formula, and could even be an early adaptation of older *čim ud bōzišn*.[237] Other hitherto unrecognized legal expressions, such as *wisē kardan* 'to summon' (to court), enhance our knowledge of Sasanian juridical language, which survived into the eighth century.[238]

Important as they are, technical terms do not suffice as a tool to solve the numerous linguistic problems that emerge in legal dealings. Although a specific legal vocabulary contributes to fewer misunderstandings and enhances a precise diction, its use does not completely eliminate the general inaccuracy of language, which remains one of the main dilemmas of jurisprudence. One of the foremost tasks of legal experts—today as in former times—is to interpret laws and regulations. These can be applied within a restrictive or extensive framework according to certain criteria that can vary from legal school to legal school. However, not only laws, but all kinds of agreements, contracts, declarations of assignment, stipulations, etc., are liable to interpretation, particularly when ambiguous formulations in documents lead to conflicting claims. The central goal is to find out the original intention of the parties involved in the legal act, notably if the phrasing of the document in question is not precise enough and

235 See Macuch 2016a, pp. 150–151.
236 On *dastwar* see also Macuch 1988b.
237 MacKenzie 1968, p. 253, and Macuch 2016a, pp. 149–150.
238 See Weber 2016a, p. 124, and Macuch 2016a, p. 156.

allows for several interpretations. In fact many of the civil disputes transmitted in the Sasanian Law-book are cases in which the wording of a stipulation or a legal document (often a will or contract) is either discussed controversially or is decisive for the outcome of a trial. It is therefore hardly surprising that Sasanian experts strove to control the language used in legal dealings by establishing a series of legal formulae as well as certain strict linguistic categories, which would enable them to assess equivocal formulations and avoid arbitrary decisions to a certain degree. Even a whole chapter of the Sasanian Law-book is dedicated to the interpretation of formulations in stipulations and documents, but there are far more cases in this work than those described in this particular division.[239]

Many of the distinctions developed by Sasanian jurists involve not only minutely defined technical terms, but common words and phrases and different grammatical forms, which were treated as formulaic expressions with specific legal implications. Although many of these elucidations may make pedantic reading today, they are nevertheless crucial for understanding how jurists tried to solve the problem of language ambiguity and how Sasanian law functioned on a daily basis. A few examples may suffice to illustrate the point.[240]

One of the remarkable linguistic peculiarities is the use of the *izāfe* in a statement of a person's will transferring a certain title or right to the next generation. In legal language an exact distinction is made between the possibility of joining nouns in the construct state with the *izāfe*, on the one hand, and the so-called 'reversed *izāfe*', in which the dependant noun (*rectum*) precedes the regent noun (*regens*) without the use of the relative particle, on the other. Although these two constructions are used with exactly the same meaning in non-legal Pahlavi literature, they have completely divergent legal implications in a juridical context. For example, the phrase *frazand ud āwādag ī Farrox* 'the children and descendants of Farrox' is interpreted in a different manner than *Farrox frazand ud āwādag* 'Farrox's children and descendants'. The first phrasing with the regular *izāfe* (*frazand ud āwādag ī Farrox* 'the children and descendants of Farrox') implies that there is a *time limit* to the disposition: only persons who have been born and already exist as heirs of Farrox at the time of the disposition are referred to. The second wording with the dependant noun preceding the regent nouns (*Farrox frazand ud āwādag* 'Farrox's children and descendants') implies *no time limit* whatsoever: not only living heirs, but even non-existant, hypothetical descendants that the person named in the disposition (Farrox) may have in the future are included in this provision.[241]

239 The title is *dar ī dādestān ēčand ī ēwāz rāy pad nāmčišt abāyēd nigerīdan* 'Chapter on several judicial cases in which particular attention should be paid to the formulation (of statements)', MHDA 16.7–25.14 (Macuch 1981, pp. 38–49; 163–172; 173–187).

240 I have discussed these linguistic peculiarities extensively in Macuch 2005b and 2015c.

241 The two full statements are: *frazand ud āwādag ī Farrox pad aswār-nibēg ma ē āwāšēnd* 'the children and descendants of Farrox should not be registered (lit: sealed) in the horseman's document (*aswār-nibēg*)' and *Farrox frazand ud āwādag pad aswār-nibēg ma ē*

The exact placing of a word in a document also has important legal implications. For example, the position of *hamē* 'always' (denoting that there should be no restriction or time limit) in dispositions transferring a title or a right to another person should immediately precede the designation of the person (or persons) to whom the title is transferred. For example, in ***hamē*** *az frazandān ī man mard-ē(w) ī pāhlom* 'always among my children the best man' *hamē* ('always') refers to the following *az frazandān ī man* 'among my children'. The implication is that the disposition refers with no time limit ('always') to the testator's children, specifically sons, one of whom with the special quality named in the will should receive the title to a certain right (in this specific case the guardianship of a fire). Most importantly it implies that different sons among the testator's children can be ranked as best qualified in different circumstances and at various periods. On the other hand, if the phrasing is: *az frazandān ī man* ***hamē*** *mard-ē(w) ī pāhlom* 'among my children always the best man' *hamē* refers to the following *mard-ē(w) ī pāhlom* implying that *a specific son* who is best qualified among the children of the testator at the time that the disposition takes effect should be chosen *once and for all* to the exclusion of all other children. The two formulations are identical with the exception of the position of *hamē*.[242]

In other examples the position of the ambiguous *tā* 'until, as long as', in relation to the personal pronoun and the object of an agreement is decisive for the legal interpretation of a statement. In other sentences a disposition stating two conditions has different implications, if a preposition (*e.g.*, *pad* or *ō*) only precedes the first condition or is repeated a second time before the second condition.[243] Moreover, the precise sequence of words in a legal formula is crucial: in the two identical formulae *dād pašt xwēš* and *pašt dād xwēš* only the sequence of the first two words is different, but they have divergent consequences. In an agreement concerning the transfer of an object into the ownership of another person the formula *dād pašt xwēš* (lit. 'the transferred contract [is her/his] own' or 'the contract of transfer [is her/his] own') implies that there is no time limit to the validity of the contract even after the death of the recipient, *giving his (or her) heirs a title* to the object of the contract. The formula *pašt dād xwēš* (lit. 'the contract [is] conveyed [as her/his] own'), on the other hand, implies that the agreement has legal effect only with respect to the person named in the contract, *excluding the heirs* of the recipient from any claims whatsoever.[244]

It was particularly important that a donor or testator use the appropriate formulaic expressions and legal terms in his will, since he would no longer be there to explain the provisions he had made when his testament became effective.

āwāšēnd 'Farrox's children and descendants should not be registered (lit: sealed) in the horseman's document', MHDA 16.11–14; for a discussion of the whole passage see Macuch 2005c, pp. 96–99.

242 Macuch 2005c, pp. 100–101.

243 See examples *ibid.*, pp. 104–107.

244 Examples *ibid.*, pp. 100–104.

Several remarkable examples have been transmitted using the words *ōwōn čiyōn* 'so as', and *čiyōn* 'as, like', which have approximately the same meaning in the daily vernacular, but completely different implications in a legal context. Employed in a will they led to meticulous distinctions, as in the following two divergent provisions:

> MHDA 20.15–21.1
> *ka gōwēd kū-m ēn xwāstag* ***ōwōn čiyōn-am*** (16) *ō pus xwāstag dād ō duxt dād ǰuttar bawēd čiyōn ka gōwēd kū-m ēn* (17) *xwāst{ag}* ***čiyōn-am*** *ō pus xwāstag dād ō duxt dād …*
>
> 'When he (= the father) declares: "This property I gave **in the same manner as** (*ōwōn čiyōn* 'so as') I gave property to the son (also) to the daughter", (then this statement) differs from when he declares: "This property I gave **as soon as** (*čiyōn* 'as') I gave property to the son (also) to the daughter"…'.

The sentence discusses the use of these two formulae in the (hypothetical?) testament of a father, who assigns a share of his estate to his daughter and to his son. The first wording uses the formula *ōwōn čiyōn* (lit. 'so as') between the designation of the two beneficiaries, son and daughter; the second one employs *čiyōn* (lit. 'as, like') between the two beneficiaries. The implications of these two formulations differ fundamentally. Subsequent explanations in the text (which I have discussed elsewhere extensively) clarify that *ōwōn čiyōn* 'so as' (with *čiyōn* as a relative adverb with a demonstrative antecedent *ōwōn*) was understood in the sense of 'in the same manner as'; *čiyōn* alone, on the other hand, was used temporally in the sense of 'as soon as; at the same time'. The implication of the first wording (with *ōwōn čiyōn*) in the will is: son and daughter receive *exactly the same share* of all the different kinds of family property (on these see Chapter III, pp. 202-230). The second phrasing (with *čiyōn*) only implies that son and daughter should receive property *at the same time*, which of course diverges radically from the intention conveyed with the first formula. Other similar examples with these formulaic expressions confirm this interpretation.[245]

Another remarkable peculiarity is the use of the ergative (or agential) construction in provisions transferring a title or a right to another person either by testament, donation or in some other manner, including the transfer of certain duties and offices (such as that of *sālārīh* 'guardianship' or *stūrīh* 'substitute succession'). The bulk of the attested cases are formulated with the ergative/agential *ku-m … (ō tō) dād*, lit. 'I gave (to you)', in the sense of 'I bestowed, bequeathed, conveyed, granted, transferred, stipulated' (usually with *ō* 'to' and the name of the recipient). Since the preterite tense is used we would expect these provisions to refer to a transfer that had already taken place in the past, but, strangely, this is definitely *not* the case in a large number of examples. On the contrary, in many instances this wording in a disposition denotes a legal act,

245 See the extensive discussion of these passages in Macuch 2015c.

which should be *implemented in the future*. The grammatical forms we would rather expect to express this intention, that is, the optative or present/future (*ē dahēd* 'should be given'; *dahom* 'I give, will give'), are in fact very seldom.[246]

It seems especially strange that a testator communicating his last will should employ the preterite to do so, although the provisions in the will would only take effect in the future after his death. There can be no doubt, however, that this exactly was the intent behind this phrasing, as a number of passages reveal, in which specific temporal instructions are added. In these the transaction specified in the provision has *not* already been carried out (as the past tense would imply), but *will take effect in the future* after the death of the donor/testator.[247] The donor/testator expressly provides that the transfer should take place *widard man* 'after my death' or *frāz az man* 'after me' (= after my demise) or *pas az 10 sāl* 'after 10 years'. According to these specifications the intent of the donor/testator is actually to transfer something not at the time the provision is made, but at some period in the future. The ergative/agential wording is chosen not only in these examples, but also in other dispositions without any further additions regarding the time of their implementation. My conclusion is that this specific formulation was required in order to avoid ambiguity with regard to the precise time when a will or donation should take effect. The last will is 'ambulatory', that is, it comes into force *not* when it is made, but from the death of the testator. In this manner it can include both property acquired by the testator *after* the will had been drawn, also beneficiaries born to him since then, excluding those who had died in the meantime. In other words: *the testator 'speaks from death'*, which is perfectly reflected in the use of the past tense in these provisions. He unequivocally determines (even without any time specification) that a disposition should take effect and be implemented *not* immediately when the document is drawn (or the oral stipulation made public before witnesses), but after his demise, either immediately or at a specific time named explicitly in the will (*e. g.*, 'after 10 years'). We may assume that the agential/ergative form in the testament (*kū-m …[ō tō] dād*, lit. 'I gave [to you]') in fact denotes the intent of transferring something in the future after the testator/donor has passed away. This seems to

246 For attestations see *ibid.*, p. 133, no. 10.

247 Examples: MHD 20.6 (Macuch 1993, pp. 155, 161): *kū-m xwāstag ī widard man ō dūdag ī man rasēd ō tō dād* 'I gave the property that will come to my family after my death to you'; MHD 90.2 (*ibid.*, pp. 570, 573): *kū-m pad be widerišnīh xwāstag pad stŭrīh ō kas dād* 'I gave property after (my) death in *stŭrīh* to (such-and-such) a person'; MHD 30.4f. (*ibid.*, pp. 221, 225): *kū-m xwāstag ī man xwēš frāz az man ō Ādurfarrbay dād* 'I gave the property which is my own after me to Ā.'; MHD 31.4 (*ibid.*, pp. 222, 226): *kū-m xwāstag ī man xwēš frāz az man ō wāhmān mard dād* 'I gave the property which is my own after me to such-and-such a man'; MHD 43. 14 (*ibid.*, pp. 302, 319): *kū-m frāz az man dād* 'I gave (it) after me (= after my death)'; MHD 88.5 (*ibid.*, pp. 561, 564): *kū-m ēw bahr frāz az man pad stŭrīh ō tō dād* 'I gave one share after me in *stŭrīh* to you'; MHDA 8.14f.,16 (Macuch 1981, pp. 29f., 121): *kū-m pas az 10 sāl ō Mihrēn dād* 'I gave it after 10 years to Mihrēn'.

be the reason for the constant use of this formulation in the will in contrast to other transfer documents in which the present/future tense (*dahom* 'I give, shall give') or optative (*ē dahēd*) is chosen with no such temporal implications.[248]

5 The concept of legal rights

Did Sasanian law develop a concept comparable to the idea expressed by the vague English word 'a right'?[249] The absence of a single equivalent term would not mean that the whole idea of legal rights protecting the individual in law (and possibly from the law) was unknown, but only that this was expressed in a different manner. In an attempt to resolve the ambiguity of the English word, Wesley N. Hohfeld has suggested to distinguish between four various forms of rights, to speak of

1. a 'claim' when there is a correlative 'duty' in someone else (as in the 'right' of a creditor to the repayment of a debt, correlating with the 'duty' of the debtor to repay the debt);
2. a 'privilege' in the absence of a correlative 'duty' (as the liberty of disposing over one's own property; the jural correlative of a 'no-right');
3. 'authority' or 'power' when a person has affirmative control over a given legal relation (as, *e.g.*, guardianship over dependent persons);
4. 'immunity', when one is exempt from the legal power or control of another (as the protection against being prosecuted).[250]

This is only a very shortened rendering of his complex analysis, to which I would like to refer the reader here, but it will suffice for our purpose of determining, whether Sasanian jurists were acquainted in some manner with the idea of a legal right. Although it would be anachronistic to transpose Hohfeld's modern categorization of rights to a pre-modern system, his precise allocations are a useful guideline for detecting comparable concepts and locutions in Sasanian law.

The most frequent term expressing the notion of 'having, enjoying a (specific) right' in the broadest sense of the word is the legal term *pādixšāy* 'authorized, empowered, entitled, privileged, allowed' (< OIr. √**xšaH* 'to rule; be lord of' + prefix *pati-*)[251], also in the compound *pādixšāy-būd* 'authorization, entitlement', the abstract form *pādixšāyīh* 'authorization, empowerment, entitlement' and the adverb *pādixšāyīhā* 'entitled, privileged, empowered' (the noun *pādixšāy* 'ruler, sovereign' is only attested in a non-legal context).[252] The verbs *pādixšāy*

248 Most illuminative is MHDA 22.17–23.6, in which theses verbal forms are contrasted. I have discussed this and other passages extensively in Macuch 2015c, pp. 133–136.
249 On legal rights see also Macuch (forthcoming b).
250 Hohfeld 1919, pp. 35–64.
251 Cheung 2007, p. 451.
252 For attestations see Macuch 1993, *Index*, pp. 723–724.

būdan 'to be entitled, authorized' and *pādixšāy kardan* 'to authorize, entitle' are repeatedly employed to refer to the existence of a specific legal title or right and the transfer of a specific title or right respectively. This locution is used extensively in all fields of law. Can it be parsed in a manner comparable to the distinctions made by HOHFELD? I contend that three of the four uses mentioned above can be detected in the legal material.

The meaning of being entitled to something in the sense of having a 'just claim' (in the sense of the assertion of a right against another member of the community or a demand for a remedy) is amply attested in the Sasanian Law-book. The expression occurs, for example, in connection with the liabilities of a community of heirs regarding the question: when does a shareholder (*hambāy*), who has paid back the total sum of a liability of the inherited estate (*abām ī pidarān* 'debt of the parents'), have the right (*pādixšāy*) to demand reimbursement from the other shareholders? The Law-book presents three case-studies: (1) A shareholder who has paid back the whole debt although the creditor has made no payment claim (*ǰud az xwāstārīh*) has the right (*pādixšāy*) to demand reimbursement from the other shareholders. (2) A shareholder offers to pay his part of the whole sum, but the creditor refuses to accept partial payment and declares that he will wait for payment by the other shareholders. If the shareholder nevertheless repays the whole debt, he has no right (*nē pādixšāy*) to demand reimbursement from the other shareholders. (3) The same creditor, who has first refused partial payment, later asks the same shareholder to repay the whole sum. In this case the shareholder has the right (*pādixšāy*) to demand reimbursement from the other shareholders.[253] Another case transmits a decision of the highest judge, the Chief Mobed (*mowbedān mowbed*): a creditor, who has lent a sum of money to two men, who have 'equal proprietary shares' (*dārišn āgenēn*) and are 'business associates' (*hamxwāstag*), has the right (*pādixšāy*) to demand payment of the whole sum from one of the two debtors.[254] The word is also employed in the context of family law: a person who provides for a minor, who is not being maintained by the father, has the right (*pādixšāy*) to confiscate the earnings (*kār-windišn*) of the father to an amount equivalent to the costs of upbringing the child.[255]

The term *pādixšāy* is also used in the sense of being entitled to a special right or 'privilege/liberty' (the jural correlative of 'no-right'). In family law the regular marriage of the arranged type is called *pādixšāyīhā zanīh* 'marriage of the privileged kind' or 'marriage with full matrimonial rights'. This form of marriage conveys a large range of distinctive rights (= privileges) to the husband (*šōy ī pādixšāy[īhā]*), the wife (*zan ī pādixšāy[īha]*) and the children (*pus/duxt ī pādixšāy[īhā]* 'son/daughter from a privileged marriage'), which are expressly

253 MHD 53.4–6; 53.6–10 (MACUCH 1993, pp. 369; 370).
254 MHD 55.11–13 (*ibid.*, pp. 386; 391).
255 MHD 33.3–6 (*ibid.*, pp. 241; 244).

excluded in the two other separate forms of matrimony.[256] The wife and children from this form of marriage can be entitled to income, which is expressed by *pad windišn pādixšāy* '(they) have a right to earnings'.[257] That the term *pādixšāy* is also used in the sense of 'liberty' to dispose over something or to enact a transaction according to one's will is apparent in the phrases 'he is entitled to give it to anyone he wants to' (*ō har kē kāmēd pādixšāy dād*) or 'he is authorized to sell it' (*pādixšāy frōxt*) or 'he is authorized to give away (someone/something)' (*be dād pādixšāy*).[258] The correlating term 'no-right', is expressed by the negation of the word, as in '(the wife) has no right to reject the command of the husband' (*az framān ī šōy be ēstād nē pādixšāy*) or 'he has no right to give away (someone/something)' (*be dād nē pādixšāy*) or 'he has no right to fell (the tree)' (*zadan nē pādixšāy*).[259]

Interestingly, the obligation or duty to perform a specific act is also expressed by the negation of the term, but in a fixed wording in the phrase *nē pādixšāy bē ka* lit. 'he/she has no right than; he/she has no (other) option but', meaning 'he/she is obliged, has the duty, is compelled to (do/say/perform something)'. This twisted formula, which explicitly makes use of the term *pādixšāy* instead of other far simpler ways of expressing the idea of a 'duty' (*e.g.*, by using words such as *frēz* or *xwēškārīh* 'obligation, duty') might even indicate that Sasanian jurists were in some vague form aware of the jural correlative between a 'right' and a 'duty'. For example, in the context of credit law one case discusses a loan contract based on real security, giving the creditor usufructuary rights to a certain amount of the produce of the mortgaged property (*grawagān*, comparable to the Roman *antichresis*).[260] The wording of the contract is discussed controversially, but one jurist maintains that, if the debtor pays back the full sum of the loan, then the creditor (lit.) 'has no (other) right/option than to accept the money' (*xwāstag ... nē pādixšāy bē ka stānēd*), that is, he is obliged to accept the payment and cannot continue to profit from the fruits of the property.[261] In one passage the son and other relatives of a deceased father are as his heirs and successors obliged to accept guardianship (*sālārīh*) over a sacred fire or a pious foundation of the father (*nē pādixšāy bē ka kunēnd* 'they have no right/option, but to perform [guardianship]').[262] In another example a daughter from a marriage 'with full matrimonial rights' (*pādixšāyīhā-zanīh*) inherits property set aside for the institution of 'substitute succession' (*stūrīh*) from the father, that is,

256 On marriage forms see Chapter II, pp. 133–147.
257 MHD 36.17 (Macuch 1993, pp. 268; 270).
258 MHD 26.10 (Macuch 1993, pp. 194; 201); MHD 33.14,15,17 (*ibid.*, pp. 241f.; 244f.); MHD 43.2 (*ibid.*, pp. 301; 318) respectively.
259 MHD 27.13 (Macuch 1993, pp. 196; 203); MHD 35.6 (*ibid.*, pp. 253; 256f.); MHD 36.14 (*ibid.*, pp. 268; 269); MHD 40.17 (*ibid.*, pp. 281; 286) respectively.
260 See Chapter IV, pp. 343–349.
261 MHD 40.1–13 (Macuch 1993, pp. 280f.; 285f.).
262 MHD 45.8–17 (*ibid.*, pp. 304f.; 321).

she receives a right of disposal over a part of the inheritance reserved for engendering offspring for the father.[263] In exchange she has the 'duty' (lit.: 'no [other] right than …') to act as the father's proxy and procreate children for him (*ān stūrīh nē pādixšāy bē ka kunēd* 'she has the duty to perform as proxy').[264]

The specific meaning of 'authority, power' is also attested for *pādixšāy*, not only in the noun 'sovereign, ruler, king', but in phrases expressing the act of conferring empowerment to someone. For example, a husband can empower his wife to enter an 'auxiliary marriage' (*čagar-zanīh*) by dismissing her from his guardianship with the formula 'I have given you the right to be guardian over yourself' (*kū-m pad xwēš-tan sālār pādixšāy kard hē*).[265] In the context of litigation the conveyance of a mandate or power of attorney is expressed with the verb *pādixšāy kardan* 'to give a mandate/power of attorney', as in 'I have been given a mandate by the person to whom you owe a debt to request and take it' (*kas kē čiš awiš tōzišn dahišn xwāst ud stad rāy az pādixšāy kard hom*).[266] In two case-studies *pādixšāy* (in *pādixšāy-būd*) is contrasted with *ēwēn* 'legal, lawful' (in *ēwēn-būd*) in the context of a transaction: if the transferor declares that he has conveyed a certain 'thing' (*xwāstag*) by sale (or some other means of transaction) to the transferee using the term *ēwēn*, then the implications are different than when he uses the term *pādixšāy* in his statement.[267] By employing *ēwēn* the transferor declares that the transaction is 'lawful, legal', but he does not explicitly confirm that he is also 'empowered' (*pādixšāy*) to enact it (as owner or possessor of the property or empowered agent). A legal transaction can be 'lawful' insofar as that it follows the required prescriptions. A statement by which the transferor confirms that he is 'entitled' to enact the transaction, on the other hand, makes him personally liable if a third party should contest this right (see the term *dastwar* below). We can conclude that *pādixšāy-būd* explicitly expresses the 'entitlement/empowerment' of a transferor to enact a transaction, whereas *ēwēn-būd* only substantiates the 'legality' of the agreement, but does not transmit any information on the question, whether he is empowered to undertake the deal. We can hence assume that in a contract of conveyance the term *pādixšāy* confirms the transferor's subjective right to undertake a transfer.[268]

Another recurring legal term is the noun *dastwar* 'authorized, entitled (person)' and its abstract form *dastwarīh* 'entitlement, authorization, empowerment, right of disposal' (in a religious context the noun usually denotes an expert in religious matters, a theologian or Zoroastrian priest). In juristic sources *dastwar* can denote a legal expert (the plural *dastwarān* often refers to a group of anonymous 'legal authorities'), but it is used far more frequently in the specific context

263 See Chapter II, pp. 163–174.
264 MHD 101.2 (Macuch 1993, pp. 614; 622).
265 MHD 3.10 (*ibid.*, pp. 68; 71).
266 MHD 76.5 (*ibid.*, pp. 510; 512).
267 MHDA 22.11–13 (Macuch 1981, pp. 46; 169); MHDA 22.8–11 (*ibid.*, pp. 45; 169).
268 On the transfer and acquisition of property see Chapter IV, pp. 301–305.

of property law. In this setting *dastwar* designates a person who has a right or title to ownership of the 'substance' (*bun*) or the 'fruits' (*bar*) or of both of these components of a corporal 'thing' (*xwāstag*).[269] The abstract *dastwarīh* denotes a person's right or entitlement to the 'thing' as in the phrase 'it is my own by that entitlement' (*kū-m pad ān dastwarīh xwēš*).[270] In legal proceedings *dastwar* is the 'legal predecessor' or 'predecessor in title' of a certain 'thing', who transfers this object by sale, barter, gift, will, etc. to another person and is obliged to defend the new owner against the claim of a third party in court (the exact counterpart of the ancient Roman *auctor*). In this specific context *dastwarīh* is '*auctor*-ship' or the act of vouchsafing for the legality of a transaction in court as the recipient's 'predecessor in title', *i. e.*, the person who previously had the right of disposal over the matter in dispute.[271]

Is a difference discernable between the use of these two most frequent expressions, *pādixšāy* and *dastwar(īh)*? It seems that *pādixšāy* is employed in a very broad sense of 'enjoying a (specific) right' and covers almost the whole spectrum of meanings differentiated by HOHFELD, when it refers to a person having a (just) 'claim', a 'privilege/liberty' or 'power', depending on the context in which it appears. The only meaning that is not attested is that of 'immunity', which might be significant, but could also be due to the fragmentary state of the material at our disposal. The word *dastwarīh* 'entitlement', on the other hand, designates in property law specifically the title (or right) to ownership of the substance or fruits (or of both elements) of a corporal 'thing' (*xwāstag*). The meaning '*auctor*-ship' in procedural law is a secondary development due to the option a third party might have to contest the legality of a specific transaction and the recipient's right to ownership. The *dastwar* as the latter's 'predecessor in title' was then obliged to procure adequate evidence of ownership and to defend the recipient in the lawsuit, or, to use Sasanian terminology, *pad dastwarīh andar ēstēd* 'he acts as *auctor*; he enters *auctor*-ship'.[272]

The notion of having specific rights by entitlement is also inherent in the term *tuwān(īg)*, lit. '(having) power, (being) capable' and its abstract *tuwānīgīh* 'powerfulness, capability' (< OIr. √**tauH* 'to be able, strong').[273] In a legal context *tuwān* has the meaning of 'legally capable' and *tuwānīgīh* of 'legal capacity, contractual capability', the right to act as an independent legal subject *sui iuris*. But the term is far more often attested in the context of obligations in the specific sense of 'solvency', the ability to pay, in contrast to *a-tuwānīgīh* 'insolvency'.[274]

269 This expression is also used in this sense as a loanword in the Babylonian Talmud, see Chapter VII, pp. 596–598; also MACUCH 2008a.
270 MHD 5.17 (MACUCH 1993, pp. 88; 92).
271 See Chapters IV, pp. 385–387, and VI, pp. 542–544; also MACUCH 2016a, pp. 150–151.
272 MHD 5.7 (MACUCH 1993, pp. 87; 91).
273 CHEUNG 2007, p. 386.
274 For attestations see MACUCH 1993, *Index*, p. 735.

The legal material provides ample evidence that Sasanian jurists developed a number of technical expressions in the context of asserting and denying claims, which can be interpreted as 'rights' locutions, including 'subjective rights' in the sense of *specific legal rights possessed by individuals, entitling them to certain privileges and forming the basis of their claims against others.* The situation is however completely different if we take 'subjective rights' to mean 'human rights' or 'rights of persons' in the modern sense of the word, that is, rights all individuals should have qua affiliation to the human race, or, as BURNYEAT has specified, 'certain minimum decencies ... due to each and every individual without their having to deserve or qualify for them; their being human is enough'.[275] There can be no doubt that this is a concept completely alien to Sasanian legal thought, as will be elucidated in the following Chapter.

6 Animal rights

One of the well-known characteristic features of Zoroastrian law is the special status given to beneficent animals of the good creation, protecting them from violence, mistreatment and neglect.[276] Is it possible to speak of 'animal rights' in this context? According to the Zoroastrian world-view the whole of creation is divided into two main groups belonging to the antagonistic powers of good and evil. These moral qualities by which humans were judged were projected in an anthropocentric view of the world to other living beings, separating animals into two antagonistic groups:

1. beneficent (*spəṇta*) animals, products of the good creation who were important for the welfare of humans, such as cattle, dogs, beasts of burden and other domestic animals living under the guardianship (*sālārīh*) of humans, and specific wild animals considered as creatures of the good creation, (the hedgehog, otter, fox, weasel, the water beaver, among others);
2. 'noxious creatures' (*xrafstar*), the collective expression for all animals either harmful to man and his crops or hideous, and hence reminiscent of the perversion of life by the Evil Spirit, such as insects (the locust, the wasp, the ant, the fly, spiders, scorpions etc.), reptiles (serpents, lizards, tortoises, etc.) and certain dangerous wild animals (such as the wolf).

The behaviour expected of a Zoroastrian towards creatures of these two groups differed radically: destroying 'noxious creatures' was regarded as a highly meritorious act (*kirbag*), whereas, in sharp contrast, offences committed against beneficent animals of the good creation were liable to punishment as 'sins pertaining to the soul' (*wināh ī ruwānīg*). Beneficent animals stood under the protection of the divine Vohu Manah/Wahman and were regarded as having souls,

275 BURNYEAT 1994, pp. 10–11.
276 On the treatment of animals in Zoroastrian law see MACUCH 2003a.

which, as the souls of humans, went to the hereafter after their demise. Slaying one was hence only permitted in the context of ritual sacrifice, which would limit destruction to the physical life of the animal and set its spirit free to depart to the hereafter.[277] All other forms of killing a beneficent animal were considered as 'unlawful' (*a-dād*). The Zoroastrian ritual knew two distinct types of animal sacrifice. The animal was either slaughtered during the actual performance of the Long Liturgy or it was slayed before the liturgy and its meat was prepared and cooked beforehand to be presented as an offering.[278]

The reasons brought forward for restricting the slaughter of beneficent animals to the ritual, are noteworthy. First, it is argued that slaying beneficent animals in the context of the ritual after stunning them with a log destroys the *druz*, but also prevents wanton slaughter; it protects animals from being killed 'unlawfully and rashly' (*a-dādīhā ud halagīhā*) and leads to 'less killing of cattle' (*kam-kušišnīh ī gōspand*). Second, the ritual prescribes stunning the sacrificial animal with a log (*čōb*) before applying the knife (*kārd*) due to 'compassion with the cattle' (*abaxšāyišn ī abar gōspand*), so that the animal may feel 'less fear and less pain' (*kam bīmīh ud kam dardīh*) and it prevents killing them 'quickly, any time one wishes to on impulse' (*zūd zūd pad har zamān ārzōg*).[279]

These explanations can be regarded as apologies of a priestly class bent on keeping to themselves the privilege of killing animals and distributing their meat to the community, but there can nevertheless be no doubt that there was a genuine concern in Zoroastrianism for the welfare of animals belonging to the good creation.[280] Caring for domestic animals under one's guardianship and behaving kindly towards them was an important moral and legal obligation, which is repeatedly stated in the sources and still heeded minutely in Zoroastrian communities up to this day. Avestan and Pahlavi sources list a large range of offences, which were punished by religious authorities in the *ruwānīg*

277 See Boyce 1975c, pp. 149f; 297f.
278 See Cantera 2022.
279 DkD 364.16–21 (DkM 466.12–18): *gōspand čōb pēš az kārd frāz burdan ud hammis ahārīg ī andar ān dar kunišn čim ān jud az nērangīg sūdārīh ī čand druz az tan pāk kardan nāmčištīg bahr ī +wēš-ahrīh ud dūš-mizagīh pad a-dādīhā ud halagīhā ud kam kušišnīh-iz ī gōspand ēk abaxšāyišn ī abar gōspand pad-iz ān rāh kam bīmīh ud kam dardīh ī-š az frāz burišn (ī) kārd ud nē halagīhā zūd zūd pad har zamān ārzōg tēzīhā ōzadan ī gōspand.* 'The reason for having to strike the cattle with a log before applying the knife—together with other matters in the same chapter—(is): besides the ritual gain of cleansing the body of several *druz* (it is) mainly because an increase of dread and bad taste (results) by (killing) unlawfully and rashly (*a-dādīhā ud halagīhā*). And killing cattle less (*kam kušišnīh-iz ī gōspand*) (is) first because of compassion (*abaxšāyišn*) with the cattle; in this way (there is) less fear and less pain (*kam bīmīh ud kam dardīh*) through the application of the knife, and it prevents the killing of cattle rashly, quickly any time one wishes to on impulse.' See also Amouzgar/Tafazzoli 2000, p. 97 (23), and (partly) Macuch 2003a, p. 171, with further references.
280 On the rules and offences regarding meat and food distribution see Macuch 2012a, pp. 247–269. On the sin of meat consumption see Farridnejad/Zeini 2024.

category according to the degree of the sin and the intention of the delinquent. These include depriving animals under one's guardianship of food; afflicting bitches who are pregnant or have just littered; bruising, beating and mutilating dogs who protect the community; injuring and slaying small and large cattle (*stōr/gōspand*) unlawfully (*a-dādīhā*); injuring beasts of burden (horses, camels, donkeys, oxen) and killing other beneficent animals. Judgement in these cases had to take into consideration, whether the offence was committed willfully and intentionally (*pad nigerišnīg*) or by negligence (*sūdagīhā*).[281] In specific cases offences could be punished according to both *ruwānīg* and *hamēmālān* categories, when an animal owned by another person was harmed or injured. In this case the delinquent was not only liable to making amendments by paying a compensation (*tōzišn*) for the sin to religious authorities, but also paid a fine (*tāwān*) to the owner of the animal. Amends also had to be made to the proprietor of an estate or court in the case of theft, if a person injured the dog protecting the property.

Can we conclude from these details that Zoroastrian law acknowledged animal rights with respect to creatures of the good creation? Although animals of this group could be killed in the context of sacrifice, there can be no doubt that both deliberate cruelty towards them and killing or harming them negligently were violations of religious precepts which were considered as *ruwānīg* offences liable to punishment according to Zoroastrian norms. The sources reveal in no uncertain terms that *domestic animals had in fact certain recognized rights*, even comparable to the limited rights of a slave or a woman under guardianship: the right to physical integrity and to live unimpaired by humans, correlating to the duty of their owners to take care of the animals under their guardianship by providing them with food and shelter and protecting them from aggressive acts. But it would be anachronistic to compare these Zoroastrian norms to the modern concept of animal rights, based on the idea that all sentient non-human beings should be protected legally due to their capacity for suffering and memory, although, as we have seen, in Zoroastrianism compassion is one of the arguments put forward for limiting the right to kill an animal to the context of the ritual. The care due to animals remains, however, within the boundaries of Zoroastrian dualism with its strict division of all creatures into the two distinct groups of good and evil, subject to diametrically opposed treatment and corresponding norms.

281 On these offences against animals see MACUCH 2003a, pp. 179–186, with further references; on offences committed wilfully or negligently see also Chapter V, pp. 411–422.

Chapter II

Legal Identity and Kinship Ties

Introductory: Sasanian elites and kinship as a central unit

The legal texts described in the first Chapter give us access to Sasanian society from a completely different perspective than most other available sources. They not only enable us to reconstruct important institutions, social structures and hierarchies, but allow insight into the strategies employed by the Sasanian elites to keep their wealth, stabilize their social standing and strengthen their authority across many generations. They are eminently important for understanding basic social and political structures as well as the scheme behind the development of certain unique features of Sasanian law and their interconnections, especially in the fields of family, property and succession. My main goal in this section (and in the next Chapter) will be to reconstruct fundamental legal institutions of family law based on this material, to discuss the impact of these practices on the social structure of the late Sasanian period (6th–7th centuries) and to show how they were used for consolidating the power of the Sasanian elite, notably the Iranian nobility and the Zoroastrian priesthood. Focusing on the vast field of kinship, I will argue that the stability of late Sasanian society was highly dependant on a well-conceived concept of the family with characteristic marriage and succession practices, not to be found in this specific combination in any other legal system. In short: I will try to show that the power of the Sasanian elite was founded to a large extent—if not uniquely—on an elaborate set of regulations forming family and kinship with far-reaching consequences which we can reconstruct in detail from the legal sources. The efficiency of the system, however, stood on feet of clay, and the same legal institutions, which were instrumental in preserving social hierarchies across the generations, were not only severely challenged in the Sasanian period (by the so-called Mazdakite upheaval), but even contributed—due to the unequal and unjust distribution of wealth—to the downfall of the Sasanian Empire itself.

What were the common interests of the two powerful elite groups, the nobility and the priesthood, and how are these represented in the legal system? There can be no doubt that by the end of Sasanian rule the Zoroastrian clergy had developed numerous institutions to its own advantage, leading to an increase in wealth and power. Besides property bequeathed to priests and fees bestowed on them for performing their central duties in the Zoroastrian ritual, enormous wealth was accumulated in pious foundations and huge estates belonging to fire temples under the tutorship (*dāštārīh*) or guardianship (*sālārīh*) of priests (which we will discuss in Chapter III, pp. 220–229). Another important means of amassing riches and consolidating power was achieved by fixing the laws of marriage and succession to the advantage of both the aristocracy and the priesthood on the basis of Zoroastrian principles. To avoid misunderstandings, I should add here, that I am by no means suggesting that *all* members of the priestly class were wealthy or powerful, there may well have been considerable differences between priests of various ranks,[1] but there is good reason to assume that those religious authorities holding higher positions in jurisdiction were both affluent and politically influential, as certain case studies reveal (for example, the trial against Mār Abā, which was initiated by the Zoroastrian priesthood, see Chapter VI, pp. 575–581). The nobility held power due to the wealth they had inherited and amassed across many generations, consisting mainly of landed property and real estate. They were interested in promoting and maintaining a legal system, which would open additional options to their advantage in the field of succession and facilitate the inter-generational transfer of property. The clergy with its explicit acknowledgement of endogamy, especially its propagation of all types of next-of-kin matrimony, including incestuous marriages within the nuclear family, was the best ally of a nobility interested in keeping their vast property together. But this was only *one* strategy among others, embedded in a large number of flexible options with which a lineage could promote its material (as well as its spiritual) interests.

In the light of these considerations, the organisation of kinship, that is, people connected to each other by common descent, seems to be far more important for our assessment of the social and political history of Sasanian Iran than hitherto assumed. Western societies today are based—at least ideally—on meritocracy rather than aristocracy, despite the prestige still connected with noble lineage and ancestry in certain circles.[2] The basic political, economic and religious units no longer consist of aristocratic kinship groups, but are rather dispersed in diverse organisations (such as political parties, lobbies, trade unions, industries, firms, associations, centres of learning, different religious creeds and sects, among others). If we take into consideration that Iranian society was structured in a completely different manner than most modern Western societies, the complex set of laws regulating marriage and family ties with a large number of

1 The remarkable discrepancy between the opulent life of the chief religious authority (*mowbedān mowbed*) and that of simple priests (*hērbed*), who lead an almost ascetic life, as they fulfil their priestly duties by irrigating the tilled land and citing the Avesta and Zand, is alluded to in a tale in *Dēnkard* 6, D3 (Shaked 1979, pp. 178–181). Although the narrative belongs to *andarz* literature and could largely be fictional, clearly containing an admonition, the gap between the living conditions of the Chief Priest, on the one hand, and the *hērbeds*, on the other, could well reflect real circumstances. See Daryaee 2009, p. 44.

2 For an introduction to kinship, family and descent from a social anthropological perspective see Fox 1967.

constructed links, suddenly makes sense. All the available sources indicate that society in Sasanian Iran was built on a hierarchical division (probably into four estates), governed by powerful kinship groups belonging to the uppermost echelons of society, who took possession of the economic resources and controlled the political and religious affairs of the State. Hence, understanding the intricacies of this far-reaching web of regulations, customs, norms and laws constituting family law, marriage and succession has crucial implications for our comprehension of the basic structure of this society. History itself allows a glimpse of what could have happened if the laws regulating family affairs (besides other branches of law) were to be changed. When the Sasanian king Kawād attempted to weaken the power of the priesthood and the nobility towards the end of the 5th century by altering the laws of matrimony in correspondence with the 'heretic' teaching linked to (the name or title) Mazdak, these radical measures led to a total collapse of the social system and became a serious threat to the reign of the Sasanian dynasty itself. Only by reinserting the previous marriage regulations and renewing the tie between the ruling house, the Zoroastrian clergy and the Sasanian aristocracy—among other measures—did Kawād's son, the famous Husraw Anōšag-ruwān, manage to ensure his reign and to restore the empire. We will return to the so-called Mazdak rebellion and its consequences in Chapter III. Let us now leave these general observations for the moment and make an attempt to reconstruct the main traits of Sasanian social hierarchy and legal identity before we turn to the laws governing marriage and succession.

1 Social organisation and hierarchy

It is well known that the division of the Zoroastrian community into three social groups or classes, to which a fourth was later added, is already mentioned in the Avesta with the sequence (1) priests (*aϑauruuan-*), (2) warriors (*raϑaēštā-*), (3) cattle-breeding farmers (*vāstriiō.fšuiiaṇt-*), (4) artisans (*hūiti-*).[3] There is no evidence on a social structure corresponding to the one in the Avesta in the Achemenid and Parthian periods, but it reappears in several late Pahlavi sources of the post-Sasanian period as well as in Persian and Arabic texts describing Sasanian Iran, with three main variations. The first variant in Pahlavi literature agrees exactly with the Avestan version, dividing society in descending order into the four estates (*pēšag*) of (1) priests (*āsrōnān*), (2) warriors (*arteštārān*), (3) cultivators (*wāstaryōšān*) and (4) artisans (*hutuxšān*). This is the formation given in the bulk of Pahlavi religious texts, with a very clear hierarchy, placing

3 See for example the first three groups mentioned in Yt 19.8 (Hintze 1994, p. 90); the artisans are included in Y 19.17 (Wolff 1910, p. 52). On the social classes in the Avesta see Benveniste 1932; on the Indo-Iranian background and tradition see Benveniste 1938 and 1969, I, pp. 279ff.

the priesthood on the highest level. Two sources equate the four groups with the microcosm of man's body, the estate of priests corresponding to the head (*sar*), warriors to the hands (*dast*), cultivators to the belly (*aškam*) and artisans, who are given the lowest rank, to the feet (*pay*),[4] while another attestations explain, why the highest station is due to the priests,[5] and elucidate the various duties (*xwēškārīh*) of the members of the four estates.[6] It is hardly surprising that these theological treatises, composed or redacted by religious authorities, should place the priesthood in the most important, uppermost position, nor is it strange that pious Zoroastrians should appear divided into in the same four groups in this sequence in the description of the righteous souls in heaven in the *Ardā Wirāz nāmag*, the Pahlavi 'Divina Commedia', representing what would have been regarded as an ideal state of affairs by the clergy.[7]

The other two transmitted versions of the social hierarchy agree in presenting four estates, but Persian and Arabic sources, based presumably on non-religious texts (possibly translations of the lost national chronicle, the *Xwadāy nāmag*[8]), convey a somewhat divergent picture of Sasanian society, correlating in the number of estates, but with remarkable discrepancies regarding their sequence and structure. The Persian *Letter of Tansar*, based on the Arabic translation of a Pahlavi original (see Chapter I, p. 52), corresponds with Pahlavi religious literature in listing the priestly class as the foremost group (after the King of Kings, who comes first), but differs by inserting the class of 'scribes' or 'secretaries' (*kuttāb*, rendering MP *dibīrān*) as the third estate between 'warriors' (second estate) and 'cultivators and artisans' (grouped together in the fourth estate).[9] Moreover, the details given in this source on the members of the four estates transmit a far livelier image, nearer to the complex reality of Sasanian times with its vast administration and bureaucracy, than the rather static formations based on the Avesta in Pahlavi religious literature. The first estate of 'religious authorities, clergy' (*aṣḥāb-i dīn*), we are told, comprises 'judges' (*ḥukkām*), 'ascetics, priests' (*zuhhād*), 'temple-guardians' (*sadana*), and 'teachers' (*muʿallimān*). The second estate of the 'military, men of war' (*muqātil*; *mardān-i kārezār*) is divided into 'knights, cavalry' (*sawār*) and 'foot-soldiers' (*pīyāda*). The most

4 *Dēnkard*, Book 4 (DkM 429.5–9) and *Škand gumānīg wizār* I.20, both cited in Tafazzoli 2000, p. 2.

5 *Dēnkard*, Book 3 (DkM 34.1–35.2; de Menasce 1973, no. 42, p. 54). The fourth group of artisans is missing here.

6 *Dādestān ī mēnōy ī xrad* 30–31 (Chapters 31–32 in the numeration of West 1885, pp. 67–69; Pāzand text in Antia 1909, pp. 308–309; Persian translation by Tafazzoli 1975 [1354], pp. 48–49).

7 AWN 14 (Gignoux 1984, pp. 166–168). For an overview of the contents of the AWN see Macuch 2009a, pp. 158–160, with further references.

8 On the 'Book of Sovereigns', the lost Pahlavi epic history of Iran, which was translated into Arabic in different versions, all unfortunately lost, but cited in diverse Arabic historiographies, see Macuch 2009a, pp. 172–181, with further references.

9 See Persian text in Darmesteter 1894, p. 214 and translation in Boyce 1968a, p. 38.

detailed enumeration of members pertains to the third estate of 'scribes, secretaries' (*kuttāb*), consisting of 'writers of treatises' (*kuttāb-i rasāʾil*), 'accountants' (*kuttāb-i muḥāsibāt*), 'recorders of judicial decisions and registrations and contracts' (*kuttāb-i aqẓiya-u siğillāt-u šurūṭ*), 'writers of biographies/chronicles' (*kuttāb-i siyar*), 'physicians' (*aṭibbāʾ*), 'poets' (*šuʿarā*), 'astrologers, astronomers' (*munağğimān*). Members of the fourth estate of 'crafts' (*mihna*) are 'merchants' (*bāzargānān*), 'farmers, cultivators' (*rāʿiyān*), 'dealers, traders' (*tuğğār*), 'other craftsmen' (*sāyir-i muḥtarafa*).[10] According to this source no member of one estate was allowed to pass to another. Only in exceptional cases, which had to be examined thoroughly by the king as well as priests (*mowbeds* and *hērbeds*), a transition from one estate to another could take place.[11]

The third variant transmitted in Arabic sources corresponds with the latter in that it counts four estates and places the 'scribes' in the third position, but it exchanges the first and second ranks, establishing 'warriors' as the uppermost group, followed by 'priests' in the second station. According to Ṭabarī the four classes, already established by the legendary king Jamšīd, were organized in the sequence of (1) 'warriors' (*muqātila*; translated by Balʿamī as *laškarīān*), followed by (2) 'theologians, jurisconsults' (*fuqahāʾ*; Balʿamī has *dānāʾān* 'sages'), (3) 'scribes' (*kuttāb*; Balʿamī has *dibīrān*) and (4) 'cultivators' (*ḥurrāṯ*; Balʿamī translates *kištārwarzān*; *pēšawarān*).[12] The same sequence with 'warriors' in the first position is transmited by Ṯaʿalibī.[13]

To sum up: three different lists of classes or estates have been transmitted representing the 'ideal model' of the Sasanian State which agree in the number of divisions, but are divergent in content and sequence (see Table 3).

Pahlavi religious literature seems to keep slavishly to the classes named in the Avesta, despite all changes that must have taken place across the centuries up to the Sasanian period. Since many of these descriptions reflect an ideal state of affairs in the sacred texts or are late redactions of the Islamic period, it can be doubted that they actually represent the social structure of the Sasanian State. The other two lists, with the 'scribes, secretaries' inserted in the third position seem to be far more realistic depictions of what we would expect of a complex

10 Darmesteter 1894, p. 214; Boyce 1968a, p. 38.

11 Besides the *Letter of Tansar* other Arabic sources list the 'scribes' as the third estate, notably al-Ğāḥiẓ, Miskawayh and the ʿAhd Ardašīr; on these attestations see Tafazzoli 2000, pp. 19–20.

12 Ṭabarī, ed. de Goeje 1879–1901, I, p. 180, and Balʿamī, ed. Bahār/Gunābadi 1962, p. 130, *apud* Tafazzoli 2000, p. 20. Firdausi's *Šāhnāma* also attributes the establishment of the estates (here: three) to king Jamšīd, albeit with the 'priests' in the first position. The name given to them in the oldest manuscript is *āsurbān*, probably a corruption of MP *āsrōnān* 'priests'; see the edition of Khaleghi-Motlagh 1988–2008, I, p. 42, verse 20. See also Benveniste 1932, pp. 132–134 (who, however, refers to later manuscripts used by Mohl 1838–1878 in his edition of the National Epic, where the name of the first estate of priests has been corrupted to *āmūzyān*).

13 Ed. Zotenberg 1900, p. 12, *apud* Benveniste 1932, p. 132.

Table 3. Representations of the social estates

Estates (*pēšag*)	Pahlavi Books (Dk; MīX; AWN)	Letter of Tansar	Arabic and Persian Sources (Ṭabarī; Balʿamī; Ṯaʿalibī)
		King of Kings (*šāhān šāh*)	
1	priests (*āsrōnān*)	clergy (*aṣḥāb-i dīn*)	warriors, military (*muqātila*; *laškarīān*)
2	warriors (*arteštārān*)	military, men of war (*muqātil*; *mardān-i kārezār*)	theologians, jurisconsults, sages (*fuqahāʾ*; *dānāʾān*)
3	cultivators (*wāstaryōšān*)	scribes, secretaries (*kuttāb*)	scribes, secretaries (*kuttāb*; *dibīrān*)
4	artisans (*hutuxšān*)	crafts (*mihna*)	cultivators (*ḥurrāṯ*; *kištārwarzān*; *pēšawarān*)

empire with a vast bureaucracy. But did the 'scribes' really constitute an individual estate with rights and duties differing substantially from those of the other two upper echelons of society, even if they were recruited from the latter as officials for the highest positions in the administration (*e. g.*, as 'secretaries of State')? Masʿūdī mentions these secretaries or 'superintendents of the archives' (*arbāb ad-dawāwīn*), who were engaged in the important task of registering landed property.[14] Al-Ḫwārezmī transmits a list of the *dīwāns*, in which they were engaged, giving the Middle Persian terms with their Arabic translations (see Table 4; mp. *dibīrag* is rendered by its arabicized form *dafīra* in all the entries).[15]

Despite the shortness of the entries, this list of registers or archives conveys an impression of the extensive bureaucracy of the late Sasanian Empire, in which a large number of scribes, besides the chief secretaries, must have been engaged. We can reasonably assume that, if there was a separate estate (*pēšag*) of scribes, it had an individual hierarchy of its own.

It is difficult to press the different types of 'scribes, secretaries' (*dibīrān*) into the 'imagined order' of the four estates. Scribes not only appear as important political figures from the very beginning of Sasanian reign in the early inscriptions, but were in certain cases themselves members of the nobility, such as A(r)štād, the 'scribe' ⟨dpywr⟩ *dibīr* in the Middle Persian version) or, more precisely, 'letter scribe' ⟨prwrtk SPR'⟩ *frawardag dibīr* in the Parthian version)

14 Masʿūdī (*Murūǧ aḏ-ḏahab*) *apud* Altheim/Stiehl 1954, p. 240.

15 Al-Ḫwārezmī (*Mafātīḥu'l-ʿulūm*); for the Arabic text see, van Vloten 1895, pp. 117–118, and Unvala 1928, p. 80. Explanations and translations of the MP terms are to be found in Unvala 1928, p. 91, and Altheim/Stiehl 1954, pp. 240–241. Note that the last register (*ruwānagān dibīrag*) is translated as *kitābat al-awqāf* (register of *awqāf*) by al-Ḫwārezmī. On pious foundations see Chapter III, pp. 220–229.

Table 4. List of *dīwāns* according to al-Ḫwārezmī

MP terms	Arabic rendering	Translation
*dād *dibīrag* (= *dafīra*)	*kitābat al-aḥkām*	Register of laws/decrees/judgements
*šahr hamār *dibīrag*	*kitābat al-bilad li-l-ḫarāǧ*	Register of the accounts of the empire/lands (the Arabic version adds: regarding taxation)
*kadag hamār *dibīrag*	*kitābat ḥisāb dār al-mulk*	Register of the accounts of the (royal) house
*ganǧ hamār *dibīrag*	*kitābat al-ḫazāʿin*	Register of the accounts of the treasury
*āxur hamār *dibīrag*	*kitābat al-iṣṭablāt*	Register of the accounts of the (royal) stables
*ātaš hamār *dibīrag*	*kitābat ḥusbānāt an-nīrān*	Register of the accounts of fire-foundations
*ruwānagān *dibīrag*	*kitābat al-awqāf*	Register of pious foundations

from the noble Mihrān family in Ray ⟨ZY mtr'n ZY MN rd-y⟩ *ī Mihrān ī az Ray* in the MP version), mentioned in the retinue of king Šābuhr I.[16] Tafazzoli mentions three *dibīr*s among the Persians in high positions, all of noble descent and aristocrats, who exercised political power in the 5th century and are named in several Arabic sources: Gōdarz, the *katib al-ǧund* (secretary of the army); Gušnasp Ādur, the *kātib al-ḫarağ* (finance secretary), Čuwānōy, the *ṣāḥib ad-dīwān ar-rasāʾil* (chief scribe).[17] Moreover, scribes were included in the favoured classes in late Sasanian society in another important respect: together with nobles and priests they were exempted from paying the poll tax (*ǧizya*) after the tax reform of Husraw I, as Ṭabarī (among others) reports:

> They imposed the poll tax (*ǧizya*) on everyone except the Noble Families (*ahl-al buyūtāt*; MP *wāspuhragān*), Grandees (*al-ʿuẓamāʿ*; MP *wuzurgān*), warriors (*al-muqātila*; MP *arteštārān*), priests (*al-harābiḏa*; MP *herbedān*), secretaries (*kuttāb*; MP *dibīrān*) and those in the king's service.[18]

According to this passage the only citizens of Ērānšahr liable to pay the poll tax (at least after the reforms of Husraw I) were commoners belonging to the fourth class (with the exception of men below the age of twenty and above the age of fifty) and religious minorities.[19] If we furthermore take into consideration that (according to other sources) plebeians (*bī-aṣl*), traders (*bāzārī*) and the

16 ŠKZ 34 (MP), 28 (Parth.); Back 1978, p. 365, *apud* Tafazzoli 2000, p. 20.
17 Tafazzoli 2000, pp. 24–25.
18 Tafazzoli 2000, pp. 26–27, and Gariboldi 2015, p. 69, with further references.
19 Gariboldi 2015, p. 69, and Altheim/Stiehl 1954, p. 40.

offspring of servants were not allowed to become scribes[20], the circumstantial evidence is overwhelming that the *dibīrān* were separated by certain rules and regulations especially from the fourth estate of commoners. But there seems to have been no strict division between the estate of scribes and the other two upper classes. Scribes, notably in higher positions as secretaries of the State, were recruited, as we have seen, from the nobility (possibly also the priesthood), retaining their rights and status as aristocrats. The small treatise *Husraw ī Kawādān ud rēdag-ē(w)* mentions 'writing' (*dibīrīh*), the activity of the scribe, among the accomplishments expected from a well-educated young man of noble descent, a most difficult skill (if we take the Pahlavi script into consideration), which would have been hardly taught to commoners of the lowest estate.[21] But given the long (and certainly not exhaustive) list of scribes in the *Letter of Tansar* and the different archives of the State cited above, in which a huge number of scribes must have been employed, there were presumably considerable differences of rank between members of this group, as may also be assumed with regard to the other two foremost 'ideal' estates (on the different ranks of priests see p. 94, fn. 1 above).

The discrepancy regarding the first estate (either 'priests' or 'warriors' in the first position) could well be due to the different sources or redactions (presumably of the *Xwadāy nāmag*) used by Arabic and Persian historiographers or to shifts in political influence and power across the centuries. Would these two divergent sequences have any historical, social and legal significance apart from political propaganda?[22] The correspondences with the Avesta (and the Indo-Iranian background) have raised doubts regarding the historical authenticity of the four-estate structure for the Sasanian period.[23] On the other hand, since the Sasanians stylized themselves as revivers of the Zoroastrian religion, basing their propaganda and ideology on two pillars, the throne (represented by the king) and the church, they might have accepted this ancient classification as a *theoretical* basis for the organization of their empire. The division into four estates obviously represents the 'ideal social order' of the Sasanian State and is an imagined construct, important for legitimizing hierarchies which were crucial for retaining social stability. The question is, how far this ideal formation, founded on the sacred texts and expanded to adapt to the changed conditions of a large empire, reflects real social and legal structures. Was the State in fact organized according to the hierarchies of the four-estate construct? Were these visible in the institutions of the empire and transposed into the law? In other words: was the Sasanian State modelled on the pattern of the Avesta or does this sequence of estates depict an important *imaginaire*, which hardly corresponds with the concrete social realities of the Iranian Empire, Ērānšahr?

20 *Apud* Tafazzoli 2000, p. 27, who states Ibn al-Balḫī's *Fārs-nāma*, p. 93. On the *dibīr* see now Gyselen/Khurshidian 2024.

21 'Husraw, son of Kawād and a Page'; HKR 10; see Azarnouche 2013, p. 45.

22 On the different redactions of the Pahlavi *Xwadāy Nāmag* 'Book of Lords' see the overview in Macuch 2009a, pp. 172–181, with further references.

23 See already Benveniste 1932, pp. 130–131.

The question is not easily answered, even though we may assume that an ideal theory of the state would definitely have had social and legal consequences by its definition of political authority and the establishment of corresponding legal institutions. The problem is that there are no references whatsoever to the ideal construct in the legal material. This is hardly surprising, given that 'imagined orders' belong to the self-evident 'certainties' of a society and are usually neither questioned nor even perceived in most cases. There are several indications in the sources, besides the material cited above, that there was in fact a strict division of the population (besides the one mentioned above), separating men of high birth, *i. e.*, the aristocracy and Zoroastrian religious authorities, from the rest of the citizens of Ērānšahr, who as commoners had divergent rights and duties, no matter whether they were Zoroastrians or adherents of another faith. A person's rank, grade and position in the State and—as we will see below—also his legal status were determined by various categories, in which the individual's standing according to birth played a crucial role, even if it was not the sole criterion. Particularly classical sources and Arabic and Persian historiographies, besides Pahlavi texts, agree that the question of a person's rank and station in society was of supreme importance and that there was a strict divide between nobles and commoners regarding legal rights and duties as well as in almost every other aspect of daily life. The Sasanian elite, belonging to the two foremost estates and engaged as officials of the State in the third estate—if we follow the ancient scheme—was obviously also privileged in real life with regard not only to social prestige, but also to proprietary rights. Hence the ideal structure of society with its division into four estates is reflected to a certain extent in several rules and regulations, separating particularly common people from the other social groups. But the model remains problematic especially with respect to the first three estates and does not suffice to describe the complex legal structures and hierarchies of Sasanian society. Moreover, the main division between nobles and commoners is by no means the only criterion for determining an individual's place in society, as will be seen in the following section.

2 The law of persons and legal status

Differences in class or rank in connection with the estate to which a man belongs are not explicitly mentioned or discussed in the legal material. This could be just coincidental or due to the fact that the compiler of our most important source, the Sasanian Law-book (see Chapter I, pp. 20–22), was not interested in assembling material on this specific topic. To a man living in the late Sasanian period the social hierarchy sketched above, dividing society particularly into nobles and commoners, must have been an unquestioned, self-evident fact of daily life. If, on the other hand, the compilation stems from Islamic times, questions of rank were presumably no longer of major interest to the surviving Zoroastrian communities striving to develop solidarity among the adherents of the faith instead of upholding social divisions. In fact, the Pahlavi texts of the *riwāyat*-type (see Chapter I, pp. 31–37) convey the impression that legal precepts applied equally to all Zoroastrians regardless of their status in society, but even in these late texts there is enough conclusive evidence pointing to the contrary, revealing that the position of a person in the community still played an important part in legal dealings.[24] Moreover, a large number of details in the individual cases discussed in the Law-book and other sources show that by the late Sasanian period Ērānšahr had developed a highly stratified society and that the legal status of a person was determined by far more criteria than the vertical divide mentioned above.

Although we do not know, whether Sasanian law developed a theory of legal personality, there can be no doubt that the question as to who (or what) was a 'legal person', that is, a subject of rights and duties, capable of legal relationships and having full legal capacity, was regarded from a completely different perspective than in modern Western legal systems. The idea that not only human persons, but also other non-human entities, comparable to modern corporations, such as charitable foundations or fire-endowments, could have legal personality as a whole does not seem to have occurred to Sasanian jurists, despite the important position of these institutions in the economy of Ērānšahr and the emergence of analogous legal problems (for example, the problem of 'ownership', which was even solved in a similar manner; see Chapter III, pp. 217–218, 228). Unsurprisingly, neither does the Sasanian concept of the 'legal person' correspond with respect to human beings to the humanistic ideal of 'free individuals', having—at least theoretically—equal rights before the law regardless of race, gender, religious beliefs, amount of property and status in the community. There was no comparable kind of equality; on the contrary, the legal rights and duties of individuals in Sasanian Iran were defined by a large range of rules and regulations, determining not only their standing in the family and society, which could only seldom be changed (except in specific cases such as the transition from slavery to freedom and vice versa), but also their legal status. We can distinguish between five basic constituent elements determining the legal position of an individual:[25]

1. birth: a person is either freeborn (*āzād*) or a slave (*anšahrīg*, *bandag*);
2. rank and station (*gāh*) in the community: a person belongs either to the nobility or is a commoner;
3. citizenship: as an inhabitant of the realm (*ādehīg*) he is either a citizen of Iran (*mard ī šahr*), subject of the King of Kings (*šāhān šāh bandag*) and Iranian (*ēr*), or a foreigner (*an-ēr*; *uzdehīg*);

24 See the discussion of two legal cases in the *Riwāyat of Ādurfarrbay*, Macuch 2017a and 2017b.

25 The following assessment is based on all the available information in the Sasanian Law-book and other later Pahlavi sources, see also Macuch 2010a.

4. religious affiliation: a person is either Zoroastrian (*weh-dēn*) or an infidel (*ag-dēn*);
5. gender and age (women and minors are often subject to the same restrictions applying to persons with limited legal capacity or without legal capacity).

These five elements of birth, rank, citizenship, religion, gender/age were crucial for establishing an individual's place in the community and his (or her) rights and duties, which could differ considerably according to the person's legal status. A large range of cross-connections between these criteria were possible, but only a freeborn man belonging to a noble family (*āzād*), of major age (*purnāy*), a subject of the King of Kings (*šāhān šāh bandag*), an Iranian (*ēr*) and a citizen of Ērānšahr (*mard ī šahr*), confessing Zoroastrianism (*weh-dēn*) was considered as a person having full legal capacity (*tuwānīgīh*).[26] All other persons had only limited legal capacity according to their standing in society or lacked rights completely, as in the case of those slaves, who were fully enslaved (it was possible in Sasanian law for a slave to be partly freed, see pp. 108–109 below). The rights and duties of all the others in this list were either restricted on grounds of low descent (as in the case of commoners) or due to dependency under guardianship (women and minors) or they were limited because of alien ethnicity and religious affiliation (foreigners and infidels) or they were only conceded under specific exceptional conditions (slaves). A separate evaluation of these different categories will help clarify the social stratifications and divergent constructions of legal personality in Sasanian jurisprudence.

Table 5. Overview: constituent elements forming an individual's legal status

Criteria	Legal status	
birth	freeborn (*āzād*)	slave (*anšahrīg*; *bandag*)
rank and station	noble (*āzād*; *wuzurg*)	commoner (*xwurdag*)
citizenship	citizen of Iran (*mard ī šahr*); subject of the King of Kings (*šāhān šāh bandag*); Iranian (*ēr*)	foreigner (*an-ēr*; *uzdehīg*)
religious affiliation	Zoroastrian (*weh-dēn*)	infidel (*ag-dēn*)
gender	man (*mard*; *mērag*)	woman (*zan*; *ziyānag*)
age	major, adult (*purnay*)	minor, underage (*aburnāy*)

26 Since no theoretical treatises on law have survived (if they ever existed), the differentiation of rights and duties along these lines is only seldom explicitly mentioned, though it is an inherent part of the law. An exception is Dd *Pursišn* 55.2, in which the legal conditions for establishing a *stūrīh* (substitute succession) are named. On this important institution see pp. 163–174 below.

2.1 Slaves and freedmen

The Sasanian law of persons is similar to that of other societies of late antiquity in that it distinguishes between the legal status of freeborn persons (men and women of noble station and plebeians) on the one hand, and slaves of both genders, on the other.[27] However, the dividing line between freedom and slavery in Sasanian Iran was not quite as strict as this division suggests, not only due to the possibility of manumission (which was known in all societies and would dramatically change the legal position of the released person), but since it was allowed to liberate part of a slave belonging to two or more masters. The slave could be manumitted by one master and kept enslaved by another one simultaneously. If the slave was partially freed in this manner, he (or she) no longer completely lacked legal and civic rights, but the strange situation emerged that the same person would have certain legal rights to the extent of the manumitted portion, but be treated as a slave with regard to the unreleased part. Another indefiniteness of legal status may be observed in litigation, when a slave, who was considered as a legal object, a 'thing' (*xwāstag*), was allowed to appear in court as a witness or even as one of the parties (plaintiff or defendant), being hereby *de facto* accepted as a legal subject. We will come back to the double standard reflected in these cases below.

Four main causes of enslavement can be deduced from the Pahlavi sources, which do not differ substantially from those in other societies of late antiquity: (1) capture as a prisoner of war or deportation; (2) descent from a slave; (3) debt bondage; (4) sale of children and other members of the family under guardianship. The first (and probably original) source of slavery, already mentioned in Old Iranian, Elamite and Babylonian texts[28], the capture of prisoners in war or deportation from another country, is apparently also the origin of the most frequent, unambiguous Pahlavi legal term for 'slave', *anšahrīg*, lit. 'outlander, foreigner'.[29] Another Pahlavi word for 'slave' with a similar provenance, *wardag*, lit. 'captive' (NP *barda*[30]) is attested in the third century Sasanian inscription of Kirdīr on the Kaʿba-ye Zardošt,[31] but *not* used, as far as I can see, anywhere as a *legal* term for 'slave' in the extant material. Despite its literal meaning, *anšahrīg* not only refers to foreigners who were enslaved, but denotes all kinds of slaves

27 On slavery in Sasanian Iran with further references see also Macuch 1981, pp. 79–84 (no. 15); 1988a, pp. 763–766, and 2010a, pp. 195–199.

28 For an overview on the Achaemenid period with further references see Dandamayev 1988.

29 The compound *an-šahrīg* with the privative prefix *a(n)-* 'un-, less-' + adj. *šahrīg* 'inhabitant, citizen, resident' (from *šahr* 'realm, empire'; Av. *xšaϑra-*) is unusual, as one would expect **a-šahrīg* before a consonant (a construction with *any* < OP *aniya-* 'other, another' is unlikely). The Armenian loan-word *anašxarhik* 'foreigner, stranger' (*ašxarh* < Ir. **xsaϑr-*) makes it likely that the term is of older provenance, though not attested in any elder source (Perikhanian 1997, p. 336; Hübschmann 1897, p. 101, no. 36).

30 Av. *varəta-* 'captive, enslaved'; Bartholomae 1904, col. 1368.

31 KKZ, line 13 (in the Middle Persian version); see Back 1978, p. 427.

of both genders and is exclusively employed in this sense. In contrast, another frequent term, *bandag* (lit. 'bound'), does not exclusively designate the 'slave' in the sense of a person without rights, but also has the two-fold meanings of 'subject' and 'servant', the former in the designation *šāhān šāh bandag* ('subject of the King of Kings'), the latter in the context of fire-foundations. The technical terms *ātaxš-bandag* ('servant of the fire') and *ādurān-bandag* ('servant of the fires') refer to free persons dedicated to the service of a Zoroastrian fire-foundation, who—far from being slaves—could belong to the highest echelons of Sasanian society with full citizen's rights. Slaves working on the property of a fire-foundation on the other hand were called *anšahrīg ī ātaxš* 'slave(s) of the fire', unequivocally calling attention to their status as slaves, *i. e.*, persons with no legal rights (on fire-foundations see Chapter III, pp. 225–229).

The second cause of slavery, descent from a slave, presumably followed the general rule that a person's status at birth was determined by the position of the parents: children of slaves were slaves. There seems, however, to have been a fundamental change in Sasanian law regarding the legal position of children born in a mixed relationship to a freeborn citizen and a slave from the time of one of the kings called Wahrām (since no date is given, we cannot be sure which one of the five kings of this name is meant; the last one reigned from 420 to 439). In an interesting passage of the Sasanian Law-book a significant alteration of the basic rule regarding children from these alliances is noted: until the reign of the said King Wahrām the status of the child followed that of the father, whereas it took the status of the mother after this period (*tā xwadāyīh ī Wahrām mardōmān anšahrīg ān xwēš bawēd ī az pidar zāyēd nē ān ī az mād* 'Up to the reign of Wahrām people gain ownership of a slave who descends [as a slave] from the father, not of the one who descends [as such] from the mother …'[32]). The theoretical background of the first rule, with the child following the position of the father, is in complete accord with both the patrilineal system of descent in Sasanian law and the corresponding sections on children of slaves from 'mixed' sexual relationships (both from a legal marriage and an illicit alliance) in Īšōʿbōxt's *Corpus Iuris.*[33] Moreover, the quoted passage continues to elucidate the first regulation by citing one of the basic tenets formulated by one of the most influential jurisconsults (and theologians) of the Sasanian period, called Sōšāns, who determined that 'the child (is) the father's own' (*waččag pid xwēš*), hence (as we may add) the status of the child, no matter whether from a freeborn man or a slave, always follows that of the father: the child is freeborn if the father is free or a slave if he is a slave. However, in contradiction to this rule, after the reign of the said Wahrām the legal position of a child from these sexual relationships changes fundamentally: 'and now they say that (the child

32 MHD 1.2–3; Macuch 1993, p. 22 (transliteration); p. 24 (translation).
33 I have discussed the different cases in the commentary to MHD 1.2–4, Macuch 1993, pp. 27–31 (no. 2). On Īšōʿbōxt's work see Chapter I, p. 48.

is) the mother('s own)' (*ud nūn gōwēnd kū mād*), that is, the child follows the status of the mother. How can we explain this fundamental change, which in fact contradicts the rule of patrilineal descent? Although the social background is not elucidated, it would not be too far-fetched to assume that sexual relationships (or marriages) between freeborn men and slave-women would have been far more frequent than those between freeborn women and slave-men. We can only speculate that giving the legal status of the father to the child in a marriage between a freeborn man and a slave-woman would not only have led to a decrease of slaves belonging to a household, but would have increased the number of heirs in an unwanted manner, giving the child of a slave under certain circumstances (*e. g.*, in a *pādixšāy*-marriage) the same rights as the free legitimate offspring of a *paterfamilias*. Seen in the light of the importance attached to rank and station in Sasanian society and the prohibition of marriages between nobles and commoners (see p. 111) with the goal of preventing the transfer of property to an inferior class, this alteration makes perfect sense. By binding the status of the child to that of the mother these children from a mixed union would be barred from inheriting from their father, but could still be freed and adopted by him if he wished to give them the status of heirs.

Besides captivity and descent from a slave, debt bondage seems to have been one of the frequent reasons for enslavement. Another word from the daily colloquial is used in this context as a legal term: *tan* (lit. 'body, person') is attested in the specific setting of loan and debt to denote a 'person/body' pledged as security, who is personally (lit. 'physically', *pad tan*) liable for a debt and could end in bondage. A person taking out a loan could offer a member of his family, particularly one of his children, as security to the moneylender, who accepted this form of security with the formulaic words: *kū-m Mihrēn (Farrox) pad tan az tō padīrift* 'I (= the creditor) accept N.N. (name of the security: Mihrēn/Farrox) as personal security (*pad tan*) from you (= the debtor)'.[34] The person pledged in this manner could be enslaved if the debtor was unable to repay the loan. It seems that this form of pledge was combined in Sasanian law with a specific type of suretyship, which is also explicitly mentioned in the Babylonian Talmud[35] (see Chapters IV, pp. 352–354 and VII, pp. 606–608). The procedure furthermore indicates that a surety who became a slave due to the insolvency of the debtor was freed and released from slavery on repayment of the debt, suggesting that the legal status of an Iranian subject could be fluent and change maybe even several times in the course of his life. Persons might easily become slaves due to debt bondage, but could also return to their original status as 'free' men. In any case, the transition between freedom and slavery, particularly if someone belonged to the lowest class of impecunious commoners, seems to have been far easier in these instances than the change from a lower social estate to a higher one.

34 MHD 57.12–58.3; Macuch 1993, pp. 393–395, and commentary pp. 401–406 (no. 11–17).
35 See Macuch 2016b.

The fourth origin of slavery mentioned above, the sale of members of the family, seems to have been far more restricted than the other causes of servitude. The only accepted reason is a state of emergency called *adwadād* (Av. *aδβadāitī-*, lit. 'leaving on the way'), in which the legal guardian of a family is definitely no longer able to support all the family members under his guardianship.[36] This technical term originally denoted the offence of 'forsaking a person under one's guardianship', but designates in this context a state of emergency consisting of 'not being able to provide maintenance; inability to maintain'. Only in this exceptional case of emergency, when a guardian is no longer able to provide food and other necessary items for those under his *manus*, is the head of a household permitted to sell his wife or his children to save them or other members of the family from starvation and death.[37]

We have no way of reconstructing the quantity of slaves in Ērānšahr, or the relation between the number of freeborn citizens and slaves, or the role the latter played in the economy of the realm, but the sources point to a large number of slaves occupied in three major areas:

1. In the household (*dūdag, kadag*). These slaves were regarded as 'things' (*xwāstag*) belonging to the 'total estate; undivided inheritance' (*abarmānd*) of a family and could be bequeathed by the *paterfamilias* together with their children as part of the residue to his heirs.
2. In agriculture. Slaves working in large estates (*dastgird*) and also in smaller units had the status of so-called *glebae adscripti*, persons 'bound to the soil'. They belonged to the land on which they worked and were alienated together with the animals if the land was sold.[38]
3. In fire foundations. Many of the large endowments had extensive property at their disposal, consisting of agricultural land, orchards, vineyards etc. Slaves working on this property were called *anšahrīg ī ātaxš* 'slaves of the fire' (not to be confused with *ātaxš-bandag* 'servant of the fire' or *ādurān-bandag* 'servant of the fires', who was not a slave, see above). We have hardly any details on their lot, but there is evidence that non-Zoroastrians (in this instance Jews) could also be employed as 'fire-slaves' (*ʿbdʾ d-nwrʾ* 'slaves/servants of the fire' in the Babylonian Talmud).[39]

Although slaves in all three areas were regarded theoretically as legal objects, subject to the will of the masters, their treatment in theses three areas must have differed considerably. We can reasonably assume that the lot of a slave working with his family in a household would have been far better in most cases than

36 See Chapters I, pp. 75–76, and V, pp. 463–467; also Macuch 2012a with further references.

37 MHD 33.6–9 and 33.13–17 (Macuch 1993, pp. 244–245).

38 MHD 18.9–10; MHDA 36.16–37.1 (Macuch 1981, pp. 80–81).

39 See Chapter VII, pp. 599–603. For further details see Macuch 2002b. On these three major areas see also Macuch 2010a.

one bound to the soil or working on a large estate. Moreover, the legal rights of the owner with respect to this 'thing' were restricted to a certain degree, placing the slave on a somewhat different level than material objects. In contrast to most other types of transactions, a Zoroastrian slave-owner was not permitted to sell his slave to a non-believer. Both the seller and the buyer were treated legally as thieves and punished according to the prescribed penalty for theft (*drōš*).[40] Moreover, a master who allowed cruel treatment (*stahm*) or bodily abuse (*zaxm*) of his slave was also subject to a penalty (*tāwān*), by which the slave was protected to a certain extent from arbitrary acts of cruelty (the same rule applied to a guardian who permitted a woman under his guardianship to be abused).[41] A master could assign the right to a *peculium* to his slave by giving him the 'right of disposal over his (own) income' (*pad windišn pādixšāy kard*), also enabling the slave to receive gifts from a third party.[42]

Strange constellations emerged particularly in litigation, revealing the double legal status of the slave as an object as well as a legal person, capable of acting in court as a witness and defendant.[43] In one remarkable case the plaintiff (*pēšēmāl*) claims that the defendant (*pasēmāl*) he has brought to court, is his slave, that is, he takes action for the return of his property by suing the 'thing' itself.[44] The most peculiar aspect of this case is that the defendant is not a freedman and does not claim to be one (in which case his legal status would have been changed, permitting the plaintiff to sue him), but declares that he belongs to another master, that is, he appears by his own statement as the property of a third party, although he is at the same time a party to the suit brought against him and therefore a legal subject. Obviously the slave was permitted to act as though he were a legal person in certain cases demanding the use of his human faculties within the limited range of litigation in legal practice, despite remaining theoretically an object of law.

Moreover, as already indicated, a large number of individual cases on slavery in the Law-book reveal that the boundary between being free and enslaved was not as rigid as this separation might imply, nor was it quite as simple to determine the exact status of a person if he/she belonged in part to both groups. The transition from one state to the other seems to have been far more fluid in Sasanian Iran than in many other legal systems of late antiquity. Moreover, it was possible to belong to both categories simultaneously. A slave could belong as joint property to different masters at the same time, who were co-proprietors or shareholders (*bahr-xwēš*), each one of them having the right of disposal of an ideal portion,

40 MHD 1.13–15 (for further references see Macuch 1993, p. 38f.).

41 MHD 1.4–6 (Macuch 1993, p. 24).

42 MHDA 3.6–13 (Macuch 1981, p. 71). On the peculiarities of this specific case see Macuch 1988a, p. 765.

43 Although legal theory takes another stand and is opposed to accepting the testimony of a slave, see MHD 98.4–5 (Macuch 1993, p. 587, and commentary, p. 591f. , no. 11).

44 MHD 107.9–12 (Macuch 1993, p. 650).

which could consist of one-half, one-third or even one-tenth of the slave. Given that the main form of holding property in a descent group consisted of joint 'ideal' shares, which obviously not only applied to landed property and real estate, but also to chattels and slaves, this is hardly astonishing. But in contrast to ancient Greek and Roman law, it led to the strange situation that a person could also be partly enslaved and partly freed to a specific extent at the same time. If one of the shareholders manumitted the slave to the degree corresponding to his portion, then the latter was liberated to the extent in which he/she belonged to that master (one-half[45], one-third[46], one-tenth[47]) with the result that that person then belonged partly to the category of freedman, partly to that of a slave. The former slave would have the rights and duties of a freedman to the extent in which he/she was liberated and his or her children would be free to the same degree. Although it stretches the imagination to understand what it would mean practically to be freed to one-tenth, this is exactly what is explicitly stated not only in the Sasanian Law-book, but also in Īšōʿbōxt's *Corpus Iuris*, based almost completely on Zoroastrian law. Legally this type of manumission implied that a certain percentage of the slave's faculties and work-force (including the rights over a *peculium*) as well as his/her children would be subject to different regulations than the part that was still enslaved. Despite the obvious legal difficulties and the fact that we have no way of knowing how frequent this kind of partial liberation was, the question remains how concrete problems emerging from this double status were resolved. There is a hint how jurists reacted to difficulties emerging from this double status in a case referring to a fire-foundation: if a master manumits one-half of a slave and assigns three-quarters of the same slave to the 'service of a fire' (*pad bandagīh ī ātaxš*) only one half (given the terminology employed here, presumably the freed part) is regarded as dedicated to the service of the fire.[48]

A slave could, of course, also be completely released from slavery, acquiring legal capacity, the right to own property and to undertake obligations on his own, which would drastically change his position in the community from that of a slave to a freedman. The terminology used in this context is decisive: the freedman became a 'subject of the King of Kings' (*šāhān šāh bandag*) and could not be re-enslaved according to one school of thought (although the opposite opinion is also stated, albeit with no information on the circumstances leading to re-enslavement).[49] A slave belonging to a non-Zoroastrian could also acquire

45 MHD 48.13–15 (Macuch 1993, p. 324); 101.11–15 (*ibid.*, p. 623); see also Īšōʿbōxt, Book V, Chapter XIII, §7 (Sachau 1914, p. 179).

46 Īšōʿbōxt, Book V, Chapter XIII, §7b (Sachau 1914, p. 179).

47 MHD 1.6–7 (Macuch 1993, p. 24); Īšōʿbōxt, Book V, Chapter XIII, §5 (Sachau 1914, p. 179, §5).

48 MHD 103.4–6; for a discussion of this passage see Macuch 2002b, p. 115f.; on fire-foundations see Chapter III, pp. 220–229.

49 MHD 20.7–10 (= 31.15–32.1; Macuch 1993, p. 161). Īšōʿbōxt, Book V, Chapter XIII, §2 (Sachau 1914, p. 177).

manumission by converting to Zoroastrianism, in which case the Zoroastrian community was even obliged to help the slave buy himself free (by a loan or other means).[50] We have no exact information on the legal position of a freedman, but can assume that it was comparable to that of a commoner belonging to the lowest class of Sasanian society.

2.2 Nobles and commoners

A person's rank and station (*gāh*) in the community seems to have been one of the most important constituent elements determining an individual's status and his/her legal rights and duties. Although only little direct evidence is transmitted in the legal material at our disposal, the details in numerous other sources, specifically Arabic and Persian historiographies, stress the fundamental distinction between nobles and commoners in the Sasanian Empire. We are informed that huge compendiums belonging to the category of *āyēn* ('regulation, custom') literature were written on the organization of the State and social institutions, including the social estates, one of which (the *Āyen-nāmag* 'Book of Regulations'), consisting of thousands of pages, was rendered into Arabic by Ibn al-Muqaffaʿ. Unfortunately it is lost, as most of his translations, but was presumably used by Arabic historiographers in their depictions of Sasanian Iran.[51] More importantly, special charters of rank (*gāh-nāmag*) were drawn, in which an individual's position was determined exactly in relation to others, including the sovereign. The *Gāh-nāmag* ('Book of Rank') was an extensive catalogue (which has not survived, but is described in Arabic literature), a kind of Who's Who, enumerating 600 high dignitaries of the empire and classifying them according to their rank and station in Sasanian society.[52] The *Letter of Tansar* confirms the registration of the nobles following a decree of the King of Kings (which one: Ardašīr, Husraw, Yazdegird, another sovereign?), in which he ordered that the 'rank and station' (*daraǧa wa martaba*) of every man should be recorded in 'books and archives' (*kitābhā wa dīwānhā*) in order to prevent the 'decadence of rank' (*taǧḥīz-i marātib*) and the mingling of nobles (*ahl-i daraǧāt*) with commoners (*ahl-i ʿamma*).[53] He gave instructions regarding almost every aspect of daily life: men of noble birth were to be distinguished from common people with regard to their 'horses and clothes, houses and gardens, women and servants'. He, moreover, set differences between various grades of nobility with regard to 'entrance- and drinking-places, sitting- and standing-places, clothes, ornaments and houses'.[54] That Sasanian aristocracy

50 MHD 1.10–13 (Macuch 1993, p. 24f., and commentary, 34f., no. 6).
51 On the translations of Ibn al-Muqaffaʿ see Gabrieli 1931–1932.
52 See Christensen 1944, pp. 62–68, with further references.
53 Persian text in Darmesteter 1894, pp. 222–223; translation Boyce 1968a, p. 44; on this source see Chapter I, pp. 52–53.
54 Boyce 1968a, p. 44.

itself was divided into several ranks is well known and already attested in the third century inscriptions of Šābuhr I at Hājjiābād and Narseh at Paikūlī, distinguishing between the *šahryārān* (local dynasties), *wāspuhragān* (noble families; princes), *wuzurgān* (grandees) and *āzādān* (freemen).[55] Narseh also includes the *kadag-xwadāy(ān)* (householders), which are missing in Šābuhr's list, in several passages of his inscription enumerating the high dignitaries of the State, either preceding or following the *āzādān*.[56] Another noble rank, that of the *dehgān(ān)* (small nobility), was probably only introduced in the 6th century by Husraw I Anūšīrwān in the course of his vast reforms after the Mazdakite upheaval. Only a man belonging to one of the higher ranks of the aristocracy had access to any State or court office of importance, as not only Persian and Arabic but also classical sources disclose.[57]

Besides all these details, which would have been superfluous if the question of social standing had not been of utmost importance, there is another significant indication that a man's station in the social construct defined his rights and duties. There is a very clear vertical divide between the aristocracy and commoners regarding property rights, transmitted in the *Letter of Tansar*, which corresponds perfectly to the legal institutions we are able to reconstruct in the fields of family and property law. This source explicitly states that the State specifically protected the proprietary rights of the aristocracy by implementing two laws decreed by the King of Kings:

1. A man of noble birth (*mardōm-zāda*) was not allowed to take a wife from among commoners (*zan-i ʿamma*). The person who did not follow this rule lost his right to inheritance.
2. Commoners (*ʿamma*) were not allowed to purchase the estates (*mustaqall wa amlāk*) of the nobles (*bozorgān*; variant: *bozorg-zadagan*).[58]

This important information agrees well with the specifics on family and property law reflected in the individual cases of the Sasanian Law-book. Interestingly, both regulations have *one and the same goal*: to prohibit the transfer of property from the nobility to commoners either indirectly by marriage, since the legitimate children of a common woman would inherit, or directly by selling the estate. If we add to these rules the numerous legal details on 'intermediary succession' (*ayōgēnīh*) and 'substitute succession' (*stūrīh*) and the artificial construction of legitimate heirs (to be described below), then it becomes quite evident that Sasanian law developed a large range of options to preserve and increase the property of its elite and took special care to avoid splitting and

55 For the Šābuhr inscription see Back 1978, p. 374.
56 The different passages of the Paikūlī inscription with these lists of dignitaries are put together for easy comparison in the conspectus given by Skjærvø 1983b, p. 46.
57 For example Procopius 1,6,13, *apud* Schmitt 2004, p. 676.
58 Persian text Darmesteter 1894, pp. 222–223; translation Boyce 1968a, p. 44.

alienating the possessions of noble lineages.[59] We may confidently conclude that Sasanian property law and its law of succession were specifically constructed to promote and protect the material interests of the aristocracy. Given that Sasanian society knew different ranks of nobles from the very beginning, as the inscriptions of Šābuhr and Narseh suggest, it seems highly unlikely that these regulations should be only late changes, resulting from the chaos produced by the Mazdakite movement in the 6th century. Moreover, the legal institutions mentioned above would have needed several centuries to develop in the manner they are presented in the late Pahlavi legal texts as an interconnected network, making it very likely that the vertical divide between aristocrats and plebeians was a real feature of Sasanian society from the very beginning (despite later possible changes and modifications in detail), and not only an element of the late Sasanian period.

The social structure described in the 'Letter of Tansar', dividing society into aristocrats of noble descent and common people of low origin, is unwittingly confirmed in Pahlavi eschatological literature, in the *Zand ī Wahman Yasn*. The question, whether this work is a late redaction of an age-old Zoroastrian eschatological source in its Sasanian garb or a far later composition, has been discussed controversially.[60] The most likely explanation of its different layers is that it is a blend of material from various ages in a redaction stemming from the Islamic period, in which the disastrous fate of Ērānšahr—before the appearance of the three Zoroastrian saviours at the end of time—is described in drastic words:

ZWY 4.33–36
(33) *xwāstag ud ⁺āzarmīgīh hamāg be ō ǰud-kešān ud ǰud-ristagān rasēd* … (35) *ud xwurdagān duxt ī āzādagān ud wuzurgān ud mow-mardān pad zanīh gīrēnd.* (36) *ud āzādagān ud wuzurgān ud mow-mardān be ō škōhīh* (*ud*) *bandagīh rasēnd ud ⁺zanīn ud xwurdag be ō wuzurgīh ud pādixšāyīh rasēnd ud a-čāragān ud xwurdagān be ō pēšgāhīh ud rāyēnīdārīh rasēnd.*

'(33) Property (*xwāstag*) and honour (*⁺āzarmīgīh*) will all go to infidels (*ǰud-kēšān*) and heretics (*ǰud-ristagān*) … (35) Plebeians (*xwurdagān*) will marry the daughters of Freemen/Nobles (*āzādagān*), Grandees (*wuzurgān*) and of Mobeds (*mow-mardān*). (36) Freemen, Grandees and Mobeds will become poor and slaves (*ō škōhīh ud bandagīh rasēnd*). And women (*⁺zanīn*) and plebeians (*xwurdag*) will reach the status of Grandees and sovereignity (*ō wuzurgīh ud pādixšāyīh rasēnd*). And the poor ones (*a-čāragān*) and the plebeians (*xwurdagān*) will obtain front rank (*pēšgāhīh*) and power (*rāyēnīdārīh*).'[61]

59 On these institutions see pp. 163–174 below. On the connection between family law and the consolidation of power in the Sasanian period see also Macuch 1995.

60 For an overview of the controversial discussion see Cereti 1995, pp. 15–17, and Macuch 2009a, pp. 152–155, with further references.

61 See the edition of Cereti 1995, p. 137 (transcription), p. 155 (translation which I have followed with only a few minor changes).

No matter, whether the ZWY was originally based on an older Avestan text or is a later, reworked product of Sasanian and Islamic times, the worst possible devastations to Iranian society imaginable to its Zoroastrian authors or redactors point to a worldview consistent with all the details listed above on the hierarchical structure of Sasanian society. According to our text the worst calamities to befall Ērānšahr were:

1. the transfer of property and social standing from the nobility and priesthood to heretics and non-Zoroastrians;
2. the intermingling of nobles, priests and commoners by intermarriage;
3. the complete reversal of the hierarchy with women, plebeians and poor people taking the place of the nobility and priesthood.

Obviously the abolishment of the crucial division between the elite (aristocrats and priests), on the one hand, and commoners (including other persons of low standing, such as women and slaves) and heretics, on the other, was regarded as one of the worst disasters to befall Ērānšahr, leading to the downfall of the social order and the destruction of the Zoroastrian church and the Sasanian State, the two ideal pillars of the Iranian Empire. This is exactly the same main objection brought forward against the egalitarian world-view of Mazdakite heresy, which would have led to the annihilation of all the legal institutions of the Sasanian State in the sixth century if it had been successful (see Chapter III, pp. 253–259). This clear division of Iranian society into two major social groups is reflected indirectly in the legal regulations we are able to reconstruct in almost every legal field of Sasanian jurisprudence.

2.3 Citizens and 'non-Iranians' (foreigners)

The late *Dēnkard*, Book 3, transmits a kind of theoretical explanation of elements 'joining and separating' (*hamīh ud ǰudāgīh*) people into four categories, beginning with the divide between Iranians and non-Iranians. Although this is definitely not a legal text, nor can be dated with certainty to a specific period (apart from its last redaction in the 9th century), it could well reflect ancient values of the priesthood, which may have been current in the Sasanian period with regard to the different inhabitants of Ērānšahr.[62] The importance of the passage lies in its clear hierarchy of groups, united by certain traits and separated from each other in accordance with their character and religious affiliation, on the one hand, and according to the grade of observance of religious precepts,

62 The use of *hād* at the beginning of the first sentence after the title could refer to the Avesta. According to Skjærvø 2010 (pp. 182–190) the particle *hād* (originally the 3rd sg. subjunctive of 'to be': 'so be it; be it as it may') is used in the *Dēnkard* primarily to introduce citations from the Avesta in Pahlavi.

notably worship and donations to the gods (*dāšn ī ēzišn*), on the other.[63] In short, four groups can be distinguished:

1. Among 'people' (*mardōmān*) there is a union (*hamīh*) of Iranians (*ērān*) because of their 'Iranian character' (*ērīg xēm*), separating (*ǰudāgīh*) them from non-Iranians (*an-ērān*) due to their 'un-Iranian character' (*an-ērīg xēm*).
2. Among Iranians (*ērān*) there is a union of Zoroastrians (*hudēnān*), who follow Zoroastrian law (*hudēnīg dād*), separating them from the adherents of evil religions (*ag-dēnan*), who follow the 'law(s) of evil religion(s)' (*agdenīg dād*).
3. Among Zoroastrians (*hudēnān*) there is a union of 'the good' (*wehān*) due to their donations to worship (*pad dāšn ī ēzišn-iz*), separating them from 'evil' persons (*wattarān*), who do not donate and worship (*pad a-dāšnīh ī an-ēzišnīgīh-iz*).
4. Among these three the highest rank (*sar*) is achieved by the union with the gods (*yazdān*) due to worship and donations (*pad ēzišn ī dāšn-iz*), separating the worshippers from the demons who should neither be worshipped nor offered donations (a reference to the priestly caste?).

Although this is not a legal text, the criteria for distinguishing Iranians from non-Iranians, Zoroastrians from non-Zoroastrians and building a hierarchy within the latter group could have well been followed on a theoretical basis for dealing with the diverse inhabitants of the Sasanian State. The information on the status of both citizens and foreigners in a juristic context is scant and although various expressions are used in legal texts for 'inhabitant' of the land (*ādehīg*), 'citizen' (*mard ī šahr*), 'subject of the King of Kings' (*šāhān šāh bandag*), 'Iranian' (*ēr*) 'non-Iranian' (*an-ēr*) and 'foreigner' (*uzdehīg*) it is almost impossible to determine the exact legal distinctions and implications of these

63 DkD 109.7–13 (DkM 143.20–144.6): *hād hamīh ud ǰudāgīh ēwēnagān was u-š ēk andar mardōmān hamīh ī abāg ērān pad ērīg xēm ǰudāgīh az an-ērān pad an-ērīg xēm. ud ēk andar ērān hamīh ī abāg hudēnān pad hudēnīg dād ǰudāgīh az ag-dēnān pad agdenīg dād. ud ēk andar hudēnān hamīh ī abāg wehān pad dāšn ī ēzišn-iz ǰudāgīh az wattarān pad a-dāšnīh ī an-ēzišnīgīh-iz. ēk sar ī ēn har sē ast hamīh ī abāg yazdān pad ēzišn ī dāšn-iz ǰudāgīh ī az dēwān pad an-ēzišnīh ī a-dāšnīh-iz.* 'That is, there are many kinds of unions and separations: One is among people (*mardōmān*) the union of the Iranians (*ērān*) because of (their) Iranian character, the separation from the non-Iranians (*an-ērān*) because of (their) non-Iranian character. And one is among the Iranians (*ērān*) the union of the adherents of the Good Religion (*hudēnān*) because of the law of the Good Religion, the separation from the adherents of the Evil Religion(s) (*ag-dēnān*) because of the law of the Evil Religion(s). And one is among the adherents of the Good Religion (*hudēnān*) the union with good persons because of (their) donations for worship (*pad dāšn ī ēzišn-iz*); the separation from the evil people because of (their) not donating to (worship) and not worshipping (*pad a-dāšnīh ī an-ēzišnīgīh-iz*). One is the foremost of these three, the union with the gods (*yazdān*) through worship as well as donations (*pad ēzišn ī dāšn-iz*); the separation from the demons by not worshipping (them) and not (giving them) donations (*pad an-ēzišnīh ī a-dāšnīh-iz*).' See also DE MENASCE 1973, p. 145, no. 140.

terms. Who was regarded as an 'inhabitant' (*ādehīg*)—was this the neutral term for every free person who lived within the borders of Ērānšahr, regardless of his (or her) creed, rank and ethnic affiliation? Who exactly was regarded as a 'citizen' and did citizenship include having a special status and specific rights comparable to, say, Roman law? Was there a legal difference between the terms *mard ī šahr* (lit. 'man of the realm'; 'citizen') and *šāhān šāh bandag* ('subject of the King of Kings')? Were the religious minorities of Ērānšahr just 'inhabitants', whereas freeborn Zoroastrians were 'citizens' and 'subjects' (as one passage suggests)? Moreover, the third and fourth basic constituent elements of legal personality, that is, citizenship and religious affiliation, can hardly be kept apart, even though they are mentioned as separate categories (see pp. 102–103). An 'inhabitant' (*ādehīg*) of Ērānšahr, who is a 'citizen' (*mard ī šahr*) and a 'subject of the King of Kings' (*šāhān šāh bandag*), seems to be always at the same time an Iranian (*ēr*) and a Zoroastrian (*weh-dēn*). The basic criteria of 'citizenship' and religious affiliation were almost synonymous with the ethnic designation 'Iranian': if a person converted from Zoroastrianism to another creed he became not only an 'infidel' (*ag-dēn*), but also an *an-ēr*, a 'non-Iranian'.[64] Hence the *an-ēr* is not always a foreigner in the ethnic sense of the word, but could also be a convert, who was regarded prior to his conversion as an 'Iranian' (*ēr*). Of course, the *an-ēr* could also be a 'foreigner' (*uzdehīg*) in the true sense of the word, that is a person from a different country or state, and the term could also be used as a synonym of *ag-dēn* ('infidel') with regard to those religious minorities (predominantly Christians and Jews) who lived for many centuries among Zoroastrians within the borders of Ērānšahr. In either case the *an-ēr* was not—or no longer—an Iranian citizen and subject of the King of Kings (*šāhān šāh bandag*). We may group the basic terms used in this context tentatively as follows:

Table 6. Inhabitants of the Empire: basic terms

Inhabitants of Ērānšahr	Citizens, subjects	Foreigners, converts, religious minorities
ādehīg ('inhabitant of the land')	*mard ī šahr* ('man of the land; citizen')	*uzdehīg* ('foreigner')
	šāhān šāh bandag ('subject of the King of Kings')	
	ēr ('Iranian')	*an-ēr* ('non-Iranian')
	weh-dēn or *hu-dēn* ('adherent of the Good Religion; Zoroastrian')	*ag-dēn* ('adherent of an evil religion; infidel')

64 See Macuch 2024a.

The fragmentary information on citizens and foreigners only enables us to sketch an incomplete picture. Of particular interest are a few short statements in the summary of the legal *nasks* in *Dēnkard* 8, in which 'non-Iranians' (*an-ēr*) are compared with other persons with limited legal capacity. As a synopsis of the Pahlavi *zand*, these passages unfortunately offer no explanations and can be only understood correctly in the light of other sources on Sasanian law. In one instance[65] the legal capacity of an *an-ēr* is contrasted with that of a woman, who normally only has limited legal capacity and has to be generally represented by her legal guardian (*sālār*) in public, particularly in legal disputes. In certain rare cases, however, if she is her own guardian (*abar tan ī xwēš sālār*), she can represent herself in court and act both as a witness (*gugāy*) and as an *auctor* (*dastwar* 'legal predecessor'), that is, as a person who vouchsafes in court for the validity of a sale (or barter) in a civil conflict.[66] A 'non-Iranian' (*an-ēr*) in contrast is neither allowed to appear as a witness, nor is he permitted to act as *auctor* in court (the passage even compares him drastically to another category of persons, to those 'deserving death', *margarzān*, who have lost all their civic rights).[67]

The comparison with the *margarzān*, however, obviously does not mean that 'non-Iranians' were completely without rights. On the contrary, even if their testimony as witness or *auctor* was not permitted in court, they could nevertheless still appear as one of the parties in a civil lawsuit against an Iranian, as we may deduce from another short passage distinguishing between disputes involving persons who did not belong to the same legal category.[68] According to this statement three kinds of civil disputes of persons with limited legal capacity involving property rights were possible:

1. litigation between an Iranian (*ēr*) (as plaintiff) and a non-Iranian (*an-ēr*) or several non-Iranians (*an-ērān*) (as defendants);
2. litigation between a non-Iranian (*an-ēr*) (as plaintiff) and an Iranian (*ēr*) (as defendant);

65 DkD 537.12–14 (DkM 708.18–20): *abar šāyistan ī zan pad gugāyīh ud +dastwarīh ka abar tan ī xwēš sālār pādixšāy pad-iz dastwarīh (ī) šōy nē šāyistan ī an-ēr ud margarzān pad ēk-iz.* 'On the admissibility of a woman as a witness and an +*auctor* when she is her own guardian (and) also (if) she is authorized by the entitlement of the husband. (On) the inadmissibility of a non-Iranian (*an-ēr*) and a person 'worthy of death' (*margarzān*) in either (function).' For a discussion of the passage see Macuch 2010a, p. 199.

66 On the *auctor* (*dastwar*) see Chapters IV, pp. 385–387, and VI, pp. 542–544; also Macuch 1988b and 2016a, pp. 150–151.

67 On the loss of civil rights in the case of a *margarzān* see MHD 97.15–98.1; 98.13–14 (Macuch 1993, pp. 582, 586 and 582–583, 587 respectively).

68 DkD 537.5–7 (DkM 708.10–11): *abar pahikārišn ī ēr abāg an-ēr abāg an-ērān an-ēr abāg ēr +bandag abāg mard ī šahr pad xwāstagīg čiš.* 'On the litigation of an Iranian (*ēr*) against a non-Iranian (*an-ēr*) (and) against non-Iranians (*an-ērān*); of a non-Iranian (*an-ēr*) against an Iranian (*ēr*); of a slave (+*bandag*) against a citizen (*mard ī šahr*) regarding an object of property.'

3. between a slave (+*bandag*) (who is *not* a citizen and hence comparable to the 'non-Iranian') and a citizen (*mard ī šahr*).

The passage suggests that 'non-Iranians' (in the extended sense described above, that is, foreigners, converts, adherents of a different religion) were accepted as persons with limited legal capacity, both as plaintiffs and defendants in court when dealing with Iranians (= citizens, subjects, Zoroastrians), just as a slave, who normally had no civil rights could under certain circumstances be accepted as a party in civil litigation involving the slave himself against a citizen (*mard ī šahr*) with full legal rights (see above p. 108). Moreover, several short passages reveal that complex legal transactions with non-Iranians could take place, that contracts and agreements were concluded and both real and personal security in the form of a pledge (*graw*) or a pawn (*nabāg/nibāg*) could be offered for a loan. In one instance people living near the borders of Ērānšahr (*marzānān*) are mentioned, who transfer a pledge (*graw*) to non-Iranians (*an-ērān*, referring in this case probably to foreigners living beyond the border) on the basis of a contract (*pašn*).[69] At the same time it is described as a grave sin (*garān wināhīh*) to deliver an Iranian (*ēr*) pledged as security (*tan*) into debt bondage to a non-Iranian (*an-ēr*).[70] But once a contract of this type had been concluded and a person handed out to the 'non-Iranian' creditor as security, the contract had to be kept. It was considered as a grave offence (*garān wināhīh*) to steal a pawn (*nabāg/nibāg*) one had stipulated for a loan from a 'non-Iranian', even if the Iranian borrower had pledged his own son (*xwēš pus*) as security to the 'non-Iranian' moneylender.[71] These passages correspond well with the information available on the Zoroastrian law of contract, which strictly forbids breach of contract, including those concluded with foreigners and infidels (see also the next section 2.4). We can deduce from these short entries that 'non-Iranians' in the extended sense of the word described above (foreigners, converts, religious minorities) were not deprived of all legal capacity, but were conceded certain rights both in litigation and in transactions with Iranians.

69 DkD 544.14–15 (DkM 717.1): *abar graw dād ī marzanan o an-eran ud pašn xwāst.* 'On people living near the boundary transferring a pledge (*graw*) to non-Iranians and requesting a contract.' For a discussion of this and the following *Dēnkard* passages see Macuch 2010a, p. 201.

70 DkD 546.18–19 (DkM 719.13): *abar garān wināhīh ī tan (ī) ēr ō an-ēr abespārdan.* 'On the great offence of delivering an Iranian person (in debt bondage, *tan*) to a non-Iranian.' On debt bondage and the term *tan* in this context see p. 106 above and Chapter IV, pp. 352–354

71 DkD 544.19–20 (DkM 717.5–6): *abar garān wināhīh ī mard nibāg az an-ērān abāz duzīdan ka-š xwēš pus.* 'On the great offence of a man stealing back a pawn (*nibāg*) from non-Iranians, (even) if it is his own son.' See Chapter IV, p. 333, on security for a loan.

2.4 Zoroastrians and infidels

That 'non-Iranians' in the extended sense of the word (foreigners, converts, infidels) were *not* completely without rights is confirmed indirectly by another important statement in the Sasanian Law-book dealing with the legal rights of infidels (*ag-dēn*) in comparison to Zoroastrians (*weh-dēn*) which shows that Sasanian law put only a few—albeit significant—restrictions on the former:

MHD 60.16–61.1
ag-dēn nē hamāg-tōzišn bē xwāstag(+-tōzišn)[72] *bawēnd. ag-dēnān bē čiyōn-šān stūr nē gumārišn ud ān čiš ī pad rāh ī zahagīh ud paywand abāyēd {... ... dār}ēnd enyā-šān abārīg dādestān ōwōn čiyōn ān ī weh-dēnān.*

'Infidels (*ag-dēn*) do not count as joint debtors (*hamāg-tōzišn*), but (only as) +part-debtors (*xwāstag-+tōzišn*). (Regarding) infidels (*ag-dēnān*): except (the rule) that a "substitute successor" (*stūr*) should not be nominated (*nē gumārišn*) for them and the thing (*čīš*) that is due in the line of offspring (*zahagīh*) and descent (*paywand*) {... ...}, all other decisions (*dādestān*) concerning them are as those regarding adherents of the Good Religion (*weh-dēnān*).'[73]

The passage is embedded in a chapter on succession and inheritance (*dar ī xwāstagdārīh*) and calls our attention to the following three major differences between the rights of Mazdeans and religious others:

1. Infidels (*ag-dēn*) cannot be held liable as joint debtors or co-debtors (*hamāg-tōzišn*), but only as part-debtors (*xwāstag-+tōzišn*). In the context of inheritance this restriction refers to joint heirs who are shareholders and jointly liable for a debt. It states that a creditor cannot claim back the whole sum of a loan from each one of the debtors if they are not Mazdeans (in contrast to joint debtors confessing Zoroastrianism). Each one of the debtors will have to be sued separately, whereas in the case of Zoroastrian co-debtors each person could be held liable for the whole debt.[74]
2. A 'substitute successor; proxy' (*stūr*) cannot be engaged by official instances for a non-Zoroastrian. The use of the verb *gumārdan* 'to nominate', in this sentence implies that the third form of engaging a 'proxy' by religious authorities is meant here: it was not allowed to nominate a *stūr* for an unbeliever, who died without leaving a legitimate heir, in order to secure the transfer of property to the next generation and the continuity of the lineage.[75] Although *stūrīh* was a thoroughly Zoroastrian institution (described in section 4.4 below) based on several unique Mazdean norms of the Sasanian period, which were unacceptable to Jews and Christians alike, it seems that

72 On the reading *xwāstag*(-+*tōzišn*) see Macuch 1993, p. 425 (n. 9).
73 Macuch 1993, pp. 409, 415; see also Macuch 2014b.
74 See also commentary Macuch 1993, pp. 425–426 (no. 9) and Chapter III, p. 253, on joint debtors and part-debtors.
75 On the institution of *stūrīh* see pp. 163–174.

Christians of noble descent were nevertheless interested in using this institution for the same reasons as Zoroastrians and sought to circumvent the religious obstacles preventing its establishment.[76] Our passage unequivocally forbids non-Mazdeans the use of this institution.

3. Further limitations regarding the right of unbelievers to inherit property from Zoroastrians by means of offspring and descent (*pad rāh ī zahagīh ud paywand*; the verb is deleted by a lacuna in the text).

All three restrictions relate to property rights in the context of inheritance. The first one reduces the options of unbelievers who inherit property together with other shareholders and are liable for debts of the decedent. As every infidel debtor is personally liable only for a part of the debt and—in contrast to Zoroastrians—not every shareholder can be sued for the whole sum, this would reduce the options of a creditor to retrieve his money (this might have even been an intended effect to put unbelievers seeking to take out a loan from a Zoroastrian at a disadvantage). The second limitation forbids religious authorities to nominate a 'proxy' for unbelievers in order to engender offspring for a man who has no male heir. This is in full agreement with Zoroastrian precepts, as only Mazdeans were encouraged and required to increase the creation of Ohrmazd in the struggle between Good and Evil by generating children (with the intended side-effect of keeping property within the Zoroastrian community and securing the continuity of affluent noble lineages). This right could by no means be conceded to followers of another faith. The third restriction concerning inheritance (with a lacuna in the text) has a similar background, forbidding unbelievers to become universal successors of a Zoroastrian.[77]

Apart from these three restrictions (which are coherent from a Zoroastrian point of view), the passage ends with the important statement that *the same laws* are to be applied to Zoroastrians and infidels alike. This ruling corresponds well with other precepts of Zoroastrianism, such as the obligation of keeping contracts with foreigners (as we have seen in 2.3 above) and infidels (as in *abāg xwēšāwandān dōstān ǰud-dēnān mardōmān mihr ma drōzēd* 'Do not break a contract with relatives, friends and those confessing another religion (*ǰud-denan*).'[78]

Even though the entries are short, the overall impression is that adherents of other faiths were treated according to clear principles which were by large acceptable to the religious minorities living in Ērānšahr. It stand to reason that the central government could not ignore the ethnic realities of the Sasanian empire

76 On the strategies of adapting this institution to Christian law see Payne 2017 and Chapter VII, pp. 620–621.

77 This restriction is confirmed in a passage of the *Hērbedestān* dealing with the property of converts to Zoroastrianism, see Macuch 2009f.

78 *Handarz ī dānāgān ō māzdēsnān* 6, Jamasp-Asana 1897–1913, p. 52. See also the similar statement in *Mihr Yašt* 1.2 *apud* Gershevitch 1959, pp. 74–75.

and the large communities of Jews and Christians, who were—according to the testimony of the Babylonian Talmud and many Syriac sources—obviously allowed to practise their own cult and even implement their own religious laws to a certain degree. This may have been one of the main reasons for the development of a comparatively peaceful *modus vivendi* between the Persian government and the Jewish and Christian communities despite persecutions from time to time.[79] A few conclusions can be reached on the position of Jewish and Christian courts within the framework of the Sasanian legal system, which we will deal with below.[80] To sum up: Non-Mazdeans (notably Jews and Christians) were conceded certain rights, including the right to follow their own religious norms (as long as they did not obstruct or defy Zoroastrian laws), to hold judgement in civil cases before their own courts (as long as they did not interfere with Sasanian jurisdiction) and to inherit property with the exclusion of the three restrictions described above.

2.5 Men and women

Besides the basic constituent of rank and status within the hierarchy of Sasanian society, the most important distinction, determining the rights and duties of the individual, was that of gender. Only a male of noble descent could attain full legal capacity (*tuwānīgīh*) under the condition that he was a citizen of the land (*mard ī šahr*), of major age (*purnāy*), mentally healthy (*ōšyār*)[81], freeborn and noble (*āzād*), a subject of the King of Kings (*šāhān šāh bandag*) and a Zoroastrian (*weh-dēn*).[82] A man fulfilling all these criteria became a person *sui iuris* after reaching the age of fifteen years, hereby attaining the right to participate in the religious and social life of the community, of serving as the head of a family or descent group, of fulfilling religious obligations and dealing with all kinds of legal transactions. As the legitimate son (*dādestān-pus*) of a *paterfamilias* or 'master of the house' (*kadag-xwadāy*) he became the direct successor of the father and was not only heir (*xwāstagdār*)[83] to the latter's property, but also inherited his name (as 'name-bearer', *nām-burdār*)[84] and place in the descent group, his standing in the community and his rank (*gāh*) in the social estate (*pēšag*). As the new head of the household (*kadag-xwadāy*) he also assumed guardianship

79 Brody 1990 and Payne 2015b, pp. 44–58, come to the same conclusions regarding the Jewish and the Christian communities respectively.

80 See Chapter VI, pp. 526–532.

81 This criterion is mentioned in REA 5.4 and could be late (possibly under the influence of Islamic law?).

82 These conditions are listed in a text from the 8th century (Dd 55.2), but the dispersed details transmitted in the Sasanian Law-book indirectly confirm that criteria similar to these must also have already been effective in the Sasanian period.

83 See references in Macuch 1993, p. 714.

84 *Kārnāmag ī Ardaxšēr ī Pābagān* I, 6.

Table 7. Overview: rights and duties of the *kadag-xwadāy* (*paterfamilias*)

Rights		Duties	
xwāstagdārīh	'proprietorship' of family property	*tōzišn ī pidarān*	responsibility to pay for 'debts of the fathers'
nāmburdārīh	status as 'name-bearer' of the family or lineage	*ruwān yazišn*	performance of 'rituals for the souls' of the deceased
gāh	'rank' (status in the community)	*nāmagānīh*	responsibility for the 'cult of the ancestors'
sālārīh 1. *dūdag-sālārīh* 2. *xwāstag-sālārīh*	guardianship (*manus*; *potestas*) 1. over the family 2. over property	*pādixšāy-zanīh*	'marriage with full matrimonial rights' (*cum manu mariti*)
		stūrīh	'substitute succession' (for another man)
		čagar-zanīh	'auxiliary marriage' (*sine manu mariti*) (to procreate children for another man)

(*sālārīh*) over the women, including wives, unmarried daughters, sisters and aunts, and minors of both sexes in the family (if there were several adult sons, usually the oldest son replaced the father as family guardian, *dūdag-sālār*, if there was no other disposition in the former's will).[85]

Despite having full legal capacity, the man was hardly less encumbered by a large range of duties than the woman. He was bound with at least as many rules and regulations to the traditions and customs of the forefathers, to the social structure of the descent group (*paywand*, *tōhmag*), the lineage (*kadag*, *xānag*) and family (*dūdag*, *nāf*), and, as a citizen of Ērānšahr, also to his sovereign, the King of Kings. As a Zoroastrian he was obliged to perform the required rituals for the soul of the deceased (*ruwān yazišn*)[86], to keep the cult of the souls of the ancestors (*nāmagānīh*),[87] and to marry and procreate legitimate children by entering a 'marriage with full matrimonial rights' (*pādixšāy-zanīh*). He was, moreover, obliged to help other co-religionists who had no children by acting as 'proxy' or 'substitute successor' (*stūr*) for them and engendering children in their name in an 'auxiliary marriage' (*čagar-zanīh*). As heir of family property (*xwāstagdār*) he was responsible for settling debts of the fathers (*tōzišn ī*

85 On inheritance see below and Macuch 2005b.
86 For references see Macuch 1993, p. 729.
87 On this term see Klingenschmitt 1971, pp. 145–150.

pidarān)[88] and managing family property (*xwāstag-sālārīh*) to the advantage of the descent group. As family guardian (*dūdag-sālār*) he was obliged to maintain all the persons under his guardianship with food, clothing and shelter, and to represent the family in all legal transactions in the public sphere, including claims against one of the persons under his guardianship.

In contrast to the adult man of noble descent, the woman as a rule did not attain legal capacity on reaching maturity, no matter to which social stratum she belonged, but ideally remained under the legal guardianship (*sālārīh*) of a man during her whole life: first under the *potestas* of the father, brother, uncle or any other male relative, who was family guardian (*dūdag-sālār*), later as *materfamilias* or 'mistress of the house' (*kadag-bānūg*) under the guardianship of her husband in a marriage 'with full matrimonial rights' (*pādixšāy-zanīh*). There were, however, in legal practice several exceptions to this rule. When a woman became a widow or entered a so-called 'consensus-marriage' (*xwasrāyēn/gādār*), in which she was *not* under the guardianship of the husband (see pp. 145–147 below), she assumed certain limited rights, which were normally denied to women, such as the right to litigate and to conduct legal transactions. In contrast to the regular marriage of the *pādixšāy*-type, which was arranged by the woman's guardian, she could choose her husband and enter this form of matrimony by herself if she was a widow or if her guardian had failed to procure a husband for her by the time she reached sexual maturity at the age of fifteen.[89] This fairly flexible regulation is hardly surprising if we take the importance attached to fertility and the procreation of children in Zoroastrianism into account. The only case, which does not seem to have been envisaged at all is that of an unmarried, single woman without children. This did probably occur, but is not mentioned anywhere in the legal material. As will be seen below, Sasanian law developed a large range of ingenious strategies to avoid this calamity, exploiting the reproductive faculties of women to the extreme by allowing various marriage forms to the purpose of increasing the number of children in affluent Zoroastrian families.

Despite their dependant status, women were not completely without rights. According to one passage, a woman could refuse a marriage arranged by her father or brother.[90] She could attain the right to dispose of her own income (*windišn*)[91] and could enter a marriage in which the husband had no title to the income of his wife (*ǰud az windišn*).[92] This, however, did not necessarily mean that she herself always had free access to these earnings, since we are informed that they went to the father, if there were no alternative arrangements.[93] Her

88 For references see Macuch 1993, p. 734.
89 See Macuch 1993, pp. 182–183 (no. 3).
90 MHD 36.9–16 (Macuch 1993, pp. 267, 269).
91 MHD 24.8–10; 33.1–3 (*ibid.*, pp. 174, 179 and 241, 243–245 respectively).
92 MHDA 1.1–2, 8–12 (Macuch 1981, pp. 21, 69).
93 MHDA 1.1–2 (*ibid.*, pp. 21, 69).

husband could make her a joint proprietor of his income, entitling her to a portion of his property, but could also cancel this privilege, if the wife was disobedient (*a-tarsag*).[94] Generally the range and limit of a woman's legal capacity was determined by her guardian both in her natal family as well as in the family of the husband.

The highest status a woman could achieve was that of *materfamilias* or 'mistress of the house' (*kadag-bānūg*) by entering a marriage 'with full matrimonial rights' (*pādixšāy-zanīh*). In the hierarchy of the household she came after the husband and had the general right to give instructions to other subordinate wives, minors and slaves who were obliged to show her obedience (*tarsagāhīh*).[95] Moreover, she was entitled to maintenance (*xwārišn ud dārišn*) and to a legal portion (*bahr ī kadag-bānūg*) of the total estate (*abarmānd*) of her husband at his demise the same size as the share of a son. Her children were all the husband's legitimate sons and daughters (*dādestān-pus, dādestān-duxt*) and entitled to inheritance (*yōhē pasčaēta*).[96]

The most important religious, legal and social duty of women was to put their reproductive faculties into the service of the men in their families and to bear children, as will be seen in the sections below on kinship, matrimony and inheritance. As wives, sisters or daughters they were obliged to act as 'intermediary successors' (*ayōgēn*)[97] of the husband, father or brother or 'substitute successors' (*stūr*) of other men in the lineage, if one of these men died without leaving a male heir. Their duty was to procreate sons, or at least one son, for the deceased by entering an 'auxiliary marriage' (*čagar-zanīh*) with another man to this purpose. The *pādixšāy*-wife remained legally the wife of her deceased husband, the daughter or sister entered a fictive incestuous (*xwēdōdah*) marriage of the *pādixšāy*-type with the father or brother, and a real *čagar* marriage in order to conceive children.[98] The sons of the *ayōgēn* (or *stūr*) were regarded as the direct legal successors and heirs of the deceased *paterfamilias.* Diverse forms of matrimony with completely different legal implications were constructed to this purpose, including incestuous and temporary marriage, which can only be understood correctly within the larger framework of Sasanian family law and kinship structure. Both marriage within the nuclear family and time-limited marriage made it possible for women to generate children for different men during their lifetimes without endangering the patrilineal principal of succession, as will be seen below.[99]

94 MHDA 1.2–6; 7.9–16 (Macuch 1981, pp. 21, 69 and 28, 99 respectively).
95 See chapter on 'disobedience' MHDA 4.12–8.2 (*ibid.*, pp. 96–99).
96 For references and details see Macuch 2005b and Chapter III, pp. 230–235.
97 For references and details see Macuch 2003b and pp. 163–174 below.
98 On the impact of incestuous marriages see Macuch 1991a and 2003b.
99 On the function of incestuous marriage see Macuch 2010c; on temporary marriage Macuch 2006 and pp. 157–162 below.

Table 8. Overview: rights and duties of the *kadag-bānūg* (*materfamilias*)

Rights		Duties	
windišn ī xwēš	'own income'	*pādixšāy-zanīh*	'marriage with full matrimonial rights' (*cum manu mariti*)
xwārišn ud dārišn	'nourishment and maintenance'	*tarsagāhīh*	'obedience' to the husband
bahr ī kadag-bānūg(īh)	'share of the *materfamilias*'	*ayōgēnīh*; *stūrīh*	'intermediary succession'; 'substitute succession'
		čagar-zanīh	'auxiliary marriage' (*sine manu mariti*) with another man (to procreate children for the *pādixšāy*-husband)

2.6 Conclusions: social stratification and legal rights

Our scrutiny of rights and duties in the Sasanian law of persons suggests that individuals were not only embedded in a strict hierarchy, but also in a complex network of social relationships by which their legal status in society was defined to a large degree. Even the Zoroastrian freeborn man of noble descent, who gained full legal capacity (*tuwānīgīh*) at maturity and was a person *sui iuris* ('of his own law'), remained tied with numerous rules and regulations to traditions, customs and religious duties as well as to the social structure of the family and as an Iranian subject to his sovereign, the King of Kings (*šāhān šāh bandag*). All other individuals discussed above had only limited legal capacity with varying privileges and obligations according to their gender, age and position in society or no legal rights whatsoever. Commoners belonging to the lower (the 4th, possibly also the 3rd)[100] estates had limited rights with regard to marriage choices and the acquisition of property and were excluded from the possibility of undertaking transactions involving real estate with the aristocracy (at least by the late Sasanian period). Foreigners (*an-ēr*) and infidels (*ag-dēn*) were accepted as 'legal persons' and not treated differently from Zoroastrians when litigating with an Iranian citizen or undertaking legal transactions, but they were *not* conceded the same rights in the area of family law, inheritance and succession. Persons under guardianship (*sālārīh*) with limited or no legal capacity (*alieni iuris* 'of another's law') encompassed women if all ages and classes, who were subject to a man's *potestas*, as well as

100 According to the second transmitted variation (with 'scribes' as the 3rd estate) discussed pp. 95–101 above.

underage children and slaves. A woman had additional limited rights only in the exceptional case of having no guardian (*a-sālār*), for example as a widow (if there was no other guardian in the family) or in a 'consensus marriage' (*xwasrāyēn/gādār*) without *manus* of the husband. However, the unmarried widow was soon placed under the family guardianship (*dūdag-sālārīh*) of another man in the lineage (a brother, uncle etc. of the deceased husband). In the 'consensus' marriage the wife could remain under the *potestas* of the father, if the marriage was time-limited (see pp. 145–147 below). A woman without guardian for a longer period was definitely the (unavoidable) exception, rather than the rule. Slaves had theoretically no legal capacity, being 'legal objects', but could be accepted under specific circumstances as legal persons in judicial practice, capable of entering litigation and giving testimony. The position of freed slaves depended on the degree of their manumission, which—in contrast to Roman law—could consist of a certain percentage of the slave (one-half, one-third, one-tenth etc.). A partly manumitted slave could hence belong to both categories of freedman and slave at the same time.

Although the available information is extremely fragmentary, a tentative reconstruction of the social hierarchy of these different groups based on the details illustrated above is feasible. Three major categories (with several subgroups) can be distinguished:

1. persons with **full legal capacity** (*tuwānīgīh*; *personae sui iuris*) of noble descent:
   - men, who fulfil *all* the following conditions:
     - freeborn and noble (*āzād*);
     - of major age (*purnāy*);
     - mentally healthy (*ōšyār*);
     - Zoroastrian (*weh-dēn*);
     - citizen of the State (*mard ī šahr*);
     - subject of the King of Kings (*šāhān-šāh bandag*);
2. persons with **limited legal capacity**:
   - 2.1. due to low descent:
     - 2.1.1. Zoroastrian freeborn men of age (*purnāy*), citizens (*mard ī šahr*), belonging as commoners to the 4th estate (possibly also to the 3rd estate of scribes);
     - 2.1.2. Zoroastrian freedmen, originally slaves, who were completely manumitted and became subjects of the king (*šāhān-šāh bandag*);
   - 2.2. due to ethnic origin, religious affiliation or gender:
     - 2.2.1. infidels (*ag dēn*);
     - 2.2.2. foreigners (*an-ēr*; *uzdehīg*);
     - 2.2.3. Zoroastrian freeborn women *without* a guardian (*a-sālār*; *e.g.*, as widows or in a *xwasrāyēn/gādār*-marriage);

3. dependant persons **under guardianship** (*pad sālārīh*; *personae alieni iuris*):
   3.1. with limited legal capacity:
      3.1.1. Zoroastrian freeborn women married to a nobleman (under guardianship of the husband, in a marriage 'with full matrimonial rights', *pādixšāy-zanīh*);
      3.1.2. Zoroastrian freeborn women married to a commoner (under guardianship of the husband; *pādixšāy-zanīh*);
      3.1.3. Zoroastrian freeborn women married in an 'auxiliary marriage' (*čagar-zanīh*) under guardianship of a member of the lineage (*not* the *čagar*-husband);
      3.1.4. Partly manumitted Zoroastrian slaves;
   3.2. with no legal capacity (with possible exceptions in litigation and giving testimony):
      3.2.1. underage children (*aburnāy*);
      3.2.2. slaves (*anšahrīg*, *bandag*) of all confessions.

The bulk of laws and regulations in the fields of family law, inheritance and property were constructed to serve the interests of the first group of persons with full legal capacity, not as individuals, but within the framework of large kinship groups and families belonging to the foremost estates of society, the aristocracy and priesthood, as will be argued in the following sections.

3 Kinship, family and descent groups

In contrast to modern Western societies, based—at least theoretically—on meritocracy, Sasanian society was founded on aristocracy, in which kinship-based social relationships were of fundamental importance and the basic political, religious, economic and territorial units consisted of descent groups.[101] As in many other societies throughout history, supreme importance was attached to the question of ancestry and descent. The prestige and power of noble families (as well as the legitimacy of the reigning dynasty)[102] were based on the quality and length of their genealogies, the strength of kinship ties and loyalties, and on legal rights and privileges derived from their position in the hierarchy of lineages and descent groups. Understanding the importance attached to kinship is crucial for reconstructing the intertwined network of rules governing family law, marriage, succession and inheritance which led to the emergence of unique legal institutions, some of which even continue to exist in an Islamic context (after having lost their relevance to the whole system) up to this day in Iran.[103]

101 Pourshariati 2008, pp. 56–160, has come to similar conclusions from a completely different perspective, using other sources. See her meticulous survey of the evidence on the major noble families in the Sasanian period.

102 On the construction of Ardašīr's genealogy see Macuch 2014 a.

Before discussing the intricacies of Sasanian kinship within the framework of family law, it will be best to begin by explaining a few general technical terms employed in Social Anthropology to distinguish various family ties as well as kinship groups and their members.[104] The term 'kinship' denotes according to its most common definition the relations between 'kin', that is persons related by real, putative or fictive consanguinity building a 'descent group', *i. e.*, a group formed on the basis of descent from an actual or assumed common ancestor. A 'descent group' consisting of members, whose relationship to each other is not only assumed, but can be actually demonstrated (*e. g.*, by concrete family ties or by a real, not only hypothetical, genealogy) is called a 'lineage'. Cultures can differ considerably in their definition of those who count as 'blood' kin, *i. e.*, people related to each other through common descent. The notion of consanguinity, of relation by blood-ties, is not necessarily bound to 'real' genetic relationships, but can be defined in different cultures in various ways, including putative and fictive forms. In the context of our topic it is important to stress three points:

1. A child is *not* necessarily regarded as a kin of *both* mother and father and their respective lineages (this is the case in contemporary Western legal systems, but not in all cultures and legal systems).
2. A consanguine need *not* necessarily be a *real* (*i. e.*, genetic) blood relative, but someone defined as such by society and law. (The *pater*, or legal father, for example, need not necessarily be the *genitor*, or actual biological father. The most obvious case, known in almost all cultures, is that of the adopted child).
3. The question of consanguinity is of supreme importance in any given society and is never treated in an arbitrary fashion.[105] It is intrinsically connected to age-old traditions, religious beliefs and social customs that shape the foundation of a community and its legal system, hence every society constructs its own specific notions of consanguinity.

Based on these differentiations social anthropologists distinguish theoretically between three major means of defining relationships in a descent group:

1. *Patrilineal* or *agnatic* (borrowed from Roman law), *i. e.*, the members of a descent group are only related through males (through the line of the father, paternal grandfather, paternal great-grandfather etc.). Inheritance of property, title, rank etc. is restricted to the children of the male members of the group.
2. *Matrilineal* or *uterine*, *i. e.*, the members of the descent group are only related through females (through the line of the mother or sister, maternal

103 Temporary marriage and the Shīʿite law of succession are two examples, which I have discussed in Macuch 2006 and 2017d; see also Chapter VII, pp. 628–637.

104 On kinship and marriage see Fox 1967, on which the following definitions and explanations are based.

105 Fox 1967, p. 34.

grandmother or grandaunt etc.). Inheritance of property, title etc. is hence restricted to the children of the female members of the group.

3. *Cognatic*, *i. e.*, members of the descent group are related to each other by both male and female links (mother and father, maternal and paternal grandparents etc.). Both children of the male and female members of the group have a right to inherit.

The patrilineal and matrilineal principles (also called *unilineal*) assign the individual to only one group and have the advantage of restricting the number of a person's heirs to those defined in this manner as relatives. These three possibilities of categorizing kinship systems are of course only theoretical types, which seldom occur in complex societies in the pure, distinctive forms described above. In advanced legal systems a unilateral (usually patrilineal) type of descent is often combined with cognatic elements. In ancient Rome, for example, although the male line determined membership in the gens and only agnates originally had access to the inheritance of a *paterfamilias*, it later became possible for a man's cognates to inherit in the absence of the former.[106] In other societies, such as the Sasanian one, as we will see, cognatic ties were not only recognized, but played an important part in securing the continuity of a lineage, despite the fact that succession was strictly patrilineal and only a male could replace the deceased head of a household completely.

With these general observations in mind, we can now attempt to reconstruct the basic features of Sasanian kinship before discussing the peculiarities of matrimony, succession and inheritance in the following sections in detail. The available information is far from exhaustive and, unsurprisingly, there is no systematic description of kinship in the sources, but taken together the dispersed details depict a coherent system in which every feature had its specific function within the larger framework of family law. Aristocratic descent groups (*paywand*, *tōhmag*) and lineages (*kadag*, *xānag*) were made up of one or several families (*dūdag*) with the collective right of disposal over family property that was to a large extent inalienable or indivisible (consisting of agricultural land, vineyards, orchards, real estate; also fire foundations and pious endowments, as will be seen below in Chapter III). This property remained for generations in the possession of the lineage and a large number of legal regulations were specifically construed to enable its undisturbed transfer from one generation to the next. The 'family' (*dūdag*) or 'house' (*kadag*, *xānag*; used also in the figurative sense of 'lineage') forming the basic unit within a larger descent group could in itself be an extensive formation. In its most simple form it consisted of a *kadag-xwadāy* 'master of the house' (or *paterfamilias*) and his wife from an arranged marriage 'with full matrimonial rights' (*pādixšāy-zanīh*), called *kadag-bānūg*

106 Nicholas 1962, pp. 248–250.

'mistress of the house' (*materfamilias*) under the guardianship (*sālārīh*) of the husband, and their children. Both sons and daughters from this type of matrimony counted as legitimate offspring and inherited from the *paterfamilias*, albeit with an important difference: in the basically patrilineal structure only the sons became the direct successors of the *paterfamilias*, whereas the daughters stepped in as 'intermediary successors' (*ayōgēn*)[107] if there were no sons. The daughter engaged as 'intermediary successor' was obliged to generate a son for the deceased head of the family and, moreover, formed a genetic or 'blood link' between a man and his male successor. Hence the Sasanian concept of the family clearly included the daughters (and other women, as will be seen below), revealing important cognatic elements, which left their mark on later legal developments.[108]

Due to several reasons family structure was only seldom as simple as in this basic model (see Fig. 1 on next page). First of all Sasanian law did not know the legal concept of primogeniture, therefore all the legitimate children from a marriage 'with full matrimonial rights' (*pādixšāy-zanīh*) were entitled to a specific portion of the inheritance, varying according to gender, daughters receiving half the share of a son. The heirs received their shares as 'ideal' portions (*a-baxt*) of the undivided inheritance (*pad abarmānd*), which consisted of different elements (to be elucidated in Chapter III). In order to avoid splitting family property the sons formed a collective partnership (*hambāyīh*) of co-inheritors or co-holders (*brād ī hambāy* 'shareholding brothers') which could also include the daughters under certain circumstances, if these remained in their natal lineage by endogamy or were engaged for one of the brothers as 'intermediary successor' (*ayōgēn*). A joint partnership was one of the best means of avoiding the division of family property into separate units (*baxtīgīh kardan*), particularly if it consisted of real estate.[109] Fire foundations and pious endowments belonging to a family were bequeathed to the heirs collectively and could neither be alienated nor split up into individual shares (see Chapter III, pp. 220–229). The concept of collective proprietary rights would support the unity of a lineage even if it was divided into smaller family units.

There is also another well-known difference between the Sasanian model of the family and that of almost all other known communities, which clearly distinguishes the Zoroastrian pattern of kinship in this period from that of almost all other legal systems: the complete lack of an incest taboo. Endogamy (*xwēdōdah*), *i. e.*, marriage within the descent group, and particularly inside the nuclear family (between mother and son, father and daughter and between siblings) was not only encouraged and praised by religious authorities as one of

107 For a discussion of this term see below pp. 163–168.

108 This basic idea of the family, explicitly including the daughters, is still very visible in the Shīʿite law of succession, see Macuch 2017d and Chapter VII, pp. 632–637.

109 Shareholding *dehgān* families are still amply attested in the eighth century Tabarestān documents, see Macuch 2017c, pp. 169, 174–176.

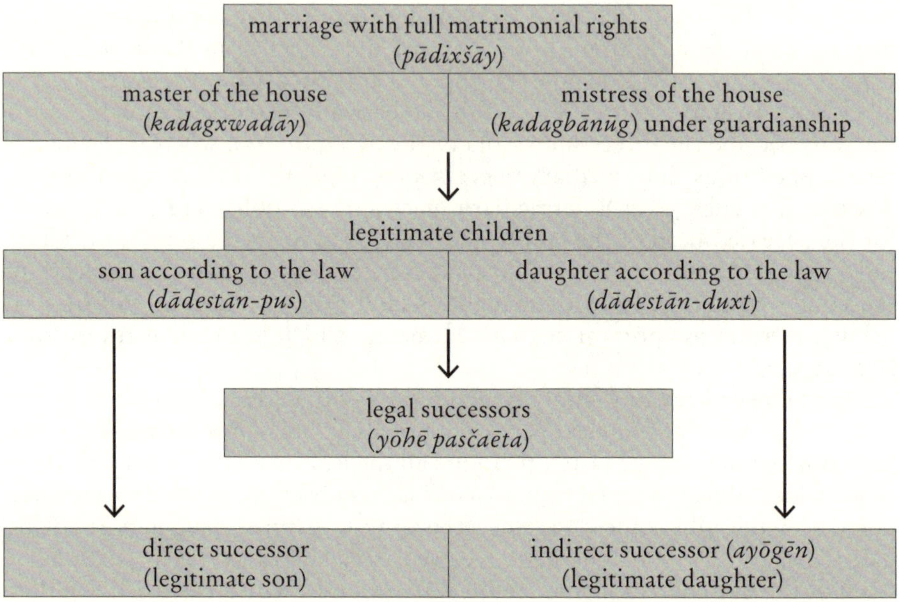

Fig. 1. Family structure: basic model

the most meritorious acts of the true Mazdean, but became one of the central ingredients of Sasanian family law. The propagation of incestuous marriage by Zoroastrian theologians and priests had far-reaching implications that led not only to 'real' marriages, especially between father and daughter and between siblings, but made important *fictive* conjugal bonds between members of the nuclear family possible. These are in fact unique and only viable in a society that accepted incest on an ideological basis and integrated it as an important element of family law into its legal system. By concluding a real (or fictive) incestuous marriage one could avoid splitting family property, since the *patrimonium* of the daughter would remain within the family. But there is far more to be said on this topic and we will return to it later (pp. 148–157 below).

Secondly, given that only a male could replace the head of a household as *kadag-xwadāy* and direct successor, assuming all the responsibilities of the deceased, it was incumbent on every *paterfamilias* to procreate sons in order to ensure the transfer of rank, status and family property and not to become 'nameless' (*abē-nām*). This obligation led to the development of a large spectrum of legal institutions with the sole function of preventing the termination of a lineage. In this context we should recall the anthropological discovery elucidated above that *no society treats the question of consanguinity in an arbitrary fashion*, but assumes its own theory of family bonds and has its own reasons for encouraging the development of certain fictive consanguineous relationships. Sasanian kinship is full of presumed consanguineous bonds to an extent that can be quite confusing (these were in fact later confused in the New Persian *Riwāyat*s). The technical terms used in this context are difficult or even impossible to translate and have overlapping meanings and cross connotations which all have to be taken into consideration if the underlying pattern is to be reconstructed correctly. The main reason for the overwhelming number of fictive ties developed in this model lies in the obligation to ensure the transmission of family property (*abarmānd*) and the continuity of the lineage (*nāmburdārīh*) on the one hand, and the performance of religious ceremonies in the name (*nāmagānīh*) of ancestors, on the other, thus linking kinship and religion inseparably to each other. Although these obligations were also known in other ancient societies, none of these went so far as to develop such an elaborate system of constructed consanguineous ties in order to avoid the extinction of a lineage.

The legal system developed two important methods of securing the continuity of a man's lineage if the deceased *paterfamilias* left no son(s). The first method was to engage his wife, his unmarried daughter or sister as an 'intermediary successor' (the technical meaning of the term *ayōgēn*, which has been explained in various ways, see pp. 163–168 below) who was obliged to put her reproductive faculties in the service of the deceased (that is, the *pādixšāy*-husband or brother or father) by entering an 'auxiliary marriage' (*čagar-zanīh*) of the *sine manu mariti* ('without guardianship of the husband') type with another man, who could be a relative or another Zoroastrian fellow-citizen. This completely different form of matrimony was exclusively conceived to engender children for a deceased man who had left no male successor. The widow of the deceased remained legally the spouse of her dead husband in *pādixšāy*-wedlock when she contracted the *čagar*-marriage and the children from this second marriage were counted as the legitimate offspring of their *pater* or legal father, that is, of the first deceased *pādixšāy*-husband, *not* of their *genitor*, the *čagar*-husband. If the daughter or sister was engaged as 'intermediary successor' a *fictive* incestuous marriage of the *pādixšāy* type was tacitly assumed between daughter and father or sister and brother with the same objective that children be generated for the deceased father or brother in an 'auxiliary marriage' (*čagar-zanīh*). The sons of the 'intermediary successor' were finally regarded as the direct legal successors and heirs of the deceased *paterfamilias*, entitled to inherit his estate and replace him in the community.

The second method of securing a man's male offspring became another characteristic institution of Sasanian jurisprudence, known by the technical term *stūrīh*, another expression that defies translation, but can be rendered by 'substitute succession', 'subsidiary succession' or 'succession by proxy'.[110] Both men and women from inside and also outside the family could be engaged as 'proxy' or 'substitute successor' (*stūr*) with the same duty to engender a son in an

110 For a discussion of the term see below pp. 169–174.

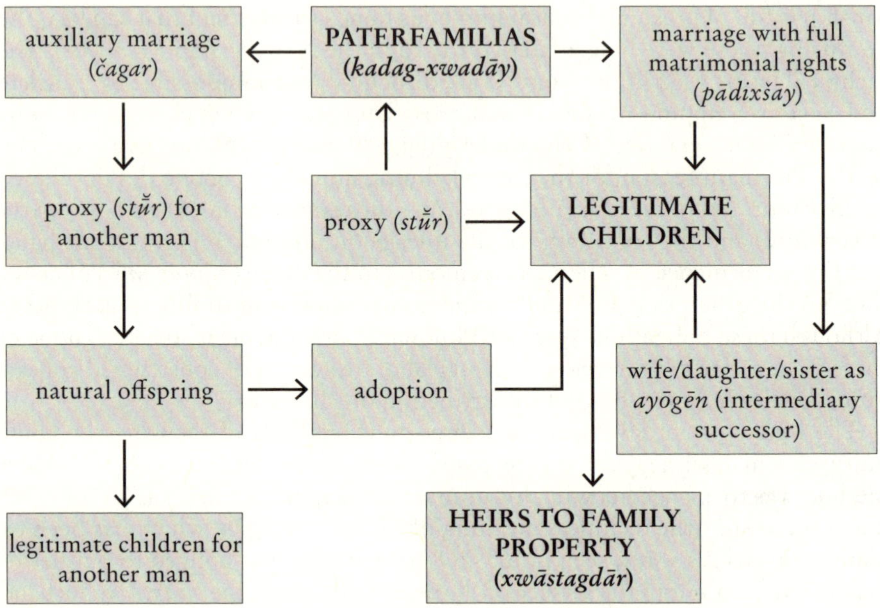

Fig. 2. Family structure: extended model

'auxiliary marriage' (*čagar-zanīh*) for the deceased *paterfamilias.* The head of a household could also act as *stūr* for another sonless man by concluding a *čagar*-marriage with the latter's widow in order to generate children for the deceased. If several children were born in this *čagar*-marriage, the husband could adopt one (or more) of his (own natural) *čagar*-children if necessary in order to secure his own succession. A large part of family property was set aside for these institutions and extensive regulations were conceived in this context to which we will return below.

Moreover, we have reason to assume that besides the regular form of marriage without a time limit both types of matrimony (*pādixšāy*- and *čagar-zanīh*) could be stipulated as *temporary* marriages, that is, they could be limited from the beginning to a certain number of years (possibly also months or even days). A third form of matrimony was known, which we have already mentioned above, the 'consensus marriage' (*xwasrāyēn/gādār*) of the type *sine manu mariti* that could be concluded on both an unlimited or on a temporary basis. In these three marriage types, which we will discuss in detail below, there does not seem to have been a limit to the wives a man could marry, with one possible exception: in the case of the arranged (*pādixšāy*-)marriage the financial means of the *kadag-xwadāy* could have set a limit to the number of wives he could take due to their status as 'mistress of a household' (*kadag-bānūg*). We are unfortunately not informed what this exactly implies, but it could have meant that separate households would have to be set up for every wife in this position.

All these details will have to be taken into consideration in a reconstruction of Sasanian kinship and family structures. We have good reason to assume that all these different types of marriages could be concluded in large aristocratic families, that the 'head of a household' (*kadag-xwadāy*) could have several *pādixšāy*-wives (depending on the extent of his wealth), besides a number of *čagar*-wives, with whom he would be married in order to procreate children for other men in 'proxy' (*stūrīh*), and other wives in 'consensus-marriage' (*xwasrāyēn/gādār*). We may furthermore assume that the institutions of 'intermediary succession' (*ayōgēnīh*) and 'substitute succession' (*stūrīh*) were observed on a large scale, that both endogamy (*xwēdōdah*) and exogamy (*bayāspān*) were practiced, that real and fictive marriages within the nuclear family were an integral part of family law, and finally, that a large range of presumed consanguineous bonds emerged which were necessary in order to guarantee the continuity of a lineage. We will attempt to bring all these specific features together in the last section of this Chapter (section 7, pp. 183–186) after discussing marriage, succession and the allocation of children separately.

4 Matrimony and succession

The emergence of different marriage types in Sasanian family law and their time-limited variants with divergent functions can only be comprehended in the context of the laws governing succession and inheritance, as we have indicated above. Polygyny (several wives) seems to have been practiced in affluent aristocratic families on a large scale due to the necessity of procreating heirs and male successors, besides fulfilling the general religious obligation of engendering numerous children in support of Ohrmazd in the battle against Evil within the larger scheme of Zoroastrian world history and eschatology. Polyandry (several husbands), on the other hand, was strictly forbidden to women due to the patrilineal model of succession linking children to the line of the father (which was however, as we have seen, combined with cognatic features). But in order to use the reproductive faculties of women to the fullest possible extent, Sasanian law found an ingenious strategy to circumvent this fundamental rule: a fertile woman could be engaged as *genetrix* for several men in the same family or in different lineages by concluding temporary marriages that would bind the woman to one man only for a specific, exactly defined period of time, after which she was free to enter another marriage. As we will see, temporary marriage was *not* a separate form of wedlock (as it is today in Shīʿite law), but a time-limited version of the three basic forms of matrimony with its own important function within the larger scheme.

4.1 Marriage types

There were only *three* basically different forms of matrimony in Sasanian law contrary to the five Zoroastrian marriage types listed in the late New Persian *Riwāyats* of the 15th–18th centuries.[111] Although this late description has been repeatedly referred to in secondary literature on Sasanian law,[112] it does *not* correspond to the information we were able to gain from Pahlavi legal texts and cannot be used as a source for reconstructing Sasanian family law. Written long after the Muslim conquest of Iran, the authors of the New Persian *Riwāyats* no longer had exact knowledge of the complex Sasanian network of marriage, succession and inheritance, nor was there any need to, given that the whole superstructure forming these institutions in the earlier period had by then completely disappeared. They defined the technical terms employed in this context according to their own altered or simplified legal usage from the 15th century onward, which also differs considerably from the descriptions and definitions in late Pahlavi literature of the 9th to 11th centuries. Hence the three original marriage types transmitted in Pahlavi legal texts (and described in the following) were expanded in these late *Riwāyats* to five: the two additional forms are designated as *ayūk/ayūkān* and *stor/star/satar*, technical terms derived from Pahlavi *ayōgēn* and *stūr* respectively, and explained as wives in two different forms of marriage.[113] We have overwhelming evidence in the Pahlavi legal sources that the corresponding terms in Sasanian law, *ayōgēn* ('intermediary successor') and *stūr* ('substitute successor') did *not* denote 'wives' in different marriages, but persons engaged as intermediary and subsidiary successors or 'proxies' within the framework of institutions created to prevent the extinction of a lineage, as already mentioned above. We will return to these institutions and their terminology later (section 4.4, pp. 163–174 below).

4.1.1 *Pādixšāy*-marriage

The regular form of wedlock, called *pādixšāyīhā zanīh* or *pādixšāy-zanīh*,[114] lit. 'privileged, authorized marriage; marriage with full matrimonial rights' of the

111 Unvala 1922, I, pp. 180–182. On these texts see above Chapter I, pp. 38–39.

112 For example, MacKenzie/ Perikhanian 1969, p. 104, no. 4, quoting Perikhanian, among others.

113 Unvala 1922, I, pp. 180–182; Dhabhar 1932, pp. 195–196. Although I have already referred to this important divergence from Sasanian law nearly forty years ago (Macuch 1981, p. 8) and repeated it later (*e. g.*, Macuch 2007b, p. 193), this late source is still being used anachronistically to describe Sasanian marriage forms.

114 < **pāti-xšā-u̯an-* from the Ir. root √**xšaH* 'to rule, be lord of' (Cheung 2007, pp. 451–452); Av. √*xšā* 'to be able, rule, be lord of', with *pati-* 'to have lordship over; to rule over' (Bartholomae 1904, cols. 551–553; Kellens 1984, p. 365, and 1995, p. 17); *pādixšāyīhā*, the adverbial form of *pādixšāy*, lit. 'entitled, empowered, authorized'. The Pahlavi term is often written with the heterogram ⟨ŠLYT'⟩. On the large range of legal uses of this term see Chapter I, pp. 85–90 above.

cum manu mariti type, was arranged by the families of the prospective spouses. Although there is no systematic description of this basic marriage type, we are comparatively well informed on its legal implications by numerous references in the Sasanian Law-book and by a model marriage contract dated to the 13th century (see Chapter I, pp. 22–23). Despite this late dating, the model contract definitely stems from the Sasanian period or is at least based on an older *Vorlage* from this period as the source of the precise clauses and legal language of the surviving model. In contrast to other marriage contracts (transmitted in the New Persian *Riwāyat*s among other texts) the model contract makes meticulous use of legal terminology, revealing exact knowledge of pre-Islamic family law with all its complex connotations, and is, moreover, a legal document in the true sense of the word in that it records precisely and in detail the rights and duties of the prospective spouses (albeit in a concise legal jargon, often including a mass of legal information in a single word, not immediately visible to a layperson who has no exact knowledge in this field).[115] Based on this source and other entries in the Sasanian Law-book we are able to reconstruct the preliminaries of marriage and other specifics of this type of matrimony fairly well, in any case to a larger extent than those of the other two marriage forms.

The prospective bridegroom first made a request (*xwast*) for the hand of the prospective bride by asking her legal guardian, usually the father, or in absence of a father, a brother or another male family member who acted as family guardian (*dūdag-sālār*) in the lineage of the bride. This formal act of proposal by the bridegroom and the acceptance (*dād* 'giving away') of the father as well as the consent of the bride are explicitly noted in the marriage contract: the groom takes the bride as his wife in *pādixšāy*-marriage in fulfilment of a 'pious act' (*pad ahlawdād*) 'by request (of the groom) and acceptance (of the bride's father)' (*pad xwāst ud dād*) and with the 'approval' (*hunsandīh*) and 'consent' (*hamdādestānīh*) of the bride.[116] The last formula, referring to the explicit 'approval and consent' of the bride seems to have been an important ingredient of the marriage contract and the Law-book confirms that the agreement of the bride was necessary for entering matrimony, but we have no way of knowing whether this was just a formal requirement or whether a woman could in fact refuse to enter a marriage endorsed and agreed to by her guardian.[117] The contract also explicitly notes the religious connotation of concluding a *pādixšāy*-marriage:

115 On the model Pahlavi marriage contract see the edition with commentary MACUCH 2007b.

116 Marriage contract, 3rd clause, MACUCH 2007b, pp. 186 and 190 (commentary p. 195f.). The New-Persian *Riwāyat*s depict vividly how the request of the groom was brought forward. This could have been similar in the Sasanian period, see UNVALA 1922, I, p. 179, l. 1ff. and the translation by DHABHAR 1932, p. 193f.

117 See also MHD 36.9–16 (MACUCH 1993, p. 269). MHD 89.15–17 (*ibid.*, p. 573) mentions a case, in which the daughter is married as a minor. On reaching majority, she does not give her consent to the marriage, but later agrees to it (unfortunately, we are not informed on the outcome of this case).

the formal act of 'giving away' (*dād*) the bride by the father is accomplished in fulfilment of a 'pious act' (*pad ahlawdād*) whilst uttering the 'triple formula' (*pad sē gōwišnīh*), presumably an allusion to the famous Zoroastrian maxim *humat*, *hūxt*, *huwaršt* ('good thought, good speech, good deeds').[118] Hence the contract underlines the notion that marriage was not only a 'solemn union' (as in Roman law)[119] but a *sacred* act, sanctioned by the priesthood, with significant religious implications. Its breach would not only have dire legal consequences in this world, but would damage the soul and lead to far graver ramifications in the hereafter. It seems that most *pādixšāy*-marriages were permanent unions and not conceived with a time-limit, but we also have conclusive evidence that a temporary variant existed in the Sasanian period in full compliance with religious norms and endorsed by the Zoroastrian clergy, as we will see below (section 4.3, pp. 157–162).

By entering this marriage the spouses (*zan ī pādixšāyīhā* '*pādixšāy*-wife' and *šōy ī pādixšāyīhā* '*pādixšāy*-husband') acquired specific rights and accepted a large spectrum of precisely defined duties, which can be summarized as follows:

1. In the case of an exogamous union, the wife left her natal lineage and the guardianship of her father (or brother or another male in the family), entered the lineage of the husband and came under his guardianship (*sālārīh*, '*manus*') or that of the husband's father.[120] Entering the lineage of the husband and coming under his *manus* had important consequences regarding the legal affiliation of the children, who would all belong to the husband's line and count as descendants, heirs and successors in his lineage. In an endogamous alliance the wife remained in her natal lineage. If the marriage was time-limited, the wife could change back to her original descent group after its termination and act as an 'intermediary successor' (*ayōgēn*) or 'substitute successor' (*stūr̆*) for a man in her original family (see section 4.4, pp. 169–174 below).
2. A wife in this status had the obligation to act as 'intermediary successor' (*ayōgēn*) for her husband, that is, she not only had the duty to produce children for her spouse as long as he lived, but also after his death, particularly if the husband left no offspring. Consequently, it was crucial that the woman should have no further obligations as an *ayōgēn*-daughter (or sister) towards her natal family in this respect. This is specifically noted in the second clause of the marriage contract: the bride should have no marital duties as a daughter (*duxtagānīh*) towards a man (father, brother) from her original family and should not be obliged to carry out

118 Marriage contract, 4th clause, Macuch 2007b, pp. 186, 190 (commentary p. 196).
119 See du Plessis/Borkowski 2010, p. 118.
120 Marriage contract, 2nd clause, Macuch 2007b, pp. 186, 190 (commentary pp. 193–195). See also MHD 5.1 (Macuch 1993, pp. 70, 73), according to which 'marriage without guardianship is not permitted' (*zanīh ǰud ǰud az sālārīh nē šāyēd*).

his 'intermediary succession' (*ayōgēnīh/ayōgānīh*) or 'substitute succession' (*stŭrīh*).[121] This statement is of supreme importance, as a woman could not be married in the *pādixšāy* status with a man outside her natal lineage if she had to perform these duties for her father or brother. In the latter case, she would be regarded as the (usually fictive) *pādixšāy*-wife of the father or brother and it would not be possible for her to enter another marriage of this type at the same time due to the strict prohibition of polyandry. By concluding a *pādixšāy*-marriage outside her original lineage all the claims other male members of her natal family might have on her reproductive faculties as an *ayōgēn* or *stŭr* are banned at least for the period in which she is married, if it is a time-limited *pādixšāy*-marriage, or forever, if the marriage is a permanent one. This duty towards the new lineage is later repeated (in the 5th clause): the wife explicitly commits herself to take on the husband's 'intermediary succession' (*ayōgānīh*), hereby obliging herself to generate offspring for the husband even after his demise (that is, in a *čagar*-marriage).[122]

3. The wife received the title 'mistress of the house' (*kadag-bānūg*), corresponding to the title of the *pādixšāy*-husband as 'master of the house' (*kadag-xwadāy*). This was a privileged position in comparison to other wives (in the *čagar* or *xwasrāyēn* status) due to her entitlement to maintenance and inheritance and the status of her children as legitimate heirs of the husband (none of the wives in the other marriage forms were conceded these rights).[123] If the 'master of the house' had several wives in the *pādixšāy*-status, each one received the title of *kadag-bānūg* with all the rights and duties of a woman in this position. We have no exact information whether there was a limit to a man's possible number of *pādixšāy* wives, but if the title *kadag-bānūg* implies that every one of these wives was conceded her own separate household, the number of women a *paterfamilias* could marry in this manner probably depended on his financial means.[124]
4. The children conceived in this marriage all counted as the legitimate offspring of the husband: *dādestān-pus* 'son according to the law' and *dādestān-duxt* 'daughter according to the law'.[125] They were his heirs and 'legal successors', called *yōhē pasčaēta* 'who (succeeds) him afterwards', a phrase taken from a lost passage of the Avesta that became a technical term in Sasanian law designating the legal successor of a *paterfamilias* in general, no matter whether succession took place directly (by the legitimate son) or through

121 Macuch 2007b, pp. 186, 190 (commentary pp. 193–195).
122 *Ibid.*, pp. 186, 190 (commentary p. 196); see also Macuch 2003b, p. 240.
123 Marriage contract, 6th clause, Macuch 2007b, pp. 186, 191 (commentary p. 196f.)
124 Two *pādixšāy*-wives are mentioned MHDA 1.2–6 (Macuch 1981, pp. 21, 69). On the rights and duties of the *kadag-bānūg* see also pp. 123–124 above.
125 All the attestations of these terms must be taken into consideration (see Macuch 1993, *Index*, p. 699).

an intermediary (the legitimate daughter).[126] Jurists distinguished between the status of the legitimate son as 'direct successor' of the father and that of the legitimate daughter as 'intermediary successor' (*ayōgēn*). Daughters in this status had the important duty to secure the continuity of the lineage if there was no male heir, besides being themselves entitled to a share in the inheritance. The legitimate sons, on the other hand, replaced the father totally as direct successors, inheriting not only his property, but also his name (as *nām-burdār* 'name-bearer') and place in the descent group (*paywand, tōhmag*), his standing in the community and his rank (*gāh*) in the social estate (*pēšag*). These implications are all contained in the 6th clause of the marriage contract, by which the husband commits himself to accept the children of his wife as his *pādixšāy*-children.[127]

5. The wife and children from this marriage were entitled to maintenance by the husband (*xwārišn ud dārišn* 'nourishment and maintenance'): the wife as long as she lived, the son until he reached majority, the daughter until she married.[128] In contrast to the other types of marriage (*čagar* and *xwasrāyēn*) the husband had full guardianship (*šōywarīh sālārīh*, lit. 'husbandly *manus*') of his wife with the obligation to take care of her material needs (*xwārišn wastarg*, lit. 'food, clothing'). He explicitly pledges in the marriage contract to maintain his wife according to his financial capacity (*tuwān-sāmānagīhā*), 'fitting (the requirements of) the times' (*āwām-passazagīhā*), and to hold her in high regard and 'well respected' (*xūb pad āzarm*).[129]
6. The wife committed herself to observe the instructions and commands of the husband (*framānburdārīh*), to be obedient (*tarsagāh/tarsagāy*)[130] and to behave dutifully (*tarsagāh warzīdārīh*) towards her spouse. In the 5th clause of the marriage contract she also pledges not to deviate from the marriage as long as she lives (*zīndag drahnāy*), nor from observing the 'Good Religion' (*weh-dēnīh*) or 'being an Iranian' (*ērīh*, that is, a Zoroastrian) or from fulfilling her religious duty as the husband's *ayōgēn* (see number 2 above).[131] The opposite of obedience (*tarsagāhīh*) is *a-tarsagāhīh* 'disobedience; undutiful behaviour', which could be sanctioned by the husband by excluding the wife from her right to inheritance or to other property.[132]

126 See specifically Chapter eleven of the Law-book, MHD 21.4–24.10 (Macuch 1993, pp. 170–191) and below pp. 163–168 on succession.
127 Macuch 2007b, pp. 186, 191 (commentary pp. 196–197).
128 See MHD 32.12–14 (Macuch 1993, pp. 240, 243) in the chapter on maintenance in the Law-book.
129 Marriage contract, 6th clause, Macuch 2007b, pp. 186, 191 (commentary pp. 196–197).
130 On this term see Macuch 1981, pp. 88–89 (no. 26).
131 Macuch 2007b, pp. 186, 190 (commentary p. 196).
132 A whole chapter of the Law-book is dedicated to the offence of *a-tarsagāhīh* 'disobedience', see MHDA 4.12–8.2 (Macuch 1981, pp. 96–99). With respect to women it was defined concisely as follows: *a-tarsagāhīh ī zanān ēn bawēd kār ī frārōn ī-š šōy framāyēd*

7. The proprietary rights of the wife and the dower to be paid by the husband to the bride[133] were recorded meticulously in the 7th clause of the marriage contract. The union could be concluded 'without (the right to the) income' (*ǰud az windišn*) of the wife.[134] This formula implied that the husband renounced his right to claim the earnings of his wife, but it did not necessarily mean that the latter could keep the income for herself. The father of the bride could retain his right to her earnings and revenue after the betrothal of his daughter (the conditions are not transmitted, but we may assume that at least part of the income the daughter was entitled to was drawn from collective family property).[135] In the 7th clause of the marriage contract the husband concedes his wife full right of disposal over the income from (her own or his?) property (*pad windišn pādixšāyīhā kard* 'she is given full entitlement to the income').[136] Furthermore, the husband commits himself to give an 'ideal' (*a-baxt*, lit. 'undivided') half (*pad do bahr ē bahr*) of his proprietary rights, corresponding to the sum of 3000 silver drachms in domestic currency, as dower to the bride. The bride declares her consent to the sum with the formulaic words: 'it (is) well approved of (and) sanctioned' (*weh sahist dōšīd*), a general formula used to express consent in legal transactions.[137] The promised sum of 3000 silver drachms is not to be paid directly in cash, but an 'equivalent' (or substitute', *guharīg*)[138] is agreed upon, consisting of an 'ideal' half of the husband's possessions of the type *bona adventitia* (in Roman law), or, using Pahlavi legal terminology, *mad ud rasēd*, lit. '(property) that has come and shall be attained'. This legal formula (discussed in Chapter I, p. 78) designates every kind of surplus income (*bar*) that the husband had already acquired (*mad ēstēd*) before entering marriage and also earnings and revenue that he will attain (*rasēd*) in the future in both categories of 'possession' (*dārišn*) and 'ownership' (*xwēšīh*).[139] The terms of the contract reveal that *pādixšāy*-matrimony included fixing a certain amount of dower (or marriage-portion, settlement) which could be substituted by giving the wife joint property rights with regard to the *bona*

nē kardan ud ān ī a-frārōn ī ne kardan gōwēd kardan ud har dō pad sē bār bawēd 'The disobedience of women is this: not to carry out the righteous act the husband commands and to perform the wrongful deed he forbids to be done and each (offence) is committed three times.' (MHDA 5.6–8: Macuch 1981, p. 96).

133 *Not* to be confused with the 'dowry', the sum paid by the bride to the husband!

134 MHDA 1.1–12 (Macuch 1981, pp. 21, 69).

135 MHDA 1.1–3 (*ibid*., pp. 21, 69).

136 On the income to which a *pādixšāy*-wife was entitled see Chapter III, pp. 251–253 and the Tabarestān document 21 (Macuch 2019b, pp. 118–125).

137 On the vast implications of the legal terminology in the 7th clause see Macuch 2007b, pp. 197–200. See also Macuch 1993, p. 454, no. 1, and Chapter IV, pp. 301–305 on transactions.

138 See attestations in Macuch 1993, p. 708.

139 On the terminology of property law see Chapter III, pp. 193–197, and Macuch 2015d.

adventitia.[140] The formulation in this clause indicates that full payment of the dower remained more or less a theoretical option as long as the marriage prevailed. But the husband also pledges to deliver a 'portion' (*ǰādag*) of the dower to his wife 'unspoilt' (*abē-āhōgīhā*) and without 'delay and obstinacy' (*spōz-iz ud wastārīh*) should she claim it for herself or should a third party put in a monetary claim against her (*xwāstārīh kunēd*).[141]

8. The *pādixšāy*-wife and children were all entitled to inheritance on the demise of the *paterfamilias*. The share of the 'mistress of the house' (*bahr ī kadag-bānūgīh*) was equivalent to that of the sons (*bahr ī pusīh*); daughters received half the share of the sons (*bahr ī duxtīh*).[142] As direct successors of the father the sons inherited his property (as *xwāstagdār* 'heir; possessor of property'), but also the responsibility for his debts (*tōzišn ī pidarān*) and guardianship (*sālārīh*) over the women and minors in the family as well as the important religious obligation to perform the required rituals for the soul of the deceased (*ruwān yazišn*) and to keep the cult of the souls of the ancestors (*nāmagānīh*). The daughter's share was either handed out on the occasion of a marriage outside the descent group as a dowry (*pēšīgān-wāspuhragān*) or remained an undivided 'ideal' (*a-baxt*) share of the total estate (*abarmānd*) if the daughter remained in her natal lineage by endogamy or was engaged as 'intermediary successor' (*ayōgēn*) for the deceased father or brother.[143]

It is strange that the marriage contract notes the precise conditions and agreements regarding the 'dower' (gift or settlement given by the husband to the bride; *donatio propter nuptias* in Roman law), but absolutely nothing on the 'dowry' (property brought into the marriage by the wife; *dos* in Roman law). Although the Pahlavi term for 'dower' (*kābēn*)[144] is not used in the contract, the 7th clause leaves no doubt that this is exactly what is meant in the text: *pādixšāy*-matrimony obviously included fixing a marriage-portion (3000 silver drachms in our contract), which was conceded by the husband to the wife herself but did not have to be paid immediately and could be substituted by giving the wife joint property rights with regard to the *bona adventitia*, as we have seen above. Moreover, we may assume from the wording of the clause that the dower was only paid in cash under certain circumstances (or else the husband would not have been obliged to commit himself to paying it without 'delay

140 Joint proprietary rights with the *pādixšāy*-wife (or wives) are also mentioned MHDA 1.2–6 (Macuch 1981, pp. 21, 69); see also Chapter III, pp. 251–253 (on partnership).

141 The details on the dower are reminiscent of the Roman *donatio propter nuptias* ('gift on account of marriage') and the Islamic *mahr*, particularly the device of the 'deferred dower'; see Coulson 1964, p. 207f., Macuch 2007b, p. 200, and below.

142 For references see Macuch 1993, p. 694.

143 On inheritance see Macuch 1981, pp. 73–77 (no. 4), and 2005b with further references.

144 Attested in the *Jamāsp-nāmag* 16 (see Bailey 1930–1932a, p. 56).

and obstinacy', if it were claimed). Interestingly, the Persian form of the word (*kābīn* 'dower') is used in the New Persian *Riwāyats*[145] as a synonym of the Arabic *mahr*, which was originally the purchase price for the wife, paid by the husband in pre-Islamic Arabia to the father of the bride or another male relative in return for receiving the bride. The Qur'ān transferred the wife from the position of a sale-object to that of a contracting party by ruling that the wife alone should receive the *mahr*.[146] Our marriage contract not only explicitly states that the bride should give her consent to the proposed amount of money, but also names her as the sole recipient of the dower, indicating that the practice of giving the dower directly to the wife was already known in Zoroastrian law. Even the device of the 'deferred dower'[147], by which the parties agreed to postpone payment of a portion of the *mahr* until the termination of the marriage, thus providing maintenance for the wife after separation, was obviously known in Iranian law according to our contract: payment of the dower remained more or less a theoretical option until it was claimed. This could have occurred on termination of the marriage, but there is no divorce clause in the contract.

After these exact regulations regarding the 'dower' one would also expect a separate clause on the 'dowry', the money or property brought by a wife to her husband on marriage (called *pēšīgān-wāspuhragān* in the Law-book; *dos* in Roman law), but this is missing.[148] There is no dowry clause in the Pahlavi document and it is probably no coincidence that it is also missing in the Sogdian marriage contract that refers to a similar (if not identical) type of matrimony in which the bride is designated as *ZNH xypδ x'n'kH p'txš'wnH wδwH* '(as) a lady possessing authority in his (= the husband's) own house'.[149] Although it is noted that the bride brings a certain property into the marriage, designated as *xypδ 'stw* 'her own share', one would expect a far more detailed description in a legal document.[150] It seems likely, as Yakubovich has inferred, that the dowry transfer was recorded in a separate document, comparable to the Late Babylonian list of items of the *nudunnû* 'dowry', and that it was generally not included in Pahlavi and Sogdian marriage contracts.[151] On the other hand, the surviving Bactrian marriage contract does list the items belonging to the 'dowry' (ναμαγγο) brought by the bride into the marriage at the end of the document.[152] The contract, however, betrays a fundamentally different concept of matrimony

145 Unvala 1922, I, p. 183, ll. 6–7; p. 423, ll. 8f. and 17f. The amount of dower to be paid by the husband is fixed in all attestations in the New Persian *Riwāyats* to the amount of *do hazār diram sīm-i sapīd-i wīžah wa do dinār zar-i surḫ-i sarah-i Nīšāpūrī* '2000 *dirhams* of pure white silver and two *dinārs* of pure red gold of the Nīšāpūr currency'
146 Coulson 1964, p. 14.
147 *Ibid.*, p. 207f.
148 On the Pahlavi term see Macuch 1981, p. 85, no. 17.
149 See the edition of Yakubovich 2006, pp. 310 and 318, with references to earlier editions.
150 Yakubovich 2006, pp. 321 and 339.
151 *Ibid.*, p. 339.
152 Sims-Williams 2000, p. 207 (glossary); 2012a, pp. 26–29 (text), l. A34–35.

Table 9. Legal implications of *pādixšāy*-marriage

husband (*šōy ī pādixšāyīhā*)	wife (*zan ī pādixšāyīhā*)
'master of the house' (*kadag-xwadāy*)	'mistress of the house' (*kadag-bānūg*)
guardianship (*sālārīh*) over wife and children	under guardianship (*sālārīh*) of the husband
duty to maintain wife and children	right of maintenance (*xwārišn ud dārišn*) by the husband
commitment to keep the wife in high esteem (*pad āzarm*)	duty to be obedient to the husband (*tarsagāhīh*)
children are legitimate successors and heirs (*yōhē pasčaēta*)	duty to bear children
wife and all children inherit ('ideal' *a-baxt*) shares (*bahr*)	right to a specific share of the inheritance in the lineage of the husband (*bahr ī kadag-bānūg*)
right to request the wife as *ayōgēn* and *stūr*	obligation to act as *ayōgēn* and *stūr* for the husband
payment of a dower to the wife	dower from the husband
right to cancel the wife's income if she is disobedient	right to her 'own income' (*windišn ī xwēš*)

in Bactrian law in two important respects: (1) the woman requested as a bride is married to two brothers, which would be impossible in Sasanian law with its strict prohibition of polyandry; (2) the wife is conceded the right to refuse another wife beside herself, which again would be impossible according to Sasanian law with its explicit encouragement of polygyny.[153] We may conclude that marriage laws in Bactria—and probably the whole underlying concept in this field—differed considerably from those in Sasanian Iran, although the basic goal of keeping family property together and a 'house' (= lineage) intact by marrying two (or more) brothers to the same wife might have been similar.[154]

4.1.2 *Čagar*-marriage

None of these regulations constituting *pādixšāy*-wedlock apply to *čagar*-matrimony[155], a technical term that defies literal translation, but can be best

153 Sims-Williams 2012a, pp. 26–29.

154 See Crone 2012, pp. 402–403, and Azad 2016, pp. 42–43, on the possible strategies behind fraternal polyandry in the Bactrian documents (pp. 42–50).

155 <**ča-kar-*, formed by reduplication of the root √*kar* 'to do, make, perform, accomplish' (Bartholomae 1904, cols. 444–448; Kellens 1995, pp. 14–15; Cheung 2007, pp. 236–238). Not to be confused with NP *čākar/čāker* 'servant, maidservant', although this

described as 'auxiliary marriage'. The function of this conjugal alliance can only be understood correctly in relation to the regular *pādixšāy* type of marriage described above, and in the context of the all-prevailing Zoroastrian obligation to procreate children: the sole purpose of this completely different type of matrimony was to engender offspring for a man who had none.[156] The *čagar*-wife (*zan ī čagarīhā*) is hence neither simply a remarried widow (as described in the New Persian *Riwāyats*),[157] nor a 'concubine',[158] nor a 'serving'[159] or 'subordinate' wife,[160] nor the wife in a 'levirate' marriage,[161] as she has been labeled in earlier studies. The main duty of a *čagar*-wife (who could be the widow, daughter or sister of the deceased) was to produce children, preferably sons, for a man (*i. e.*, the deceased husband, father or brother) who had no legal male successor; in the Sasanian period particularly for affluent members of the aristocracy, who had the means of financing the institution needed to rear and support the wife and her children, called *stūrīh* ('substitute succession'). Both men and women were obliged to accept and carry out this important task. As we have seen above, the widow in a *pādixšāy*-marriage was committed by contract to act as an 'intermediary successor' (*ayōgēn*) for her husband if he died without leaving at least one male successor. On his demise the wife remained legally the spouse of her husband if the marriage had not been time limited or terminated before his death. In order to generate heirs for the deceased husband she entered a *čagar*-marriage with a relative in the lineage of the husband or—in absence of an appropriate male candidate—with a Zoroastrian man from outside the lineage. The children engendered in this marriage all belonged to their legal father, the first *pādixšāy*-husband, counted as his legitimate heirs and successors (sons as direct successors; daughters as intermediary successors according to the rules prevailing in Sasanian family law). If the widow could not fulfil this obligation towards her *pādixšāy*-husband (due to different reasons, such as lack of

form with the long vowel is (mistakenly?) also used in the New Persian *Riwāyats* besides *čakar*/*čagar* for this type of marriage (see Unvala 1922, I, p. 181, last line, and p. 183, l. 15); on *čakar* and *čākar* see also Bartholomae 1910, pp. 7–8, and Klingenschmitt 1971, p. 124.

156 Klingenschmitt 1971, p. 120, is the only scholar who has defined this marriage precisely in the past as 'Einrichtung zur Zeugungshilfe für einen zeugungsunfähigen Mann' (albeit without going into its specifics within the framework of Sasanian family law).

157 Persian text Unvala 1922, I, pp. 184–187; translation Dhabhar 1932, pp. 198–202.

158 Bartholomae 1910, p. 7: 'Nebenfrau , Konkubine'.

159 West 1880, p. 323: 'handmaid, serving wife, concubine'

160 Tavadia 1930, p. 137 (10.21): 'subordinate wife'.

161 Perikhanian 1997, p. 346: '*čakar, čakarīh* "levirate marriage"'. This definition is far too narrow; *čagar* does *not* simply designate the marriage between a widow and her husband's brother as in the levirate of Jewish law (although the Pahlavi technical term also includes this type of matrimony), but rather denotes the conjugal alliance of the widow or sister or daughter of a deceased *paterfamilias* with *any suitable man* inside or outside the lineage of the deceased to the purpose of producing offspring for the latter.

Table 10. Comparison of *pādixšāy*- and *čagar*-matrimony

pādixšāy-marriage	*čagar*-marriage
cum manu mariti: husband has guardianship (*sālārīh*) over wife and children	*sine manu mariti*: husband has *no* guardianship (*sālārīh*) over wife and children
children are legitimate successors and heirs of the father (*yōhē pasčaēta*)	children are *not* legitimate heirs of the natural (*čagar*-)father
wife has the right to maintenance (*xwārišn ud dārišn*)	wife has *no* right to maintenance
spouses inherit from each other	spouses do *not* inherit from each other
wife is obliged to bear children for the husband	wife is obliged to bear children for her former (*pādixšāy*-)husband
wife is obliged to act as *ayōgēn* (and *stūr̆*) for the husband	*no* obligations of the wife as *ayōgēn* (or *stūr̆*) towards the (*čagar*-)husband
duty of the wife to be obedient (*tarsagāh*) towards the husband	*no* duties of the wife towards the (*čagar*-)husband

fertility, old age, etc.) or had died in the meantime, one of the women in the lineage of the deceased *paterfamilias*, a daughter or sister, could be engaged as 'intermediary successor' (*ayōgēn*) for the father or brother with exactly the same implications: the obligation to procreate children for the father or brother in a *čagar*-marriage (in which the wife counted legally as the fictive *pādixšāy*-wife of the father or brother). The guardian (*sālār*) of these women was a male relative from the lineage of the deceased man, who was *not* at the same time the *čagar*-husband. If none of these women were available, a man from the lineage of the deceased *kadag-xwadāy*, a brother, uncle, cousin, an adopted son, or any other man the *paterfamilias* may have had appointed in his will as *stūr̆* was obliged to act as 'substitute successor', enter a *čagar*-marriage and engender offspring for the deceased man.

In short: *čagar*-marriage was a kind of 'auxiliary marriage', in which presumed consanguineous bonds prevailed to the extreme due to the specific, exactly defined purpose of this conjugal alliance. Unsurprisingly, none of the rules governing *pādixšāy*-wedlock applied to *čagar*-marriage and were even diametrically opposed to these: (1) the *čagar*-husband had *no* guardianship (*sālārīh*) over the wife and children; (2) the children did *not* count as the legitimate offspring of their natural *čagar*-father (*genitor*), but of their legal (*pādixšay*-)father (*pater*); (3) they were *not* the legitimate successors and heirs of the natural father; (4) the wife had *no* right of maintenance or inheritance; (5) she had *no* duties towards the *čagar*-husband, was neither obliged to bear him children, nor to be subservient to him. The woman who had entered a *čagar* union in her function as 'intermediary successor' (*ayōgēn*) and 'substitute successor' (*stūr*) as well as the children born in this marriage were maintained by a portion of the inheritance (called *bahr ī stūrīh* 'portion for substitute succession') set aside specifically for this purpose from the property belonging to the lineage of the deceased *pādixšāy*-husband.[162]

In a complex society such as the Sasanian one it comes as no surprise that in exceptional cases, notably emergences, the general provisions described above were not heeded in practice. As a rule, the *čagar*-husband was not obliged to provide for his wife and her issue, since they were maintained by the property set aside specifically for the institution of 'subsidiary succession' (*stūrīh*) in the family of the deceased *pādixšāy*-husband. We are however informed that in cases of need, the *čagar*-father had the obligation to maintain his natural offspring and was, vice versa, provided for, if necessary, from the share of the inheritance due to the wife and children.[163]

4.1.3 *Xwasrāyēn/gādār*-marriage

This third type of legal matrimony, which can be best described as 'consensus marriage', in turn differs substantially from the two other forms illustrated above. The technical terms transmitted in this context do not originally designate the marriage itself, but are specific expressions for the husband and wife distinguishing this type of marriage from the two other forms of matrimony. Whereas the 'husband' is otherwise called *šōy*, in the consensus marriage the corresponding term is *gādār*,[164] lit. 'lover', and the 'wife' is not *zan* (as in the other two marriage types), but *xwasrāyēn*,[165] lit. 'having her own *manus*', meaning that the woman is her own legal guardian. The phrase *gādār kardan*

162 References to and quotations from the Pahlavi sources can be found in Klingenschmitt 1971, pp. 114–125, and Macuch 1981, pp. 100–113.

163 MHD 32.15–33.1 (Macuch 1993, pp. 240, 243).

164 The expression is an agent noun from *gādan*, *gāy-* 'to have sexual intercourse, copulate with, *coire*' (MacKenzie 1971, p. 34; from the root √**gaH* 'to copulate with', Cheung 2007, p. 94).

165 Written ⟨hwsl'yn'/hwsl'ywn⟩ which can be read both as *xwasrāyēn* and *xwasrāyūn* (*xwasrāy-* with either the suffix *-ēn* or *-ūn* respectively). Perikhanian 1970, p. 350f., explains the word as **xvatsrāy-īwn* 'self-conveyance; entrusting oneself', deriving it from the base √*srāy* 'lean, rely upon; entrust' (Bartholomae 1904, col. 163/: *sray-* ; Kellens 1995, p. 66: *srī*; Cheung 2007, p. 351: **srai* ; Av. *sri-*). Klingenschmitt 1971, p. 168, no. 8 (and 2000, p. 225), has the far more convincing etymology, explaining the word as (*xwasrāyēn*) <**x^{v}asaraenī-* from **hu̯a-sar(a)* 'eigene Munt habend' (having one's own *manus*) + feminine suffix **-ai̯nī-* (>*-aēnī-*>*-ēn*). This explanation corresponds not only exactly to the details we are able to derive from the texts on this type of marriage, but is also reflected in the designation of the wife in the New Persian *Riwāyats* as *ḫod-sālār-zan* 'woman who is her own guardian' (besides *ḫod-aš rāy zan* 'woman who [gives] herself', Unvala 1922, II, p. 182, l. 1, and *ḫod-sarāy*, *ibid.*, p. 181, l. 3) and explained as 'she (who marries) without the consent of her parents …', see Unvala 1922, II, p. 184, l. 3; Dhabhar 1932, p. 198.

(lit. 'to take a lover') is *not* simply a synonym of *gādan*, but designates the stipulation of this specific form of wedlock: 'to enter a consensus marriage' (parallel to *šōy kardan* 'to take a husband, enter matrimony').[166]

Despite these striking differences in terminology (which in fact highlight the exceptional status of this probably rather rare alliance), this was a legitimate marriage, accepted by juristic and religious authorities, although it was concluded without permission of the woman's guardian and based solely on the will and acceptance of husband (*gādār*) and wife (*xwasrāyēn*). Whereas *pādixšāy*- and *čagar*-marriages were arranged unions conceived to the specific purposes we have elucidated above, this third type was solely founded on the mutual agreement of the spouses. Given the important role of the guardian in Sasanian law, it seems strange that this kind of independent action on the part of a woman should have been tolerated, but on the other hand 'consensus marriage' seems to have closed a legal gap that would have otherwise ensued in at least two cases (both attested in the legal material):

1. If a young girl's guardian failed to contrive a marriage for her in due time after she had reached puberty (or, according to another passage, 15 years of age), she could choose a husband herself.[167]
2. If a widow with *no* guardian and *no* obligations whatsoever towards her deceased husband (as an 'intermediary successor', *ayōgēn*, or 'substitute successor', *stūr*) wished to marry again, she could do so by entering this type of marriage.[168]

It was incumbent upon every Mazdean to marry and procreate as many children as possible, hence a solution had to be found for these exceptional cases, in which a young girl or a widow could not rely on a guardian to procure a husband for them. This does not necessarily mean that this specific manner of choosing a spouse was an invention of Sasanian jurisprudence (or was even unduly encouraged by legal authorities); it could well have been a surviving remnant of older

166 On this expression and its connection to the 'consensus marriage' see Macuch 1981, 89–95, no. 31, with quotations from and references to the sources. On the important passage REA 43.2 see specifically Macuch 1985, pp. 198–200; on the legal terminology 2005b, p. 382, and Chapter I, pp. 78–79.

167 See for example DkM 714.22–715.3 and REA 43.2. Both passages are transliterated and translated in Macuch 1981, pp. 90 and 92 respectively; the whole text of REA 43.2 in Macuch 1985, pp. 198–199 (Safa-Isfehani's 1980 translation of the REA passage, p. 288, is wrong and misleading). That this is not a late marriage type, but was already known in the Sasanian period, is confirmed by MHD 24.7–10 (Macuch 1981, p. 95; and 1993, p. 179) and MHD 33.1–3 (Macuch 1981, p. 94; and 1993, pp. 243–244.).

168 For example REA 5.24–25 (transliterated and translated in Macuch 1981, p. 93) and RAF 73 (on this remarkable text see the extensive discussion in Macuch 2017a).

forms similar (or even historically identical) to two different types of matrimony in ancient Indian law.[169]

The legal implications of consensus marriage were partly similar to the *čagar* type in that (1) the wife was not under guardianship of the husband, (2) the children were not legitimate heirs of their natural father, and (3) the wife was neither entitled to maintenance, (4) nor to inheritance. But it differed from *čagar*-marriage in two very important respects: (5) if the wife was a widow she was *not* obliged to engender children for a former (*pādixšāy*-)husband; if children were born, these were *not* regarded as the latter's legitimate offspring, and (6) it was a marriage concluded only by the *mutual agreement* of the man and woman involved, without the consent of the young girl's or the widow's guardian. If a re-married widow (second case above) bore a son in consensus marriage and this son became guardian (*sālār*) in the family of the woman after reaching maturity, he could change his mother's status by giving her to her *gādār*-husband in *pādixšāy*-matrimony.[170] As the two other marriage types the 'consensus marriage' could also be concluded on a temporary basis (see section 4.3 below).[171]

Table 11. Comparison of *čagar*- and *xwasrāyēn/gādār*-matrimony

čagar-marriage	*xwasrāyēn/gādār*-marriage
sine manu mariti: husband has no guardianship (*sālārīh*) over wife and children	*sine manu mariti*: husband has no guardianship (*sālārīh*) over wife and children
children are not legitimate successors and heirs of the father	children are not legitimate successors and heirs of the father
wife has no right to maintenance (*xwārišn ud dārišn*)	wife has no right to maintenance
spouses do not inherit from each other	spouses do not inherit from each other
wife is obliged to bear children (as *ayōgēn* and *stūr*) for her former (*pādixšāy*-)husband	wife is *not* obliged to bear children for a former (*pādixšāy*-)husband
concluded *with* consent of the woman's guardian	concluded *without* consent of the woman's guardian

169 There could be a possible connection to the *svayaṁvara* (choice of spouses) and *gāndharva* (love marriage) in Indian law (see Jolly 1896, pp. 50–51).

170 According to REA 43.2, on this passage see extensively Macuch 1985, pp. 198–200 (there is unfortunately a printing mistake pp. 199–200: the last two lines p. 199 and the first line of p. 200 have been mixed up).

171 For references to and quotations from the Pahlavi sources see Macuch 1981, pp. 89–95 (no. 31). On temporary marriage see pp. 157–162 and Macuch 2006.

4.2 Exogamy (*bayā̆spān*), endogamy and marriage within the nuclear family (*xwēdōdah*)

Another technical term causing confusion in the past is attested in the context of the first (*pādixšāy*) and the third (*xwasrāyēn/gādār*) type of matrimony and has been read and interpreted divergently due to various spellings in the sources.[172] The most likely readings for the two major variant spellings (ending in either *-stān* or *-spān*) are: (1) *bē-āstān*, lit. 'out of the threshold; away from the house'; (2) *bayāspān*, lit. 'messenger' or '*Baga*-bride'; (3) *bayaspān*, lit. '*Baga*-union, divine alliance', but a definite etymology still cannot be suggested, despite several efforts to explain the provenance of the word.[173] Whereas the first reading agrees well with the interpretation of the term suggested here as 'exogamy' (that is, matrimony outside one's natal lineage), the second reading *bayaspān/bayāspān*—apart from being the *lectio difficilior*—seems to be more likely, due to its possible etymological relation to Sogdian *βagānīpš/βagānīšp* 'bridegroom', lit. '*Baga*-son; son in/by the *Baga*-rites' (see fn. 173). Not only the provenance of the enigmatic word has been explained differently, but also its technical meaning as: 'a girl married for the

172 The most frequent are: (1) ending in *-stān*: ⟨bgʾstʾn⟩, ⟨byʾstʾn⟩ which can also be read ⟨bšstʾn⟩ (MHD 21.9; 41.10); (2) ending in *-spān*: ⟨byšspʾn⟩ ⟨bygʾspʾn⟩ (REA 31.2,10), ⟨bwšspʾn⟩ (REA 31.11), ⟨bgʾspʾn⟩ ⟨bšspʾn⟩ ⟨byšpʾn⟩ (REA 31.12, 13,14; a list of the different spellings in the original Pahlavi script can be found in CARLSEN 1984, p. 115, and SUNDERMANN 1998, p. 121).

173 BARTHOLOMAE 1918–1923, V, pp. 30–31, disregarding the forms in *-stān* as an adjustment to those in *-spān*, reads *baydēspān*, from *bay* 'god' and **dēspān* 'messenger' (Armenian loan-word *despan*), 'Götterbote' ('god's messenger') and explains *frazand ī baydēspān* 'Götterbotenkind' (child sent by the gods) as a designation for a child born in a marriage not authorized by the woman's guardian. PERIKHANIAN 1970, pp. 349–350 (referring to HENNING's 1965 explanation of the Sogdian word βγʾnyšp, βγʾnypš, βγʾnpš as 'wedding', a compound he explained literally as '*Baga*-union') reads *bayaspān* <**bagaspāna-* (*baga-* + base *spā̆n-* 'unite, associate, connect, bind') with the meaning 'marriage union, wedlock'. SCHWARZ 1974, however, later established the meaning of the Sogdian word referred to here beyond doubt as 'bridegroom', not 'wedding' (referred to by PERIKHANIAN 1997, p. 343). CARLSEN 1984, pp. 120–121, reading *bayāspān*, argues that the term means basically 'messenger', as BARTHOLOMAE had suggested, and designates 'a girl who marries for the first time'. Another possible reading, based on a suggestion by SHAKI 1975, p. 231, is taken up by SUNDERMANN 1998, p. 124: *bē-āstān* 'out of the threshold' as an expression for 'out of the house', *i.e.*, 'separated from (her) own family', which in his opinion could 'well be said of a girl who becomes a member of her husband's family without the blessing of her guardian' (*ibid.*, p. 124). Discussing other possibilities, SUNDERMANN argues that if one reads **bayāspān* (in the sense of a girl who is married without the consent of her guardian) the word should be somehow related to the Sogdian word for 'bridegroom' (quoted above): *byʾ(ny)pš* 'Baga-son; son of the god Baga' or 'divine son', which had become by the time of the Sogdian Ancient Letters a general form of address for 'husband' (SUNDERMANN 1998, p. 125), and reconstructs an OP **bagāpuça-* 'divine son' and a corresponding **bagā̆puçānī-* ('bride' as a specific designation for the girl, who marries on her own) > MP **bayā̆psān* > **bayā̆spān* (by metathesis; *ibid.*, pp. 127–128).

first time'[174] or 'girl or woman who is not given … to her husband by her father or brother or any other authorized member of her family but who becomes a member of her husband's family as the partner, the mate of her bridegroom'[175] or 'technical term designating one of the varieties of marriages *sine manu mariti*'.[176]

None of these definitions is convincing if we take all the attestations of the term into consideration. It is used in our oldest legal source, the Sasanian Lawbook, with the expression for 'daughter' (*duxt ī bayăspān* '*bayăspān* daughter' and *duxt ī bayăspān-dād* 'daughter born in *bayăspān*'), but—true to the essence of this text—the two passages in which it occurs are not conclusive and do not offer any kind of explanation.[177] Significantly, the only comprehensive description (to be found in the REA 31.10–14) does *not* correspond to the interpretations in the studies quoted above. Although this text does not offer any exact definition either, but rather presents four cases, the context in which the word appears, is clear enough and reveals an important detail, hitherto ignored in all attempts to explain it: in all four instances the bride 'leaves' (*šawēd* or *bērōn šawēd*) her natal lineage (*xānag*, the 'house' of father or brother) when she marries and no longer belongs to her original descent group, that is, as we may conclude, the *conjugal alliance is an exogamous* one. The four described cases are:

1. Father (or brother) arrange a *pādixšāy*-marriage for their daughter (or sister): when the bride 'leaves the lineage (*xānag* "house") of the father (or brother) and enters the lineage (*xānag* "house") of the husband, (then) it/she is (regarded as) *bayăspān*' (*az xānag ī pid ayāb … az xānag ī brād ō xānag ī šōy šawēd bayăspān bawēd*).[178]
2. After reaching the age of 15 years the daughter (or sister) 'leaves according to her own wish the lineage ("house") of the father or brother' (*xwad kāmagīhā az xānag ī pid ud brād bērōn šawēd*) 'without authorization of the father or brother' (*abē-dastwarīhā ī pid [ud] brād*) and concludes a 'consensus marriage' (*gādār kunēd*). When the bride 'has approached the

174 Carlson 1984, p. 120, whose interpretation is too far-fetched and not supported by any source.

175 Sundermann 1998, p. 126f., does not take the important attestation REA 31.10 into consideration. Contrary to his explanation, the term is used here explicitly in the context of *pādixšāy*-marriage, which was always arranged by the guardian (usually father or brother) of the bride (see the first case described below). Moreover, in the second case mentioned in this context, that of a consensus marriage, the bride did *not* become a member of the husband's family by changing into his lineage.

176 Perikhanian 1997, p. 343 (under *bayaspan*). This definition is also contradicted by the explicit reference to *pādixšāy*-marriage in REA 31.10, which was always *cum manu mariti*.

177 MHD 21.9 (Macuch 1993, pp. 170, 175); 41.10 (*ibid.*, pp. 300, 316). Although the latter passage contains a reference to *xwasrāyēn/xwasrāyūn* (see pp. 145–147 above), it is not conclusive, since not only the consensus marriage, but also the *pādixšāy* one is mentioned in the context of *bayăspān* (see below).

178 REA 31.10 (Anklesaria 1962, p. 112; Safa-Isfehani's 1980 translation, pp. 212–214, is unreliable and misleading).

husband (*ka ō nazdīk ī gādār šud*), (then) it/she is (regarded as) *bayăspān*' (*bayăspān bawēd*).[179]

3. The 15 year old daughter (or sister) 'leaves without the consent of the father or brother' (*a-kāmagīhā [ī] pid ud brād bērōn šawēd*) and 'enters a "consensus marriage" (*gādār kunēd*), (then) it/she is (regarded as) *bayăspān*' (*bayăspān bawēd*).[180]
4. The daughter or sister have reached the age of 15 and are 'in need of a husband' (*šōy abāyēd*), but the father or brother do 'not provide a husband for them' (*ō šōy nē dahēnd*) and are therefore 'sinful' (*wināhgār*). If she enters a 'consensus marriage' (*ka gādār ī frāz kunēd*), (then) it/she is (regarded as) *bayăspān*" (*bayăspān bawēd*).[181]

We may draw three important conclusions from these cases. First of all, *bayăspān* does *not* refer to a young girl or woman who chooses her own spouse: as we have seen, another technical term is used for the bride in this case, namely *xwasrāyēn/ūn* ('having her own *manus*', see 4.1.3, pp. 145–147). It is not only highly improbable that two different terms should denote exactly the same legal issue, but, more importantly, the first case cited above explicitly mentions a *pādixšāy*-marriage *cum manu mariti* in the context of *bayăspān*, that is, a marriage which was always arranged by the girl's guardian (father or brother) and hence contradicts this explanation. Not the choice of the bride is the significant feature in this context, but the fact that the girl 'leaves' her original 'house' (= lineage) and does not remain in her natal group, but changes into that of the husband by 'entering' his lineage (*ō xānag ī šōy šawēd*) under his guardianship. Second, cases two to four all describe variant motivations for a girl to conclude a 'consensus marriage' (using the expression *gādār kardan*, see 4.1.3, pp. 145–147): the young girl 'leaves' her natal lineage 'according to her own wish' (*xwad-kāmagīhā*) without authorization (*abē-dastwarīhā*) of her guardian, or she 'leaves' without the consent (*a-kāmagīhā*) of the guardian, or she is 'in need of a husband' (*šōy abāyēd*), but has not been married by her guardian, and enters a 'consensus marriage', parting from her original descent group. In contrast to *pādixšāy*-marriage, however, the girl neither enters the lineage of the husband, nor is she under his guardianship, hence the children born in this form of wedlock cannot be claimed by any lineage: a son born in consensus marriage is 'nobody's son' (*pusarīh ī kas nēst*).[182] The third remarkable feature is that from the three variant marriage types only *čagar*-wedlock is not mentioned in this context. The reason may be easily detected: this specific conjugal alliance does not fit into the description of *bayăspān* as an exogamous union. In *čagar*-marriage the bride remained in the lineage of

179 REA 31.12 (Anklesaria 1962, p. 113).
180 REA 31.13 (*ibid.*, p. 113f.).
181 REA 31.14 (*ibid.*, p. 114).
182 According to REA 43.2 (transcribed, translated and commented in Macuch 1985, p. 198ff.).

her deceased *pādixšāy*-husband under the guardianship of one of the members of his family. She could never 'leave' the lineage of the deceased husband due to the specific function of this institution as an auxiliary marriage. Taking all these aspects into account, the technical meaning of *bayăspān* may be confidently established as a conjugal bond *outside* the natal lineage of the bride. Originally the term may have denoted either the bride herself: lit. '*Baga*-bride, divine bride' for a woman who enters an exogamous union, 'leaving' her original lineage (as *pādixšāy*- or *xwasrāyēn*-bride), or it is the expression for this type of alliance outside the group itself, that is 'exogamy' (lit. '*Baga*-union, divine union'). I assume that the term was used in the latter sense in contrast to the well-known term for 'endogamy' (*xwēdōdah*/*xwēdōdād*).

Differentiating between conjugal alliances within and without the descent group was crucial in Sasanian family law due to the divergent implications of these two different types of marriages, particularly with regard to succession and inheritance. Both exogamy and endogamy were known, but marriage within the family or descent group seems to have been the preferred variant at least in aristocratic and priestly circles. Moreover, one of the most prominent features of Zoroastrian law, distinguishing it from almost all other societies of late antiquity, was the complete lack of regulations prohibiting marriages between members of the nuclear (or conjugal) family, which were strictly forbidden in most—when not all—other legal systems. There is plenty of evidence in both foreign and Iranian sources on marriages within a lineage, including incestuous ones between mother and son, father and daughter, brother and sister. In a large number of late Pahlavi texts these unions are placed in a religious context and praised as the most meritorious and virtuous deeds, suggesting that conjugal bonds between members of the elementary family were not only allowed, but even encouraged by religious authorities as the best possible connection between husband and wife. The reliability of these late, primarily religious texts has been debated in several studies, questioning the idea that Zoroastrian priests of the 9th and 10th centuries strove to save an age-old custom and that marriages within the nuclear family were concluded on a large scale in Iranian societies in the pre-Islamic period.[183]

183 The question has been discussed since the 19th century due to three main reasons: (1) Incestuous relationships are not accepted or allowed by contemporary Zoroastrians. The parsis understandably also denied their existence in the past, not wanting their faith to be associated with a practice that must seem abhorrent and completely alien to them (Sanjana 1888 and Katrak 1965; refuted by Hübschmann 1889 and Klima 1966). (2) The controversy was spurred on by the long-lasting (but faulty) theory promoted by social anthropologists that there is no culture without an incest taboo, aside from certain exceptions regarding the ruling dynasty or certain influential groups such as nobles and priests, or as part of the ritual in certain cults (but see also Spooner 1966; Fox 1967, p. 31; Sidler 1971; Shepher 1983 who take a more differentiated view). (3) The foreign sources and the Avestan and late Pahlavi material have been interpreted differently with divergent results, leading to three major explanations: (a) Foreign sources describing incest in Iran tend to simplify and misinterpret cultural phenomena diverging from their own mores.

Although these questions have been discussed controversially with divergent results, from a legal point of view there can be absolutely no doubt that endogamy, including marriages within the elementary family, fulfilled an important function in Sasanian family law, notably as common strategies to maintain the lineage and its property.[184] In this context it is crucial to stress that the well-attested term *xwēdōdah/xwēdōdād* (< Av. *x*ᵛ*aētuuadaϑa-*),[185] 'next-of-kin marriage', does *not* refer exclusively to the incestuous type of matrimony, but to endogamy on a larger scale. The intra-familial variant comprising marriages between mother and son, father and daughter and siblings was only *one* form of 'next-of-kin' wedlock, albeit the closest possible one and the one most praised in religious texts. This is made quite clear in several sources, listing different possible *xwēdōdah*-connections:

1. between relations (*abāg nabānazdištān*);
2. between close relations belonging to the next-of-kin (*andar nabānazdištān ō abāg nazdpaywandān*);
3. between 'the nearest relations' (*nazdpaywandtar*), listed precisely as:
   (a) father and daughter (*pid ud duxt*);
   (b) son and mother (*pus ud burdār*, lit. 'bearer', *i. e.*, natural mother);[186]
   (c) brother and sister (*brād ud xwāh*).[187]

This list of possible 'next-of-kin' unions shows that there was *no separate* expression for 'incest' in Pahlavi literature, but that marriage within the nuclear family was inherent in the term *xwēdōdah*, best rendered by 'endogamy'. This is in fact exactly what we would expect in a society with no ban on these relationships:

(b) The significance of *xwēdōdah* was stressed in the post-Sasanian period as a strategy to encourage endogamous alliances within the Zoroastrian communities in order to preserve them within an increasingly hostile Muslim environment. (c) The praise *xwēdōdah* receives in later texts can be explained as reluctance on the part of the Mazdeans to enter these marriages, causing the clergy to acclaim them in this exaggerated manner (West 1882, pp. 389–430; Hübschmann 1889; Frye 1985; Herrenschmidt 1994; Panaino 2006). On the main questions regarding incestuous relationships see Macuch 1991 (with references to the vast secondary literature on this subject). For an extensive recent overview see Skjærvø 2013. Frandsen 2009 (who is not an Iranist) is full of elementary mistakes, hence unreliable.

184 On marriage within the nuclear family in a legal context see Macuch 2010c with references to the sources.

185 Bartholomae 1904, col. 1860; from *x*ᵛ*aētu-* 'family, kin' + **vadaϑa-*, from the base √*vad* 'to carry, lead (away); to marry (a wife)' (*ibid.*, col. 1343f.; Kellens 1995, p. 49; Cheung 2007, p. 200).

186 The same exact terminology (with *burdār* 'bearer' for 'natural mother, *genetrix*') is employed in both DkM 72.3–11 and PRDd 8d1 (Williams 1990, I, p. 53) in order to avoid misunderstandings. The usual term for 'mother', *mād*, could also be used in a figurative sense to designate other wives of the father (just as *pid* could be used of both the natural and the legal father). By choosing *burdār* the text explicitly points to a person's *genetrix* in contrast to all other women in the family who could also be called 'mother'.

187 DkM 72.3–11, quoted and translated in Macuch 2010c, pp. 135–136.

there was no need of a special term, since marriages between members of the nuclear family were allowed within the general rule of endogamy and did not have to be treated as an exception. Moreover, the negative connotation of our word 'incest', which usually refers to a legally forbidden sexual connection, does not apply to the Iranian word: these alliances were perfectly legal forms of matrimony; *xwēdōdah* does not refer to (illegal) sexual relationships, but to legitimate conjugal unions both within the elementary family as well as inside the larger family or lineage.

Although the term itself is not attested in the Sasanian legal material (which could be purely coincidental or due to the fact that *xwēdōdah* is a religious, not a legal term) incestuous marriages are expressly referred to in a juristic context. The Law-book bears witness to two forms of wedlock within the nuclear family: between father and daughter and between brother and sister (only marriage between mother and son is not attested, which could again be purely coincidental, or due to the specific legal function of endogamy within the framework of secondary succession, to be discussed below). Significantly, these unions are not described as exceptions or special cases, but are alluded to in the context of completely different legal problems regarding inheritance and the transfer of property, resulting from the double (or eventually triple) status of the persons involved. The main problems discussed in these cases are:

1. Does a daughter who is at the same time the wife of a *paterfamilias* receive two portions as her share of the inheritance: the one bequeathed to the wife (*bahr ī zanīh*) as well as the portion of the daughter (*bahr ī duxtīh*), or does she only receive the share of the wife (which is twice the share of the daughter)?[188]
2. Does a daughter who is the wife of the *paterfamilias* receive two objects (a golden and a silver one), which he had bequeathed (in his will) separately to his wife and daughter respectively, or does she only receive the golden one left to the wife?[189]
3. A *paterfamilias* leaves two pieces of land ascribed to the institution of 'substitute succession' (*stūrīh*) to each first born child of his son and daughter: what are the legal consequences of this disposition if his son and daughter marry each other?[190]
4. The *paterfamilias* bequeaths a certain property to his son on the condition that he enter matrimony with his daughter (the son's sister): what are the legal implications if the son does not marry his sister?[191]

188 MHD 11.8–14; English translation Macuch 2010c, p. 137. For a full discussion of this passage, see Macuch 1993, pp. 347–348. On inheritance see Macuch 2005b.
189 MHD 104.9–11 (Macuch 1993, pp. 618, 626; English translation Macuch 2010c, p. 137).
190 MHD 105.5–10 (Macuch 1993, pp. 640, 647; English translation Macuch 2010c, pp. 137–138).
191 MHDA 18.7–12 (Macuch 1981, pp. 41, 164–165; English translation Macuch 2010c, p. 138).

These remarkable passages not only reveal that marriages within the nuclear family were common in the Sasanian period, but that concrete legal difficulties could arise due to the double or triple status of family members as daughters, sisters and wives. In assessing these cases, however, several characteristic features of Sasanian law have to be taken into account, which point to a far more complex state of affairs than immediately visible in these passages.

Far more important from a legal perspective than 'real' conjugal bonds within the nuclear family were 'fictional' alliances based on the *theoretical* possibility of entering an incestuous marriage. In fact, 'intermediary succession' (*ayōgēnīh*, and to a certain extent also 'substitute succession', *stūrīh*), both characteristic strategies of securing the continuity of a man's lineage, would have been impossible to implement without this basic rule allowing matrimony between close relatives. As we have seen, if a *paterfamilias* left no male heir and no wife on his demise, either his daughter, if he had one, or—in absence of a daughter—his sister were obliged to act as 'intermediary successor' and engender a son for the deceased by entering a *čagar*-marriage with another man. The children of the daughter or sister were all legitimate heirs of the deceased *paterfamilias* exactly in the same manner as the offspring born by a *pādixšāy*-widow acting as *ayōgēn* would be (see pp. 163–168 below). In these instances, the daughter or sister of the deceased were treated legally *as if* they had entered a marriage of the *pādixšāy*-type with the father or brother respectively.[192] These unions between father and *ayōgēn*-daughter or brother and *ayōgēn*-sister were only *theoretical constructs* and could (at least in most cases) never be consummated, but the important point is that they were based on the legality of incestuous matrimony. The main purpose of this highly theoretical construction, founded on the model of the arranged marriage of the *pādixšāy*-type in combination with guardianship (*sālārīh*) of the husband over the wife, was to guarantee the assignment of the children born by the 'intermediary successor' to their legal father instead of the natural one. In order to achieve this goal a marriage *cum manu mariti* between the legal parents had to be tacitly assumed, linking the daughter or sister in fictive matrimony to the *paterfamilias*.

In attempting to determine the impact of the closest type of next-of-kin matrimony two other aspects of Sasanian family law will also have to be taken into consideration: first, the largely constructed nature of consanguineous bonds, resulting from the artificial assignment of children born in the two institutions of secondary succession (*ayōgēn[īh]* and *stūrīh*); and, second, the possibility of concluding temporary marriages. As to the first feature, a number of children born in 'intermediary succession' or 'substitute succession' were not the natural offspring of a *paterfamilias*, but counted as his legal children, who could also intermarry. Hence, to a certain extent marriages

192 Discussed more thoroughly in Macuch 2003b, p. 241f., and 2010c.

between so-called siblings were not incestuous at all, since their status within the lineage was a legal construction and they were not necessarily related to each other biologically by the same natural parents (on the status of children see pp. 175–177 below). As to the second point, temporary marriage is expressly linked to the practice of *xwēdōdah* in several passages, calling our attention to the fact that next-of-kin (and incestuous) unions could be limited to a certain period of time, thus facilitating the fulfilment of this religious obligation (which Zoroastrians seem to have been only reluctant to comply with, as several Pahlavi and foreign sources suggest).[193]

To sum up, from a legal point of view we may differentiate between various types of matrimony within the nuclear family (as one variant of endogamy), distinguishing following forms:

1. 'Real' marriages between father and daughter as well as brother and sister, explicitly attested in the Sasanian legal material in passages dealing with inheritance and the transfer of property.
2. Temporary incestuous marriages with a time-limit (of one to four years according to the sources; ten years in a *čagar*-marriage; see pp. 157–162 below).[194]
3. 'Fictive' incestuous alliances within the framework of 'intermediary succession' (*ayōgēn*) (perhaps also of 'substitute succession'), theoretically uniting the woman fulfilling these duties in *pādixšāy*-matrimony with the deceased *paterfamilias*.
4. Marriages between siblings who had the same *pater*, without having the same *genitor*, belonging to the same nuclear family only in a constructed legal sense.[195]

As we have seen, endogamy within the descent group (*abag nabanazdištān* 'with relatives') consisted of far more conjugal possibilities than only (real or fictive) marriages between members of the nuclear family. Although these are not explicitly enumerated in Pahlavi texts in the context of *xwēdōdah*, miraculously an illuminating list of matrimonial unions in Syriac legal literature has survived, which can be used to reconstruct in detail different kinds of next-of-kin marriages in the Sasanian period. This list is conserved in the tractate on forbidden conjugal alliances (and in the canonical letters) of Mār Abā, the Catholicos of the Church of the East in the 6th century (from 540 to 552), during the reign of Husraw Anōšag ruwān (531–579).[196] His tractate on marriage law is particularly interesting, since he was a convert to Christianity from Zoroastrianism, was well versed in Sasanian jurisprudence and worked prior to his conversion as a high official of the State in the service of the King. After his conversion he

193 Macuch 1991 with references to the sources.
194 For references to the sources see Macuch 1991, p. 153, no. 83, and 2006, pp. 593–594.
195 For more details see Macuch 2010c.
196 See Sachau 1914, pp. 258–285; Braun 1915, p. 200f., no. 1.

retained the Zoroastrian legalistic approach to religious matters from his former religious affiliation and formulated the first Christian marriage law in direct opposition to Sasanian law, thus unintentionally giving us detailed insight into Zoroastrian marital relationships within the descent group.[197] He not only confirms the dispersed information on endogamy in Pahlavi texts, but provides an extensive list of different possible marriage bonds, which were legitimate in Zoroastrian law, but forbidden to Christians. These were (according to Mār Abā's marriage tractate and his third canonical letter) conjugal unions with the following women:

1. one's mother;
2. the wife of the father;
3. one's sister;
4. one's daughter;
5. the daughter of the son (= niece);
6. the daughter of the daughter (= niece);
7. the daughter-in-law;
8. the wife of the brother (= sister-in-law);
9. the wife of the paternal uncle;
10. the sister of the mother (= maternal aunt);
11. the sister of the father (= paternal aunt);[198]
12. the step-daughter;
13. the step-granddaughter.[199]

Although Mār Abā only refers once (in the first case of a person's mother) in his discussion to the customs of the Persians, it is very likely that this list of conjugal relationships forbidden in Christian law was inspired by current endogamous practice among the Zoroastrians of the Sasanian period, with which he was well acquainted. His Christian marriage rules not only forbade matrimony between members of the nuclear family (numbers 1, 3 and 4 above), but also all other possible next-of-kin combinations between consanguins, no matter whether they were related by 'blood' in a genetic sense (numbers 5, 6, 10, 11) or merely defined as such (numbers 2, 7, 8, 9, 12, 13).[200] All these different possibilities of entering legal matrimony with a person inside one's own lineage were crucial for upholding the Sasanian system of inheritance and succession, particularly the important institutions of secondary succession, *ayōgēn(īh)* and *stŭrīh*, both founded on the legality of matrimony between near relations. Mār

197 On Mār Abā's vita and the trial against him see Macuch 2014c with further references. On his legal work see Chapter I, p. 47 above.

198 The list is in Sachau 1914, pp. 260–261, and elucidated in §§2–11 (pp. 261–279).

199 The last two forms are added here following Mār Abā's third canonical letter, see Bedjan 1895, pp. 282–283; Braun 1915, p. 201; see also Macuch 2014c, pp. 52–53.

200 There could of course be cross-connections and the women in these cases could also be 'blood'-relations, belonging to the same lineage.

Abā's rejection of these unions (among other grave offences) was regarded as serious meddling in the legal affairs of the State by Zoroastrian religious and legal authorities and led to a prolonged trial against the Catholicos, in which he was accused of several illegal acts. Among these he is also charged of expelling (converted) Christians from the church who had previously acted according to Zoroastrian law by marrying their mother-in-law, their daughter-in-law, the wife of their uncle or two sisters (and did not dissolve these marriages after conversion).[201] It seems that Mār Abā's marriage law was a direct and complete refutation of Zoroastrian family law, forbidding not only next-of-kin marriages (*xwēdōdah*), but also polygyny, two of the most important prerequisites of the Sasanian kinship system.

To sum up: both exogamy (*bayǎspān*) and endogamy (*xwēdōdah*) were practised, but there can be no doubt that endogamy, including both 'real' and 'fictive' marriages within the nuclear family, was encouraged in Zoroastrianism and enabled the emergence of unique institutions of secondary succession, crucial for preserving and stabilizing the *status quo*. From a legal perspective these measures had two main objectives, both in the interest of the nobility and priesthood: (1) to guarantee the continuation of the lineage and (2) to prevent the partition and fragmentation of family property by keeping it within the descent group.[202]

4.3 Temporary marriage

Marriage with a clearly defined time-limit was another significant ingredient of Sasanian family law. It is important to stress that this was *not* a separate form of matrimony comparable to the three types (*pādixšāy*, *čagar* and *xwasrāyēn/gādār*) we have discussed above. These marriage forms were differentiated because of their divergent legal functions within the overall scheme of family law, whereas temporary marriage was more of a strategy than an individual form of marriage, conveying flexibility to an otherwise rigid system. All three types of matrimony could be concluded on a temporary basis with the goal of making a fertile woman available to several men during her lifetime and enabling her to engender offspring for more than one husband or lineage (this applies to the two regular forms of matrimony, *pādixšāy* and *čagar*; in the context of 'consensus marriage' the main reason seems to have been another one, see below). In the light of the general Zoroastrian precept to procreate children and its implementation in Sasanian family law, temporary marriage seems to have been a necessary concession within a patrilineal system prohibiting polyandry. A rule forbidding a fertile woman—no matter how urgently she might be needed

201 Mentioned in his Vita, see Bedjan 1895, p. 234; Braun 1915, p. 200ff.; Macuch 2014c, p. 52; on the trial against him see also Chapter VI, pp. 573–581.
202 Īšōʿbōxt, Book I, chapter III (Sachau 1914, p. 37) in fact confirms exactly this conclusion.

in another family—to engender children for two (or more) men in her lifetime would have contradicted the general concept of matrimony in Sasanian law. By allowing marriage to be concluded for a specific limited period, the reproductive faculties of a woman could be used successively (but *not* simultaneously!) to the advantage of several husbands or lineages. We may furthermore conclude, that this is the main reason why no specific legal term is attested for temporary marriage: it was an inherent part of the system, fulfilling its own important function within the framework of family law, *not* a distinct and individual legal institution (in contrast to the Shīʿite *mutʿa* or *ṣīġe*, to be discussed in Chapter VII, pp. 628–632 below).

Although no separate technical term denotes temporary unions due to this background, several passages in the legal material leave no doubt that marriages could be and were concluded on a time-limited basis. Different lengths are recorded, reaching from the rather long period of ten years to shorter time-spans of four, two, three and one year(s) in the Pahlavi material (a foreign source, the Babylonian Talmud, even refers to one day in this context).[203] The following formulae are transmitted:

1. Ten years:
   - 'If a woman gives herself in marriage to a man for ten years' (*ka zan-ē[w] tā 10 sāl tan pad zanīh ō mard-ē[w] dahēd*).[204]
   - 'For ten years I am your wife' (*tā 10 sāl zan ī tō hom*).[205]
   - 'For ten years I have given myself to you in marriage' (*kū{-m tā 10 sāl} tan pad zanīh ō tō dād*).[206]
   - 'For ten years I have given myself in marriage to Mihrēn' (*kū-m tā 10 sāl tan pad zanīh {ō Mi}hrēn dād*).[207]
2. Three years:
   - 'For three years she has entered a marriage with me' (*sāl 3 ō zanīh ī man mad*).[208]
   - 'For three years she has entered a marriage with Kērēn' (*sāl 3 ō zanīh ī Kērēn mad*).[209]
3. One, two, three or four years (with regard to next-of-kin marriage):
   - 'He who maintains next-of-kin marriage for one (two, three or four) year(s)' (*kē ēw [dō, sē, čahār] sāl xwēdōdah pad zanīh dārēd*).[210]

203 *Yoma* 17b and *Yevamot* 37a–b (quoted Macuch 2006, p. 589); on temporary marriage in the Talmud see Elman 2019a.
204 MHD 87.17 (Macuch 1993, pp. 561, 564).
205 MHD 23.2 (Macuch 1993, pp. 172, 177).
206 MHD 87.2f. (*ibid.*, pp. 560, 563).
207 MHDA 2.8 (Macuch 1981, pp. 22, 70).
208 MHD 83.13f. (Macuch 1993, pp. 539, 542).
209 MHD 83.14 (*ibid.*, pp. 539, 542).
210 PRDd 18.7–19.2 (Williams 1990, I, p. 58f., II, p. 15, nos. 8h1–8h3. See also Macuch 2006, p. 594).

Interestingly, all the Pahlavi sources allude to temporary marriage for a longer period, reaching from one year (the minimum time needed to conceive and carry a child to full term) up to 10 years (the time-span necessary for rearing a child). Since the main objective of the two regular marriage types, *pādixšāy* and *čagar*, was the procreation of children and legitimate heirs for the lineage of the *paterfamilias*, one would in fact expect a time-limited variant of either of these unions to take into account the minimum time-span necessary for performing this task in the marriage contract (as in the cited formulae). On the other hand, marriage for a short period of one day, mentioned in the Babylonian Talmud, obviously had another purpose, which could point to one of the uses (or: misuses) of the 'consensus' (*xwasrāyēn/gādār*) type of matrimony for sexual enjoyment (comparable to the Shīʿite *mutʿa/ṣīġe* that can also be concluded for one day and is hence often regarded as prostitution by Sunnite jurists, see below Chapter VII, pp. 628–632).

Unfortunately, none of all this is stated explicitly in the texts, but the precise use of legal terminology in passages referring to temporary marriage leaves no doubt that this form of matrimony was an important option in all three possible conjugal alliances. The attested cases point unequivocally to the three different types of marriage, although these are not expressly named in the texts. The reason is that the cross-connections between the technical terms used in this context and the marriage type they refer to were all well known to trained jurists and did not have to be elucidated (following the rule that legal precepts should be short, precise and to the point). A reconstruction of the underlying institutions allows the following conclusions:[211]

1. *Pādixšāy*-marriage. In two instances the term *ayōgēn* ('intermediary successor') is mentioned in connection with a marriage limited to ten years. As we have seen above, only the wife in a *pādixšāy*-marriage (or the daughter or sister acting as a 'fictive' *pādixšāy*-wife) is obliged to act as 'intermediary successor' (*ayōgēn*) for the husband. In the first case (MHD 87.2–3), the wife has the duty to perform this task for her husband if he dies childless within the time-span of the union, that is, ten years. This obligation presupposes a marriage *cum manu mariti*. In the second case (MHD 23.1–4) a daughter who has entered a temporary marriage for ten years with the consent of her father, can only act as *ayōgēn* for the deceased father *after* her marriage has expired (since, as we may add, she would be 'intermediary successor' of the husband within the time-span of the marriage and cannot perform this task for two men at the same time).[212] The terminology clearly and unequivocally points to a time-limited form of *pādixšāy*-marriage—no further elucidation was needed for schooled jurists of the Sasanian period.

211 The philological and contextual problems in these texts have been discussed extensively in Macuch 1985 and 2006.
212 Macuch 1985, pp. 194–197, and 2006, pp. 591–592.

2. *Čagar*-marriage. The institution of 'substitute succession' (*stūrīh*) was based, as we have seen, on the possibility of concluding a marriage of the type *sine manu mariti*, in which children could be generated for a deceased *paterfamilias*. A woman or man installed as 'substitute successor; proxy' (*stūr*) would enter this type of 'auxiliary marriage' in order to perform this task. According to several attestations (*e. g.*, MHD 50.1–3; 96.8–10) a *stūrīh* could be limited to a certain number of years (in these instances ten years). We may confidently conclude that an 'auxiliary marriage' could be restricted to exactly the same period of time, since the *čagar*-wife was kept by the income of the property set up for this institution and would have no means of maintenance after the *stūrīh* expired. We may hence infer, that these passages refer to a time-limited variant of this type of marriage.[213]
3. *Xwasrāyēn/gādār*-marriage. The 'consensus' marriage of the *sine manu mariti* type could be concluded (without consent of the woman's guardian) according to MHD 24.7–10 both on a permanent basis (*az ān ī hamēīg*, lit. 'of the for-ever-type') or on a temporary basis (*nē az ān ī hamēīg*, lit. 'not of the for-ever-type') with different consequences: in a time-limited marriage the guardianship (*sālārīh*) of the father and the right of the daughter to a share of the total inheritance (*abarmānd*) would not change, whereas in a permanent marriage she would lose this right and the father would no longer have a title to the income of the daughter. The passage unambiguously refers to this type of wedlock by its terminology using the formula *gādār kardan* 'to enter a consensus marriage', denoting the conclusion of a *xwasrāyēn/gādār*-marriage, instead of *šōy kardan* 'to marry, take a husband', the formula employed in the context of the two other forms of matrimony.[214]

The intriguing question is: why could all three types of matrimony—besides the permanent variant—also be contracted on a time-limited basis? As so often in the available legal material, the answer to this question can only be found indirectly. One of the discernable reasons for creating a time-limited version of the *cum manu mariti* marriage seems to be the meritorious deed of giving one's own wife to another man who had no wife and children for a specified period in order to enable this man to accomplish his duty as a Zoroastrian and generate offspring. Although the *pādixšāy*-marriage was perceived (at least theoretically) as a permanent union, which did not even end with the death of the husband, but survived beyond the grave as an 'eternal deed' (*kār ī frašgirdīg*)[215], enabling the widow of a deceased husband to procreate legitimate children for the latter even after his death, obviously there were cases, in which a temporary form of this marriage was advantageous. One of these is mentioned MHD 101.4–8: a

213 Macuch 1985, pp. 200–201, and 2006, p. 592.
214 Macuch 1985, pp. 197–200; 2006, p. 593. On the terminology see above pp. 145–147.
215 REA 31.3 (Macuch 1985, p. 202).

husband is entitled to give his *pādixšāy*-wife to another man who, by no fault of his own, is 'in need of a wife and children' (*pad zan ud frazand niruzd*) and has 'brought forward a legal request for the wife' (*xwāhišn ī zan dādīhā kard ēstēd*). The consent of the wife for this transaction is not necessary.[216] We may assume that this kind of interim marriage was concluded as a perfectly legal *pādixšāy*-union with guardianship of the husband over the wife and children for an exactly defined time-span and that the wife returned to her original husband after accomplishing her duty to generate children for the interim spouse. It could not have been concluded as a *čagar*-marriage *sine manu mariti*, since the children would not belong legally to the new husband in this case, but to the former one. The only possible marriage to this purpose, agreeing with the rules of family law, is the *pādixšāy* one. We may furthermore infer that temporary marriage opened addition options: the reproductive faculties of women could be used to the advantage of several men or lineages, whereas a permanent marriage tied a woman to only one husband or lineage. As we have seen in the cases described above, a woman could be engaged as 'intermediary successor' (*ayōgēn*) for her husband in a temporary marriage for a specific, exactly determined number of years in the marriage contract (10 years in the attested cases), but then return to her original lineage and serve as *ayōgēn* for her father (or brother).

As to the *čagar*-marriage, a time-limitation agrees perfectly with the main purpose of this type of 'auxiliary' matrimony. Since its only purpose was to engender offspring within the institution of 'substitute succession' (*stūrīh*), for which a certain part of family property was specifically set apart (see Chapter III, pp. 213–219), we may even assume that the temporary form was the regular type of marriage, at least in cases in which the institution was limited to a certain number of years (10 years in the passages cited above). As we have seen, the *čagar* wife remained legally the spouse of her former *pādixšāy*-husband, hence this marriage type was *per definitionem* also an interim marriage, albeit with completely different implications than the *pādixšāy* one regarding the affiliation of the children.

The 'consensus' marriage (*xwasrāyēn/gādār*), on the other hand, was neither an arranged marriage as the two other types, nor was it explicitly conceived to procreate children and legitimate heirs for a specific lineage. It seems that the temporary variant of this specific marriage type had a completely different function, that of limiting an alliance which was not approved of by the guardian of the bride, and of turning an otherwise illegal sexual relationship into a legal one. The Talmud-passage referred to above explicitly alludes to temporary marriage among the Persians for the duration of only one day, which could well be a reference to the 'consensus' type of matrimony.[217] We have of course no way of determining how frequent these marriages were, but the passage does recall the Shīʿite institution, in which contracts for one day are permitted.

216 The text is cited and discussed in Macuch 2006, pp. 591–592.
217 The passage is cited in Macuch 2006, p. 589.

Temporary marriage was not only a useful device in these instances, but also a convenient institution for enticing Zoroastrians to enter next-of-kin matrimony, as we may conclude from passages on *xwēdōdah* in the late Pahlavi texts. These marriages could also be contracted on a time basis (one, two, three and four years are mentioned), thus enabling Mazdeans to marry within their lineage without having to enter a permanent union.[218] This would in fact confirm reports in foreign sources, describing—paradoxically—the reluctance of Zoroastrians to marry their relations, particularly members of the nuclear family.[219] Devising a time-limited form of *xwēdōdah* could have been an important strategy to facilitate the fulfilment of this obligation, which is, unsurprisingly, never described in terms of a legal advantage for noble lineages (as a means of keeping family property from being partitioned), but as an important religious duty, incumbent on all Zoroastrians, no matter to which social class they belonged.

To conclude: temporary marriage conveyed flexibility to family law and extended the possible marital options in this field to the advantage of affluent noble descent groups. By enabling women to be married to several men in different phases of their lives, the unwritten rule in every patrilineal society, that a woman could only be conjugally united to one man at a time, was both confirmed and circumvented in an efficient manner. A woman's guardian could arrange a marriage for her outside her natal lineage for an exactly defined timespan with all the rights and duties of a *pādixšāy*-wife, including the obligation to act as 'intermediary successor' for her husband. After the temporary marriage expired, she could re-enter her original lineage and put her reproductive faculties at the disposal of her natal family and act as 'intermediary successor' (*ayōgēn*) for her father or brother or as 'substitute successor, proxy' (*stūr*) for another relative in a *čagar*-marriage. The reversed sequence was also possible: she could be first married in a next-of-kin union (*xwēdōdah*) to a relative or in a 'real' or 'fictive' marriage to her father or brother for an exactly defined number of years and later enter wedlock outside her original lineage (*bayāspān*) after expiry of the first marriage contract. In short: temporary marriage opened the important option of using the fertility of a female to the fullest possible degree in the two basic forms of matrimony, without having to give up the patrilineal principle of descent.[220]

218 For example PRDd 18.7–19.2 (cited in Macuch 2006, p. 594).

219 On these attestations see Macuch 1991a.

220 Temporary marriage belongs—in my conviction—to the age-old traditions of the Iranians and is, despite all the changes that took place after the downfall of the Sasanian legal system, definitely a precursor of the Twelver-Shīʿite *mutʿa* or *ṣīġe*, a form of marriage completely alien to the general concept of matrimony in Islamic (Sunnite) law (see Chapter VII, pp. 628–632 below).

4.4 Intermediary succession (*ayōgēnīh*) and substitute succession (*stūrīh*)

These two major methods of securing the continuity of a man's lineage, particularly if the deceased *paterfamilias* left no male successor, were—to judge by the amount of space conceded to them and the large number of cases discussed in the Sasanian Law-book and other Pahlavi sources—significant institutions of family law, crucial for upholding the hierarchy with its division into nobles and commoners and the social system as a whole (the term *stūrīh* is also used in the context of fire-foundations, which will be discussed in Chapter III, pp. 213–219). They were probably originally created as a means to ensure the inter-generational transfer of family property within a lineage, but evolved in the course of Sasanian history into two of the most important methods of preserving powerful aristocratic lineages with tremendous and enduring impact on the structure of the family and of Iranian society in general, reaching far into Islamic times and leaving their trace in Nestorian-Christian law as well as in the Shīʿite law of succession (which differs fundamentally from that of Sunnite law, see Chapter VII, pp. 632–638).

In the ideal case, there would in fact be no need of these institutions. The head of a family would generate his successor(s) himself in *pādixšāy*-wedlock and the natural children from this marriage would all count as his legitimate offspring, as *dādestān-pus* 'legitimate son' (lit. 'son according to the law') and *dādestān-duxt* 'legitimate daughter' (lit. 'daughter according to the law'). Both sons and daughters were entitled to shares in the inheritance and, moreover, counted as legitimate successors of the father, as *yōhē pasčaēta* 'who (succeeds) him afterwards', a phrase extracted from the Avesta, which became a technical term for the 'legal successor' of a *paterfamilias* in general, no matter whether it referred to a son or a daughter.[221] The original Avestan context is unknown and one could speculate that the use of this simple phrase to denote a man's 'successor' stems from an early, pre-Sasanian period of Zoroastrian law, in which both male and female children of the *paterfamilias* had the same succession rights. However, the provenance of the phrase is not explained and this assumption could be entirely wrong, if we take into consideration that Avestan passages or words are often cited in Pahlavi literature out of context by theologians and jurists in order to convey legitimacy to a preferred legal concept or argument.[222] But no matter how the question of succession was handled in earlier times, by the Sasanian period jurists definitely distinguished between the status of sons and daughters: only the legitimate son

221 MHD 21.4, 14, 22.1, 3, 8 (Macuch 1993, pp. 175–176). On inheritance see Macuch 2005b and Chapter III, pp. 230–245 below. On the difference between the terms *yōhē pasčaēta* 'successor' and *xwāstagdār* 'heir' see Chapter III, pp. 206–207.

222 See for example Macuch 2017a, pp. 263–264.

counted as the *direct successor* of the father, whereas the daughter was accepted solely as *intermediary successor.* The technical term used for the daughter in this case (as well as for the wife or the sister in this function) is another expression that has been read and explained divergently in the past, but in fact defies translation despite various explanations and etymological suggestions: *ayōgēn/ayōkēn* designates the female serving as 'intermediary successor', and the abstract form (only attested in late Pahlavi texts) *ayōgēnīh/ayōkēnīh* the 'institution of intermediary succession' (which overlaps to a certain extent with that of *stūrīh*, which might be the reason, why an abstract form of the term is missing in the earlier legal material).[223]

223 The first transcription (*ayōgēn*), which is the form used in the present survey, follows the etymology suggested by KLINGENSCHMITT (1971, p. 168, no. 10, and 2000, p. 225f.), who translates 'Erbtochter (auch „Erbschwester")' (daughter or sister who inherits) from Av. **aiiūγaēnī-* (or **aiiaoγaēnī-*), an extension of **ai̯ug-* or **ai̯au̯gā-* 'unbound, without siblings' + feminine suffix *-aēnī-* (a suffix also to be found in *xwasrāyēn*, if the reading with *-ēn* is correct, see above fn. 165), compare OIr. *ayugū-* 'girl, who is the only daughter of a mother'. Although several arguments can be brought forward against this etymology, it nevertheless still seems to be the most likely one. But it should be noted that it does *not* explain the spelling with double ⟨kk⟩, nor does it correspond to the transmitted Pāzand form of the word *aēuuō.kaē* (Dd 53.13); moreover the *ayōgēn* is by no means always the only daughter, but designates every female successor within a lineage, including wives, sisters and daughters. Another possible, but purely speculative etymology, (suggested to me personally by ILYA GERSHEVITCH), which has the advantage of taking the spelling with double ⟨kk⟩ into consideration, is derived from a reconstructed **āyauka-+kaniiā* 'joining girl; girl who (is) a link' from the root √*yu* 'to join, (re)bind, hold' (KELLENS 1995, p. 47; CHEUNG 2007, p. 215, under **i̯au¹*) with preverb *ā-* (> *ā-yau-ka*) + *kaniiā* ('girl' from *kanī+ā-*; MP *kanīg*), which would become **āyōk-kēn* > *ayōkēn* in Middle Persian. As so often with unattested reconstructions, we have reason to doubt this explanation, although it accounts for the double ⟨kk⟩. Numerous readings, translations and connotations have been suggested for the term, which is attested with variant spellings in Pahlavi literature: (1) ⟨'ywkkyn'⟩ (with double ⟨kk⟩) is the most frequent one in the Law-book (almost everywhere, particularly in the chapter dedicated to this subject, MHD 21.4–24.10, with two exceptions, MHD 22.12 and 25.5, where it is written with one ⟨k⟩); (2) ⟨'ywkyn'⟩ in later Pahlavi texts (*e. g.*, REA 1.2; 18.18,19,10; 23.19); (3) ⟨'ywk'nyh⟩ (in the Model Marriage Contract, JAMASP-ASANA 1897–1913, 141.11 and 142.2); (4) ⟨'ywk'yn'⟩ (Dd 55.8; 57.3); (5) *aēuuō.kaē* in Avestan letters (Dd 53.13). In the New Persian *Riwāyats* we encounter the following forms in Arabic script: (1) *ayūk*; *zan-e ayūk*; *doḫtar-e ayūk*, *nekāḥ-e ayūk*; *ayūk-zan* (UNVALA 1922, I, 180.7,9,10; 1; 184.5,184.6,8;187.8); (2) *yūkī zan* (*ibid.*, 180.11); (3) *yūkan-zanī*; *yūkan-zan* (*ibid.*, 180.12; 188.16). The oldest explanation of the word as 'Nadelgeld' (pin-money) by BARTHOLOMAE (1918–1923, V, p. 28, who did not suggest any reading) can be safely discarded due to definitions of the term excluding this interpretation in late Pahlavi texts, to which this brilliant scholar had no access at the time he was working on the legal material. DHABHAR (1932, p. 187) in his (by now completely outdated translation) of Dd 58, bases his reading *ayōk-āyīn* 'only daughter' (without further explanation) on the form transmitted in the New Persian *Riwāyats*. DE MENASCE (1964a, pp. 36, 42, 57–58) reads *ēvakēn* and explains the term as 'fille « unique » … (ou la sœur unique dans certain cas) même ayant pris mari est tenu pour la femme « autorisée » (*pātixšāyīhā*) de son père, de même que les enfants

This legal term is employed in all attestations (including Pahlavi texts of the post-Sasanian period) exclusively of women, who formed a—real or constructed—'blood' link between a man and his prospective male legal successor and had the obligation to engender a male heir for the deceased. Three groups of women are named explicitly in this context:

---

qui naîtront d'elle seront les enfants autorisés de ce même père ...'. PERIKHANIAN (1970, pp. 351–353) initially understands the term as the Pahlavi rendering of a lost Avestan term, which she reads ⟨'ynwkkyn : 'ynwkk'yn⟩ (*i. e.*, **ēnōkēn*) from an Av. **aēnō.kaēnā-* 'expiator, redeemer' (of her father's sin of dying *a-puϑra-*, sonless), and explains: 'The literal meaning of *aēnō.kaēnā- ī pit/brat* may be established as "redeemer, expiator of her father/brother", while its technical meaning is "*epikleros* daughter/sister."'(*ibid.*, p. 353). This analysis is hardly convincing, not only due to the far-fetched etymology, but also to the discrepancy between her reading of the word and the Pāzand-form *aeuuō. kaē* (Dd 53.13), which might represent *aēiiō.kaē* (due to the similarity of the letters ⟨i⟩ and ⟨u⟩) but never **aēnō.kaē(nā-)*. PERIKHANIAN later (1997, pp. 412–413) abandons both her original reading and etymology and adheres to the explanation provided by KLINGENSCHMITT cited above; MACKENZIE's **ēnōkēn* (< Av. **aēnō.kaēnā-*) 'heiress', in his *Pahlavi Dictionary* (1971, p. 30), based on PERIKHANIAN's first reading, is hence a ghost-word. A completely different explanation of the word derives from the puzzling sequence of terms in the heading of the chapter on *ayōgēn* in the Sasanian Law-book, MHD 21.4–5, which reads: ⟨BB' Y 'ywkkyn' *yōhē pasčaēta* 'ywkh ps'cyt'⟩ (MACUCH 1993, p. 170). This strange sequence begins with *dar ī ayōgēn* ('Chapter on *ayōgēn*'), followed in Avestan script by *yōhē pasčaēta* ('who [succeeds] him afterwards'), which in turn seems to be rendered (inaccurately) in Pahlavi letters as ⟨'ywkh ps'cyt'⟩, **a yōk h(ē) pasčaēta* (or **a-yō-h(ē) pasčaēta*, if we take into consideration that ⟨wk⟩ renders the long vowel ⟨ō⟩ in Avestan words written in Pahlavi script). SHAKI (1971, p. 332, and 1975, p. 228), based on this sequence, assumes that the Pahlavi term is derived from the Avestan phrase *yōhē pasčaēta*, denoting the 'legal successor', that is: *yōhē* (*pasčaēta*) > *ayōk-hē* > *ayōkēn*. Although I once even endorsed this interpretation (MACUCH 1981, p. 104, fn. *), I am no longer convinced that it is correct and would rather assume that the whole sequence is a construction, maybe a popular etymology or a pseudo-scholarly explanation, attempting to derive the Pahlavi word from the Avestan technical term for 'successor'. The main problem in SHAKI's explanation is (besides the spelling with double ⟨kk⟩, which is not accounted for) the initial ⟨'⟩. If the Pahlavi word was in fact derived from *yō hē* (*pasčaēta*), then ⟨'⟩ can only be the privative prefix: **a-yōk-hē* (or **a-yō-hē*) 'who (succeeds) him *not* (afterwards); *un*-successor', which does not make sense, even if it is only employed with reference to women (who could, on the contrary, be a man's successor, if only indirectly). Sasanian jurists probably had no idea of the provenance of the Pahlavi technical term, but they could have constructed the two legal expressions in juxtaposition in the quoted heading to describe the content of the chapter explicitly discussing women, who served as 'intermediary successors': 'Chapter on *ayōgēn*-successors (*yōhē pasčaēta*) (that is:) un-(usual) successors (**a-yohē pasčaēta*)'. This is of course purely speculative, but the idea that *ayōkēn/ayōgēn* should have been deliberately invented or derived from the Avestan words is far too problematic and we should rather assume that it was an ancient legal term, whose provenance was no longer known, but somehow connected by Sasanian jurists to the Avestan elliptical phrase used as a technical term for 'successor'.

1. wives: specifically the *pādixšāy*-wife,[224] the *čagar*-wife,[225] the wife in a temporary marriage;[226]
2. daughters: specifically the unmarried daughter;[227] the daughter who had been placed under the guardianship of a fellow-citizen;[228] the daughter from an exogamic union (*duxt ī bayăspān*);[229] the daughter from a marriage of the *čagar* type;[230]
3. sisters in general:[231] specifically the sister in a joint partnership (*andar hambāyīh*) with an unmarried brother who has no offspring;[232] the sister who is under guardianship (*sālārīh*) of a brother.[233]

All these cases refer to women who were obliged to serve as 'intermediary successors' with the duty to produce progeny for their husbands, fathers or brothers in an 'auxiliary' (*čagar*) marriage, concluded specifically to this purpose. In order to use the reproductive faculties of the females, who were either born in the lineage or included into it by a *cum manu mariti* marriage, the strict rule of patrilineal descent, accepting only males as legal successors of the *paterfamilias*, was successfully combined to the advantage of the descent group with cognatic features, enabling the women to be engaged in the crucial task of procreating legal offspring. The children of the *ayōgēn*-women counted as legitimate heirs and successors of their *pater*, the deceased *paterfamilias*, not of their *genitor* (the *čagar*-husband—who could, however, adopt his own natural children if he was himself in need of progeny). As we have seen above, the daughter or sister installed as 'intermediary successor' counted theoretically as the fictive *pādixšāy*-wife of father or brother (in a *xwēdōdah*-marriage) with the same legal consequences regarding the affiliation of the children. Although these women received a share of the inheritance and were maintained during the period of rearing the children by a part of the property set aside specifically to this purpose (on *stŭrīh*-property see Chapter III, pp. 213–219), only the sons of the 'intermediary successor' were finally regarded as the direct heirs of the deceased *paterfamilias*, entitled to act as his successors and replace him in the community. If the 'intermediary successor' only had daughters, one of these (usually the oldest) was obliged to continue the duty of her mother as *ayōgēn* for

224 Dd 55.7 (see Appendix I, pp. 648–649); see also the *pādixšāy*-marriage contract, clauses 2 and 5 (Macuch 2007b, p. 190; MacKenzie/Perikhanian 1969, p. 105, has a completely misleading translation of these paragraphs).
225 MHD 49.2–3 (Macuch 1993, pp. 308, 325).
226 MHD 87.2–3 (*ibid.*, pp. 560, 563).
227 MHD 23.1–4; 89.17–90.1 (*ibid.*, pp. 172, 177 and 570, 573 respectively); Dd 53.13; 57.3; REA 18.18; 23.7ff.; 31.8; 44.2–3.
228 MHD 22.10–12 (Macuch 1993, pp. 171, 177).
229 MHD 21.8–10 (*ibid.*, pp. 170, 175).
230 REA 23.19–24.
231 MHD 22.9–12; 22.13–23.1 (Macuch 1993, pp. 171f., 177); REA 1.3; 31.9.
232 MHD 23.4–7 (*ibid.*, pp. 172, 177).
233 MHD 23.6–10 (*ibid.*, pp. 172, 178).

her legal grandfather. The son who was finally born could theoretically even be separated from his legal father by several generations, although one can assume that this would have rather been the exception than the rule.

Interestingly, this is in fact the cultural and legal background of the Frēdōn saga in its Pahlavi version (as narrated particularly in the *Bundahišn* and in the *Abdīh ud sahīgīh ī Sīstān*;[234] also transmitted in Firdausi's *Šāhnāma*, albeit in a simplified form). In the Pahlavi version Frēdōn's son Ērēj, who in the saga inherits Ērānšahr and is murdered by his brothers, is separated from his heir and legal successor Manuščihr by a chain of eight daughters serving as 'intermediary successors', each of whom engenders a daughter until the desired male heir is finally born.[235] Although the texts do not use the legal term (neither would one expect them to in an epic narrative), the important point is that even family ties in a constructed genealogy would have to conform with Zoroastrian cultural, social and legal norms in order to be credible. The whole construction only makes sense within the framework of the Sasanian law of succession with its specific institutions of cognatic descent, making use of the *ayōgēn* to preserve a lineage. The same may be said of the legends and tales surrounding the lineage of Ardaxšēr, the founder of the Sasanian dynasty: according to the (constructed?) genealogy transmitted in the *Bundahišn* his mother was the daughter of Sāsān, who—according to the *Kārnāmag*—was a descendant from the line of Darius, the last Achaemenid or (in the Iranian epic) Kayanian king. This genealogy only makes sense if we assume that Sāsān's daughter was regarded as her father's 'intermediary successor' (*ayōgēn*), who gives birth to Ardaxšēr, the legitimate successor of Sāsān, in an 'auxiliary' marriage with Ardaxšēr's natural father Pābag, who later adopts him as his son. This construction is perfectly consistent with Sasanian family law, representing Ardaxšēr as the sole legitimate successor in an ancient line of kings, being connected to them by 'blood', hence the only person fit to rule over Ērānšahr.[236]

The women engaged as 'intermediary successors' were categorized in the Sasanian law of succession as 'natural proxies' (*stŭr ī būdag*) of the men they were serving in this function. The Sasanian Law-book distinguishes exactly between the two institutions of *ayōgēn(īh)* and *stŭrīh*, which are brought together (or maybe confused to a certain extent) in later Pahlavi sources of the post-Sasanian period. The term *ayōgēn-stŭr*, which combines the two words to designate a woman engaged in the task of 'intermediary succession by proxy', is only attested in post-Sasanian Pahlavi texts, not in the Sasanian material.[237] Although both institutions were developed for the same reason, that is, to generate

234 GrBd 35.11–16 (Anklesaria 1956, pp. 294–295; Pakzad 2005, pp. 392–394) and Pahlavi Texts 25,4–6 (Jamasp-Asana 1897–1913, pp. 25, 4–6).
235 On these narratives see Macuch 2016c, p. 314, fn. 26. On the legal background of the Frēdōn saga see Macuch 2020a.
236 On the divergent narratives regarding Ardaxšēr's genealogy see Macuch 2014a.
237 REA 1.2; 2.1; Dd 55.7 (Appendix I, pp. 648–649).

offspring, the different terminology and the details in the Law-book seem to indicate that they were originally separate strategies of preserving a lineage and that the institution of *ayōgēn(īh)* was older than *stū̮rīh*.

This second (or extended) method of securing the continuity of a lineage, denoted by the technical term *stū̮rīh*, became another characteristic institution of Sasanian family law, which I have rendered (without attempting a precise translation) by 'substitute succession', 'subsidiary succession' or 'succession by proxy (*stū̮r*)'. The etymology and exact meaning of the expression has been discussed controversially in the past with divergent results, but its technical use in the context of family law is described in a large number of cases and can be reconstructed relatively well.[238] The institution could have possibly developed as an extension

238 The term is always written ⟨stwl⟩, the abstract form ⟨stwlyh⟩ which can be read with either a long vowel as *stūr(īh)/stōr(īh)* or a short one: *stur(īh)/stor(īh)*. In the New Persian *Riwāyats* it is always written defectively ⟨str⟩ in the Arabic script which would point to a short vowel (*stor/star/ster*). Dhabhar (1932, p. 195) in his edition of these texts transcribes *satar* in the chapter on different kinds of marriages, without attempting a translation ('*satar*-wife'). West (1882, p. 188), on the other hand, in his (antiquated) edition of Dd does not suggest a reading, but renders the abstract form by 'adopted-sonship', a (wrong) translation which is taken up by most later Parsi scholars. Bartholomae (1918–1923, III, p. 48; IV, p. 51; V, pp. 9, 18), reading *stūr* and *stūrīh*, has 'Verwalter' (curator, administrator) and 'Cura, Pflege, Verwaltung' (trusteeship, administration) respectively, which is in turn adapted by de Menasce (1964a, p. 57): 'administrateur, tuteur'. Perikhanian (1970, pp. 353–357) prefers to adapt the technical term without attempting a translation, but describes the institution as that of 'subsidiary succession' and suggests that there is a 'correlation *stūrīh* : *čakarīh* as that of "class word" : "special designation"', rendering the latter by 'servant' or 'service' (NP *čākar*, Osset. *cayar* 'slave'): 'The widow who entered a levirate marriage as *stūr* of her late husband was considered by the ancients to be "in the service" of the latter's succession' (*ibid.*, p. 357). She mentions the Armenian loan-word *struk* 'slave' and its derivatives: *strkutʿiwn* 'slavery, servitude', *strkanam* 'become enslaved', and suggests (*ibid.*, fn. 20) that Old Iranian personal names containing the (obscure) element *stura-* could be elucidated by 'a comparison with MIr. *stū̮r* "attendant, servant"' (*e.g.*, *Baēšatastura-* 'Healer's attendant', 'one who is in the service of the H.'), and 'other possible shades of meaning of Iran. *stū̮ra-* (base *stā*): "one who is standing by; supporter, helper, protector"'. Klingenschmitt (1971, pp. 136–142) assumes that the Pahlavi technical term is a loan-word from Av. **stūiriia-*, an *-iia-* derivative from an indeterminable base, attested only as acc. sg. *stūirīm* in a single Avestan phrase in RAF, *Pursišn* 75.4: *nōit̰ vaŋhō ahmāt̰ š́iiaoϑnəm vərəziieiti … frāiiō.humatahe frāiiō.hūxtahe frāiiō.huuarəštahe* ***stūirīm*** *upascinkaiiōit* (according to ms. G, or: *upasca. kaiiōit*, according to ms. TD 2) (*ibid.*, p. 136) '(Wer als Adoptivsohn von der Adoption zurücktritt,) tut keine bessere Handlung, als wenn er das ***stūiriia-*** eines *aṣ̌a*haften Mannes, dessen Gutgedachtes überwiegt, dessen Gutgesprochenes überwiegt, dessen Gutgetanes überwiegt, zerstörte.' (*ibid.*, p. 142) ([Who as an adopted son withdraws from adoption] does not perform a better act than as if he would destroy the *stūiriia-* of a righteous man, whose good thoughts prevail, whose good speech prevails, whose good deeds prevail). He compares Av. **stūiriia-* with OIr. *sthūrá-*, *sthūlá-* 'thick, large, solid, firm, strong', but questions a possible connection due to the discrepancy of meaning: '**stūra-* im Sinne von „potent, zeugungsfähig?"' (*ibid.*, p. 138) (**stūra-* in the sense of 'potent, fertile, procreative?'), and OIr. *sthū̮ri-* 'einspännig, mit einem Zugtier bespannt

of *ayōgēn* practice due to several reasons. First of all, given the significance of noble descent in the Sasanian period, other methods of preserving the lineage had to be found if there was no suitable female who could build a link between a man and his legal successor. Moreover, the head of a household could have preferred to appoint another person of his choice as 'proxy' in his last will (in order to spare the females of the lineage or on other grounds). Finally, in absence of an appropriate female or an appointed proxy, legal authorities could have detected the possibility of taking influence and controlling the inter-generational transfer of property by choosing a *stŭ̄r* among those deemed 'most worthy' (*sazāgtar*).

The *stŭ̄r* is explicitly designated in late Pahlavi literature as a *guharīg* 'proxy, substitute' for a Zoroastrian (*weh-dēn*) noble man (*āzād*) who is a subject of the King of Kings (*šāhān šāh bandag*) and dies without a male heir, leaving a property worth at least 60 'profit-earning' (*barōmand*) stater (*stēr*).[239] According to the Law-book the two main conditions entitling a man to the establishment of a *stŭ̄rīh* in the Sasanian period were, first, adherence to the Zoroastrian religion as a citizen of Ērānšahr, and, second, the existence of property consisting of a minimum sum (of 60 'profit-earning' stater)[240] set aside specifically for the

(vom Wagen)' (*ibid.*, p. 139) [harnessed with one draft animal; one-animal (carriage)], which is also used in the figurative sense of 'mit keinem Genossen versehen' [having no companion] in the sense of 'zu einem einspännigen Haushalt oder zu einer einspännigen Person gehörig, zu einem Haushalt ohne Nachkommenschaft gehörig' (*ibid.*, p. 139) [belonging to a household or person of one; belonging to a household without offspring]. Buyaner 2014 refutes the latter explanation and offers another solution to the etymological problem. He questions Klingenschmitt's reconstruction of the *hapax legomenon* (acc. sg.) *stūirīm* as an *-iia-* derivative (**stūiriia-*) and suggests an affiliation with the group of words designating relatives of the second degree in **-u̯i̯a-*, proposing a different derivation: **stṛ-/star-*: **stūiriia-* < OIr. **stṛu̯i̯a-* (*ibid.*, p. 701). The common etymon of the Avestan word as well as of Pahlavi *stur* (to be read in this case with a short vowel) and NP *s(a)tar* would be **stṛ-/star-*, which he renders as 'der junge bzw. zugeordnete Hausgenosse' (*ibid.*, p. 703) [the young or allocated house companion]. Buyaner compares the word with the Slavic terms for adopted family members, reconstructing an Old Slavic **steru̯* and tracing the origin of both expressions to a common IE **ster-* 'der Junge' (young man), the corresponding masculine form to feminine **stēr-ih₂* ‚die Junge' (young woman; OInd. *strī́* 'woman', Av. *strī* 'woman, young woman', Greek στειρα 'the infertile, barren woman, or: who has not yet given birth') (*ibid.*, p. 705; an overview of the development of these terms in Old Indian, Iranian and Slavic is on p. 706). The term also occurs in the Bactrian documents, translated by Sims-Williams (2000, p. 174) as 'servant, vassal': 'αβηστορογοπαδδιστο adj. "without the obligations of a vassal" < αβη- + ²στορογο (<*sturaka-?) "servant, vassal", Arm. *strowk* "slave, vassal"' (with reference to Perikhanian 1970, pp. 353–357).

239 These conditions are repeatedly mentioned in various scattered passages of different works, but summarized best in the overview Dd 55.2, see Appendix I, pp. 647–648.

240 The Sasanian Law-book has a number in this context which I have previously read as 80 (*stēr*/stater), whereas other Pahlavi sources all have 60. However, as Weber 2008b, p. XXIV, has been able to show, a small hook before an amount of money is an abbreviation for *stēr*/stater, hence the number should in fact be read S[tater] 60 (instead of 80, which looks identical).

purpose of maintaining the person installed as *stūr* and his or her progeny until the children came of age or for a certain limited period (ten years are often mentioned).[241] Three types of 'proxies' or 'substitute successors' are differentiated in the Pahlavi sources, which seem to reflect the development described above:

1. 'Natural proxy' (*stūr ī būdag*). This term is used exclusively of the *ayōgēn*-women, that is, the *pādixšāy*-wife of the deceased *paterfamilias*, his unmarried daughter or sister, who are obliged to put their reproductive faculties as 'intermediary' and 'substitute successors' in the service of the descent group to which they belong legally: their natal lineage, in the case of the daughter or sister; the lineage of the husband, in the case of the *pādixšāy*-wife. To underline this double function the compound *ayōgēn-stūr* designates these women in late Pahlavi texts, which could, however, be a late invention bringing both terms together, since it is not attested in this form in the Sasanian material.[242] If several women were available, the 'most suitable' or 'more fitting' (*sazāgtar*) was engaged, but divergent opinions are transmitted in this respect. According to the Law-book the most appropriate are: (a) the oldest daughter;[243] (b) (in contradiction to the latter ruling) the youngest daughter;[244] (c) the daughter who marries last;[245] (d) the daughter from an exogamous union (*bayǎspān*);[246] (e) the oldest sister.[247]
2. 'Appointed proxy' (*stūr ī kardag*). A man could appoint another person in his testament to act as his substitute successor, hereby releasing the women in the family from the duty of continuing his line. This person could be both male or female, an adopted son (*pus ī padīriftag*; who could also be a natural *čagar*-child of the *paterfamilias*), another relative belonging to the lineage of the *paterfamilias*, or any other fellow-citizen according to the stipulation of the deceased. If a male was appointed as 'proxy', he became at the same time the 'natural guardian' (*dūdagsālār ī būdag*) of the family, in which he was engaged as *stūr*.[248]
3. 'Nominated proxy' (*stūr ī gumārdag*). If the *paterfamilias* fulfilled the conditions mentioned above, leaving an estate of a minimum value of 60 'profit-earning' staters, but had neither a *pādixšāy*-wife, nor daughter or sister, nor a shareholding brother (*brād ī hambāy*) and did not appoint another person as 'proxy' in his will, then a *stūrīh* had to be established

241 Scattered in various passages—all references should be taken into consideration, see index under *stūr(īh)* in Macuch 1993, pp. 731–732.
242 Dd 55.7; see Appendix I, pp. 648–649.
243 MHD 41.10–13; 41.15 (Macuch 1993, pp. 300, 316).
244 MHD 46.15–47.2 (*ibid.*, pp. 306, 322).
245 MHD 41.10–13 (*ibid.*, pp. 300, 316).
246 MHD 41.9–10 (*ibid.*, pp. 300, 316).
247 MHD 41.10–13 (*ibid.*, pp. 300, 316).
248 MHD 26.10–12 (*ibid.*, pp. 194, 201). On guardianship see below pp. 177–183.

by official authorities. In the Sasanian period this seems to have been an important responsibility in cases involving larger properties or esteemed families. Judges in civil service (*dādwarān*) are obliged to nominate a 'proxy' and a congregation of *mowbeds* following instructions of the King himself is mentioned, suggesting that the institution was both socially and politically significant.[249] In the post-Sasanian material, the task of appointing a 'proxy' is collectively attributed to 'religious authorities' (*padān ī dēn*).[250] These officials were, however, not completely free in making their choice, but followed a specifically established sequence, usually giving priority to the women of a family: for example, the daughter of the brother counted as 'more suitable, fitting' (*sazāgtar*) than the son of the brother.[251] Given the importance attached to the continuity of a lineage, the question of engaging the 'most suitable' person as *stūr*, seems to have caused numerous controversies, which are discussed in several cases in the Law-book with divergent solutions.[252] The suitability of a *stūr* is also questioned in an original document of the eighth century, Tab. 28, revealing how important this institution remained even after the Muslim conquest of Iran (see Appendix XIV, pp. 731–734).

Apart from the first type (*stūr ī būdag*), exclusively referring to women, both males and females from inside and outside the family could be installed as *stūr* with the difference that a male could serve as 'proxy' for several other men, whereas a woman—in perfect consistency with the patrilineal principle of descent—could only be engaged in one family at a time. A female could become 'proxy' even if she was underage and also if she was already married, but did not act as *stūr* for another person (in the latter case her marriage could only continue as a *čagar*-marriage).[253] The *stūrīh* could, however, be limited in time (10 years are often mentioned),[254] which would open additional options for engaging fertile women for this task. After fulfilling the first obligation as 'proxy' (in a time-limited *čagar*-marriage), a female could serve as *stūr* for another man. These two possibilities of utilizing women seem to be meant by two technical terms, which are not explained, but refer explicitly to females: *tan-stūr* 'physical proxy', and *zīndag-stūr* 'proxy for life'.[255] The former seems to designate a woman who acts as *stūr* only for a certain limited period, whose 'body' (*tan*), as it were, is used to procreate a male successor within a restricted period, whereas

249 MHD 43.14–16; 49.15–17 (Macuch 1993, pp. 302, 319 and 309, 325 respectively); MHDA 14.9–11; 26.11–16 (Macuch 1981, pp. 36, 113 and 50, 189 respectively). On the political relevance of the institution see also Macuch 1995.

250 Dd 57.5; see Appendix I, pp. 650–651.

251 Dd 55.6 (Appendix I, pp. 647, 649); see also Macuch 1995, pp. 154–157, with further references.

252 See specifically chapters 19, 33 and 36 on *stūrīh* (MHD 41.1–53.3; 81.1–82.17; 87.1–88.17).

253 One of these cases is discussed in REA *Pursišn* 1.

254 See *e.g.*, MHD 50.1–3; 96.8–10 (Macuch 1993, pp. 309, 326 and 606, 609 respectively).

255 MHD 46.14–15; 48.10–11 (*ibid.*, pp. 306, 322 and 308, 324 respectively).

the latter expression most likely refers to a woman, who is installed as 'proxy' as long as she lives, 'for life' (*zīndag*). These two options could have been an important ingredient of family law, if we assume that the number of aristocratic females among the noble dynasties who were deemed as fitting candidates for procreating offspring was rather limited. A woman who was a slave (*bandag*), a servant (*paristār*), a non-Iranian (*an-ēr*), an adherent of another religion (*ag-dēn*) or had committed a *margarzān*-offence ('worthy of death') was *not* suited to be *stūr*.[256] The conditions listed for the man are partly similar: to be eligible for the task he must be Zoroastrian (*hu-dēn*), sane (*ōšyārag*), a subject of the King of Kings (*šāhān šāh bandag*), potent (*frazandēmēdag*) besides being free of any sin or offence of the *margarzān* type.[257]

As a rule a man's *čagar*-children could not be engaged for him as 'proxy', since they belonged legally to their *pādixšāy*-father and counted as the latter's offspring, but exceptions were possible and even seem to have been frequent.[258] If a man had several *čagar*-children, but no *pādixšāy*-offspring, he could adopt one or several of his sons and arrange for them in his will to be engaged as *stūr* (of the *kardag* type). One of his *čagar*-daughters could even serve as his 'intermediary successor' after being adopted. Several cases involving the problem of the legal affiliation of the children are discussed in the Law-book, for example, the question, whether *all* the children (including daughters) should count as the heirs of their legal (*pādixšāy*-)father or only the sons, or whether a *čagar*-father was allowed to adopt his natural *čagar*-children into the *pādixšāy* status.[259] Despite all theoretical difficulties (and practical controversies), these children seem to have been indeed engaged as 'proxies' for their natural fathers after adoption and both the *čagar*-son and the *čagar*-daughter are explicitly mentioned in this context.[260] A late Pahlavi text even specifies the sequence of suitable *čagar*-children with the oldest son in the first place, followed by the second oldest son. As to the daughters, if there are several, one of them becomes *ayōgēn-stūr* of the natural father, but if there is only one daughter, she can only become *stūr* if her mother is still alive.[261] The latter condition is particularly interesting: the mother, who is referred to here, is actually the person serving as *stūr* for her (real or fictive) *pādixšāy*-husband, who is the legal father (*pater*) of all the children she generates in the *čagar*-marriage. If the issue consists of only one female, this daughter would have the duty to continue the lineage of her *pater* as 'intermediary successor' (*ayōgēn*) if the mother serving as *stūr* dies, and could not be

256 MHD 43.9–11 (*ibid*., pp. 302, 318); best summarized Dd 56.4 (see Appendix I, p. 650).
257 Dd 56.2 (see Appendix I, pp. 649–650).
258 MHDA 14.9–14 (forbidding to nominate *čagar*-children as 'proxies' or guardians; Macuch 1981, p. 143).
259 See *e.g.*, MHDA 40.11–14 (Macuch 1981, pp. 67, 224).
260 MHD 42.11–12 and 48.3–7 (Macuch 1993, pp. 301, 317 and 307, 323 respectively). See also REA 23.11.
261 REA 23.17–24.

engaged in this function for her *genitor*, the *čagar*-father. But if the mother is alive and still serves as 'proxy' in the described manner, then the daughter could act as *ayōgēn* for her natural father. In this context it is important to recall that a *stū̆rīh* could be established on a temporary basis, hence enabling the daughter to serve as 'intermediary successor' for both her *pater* and *genitor*, if necessary, in different phases of her life.

Besides being an important ingredient of Sasanian family law, *stū̆rīh* was also regarded as one of the most meritorious religious institutions, repeatedly mentioned in Zoroastrian texts of the post-Sasanian period. Mismanagement and abuse of 'substitute succession' was liable to punishment, refusal to carry out the tasks of a *stū̆r* after accepting the assignment counted as an offence 'worthy of death' (*margarzān*) after the timespan of a year[262] and 'destroying substitute succession' (*stū̆r-škenišnīh*; *stū̆rīh be škenēd*) is listed among the *margarzān* sins in late Pahlavi texts.[263]

In accordance with the purpose of this institution, the *stū̆r* never had access to the substance (*bun*) of the property set up specifically for generating offspring in 'substitute succession' (*pad stū̆rīh*; see Chapter III, pp. 213–219). Only the sons and daughters of the 'proxy' could inherit property from their legal father, but the *stū̆r* was entitled to maintenance and could use the income (*bar*) of this property for her (or his) expenses during the period of raising the children. The sum paid for the daily expenses of the 'proxy' (besides the remuneration of the legal guardian of the family, *dūdag-sālār*) is designated by the phrase *srēnag/sēnag masāy ud bāzā masāy*, lit. 'the size of a buttock/breast and size of a forefoot'.[264] This expression, derived from Av. *sraoni.masah-* 'the size of a buttock' and **bāzu.masah-* 'the size of a forefoot' (with *sēnag* 'breast', as a late variant of the original *srēnag* 'buttock'), denotes the daily ration of a mature, blameless man, which was originally paid in kind by meat rations from the front and hind parts of a slaughtered animal.[265] In this late phase of Zoroastrian law, the phrase should not to be taken literally, but rather as a technical term for the daily amount of sustenance due to persons acting as *stū̆r* or guardian (*sālār*, see below), which did not have to be paid specifically in

262 MHD 16.12–14; 82.12–14 (Macuch 1993, pp. 141, 144 and 531, 533 respectively).

263 PRDd 41.1 (Williams 1990, I, p. 157; II, p. 69; his translation of *stū̆r škenišnīh* as 'to break adoption' is wrong) and Dd 59.3 *stū̆rīh be škenēd* (West 1882, p. 193, is by now completely outdated; his rendering of *stū̆rīh* by 'adoption' is wrong); on this passage see Appendix I, pp. 652–653. On *stū̆r-škenišnīh* see also Chapter V, pp. 461–462.

264 See e. g., REA 18.10: *u-š pad uzōnag ī rōzgarīh (ī) im stū̆rīh rāyēnīdan sēnag masāy ud bāzā masāy wastaragīg wahāg čiyōn ān ī dūdag-sālārīh nibišt xwēšīhēd*. 'For the daily expenses of engaging herself/himself in "substitute succession" (*stū̆rīh*) (a daily ration) "the size of a buttock and the size of a forefoot" (and) the price of clothing—as it is written on family guardianship—become her/his (= the *stū̆r*'s) own.' See also REA 18.12; both de Menasce 1964a, p. 41, and Safa-Isfehani 1980, p. 134, have not understood the technical terms and have impossible translations.

265 On the provenance of this phrase see Chapter I, pp. 76–77 above.

meat rations. Late Pahlavi texts give the following equivalents in money: (1) a daily amount (*har rōzag šabān*) of three-fifths (*sē-panǰ ēk*) of one full drachm (*drahm-ē ī purr*);[266] (2) four staters every month, corresponding to sixteen full (*purr*) drachms.[267]

Substitute succession became one of the most significant institutions of family law in the Sasanian period and was widespread—as we have reason to assume—among the affluent nobility and the clergy. Not only families lacking offspring, but *every* head of a household with a certain amount of property at his disposal was legally obliged to establish at least one *stūrīh*, preferably two or more. Even if a man had several legitimate sons and daughters, he would nevertheless set apart a part of his property for this purpose in order not to risk remaining 'without name' (*abē-nām*) at his demise should none of these children reach maturity. He had the right to establish several *stūrīh*s and could install two (or more) proxies if he had the means to finance them.[268] According to the Law-book a man even had a right to a proxy if the portion of property in *stūrīh* did not suffice for the upkeep of the persons involved.[269] The importance attached to this institution is hardly surprising if we take into consideration that mortality rates among children were high, and a long list of dangers, including fatal illnesses, violent conflicts, war, death at childbirth, etc., could decimate a man's offspring, leaving him without a legitimate successor, who could continue the lineage and assume his place in the social hierarchy with all the social and religious rights and duties of a *kadag-xwadāy*. The best means of ensuring that a 'name-bearing child' (*frazand ī nām-burdār*) would always be there was provided in Sasanian law by the creation of *stūrīh*.[270]

266 According to REA 5.15: *mizd ī dūdag-sālārīh sēnag masāy ud bāzā masāy ud wastaragēn wahāg rāy har rōzag šabān-ē sē-panǰ ēk ī drahm-ē ī purr xwēšēd.* 'As remuneration for (exercising) family-guardianship "the size of a buttock and the size of a forefoot" and the price of clothing, three-fifths of a full drachm, become his own on a daily basis (*har rōzag šabān*).' REA 23.30: *andāzag ī ān sēnag masāy bāzā masāy pad rāh ī dūdag-sālārīh ān-iz ī stūrīh ī dēnīg har rōz ud šabān rāy sē-panǰ ēk ī drahm ī purr.* 'The amount of (remuneration) "the size of a buttock and the size of a forefoot" due to (exercising) family-guardianship and religious "substitute succession" (*stūrīh ī dēnīg*) (is) three-fifths of a full drachm on a daily basis (*har rōz šabān*).'

267 Dd 55.7 (see Appendix I, pp. 648–649).

268 See particularly MHD 50.6–7 and 50.7–12 (Macuch 1993, pp. 310, 326). On the political significance of the institution see Macuch 1995.

269 MHD 50.5–6 (Macuch 1993, pp. 310, 326).

270 The *stūrīh* shows certain similarities to the English trust and the *fideicommissum* of Roman law, but also significant divergences. As an essential ingredient in the overall network of Sasanian family law *stūrīh* is intricately interwoven with other specific elements of kinship and succession, hence defies—as one component within this complex framework—comparison with similar institutions of other legal systems (see below section 7 of this Chapter). This said, affinities may be detected to the Roman *fideicommissum*, a testamentary instruction to an heir or legatee that emerged originally in order to enable a testator to circumvent restrictions on legacies and to ignore certain fundamental principles of the ordinary law of succession. In its developed form the most important

5 Categorization of children

Due to these various legal institutions, which were all obviously created to perpetuate descent groups, kinship structure had become rather complex by the late Sasanian period. The head of an affluent family, who could afford separate households, would not only have one 'privileged' wife, but several ones in order to fulfil his Zoroastrian obligation of generating children and securing the lineage. The offspring from these *pādixšāy*-wives all counted as the legitimate sons and daughters (*dādestān-pus* 'son according to the law'; *dādestān-duxt* 'daughter according to the law') of the *kadag-xwadāy*, the relationship between the siblings and half-siblings being that of 'legitimate brother' (*dādestān-brād*) and 'legitimate sister' (*dādestān-xwāh*).[271] He would furthermore be obliged to act as *stūr̆* for other Zoroastrian men (from inside or outside his own lineage) and to enter one or several 'auxiliary' marriages in order to generate children for them in proxy. The offspring from these *čagar*-marriages counted as his natural issue (*frazand ī tanī[g]zād*[272]) but not as his legitimate children. He could, however, change their status by adopting one or several of these children, who could become either his direct successors or be engaged as 'substitute' or 'intermediary' successors. This could also have applied to children from a 'consensus' marriage, who are, however, not mentioned in this context. Hence the technical expressions for 'legitimate son/daughter' (*dādestān-pus/duxt*) did not simply designate a man's children from a *pādixšāy*-marriage, but every legitimate child, also those from an 'auxiliary' or 'consensus' marriage, who had been adopted by the *paterfamilias*. Similarly, the progeny born for a man after his demise in a *čagar*-marriage of his 'privileged' wife or of his daughter or sister as *ayōgēn* or of another person engaged as *stūr̆* counted automatically as his legitimate offspring. Other terms for the children generated in these two institutions of

use of the *fideicommissum* was to enable the transfer of property or a fixed part of it according to the wishes of the testator (either immediately or at some later time) from the first recipient to another legatee (the *fideicommissarius*), who could be male or female, a member of the family or outside the family, also a person not yet born. By immobilizing this property in a trust the testator could retain control of its transfer beyond the first recipient, even in perpetuity (see Nicholas 1962, pp. 267–270; Kaser 1986, pp. 342–346). Although the idea of tying up property in a trust to be transferred to a future heir or legatee is similar, the parallels practically end here. The Roman institution was not created to provide heirs, nor was it an integral part of a larger scheme to ensure the continuity of kinship groups, nor did it have religious significance, enabling exceptions (a *stūr̆īh* could also be established for a man whose property did not reach the required minimum amount) and particularly visible in fire foundations of the *stūr̆īh* category (see Chapter III, pp. 213–219). Moreover, an important tool for the conception of *stūr̆īh* was the possibility of 'owning' the fruits in perpetuity (*bar xwēšīh*), a concept foreign to Roman law, as will be seen in the next chapter.

271 See index in Macuch 1993, p. 698f., for references.

272 The term is attested in REA 8.3.

secondary succession (*stūrīh* and *ayōgēnīh*) are transmitted as *andar dūdag zād*[273] 'born in the family' and—with regard to the issue of the daughter as 'intermediary successor'—*duxt-dād*[274] 'born of the daughter', both underlining the idea that these descendants belonged legally to the lineage, even if they were not necessarily the natural issue of a *paterfamilias*.

Taking these variants into consideration, we may distinguish between four different, but partly overlapping, types of children in a family:[275]

1. The natural *and* legal offspring of a *kadag-xwadāy* from a 'privileged' (*pādixšāy-*)marriage: both *dādestān-pus/duxt* 'legitimate sons/daughters' and *frazand ī tanīgzād* 'natural children', who counted as his direct successors (*yōhē pasčaēta*) in the case of the sons, or as 'intermediaries' (*ayōgēn*), in the case of the daughters.
2. The legal offspring (*dādestān-pus/duxt*) generated for the *paterfamilias* in one of the institutions of secondary succession (*stūrīh*; *ayōgēnīh*) in an 'auxiliary' (*čagar*) marriage, also called *andar dūdag zād* 'born in the family' and *duxt-dād* 'born of the daughter', who counted as successors (*yōhē pasčaēta*) and heirs of the legal father.
3. The natural children (*frazand ī tanīgzād*) from an 'auxiliary' (*čagar*) marriage of the *paterfamilias* acting as *stūr* for another man, and those generated by him in 'consensus' (*xwasrāyēn/gādār*) marriage, who did *not* count as his legitimate progeny.
4. Adopted sons and daughters (*pus/duxt ī padīriftag*). Children of this category could also belong to the third group, since a man could under certain circumstances—when sufficient successors had been generated for the legal father—adopt his natural *čagar*-children (possibly also those from a 'consensus' marriage), hereby changing their status to that of his legitimate heirs. Another man's children from a 'privileged' (*pādixšāy*) marriage could also be adopted if the legal father agreed to the procedure. Instead of (or: besides) receiving direct succession rights, the adopted son could be installed as *stūr ī kardag* 'appointed proxy' (see p. 170) by his adoptive father and act as 'natural guardian' (*sālār ī būdag*) in his adoptive family for this period (see pp. 179–180). In this case the children of the adoptive son would receive full succession rights. This seems to be the background of a case in which a son from a 'privileged' marriage remains in his natural family, retaining existing

273 Macuch 1993, pp. 338–339 (no. 10).
274 Macuch 1993, pp. 330–331 (no. 2).
275 A similar division in Nestorian-Christian family law is probably based on Sasanian law, despite the fact that the former explicitly refutes Zoroastrian family law and secondary succession (at least theoretically, but not necessarily in practice, see Chapter VII, pp. 620–621). Īšōʿbōxt's categorization of children distinguishes between three groups: (1) *b-nāmusā* 'according to the law'; (2) *b-kyānā* 'according to nature' and (3) *b-qūbālā* 'through adoption'. Sachau 1914, pp. 114–115, IV, § 1.

succession rights, but is at the same time the adoptive son in another one.[276] Unfortunately the exact consequences are not transmitted, but engaging the adopted son as 'proxy' (or an adopted daughter as 'intermediary successor') would correspond well with the purpose of these institutions (see particularly p. 172). It is not too far-fetched to assume that 'sharing' one's legitimate son with another Zoroastrian 'in need' of a successor was a similarly virtuous deed as—in the attested case of—giving one's 'privileged' wife to a fellow-Zoroastrian in an interim marriage in order to support him in fulfilling his religious duty, enabling him to generate children (see pp. 159–161).

6 Guardianship (*sālārīh*)

One of the major duties of the head of a household was to act as guardian (*sālār*)[277] over the dependant members of the family, who lacked full legal capacity, that is, all women, including wives, unmarried daughters, sisters and aunts, minors of both sexes, disabled and aged persons, as well as over all forms of family property, notably real estate, slaves, animals, sacred fires and religious endowments belonging to the lineage.[278] It was the guardian's task to maintain all persons under his guardianship with the daily necessities, food, clothing and shelter, to take good care of the domestic animals, to feed them regularly and protect them from harm (failing in this respect counted as an offence of the *adwadād* type, see Chapters I, pp. 75–76, and V, pp. 463–468; on animal rights see Chapter I, B, pp. 90–92).[279] Another major function was to administer the property and to manage the affairs of the family, which he represented in the public sphere, dealing with legal transactions, lawsuits and claims. The guardian furthermore assumed important religious duties for the lineage, arranging for the performance

276 MHD 70.12–16 (Macuch 1993, pp. 465, 469). Unfortunately the case is not very clearly presented (the question being here another one, namely, which one of an adopted son's ascendants would act as his 'proxy' on the son's demise, if he belongs to two families: the father from the original family or the adoptive father?). Although it is not mentioned, it seems logical that the son would have received additional succession rights in his adoptive family, which could have been, however, restricted to acting as appointed 'substitute successor/proxy' (*stūr ī kardag*) for the adoptive father and taking over 'guardianship' (*sālārīh*) of the family for this period. Roman law also knew the difference between *adoptio plena* (full adoption) and *adoptio minus plena* (restricted adoption), which can however only superficially be compared to the Sasanian institution, since the unique options of the *stūrīh* institution are of course missing in the Roman system (despite similarities to the *fideicommissum*, see above, fn. 270). For an overview on Roman adoption with further references see Nicholas 1962, pp. 77–79, and du Plessis/Borkowski 2010, pp. 132–135.

277 On *sālār* 'princeps' (and *sālārīh* 'principatus') designating in family law the 'guardian', a person who has *potestas* (authority) see Bartholomae 1910, p. 8.

278 On the different forms of property see Chapter III, pp. 202–219.

279 On the treatment of animals in Zoroastrian law see Macuch 2003a.

of the required rituals for the souls of deceased family members (*ruwān yazišn*)[280] and keeping the cult of the souls of the ancestors (*nāmagānīh*).[281] At the demise of the *paterfamilias* his legal successor, usually the oldest son of legal age—if there was no other disposition in the father's will—assumed guardianship over the dependant family members and over the various assets of the household in the four basic categories of property (in ownership, in possession, in *stūrīh* and 'for the soul', see Chapter III, pp. 202–220). These two main areas of guardianship, over family members and property, could in turn be divided under specific circumstances into two separate categories, called *dūdag-sālārīh* 'family guardianship' and *xwāstag-sālārīh* 'guardianship of property', for example, when guardianship of a fire or pious endowment was explicitly bestowed on a female, who could never be family guardian (*dūdag-sālār*) being subject to lifelong guardianship herself, but could be engaged as *xwāstag-sālār* for a specific sacred fire or endowment (see below).

The replacement of a *paterfamilias* as guardian of the family and its property was regulated exactly. This was obligatory if the head of a household was absent for a longer period of time or passed away. A guardian had to be installed in the following cases: (1) when there were women, underage children and disabled persons in the family; (2) when a sacred fire was in the care of the family; (3) when another kind of pious endowment 'for the soul' (*pad ruwān*) had been founded by the *kadag-xwadāy* himself or another member of the family under his guardianship; (4) when a person (a woman or an underage son) was installed as 'proxy' (*stūr*), who could not be his/her own guardian.[282] As a rule, guardianship could only be practised by a mentally sound (*ōšyār*) male of full legal age (at least 15 years old),[283] but there is a noteworthy exception—at least according to the opinion of one group of jurisconsults—in the case of sacred fires and pious endowments, which could also be placed under the guardianship of a woman (only as *xwāstag-sālār* 'guardian of property'), if she was the founder herself or was designated as custodian by the founder.[284] Moreover, separating guardianship of the property (*xwāstag-sālārīh*) from family guardianship (*dūdag-sālārīh*) seems to have been a convenient device to permit individuals, who were themselves usually under guardianship (particularly underage children and women), to settle debts and liabilities of the *kadag-xwadāy* after his demise, even before a new male guardian was engaged (see also below).[285]

280 For references see Macuch 1993, p. 729.

281 On *nāmagānīh* see Klingenschmitt 1971, pp. 145–150.

282 The establishment of guardianship is discussed extensively in the Law-book, see references Macuch 1993, pp. 702 and 730. General descriptions of the institution are to be found in REA 5.1–30 and Dd 55.4–8 (see below Appendix I, pp. 647–649). On guardianship over women and minors who are *stūr* in a family see MHD 49.4–8 (Macuch 1993, pp. 308–309, 325).

283 REA 5.4.

284 MHD 14.1–2; 25.8–11; 27.12–14; 36.6–12; Hēr. 5.4. All passages are discussed in Macuch 2009c, pp. 269–271.

Besides these two possible forms of guardianship (*dūdag-sālārīh* and *xwāstag-sālārīh*), three different types of guardians are distinguished in the legal material according to the manner in which they are chosen and the sequence of their suitability (*sazāgīh*). If the *paterfamilias* had no legitimate son of full legal age, who would immediately assume responsibility for the family at his demise, another close male relative (*e. g.*, a share-holding brother) was obliged to take over as 'natural guardian'. The *paterfamilias* also had the option of appointing a specific person or several persons as guardian(s) in his will, sometimes only for a limited period until one of his minor legal sons came of age and immediately assumed guardianship. In the absence of both types, an appropriate man had to be nominated for the task by judicial authorities. Interestingly, the terms employed in this context correspond exactly to the three categories of *stŭrīh* described above (pp. 170–171). Could this symmetry indicate that the two institutions were conceived as parallel constructs or was one theoretical model based on the other? Guardianship may have been the more ancient institution, if we assume that *stŭrīh* developed later as an extension of *ayōgēnīh* and was moulded on the pattern of *sālārīh*. Unfortunately the question is not addressed and there are no clues that could help us find a solution, but the correspondence is striking and probably not coincidental.

The similarity of these categories to those of the comparable institution of *tutela* in Roman law is another aspect that should be mentioned, but the congruities are more likely due to parallel developments, especially if we take the divergences between the two systems into account. In Sasanian law one and the same term, *sālārīh* 'guardianship', is used for the institutions differentiated in Roman law as *potestas* (or *patria potestas*, the authority of the *paterfamilias* over his descendants), *manus* (the subordinate marital relation of a wife 'in the hands', *i. e.*, in the legal control, of the husband), *tutela* (guardianship over children and women not *in potestate*) and *cura* (curatorship, guardianship outside the main forms of *tutela*). Moreover, Sasanian law does not differentiate between guardianship over minors (*tutela impuberum*) and women (*tutela mulierum*).

The three types of guardians in Sasanian law, who could assume responsibility after the demise of the *paterfamilias*, are transmitted as:

1. 'Natural guardian' (*sālār ī būdag*; comparable to *tutor legitimus*). According to the Law-book these are: (a) the *padixšāy* son of the *paterfamilias*; (b) his adopted son (*pus ī padīriftag*); (c) the man, who is installed as 'appointed proxy' (*stŭr ī kardag*) of the *paterfamilias*; (d) a brother of the latter, who is share-holder (*brād ī hambāy*).[286] Although the adopted son is also named in this context, controversial opinions are transmitted on the matter and he was obviously not accepted by all legal schools or jurisconsults (on the legal

285 MHD 31.8–15 (Macuch 1993, pp. 222–223, 226–227).
286 MHD 26.10–11 (Macuch 1993, pp. 194, 201).

implications of adoption see pp. 176–177 above).[287] By combining the information on 'substitute succession' (*stūrīh*) and guardianship, we may however infer that the adoptive son, who was appointed as 'proxy' (*stūr ī kardag*) by the head of a household, would at the same time be engaged as guardian after reaching maturity (see p. 170 above; this could also be the reason why both the adoptive son and *stūr ī kardag* are mentioned in the sequence of suitable candidates for 'natural' guardianship just quoted). In later Pahlavi texts the requirements are simplified, only denoting the son or the natural son (*pus ī tanīgzād*) who has reached maturity with fifteen years.[288]

2. 'Appointed guardian' (*sālār ī kardag*; comparable to *tutor testamentarius*). This person is usually a male (with the sole exception of guardianship over a sacred fire or a pious foundation, for which also a female could be engaged according to one legal school, see above), who is appointed by the head of the household himself either in his will or by a separate statement.[289] The *paterfamilias* was also free to appoint two guardians.[290]
3. 'Nominated guardian' (*sālār ī gumārdag*; comparable to *tutor dativus*). If no person of the two first categories was available, judicial authorities chose the man 'most suited' (*sazāgtar*) to carry the responsibility of guardianship, generally the 'nearest relative' (*nazdīk paywandtar*) of the *kadag-xwadāy*.[291] An—unfortunately imprecise—late Pahlavi text gives the following sequence of the most suitable men: (a) the natural father (of the *paterfamilias* if he was born in an 'auxiliary' marriage; *pid ī čagar*); (b) his oldest brother; (c) his (*čagar?*) son;[292] (d) other near relatives (*abārīg paywand ī nazdīktar*). Choosing an appropriate guardian to replace the *kadag-xwadāy* seems to have been—besides appointing a *stūr*—one of the significant tasks of high-ranking judicial officials in the Sasanian period. According to the Law-book the *mowbed*, who was not only a religious, but also a legal authority with a higher position in the judicial hierarchy than the officials called *dādwar ī keh* 'minor judge' and *dādwar ī meh* 'major judge', was responsible for selecting the guardian; in another passage a congregation of *mowbed*s, following orders of the sovereign, dealt with the

287 MHD 26.12; 69.9–10 (*ibid.*, pp. 194, 201 and 463, 467 respectively).
288 REA 5.5; Dd 57.5 (see Appendix I, pp. 650–651).
289 MHD 25.11, 13f.; 27.4f.; 28.2 (Macuch 1993, pp. 193, 200 and 195, 202, and 196, 203 respectively). For an overview see REA 5.3 and Dd 57.5 (Appendix I, pp. 650–651).
290 MHD 28.12–13 (Macuch 1993, pp. 197, 204).
291 REA 5.8, 9; 6.2.
292 Dd 55.6 (Appendix I, pp. 647, 649). Both mss. have ⟨BRTH̱⟩ *duxt* 'daughter' here instead of ⟨BRH̱⟩ *pus* 'son', which is definitely a mistake due to the similar spelling of the two words. The whole passage seems to be corrupt or at least imprecise, since the daughter could not be appointed as guardian (with the sole exception mentioned above), whereas the legal son of a *paterfamilias* would count as 'natural guardian' and need not be nominated by judicial authorities; but maybe the *čagar*-son is meant (who could be chosen as guardian, if he had been adopted by the deceased *paterfamilias*).

matter.[293] Obviously even the king himself could be involved in appointing guardians (and 'proxies'), enabling the State to take direct influence on the management of the vast estates belonging to the property of affluent lineages. The procedure evidently lost its political and social significance in the post-Sasanian period, but was still regulated precisely. Although religious instances (*padān ī dēn*)[294] are still the preferred authorities for selecting an appropriate guardian, a distinguished Zoroastrian layman of good repute could also assume this task, if a priest was not available. A candidate for guardianship could be proposed by a family member or could apply himself for appointment to one of the authorities in charge. A sequence of persons to whom one could apply for nomination in the post-Sasanian period is transmitted in descending order: (a) religious authorities: *rad*, *mowbed* and *dastwar*;[295] (b) the warden of a Wahrām fire (*ātaxš-madār*);[296] (c) the diligent student of a Mazdean priest (*mard ī āsrōn hāwišt*);[297] (d) a respected Mazdean layman (*mard ī weh-dēn*).[298] The nomination was recorded in a document (*nāmag*) obliging the guardian to manage the affairs of the household 'in the best interests of the family' (*pad dūdag sūdōmandīhātar*) following the 'highest values (or laws) of the Good Religion' (*weh-dēn dādestānīhātar*).[299]

Besides providing maintenance for the dependent members of the family, the major function of the legal guardian was to protect the proprietary interests of his wards by managing family property to his best ability, making investments and appropriate purchases, taking out loans, paying and collecting debts, and representing the family in litigation.[300] Despite his wide powers of management, restrictions were placed on all transactions, which could cause damage to the family or to its property. This seems to be the background for including the mistress of the house (*kadag-bānūg*) in legal proceedings although she would normally be represented by her husband or legal guardian in court. In a large

293 MHDA 14.10–12; 26.11–16 (Macuch 1981, pp. 36, 143 and 50, 189 respectively). On the significance of this procedure see also Macuch 1995.
294 Dd 57.5 (see Appendix I, pp. 650–651).
295 REA 5.10 (Safa-Isfehani's edition of 1980, here pp. 30–32, is totally unreliable).
296 REA 5.11; *ātaxš-madār*, lit. 'fire-comer' (a compound with the agent noun *madār* from *madan* 'to come'), is probably a technical term designating some kind of warden of a Wahrām fire, mentioned in the same passage, that is, a person whose task it was to take daily care of a sacred fire of the highest category, supplying it with fuel and keeping it 'ever-burning' (*hamēšag-sōz*). I know of no other attestation of the word. Both translations of this passage by de Menasce 1964a, p. 38, and Safa-Isfehani 1980, p. 32, are impossible.
297 REA 5.12.
298 REA 5.13.
299 REA 5.14.
300 These various obligations are described in numerous passages of the Law-book, *e.g.*, MHD 14.7–12; 15.12–14; 16.14–17; 67.3–13; 75.12–14 (Macuch 1993, pp. 131f., 143, 144, 451, 504 respectively).

number of cases the *kadag-bānūg* as a widow plays a prominent role in litigation, notably in disputes over debts and liabilities of the family, and takes legal action or is sued together with the guardian, effecting the outcome of the trial (interestingly, one of these cases mentioning the name of a woman as one of the claimants, possibly a *kadag-bānūg*, is documented in the original court records from Tabarestān).[301] Another restriction recorded in the legal material regards the incapacity of the guardian (including the husband) to refuse gifts or donations to the children or women under his wardship: his rejection is null and void, the transaction takes place nonetheless (in the case of the minor after he or she has reached maturity).[302] The guardian was furthermore expected to protect his wards and prevent violent acts against them, being subject to a fine (*tāwān*) if a third party wounded or injured a woman or a slave under his guardianship with his knowledge, under his 'surveillance and observation' (*pad dīd ud wēnišn*).[303] He was obliged to continue to provide maintenance for women under his guardianship and slaves under his control, if they were suspected of having committed an offence (*pad wināh warōmand*), and to pay the costs for arranging an ordeal (*pad passāxtan*) by which their innocence or guilt could be revealed.[304]

The guardian was entitled to daily sustenance in exchange for his services to the family if he had received no share in the inheritance of the *paterfamilias*. The legitimate, mature son, who became immediately guardian of the *būdag* type after the demise of the *paterfamilias*, would receive no further remuneration, but any other legal guardian without succession rights, particularly of the nominated type (*sālār ī gumārdag*), was entitled to daily provisions from the income of family property. As elucidated above, the technical phrase *srēnag/sēnag masāy ud bāzā masāy*, lit. 'the size of a buttock and size of a forefoot' denoted the daily ration of a mature man, referring originally to meat rations, which were taken as a measure for calculating the quotidian nutriment of a mature man (Av. *sraoni.masah-* 'the size of a buttock'; **bāzu.masah-* 'the size of a forefoot'), consisting of two pieces (from the front and hind parts) of a slaughtered animal.[305]

The obligations of a legal guardian ended automatically, when a legitimate son of the deceased *paterfamilias* reached maturity and took over the affairs of the family as 'natural guardian' (*sālār ī būdag*).[306] A guardian could be removed from

301 For example MHD 13.6–13; 15.3–7; 16.1–2, 5–10 (Macuch 1993, pp. 130f., 142, 143f. respectively). On the Tabarestān court records see Macuch 2016a (here: p. 159).

302 MHD 19.7–10 (Macuch 1993, pp. 154, 160).

303 MHD 1.4–6 (*ibid.*, pp. 22, 24).

304 MHD 33.11–13 (*ibid.*, pp. 241, 244).

305 MHD 27.2–4 (*ibid.*, pp. 195, 202); also REA 5.15: *sālār ī gumārdag sēnag/srēnag masāy bāzā masāy ōh bawēd* 'the nominated guardian receives (a daily ration corresponding to) "the size of a forefoot and the size of a buttock".' (Unreliable translations by de Menasce 1964a, p. 38, and Safa-Isfehani 1980, p. 34). On the monetary equivalent of the phrase see pp. 173–174 above; on its provenance also Chapter I, pp. 76–77.

306 MHDA 32.9–13 (Macuch 1981, pp. 58, 215); REA 5.18: *ka-š pus ō purnāyīh mad im dūdag-sālār az dūdag-sālārīh guharīg ud dūdag-sālār ān pus bawēd* 'When the son has

office before his term came to an end, if he proved to be untrustworthy (due to maladministration, dishonesty or negligence) or caused a damage worth at least three stater (according to a late Pahlavi text), but could be installed officially again, if he paid for the loss within the timespan of a year.[307] The son as 'natural guardian' did not lose guardianship in this case, but if he did not replace the loss—following the notion that a person in this position should act according to the best interests of his wards—another man was nominated as guardian for the underage children.[308]

7 Family law: a refined network of institutions

The most striking feature of Sasanian family law is the consistency of the system, in which every single trait complements the other elements, fitting perfectly into an overall pattern. This is astonishing if we infer that these institutions evolved gradually across a long period of time, but is maybe less surprising if we attempt to understand their common purpose. In fact, none of the institutions described above can be comprehended on its own without reconstructing the general framework, in which every single component fulfils an important function as a significant part of a larger coherent structure. The interdependent parts of this complex mosaic (of which only several random pieces have survived in the legal material) can be best understood by systematizing the information on the different forms of matrimony described above. These can be divided into three major, interconnected sections:

Table 12. Overview: matrimonial options

A: Marriage types	B: Permitted alliances	C: Duration of matrimony
1. 'privileged' (*pādixšāy*) 2. 'auxiliary' (*čagar*) 3. 'consensus' (*xwasrāyēn/gādār*)	1. endogamous, including the nuclear family (*xwēdōdah*) 2. exogamous (*bayăspān*)	1. permanent (*ān ī hamēīg*) 2. temporary (*nē ān ī hamēīg*)

Every one of the three forms of matrimony listed in column A could be combined with one of the two options listed in columns B and C: a 'privileged' marriage could be concluded within the lineage, including the closest members of the elementary family, or outside the lineage, either permanently or temporarily. The same options were open for conjugal unions of the 'consensus' and 'auxiliary' type. In the latter case the *čagar*-wife could be married to a man outside the descent group (permanently or temporarily), if no appropriate man

reached maturity the family guardian is replaced and that son becomes family guardian' (see also *ibid.*, p. 228).

307 MHD 28.17–29.3 (Macuch 1993, pp. 197–198, 204–205); REA 5.27–29.

308 MHD 28.15–17 (Macuch 1993, pp. 197, 204).

was available inside the group, although she herself and her children always remained legally in the lineage of the deceased *pādixšāy*-husband (as elucidated above, *čagar*-marriage cannot be designated as a 'levirate' type of matrimony, since the husband was not necessarily the brother—or another near relative—of the deceased, even if this was the preferred option, see pp. 142–145).

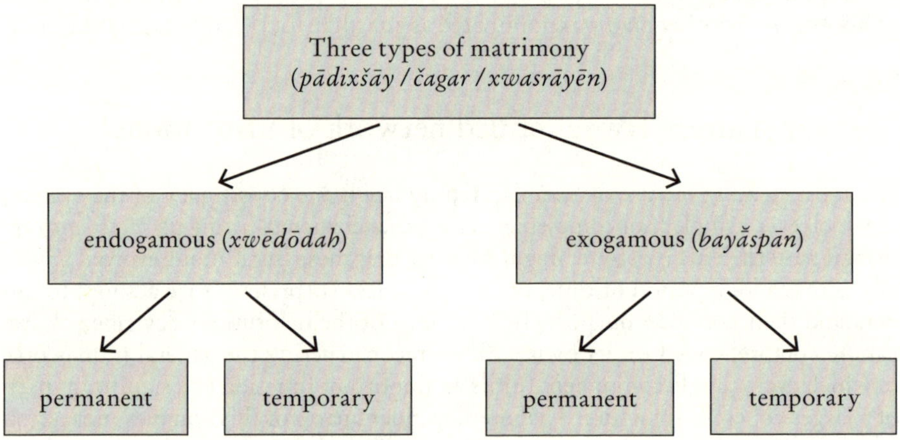

Fig. 3. Potential cross-combinations in marriage law

These various possible cross-combinations conveyed versatility to marriage law, which was based theoretically on the Zoroastrian cosmological world view of limited history, during which every Mazdean had the religious duty to generate numerous children for the battle against Evil in order to promote the victory of Ohrmazd and enable the Restoration (*frašgird*) of the world at the end of limited time.[309] The Sasanian system of patrilineal descent, on the other hand, followed the basic unwritten rule, that a woman could be married to only one man at a time, restricting her reproductive faculties to this one man. By introducing the various options described above the system extended its means of exploiting female fertility for different men and lineages. Patrilineal succession was extended by cognatic features, such as 'intermediary succession' (*ayōgēnīh*), permitting females to continue the lineage in absence of a male, and several significant additional elements, such as different marriage forms, endogamy within the nuclear family, time-limited marriage and the possibility of generating children for a man 'in proxy' (*stūrīh*). By introducing these diverse options marriage law took on an astonishing grade of flexibility, unknown in most other legal systems based on the patrilineal principle of descent. For example, a young

309 On the Zoroastrian time conception see Rezania 2010 (with further references) and Panaino 2015, pp. 238–241.

girl could enter an arranged exogamous (*bayăspān*) alliance of the 'privileged' type on a temporary basis (for one, two, three or ten years), joining the lineage of her husband for this period with all the legal implications of *pādixšāy* matrimony. After the marriage expired, she could re-enter her natal lineage and act as 'intermediary successor' (*ayōgēn*) for her father or brother in a 'fictive' *pādixšāy*-marriage of the *xwēdōdah* type or as 'proxy' (*stūr*) for another relative by generating children in *čagar*-wedlock. The reversed sequence was also possible: she could first act as *ayōgēn* or *stūr* in her natal lineage within a certain time limit and later enter a conjugal union of the 'privileged' type in another descent group. By combining the various options in columns A, B and C a flexible scheme was created, which enabled the utilization of female reproductive faculties to an optimal degree without having to give up the patrilineal line of descent.

Flexibility is likewise one of the main features of 'substitute succession', enabling the establishment of both permanent and time-limited *stūrīhs* (the latter often restricted to ten years, the period needed to rear a child). Although we are not very well informed on the specifics of the latter option, the adaptability of the system is reflected in its technical terminology, which distinguishes between *tan-stūr* (lit. 'physical proxy'), referring to a woman, who is engaged as temporary 'substitute successor', and *zīndag-stūr* (lit. 'life-long proxy'), a woman, who is permanently engaged as 'proxy' for a specific man as long as she lives (*zīndag*) (see pp. 171–172). Obviously Sasanian law found an escape from the general rule that a woman—in contrast to a man—could only be *stūr* for one family at a time by creating the temporary *tan-stūr*, whose engagement ended with the birth of a legitimate successor and could hence, as we may conclude, serve later as 'proxy' in another family, despite the restrictions put on females. In short: all these institutions of family law are logical and indispensible pieces of a huge network, in which *every part is a necessary ingredient complementing the other elements, enabling both men and women to perform their duty of procreation to the fullest possible degree within patrilineal descent*. The ingenious adaptability of this scheme with regard to men and women may be schematized as follows:

Table 13. Strategies enabling versatility within the framework of patrilineal descent

man	woman
Polygyny (unlimited number of wives in *pādixšāy*, *čagar* and *xwasrāyēn*/*gădār* status with and without guardianship)	Time-limited marriages (of all three types sequentially)
'Proxy': *stūr* for another man or for several other men in *čagar*-marriage(s)	'Intermediary successor' (*ayōgēn*) or 'proxy' (*stūr*): on a permanent basis (*zīndag-stūr*) or temporarily (*tan-stūr*)
Several wives and households simultaneously	Several husbands and change of lineages sequentially

At the beginning of this Chapter we asked whether family law and kinship ties had an impact on the hierarchical structure of Sasanian society. We asked how kinship was shaped, to which purpose specific institutions of family law were created and how they promoted the interests of the Sasanian elite, the Zoroastrian clergy and the nobility. Having elucidated the complex network of interdependent institutions in this field, we may now take stock of the results of this study. Most of the fictive ties, temporary institutions and constructed consanguineous bonds determining the structure of kinship in Sasanian Iran would have been impossible in a society without a Zoroastrian background, its basic concept of life and fertility and its encouragement of endogamy, specifically incestuous marriages within the nuclear family. But it is by no means pure coincidence that the ideological foundation, upon which the laws of marriage and succession were built, corresponds so well with fundamental social and economic interests of the land-owning aristocracy. By supporting a kinship system based on a large number of fictive consanguineous bonds and creating different options for generating legitimate offspring for wealthy families, Sasanian family law opened more alternatives to ensure the continuity of a lineage than any other known system of late antiquity. The intricate network of institutions we have discussed, the three different forms of matrimony with their various potential cross-combinations, the possibility of entering both real and fictive incestuous marriages as well as temporary marriages, and the additional options of 'intermediary succession' and 'substitute succession' all enabled flexibility within a patrilineal system bent on producing male successors for affluent aristocratic descent groups. This is a coherent scheme, in which every detail in this set of laws is a necessity and a logical consequence of the main rule, namely that the lineage must be preserved under all circumstances. At the same time these regulations aim at securing the intergenerational transmission of property and reducing the danger of splitting real estate, not only by encouraging endogamy and incest, but also several other devices, which will be discussed in the next Chapter.

Chapter III

Property and Inheritance

Introductory: Descent groups and property law

Our reconstruction of the social hierarchy and the kinship system of the Sasanian Empire in the last Chapter revealed how legal identity and family ties were construed to serve the immanent interests of powerful lineages. Particularly family law with its diverse marriage forms and interconnected institutions of secondary succession played a crucial role in preserving the vast property of the Sasanian elite by securing the continuity of the lineage and ensuring the intergenerational transfer of property. As we have noted, the power of the aristocracy was based to a large extent on its assets, on wealth accumulated across many generations, consisting mainly of landed property and real estate, which was divided into separate categories according to specific legal criteria to be described below. Besides the institutions and options we have already discussed, Sasanian law offered additional ingenious devices to avoid splitting the property of a family, although all the legitimate children of a *paterfamilias* (besides his *pādixšāy*-wife) had a title to a portion of the inheritance. Several strategies were developed in this field to preserve and increase the property of a lineage, not only to the advantage of the aristocracy, but also of the Zoroastrian priesthood, which was given access to a specific part of a family's possessions by various means. The clergy profited not only from a portion of family property set aside specifically for rites and ceremonies to be performed regularly for family members and the souls of the ancestors, but also notably from pious endowments and fire temples founded by the nobility, some of them huge establishments with their own individual infrastructure, including landed property, animals and slaves. Although these foundations remained a distinctive part of family property, they could be placed under the tutorship (*dādwarīh*) or guardianship (*sālārīh*) of priests, who became beneficiaries of these endowments besides the other members of the family. This was a system obviously conceived to the advantage of the two uppermost social classes, combining the characteristic Sasanian institutions of marriage and succession with specific proprietary rights and laws aiming to preserve the wealth of aristocratic and priestly descent groups. We have good reason to assume that the privileges offered by the system to nobles and priests excluded a large section of the population and that this exclusion finally led to the 'heretical' upheaval connected with the name or title of Mazdak at the end of the fifth century. Although it was—according to several foreign and late Iranian sources—the King himself, who in an attempt to weaken both priesthood and nobility made crucial changes in family and property law, these alterations inadvertently led to the collapse of the entire social and legal system and threatened the very existence of the royal family itself. Interestingly the dramatic consequences of this 'heretical' movement, which was finally eliminated by the famous King Husraw Anōšag-ruwān, are described in a late Pahlavi source (*Dēnkard* 3 and 7; see Appendix IV) using Sasanian legal terminology with full knowledge of all its complex implications. This important source, which gives unique insight into the dire consequences of the Mazdakite upheaval from the perspective of both the Zoroastrian priesthood *and* Sasanian law by the use of legal language, has hardly been given the attention it deserves in the numerous studies on this uprising. After discussing the main concepts and institutions of property law and inheritance at the end of this Chapter we will summarize the most remarkable passages of this text, which unwittingly reveals the central role of jurisprudence in upholding social discrepancies and indirectly confirms the privileged position of the upper classes of Sasanian society in all legal fields.

1 Fundamental concepts

One of the most important instruments of law—as described in Chapter I, pp. 72–85—is the use of an individual legal jargon and of precisely defined technical terms to describe, categorize and discuss complex juristic matters in all fields of jurisprudence. As no systematic description of any area of property law (including inheritance) has survived, our main clue to reconstructing this field—at least to a certain extent—is the precise and consequent use of legal language. The professional argot of property law is not only clearly distinguished from the daily colloquial and the language of other literary genres, but is short and to the point, often comprising a mass of information in a single technical term or phrase with a large range of implications which can be only be assessed correctly if the juristic background and its various cross-connotations are known. But although legal vocabulary is utilized in all instances with meticulous precision, it is hardly ever explained, nor are the institutions elucidated to which the terms refer. We have no way of knowing, whether this deficit is due to the sparseness of our Iranian sources or whether Sasanian jurisconsults lacked the sophistication of their Roman colleagues in this respect. There can, however, be no doubt that Iranian property law was built on several fundamental distinctions, which are reflected in the casuistic of the sources. No matter how far jurisprudence was intellectualized, it is obvious that Iranian jurists dealt with matters in the field of property (and obligations, see next Chapter) according to clearly defined concepts of a highly abstract nature. Since neither the technical terms nor the legal ideas forming them are explained, our first main task in the context of property law will be to reconstruct the major distinctions in this field and to piece together the basic concepts of property law and inheritance. As will be seen, Sasanian property law distinguished between certain fundamental categories also known in other legal systems of late antiquity, particularly Roman law, but not always identical with these.

1.1 Terminology and types of property (*xwāstag*; *xīr*)

No classification of property has survived comparable, say, to that in the 'Institutes of Gaius' (mid-second century AD) for Roman law, but it is clear that Iranian jurists had developed a well-defined, coherent concept of property by the late Sasanian period. The basic ideas are apparent in the division of property in different, strictly separated categories, distinguished by the meticulous use of technical terms, which are never confused or blurred. Here we may detect remarkable similarities to Roman law, but also important characteristic differences, which make borrowings in most cases very unlikely. In Roman law the most frequently employed term in this context, *res*, is an elusive word with the primary meaning of 'thing', *i. e.*, a physical object (such as a chair, table, a house, a piece of land), which was later also used of abstract 'things' (such as a debt, a right of way, etc.) and came to designate any asset that had economic value.[1] In the context of property law *res* is employed with three main meanings (following M. Kaser):

1. (in a narrow sense:) the individual, limited, legally independent corporeal thing or physical object;
2. (in a wider sense:) everything that can be the object of a (private) right or of civil litigation ('legal object');
3. a property as a whole (*patrimonium*, *bona*).[2]

These three uses of *res* correspond—remarkably—almost exactly to the Middle Persian expression *xwāstag*,[3] which takes on the meaning 'thing' in a legal context, referring to any legal or physical object having economic value (as opposed to 'legal subject', a person with legal capacity). The similarities between the two terms are in fact striking and the—as yet unanswerable—question is, whether this is pure coincidence due to a parallel, but independent development

1 See du Plessis/Borkowski 2010, p. 151, and Nicholas 1962, p. 98.

2 Kaser 1986, p. 90: '*Res* kann in der Rechtssprache dreierlei bedeuten: bald im engeren Sinne die einzelne, abgegrenzte, juristisch selbständige körperliche Sache, bald im weiterem Sinn alles, was Gegenstand eines (privaten) Rechts oder eines Zivilprozesses sein kann (Rechtsobjekt …); zuweilen ein Vermögen als ganzes (*patrimonium*, *bona*), also einen Inbegriff geldwerter Gegenstände.'

3 The noun (ending in the suffix *-ag*) is derived from *xwāstan*, *xwāh-* (OIr. √**xu̯az* 'to want, desire, wish', Henning 1933, p. 187; Cheung 2007, p. 459f.) with a large range of meanings: (1) 'to wish, will, desire'; (2) 'to call, summon'; (3) 'to ask, claim, demand"; (4) 'to seek, search, look for, ponder, strive to attain' (Nyberg 1974, p. 221f.).

of property law in both systems, or to some kind of exchange of ideas. In a legal context *xwāstag* denotes:

1. a 'thing, object' with a range of meaning that comprises corporeal objects of a completely different nature, encompassing immovable property (real estate, a piece of land, orchards, trees, canals, houses etc.) and movable property (goods and chattels, cattle, animals, slaves, jewellery etc.);
2. in a wider sense 'object of dispute; matter in dispute; subject-matter of a dispute', designating everything that could be the object of civil litigation;
3. in a general sense 'property, wealth, object of value' as a whole, including the complete mass of inherited and inheritable family property (*abarmānd*).[4]

It is also employed in a fourth sense, that of 'money', which is however clearly distinguished from the other three usages by its spelling in the Pahlavi script. In contrast to *xwāstag*, written eteographically ⟨hw'stk'⟩, with the three meanings given above, *xwāstag* 'money' is always written with the ideogram ⟨NKSY'⟩ in legal texts and documents in order to distinguish it exactly from the homonym. This differentiation by the use of the ideogram has been recently confirmed by the Tabarestān documents, in which the two words are kept apart by the means of these two different spellings.[5] This distinction is kept meticulously in the original documents in the Pahlavi cursive script and in all the legal sources of the Sasanian period, particularly the Law-book, but in late Pahlavi texts of the Islamic period the two spellings are sometimes confused, due presumably to the vulgarization of legal language, and, doubtlessly, also to copyists' mistakes or lack of legal training.

Attestations of *xwāstag* in the threefold sense of *res* are abundant in legal texts, also in specific combinations or formulae, which modulate or specify the meaning of the word (notably in connection with the terms *mad* and *rasēd*, as will be seen below). In certain cases it is difficult to distinguish between the first and the third use of the word ('thing' and 'property') as in *xwāstag ī xwēš*[6] 'property/thing in ownership' or *xwāstag ī kasān*[7] 'property/thing belonging to a (third) party'; *xwāstag ī man xwēš*[8] 'property/thing in my ownership', whereas the specific meaning of (immovable) 'property' is apparent in *xwāstag ī āgraw*[9] 'mortgaged (substance of) property, hypotheca' (on this technical term see Chapter IV, pp. 336–342) or *xwāstag ī pidar/pidarān*[10] 'estate of the father/ancestors'. The

4 On this term see below; for attestations see Macuch 1993, p. 713f.

5 On ⟨NKSY'⟩ *xwāstag* 'money' see particularly Tab. 17.5; 17.13; 17.8–11; 18.7 (Macuch 2017c, p. 186). On this word in legal texts and in other Pahlavi documents in the cursive script see also Macuch 2008b, p. 264f.

6 MHD 17.4 (Macuch 1993, pp. 151, 157); MHD 30.1 (*ibid.*, pp. 220, 224).

7 MHD 38.1f. (Macuch 1993, pp. 278, 282).

8 MHD 17.4 (Macuch 1993, pp. 151, 157); MHD 20.16f. (*ibid.*, pp. 156, 161); MHD 31.4 (*ibid.*, pp. 222, 226); MHD 54.11 (*ibid.*, pp. 374, 377); MHD 68.4 (*ibid.*, pp. 448, 452).

9 MHD 38.13 (Macuch 1993, pp. 278, 283).

10 MHD 26.7 (Macuch 1993, pp. 194, 201); MHD 59.12 (*ibid.*, pp. 408, 413); MHD 62.13 (*ibid.*, pp. 411, 417).

second use of the word as 'object of dispute; matter in dispute' is predominant in the context of litigation, as in: *pēšēmāl pad xwāstag … ud pasēmāl anbasān*[11] 'the plaintiff … and defendant (are) in disagreement regarding the matter in dispute'; *pad ān xwāstag pad any šahr hamēmāl hēnd*[12] 'they are opponents regarding the object of dispute in another region' or *pad xwāstag saxwan guftan*[13] 'to make a statement (in court) regarding the matter in dispute' and *pad xwāstag pahikārdan*[14] 'to enter litigation regarding the object of dispute'.

Another term, *xīr* 'thing, object, matter (in dispute), property' seems to have been also used in the threefold sense of *xwāstag*, but is not employed as frequently as the latter expression. In the Law-book *xīr* usually takes on the meaning of 'property, possessions, belongings, goods', particularly together with *xwāstag* in the expression *xīr ud xwāstag* 'goods and property' designating the whole range of a man's possessions (*xīr ud xwāstag ī xwēš* 'one's own goods and property'[15]; compare *xīr ī xwēš*[16] 'one's own assets'). It is attested in the context of family property as *xīr ī dūdag*[17] 'property of the family', and with regard to the individual shares of the family members in *xīr ī pus, duxt, zan ī pādixšāyīhā*[18] 'property of the son, daughter (and) *pādixšāy*-wife'. In the context of fire endowments the term designates the assets (land, orchards, vine-yards, villages, etc.) assigned to the upkeep of a sacred fire by the founder: *xīr ī ātaxš*[19] 'property of the fire' (on fire foundations see pp. 220–229 below).

The similar usage of Latin *res* and Pahlavi *xwāstag* in the context of property law reveals a congruent tendency in both systems to deal with matters regarding property on an abstract level. The term *xwāstag* with the basic legal meaning of 'thing' can refer to all physical objects (in litigation also to abstract 'things', such as the right to utilize a water canal or to reclaim a loan), without specifying the individual qualities of the object in question. This broad range of meanings encapsulated in a single word designating anything that had an economic value and could be the issue of a legal dispute presumably enabled jurists to extend their view beyond limited discussions of particular cases and to find general solutions to legal problems. Although in the transmitted material the focus is on individual cases, not on theoretical reflections, the high level of abstraction is apparent in the division of every 'thing' into two main categories: (1) the 'substance, capital, principal, base' (*bun*), on the one hand, and (2) its

11 MHD 9.12 (Macuch 1993, pp. 103, 106).
12 MHD 6.7f. (*ibid.*, pp. 88, 92).
13 MHD 12.16 (*ibid.*, pp. 117, 120).
14 MHD 7.4 (Macuch 1993, pp. 89, 93).
15 MHD 32.16 (*ibid.*, pp. 240, 243).
16 MHD 30.7 (Macuch 1993, pp. 221, 225); MHD 95.17 (*ibid.*, pp. 606, 609); MHD 103.7,10 (*ibid.*, pp. 617, 625).
17 MHD 15.11 (Macuch 1993, pp. 139, 143); MHD 96.1 (*ibid.*, pp. 606, 609); MHD 107.4 (*ibid.*, pp. 642, 649).
18 MHD 32.16f. (Macuch 1993, pp. 240, 243).
19 MHD 34.1 (Macuch 1993, pp. 252, 255); MHD 93.4 (*ibid.*, pp. 593, 598).

'fruit(s), increase, product' (*bar*) or 'income, interest' (*windišn*, *waxš*, *waxt*), on the other. This basic division of 'things' into the two categories of 'substance' and 'fruit' was one of the most important fundamental distinctions with consequences, which went far beyond parallel categorizations in Roman Law and had significant implications in all areas of property law as we will see below.

Another basic distinction was made between family property handed down from the forefathers, and possessions transferred to a person (or family) by a third party and those acquired by a person him/herself. We may hence suggest a division of property into three basic types according to the form of its transfer (as inheritance, donations or income), following the terminology used in this context:

1. Possessions (comprising the 'total estate') of a family, which had been passed down from the ancestors (*abarmānd ī pidar/pidarān*, lit. '[property that] has remained from the father/ancestors; patrimonial estate').[20]
2. Property assigned to a person (or several persons) by transactions within a family or of a third party (*dād* 'transmitted property, gift, donation').[21]
3. Property acquired by a person during his/her lifetime (*handōxt ī xwēš* 'one's own acquisition'; *handōzišn ud windišn* 'acquisition and earnings').[22]

The two latter means of acquiring property by transfer (purchase, barter etc.) or gifts and donations on the one hand, and by earnings, revenue and interest on the other hand, were also called collectively *mad ud rasēd*, lit. 'has come and shall arrive', derived from the verbs *madan* 'to come' and *rasīdan* 'to arrive', possibly a shortened form of an original formula—as we may conclude from other attestations cited below—such as **xwāstag ī mad ud ān ī rasēd* 'the thing/property that has come and shall be acquired'.[23] The expression designated every kind of surplus income (*bar*) not belonging initially to the first category of property inherited from the ancestors, comparable to *bona adventicia* in classical Roman law. The two words could be used together as one expression *mad ud rasēd* (without *xwāstag*) to denote an income or revenue received in the past (*mad* 'has come', referring to an income that has been acquired before a contract stipulating the transfer of a specific property or of inheritance takes effect), as well as an income a person expects to achieve in the future (*rasēd* 'shall be attained'; such as rent for a leased piece of land or interest for a loan). They could also be used separately with the term for 'thing, property', as in *xwāstag ī ō xwēšīh mad*[24] 'property/thing that has come into one's ownership' or *xwāstag ī*

20 For attestations see MACUCH 1993, p. 686.
21 *Ibid.*
22 MACUCH 1993, p. 711.
23 On the derivation of these terms see above, Chapter I, p. 78. The shortened formula *mad ud rasēd* is attested in MHD 20.8 (MACUCH 1993, pp. 155, 161) and MHD 31.16 (*ibid.*, pp. 223, 227).
24 MHD 7.1 (MACUCH 1993, pp. 89, 93).

ō man rasēd[25] 'thing/property that will come to me', besides *xwāstag ī ō xwēšīh ī man rasēd*[26] 'thing/property that will come into my ownership'. If we follow this line of thought another simplified classification of property into two major categories according to the manner of its acquisition (by inheritance or otherwise) might be taken into consideration:

1. the total (residuary) estate of a family, passed down from the forefathers (*abarmānd ī pidar/pidarān*, lit.'[property that] has remained from the father/ancestors');
2. property acquired by *any* kind of transfer, by donations (*dād*), acquisitions (purchase, barter) as well as by a person's own earnings (*mad ud rasēd*, lit. '[property that] has come and shall be attained').

No matter which one of these divisions (into three or two categories) we take as a basis, one of the fundamental distinctions in Sasanian property law was that between the patrimonial or 'total estate' (*abarmānd*) of a lineage or family, inherited from the ancestors and passed on to future generations, consisting in turn of various categories of property, on the one hand, and the increase of this property achieved by different means, on the other.

Table 14. Overview: basic division of property (*xwāstag, xīr*)

Patrimonial estate of a descent group	Income	
abarmānd ī pidarān ('total estate of the forefathers')	(*xwāstag ī*) *mad ud rasēd* ('[property that] has come and shall be attained')	
	dād ('gift, donation, transmitted property)	*handōxt ī xwēš* ('one's own acquisitions') – *handōzišn* ('acquisitions') – *windišn* ('income, earnings')

1.2 Possession (*dārišn*) and ownership (*xwēšīh*)

Another crucial distinction between two main forms of proprietary rights, known in Sasanian law as in other advanced legal systems, is the difference between 'ownership' and 'possession'. Generally 'ownership' is not easily defined, given the large range of possible relations a person can have to a material object and the initial relativity of the concept as a right that could be restricted by the rights of others, of co-partners, co-inheritors, neighbours, the public, the state, etc., since earliest times. But despite these possible limitations, 'ownership' is

25 MHD 17.2 (*ibid.*, pp. 151, 157).
26 MHD 17.6 (Macuch 1993, pp. 151, 157); MHD 20.14 (*ibid.*, pp. 155, 161).

considered in most sophisticated legal systems as the permanent, plenary right to exclusive enjoyment of a thing, the right to use, possess and dispose of a specific property, to deal with it according to one's wishes and to prevent others from interfering. In short, 'ownership' is explained as the most extensive private right a person can have with respect to a physical object, as the 'complete (or all-encompassing) control over a thing'.[27] 'Possession', on the other hand, is the actual physical control of a specific property,[28] which can, but does not necessarily include ownership, such as the right to occupy and live in a rented house, or to till a leased piece of land. The *de facto* possession of a thing (a rented house, leased land, a pawned object) is distinguished from the all-encompassing right of 'ownership', despite possible restrictions that could be put on the latter (by mortgage, lease, other charges). Although 'possession' can be seen *prima facie* as evidence of 'ownership' (notably in the case of movable objects), these two terms denote completely different legal concepts. 'Possession' might even be unlawful, for example in the case of an illegally occupied house or a stolen object.

The definitions of these two basic concepts are derived in many modern legal systems from classical Roman law, which differentiates precisely between *dominium* (later also *proprietas*) 'ownership' on the one hand, and *possessio* 'possession, holding, tenure', on the other, in the sense described above. Roman legal theory of the classical period defines 'ownership' (*dominium*, *proprietas*) as a person's total, undivided and permanent right to deal with an object in any manner he chooses to. It is the most extensive private right a person can have with respect to a material object, giving that person full power of disposal, which can be limited in certain respects, but is not restricted from the outset.[29] In other words: 'ownership' is defined as an 'absolute' or 'real right', which can be defended on this ground against any possible claims others might bring forward. 'Possession' (*possessio*), on the other hand, only states that a person has physical control over a specific property, no matter whether (s)he is lawfully entitled to it or not. The concept of 'absolute ownership' in most Western legal systems, giving the owner exclusive rights, is a remnant of Roman legal theory, an abstraction on a highly theoretical level, which deliberately ignores the large range and variety of possible legal relations between legal subjects and objects. It has been observed that it does not correspond with social reality, particularly in the case of landed property, where the economic utilization of the land and unrestricted ownership are in most ancient (also medieval and many modern) societies only rarely in one and the same hand.[30] It is therefore hardly surprising that Sasanian law developed a different method of dealing with complex owner-

27 Avenarius 1985, p. 108: 'Eigentum ... ist das umfassende Herrschaftsrecht über eine Sache.' On the difficulties of defining ownership see also Herzog 1936, I, pp. 69–71.
28 Avenarius 1985, p. 64: 'Besitz ... ist die tatsächliche Gewalt einer Person über eine Sache.'
29 See Kaser 1986, p. 103ff; Liebs ²1982, p. 148ff.; Wieacker 1961, p. 187.
30 See particularly Wieacker 1961, pp. 187–221, on the development of the concept of 'ownership' in Roman law.

ship rights, which were closer to the reality of the distribution of property than those of classical Roman law.

A basic differentiation between 'ownership' and 'possession' can also be observed in Iranian texts, although the Sasanian notion of 'ownership' presumably did not correspond exactly to the abstract concept developed in classical Roman law, as described above. Jurists distinguished precisely between 'ownership' (*xwēšīh*), that is, a person's title to a certain 'thing' (*xwāstag*) giving him full power of disposition and alienation, on the one hand, and 'possession, holding, tenure' (*dārišn*), the immediate *de facto* possession of a 'thing' which could, but did not necessarily include ownership, on the other.[31] Given the importance of keeping these two fundamental concepts apart, the terms are always used with meticulous precision in a legal context and never confused: *xwēšīh* is always 'ownership' (as in *xwāstag pad xwēšīh* 'property in ownership'[32]; *xwēšīh ī xwāstag* 'ownership of property'[33]; *xwāstag ī pad xwēšīh ī xwēš* 'property in one's own ownership'[34]; *xwēšīh ī xwēš* 'one's own ownership'[35]). 'Possession', on the other hand, is always *dārišn* (or *xwāstag dārišn*[36] and *dārišn ī xwāstag*[37] 'possession of property') in the described sense. It was crucial to be precise, since Sasanian property law developed a large range of proprietary rights based on the fundamental distinction between 'ownership' and 'possession' with regard to both the 'substance' (*bun*) of a material thing as well as to its 'fruit, income, increase' (*bar*), as will be seen below. The verbs in this context are also employed with meticulous precision: *dāštan*[38] or *pad dārišn dāštan*[39] is always 'to possess, hold', 'to hold in possession'; whereas 'to own' is without exception always *pad xwēšīh dāštan* (lit. 'to possess in ownership', 'to own'[40]).

Despite the similar definitions, we have good reason to assume that—in contrast to classical Roman law—'ownership' was not considered as an 'absolute' or 'real right' in Sasanian law, giving the owner a legally protected title to a thing that could be defended on this ground alone against other contenders. As experts on Roman law have maintained, this abstract definition of ownership in *classical* Roman jurisprudence as an 'absolute right' was a relatively late development, which had not yet taken root in *ancient* Roman law.[41] Interestingly, the clue to comprehending the initial concept of ownership in both legal systems

31 All attestations of the two terms must be taken into consideration, see Macuch 1993, pp. 700 (*dārišn*) and 715 (*xwēšīh*), with references to the passages, in which they occur.
32 MHD 90.10 (Macuch 1993, pp. 571, 574).
33 MHD 91.4 (*ibid.*, pp. 579, 584).
34 MHD 5.4 (*ibid.*, pp. 87, 91).
35 MHD 76.11 Macuch 1993, pp. 510, 512).
36 MHD 15.15, 16.1 (*ibid.*, pp. 140, 143).
37 MHD 39.15 (*ibid.*, pp. 280, 284f.).
38 For attestations see Macuch 1993, p. 701.
39 DkM 725.5.
40 MHD 10.17; 41.17 (Macuch 1993, pp. 115, 118 and 300, 316 respectively).
41 Particularly Wieacker 1961, p. 208f.; see also Kaser 1986, p. 104f.

can be found in disputes regarding proprietary rights in civil litigation. In the *pre-classical* period of Roman law lawsuits concerning property (the *legis actio sacramento in rem*)[42] were not decided on the basis of a party's absolute right of ownership, but because one of the litigants proved to have a 'better right' to the property. The defendant could attempt to prove the legality of his title against the plaintiff and free himself from responsibility in cases of fraud by naming his legal predecessor (*auctor*), that is, the person, from whom he had acquired the object of dispute. The judge could only decide, which one of the opponents had brought forward *better* proof of ownership, but he could not dismiss the suit on the ground that neither the plaintiff nor the defendant was the owner of the disputed object. A third party could also lay claim to the object and prove to have an even better right than the litigant who had won the suit. The procedure reveals that ownership in *ancient* Roman law was considered as a 'relative right', not as the 'absolute right' of later *classical* Roman jurisprudence, giving the owner full legal protection against claims of others.[43]

This manner of dealing with disputes regarding property in ancient Roman litigation has an exact parallel in Sasanian jurisprudence. Two parties, who both claimed to have the same title to a certain thing and filed a suit, were obliged to present judicial evidence of their claim to the judge. Proof could be offered by presenting written documents (which had to be evaluated), by the statements of witnesses, by taking the oath or by calling one's 'legal predecessor'.[44] The common procedure in the context of proprietary rights—which has been recently confirmed by the Tabarestān documents—was to summon one's 'predecessor in title' (*dastwar*), the person from whom one had acquired the object of dispute by sale, barter, gift or any other kind of transaction.[45] The function of the 'predecessor' was exactly the same as in ancient Roman law: both the Roman *auctor* and the Sasanian *dastwar* had to guarantee that the defendant had acquired the property lawfully and had a legal title to it. Moreover, in both systems *auctor* and *dastwar* were obliged to defend the alleged proprietor (the defendant) in court and to help him dismiss the claim of the plaintiff.[46]

Comparing the two systems has important consequences for our comprehension of the Sasanian concept of ownership. Legality of ownership depended on the ability of the potential owner to prove his legal title (*dastwarīh*) by specifying the manner in which the disputed object had come into his possession, whether it was 'inherited from the forefathers' (*az pidarān abar mānd*) or acquired by other means.[47]

42 Kaser 1986, pp. 104f., 124f., 194f.

43 See Wieacker 1961, pp. 208–210, and Kaser 1986, pp. 104–105.

44 On civil litigation see Chapter VI, pp. 533–569.

45 On the evidence of the Tabarestān texts see Macuch 2016a, pp. 150–151. On the Sasanian *dastwar* see also Chapter IV, pp. 385–387, and Macuch 1988b and 2008a.

46 On the procedure in Roman law see Wieacker 1961, p. 209; Kaser 1986, p. 125; Liebs ²1982, p. 228f.; Manthe 2000, p. 25f.

47 MHD 95.11 (Macuch 1993, pp. 605, 608).

By revealing—to use Sasanian legal terminology—'which kind of ownership' (*čē ēwēnag xwēšīh*)[48] was in effect, a person could prove his title and be accepted as owner—but only as long as he was not dispossessed by another person with 'better proof'. Due to the difficulties involved in proving ownership (which might have been possibly easiest and most convincing if the object in question had been in possession of the family for a longer period), the Sasanian theory seems to have been similar to that of *ancient* Roman law: ownership was considered as a 'relative right', *not* as the 'absolute right' of *classical* Roman jurisprudence and other legal systems derived from the latter. This does not necessarily point to a generally lower level of legal sophistication. We have good reason to assume that Iranian jurists developed other abstract categories and acknowledged the two main elements of ownership: (a) the right to the general uses of a thing (as elucidated above), and (b) the permanence of that right, including inheritability.[49] The meticulous use of the terminology of 'possession' and 'ownership' in the texts indicates that jurists were not only conscious of the profound difference between these concepts, but developed at least two important types of property (*pad stŭrīh* and *pad ruwān*, to be discussed below) based on the fundamental distinction between these two divergent proprietary rights. They furthermore introduced other categories, based on the complexity of ownership rights, which were nearer to the concrete distribution of property in Ērānšahr, revealing an efficient and astoundingly coherent system.

1.3 Substance (*bun*) and fruit (*bar*)

Despite—or maybe due to—the Iranian perception of ownership as a 'relative right' (at least with regard to property, which was *not* inherited from the forefathers, as elucidated above), Sasanian jurists found another method of distinguishing between different proprietary rights by dividing every legal object (*xwāstag*) into two main parts: the 'substance, capital, principal, parent thing, base, core assets' (*bun*)[50], on the one hand, and its 'fruit, produce, increase, income, profit, revenue' (*bar*)[51], on the other. The fruits or income of a thing encompass both the natural produce of land and livestock as well as rent and other types of profit, called also *windišn* 'income, earnings', and *waxš*, *waxt* 'increase, interest'. These or similar distinctions are of course also known in other legal systems, but the right to 'own' the 'fruit(s)' (*bar*) of a 'thing' in perpetuity (in the sense of 'ownership' described above) apart from the 'substance' (*bun*), and

48 MHD 9.15, 10.7, 95.11 (*ibid.*, pp. 102–103; 106–107, 608 respectively); DkM 707.22.
49 According to Herzog 1936, p. 71.
50 Av. *bŭna*- 'basis, ground, depth' (Bartholomae 1904, col. 968f.).
51 From *burdan*, *bar*- 'to carry, bear' (OIr. √**bar* 'to bring, carry'; Cheung 2007, pp. 6–10; Av./OP √*bar*, Bartholomae 1904, col. 933ff.; Kellens 1995, p. 37f.).

the meticulous precision with which these two elements of a material thing are kept apart in classifications of property are unique characteristics of Iranian law.

The terms are usually used as abstract categories in the juristic texts and not explained, but we may draw several conclusions from the context in which they are attested in legal literature. The main feature, setting the concept apart from Roman law and many other legal systems, is that ownership of these two parts of a material thing could be separated: the 'owner of the substance' (*bun-xwēš*)[52] could be a different person from the one who owned its product or increase, the 'owner of the fruit' (*bar-xwēš*).[53] It is important to note that 'ownership of the fruit' (*bar-xwēšīh*) has another quality than mere *usufruct*, lit. 'use of the fruit', that is, the right to enjoy the produce of property belonging to another person and to take its fruits (for example, the right of the tenant or lessee to enjoy the crops of agricultural land or the fruits of trees in an orchard), or *antichresis*, the right of the creditor to the fruits of a pledged or mortgaged property instead of interest (called *bar-xward*, *bar burd* or *bar grift*, see below).[54] The crucial distinction lies in the inheritability *in perpetuum* of *bar-xwēšīh*, which enabled the development of legal institutions based on the permanence of 'ownership of the fruit(s)', in contrast to lease, usufruct, *antichresis*, and other agreements of a similar kind. Although the right to usufruct can also be inherited, it is terminated by expiry of the agreed period of time and does not become a permanent element of a person's (or a family's) estate. In contrast, permanence and inheritability of the income are exactly what the term *bar-xwēšīh* implies, as we may conclude from complex legal institutions founded on the possibility of owning the fruits in perpetuity. Although the close affinity of usufruct to ownership was also noted in Roman law, it was finally recognized in the latter as a servitude, that is, a proprietary right involving the use of another person's property, and did not lead to a concept comparable to that of Iranian law, as described below.[55]

52 MHD 37.14; 39.12; 39.12–15 (Macuch 1993, pp. 277, 282 and 280, 284 respectively); MHDA 15.3; 30.16; (Macuch 1981, pp. 37, 144 and 55, 209 respectively); DkM 709.7 (*bun-xwēšīh*). MHD 12.15 (Macuch 1993, pp. 117, 120).

53 MHD 37.14–15; 90.9 (Macuch 1993, pp. 277, 282 and 571, 574 respectively); MHDA 2.5 (Macuch 1981, pp. 22, 70). In all of these passages the correct translation of *bar-xwēš* should be: 'owner of the fruit(s)' instead of 'Nutznießer' or *usufructarius*! Since the terms are not explained, I only became fully aware of the fundamental difference between the two concepts of *bar-xwēšīh* and *bar-xward* after having completed work on the two editions of the Law-book.

54 On these differentiations and a possible parallel in Talmudic law see Macuch 2015d and Chapter VII, pp. 603–606. Antichresis denotes in Roman law an agreement by which the debtor provides security for a loan by giving the creditor the permission to use the fruits of a property in lieu of interest. Sasanian law knew a similar kind of mortgage, called *grawagān(īh)*, see Chapter IV, pp. 343–349.

55 See du Plessis/Borkowski 2010, pp. 159 and 166, and Nicholas 1962, p. 139, fn. 1.

This precise distinction between ownership of the substance, on the one hand, and ownership of the fruits, on the other, was not only crucial for categorizing different types of inheritable family property (*abarmānd*), but was also taken into account in transferring (*dād*) real rights. Transactions could be restricted to one of these two parts of a material thing: an individual could be the 'owner of the income' (*bar-xwēš*) of a specific property without having a title to its substance or principal (*bun*). For example, a person could transfer the title to a vineyard (*dastgird raz*) to another individual without conveying proprietary rights to the land (*zamīg*) upon which the vine was planted.[56] Trees, the land on which they were planted, and their fruit could also be dealt with as separate entities and be transferred separately: a person could become the owner of a date-palm or an olive tree without having a title to the land (*zamīg*) or the fruits (the dates or olives) which in turn could be transferred to another person either in ownership or as usufruct.[57]

Although the two technical terms are used frequently, only a few concrete cases are noted in the Pahlavi legal texts, which usually discuss these words on an abstract level. Several examples are to be found in the Tabarestān records, but, unsurprisingly, *bun* is used here (and in the documents of the 'Pahlavi Archive') with a very concrete meaning, not in the abstract, theoretical sense elucidated above. The word designates specifically some kind of (inalienable?) permanent collective property of the village of **Asp-gurd* (read previously as **Haspin-raz*)[58] in whose archive the Tabarestān documents were presumably kept. This collective property consisted of agricultural land, of vineyards (Tab. 13)[59] that could be leased to farmers, peasants and cultivators, orchards (olive-trees, Tab. 18 and 24)[60] that could be mortgaged as security for a loan, also money (Tab. 18)[61] that could be granted as a loan and waterways (or *qanāts*) used for irrigating the crops (Tab. 17).[62]

56 MHDA 20.11–15 (Macuch 1981, p. 167, and 2008a, p. 132f.).

57 Date-palms (muγ ⟨DLR'⟩) and their fruit (bar) are mentioned MHD 102.14–15 (Macuch 1993, p. 624, and 2008a, p. 133).

58 On the revised reading of the name of this village see Weber 2020a, p. 175 (also Macuch 2020b, p. 196, fn. 3).

59 Macuch 2017c, pp. 167–172.

60 Macuch 2017c, pp. 183–188 (Tab. 18) and Macuch 2019b, pp. 132–146 (Tab. 24). Both documents suggest separate ownership of olive trees with their product, *zayt*, on the one hand, and of the land, *zamīg*, on which they were planted, on the other. The olive-yields of trees on different parcels of land belonging to various families are mortgaged by the debtor as security for a loan.

61 Macuch 2017c, pp. 183–188.

62 Macuch 2017c, pp. 189–190 (Tab. 17). Taking the evidence of the documents from the 'Pahlavi Archive' into consideration, Weber 2017a (p. 135, fn. 9) explains *bun* as 'a form of inventory holding of the community which contained corn, oil and other things of daily maintenance'. As I have already pointed out elsewhere (Macuch 2022a, pp. 134 and 137) both abstract and concrete meanings of *bun* ('substance'; 'inventory holding') make sense if we assume—as the Tabarestān documents suggest—that it designates

In the Law-book the term *bun-xwēšīh* 'ownership of the substance' is employed in one remarkable instance in a lawsuit involving two men who claim one and the same woman as their wife. The striking solution of this dispute is to confirm the liaison between the woman and the man, who already has her, 'since "possession" (*dārišn*) is certain, whereas "ownership of the substance" (*bun-xwēšīh*) is uncertain' (*čē dārišn ēwar ud bun-xwēšīh warōmand*).[63] The reasoning in this judgement allows two conclusions: the terms 'possession' and 'ownership' were not only used of material things, but of persons in legal dependency (besides slaves), underlining the hierarchical relationship of a man to his wife and children (in another passage the same terminology is used with respect to the latter: *waččag pid xwēš* 'the child is the father's own').[64] The case moreover stresses the difficulty of proving ownership rights if there were no valid documents, legal predecessors or witnesses to provide evidence.

The division of 'things' into *bun* and *bar* led to the development of complex institutions founded on the distinctions we have described. A large section of family property was expressly set apart for two purposes, 'for substitute succession' (*pad stūrīh*) and 'for the soul' (*pad ruwān*), both based on the fundamental distinction between ownership and possession of substance and fruit, as will be seen below. The substance (*bun*) of the property in *stūrīh* and of property belonging to family foundations 'for the soul' (pious endowments and sacred fires) remained in the possession (*dārišn*) of the heirs, but it was bound to certain fixed purposes and hence *not* part of property in ownership (*xwēšīh*). The heirs had, however, as a rule a permanent and inheritable right to the income (*bar*) of the property in both institutions if there were no explicit restrictions or time limits in the will of the deceased. We have good reason to assume that this kind of permanent title to the income is meant with 'ownership of the fruit' (*bar-xwēšīh*), which was distinguished both from *bun-xwēšīh* 'ownership of the substance' as well as from the right to usufruct, called *bar-xward* (or, with the verbs *burdan*

property of the village whose 'substance' (*bun*) was held by shareholders enjoying a collective right to the produce of this property (crop yields, corn, wheat, wine, olives, oil processed from olives, etc.) with shares corresponding to their 'ideal' (*i.e.*, undivided) portions of the cultivated lands, orchards, vineyards etc. Specific products of this land seem to have been collected in some kind of central repository or inventory of the village, also called *bun*, until they were apportioned among the shareholders or used for some other purpose. Several documents of the 'Pahlavi Archive' indicate that the shareholders or partners had specific 'accounts', called *mar*, in the *bun* from which payments and other transactions were undertaken under the supervision of an official called *bunbān* 'custodian of the *bun*' (on *bunbān* see Weber 2016b, p. 187). On *bun* in the Tabarestān documents see also Macuch 2017c, pp. 168–169, with further references; on this term in the documents of the 'Pahlavi Archive' and in the Bactrian legal documents (βονο and βοναγο) see also Macuch 2008b, pp. 255–260. For attestations of the word in the Bactrian documents see Sims-Williams 2000, p. 187.

63 MHD 12.15 (Macuch 1993, pp. 117, 120).

64 MHD 1.3 (*ibid.*, pp. 22, 24).

and *griftan* instead of *xwardan*, also *bar burd* or *bar grift*) 'use of the fruit(s)'. The precise use of this terminology allows several conclusions:

1. Sasanian legal theory distinguished clearly between *two different proprietary rights* with respect to the *income* of property:
   (a) the *permanent*, *inheritable right* of a family to the fruits of a specific property, called *bar-xwēšīh* 'ownership of the fruit(s)' (for example, in regulations regarding *stūrīh* and *ruwān* property);
   (b) the restricted right to the fruits for a certain specified period (lease, *antichresis*, etc.): *bar-xward* (or *bar burd*; *bar grift*) 'use of the fruit(s), usufruct'.[65]
2. The right designated as *bar-xwēšīh* was regarded as a *separate form of ownership*, to be distinguished from 'ownership of the substance' (*bun-xwēšīh*), but having similar legal implications with respect to permanency and inheritability.

These terms are always employed with meticulous precision, suggesting that Sasanian jurists distinguished theoretically between four basic proprietary rights and that versatile combinations of these different elements were possible:

Table 15. Basic proprietary rights

Material thing (*xwāstag*)	Ownership (*xwēšīh*)	Possession (*dārišn*)
Substance (*bun*)	*bun-xwēšīh* 'ownership of the substance'	(*bun-*)*dārišn*; *dārišn* (*ī bun*) 'possession of the substance'
Fruit (*bar*)	*bar-xwēšīh* 'ownership of the fruits'	*bar xward* (*bar burd*; *bar grift*) 'use of the fruits, usufruct'

The underlying idea that ownership of the fruits can be a proprietary right in itself, to be distinguished from mere usufruct and independent of ownership of the principal, allows flexibility in an area which would otherwise have been bound by too many regulations and restrictions. The concept is demonstrated perfectly by the various ingredients of family property. The 'total (patrimonial/residuary) estate' (*abarmānd*) of a family, including substance and income, was bequeathed as a rule—to which exceptions were possible—as joint possession (*dārišn*) to the heirs, called *xwāstagdār*, lit. 'possessor(s) of property'[66], a technical term which captures precisely the essential idea: the heirs had joint proprietary rights and were usually shareholders of the substance (*bun*), but were not

65 On *bar-xward* see MHDA 7.8 (Macuch 1981, pp. 29, 99); *bar burd* MHD 9.5; 34.11; 48.2; 49.14; 53.14 (Macuch 1993, pp. 102, 105; 253, 256; 307, 323; 309, 325; 373, 376 respectively); *bar grift/gīrēd* MHD 38.3,4 (*ibid.*, pp. 278, 283).

66 See below pp. 206–210.

owners in the sense of the word described above. By receiving a title to 'ownership of the fruit' (*bar-xwēšīh*) of a large section of the estate 'in possession' (*pad xwāstagdārīh*) of the family, including specifically those elements that were immobilized in the institutions of *stūrīh* and 'for the soul' (*pad ruwān*), the heirs obtained the right of disposal of the income of this property, which remained in the descent group and could be utilized for the upkeep and to the advantage of the family. Besides having a right to a specific share in joint property, an heir could also be 'owner of the substance' (*bun-xwēš*) of a specified portion of the inheritance (a piece of land, a house, a slave, an animal, jewelry, etc.), which had been bequeathed to him/her expressly in the form of ownership (*pad xwēšīh*) in the will of the *paterfamilias* (*kadag-xwadāy*). Hence specific segments of family property could be passed on in separate categories, conferring ownership of the substance or of the income. If the right to the fruits was not permanent or inheritable or if an agreement existed that it should be terminated at a fixed period (in the case of a lease or *antichresis*), then the heir(s) only had 'use of the income' (*bar-xward*), in contrast to 'ownership of the income' (*bar-xwēšīh*). The concept is simple (at least in theory if not necessarily in practice), but coherent and flexible, and could have had some impact on theoretical discussions as well as legal practice in other contemporary legal systems (*e.g.*, in Jewish law according to the evidence of the Babylonian Talmud).[67]

Table 16. Substance and fruit: fundamental distinctions

xwāstag ('thing, property')			
bun ('substance')		*bar* ('fruit')	
bun-xwēšīh ('ownership of the substance')	*(bun-)dārišn* ('possession of the substance')	*bar-xwēšīh* ('ownership of the fruits')	*bar-xward* ('use of the fruits; usufruct')

2 Basic components of a family's total patrimonial estate (*abarmānd*)

The division of every 'thing' capable of producing income (*barōmand*) into the basic categories of *bun* and *bar* and the distinction between ownership and possession of these two parts of a 'thing' were the legal tools for the formation of various elements of family property crucial for preserving the material prosperity of aristocratic and priestly lineages across a long period of time. As in other

67 On the debate in the Bavli see Macuch 2015d and Chapter VII, pp. 603–606; on the use of the legal terms in a theological context see Zeini 2024.

fields, there is no systematic description of this area. The following is hence an attempt to reassemble the various components comprising a family's estate based on diverse case studies involving problems of succession and the intergenerational transfer of property.

The central expression in the context of inheritance is *abarmānd*, an amply attested term, whose exact meaning is by no means easy to determine despite its frequent usage in both legal and other texts and its clear etymology from *abar* + *mānd*, lit. '(that which is) left over, has remained'.[68] It has been rendered by 'residuary wealth';[69] 'surplus property';[70] 'residue';[71] 'privilege; special type of inheritance;'[72] 'inheritance, heritage, heredity';[73] 'residuary legacy';[74] 'succession, inheritance; successor, heir (masc. and fem.)'.[75] Although the general translation 'inheritance, residue, residuary legacy, heritage' fits in well with the literal meaning of the word and its usage in both legal and non-legal texts, several puzzling attestations in a juristic context indicate that it was employed in a precise technical sense that is not visible in these general translations. Bartholomae already realized in his study of the technical meaning of the word that the common translation 'Erbschaft, Nachlaß' [inheritance, legacy],[76] did not correspond well with several passages, in which the word refers to property transferred to a son or other potential heirs during the lifetime of a *paterfamilias*.[77] Although his

68 < *abar* 'over, on, upon, up' + *mānd*, from *māndan*, *mān-* 'to remain, stay, wait, dwell', base Ir. *(*d*)*mān* 'to remain, dwell'; Av. √*mān* (*mąn*); OP √*mān* (Cheung 2007, pp. 73–75); √^{2}*man* (Bartholomae 1904, col. 1124; Kellens 1995, p. 42); on the uses of *abar* see Durkin-Meisterernst 2014, pp. 299–306. Herzfeld's attempt to derive the word from an unattested OP **māndā-* '*Dienstpflicht' [official duty] (*apud* Zaehner 1940, p. 35) is hardly convincing. That the basic meaning of *abarmānd* is '(that which is) left over/has remained' can also be assessed from the amply attested *abar* (...) *mānēd*, lit. '(it) remains (to), is bequeathed (to), is inherited', 3rd sg. pres. of the verb *abar māndan* (written ⟨MDM KTLWNtn'⟩); for attestations see Macuch 1993, Index, p. 719.

69 West 1894, p. 60 (45), in his translation of the summary of the legal *nasks* in *Dēnkard* 8.

70 West 1894, p. 113 (13).

71 West 1894, p. 113 (16).

72 Bailey 1930–1932a, p. 81.

73 Zaehner 1940, p. 36f., who revives Darmesteter's 'héritage' based on non-legal literature, which had been previously contested by Bartholomae 1918–1923, V, in a study dedicated to this word in Sasanian law ('Der Begriff *apармand*'), see below.

74 Shaki 1971, p. 341.

75 Perikhanian 1997, p. 337. The second translation of the word as 'successor, heir' (also propagated by Shaki 1975, p. 233f., no. 31) is wrong. It is based on the use of *abarmānd* with *bawēd/ōh bawēd* in *duxt abarmānd ī pid nē bawēd* (MHD 22.3), which, however, should be rendered, according to the parallel passage *duxt abarmānd ī az pidar ... nē bawēd* (MHD 62.12), as 'the daughter does not receive the total (residuary) estate of the father.' On the use of *ōh bawēd/nē bawēd* in this sense compare *sālār ī gumārdag sēnag masāy ud bāzā masāy ōh bawēd* (MHD 27.2) 'the nominated guardian receives (a daily ration corresponding to) 'the size of a forefoot and the size of a buttock'; on the expression for 'daily ration' see Chapters I, p. 76, and II, pp. 173–174. See also Macuch 1993, pp. 420–421.

76 Bartholomae 1918–1923, III, pp. 17 and 64; V, p. 4.

77 *Ibid.*, V, pp. 9–20. On this option see pp. 207 and 238–239 below.

final explanation of *abarmānd* as 'eine Sonderzuwendung aus dem väterlichen oder Familienvermögen an ein Familienmitglied' [a special gratuity from the property of the father or the family to a member of the family], comparable to the Roman *praecipuum*[78] or '*donatio* (vornehmlich *mortis causa*)'[79] is wrong, he was right to assume that the word has a precise legal meaning that is not covered by the common translation as 'residue, inheritance, legacy'.

The specific meaning of *abarmānd* can be derived from passages of the Lawbook in which it appears in juxtaposition to other well-known technical terms: in one instance *pad abarmānd* is contrasted to *pad bahr* 'in portions, shares', indicating two possibilities of bequeathing family property: either

1. as a whole (*pad abarmānd*), encompassing different categories of property (to be described below) which were *not* partitioned between the heirs, but held by them jointly as shareholders (*hambāy*), each person having an 'ideal' portion at his/her disposal; or
2. partitioned into separate shares (*pad bahr*).[80]

The first option, which was the usual form of bequeathing family property (and for specific categories of property the only option), implies that *abarmānd* denoted the *entirety* of a family's estate, encompassing property subject to different provisions, parts of which were *not* (or could not be) partitioned, whose substance (*bun*) was transferred more or less intact as a whole across several generations.[81]

In another instance *pad abarmānd* is contrasted with *pad xwēšīh* 'in ownership', pointing to another important feature of the patrimonial estate: it could *not* be bequeathed in its entirety in the category of ownership.[82] Moreover, *abarmānd* is basically distinguished from property acquired by a person during his/her lifetime (*xwāstag ī man handōzam* 'property that I acquire'), as already noted above.[83] Apart from these passages other attestations of the word[84] in a legal context suggest that *abarmānd* was a technical term with *two major overlapping meanings*, both in perfect correspondence with the literal sense of the word as '(that which is) left over, has remained':

1. property that has been passed down from the forefathers, comprising a family's 'total patrimonial estate', consisting of the four different components described below (to be distinguished from new acquisitions);

78 *Ibid.*, V, p. 19.
79 *Ibid.*, V, p. 53.
80 MHD 61.3–5; 61.5–7 (Macuch 1993, pp. 409f., 415; see also commentary on pp. 419–421, n. 2).
81 These components are indicated in MHDA 21.2–5 (Macuch 1981, pp. 44, 167).
82 MHD 90.16 (Macuch 1993, pp. 571, 574).
83 MHDA 2.3 (Macuch 1981, 22, 70). See pp. 192–193 above.
84 All the attestations should be taken into consideration, see Macuch 1993, Index, p. 686.

2. 'residue, residuary legacy, inheritance', property that is left by the *kadag-xwadāy* to be passed on to the next generation after legacies and bequests have been met and debts have been paid.

Both meanings are intertwined and inseparable: *abarmānd* designates the *complete mass of a family's collective estate, consisting of different elements*, which have been transferred from the forefathers to the present generation as a unity and in the ideal case will continue to be handed down as *an undivided whole* to the heirs as shareholders (*hambāy*) after the payment of debts, liabilities and other expenses.

The 'total (patrimonial/residuary) estate' (*abarmānd*) of an affluent lineage, administered by the head of a household (*kadag-xwadāy*), consisted of four major categories, subject to different legal provisions based on the distinctions between 'possession' and 'ownership' and 'substance' and 'fruit' which we have described above. These different forms of proprietary rights were labeled (using Sasanian legal terminology):

1. *pad xwāstagdārīh* (lit. 'in hereditary possession'): property over which the successor(s) and heir(s) (*xwāstagdār*) have (limited) proprietary rights as holder(s);
2. *pad xwēšīh* ('in ownership'): assets transferred with ownership rights to the heir(s) and legatee(s);
3. *pad stūrīh* ('in trust; for substitute succession'): property set apart in a kind of trust for two purposes: (a) for maintaining 'substitute succession' (see Chapter II, pp. 169–174); (b) for preserving a consecrated fire (discussed below pp. 217–219);
4. *pad ruwān* ('for the soul', also: *ruwān ray* and *pad ruwān dāštan* 'for keeping the soul'): property reserved for pious and religious purposes (including 'pious gifts', *ahlawdād*, and sacred fires, *ādur/ātaxš*).

The first two expressions denote different types of proprietary rights (possession and ownership), whereas the latter two categories refer to property specifically reserved for legal institutions crucial to the continuity of a lineage and the preservation of its material means, whose principal (*bun*) was held by the heirs in possession and was as a rule inalienable. It seems that a large amount of family property bequeathed as *abarmānd* was bound to these specific purposes, whereas only a small part was transferred to the heirs with ownership rights, as the distribution of these four elements (illustrated in the following diagram, see Fig. 4) suggests.

These various categories constituting the total (patrimonial/residuary) estate of a family were subject to different regulations, which we will now attempt to scrutinize separately.

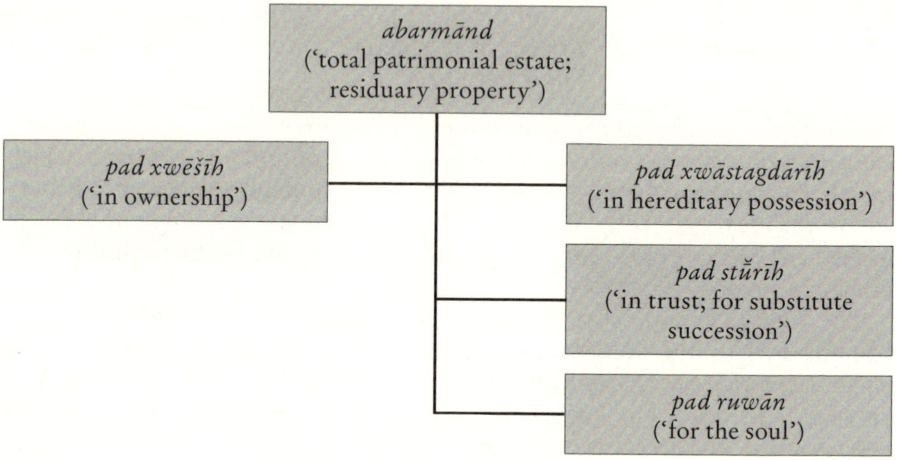

Fig. 4. Overview: components of a family's 'total (patrimonial/residuary) estate'

2.1 Hereditary possession (*xwāstagdārīh*)

A large part of a family's estate consisted of property 'in (hereditary) possession', called *pad xwāstagdārīh* in most legal texts (another attested form is *xwāstagdārišn*, lit. 'possession of property', if this is not a spelling mistake).[85] This technical term designates a family's collective property, encompassing real estate, movables and immovables, which in the ideal case were bequeathed as a unity (*i.e.*, not partitioned) to the next generation and were held by the heirs in joint possession. The concept behind the expression seems to be that of the family (or lineage) as a self-perpetuating entity, whose transitional head, the *kadag-xwadāy*, and later his successors are more or less trustees, not owners, of family property. The technical term for 'heir', *xwāstagdār*, lit. 'possessor of property'[86] (also *abarmānd-xwāstagdār*, lit. 'possessor of the total residuary estate')[87] reflects the basic idea that the heirs were as a rule not owners of the substance (*bun*) of a family's collective property, but succeeded to undivided

85 For attestations see Macuch 1993, Index, p. 714. The form *xwāstagdārišn* occurs in the title of the chapter dedicated to the topic of inheritance (MHD 59.11), but it could be a mistake for the pl. *xwāstagdārān* ('heirs'), which is written similarly (compare MHD 58.15 and 59.11, in which *xwāstagdārišn* is definitely a misspelling of *xwāstagdārān*).

86 < *xwāstag* 'thing, property' + *-dār* 'holder, possessor' < *-dāra-* (Ir. base √**dar*, Av. √*dăr*, OP √*dār* 'to hold, keep, maintain, have', Bartholomae 1904, col. 690; Kellens 1995, p. 27f.; Cheung 2007, p. 57; MP *dāštan*, *dār-*).

87 MHD 2.4f. (Macuch 1993, pp. 40, 42).

(*a-baxt*) shares and had a title to the income (*bar*). The word has a somewhat different colouring than *yōhē pasčaēta*, lit. 'who (follows) him afterwards'. This Avestan phrase denoting a man's 'successor' stresses another aspect of succession, namely the duty of *continuing the lineage*, a task incumbent on both male and female heirs (the latter as *ayōgēn* or *stūr ī būdag*).[88] The term *xwāstagdār*, on the other hand, emphasizes the *material aspect* of succession: the heirs become the 'possessors' of family property in perpetuity, replacing the head of a household as the person responsible for the estate as a whole, assuming all the rights and duties of the latter, including the important obligation of repaying debts and liabilities of the family.[89] The term moreover designates not only the natural heirs of a *paterfamilias*, his legitimate sons and daughters, but every legatee named by the former, *e.g.*, fellow-citizens (*mard ī šahr*) from outside the family.[90] In contrast to the son, who succeeds automatically as *xwāstagdār* to the father (if he does not expressly reject succession), a fellow-citizen has to explicitly declare that he is willing to take possession of the property assigned to him, hereby assuming all the duties of an heir.[91] A daughter could receive the same successional rights in this category of property as a son—at least according to legal practice (*pad kardag*) if not in legal theory—with the same implications, notably to cover the family's liabilities.[92]

The head of a household could install a son or another person as *xwāstagdār* during his lifetime, hereby transmitting the obligation to repay debts and liabilities to his successor(s).[93] In the ideal case the substance (*bun*) of family property, belonging collectively to all the heirs and legatees (*xwāstagdārān*), was inalienable (with the exception of property in ownership and partitioned residue), but this rule did not apply in cases of large debts, which could not be repaid by the income (*bar*) of family property alone. The son, who accepted the 'total (residuary) estate' (*abarmānd*) of a family took full responsibility for all the liabilities of the father as 'joint and several debtor' (*hamāg-tōzišn*), *i.e.*, he assumed the obligation to satisfy the claims of potential creditors with all the property at his disposal (this applied as a rule to property in the categories of *pad xwāstagdārīh* and *pad xwēšīh*, but not to the *stūrīh* or *ruwān* types, see below).[94] If the deceased had several sons, who became his heirs as shareholders of the estate in the category of *xwāstagdārīh*, all of the sons took full responsibility for the liabilities of the father as 'joint and several debtors' (*hamāg-tōzišn*), *i.e.*, each one

88 See Chapter II, pp. 163–174.

89 On these obligations see the chapter on inheritance in the Law-book, MHD 59.11–63.5 (Macuch 1993, pp. 408–432).

90 MHD 60.5–7; 61.11–12 (Macuch 1993, pp. 409, 414 and 410, 416 respectively).

91 MHD 61.9–11, compare 60.7–8 (Macuch 1993, pp. 410, 415 and 409, 414 respectively).

92 MHD 61.16–62.2; 62.12–15 (Macuch 1993, pp. 410, 416 and 411, 417 respectively). On legal practice (*kardag*) versus legal theory (*čāštag*) see Chapter I, pp. 66–71.

93 MHD 61.1–5; 61.5–9 (Macuch 1993, pp. 409f., 415).

94 MHD 59.12–16 (*ibid.*, pp. 408, 413). The next sentence (MHD 59.16–17) implies that a single son could only inherit property in the category of *xwāstagdārīh*.

of them could be charged by the creditor(s) for the whole debt.[95] The heir (son or daughter) who satisfied the claim(s) of the creditor(s) could in turn ask his/her co-heirs for repayment in proportion to their individual shares.[96] (This does not apply in the case of property bequeathed as *ahlawdād* in the category of *ruwān* property: in this instance the heirs are only 'part-debtors', *xwāstag-tōzišn*, *i.e.*, they can be charged only in proportion to their individual shares, *bahr-marīhā*).[97] If a *pādixšāy*-son was explicitly re-installed (by legal authorities?) as *abarmānd-xwāstagdār*, he alone took full responsibility for all the liabilities of the parents and could not reclaim payment from the other partners/heirs (*hambāyān*) (at least according to the statement of a jurisconsult named Xwadāybūd ī Dibīr).[98] An unmarried daughter who still belonged to her natal lineage and received property in the category of *xwāstagdārīh* had the same obligations as the son(s). After entering marriage she would lose her earnings as a shareholder, but she remained obliged to cover successional liabilities by hypothecating her possessions (*pad rāh ī āgrawīh*).[99] The daughter who was the only child assumed full liability for all the debts of the family, regardless of her status as an unmarried or married woman.[100] As a single child, the daughter would be engaged as 'intermediary successor' or 'natural proxy' (*ayōgēn* or *stūr ī būdag*) and have a title to the income of *stūrīh*-property, but would only inherit the 'total (residuary) estate' (*abarmānd*) as a last resort, if there were no other male relatives to take over (this procedure was labeled *pad rāh ī a-kasīh*, lit. 'by means of having no relations').[101] Fellow-citizens appointed as *xwāstagdār* by the testator, on the other hand, were only regarded as 'part-debtors' (*xwāstag-tōzišn*), that is, they were only obliged to contribute to the payment of debts in proportion to their share of the property.[102] Interestingly, one passage in this context also mentions adherents of other religions (*ag-dēn*, predominantly Christians and Jews in the Sasanian period) in

95 MHD 60.5–6 (Macuch 1993, pp. 409, 414).

96 MHD 59.12–14; 62.16–63.1 (*ibid.*, pp. 408, 413 and 411f., 417 respectively).

97 MHD 60.1–5 (Macuch 1993, pp. 408f., 413f.). On the specifics of *ruwān* property see below pp. 220–229.

98 MHD 2.4–6 (Macuch 1993, pp. 40, 42). The formulation of the first part of the sentence is not conclusive: *ka tōzišn ī pidarān abāz ō pus (ī) pādixšāyīhā pad abarmānd-xwāstagdār dahēnd ...* 'If they return (the obligation to pay) the liabilities of the fathers to the *pādixšāy*-son as *abarmānd-xwāstagdār* ...' could possibly refer to some kind of official or legal authority obliging the son to repay the debts of the father (after another beneficiary or heir installed as *xwāstagdār* had refused to do so?). On the term *hambāy* see below pp. 245–253.

99 MHD 62.12–15 (Macuch 1993, pp. 411, 417). On *āgrawīh* 'mortgage of the substance (*bun*), hypotheca' see Chapter IV, pp. 336–342.

100 MHD 63.3–4 (*ibid.*, pp. 412, 418).

101 MHD 62.10–12 (Macuch 1993, pp. 411, 417). The same phrase is used of the mistress of the house (*kadag-bānūg*), who inherited the total estate (*abarmānd*) of the husband only if there were no other relatives to whom it could be passed on (MHD 62.8–9; *ibid.*, pp. 411, 417).

102 MHD 60.6–7 (Macuch 1993, pp. 409, 414).

this context. Shareholding heirs in these cases could as a rule—in contrast to Zoroastrian co-heirs, but similar to fellow-citizens established as successors—only be made liable as 'part-debtors' (*xwāstag-tōzišn*), not as 'joint and several debtors' (*hamāg-tōzišn*) with the consequences already described above.[103]

Can anything concrete be said of a family's assets transmitted *pad xwāstag-dārīh*, besides the obvious fact that they did not belong to the category of ownership and were distinguished from *stūrīh*- or *ruwān*-property? Although the Law-book does not specify these, it would not be too far-fetched to assume that property 'in possession' could consist of various elements. These presumably included property granted to the family as a lease (*tāg*), (land, orchards, vineyards, as in the Tabarestān documents)[104] which was held 'in possession' either for a limited time or in perpetuity (comparable to the Roman agricultural lease called *emphyteusis*), requiring the payment of a periodic sum or rent.[105] Another component could have consisted of immovable property belonging to the crown (*šāhīgān*) which was granted—according to one passage—in perpetuity to *aswārān* 'horsemen', equestrians or knights belonging to the higher ranks of Sasanian society, in exchange for military services. After the demise of the *aswār* the heirs (*xwāstagdār*) could take conditional possession of this land in exchange for paying yearly taxes.[106] Property 'in possession' could have also included the fruits (*bar*) of assets held as security for a loan in lieu of interest (by *grawagānīh* 'mortgage of the fruits', corresponding to the Roman *antichresis*).[107]

In the context of real security the term *xwāstagdār* is also attested in two complex documents from Tabarestān (Tab. 18 and 24) involving loan-contracts, in which the fruits of specified 'olive trees' (*zayt*) are mortgaged as *antichresis*. Both documents record these 'olive trees' in exact lists, naming meticulously all the proprietors of the land on which the trees are planted. According to Tab. 18, several of these trees are on 'the land of the heirs of men, who are not shareholders' (*zamīg ī xwāstagdārān ī mardān ī a-ǰomāyīg*) and on 'the land of the men, who are heirs of the men called Dērā' (*zamīg ī mardān ī xwāstagdārān ī mardān ī Dērā nām*).[108] Similarly, in Tab. 24 one group of olive trees is on the 'land of the heirs' (*zamīg ī xwāstagdārān*), another group on that of the 'esteemed sons and heirs' (*pusarāwandān ud xwāstagdārān*) and the 'heirs of the men called Wahmanpanāh' (*xwāstagdārān ī mardān ī Wahmanpanāh nam*).[109] Although

103 MHD 60.16–61.1 (*ibid*., pp. 409, 415).
104 See Macuch 2017c with further references.
105 On leasehold see Chapter IV, pp. 367–372.
106 See Macuch 2005c, p. 97f. with further references.
107 On this type of security see Chapter IV, pp. 313–349.
108 Tab. 18.10 and 18.14. The whole document is edited in Weber 2017a, pp. 151–154, and commented in Macuch 2017c, pp. 183–188; on this important document see also Macuch 2017b.
109 Tab. 24.6,7,8,9,10,13,14,18; Tab. 24.5 and Tab. 24.16 respectively. The whole document is edited in Weber 2019b, pp. 102–110, and commented extensively in Macuch 2019b, pp. 132–146.

the term is not explained in either of the texts, the context clearly points to land (*zamīg*) in the collective possession of the 'heirs' of several larger families as shareholders, whose names are listed in the documents.

Despite these details on hereditary possession in the Law-book and the Tabarestān documents, the information on *xwāstagdārīh*—as on other legal matters—remains fragmentary and is far too abstract to allow exact comparisons with other legal systems.[110] In contrast to the category of property 'in ownership' (*pad xwēšīh*), the standard regulation for holding property 'in hereditary possession' (*pad xwāstagdārīh*) provided that the heirs became shareholders and had a title to the income (*bar*) of a family's collective property in proportion to their individual shares. Since the *xwāstagdār* also assumed responsibility for the debts of the family, the right to the fruits could exceptionally be expanded to the substance (*bun*) in emergences, including the payment of extensive liabilities.

2.2 Property 'in ownership' (*pad xwēšīh*)

Property held or bequeathed 'in ownership' (*pad xwēšīh*) is explicitly distinguished in several passages of the Law-book from the categories of property 'in possession' (*pad xwāstagdārīh*), 'for pious purposes' or 'for the soul' (*pad ahlawdād*; *pad ruwān*) and 'for substitute succession' (*pad stūrīh*). One would search in vain in Pahlavi legal texts for a definition of these expressions, but the different components of an affluent family's estate are contrasted in several passages offering a few distinctions: (1) In intestate succession the son (as universal

110 Despite the identical wording, *xwāstagdārīh* does not seem to correspond to *bonorum possessio* ('possession of property') in Roman law, a scheme introduced by the Praetor to correct the drawbacks of civil-law succession, which was originally based on a strong agnatic concept, excluding cognates from succession. By granting *bonorum possessio* the Praetor could remedy the flaws from agnatic succession, allowing persons other than heirs (such as descendants from the female line, who were originally excluded from inheritance) to take possession of the property (Nicholas 1962, pp. 243–250; du Plessis/Borkowski 2010, pp. 208–211; Kaser 1986, p. 301f.). The whole background is different in Sasanian law due to the importance attached to cognatic ties, the preference of endogamy within a descent group (including the nuclear family), the creation of temporary marriage and the institutions of intermediary and substitute succession, in which the female line plays a dominant role. Sasanian law not only accepted cognatic links, but assigned the important task of reproduction to the females in their natal lineage, construing an elaborate system of marriage and succession to combine patrilineal descent with cognatic elements. Although a *xwāstagdār* could also be installed from among fellow-citizens (*mard ī šahr*) outside the family there is absolutely no proof—in contrast to the *bonorum possessor* of Roman law—that any kind of official instance (comparable to the Roman Praetor) apart from the head of the family himself, was involved in this act (MHD 2.4–6, the only passage which could possibly indicate the involvement of a legal authority, is inconclusive, see fn. 98 above).

successor of the father) inherits family property as a rule as 'hereditary possession' (*pad xwāstagdārīh*; with the implications described above) with the exception of property expressly bequeathed to him (by testament or grant) 'in ownership' (*pad xwēšīh*) or "for pious purposes' (*pad ahlawdād*).[111] (2) In testamentary succession, the wording of the will is decisive: property bequeathed to the son without exact specification (using the verb *dādan* 'to give': *kū-m xwāstag ō pus dād* 'I have given this property to the son') is held by the heir 'in (hereditary) possession' (*pad xwāstagdārīh*), but if the father specifically bestows property on his son 'in ownership' (with the words: *kū-m pad xwēšīh dād* 'I have given it in ownership'), then the heir has different rights with respect to this specific property.[112] (3) Property *pad xwēšīh* is furthermore distinguished from *pad stŭrīh*, constituting another distinct part of a family's total property, whose substance (*bun*) was just as inalienable as that of property 'for pious purposes' (*pad ahlawdād*) or 'for the soul' (*pad ruwān*).[113]

If we take all the attestations of the term into consideration, the notion of *xwēšīh*—in contrast to *dārišn*—involves enjoyment of a number of exclusive rights over property bequeathed in this manner: the right to use it privately, to keep it apart from the joint-property of the family and to alienate it (by sale, barter or donation) at one's own discretion.[114] In contrast to the category of *pad xwastagdārīh*, the person who was both *bun-xwēš* ('owner of the substance') and *bar-xwēš* ('owner of the fruit'), had the right to dispose of both the principal and the income of this property according to his (or her) own will (*kāmag*). This also applied apparently to women who had previously received authorization from their husbands to own property.[115] Apart from the 'total (patrimonial) estate' (*abarmānd*), the head of a household could transfer assets acquired during his lifetime (*handōxt ī xwēš* 'one's own acquisitions' or *mad ud rasēd* '[property that] has come and shall arrive') as a gift to his children or wives during his lifetime or bequeath it to them by testament expressly as *xwēšīh*-property, giving the recipient(s) full ownership rights. Gifts and donations from a third party to certain members of the family (including

111 See specifically MHD 61.14–15 (Macuch 1993, pp. 410, 416).

112 MHD 62.6–7 (*ibid.*, pp. 411, 417). On the wording of the testament (with the agential or ergative construction) see Macuch 2015c and pp. 83–85 above.

113 All the attestations of these terms should be taken into consideration; distinctions are indicated in MHD 21.17 (Macuch 1993, pp. 171, 176); 52.2 (*ibid.*, pp. 312, 328), MHDA 21.2–3 (Macuch 1981, pp. 44, 167, and 2015c, p. 136) and DkM 749.4 (*abar xwāstag ī pad xwēšīh ud ān ī pad stŭrīh ō nabānazdištān rasēd* 'On property which is bequeathed in ownership and that, which is bequeathed in *stŭrīh* to the relatives').

114 For attestations of the term see Macuch 1993, Index, p. 715; on 'ownership' and 'possession' see pp. 193–197 above.

115 See for example MHDA 4.5–10 (Macuch 1981, pp. 24f., 72) in which the transfer of a gift into the ownership of a woman (with the consent of the husband) has different implications than its transfer as mere possession.

women) could be granted in this category, conveying the right to exclusive ownership, if the donor confirmed that the object was his own (by the words *xwāstag ī man xwēš* 'the thing that is my own') and expressly transferred it to another person's ownership (*tō xwēš* '[shall be] your own') or by using the formula *pad xwēšīh*.[116]

Due to the concept of 'ownership' as a 'relative right' (in contrast to the 'absolute right' of classical Roman law)[117] Sasanian law distinguished between hereditary—or at least older—ownership rights and those acquired recently by a legal transaction (purchase, barter, gift or donation). As a rule a beneficiary was obliged to reveal how a specific object had come into his or her ownership (*čē ēwēnag xwēšīh* 'what kind of ownership')[118] and to provide evidence if his/her title was contested by a third party. Property in hereditary ownership or to which the owner had some other kind of ancient, vested right was called *pad xwēšīh ī xwēš* 'in my own ownership', a formula stressing the fact that this specific property had *not* been recently acquired by a legal transaction, but was an inherent part of the person's personal estate.[119] In contrast to this type of ownership (which had to be proved by other means, *e. g.*, by testament or witnesses), recently acquired ownership rights (by sale, barter etc.) were defended in court by summoning the potential owner's 'legal predecessor' (*dastwar*), who was obliged to confirm that he was entitled to this object prior to its transfer and to defend the new owner against claims of a third party.[120]

Although almost all these cases are described in abstract terms, we can draw a few conclusions as to the type of property referred to in these passages. Private ownership seems to have included not only the personal property of the members of a household, consisting mainly of movables (clothing, jewelry, ornaments, arms, weapons and private items of daily use, etc.), but also other valuable objects of all kinds, including slaves and animals, as well as immovables (houses, vineyards, orchards, farming land) and real estate. But despite the possibility of *bun-xwēšīh* ('ownership of the substance') in these cases, we have reason to assume that the bulk of a wealthy family's estate remained either in the category of *xwāstagdārīh* or was immobilized as *stūrīh* or *ruwān* property, restricting the ownership rights of the heirs to the fruits (*bar-xwēšīh*). This would leave a large part of the substance of family property intact to be transferred to the next generation.

116 For example MHD 17.4 (Macuch 1993, pp. 151, 157); MHDA 4.5–10 (Macuch 1981, pp. 24f., 72).
117 See above, pp. 195–196.
118 MHD 9.15; 10.7; 95.12 (Macuch 1993, pp. 103, 106; 104, 107; 605, 608 respectively); DkM 707.22.
119 Particularly MHD 5.4 (Macuch 1993, pp. 87, 91) and 76.11 (*ibid.*, pp. 510, 512).
120 See Chapters IV, pp. 385–387, and VI, pp. 542–544.

2.3 Property 'in trust; for substitute succession' (*pad stŭrīh*)

Property of this category was the economic basis of 'substitute succession' (*stŭrīh*), the institution derived to generate heirs for a sonless man described in Chapter II (pp. 169–174). Possessions reserved to maintain the 'proxy' (*stŭr*, or 'proxies' in the case of several *stŭrīh*s) and all of the children born in this context were tied up in a kind of trust and had to be large enough to provide an income over a long period of years, at least until the heir(s) came of age and could take possession of the patrimonial estate. Interestingly, *stŭrīh*-property could also be reserved for another purpose: to sustain a consecrated fire, established by the *paterfamilias* for the spiritual wellbeing of the family. Despite numerous case studies discussing legal problems both in the Law-book and in later Pahlavi sources, property in *stŭrīh*—with one exception—is never explicitly named or restricted to certain parts of a family's estate. The institution was so well known and widespread that there was obviously no need for explanations. The sole condition named in the sources, namely that *stŭrīh*-property must be 'fruitful' or 'profitable' (*barōmand*), suggests that it could include all kinds of assets yielding some kind of revenue to maintain the persons engaged in procreation or—as the case may be—in preserving a sacred fire: *e. g.*, agricultural or farming land, orchards and vineyards (crop-yields), real estate and houses (lease or rent), money (interest), animals and slaves (work-force; products; offspring). The only property referred to explicitly as *stŭrīh*-property is a sacred fire (*ātaxš*; also a *Wahrām* fire), which seems strange on first sight, since a fire does not yield any kind of (material) profit on its own.[121] But we have reason to assume that these passages do not just allude to sacred fires, but to fire foundations, which were equipped with—at times vast—estates and other income producing property, including slaves and animals, all dedicated to providing for the upkeep of the sacred fire. Fire foundations could be established in two manners, both of which gave the beneficiaries only access to the revenue of the property, but not to its substance: (1) as *stŭrīh*-property (to which we will return presently); (2) as property 'for the soul' (*pad ruwān*; which will be discussed under 2.4, pp. 220–229 below).

The minimum value of *stŭrīh*-property 'yielding revenue' (*barōmand*) is fixed at 60 staters in late Pahlavi texts or possibly, according to the Law-book, 80 staters, but the latter sum can be read as 60 (instead of 80) if the first sign in the row of numbers represents an ⟨s⟩, the abbreviation of *stēr*, as it is attested in Pahlavi documents in the cursive script.[122] In affluent families, however, property in *stŭrīh* could have well been far more worth than the minimum sum of 60

121 MHD 46.2–4 (Macuch 1993, pp. 305, 321); compare MHDA 39.1–8 (Macuch 1981, pp. 65f., 222).

122 On the abbreviation ⟨s⟩ for *stēr* see Weber 2008b, p. XXIV. The minimum sum of 60 staters seems to be confirmed indirectly in a passage of the Law-book: a man bequeaths 'a share' (*ēw bahr*) of family property as *stŭrīh*-property on his demise to a person without specifying the exact amount. The legacy is altogether worth 90 staters, hence the

staters and it could have included several of the different kinds of assets listed above. Moreover, as we have already elucidated in the last chapter, a man had the right to establish several *stūrīh*s and to install two or more proxies in order to secure his succession.[123] This seems to have been the standard procedure in wealthy families—even if several potential heirs had already been born—in order to ensure the continuity of the lineage should none of these descendants outlive the *paterfamilias*. Remarkably, a man even retained this right to a proxy if the portion of property in *stūrīh* did not suffice for the upkeep of the persons involved (we are not informed on how they should be maintained in this case) and even if the family's financial liabilities were just as extensive as the value of the property reserved for 'substitute succession' (the argument for the latter decision being: one should always take into consideration that a family could acquire further property in the future or could be released entirely from debt).[124]

Property tied up in *stūrīh* was as a rule inalienable (with possible exceptions in the case of debt); neither the immediate heirs, nor persons engaged as 'proxies' (*stūr*) for the head of a household had access to its 'substance' (*bun*), which, however, remained in the collective possession of the family as a separate component of its 'total (patrimonial/residuary) estate' (*abarmānd*). The proxies were entitled to remuneration (called *srēnag/sēnag masāy ud bāzā masāy*[125]) and to 'ownership of the fruits' (*bar-xwēšīh*) of *stūrīh*-property, if they were family members or explicitly installed by testament (*stūr ī kardag*).[126] Although we are not very well informed on the rights of the persons involved, this choice of words (instead of 'usufruct', *bar-xward*) indicates that a *stūrīh* could be fixed in perpetuity as a permanent part of a family's estate and was not necessarily limited to a specific number of years or to a certain person as proxy. This is in fact confirmed by the possibility of passing the obligations of *stūrīh* together with the property reserved for it to the next generation: if a person engaged as *ayōgēn-stūr* or *stūr* did not produce the desired male heir for the *paterfamilias* or only generated daughters, then this duty was transferred to one of these daughters (as *ayōgēn* 'intermediary successor') or to another person designated in the will as proxy (*stūr ī kardag*).[127] This second (or third, fourth etc.) proxy

recipient receives two shares out of three as his portion in *stūrīh*, corresponding to the value of 60 staters (MHD 88.5–6; Macuch 1993, pp. 561, 564).

123 See Chapter II, p. 174; MHD 50.6–7 and 50.7–12 (Macuch 1993, pp. 310, 326).

124 MHD 50.5–6; 109.6–8 (Macuch 1993, pp. 310, 326 and 644, 651 respectively).

125 On this phrase see Chapter II, pp. 173–174.

126 See, *e.g.*, MHD 90.9: *stūr ī kardag bar-xwēš* 'the appointed proxy (is) owner of the fruit' (Macuch 1993, pp. 571, 574; I had translated the term *bar-xwēš* by 'Nutznießer (*usufructarius*)' instead of the correct 'owner of the fruit', still being unaware at that time of the important difference between the two concepts of 'usufruct' and 'ownership of the fruits' in Sasanian law). On the remuneration of the *stūr* see Chapter II, pp. 173–174.

127 On these terms and the obligations of the women engaged as *ayōgēn* or *ayōgēn-stūr* see Chapter II, pp. 163–174. The transfer of *stūrīh*-property together with the obligation to generate heirs to the *ayōgēn*-daughter of a person engaged as *stūr* is described in

inherited—together with the obligation to procreate an heir—also the right to 'ownership of the fruits' of *stŭrīh*-property from his or her predecessors. On the other hand, expressly limited *stŭrīh*s are also attested (we have already mentioned 10 years above) and seem to have been frequent, also those restricted to a certain person as proxy: the formula explicitly restricting the duration of the institution or the sequence of beneficiaries is: '*stŭrīh* should not be held in succession' (*stŭrīh nē pad raft dārišn*).[128] Here again Sasanian law shows remarkable flexibility, allowing a large range of variations corresponding to the financial means of a lineage as well as to the personal preferences of the head of a household.

According to a late Pahlavi Riwāyat text, ownership of the property held in *stŭrīh* finally went to the designated beneficiaries, the legitimate heir or heirs of the *kadag-xwadāy* born of the *stŭr*: (1) if the proxy had only one son (*stŭrīg-pus*), this son received ownership rights (*pad xwēšīh*) over *stŭrīh*-property after reaching maturity (at fifteen years of age);[129] (2) if the proxy had several children, sons and daughters, the eldest son became family guardian (*dūdag-sālār*) after reaching maturity and all the heirs received ownership rights over *stŭrīh*-property in proportion to their residuary shares of the estate as sons and daughters (the daughter obtaining half the portion of a son, see below pp. 232–233).[130] That is, once the beneficiaries, the children of the proxy, reached maturity and took control of *stŭrīh*-property they became owners and there was no more need to retain the institution. But we should bear in mind that this is a very late text which reflects not only the drastically changed situation in the Islamic period, but simplifies procedures, ignoring different options, which might have been current in Sasanian times. Given the versatility of the legal system, it would not be too far-fetched to assume that a specific part of a family's total estate remained tied to *stŭrīh* purposes for the next generations after

---

some length in REA *Pursišn* 18 (Safa-Isfehani 1980 has completely misunderstood the whole *Pursišn*. Her translation of the whole text is unreliable).

128 MHDA 39.2–3 (Macuch 1981, pp. 65f., 222) with respect to the *stŭrīh* of a sacred fire, see below; REA 18.17 (Safa-Isfehani 1980, p. 138, has a wrong translation).

129 REA 18.14–15: (14) *agar zan pad im stŭrīh kunēd ud u-š frazand zāyēd agar pus stŭrīg pus ī ōy kē-š stŭrīh az-iš padīrift ested* (15) *ka pus ō dād ī panǰdahsālag mad ēg-iš rāyēnīdan ī im stŭrīh bowandagēnīdan ud xwāstag ī stŭrīh be ō im pus rasēd pad xwēšīh be awiš abespārišn*. '(14) If he (= the proxy) takes a wife during this *stŭrīh* and a son is born, if it (is) a son, (then) he (is) the 'son in proxy' (*stŭrīg-pus*) of the one, whose *stŭrīh* he (= the proxy) had accepted from him. (15) When the son has reached the age of fifteen, (then) the management of this *stŭrīh* has come to an end and the property in *stŭrīh* goes to this son: it should be given to him in ownership.' (Wrong Safa-Isfehani 1980, p. 136).

130 REA 18.19: *agar pus ud duxt ēčand bawēnd ka ēk az pusarān ō panǰdahsālagīh mad dūdag-sālār ī* (ms.: *dūdagsālārīh*) *awēšān pus duxt bawēd u-šān xwāstag ī stŭrīh pusīhā ud duxtīhā xwēšīhēd*. 'If there are several sons and daughters, when one of the sons has reached the age of fifteen, (then) he becomes the family guardian of those sons and daughters and the property in *stŭrīh* is owned in proportion to (the shares of) the son and the daughter.' (Wrong Safa-Isfehani 1980, p. 138).

the beneficiaries took possession of it (or ownership of parts of it), and that the complete dissolution of the institution was only one possible option among others. *Stŭrīh*-property dedicated to the upkeep of a sacred fire seems to have been subject to different regulations altogether (see below).[131]

Several legal similarities may be detected between *stŭrīh*- and *ruwān*-property (specifically of the type fixed in a pious endowment): (1) the substance was as a rule bound to the purpose of the institution and inalienable (with the sole possible exception of extensive liabilities of succession, which could be only met by using the principal, *e.g.*, by hypothecating it); (2) the proxies, trustees, legatees, heirs and beneficiaries were as a rule 'owners of the fruit' (*bar-xwēš*) or had a right to usufruct (*bar-xward*); (3) the legal formulae for establishing these institutions were identical: *paydāg kardan* 'lit. 'to reveal, make visible, obvious', in the sense of 'to establish, settle, found' and (more seldom) *paydāgēnīdan*, lit. 'to reveal',[132] are the verbs employed in this context: *kū-m ēn xwāstag pad stŭrīh paydāg kard* 'I have established this property for substitute succession';[133] *kū-m xwāstag ruwān rāy paydāg kard* 'I have established property for the soul'.[134] It was even possible to dedicate property to both purposes alternately every second year. In one remarkable instance a father bequeaths a 'thing'/property (*xwāstag*) worth 60 (or 80) staters, that is, the minimum sum required for a *stŭrīh*, alternately 'for substitute succession' the first year and 'for the soul' the second year (*kū-m har 2 sāl sāl ī nazdist stŭrīh ud sāl ī dudīgar ruwān rāy paydāg kard* 'I have established it alternately every two years the first year for *stŭrīh* and the second year for the soul'). The testator could thus dedicate the revenue of the same property on a rotating basis to the two—religiously significant and interrelated—purposes of securing his succession and the continuity of the lineage (*stŭrīh*), on the one hand, and redeeming his soul (*ruwān*), on the other.[135] In both cases the substance (*bun*) of this property would be inalienable and tied to the specific objectives defined in the will or document.

131 'Destroying substitute succession' (*stŭr-škenišnīh*) was regarded as a *margarzān* sin, see Chapter V, pp. 461–462. On the similarities and differences to the fideicommissum in Roman law see p. 174, fn. 270.

132 MHD 45.5 (Macuch 1993, pp. 304, 320).

133 See, *e.g.*, MHD 44.16 (Macuch 1993, pp. 304, 320); compare MHD 42.3f.; 45.2: *pad stŭrīh paydāg kunēd* (*ibid.*, pp. 300, 316 and 304, 320 respectively); 45.9: *xwāstag pad stŭrīh paydāg kard* (*ibid.*, pp. 304, 320); 47.8: *pad stŭrīh ī xwēš paydāg kard* (*ibid.*, pp. 306, 323).

134 See, *e.g.*, MHD 34.12; 35.4 (Macuch 1993, pp. 253, 256); compare MHD 34.13: *xwāstag ī-m ruwān rāy paydāg kard* (*ibid.*, pp. 253, 256).

135 MHD 46.4–9 (Macuch 1993, pp. 305, 321; 'Drachmen' added in the translation should be corrected to 'stater'). In this interesting case the father 'has not determined, who should possess the property dedicated' to *stŭrīh* (*ān xwāstag dāštan rāy framān nē dād*), but he has heirs, both son and daughter. We may therefore conclude that establishing a *stŭrīh* in this instance was not a necessity, but a precautionary measure. According to the rules of intestate succession, the daughter is engaged as *stŭr* (for which preferably women were chosen) with the right to the revenue of the property one year, whereas

The religious significance of the institution is particularly apparent in the possibility of establishing the equipment dedicated to the care of a consecrated fire as *stūrīh*-property. Sacred fires and fire foundations (possibly also other pious endowments) were obviously subject to special regulations, which set them apart from other legal objects. They may even have been considered as non-human legal entities in their own right, having juristic personality to a certain degree, capable of enjoying and being subject to legal rights and duties. Although it is highly unlikely that Sasanian law developed a theory of the (non-human) juristic person, several significant entries indicate that sacred fires had in fact a special status, comparable to that of a natural person, a human being. For example, a fire is entitled to 'nourishment', *i.e.*, fuel, three times in the summer and twice in the winter, just as often as a 'righteous man' (*mard ī ahlaw*) is entitled to a meal. Withdrawing fuel from a fire and not giving food and drink to a Zoroastrian are both considered as an offence of *adwadād* 'withholding nourishment' and liable to punishment.[136]

Another remarkable feature of the consecrated fire (in this case a Wahram fire) is that it could own property. We are fortunate that the exact wording of a document has survived in the collection of the Law-book, in which the foundation of a fire by a certain Dādgušnasp ī Šahr ī Zādaragān is declared by him as follows: 'I have seated a fire as a Wahrām fire in its proper place (*dādgāh*) and have given this property (*xwāstag*) to my *stūrīh* and as ownership (*xwēšīh*) for the upkeep of the fire to the fire (itself)' (*kū-m ātaxš-ē pad wahrāmīh ō dādgāh nišāst ud ēn xwāstag pad stūrīh ī man ud xwēšīh ī ātaxš dāštan ō ātaxš dād*).[137] We are furthermore informed that this remarkable founding document was sealed by Wehšābuhr, the chief judicial authority himself, who was presumably *mowbedān mowbed* in the first half of the 6th century under Husraw I.[138] Hence this was definitely a legally sanctioned procedure by the sixth century. As we will see in the next section (pp. 225–229), consecrated fires were equipped with property 'yielding revenue' (*barōmand*) that could consist—in the case of large foundations—of huge estates, dedicated to the maintenance of priests and other persons involved in the preservation of the fire. In the cited document the founder furnishes the sacred fire he has seated in its most prominent, 'highest' form (*ātaxš Wahrām*) in a duly constructed sanctuary (*dādgāh*)[139] with property, which he places in his own *stūrīh*, but dedicates in ownership (*xwēšīh*) to the fire itself, or, in other words, the founder and his family retain the right to the fruits of

the son—as guardian of both the property and the family (*dūdag ud ān xwāstag sālār*)—holds the property 'for the soul' the ensuing year, that is, daughter and son are alternately entitled to the property as *bar-xwēš* with the corresponding rights and duties.

136 FīO XXVb (Reichelt 1900–1901, II, p. 209.1–7; Klingenschmitt 1968, no. 711); on this passage see Macuch 2012b, p. 528; on the *adwadād* offence see also Macuch 2012a, Chapters I, pp. 75–76 and V, pp. 463–468.

137 MHDA 39.5–7 (Macuch 1981, pp. 66, 222).

138 On the dating of Wehšābuhr see Macuch 2017a, pp. 265–269.

139 On the Zoroastrian cult of fire see Boyce 1968b and 1975a, and Stausberg/Karanjia 2015 (with further references).

this property (as *bar-xwēš* or in usufruct, *bar-xward*), whereas the consecrated fire itself is 'owner of the substance' (*bun-xwēš*). The precise wording suggests that a sacred fire was in some manner considered as an individual legal entity, capable of owning property, comparable—if not identical—with the concept of the juristic (or artificial) person in contemporary legal systems (*e.g.*, a corporation in contrast to a 'natural person'). But this was obviously not the only option: another passage states that the '*hambaragān* own the Wahrām fire' (*ātaxš ī Wahrām hambaragān xwēš*) and that several documents with this judgment are to be found in the 'archive of the fire of Hurām-Ardaxšēr' (*nāmag-niyān ī ātaxš ī Hurām-Ardaxšēr*) in Xabr, a village (*deh*) in the province (*nahang*) of Ardaxšēr-Xwarrah.[140] Unfortunately the decisive term *hambaragān*, lit. 'joint partners of the fruit(s); shareholders of the income',[141] is not explained: it could either refer to the co-beneficiaries of a Wahrām fire (who were determined by the founder) or to the persons responsible for assembling, consecrating and seating the fire in its sanctuary.[142] In any case, Sasanian law appears to have been flexible in the question of ownership of a consecrated fire and the matter could be resolved (1) by bestowing ownership on the fire itself and placing the fire in the founder's *stūrīh*; (2) by determining the founders or beneficiaries as owners, albeit only as *hambaragān* 'co-partners/shareholders of the income (*bar*)' (*not* as owners of the substance, *bun-xwēš*, *i.e.*, the fire itself). In fact, these two options do not contradict each other. The fire could well have been considered theoretically as owning itself (as *bun-xwēš*), whereas the co-beneficiaries of the income (*ham-baragān*) of the property of the fire would only be joint owners of the fruits (as *bar-xwēš*).

140 MHD 78.12–14: *ātaxš ī Wahrām hambaragān xwēš nāmag kē ēn and dādestān az-iš paydāg pad nāmag-niyān ī ātaxš ī Hurām-Ardaxšēr ī Ardaxšēr-Xwarrah nahang Xabr Hurām-Ardaxšēr deh nišast dārēnd* 'The joint-partners/shareholders of the income (*hambaragān*) own the Wahrām fire. Documents revealing many judgements on this (issue) are kept in the archive of the fires established in Hurām-Ardaxšēr in Xabr, a village of Hurām-Ardaxšēr, in the province (*nahang*) of Ardaxšēr-Xwarrah.' (Macuch 1993, pp. 517f., 520f.). On *nāmag-niyān* 'archive, repository' see fn. 191 below. Ardaxšēr-Xwarrah, called here *nahang* ('province'; on this term see Gyselen 2019a, p. 11), is the name of one of the five administrative divisions (*kūra*) of Pārs in the south-west under the Sasanians; Xabr the name of a town or village south of Shīrāz; on the geographical names in the Law-book see de Menasce 1964b [= 1985, pp. 81, 86, 88].

141 Plural of *ham-barag* 'joint partner/co-partner/shareholder of the fruit(s)' < *ham-bar-ag-ān* with suffixes *-ag* (Durkin-Meisterernst 2014, pp. 155–157; §§295–297) and (plural) *-ān* (less likely is a derivation from *ham-bar-agān* 'pertaining to, relating to the *hambar* 'co-partner/shareholder of the fruit[s] with *-agān*, as in *ruwānagān*; *nāmagānīh*; *grawagān*). The term also occurs in connection to land: *zamīg ī hambaragān* 'land of co-partners/shareholders of the fruits' (or 'land pertaining to co-partners/shareholders of the fruits'), *i.e.*, land in possession of joint partners with a title to usufruct or ownership of the fruits (MHD 19.6 and 85.8; Macuch 1993, pp. 154, 159, and 549, 552 respectively).

142 The *ātaxš ī Wahrām* was a fire of the highest category, which was established by collecting fires from sixteen different sources, purifying them with the appropriate rituals and placing them in a sanctuary constructed to this purpose, called *dādgāh* (MHD 26.17–27.1,7; 94.5; Macuch 1993, pp. 195, 202 and 594, 597 respectively).

Prima facie the possibility of equipping a consecrated fire with property, which remains in one's own *stūrīh*, seems strange, if we assume—following the bulk of the descriptions—that the main purpose of the latter institution was to ensure the survival of a lineage. Trusteeship of a sacred fire, one might assume, must have had another objective. But if we take the religious background of these regulations into consideration, affinities may in fact be detected between these two forms of *stūrīh* dedicated to (1) the continuity of a lineage and (2) the preservation of a sacred fire. Both acts were religiously significant and theologically linked to the cosmological purpose of world history. The central position of fire in the Zoroastrian cult is well known;[143] likewise the precept of increasing humankind. Procreating children, observing the rituals, founding and consecrating fires, keeping them intact and 'ever-burning' (*hamēšag-sōz*) up to the Restoration (*frašgird*) were all important duties of the Mazdean. A theological passage of the *Dēnkard* explicitly places the most praised form of marriage, endogamy (*xwēdōdah*), in a cosmological context, explaining it as a continuous transmission of 'strength' or '(creative) power' (*nerog*) from one generation to the next up to the final victory against the evil forces at the end of limited time and the Restoration (*frašgird*) of the world.[144] The *stūrīh* institution was obviously one of the legal instruments enabling Zoroastrians to fulfil two of these important religious obligations by providing the financial means to increase the number of children and continue the lineage, on the one hand, and to sustain a consecrated fire, on the other, both 'up to *frašgird*'.

Apart from the possibility of owning property discussed above, two further regulations characterize a sacred fire: (1) property dedicated to the fire in *stūrīh* could '*not* be held in succession' (*stūrīh nē pad raft dārišn*), that is, the heirs of the founder did not inherit this property in the ordinary sequence of succession;[145] and (2) the founder of a consecrated fire (of the Wahrām type) dedicated to his family, could himself be nominated by official instances as its trustee (*stūr ī gumārdag*) (this would have been impossible in the case of *stūrīh* established to generate offspring).[146] These two directives suggest that *stūrīh*-property reserved for a sacred fire was subject to specific restrictions, possibly due to its religious significance. Although it remained a separate category of a family's 'total (patrimonial/residuary) estate' (*abarmānd*), the usual rules of succession did not apply and the trustees (from among members of the family, as we may assume) were chosen by judicial or religious instances.[147] There must have been a difference between sacred fires in *stūrīh* and fire foundations belonging to the *ruwān* category, but this is unfortunately not elucidated in the sparse legal material.[148]

143 See Boyce 1968b, 1975a, and Stausberg/Karanjia 2015, pp. 371–372 (with further references).
144 DkM 72.3–11. On this text see Macuch 2010c, p. 135.
145 MHDA 39.2–3 (Macuch 1981, pp. 65f., 222).
146 MHDA 39.7–8 (Macuch 1981, pp. 66, 222). On the legal terminology used in this passage see Chapter II, pp. 170–171.
147 On the sequence of persons eligible to be chosen as *stūr* see Chapter II, p. 171.
148 On the 'foundation deed' see Chapter IV, pp. 275–279.

2.4 Property 'for the soul' (*pad ruwān*)

Concern for the wellbeing of the souls of the living as well as the departed was one of the foremost features of Zoroastrianism. Every mature Mazdean was held responsible for the fate of his own soul, which he could determine positively by performing good deeds (*kirbag*), financing righteous gifts (*ahlawdād*) and pious foundations (*ruwānagān*), holding the prescribed rituals, observing the required rites for deceased family members and keeping the cult of the souls of the ancestors (*nāmagānīh*). The ritualization of daily life must have produced considerable costs, as only priests could perform certain prescribed liturgies and tend consecrated fires, as well as execute other tasks deemed important for the survival of the community, such as slaughtering and sacrificing animals.[149] Consequently a—presumably—large part of family property was specifically set apart for financing the performance of rites and ceremonies, as well as other pious and charitable acts for the benefit of the souls of the living and the departed, which could also include persons from outside the family. Flexible as Sasanian law was, family property reserved for the 'preservation, or salvation, of the soul' (*pad ruwān dāštan*) could be used for various purposes, which we may divide into two main categories:

1. funds set aside for charitable deeds (*ahlawdād*) as well as for rituals, ceremonies and liturgies (*pad ruwān yazišn*), to be performed for the souls of the departed on a regular basis;
2. property tied up in charitable foundations 'pertaining to the soul' (*ruwānagān*) or dedicated (as *xīr ī ātaxš* 'property of the fire') to the upkeep of sacred fires (*ādurān ātaxšān*).

Both types of *ruwān*-property were bound to religious objectives. Its exact utilization within this framework could be determined by testament or in a separate document, but as a rule the substance of property reserved for the soul could neither be alienated, nor encroached upon or changed into another category of family property (exceptions were however possible in the case of debt).[150] Moreover, charitable foundations (*ruwānagān*) and fire endowments (*ādurān ātaxšān*), based on property yielding revenue (*barōmand*), were not only founded for the salvation of a person's soul, but also intended to secure an income for the children and descendants of the founder in perpetuity (as *bar*-

149 Only priests were allowed to kill animals 'lawfully' (*dādīhā*), see Chapter I, pp. 90–92, and Macuch 2003a (with further references). As already mentioned, the daily ration of a Zoroastrian was calculated on the basis of pieces of meat from a slaughtered animal. The meat portions were distributed in the community by the priests after sacrificing the animal according to certain criteria. On animal sacrifice see Cantera 2022; on food distribution see Macuch 2012a, pp. 247–269.

150 See MHD 70.16–71.2 (Macuch 1993, pp. 465f., 469); MHD 31.8–15 (*ibid*., pp. 222f., 226f.) discusses a specific case referring to a sacred fire, albeit of the lowest type (*ādurōg*).

xwēš 'owners of the fruit'). Although these establishments are often alluded to in legal literature, this is usually done in an abstract form, which does not offer enough details. Additional information on concrete pious foundations can be found, however, in several other sources, which shed light on the significance of these institutions not only from a religious perspective, but also from a legal, social and economic point of view. These foundations could be small family affairs, but also huge institutions with their own infrastructure, encompassing agricultural land, villages, orchards, vineyards, slaves and animals, besides priests, guardians, servants and other persons (including women and children) all occupied in maintaining the endowment and living by its profits. The general term for these endowments is *ruwānagān*, lit. 'relating to the soul', and is attested in an Arabic source, the *Mafātīhu'l-ʿulūm* of al-Ḫwārezmī, in which a 'register of religious foundations' (*rūwānakān dafīra*, *i.e.*, MP **ruwānagān dibīrag*) is mentioned and translated by *kitābat al-awqāf*. Although no further details are conveyed in this source, we may note that al-Ḫwārezmī uses the plural form of the Arabic *waqf* to translate MP *ruwānagān*, hereby drawing a parallel between the Islamic foundation and its Zoroastrian predecessor.[151] The Sasanian *ruwānagān* was well known and seems to have had significant impact on the legal structure of the Islamic *waqf*, which emerged in the formative period of Islamic law, as will be argued in Chapter VII, pp. 622–627.[152]

Three different modes of endowing an estate or funds for the salvation of a person's soul are referred to in a chapter of the Law-book.[153] Property could be settled or founded (*paydāg kard*)[154]

1. for religious services (*yazišn*) to be held by priests for the souls of the departed;

151 The term *ruwānagān* (< *ruwān* 'soul' + *-agān* 'relating to, pertaining to'; on the suffix see Durkin-Meisterernst 2014, p. 158) is also attested in Manichaean texts and designates the services of the Hearers (*niyōšāgān*; *auditors*), the lowest level of the Manichaean hierarchy, for the benefit of the Elect (*wizīdagān*; *electi*), the next higher level in the hierarchy. The word is most probably adapted from Zoroastrian usage, as so many other Manichaean technical expressions in Iranian texts, but employed of course in a completely different religious context. For attestations of the Manichaean term and further references see Durkin-Meisterernst 2004, p. 297: '"things of/for the soul", soul-work, *i.e.*, gifts (esp. food) by Hearers to the Elect, "alms"'. On al-Ḫwārezmī's list see Chapter II, p. 99.

152 See also specifically on the Sasanian foundation Macuch 1991b and 1994a; on the allusion to the pious foundation in the Babylonian Talmud Macuch 2002b; for a comparison with the Islamic *waqf* see Macuch 2009d and recently Jokisch 2017.

153 MHD 34.1: *dar ī yazišn ud nihādag ī abar xīr ī ātaxš ud xwāstag ī ruwān nihād paydāg kard* 'Chapter on religious services and the foundation, which is established for the property of the fire and the property founded for the soul' (Macuch 1993, pp. 252, 255). The title is problematic and has been translated divergently, see references *ibid.*, p. 258 (n. 1). I had argued for a different translation in the quoted edition, but now prefer to stick to the text without any emendations whatsoever.

154 On *paydāg kardan* (lit. 'to reveal, make obvious, visible'), the technical term for 'to establish, settle, found', see p. 216 above.

2. for financing a foundation (*nihādag*)[155] for the 'property of a fire' (*xīr ī ātaxš*);
3. for 'fixing property (as endowment) for the soul' (*xwāstag ī ruwān nihād*).

The precise use of the funds or possessions dedicated to this purpose (called *xwāstag ī ruwān* 'property of the soul')[156] was determined in the will of the testator or in a separate document (called *pādixšīr* in the inscriptions of Šābuhr I and the High Priest Kirdīr, who also employs another term to be read either ⟨GT-y/GTk⟩ *nāmag* or ⟨gt/gtk⟩ *gitt*, *gittag* for 'foundation deed')[157] by using specific formulae. If the testator employed the words *ruwān yazišn rāy* ('for religious services for the soul'), the funds were exclusively utilized for performing the appropriate post-mortem rites and ceremonies either for the decedent himself or for persons explicitly named in his will or in the document.[158] Religious services a man financed for the souls of other men (*yazišn ī pad ruwān ī mard*) were considered as also benefitting his own soul.[159]

On the other hand, if the testator or founder used the formula *ruwān rāy* (or *pad ruwān*) 'for the soul', the endowed property was not explicitly tied to post-mortem rituals, but could be used for any purpose deemed 'most beneficial for the soul' (*ruwān rāy sūdōmandtar*), including all kinds of charitable acts (*ahlawdād*).[160] We may assume that these funds could finance alms for the poor and needy, in the case of larger sums also objects of public utility (roads, bridges, irrigation canals) or they could be employed—if the property yielded revenue (*barōmand*)—for establishing a pious foundation (*ruwānagān*) or for furnishing a sacred fire with income-producing property, called *xwēšīh ī ātaxš* '(property in) ownership of the fire',[161] or *xīr ī ātaxš(ān)* 'property of the fire(s)'.[162] As will be seen below in the case of King Šābuhr I, these different options could be combined: besides contributing to the upkeep of a consecrated fire, the surplus (*bar*) of property dedicated to a fire foundation (in this case specifically cattle) could be used for financing religious ceremonies and rituals for the souls of the

155 The precise technical meaning of *nihādag* (lit. 'set, placed down'), probably 'establishment, foundation, endowment, deposit', is still a matter of debate, despite the obvious etymology (from *nihādan*, *nih-* 'to place, put, establish, deposit'; MacKenzie 1971, p. 59; Nyberg 1974, p. 138; Av. *ni-dā-* 'set down, place down'; Bartholomae 1904, col. 721; Kellens 1995, p. 29; base **daH²* 'to place, put', Cheung 2007, p. 45f.).

156 MHD 34.1; 71.2 (Macuch 1993, pp. 252, 255 and 466, 469 respectively).

157 Both terms are attested on the Kaʿba-ye Zardušt at Naqš-e Rostam; for attestations see Gignoux 1972a, pp. 31, 62; KKZ §02 (Back 1978, p. 389); ŠKZ §35 (Huyse 1999, I, p. 48); on the possible etymology of *pādixšīr* (<**pāti-xša(i)θr-iya-* 'authoritative document'?) see Huyse 1999, II, p. 111, with further references. On ⟨GT(k)⟩ *nāmag*, or ⟨gtk⟩ *gitt(ag)* and foundation deeds in general see Chapter IV, pp. 275–279.

158 MHD 34.3–4; 35.9–36.1 (Macuch 1993, pp. 252, 255 and 253f., 257 respectively).

159 MHD 35.16–17 (*ibid.*, pp. 254, 257).

160 MHD 34. 4–6; 34.12–15 (*ibid.*, pp. 252, 255 and 253, 256 respectively).

161 MHDA 39.5–7 (Macuch 1981, pp. 66, 222).

162 MHD 34.1; 93.4 (Macuch 1993, pp. 252, 255 and 593, 596 respectively); MHDA 27.1,3 (Macuch 1981, pp. 51, 189).

founder and the beneficiaries named in the founding document. But the founder/testator could also provide that *ruwān*-property be exclusively utilized for other purposes than religious liturgies and rituals by choosing the formula *ēn xwāstag ruwān rāy yazišn nē paydāg … kard* 'this thing/property is founded 'for the soul', *not* for religious ceremonies', hereby specifying that it is reserved for one of the other charitable acts, for establishing a pious foundation or preserving a fire.[163]

Ruwān-property could be set apart both for the benefit of one's own soul as well as the souls of friends and relations with the words: *ruwān ī xwēš ud anī-z kas rāy* 'for (my) own soul and another person's' or *pad ruwān ī xwēš ud Mihrēn dāštan rāy* 'for preserving my own soul and the soul of Mihrēn' (*i.e.*, such-and-such a person, N.N.).[164] The disposition of the founder also contained a provision forbidding another person to alienate the property dedicated to the salvation of the soul: *Mihrēn ud ān-iz kas ān xwāstag frōxt ud be dād nē pādixšāy* 'Neither Mihrēn nor any other person is authorized to sell or give away that property', specifying that this property was immobilized and could not be sold, bartered or donated (to another purpose than that named by the founder, as we may add). The founder had the right to assign guardianship (*sālārīh*) or trusteeship (*dāštārīh*) of the foundation to a person he chose, who could—but did not necessarily have to—be a member of his own family, with the words: *kū-m … dāštan rāy framān dād* 'I have willed it (to such-and-such a person) to be held'.[165] In case no particular person was named as a guardian or trustee in the endowment deed of the founder, his son or other relations were obliged to serve as guardians (*sālār*).[166] In this manner the *xwāstag ī ruwān* remained in the founder's family and was bequeathed as a distinct part of the total patrimonial estate (*abarmānd*) of the deceased to his descendants, even though the latter had *no* right of ownership of the substance (*bun-xwēšīh*) and were *not* authorized to change its legal status.

Besides smaller family foundations, endowments of a public character, such as fire-temples, irrigation canals or roads and bridges, intended to benefit the community, could be financed by the property set apart for the soul. From the evidence of the Law-book we can deduce that these pious foundations could again be divided into two main categories:

1. endowments consisting only of a principal, or base (*bun*), which could not be increased and yielded no profit (*a-bar*), *e. g.*, roads, bridges etc.;
2. foundations that were surplus producing (*bunōmand*), such as property donated to fire-temples, consisting of cultivated land, cattle and slaves, villages, vineyards and orchards.

163 MHD 35.2 (Macuch 1993, pp. 253, 256).
164 MHD 24.17–25.1 and 25.2–5 (Macuch 1993, pp. 192f., 199 respectively). The names Mihrēn and Farrox in the Law-book do not designate specific individuals, but are used in the sense of Numerius Negidius (N.N.) and Aulus Agerius (A.A.) in Roman legal texts.
165 MHD 27.12–14 (Macuch 1993, pp. 196, 203).
166 MHD 29.9–11; 45.15–17 (*ibid.*, pp. 198, 205 and 305, 321 respectively).

As an example for a foundation of the non-profitable kind (*a-bar*), we have evidence in an inscription of the famous 5th century prime minister Mihr-Narseh from Gōr (modern Fīrūzābād), in which he praises himself for having built a bridge for the benefit 'of his own soul' (*ruwān ī xwēš rāy*) at his own expense and asks those who cross the bridge to give him their blessing.[167] This was certainly not the only type of non-profitable foundation (if the bridge indeed belongs in this category; a fee or tax might have been charged for the right to cross the bridge, producing income). As a rule the funds dedicated to the construction of an endowment of the *a-bar* type were divided in order to meet the expenses: the *bun*, or principal, consisted of the portion of the property which was left after the payment of 'taxes and duties' (*harg bār*) and the reservation of a certain amount for the maintenance of the substance (*uzēnag ī pad bun*) and the payment of the guardians and administrators (*mizd ud rōzīg ī sālārān*).[168] We know that the same Mihr-Narseh also established foundations of the profitable type, since he founded five fire-temples, bestowing them with considerable property, and was himself engaged in the 'service of a fire' (*bandagīh [ī] ātaxš*), as we will see presently.

As to the second type of surplus producing foundations (*barōmand*), only the income (*bar*) was spent on their upkeep, for taxes and the payment of the guardians and trustees. The profit, which remained after meeting these expenses, was spent for the pious purposes specified by the founder (offerings, liturgies, other works of charity); the rest went to the founder and his family or to the beneficiaries named in the endowment deed and their heirs.[169] It seems that—apart from religious piety—one of the main reasons for establishing a pious foundation of the second type was to secure an income for one's own children and descendants or those of other family members and friends. The heirs and beneficiaries were 'owners of the income' (*bar-xwēš*) in perpetuity (again, exceptions were possible) and the principal of the foundation remained a distinct part of family property, although its legal status could not be changed.[170] If the founder assigned possession (*dāštan*) of the foundation to a person outside his own family, the principal (*bun*) was transferred, but remained bound to the purpose defined by the founder, whereas the beneficiary and his descendants received ownership rights of the income (*bar*).[171] However, if the beneficiary or his heir(s) committed an offence, guardianship (*sālārīh*) of *ruwān*-property reverted to the family of the founder.[172] The founder could also engage a woman (*e. g.*, his own wife or his daughter) as guardian (*sālār*) of property reserved for the soul or for a sacred

167 See the edition by Henning 1954a [= 1977].

168 MHD 34.2–3 (Macuch 1993, pp. 252, 255).

169 MHD 24.12–25.8; 34.2–3 (*ibid.*, pp. 192f., 198f. and 252, 255 respectively).

170 MHD 24.16–25.5; 46.4–9 (*ibid.*, pp. 192f., 199f. and 305, 321f. respectively).

171 MHD 35.3–6; 24.13–16; 25.2–5; 25.17–26.1 (*ibid.*, pp. 253, 256f.; 192f., 199f.; 193f., 200 respectively).

172 MHD 29.3–6 (Macuch 1993, pp. 198,205).

fire[173]—the only case in which a female could be appointed as 'guardian of property' (*xwāstag-sālār*), but this was apparently a matter of debate among Sasanian jurists.[174] A woman who endowed a fire also became its guardian, but guardianship would be passed on to the woman's husband, if she married subsequently.[175] Tying up property in this manner seems to have offered two major advantages: (1) the principal (*bun*) could not be split into individual shares and remained whole at the time of succession, even if the heirs and legatees opted for partition (*baxtīgīh kardan*) of the rest of the inheritance; and (2) pious foundations were presumably safe from confiscation by government authorities while perpetually producing income for the heirs and beneficiaries.

Fire endowments of all sizes were the most significant and widespread institutions in the category of profitable foundations 'for the sake of the soul', as we may conclude from other non-legal sources.[176] In his great inscription on the Kaʿba-ye Zardušt Šābuhr I claims to have established a fire named Husraw-Šābuhr for his 'own soul' (*pad amā ruwān* in the MP version)[177] and another four fires for the souls of members of the royal family: a fire named Husraw-Āduranāhīd 'for the soul' of the queen, his wife and daughter, Āduranāhīd (*pad Āduranāhīd bānbišnān bānbišn amā duxt ruwān*); and three fires 'for the souls' of his sons. According to the Law-book, sacred fires were furnished with income-producing property, called *xwēšīh ī ātaxš* 'property in ownership of the fire',[178] *xīr ī ātaxš(ān)* 'property of the fire(s)'[179] or simply *ādurān ud ātaxšān* 'of the fires'.[180] Šābuhr also claims in his inscription to have assigned property to the five fires and to have drawn a document (*pādixšīr*), specifying the use of its income. The extent of the property is not specified in

173 MHD 27.12–14 (*ibid.*, pp. 196, 203).

174 MHD 110.2–3 (*ibid.*, pp. 645, 652) refutes the possibility of engaging a woman as guardian. On guardianship and the difference between the two types of *xwāstag-sālārīh* and *dūdag-sālārīh* see above Chapter II, pp. 177–178.

175 MHD 25.5–8 (Macuch 1993, pp. 193, 200); MHDA 14.1–4 (Macuch 1981, pp. 36, 143).

176 Three classes of fires are distinguished in the Law-book: (1) the consecrated fire of the highest category, *ātaxš ī Wahrām/ātaxš Wahrām*, which was established by collecting fires from 16 different sources, purifying them by performing the appropriate rituals and placing them in a sanctuary constructed to this purpose, called *dādgāh* (MHD 26.17–27.1,7; 94.5); (2) a general category, which is not clearly specified, called *ātaxš* (attestations, see Macuch 1993, Index, p. 692); (3) a minor fire called *adurōg* 'little fire', which did not have to burn in a *dādgāh* and was in most cases a family fire (attestations *ibid.*, p. 688). Although all these sacred fires were administered by a guardian (*sālār*) and endowed with property the extent of the estate donated to them must have differed considerably. On these fires see Boyce 1968b and 1975a.

177 ŠKZ § 33 (Huyse 1999, I, p. 46).

178 MHDA 39.6; (Macuch 1981, pp. 66, 222).

179 MHDA 26.13; 27.1,3 (*ibid.*, pp. 50f., 188f.); MHD 34.1, 93.4 (Macuch 1993, pp. 252, 255 and 593, 596 respectively).

180 MHDA 16.4 (only *ātaxšān*; Macuch 1981, pp. 38, 145); MHD 50.3 (Macuch 1993, pp. 310, 326).

the inscription, but can nevertheless be deduced from the tremendous surplus of one thousand lambs yearly, which belonged legally to the founder and his heirs. In the following part of the inscription Šābuhr gives exact instructions as to the amount of offerings to be made from this surplus: one lamb together with a specified amount of bread and wine daily for the salvation of his own soul and another lamb daily together with the same specified amount of bread and wine for the wellbeing of the souls of members of the royal family whose names are listed in the text. The rest of the surplus was to be offered for the benefit of the souls of a third group of dignitaries who lived under the dominion of Šābuhr's ancestors, Pābag and Ardaxšēr, and those who served under Šābuhr himself.[181]

These details reveal that fire foundations could be furnished with property of a considerable size and that the *xwēšīh* or *xīr i ātaxš(ān)* could produce a huge surplus, capable of maintaining a large number of persons engaged in the service of the fire as well as the heirs and descendants of the founder. Besides priests and guardians (*sālār*) or trustees (*stūr*), the personnel of a large fire endowment consisted of so-called 'servants of the fire' (*bandag ī ātaxš* or *ādurān-bandag*),[182] who were laypersons (also women, as in the case of Mihr-Narseh's wife, see below) and could be even high dignitaries of the State (for example the prime minister Mihr-Narseh himself). On the lowest level of the hierarchy, 'slaves of the fire' (*anšahrīg ī ātaxš*) laboured on the vast property belonging to a fire foundation. These were not necessarily Zoroastrians and we have in fact evidence that under Pērōz, son of Yazdegird II (459–484 CE), the children of Jews from Isfahān were transported to work on the estates of the fire-temple of *Srōš ādurān* in Harwān.[183] Details on the 'property of the fire' are provided in another later source. The Arabic historian Ṭabarī reports that the famous fifth century prime minister Mihr-Narseh, who is also mentioned in the Law-book as a 'servant of the fire',[184] founded two fire-temples for himself (called Mihr-Narsiyān and *Frāz-marā-āwar-xudāyā* 'Bring me forth, O Lord'[185]) as well as three fire-temples for his three sons Zurwāndād, Kārdār and Māhgušnasp, who were themselves high dignitaries under King Bahrām

181 ŠKZ §§33–50 (HUYSE 1999, I, pp. 46–63).

182 For attestations see MACUCH 1993, Index, pp. 688 (under *ādur*) and 692 (under *ātaxš*).

183 On this report by Hamza Iṣfahānī and on the personnel of fire foundations, mentioned as 'bd' dnwr' 'servant/slave of the fire' in the Babylonian Talmud, see MACUCH 2002b, p. 126f., and Chapter VII, pp. 599–602. On the difference between *bandag* and *anšahrīg ī ātaxš* see specifically MHD 1.7–10 (MACUCH 1993, pp. 22, 24) and Chapter II, pp. 104–105.

184 MHDA 39.11–17 (MACUCH 1981, pp. 66, 223).

185 NÖLDEKE 1879 [= 1973], p. 111, n. 7, observed that the Arabic explanation of this name ('Komm zu mir her, O Herr!' in NÖLDEKE's rendering) is not a correct translation. The name of the fire-temple ('Bring me forth, O Lord') is presumably a plea to the Lord for help for the soul in passing to the hereafter. The name—if it is transmitted correctly—would in fact very well suit the purpose of an endowment for the salvation of the soul of the founder (MACUCH 2002b, p. 122, fn. 47).

Gōr (421–439).[186] He established four villages near his birthplace Abruwān and provided each of them with a fire-temple for himself and his three sons, bearing their names (Zurwāndādān, Kārdārān, Mahgušnaspān). The passage suggests that Mihr-Narseh had founded these fires as pious endowments with vast property to the same purpose described in the Law-book and in the inscription of Šābuhr I. These fire-temples were equipped with three gardens, in each of which he planted 12,000 trees: date trees in the first, olive trees in the second and cypresses in the third. The villages remained together with the gardens and fire-temples in the hands of Mihr-Narseh's heirs and descendants.[187] According to the Law-book, Mihr-Narseh also assigned his wife and children to the service of the fires (*pad ādarwaxšīh ud bandagīh ... be dād*), hereby securing an income for these members of his family, besides his three sons.[188] Obviously the villages and gardens founded by Mihr-Narseh were donated to the foundations as 'property of the fire' and their presumably huge income was utilized for two main purposes: (1) for the payment of the priests, attendants and servants engaged in the upkeep of the fires, and (2) to provide a livelihood for the founder's relations and heirs in perpetuity as *bar-xwēš* ('owners of the income').

Although the property assigned to fire endowments was certainly not always as immense as in the cases of Šābuhr and Mihr-Narseh, we have reason to assume that certain fire-temples had huge possessions at their disposal and that they played an important part in the economy of Ērānšahr. Foundations were registered in a special State department called the *dīwān ī kardag(ān)* 'archive for religious institutions',[189] which also controlled the management of property dedicated to the fire, the *xīr ī ātaxšān*. The foundation deeds, called *pādixšīr*, *mādayān* or ⟨GTk/gtk⟩ *nāmag/gittag*, in which the provisions laid down by the founder were recorded,[190] were kept in individual 'repositories' or 'archives' (*nāmag-niyān*) in the regions in which the consecrated fires were seated.[191] In the third century the high priest Kirdīr praises himself as the important authority put in charge of the religious foundations of Šābuhr I.[192] By the late Sasanian period, as we are told in the Law-book, three high officials were responsible for the administration of matters related to fire foundations, two of which were at the same time religious dignitaries, the *mowbed* and the *rad*. Both were in charge of levying taxes (*sāk/nisāk*) on the property of the fire; the *rad* also controlled

186 On Mihr-Narseh's sons see Macuch 2002b, p. 122, fn. 48.
187 Nöldeke 1879 [= 1973], p. 111f.
188 MHDA 40.3–5 (Macuch 1981, pp. 67, 223).
189 MHDA 27.2; 37.5 (*ibid.*, pp. 51, 189 and 63, 220 respectively).
190 On the technical terms and provisions included in the foundation deed see Chapter IV, pp. 275–279.
191 MHD 78.11–14 (Macuch 1993, pp. 517f., 520). On this passage see above, p. 218, fn. 140. On *nāmag-niyān* < *nāmag* 'document' + **nidāna*- 'treasury, depository', MMP ⟨nyʾn⟩ *niyān* 'treasure, store' (Durkin-Meisterernst 2004, p. 252); Skr. *nidhāna*- 'treasury, repository', Khot. *nyanaa*- 'treasury' (see Macuch 1993, p. 526f., n. 8, with further references).
192 KKZ § 03 (Back 1978, pp. 390–391). On Kirdīr see Chapter IV, pp. 276–277.

other transactions and the use of the surplus (*mad*) with the exception of endowments belonging to royal property (*šāhīgān*). Interestingly, the endowments of the king and members of the royal family were at this late period (6th or 7th century) no longer under the control of a religious authority, but of a State official, the *āmārgar* ('calculator, accountant'), a kind of treasurer or fiscal administrator, who was appointed by the king.[193] These transactions were recorded in an 'account relating to the fire', **ātaxš hamār(/āmār) dibīrag*, the name of which has survived (as *ātaš hamār dafīra*) in al-Ḫwārezmī's *Mafātīhu'l-ʿulūm*.[194] The surplus of 'property of the fire' could be further increased by giving loans and taking interest. We are informed that it was not possible to be released from 'a loan from (the property of) the fires' (*abām az ādurān ud ātaxšān*).[195] The income from fire foundations could moreover be utilized to pay for the work of scribes involved in drafting court transcripts and records. These costs were later reclaimed from the plaintiffs and defendants (possibly at a considerable rate of interest).[196] Unsurprisingly, it seems that augmenting the earnings of religious foundations was considered as an important duty and that various means were found to increase this income, which financed not only the personnel of these institutions and the families of the founders, besides other beneficiaries, but also other activities in the judicial sphere, depending on the size and purpose of the foundation.

Taking all these details into consideration, it seems that there were considerable differences between the various foundations mentioned in the sources, not only in size and impact, but also with regard to their legal status. Although Sasanian law does not differentiate between two types, comparable to the Islamic family foundation (*waqf ahlī*) and the public institution (*waqf ḫairī*), we may already detect these two variants in the Sasanian material, albeit without the legal distinctions separating the two forms in Islamic law.[197] It is not too far-fetched to assume that the huge income producing fire foundations (possibly also other pious endowments) of the *ruwān* type were somehow regarded as individual legal entities, subject to specific regulations, setting them apart from other kinds of property. As we have seen in the context of fires founded for *stūrīh*, the larger foundations seem to have been even considered in some form as juristic persons, capable of owning property and of enjoying other legal rights and duties (this is definitely attested for the *ātaxš Wahrām*, the highest form of consecrated fire).[198] They remained, however, linked to the fam-

193 MHDA 26.12–14; 26.17–27.4 (Macuch 1981, pp. 50f., 189). On the *āmārgar* see also Macuch 2014c, p. 48 (and fn. 11 with further references) and Chapter VI, pp. 512–514.

194 Edition van Vloten 1895 [= 1968], p. 118; see also Chapter II, p. 99.

195 MHD 50.3 (Macuch 1993, pp. 310, 326).

196 MHDA 16.4–5 (Macuch 1981, pp. 38, 145). See Chapter VI, pp. 585–587.

197 This differentiation in Islamic law was presumably a late development, see Chapter VII, pp. 622–623.

198 MHDA 39.5–7 (Macuch 1981, pp. 66, 222); on this passage see above, pp. 217–218.

ily of the founder or the beneficiaries both by the purpose of the foundation (religious ceremonies, offerings, other charitable acts for the salvation of the souls of the founder and other beneficiaries) and by the devise of *bar-xwēšīh*, giving the heirs a perpetual, inheritable right to the income. Smaller family foundations with less revenue were an inalienable integral element of the family's total (patrimonial/residuary) estate (*abarmānd*), either in the *stūrīh* or in the *ruwān* category of property.

2.5 Conclusions

The total patrimonial estate (*abarmānd*) of a wealthy family group, passed down from the ancestors and transferred to the next generation, consisted of various elements subject to different legal regimes, which we can divide, following Sasanian terminology, into at least four categories: property (1) 'in possession' (*pad xwāstagdarīh*), (2) 'in ownership' (*pad xwēšīh*), (3) 'for subsidiary succession; in trust' (*pad stūrīh*) and (4) 'for the soul' (*pad ruwān*). The underlying concept behind all the regulations described above seems to be that of the lineage or family group as a self-perpetuating organism, whose transitional head, the *kadag-xwadāy*, was more of a trustee and administrator than an owner of the substance (*bun*) of the estate, albeit with a wide range of powers and the important obligation to preserve and increase the property of the forefathers. These rights and duties were passed on to the heirs, who were as a rule 'possessors' (*xwāstagdār*) and 'shareholders' (*hambāy*), including women (predominantly daughters, but also sisters and wives), or 'associate brothers' (*brād ī hambāy*) with 'ideal' (*a-baxt*, lit. 'undivided') portions and joint proprietary rights. This form of devolution of property as an undivided whole, consisting of the various components described above, was called *pad abarmānd* 'total (patrimonial/residuary) estate bequeathed as a whole'. On the other hand, Sasanian law was flexible enough to allow partition of the estate or parts of it, if it became necessary (*e. g.*, in the case of debt) or if this was requested by the heirs and legatees. Hence, apart from the devolution of property as a whole (*pad abarmānd*), another option was to divide the residue into separate legal shares (*pad bahr* 'in shares' or *pad ǰud bahr* 'in separate shares'). By accepting succession the heirs and legatees took full responsibility for debts and liabilities of the family, which gave them in this exceptional case the right to hypothecate (*āgraw kardan*) or even alienate the substance in emergences. With the separation of ownership rights into *bun-xwēšīh* and *bar-xwēšīh* two basic forms of perpetual legal entitlement to property were created, which opened several important options for keeping a family's total estate intact. The heirs and legatees were 'owners of the fruit' (*bar-xwēš*) of a large section of the estate 'in possession' (*pad xwāstagdārīh*) of the family, besides those assets that were immobilized in the institutions of *stūrīh* and 'for the soul' (*pad ruwān*), without having ownership rights of the principal (*bun-xwēšīh*). But an heir or beneficiary could also become 'owner of the substance' (*bun-xwēš*) of a certain portion of property assigned to him or her by the testator expressly 'in ownership' (*pad xwēšīh*). Of these four basic categories of family property the heirs only had full right of disposal over the second type of 'property in ownership', whereas ownership rights of the other three types comprising the total estate were from the outset restricted to the fruits (*bar-xwēšīh*). Thus in the ideal case the bulk of family property remained whole and un-fragmented; the heirs had access to its vast income as shareholders, but either only a limited right to alienate the substance (in the case of property of the first category, *pad xwāstagdārīh*) or no right whatsoever (in the case of *ruwān* or *stū̆rīh* property).

Table 17. Overview: proprietary rights of the heirs

abarmānd 'total patrimonial (residuary) estate'		Type of proprietary rights	
pad xwāstag-dārīh	property 'in possession'	*bar-xwēšīh*	'ownership of the fruits'
		dārišn (ī bun)	'possession' of the substance
		hambāyīh	'shareholding' (collective proprietary rights)
pad xwēšīh	property 'in ownership'	*bun-xwēšīh*	'ownership of the substance' (individual right)
pad stū̆rīh	property 'for subsidiary succession; in trust'	*bar-xwēšīh*	'ownership of the fruits' (bound to the purpose of the institution)
pad ruwān	property 'for the soul'	*bar-xwēšīh*	'ownership of the fruits'
		hambāyīh	'shareholding' (collective proprietary rights)

3 Inheritance

As we have seen, inheritance involved the transfer of the total patrimonial estate of a family, consisting of the elements described above, to relatives, dependents and beneficiaries, with the obligation of settling debts and obligations of the forefathers (*abām ī pidarān*). How this was done exactly, whether there were compulsory rules, limiting the options of a *kadag-xwadāy* (or another deceased person) or whether the decedent had a more or less unrestricted right to determine the devolution of family property after his death, are questions, to which we can only sporadically find answers in the legal material. A systematic description is lacking, as in many other areas of law, but we can definitely ascertain that Sasanian law knew both intestate succession, following fixed rules that can be reconstructed to a limited degree from the scattered material, as well as the transfer of property based on the last will of the deceased to those he might personally prefer. Several distinctive characteristics of the Sasanian law of inheritance and succession have already been discussed, notably the status of both sons and daughters as successors, *yōhē pasčaēta* 'who (follows) him afterwards' and heirs, *xwāstagdār* 'possessor(s) of property', albeit with different rights and duties,[199] and the immobilization of the substance (*bun*) of property reserved for 'substitute succession' (*stūrīh*) and 'for the soul' (*pad ruwān*).[200] Property of these two last categories was tied to the specific purposes described above and could—as a rule—not be transferred to another function by testament, although exceptions in cases of emergency or debt seem to have been possible.

3.1 Intestacy

If a deceased *kadag-xwadāy* left no will, all his legitimate children, sons and unmarried daughters (*dādestān-pus* 'son according to the law' and *dādestān-duxt* 'daughter according to the law'), from a 'privileged marriage' (*pādixšāy-zanīh*) and the wife (or wives) from this form of matrimony were entitled to inheritance and received an ideal legal portion (*bahr*) of the total estate (*abarmānd*). As Sasanian law knew no right of primogeniture (right of the first born), all the legitimate sons became joint universal successors of the deceased and replaced him totally, inheriting not only his property, but all the latter's rights and duties, including the important obligation to conduct the obligatory religious rites and ceremonies and to keep the cult of the ancestors (*nāmagānīh*).[201] The vast material on guardianship (*sālārīh*) further suggests that the son, who became family guardian (*dūdag-sālār*), usually the eldest or the first son to reach maturity after the demise of the *kadag-xwadāy*, was put in charge of administrating the property to the advantage of all family members and was made responsible for the execution of the post-mortem rites and other religious ceremonies.[202] If the deceased left no male successor, one of his daughters (the eldest one or one who was not married) or his wife, or—if these were non-existent—one of his sisters became 'intermediary successor' (*ayōgēn*) with the consequences already described above (Chapter II, pp. 163–168).

199 On the difference between these two terms see pp. 206–207 above; on *yōhē pasčaēta* see Chapter II, pp. 137–138.
200 See pp. 213–229 above.
201 On these obligations see pp. 206–210 above.
202 All attestations should be taken into consideration, see Macuch 1993, Index, p. 702. On guardianship see Chapter II, pp. 177–183.

The distribution of the legal shares (*bahr*) to which the heirs were entitled in the case of intestate succession is not transmitted consistently in the sources. Īšōʿbōxt, whose *Corpus Iuris* is largely based on Zoroastrian jurisprudence, has established the norm for the Christian community of Pars as follows: the sons and the wife of the deceased are allotted equal portions of the inheritance, whereas unmarried daughters, who still live in the house of their father, receive half the amount of the former. Married daughters are not entitled to a share, as they have already received their ration of the father's estate as dowry on entering matrimony.[203] As the rules and regulations in Īšōʿbōxt's work correspond largely to Sasanian law we would expect this arrangement to be taken from the latter, even if the Christian concept of the family diverges from the Zoroastrian one.[204] The Sasanian Law-book repeatedly discusses questions pertaining to the individual portions of the heirs, but does not inform us on matters well known to jurists, such as their proportional shares. There are, however, a few details in late Pahlavi literature as well as in the New Persian *Riwāyat*s, which, taken together with the information in the Law-book and Īšōʿbōxt's statements, allow the following tentative reconstruction:

- the legitimate *pādixšāy*-sons of the deceased received equal portions of the 'son's share' (*bahr ī pus/pusīh*);[205]
- the share of the wife (or wives) in *pādixšāy*-status was either twice as large as that of a son[206] or corresponded exactly to that of a son[207] (*bahr ī kadag-bānūg* 'share of the mistress of the house' or *bahr ī zanīh* 'share of the wife');[208]
- unmarried *pādixšāy*-daughters were entitled to half the portion of their brothers or mother (*bahr ī duxt/duxtīh* 'share of the daughter');[209]
- married daughters were no longer entitled to a share, as they had already received their portion of the father's estate in advance as 'dowry' (*pēšīgān-wāspuhragān*);[210]

203 Sachau 1914, p. 95 (§§ 1–4). On Īšōʿbōxt's Corpus Iuris see Chapter I, p. 48.

204 Richard Payne has recently shown convincingly that Zoroastrian law was in fact adapted to a far larger degree even in this legal branch among Christians of the Persis than hitherto realized. In their refutation of Zoroastrian family law and marriage practices both Mār Abā and Īšōʿbōxt indirectly confirm that Christians did in fact practice the characteristic Zoroastrian institution of 'substitute succession' (*stūrīh*), albeit in the disguise of the levirate, see Payne 2017 and Chapter VII, pp. 620–621.

205 According to the *Dādestān ī dēnīg* (Dd 61.4; for a translation of this passage see Appendix I, pp. 654–656). *bahr ī pus/pusīh* 'share of the son' is attested MHD 51.13 (Macuch 1993, pp. 312, 327), 62.5 (*ibid.*, pp. 411, 416), 90.17 (*ibid.*, pp. 571, 574).

206 Dd 61.4 (Appendix I, pp. 654, 656).

207 According to Īšōʿbōxt, Book IV, Chapter I, § 1 (Sachau 1914, p. 95).

208 For attestations of the terms see MHD 44.11, 13 (Macuch 1993, pp. 303, 320); 52.12 (*ibid.*, pp. 313, 328); MHDA 6.7 (Macuch 1981, pp. 27, 97).

209 New Persian *Riwāyats* (Unvala 1922, vol. I, p. 188.10–12; Dhabhar 1932, p. 203); Īšōʿbōxt, Book IV, Chapter I, § 1 (Sachau 1914, p. 95); Dd 53.9 (translation see Macuch 1981, p. 75); *bahr ī duxt/duxtīh* is attested MHD 44.10 (Macuch 1993, pp. 303, 319); 51.15 (*ibid.*, pp. 312, 328).

- crippled, blind, or otherwise disabled sons and their mother were granted twice the share of a healthy son;[211]
- disabled daughters received the share of a son.[212]

Children and wives from the two other forms of matrimony, the 'auxiliary marriage' (*čagar*) and the 'consensus marriage' (*xwasrāyēn/gādār*), were not entitled to any part of the deceased's estate, if the latter had not previously changed their status into that of *pādixšāy*-wife and children. If the *kadag-xwadāy* had adopted his *čagar*-children and altered the status of his wife, then both were entitled to the same shares of the inheritance as his *pādixšāy*-wife and children.[213] This form of adoption or change of status, however, was discussed controversially and another entry explicitly refutes the possibility of adopting one's *čagar*-children and altering the position of the *čagar*-wife in this manner—in full accordance with the purpose of this marriage.[214] Several legal problems might have emerged from adoption, which are unfortunately not discussed in this specific context, but can be deduced from other passages, revealing that an adopted son was entitled to inheritance, if he had previously accepted adoption,[215] whereas

210 According to Īšōʿbōxt, Book IV, Chapter I, § 1,4 (Sachau 1914, p. 95); on *pēšīgān-wāspuhragān* 'dowry' see Macuch 1981, p. 85f. (no. 17).

211 Dd 61.4 (Appendix I, pp. 654, 656); the New Persian *Riwāyat*s grant only one share to the mother in this case (Unvala 1922, vol. I, p. 188.12–13; Dhabhar 1932, p. 203); Īšōʿbōxt grants only one and a half shares to the disabled son (Sachau 1914, p. 125, § 4).

212 Only Īšōʿbōxt, Book IV, Chapter VII, § 4 (Sachau 1914, p. 125). This might have been a specific regulation of Christian law.

213 MHDA 40.11–14 (Macuch 1981, pp. 67, 224) according to the legal authority Pusānweh ī Burzādurfarrbay. He states that changing the position of the *čagar*-children and wife into *pādixšāy* status should be judged as a regular form of adoption: in this case the children would be treated as if they had been adopted (*ōwōn čiyōn pad pusīh ud duxtīh padirīft hē* 'as if they were adopted as son and daughter') and the wife 'would inherit the property (of the husband) as if she were a *pādixšāy*-wife' (*zan xwāstag ī ka pādixšāyīhā hē abar mānēd ud awiš rasēd*). According to MHDA 35.12–13 (Macuch 1981, pp. 61, 219) the adoption of *čagar*-children was officially confirmed and recorded in numerous cases. This was also legal practice in the region of Darabgird (MHD 70.9–12; Macuch 1993, pp. 465, 468f.). This procedure is confirmed for the post-Sasanian period by REA 23.3, 15: the *čagar*-wife and children are excluded from inheritance and the *čagar*-husband cannot inherit from his wife, but a husband can change the status of his wife and children to that of *pādixšāy*, thus giving them access to his estate after his demise (REA 23.13–14, 16; for a translation of these passages see Macuch 1981, p. 106f.). Questions of inheritance seem to have been handled in a flexible manner, taking the concrete social situation of a family into consideration, in both the Sasanian period and in the Zoroastrian communities of later times (see next fn. 214); for an extensive discussion of a remarkable example see Macuch 2017a.

214 MHDA 40.9–11 (Macuch 1981, pp. 67, 224), according to a resolution of the assembly of *mowbeds*, recorded in the *dīwān* of Ardaxšēr-Xwarrah, stating that the declaration of a man wishing to give his *čagar*-wife and children *pādixšāy*-status is 'null and void' (*pad kār nē dārišn*). Legal practice in other regions, *e.g.*, Darabgird, diverged evidently in the Sasanian period (see fn. 213 above).

215 MHD 70.3–5 (Macuch 1993, pp. 464, 468).

an adopted daughter was not.[216] The *xwasrāyēn/gādār*-children and wife were not entitled to inheritance, but their status could be changed to *pādixšāy* under certain (controversially discussed) circumstances according to the few passages dealing with this marriage form in late Pahlavi texts.[217]

All heirs received their shares as 'ideal' portions (*a-baxt*, lit. 'undivided') of the total estate (*pad abarmānd*), consisting of the different elements described above. The sons entered into a partnership of 'shareholding brothers' (*brād ī hambāy*) or 'shareholdership' of co-heirs (*hambāyīh*), which could also include the *pādixšāy*-widow(s) (*kadag-bānūg* 'mistress of the house') of the deceased and the daughters under certain circumstances (if they were not married outside their lineage or had entered an incestuous marriage, *xwēdōdah*, or could be engaged as 'intermediary successor', *ayōgēn*, for their father or brother in their natal lineage). The Law-book, concerned with solving concrete legal problems, does not elucidate the system, but it does mention en passant various groups of shareholders (*hambāy*), allowing us to discern a large range of different constellations: besides brothers (*brād ī hambāy*), shareholders could be brothers and sisters;[218] the son and the 'mistress of the house' (*kadag-bānūg*);[219] the son, daughter and 'mistress of the house';[220] the 'mistress of the house' together with both underage and adult sons and daughters;[221] two daughters;[222] a daughter together with the family of the son (*dūdag ī pus*).[223] These random examples were certainly not the only possible groupings, but they suggest that joint partnership of heirs was frequent and by no means restricted to a man's sons. Shareholding was, moreover, one of the best means of keeping a family's 'total estate' (*abarmānd*) intact and avoiding the division of common family property into small units. But if the heirs came to an agreement that their ideal shares should be partitioned into separate portions (*baxtīgīh kardan*), parts of the estate could be divided among the recipients with the exception of the substance (*bun*) of property tied up in trust, 'for substitute succession' (*pad stūrīh*), and 'for the soul' (*pad ruwān*). If there was no agreement in this respect, a division could nevertheless be undertaken under the condition that the sons in favour of parti-

216 MHD 70.2–3 (*ibid.*, pp. 464, 468).

217 On this marriage type see Chapter II, pp. 145–147; also MACUCH 2017a, p. 262, for a comparison between the *čagar* and *xwasrāyēn* forms of matrimony with further references. REA 43.2 mentions an interesting option: the son from a *xwasrāyēn/gādār*-alliance can transfer—after reaching maturity and becoming family guardian—guardianship over his mother to the mother's husband, hereby changing the marriage into a *pādixšāy*-one (for a translation and discussion of this passage see MACUCH 1985, pp. 198–200).

218 MHD 22.3–6 (MACUCH 1993, pp. 171, 176); 23.4 (*ibid.*, pp. 172, 177); 23.10–17 (*ibid.*, pp. 173, 178).

219 MHD 88.7–8 (MACUCH 1993, pp. 562, 564).

220 MHD 88.14–17 (*ibid.*, pp. 562, 565).

221 MHD 51.16–52.1 (*ibid.*, pp. 312, 328).

222 MHD 41.16–17 (*ibid.*, pp. 300, 316).

223 MHD 23.17–24.2 (MACUCH 1993, pp. 173, 178).

tioning accept guardianship (*sālārīh*) of the minors, disabled and infirm members of the family and of the property as a whole.[224] Another option was that those heirs, who did not vote for partition, remain joint partners with the corresponding privileges: for example, a sister would be engaged as 'intermediary successor' (*ayōgēn*) for her shareholding brother if it became necessary that she continue the lineage, not for the brother who advocated for division.[225]

3.2 Testament

The rules which applied in the case of intestate succession could be changed by three means:

1. by the last will (*handarz*) of the decedent;
2. by testamentary contract (*paymān*) (this seems to be meant in the passages using this expression—which denotes all kinds of contracts in the context of the intergenerational devolution of property);
3. by gifts (*dād*) made in contemplation of death (*donatio mortis causa* in Roman law).

To judge by the short statements in the Law-book, the testamentary contract (*paymān*) was a will in form of a contract concluded during the lifetime of the testator with his heirs or beneficiaries, specifying the exact conditions under which the latter would inherit a specific share of the testator's estate after his demise. In contrast to the regular will, the testator could appoint successive heirs by this devise: he could provide that (a portion of) his estate be given to a certain person for life, then be transferred to another one after the death of the first recipient.[226] This procedure allowing the testator to determine successive heirs is not attested in the context of the regular will (*handarz*). Gifts and donations made in contemplation of death (*donatio mortis causa*) which did not take effect until after the demise of the donor, were presumably also known in Sasanian law, but it is difficult to separate them from the other two means of devolving property, especially as no specific legal expression is transmitted in this context

224 MHD 52.17–53.3 (*ibid.*, p. 367, no. 63).
225 MHD 22.13–23.1 (*ibid.*, pp. 172, 177).
226 MHDA 24.14–25.1 (Macuch 1981, pp. 48f., 171): In this case the testator (Farrox) provides that his wife (Zanbūd) should receive an entire portion of the inheritance for life if she produces a child, but only half a portion, if no child is born (corresponding to the regular share of the *kadag-bānūg* if there is no testament, as described above). After her demise the same property should pass to another man (Mihrēn). This disposition in the testamentary contract is interpreted as follows: The second recipient (Mihrēn) only has an entitlement to a portion corresponding exactly to that of the wife (Zanbūd), *i.e.*, to an entire share if a child has been born, but only to half a share in the opposite case (see also commentary Macuch 1981, p. 187, no. 59). MHD 108.8–11 (Macuch 1993, pp. 643, 650f.) is fragmentary. Both passages are far too sparse to allow precise conclusions.

(the general term *dād* 'gift, donation' is used of all kinds of gifts, also those *inter vivos*, which were fully operative in the donor's lifetime). Most entries in this field are mainly concerned with interpreting the words of the testator/donor, than explaining the exact circumstances of the transfer or formulating general rules, as the examples cited below will demonstrate.

The only technical term employed with the meaning of 'last will, testament' is *handarz*, despite SUNDERMANN's suggestion that *abestāg*, which occurs in two sentences of the Law-book, should also be interpreted in this sense. His argumentation relies on a single problematic passage of this text, which can, however, be explained quite differently and in my opinion does not prove on its own that *abestāg* was used with this specific meaning or in this context.[227] A

227 SUNDERMANN 2001, following a suggestion by HENNING, construes a connection between MP *abestāg* 'Avesta' and Sogd. *(ə)pštāwan* 'order, recommendation' (a derivative of *ʾpšty-* 'to order'), proposing that the MP word should be understood in the sense of 'testament', based on MHD 48.15, which begins as follows: *ast kē guft kū az wāhmān abestāg ēdōn paydāg kū …* 'There is one (commentator) who said: "in the *wāhmān abestāg* it is revealed …"' (for the whole sentence see MACUCH 1993, pp. 308, 324). He argues that the word *wāhmān* 'so-and-so' in this context is problematic if we retain the meaning 'Avesta' for *abestāg* and suggests to translate the latter as 'testament', based on the Sogdian word (*i.e.*, 'in the testament of so-and-so it is revealed'). Although the meaning might fit in here, he ignores the only other attestation of *abestāg* in another passage of the Law-book, which excludes this interpretation: MHD 14.17–15.1: *pad margarzān pad-iz ēk azišmānd sar brīd abāyīdan az abestāg paydāg* 'In the case of a crime "worthy of death" the necessity of cutting off (the delinquent's) head on (the occurrence of) only one obstruction of justice is revealed in the Avesta' (on *azišmānd* 'obstruction of justice' see Chapter VI, pp. 561–569). Besides the problematic etymological derivation (which has been refuted by BELARDI, see overview in CIANCAGLINI 2008, p. 98) it seems rather unlikely that *abestāg* should have been employed with two different meanings in the same text, given that technical terms are used with meticulous precision in the legal material. These two entries in the Law-book do, however, point to another, far more extensive use of the term 'Avesta' than in the late Pahlavi texts. The latter distinguish between the Old Iranian text and its Pahlavi version in the phrase *abestāg ud zand* 'Avesta and (its Pahlavi) exegesis', but in our two passages there is no distinction between original and translation: *abestāg* designates here not only the Old Iranian sacred text, but includes its Pahlavi version, consisting of translation and commentary (*zand*), as we may conclude from the context of the quoted passages. Both sentences refer to contemporary Sasanian law, using Pahlavi legal terminology, which could not have stood in the original Old Iranian text, but only in its translated version or in the commentary (*e.g.*, *azišmānd* 'obstruction of justice' in the entry cited above or the characteristic Sasanian institution of *stūrīh* in the passage SUNDERMANN quotes). That there were several Pahlavi versions of the Avesta, not only one, is revealed in Dk V.24.12 (*čand zand* 'several/diverse exegeses'; AMOUZEGAR/TAFAZZOLI 2000, nr. 12, pp. 82–83) and by the diverse commentaries to the *Wīdēwdād*, the rediscovered *Zand ī fragard ī juddēwdād* and the commentary of Mēdōmāh, *Juddēwdād ī Mēdōmāh* (on these texts see Chapter I, pp. 29–30). This would also explain a phrase such as *wāhmān abestāg* 'the Avesta of so-and-so' (or should we read *⁺wahman abestāg*? 'the Avesta of ⁺Wahman'?), which could have referred either to an unspecified Pahlavi version of the sacred text (whose exegete is unnamed), or, in the second case, to the version of a specific exegete called ⁺Wahman. On *abestāg ud zand* see also CANTERA 2004, pp. 1–13.

large number of cases exemplify the alterations a testator could enforce by will under the condition that the will is made in good health (*tan-drustīh*) and full consciousness (*ōšyārīh*).[228] Besides diminishing the individual shares of his regular *pādixšāy* heirs by adopting his *čagar-* and *xwasrāyēn*-children, as already mentioned above, he could entitle his wives and daughters to larger or lesser portions of the inheritance in his will or appoint other relatives or beneficiaries outside his own family as heirs and legatees.[229] A few restrictions are discernable, which might have been disputed in detail. One entry explains that if a testator had only one son, then this son could only inherit property in form of 'possession' (*pad xwāstagdārīh*), no matter which type of property the testator had specified in his will.[230] This might have only applied to the case of a *single* son, as he was obliged to take both benefit and burden as *xwāstagdār*, inheriting as sole heir not only a family's assets, but also the entire responsibility for debts and liabilities. According to other passages however—and in contrast to the former statement—the testator could specify precisely the category of property he wished to bequeath to his son(s or heirs): 'in ownership' (*pad xwēšīh*) or 'as pious gifts' (*pad ahlawdād*), then these parts would *not* be passed on in the category of 'possession' (*pad xwāstagdārīh*).[231] Another restriction is noted with respect to the daughter: no matter what the will of the father states, a daughter is only entitled to a share (*bahr*) of the property, not to the whole estate, but the testator can determine the size of this share and bequeath property to her 'in ownership' (*pad xwēšīh*).[232] The head of a household could also assign gifts from his acquired property to beneficiaries of his choice during his lifetime, providing in his will that the donation should be taken into account at the time of the distribution of property among the heirs in order to avoid disadvantaging the other recipients. The formulaic phrase employed in this case runs: *pad bahr hangārišn az bahr hangārišn* 'to be taken into account regarding the share; to be deducted from the share'.[233] The phrase determines that when the will takes effect the share of this beneficiary is to be reduced in accordance with the value of the donation he has already received during the lifetime of the testator.

Due to problems arising from the general inaccuracy of language, most of the entries on testamentary succession in the Law-book are dedicated to the interpretation of the exact meanings of equivocal formulations in the testator's last will (some of these have been discussed above). By using the appropriate legal formulae

228 This is implied indirectly in Dd 53.2 (see Appendix I, pp. 641–644).
229 See particularly Chapter 23 of the Law-book, MHD 59.11–63.5 (Macuch 1993, pp. 408–418).
230 MHD 59.16–60.1 (Macuch 1993, pp. 408, 413). On the various types of property see above pp. 205–206; on *pad xwastagdārīh* see pp. 206–210.
231 MHD 61.14–15 (Macuch 1993, pp. 410, 416); 62.6–7 (*ibid.*, pp. 411, 417). On these terms see pp. 205–206 above.
232 MHD 61.12–14 (Macuch 1993, pp. 410, 416).
233 MHD 61.14–62.2 (*ibid.*, pp. 410f., 416).

and correct expressions the testator could reduce arbitrary interpretations to a minimum and facilitate legal decisions if conflicts arose among the heirs and legatees. I have already mentioned the use of the agential/ergative construction in the will, donation or testamentary contract (*kū-m ... [ō tō] dād*, lit. 'I gave, I have given [to you]') to express the intent of the testator to transfer property *after* his death (Chapter I, pp. 83–85). The will is ambulatory, *i. e.*, it is revocable up to the death of the testator and does not take effect from the time it is made or at a specific period during the lifetime of the testator, but from his demise. This seems to be reflected in the use of the preterite in that the testator 'speaks from death'. This particularity of legal language was well known to jurists and is not explained in any of the extant texts, but can be deduced from numerous attestations in the Law-book in connection with the transfer of property, which, taken all together, lead to this conclusion. In one example the use of the present tense is explicitly contrasted with the ergative/agential form in a case with the following background: a person expresses his wish to bequeath or donate a thing in his property (or a part of his property) to a recipient (A), naming at the same time a condition in connection with the coming of age of another beneficiary (B), called 'lad' (*rēdag*, presumably an underage male successor of the testator/donor).[234] Three different formulations are discussed, which have completely different legal consequences:

1. The testator/donor uses the ergative/agential construction (*kū-m ... ō tō dād*; in connection with the ambiguous *tā* 'as long as, until' + *purnāy* 'of age' or *aburnāy* 'underage'): 'Until the lad comes of age ... I gave this thing to you' (*kū-m tā rēdag purnāy bawēd... ēn čiš ō tō dād*) or: 'As long as the lad (is) underage I gave this thing to you' (*kū-m tā rēdag aburnāy ēn čiš ō tō dād*). Both provisions have the same implication, namely that beneficiary B (the 'lad' or male successor of the testator) must be still underage at the time when the disposition takes effect, *i. e.*, *at the death* of the testator/donor. Recipient A only

234 MHDA 22.17–23.6: *ka gōwēd kū-m tā rēdag purnāy bawēd ayāb gōwēd kū-m tā rēdag aburnāy ēn čiš ō tō dād har dō ē(w) ēwēnag. ud ka gōwēd kū tā rēdag aburnāy ēn čiš ō tō dahom juttar bawēd čiyōn ka gōwēd kū tā rēdag purnāy bawēd ēn čiš ō tō* ⁺*dahom* (ms.: *dād*) *čē ka gōwēd kū tā rēdag aburnāy ēn čiš ō tō dahom ēg-iš pad gyāg be dahišn u-š hangām tā rēdag purnāy bawēd xwēš u-š pas nē xwēš. ud ka gōwēd kū tā rēdag purnāy bawēd ō tō dahom ēg-iš pēš az purnāyīh ī rēdag be dahišn u-š hamēwēn xwēš.* 'If he declares: "Until (*tā*) the lad comes of age" or says: "As long as (*tā*) the lad (is) underage I gave this thing to you (*kū-m ... ō tō dād*)", (then) both (statements) have the same (implications). And if he declares: "As long as (*tā*) the lad (is) underage I give (*dahom*) this thing to you", (then) it differs from if he says: "Until (*tā*) the lad comes of age I give (⁺*dahom*) this thing to you". Because if he declares: "As long as (*tā*) the lad (is) underage I give (*dahom*) this thing to you", then he (= the donor) has to give it on the spot (= immediately; *pad gyāg*) and during the timespan until the lad comes of age it is his (= the recipient's) own and afterwards it is not his own. And if he declares: "Until (*tā*) the lad comes of age I give (*dahom*) it to you", then it has to be given before the coming of age of the lad and it is his (= the recipient's) own to the same extent (*hamēwēn xwēš*).' (MACUCH 1981, pp. 46, 169f.); PERIKHANIAN 1997, p. 287, has a completely different translation.

has access to this property after the death of the testator as long as beneficiary B (the 'lad') is a minor. This makes perfect sense in a will or testamentary contract, since underage children had no legal capacity and stood under the guardianship of a person who would also manage family property until the legitimate heir and successor came of age and was able to take charge of family affairs.

2. The testator/donor makes use of the present tense (*dahom* 'I give'; in connection with the ambiguous *tā* 'as long as, until' + *aburnāy* 'underage'): 'As long as the lad (is) underage I give this thing to you' (*tā rēdag aburnāy ēn čiš ō tō dahom*). This wording implies that the transfer of property to the recipient A takes effect *immediately* (*pad gyāg*, lit. 'on the spot') when the provision is made and that A's ownership of the property is temporally limited: it ends when B (the 'lad' or male successor of the testator) comes of age. In contrast to the first formulation, recipient A has immediate access to the property, but only as long as beneficiary B is still underage.
3. The third formulation with the present tense (*dahom* 'I give' + *tā* 'as long as, until' + *purnāy* 'of major age') has again different implications: "Until the lad comes of age I give this thing to you (*tā rēdag purnāy bawēd ēn čiš ō tō* ⁺*dahom*).[235] In this case the property is to be transferred to recipient A *at some period before* beneficiary B (the 'lad' or male successor) comes of age; the property remains in the ownership of both beneficiaries (A and B) to 'the same extent' *(hamēwēn xwēš)*.[236]

Nota bene, only the first wording makes use of the ergative/agential form, *i.e.*, only this variant takes effect *after* the death of the testator, whereas the other two provisions using the present tense are both operative during the lifetime of the donor and refer to a temporary transfer of proprietary rights (number 2) or a conditional gift (number 3).[237]

235 Ms. ⟨YHBWNt⟩ *dād* (MHDA 23.3) corrected in accordance with the correct form ⟨YHBWNm⟩ *dahom* given a few lines later in the repetition of this wording MHDA 23.5 (*tā rēdag purnāy bawēd ō tō dahom*).

236 On the legal meaning of *hamēwēn* 'to the same extent; with equal shares' see Macuch 2015c, p. 140, fn. 22.

237 Another peculiar (and unfortunately elliptical) sentence could possibly have the same background, albeit with the difference that the use of the past participle is contrasted with that of the present tense with similar implications: MHDA 12.8–9: *nāmčištīg dād ē(w) a-š xwāst nē abāyēd ud nāmčištīg dahom* (*ud*) *nāmčištīg ē(w) dād ē(w) dahom ā-š hamē be xwāst abāyēd* '(If a transaction is formulated by the words:) "This particular (thing is) given", then it cannot be requested; (but if the statements are:) "I give this particular (thing)" (or) "I give this particular gift", then it can be requested at any time (*hamē* "always").' (Macuch 1981, pp. 34, 125). I take these cryptic entries to mean that the implementation of a statement or will formulated with the past participle (*dād*) is bound to a fixed time (death of the donor/testator), whereas a donation, gift (or any other kind of transfer) using the present tense (*dahom*) can be requested by the beneficiary at any time (s)he chooses (by the words *andar abāyēd* 'it is needed', which could explain the use of the verb *abāyistan* in this context, see Chapter IV, pp. 301–305).

Another remarkable example of linguistic precision in a will has also been already mentioned: the minute differentiation between formulations using *čiyōn* 'as, like' and *ōwōn čiyōn* 'so as'. The formulaic expression *ōwōn čiyōn* 'so as' between the designations of the beneficiaries was understood in the sense of 'in the same manner as'. If a father assigned property to his daughter 'in the same manner as' to his son, *i.e.*, using these specific words in his will, this meant that he bequeathed to his daughter shares corresponding *exactly* (*rāst*) to those of his son. The disposition was taken to refer to all categories of the 'total estate': property 'in ownership', for 'substitute succession' and 'for keeping the soul'. The exact share of the daughter was moreover calculated by also taking those portions of the property into account that had been already given to the son *before* the will came into force. On the other hand, a disposition with the formula *čiyōn* 'as' alone between the designations of the beneficiaries was interpreted in the temporal sense of 'as soon as; at the same time'. By this specific wording the testator determined that the estate should be transferred *simultaneously* to son and daughter after his death. Both recipients were to receive property to the same extent, but—in contrast to the wording with *ōwōn čiyōn*—the provision *excludes* those portions of the total estate from the calculation of the daughter's share, which were already transferred to the son *before* the implementation of the will.[238]

From the point of view of our topic the most remarkable entries in the will or testamentary contract are those regarding the transfer of landed estates (*dastgird*), land (*zamīg*, *gil*) and houses (*xānag*, *kadag*) which could also have been the model for all other kinds of business transactions (especially for the sale of immovable property).[239] Any fixtures on the land, estate or building were conveyed together with the main property, including all assets inside its borders (animals and slaves working and residing on the property) or accessories (everything belonging to a house, *e.g.*, doors, windows, keys etc.) as well as water canals (*kahas*) operating within and outside the borders of a plot of land. In the context of estates (*dastgird*) we find four possible formulations and their consequences involving the transfer of landed property by will, testamentary contract or by gift in contemplation of death (*donatio mortis causa*):[240]

1. The simple provision 'I gave this estate to you' (*kū-m ēn dastgird ō tō dād*) in itself implies that all assets belonging to the estate are conveyed to the recipient (*ān dastgird ud har čē pad ān dastgird dāšt ēstēd dād bawēd* 'the estate itself and everything that is held in possession by that estate is transferred').[241]

238 See also Chapter I, p. 83. For an extensive discussion of these (and other) cases see Macuch 2015c.

239 On barter and sale see next Chapter, pp. 372–389.

240 All provisions make use of the ergative/agential construction *kū-m … dād* 'I have given, I gave', the grammatical form denoting a transaction that will take place after the demise of the testator or donor, as elucidated above and in Chapter I, pp. 83–85.

241 MHD 18.6–7 (Macuch 1993, pp. 152, 158).

2. The next formulation is somewhat more detailed: 'I gave this estate and everything that is held in possession by the estate to you' (*kū-m ēn dastgird ud har čē pad ēn dastgird dāšt estēd ō tō dād*). This wording implies that animals (*stōr*) and slaves (*anšahrīg*) who live and work on the estate and are bound to the soil (so-called *glebae adscripti*, slaves who were engaged in cultivating the land and belonged legally to the plot on which they worked) are transferred with the estate to the recipient (*stōr ud anšahrīg-ēw kē kār ān gyāg kunēd dād bawēd* 'an animal and slave, who work in that place, have been given').[242] This seems to have been the generally accepted procedure in the late Sasanian period, as it is confirmed by the highest legal authority himself, the Chief Mobed (*mowbedān mowbed*) Wehšābuhr under the Sasanian king Husraw I in the first half of the 6th century. A provision in his last will (*handarz*) is recorded in the Law-book, stating that the slaves (*anšahrīgān*) residing on the estate he has bequeathed to his heirs and legatees are to be conveyed to these together with the estate.[243]
3. The third wording is not just a variation of the second one, as it has different consequences (which might, however, also include the ones in the second variant): 'I gave to you this estate together with everything that is included in it' (*kū-m ēn dastgird az har čē-š andar hămist ō tō dād*) implies that a title deed (*wizīr*) documenting a legal title to the estate is transferred together with all the assets belonging to the estate outside its borders, as well as a water canal (*kahas*) operated from within the estate and running through another plot of land.[244] The same formulation is interpreted more generally in another passage of the Law-book, explaining that besides the estate itself another thing or property (*xwāstag*) that could be requested on the basis of the title deed (*wizīr*) of the estate is conveyed to the beneficiary.[245]

242 MHD 18.9–10 (Macuch 1993, pp. 153, 159). On slaves engaged in agriculture see also Macuch 1981, p. 80.
243 MHDA 36.16–37.1: *abāg ān ī abar handarz ī ham Wehšābuhr pad dād ī dastgird pad gōwišn ī ham Wehšābuhr nibišt kū az anšahrīgān ī-š andar mānēnd hămist ōwōn ē bawēd* 'Together with (the provision) in the testament of the same Wehšābuhr regarding the transfer of an estate, written according to the statement of the same Wehšābuhr: "It shall take effect together with the slaves residing in it".' (Macuch 1981, pp. 63, 220). On the dating of Wehšābuhr see Macuch 2017a, p. 269.
244 MHD 18.10–13: … *wizīr-iz ē(w) ī andar ān dastgird ested ud xwāstag-iz-ē(w) ī pad any gyāg pad wizīr šāyēd āštan ud kahas-ē(w) ī az ān gyāg rāyēnīd ēstēd ud kār pad abārīg gyāg kuned dad bawēd* '… a title deed made for that estate and also a thing in another place that should be held in possession by the title deed and a water canal which is operated from that place and works in another place is given.' (Macuch 1993, pp. 153, 159). On *wizīr* 'title deed' see Chapter IV, pp. 268–270.
245 MHDA 34.3–6: *ka gōwēd kū-m ēn dastgird az har čē-š andar hămist ō tō dād wizīr-iz-ē(w) ī pad ēn dastgird ēstēd ud xwāstag-iz-ē(w) ī pad any gyāg pad ān wizīr sayed xwāstan dād bawēd* 'If he states: "I gave to you this estate together with everything that is included in it", (then) a document (= title deed) made for this estate and a thing that can be requested by that document is (also) given.' (Macuch 1981, pp. 60, 217).

4. The fourth entry is a variant of the third one in that it expressly names two beneficiaries as the recipients with corresponding implications: 'This estate together with everything that is included in it I gave to you and that estate to you' (*kū[-m] ēn dastgird az har čē-š andar hămist ō tō ud ān dastgird ō tō dād*). Each of the two recipients receives a separate estate and a corresponding title deed (*wizīr*), but each of the two is only entitled to one-half of any property in one of the estates that could be requested on the basis of the title deed by the other recipient and only one-half of a water canal operating in both estates, that is, they are equal shareholders of any assets belonging to both estates.[246]

The entries referring to buildings (*xānag, kadag*) confirm that all things explicitly and implicitly bequeathed in conjunction with the main property were included in the transfer. This is elaborated in one of the seldom cases, in which a simple provision is explained in detail: If the testator (donor) states 'I gave you this house' (*kū-m ēn kadag ō tō dād*), then this implies that all fixtures and accessories belonging to this specific house are transferred (not only the walls and roof, as we may add). These include the house (or hall) itself (*srāy*), columns (*stūn*), windows (*rōzbānag*), doors (*dar*), keys (*kilēl*), the storehouse (*hamābēr*) and the well in the storehouse (*čāh ī pad hamābēr*).[247] If the testator (donor) provides 'I gave you this house to hold as a place of residence' (*kū-m ēn xānag pad mānišn dāštan ō tō dād*), this wording implies that the house will be transferred into the ownership of the recipient without any time limitation (*ǰāwēdānīg* 'perpetually).[248] Both quoted formulations are precise in that they refer to a specific building by the use of the demonstrative pronoun *ēn* 'this', *i.e.*, *ēn kadag* or *ēn xānag* 'this (specific) house', which has different implications than an imprecise provision (with the indefinite article *-ē[w]*) referring to 'one house' (*xānag-ē[w]*), as we are informed in another passage recording the decision of the jurisconsult Pusānweh, son of Āzādmard. If the testator/donor has declared: 'I gave you one house' (*kū-m xānag-ē[w] ō tō dād*) and this statement refers to a 'part' (*ast-ē[w]*) of a building complex, then—according to the interpretation of the quoted jurist—the 'foundation building' or 'ground building' (*bun*) is transferred to the recipient.[249] The use of *bun* to designate a

246 MHD 18.13–17: ... *ēn dastgird ō ōy ud ān dastgird ō ōy dād bawēd wizīr-iz ē(w) ī andar ēn dastgird kard ēstēd u-š xwāstag-ē(w) ī pad ān dastgird pad-iš šāyēd dāštan ud kahas-ē(w) ī az gyāg rāyēnīd ēstēd ud kār pad ān gyāg kunēd nēm ō ōy ud nēm ō ōy dād bawēd* '... this estate is given to him and that estate to him; a title deed made for this estate and also a thing in the other estate that should be held in possession by it (= the title deed) and a water canal which is operated from that place and works in that place is given half to him and half to him.' (Macuch 1993, pp. 153, 159).

247 MHD 18.17–19.2 (Macuch 1993, pp. 153, 159).

248 MHD 19.2–3 (*ibid.*, pp. 153, 159).

249 MHD 19.3–5: *ka gōwēd kū-m xānag-ē(w) ō tō dād ... ka-š ast-ē(w) bun dād bawēd* 'If he declares: "I gave one house to you" ... if it is a part (of a building complex) (then) the ground building is given.' (*ibid.*, pp. 154, 159).

kind of 'foundation building' or 'ground building' (the exact meaning of which is unfortunately not explained) is reminiscent of the controversially discussed term *bun-xānag* ('foundation-house' according to HENNING)[250] in the Kirdīr inscriptions[251] and the corresponding Bactrian expression *βονο καδγο*,[252] which have been translated as '(personal) estate' and '(family) estate' respectively in more recent publications.[253] Although the exact meaning of the term eludes us, it seems that the older interpretation of *bun-xānag* as 'foundation-house' by HENNING would be (at least in the light of the quoted passage of the Law-book) nearer to the point than many of the suggestions made in later publications.[254] The cited passage suggests that a 'house' (*xānag*) in the concrete sense of the word is meant, with *bun* possibly designating the original edifice in a larger complex of buildings.

A distinction was presumably made between 'estates' (*dastgird*) and 'land' (*zamīg*), as we can conclude indirectly by entries involving the devolution of 'land'. It seems that the term *dastgird* referred to a clearly defined parcel of land with fixed borders, consisting of land that was already cultivated and used for agriculture, including water canals, roads and buildings (in which slaves and animals working on the premises or overseers could reside), whereas *zamīg* (or *gil*, lit. 'soil') could designate any plot of land that had not yet been developed in this manner (provided it is not expressly characterized otherwise, as in *zamīg ī kišwzār* 'cultivated land'[255]). This seems to be the background of a difficult passage in the Law-book bequeathing the transfer of 'land' with the words 'I gave land to you' (*kū-m zamīg ō tō dād*). In contrast to the wordings cited above, this specific formulation neither makes use of the demonstrative pronoun *ēn* 'this' (which specifies the object of transfer) nor of the indefinite pronoun *-ē(w)* 'one' (referring to only a part of a larger complex) in connection with the word *zamīg* 'land', but refers to a plot of land as a whole. Consequently, this wording implies, as we are told, that the 'land' is bequeathed 'in one piece, as a whole' (*ēw-kardagīhā*) to the recipient, that is, it is not partitioned or parcelled, but transferred as an undivided unit.[256] The specifics of this land 'in one piece' (*ēw-kardagīhā*) are then listed as follows:

250 HENNING 1957, p. 1.
251 KKZ 3 and KNRm 7 (BACK 1978, p. 391).
252 Bactrian documents J6, 5', 6'; L6, 9 (in SIMS-WILLIAMS 2000).
253 HUYSE 1998, p. 116; SIMS-WILLIAMS 2000, p. 187, respectively.
254 On the corresponding term *bun-kadag* in documents in the Pahlavi cursive script (compare Bactrian *βονο καδγο*) see MACUCH 2008b, pp. 255–257, with further references.
255 As in Tab. 18.8: *az ān man xwēš zamīg ī kišwzār ēw-kardag* 'From the cultivated land of my own in one piece' (MACUCH 2017c, p. 185). On *dastgird* see now PANAINO 2022a.
256 MHD 19.5–7 (MACUCH 1993, pp. 154, 159). The terms *zamīg ī ēw-kardag* 'land in one piece' and *zamīg ī kišwzār ēw-kardag* 'cultivated land in one piece' also occur in Tab. 18.8, 12, 17 (albeit without definitions; see MACUCH 2017c, pp. 183–188).

1. It does not belong to 'co-partners/shareholders of the fruits/income' (*hambaragān*)[257] or other persons (*i.e.*, the recipient does not receive only a share of this plot of land in a partnership with a title to the fruits, but the whole unit).
2. It is not cultivated, there is no waterway carrying water to another property (*ǰō[y] kē āb ō any xwāstag barēd*), no houses (*kadag*), no roads (*rāh*) and, consequently also no overseers or supervisors (*sālār*). In other words, if we take all that has been said on the *dastgird* into consideration: this 'land' (*zamīg*) is *not* an 'estate' (*dastgird*), but as yet an uncultivated plot in an undivided unit that still has to be developed.

These are by far not the only examples of semantic sophistry from this branch of law, which is still open to study, but they reveal impressively that great care was taken to understand wills and to implement the exact wishes of the head of a household, when these were compatible with the important principles upon which the laws of property and succession were built.

The legal heirs could contest the will, if they claimed that the testator was suffering from a fatal illness (*dardōmandīh*) and was not fully conscious (*nē ōšyār*) at the time it was made. This is not explicitly said in the Law-book, but in a late Pahlavi text the case of a wealthy man is discussed, who obviously had no son and conveyed his entire estate during a fatal illness to one of his daughters, although there were several other women in the family, wives, daughters and sisters, who were also entitled to inheritance.[258] The commentary implies that—in contrast to a fully conscious person (*andar ōšyārīh*)—a testator who is fatally ill (*andar dardōmandīh* ⁺*nigūn be widerišnīh* 'during an illness close to death') is not authorized to make dispositions regarding his entire estate, but he may provide for the repayment of a debt (*abām*) and for the maintenance of persons under his guardianship (*sālārīh*), his wive(s), underage children, father or other aged individuals (*zarmān*).[259] During an 'illness that is not fatal' (*dardōmandīh nē pad widerišnīh*) and in full consciousness (*andar ōšyārīh*), on the other hand, he is authorized to dispose over the estate according to his wishes.[260] The decisive factor is consciousness: if a lack of awareness on the part of the testator could be reasonably assumed, then the provisions made in a will, were, with the exception of those listed above, null and void (*nē awestwār ud nē wāwar*, lit. 'unreliable and invalid'), and could be successfully contested by the legal heirs.[261]

We are not very well informed on the right to renounce a bequest and the circumstances in which the heirs and legatees could disclaim the inheritance or refuse to take possession of it. According to the legal school of Pēšagsīr, the

257 On this term see fn. 141 above.
258 Dd 53 (for the whole *Pursišn* see Appendix I, pp. 641–646).
259 Dd 53.6 (Appendix I, pp. 642, 644)
260 Dd 53.7.
261 Dd 53.8.

son of the decedent became automatically his heir (*xwāstagdār*) if he did not expressly renounce the inheritance, implying indirectly that renouncement was a possible option (in contrast, a fellow citizen, *mard ī šahr*, installed by the decedent as *xwāstagdār*, inherited only on the condition that he expressly accept the inheritance).[262] The *Corpus Iuris* of Īšōʿbōxt employs an Iranian loan-word in this context, the technical term *abēsaxwan* 'without claim' (lit. 'without word/speech' < *abē*+*saxwan*), and its abstract *abēsaxwanīh* 'waiver, renunciation', terms also attested in the Bactrian legal texts.[263] In the Law-book the fixed formula *az … abēsaxwan būdan* 'to renounce, waive a claim (to something)' generally designates the renouncement of any kind of claim or the refrainment from exercising a legal right in any legal context, not only that of inheritance. A specific case involving donation and inheritance is discussed in a single passage: a *paterfamilias* entitles his *pādixšāy*-wife in a written document (*wizīr*) to give a specific 'thing' (*xwāstag*) to a person of her choice, but—in contrast to the document—provides in his last will (*handarz*) that it should be transferred to a person he has chosen himself. Despite this disposition the wife retains the right to make the donation, even if she consents to the last will of the husband and has 'renounced the claim to that thing' (*az ān xwāstag abēsaxwan būd ēstēd*)".[264] No explanation or legal justification is given for this decision, but we may assume that the first document (*wizīr*) entitling the wife to make the donation remains in full force and effect despite the disposition in the husband's testament (*handarz*) and even despite her own renouncement of this right.

4 Joint property (*hamxwāstagīh*) and partnership (*hambāyīh*)

In accordance with the basic concept of the family group or lineage as a self-perpetuating organism the heirs inherited as a rule (to which exceptions were possible) from the *kadag-xwadāy* the undivided patrimonial estate (*abarmānd*), consisting of the different elements described above, as joint proprietors (*hamxwāstag*) and 'partners, companions, associates, shareholders' (*hambay*). As we have seen, not only the male heirs became co-proprietors (*brād ī hambāy* 'shareholding brothers'), but also the women, wives, unmarried daughters and sisters of the deceased, who together with the sons received 'ideal' (*a-baxt*, lit. 'undivided') shares of the total patrimonial estate (*abarmānd*) corresponding to their legal portion of the residue.

262 MHD 61.9–11 (Macuch 1993, pp. 410, 415).

263 On the formula *az … abēsaxwan būdan* and the use of the loan-word *abesaxwan(īh)* in Syriac and Bactrian legal texts see Chapter VII, pp. 611–614.

264 MHD 64.2–7 (Macuch 1993, pp. 434, 437; Macuch 1989, pp. 155–156); see also below Chapter VII, p. 612.

Besides this type of shareholding based on inheritance, a partnership could also take rise in joint acquisition or by an agreement between two or more persons to co-operate for a joint commercial venture or another common purpose. A number of technical terms are transmitted in this context, which make it rather likely that Sasanian law distinguished exactly between various forms of partnership and shareholding, but here again, as in many other fields, the available information is so fragmented that basic concepts can hardly be detected. The general term for 'partnership, companionship, *societas*' is *hambāyīh*[265], which seems to refer to any type of associate partnership, both of heirs and other co-proprietors as well as persons involved in joint ventures. A distinction seems to have been made between partners within the family group, usually the heirs and beneficiaries called *brād ī hambāy* 'shareholding brother(s)', and associates outside the family, called *hambāy ī dēnīg*, lit. 'religious partner(s)', presumably the designation for any adherent of the Good Religion with whom one has formed some kind of *societas* or company.[266] Another word which in fact has the general meaning of 'man, young man', *mērag*, and in the bulk of attestations designates a young husband (as the counterpart to *ziyānag* 'young woman, wife'), seems also to have been used in this context as a specific technical term for 'business partner, associate, *socius*', as we have good reason to assume from a few entries (which would otherwise be enigmatic).[267] Nyberg, attempting to bring the two meanings together (based on Bartholomae) has in my opinion the best definition of the term as 'a (young) man standing in personal association (through family ties or partnership) with another'.[268]

In compliance with the basic distinction between the two elements of a corporeal thing (*xwāstag*), consisting of 'substance' (*bun*) and 'fruits' (*bar*), and the difference between possession (*dārišn*) and ownership (*xwēšīh*), we can furthermore distinguish between various kinds of partnership according to the terminology employed in this context. These can be grouped into the following basic types (with partly overlapping rights and duties):

1. Joint proprietors (*hamxwāstagān*)[269] who are co-owners of a specific property with two variations: (a) *pad āgenēn xwēš* 'in joint ownership'[270] with exactly

265 < *hama* 'joint, together' + *bāga-* 'share, portion' (Bartholomae 1904, col. 952); OIr. **hama-bāga-* 'shareholder, companion, partner'; Aram. hnbg' 'partner' (Hinz 1975, p. 115); on Syr. *habbāḡā* and Mand. *hambaga* 'enemy, adversary' see Ciancaglini 2008, p. 160.

266 MHD 23.15; 24.2. On this term see Macuch 1993, pp. 189–190 (no. 15).

267 This has been already recognized perceptively by Bartholomae 1918–1923, IV, p. 50ff., 'Geschäftsfreund'; on *mērag* in this sense see particularly MHD 93.14–94.2 (Macuch 1993, pp. 594, 597) and MHDA 14.7–9 (Macuch 1981, pp. 36, 143); see also commentary, *ibid.*, pp. 156–157.

268 Nyberg 1974, p. 132.

269 MHD 1.17; 53.4, 86.5, 9, 10, 11.

270 MHD 12.10; 51.4; 55.15; 56.13.

equal shares (in contrast to *ǰud ǰud xwēš* '[having] separate ownership');[271] (b) with divergent shares, paraphrased as *mard dō xwēš*[272] '(in) the ownership of two men' or *ī-š az any mard hammis xwēš* 'who has ownership together with other men'.[273]

2. Joint proprietors (*hamxwāstagān*) who are co-possessors (*pad āgenēn dārišn* 'in joint possession),[274] of the fruits with equal shares (as *bar-xwēš* 'owners of the fruit', without being necessarily owners of the substance).
3. Co-partners of the income (*hambaragān*),[275] shareholders who have access to the fruits of the income (either in perpetuity as *bar-xwēš* or for a limited time as usufruct, *bar-xward*). Shareholders of the income or profit are also denoted as *hamwindišn*[276] '(having) joint earnings, income' and *hamwaxš*[277] '(having) joint interest, increase'. Shareholders with exactly equal shares of the income are *āgenēn hamwindišn* '(having) joint income with equal shares'.
4. Co-sureties (*hampāyandān*),[278] partners who have taken up a loan together and provide suretyship for each other as security for the debt.

Although these terms indicate that there were different forms of partnership, an underlying concept of *hambāyīh* is difficult to reconstruct (if there was one), apart from the fundamental distinctions already elucidated above. But the individual cases discussed in the Law-book illustrate the social and economic significance of partnership and shareholding, besides revealing how a *societas* functioned in practice, even though many legal aspects are missing. In the following we will attempt to specify these four kinds of partnership in greater detail.

The first type in which the partners are 'joint proprietors' (*hamxwāstag*) and 'co-owners with equal shares' (*pad āgenēn xwēš*) is elucidated in a remarkable sentence of the Law-book, conveying a decision of general principle of the highest legal authority, the *mowbedān mobed* (unfortunately the name of this specific authority is not transmitted, so that an exact dating is not possible).[279] The main issue of this passage is how to interpret the wording of loan contracts,[280] but the second part transmits indirectly a legal definition of the technical expression *pad āgenēn xwēš*. The use of this formulation in a contract unequivocally

271 These two expressions, *āgenēn xwēš* and *ǰud ǰud xwēš*, are contrasted MHD 12.10 (Macuch 1993, pp. 117, 120).
272 MHD 55.15.
273 MHD 86.2–3.
274 MHD 24.17; 25.5; 26.17.
275 MHD 19.6; 78.12; 85.8. On this term see also p. 218 and fn. 141 above.
276 MHD 23.12; MHDA 1.3,1,12, 3.2.
277 MHD 51.2.
278 MHD 2.1; 56.1,3,8,9,10.; 57.1,6; 59.4. On this term see also Chapter IV, pp. 349–359.
279 MHD 55.11–17 (Macuch 1993, pp. 386, 391).
280 Contracts and transactions will be discussed in Chapter IV.

implies that the partners who are 'co-owners' have *identical shares* of the joint property and are hence equally liable for repaying debts. The decision of the Chief Mobed was obviously necessary in order to determine 'once and for all' (*ǰār-ē[w]*) how the courts should interpret another similar (but not identical) formulation used in loan contracts: if the contract has: 'this property is in the ownership of two men' (*ēn xwāstag mard dō xwēš*) this in fact only states that the two men (= debtors) are co-owners, but does not convey any information on the proportion of their shares (*nē paydāg kū čand ōy ud čand ōy* 'it is not clear, how much belongs to one, how much to the other'). In his decision of principle the highest legal authority decrees that this wording should be regarded as equivalent to the contract using the precise words: 'It is in their joint ownership' (*kū-šān pad āgenēn xwēš*). The latter wording (with *āgenēn*) implies that the parties have proportionally exactly identical (*rāst*) shares and are hence both liable for repaying a debt they have jointly taken up to the same extent. The former wording (without *āgenēn*) does *not* imply equal shares of the partners, but is to be interpreted in exactly this sense according to the decision of the Chief Mobed, no matter how large the individual portions of the parties might be.[281] We can infer from this (somewhat twisted, but revealing) entry that in Sasanian legal terminology *āgenēn xwēš* '(having) co-ownership' or *pad āgenēn xwēš* 'in co-ownership' refers explicitly to a type of partnership in which *all the parties own exactly equal shares* of the joint property and share equally in both profit and loss.

In other attestations of the term the partners are 'co-owners' (*āgenēn xwēš*) of sheep (*gōspand*)[282] and a sacred fire (*ātaxš*). In the latter case the partners are heirs, a son and a daughter, who both hold equal shares of the estate as *hamwaxš* '(having) joint interest, income'. If they partition the estate (*pad baxtīgīh kunēnd*) and the family later receives a donation of property (*xwāstag*) which cannot be partitioned, such as a sacred fire, this property remains in their co-ownership (*āgenēn xwēš*; as *bar-xwēš*, as we may add) and son and daughter have both either equal shares (*bahr*) or are both engaged equally in upholding and keeping (*dāštārīh*) the sacred fire.[283] Another remarkable entry, quoting the jurisconsult Rādohrmazd, implies that every acquisition of one of the partners in a co-ownership with equal shares (*āgenēn xwēš*) belongs jointly to both. In this specific case an exception is noted: property acquired by one of two partners is held in ownership jointly by both, but a woman/wife (*zan*) acquired by

281 See also commentary on this sentence in Macuch 1993, pp. 396–398 (no. 3).
282 MHD 12.10 (Macuch 1993, pp. 116, 120).
283 MHD 51.4 (Macuch 1993, pp. 311, 327). The reading of this passage is uncertain, as there is a lacuna before *ātaxš*, in which a qualifying word might have stood (such as *xwāstag ī ātaxš* 'property of the fire'?). The problem of ownership of a sacred fire has been already discussed above (pp. 217–218, 228); the main point is that the fire (and its property) could not be partitioned between the heirs, but was an undividable and inalienable component of family property. See also commentary in Macuch 1993, p. 364, no. 58.

one man, belongs to the partner who is 'the good/better one' (*ōy ī weh*). Within the framework of Sasanian marriage law, prohibiting polyandry, this decision is comprehensible, but, interestingly, the woman/wife does not automatically revert to the partner, who has originally acquired her, but rather to the man deemed more suitable according to Zoroastrian norms. This ruling suggests that the jurisconsult sought to retain the basic idea of co-ownership of property of the type *āgenēn xwēš*, which gives every partner equal shares and equal access to acquisitions, as far as possible without violating other religious and legal norms.[284]

Another formulation in a passage on 'joint proprietors' (*hamxwāstagān*) refers to joint ownership with the words: *xwāstag ī-š az any mard hammis xwēš* 'property which is his own together with other men'.[285] If we take the distinction elucidated above (between the use of *xwēš*, on the one hand, and *āgenēn xwēš*, on the other) into consideration, this phrase would indicate that the partners here are co-owners, but do *not* have equal shares (since having identical shares would be designated by the precise *āgenēn xwēš*). The associates in this case jointly own a house (*xānag*), a water channel (*kahas*) and another (not specified) property (*xwāstag*). We are not informed, how this partnership emerged (by joint acquisition, gift or inheritance?), but the co-owners have initially agreed to share any repair costs (*uzēnag*) that might come up for the joint property (despite their divergent shares, as we may add). If one of the partners advances the payment for repairs and the others later refuse to reimburse him, the partner who has made the payment in advance is entitled to demand a compensation (*guharīg*) from the others and to retain their shares (of the income?) as a pledge (*pad grawīh*) until he has been compensated.[286]

Taking all these entries into consideration we can conclude that the first type of *societas* noted above (joint proprietors, who are co-owners) encompasses two kinds of associations:

1. in which the parties have equal shares (*āgenēn xwēš*) and equal access to acquisitions;
2. in which the parties have divergent shares (*mard dō xwēš*), but are treated as having equal shares in cases of debt and liability (according to the decision of general principle of the Chief Mobed).

The first type of partnership involving co-possession (*pad āgenēn dārišn* 'in joint possession [with equal shares]') is, unsurprisingly, mainly mentioned in the context of property dedicated to a religious purpose 'for the soul' and sacred fires, which remained in the possession (*dārišn*) of a family, but were bound to

284 MHDA 4.4–5 (Macuch 1981, pp. 24, 72).
285 MHD 86.2–3.
286 MHD 86.2–15 (Macuch 1993, pp. 550, 553f.). On the pledge/pawn (*graw*) see Chapter IV, pp. 326–336.

the functions laid down by the founder. If a man determines by testament that a specific property should be dedicated to the salvation of his soul (*ruwān rāy*), then his wife and children hold it jointly in possession with equal shares (*pad āgenēn dārišn*).[287] If there is no last will and a man has founded a certain property for his own soul and the soul of another person without determining the right of possession (*dāštan rāy framān nē bawēd*), then the heirs of both families hold it jointly with equal shares (*pad āgenēn dārišn*).[288] A third passage is concerned with the guardianship (*sālārīh*) of a sacred fire (*ātaxš*) in the case that the (deceased) founder has not explicitly determined a guardian: if the founder has two sons, who are of the same age and both 'equally diligent in the practice of religion and virtuous' (*pat dēn kardārtar ud weh hāwand*), then both sons will hold the fire jointly in guardianship with equal shares (*pad āgenēn dārišn*).[289] All these entries on 'joint possession' comply with the laws governing this category of family property 'for the soul', usually giving the heirs and beneficiaries as partners joint access to the fruits in perpetuity (*bar-xwēšīh*), but no right to change the status of the substance (see above pp. 220–229).

The third type of *societas*, that of co-partners or shareholders of the income (*hambaragān*), is likewise attested in connection to a sacred fire (of the Wahrām type), as we have already noted above,[290] and of land: *zamīg ī hambaragān* 'land of co-partners/shareholders of the fruits'. The latter expression designates land belonging to associates who have either a title to its usufruct or are owners of the crops (we have already discussed the contrast to *zamīg ī ēwkardagīhā* 'land in one piece', *i.e.*, land that is not partitioned or parcelled).[291] The term also occurs in a short chapter dedicated to questions involving the partnership (*hambāyīh*) of a water channel (*ǰōy-kahas*), which usually ran through several estates and was not restricted to one plot of land.[292] It is not quite clear, whether a construction comparable to the underground cannel, a *qanāt*, is meant, but the *kahas* seems to have been a more complex building than a simple water way, since we are informed that it was dug up to 'the height of an ear' (*gōš-bālāy*). In this passage a person digs a water channel in this manner on his own land or on the land of 'co-partners of the fruits' (*hambaragān*). Proprietors of the adjacent estates, who also profit from the water channel, are not allowed to dig another channel within the borders of the field (*nindār dašt*) on which the channel was dug without the consent of the channel owner and outside the borders of the field (*bērōn dašt*) only if the latter does not suffer a loss.[293] Two men who construct

287 MHD 24.16–17 (Macuch 1993, pp. 192, 199).
288 MHD 25.2–5 (*ibid.*, pp. 193, 199f.).
289 MHD 26.15–17 (*ibid.*, pp. 195, 202).
290 See pp. 217–218 above.
291 MHD 19.6 (Macuch 1993, pp. 154, 159). See also above pp. 243–244.
292 MHD 85.8 (Macuch 1993, pp. 549, 552).
293 On *dašt* 'plain; the cultivated fields, or part of these, surrounding a village' see Lambton 1953, p. 426. This is very similar to the *qanāt* regulations in Islamic law, forbidding the

a water channel together as partners are both usufructuaries, but if one of the parties interrupts the work or refuses to expand the construction (*āb abzūdan*, lit. 'to increase the water') he loses his share of the increase (*abzōn bahr*) to the other partner (on the technical term *abzōn* '(total) surplus, increase' see below).[294] These entries offer no definitions, but it would not be too far-fetched to assume that any kind of co-operation or joint venture leading to profit (as the digging of a water channel) could take the form of a *hambāyīh* based on common income.

Partnerships of this third type with joint earnings could include women as usufructuaries. The term *hamwaxš* '(having) joint increase' occurs only in a single entry referring to the partnership of a man's heirs, son and daughter, who are bestowed with equal shares of the income, as we have already noted above.[295] Another expression, *hamwindišn*, *hamwindišnīh* '(having) joint earnings, income' is employed with and without the elucidating *āgenēn*: *āgenēn hamwindišn* refers to an association with exactly *equal shares* of the income,[296] whereas *hamwindišn* alone denotes a partnership of the income with *divergent shares*. The latter is attested in the context of partnerships between husband and wife highlighting the economic options of women who were given a share (albeit not an equal one) of the profits of their husband's estate. We have seen in the context of the *pādixšāy*-marriage that a husband could convey to his wife the right of disposal over earnings from (his or her own) property (using the words *pad windišn pādixšāyīhā kard* 'she is given full entitlement to the income').[297] If a husband has two *pādixšāy*-wives and makes them both joint partners of his earnings by contract (*paymān*) with the words: 'I have made you and you co-partners of the income' (*kū-m tō ud tō hamwindišn kard hē*), this does *not* imply that the wives are co-usufructuaries, but that every wife is a separate (*ǰud ǰud*) joint partner of the husband. The wives have among themselves separate incomes (*ǰud windišn*) and are not permitted to change the terms of the partnership with the husband, which is the sole prerogative of the latter.[298] The husband can revoke the association or his wife's right to income on grounds of disobedience (*atarsagāyīh*), but the wife is given the option of defending herself against the allegation of insubordination.[299]

We are not informed in the Law-book, how exactly a wife could defend her rights against allegedly false accusations, but a remarkable document in the Tabarestān collection seems to describe precisely one of these cases. In Tab. 21

construction of a second *qanāt* within the borders (*ḥarīm*) of a field; see also commentary to this sentence in Macuch 1993, pp. 556–557.

294 MHD 85.11–16 (Macuch 1993, pp. 549, 552).

295 MHD 51.2; see p. 247 above.

296 This interpretation is indirectly confirmed by MHDA 3.1–6 (Macuch 1981, pp. 23, 71).

297 See Chapter II, p. 139 above.

298 MHDA 1.3–6 (Macuch 1981, pp. 21, 69).

299 MHDA 3.13–17; 4.2–4; 5.15–6.1; 6.5–7 (Macuch 1981, pp. 24, 72; 26f., 97 respectively). See also commentary *ibid.*, pp. 88–89 (no. 26).

Table 18. Overview: terminology of partnership and shareholding (*hambāyīh*)

<table>
<tr><th colspan="2">General terms</th><th colspan="2">Particular types</th></tr>
<tr><td rowspan="3">brād ī hambāy</td><td rowspan="3">‘shareholding brother’ (within a family group)</td><td colspan="2">hamxwāstag(ān) ‘joint proprietor(s), co-proprietor(s)’</td></tr>
<tr><td>(pad) āgenēn xwēš</td><td>‘(in) joint ownership’ (with equal shares)</td></tr>
<tr><td>ī-š az any mard hammis xwēš</td><td>‘(in) ownership together with other men’ (with divergent shares)</td></tr>
<tr><td rowspan="2">hambāy ī dēnīg</td><td rowspan="2">‘religious partner’ (business associate, companion outside the family group)</td><td>mard dō xwēš</td><td>‘(in) ownership of two men’ (with divergent shares)</td></tr>
<tr><td>(pad) āgenēn dārišn</td><td>‘(in) joint possession’ (with equal shares)</td></tr>
<tr><td>mērag</td><td>‘business associate, companion, socius’ (lit. ‘young man’)</td><td colspan="2">hambarag(ān) ‘co-partner(s) of the fruits, shareholder(s) of the income’</td></tr>
<tr><td colspan="2" rowspan="4"></td><td>hamwaxš</td><td>‘(partner with) joint interest’</td></tr>
<tr><td>āgenēn hamwindišn</td><td>‘(partner with) joint income’ (with equal shares)</td></tr>
<tr><td>hamwindišn</td><td>‘(partner with) joint income’ (with divergent shares)</td></tr>
<tr><td colspan="2">hampāyandān ‘co-surety’ (in a societas of co-debtors)</td></tr>
</table>

a father files a complaint (*garzišn*) against his own son-in-law who has stopped payments to his wife, the *pādixšāy*-daughter of the complainant. The father (a scribe, named Farroxgušnasp) accuses the husband (called Yazdfarrox) of cutting the maintenance and income of his daughter (called Yazdweh) because of a false accusation (*mihōxt*) against her, which, according to the father, is groundless (*abēčim*). He confirms that his son-in-law was married for several years to his daughter and maintained her as ‘one of his own’ (*pad ēk ī xwēš*) before the false accusation came up. The document then includes a list of the various earnings and payments to which this *pādixšāy*-wife is legally entitled (either by marriage contract or by partnership contract with the husband). The income is collectively called *abzōn* ‘increase, growth, surplus’ and consists of five elements, which are—due to the limited and concise content of these texts—not explained, but can be translated tentatively as: (1) ‘(daily) ration’ (*rōzīg*), (2) ‘extra allocation’ (*padēxīh*; lit. ‘prosperity’), (3) ‘work-based/related income’ (*kār-wahāg*, lit.

'work-value'), (4) 'clothing' (*paymōzan*), (5) 'surplus' (*abzūd*). Of these five components only *rōzīg* '(daily) ration' (either referring to quotidian food or used as a general term for 'ration, sustenance')[300] and *paymōzan* 'clothing' are self-explanatory; the other elements denote specific types of income, which cannot be precisely determined without further information, but we can draw the important conclusion that the terms *abzōn* and *abzūd* (presumably synonymous in the daily colloquial) were distinguished in legal language. Whereas *abzōn* denotes the total income to which the wife is entitled, consisting of the five different elements noted above, *abzūd* designates only *one* component of this income, referring presumably to a specific type of surplus.[301]

The fourth type of partnership, *hampāyandānīh* 'co-suretyship', takes form when two or several debtors take up a loan together and agree to act at the same time as sureties for each other. As we will elucidate in the next chapter in the context of credit law and personal security, the technical term *hampāyandān* is used of co-debtors who warrant for each other, giving the creditor the option to sue any one of the debtors for the whole sum. Sasanian law distinguished between co-debtors and co-sureties: co-sureties (*hampāyandān*) were 'joint and several debtors' (*hamāg-tōzišn*), *i.e.*, every debtor was liable for the total amount of the debt, whereas co-debtors, who did *not* warrant for each other, were only 'part debtors' (*xwāstag-tōzišn*). Every 'part debtor' was only liable for his own share of the loan and could be sued by the creditor only with regard to this proportional share.[302]

5 Social consequences of property law and the Mazdakite upheaval

All the details we have pieced together on the various categories of property constituting the patrimonial estate of rich families and the intricate rules regarding the continuity of a lineage lead us back to the main question posed at the beginning of this Chapter: *why* were these institutions established, and – if our initially formulated hypothesis is correct—*how* did they promote the interests of the Sasanian elite, the wealthy Zoroastrian clergy and the nobility? We have already noted, that there seems to be a close affinity between this specific categorization of patrimonial property into four distinguishable elements and the fictive ties and constructions determining the structure of kinship discussed in Chapter II. Given that endogamy, even of the incestuous type within the 'nuclear family', was preferred, that extensive fictive consanguineous bonds could

300 On the use of *rōzīg* as a general term for 'ration, sustenance' (not only in its literal sense of 'daily ration') see Weber 2008b, pp. XXIX–XXXI.
301 For an extensive discussion of Tab. 21 see Macuch 2019b, pp. 118–125.
302 See Chapter IV, p. 356.

be construed, and that intermediary or substitute successors were engaged if a *paterfamilias* left no direct (male) heir, we can safely conclude that the construction of fictive kinship bonds with this unparalleled range is not just an inexplicable peculiarity of Sasanian law, but that it served the economic interests of the land-owning social elite. These laws were obviously implemented in order to ensure the intergenerational transfer of property, just as the division of the patrimonial or family estate into several inalienable categories prevented its undesired partitioning and fragmentation into small units. In short, the total patrimonial estate (*abarmānd*) of a wealthy family or lineage was held intact by two means:

1. by ensuring the continuity of the lineage in accord with the elaborate rules constituting family law (including polygyny, real and fictive incestuous marriages, time-limited matrimony, and 'intermediary' and 'substitute succession', as we have seen in Chapter II), and
2. by limiting the access of the heirs and legatees to the substance (*bun*) of property, whilst giving them full access to the income (*bar*) in perpetuity by the devise of *bar-xwēšīh* 'ownership of the income'. Alienating large parts of the estate, *i.e.*, those assets belonging to the first, third and fourth categories of property described above, became almost impossible.

Thus the pre-eminence of an affluent Sasanian elite was ensured across a long period of time by the transmission of the family estate in this specific form in alliance with the institutions created to avoid the termination of a lineage.

We also have good reason to assume that the system was to the advantage of the upper stratum of the Zoroastrian priesthood, as the clergy could profit considerably from at least two categories of a family's total estate: property 'in trust or for substitute succession (*pad stūrīh*)' and 'for the soul' (*pad ruwān*). Besides the descendants of noble families, Zoroastrian priests had access to the income of larger endowments (*ruwānagān*) established 'for the soul': they could act as administrators (*sālār*) of the charitable foundations, notably the larger fire endowments for whose preservation they were responsible as 'keepers' (*pad dāštārīh*), and they of course performed the numerous obligatory Zoroastrian rites and rituals as well as the post-mortem ceremonies of *nāmagānīh* for the souls of the deceased ancestors. For the latter two tasks they were paid from the income of that part of *ruwān*-property explicitly reserved for this purpose in two main sub-categories, called *pad ahlawdād* 'for charitable purposes' and *pad ruwān yazišn* 'for religious ceremonies for the soul'. Furthermore, the clergy was also involved in selecting 'proxies' of the 'nominated' type (*stūr ī gumārdag*) if neither of the other two types of *stūr* were available. Religious authorities (*padān ī den*) or a congregation of *mowbeds* chose from among the relatives of the deceased the 'proxy' deemed 'most fitting' or 'most worthy' (*sazāgtar*) according to an established sequence from which they could, however, deviate. This important right opened additional options of taking influence on the nobility and participating in the devolution of property after the death of a *kadag-xwadāy*.[303]

These details leave the impression that almost all the rules and regulations transmitted in these two branches of law were adjusted to the specific needs of wealthy noble and priestly families belonging to the two uppermost social estates. As we have already noted, the divergent status of nobles and commoners is revealed not only in the various customs governing daily life, established to visibly distinguish these two groups, but particularly in laws protecting the proprietary rights and privileges of the aristocracy. This exactly is the context in which the two important regulations transmitted in the 'letter of Tansar' should be considered:

1. A man of noble birth is not allowed to take a wife from among commoners. Who did so nevertheless, lost his entitlement to inheritance.
2. Commoners are not allowed to purchase the estates of the aristocracy.[304]

Both legal provisions have one and the same goal: to hinder the transfer of property from the nobility to commoners either indirectly by marriage (of the *pādixšāy*-type), since the legitimate children of a common woman would inherit in this case, or directly by selling parts of their estate. If we add to this rule the many details on the artificial construction of legitimate heirs, then it becomes quite evident that Sasanian law developed numerous options to preserve and increase the property of its elite and paid special attention to avoid splitting and alienating it.

The care taken to promote the economic interests of the nobility in this manner does not imply, however, that the patrimonial estate was always kept together and never partitioned, although shareholding does seem to have been the preferred and widely practised variant (this did not change after the fall of the Sasanian empire, as the Tabarestān documents show spectacularly).[305] Several cases reveal, on the contrary, that the heirs and legatees could request the division (*baxtigīh kardan*) of a family's estate—with the exception of *stūrīh* and *ruwān* property—in the event of succession if it was preferable to joint possession. We have however good reason to assume that the extent of patrimonial property differed considerably between the lower and higher strata of the nobility and that the economic basis of affluent lineages was not necessarily endangered by partition, if the estate was large enough (see for example the extensive properties dedicated by Mihr-Narseh to fire foundations alone).[306] Sasanian law was in any case flexible enough to allow several options.

Another possible discrepancy in the Sasanian model should be referred to here. Even if the estate was *not* divided among the heirs: how would the procreation of numerous children based on Zoroastrian doctrine—serve the interests

303 On the impact of Zoroastrian family law on power relations see also Macuch 1995.
304 See Chapter II above, pp. 111–112; on the 'Letter of Tansar' see Chapter I, p. 52.
305 See particularly Tab. 18 (Macuch 2017c, pp. 183–188) and Tab. 24 (Macuch 2019b, pp. 132–146).
306 See pp. 226–227.

of the elite, given that there would be a substantial increase of shareholders from one generation to the next? Even if the bulk of ancestral property remained inalienable and was not partitioned, would there not be too many shareholders after several generations? Would it not have been easier instead to establish primogeniture and determine one (male) heir as proprietor and successor to avoid fragmentation? There is too little material in the texts to answer these justified questions, but we can attempt an assumption. Too many shareholders might have been a problem after a while for a smaller estate, but we should also take into account that the mere existence of the described institutions of secondary succession point to a different situation in Iran in late antiquity. They would hardly have been necessary if conceiving and rearing children up to maturity would have been an easy task in this period.[307] Moreover, despite polygyny and huge harems, the number of women eligible for procreating legitimate children for the aristocracy was obviously restricted to noble families (see the regulation quoted in the 'Letter of Tansar' above) with the result that, although a man could (and was obliged to) generate a large number of children with different wives only a few from 'privileged' (*pādixšāy*) marriage or from one of the institutions of secondary succession (*ayōgēnīh* and *stūrīh*) would have been entitled to inheritance. Children from the other marriages would *not* inherit and be regular shareholders, even if they could be included in the father's will and also receive maintenance if necessary. Be it as it may, despite this possible obstacle in the case of smaller family estates the Sasanian model seems to have been effective as long as it was not contested by the underprivileged mass of population belonging to the lower classes of Sasanian society.

In the light of this unbalanced legal system, bent on promoting the interests of wealthy and powerful descent groups, the rebellion connected with the name (or title) of Mazdak towards the end of the 5th century comes to mind. This well-known and often discussed movement flared up under the Sasanian King Kawād (488–531) at the end of the 5th century, was initially supported by the King, but suppressed towards the end of his reign at the beginning of the 6th century by his famous son Husraw Anūšīrwān (531–579 CE), one of the most widely acclaimed kings of the Sasanian dynasty, possibly because of his reforms in the aftermath of this famous upheaval.[308] It seems that Mazdakite doctrine

307 We tend to forget in an age of population explosion that mortality rates among children were rather high in earlier centuries before the progress of medicine in the 20th century. As already noted in the section on *stūrīh* (Chapter II, pp. 169–174), not only stillborn babies and a large range of fatal illnesses during childhood, but also violent conflicts, privatized feuds, strife and war could decimate a man's legitimate offspring before the children reached maturity.

308 So much has been written on the Mazdakites that would be impossible to mention all studies. The most important are Christensen 1925; Altheim/Stiehl 1954; Klima 1957 and 1977; Sundermann 1977 and 1988; Yarshater 1983; Crone 1991 and 2012 (especially chapter 18, pp. 439–450); de Blois 2012 and 2015; Macuch 2015b and 2021.

was based on an older interpretation of the sacred Zoroastrian texts according to a certain Zarādušt, son of Xurrag, or—according to *Dēnkard* 3—Zarduxšt, son of Xrōsag. Several sources indicate that Zarādušt/Zarduxšt belonged to the Zoroastrian establishment, was possibly a contemporary of Mani (3rd century) and originally a Mazdean priest, a *mowbed* or even Chief *mowbed*, from Fasā in Fārs, who was the founder of a new religious and social interpretation of Zoroastrian precepts, on which later Mazdakite doctrine was based.[309] Mazdakite social and religious teaching is described in several sources, particularly in aš-Šahrastānī's famous book on sects,[310] and represents the revolutionary idea that all means of subsistence on earth should be divided equally and that women and property should be shared by all alike. This concept that has been denoted as a form of 'communism' has, however, a religious background with the main objective to abolish quarrels and controversies among men. According to Mazdakite social doctrine (which was part of an astrological and, presumably, esoteric system), these were all the result of an unequal distribution of wealth and women, the main reason for hatred, strife and disputes.

Several remarkable passages dealing with the social and legal consequences of Mazdakite teaching have survived in the 9th century *Dēnkard* (III.5.1–2 and VII.7.22–25; see Appendix IV), which indirectly confirm all that has been said on the social and political significance of Sasanian family and property law and its promotion of the interests of the aristocracy and clergy to the detriment of commoners, the mass of the population. Although the *Dēnkard* is comparatively late, we have good reason to assume that the entries on Mazdakism are far older, possibly based on an elder *Vorlage* from the Sasanian period, as so much of late Pahlavi literature. As I have argued elsewhere, the significance of these passages lies in the meticulous use of legal language. Technical terms are employed not only with minute precision, but with full knowledge of all their legal implications, which makes it likely that these pieces were taken from an original text on the Mazdakites written at a time when Sasanian jurisprudence was still a widely practised and well-known discipline.[311]

The viewpoint of these entries is that of orthodox Zoroastrianism: Mazdakite teaching is seen as a dangerous heretical doctrine, which caused the complete downfall of all the important legal and social institutions of the Sasanian State. The consequences leading to the total collapse of the legal and religious system are embedded in Zoroastrian theology and presented in a drastic manner, but at the same time in the short and concise form of juristic treatises, using

309 Yarshater 1983, p. 995; Crone 1991, p. 24. On the name see also Dk III.5.1–2 (Appendix IV, pp. 669–671).

310 aš-Šahrastānī, *Kitāb al-milal wa-n-niḥal*; translation by Gimaret/Monnot 1986, pp. 663–666.

311 For an extensive discussion of these passages see Macuch 2015b; on the esoteric and astrological aspects of Mazdakite doctrine see Macuch 2021 with further references. The texts are assembled in Appendix IV, pp. 669–673.

the appropriate technical vocabulary, which had no need of explanations. Why the Mazdakites were regarded as the 'most heretical of heretics' (*ahlomōyān ahlomōy*) becomes quite evident from this legalistic perspective if we scrutinize the main accusations against them in the light of Sasanian law. The heretical practices listed in these two extracts refer mainly to the immense social and legal consequences of Zarduxštī/Mazdakite doctrine, which we may summarize as follows:

1. The Zarduxštīs/Mazdakites do not accept the central role of the Zoroastrian priesthood in the context of the ritual. They give the share (*bahr*) normally due to priests for the performance of religious rites (*kardārīh*) to their own followers (*xwēšān*) and ignore the important rules of food-distribution. (Orthodox teaching distinguishes between various categories of recipients according to their rank in society, between those who are 'worthy', *arzānīgān*, and 'inferior persons', +*niyuruzdān*, as well as those, who are entitled to maintenance 'by law', *dādīhā*, and those who are 'beneath entitlement by law', *frōd az dādīhā*. Moreover, the portions of meat to be allotted and the number of meals per day are determined precisely.) The Mazdakites hereby 'fatten' their own followers (*bahr ō xwēšān dahēnd xwarišn fšōnēnēnd* 'they give shares to their own (and) use food for fattening', a direct reference to Y XI.1f.).[312]
2. They have destroyed the traditional hierarchy of society and the State by abolishing the differences between the ranks and stations of nobles and commoners (*gāh ud pāyag ī mardōm agārēnīdan*). They do not heed Zoroastrian marriage laws, based on patrilineal descent, but practice matrilineal descent (*paywand pad mādarān*). They have eliminated the institution of 'substitute succession' (*stūrīh*) and the cult of 'name-preservation' (*nāmagānīh*) of the ancestors.
3. They do not keep the laws of inheritance. They ignore ownership of hereditary property (*wāspuhragān xwēšīh*), hereby causing the decrease of property (*gēhān*) and material substance (*mādag*) of the lineages. They buy females like small cattle and treat both them and family property (*ān-iz ī zahag pus brād* "that which belongs to the offspring, sons [and] brothers") as one would treat the usufruct of property (*bar*), *i.e.*, they keep both females and property in joint possession (*hamīh*).
4. They have annihilated the laws of ownership (*xwēšīh*) and possession (*dārišn*), hereby destroying the very basis of the legal system upon which the State is founded.
5. They do not heed procedural laws and jurisdiction (*dādwarīh*). They do not give oaths (*war*) on principle, even if this could lead to acquitting an accused person (*bē bōxtēd*), and they are contract-breakers (*mihrōdruǰ*).

312 On the rules of distributing food according to Zoroastrian precepts see Macuch 2012a; on the allocation of meat see also Macuch 1990. On the reference to Y XI.1f. see Macuch 2015b, pp. 159–164.

In the light of the Sasanian legal system these Mazdakite practices must have been considered as truly earth shattering and a serious threat to the powerful elites of Sasanian society. The total destruction of the State is illustrated dramatically by showing that the Mazdakites wilfully eliminated all the institutions that guaranteed the supremacy of the two most influential classes of society, the nobility and the priesthood, by two means:

- by undermining the ritual authority of the Zoroastrian clergy; and
- by refuting *all branches of jurisprudence*, encompassing family law, property law and procedural law.

To conclude, we have seen that the Iranians developed a highly complex set of laws with the aim of settling the transfer of property across generations in a manner profitable to the wealthy notables of Sasanian society. The complex legal design of Sasanian kinship groups with their fictive alliances and artificial constructions of consanguinity was an important device to maintain the vast wealth and the social predominance of the aristocracy and the clergy, even if the former goal might have been at times difficult to achieve in the case of smaller estates due to the practice of shareholding. The main point is, however, that the whole construction depicts a coherent system, in which every detail in this set of laws is a necessity and a logical consequence of the main rule, namely that the lineages and their vast property, or—in other words—the established social and economic hierarchy of the State, which guarantees the balance of power between the dominant groups, must be preserved under all circumstances.

By the end of Sasanian rule the legal system had become so complex, that it must have been impossible to change any part of it from within without creating havoc, as the Mazdakite upheaval demonstrates. Our survey of family and property law reveals clearly why any fundamental change with regard to the distribution of property had to begin with an alteration of the laws of marriage and succession, as King Kawād, seeking initially to support the movement, obviously recognized when he—according to almost all sources—changed the laws of matrimony. It would not be too far-fetched to assume that the unequal distribution of property and wealth between the Sasanian elite and the mass of the population was even one of the reasons why Iran could be so easily conquered by the Arab Muslims in the 7th century: the majority of Iranian soldiers probably did not have much to fight for. The reforms of Husraw Anūšīrwān in the 6th century did not suffice to alter the injustices of the social system fundamentally, especially as he was forced to re-insert the marriage and succession laws the Mazdakites had abolished, hereby reinstating the traditional hierarchies. Thus—paradoxically—it seems that this intricate set of laws supporting the privileges of the elite, developed across many centuries, had become crucial for the preservation of the Sasanian State, but at the same time finally contributed to its downfall.

Chapter IV

Contracts and Obligations

Introductory: the significance of the contract in Zoroastrianism

Keeping contracts was considered as one of the most important responsibilities of the Zoroastrian. Fulfilling obligations, which might ensue from all types of deeds, oral and written agreements, business and marriage contracts, pacts and treaties, was not only a legal requirement, but a significant religious duty, which took place under the surveillance of the god of the covenant, Mithra (MP Mihr). The Avestan common noun *miϑra-* (MP *mihr*) 'contract, deed, pact, covenant' is identical with the name of the god Mithra and the origin of this well-known, multi-functional Indo-Iranian god has been convincingly explained (albeit not without contradiction) as the personification of the immanent power that lies in contractual agreements.[1] Entering a contract, that is, a voluntary, binding agreement between two or more parties, was originally regarded as a religious act, enforced by prescribed formulae spoken aloud by the contracting parties, binding them to the promise or agreement with a force far greater than judicial institutions alone could warrant.

As has been observed, there are several allusions to the basic function of Mithra as god of contract (or, due to the religious connotation, lord of the covenant)[2] in *Yašt* 10, the Avestan hymn dedicated to this deity. In the hymn Ahura Mazdā admonishes Zarathustra to never become a contract-breaker (*miϑrō.druj-*), to keep contracts with both the righteous 'adherents of *aša*' (*ašauuan-*) and the deceitful 'adherents of *druj*' (*druuaṇt-*), as the contract applies to both.[3] Another passage of the hymn ranks the partners of an agreement

1 Meillet 1907 was the first to establish Mithra's original competence as god of the contract, followed by Gershevitch 1959, p. 43, and others; for an overview of the scholarly debate see Boyce 1975c, pp. 24–27; on Mihr as judge see Shaked 1980; for a recent discussion of the immense religious implications of Mithra as god of contract see König 2022b, pp. 401–431.

2 Boyce 1975c, p. 25.

3 Yt 10.2; see Gershevitch 1959, pp. 74–75, and commentary pp. 151–157. A similar statement is transmitted in the *andarz*-text *Handarz ī dānāgān ō māzdēsnān* 6 (Jamasp-Asana 1897–1913, p. 52): *abāg xwēšāwandān dōstān ǰud-dēnān mardōmān mihr ma drōzēd* 'Do not break a contract (*mihr*) with relatives, friends and those confessing another religion (*ǰud-dēnān*).' This religious precept seems to be one of the basic reasons for the more or less peaceful coexistence between Zoroastrians and the large communities of Jews and Christians in the Sasanian empire, see Macuch 2014b.

or contract according to a 'curious scale',[4] bearing witness to the large range of possible contractual (or rather: quasi contractual) connections between various persons and groups in the Avestan period: these encompass (in ascending sequence of importance) deeds between two friends, two fellow-citizens or (business) associates, the marriage contract between husband and wife, agreements between two fellow-students, between disciple and teacher, between son-in-law and father-in-law, between brothers, between father and son, as well as treaties concluded between two countries.[5] Unsurprisingly, at this early stage no distinction is made in this list of mutual agreements between social arrangements, *i. e*, the unwritten norms and self-evident reciprocal moral duties forming relationships between members of a family (or extended family, including the relationship between teacher and student), on the one hand,[6] and the (legally enforceable) contract between persons (friends, fellow-citizens, partners, husband and wife) or the (binding) treaty between countries, on the other. This ranking ends with the most important 'contract' of all, that of the 'Mazdayasnian Vision/religion' (*miϑrō yō daēnaiiā̊ māzdaiiasnōiš*).[7] Whatever might have been meant originally by this statement (presumably the obligations resulting from the bond between Ahura Mazdā and his adherents), in the Pahlavi texts the conflict between Ohrmazd and Ahriman was depicted as taking place within the framework of a 'contract' (*pašn*; *paymānag*) between the two adversaries. This 'contract', restricting the battle between good and evil to 'limited time', a period of 9000 (or 12000) years, had been suggested by Ohrmazd in his omniscience (*pad harwisp-āgāhīh*), knowing that victory will be his at the end of this period, and was accepted by Ahriman (*pad ān paymānag hamdādestān būd* 'he agreed to that contract'), who could not foresee the final outcome of the combat (*a-wēnag-fražāmīh rāy* 'due to not seeing the end').[8] This is a truly remarkable description of the procedure involved in concluding a contract, which only comes into existence when one party makes an offer that is explicitly accepted by the other one, thus forming a binding agreement. The idea of an offer (by Ohrmazd) and its acceptance (by Ahriman) is reminiscent of formal juristic dealings in Sasanian law forming a contract or obligation and was presumably based on legal practice (see below, pp. 301–305).

4 Gershevitch 1959, p. 26.
5 Yt 10.116–117; Gershevitch 1959, pp. 130–132, and commentary pp. 266–268.
6 Moral claims also received partial legal recognition as *obligationes naturales* 'natural obligations' in an advanced state of Roman law, *apud* Herzog 1939 [= 1980], p. 3; see below p. 307.
7 Yt 10.177; Gershevitch 1959, pp. 130–132; on *daēnā-* 'Vision' and its relation to 'religion' see Cantera 2013, pp. 127–131, with further references.
8 GrBd 1.24–28 (Pakzad 2005, pp. 12–13); similarly WīZ 1.8–11 (Gignoux/Tafazzoli 1993, pp. 30–33); see also König 2022b, pp. 415–417. For an overview of time concepts in Zoroastrianism see Boyce 1975c, pp. 285–293; for an extensive discussion of the idea of time in Zoroastrianism see particularly Rezania 2010 and Panaino 2003a, 2003b and 2007 with further references.

The religious significance of keeping contracts (*miϑra-*, MP *mihr*, in the restricted sense of the word as a voluntary, binding agreement) is also emphasized in the fourth chapter of the *Wīdēwdād*, which offers an overview of their different types in the Avestan period, dividing them into six categories.[9] The first two are (1) the verbal contract (Av. *vača.hina-*, rendered by MP *pad gōwišn*) and (2) the contract by handshake (Av. *zasta.maršta-*, rendered by MP *dast-mušt*). These are followed by a sequence of another four types, which are distinguished in ascending order according to the value of the property involved (or the pledge or mortgage offered as security): (3) 'the size of small livestock (a sheep or goat)' (Av. *pasu.maza-*, rendered by MP *pah-masāy*, the equivalent of three stater according to the Pahlavi gloss);[10] (4) 'the size of large livestock or cattle (a cow, ox, horse or another beast of burden)' (Av. *staorō.maza-*; MP *stōr-masāy*, the equivalent of twelve stater according to the Pahlavi gloss); (5) 'the size of a man' (Av. *vīrō.maza-*; MP *wīr-masāy*, the equivalent of five-hundred drachms):[11] (6) 'the size of a piece of land' (Av. *daŋhu.maza-*; MP *deh-masāy*, corresponding to more than five-hundred drachms: *wēš az panǰ sad drahm*).[12] Each of these contracts was binding, but could be invalidated or confirmed by the following category, *i. e*, type one could be replaced by type two, type three by type four, etc. As we have seen, all contracts, also with foreigners and adherents of other faiths, had to be kept; breach of contract (Av. *miϑrō.druj-*; MP *mihrōdrujīh*) was regarded as one of the most heinous offences to be atoned for (according to the interpretation in the Pahlavi commentary) not only by the contract-breaker himself, but also by following generations.[13] Hence the basic

9 Vd 4.2; for the Pahlavi translation see Moazami 2014, pp. 100–101.

10 One stater (*stēr/satēr*) is the equivalent of four drachms (*drahm*), the silver coinage of the Sasanians, according to Šnš 1.2 (Tavadia 1930, p. 28; see also Moazami 2014, p. 101, fn. 1).

11 In contrast to the preceding and following Pahlavi glosses the exact currency (whether stater or drachms) is not specified here, but we can assume that drachms are meant, since the value of the next higher category of security, a 'piece of land', is explicitly given in the latter currency as worth 'more than five-hundred drachms' and this sum is repeated in the similar passage PRDd (see next footnote).

12 This list is repeated in a late Pahlavi text, the *Pahlavi Riwāyat accompanying the Dādestān ī dēnīg*, Chapter 12, bearing witness to the longevity of Zoroastrian norms regarding contractual obligations, but also to the changes which occurred across the centuries. Here we find (1) the 'verbal contract' (*pad saxwan* 'by speech') rendered by the Pahlavi term *pašt*, (2) the contract 'by hand-shake' *ān kē dast sāyēd* 'he who shakes hands'. The following four categories also correspond to the Avestan text, defining the contract by its worth (or: by the value of the offered security), but, interestingly—probably due to a change of legal norms regarding the pledging of persons—the list does not mention the 'man' (number 5), but only his value of 500 drachms. The four next categories are defined by this corresponding list of securities: (3) 'a sheep' (*gōspand*); (4) 'cattle' (*stōr*); (5) '500 drachms' (*panǰ sad drahm*); (6) 'a village' (*deh*) (Williams 1990, I, pp. 74–77; II, pp. 24–25).

13 This exactly is the background of the curse placed upon the Mazdakites at the end of the sentence on this 'heresy' in Dk 7 (quoted in Appendix IV): *awēšān pad-iz frazandān druzēnd kū-šān mihrōdruǰ abar rasišn ud pad-iz ān ī xwēštan* 'They lie through their children {*i. e*, (the sin of) the contract-breaker (*mihrōdruǰ*) must come upon them and upon their kindred (*xwēštan*)!}.'

idea that 'contracts must be kept' was as crucial to Iranian law from ancient times, as the corresponding principle of *pacta sunt servanda* in Roman jurisprudence.

By the late Sasanian period this field of law had become far more complex, but it seems that the Avestan expressions were kept as technical terms for specifying the value of property (not only in legal disputes resulting from non-performance of contract, but also in other cases).[14] The use of words retained from the Avesta underlines the continuing religious connotations of jurisdiction in general, but in the sequel, as in other fields, the Iranians developed a far more sophisticated law of obligations that seems to have adapted several features from other ancient Near Eastern cultures and in turn left its trace in other legal systems of late antiquity. The word *mihr*, associated with the god Mihr, continued to be used in Pahlavi texts as the common word for 'contract' in a general sense, but a large range of other technical terms designating agreements, contracts, deeds and documents emerged, the precise meanings and implications of which still have to be determined.

1 Technical terms for contracts and other documents

Consistent with the economic development written contracts and documents of all kinds recording a large range of legal transactions were in use by the late Sasanian period, besides the stipulation or verbal contract with or without witnesses, for which different terms are transmitted in the texts. As in other legal fields, the information is sparse and dispersed across several sources, mostly in complex case studies, as in our main source, the Sasanian Law-book, but without definitions, not to mention any kind of systematic survey.[15] The lack of explanations in this field is an obstacle difficult to overcome, as many of these terms can refer to a large scope of undertakings, if they are not exclusively attested within a specific branch of law or in an elucidatory context. Hence the following tentative attempt to specify the most frequent expressions can only be provisional until a more in-depth study is undertaken.

14 As in MHD 8.12: *ka-iz mādag az ⁺vīrō mazō* ⟨wyıwk' mzd⟩ *kam ēg-iz sāl drahnāy zamān dahišn* 'Even if the (value of) the (disputed) object (is) less than *vīrō.mazō* [= 500 drachms] a date (for the trial) should be appointed within a year' (Macuch 1993, pp. 90, 95; the second component of the word is written ⟨mzy/d/g⟩ which seems to be a mix-up of *mazō* with *mizd* 'reward, pay'). Perikhanian 1997, pp. 42–43, has a completely different translation of this passage due to her reading '*nērok ud mizd*' (instead of *vīrō. mazō*, besides other emendations of the text). The MP form *wır-masāy* is also attested DkM 715.7 with reference to a woman (presumably a slave-woman): *ka abāg dēn ī māzdēsnān hamwāz be būd ā-š pas dāsᵃr dahišn ī wır-masāy zan* 'If he (= a convert?) complied with the (rules of the) Mazdean religion, then a woman worth *wīr-masāy* [= 500 drachms] should be given to him as a gift.'

15 In contrast to family law, there are only a few—moreover, often enigmatic—passages on contracts and loans in late Pahlavi literature, see for example Macuch 2017b.

In the proposed translations, or rather interpretations, of the terms, 'contract' is employed in its common legal usage referring to a voluntary agreement between two or more parties, creating a legally enforceable obligation. The distinctive feature of the contractual obligation is that it is usually—when not always—based on the consent of the parties involved. 'Stipulation' refers to the verbal contract, which could be concluded without witnesses (under the surveillance of the god Mihr or with Ohrmazd as the only witness)[16], but was presumably often confirmed—following the rules of offer and acceptance described below—in the presence of witnesses, usually three persons or a judicial official in his area of competence.[17] 'Testamentary contract' designates a will in form of a contract, concluded during the lifetime of the testator with the beneficiaries, in which the testator could appoint successive heirs.[18] A 'document of conveyance' records the intention of one person to transmit property (by sale, barter, donation, gift etc.) to another; a 'promissory note' contains a promise by the maker to pay on demand or at a fixed time a certain sum to another person or to a third party assigned by the latter; a 'mandate' is an authorization given to another person to do certain things or to take some course of action. The term 'title deed' designates a document confirming ownership of landed property; the 'foundation deed' is a record of the endowment of a pious foundation or a sacred fire and the specific conditions laid down by the founder.

1.1 *pašn*, *pašt*

In a legal context *pašt* is far more frequently attested than *pašn* with the same meaning of 'contract, bond, agreement'. These expressions denoted originally the 'verbal contract', corresponding to the first type of contract mentioned in the Avesta, *vača.hina-* 'verbal contract', explained as *pad gōwišn* (in the Vd) and *pad saxwan*, *i. e*, contract 'by speech', in the similar passage PRDd, based on the Vd or another Avestan *Vorlage* (correlating with the *stipulatio* in Roman law and the simple 'parol contract' in English law).[19] In our extant legal sources, however, *pašt* does *not* exclusively denote the verbal contract, as we may conclude from

16 See Introductory to this Chapter above, pp. 260–263, and Bartholomae 1916–1925, II, p. 4, fn. 1.

17 On the Roman stipulation see fn. 207 below.

18 On the testamentary contract see Chapter III, pp. 235–236.

19 Vd 4.2 and PRDd, Chapter 12.1 (Williams 1990, I, pp. 74–77; II, pp. 24–25); on these passages see Introductory to this Chapter, pp. 260–263, and fn. 12 above. From the Iranian root **pas* 'to bind, tie', Av. √*pas* (*paš*) 'to bind, tie' (Cheung 2007, p. 299). On *pašt* see also Bartholomae 1916–1925, II (subtitle: 'Der Verbalkontrakt im sasanidischen Recht'), pp. 3–15, who perceptively recognized the correspondence between the Avestan and the Pahlavi terms, but did not take the later development into consideration. On the stipulatio see fn. 207 below.

two perceptions: (1) the word is also used in legal formulae in a testamentary contract (*paymān*), which was recorded in written form;[20] and (2) *pašt* is at times confused with the similarly written *nibišt* 'written record/document' (the only difference between the two is a preceding stroke in *nibišt*, which can be read ⟨W⟩ *ud* if the following word is *pašt*, *i. e*, either ⟨npšt'⟩ or ⟨W pšt'⟩).[21] A variant *pušt*, lit. 'back, support, protection', is also transmitted in the phrase *pušt ud paymān* 'stipulation and contract',[22] but as this seems to be the only attestation in this context, it could be a mistake for *pašt* (in the hendiadys *pašt ud paymān* 'stipulation and contract', maybe due to a mix-up with the phrase *pušt ud panāg* 'support and protection'?). In a legal context *pašt* is used of the following types of undertakings:

1. a verbal agreement (or stipulation) between bridegroom and bride on her share of inheritance or on the dower to be paid to the bride prior to the drawing up of the marriage contract, which was also recorded in this document (clause 7 of the model marriage contract);[23]
2. a (verbal?) contract of sale (with a guarantee to keep the purchased item 'undamaged and intact', *drust dārišnīh*, until it is delivered to the purchaser);[24]
3. a testamentary contract (apart from the regular will) that transfers ownership of property from one person to another at a fixed time in the future;[25]

20 In the formulae *pašt dād xwēš* and *dād pašt xwēš*; see in the following list number 3 below and Chapter I, p. 82.

21 This seems to be the case in MHD 6.13–14 (Macuch 1993, pp. 88, 93; see fn. 24 below) and possibly also in the heading of a chapter on *dar ī nēm bahr ud arz ī andar xwāstag kē nibišt* (or: *pašt*) *abar kunēnd* 'The chapter on one half of the share and the value of a thing, for which a written record (*nibišt*) (or: contract, *pašt*) has been made' (MHD 53.11, *ibid.*, pp. 373, 376).

22 MHD 71.8 (Macuch 1993, pp. 477, 479); on the heading of this chapter in which the phrase occurs see fn. 28 below.

23 MHDA 7.6–7 (Macuch 1981, pp. 28, 98): *xwāstag ī-š … pad pašt ī abāg mād kard dastwarīh xwēš šāyēd būd …* 'the property, to which … according to the stipulation made with the mother (= bride/wife) she should have an entitlement …'. On clause 7 of the marriage contract see Macuch 2007b, transcription and translation pp. 190–191; commentary pp. 197–200.

24 MHD 6.13–14. I have previously read ⟨npšt'⟩ *nibišt* 'written record', instead of ⟨W pšt'⟩ *ud pašt* in this sentence (Macuch 1993, pp. 88, 93), which is of course also possible, but I now prefer the latter variant: *kū mard dō agenēn xwāstag-ē(w) ō mard frōxšēnd ud pašt kunēnd kū drust dārēm …* 'If two men sell together an item to a man and make a contract: "We will keep it undamaged" …'; see the similar passage with *paymān* instead of *pašt*, MHD 64.10–15 (Macuch 1993, pp. 434, 437); compare also MHD 93.11–14 (*ibid.*, pp. 593f., 596f.), which probably also refers to a contract of sale, see commentary, *ibid.*, pp. 601–602 (n. 5).

25 MHDA 10.13–11.10 (Macuch 1981, pp. 32f., 124). This is a difficult passage discussing the legal implications of two different formulations in the testamentary contract: *pašt dād xwēš* or *dād pašt xwēš*. On these see Chapter I, p. 82; see also MHDA 18.11–12 (Macuch 1981, pp. 41, 165): *abāz ō pašt ī pas ēstēd* 'the last (clause of the) contract is decisive'; possibly also MHDA 40.16 (*ibid.*, pp. 67, 224); on the testamentary contract (*paymān*) see Chapter III, pp. 235–236.

4. a document of conveyance (other than a will) or a promissory note that transfers ownership of a specified thing to another person;[26]
5. a (verbal?) contract of adoption;[27]
6. an unspecified contract (of loan, barter, sale?) between two parties stating the self-commitment of both or of one of the parties to fulfil the contract or to pay a fine (*tāwān*) on non-performance.[28]

1.2 *paymān*, *paymān-nāmag*

This is the most frequently attested word for 'contract, binding agreement' (in the Tabarestān documents: *paymān-nāmag*), besides *pašt* and *wizīr*, in both legal and non-legal literature, referring to a large range of different kinds of agreements.[29] It is often used with the verb *kardan* (*paymān kardan* 'to make, draw up, conclude, enter a contract'), and designates:

1. a loan contract; examples include: contracts concluded on the basis of a security: by mortgaging the fruits of a property (*grawagān*);[30] or by pledging (*graw*) an estate (*dastgird*) or a slave (*anšahrīg*)[31] or an item of specific value;[32] or on the basis of a suretyship (*pāyēn[d]ānīh*)[33] or of co-sureties (*ham-pāyēn[d]ān*);[34] other examples specify interest (*waxš*) and compensation 〈'nw'n〉[35] or the assignment of a pledge to the moneylender in the case of non-performance of contract;[36]
2. a contract of sale (with a guarantee to keep the purchased item 'undamaged and intact', *drust*, until it is delivered to the purchaser);[37]

26 MHD 17.1–4 (Macuch 1993, pp. 151, 157); 20.16–21.3 (*ibid.*, pp. 156, 161).
27 MHD 42.9–10 (*ibid.*, pp. 301, 317).
28 The whole chapter MHD 71.8–72.13 (Macuch 1993, pp. 477–480) with the misspelling or variant (?) *pušt* (instead of *pašt*): *dar ī* 〈'nw'n〉 *ud tāwān dahišnīh ud ahlawdād ud a-tuwānagīh-iz ī andar pušt/pašt ud paymān* 'Chapter on compensation and paying a fine and (giving) a pious gift and also on the incapacity (to fulfil) stipulations and contracts (*pušt/pašt ud paymān*).'
29 The term also has the meaning of 'measure' (besides 'moderation, modesty') and is derived from **pati-* + √*māy* 'to measure'.
30 MHD 40. 5–13 (Macuch 1993, pp. 280, 285): *ka Ādurfarrbay az Mihrēn abām stānēd ud xwāstag grawagān ud paymān kunēd* … 'When A. takes out a loan from M. and mortgages property as antichresis (*grawagān*) and concludes a contract …'.
31 MHD 38.13–17 (Macuch 1993, pp. 279, 283).
32 MHD 67.3–13 (*ibid.*, pp. 447, 451).
33 MHD 56.15–17 (Macuch 1993, pp. 387, 393); 58.4–9 (*ibid.*, pp. 389, 394); 59.1–6 (*ibid.*, pp. 390, 395). On the different kinds of suretyship see pp. 349–359.
34 MHD 55.17–56.5 (Macuch 1993, pp. 386, 391f.): *ka gōwēd kū mard 3 az man abām stad paymān kart kū hampāyēn(d)ān hēm* … 'When he (= the creditor) says: "Three men took out a loan from me and made a contract: 'We are co-sureties …'."'
35 MHD 30.8 (Macuch 1993, pp. 221, 225; the same sentence is repeated MHDA 12.17).
36 MHD 54.5–11 (*ibid.*, pp. 374, 377).
37 MHD 64.10–15 (Macuch 1993, pp. 434, 437).

3. a marriage contract (*paymān ī zanīh* according to the model Pahlavi marriage contract);[38]
4. an unspecified contract (of loan, barter, sale?) between two parties stating the self-commitment of both or of one of the parties to fulfil the contract or to pay a fine (*tāwān*) on non-performance;[39]
5. a letter of attorney or mandate, authorizing a person to convey ownership of property to a third party (*e. g.*, a husband authorizes his wife who is his associate partner to assign ownership of a 'thing' to a person of her choice);[40]
6. a testamentary contract (apart from the regular will) that transfers ownership of property from one person to another at a fixed time in the future;[41]
7. a document of conveyance (other than a will) or a promissory note that transfers ownership to another person, assigning the choice of the property up to an exactly specified value to the receiver.[42]

In contrast to *wizīr* the term *paymān* does not always seem to denote a written contract or a sealed document, but the evidence does not allow a definite conclusion. In the Tabarestān documents the more precise *paymān-nāmag*, lit. 'document of contract', *i. e*, 'written contract', is used of the *officially sealed document* bearing the seal of a legal authority, besides other seals, in order to make it 'legally binding' (*ēwarīh rāy*; in all attestations we find: *ēn paymān-nāmag … āwišt* 'this document of contract … was sealed', followed by the names of the promisor or contractors and at least one legal authority). The examples refer to (a) an unilateral

38 Clause 10 of the *pādixšāy*-marriage contract: *ud im wahmān ī wahmān pad čē ham-dar abārīg čiyōn paymān ī zanīh būd kē xwēškārīh būd pursīd xwast ud wizōst ud abarmad* (*kard?*) *hom* 'And I, (the present) K., son of L., whose duty it was to carry out an investigation on other matters relevant to the marriage contract, have examined (these) and (*drawn*) a disposition (*abarmad*).' (See Macuch 2007b, pp. 190, 191).

39 MHD 6.15–16 (Macuch 1993, pp. 88f.; 93): *ka mard dō abāg mard dō paymān kunēnd kū ēn čiš kunēm agar ǰuttar kunēm tāwān dahēm …* 'If two men conclude a contract with two men: "We will perform this thing, if we act otherwise, we will pay a fine …"'; and the whole chapter MHD 71.8–72.13 (*ibid.*, pp. 477–480) on, among other topics, *pušt/pašt ud paymān* 'agreements and contracts' see above fn. 28.

40 MHD 4.4–9 (Macuch 1993, pp. 69, 72): *ka mard zan hambāy ud ēn-iz paymān kunēd kū ēn xwāstag ōy kē tō xwēš hūd gōwē xwēš ēd bawēd …* 'When the wife of a man (is his) partner and he gives (her) a letter of attorney/mandate (*paymān*): "This thing shall be the own of that (person) to whom you assign it in ownership" …'. The term *wizīr* is also used in this context, see section 1.3 below.

41 MHD 20.11–12 (Macuch 1993, pp. 155, 161): *ka mard-ew abāg Farrox paymān kunēd kū m ēn xwāstag* (*pas*) *az dah sāl ō tō dād …* 'If a man makes a "(testamentary) contract" with Farrox: "I will have given this thing to you (after) 10 years …"'; possibly also MHD 108.8–11 (*ibid.*, pp. 643, 650f.); on the legal implications of the formulation *kū-m … dād* see Chapter I, pp. 83–85; on the testamentary contract see Chapter III, pp. 235–236.

42 MHD 54.11–15 (Macuch 1993, pp. 374, 377): *ka Farrox abāg Mihrēn payman kard kū xwāstag ī man xwēš ud tō gōwē* (*čand*) *arzēd 200 wahāg arzēd tō xwēš …* 'When F. has made a contract (= document of conveyance) with M.: "The property that is my own and you designate up to the value of 200 (drachms?) (shall be) your own …"'

contract containing the self-commitment of the defendant to fulfil an obligation towards the plaintiff;[43] (b) loan-contracts with and without real security.[44] Maybe the need was felt to specify the *officially sealed* document as *paymān-nāmag* in contrast to *paymān* alone, which could refer to both the verbal and written contract, but was confirmed only by the seals of witnesses, not necessarily by the seal of an official instance (on the use of seals see below pp. 286–301).

1.3 *wizīr*

Determining the exact meaning of this expression can at times be problematic due to its use in a twofold sense in Sasanian law to designate: (1) the 'judgement, sentence, decision' of a judge or another judicial authority (besides *dādestān* 'judgement, sentence'); (2) a written 'document' or 'contract' (which in this second use definitely does *not* only refer to the documentation of a judgement, as one might rashly assume). The second meaning of 'document, contract' is easily determined, when *wizīr* is attested with the verb *āwištan* 'to seal' (usually written with the ideogram ⟨HTYMWNtn'⟩ as in *mard 3 xwāstag* ⟨NKSY'⟩ *abām stānēnd wizīr āwāšēnd* 'three men take out a money loan and seal a contract)'.[45] Sasanian jurists do not seem to have been confused by the double meaning of the term, but we can occasionally be mistaken, having to detect its exact sense by the context in which it appears. For example, *wizīr kardan*, lit. 'to make *wizīr*', can mean both 'to draft a document/contract' as well as 'to reach a judgement/decision': the phrase definitely has the former meaning in *wizīr ī andar ēn dastgird kard ēstēd* 'a document, which has been drafted for this estate',[46] but the latter in *dar ī wizīr kard ī pēšag-sālārān ud hunsandīh ud a-hunsandīh ī pad wizīr* 'Chapter on reaching a judgement on the part of the 'leaders of the guild' and approval or disapproval with the judgement'.[47] The case studies in the Law-book suggest that *wizīr* was used of the following documents:

1. a contract for a money loan (*xwāstag abām*) or, more precisely, *wizīr ī abāmdān* 'loan contract', which was sealed by the contractors, hence legally enforceable (as in the first example quoted above);[48]

43 Tab. 15.14–16 (Macuch 2017c, pp. 180–182).

44 Tab. 17.16–18; 18.26–27 (Macuch 2017c, pp. 188–191; 184, 186 respectively); see pp. 320–323 and 345–349 below; Tab. 26 (Macuch 2022b, pp. 167–170).

45 MHD 2.1 (Macuch 1993, pp. 40, 42); with *āwištan* see also MHD 20.13; 30.15,17; 31.10,11; 38.7; 107.3; MHDA 6.14. On the distinction between *xwāstag* 'money', always written with the heterogram ⟨NKSY'⟩, and *xwāstag* 'res; thing, object, property', written eteographically ⟨hw'stk'⟩ see Macuch 2008b, pp. 264–265, and Chapter III, p. 190.

46 MHD 18.15 (Macuch 1993, pp. 153, 159).

47 MHD 2.17 (Macuch 1993, pp. 54, 56). The context of the whole chapter should be taken into consideration to determine the precise meaning of *wizīr kardan* here; compare also MHD 3.6. Both meanings are abundantly attested in the Law-book (see *ibid.*, Index, pp. 738–739).

2. a title deed or document of a landed estate (*dastgird*), proving a person's ownership, in which all the assets belonging to the estate, including those outside its borders and passing through the land (such as a water canal), were recorded (as in the second example quoted above);[49]
3. a document of conveyance (other than a will) that transfers ownership from one person to another (examples are: the gift of a father to his underage child or of a husband to his wife;[50] assignment of property by the founder to a fire foundation of the *ādurōg* type);[51]
4. a letter of attorney or mandate, authorizing a person to convey ownership of property to a third party (*e.g.*, a husband authorizes his wife to assign ownership of a 'thing' to a person of her choice);[52]
5. a marriage contract (which could be *wizīr ī ēwar*, a 'valid, authentic, reliable document', or *wizīr ī warōmand*, an 'uncertain, disputable document' according to the evaluation of the seals it bears).[53]

48 MHD 2.1 (Macuch 1993, pp. 40, 42); see also MHD 38.7 (*ibid.*, pp. 278, 283): *ka Farrox pad abām stad ī xwāstag* ⟨NKSY'⟩ *ud grawagānīh ī xwāstag andar Mihrēn wizīr awašēd* 'When Farrox seals a contract for taking up a money loan and granting property as an antichresis with Mihrēn …'; *wizīr ī abāmdān* 'loan contract' is attested MHD 78.17 and 100.3; *abāmdān wizīr* with the same meaning MHD 107.3; *wizīr* is also attested Tab. 24.28 in the context of a loan, for which an antichresis (*grawagānīh*) has been granted as security, consisting of the crops (olives) of olive trees. The exact amount of yields of every single mortgaged tree is listed meticulously in this spectacular document, called *zaytēn wizīr* 'olive (or: olive tree) document', bearing the seals of all persons involved in the transaction as well as legal officials; see Weber 2019b, pp. 102–110, and Macuch 2019b, pp. 132–146. The whole text of this document is in Appendix X, pp. 704–710.

49 MHD 18.15 (Macuch 1993, pp. 153, 159); see also MHD 18.11f.: *wizīr-iz ēw ī andar ān dastgird ēstēd* 'also a document drawn for that estate' (*ibid.*); and MHDA 34.2–5 (Macuch 1981, pp. 60, 217), stating that the conveyance of a 'title deed' (*wizīr*) implies the transfer of the land itself.

50 MHD 20.13 (Macuch 1993, pp. 155, 161): *ka pid pad aburnāyag ayāb šōy pad zan wizīr āwašēd kū xwāstag ī ō xwēšīh ī man rasēd tō xwēš …* 'If a father seals a document for his underage child or a husband for his wife (stating): "The thing which will come into my ownership (is) your own …"'; compare MHD 30.15 (*ibid.*, pp. 221, 225): *wizīr ī mard andar zan ud frazand āwāšēd* 'the document a man seals for his wife and child'

51 This can be deduced indirectly from the case discussed MHD 31.8–15 (Macuch 1993, pp. 222f., 226): *u-š pas ādurōg nišāst ud xwāstag hamāg awiš dād ud nē wizīr āwišt …* 'and afterwards he established an *ādurōg*-fire and gave all (his) property to it, but did not seal a document …'.

52 MHD 64.2–9 (Macuch 1993, pp. 434, 437): *ka kadag-xwadāy andar zan ī pādixšāyīhā wizīr āwāšēd kū ēn xwāstag ōy kē tō xwēš rāy gōwē xwēš ēd bawed* 'When the master of the house seals a document (= letter of attorney) for (his) privileged wife: "This thing shall be the own of that (person) to whom you assign it in ownership" …'

53 MHD 32.4–10 (Macuch 1993, pp. 223, 227). Seals did not all have the same validity, but had to be evaluated according to specific criteria, see below pp. 296–301 (discussing also this passage).

In all these cases the *wizīr* is a *written and sealed* document, as opposed to a verbal disposition, agreement, deed or contract, suggesting that this term was used of recorded transactions, which were in certain cases also registered in one of the State archives: fire-foundations were registered in archives, called *nāmag-niyān* 'deposit of documents', in the districts in which the fires were established (see below under *nāmag*) and *dīwān ī kardagān* 'archive for religious institutions' or **ātaxš hamār dibīrag* 'account relating to the fire'. There was also a register of other endowments 'for the soul' (*pad ruwān*)[54] as well as for estates belonging to the crown, *šāhīgān*, and presumably also one for other landed property. Recording and sealing legal transactions must have been the standard procedure for most of the larger dealings, but not all documents bearing seals were of the same value. The seals in turn had to be evaluated according to specific criteria, which will be discussed below. Identical copies (*hampaččēn*) were drawn of the original version (*mādagwar*) of the document and we may conclude from random entries that every contracting party or—in the case of a 'document of conveyance' or 'mandate'—every recipient, besides the conveyor, received an identical copy of the *wizīr*.[55]

1.4 *dib*, *nibēg*, *nāmag*

These three terms denote exclusively the *written* document (not necessarily contractual agreements). The first expression, *dib* 'document, writ, transcript', refers in a legal context to the following types of documents:

1. a transcript or protocol of proceedings from a legal case (recording the obstruction of justice, *azišmānd*, on the part of one or both litigating parties;[56] sealed with an official seal);[57]
2. the recorded sentence of a judge[58] or of another State official in his area of competence;[59]
3. an edict of public officials or judicial authorities;[60]
4. generally any kind of written and sealed document.[61]

54 On the **ruwānagān dibīrag* 'archive of religious foundations' and the other terms see Chapter III, p. 221.

55 According to MHDA 33.15–17 and 33.17–34.1 (Macuch 1981, pp. 59, 216f.) if there were two recipients or the share given to a recipient by the conveyor of a certain property was of a different size than the part that he retained, the person with the larger portion received the original version (*mādagwar*) of the document of conveyance (*wizīr*) and the one with the smaller portion was given the copy (*hampaččēn*).

56 MHDA 14.1 (Macuch 1981, pp. 36, 143).

57 MHD 100.7–15 (Macuch 1993, pp. 613f., 621f.).

58 MHDA 14.6 (Macuch 1981, pp. 36, 143); 26.5 (*ibid.*, pp. 50, 188).

59 MHDA 28.2–3 (*ibid.*, pp. 52, 190f.).

60 MHDA 38.16–17 (Macuch 1981, pp. 65, 222): *dib ī pādixšāy kard ud xwēškārīh nāmag ī kār-framān ī šahrīhā* ... 'the authorized edict and document on the specific duties of the

The second term *nibēg* specifically designates the 'template' or 'original' record, on which a document of conveyance (*nāmag*) is based.[62] In the compound ⟨PRŠY' npyk'⟩ *aswār-nibēg* 'horseman's document' it is a technical term for a legal certificate recording a grant bestowed to an *aswār* 'equestrian, horseman, knight', by the King for military services.[63] The *aswārān* are described in Arabic texts as equestrians belonging to the higher ranks of Sasanian society who at the time of Husraw I received military equipment from the King and were exempt from paying taxes in exchange for rendering military service in the army, which, according to the *Dēnkard* and the letter of Tansar, consisted of two main groups, the *⁺aswārīh* 'cavalry' and *paygīh* 'infantry'.[64] The names of the knights and the brands of the horses were registered in diverse archives (*dafātir*), listed by al-Yaʿqūbī as *dīwān al-maqātila* 'archive of soldiers', *dīwān al-ʿaṭāʾ* 'archive of pay', *dīwān al-ʿarḍ* 'archive of pay', among others.[65] According to the Law-book the *aswārān* were given some kind of grant (not specified in the text) consisting probably of land belonging to the crown for financing their costly military equipment (*pad ēmōzan hangārišn* 'to be taken into account for the equipment').[66] The knight had lifetime possession of the grant, but he was not the owner, and the land conveyed to him was returned to the royal treasury (*šāhīgān*) at his demise. The grant could, however, also be transferred to the heirs (*xwāstagdār*) of the *aswār*, under the condition that they pay yearly taxes corresponding to the value of the equipment until the grant was returned to the royal treasury. The technical term *aswār-nibēg* 'horseman's document' presumably designates this legal deed, stating the name and rank of the horseman as well as the transaction of the grant and its conditions.[67]

Another compound, ⟨dsṭ-npyk⟩ *dast-nibēg*, lit. 'handwritten record' is attested in a document from the Pahlavi Archive (Berk. 149.9).[68] As Weber has perceptively remarked, it is the equivalent of ⟨dstnypyk⟩ *dast-nibēg* in the Parthian version of the Šābuhr inscription (ŠKZ 30), in which the expression occurs at the very end of the inscription in connection with the signature of the scribe: *dast-nibēg im man Hormizd dibīr Šilag dibīr puhr* 'this (is) the handwritten record by me, the scribe

public official (*kār-framān*) of the provinces.' The term *kār-framān* is attested in the two senses of (1) a 'public official' of the State (who is bound by instructions in his specific area of competence) and (2) the 'official authority' of the State (as in *muhr ī pad kār-framān dāštan* 'seal for exercising official authority') See Macuch 1993, pp. 357–358.

61 MHDA 7.2–3 (Macuch 1981, pp. 28, 98); 29.15; 30.1 (*ibid.*, pp. 54f., 193); MHD 84.2 (Macuch 1993, pp. 539, 542); 102.15–16 and 103.3–4 (*ibid.*, pp. 616f., 624).

62 See MHD 110.13 (Macuch 1993, pp. 645, 652): *bē ka nāmag pad nibēg ī Ādurfarrbay ēnyā nē šāyēd* 'unless the document (is) based on the template of A. it is not valid'.

63 MHDA 16.11, 13, 15f.; 17.1; 19.3–5 (Macuch 1981, pp. 39, 163; 42, 165 respectively).

64 See Tafazzoli 2000, p. 12ff., with further references.

65 See Altheim/Stiehl 1954, p. 135ff., with further references

66 MHD 77.6–9 (Macuch 1993, pp. 516, 519).

67 For a discussion of these passages see Macuch 2005c, pp. 96–98.

68 Weber 2015, pp. 34–36.

Hormizd, son of the scribe Šilag'.[69] Berk. 149 is a completely different kind of text, documenting a concrete case involving the return of spoiled (?) goat meat that had been delivered to the household of the *ōstāndār* (governor of a province) to the supplier. Similarly, *dast-nibēg* is attested at the end of the short document together with the signature of a person in the household of the *ōstāndār* responsible for recording goods. WEBER reads: *dast-nibēg ēk-pušt* (?) *kard* 'the food-taster/*praegustator* (?) made the handwritten record'.[70] Since all texts were handwritten in this period, it seems reasonable to assume that this expression did not just denote any kind of written text, but served a specific purpose. To judge by these two—not very instructive—attestations, *dast-nibēg* seems to designate the template (or original record) of a text or document (as opposed to a copy) that was taken down personally by the person who notes his name or position in the text. By noting his name the scribe signs the text, taking personal responsibility for its content.

The term *nāmag* 'writ, record, letter' denotes generally any kind of *written* record, when employed alone. In the context of legal proceedings as the second part of a compound it is a technical term designating a 'court transcript' or 'protocol', such as *saxwan-nāmag* 'protocol of statements' (in civil proceedings), *pursišn-nāmag* 'protocol of interrogation' (in criminal proceedings), *uzdād-nāmag* 'transcript of proceedings' (an unexplained document accompanying the *pursišn-nāmag*), and *yazišn-nāmag* 'protocol of recitation' (record of the procedure of oath-taking). In the Tabarestān documents two further transcripts or protocols are mentioned, the *zastbūd-nāmag* 'protocol of interrogation'[71] and *wizōst-nāmag* (or: *wizōstan-nāmag*) 'protocol of investigation'[72] without further explanations. Moreover, *nāmag* could be the correct reading of the ideogram ⟨GTk'⟩ (if it is indeed a ideogram and not a Semitic loan-word, to be read ⟨gtk'⟩ *gittag*), since it also refers in the context of legal proceedings to a court transcript or protocol (see pp. 275–279).[73]

The *xwēškārīh nāmag* 'document on the area of competence, document on specific duties' is a kind of treatise or documentation specifying the field of expertise or sphere of responsibility (*xwēškārīh*) of judicial authorities.[74] In family

69 HUYSE 1999, I, p. 63, § 51.

70 The reading ⟨'ywkpušṭ⟩ *ēk-pušt*, lit. 'having the only protection', has been proposed by WEBER 2015 (p. 35), who interprets the word as a title designating the 'food-taster', a kind of *praegustator* or person responsible for examining the victuals supplied to the household of an *ōstāndār*. Alternatively, given the numerous ambiguities of the Pahlavi cursive script, one could assume that the letters between *dast-nibēg* and *kard* stand for a name, as in the Šābuhr inscription.

71 Tab. 23.22 (MACUCH 2017c, p. 175, with further references).

72 Tab. 13.11 (*ibid.*, p. 171); Tab. 22bis.14 (MACUCH 2022a, p. 147).

73 Tab. 7B.3 (WEBER 2016a, pp. 136, 138–139). On the legal terms see also MACUCH 2016a, p. 154, and 2017c, pp. 171, 175. On the transcripts or protocols see also Chapter VI.

74 On *xwēškārīh nāmag ī kār-framān ī šahrīhā* 'document on the area of competence of the public official (*kār-framān*) of the provinces' see fn. 60 above. MHDA 25.15–30.5 (MACUCH 1981, pp. 49–55; 188–193) a whole chapter is dedicated to the competences (*ēwarīh*) of judicial authorities (*kārdārān*).

law the *hišt-nāmag* 'certificate of divorce' documents the legal separation of (*pādixšāy-*)spouses, noting that the wife is released from the guardianship (*sālārīh*) of her husband and subsequently dismissed from the marriage.[75] In contractual law the precise *paymān-nāmag* 'document of contract' (instead of *paymān* alone) denotes explicitly the *written* contract that was sealed not just by the promisor or one or both contractors, but also by a judicial authority and was hence 'legally binding' (see section 1.2 above under *paymān*). As the first part of a compound, the word is attested in *nāmag-niyān* 'deposit of documents', referring specifically to an archive of documents of registered fire foundations.[76] The documents of the 'Pahlavi Archive' also refer to a *nāmag ī nēk* (if this reading is correct) always written ⟨GṬk' Y nywk'⟩, lit. 'good (= valid?) document', in several texts (see pp. 278–279).

1.5 *abarmad*

This technical term, written both ⟨'plmt'⟩ and ⟨MDMmt'⟩, is attested in the Law-book and the Pahlavi marriage contract and presumably with the same meaning in *Dēnkard* 3 and 4. It obviously designates some kind of official document containing an order, disposition, injunction or decree, sanctioned and sealed by high religious authorities (*pahlom dēn burdārān*), judges (*dādwarān*) and other legal/religious dignitaries (*radān*). In two passages of the Law-book it is attested with the verb *kardan* 'to make, draw, prepare, record'. An *abarmad ī radān* 'order, decree of the *radān*' is mentioned in the context of property belonging to the Farrbay fire: (MHD 103.9) *pad abarmad* ⟨'plmt'⟩ *ī radān pad xīr ī Ādur ī Farrbay kard nibišt ēstēd* 'in the order/decree that the *radān* drew with regard to the property of the Farrbay fire it is written ...'.[77] Another passage mentions an *abarmad* drawn by judges (*dādwarān*) in the context of determining a 'proxy' (*stūr*): (MHD 49.16–17) ... *ka dādwarān abarmad* ⟨'plmt'⟩ *kard az ān ī ka dādwarān abarmad* ⟨MDMmt'⟩ *kard frāz stūr ī Mihrēn ud xwāstag awiš ōh abespārišn* '... when the judges have drawn the disposition/order, (then) from that moment on, in which the judges have drawn the disposition/order she is the *stūr* of Mihrēn and the property has to be given to her'.[78]

75 MHD 87.10 (Macuch 1993, pp. 561, 563): *pad hišt-nāmag naxust sālārīh hanjāmēnd ud pas hišt nigerīdan* 'in the divorce-certificate first the (matter of) guardianship is determined and then the divorce is to be considered'.

76 MHD 78.12–13 (Macuch 1993, pp. 517f., 520f.) refers specifically to an archive of the fire documents of Huram-Ardaxšēr (*nāmag-niyān ī ātaxš ī Hurām-Ardaxšēr*) in Xabr, a village in the district of Ardaxšēr-Xwarrah. On the geographical names see de Menasce 1964b. On *namag-niyān* see Macuch 1993, p. 526, fn. 8, with further references.

77 Macuch 1993, pp. 617, 625.

78 *Ibid.*, pp. 309, 325.

In the tenth clause of the model Pahlavi marriage contract *abarmad* seems to designate an additional document, a supplement to the marriage contract: *ud im wahmān ī wahmān pad čē ham-dar abārīg čiyōn paymān ī zanīh būd kē xwēškārīh būd pursīd xwāst ud wizōst ud abarmad* ⟨MDMmt'⟩ (*kard*) *hom.* 'And I, (the present) so-and-so, son of so-and-so, whose duty (*xwēškārīh*) it was to carry out an investigation (*pursīd xwāst*) on other matters relevant to the marriage contract, have examined (these) and (drawn) a disposition (*abarmad*)'.[79] This clause of the model contract, written in the first person, renders the statement of a scribe (presumably the scribe who wrote the marriage contract) or another official whose responsibility it was (*kē xwēškārīh būd*) to examine 'other matters relevant to the marriage contract' (*pad čē ham-dar abārīg čiyōn paymān ī zanīh būd*) and to prepare an *abarmad*. As I have assumed in my edition of the marriage contract, *abarmad* here probably designates a separate document containing an additional settlement with specifics on the 'dowry' (the money or property brought by a wife to her husband on marriage, MP *pēšīgān-wāspuhragān*, comparable to the Roman *dos*). The 'dowry' is, strangely, not mentioned at all in the Pahlavi model marriage contract, which only contains specifics on the 'dower' (the marriage-portion or settlement to be paid by the husband to the wife; MP *kābēn*, NP *kābīn*, corresponding roughly to the Roman *donatio propter nuptias* and the Islamic *mahr*; clause 7 of the marriage contract). Significantly, none of the three surviving Iranian marriage contracts in Sogdian, Bactrian and Pahlavi have a passus on the 'dowry'. We may hence assume (with Yakubovich, editor of the Sogdian marriage contract) that the dowry was recorded in a separate document, comparable to the lists of items of the *nudunnû* (dowry) from late Babylonian times.[80] The disposition called *abarmad* in clause 10 might designate this supplementary document containing specifics on the dowry (or other items not listed in the marriage contract).

The same technical term is attested at the end of *Dēnkard* 3 (DkD 317.22; DkM 407.10) as *abarmad* ⟨MDMmt'⟩ *ī pahlom dēn burdārān* 'the *abarmad* of the foremost religious leaders', and in *Dēnkard* 4 in the well-known narrative on the collection and authorization of Avestan texts by the high-priest Tansar/Tōsar under King Ardaxšēr I: (DkD 321.9–11; DkM 412.11–14) *ōy bay Ardaxšēr ī šāhān šāh ī Pābagān pad rāst dastwarīh Tansar/Tōsar ān-iz hamōg ī pargandag ud hamāg ō dar xwāst Tansar/Tōsar abarmad* ⟨MDMmt'⟩ *ān ī ēk frāz padīrift ud abārīg az dastwar hišt.* 'His late majesty Ardaxšēr, King of Kings, son of Pābag, in order (to achieve) true authorization summoned Tansar/Tōsar, likewise those with the dispersed (texts of the Avesta) and all (religious authorities) to (his) palace. The *abarmad* of Tansar/Tōsar adapted one (version) and dismissed the other (texts) from the authorized (canon).' In all previous renderings of this passage the word has been understood as a

79 Macuch 2007b, pp. 190, 191 and 201 (commentary).
80 *Ibid.*, pp. 199–201; Yakubovich 2005 and 2006.

verbal form (*abar mad*).[81] But to judge by all the other passages quoted above, *abarmad* in *Tansar/Tōsar abarmad* 'the decree/injunction of Tansar/Tōsar' is most likely a noun, a technical term denoting some kind of official document by which the high priest authorized the official canon of Avestan texts under Ardaxšēr I.

1.6 *nāmag/gitt(ag)* ⟨GT(k); gt(k)⟩; *pādixšīr*, *mādayān*

As we have already noted in the last Chapter these three technical terms for foundation deeds of fire endowments are attested in the third century inscriptions of Šābuhr and Kirdīr. The first term could be a ideogram ⟨GT(k)⟩ (for *nāmag*) or a loanword ⟨gt(k)⟩ from the Semitic, to be read *gitt(ag)* (Akk. *giṭṭu* 'tablet, receipt, certificate, document, deed written on parchment'; Syr. *geṭṭā* 'testament', Heb. *geṭ* 'document, certificate, bill of exchange, bill of divorce'). Henning was the first to suggest a borrowing from Syr. *geṭṭā* 'testament', Akk. *giṭṭu*, to be read *gett* due to its provenance from the Syriac.[82] This reading was corrected by Szemerényi to *gitt*, based on the Armenian loanword *ktak* 'testamentum, foedus' (< *gitt-ak*, which in turn could have been transmitted to Armenian by means of the Iranian loanword).[83] Although Armenian has adapted numerous Iranian loanwords, specifically technical terms, the reading of this word remains problematic. The expression is also attested in the Lawbook (always written ⟨GTk/gtk⟩, never ⟨GT'k⟩, as Perikhanian has it),[84] in the texts of the 'Pahlavi Archive' as ⟨GṬk'/gṭk' Y nywk'⟩ *nāmag/gittag ī nēk*,[85] lit. 'good (= valid?) document', and in the Tabarestān documents. Especially the attestations in the latter texts seem to point to an ideogram to be read *nāmag* rather than a loanword. In Tab. 7B.3 the formulation *pasēmāl ī abar ēn nāmag* (written: ⟨GTk⟩) *nibišt* 'the defendant, who has been recorded in this protocol' correlates exactly with *pēšēmāl ī abar ēn nāmag* (written: ⟨n'mk'⟩) *nibišt ēstēd* 'the plaintiff, who has been recorded in this protocol' (Tab. 6B.4–5; 8A.3–4). Since both phrases are identical, apart from the spelling of ⟨GTk⟩ and ⟨n'mk'⟩ (and of course the 'defendant' in the first case and the 'plaintiff' in the second), we have good reason to assume, following Weber, that ⟨GTk⟩ is an ideogram

81 From *abar madan* 'to appear, assume command, supervise, come upon, cope with, comprehend, befall, take control, assail, come upon, superintend'. *Tansar/Tōsar abar mad* has been previously rendered as: 'Tansar set about his business' (Zaehner 1955, p. 8; Boyce 1979, p. 103); 'Tansar siegte' (Tavadia 1956, p. 55); 'Tōsar assumed command' (Shaki 1981, p. 118) among others.

82 Henning 1954b, p. 41, no. 3.

83 Szemerényi 1970, p. 420.

84 Perikhanian 1997, p. 362.

85 Berk. 38, 46, 62, 97, 121, 231 (according to Weber 2019c, pp. 97–98); see also Berk. 62 (Weber 2020b, pp. 153–155); Berk. 77 (Weber 2015, pp. 32–33), Berk. 138 (Weber 2019c, pp. 97–98) and Berk. 231 (Weber 2017b, pp. 130–137).

for *nāmag*.[86] In this case the term definitely has the meaning of 'court transcript, protocol'. One could, however, argue that a general word like *nāmag*, which is used of all kinds of written records (including letters) would not be appropriate as a technical term for one of the presumably most prestigious and important documents of the Sasanian age, the foundation deed of a fire endowment. But this exactly could be the reason, why another spelling (as ideogram) was used in order to distinguish it—at least in writing—from other kinds of *nāmags* (just as ⟨hw'stk'⟩ *xwāstag 'res'* is distinguished from ⟨NKSY'⟩ *xwāstag* 'money' by the spelling alone).[87]

In his inscriptions in *Naqš ī Rağab*, *Sar Mašhad*, *Naqš-e Rostam* and on the *Kaʿba-ye Zardušt* Kirdīr, who held the important religious office of High Priest under four Sasanian kings in the third century, uses these three unexplained technical terms for documents imprinted with his official seal as *hērbed* under Šābuhr I,[88] as *mowbed* under Ohrmazd I,[89] and as *hamšahr mowbed ud dādwar* 'Mobed and Judge of the Empire' under the kings Wahrām I and II.[90] Kirdīr takes pride in reporting that during his office under these kings the cult of the gods was increased and a large number of Wahrām-fires, *i. e*, consecrated fires of the highest category, were established (*was ādur ī Wahrām nišāst*) for which foundation deeds, called ⟨GT(k)/gt(k)⟩ *nāmag/gitt(ag)*[91] and *pādixšīr*, were sealed (as already noted, the latter term for this document is also used in Šābuhr's inscription on the *Kaʿba-ye Zardušt*).[92] These terms together with a third one, *mādayān*, are repeatedly mentioned in his inscriptions for presumably three types of official documents bearing his personal seal with one of the corresponding titles bestowed on him by the four kings, usually in the sequence *nāmag/gitt(ag)* ⟨GT(k)/gt(k)⟩ *ud pādixšīr ud mādayān*.[93] The inscriptions end with Kirdīr's statement that they were written, so that anyone who saw these documents, *i. e*, '*pādixšīr*, *mādayān* or *nāmag/gittag* or any other document (*ayāb any nāmag*)', might know that he, Kirdīr, was the one (with all the authority bestowed upon him by the kings themselves) who had

86 See Weber 2016a, pp. 136, 138–139. Could this possibly also be the correct form for the heterogram given in chapter 15 of the *Frahang ī Pahlavīg* for *nāmag*, ⟨KT'⟩ (besides ⟨MGLT'⟩) which has been read ⟨KTYB̲⟩ by Nyberg 1988, pp. 12, 47, 85?

87 See Chapter III, p. 190.

88 With the title: *Kirdīr ī hērbed* 'K. the *hērbed*'; KKZ § 03; KNRm § 08 (Back 1978, p. 393).

89 With the title: *Kirdīr ī Ohrmazd mowbed* 'K. *mowbed* of Ohrmazd'; KKZ § 04; KNRm § 11 (Back 1978, p. 396).

90 With the title: *Kirdīr ī bōxt-ruwān ī Wahrām ī Ohrmazd mowbed* 'K., redeemer of Wahrām's soul, *mowbed* of Ohrmazd'; KKZ § 08–09 (Back 1978, pp. 410–411).

91 KKZ § 14, KNRb § 24 (Back 1978, pp. 431, 483 respectively).

92 For attestations see Gignoux 1972a, pp. 31, 62; KKZ § 02 (Back 1978, p. 389); ŠKZ § 35 (Huyse 1999, I, p. 48); on the possible etymology of *pādixšīr* (< **pāti-xša(i)θr-iya-* 'authoritative document'?) see Huyse 1999, II, p. 111, with further references. See also Chapter III, p. 227.

93 KKZ § 03, 05, 07, 10; KNRm § 07 (Back 1978, pp. 391–392, 398, 404).

sealed them.[94] If we take the importance of official seals into account, Kirdīr is telling us that these foundation deeds bearing his seals were legally binding and incontestable.

This specific use of ⟨GTk'/gtk'⟩ *nāmag/gittag* in the context of fire endowments is confirmed by several passages of the Law-book, in which the term designates the 'foundation deed', containing specific provisions of the founder regarding the endowment. In MHDA 36.11–12 a certain Ādurbād, son of Mardbūd, founds a fire (*ātaxš*) for his own soul (*pad ruwān ī Ādurbād*). He assigns guardianship (*sālārīh*) of the fire to his sister and wife Dādxwaš and provides that guardianship should be transferred to a certain Farroxgyān after her death and to another person after the latter's demise. This testamentary contract designating the guardians of the fire becomes an integral part of the foundation deed, which is then confirmed by an official seal: 'Husraw, who was *čāšān*, sealed the *nāmag/gittag* with the seal of Warangohrmazd (for) the fire of Ērān-Xwarrah and included the disposition of Ādurbād on his demise into the *nāmag/gittag*' (*pad muhr ī Warangohrmazd ādur ī Ērān Xwarrah Husraw ī čāšān būd nāmag/gittag* ⟨GTk'/gtk'⟩ *āwišt ud framān-iz ī Ādurbād pad ōšagān ō nāmag/gittag* ⟨GTk'/gtk'⟩ *burd*).[95]

In another passage the foundation deed of the Chief Judge of the State (*šahr dādwarān dādwar*), named Farroxgyān ī Zarduxštān, is mentioned: 'in the *nāmag/gittag* of Farroxgyān ī Zarduxštān, who was the Chief Judge of the State, was written, sealed on both sides …' (*abar nāmag/gittag* ⟨GTk'gtk'⟩ *ī Farroxgyān ī Zarduxštān ī šahr dādwarān dādwar būd dō-wardān āwišt ēstēd ōwōn nibišt …*).[96] The document then records the words of the Chief Judge, noting that he has established the highest form of consecrated fire, a Wahrām fire, and will keep it in his 'possession' (*dārišn*) until 'house and dwelling' (*kadag ud man*) have been built for it: 'I have, in order to fulfil my own (religious) duty and because of the good deed of founding that fire sooner, established the fire as a Wahrām fire in its proper place. Because of this I am holding the fire in my possession until house and dwelling have been provided for the fire' (*kū-m ō xwēš kardan kār ud kirbag ī az ahy nišāst ī ān ātaxš rāy ān ātaxš pad wahrāmīh ō dādgāh nišāst az ān čiyōn-am tā kardan ī kadag ud mān ī ān ātaxš andar dāšt*). The foundation deed specifies that the fire will then be transported (lit. 'led', *nayīhēd*) to its 'house and dwelling' (*kadag ud mān*), *i. e*, altar and temple, when these have been provided, but remain in the 'possession' of the Chief Judge: 'I hold it (= the fire) by that document (*dib*), as deemed proper' (*andar an dib čiyōn abāyēd dārum*).[97]

94 KSM § 57; KKZ § 16; KNRb § 26 (*ibid.*, p. 484).
95 MHDA 36.11–12 (Macuch 1981, pp. 62, 221).
96 MHD 110.5–6 (Macuch 1993, pp. 645, 652).
97 The idea that a Wahrām fire was housed in a *kadag ud mān* 'house and dwelling' is reminiscent of the common Latin word for the home of a divine image or statue, *aedes* (rather than *templum*), which means simply 'house'; see Beard 2008, p. 285.

A third attestation of the term occurs in a passage already discussed in the last Chapter citing the foundation deed (GTk'/gtk') of a Wahrām fire, established by a certain Dādgušnasp ī Šahr ī Zādaragān, that was confirmed and sealed by the Chief Mobed (*mowbedān mowbed*) Wehšābuhr personally.[98] The document states the words of the founder, who conveys property into the 'ownership' (*xwēšīh*) of the fire itself for its upkeep, and to his (*i. e*, the founder's) *stūrīh*, giving the beneficiaries from inside and outside his family access to the income of this property, without ownership rights of the substance. (On the legal implications of this disposition see Chapter III, p. 217).

To conclude, in the 3rd century inscriptions of Kirdīr three terms, *nāmag/gitt(ag)* ⟨GT(k)/gt(k)⟩, *pādixšīr* and *mādayān* designate the 'foundation deed' of a fire endowment. Only the first term, to be read either *nāmag* (if it is an ideogram) or *gittag* (if it is a loanword) is attested in the Law-book, citing directly from these foundation deeds by which we may deduce that this term designated a document recording the specific provisions of a fire endowment.[99] These included: (1) dispositions of the founder regarding guardianship (*sālārīh*) of the fire across several generations (in the form of a testamentary contract); (2) assignment of property for the upkeep of the fire to the 'ownership' (*xwēšīh*) of the fire itself and to trusteeship (*stūrīh*) of the founder (giving the latter's heirs access to the fruits of this property, but not to its substance); (3) the confirmation that the fire, after being transported to its own altar and temple ('house and dwelling', *kadag ud mān*), continued to be in the 'possession' (*dārišn*) of the founder. Predictably all the specifics of Sasanian property law and its precise distinctions between different proprietary rights described in Chapter III are confirmed by these details on the foundation deed.

The other technical term we have mentioned above, ⟨GṬk'/*gṭk*' Y nywk'⟩ *nāmag/gittag ī nēk*, lit. 'good (= valid?) document', denotes in texts of the 'Pahlavi Archive' a specific kind of written document containing transfer lists of various products and livestock. Berk. 62[100] (from the early Islamic period) records the transfer of wheat (*gandum*), sheep (*gōspand*), piglets (*xūkčak*), birds/hen (*murv*), oxen/cows (*gāw*) and flour (*ārd*) to various recipients. Interestingly, in this long list two of the animals (sheep) are expressly dedicated to the deity of contract, Mihr (lines 8–9): *dāšn ī pad bay ī Mihr rāy gōspand 2* '(as) a gift for the deity Mihr: two sheep', a provision which might be connected to the offerings to deities within the framework of a fire foundation. Berk. 138[101] contains a list

98 MHDA 39.3–4 (Macuch 1981, pp. 66, 222): *pad nāmag/gittag* ⟨GTk/gtk⟩ *ī Dādgušnasp ī Šahr ī Zādaragān kard ud pad muhr ī Wehšābuhr mowbedān mowbed āwišt pad gōwišn ī Dadgušnasp ōwōn nibišt* 'in the *nāmag/gittag* that Dādgušnasp ī Šahr ī Zādaragān made and that was sealed with the seal of Wehšābuhr, the Chief Mobed, according to the statement of D. is written …'.

99 On these see also Chapter III, p. 227.

100 Weber 2020b, pp. 153–155.

101 Weber 2019c, pp. 97–98.

of transferred male and female *gōspand* (small livestock, sheep), and goats (*buz*). Berk. 231[102] consists of two parts: part A lists the income of a carpenter (*durgar*, according to WEBER's reading) named Zādōy who works for an affluent entrepreneur called Windād-Burzmihr[103] during the timespan of two years; part B presents an overview of Zādōy's investments in these two years. The shortest of these records, Berk. 77[104], is rather obscure, but seems to refer to authorities who control the collective property registered in the central repositories (*bunān*) of settlements and villages.[105] Due to the nature of these texts the term *nāmag/gittag ī nēk* is not explained, but it seems to designate some kind of official document (with *nēk* in the sense of 'proper, faultless, valid'), in which the transfer of agricultural products and livestock, and other expenses and investments, also transactions involving the collective property in the central repository (*bun*) of a village, were taken down to a specific purpose (possibly in the context of taxation, but this is only a conjecture; there is too little context to attempt any reasonable conclusions on the purpose of these lists).

1.7 *čak*, *pădirāy*, *ayādgār*

These three terms occur repeatedly in the original documents in Pahlavi cursive script, particularly in the shorter economic texts of the 'Pahlavi Archive'. The most frequent term, *čak* 'document, note, entry, cheque, payment entitlement', is also known from the Sasanian Law-book where it is, however, employed in a different context, that of procedural law, in the sense of 'note/entry in a transcript (of proceedings)'.[106] According to the rules of procedure the litigants in a civil trial were obliged to enter a statement in the transcript (or protocol) of proceedings (*saxwan-nāmag*) if the opposing party failed to appear in court in order to record that the opponent was absent and hence not taking legal action. This act is called *čak dādan*, lit. 'to make an entry, to place on record', as in: *saxwan pad nē āmad čak dahišn* 'the statement "he has not come" is to be placed on record'[107] and *saxwan pad nē rāyēnēd čak dahišn* 'the statement "he is not taking legal action" is to be placed on record'[108] (see also Chapter VI on civil proceedings, p. 538). The *čak*, in this case 'note, entry', seems to have been simply a statement integrated in the court transcript, the *saxwan-nāmag*,

102 WEBER 2017b, pp. 130–136.
103 On the entrepreneur Windād-Burzmihr, who is mentioned in numerous documents, see WEBER 2019a.
104 WEBER 2015, pp. 32–33.
105 On *bun* in this sense see MACUCH 2017c, pp. 168–169, and 2022b, p. 163, with further references.
106 MACUCH 1981, pp. 153–155, no. 23.
107 MHD 73.16f.; 74.7 (MACUCH 1993, pp. 490, 493 and 491, 493 respectively).
108 MHD 74.3 (*ibid.*, pp. 490, 493). For further examples see MACUCH 2008b, pp. 260–261.

In the Tabarestān records and the texts of the 'Pahlavi Archive', however, *čak* designates a separate type of document. The word is of Chinese origin (*tsʾə*, Middle Chinese *tṣak* 'writing tablet, list, document, diploma'), as MacKenzie has elucidated in his edition of the Khwarezmian legal material in the *Qunyat al-Munya* in the context of Khwar. 'čk [*čik*], deed (of divorce)'.[109] It was most likely brought from Central Asia by Sogdian merchants across the Silk Roads (see section 4.3 on sale below, pp. 372–387) and adapted into a large range of Iranian languages: Sogd. *cʾk /čak/* 'document';[110] Bactr. σακο 'document, receipt';[111]; MP *čak* 'document, note, entry, receipt';[112]; NP *čak* 'the written and signed sentence of a judge or magistrate; a draft or cheque for a salary or pension; an obligation, deed, bond, note';[113] and via New Persian into Arab. *ṣakk* 'document of authorization, cheque'.[114] The Arabic term is explained by al-Ḫwārezmī as an 'inventory (*ʿamal*) prepared for every issue of pay; it contains the names and total number of all those entitled to receive something, together with the amount of cash needed for this, and the ruler puts his official mark (*yuwaqqiʿu*) at the end of it, giving authority for the payment of the salaries'.[115] It has entered most European languages as 'check, cheque, Scheck etc.', retaining its meaning in the context of trade and other transactions as a written document specifying the amount of payment (either in kind or in money) to be given to a person for a specific item, product, service or performance.

The term appears most frequently in the shorter documents of the 'Pahlavi Archive' listing agricultural products, rations for feeding animals and other items to be transferred to another person or household named in the text. The designation of the document and the name of the recipient or the title of the official who seals it is usually noted at the end of the text in the fixed formula *čak* + name/title + *āwišt* 'NN has sealed the *čak*', as in: *čak Yazdānpādār āwišt*;[116] *čak Farroxān āwišt*;[117] *čak Frāy āwišt*,[118] or: *čak ōstāndār āwišt*[119] 'the *ōstāndār* (= governor of a province, *ōstān*) has sealed the *čak*'.[120]

109 MacKenzie 1990, p. 109; see also p. 90, nos. 96, 100.
110 Livshits 2007, p. 179. This important attestation in the Mugh document A-13 was still unknown to MacKenzie 1990, p. 90, who (wrongly) wrote that the term is not attested in Sogdian.
111 Sims-Williams 2007, p. 262.
112 Weber 2008b, pp. 38–39; Macuch 2008b, pp. 260–261, with further references.
113 Steingass 1892, p. 396.
114 Wehr 1956, p. 472; also MacKenzie 1990, p. 90, nos. 96, 100.
115 *Apud* Bosworth 1969, p. 125.
116 Berlin 16.9–11 (Weber 2008b, pp. 72–75; revised: Weber 2016c, pp. 70–71); Berk. 33B.8 (Weber 2014b, 50.51); Berk. 106.9 (Weber 2014b, pp. 58–59); Berk. 220B.10 (Weber 2014b, pp. 62–65).
117 Berlin 35.5 (Weber 2008b, pp. 147–150).
118 Berk. 6.9 (Gignoux 2010, pp. 98–99; Weber 2022c, pp. 534–535); Berk. 10.11 (Gignoux 2010, pp. 96–97); Berk. 235.6 (*ibid.*, pp. 100–102).
119 Berk. 32.7–9 (Weber 2014b, pp. 48–49); Berk. 85.12–13 (Gignoux 2010, pp. 106–107); Berk. 142.12–14 (Weber 2022b, pp. 324–327).

The *čak* is also mentioned in two complex legal documents from Tabarestān, allowing further conclusions. Tab. 20[121] is an administrative letter sent by an official (named Kurrag) to another official (named Dādēnbōxt) containing a request to issue a *framān* '(payment) order', on the basis of a *čak* 'payment entitlement'. The recipient of the payment is a (frequently mentioned) scribe named Farroxgušnasp, who has offered his own horse for cultivating the soil of a piece of hard ground or fallow land, which could not be tilled appropriately due to several reasons (among these the previous use of a donkey for tillage). The *čak* determines that the said Farroxgušnasp should receive 10 *grīw* of the produce of the land in the following year in return for this service. The recipient of the letter, the official named Dādēnbōxt, is instructed to release a corresponding payment order (*framān*) following the directives in the *čak*. This remarkable document implies that at least two officials were involved in these financial transactions: one who confirmed that a person was entitled to payment by issuing a *čak* (according to one case noted above, this official was the governor, *ōstāndar*, of a Province), and another official who issued the payment order (*framān*) on the basis of this *čak*.

According to another document (Tab. 26)[122] from the year 107 PYE (= 758/759 CE) a money-borrower takes out a loan, which he intends to repay by means of a *čak* that he is expecting to receive for the past year (106 PYE). He complains that this *čak* for the year 106, enabling him to repay the debt, has not been furthered to him yet. As Tab. 20 suggests (see above), the *čak* was a prerequisite for issuing a payment order (*framān*), which was presumably released by the central administration of the province (located according to the Tabarestān documents in the residence of the commander or king of Parišwārgar in *Halīg).[123] In our case the *čak* or 'payment entitlement' relates to the rent (*tāg*) of a leased piece of land, possibly in the collective ownership of landlords, *dehbedān*, who are mentioned in line 12. The money-borrower is one of these landlords expecting a *čak* in which his share of the rent (*tāg*) for the past year is specified.

Another frequent term denoting a specific type of document in the texts of the 'Pahlavi Archive' has been read by Dieter Weber as *pădīrāy* (< *păti-grāba-) 'Empfangsbestätigung' ('receipt, receipt confirmation, acknowledgement of receipt').[124] To judge by the content in which the word appears, the *pădīrāy* is a document by which the recipient of a payment confirms that he/she has received a specified amount of money or a certain item or product. These two types of document, *čak* and *pădīrāy*, obviously serve different purposes and were utilized in different phases of a transaction. Whereas the *čak* verifies that

120 On the formal structure of checks and specifically the use of *dād* in this context in the sense of a shortened infinitive 'to be given, is to give' see now Weber 2022c, pp. 534–537.

121 On the content of this document see Macuch 2022a, pp. 141–143 (the whole document is in Appendix XV, pp. 735–736).

122 See Macuch 2022b, pp. 167–172 (the whole document is in Appendix XV, pp. 736–737)

123 On the historical background of these documents see Macuch 2024c.

124 Weber 2008b, pp. XVI; 20–21; for a list of documents of the *pădīrāy* type see p. XIX.

a person is officially *entitled* to a specific payment, the *pădīrāy* confirms that the recipient has indeed *received* the payment. The latter type of document has a specific form, usually (but not always)[125] beginning with the 1st sg. pres. of the verb *padīriftan* 'to receive, accept': *padīrēm* 'I receive', either as the first word of the document or in one of its first lines, by which the recipient, whose name is given in the text, explicitly confirms that he/she has obtained a payment in money or kind.[126] Another characteristic feature is that the *pădīrāy* is sealed either by the recipient himself/herself[127] or by a so-called 'witness-seal' (*gugāy-muhr*) or 'witness-seals' (*gugāy-muhrīha*; *gugāy-muhrān*), presumably seals of reliable witnesses to the transaction, who are named in the text and confirm the document.[128] Depending on the person(s) who seal(s) the *pădīrāy* two different formulae appear at the end of the document:

1. The recipient seals the receipt himself/herself: *pădīrāy*—name of the recipient—*āwišt*; *e. g.*: *pădīrāy mādar ī Xusrōyān āwišt* 'The mother of Xusrōyān has sealed the receipt';[129] *ēn pădīrāy Frāy āwišt* 'Frāy has sealed this receipt'.[130]
2. The receipt is sealed by witness-seals: *pădīrāy*—name of the recipient—*pad gugāy-muhrīhā ī*—name on the witness-seals—*āwišt*; *e. g.*: *pădīrāy Dādēn-Windād pad gugāy-muhrīhā ī Weh-[...] āwišt* 'Dādēn-Windād has sealed the receipt with the witness-seals of Weh-[...]';[131]; *pădīrāy Mihrōy pad (gug) āy- muhrīhā ⟨ī⟩ Pērōz-Mihr ī pēšēnīg (?) āwišt* 'Mihrōy sealed the receipt with the witness-seals (of) Pērōz-Mihr, the former (?)';[132] *pădīrāy Wahman-Ohrmazd pad gugāy-muhrīhā ⟨ī⟩ Dēn-[...] āwišt* 'Wahman-Ohrmazd sealed the receipt with the witness-seals (of) Dēn-[...].'[133]

The expression *gugāy-muhr* 'witness-seal' is not explained, but, to judge by the evidence of other sources, it designates the private seal of a witness, who is not an official of the State, but whose trustworthiness has been established by official instances. Documents with the seal imprints of trustworthy witnesses could hence be treated as reliable and valid, even if they were not confirmed and made 'legally binding' (*ēwarīh*) by the personal seal of an official or by an administrative seal. On the different types of seals and their evaluation according to specific criteria see section 2 below (pp. 286–301).

125 An exception is document 38 in the Berlin collection, see *ibid.*, pp. 158–159.
126 See the examples in Weber 2008b, documents 4, 5, 23, 28, 37.
127 The recipient in Berlin 5 is a woman: *mādar ī Xusrōyān* 'the mother of Xusrōyān', who also seals the **pădīrāy* (*ibid.*, p. 25).
128 The singular is attested in Doc. 13.9 (Weber 2008b, p. 61); the plural form, *gugāy-muhrīhā* or *gugāy-muhrān*, is more frequent, as in the examples quoted below; on this term see also Macuch 2008b, pp. 261–262.
129 Weber 2008b, Berlin Doc. 5.8–9 (p. 25).
130 *Ibid.*, Teheran C. 7–8 (p. 172).
131 *Ibid.*, Berlin Doc. 28.7–8 (p. 119); compare Doc. 4.4–6 (p. 19).
132 Weber 2008b, Berlin Doc. 37.7–12 (p. 155).
133 *Ibid.*, Teheran G.6–9 (p. 179).

Another frequent technical term in the records of the 'Pahlavi Archive' for a specific type of document is *ayādgār* 'memorandum, memoir', a word also well known as the designation of a literary genre in Pahlavi literature.[134] In the documents the term seems to denote a separate or additional record or register of undertakings, often (but not always) based on transactions noted in the two document types we have discussed above, the *čak* 'cheque, payment entitlement' and the *pădīrāy* 'receipt'. As both Gignoux and Weber have elucidated, the following recurring formula in the *ayādgār* refers usually to either one of these document types or to both:

> *abar čak* (or: *pădīrāy*; or: *čakīhā ud pădīrāyīhā*) *kē ēn ayādgār awiš wirāst ud nibišt ēstēd…* 'on the basis of the cheque (or: receipt; or: the cheques and receipts) for which this memorandum has been prepared and written …(a specific transaction is undertaken).'[135]

The formula indicates that the *ayādgār* was, as the literal meaning of the word suggests, a record or memoir of a transaction, which was authorized and carried out on the basis of another document, often a *čak* or a *pădīrāy*, or several 'cheques and receipts' (*čakīhā ud pădīrāyīhā*). This document was obviously scrolled and held together by a tie (*band*), which was sealed either:

1. by a 'witness-seal' (*gugāy-muhr*) or several 'witness-seals' (*gugāy-muhrīhā*), as in: *band ī ēn ayādgār amāh pad gugāy-muhr ī Māhdād-Weh ī Māhānān āwišt* 'We have sealed the tie of this memorandum with the witness-seal of Māhdād-Weh ī Māhānān';[136] or *band ī ēn ayādgār Mihrbandag pad gugāy-muhrīhā ī Māhpērōz ī Noxzādān und Aspbād āwišt* 'Mihrbandag sealed the tie of this memorandum with the witness-seals of Māhpēroz, son of Noxzād, and Aspbād';[137] or
2. by the seal of a high official, such as the *ōstāndār*, the governor of a province (*ōstān*), as in: *band ī ēn ayādgār pad muhr ī ōstāndār āwišt* 'The tie of this memorandum has been sealed by the seal of the *ōstāndār*';[138]or *band ī ēn ayādgār ōstāndār āwišt* 'The *ōstāndār* has sealed the tie of this memorandum'.[139]

The Sasanian Law-book only mentions an *ayādgār hampaččēn* 'copy of a memorandum', in the context of criminal law. This document was imprinted with

134 For an extensive discussion of this type of document see Gignoux 2019 with further references.

135 Gignoux and Weber have slightly divergent translations of this phrase. Compare Gignoux 2019, p. 128 (examples on pp. 130, 131, 133, 134, 135); Weber 2008b, p. XVI (examples: pp. 61, 143; revised reading: Weber 2019c, pp. 105–106); Weber 2020–2021, examples: pp. 52, 61, 67.

136 Weber 2008b, Berlin Doc. 13.8–11 (p. 61).

137 Weber 2020–2021, Berk. 226.5–8 (p. 61).

138 Weber 2020b, Teheran Doc. 1.6–9 (pp. 161–163).

139 Weber 2008b, Berlin Doc. 34.7 (p. 143); revised reading of the document: Weber 2019c, pp. 105–106.

the seal of the highest religious and judicial authority, the *mowbedān mowbed* Wehšābuhr, and contained a decree of the Chief Mobed regarding the obligation to take down the court transcript called *pursišn-nāmag* 'record of interrogation', in the case of a criminal offence and to note the punishment of the delinquent at its end.[140]

Table 19. Overview: contracts and documents

Pahlavi term	Type	Specific documents
abarmad	disposition, order, instruction, injunction, decree	– instruction of the *radān* regarding the property of the Farrbay fire – disposition of the judges (*dādwarān*) regarding the establishment of a 'proxy' (*stŭr*) – supplementary document to the marriage contract (with specifics on the dowry?) – decree of the foremost religious leaders (*pahlom dēn burdārān*) – decree of the high priest Tansar/Tōsar authorizing the official canon of Avestan texts
ayādgār	memorandum, memoir	– decree of the Chief Mobed – record of a transaction, authorized and carried out on the basis of another document (often a *čak* or *pădīrāy*)
čak	1. note, entry in the *saxwan-nāmag* 2. document, cheque, payment entitlement	– entry of a litigant recorded in the transcript or protocol of civil proceedings – document specifying the amount of payment due to a person for a specific item, product, service or performance
dib	court transcript 1. edict 2. sealed document	– transcript or protocol of legal proceedings – recorded sentence of a judge – edict of State officials
⟨GTk/gtk⟩ *nāmag/ gittag*	1. foundation deed 2. court record	– document containing the specifics of a pious (fire) endowment – transcript of a legal case – *nāmag/gittag ī nēk* 'good' (= valid?) document (registering the transfer of products and livestock and other transactions)

140 MHDA 34.6–9 (Macuch 1981, pp. 60, 217). On the *ayādgār* of the *mowbedān mowbed* see also pp. 574–575 below.

Pahlavi term	Type	Specific documents
mādayān	foundation deed	– document containing the specifics of a pious endowment
nāmag	1. any written document; 2. (as second element of a compound): (a) court transcript; protocol (b) sealed document	– *hišt-nāmag* 'certificate of divorce' – *nāmag-niyān* 'deposit of documents', (archive of documents of registered fire foundations) – *paymān-nāmag* 'document of contract' – *pursišn-nāmag* 'protocol of interrogation' – *saxwan-nāmag* 'protocol of statements' – *uzdād-nāmag* 'transcript of proceedings' – *wizōst(wizōstan)-nāmag* 'protocol of investigation' – *xweškārīh nāmag* 'document on the area of competence' (of a judicial authority) – *yazišn-nāmag* 'protocol of recitation' (of taking the oath) – *zastbūd-nāmag* 'protocol of interrogation'
nibēg	1. template (original record) 2. certificate	– *aswār-nibēg* 'horseman's document' (legal certificate of an equestrian) – *dast-nibēg* 'handwritten record' (template containing the name [= signature] of the scribe)
nibišt	any written document	
nibištag[141]	bill of indictment	– formal written document noting the charges in a criminal case before the hearings begin in court
pādīrāy	receipt; receipt confirmation; acknowledge-ment of receipt	– document confirming the receipt of a pay-ment, sealed by the recipient or by 'witness-seals' (*gugāy-muhrīhā/gugāy-muhrān*)
pādixšīr	foundation deed	– document containing the specifics of a pious endowment
pašn	contract, bond	– contract with non-Iranians
pašt	1. verbal or parol contract (stipulation) 2. written contract	– agreement between bridegroom and bride prior to the marriage contract – contract of sale – testamentary contract – document of conveyance contract of adoption

141 Not to be confused with the very general *nibišt*. The technical term *nibištag* designates specifically the 'bill of indictment' in a criminal trial, as we may conclude from its recurring attestation in this specific context; see Chapter VI, pp. 573–574.

Pahlavi term	Type	Specific documents
paymān	1. verbal or parol contract (stipulation) 2. written contract	– loan contract – contract of sale – marriage contract – letter of attorney or mandate – testamentary contract – document of conveyance
paymān-nāmag	written contract sealed by a legal authority	– unilateral contract – loan contract
wizīr	1. sealed contract or document 2. title deed	– loan contract – marriage contract – title deed of an estate – document of conveyance – letter of attorney or mandate

2 The function of seals

Seals were utilized in all fields of administration and jurisprudence, not only in the context of validating documents and contracts. A comparatively large amount of original seals and bullae from the Sasanian period have survived, enabling the reconstruction of the geographical administrative divisions of the Sasanian empire and the functions of State officials within this framework in a number of extensive studies based on these primary sources.[142] Despite their importance the information to be gained from the seals themselves and their impressions is limited, but their particular functions in jurisprudence are illustrated in several case studies of the Law-book mentioning various categories of seals, the evaluation of sealed documents according to specific criteria, and the use of seals in civil and criminal litigation.[143]

Generally three different categories of seals can be distinguished according to their owners or users and their functions:

1. seals of private individuals who were not necessarily (but could have also been) State officials;

142 See particularly Gyselen 1989, 2002a, 2007, 2019c, 2024a, 2024b, 2024c and her recent monograph (2019a, with numerous bibliographical references); also Gignoux/Gyselen 1982. For a full list of Gyselen's publications in this field (up to 2016) see the Festschrift in her honour, ed. by Cannuyer 2016, pp. xvii–xxvi. A list of Gignoux's publications on seals (up to 1995) is in the Festschrift in his honour, ed. by Gyselen 1995, p. 12.

143 On the use of seals see Macuch 1997; on the important information to be gained by seals see the forthcoming monograph by Purwins (*Der Aufbau des Sasanidenstaates*).

2. personal seals of State officials on which the official's function or title (also honorary titles) and his proper name were engraved;
3. anonymous administrative seals, bearing only the name and place of the administration, but no personal names.

Evaluating seals was obviously an important task in civil litigation, as both opponent parties could present sealed documents and contracts as evidence to the judge. The courts developed several criteria by which seals were judged to be 'reliable' (*ēwar*), 'valid' (*wāwar*), 'genuine' (*wizurd*), on the one hand, or 'doubtful, untrustworthy, unreliable' (*warōmand*), on the other. Even seals belonging to the 'reliable, valid, genuine' category could be contrasted with each other in order to determine their trustworthiness. The evaluation of seals was apparently not restricted to the seals of private individuals, but could also become necessary if a document was imprinted with an administrative or personal seal that was no longer in use and had been replaced in the meantime by another type of official seal.

2.1 Seals of private individuals

Seals belonging to private individuals are mentioned in a number of passages dealing with civil litigation from which we can deduce that these 'private seals' (as opposed to seals of State officials) were used to confirm documents of different kinds, contracts, testaments, bills of sale, barter or rent, etc. The seals are not described, so we do not know whether the proper names of the owners were engraved on them. A large number of seal impressions with images of birds, animals and other items without any writing have survived, which could well have been used as private seals. On the other hand, it seems likely that names were also engraved on private seals, as it would have been difficult for a judge to evaluate a document with the seal imprint of a private individual (as either 'reliable, valid, genuine' or 'doubtful, untrustworthy, unreliable') if the seal bore no name. The process of evaluation will be discussed in detail below (see section 2.4), but the statements of the litigants could also be decisive, as illustrated in one of the cases: in a lawsuit the plaintiff presents to the court as evidence 'a document sealed by the defendant' (*nāmag-ē[w] ī pad muhr ī pasēmāl*) in order to prove his claim. The exact nature of the claim is not elucidated, but we can assume that the documentary evidence consists of some kind of contract (*e. g.*, a loan-contract, bill of sale or rent) and that the defendant is being sued for breach of contract. The defendant denies having used this seal at the time when the document had been drawn or afterwards with the words: 'the seal with which (the document) has been sealed was not in use at all at that time (and) it did not return to me' (*muhr ī padiš āwišt andar an ē hēčīn nē pad miyān būd abāz ō man nē mad*), that is, he denies having concluded a contract with the plaintiff and hence being bound to an obligation, as his opponent claims. The judges (whose names are given as Māhādur-Frāygušnasp, a *mowbed* in Ardaxšēr-Xwarrah, and Zurwāndād) nevertheless decide to treat the document 'as a valid (one)' (*pad ēwarīh*), *i. e*, they rule the case in favour of the plaintiff, reasoning that it is manifest (*paydāg*) that the defendant—contrary to his statement—did in fact use the same seal later after the document in question had been drawn.[144] In another case the private seal of a witness on a document is accepted as a *muhr ī wāwarīgān* 'valid seal', although as a rule only documents with official seals were treated as reliable evidence of the *wāwar* type (on this case see below).[145]

The courts took great care in identifying private seals, as entries dealing with the responsibilities of State and court officials indicate. The *frēzwān* (lit. 'duty fulfiller') was a kind of policeman or commissioner responsible for the detention and identification of persons involved in legal proceedings (*tan āšnāg kardan*, lit. 'making the person known') and ascertaining their seals in court (*muhr padīriftan* 'accepting the seal').[146] The second expression is not explained, but it probably means that the *frēzwān* was in charge of examining the authenticity of private seals and deciding, whether they in fact belonged to the parties involved in litigation and could be accepted in court or not. In an age without identity cards it was crucial to establish the identities of the litigants and their seals as exactly as possible. This also seems to be expressed in connection with the duties and competences of the judge (*dādwar*), who has, as we are informed, the duty to ascertain whether the name and the seal of a person in a lawsuit (or on trial) correspond to each other: this at least seems to be the meaning of the strange word list *hamtanīh ud hamnāmīh ud hammuhrīh*, lit. 'same person and same name and same seal'.[147] The judge is, moreover, obliged to check the references given on behalf of the person and the seal of the litigant or witness: *tan ud muhr kū kē pad āšnāg guft* 'person and seal: who identified (them)?'.[148] This technical phrase *pad āšnāg guftan*, lit. 'to declare as known', 'to identify', or, more precisely, 'to establish the identity (of a person/seal)', is also attested in several Tabarestān documents in this exact sense. The name of the witness, who establishes or vouchsafes for the identity of a party and his seal, was included in the documents: 'this document of contract was sealed according to the identification of one called Yazdānwindād' (*ēn paymān-nāmag pad āšnāg guft ī Yazdānwindād nām ... āwišt*);[149] 'this document of contract was sealed according to the identification of Dērā' (*ēn paymān-nāmag pad āšnāg ī Dērā ... āwišt*);[150] 'this document of contract was sealed according to the identification of

144 MHD 99.3–8 (Macuch 1993, pp. 612, 620).

145 MHD 93.11–14 (*ibid.*, pp. 593f., 596f.); see p. 297 below.

146 MHDA 30.3–5 (Macuch 1981, pp. 55, 193). On the *frēzwān* see also *ibid.*, pp. 202–204 (no. 48) and Chapter VI, pp. 518–519.

147 MHDA 26.2–3 (Macuch 1981, pp. 50, 188); on the *dādwar* see Chapter VI, pp. 496–503.

148 MHDA 26.5–6 (Macuch 1981, pp. 50, 188).

149 Tab. 15.14–16 (Macuch 2017c, pp. 180–181).

150 Tab. 17.16–18 (*ibid.*, p. 189).

Wangird the scribe' (⟨ēn⟩ paymān-nāmag pad āšnāg guft ī *Wangird ī dibīr … āwišt*).[151] Each one of the witnesses named at the end of the three documents (Yazdānwindād, Dērā and *Wangird the scribe) confirms the identity and the seal of the promisor (borrower, debtor) who accepts an obligation (to return a certain item in Tab. 15; to repay a loan in Tab. 17 and 18) and validates the document with his private seal.

Private seals were also used in civil litigation to confirm the transcripts of court proceedings and to authorize representatives, advocates and intercessors acting on the behalf of the litigants. In civil cases the transcript (*saxwan-nāmag* 'record of statements') containing the statements of the plaintiff and the defendant had to be confirmed with the seals of all litigants.[152] Since legal action was taken on the basis of the *saxwan-nāmag* the plaintiff could refrain from sealing the transcript (*muhr nē brīdan*) before the defendant appeared in court and made his statement.[153] If the defendant failed to attend the hearing at the scheduled date his absence was considered as an obstruction of justice (*azišmānd*) on his part and was punished according to the value of the disputed object (after the third obstruction the defendant invariably lost the case).[154] If two defendants had been sued and one of them was absent at the time when the statements of the litigants were recorded, the *saxwan-nāmag* applied only for the defendant who had appeared in court, made his plea and sealed the transcript.[155] These passages imply that private seals were used to validate the recorded statements of the litigants, that the transcript was invalid (*a-wāwarīgān*) for a litigant who had not explicitly confirmed it with his private seal and that legal proceedings could only be pursued on the basis of a sealed *saxwan-nāmag*. This at least seems to have been the usual procedure. But as the Law-book also records opinions of different legal schools and controversial rulings, another passage discloses, on the contrary, that the judge (*dādwar*) is authorized to instigate legal proceedings even if the *saxwan-nāmag* and other documents used in the lawsuit have not been sealed by the plaintiffs (*pad āwišt ī pēšēmālān nē kard ēstēd*).[156] This passage, however, does not explicitly refer to a civil case and could mean that the judge had the right to continue legal action in the interest of the State (*e.g.*, if the defendant was suspected to be involved in a criminal offence) even if the original plaintiff renounced his claim by not sealing the *saxwan-nāmag* (which would normally effect a stay of proceedings).

An advocate or intercessor (*jādag-gōw*) acting on behalf of a party in court received power of attorney by the seal of the litigant he represented, as we may

151 Tab. 18.26–27 (*ibid.*, p. 184).
152 MHD 73.13–74.5 (Macuch 1993, pp. 490, 493).
153 MHD 73.10–12 (*ibid.*, pp. 490, 493).
154 MHD 10.12–12.17 (*ibid.*, pp. 113–120). On *contumacia* or obstruction of justice see Chapter VI, pp. 561–569.
155 MHD 74.1–5 (Macuch 1993, pp. 490, 493).
156 MHDA 28.7–10 (Macuch 1981, pp. 53, 191).

conclude indirectly from a curious passage dealing with a conflict of interest, when one party seeks to represent the opposing party. This is, of course, as in present law-systems not permitted. The plaintiff, we are informed, is not authorized to intercede on behalf of the defendant, even if he has a mandate confirmed by the seal of the defendant (*pad muhr ī pasēmāl*). A witness of the case, on the other hand, may act as intercessor, if this is accepted by both parties.[157] Another short passage states that an intercessor is not allowed to act on the basis of a mandate bearing his own seal (*pad muhr ī xwēš*), indirectly underlining the reasonable assumption that an advocate needed a mandate authorized by the seal of the party he sought to represent.[158]

As these random entries reveal, the seals of private individuals, who were not necessarily—but could also have been—State officials, were used in Sasanian jurisprudence to confirm legal deeds and contracts out of court. The sealed documents could be presented as evidence if one of the parties took legal action, but the court was obliged to examine the validity of the seals and ascertain that they indeed belonged to the individuals as claimed. In civil litigation, moreover, the opponents used private seals to confirm their statements in the transcript of court proceedings, the *saxwan-nāmag*, and to authorize representatives or intercessors with their mandate. We have no evidence whatsoever on the use of private seals in criminal cases. The procedure was a completely different one and the transcript in criminal proceedings, the *pursišn-nāmag* 'record of questioning (or investigation)', seems to have been a very one-sided document, recording mainly charges against the accused, but we cannot discard the possibility that documents imprinted with private seals could be also used as evidence in these cases.[159]

2.2 Personal seals of officials

Seals engraved with the title and the proper name of a legal official are most likely referred to in several Tabarestān documents in a technical phrase stating that the respective document has been sealed by the seal of so-and-so to make it 'legally binding' (*ēwarīh rāy … muhr abar nihād*). The names of the officials are always recorded in this context: *ēwarīh rāy *Kōfāhr muhr abar nihād* 'to make it legally binding *Kōfāhr placed his seal upon it';[160] *ēwarīh rāy Farroxzād muhr abar nihād* 'to make it legally binding Farroxzād placed his seal upon it';[161] *ēwarīh rāy* (… *muhr abar nihād*) 'to make it legally binding (… placed his seal upon it)'.[162] The

157 MHD 76.1–3 (Macuch 1993, pp. 502, 505).
158 MHD 106.11–12 (*ibid.*, pp. 641, 649).
159 See Chapter VI, pp. 574–575.
160 Tab. 15.16–17 (Macuch 2017c, p. 180).
161 Tab. 18.28 (*ibid.*, p. 184).
162 Tab. 17.19 (*ibid.*, p. 189; There is a lacuna in the document, but there can be no doubt that the gap must be filled in as suggested).

phrase implies that a document was only considered as 'reliable, legally binding' (*ēwar*) if it was confirmed by the personal seal of a legal official bearing his name, but we must keep in mind that the Tabarestān documents were written in the eighth century at a time when a central State administration no longer existed. In the Law-book, which cites directly from a large number of various Sasanian sources, anonymous administrative seals seem to have had the same effect of conveying 'reliability, validity' to a document, but were—in contrast to 'personal' seals—not bound to the person of a certain official and could be employed by different authorities working in the State administration or in law courts, as we will see below.

The personal seal of the highest religious and legal dignitary of the State, the Chief Mobed, is mentioned in the Law-book in connection with an edict prescribing the correct procedure in criminal proceedings. The compiler cites from the 'copy of a memorandum' (*ayādgār hampaččēn*) written by the *mowbedān mowbed*, the infallible highest legal authority of the State (besides the King himself), whose judgement could not be questioned or contested.[163] The document in question had been written and authorized by the seal of Wehšābuhr (*pad-iz muhr ī Wehšābuhr ī mowbedān mowbed būd āwišt*), presumably the same Chief Mobed who presided over the commission engaged with fixing the canon of the Avesta under Husraw Anūšīrwān.[164] The memorandum, prescribing how to proceed in criminal cases regarding crimes 'worthy of death' (*margarzān*), presumably conveys a decision on principle of the highest legal authority, which was binding on lower judicial instances. It states that in criminal litigation a transcript of court proceedings, a *pursišn-nāmag* 'record of questioning (or investigation)' should be written in all cases and the punishment of the accused should be recorded at its end.[165] Copies (*hampaččēn*) of this presumably important document were authenticated by the personal seal of the *mowbedān mowbed* and, as we may assume, sent to the provinces to be observed by the judicial authorities.

The same source also mentions another 'copy of a memorandum with the seal of the Chief Mobed' (*ayādgār hampaččēn ī pad-iz muhr [ī] mowbedān mowbed*) written at the command of the sovereign (*šāhān šāh*). This enigmatic document is concerned with a completely different matter, presumably that of calculating certain dates in correlation with the Zoroastrian millenary scheme of cosmic history. Taken out of context (as most entries of the Law-book) the sentence is difficult to understand, but it could be an attempt to determine the dates of

163 See Chapter VI below, p. 574.
164 On the dating of Wehšābuhr see Macuch 2017a, pp. 266–269, with further references.
165 MHDA 34.6–9 and 34.10–13 (Macuch 1981, pp. 60, 217). Crimes 'deserving death', which were prosecuted by the State, are, according to MHDA 34.9–13, blasphemy (*yazdān-dušmenīh*), rebellion (*xwadāy-dušmenīh*), heresy (*ahlamogīh*), contract-breaking (*mihrōdrujīh*), 'falsehood' (*drōzanīh*) and 'lying' (*a-rāst gōwišnīh*); on criminal offences see Chapter VI, pp. 489–494.

the ancestors of the Sasanian king Husraw I and that of other high dignitaries, who lived in the 'tenth century' (*satō.zim ī dahom*), possibly referring to the last century of the millennium of Zoroaster, the years 9000–10000 according to the *Bundahišn*, within the framework of the Zoroastrian time cycle.[166]

Another problematic passage of the Law-book might also refer to the personal seal of an official, but if this were indeed the case, the sentence would, strangely, suggest that officials other than the individual whose proper name was engraved on the seal could utilize this official's personal seal.[167] The passage deals with the foundation deed of a certain Ādurbād, son of Mardbūd, who has founded a sacred fire 'for the soul' (*pad ruwān*) and lists the names of family members to whom guardianship of the fire, called 'the fire of Ērān-Xwarrah' (*ādur ī Ērān-Xwarrah*), should pass after the death of the founder. It continues with the words: 'Husraw who was *čāšān* sealed the foundation deed regarding the fire of Ērān-Xwarrah with the seal of Warangohrmazd' (*pad muhr ī Warangohrmazd*

166 MHDA 38.6–12 (Macuch 1981, pp. 64f., 221f.): *abāg ān ī abar ham ayādgār hampaččēn ī pad-iz muhr* (*ī*) *mowbedān mowbed pad gōwišn ī šāhān šāh nibišt kū agar Yazdegird andar satō-zim ī dahom pad panǰāhag ī pēš būd xwadāyīh-iz* (*ī*) *ōy bay anōšag-ruwān pidarān amā* ⁺*frahixt* (ms.: *frahist*) *ud ān ī andar ān satō.zim būd ud agar pad panǰāhag ī pas būd Hudād-iz ud Farrbay ud Ādurbōzēd* (*ud*) *Ādurbād ī Zarduxštān andar ān satō. zim pad pādixšāyīh ēstād hēnd agar ōwōn čiyōn nibišt ēstēd panǰāhag ī pēš ān guft ēstēd ī abdom uzīd.* 'Together with that which is written in the same copy of the memorandum, sealed with the seal of the Chief Mobed, at the behest of the King of Kings: If Yazdegird was (= lived) in the tenth century during the first fifty years, (then) we are taught of the reign of his late majesty Anōšag-ruwān's ancestors and that which is in the same century. And if he (= Yazdegird) lived during the latter fifty years, (then) Hudād and Farrbay and Ādurbōzēd and Ādurbād ī Zarduxštān achieved authority during that century. If it has been written thus, (then) the latter fifty years are those (years) that have last passed.' The names of the Chief Mobed and the King who ordered the memorandum are not transmitted, but this remarkable passage refers explicitly to Husraw I (531–579 CE) by his famous epithet *ōy bay anōšag-ruwān* 'his late majesty of immortal soul', and to one of the three kings named Yazdegird. The question in our passage is: did Yazdegird live during the first fifty years (*pad panǰāhag ī pēš*) of the 'tenth century' (does this refer to the last century of the 'millennium of Zoroaster', *i. e.*, 9000–10000 within the Zoroastrian time scheme?) or during the latter fifty years (*pad panǰāhag ī pas*)? According to our sentence, Husraw's dates should be calculated in relation to those of Yazdegird, but which one of the three kings named Yazdegird is meant? As I have already noted earlier (Macuch 1981, p. 232, n. 51) two of the high dignitaries named in the text, Ādurbōzēd and Ādurbād ī Zarduxštān, were Chief Mobed and *rad* respectively under the first Yazdegird (399–421 CE), but it cannot be excluded that the text alludes to Yazdegird II (439–457 CE). Setting the dates of the two kings (Husraw I and Yazdegird) and of four high dignitaries (Hudād, Farrbay, Ādurbōzēd and Ādurbād ī Zarduxštān) in relation to each other might have been of great importance for determining the exact position of these authorities within the framework of the Zoroastrian time cycle. On Zarathustra's millennium see Boyce 1975c, pp. 285–290; on human and divine time in the Zoroastrian cosmology see Panaino 2003; on the astronomical conference of the year 556 under Husraw Anōšag-ruwān see Panaino 2010 with further references; on the concept of time in Zoroastrianism extensively Rezania 2010. On this passage see also Panaino 2022b, p. 41, fn. 60.

167 MHDA 36.6–12 (Macuch 1981, pp. 62, 219f.).

ādur ī Ērān-Xwarrah Husraw ī čāšān būd gittag/nāmag āwišt).[168] This last entry suggests that the official called Husraw did not use his own seal, but that of another official, called Warangohrmazd, to confirm the foundation deed, but the passage could also be interpreted differently, if we assume that Warangohrmazd is not the name of an official, but of a district.

2.3 Administrative seals

Anonymous administrative seals on which only the name and place of the administration were engraved, were called collectively *muhr ī pad kār-framān dāštan* lit. 'seal(s) for exercising command'[169], as we may conclude from the evidence of the primary sources in combination with one of the most frequently quoted and controversially discussed passages of the Law-book:

> MHD 93.4–9
> *muhr ī pad kār-framan dāštan ān ī mowbedān ud āmārgarān fradom pad framān ī Kawād ī Pērōzān ud ān ī dādwaran fradom pad framān ī Husraw ī Kawādān ka muhr ī mowbedān ī Pārs kand mowbed nē pad nām ī mowbedīh bē pad nām ī driyōšān ǰādag-gōwīh xwand nibišt ud pad ān čim abar muhr ī hamgōnag kand ēstēd.*
>
> 'The "seal for exercising command" (*muhr ī pad kār-framān dāštan*): that of the *mowbeds* and the *āmārgars* was first (made) on the orders of Kawād, son of Pērōz, and that of the judges (*dādwarān*) was first (made) on the command of Husraw, son of Kawād. When the seals of the *mowbeds* of Pārs were engraved, (then) the appellation *mowbed* was not written (on them) with the title (of) *mowbedīh*, but with the title (of) *driyōšān ǰādag-gowīh* ("Intercession for the Poor"). And because of this reason (this title) has been engraved on seals of the same type.'[170]

I have already commented on this passage and the confusion it has caused, but it will be useful to repeat a few observations here. The sentence begins with the statement that administrative seals for officials in the positions of *mowbed* and 'calculator' (*āmārgar*) were first introduced by the Sasanian monarch Kawād ī Pērōzān, those for officials in the position of 'judge' (*dādwar*) by his son, Husraw ī Kawādān.[171] The title of *mowbed* was first replaced on administrative seals by the title *driyōšān ǰādag-gōw* 'Advocate of the Poor' in the province of Fars from whence it was extended to other provinces. The sentence does *not* imply that administrative seals engraved previously with the title *mowbed* vanished from

168 On ⟨GTk/gtk⟩ *nāmag/gittag* 'foundation deed' see pp. 275–279 above.
169 MHD 93.5 (Macuch 1993, pp. 591, 596); 100.6,10,14 (*ibid.*, pp. 613f., 621f.9).
170 Macuch 1993, pp. 591, 596. This sentence has been discussed by de Menasce 1963, Shaked 1975, Gignoux 1976, Sundermann 1976, Garsoïan 1981, Gyselen 1989, pp. 31–34, and Macuch 1997, p. 83.
171 On the competences and positions of these authorities in the legal and administrative system see Chapter VI, pp. 496–518.

the scene once the title *driyōšān ǰādag-gōw* was introduced. It only states that at a certain time during the reign of Husraw Anuširwān seals being engraved for the *mowbed*s of Fars (*ka muhr ī mowbedān ī Pārs kand*) received another inscription. It would be absurd to deduce that the institution of the *mowbed* no longer existed whilst all evidence points to the contrary or that seals engraved with this title were from then on no longer used or valid. Moreover, no part of the passage implies explicitly that seals with the new title *driyōšān ǰādag-gōw* remained confined to Fars. The problem is—as so often in the Law-book—that the last part of the sentence is open to different interpretations: *ud pad ān čīm abar muhr ī hamgōnag kand ēstēd* 'and because of this reason (= because the title *mowbed* was replaced by *driyōšān ǰādag-gōw* in Fars) it (= the new title) was engraved on seals of the same type' could mean:

1. the title *driyōšān ǰādag-gōw* replaced the title *mowbed* on (all?) seals of the administrative type (in Fars); or
2. the title *driyōšān ǰādag-gōw* was also engraved on seals of the administrative type (in other regions).

The second interpretation is the only one that takes the available evidence of the primary sources, the seals themselves, into consideration, since seals engraved with the new title were in fact issued and in use in different provinces of the empire, not only in Fars. As Gignoux and Gyselen have shown, a large number of these anonymous administrative seals with the inscription *driyōšān ǰādag-gōw ud dādwar or ǰādag-gōw dādwar ī driyōšān* 'Advocate of the Poor and Judge' were utilized in at least 16 different administrative districts, including those located in Fars, but also in other regions of the realm (Abaršahr, Ādurbadagān, Ardaxšēr-xwarrah, Bīšābuhr, Ērān-Xwarrah-Šābuhr, Gēlān, Gurgān, Hamadān, Husraw-šād-Kawād, Māsabadān, Ray, Staxr, Wālaxšfarr and Weh-Ardaxšēr).[172]

The quoted passage is an important source for dating the emergence of anonymous administrative seals, which were apparently not bound to a specific person or dignitary, but only to an office. As Kawād and Husraw I were the first to introduce these seals, according to our text, these changes might have been part of a scheme of the two monarchs to divert power and influence from the nobility and the clergy by placing more emphasis on the State offices created by the king. The initiation of a seal with the imprint *driyōšān ǰādag-gōw ud dādwar* could have even emerged in the wake of the Mazdak upheaval and been inspired by the fundamental critique of the Mazdakites regarding the unequal distribution of wealth and the hierarchical division of society.[173] By replacing the title *mowbed* on the seals with that of 'Advocate of the Poor and Judge' the

172 See Gignoux 1976, pp. 104–106, and Gyselen 1989, pp. 31–33; for attestations see Gyselen 2019, p. 364 (index).

173 On the Mazdak movement see Macuch 2015b (with further references) and Chapter III, pp. 253–259.

King would have skilfully presented the judges in his administration (as well as himself) as protectors of the poor, without giving the clergy any cause to complain, for the new title would correspond exactly with the self-image of the Zoroastrian priesthood as intercessors for the *driyōšān* (Av. *drəgu-*, *driγu-*), the true original disciples of Zarathustra.[174] All this is mere speculation, but it fits in well with the reforms initiated by Husraw I.

Besides possible strategic reasons for creating anonymous seals, this type of seal apparently had the advantage that it was not necessarily bound to an administrative district. According to an illuminating sentence in the Law-book, officials in the position of *mowbed* and *dādwar* working in another province (*šahr*) or district (*tāsūg*) than the one to which they were originally assigned, could use the administrative seals (*muhr ī pad kār-framān dāštan*) of their own region in order to validate documents if they had the authorization to use these seals.[175] A concrete example from legal practice is also transmitted: a transcript from criminal proceedings (*pursišn-nāmag* 'record of interrogation'), written in the 26th year of King Husraw, son of Ohrmazd (*i.e.*, Husraw II, 590–628 CE), in the province of Ardaxšēr-xwarrah under the administration of the *ōstāndār* Māhādur, was prepared by the *mowbed* of Ohrmazd-Ardaxšēr (called Frāyzarduxšt), but sealed in Gōr with the administrative seal of the same *mowbed* of Ohrmazd-Ardaxšēr (Frāyzarduxšt), who had written the transcript.[176] This seems to point to the curious fact that these anonymous seals were not necessarily bound to the administration of the province or district for which they were originally made, but could also be used by the officials who had the authorization to use administrative seals in other regions. But if we keep in mind that the compiler of the Law-book was interested in recording the most complicated, controversial and even curious cases, this might not have been the normal procedure, but rather an exception to the rule. It is also possible that the use of an administrative seal by an official in a different district was restricted to criminal proceedings as in the described case.

Court recordings in both criminal and civil proceedings were confirmed by administrative seals. The official, who wrote the 'record of questioning' (*pursišn-nāmag*) in criminal litigation, sealed the document with the administrative seal of his district, as we have seen above. In civil cases the administrative seal of the district in which the proceedings took place was added to the private seals of the parties (who had already sealed the *saxwan-namag*) in the preliminary hearing. A concrete example from legal practice under the reign of King Ohrmazd (which one of the five monarchs with this name?) refers to a civil case in which the *dādwar* of Gōr sends the transcripts or protocols (*dib*) with the statements

174 On MP *driyōš* and Av. *drəgu-*, *driγu-* (Bartholomae 1904, cols. 777–778) see Colditz 2000, pp. 171–189, with further references.
175 MHD 100.5–7 (Macuch 1993, pp. 613, 621).
176 MHD 100.7–11 (Macuch 1993, pp. 613f., 621).

of the litigants to the *mowbed* of Ardaxšēr-xwarrah. We are not informed to which purpose (possibly the documents were sent to the next instance), but the passage continues to confirm that these court records containing the statements of the opponents were sealed with their private seals and with the 'administrative seal of the (law) courts of Xūnābagān' (*pad muhr ī Xūnābagān mānān pad kār-framān dāštan*) by a representative of the law courts called Anōšzād.[177]

Officials received the authorization to use administrative seals by a document called *muhr-dād* '(document of) seal transfer', as a short passage dealing with the rights of the *mowbed* and the *dādwar* seems to suggest.[178] These officials, it states, have the right to keep their seals if they are replaced (*az kār guharīg kard*) until the *muhr-dād* has been sealed (*tā muhr-dād āwišt*), but they are not allowed to give back their seals to a former official. This appears to mean that the authorization of the *mowbed* and *dādwar* to use seals remained valid as long as the document assigning these seals to their replacements (the *muhr-dād*) had not yet been issued.

2.4 Evaluation of seals

As courts often ruled on the validity of documents, particularly in civil cases, one of the crucial problems to be solved was how to evaluate a document presented as evidence for a claim. The validity of a document was self-evident (*paydāg*) if was imprinted with the personal seal of an official or an anonymous administrative seal of one of the State administrations or law-courts. These official seals were as a rule classified as *muhr ī wāwarīgān* 'valid seal',[179] *muhr ī ēwar* 'reliable, legally binding seal'[180] or *muhr ī wizurd* 'genuine seal'.[181] All these terms denoted seals which would usually provide solid proof for the legal validity of a document, but there seems to be a slight difference between the two latter terms: a personal or administrative seal, which was currently in use and effective, was assessed as a *muhr ī ēwar*, whereas *muhr ī wizurd* was used of a seal that was older and no longer in use. As we will see below, the assessment of documents with one of these two types of seals was discussed controversially.

Important information on the validity of seals and the evaluation of documents can be gained from the Corpus Iuris of Īšōʿbōxt. The entries not only correspond to the details available in the Sasanian Law-book on the classification of seals, but are of invaluable help for understanding unexplained allusions in the

177 MHD 100.11–15 (*ibid.*, pp. 614, 622). Xūnābagān was possibly a district in the town of Gōr, which was situated in the region of Ardaxšēr-xwarrah in the province of Pārs. On the geographical names see de Menasce 1964b.

178 MHDA 12.13–17 (Macuch 1981, pp. 34, 141, with a slightly different interpretation of this passage).

179 MHD 93.12; 99.1 (Macuch 1993, pp. 593, 596f., and 612, 620 respectively).

180 MHD 32.4 (Macuch 1993, pp. 223, 227).

181 *Ibid.*

Pahlavi texts. According to this source, documents were distinguished according to the reliability of their seals into 'valid' and 'doubtful' ones (*šṭārā šarrīra wa-d-bə-pušākā*).[182] A valid document (*šṭārā men šarrīrā*) is that which is sealed by officials of the State: 'persons who are chosen and employed by the church or by the sovereigns (*malkē*) and the magistrates (*šalliṭānē*)'. A doubtful document (*d-bə-pušākā*), however, is only sealed by the witnesses of a transaction. In the Syriac translation of Īšōʿbōxt's text—written originally in Pahlavi—the expression *šarrīrā* 'firm, valid' renders MP *wāwarīgān* 'valid, true, trustworthy', a term attested, besides the Law-book, in the *Dēnkard* and as an Iranian loan-word in the Babylonian Talmud in this sense in a definitely legal context.[183]

Two passages of the Law-book refer explicitly to the *muhr ī wāwarīgān* 'valid seal'. The first case deals with a person who has entered into a contract (*pašt*) with another person.[184] We are not told which kind of contract has been concluded, but the sentence suggests that the deal involves the transfer of an object and hence most likely refers to a bill of sale, barter or rent. The first party to the contract (vendor) commits himself to showing a document (*nāmag*) sealed with a *muhr ī wāwarīgān* in order to prove that he is entitled to the object he has agreed to transfer to the second party (purchaser). Instead, he presents a document sealed by a witness to the former transaction by which he, the vendor, became the owner (or possessor) of the object. The text continues with the statement that the procedure is to be regarded as 'proper' (*xūb*) if the seal of the witness in question has been assessed as a 'valid seal' (*muhr ī pad wāwarīgānīh padīrift ēstēd* 'a seal which has been accepted as a valid one').

This important passage reveals that Sasanian courts not only accepted documents with official seals, but could also admit those with the private seals of witnesses as substantial evidence after having assessed them according to certain criteria. These are not listed in the Law-book, but Īšōʿbōxt fortunately describes the procedure of evaluation exactly: 'If the valid document is produced in court, it is used as evidential. However, in the case of a document sealed by witnesses we carry out an investigation. If the witnesses who have sealed the document are religious and known as God-fearing men by all in the region and the community concerned and have a good reputation, then we use such a document as a valid one. But if this is not the case, we use it as a doubtful one.'[185] We can reasonably infer that Īšōʿbōxt adapted this procedure from Sasanian legal practice and that piety and a good reputation, based on Zoroastrian moral standards, were the exact criteria by which the courts assessed the trustworthiness of witnesses and, hence, of documents confirmed with their private seals.

182 Īšōʿbōxt, Book VI, Chapter II, § 1 (Sachau 1914, pp. 187–189).
183 On this term in the Babylonian Talmud see Macuch 1999, pp. 92–98, and Chapter VII, pp. 592–594.
184 MHD 93.11–14 (Macuch 1993, pp. 593f., 596f.). For an English translation of this sentence see Macuch 1999, p. 95.
185 Īšōʿbōxt, Book VI, Chapter II, § 1b (Sachau 1914, pp. 187–189).

A technical term, which seems to denote exactly this type of private seal used by witnesses to verify a transaction, is transmitted in several original Pahlavi documents (from the so-called 'Pahlavi Archive'), the compound *gugāy-muhr*, lit. 'witness-seal', and its plural forms *gugāy-muhrān* and *gugāy-muhrīhā*.[186] Due to the concise nature of these texts (mostly payment orders and receipts) an explanation of the term is not to be expected, but its use in connection with different types of documents and the verb *āwištan* 'to seal' seems to allow no other interpretation.[187] Moreover, an almost idential term (with the abstract ending *-īh*) is attested in the Law-book (a passage already alluded to above), *gugāyīh muhr* 'witness seal, testimonial seal' in the context of a lawsuit, in which one of the litigants brings forward documentary evidence: '... if he (= the litigant) presents a document (*nāmag*) with the seal of him, whose witness seal (*gugāyīh muhr*) has been accepted as valid (*pad wāwarīgānīh*), (then this is) proper.' (*... ka pad muhr ī ōy* ⁺*kē pad gugāyīh muhr ī pad wāwarīgānīh padīrift ēstēd nāmag āwarēd xūb*).[188] That is, the court admits as reliable evidence a document with the personal seal of a witness, who has been approved of as trustworthy according to the procedure described above.

The plural forms *gugāy-muhrān/muhrīhā* 'witness-seals' and *wāwarīgān muhrān* 'valid seals' draw our attention to the fact—now also confirmed by the Tabarestān records—that documents could be imprinted with several seals.[189] A document a person has sealed with his own seal (*nāmag ī mard pad muhr ī xwēš*) can be considered as reliable evidence if it has also been certified with one of the 'valid seals' (*ka-š any-iz muhr ī wāwarīgān muhrān abar ēstēd* 'if it is also imprinted with another seal of the valid seals'). This type of document with several seal imprints is dealt with as 'reliable, trustworthy, legally binding' (*pad ēwarīh kār az-iš kardan* 'it is treated as binding'). Correspondingly, several of the Tabarestān records are sealed not only by the promisor or contractors, but also with the personal seal of a legal authority to make them 'legally binding' (*ēwarīh rāy*).[190] All these attestations lead us to the conclusion that *muhr ī wāwarīgān* (*wāwarīgān muhrān*) denoted seals of legal authorities and officials that were *per se* valid, but that the term could also be used of private seals of witnesses (*gugāy-muhr*) whose reputation had been investigated and approved of by the court.

186 Weber 2008b, pp. 21–22 (Dok. 4.5; 13.9; 23.9; 28.7; 37.9; 38.16; also Teheran G7) and Macuch 2008b, pp. 261–262. On these terms see also pp. 282–284 above.

187 See, *e.g.*, Dok. 4.4–6: *pădirāy ... pad gugāy-muhrīhā ... āwišt* 'the receipt ... was sealed with the witness-seals' (Weber 2008b, p. 19); Dok. 13.9–11: *band ī ēn ayādgār amāh pad gugāy-muhr ī Māhdād-Weh ī Māhānān āwišt* 'we sealed the binding of this memorandum with the witness-seal of Māhdād-Weh, son of Māhān' (*ibid.*, p. 61); Dok. 23.8–10: *pădirāy pad gugāy-muhrān ī Māh-Pērōz āwišt* 'the receipt was sealed with the witness-seals of Māh-Pērōz' (*ibid.*, p. 99).

188 MHD 93.13–14 (Macuch 1993, pp. 594, 596f.).

189 MHD 99.1–3 (*ibid.*, pp. 612, 620).

190 For attestations see above under personal seals of officials, pp. 290–293.

The other two technical terms denoting trustworthy seals, *muhr ī ēwar* 'reliable seal' and *muhr ī wizurd* 'genuine seal', are contrasted with each other in a complicated case involving the evaluation of documentary evidence brought forward by two men who both claim to be married to the same woman.[191] As usual, we are not told how the uncertain legal status of the woman arose in the first place, but can assume that she had been married to one of the two men first (in a marriage of the *pādixšāy*-type?) and had been released by her husband for a certain time in order to enter an interim marriage (of the *pādixšāy*-type) or an auxiliary marriage (of the *čagar*-type) with the other man to provide one of these men with children. This description is purely hypothetical, as the background is not elucidated in the Law-book, but the whole matter could, of course, simply be a case of polyandry, which—in sharp contrast to polygyny—was forbidden in Sasanian law. Be it as it may, both men present documentary evidence with different seal imprints to prove their legal claims to the woman: one of the marriage documents is sealed with a *muhr ī ēwar*, a 'reliable, binding seal', presumably by an official of the State; the other document is older and is confirmed by a 'genuine seal' (*muhr ī wizurd*) which was formerly in use (*ī pēš az ān*). The decision that follows is astonishing: the first document with the *muhr ī ēwar* actually in use is evaluated as a *wizīr ī ēwar* 'valid, reliable, legally binding document'; whereas the second one with the older seal is only a *wizīr ī warōmand* 'unreliable, doubtful document', despite the fact that the document is sealed with a 'genuine seal'. But this does not necessarily mean that the court is obliged to render a verdict in favour of the man with the former document. The sentence continues to discuss two different possibilities:

1. The two men put their claims forward independently (*ǰud ǰud*) against the woman, *not* in a lawsuit against each other. If the woman does not explicitly state that she is the wife of the man with the (older) 'doubtful document' (*wizīr ī warōmand*), then the case can be ruled in two different ways: according to one jurisconsult, she belongs to the man with the older document, although it has been evaluated by the court as 'doubtful' (*wizīr ī warōmand*); according to the second jurisconsult, she has to be given to the man with the 'valid document' (*wizīr ī ēwar*).
2. The two men sue each other regarding the woman (*mard ēk abāg did*). In this case there is only one possibility of deciding the lawsuit in favour of the man who presents the 'valid document' (*wizīr ī ēwar*).

This exceptional case (which might not be purely hypothetical) allows several conclusions with regard to the assessment of seals as well as the legal reasoning involved in evaluating documents. First, documents with a 'genuine seal' (*muhr ī wizurd*) no longer in use were categorized as 'doubtful' (*warōmand*), although they had been confirmed by legal officials at a former period. Second, the court

191 MHD 32.4–10 (Macuch 1993, pp. 223, 227).

Table 20. Overview: terminology relating to seals

Seals of private individuals	
gugāyīh muhr	witness seal; testimonial seal
gugāy-muhr	witness-seal
hamtanīh ud hamnāmīh ud hammuhrīh	'same person, same name, same seal' (process of ascertaining a person's identity and the conformity of his name and seal)
muhr brīdan	to engrave (a document) with one's seal
muhr ī padiš āwišt	the seal with which it (= the document) is sealed
muhr ... pad āšnāg guftan	to identify, vouchsafe for a seal
muhr padīriftan	to accept a seal (on a document as evidence in court)
pad āšnāg guft ī... āwištan	to seal (a document) according to the identification of (so-and-so; name of the witness)
pad āwišt ī pēšēmāl/pasēmāl	sealed by the plaintiff/defendant
Personal seals of State officials	
ēwarīh rāy ... muhr abar nihād	'(so-and-so) placed (his) seal upon it to make it legally binding'
pad muhr ī ...	'with the seal of (so-and-so; name of an official)'
Administrative seals	
driyōšān jādag-gōw ud dādwar	Advocate of the Poor and Judge (title)
muhr ī pad kār-framān dāštan	seal(s) for exercising command
muhr-dād	(document of) seal transfer
Evaluation of seals	
muhr ī ēwar	reliable (= trustworthy, legally binding) seal (official seal currently in use)
muhr ī warōmand	unreliable, doubtful seal
muhr ī wāwarīgān	valid seal
muhr ī wizurd	genuine seal (older official seal, no longer in use)

could accept the 'doubtful document' (*wizīr ī warōmand*) as solid proof only if it was *not* provided as counter-evidence to a 'reliable, valid document' (*wizīr ī ēwar*). If both documents were brought forward as evidence in one and the same lawsuit, the party with the 'valid document' (*wizīr ī ēwar*) inevitably won. We can moreover infer that the categories 'valid' (*ēwar*) and 'doubtful' (*warōmand*) applied not only to documents with the seal imprints of private persons and witnesses, but also to those of the official type. If the seal of an official was no longer in use, the document in question could be categorized as 'doubtful', notably if contrasted as evidence against a document sealed with a recent 'valid' seal.

To conclude, seals were apparently of central importance in Sasanian jurisdiction. In civil litigation private seals were utilized by the parties to validate their statements in the transcript of a lawsuit (*saxwan-nāmag*), to provide a representative or advocate with a mandate, and to confirm documents written out of court (bills, contracts, testaments) which could be used as evidence in court. Besides these private seals, documents were confirmed with the personal seals of officials in order to make them 'legally binding' (*ēwarīh rāy*). The personal seal of the highest judge, the Chief Mobed, authenticated the copies (*hampaččēn*) of memoranda (*ayādgār*) containing decisions on principle, which were sent out to the provinces and were binding on lower instances. Anonymous administrative seals validated documents and court recordings both in civil proceedings and in criminal cases. These seals were not necessarily bound to the province or district for which they were originally designed, but could be used—at least in criminal litigation—by authorized officials to confirm court transcripts written in another region. Finally, documents confirmed by private and administrative seals could be subject to the evaluation of the court and were assessed according to specific criteria as 'reliable, valid' (*ēwar, wāwarīgān*) or 'unreliable, doubtful' (*warōmand*). As a rule documents with the seal imprints of officials of the State were considered as 'valid', but if the seal in question was old and had been replaced in the meantime by another type, the document could also be evaluated as 'doubtful', particularly if it was presented as counter-evidence to a document confirmed by a recent official seal. On the other hand, documents sealed with the private seals of witnesses, normally regarded as 'doubtful', could be accepted as 'valid', if the reputation of the individuals had been examined and approved of by the court.

3 Transfer and acquisition of property

As in other legal systems, property could be transferred for a specified term or in perpetuity by the means of sale (*frōxš*), barter (*guharēn*), lease (*tāg*), donation (*dād*), gift (*dāšn*), acquisition by marriage or inheritance, as security (*graw*) for a loan (as pledge, lien, deposit or mortgage; *āgrawīh* 'hypothec', or *grawagān* 'antichresis'). Apart from transmission by right of inheritance (*pad abarmānd*) which was subject to different rules already described above, the transfer of all other proprietary rights 'by conveyance' (*pad dād*) took place in a formal procedure, reminiscent of the religious foundation of all legal acts and the inherent sacred power of the spoken word. The legal background of this procedure, which was regulated minutely in Sasanian law, seems to be based on two perceptions:

1. the observation that there is a fundamental difference between conveying an object for a limited period (*e. g.*, as a loan, pledge, deposit or other form of security), on the one hand, and transferring it to another person with a full title (either in ownership of the fruits, as *bar-xwēš*, or in ownership of the substance, as *bun-xwēš*), on the other;
2. the notion that in both cases a contract in the strict sense of the word, *i. e*, a binding, legally enforceable agreement between two parties, only came into being, when both parties gave their consent.

The procedure (in presumably all forms of transfer) consisted of an offer made by the person willing to transfer an object or enter a contract (the offeror or transferor), which was accepted (or refused) by the other receiving party (the offeree or transferee). The type of right being transferred (*i. e*, in possession or ownership, as pawn or mortgage, time-limited or in perpetuity) and the conditions of the transfer had to be specified in each individual case, but the procedure conveying these rights was formalized and generalized, encompassing all kinds of property (land, real estate, houses, silver and gold, money, slaves and a person's personal income are mentioned in this context). The conditions that had to be fulfilled in order to generate a binding contract and to transfer property legally are illustrated in several case studies in the 'Chapter on the approval and compliance with the will (of the conveyor)' (*dar ī sahišn ud kāmag dōšīd*) among several other dispersed passages in the Law-book.[192] The main components of the procedure can be summarized as follows:

1. The transferor or conveyor (donor) had to have the right to dispose of the object, corresponding to the manner and extent to which he himself was entitled to ownership (*čē ēwenag xwēšīh* '[according to] the manner of ownership'). That is, he could not offer a thing to which he himself had no title or, if he only had a limited title, exceed this right of disposal. He could either name the recipient directly or delegate this right to a third party, giving the latter the power of agency to the extent specified in his statement.
2. The recipient or acquirer (donee) had to have the right of acquisition, that is, he had to have legal capacity according to the rules set above (see Chapter II, pp. 101–103). Legally dependent or subordinate persons (women, underage children, slaves) and persons with limited legal capacity (members of the lower estates, foreigners, infidels) were subject to different regulations, depending on their status. In the case of women, underage children and slaves usually the legal guardian (*dūdag-sālār*) or master (*xwadāy*) had to give his consent to the transfer. As a general rule, all transactions to the benefit of the family were sanctioned.[193] But there are exceptions, since the capacity of the *installed* legal guardian (of the *kardag* or *gumārdag* type, who was, nota bene, not the *paterfamilias*) to accept transactions for the family was

192 MHD 66.2–68.17 (Macuch 1993, pp. 446–453).
193 MHD 66.13–14 (*ibid.*, pp. 447, 451).

limited.[194] His authorization in this respect definitely came to an end, when a son reached maturity and took over as family guardian. The son together with the other mature heirs as shareholders, including the mistress of the house, then decided whether they were willing to accept an offer or to refuse it.[195] Moreover, according to the 7th clause of the marriage contract, a bride could also agree to (or refuse) the dower offered by the bridegroom, despite her dependent legal status as a woman (see below, p. 305).

3. The transferor or conveyor declares his will (*kāmag*) to convey a specific object to the recipient on the condition that the latter officially declares his approval (*sahišn*) of the transaction and accepts the terms of the offer. This procedure took place in the presence of witnesses, of which usually three were necessary in legal transactions, or, in the presence of a legal official, or—presumably in rare cases—of the head of the Zoroastrian Church, the *mowbedān mowbed*, the most trustworthy witness, whose word was incontestable.[196] The prescribed formulae to be spoken by the transferor to the recipient (referring to the offer) were: *ān ī tō sahēd* 'that which you approve of' (or as variants:) *ān ī tō kāmēd* ('that which you desire'); *ān ī tō passandē* ('that which you approve of') or *ān ī tō abāyēd* (or: *ān ī tō andar abāyēd* 'that which you have need of').[197] If the statement of the offeror was recorded without witnesses the written document was valid after having been sealed by the offeror. The verbal offer, we are informed, could not be repealed, as it had been undertaken in the presence of witnesses, but the written offer without witnesses could be revoked as long as the document had not yet been sealed.[198]
4. The transaction was only valid if the recipient (offeree or donee) gave his consent (*sahišn*; *padīrišn*) to the offer, by accepting with the words: *dōšīd* 'it is sanctioned' or *kāmag dōšīd* 'the will (of the transferor) is sanctioned' or *andar abāyed* 'it is necessary'.[199] If he was not willing to accept the offer, he

194 On the different types of family guardianship see Chapter II, pp. 177–183 above.
195 For example, in one specific case (MHD 67.3–13; Macuch 1993, pp. 447, 451f.) the conveyor is a debtor who has taken out a money loan of 200 (drachms?) from two men (Farrox and Mihrēn), pledging to transfer from his ownership to the creditors an object of their choice either in ownership (*pad xwēšīh*) or as antichresis (*pad grawagānīh*) according to their decision if he does not fulfil the contract. One of the creditors (Mihrēn) passes away and the other one (Farrox) becomes the legal guardian of the family of the former, in which there are underage children. The question is, whether Farrox is permitted to accept the offer for the underage children, if one of them or all of them reach maturity at this period or not. It is discussed controversially, but the preferred procedure seems to have been (according to the last sentence of this passage) to let the shareholders, the son and daughter, who have come of age, and the mistress of the house decide together, whether they are willing to accept the pledge or not.
196 MHDA 10.10–13 (Macuch 1981, pp. 32, 123f.).
197 MHD 66.3–5 (Macuch 1993, pp. 446, 450).
198 According to MHDA 10.10–13 (Macuch 1981, pp. 32, 123f., see also introduction, p. 11).
199 See Macuch 1993, p. 454, no. 1, with further references; all attestations should be taken into consideration; for the last (and most frequent) formula see *ibid.*, Index, p. 686.

could refuse with the words *andar nē abāyēd* 'it is not necessary; there is no need'.[200] Transfer of property only took place in the former case, when the recipient publicly declared his acceptance, called *padīrišn paydāgēnīdan* 'to declare (lit. "reveal") acceptance', by which a binding contract between offeror and offeree came into being.[201]

The acceptance of a transaction did not have to take place immediately. In verbal agreements and contracts of sale and barter three nights could be conceded to both the offeror and the offeree in which the former could withdraw his offer and the latter could think it over before accepting the sale or barter (exceptions to this rule are also attested).[202] In other specific cases (presumably regarding a loan), acceptance of an offer (of a pawn or pledge in lieu of re-payment) could even be delayed by several years.[203] The seller (or barterer) was compelled to guarantee that he had the right to sell and to even defend the title of the buyer (or recipient) in court should a third party claim possession of the acquired object. As the 'legal predecessor' (*dastwar*) of the buyer he was obliged to appear in court and give testimony in favour of the latter in a procedure which was also known in ancient Roman law (the *actio auctoritatis*).[204] Indirect evidence indicates that larger transactions involving real estate were documented and sealed by witnesses to the transaction or official instances, and that documents with official seals were regarded as the most reliable evidence in cases of dispute (see above section 2.4).[205]

200 Macuch 1993, p. 163, no. 4, with further references.

201 For attestations see *ibid.*, Index, p. 726.

202 MHDA 11.17–12.7 (Macuch 1981, pp. 33f., 125); a specific case, in which a husband authorizes his wife to undertake a barter, is transmitted MHD 37.1–10 (Macuch 1993, pp. 273, 274; see also Commentary, p. 275, no. 2).

203 In one interesting case (MHDA 11.12–15), presumably in the context of a loan, the conveyor (= debtor) Farrox concludes a contract (*paymān*) with the recipient (= creditor) Mihrēn, offering a pawn to the latter (which would pass into ownership of the creditor in case of non-fulfilment of contract) with the formulaic words *ēk ī tō andar abāyēd*: 'from the slaves that are my own (*anšahrīg ī man xwēš*) one that you have need of (*ēk ī tō andar abāyēd*) (shall be) your own (*tō xwēš*)'. If Mihrēn (the creditor) gives his consent with the formulaic *andar abāyēd* ' it is necessary' after ten years (*pas az 10 sāl*), then not only the slave, but a child that might have been born of that slave within these 10 years (a female is obviously meant) also goes to (the creditor) Mihrēn (see Macuch 1981, pp. 33, 124f.).

204 On *dastwar* (= Roman auctor) see Chapters IV, pp. 385–387 and VI, pp. 542–544 with further references. On the procedure in ancient Roman law see Liebs 1982, pp. 228–229, and Kaser 1986, pp. 194–195.

205 Interestingly, the same formulae are also used in the context of the transfer of a woman from one man to another within the framework of family law and marriage (see also the clause in the marriage contract discussed below). In one remarkable case a man dismisses his wife from marriage and guardianship in order to enable another man to fulfil his duty as a righteous Zoroastrian, to marry and engender children. The latter accepts marriage, but refutes guardianship (*pad sālārīh andar nē abāyidan gōwēd* 'he declares that he has no need of guardianship'). In this case the dismissal from (the first) marriage is null and void (*kar nēst*) and the transfer of the woman does not take place. This case is compared to that of a transferee who refuses to accept a transaction by uttering the same formula: *ōwōn*

The procedure described above consisting of offer and acceptance is also attested in the clause on the dower (or marriage-portion, settlement) in the model Pahlavi marriage contract we have already discussed above in the context of matrimony (Chapter II, p. 135), using the formulae prescribed in the Law-book. The seventh clause of the contract, regulating the dower to be paid by the husband to the bride, first states that the bridegroom gives the bride 'full entitlement of the income' (*pad windišn pādixšāyīhā kard*). Both bride and bridegroom then agree by contract (*az paymān*) on the dower, consisting of an 'ideal' (*a-baxt*) half (*pad do bahr ē bahr*) of the bridegroom's property corresponding to the sum of 3000 silver drachms in domestic currency after the bride has given her consent to the offer by the bridegroom, using the terminology elucidated above: the clause states explicitly that the sum of 3000 drachms has been 'approved of (*weh sahist*) by F. G. (= the bride) (and) sanctioned (*dōšīd*) (by her)'.[206] This seems to have been the standard procedure for all forms of larger transactions, including dispositions *mortis causa* and other dealings, which were carried out on the basis of mutual agreements as well as verbal and written contracts (though this is not always expressly stated in the sources).[207]

Table 21. Transfer of property: legal formulae

Words spoken by the transferor (offeror/donor)		Words spoken by the recipient (offeree/donee)	
ān ī tō (andar) abāyēd	'that which you have need of'	*andar abāyēd*	'it is necessary'
ān ī tō kāmēd	'that which you desire'	*andar nē abāyēd*	'it is not necessary; there is no need'
ān ī tō passandē	'that which you approve of'	*dōšīd*	'it is sanctioned'
ān ī tō sahēd	'that which you approve of'	*kāmag dōšīd*	'the will (of the transferor) is sanctioned'
		weh sahist	'it is approved of'

bawēd čiyōn kē pad xwāstag ī awiš dahēnd andar nē abāyidan gōwēd dād nē bawēd 'it is as if someone declares with respect to a property granted to him that he has no need (of it), (then) it is not transferred' (MHD 4,14–5,3; Macuch 1993, pp. 70, 72f.).

206 On *im wahmān ī wahmān ī rāy weh sahist dōšīd* 'which has been approved of by F. G. (= the bride) (and) sanctioned (by her)' see Macuch 2007b, transcription and translation of clause 7 pp. 190–191; commentary pp. 197–200.

207 The procedure (despite divergences) is reminiscent of the formalities of the stipulation in Roman law. A *stipulatio* or 'verbal contract', originally a promise of payment of debt, later used of different kinds of contracts, was concluded by the oral exchange of a question of the *stipulator* (or creditor) and answer of the *promissor* (or debtor). The *stipulator* asked formally: *spondesne?* ('do you solemnly promise [to pay]?'); the *promissor* answered *spondeo* ('I solemnly promise'), a formal act by which a binding contract came into being (see Nicholas 1962, pp. 159, 193; Kaser 1986, pp. 45–47).

4 Transactions and obligations

We have mentioned the religious significance of keeping contracts as one of the important components of Zoroastrian law in the Introductory to this Chapter. In the Mihr Yašt duties resulting from all kinds of contracts as well as from interpersonal relationships, stood under the protection of Mithra, god of the covenant. A breach of contract was hence not only a matter to be settled by the courts, but a grave offence that could also be punished according to the *wināh ī ruwānīg* ('sins pertaining to the soul') category of transgressions.[208] The available material is of course fragmentary, but the important religious dimension of contract law is hardly a subject matter of the Sasanian Law-book, which is invariably concerned with cases belonging to the *wināh ī hamēmālān* ('offences regarding opponents') category of transgressions. The entries discuss concrete cases, focusing on the wordings of agreements and contracts, legal formulae and the means of securing obligations (as in other lost works or compilations of this legal genre, a few of which are mentioned in the Law-book). In dealings with non-Zoroastrians, however, the religious aspect reappears, forbidding specific transactions with adherents of other faiths, although the general rule that contracts, once they were concluded, had to be kept also applied in these cases.

Due to the nature of these entries and the lack of precise explanations, it is often impossible to decide, whether the transactions referred to are based on contractual obligations or have a different background (*e. g.*, a provision in a will or a gift or donation). In Roman law the concept of *obligatio* has been defined in Justinian's *Institutes* as: '... a legal tie which binds us to the necessity of making some performance in accordance with the laws of our State',[209] and elucidated by scholars of Roman law as 'a legal relationship between persons marked by rights and their correlative duties', 'a bond by which one party is bound, and the other entitled, to some act or forbearance ...'[210] and 'a tie between two parties of such a nature as to confer on the one a power of compelling by action the other to give, do or furnish something ...'.[211] According to the Roman jurist Gaius obligations arise either (1) from contract (*ex contractu*) or (2) from delict (*ex delicto*), to which Justinian's *Institutes* later adds two further types, (3) 'obligations similar to those arising from contract' (*quasi ex contractu*), (4) 'obligations similar to those arising

208 On these two categories of Zoroastrian Law see above, Chapters I, pp. 61–63 and V, pp. 400–401.

209 '*Obligatio est iuris vinculum quo necessitate astringimur alicuius solvendae rei secundum nostrae civitatis iura*' *apud* Kaser 1986, p. 148, and dalla Massara 2017, p. 154; translation according to du Plessis/Borkowski 2010, p. 249. Alternative translations *apud* Herzog 1939 [= 1980], II, p. 1: 'An obligation is a tie of law which binds us according to the rules of our civil law, to render something' (Sandars) or (somewhat more freely) 'An obligation is a legal bond, by virtue of which, according to the law of the country, we are compellable to do or forbear doing something.' (Webb).

210 Nicholas 1962, pp. 286 and 159 respectively.

211 Sandars *apud* Herzog 1939 [= 1980], II, p. 2.

from injuries' (*quasi ex delicto*).[212] The type of obligations resulting from contract (with which we are concerned here) are divided by Gaius (followed by Justinian) into four kinds, resulting (1) from *re* 'by the thing' ('when the actual receipt of a thing under certain conditions imposed the necessity of fulfilling those conditions'); (2) *verbis* 'by word of mouth' ('obligations created by promises uttered in a form stereotyped by legal custom'); (3) *literis* 'by writing' (obligations arising from 'a written agreement made in the fixed legal phraseology'); (4) *consensu* 'by consent' (by agreement of the involved parties).[213] An agreement, which did not correspond to either of these categories, was not a contract, but a pact (*pactum*) that did not take full legal effect, although some pacts acquired full or partial legal recognition in an advanced stage of Roman law (to the latter belonged the *obligationes naturales* 'natural obligations' or moral claims, already mentioned above, which were not legally enforceable but could have legal consequences).[214]

Legal relationships between two or more persons creating an obligation by contract are definitely attested in Sasanian law, particularly in credit law and other business transactions, but a theoretical framework comparable to that of Roman law (however 'untidy' this construct may be)[215] is missing in the fragmentary Iranian texts. The important religious connotations of the contract would suggest an approach similar to the Roman concept of a 'legal tie' (*vinculum iuris*) or bond between persons, creating a binding duty, protected by the god Mithra, but a corresponding theory does not seem to have been developed in Iranian jurisprudence (of course we cannot know for sure, given the sparse material). We can, however, infer that, as in Roman law, obligations resulted either from contract or delict and that the same twofold consequences arose: a duty on the part of the person assuming the obligation and a corresponding right in the other person to enforce that duty by taking legal action, which could result in some kind of compensation or payment for damages. The nearest equivalent to *obligatio*—albeit with a religious provenance and lacking the intricacies of Roman legal theory—is *tōzišn*[216] 'atonement, pecuniary penalty, financial obligation, duty to

212 Nicholas 1962, p. 158f.; Herzog 1939 [= 1980], II, p. 2; du Plessis/Borkowski 2010, pp. 251–252; Kaser 1986, pp. 177–178.

213 Quotations from Herzog 1939 [= 1980], II, pp. 2–3; see also Kaser 1986, p. 178.

214 Herzog 1939 [= 1980], II, p. 3, and du Plessis/Borkowski 2010, pp. 250–251. According to Nicholas 1962 *pactum* designated originally an agreement not to sue, extinguishing any obligation arising from injury (*ex delicto*). The meaning of the term was later widened to mean any agreement, and 'there was coined the maxim … that a bare pact (*i. e*, an agreement which does not fall within the limits of any recognized contract) begets a defence, but no action' (*Nuda pactio obligationem non parit sed parit exceptionem*) (pp. 191–192).

215 A critique of the system by du Plessis/Borkowski 2010, pp. 252–253.

216 A verbal noun in *-išn* from *tōxtan*, *tōz-* with the basic meaning 'to atone, expiate' (Nyberg 1974, p. 194; MacKenzie 1971, p. 83); Ir. √*tauǰ^{1} 'to (re)pay, pay back (a debt, fine, vel sim.), expiate' (Cheung 2007, p. 388). On the religious provenance of the word in the context of atoning for a sin or offence committed against Zoroastrian precepts see Chapter V, pp. 400–403. It is used in a legal context mainly in the sense of 'to pay a fine,

pay, liability', also 'debt' and 'fine' with *wizārdan* 'to pay' and in the hendiadys *abām ud tōzišn* 'debt and liability'.[217] As in Roman law, *tōzišn* designates both the obligation arising from contract as that arising from a 'wrongdoing', a sin, injury or offence to be atoned for in form of a pecuniary penalty. The origin of the term is to be found in the religious context of atoning for sins: in the *Wīdēwdād* (Vd 3.38,39; 8.107) *tōzišn* translates Avestan *čiϑā-* 'atonement, expiation'[218] and (Vd 18.68) Av. *paititiš* 'expiation'.[219] In the Pahlavi glosses to the translations of these passages *tōzišn* is explained by Sasanian commentators as the penalty for a sin or offence in form of a monetary fine (*pad xwāstag* 'in money'), reflecting the use of the word in a juristic context.[220] Similarly, in the Pahlavi legal texts the stress lies on the *financial* aspect, on the duty to effect a payment, to repay a loan according to the terms of a contract (*abām tōzišnīh* 'payment of a debt')[221] or to recompense an injured person by paying a fine or compensation (*tāwān*) as penalty for the injury or offence.[222] The person who has committed himself by contract to fulfil an obligation is labeled *tōzišnōmand*, lit. (person) 'liable for payment; debtor';[223] the recipient (in a single late attestation) *tōzišn-xwēš*, lit. 'owner of the payment; creditor' (but see also other phrases denoting the debtor and creditor in the overview table 22 below).[224] Obligations, which were passed on to the heirs and legatees together with the total patrimonial estate (*abarmānd*), were called *tōzišn ī pid/pidar* 'liabilities of the father'[225] or *tōzišn ī pidarān* 'liabilities of the parents/forefathers',[226] (also *abām ī pidarān* 'debt[s] of the forefathers').[227] In two compounds the exact type of obligation arising from a liability or debt is specified: by the technical terms *hamāg-tōzišn* 'joint and several debtor' and *xwāstag-tōzišn* 'part-debtor'. A person in a partnership (*e.g.*, in a community of heirs or any other kind of business association) who is liable as *hamāg-tōzišn* 'joint and several debtor' can be either jointly charged together

settle/repay a debt; give back, return anything borrowed'; on the suffix *-išn* see Durkin-Meisterernst 2014, p. 170, § 338.

217 MHD 29.13,15 (Macuch 1993, pp. 220, 224); MHD 30.16 (*ibid.*, pp. 221, 225); on *abām* see pp. 310–319.

218 Bartholomae 1904, cols. 585–586 (''Busse, Sühne' einer Übeltat, usw. durch Geld-, Vermögensstrafe').

219 On *paititiš* see Buyaner 2016, p. 48.

220 For the Pahlavi version of these passages see Moazami 2014, pp. 90–91, 266–267, and 422–423 respectively.

221 MHD 61.2, 8 (Macuch 1993, pp. 409, 415).

222 See, *e.g.*, DkM 715.9: *tōzišn ī pad tanāpuhr* 'the atonement/penalty for a *tanāpuhr* offence'; on this offence or grade of sin see Chapter V, pp. 477–481.

223 MHD 68.17 (Macuch 1993, pp. 449, 453); 76.17 (*ibid.*, pp. 511, 513); 83.6 (*ibid.*, pp. 538, 541); DkM 703.20; see also next fn.

224 DkM 772.16f.: *wināh ī tōzišn-xwēš andar tōzišnōmand* 'the offence of the recipient of a payment (lit. "owner of a payment") against the (person) liable for payment.'

225 MHD 16.1, 4 (Macuch 1993, pp. 140, 143); 63.2 (*ibid.*, pp. 412, 418).

226 MHD 2.4 (Macuch 1993, pp. 40, 42); 13.1 (*ibid.*, pp. 127, 130); 86.15 (*ibid.*, pp. 551, 554); MHDA 32.6 (Macuch 1981, pp. 57, 215).

227 MHD 53.6 (Macuch 1993, pp. 369–370); DkM 713.20; 714.1.

with his partners (*e.g.*, co-heirs or business associates) or individually to repay the whole debt. Every one of the joint debtors is obliged to take full responsibility for satisfying the claims of the creditor(s) and it is left to the person who has been charged to recover from his co-partners the sum for which they are jointly liable.[228] As *xwāstag-tōzišn* 'part-debtor', on the other hand, a person in a partnership can only be charged in proportion to his individual share (*bahr-marīhā*) of the whole sum, but not for the entire debt or liability.[229]

Other frequent technical expressions and phrases, emphasizing the basic meaning of the term as 'financial obligation, liability, payment' are: *tōzišn dādan/kardan* 'to effect a payment';[230] *tōzišn hištan* 'to remit, abate, cancel an obligation';[231] *ō tōzišn madan/rasīdan*: 'to be due for payment';[232] *tōzišn xwāstan* 'to request, claim, demand a payment';[233] *tōzišn wizārdan* 'to make payment for a liability/debt'.[234] Due to the lack of a recognizable theoretical construct, we will attempt in the following to scrutinize the concrete legal transactions described (or often only mentioned en passant) in the texts, besides the contracts on which they are based and the legal consequences arising from these undertakings, as far as they can be reconstructed. In the legal texts three main issues are addressed:

1. the precise implications of specific formulations and formulaic words (*certa verba*) in all kinds of legal transactions (dispositions, wills, agreements and contracts);
2. various forms of security (personal and real) as means of ensuring the fulfilment of contractual obligations;
3. enforcement of contractual obligations by taking legal action.

228 MHD 59.12–16 (Macuch 1993, pp. 408, 413); 60.5–6 (*ibid.*, pp. 409, 414); on the responsibilities of the heirs with regard to the liabilities of the father see also Chapter III, pp. 206–210.

229 MHD 60.1–5 (Macuch 1993, pp. 408f., 413f.); 60.6–7 (*ibid.*, pp. 409, 414); see also Chapter III, pp. 207–209.

230 As in: *az dūdag tōzišn be kunišn* 'on the part of the family a payment must be made' (MHD16.14, Macuch 1993, pp. 141, 144); *tōzišn dahišn* 'a payment must be given' (MHD 76.4, 6; *ibid.*, pp. 510, 512).

231 Examples: *tōzišn hišt* (*nē hišt*) *bawēd* 'the obligation/payment is (is not) cancelled/abated' (MHD 2.5, 8,9,10,12; Macuch 1993, pp. 40–41, 42–43).

232 Examples: *tā wizārdan … ō tōzišn mad* 'until the payment … is due' (MHD 78.1; Macuch 1993, pp. 517, 520); *tāwān ō tōzišn … (ōh) rasēd* 'the fine is due for payment' (MHD 6.17; 72.5; *ibid.*, pp. 89, 93; 478, 480 respectively); *o tōzišn nē rasēd* 'it will not be due for payment' (MHD 109.15; *ibid.*, pp. 644, 651).

233 Examples: *ka tōzišn az dūdag xwāst* 'if he has demanded a payment from the family' (MHD 15.4; 63.3; Macuch 1993, pp. 139, 142); *ka tōzišn ō dūdag xwāhēd* 'if she claims a payment for the family' (MHD 15.9,10; *ibid.*, pp. 139, 142); *az payan(d)ān tōzišn xwāhēd* 'he requests payment from the surety' (MHD 57.9; *ibid.*, pp. 388, 393).

234 Examples: *wizārdan abāyestan ī tōzišn* 'the necessity of effecting payment for the liability' (MHD 13.10; Macuch 1993, pp. 127, 130); *kas pad tōzišn wizārdan andar nē ēstēd* 'nobody takes over the payment of the debt' (MHD 99.16; *ibid.*, pp. 613, 621); *ka tōzišn pad nagīrā(y)īh wizārēnd* 'if they make the payment whilst denying the debt' (MHD 102.13; *ibid.*, pp. 616, 624).

Table 22. Overview of terminology: *tōzišn*

Technical terms		Transactions		Persons involved	
abām ud tōzišn	debt and liability	*ō tōzišn madan/ rasīdan*	to be due for payment	*hamāg-tōzišn*	joint and several debtor
dūdag tōzišn	liabilities of the family	*tōzišn dādan/ kardan*	to effect a payment	*kas kē čiš awiš tōzišn dahišn*[235]	creditor (lit. 'person to whom a payment must be given')
tōzišn	financial obligation, liability, payment	*tōzišn hištan*	to remit, abate, cancel an obligation	*mard kē ō kas tōzišn dahišn*[236]	debtor (lit. 'man who owes a payment to a person')
tōzišn ī pidar(ān)	liabilities of the father/ forefathers	*tōzišn wizārdan*	to make payment for a liability/ debt	*ōy kē xwāstag tōzišn*[237]	debtor (lit. 'he who must pay the money')
		tōzišn xwāstan	to request, claim, demand a payment	*tōzišnōmand*	debtor (lit. 'liable for payment')
				tōzišn-xwēš	creditor (lit. 'owner of the payment')
				xwāstag-tōzišn	part-debtor

4.1 Loans and credit law (*abām/abāmdān*)

In correspondence with their importance in a complex economy, loans (transactions by which goods are lent or money given to another person on condition of return or repayment) are often (if not extensively) discussed in several sources in the context of commerce as well as agriculture, the two main means of sustenance. The development of credit law was a crucial prerequisite for the promotion of wide-reaching commercial activities of artisans, merchants and traders in the Sasanian empire (see below section 4.3), but it also played an important part in the rural communities, as both Sasanian and post-Sasanian

235 MHD 76.4f. (Macuch 1993, pp. 510, 512).

236 MHD 30.1 (*ibid.*, pp. 220, 224).

237 MHD 89.8–9 (*ibid.*, pp. 569, 572; *xwāstag* written here as heterogram ⟨NKSY'⟩ 'money').

sources disclose. Promoting farming and agriculture was one of the two central precepts of Zoroastrianism: by cultivating the land, tilling the ground, fertilizing the soil, reaping the harvest and producing crops a person contributed to the promotion of life and the support of Ohrmazd's good creation (the other central precept was the procreation of children, as we have seen above).[238] Affluent members of society, particularly the nobility with their extensive landed estates, could contribute to these religious requirements by sustaining agricultural activities (not only to their religious advantage, but also to their own financial profit). This could be—and was probably often—done from a distance by leasing parcels and giving loans to peasants and farmers, who cultivated the fields and produced the crops and were sometimes forced—as in later centuries—to borrow money in order to be able to continue their work, to supply livestock and agricultural implements, for seed and other expenses. Accordingly the most frequently mentioned form of security for a loan was the mortgage of the fruits or *antichresis* (MP *gruwagānīh*), consisting usually of the next harvest, with rates of interest (if interest was taken) based on a calculation of the average crop yields per year.[239] Besides the—more or less abstract—case studies in the Sasanian Law-book mentioning (noble) families (*dūdag*) as both debtors and creditors, the Tabarestān documents and other Pahlavi sources reveal that granting and taking out loans belonged to the regular undertakings of individuals from different layers of society.[240] Larger pious institutions and foundations also granted loans to increase their funds, as we have already mentioned in the context of religious endowments ('property for the soul').[241]

Credit law seems to have been a rather well developed field, but there is no systematic description and—as in other areas—the basic concepts will have to be reconstructed from random entries and case studies. Originally there was presumably only an undifferentiated idea of debt, which could comprise any corporeal thing or sum of money a person owed another person, no matter how this obligation came into being. In early Roman law a debt could arise because of an injury a person caused another person or because of damaging or stealing another person's property, or due to a formal act (promise, agreement, contract), or because one person had conveyed to the other a corporeal thing or a sum of money which the other was not entitled to retain. As we have already mentioned above, four types of debts or obligations were differentiated later in Roman law into those arising (1) from delict (*ex delicto*); (2) from contract (*ex contractu*); (3) (debts) similar to those from contract (*quasi ex contractu*), and (4) '(debts)

238 On Zoroastrian ethics see overview in Cantera 2015.
239 For examples see Macuch 2017b, 2017c and below.
240 For example, in Tab. 18 the moneylender is a scribe called Farroxgušnasp; the borrower an artisan, a shield-maker called Dēlgušnasp (see Macuch 2017c, pp. 183–188, and below, pp. 345–349).
241 See p. 228 above.

similar to those from delicts' (*quasi ex delicto*).[242] Although the development might have been quite different in Iran, we can detect a vague similarity in the initial connection of loans and sins or injuries and criminal acts: refusing or failing to return a loan (or its equivalent) was categorized from early times as a delict causing loss or damage to the lender, comparable to theft and robbery, and was punished accordingly. Our oldest (Avestan) source on loans (in chapter four of the *Wīdēwdād*) uses the terms 'thief' (*tāiiu-*) and 'robber' (*hazaŋhan-*) to denote the borrower, who is either unable or refuses outright to return a loan:

> Vd 4.1
> *yō naire nəmaŋhən̨te nōit nəmō paiti.baraiti tāiiuš nəmaŋhō bauuaiti hazaŋha nəmo.barahe aēšąmcit̰ iϑra vā asni iϑra vā xšafne maēϑanahe xᵛāi pairi.gəruuaiieite.*
>
> 'Who does not give back a loan to the creditor, becomes a thief of the loan, a robber of the creditor, as one who by day or by night takes the property of the house for himself.'[243]

The Avestan text is translated into Pahlavi (with glosses in square brackets) as:

> *kē ō mard ī nihišnōmand [čiš abāyēd dādan] ā-š nē nihišn abāz barēd [kū-š nē dahēd] duz ī nihišn bawēd [ān ī-š pad ēn menišn stānēd kū abāz nē dahom] apparag ī nihišn ⁺kē barišn [ka xwāhēd gōwēd ay hast-am u-t nē dahom].*
>
> 'Who to the creditor (*nihišnōmand*) [(to whom) a thing must be given] does not give back a loan (*nihišn*) [he does not give it] is a thief of the loan [one who takes it with this intent: "I will not give it back"], a robber of the creditor (*nihišn kē barišn*) [when he (= the creditor) requests (the loan) he (= the debtor) says: "I have it, but will not give it to you]."'[244]

242 Nicholas 1962, p. 159, Herzog 1939 [= 1980], II, p. 2; du Plessis/Borkowski 2010, pp. 251–252; Kaser 1986, pp. 177–178, and pp. 306–307 above.

243 The terminology in the Avestan passage refers definitely to a loan (this is not quite clear in the Pahlavi translation and commentary, hence the divergent translation of Moazami 2014, p. 99): ²*nəmah-* 'loan, credit' (Bartholomae 1904, col. 1070, 'Darlehen'); *nəmaŋhant-* adj. 'giving a loan' (*ibid.*, col. 1069, 'ausleihend'); *nəmō.bara-* adj. 'who gives a loan, creditor' (*ibid.*, col. 1071, 'der ein Darlehen gibt'). Bartholomae has translated the whole sentence in his *Altiranisches Wörterbuch* (1904) in two parts, the first section col. 1070 (under ²*nəmah-*), the second one col. 34f., under *aēšā-* 'Vermögen' (capability, property) in the second sense of 'Habe, Eigentum' (property, ownership).

244 The Pahlavi translation of Av. ²*nəmah-* 'loan, credit' is *nihišn*, written ⟨nhšn'/nydšn'⟩, a verbal noun derived from *nihādan*, *nih-* 'to put, place, establish'. The verb is used in Pahlavi texts as a technical term in the field of credit law to designate (1) the placing of a pawn or pledge (*graw*) as security (*pad graw be nihēd* 'he deposits sth. as pledge', MHD 37.12, Macuch 1993, pp. 277, 282); (2) the establishment of a pious institution (with *nihādag* 'foundation': *nihādag nihēd* 'he establishes a foundation' [MHD 34.7,8]; *xwāstag ī ruwān nihād* 'property founded for the soul' [MHD 34.1; Macuch 1993, pp. 252, 255]; see also Bartholomae 1916–1925, II, p. 9; on nouns ending in the suffix *-išn* see Josephson 1998, p. 88, *apud* Durkin-Meisterernst 2014, p. 170, § 338 and fn. 49). The Pahl. *nihišn ⁺kē barišn* ⟨nyd'šn MN(W) blšn'⟩ obviously translates Av. *nəmō. bara-* adj. 'who gives a loan, creditor' (Bartholomae 1904, col. 1071, 'der ein Darlehen gibt'). The Pahlavi word has been mixed up in several manuscripts with *niyāyišn*, written

The Pahlavi commentary elucidates:

> *ēn az abestāg paydāg ān bawēd ka gōwēd ay čiš dah ud tō-iz ka abāyēd ā-t dahom ud pad ēd menišn be stānēd kū abāz nē dahom ka kas nē dānēd pad hās^{a}r duz ud ka kas dānēd pad hās^{a}r apparag ka xwāhēd gōwēd ay nēst-am pad gyāg duz ka gōwēd ay hast-am u-t nē dahom pad gyāg duz ī duzān ud apparag ī apparagān frēzwānīg u-š band ud drōš.*
>
> 'This is revealed in the Avesta: This is in effect: When (a person) says: "Give (me) this thing and when it is needed by you (*tō-iz ka abāyēd*) I will give (it/the equivalent) back" and he takes out (the loan) (*be stānēd*) with the intention "I will not give (it) back": if no one knows, (then) he is within the (timespan) of a *hās^{a}r* a thief (*duz*), and if someone knows, he is within the (timespan) of a *hās^{a}r* a robber (*apparag*). When he (= the creditor) requests (the loan) (and) he (= the debtor) says "I do not have it", (then) he is immediately a thief (*duz*); if he says "I have it, but will not give it to you", (then) he is immediately the chief of thieves, the chief of robbers; (punishment by) both fetters/incarceration and brand/mutilation (*band ud drōš*) (is) obligatory.'

The Avestan terms for 'robber' (*hazaŋhan-*)[245] and 'thief' (*tāiiu-*)[246] and the corresponding Pahlavi terms *appar(ag)* and *duz(d)* respectively were connoted with offences committed in public (in the open; with witnesses) and those committed in private (in seclusion; without witnesses), in accordance with the definition of the 'robber' as a person, who steals openly, and the 'thief' as one, who steals stealthily (this distinction also applied in the context of sale and barter, as will be seen below).[247] These terms were not only employed in criminal law, but transposed to other legal fields, specifically contract law, in which they were used in a figurative sense to designate contractors who did not keep their contractual obligations. In the context of 'breach of contract' (*mihrōdrujīh*) transgressions were punished (at least in an early phase of Zoroastrian law, but also in specific cases in the Sasanian period)[248] according to the penalty for robbery ('stealing openly') if the deal had been agreed upon in public, in the presence of witnesses, and according to the penalty for 'theft' ('stealing secretly') if the deal had been closed in private, without witnesses. The use of these expressions established the procedure and the penalty in parallel cases, which did not necessarily have

⟨nyd'dšn⟩, 'prayer, praise', which renders Av. ^{1}*namah* 'praise, homage' (Bartholomae 1904, col. 1069, 'Verehrung, Ehrerbietung, Huldigung, Ehrfurcht[sbezeigung]'). This is the reading Moazami 2014, p. 99, has adapted, which, however, makes no sense in this context.

245 Bartholomae 1904, col. 1799 (with references to the sources).

246 *Ibid.*, col. 647 (with references to the sources).

247 This idea is expressed in several Avestan texts and in the Pahl. *zand*. See for example Nēr. 15.4 (on this passage see Chapter V, pp. 434–437). On the basic distinction between 'thief' and 'robber' in the context of sexual transgressions see also Hēr. 6.6 (Kotwal/Kreyenbroek 1992, pp. 42–45). On the punishment for theft (and robbery?) *band ud drōš* 'fetters/incarceration and brand/mutilation' see Chapter V, pp. 441–442.

248 See the examples quoted in the context of sale and barter below, pp. 381–382.

to do with theft or robbery in a concrete sense at all, but were judged according to the circumstances in which the offence was committed: in public or private, with or without witnesses.

In the ancient procedure described in the cited passage Vd 4.1 the borrower (or debtor) who does not give back the loan (not necessarily a money-loan) is classified—according to the Pahlavi commentary comporting the interpretation of the Sasanian exegetes—as a 'thief' if there are no witnesses to the agreement or transaction (*ka kas nē dānēd* 'if no one knows') or as a 'robber' if there are witnesses (*ka kas dānēd* 'if someone knows'). A similar categorization applies when the lender (or creditor) requests that the loan be returned: if the borrower (debtor) either denies the loan or is unable to return it (*nēst-am* 'I do not have it' can imply both) he is considered a thief; if he concedes that he has (received) the loan, but refuses to return it (*hast-am u-t nē dahom* 'I have it and will not give it to you'), then he is regarded as both thief and robber (*duz ī duzān ud apparag ī apparagān* 'the thief of thieves and the robber of robbers'). Within the framework of this scheme, denying or not returning a loan is an offence equivalent to theft, admitting the debt, but refusing to return it, a grave offence equivalent to both theft and robbery.

We can furthermore detect two important developments in credit law by comparing the (rather elementary) Avestan text with its Pahlavi exegesis in both the translation (with its elucidating glosses) and the commentary. First, the Avestan original does not mention any kind of agreement or contract between the borrower and lender (it only states very briefly 'who does not give back a loan to the creditor', *yō naire nəmaŋhəṇte nōit nəmō paiti.baraiti*). The Pahlavi commentary, on the other hand, stresses the fact that an agreement has been reached between the two parties: the borrower (debtor) explicitly acknowledges taking out a loan as well as his obligation to return it ('Give this thing and when it is needed by you I will give it back', *čiš dah ud tō-iz ka abāyēd ā-t dahom*). The borrower (debtor) accepts to give the thing back, when the lender (creditor) requests it by expressing his 'need' (*abāyēd*) that it be returned (using the same terminology employed in formulae creating a contract, as elucidated above).[249] According to the Pahlavi commentary the loan is based on a unilateral contract[250] deriving from a formal act (the declaration on part of the borrower/debtor), whereas the Avestan original leaves this question open. In an early phase of law there was presumably no distinction between a loan based on a formal agreement between two parties and an informal transfer of a corporeal thing or money on part of one party to the other, whereas the formal agreement became crucial for the enforcement of

249 See section 3 of this Chapter above on transfer and acquisition of property, pp. 301–305.

250 That is, a contract, which generates only rights in one party and duties in the other: the lender has a right to the repayment of the loan, but no duties, whereas the borrower has the duty to repay the loan, but no rights (as opposed to a bilateral contract, which produces reciprocal obligations, each party having both rights and duties as, for example, a sale contract).

contract in the Sasanian period. Second, in the Avestan version the intention of the borrower (debtor) is *not* addressed, whereas the Pahlavi version expressly states that 'he takes out (the loan) with the intention "I will not give (it) back"' (*pad ēd menišn be stānēd kū abāz nē dahom*). By the Sasanian period taking the intent of the borrower into consideration was regarded as such an important element in judging these cases that it is even included in the corresponding gloss to the Pahlavi translation of the Avestan text, not only in the commentary: the borrower is only considered as a thief, when he has taken out a loan *with the intention* (*pad ēd menišn*) of not returning it (but *not* if he is insolvent or unable to keep the payment deadline in the case of a money-loan, or, in the case of a borrowed physical object, if he has some other plausible reason for not returning it). In short, it seems that in the period between the composition of the Avestan text and the Sasanian exegesis two important developments took place:

1. Informal loans and those based on a *formal act* (statement of the borrower) creating an enforceable (unilateral) contract were differentiated.
2. Failure to carry out the obligations under contract, *i. e*, to return the loan immediately on request of the lender or on a fixed date, was not inevitably a breach of contract and judged as such, but took the special circumstances of the case, particularly the *intention* of the borrower, into account.

The term *nihišn* in this text (which translates Av. ²*nəmah-* 'loan, debt') might have been used predominantly in renderings of the Avestan word, since it is not attested in this sense as a technical term in the available Pahlavi legal sources. But to judge by the basic meaning of *nihišn* (something that is 'put, placed, laid down, established')[251] the word could have designated a specific type of loan (a money loan does *not* seem to have been meant in the quoted passages), for example, the (possibly gratuitous) loan of a corporeal thing (a tool, item, animal or slave) for use, which had to be returned on a specified date, or a kind of deposit (a thing given to another person for safekeeping to be returned on demand). The term could have been a general expression for 'bailment', that is, the transfer of personal property by the owner (the bailor) to another person (the bailee) in trust for a specific purpose (such as transferring goods to carriers for transport, to warehousemen for custody, to artisans for embellishment or repair; borrowing, lending, keeping animals or slaves for hire, etc.).[252] The bailor remains the

251 Not to be confused with the frequent *nihādag* 'foundation, deposit', derived from the same verb *nihādan*, *nih-* 'to put, place, establish' (Macuch 1993, p. 258, no. 1); see also fn. 241 above.

252 An interesting case of bailment is transmitted in Tab. 15: a shield-maker, called Dēlgušnasp, is sued by a scribe, called Farroxgušnasp, for not returning a shield, belonging to the latter, that had been conveyed to the artisan to be embellished by the image of the 'face of the sun' (or winged solar disk, *xwarənah-*). The shield-maker commits himself to returning the shield at a specified date and agrees, furthermore, to deliver two shields to Farroxgušnasp if he fails to keep the date of delivery (see Macuch 2017c, pp. 180–182).

owner and has the right to demand return of the goods or direct their delivery to another person at the end of the period of bailment; the bailee acquires neither ownership, nor possession, but only physical control for the agreed period.[253] Without further attestations, however, the exact technical meaning of *nihišn* remains uncertain (if it indeed did have a specific meaning in Sasanian law and was not only used in the general sense of 'loan' in translations of the Avesta).

In Pahlavi legal texts the usual expression for 'loan, debt' is the amply attested *abām*, besides *tōzišn* 'liability, obligation, payment, debt' (which we have already discussed above, section 4, pp. 306–310), and the less frequent *abāmdān* (lit. 'containing, holding, involving, comprising a loan'?).[254] The latter word is a late compound (with the suffix *-dān* < **-dāna-* 'vessel, receptacle, container'),[255] which might have had a specific technical meaning, referring maybe to a certain type

253 Comparable to the loan contracts differentiated in Roman law as commodatum (consisting of a gratuitous loan of a thing, usually a movable, for use, to be returned at the end of the loan) and depositum (goods handed over for safekeeping), see du Plessis/Borkowski 2010, pp. 298–302.

254 For attestations of *abām* and *abāmdān* see Macuch 1993, Index, p. 685. Different suggestions have been made for the etymology of this word (written ⟨ʾpʾm⟩), which is attested in several Iranian languages with the meaning of 'loan, debt' (Parth. ʾbʾmyẖ; BSogd. pʾmytʾy; pʾmytk; pʾmʾytk; Bactr. βαμδδιγο; see Cheung 2007, p. 178, for references) and NP *āvām/avām* (Steingass 1892, p. 117), *vām* (*ibid*., p. 1453) and *fām* (*ibid*., p. 905). Bartholomae (1918–1923, I, p. 43) reading *āpām*, assumes that there were two early Iranian forms of the term with the same last element, but two different preverbs: (1) **ā-i̯āma-* and (2) **upa-i̯āma-*, both meaning 'taking as one's own, seizing sth.; availing oneself of sth.' ('Ansichnehmen'; with reference to OP *āyasatā* [impf. ind. med. 3sg.] 'he availed himself of [troops]; he seized [lands]'; Bartholomae 1904, col. 1263, under 3) from Ir. √**i̯am* 'to hold; to stretch, reach out' (Cheung 2007, p. 211), Av. √^{1}*yam* 'to hold, grasp' (Bartholomae 1904, col. 1262; Kellens 1995, p. 46). He assumes that the second form, Ir. **upa-i̯āma-*, became MP **apām/*awām* > NP *vām*, and the first form Ir. **ā-i̯āma-* > MP **āi̯ām*, by adjustment ('Ausgleich') to the synonymous term > *āpām* > NP *āvām*. Similarly Klingenschmitt 1968, no. 722, argues that ⟨ʾpʾm⟩ and ⟨ʾpytkʾ⟩ 'borrowed' ('geliehen', in DkM 762.1ff.) belong together and both are derived from the root √*i̯am* with the preverb *apa-* or *upa-*: **a/upa- i̯āma-*, **a/upa-i̯ata-*. MacKenzie 1974, however, has explained the term ⟨ʾpytkʾ⟩, which he reads *apēdag*, differently: as derived from *apa-* + √*i* 'go away, apart', *i. e*, **apa-ita-ka-* 'gone apart', 'lost from its rightful place (property), stray (animal)', a meaning which seems to be confirmed by the long chapter on 'stray' animals, *apēdagānestān*, in *Dēnkard* 8 (DkM 762.1–766.2), thus indirectly contradicting Klingenschmitt's translation of ⟨ʾpytkʾ⟩ as 'borrowed'. Nyberg 1974 (p. 22) reading *apām*, explains the word from OIr. **apamna-* 'that which a p. (the lender) has to obtain (from the borrower), middle pt. of Av. *ap-*' ('to reach, to attain'; Bartholomae 1904, col. 70). The most likely derivation of the word has been suggested by Sims-Williams 2000, p. 185, and Cheung 2007, p. 177f. with references: from the IE root **H^2mei* 'to (ex)change'; Ir. √**Hmai*^{2} 'to change', Av. √*maii* + preceding **apa-* (in correspondence with Sanskrit √*may* 'to exchange, change' *[+*apa-] apamítya-*, *apāmítya-* 'something borrowed, debt').

255 On *-dān* and for other examples with this suffix see Durkin-Meisterernst 2014, p. 184, §368.

of loan, as in *xwāstag* ⟨NKSY'⟩ *ī abāmdān* 'loaned money, money debt'.[256] Another possible explanation is that the term designated a (money) loan granted in exchange for some kind of real security, a pawn or pledge (*graw*), which the lender had to return to the borrower, when the debt was repaid. This in any case is the background of a dispute, in which the moneylender (pledgee) refuses to return a pawn to the debtor (pledgor) on repayment of the debt, denying both the loan and the pledge: *az abāmdān ud grawīh nagīrā(y)* 'he refutes the debt and the pledge'.[257] But it is by no means certain that *abāmdān* exclusively referred to a money loan. Unfortunately none of the attestations of *abāmdān* are conclusive; the terms *wizīr ī abāmdān* and *abāmdān wizīr* 'loan contract; document of debt' (lit. 'document containing a loan') could have been in use for any kind of loan contract.

The most frequent term *abām* could also have been in use for all types of loans, but in the available sources it refers particularly to money loans (both with and without security). A formal classification of loan contracts (comparable to the 'real contracts' of Roman law) is not recognizable and does not seem to have existed.[258] This is in fact hardly surprising given the basic Zoroastrian idea that any (seriously intended) agreement is a contract, independent of its form or content, as we have seen above. Both informal and formal agreements were considered in religious law as contracts, protected by the lord of the covenant, Mithra, but in the further development of jurisprudence a distinction between the two became necessary in order to create legally enforceable agreements, which could not be easily denied or contested by one of the parties. The formal procedure described above of offer and acceptance (section 3 above, pp. 301–305) and the use of specific legal terms and formulae were indispensible

256 MHD 40.8f. (Macuch 1993, pp. 280, 285), MHD 89.8 (*ibid.*, pp. 569, 572). On the use of the ideogram ⟨NKSY'⟩ *xwāstag* with the exclusive meaning of 'money' in legal texts see p. 190 with further references.

257 MHD 102.1 (Macuch 1993, pp. 615, 623). On *abāmdān* see also MHD 78.17 (*ibid.*, pp. 518, 521); MHD 100.3 (*ibid.*, pp. 613, 621); MHD 107.3 (*ibid.*, pp. 642, 649). Most attestations, such as *abāmdān ī ēwar* 'legally binding loan' (MHD 3.3; *ibid.*, pp. 54, 56), are not conclusive.

258 On Justinian's classification into four types of real contracts or contracts *re* ('by the transfer of a thing': *mutuum*, *commodatum*, *depositum*, *pignus*) see Nicholas 1962, pp. 167–171, and du Plessis/Borkowski 2010, pp. 296–305 (besides the contract *litteris* 'by written record', pp. 304–306). The common characteristic of contracts *re* is that 'an obligation arises not from agreement alone, thought agreement is essential, but from the delivery of a *res corporalis*' (Nicholas 1962, p. 167). As far as I can see, only the Roman *pignus* 'pledge', a contract transferring property as security from the borrower to the lender by way of mortgage, can be compared to the Iranian 'pledge' (*graw*). Other forms of loans, or rather security for loans, denoted by the Iranian terms *passandārīh* 'deposit, pledge' (chosen by the moneylender; lit. 'holding a thing approved of'), and *jamdārīh* '(movable) pledge' (lit. 'holding a vessel') were evidently known in Sasanian law, but the material is far too sparse to allow any exact differentiations or comparisons (*e. g.*, with the Roman *depositum* or *commodatum*). The two Iranian terms are attested MHD 83.3–6 (Macuch 1993, pp. 538, 541); see also below, pp. 334–335.

tools for enabling the precise interpretation of contractual agreements as well as facilitating adjudication in cases of dispute. The terms *tōzišn* 'liability, obligation, payment' and *abām* 'loan, debt' are at times used synonymously (as in *tōzišn ī pidarān*, besides *abām ī pidarān* 'liabilities/debts of the forefathers', or *abām ud tōzišn* 'debt and liability'); *tōzišn*, however, usually stresses the financial obligation, the duty to effect a payment, as in *abām tōzišnīh* 'payment of a debt' and (using the corresponding verb) *abām tōxtan* 'to repay a debt'. The following technical terminology is attested with *abām* and *abāmdān* (on *tōzišn* see pp. 307–309 above):

Table 23. Overview of terminology: *abām*, *abāmdān*, *nihišn*[259]

Technical terms		Transactions		Persons involved	
abām ī pidarān	debts of the forefathers	*abām abāz dādan*	to pay back a loan	*abām-dādār*[260]	lender, creditor (lit. 'loan giver')
abām tōzišnīh	payment of a debt	*abām dādan*[261]	to pay (back) a loan	*abāmōmand*[262]	borrower, debtor
abām ud tōzišn	debt and liability	*abām hištan*[263]	to release from debt; grant a debt relief; remit a debt	*abām-xwēš*[264]	lender, creditor (lit. 'loan-owner')
abāmdān ī ēwar	legally binding loan	*abām stadan*	to take out a loan	*ān kē abām be dād*[265]	lender, creditor (lit. '[person] who granted the loan')
abāmdān wizīr; *wizīr ī abāmdān*	loan contract; document of debt	*abām tōxtan*	to repay a debt	*mard/mērag/ān kē abām stad/stānēd*[266]	borrower, debtor (lit. '[man] who took/takes out a loan')

259 For attestations in the Law-book see Macuch 1993, Index, p. 685, under *abām* and *abāmdān*. References to other texts and specific passages of the Law-book are given in the commentary to the translation.
260 RAF, *Pursišn* 68; on this passage see the extensive discussion in Macuch 2017b.
261 Tab. 18.5–7 (see Macuch 2017c, p. 183).
262 DkM 767.15,18,22; 770.4,8,10; 769.17.
263 MHD 2.7 (Macuch 1993, p. 40).
264 DkM 767.15,17,19; 770.4f., 10; 769.17.
265 MHD 2.1–2 (Macuch 1993, pp. 40, 42).
266 RAF 68 (see Macuch 2017b, pp. 357–358).

Technical terms		Transactions		Persons involved	
xwāstag ⟨NKSY'⟩ *ī abāmdān*	loaned money; money debt	*abām xwāstan*[267]	to demand (payment of) a debt		
nihišn[268] (Av. ^{2}*nəmah-*)	loan, credit (gratuitous loan, deposit, bailment?)			*mard ī nihišnōmand* (Av. *nəmaŋhant-*)	lender, creditor
				nihišn +*kē barišn* (Av. *nəmō. bara-*)	lender, creditor

The bulk of the entries in the Sasanian Law-book are concerned with disputes regarding the existence of a debt or lawsuits relating to the particular terms of a contract, liabilities of the family (*dūdag tōzišn*) and of the father/forefathers (*tōzišn/abām ī pidar/pidarān*), the position of joint debtors (*hamāg-tōzišn*), release from debt (*abām hišt*), and security for the loan (real and personal). These case studies discuss specific problems highlighting particular details of credit law, but the passages are far too concise and dispersed to allow a complete reconstruction of this rather complex field.

4.1.1 The loan contract without security

Neither the form nor the crucial requirements of a loan contract are elucidated (besides the basic rule that there must be an agreement based on offer and acceptance to make a contract, as noted in section 3 above), but our evidence allows the conclusion that different variants were possible: the agreement could be verbal (correlating to the Roman *stipulatio*) in the presence of witnesses or (particularly in the case of a gratuitous loan) without witnesses; the terms of the contract could be recorded and sealed by the contractors alone or including witnesses; the loan could be officially documented in written form and sealed with the seal of an official authority (this was presumably the usual procedure if a security was agreed upon, often in form of mortgage of the fruits of a specific property). A money loan could be granted with or without interest (*wuxš*). Besides these variations, generally two types of loan contracts can be distinguished:

1. loans based on real or personal security (which will be discussed under 4.1.2); and
2. loans granted without security (with which we are concerned in this section).

267 MHD 30.2 (Macuch 1993, pp. 220, 224).
268 Vd 4.1 (see pp. 312–316 above; also fn. 243 and 244).

Original examples for both these types of written and sealed contracts concerning money loans have fortunately survived in the Tabarestān collection, giving us rare insight into the exact wording of these documents, as will be seen below. Although this is not explicitly said, we can, moreover, reasonably infer from several case studies that the loan contract was a unilateral contract generating rights in one party (the lender) and duties in the other (the borrower): the lender had a right to the repayment or return of the loan, but no duties; the borrower had the duty to repay or return the loan, but no rights (in contrast to a bilateral contract—*e. g.*, a sale contract—which creates mutual obligations, each contractor having both rights and duties). As already elucidated above, two technical terms are employed for the written loan contract, *paymān* and *wizīr*, but whereas *paymān* can refer to both the verbal and the written agreement, *wizīr* (or, more precisely, *wizīr ī abāmdān* and *abāmdān wizīr* 'loan contract') is used exclusively of the written contract, confirmed with the seals of the promisor (or the contractors) as well as witnesses and official instances.[269]

In the Tabarestān texts the written contract is qualified somewhat more precisely by the compound *paymān-nāmag* 'document of contract', which explicitly denotes a scripted text, specifically a loan contract with the seal imprints not only of the promisor (or contractors) and witnesses, but of at least one legal authority in order to make it 'legally binding' (*ēwarīh rāy*).[270] Was there a difference between the written and sealed loan contracts called *paymān-nāmag* and *wizīr*? We can only speculate on the basis of the few surviving records that the former term was used of written contracts involving smaller transactions (as in Tab. 17 and 18, both loan contracts, discussed below), whereas *wizīr* might have been reserved for elaborate documents, involving larger loans and a considerable number of persons, as well as other matters that had an impact on the whole community, not only on the contractors themselves, as Tab. 24, a document called *zaytēn wizīr* 'olive (or: olive tree) document'. This complex document not only records meticulously the mortgage of fruits (*antichresis*) for a loan (in this case olives from different olive trees on a large number of parcels belonging to different families in two villages), it also affects the villages as a whole, as it contains the request of the parties to re-evaluate the produce of the trees after an earthquake.[271]

The exact form of a written contract (*paymān-nāmag*) recording a money loan without security, is illustrated by a surviving sample from Tabarestān. There can be no serious doubt that the Tabarestān documents are based on Sasanian law despite their late date (8th century), that they apply the same rules and regulations, use exactly the same technical terminology and generally

269 For attestations see p. 269, fn. 48.

270 Tab. 17.16–19; 18.26–28 (Weber 2017a, pp. 155–157; 152; and Macuch 2017c, pp. 189–190; 184 respectively).

271 The whole text of Tab. 24 is in Appendix X, pp. 704–710; for an extensive discussion of this impressive document see Macuch 2019b, pp. 132–146. See also p. 349 below.

continue Sasanian legal practice, even if there might have been a few minor changes over the decades after the downfall of the Sasanian empire due to the shift in power. We have hence good reason to assume that these original documents reflect to a large extent the legal practice of the Sasanian period and can be appropriately used to reconstruct some of the basic elements of credit law, especially in comparison with the case studies in the Sasanian Law-book. As most of the Tabarestān documents are concerned with matters of a village called *Asp-gurd, the texts presumably stem from an archive kept either in this village itself or in *Halīg, the place of residence of the 'Commander of the East' (*Xorāsān-spāhbed*) who is mentioned (as the sovereign or governor of Tabarestān) in Tab. 17.[272] In this specific loan contract the borrower or debtor is a man named Xwāst-Dēlān, son of Hormizd from the 'house' (*xānag*, *i. e*, 'lineage') of Dēl-Dēlān, resident in the village of *Asp-gurd. The moneylenders or creditors are men (*mardān*) belonging to an affluent family called Farrox-Xusrō from the same village (the same family reappears in Tab. 24). The borrower explicitly confirms that he is taking out a loan of 4 staters in the presence of (the official representing?) the 'Commander of the East' and other witnesses (or official representatives of the village) called 'the Elders' (*mehtarān*). He agrees to give back the whole sum on a specified date in the presence of the said 'Elders' to the creditors. He furthermore obliges himself to pay a fine (or interest, but neither *waxš* 'interest', nor *tāwān* 'fine' are used here) of 2 staters, 2 drachms if he fails to repay the whole sum on the fixed date, and, interestingly, an additional drachm 'for the water of the substance' (*bun āb*), a term that presumably relates to the upkeep of irrigation canals leading through several plots of land belonging to the collective property (*bun*) of the village.[273] On further default the debtor agrees to pay an additional fine or compensation (*tāwān*) of 4 staters to the creditors (that is, to double the sum of the loan). The contract (*paymān-nāmag*) is confirmed with the seal of the debtor. Seal and person are identified by the treasurer (*ganǰwar*) from the same village and the contract is sealed with an official seal of a legal authority (the name is missing due to a lacuna in the text) to make it legally binding (*ēwarīh rāy*).

The document enables us to reconstruct the (more or less) basic components of a written loan contract for which the debtor has offered no security (but this

272 For the original document and an extensive philological and contextual commentary see Weber 2017a, pp. 155–157, and Macuch 2017c, pp. 189–190; a transcription and translation of the text is in Appendix X, pp. 700–701. On the *Xorāsān-spāhbed* 'Commander of the East', the title of one of the four great Sasanian generals or commanders in charge of the military, see Gyselen 2001; on this title in the Tabarestān documents see Macuch 2024c). The name of this village was tentatively read by Weber as *Haspīn-raz, but later revised to *Asp gurd (see Weber 2020a, p. 175).

273 On irrigation canals see the corresponding chapter in the Sasanian Law-book, MHD 85.7–86.17 (Macuch 1993, pp. 549–559); on *bun* see Chapter III, pp. 197–202.

was certainly not the only conceivable form and we can assume that different variations were possible):

Table 24. Loan contract without security

	Basic elements of the contract	Particulars of Tab. 17[274]
1.	Exact date of recording	Day *Xwar*, month *Hordād*, year 77 PYE (= 728/729 CE)
2.	Name, affiliation, place of residence of the debtor	Debtor: Xwāst-Dēlān, son of Hormizd, from the house of Dēl-Dēlān; Residence: village of *Asp-gurd,
3.	Statement of the debtor (promisor): – confirmation of the obligation – total sum of the loan – name of the creditor(s) – place of residence of the creditor(s) – witnesses (officials) – specified date of repayment – fine (interest) to be paid to the creditor(s) on default – compensation (*tāwān*) to be paid on further default	Xwāst-Dēlān declares: – 'I have an obligation regarding money, 4 staters, which …I take' (*xwāstag* ⟨NKSY'⟩ *arz s[atēr] 4 ī sazēd … ī …stānēm…*) – 4 staters – men called Farrox-Xusrō (*mardān ī Farrox-Xusrō nām*) (= lineage of Farrox-Xusrō) – village of *Asp-gurd – 'the Elders' (*mehtarān*) – day *Ardwahišt*, month *Tīr*, year 77 PYE – 2 staters, 2 drachms, one additional drachm for the water of the *bun* – 4 staters
4.	Name, profession and residence of the witness who identifies the debtor and his seal	Dērā, treasurer (*ganǰwar*), resident in *Asp-gurd
5.	Seal of the debtor (promisor)	Sealed by Xwāst-Dēlān
6.	Seal of an official to make the document legally binding (*ēwarīh rāy*)	Sealed by (lacuna in the text; name of an official)

Although obviously no security had been granted for the loan in Tab. 17, the interests of the creditors were safeguarded by the testimony of reliable witnesses (the 'Elders', or, if *mehtar* is a synonym for *wuzurg* 'Grandee(s)', nobles residing in the region), in whose presence the transfer of the money took place, and by the written document itself, sealed by the debtor and, most importantly, by an official authority to make it 'legally binding' (*ēwarīh rāy*). The seal of an official was a crucial element of the written contract enabling a creditor to prove beyond doubt that a payment obligation indeed existed (on the function of seals see above pp. 286–301).[274]

A written and sealed contract for a loan without security does not seem to have been necessarily the norm, as we may conclude from the large number of cases in the Law-book in which one of the main problems in a lawsuit was to prove the existence (or non-existence) of a liability (these cases caused legal problems, but were obviously of special interest to the compiler of the Law-book and might not represent the usual procedure). The problem is particularly discussed in the context of liabilities of succession after the demise of a *kadag-xwadāy*, when a family, represented by the legal guardian together with the widow of the deceased, the *kadag-bānūg*, is involved in a lawsuit regarding an obligation, either as debtor or as creditor. If the opposing party denied the liability, the main point was to prove that a claim indeed existed: *abām būd paydāg kunišn* 'the existence of a debt has to be proved'. Under certain circumstances the alleged creditor was obliged to present some kind of 'reliable, certain, binding' (*ēwar*) proof that his claim was legitimate (see below pp. 360–364).[275] We have, however, good reason to assume that a written contract, containing the exact terms of an agreement, was a necessity (and probably the norm) if a money loan was based on real security, especially if the fruits of a property were mortgaged, as will be seen in the next sections.

4.1.2 Real and personal security

Different forms of securing debts with the primary purpose of ensuring the repayment of a loan are known and practised in all advanced legal systems. A person, who lends money (the lender or creditor) to another individual (the borrower or debtor) could request some kind of additional guarantee for the loan instead of just having to trust the borrower and to rely on his willingness and ability to return the money (the principle debt with or without interest) on a specified date. The moneylender would wish to be protected against loss, against the possibility that the borrower might be insolvent or inaccessible when called upon to repay the debt. The debtor would usually have to provide some kind of guarantee or security for the borrowed sum, which could be, in legal terms, either real or personal.[276] Real security grants recourse to an identified property or fund of the debtor, entitling the creditor to retain or recover this property and also to sell it in satisfaction of the debt. Forms of real security known in Sasanian law—as in many other legal systems—are pledge (or pawn), deposit, mortgage and hypothec. Personal security, on the other hand, permits a creditor to look to a third party for satisfaction, that is, he is given additional

274 The whole text is in Appendix X, pp. 700–701.
275 MHD 15.12–16.1 (Macuch 1993, pp. 140, 143). See also below, p. 362.
276 On real and personal security in Roman law see Nicholas 1962, pp. 149–151.

recourse to another person or several other persons (the surety or sureties). The surety (or guarantor/warrantor) commits himself to guarantee in some form for the debtor, hereby extending the group of persons against whom the creditor can assert his claims, increasing his chances of recovering the loan. In Sasanian law guarantee or suretyship could take a variety of different forms, which presumably reflect different stages in the historical development of personal security, but obviously all continued to exist side by side in the Sasanian period and can be differentiated according to the formal words used in loan contracts.

These diverse methods of securing a loan are all attested in the legal sources by specific terms, which distinguish precisely between different kinds of real security, on the one hand, and personal security, *i. e*, suretyship in its diverse forms, on the other. The term *graw*, *grawīh* 'pledge' or 'pawn' (comparable to *pignus* in Roman law), designates an item of property (both movable or immovable, also an animal or slave) transferred by the borrower (pledgor) to the lender (or pledgee/pledge-holder) as security for the payment of a debt or performance of an obligation (the term is often attested in the context of legal proceedings).[277] The lender or pledgee (*grawdār*) is entitled to hold the pledge in his possession until payment (or performance of contract) and to sell it if the debtor (pledgor) fails to repay the loan at a specified date. The pledged item remains, however, in the ownership of the debtor/pledgor until it is sold and he is entitled to redeem it by fulfilling his obligations towards the lender/pledge-holder (by repaying the loan or performing in some other manner according to the terms of the agreement). Besides *graw* other expressions taken from daily usage are employed as technical terms to designate this type of security, such as *ǰām*, *ǰāmag* (lit. 'vessel, goblet'), *ǰāmdārīh* (lit. 'holding a vessel') for a 'movable' pledge or deposit (in contrast to an immovable security); *nibāg/nabāg* 'hostage', used of a person or 'living' pawn, and *passandārīh*, (lit. 'holding a thing approved of'), a pawn or deposit that had been chosen by the creditor. These terms are only mentioned *en passant* and not explained, but they seem to have originally designated certain items or persons that were usually pawned, in any case forms of security very similar (if not even identical) to the *graw* (which will be discussed in section 4.1.2.1 below).

Two other different types of mortgage were known: *āgraw* (or with the abstract ending, *āgrawīh*; comparable to, but not necessarily identical with, the *hypotheca*)[278] was a promise of title regarding the substance (*bun*) of a specified property of the debtor (mortgagor). It seems that, in contrast to *graw*, the mortgaged item (consisting of land, houses or real estate, but also chattels) was

277 On *pignus* 'pledge, pawn' see du Plessis/Borkowski 2010, pp. 302–303; Nicholas 1962, pp. 151–152.

278 On the development of the *hypotheca* in Roman law from *pignus* see du Plessis/Borkowski 2010, pp. 303–304; Nicholas 1962, pp. 152–153.

not transferred to the creditor (mortgagee), but remained in the possession (and ownership) of the borrower (mortgagor). The lender (mortgagee) was only entitled to take possession (and ownership) of the 'substance' under mortgage (land, house, estate, animal, slave, trees etc.) in the event of a default, *i. e*,, if the debtor failed to repay the loan on time (the exact rights of the creditor are, however, difficult to extract from the sparse material). Another technical term used in the context of *āgraw(īh)* is *pēš-tōzišnīh*, lit. 'advance payment, prepayment', another undefined word, which could denote an idea similar to that of a 'charge' in this specific context, a type of security (created by the deposit of a title document or another document recording the security provided by the debtor) conferring legal rights on the creditor which prevailed over claims others might put forward (including heirs and beneficiaries) with regard to the mortgaged property (see pp. 339–340 below).

The *āgraw(īh)* type of mortgage was distinguished from the *grawagān*, *grawagānīh* (or *antichresis*), by which only the produce (*bar*) of a certain property was mortgaged. The creditor (mortgagee, *grawagāndār*) only had access to the fruits of the mortgaged property, consisting usually of the harvest of agricultural land, crop yields of trees (olive trees and date palms are mentioned) or vineyards, but also the rent of a house, the produce of an animal, the work force of a slave, among others. The creditor (mortgagee) had the right to a certain amount of the fruits of this property in lieu of interest (and in repayment of the debt), but the legal status of the principal or substance (*bun*) itself remained unchanged and was not included in this—presumably frequent—form of securing a loan. These three main forms of real security (*graw*, *āgraw* and *grawagān*) are distinguished meticulously in the sources as various means of ensuring the performance of a loan contract in accordance with the provisions put down in the agreement.

If the debtor provided personal security, the obligations of the surety or sureties (*pāyandān*) could take different forms according to the formulae employed in the loan contract. The surety (or warrantor/guarantor) could be required to guarantee that the debtor will remain in his place of residence and be readily accessible for the creditor, or he could be obliged to deliver the debtor (or another person agreed upon in the contract) to the creditor. Other forms of security, still current in modern legal systems, were the indemnity and guarantee: the surety could be charged directly for the debt by the lender (according to an agreement comparable to the indemnity) or he could have a secondary obligation to satisfy the creditor only if the principal debtor was in default (as in the guarantee). In the latter case the surety could only be held responsible for payment if the debtor failed to fulfil his obligations towards the creditor. Several debtors in a partnership (*hambāyīh*) could also agree to act at the same time as co-warrantors (*ham-pāyandān*). In this case they were jointly liable and the creditor could demand full payment from any of the persons under contract, who could in turn demand regress from the other joint debtors.

Table 25. Overview of terminology: real and personal security

Real security		Personal security	
āgraw, *āgrawīh*	*hypotheca*; mortgage of the substance (*bun*)	*ham-pāyandān*	co-warrantor; co-guarantor; co-surety; joint surety
graw, *grawīh*	pledge, pawn	*ham-pāyandānīh*	co-warranty; co-guarantee; joint suretyship
grawagān, *grawagānīh*	*antichresis*; mortgage of the fruits (*bar*)	*pāyandānīh*	suretyship, guarantee
grawagāndār	mortgagee, mortgage-holder (of a *grawagān*)	*pāyandān*	surety, guarantor, warrantor
grawdār[279]	pledgee, pawnee, pledge-holder (of a *graw*)		
ǰām, *ǰāmag*, *ǰāmdārīh*	(movable) pledge, pawn, deposit		
ǰāmdār	pledgee, pawnee, pledge-holder (of the movable pawn; *ǰām*)		
nibāg/nabāg	(living) pledge, pawn, hostage		
passandārīh	deposit, pledge (chosen by the creditor)		
pēš-tōzišnīh	advance payment, prepayment; charge		

4.1.2.1 The pledge or pawn (*graw*)

As we have already noted, several technical terms are used in this context, but the general expression for an item of the borrower's movable or immovable property, which was transferred by the borrower (either directly or by means of a sealed document) as security to the lender is *graw*.[280] This in any case is the term usually employed in the more or less abstract discussions of the Lawbook, but a few concrete objects that were transferred as pawns are also mentioned. These include movables, such as *ǰām*, *ǰāmag* 'vessel, goblet, chalice' (a term which was, however, also used in the figurative sense of 'movable pawn',

279 DkM 708.21.

280 From the Iranian root √**grabH* 'to grab, seize, take' (Cheung 2007, p. 119ff.); Av./OP √*grab* 'to grab, seize, take' (Bartholomae 1904, col. 526–528; Kellens 1995, p. 20f.); Armenian loan-word *graw* 'pledge, pawn' (Hübschman 1897, p. 131); NP *girau* 'a wager, stake, bet, pledge, pawn, deposit, earnest' (Steingass 1892, p. 1085).

see below), 'living' beings (*uštānōmand*), *i. e*, animals and slaves (*anšahrīg*) and persons taken as hostage (*nibāg/nabāg*), as well as immovable property, consisting of land (*zamīg*) and estates (*dastgird*). The borrower retained ownership of the *graw*, but the lender received legal possession until the loan was fully paid, although we can assume that the borrower could keep physical control of the pledged item in certain cases, particularly if it consisted of immovable property, a piece of land (*zamīg*) or an estate (*dastgird*), the produce of which was mortgaged, as we may conclude from the following statement:

> MHD 85.4–5
> *ka zamīg-ē(w) graw kunēd u-š pas xānīg andar ahe(n)zēd xānīg-iz grawagāndār dārišn.*
>
> 'If he (= the borrower) pledges (*graw kunēd*) a (piece of) land and then draws up a source (of water) on it, then the source is also in the possession (*dārišn*) of the mortgagee (lender, *grawagāndār*).'[281]

Short as it is, this sentence conveys several important details. It first informs us, that not only movables, but also immovable property (in this case land, *zamīg*) could be pledged, second, that the borrower retained physical control of the land, since he had the possibility of drawing up a source of water on it after pledging it, and finally, that the creditor or mortgagee (*grawagāndār*), who received the pledge also acquired possession (*dārišn*) of the water source (*xānīg*) drawn up by the borrower, even though the source was provided after concluding the loan contract. We can further assume that the transfer of an immovable pawn, as in this case, took place by some kind of written and sealed document, which—to judge by the technical term used here—gave the mortgagee (*grawagāndār*), the right to use the fruits (*bar*) or part of the produce of the land instead of interest and (or) in repayment of the loan (on documents recording *grawagān*-mortgage see section 4.1.2.3, pp. 343–349 below).

The exact wording of a loan contract allows further conclusions. In this case the borrower transfers possession of the pledge (*graw*) consisting of an estate (*dastgird*) and a slave (*anšahrīg*, who presumably works on the estate) as security to the lender and agrees that the latter should be granted ownership of the mortgaged property if the debt is not repaid on a specified date, using the following words in the loan contract (*paymān*):

> MHD 38.14–16
> *uzid ān zamān ka ān xwāstag* ⟨NKSY'⟩ *nē wizārd ēstēd ān dastgird ud anšahrīg ōy xwāstag* ⟨NKSY'⟩ *rāy to xwēš*
>
> 'When the (contractual) date passes, if that money has not been paid, (then), due to the money(-loan), the estate and the slave (are) your own (*tō xwēš*).'[282]

281 Macuch 1993, pp. 281, 286.
282 Macuch 1993, pp. 279, 283. Compare MHD 89.11–15 (*ibid.* pp. 570, 573) with a similar statement in the loan contract: *ka xwāstag* ⟨NKSY'⟩ *ī Farrox az Mihrēn abām stad ud pad zamān ī nāmčišt dād rāy ud ēn-iz paymān kard kū agar pad zamān dahom ēnyā*

The borrower explicitly agrees in this statement to grant ownership of the security (the estate, *dastgird*) and the collateral (the slave, *anšahrīg*) to the moneylender if he fails to repay the loan on a specified date. Was the lender usually (or always) entitled to (immediate) ownership on default of the borrower or did the latter have to expressly agree to these terms by including a corresponding statement? Our sources do not allow any general conclusions, but in this specific case (and MHD 89.11–15, see fn. 282) the statement of the debtor clearly allows immediate or automatic foreclosure, that is, the mortgagor (borrower) loses ownership of the mortgaged property to the lender if he fails to keep the specified payment date. The precise wording of the contract would rather indicate that the right of the lender to acquire ownership of the pawn by foreclosure had to be expressly conceded by the borrower. Otherwise the lender would only retain possession until the debt was paid, but not ownership, even if the debtor missed the deadline (this, in any case, seems to have been the procedure in cases of *grawagān*-mortgage, but there were exceptions, see below). Our sentence (referring to a contract that allows automatic foreclosure) continues to discuss a specific case in which one part of the pawn, namely the slave (*anšahrīg*) assigned as collateral (?), perishes before the contractual date: in this case the lender has both the right to take ownership of the mortgaged estate or to keep it as a pawn until the loan has been repaid. As this passage is included in a chapter on *antichresis* (*grawagānīh*), we can furthermore infer that the lender would have had a right to the produce of the estate, on which the slave worked (on *glebae adscripti*, slaves bound to the soil, see Chapter II, p. 107 above). The death of the slave would reduce or terminate completely the income granted as interest or part-payment of the debt, hence changing the terms of the contract and permitting the lender (mortgagee) to choose between the two options of either taking ownership of the estate or continuing to keep it as mortgage with a right to the fruits (on *antichresis* see section 4.1.2.3, pp. 343–349 below).

Foreclosure, *i. e*, the loss of the pledged property in default of payment, was not necessarily final even in severe cases of misconduct on the part of the debtor, as we may conclude from another passage. In this specific instance the owner of the pledged property (*ōy kē xwāstag xwēš*), *i. e*, the debtor (pledgor), steals the pledge from the creditor (pledge-holder). Although the stolen property is not concretely named in the sentence, we can assume that it must have been a movable pledge, *e. g.*, an animal or a slave, whose produce or work force was mortgaged (the term *grawagānīh* is used). In this case the debtor loses the pledge to the *radān* (*xwāstag ō radān appār*), the legal authorities in charge of adjudicating these cases (particularly theft). The *rad* has in turn the discretion to allow

xwāstag ⟨hw'stk'⟩ *tō xwēš.* 'When F. has taken out money as a loan from M. and has made a contract regarding the date of payment and the (following statement): "When I give it (= the money) back on time (it is not), otherwise the property (is) your own."' On the construction with *agar* (or *ka*) … *ēnyā* 'if (not) … otherwise' see Macuch 1993, pp. 576–577, no. 8.

the debtor to reopen foreclosure (despite the theft, which was considered as a grave offence)[283] and to regain his property by settling the debt. The statement of the *rad* reopening foreclosure is addressed to the debtor as follows:

MHD 38.11
drahm be wizār ud xwāstag abāz stān čē man xwēš.
"Pay the drachms and take back the property, as it is my own."[284]

These words spoken by the *rad* unfortunately do not transmit clearly, whether the *rad* is as legal authority himself the (temporary) owner of the pledge (until the case is resolved) or rather speaks in the name of the creditor, who has taken ownership of the security (both could be meant by *man xwēš* 'my own'), but they leave no doubt that the debtor is given the option to retrieve ownership of the mortgaged property by repaying the loan, despite the offence he has committed. The creditor likewise loses possession of mortgaged property to the legal authorities (*ō radān appār* 'it [is] lost to the *radān*') if he commits an offence regarding this property, but he nevertheless retains his right to the payment of the debt.[285] If the pledge was lost (*graw apēdag bawēd*) after being transferred to the creditor, he could not ask for a replacement or a substitute (*guharīg*) from the debtor, but if a judge (*dādwar*) confirmed the claim of the creditor, the latter was entitled to a replacement.[286]

The borrower had various options to avoid losing the pawn. He could redeem the pledge by repaying the debt in instalments instead of giving back the whole sum at once: for 'every drachm he pays' (*har-ē[w] drahm ī be wizārēd*) a corresponding equivalent (*marīhā čand*) of the pledged property 'has to be released from pledge' (*az grawīh be hilišn*).[287] The debtor could, moreover, authorize a third party to redeem the pledge as long as it was still in his ownership[288] with the words:

283 See DkD 544.14–20/DkM 717.1–6: *abar garān wināhīh ī mard nibāg az an-ērān abāz duzīdan ka-š xwēš pus* 'and on the great sin of a man stealing back a pawn/hostage (*nibāg*) from non-Iranians, (even) if it is his own son'. This passage revealing that family members could also be offered as security, is translated and commented below, p. 333 (see also section 4.1.2.4 on suretyship, pp. 349–359).

284 MHD 38.9–11 (Macuch 1993, pp. 278, 283).

285 MHD 89.3–5 (Macuch 1993, pp. 567, 572).

286 MHD 39.17–40.1 (Macuch 1993, pp. 280, 285). The term *apēdag* 'lost' is used prominently of animals in a section of the *Dēnkard* translated and commented by MacKenzie 1974 (*pah ī apēdag* 'stray sheep'; *pah ud stor ī apēdag* 'a stray sheep or larger animal'; *apēdagdār* 'finder-cum-keeper'). On the pledging of animals see also Īšōʿbōxt, Book V, Chapter VII, § 10 (Sachau 1914, p. 159).

287 MHD 85.2–4 (Macuch 1993, pp. 281, 286).

288 According to MHD 38.1: *padixšāy kardan pad čiš ī xwēš kār* 'granting authorization is (only) effective with regard to a thing in one's ownership'. That is, the debtor can only authorize a third person to redeem a pawn as long as he is still the owner and it has not yet been sold by the creditor or transferred into his ownership in satisfaction of the debt (Macuch 1993, pp. 278, 282).

MHD 37.15–16
kū-m drahm wizārdan ud ēn xwāstag az graw abāz wēxtan rāy Mihrēn pādixšāy kard.

'I have authorized Mihrēn to pay the drachms and to redeem this property from pledge.'[289]

If the person authorized by the pledgor (debtor) paid back the debt, the loan contract was considered as fulfilled and the pledge released by the creditor, but the authorized person was in turn entitled to retain possession of the pledge (*pad grawīh dāštan pādixšāy*) until the debtor reimbursed his expenses.[290]

Another method the creditor could employ to retrieve a loan was to re-pledge the mortgaged property. If the debtor (as the owner of the pledge) gave his consent, the creditor could in turn mortgage the property he had taken as a pledge (or part of it) as security to a third person in exchange for the sum he had lent to the debtor. In order to take back the mortgaged property, the debtor would then pay the debt directly to the second mortgagee, not to the original creditor.[291] In a case discussed in the Law-book the 'owner of the substance' (*bun-xwēš*) of a certain (unnamed) property takes out a loan and pledges the usufruct (*grawagānīh*) of this property (consisting *e.g.*, of crop yields; the fruits of olive-trees; the wine from a vineyard, the work force of a slave or animal, etc.) as security for the debt. The debtor (or *bun-xwēš*) fails to repay the loan on the contracted date, but he agrees, that the creditor re-pledge the *antichresis* to a second mortgagee to cover payment of the debt. If the debtor wishes to take back possession (*dārišn*) of the mortgaged property, then the first mortgagee (creditor) is legally authorized (*pādixšāy*) to refer him (the debtor) to the second mortgagee with the words *drahm xwad wizār xwāstag xwad wēz* 'Pay back the money yourself! Redeem the property yourself!', that is, the debtor is told to address the second mortgagee directly and redeem the security from the latter.[292]

289 Macuch 1993, pp. 277, 282.

290 See also MHD 38.1–3 (Macuch 1993, pp. 278, 282).

291 This is the exact procedure also described in Īšōʿbōxt, Book V, Chapter VII, § 16 (Sachau 1914, p. 163) and § 11 (4th paragraph; Sachau 1914, p. 161). Both paragraphs are cited in Macuch 1993, p. 288.

292 This is a difficult passage, which I am citing in full: MHD 39.12–16: *ka bun-xwēš drahm kē xwāstag padiš graw pad zamān ī nāmčišt bē dād rāy abāg ān mard paymān kunēd ayāb ka grawagāndār drahm xwāhēd abāz nē dahēd ud pas grawagāndār andar +āgāhīh ud dānišn ī bun-xwēš xwāstag graw kunēd ud agar ēw-bār grawagāndār xwāstag graw kunēd bun-xwēš dārišn ī xwāstag ī xwāhēd grawagāndār pādixšāy ka gōwēd kū drahm xwad wizār xwāstag xwad wēz.* 'When the owner of the substance (= borrower/debtor) makes a deal with a man (= creditor/mortgagee/mortgage-holder) regarding a specific deadline for (re)payment of money (*drahm*) for which a thing was given in pledge or when the mortgagee (creditor) requests the money (owed) and (the debtor = owner of the substance) does not return it, and then the mortgagee with the awareness and knowledge of the owner of the substance (debtor) makes the (same) property over in (some)

Although the debtor retained ownership of the pledge, he was not allowed to alienate it as long as it was in the possession of the creditor. However, in specific cases (of emergency or when another debt had to be paid and the debtor had no other property) a distinction was made between the property mortgaged as *hypotheca* (*āgraw*) and the *antichresis* (*grawagān*): the borrower was *not* allowed to sell the former (the substance of which was mortgaged), but he could, if need be, sell the latter, as only the fruits had been mortgaged (see below under *āgraw*).[293] In correspondence with this ruling, a debtor could manumit his slave during the period in which the work force of the latter was mortgaged as *antichresis* (*grawagānīh*). If his master (the debtor) was *not* insolvent and paid back the sum for which he had transferred the slave as security to the creditor, the slave was immediately (*pad gyāg* 'on the spot') considered as free (*āzād*). The slave himself could supply the money for his manumission, but the creditor could continue to hold him as a pledge until the whole sum had been paid.[294]

Other technical terms in this context evolved from the designations of concrete items that could be offered as *graw*. As we have alredy noted above, *ǰām*, *ǰāmag*,[295] lit. 'vessel, goblet, chalice', denotes one of the (probably usual) objects that could be pledged as security, but it also stands figuratively for all kinds of 'movable' pawns (as opposed to immovables); *ǰāmdār*, lit. 'vessel-holder', for the 'pawnee, pledgee' (besides *grawdār*). A passage of the Law-book discussing a lawsuit reveals clearly that *ǰām* (written ⟨M'NH⟩) was employed (in its concrete or figurative sense) for a pawn that had been conveyed into the possession of the lender (pledgee), but had to be transferred back to the borrower, when the debt was fully paid. In this case the debtor is the plaintiff, who sues the creditor for not returning a pledge after the loan had been repaid with the words:

MHD 101.17–102.1
kū-m ǰām ē(w) ī pad 10 pad tō graw kard ud 10 be padīr ud ǰām abāz dah

---

pledge (of his own), and—since the mortgagee makes the property over in pledge (and) the owner of the substance (debtor) requests the possession of the property (in pledge)—then the mortgagee is authorized to say: "Pay back the money yourself! Redeem the property yourself!"' (Macuch 1993, pp. 280, 284f.).

293 MHD 38.11–13 (Macuch 1993, pp. 278, 283). The sentence is discussed p. 337 below.

294 MHD 39.2–5 (Macuch 1993, pp. 279, 284).

295 The form *ǰām* (Av. *yama-*, Bartholomae 1904, col. 1264, 'Glas, Glasgefäss' [glass, glass vessel]), when used as a technical term for 'pledge, pawn', is always written either ⟨yy'm⟩ (with double ⟨yy⟩ as in DkM 710.16, 715.15, 716.16; and MHD 83.4 in ⟨yy'md'l⟩ *ǰāmdār*, also DkM 713.15, 16) or as a heterogram ⟨M'NH⟩ (MHD 101.17, 102.1, 2). Since the heterogram corresponds exactly to the word used in Īšō'bōxt's Law-book (Book V, Chapter VII; Sachau 1914, pp. 154–165), Syr. *mānā*, for 'pawn, pledge', we can assume that the technical term for 'pawn' in the Pahlavi original of this work was *ǰām* (possibly written as a heterogram). Was there a distinction between *ǰām* (written ⟨yy'm⟩ or ⟨M'NH⟩) and *ǰāmag* (written regularly ⟨y'mk⟩)? If so, it is not easily detected, as the latter term seems to be used in exactly the same sense of '(movable) pawn, pledge' (MHD 73.10; MHDA 26.4, 8; 27.11; 30.12, 13; DkM 725.17).

> 'I have pawned (*graw kard*) a vessel (= movable pawn, *ǰām*) for (a loan) of 10 (st./dr.): take the 10 (st./dr.) and give back the vessel (= movable pawn).'[296]

The term is also attested in *Dēnkard* 8 in several passages, which, taken together, shed light on the twofold use of this expression, despite the short synoptic character of the entries:

> DkD 541.17–18 (DkM 713.15–16)
> *abar ǰām nihādan ǰāmdār ud ǰām 2 pēš be nihād abar pahikārdan ī pad ǰāmdār čē andar im dar.*
>
> 'On depositing a vessel (= pledge, *ǰām*) with the vessel-holder (= pledgee, *ǰāmdār*) and (on) depositing two pledges in advance; on litigating with the vessel-holder (= pledgee, *ǰāmdār*) and that which (is) in this chapter.'
>
> DkD 544.9–11 (DkM 716.16–18)
> *abar čiyōn nihādan ī uštānōmand pad ǰām ud ka pad a-wināhīh ī ǰāmdār be mīrēd u-š rēš pad kār ud čē andar im dar.*
>
> 'On how to deposit an animated being (*uštānōmand*) as pawn (*ǰām*) and (on the consequences) when it dies without guilt on the part of the pledgee (*ǰāmdār*) and (when) an injury (*rēš*) has taken place (*pad kār*) and that which (is) in this chapter.'

While *ǰām* could still have its original concrete meaning of 'vessel' in the first passage, it becomes quite clear that it is employed in a figurative sense in the second one, as it is explicitly used of an 'animated' or 'living' being (*uštānōmand*), *i. e*, an animal or slave. The summary given here obviously refers to a chapter discussing the legal consequences if a living pledge perishes during the period in which it is transferred to the pledgee (*ǰāmdār*). It furthermore implies that the legal consequences for the pledgee would have been different, depending on his conduct towards the pawn and on whether an injury (*rēš*) had caused its death. This would presuppose a duty to safeguard the property transferred as security.

Another term which seems to have be used particularly of the 'living' pawn or 'hostage', *i. e*, a person held as security, is *nibāg/nabāg* (written ⟨np'k⟩), which does not occur in the Law-book, but is attested in *Dēnkard* 8 and in the Paikuli inscription as well as in Sogdian np'k, Parthian nyp'k, Bactrian ναβαγο, νιβαγο, Khotanese *nvī-* and NP *navā* with the same meaning.[297] One of the passages in the concise synopsis of the *Dēnkard* is, as far as I can see, the only longer entry in which this word occurs:

296 Macuch 1993, pp. 615, 623.

297 See Sims-Williams 2000, p. 206 (< *ni-pāka-*; Ir. **paH¹* 'to protect, guard, pasture', Cheung 2007, p. 288f.) and Skjærvø 1983a, p. 114. In the Bactrian texts the term refers to both an object as pledge or pawn (immovable property in L21', V24 and W20; Sims-Williams 2000, pp. 67–68; 118–119; 130–131 respectively), as well as to a person or hostage (a slave in P8; *ibid.* pp. 83–84; the son of one of the contractors in ac4, *ibid.* pp. 152–153). On np'k in the Sogdian marriage contract see Livshits 2015, p. 25, and commentary p. 33.

DkD 544.14–20 (DkM 717.1–6)
abar graw dād ī marzānān ō an-ērān ud pašn xwāst ud abar čiš-iz nē [nē] arzistan ī an-ēr arzōmand ud abzōnīg arz būd ī ka pad (ni)bāg be (ō) ērān dahēnd ud frāy arzīh ī tigl-ē(w) ka pad gyāg ī nibāg pad graw az an-ērān be stānēnd čiyōn dāštan ī har 2 ud abar garān wināhīh ī mard nibāg az an-ērān abāz duzīdan ka-š xwēš pus.

"On people living near the boundary (*marzānān*) transferring a pledge (*graw*) to non-Iranians and requesting a contract. And on not evaluating (*nē arzistan*) a thing which (is) valuable to the non-Iranian (*an*-ēr) and is increased in value, when they transfer it for a hostage (*nibāg*) to Iranians. And on the greater value of a youth (*tigl-ē[w]*)[298] when he is taken in place of a hostage (*nibāg*) as pawn (*graw*) from non-Iranians; on how (it is) to possess (*dāštan*) both. And on the great sin of a man stealing back a hostage (*nibāg*) from non-Iranians, (even) if it is his own son."

This remarkable (but unfortunately far too short) summary reveals, unsurprisingly, that legal transactions between Iranians (*ērān*) and non-Iranians (*an-ērān*) took place and that these were subject to specific rulings, which are only rudimentarily transmitted in this text. It first informs us that contracts (*pašn*) could be drawn between persons living near the boundary of Iran (*marzānān*) and foreigners or subjects of other countries (*an-ērān* seems to be used in this sense here) involving legal undertakings for which a pledge (*graw*) was transferred as security.[299] Unfortunately the next passages mentioning hostages (*nibāg*) are far too concise to allow precise conclusions. They could belong to the same legal field of security, as especially the last part of this sentence seems to indicate, but could also include rules on taking and releasing all kinds of hostages, including persons taken captive (to be returned against ransom money) or prisoners of war. Hostages were obviously taken by both sides and released by specific transactions, which could be perchance disadvantageous for one of the parties involved (if my understanding of the text is correct): (1) A hostage (*nibāg*) (taken by an Iranian) is released to a non-Iranian in exchange for a valuable object, which rises in value after being transferred, but the object had not been evaluated according to its worth. (2) Iranians take a young man as a pawn (*graw*) in replacement of a hostage (*nibāg*), but the youth is more worth (*frāy arz*) than the hostage. What are the legal consequences, when both (the pawn and the hostage) are held in possession (*dāštan*)? We can only speculate on the background of these two difficult

298 This word, written ⟨tgl⟩, does not seem to have been detected so far in any other Pahlavi text. The spelling corresponds exactly with that of *tigr* 'arrow', which cannot be meant in this context by any stretch of the imagination. The reading suggested here is based on NP *tigl* 'a handsome youth' (Steingass 1892, p. 320), but is doubtful.

299 The Law-book confirms these transactions with non-Iranians (*an-ērān*). According to MHD 38.1–3 a person who buys back (*abāz xīrēd*) a thing (*xwāstag*) (presumably a pawn belonging to an Iranian) from non-Iranians (*an-erān*) is entitled to keep it as a pawn (*pad grawīh dāštan*) until the sum he has paid (*ān ī be wizārd*) is given back to him by the owner of the property (see Macuch 1993, pp. 278, 282). On *ēr* see Chapter II, pp. 113–117.

passages, but the problem referred to here seems to have been that of overreaching or taking advantage of a foreign business partner and the legal consequences that followed for the parties involved (which are not transmitted due to the synoptical character of the text). The final passage is the only conclusive one: (3) A man is not permitted to steal back (*abāz duzīdan*) a hostage (*nibāg*) he has transferred to non-Iranians, even if it is his own son. The (unexplained) idea behind this last statement is clear enough: the Zoroastrian is obliged to honour contracts under all circumstances, also those with foreigners and non-Zoroastrians. Once a deal requiring a security is closed with a non-Iranian and a person has been transmitted as a pawn or hostage, the contract has to be observed, despite the fact that delivering an Iranian to a non-Iranian is generally considered as a 'grave offence' (*garān wināhīh*).[300] This is not necessarily a contradiction to our statement, since stealing the hostage is likewise regarded as a 'grave offence' (*garān wināhīh*), *i. e*, a breach of contract, even in the case of an Iranian father who has transferred his own son to a foreign (or: non-Zoroastrian) business partner as security.

The term *passandārīh*[301] occurs only in one passage of the Law-book together with *grawagānīh*, '*antichresis*', and *ǰāmdārīh* '(movable) pawn', in the context of lawsuits on loans and property issues, in which the sued party (defendant) has to reveal how he gained ownership of the disputed property. The statement of the defendant can contain the following explanations:

> MHD 83.4–5
> *ka az kas bērōn pad grawagānīh ayāb pad passandārīh ayāb pad ǰāmdārīh ayāb pad any ēwēnag man dāšt ō xwēšīh ī man mad.*
>
> 'When I held it (= the disputed object) from (that) person as an *antichresis* (*grawagānīh*) or as a (chosen) pawn (*passandārīh*) or as a (movable) pawn (*ǰāmdārīh*) or in some other manner, it (then) came into my ownership.'[302]

Although the word is not defined, the three statements explaining the acquisition of ownership all point originally to some form of pledge or mortgage (*grawagānīh*, *passandārīh*, *ǰāmdārīh*) in the course of which the pledgee (defendant) gained ownership of the mortgaged object due to the default of the debtor (plaintiff). We can therefore conclude that *passandārīh* was some kind of pledge or deposit comparable to the other two types of security named in the text. It would not be too far-fetched to assume that the term evolved from one of the formulae spoken in the formal act of conveyance, which in this case would have allowed the recipient (pledgee/creditor) to choose an object of his liking as

300 According to DkM 719.13: *abar garān wināhīh ī tan (ī) ēr ō an-ēr abespārdan* 'On the great offence of delivering an Iranian person (in debt bondage, *tan*?) to a non-Iranian'. On the technical meaning of the ambiguous term *tan* see below, pp. 352–354.

301 From *passand-* 'to like, approve'+ *dār(īh)* 'holder (holding), keeper (keeping)' (**pati-+*sand* 'to appear, seem [good]; Cheung 2007, p. 332; on *-dār* see Durkin-Meisterernst 2014, p. 185).

302 Macuch 1993, pp. 538, 541.

a pledge. As elucidated above, the transferor (in this case, the debtor) declared his will to transfer an object (pledge) approved of by the transferee (creditor) with the words *ān ī tō passandē* ('that which you approve of'). If the abstract *passandārīh* (lit. 'holding that which is approved of') was derived from this formula, then it designates a pawn explicitly chosen and accepted by the creditor.[303]

To sum up: *graw* is the general expression for 'pawn, pledge', which in turn can be specified by the terms *ǰām/ǰāmdārīh* for 'movable pledge', *nibāg/nabāg* for 'living, animated pledge, hostage' and *passandārīh* for a 'pledge chosen by the creditor'. Due to the sparse material we have no means of discerning, whether there were any significant legal differences between the various types of pledges represented by these terms.

Table 26. Overview of terminology: *graw, grawīh*

az graw abāz wēxtan[304]	to redeem the pledge (always referring to an action performed by the debtor)
az grawīh hištan[305]	to release from pledge (always referring to an action performed by the creditor)
az xwāstag ī graw abēsaxwān būdan[306]	to forego, renounce the pledged property (action performed by the creditor)
graw abāz rasēnīdan[307]	to bring back a pledge/pawn
graw abāz stadan[308]	to take back a pledge/pawn
graw abespārdan[309]	to transfer a pledge/pawn
graw kardan[310]	to pledge/pawn (something)

303 The words of the debtor, allowing the creditor(s) to choose a pawn for the loan are transmitted in MHD 67.3–6: *kā Ādurfarrbay xwāstag* ⟨NKSY'⟩ *200 az Farrox ud Mihrēn abām stānēd ud paymān ēdōn kunēd: kū kā ān xwāstag* ⟨NKSY'⟩ *nē wizārd ēstēd ašmā xwāstag* ⟨hw'stk'⟩ *ī man xwēš ān ī ašmā sahēd and čand 200 wahāg arzēd pad xwēšīh ayāb pad grawagānīh ōwōn čiyōn ašmā sahēd abāz grift pādixšāy* … 'If A. takes (a sum of) money of 200 (dr/st) from F. and M. as a loan and makes a contract: "If that money is not paid, you are authorized to retain a thing which is my own that you approve of (*ān ī ašmā sahēd*) worth 200 (dr/st) in ownership or as a pledge (*pad grawagānīh*), as it seems appropriate to you" …' (Macuch 1993, pp. 447, 451). Although here the formula *ān ī ašmā sahēd* 'that which you approve of' is used instead of **ān ī ašmā passanded* ('that which you approve of') the meaning of these formulae and the legal procedure are identical. On the formal procedure and the prescribed phrases see pp. 301–305 above.

304 MHD 37.15 (Macuch 1993, pp. 277, 282).

305 MHD 39.9; 40.2ff. (Macuch 1993, pp. 279, 284; 280, 285 respectively.).

306 MHD 89.6 (Macuch 1993, pp. 569, 572).

307 DkM 732.11.

308 DkM 732.5.

309 MHD 11.1, 6, 9; 12.6; 15.5 (Macuch 1993, pp. 139, 142).

310 For attestations see index Macuch 1993, pp. 706–707.

grawīh wišuft (*nē wišuft*) *bawēd*[311]	the (right to) the pledge has expired (not expired)
pad graw abāz griftan[312]	to hold back as pledge
pad graw/grawīh dāštan[313]	to keep as pledge
pad graw/grawīh griftan[314]	to take as pledge
pad graw nihādan[315]	to deposit as pledge
pad graw stadan[316]	to take as pledge
xwāstag ī pad kas graw[317]	object/property pledged to a person

4.1.2.2 *Hypotheca* or mortgage of the substance (*āgraw*)

The distinction between the two main types of mortgage, *āgraw/āgrawīh*[318] ('mortgage of the substance'), on the one hand, and *grawagān/grawagānīh* ('mortgage of the fruits', *antichresis*), on the other, correlates with the division of ownership into the two basic forms of *bun-xwēšīh* ('ownership of the substance') and *bar-xwēšīh* ('ownership of the fruits') and the possibility of having separate proprietary rights over the substance and fruits of a corporeal thing (*xwāstag*), as elucidated in the chapter on property and inheritance above.[319] The *āgraw* type is unfortunately far less documented than the *grawagān* (for which we now even have valuable evidence in the Tabarestān records), but although the former term has been interpreted in a completely different manner in the past, there can be—in my opinion—no doubt that the only correct interpretation of its technical meaning is 'mortgage of the substance, hypothec'.[320] This explanation is in fact even transmitted in the Law-book in a passage explicitly contrasting the two forms of mortgage with each other (embedded in a longer sentence, in which the crucial statement is):

311 MHD 37.13 (Macuch 1993, pp. 277, 282).
312 MHD 99.17 (Macuch 1993, pp. 613, 621).
313 MHD 37.12; 89.4 (Macuch 1993, pp. 277, 282; 569, 572 respectively).
314 MHD 7.17; 12.13; 14.13 (Macuch 1993, pp. 90, 94; 117, 120; 128, 132 respectively).
315 MHD 37.12 (Macuch 1993, pp. 277, 282).
316 DkM 717.4–5.
317 MHD 38.11–12 (Macuch 1993, pp. 278, 238).
318 < **ā+grab-*; Ir. **grabH* (Cheung 2007, p. 119ff.); Av./OP √*grab* 'to grab, seize, take' (Bartholomae 1904, col. 526–528; Kellens 1995, p. 20f.).
319 See Chapter III, pp. 197–202.
320 Perikhanian 1997, p. 334, has two completely different readings and interpretations of this word, written ⟨'glwb'⟩: (1) '*agraβ*: "an unpledged thing, one free from hypothec"' (*graβ* with the privative prefix *a-*; in MHD 38.13 and 40.4), and (2) '*āgraβ*: "subject to seizure (for the settlement of a debt)"', besides '*āgraβīh*: "seizure (in settlement of debts)"' (in MHD 89.9 and 29.12, 62.15 respectively). Both interpretations are in my opinion untenable, see also fn. 322 below.

MHD 40.3–4
ka grawagān kunēd bar grawagān kard bawēd ud ka āgraw kunēd bun āgraw kard bawēd

'If he (= the borrower) mortgages the usufruct (*grawagān kunēd*), (then) the produce (*bar*) has been mortgaged and if he (= the borrower) mortgages the principal (*āgraw kunēd*), (then) the substance (*bun*) has been mortgaged.'[321]

The difference between the three basic forms of real security, *graw* and *āgraw*, on the one hand, and *grawagān*, on the other, can also be deduced indirectly from another passage addressing the question, whether a debtor (as pledgor/mortgagor) is entitled to sell a thing he has pawned or mortgaged if he has no other property:

MHD 38.11–13
mard xwāstag ī-š pad kas graw frōxt nē pādixšāy ān bawēd ka-š any-iz xwāstag nēst čē xwāstag ī āgraw frōxt nē ud ān ī grawagān frōxt pādixšāy

'A man is not entitled to sell a thing which he has pawned to a person (*pad kas graw*). This is (in force) even when he has no other property, since one is not entitled to sell the thing, the substance of which is mortgaged (*xwāstag ī āgraw*), but one is entitled to sell the thing, the fruits of which are mortgaged (*grawagān*).'[322]

This short passage contains a remarkable amount of important information, allowing several conclusions. The first statement informs us (unsurprisingly) that a man who has pawned or pledged a thing as security for a debt is not entitled to sell it. The term used here is *graw* 'pledge, pawn', which—as we have seen above—designates an item (a corporeal thing; a piece of land, an estate, a chattel, an animal, slave, etc.) transferred by the borrower to the possession of the lender (pledgee/pawnee), but remaining in the ownership of the former. The debtor retains the right to redeem this item by repaying the loan, but he has no right to sell it as long as it is pawned (only the creditor/pledgee may sell the pawn on default of the debtor). This prohibition is effective even if the debtor has no other property (to pay off another debt or perform some other obligation, as we may add). The most interesting part of this passage is the explanation in which the pawn (*graw*) is compared with the other two frequent forms of security, *āgraw* and *grawagan*. The reason why the debtor may not sell the pawn (*graw*), we are told in the typically concise manner of the Law-book, is that this form of security

321 Macuch 1993, pp. 280, 285. Perikhanian 1997, p. 109, has a completely different translation of this passage due to her divergent interpretation of the term *āgraw*, see fn. 320 above.

322 Macuch 1993, pp. 278, 283. Perikhanian 1997, pp. 106, 107, reading *'agraβ'* ('unpledged thing') has a grammatically impossible translation of the last part of this sentence: '... *xvāstak ī agraβ frōxt nē (ud) ān ī graβagān frōxt pātixšay*' (p. 106) '...it is permissible to sell only an unpledged thing but not a pledged (one)' (p. 107). If we follow her (wrong) reading of the term as *agraβ* ('unpledged'), a grammatically correct translation would be: '... it is not permissible to sell an unpledged thing and it is permissible to sell a pledged one', which does not make any sense at all in this context describing the rights of the debtor! See also fn. 320 above.

is comparable to hypothecated property (the substance of which is mortgaged, *xwāstag ī āgraw*). That is, in both cases (*graw* and *āgraw*) the debtor promises the substance or principal (*bun*) of a certain item (a piece of land, a house, an orchard or specified trees, an animal or slave, etc.) to the creditor as security, hence—as we may add—implicitly agrees to give up his 'ownership of the substance' (*bun-xwēšīh*) if he does not settle the debt on time. On the other hand, if the debtor only mortgages the fruits (*bar*) of a property as *antichresis* (*grawagān*; *e. g.*, the crop yields of a piece of land, the rent of a house, the fruits of specified trees, the work force of an animal or slave), he has only granted a right of usufruct (*bar-xward*) to the creditor (*i. e*, the right to take the produce of a certain property in lieu of interest and in repayment of the debt), but the latter has no right to seize the substance (*bun*) of the property itself (an exception seems to be an agreement giving the mortgagee the explicit right to automatic foreclosure, as discussed above, p. 328). Moreover, the debtor has neither promised to give up his right to 'ownership of the substance' (*bun-xwēšīh*), nor to 'ownership of the fruits' (*bar-xwēšīh*), but only his right to usufruct (*bar-xward*). As several case studies in the Law-book and the Tabarestān documents demonstrate, these two variants of ownership rights ('ownership of the substance' and 'ownership of the fruits') could belong to different persons. Hence, the debtor (or another 'owner of the substance', *bun-xwēš*) could sell a property whose produce is mortgaged (perhaps to fulfil other obligations) despite the mortgage. The further consequences of this ruling are not discussed: did the creditor/mortgagee retain his right to usufruct? This was presumably the case, as we may conclude from the sources discussed below on *antichresis* (see the next section).

Another difficult passage dealing with the remittance or cancelation of a money debt confirms indirectly this interpretation of *āgraw*:

> MHD 89.8–9
> *mard xwāstag* ⟨NKSY'⟩ *ī abāmdān agar az xwāstag* ⟨hw'stk'⟩ *ī ōy kē ān xwāstag* ⟨NKSY'⟩ *tōzišn abēsaxwan bawēd hišt čē xwāstag* ⟨hw'stk'⟩ *pad abām āgraw*
>
> 'A man's money debt (*xwāstag ī abāmdān*) is cancelled (*hišt*) if he (= the creditor) renounces (*az … abēsaxwan bawēd*) the property of the debtor (*ōy kē ān xwāstag tōzišn* "he who must pay the money"), since the property (is) a hypothec (*āgraw*) for the debt.'[323]

This sentence, although somewhat contorted, is a fine example of concise legal jargon and the precise use of the technical terms we have already discussed above (and elsewhere).[324] Its statement is clear enough: If the moneylender waives his

323 Macuch 1993, pp. 569, 572. Perikhanian 1997, p. 209, has again a completely different translation, see also fn. 320 above.

324 On ⟨NKSY'⟩ *xwāstag*, always 'money' in a legal text, if written as a heterogram, but '*res*, thing, property', if written eteographically ⟨hw'stk'⟩, see p. 190; on *tōzišn* 'obligation, payment' see pp. 307–310; on *az … abēsaxwan būdan* 'to renounce, forego, cancel (a right)' see Macuch 1993, pp. 51–52, no. 10; Macuch 1989 and Chapter VII, pp. 611–614.

right to take ownership of the borrower's property, which has been hypothecated (*āgraw*) as security for the loan, this implies that the debtor has been released from his debt. Another entry discussing the same question, but with *graw* instead of *āgraw*, permits us to compare these two forms of real security:

MHD 89.5–6
ka az xwāstag ⟨hw'stk'⟩ *ī graw abēsaxwan bawēd ēg-iš drahm nē hišt bawēd*
'If he (= the creditor) renounces the pledged thing (*xwāstag ī graw*), then (the payment of) the drachms is not cancelled (*nē hišt bawēd*).'[325]

In sharp contrast to the preceding passage, the moneylender does *not* dispense with the repayment of a loan if he foregoes his right to taking a pawn or pledge (*graw*) as security; the borrower is *not* released from his obligation to repay the debt. This seems to be one of the main differences between *graw* and *āgraw*, although both refer to the substance (*bun*) of a specified property: the creditor can forego his right to take a pawn (*graw*), without losing his right to repayment, but if he waives his claim to the hypothecated property (*āgraw*) of the debtor this implies that he has released the latter from his obligations. The legal background of these completely different implications is not transmitted, but we can attempt to reconstruct the reasoning behind these rulings. If the borrower offered a pawn (*graw*) as security, this required that the pawn be transferred (directly or by document) into the possession of the lender (whilst remaining in the ownership of the debtor). The lender could refrain from taking a pawn as security, which, however, did not mean that the borrower was released from debt. The hypothec (*āgraw*), on the other hand, was a mere charge, consisting of a promise of rights in a specified piece of property, which was not transferred, but remained in both ownership and possession of the borrower and only became effective in the event of non-fulfilment of contract on the part of the latter. If the lender waived his right to take the hypothecated property instead of payment, this was regarded as equivalent to releasing the borrower from debt. A similar distinction between two forms of pledge is made in Īšōʿbōxt's Law-book with regard to immovable property, as Sachau has perceptively noted: one form with *traditio*, in which the pledge is transmitted to the creditor(s) (it is 'in their hand', *b'īdayhōn*, corresponding to *graw*, the term that presumably stood in the Pahlavi original of this work), the other without *traditio*, in which the creditor only holds a document (*ktāḇā*) recording the security (corresponding to the *āgraw* type of mortgage).[326]

In the context of *agraw(īh)* another technical term is employed that could be connected in some manner with this type of mortgage. The expression *pēš-tozišnīh*, lit. 'advance payment, prepayment', is attested in two difficult sentences of a short chapter in the Law-book with the heading: 'Chapter on mortgaging

325 Macuch 1993, pp. 569, 572.
326 See Īšōʿbōxt, Book V, Chapter VII, particularly §2 (Sachau 1914, pp. 154–155, and especially his commentary p. 327). It is remarkable that Sachau perceived this distinction although he had no knowledge of Sasanian law. See also below.

the substance (*āgrawīh*); whether granting an advance payment (*pēš-tōzišnīh*) is permitted or not permitted'.[327] The two passages with this term discuss the question, whether an 'advance payment' should be granted from property that has been bequeathed by the head of the family and already transferred to the heirs or other beneficiaries.[328] Both passages are rather abstract, but if we take the context of the whole chapter into consideration, we can reasonably infer that *pēš-tōzišnīh* denotes an obligation deriving from a loan (*abām*) or from the grant of a pious gift (*ahlawdād*) and had to be settled *before* other dispositions of a *paterfamilias* came into force and his heirs and beneficiaries took possession of the estate. Although the connection to *āgraw*-mortgage is not explained anywhere (despite the title of this chapter) *pēš-tōzišnīh* in this specific context seems to express an idea similar (but not necessarily identical) to the 'charge', a form of security protecting the creditor (chargee) by giving him the right to payment from the sale of the mortgaged property in priority to claims other (unsecured) creditors might have against the debtor or, as in our chapter, also in priority to any rights resulting from inheritance. The charge would have been documented by a deposit given to the creditor consisting presumably of a document recording the security or a title deed proving that the debtor was the owner of the mortgaged property.[329]

Although all these entries are rather concise and abstract, taken together they make it rather plausible that *āgraw* was a kind of hypothec, comparable maybe to a certain extent to the *hypotheca* of Roman law, a further development or

327 MHD 29.12–13: *dar ī āgrawīh pēš-tōzišnīh dād pādixšāy būd pādixšāy nē būd* (Macuch 1993, pp. 220, 224; see also commentary on p. 228f., no. 2). Perikhanian 1997, p. 382, has a completely different explanation of this term, which she reads *paštōžišnīh*⁺ (in the text, pp. 86, 88 and 90, although she also has the reading *pĕ̄š-tōzišnīh* in the glossary, p. 382) and explains it as 'the settlement of the debt of a head of household or relinquisher by his heir or by persons having acquired his estate'. For the formation she refers to Parth, *p'šn'm* 'memory, commemoration' (lit. 'after-name'), MP, NP *pašiman*, *pižman* 'repentence' (citing also other Iranian languages). This explanation is closely connected with her understanding of *āgraw* as 'subject to seizure (for the settlement of a debt)', *ibid*., p. 334, which in my opinion is wrong, see fn. 320 above. The term is, moreover, always written ⟨pyštwcšnyh⟩ with ⟨y⟩, excluding a reading as ⁺*paštōzišnīh*.

328 In the first sentence (MHD 30.17–31.2) we are informed that the status of property that has been already transferred into the possession (*xwāstag kē dārišn be kard*) (of heirs and beneficiaries) should not be reversed ('brought back', *abāz nē āwarišn*) in order to supply an 'advance payment' (*pēš-tōzišnīh*) for certain obligations resulting from debt, such as interest (*waxš*) and compensation ('nw'n) and similar claims (Macuch 1993, pp. 222, 226; see also the commentary, p. 232, no. 14). The second passage (MHD 31.2–3) states that an 'advance payment' (*pēš-tōzišnīh*) only takes effect (*kār*), when possession of the property has not yet been transferred (*ka xwāstag dārišn be nē kard*) (to the heirs and beneficiaries). But there are three important exceptions, that is, in these cases an 'advance payment' is made even if the property has already been transferred: (1) when a debt (*abām*) has to be paid; (2) when the property has been granted as a pious gift (*ahlawdād*); (3) when the proprietor has committed a *margarzān*, an offence worthy of death (Macuch 1993, pp. 222, 226; see also the commentary, pp. 232f., no. 15).

329 Compare Īšōʿbōxt, Book V, Chapter VII, §3b (Sachau 1914, pp. 156, 157).

modified and more flexible form of *pignus* ('pawn, pledge'). The similarities are in any case striking: whereas *pignus* involved a transfer of possession, the hypothec gave the creditor only 'a right *in rem* over another's property' (*ius in re aliena*) and was a simple charge. This form of security came to be used mainly in mortgages of land (although it could also be applied to chattels) and had the advantage that the borrower could take out successive mortgages on the same piece of property, whereas only one loan at a time could be secured by *pignus*. Before a system of land registration was developed (in 472 CE), successive mortgages could give rise to legal conflicts, when potential buyers or creditors were unaware that the property was burdened by a hypothec or already charged for its whole worth. Moreover, the possibility of securing more than one loan on the same property led to the development of rules regulating the sequence of charges. The basic rule was initially that the earliest charge had priority over later ones, but these were altered and extended in the late Empire, giving precedence to formal charges, which were officially registered or witnessed, over informal ones.[330]

It would not be too far-fetched to assume that similar problems had to be dealt with in Iranian law with rules corresponding by and large to those of Roman law, although none of these are transmitted in the Pahlavi texts. Chapter VII of Book five on credit law and pledge in Īšōʿbōxt's Law-book, however, does discuss several cases involving the claims of creditors with and without security.[331] Īšōʿbōxt distinguishes between movable and immovable pledges, differentiating furthermore between the pledge that is transferred to the creditor(s), which is 'in their hand' (*b'īdayhōn*; corresponding to *graw*) and the mortgage that is recorded in a written document (*ktāḇā*) but *not* transferred (property over which the creditor had a charge, presumably *āgraw* in Sasanian terminology, or hypothec). The latter form of mortgage is treated in a few case studies that broach the issue of the priority of charges with regard to pledged immovable property (a field or a house) that has *not* been transferred to the creditor(s):[332] (1) Several creditors have claims (against the same debtor), but only the first one (in time) has a document recording the pledge. He is empowered to take back the whole principal, excluding interest, from the mortgaged property (before other creditors are satisfied).[333] (2) Several creditors, with and without security, have claims. The first creditor (in time) who has a document recording the pledge is entitled to satisfy his claim before the other creditors.[334] (3) Two creditors both have documents recording the pledge. They share the pledged property in accordance with their claims.[335]

330 On the development of the hypotheca see NICHOLAS 1962, pp. 151–153; and DU PLESSIS/BORKOWSKI 2010, pp. 303–304.
331 See SACHAU 1914, pp. 154–165.
332 SACHAU 1914, pp. 326–330, has discussed the whole content of this chapter in his commentary.
333 Īšōʿbōxt, Book V, Chapter VII, § 2c (SACHAU 1914, pp. 154–155).
334 Īšōʿbōxt, Book V, Chapter VII, § 3b, first sentence (SACHAU 1914, pp. 156–157).
335 Īšōʿbōxt, Book V, Chapter VII, § 3b, second sentence (SACHAU 1914, pp. 156–157).

Although these passages leave many questions open, we can at least surmise to a limited extent how the question of successive mortgages was regulated:

1. Formal charges with a document of hypothecation were given priority over informal ones.
2. The earliest creditor with a document of hypothecation was privileged over other creditors without security.
3. Two creditors with documents of hypothecation were both entitled to share the proceeds from the mortgaged property in accordance with their claims against the debtor.

These regulations were presumably based on Sasanian law, although Christian law in Iran might have differed in specific details, since Īšōʿbōxt distinguishes between the decisions of 'worldly judges' (following Sasanian law) and those of the 'judges of the Church'. Moreover, some of these decisions are based—as we are explicitly told at the end of §2—on legal practice (*bᵊ-mparnsānūṯā*) rather than legal doctrine (*bᵊ-dīnā*), which might also have been somewhat different in Zoroastrian and Christian law. But despite possible divergences in practice the theoretical observations in Īšōʿbōxt definitely reflect Sasanian law. The two terms used in the Syriac text, *bᵊ-mparnsānūṯā*,[336] '*via administrationis*', and *bᵊ-dīnā* '*ex lege*', translate MP *pad kardag* 'according to (legal) practice' and *pad čāštag* 'according to doctrine' respectively. These two Pahlavi terms are presumably the exact words that stood in the original Middle Persian version of this text.[337]

Table 27. Overview of terminology: *āgraw*, *āgrawīh*

āgraw kardan[338]	to hypothecate the substance (*bun*) of property
pad rāh ī āgrawīh[339]	by means of hypothecating the substance (*bun*) of property
xwāstag ī āgraw[340]	hypothecated property; mortgage of the substance (*bun*)
xwāstag pad abām āgraw[341]	the property (is) a hypothec for the debt

336 On Syriac *mparnsānuṯa* 'management, administration' see Payne Smith 1903, p. 292; from the root PRNS 'to take the oversight, manage, rule, administer (property)', Payne Smith 1903, p. 462.

337 Īšōʿbōxt, Book V, Chapter VII, §2 (Sachau 1914, pp. 154–155). On *bᵊ-dīnā* see also Sachau's introduction, p. XII, on *bᵊ-mparnsānūṯā* see introduction, p. XIV. Sachau, however, had no knowledge of the corresponding categories and terms in Sasanian law, hence does not mention them. On *kardag* and *čāštag* as instruments of law see Chapter I, pp. 66–71 above.

338 MHD 40.4 (Macuch 1993, pp. 280, 285).

339 MHD 62.15 (Macuch 1993, pp. 411, 417).

340 MHD 38.13 (Macuch 1993, pp. 278, 283).

341 MHD 89.9 (Macuch 1993, pp. 569, 573).

4.1.2.3 *Antichresis* or mortgage of the fruits (*grawagān*)

The *antichresis* or *grawgān/grawagān(īh)*,[342] by which only the fruits (*bar*) of a property were provided by the debtor as a security for a loan (in contrast to *āgraw[īh]*, by which the substance was mortgaged), seems to have been a frequent kind of mortgage, to judge by the entries in the Law-book and the Tabarestān documents. As elucidated above, ownership of every 'thing' (*xwāstag*) could be separated into the two basic forms of *bun-xwēšīh* ('ownership of the substance') and *bar-xwēšīh* ('ownership of the fruits'), giving different persons access to these two components of a physical object. By means of *grawagānīh* the owner of the fruits (*bar-xwēš*) could mortgage these independently of the owner of the substance (*bun-xwēš*) by transferring the right to usufruct (*bar-xward*) to the creditor (mortgagee) until the loan was fully paid. The creditor received the right to take the produce of this property as payment or in lieu of interest or both. If the debtor failed to fulfil his obligations by a specified date he could only lose 'ownership of the fruits', but retained—if he was also 'owner of the substance' (which was not necessarily always the case, as we will see below)—his right to the principal.

Most of the passages on *grawagānīh* in the Law-book (and in later Pahlavi texts)[343] are more or less abstract discussions of problems arising from *antichresis*, but we can conclude from the few concrete surviving examples that any corporal 'thing' yielding some kind of income (*barōmand*) could be mortgaged in this manner.[344] The produce from immovable property, such as crop yields, the fruits of specified trees in orchards (*e.g.*, olive trees), grapes and wine from vineyards, the rent of a house or estate, but also the income produced by movable property, by the work force of slaves and animals, could be granted as *grawagān* security. In most cases, particularly involving landed property and houses, the difference between 'substance' and 'fruit' (the land itself and its crops; the house and its rent, etc.) would have been self-evident, but if a living pledge was involved, the question could arise, whether the offspring of an animal or a slave, born during the pledge, was to be considered as *bar* or *bun*. A passage in Īšōʿbōxt clarifies the matter: the progeny of pledged animals (sheep, goats and camels) and female slaves counts as 'substance' (Syr. *ʿeqārā* 'root', the

342 ⟨*graw+-gān/-agān* from the root Ir. **grabH*; Av./OP √*grab* 'to grab, seize, take' (Bartholomae 1904, col. 526ff.; Kellens 1995, p. 20f.; Cheung 2007, p. 119ff.); Armenian loan-word *grawakan* 'pledge, hostage, bet' (Hübschmann 1897, p. 131); MMP *grawgān/grawagān* 'pledge, security' (Durkin-Meisterernst 2004, p. 164); NP *giraugān* 'a wager, stake' (Steingass 1892, p. 1085). On the suffix *-gān/-agān* see Durkin-Meisterernst 2014, pp. 158–159.

343 For the discussion of an example from the *Pahlavi Rivāyat of Ādurfarrbay and Farrbay-Srōš* see Macuch 2017b.

344 A whole chapter of the Law-book is dedicated to antichresis (MHD 37.11, Macuch 1993, pp. 277–298) but other forms of mortgage are also discussed in several passages, which we have already cited above.

equivalent of MP *bun*), and *not* as 'fruit' (*pīʾrā*, the equivalent of MP *bar*).[345] The offspring remains in the ownership of the debtor, but can be raised and provided for by the creditor, if he has actual control of the pledge (this is usually the case, when the work force of animals and slaves is mortgaged). The debtor, as the owner of the animal or slave, is in turn obliged to reimburse all costs involved in rearing the progeny, to recompense the creditor for the loss of the pledge's work force due to pregnancy and birth, and to remunerate the efforts undertaken by the creditor to care for the newborn child or animal.[346]

Another remarkable passage in the chapter on *antichresis* in the Law-book refers to the mortgage of trees and elucidates the legal implications of pledging trees, which bear fruits and those that are fruitless. Nota bene, usually a pledge (*graw*) involves the transfer of the pledged object into the possession of the pledge-holder (and ownership of the substance on default of the debtor), whereas *grawagān* only concedes a right to the usufruct, but (as so often in the problematic case studies of the Law-book) the statements here seem to address the reversed cases: Should the pledge-holder (*grawdār*) receive ownership of the tree itself (*i. e*, of the substance, as he would be normally entitled to), if it bears fruit, or only of the fruits? And how can the *ususfructarius* or mortgagee (*grawagāndār*) with a right to usufruct be satisfied if trees are mortgaged which yield no fruits? The ensuing problems are solved as follows:[347]

1. The debtor pledges a tree (*graw kunēd*) bearing fruits (*bar*). On default of the debtor the pledge-holder (*grawdār*) receives only ownership of the fruits.
2. A tree mortgaged as *antichresis* bears no fruit and does not regrow, when it is felled (such as the cypress). The *ususfructarius* (pledge-holder, *grawagāndār*) has a claim to the felled tree.
3. The pledged tree grows again, when it is felled (such as the plane or date tree). The *ususfructarius* (pledge-holder, *grawagāndār*) has a claim to both the felled and the regrown trees.

345 On *pīʾrā* 'fruit' see Payne Smith, p. 433; *ʿeqārā* 'root' (*ibid.* p. 426). Sachau 1914, pp. 160–161 (§ 10).

346 Īšōʿbōxt, Book V, Chapter VII, § 10 (Sachau 1914, pp. 158–161).

347 MHD 40.13–17: *ka draxt-ē(w) graw kunēd kē bar hast grawdār ēwāz bar xwēš ka-š bar nēst agar ka zanēnd abāz nē rōyēd čiyōn sarw grawagāndār ēwāz hambāhišn agar ka zanēnd abāz rōyēd čiyōn ⁺čanār ud xorma hambāhišn ud abzōn xwēš tā ān ī ka andar abzōn ēstēd bē honsandīh ī ōy kē graw kard ēg-iš zadan nē pādixšāy u-š abzōn-ız andar grawīh ē(w) wahāg ayāb guharīg stānišn.* 'If he (= the pledgor/debtor) pledges (*graw kunēd*) a tree, which has fruit, (then) only the fruits (become) the pledgee's (= creditor's; *grawdār*) own. If (the tree) has no fruit (and) does not grow (again), when it is felled, such as the cypress, the mortgagee (= creditor; *grawagāndār*) only (receives) the felled (tree). If it (= the tree) grows (again), when it is felled, such as the plane tree or the date tree, then (both) the felled (tree) and the regrown (tree) (are his) own. As long as (the tree) is in growth, he (= the mortgagee/creditor) is not entitled to fell it without the consent of the mortgagor (= debtor; *ōy kē graw kard*) and he (= the mortgagee) should take the remuneration and compensation from the (tree) that is regrown during the pledge (*andar grawīh-ēw*).' (Macuch 1993, pp. 281, 286).

4. The pledge-holder needs the consent of the debtor (pledgor) to fell the tree as long as it is in growth. The tree that has grown anew during the duration of the pledge is used to satisfy the claims of the creditor to remuneration (*wahāg*) and compensation (*guharīg*).

As many of the passages of the Law-book, this sentence seems to discuss exceptional cases, in which the strict normative distinction between *graw(īh)* and *grawagān(īh)* could not be kept in legal practice: the *grawdār* (who usually has access to the substance) is satisfied in this case by the fruits alone; the *grawagāndār* (who normally only has a right to usufruct), on the other hand, is satisfied by the substance of the mortgaged property (tree), if no fruits exist.

Trees were in fact mortgaged as *antichresis*, now spectacularly attested in two of the original documents from Tabarestān, revealing exactly how the *grawagān* type of security was fixed in the loan contract.[348] Every single mortgaged tree is meticulously listed in the written contract (*paymān-nāmag*), giving the name of the land or estate, on which each tree is located, the owners of every piece of land and the expected yearly crop yields of the trees. In Tab. 18 the borrower or debtor is a man named Dēlgušnasp, a shield-maker (*spargar*), son of Dērā, from the 'house' (*xānag*, *i. e*, 'lineage') of Dēl-Dēlān, resident in the village of *Asp-gurd (the same shield-maker is also mentioned in Tab. 15).[349] The moneylender is a scribe called Farroxgušnasp from the same village. The debtor takes out a loan of 6 staters and one drachm in the presence of an official authority (representing the 'King of Parišwārgar in *Halīg'). The contract notes that the money granted as a loan constitutes a share (*ǰādag*) in the 'substance' (*bun*) of the village of *Asp-gurd. The debtor offers the crop yields of olive-trees (*zayt*) as security for the loan. These olive-trees are on three 'undivided' estates (*ēw-kardag*; lit. 'in one piece'), consisting of cultivated land (*zamīg ī kišwzar*). Each one of these three estates, on which the olive-trees are located, is in the collective property of four different shareholder families, in one case of 'heirs' (*xwāstagdār*) from different non-shareholder families. The document groups the olive-trees on the estates into three sets of four trees each according to the measure (*sāmān*) of their olive yields (we will return to these lists later). The usufruct of the listed olive trees is mortgaged (*grawagān*) until the loan is paid back. The creditor is obliged to keep the property intact (*drustīh*). The contract contains a clause

348 As elucidated above (Chapter I, pp. 18–20), these newly discovered documents (dated to the eighth century) are obviously based on Sasanian law, use the same legal terminology and generally continue Sasanian legal practice. Most of the Tabarestān documents stem either from an archive of a village called *Asp-gurd or from *Halīg, the place of residence of the King of Parišwārgar, a title which replaces that of 'Commander of the East' (*Xorāsān-spāhbed*), the military governor of Tabarestān, in later documents (on the historical background of the Tabarestān documents see Macuch 2024c).

349 For the original document and an extensive philological and contextual commentary see Weber 2017a, pp. 150–154, and Macuch 2017c, pp. 183–188; a transcription and translation of the whole text is in Appendix X, pp. 701–703.

stating that the agreement cannot be contested by any one of the contractors or by a third party. Moreover, the debtor obliges himself to pay back the loan immediately if the creditor suffers a loss (*zyān*) and to double the sum (to 12 staters, 2 drachms) if he fails to perform. The contract is confirmed with the seal of the debtor, who is identified (*pad āšnāg guft*) by a certain *Wangird, son of Dērā, a scribe from the village of *Asp-gurd (possibly the brother of the debtor, since the name of the father is identical). It is furthermore sealed with an official seal (of a legal authority called) Farroxzād to make it legally binding (*ēwarīh rāy*).[350]

Following the details in this document, the basic components of a loan contract with *grawagān* security can be reconstructed as follows (individual variations were presumably possible):

Table 28. Loan contract with *grawagān* security

	Basic elements of the contract	Particulars of Tab. 18[351]
1.	Exact date of recording	Day *Aštād*, month *Ādur*, year 101 PYE (= 752/753 CE)
2.	Name, affiliation, profession, place of residence of the debtor	Debtor: Dēlgušnasp, son of Dērā, from the house of Dēl-Dēlān; shield-maker; Residence: village of *Asp-gurd
3.	Statement of the debtor (promisor): – confirmation of the obligation – total sum of the loan – name of the creditor, profession – place of residence of the creditor – provenance of the loan – security provided for the loan – type of security – duration of the security	Dēlgušnasp declares: – 'It is my obligation to give (back) money, a loan of 6 staters [and one drachm] ...' (*man xwāstag* ⟨NKSY'⟩ *arz sazēd s(atēr) 6 [drahm 1]... abām dādan...*) – 6 staters, 1 drachm – Farroxgušnasp; scribe – village of *Asp-gurd – a share in the collective property ('substance', *bun*) of the village of *Asp-gurd – crop yields (*āhang*) of three sets of four olive trees (*zayt*) on three estates – *antichresis* (*grawagān*) in favour of the creditor Farroxgušnasp – until the sum of 6 staters, 1 drachm is repaid

350 On the function of seals see pp. 286–301 above and MACUCH 1997.
351 The whole text is in Appendix X, pp. 701–703.

Basic elements of the contract		Particulars of Tab. 18[351]
3.	– duties of the creditor – incontestability of the contract – liability of the debtor for losses of the creditor – compensation to be paid on non-performance of contract	– to keep the mortgaged property intact (*drustīh*) – whosoever disputes the terms of the contract is without expedient (*abēzār*) – commitment of the debtor to return the loan on demand of the creditor if he suffers a loss (*zyān*) – twice the amount of the loan: 12 staters, 2 drachms
4.	Name, profession and residence of the witness who identifies the debtor and his seal	*Wangird, son of Dērā; scribe, resident in *Asp-gurd, from the house of Dēl-Dēlān
5.	Seal of the debtor (promisor)	Sealed by Dēlgušnasp
6.	Seal of an official authority	Sealed by Farroxzād to make it legally binding (*ēwarīh rāy*)

The most remarkable part of this document reveals how the olive trees provided as security were recorded. As already noted in the overview, they are listed in three sets of trees according to the amount of crop yields they provide. The trees were located on three different pieces of collective property, which was not divided among the proprietors (the land is *ēw-kardag* 'in one piece'; *i. e*, the shareholders had ideal shares) belonging to different persons or families. The exact location of each tree is noted and the proprietors of the land named. These precise lists can be schematized as follows:

(1) First set of olive-trees (lines 8–12), yielding 9 *kabīz* of olives (a *kabīz* corresponds to one-tenth of a *grīw*, the measure for solid matters)[352]:

Number of olive-trees	Designation of the land, on which the olive-trees grow: *Taxlīh* (l. 8)
one	'the canyon' (*darrag*) belonging to the debtor (ll. 8–9)
one	land of the 'heirs' (*xwāstagdārān*) of non-shareholders (l. 10)
one	land of Farroxgušnasp (l. 11)
one	land of Windāspagān (l. 12)
Sum of yields (*āhang*)	9 *kabīz*

352 On *grīw* 'a grain measure, modius, peck' (< OP **grīva-*) see Bailey 1930–1932b, p. 589; on the Armenian loanword *griv* see Hübschmann 1897, number 151, and Hübschmann 1895, p. 181; on Syriac ⟨gryb'⟩ *grīḇā* 'measure of capacity, especially for grain; then the piece of land sown with that measure' see Ciancaglini 2008, p. 146, with further references. According to Hinz (1973, p. 101) OP **grīva-*, Elam. *ki-ri-ma* or *kur-ri-ma* or

(2) Second set of olive-trees (lines 13–16), yielding 8 *kabīz* of olives:

Number of olive-trees	Designation of the land, on which the olive-trees grow: *Dašt-sag-kam-ī-ul* (l. 13)
one	land of the heirs of Dērā (l. 14)
one	joint land of Dēlxwašīh and another man (l. 15)
one	joint land of Āzādmard and another man (l. 15bis)
one	land of Dadōy (l. 16)
Sum of yields (*āhang*)	8 *kabīz*

(3) Third set of olive-trees (lines 17–20), yielding 3 *kabīz* of olives:

Number of olive-trees	Designation of the land, on which the olive-trees grow: *Pid* (l.17)
one	land of Windāspagān (l. 18)
one	land of Yazdāngird (l. 18)
one	land of Gōr (l. 19)
one	land of Xwaršēd (l. 20)
Sum of yields (*āhang*)	3 *kabīz*

The first group of olive-trees produces 9 *kabīz* of olives (lines 8–12 of the contract); the second group 8 *kabīz* (lines 13–16); the third group only 3 *kabīz* (lines 17–20), or if we choose a more comprehensive schematic representation:

Crop yields	Number of olive-trees on 'undivided' (*ēw-kardag*) land
9 *kabīz*	four on the land called *Taxlīh* (lines 8–12)
8 *kabīz*	four on the land called *Dašt-sag-kam-ī-ul* (lines 13–16)
3 *kabīz*	four on the land called *Pid* (lines 17–20)
Sum: 20 *kabīz* (= 2 *grīw*)	twelve olive-trees

These lists are presumably based on a calculation of the yearly crop-yields of olives that are mortgaged (*grawagān*) to the measure specified in the contract (20 *kabīz* = 2 *grīw*) until the loan is repaid.

---

ik-ri-maš or *ik-ri-ma*, corresponds to Akkadian *bar* (9,7 litres); NP *garī* 'any standard of measure, whether for land, cloth, grain, liquids, or time', and *girīb* 'a land measure' (Steingass 1892, p. 1086); Arab. *ğarīb* is according to Steingass 1892, p. 361, 'a corn-measure equal to four qafīz' (= *kawīž* 'a measure, bushel; a medlar', Steingass 1892, p. 1065; on *qafīz* 'a measure of 12 *ṣā*ʿ or about 8 *makākīl*' see Steingass 1892, p. 982); the corresponding MP *kabīz* was, however, only one-tenth of a *grīw* (MacKenzie 1971, p. 47).

Another original document attesting *grawagān* security for a loan is Tab. 24, which is, however, more than just a loan contract and far more complex than Tab. 18. As I have discussed this difficult text extensively elsewhere, it will suffice to note that the fruits of olive trees are also granted as security for a loan in this document (called *zaytēn wizīr* 'olive' or 'olive tree document') in exactly the same manner, meticulously recording every single tree and its exact location on land belonging to different families. The document lists nine sets of olive trees in exactly the same manner as described above and their produce in olives, to which the creditors (in this case a family called Ātaxšbōyān) have a right of usufruct due to a loan, for which the crop yields of these trees (the olives) are mortgaged as *antichresis* (*grawagān*, line 26 of the document).[353]

Table 29. Overview of terminology: *grawagān*, *grawagānīh*

anšahrīg pad grawagān[354]	slave whose work force is mortgaged
grawagan kardan[355]	to mortgage the fruits, to establish an *antichresis*
grawagāndār[356]	pledge-holder, pledgee, mortgagee (of the fruits)
grawagānīh ī xwāstag[357]	mortgaging the fruits of a property
ōy kē grawagān andar nihēd[358]	pledge-holder, pledgee, mortgagee (of the fruits)
pad grawagānīh dāštan[359]	to hold as *antichresis*
xwāstag ⟨hw'stk'⟩ *ī grawagān*[360]	property whose fruits are mortgaged, *antichresis*
xwāstag ⟨NKSY'⟩ *ī grawagānīh*[361]	money paid for mortgaged property

4.1.2.4 Suretyship (*pāyandānīh*)

Besides these different types of real security, another method of safeguarding a loan could consist of providing personal security or suretyship, which could take a variety of forms. As already noted above, suretyship permits a creditor to look to a third party for satisfaction, hereby extending the circle of persons against whom the creditor has recourse should the debtor be insolvent or unwilling to fulfil the loan contract on time. The surety (or guarantor/warrantor)

353 The whole text is included in Appendix X, pp. 704–710. For a discussion of this difficult document see MACUCH 2019b, pp. 132–146.
354 MHD 39.5f. (MACUCH 1993, pp. 279, 284).
355 MHD 39.9f.; 40,3; 104.4 (MACUCH 1993, pp. 279, 284, 280, 285; 618, 626 respectively).
356 MHD 37.11,13,16f.; 39.5,7,8,13,14,16,17; 40.15; 85.5; 89.3; 104.4 (MACUCH 1993, pp. 277, 282; 279f., 284f.; 281, 286; 569, 572; 618, 626 respectively).
357 MHD 38.7 (MACUCH 1993, pp. 278, 283).
358 MHD 104.5 (MACUCH 1993 618, 626).
359 MHD 40.6,7,10,12; 83.4 (MACUCH 1993, pp. 280, 285; 538, 541 respectively).
360 MHD 38.3 (MACUCH 1993, pp. 278, 283).
361 MHD 39.3f. (MACUCH 1993, pp. 279, 284).

guarantees in some form for the debtor, either by taking responsibility for delivering the debtor to the creditor, or by providing a compensation or accepting (primary or secondary) liability for repayment of the debt. It will come as no surprise that—as in many other areas discussed in this chapter—no explanations of personal security have survived, but the terms designating the 'surety, guarantor, warrantor' (*pāyandān*, *pāyēn[d]ān*) and 'suretyship, guarantee, warranty' (*pāyandānīh*, *pāyēn[d]ānīh*) are attested in several illuminating passages of the Law-book which allow wide-reaching conclusions on this area of credit law.[362] To judge by the diverse formulations in the contracts, Sasanian law distinguished between various types of suretyship according to the formulaic words spoken by one of the principal contractors (the debtor or creditor) or the surety himself. Specific wordings could extend or limit both the commitment of the surety as well as the rights of the creditor. Another important feature is revealed by the existence of archaic types of suretyship, presumably the relicts of a distant past, beside other more recent forms, which might have only emerged in the (late?) Sasanian period. The statements of the involved parties with regard to personal security enable us to reconstruct to a limited degree, first, the divergent implications of different formulations in the contract and the underlying types of security, and, second, the historical development of suretyship, from its most simple forms (leading to debt bondage and enslavement) to the accessory type (in which the surety only pays in lieu of the principal debtor). These different forms of suretyship most likely represent subsequent stages in the historical

362 This technical term is written variously as: ⟨p'ynd'n⟩ (MHD 102.13); ⟨p'yn'n⟩ (MHD 2.8; 89.2); ⟨p'yyn'n⟩ (MHD 56.5,17; 57.2,6,8; 59.3,6); ⟨p''n'n⟩ (MHD 2.9,11,12); with the abstract ending: ⟨p'yyn'nyh⟩ (MHD 55.10; 56.6,16; 57,15) and ⟨p'yynd'nyh⟩ in the model Pahlavi marriage contract (Jamasp-Asana 1897–1913, p. 143, line 6 and 9; ms. MK fol. 145a, 20, and fol. 145b, 1, see edition of the contract Macuch 2007b, p. 186, clauses 8 and 9;); with *ham-*: ⟨hmp'n''n('n)⟩ (MHD 2.1); ⟨hmp'yyn'n('n)⟩ (MHD 56.1,3,8,10; 57.1,6; 59.4); ⟨hmp'yyn'nyh⟩ (MHD 55.10); on the different spellings see also Macuch 1981, pp. 223–227 (no. 4). Bailey (1930–32a, p. 83) has read the word as '*passoxv* (**pati-sahva(n)*: (1) speaking in reply (2) speaking for' with the technical meaning of 'surety'. Despite the well-known ambiguities of the Pahlavi script (⟨s⟩ can be read instead of ⟨yy⟩ and ⟨w⟩ instead of ⟨n⟩) it is unlikely that a well-known word as *pāsox/passox* 'reply, answer' (always written ⟨p'shw'/pshw'⟩) should be misspelt or rendered in so many different ways and, moreover, that this word would be used as a legal technical term with two different meanings: *pāsox* in the context of litigation designates the 'response' or 'statement of reply' of the defendant in a lawsuit to the claim of the plaintiff. If we keep to the readings suggested above, the word for 'surety' can be read **pāyandān*, **pāyanān* or **pāyēn(d)ān*. The tentative reading adapted here follows NP *pāyandān* 'a security, surety, cautioner, sponsor; a hostage; a pledge'; *pāyandānī* 'security, pledge, caution', with *kardan* 'to give surety' (Steingass 1892, p. 236). If this is the correct reading, the noun is presumably a late derivation from the Ir. root **paH*[1] 'to protect, guard, pasture' (Cheung 2007, pp. 288–289); Av./OP √[1]*pā* 'to protect' (Bartholomae 1904, col. 885–886 ; Kellens 1995, p. 34); MP [1]*pādan*, *pāy-* 'protect, watch, defend' (MacKenzie 1971, p. 62), from the present stem *pāy-* + suffixes *-an-* (or *-ēn-*) + *-dān*. On the suffixes see Durkin-Meisterernst 2014, p. 189, §389, and 184, §368, respectively.

development of personal security, which were, however, still all current and used side by side in the Sasanian period.[363]

The historically most ancient form of personal security might be represented in a loan contract (*paymān*), in which the person who guarantees for a loan as surety declares:

> MHD 58.4–5
> *ka tō Mihrēn xwāhē Mihrēn ō tō abespārom* ēnyā *200 be dahom*
>
> 'When you request Mihrēn I will deliver Mihrēn to you, otherwise I will pay 200 (st./dr.)'.[364]

The long sentence, in which it occurs (unfortunately one of those twisted passages, which presuppose more than they explain) is transmitted in the section dedicated specifically to the topic we are concerned with, under the title 'Chapter on co-suretyship and suretyship and partnership' (*dar ī ham-pāyandānīh ud pāyandānīh ud hamhāyīh*).[365] The surety (given the name Farrox in the text, whose statement we have cited), guarantees that he will deliver a person named Mihrēn (who is either the principal debtor or another person provided as security) to the creditor (called Ādurfarrbay), when the creditor asks him to, or will pay back the debt himself if he fails to do so.[366] The main information to

363 I have discussed Sasanian suretyship in the context of a passage of the Babylonian Talmud in Macuch 2016b.

364 Macuch 1993, pp. 389, 394.

365 MHD 55.10 (Macuch 1993, pp. 386, 391).

366 MHD 58.4–9: *ka Farrox abāg Ādurfarrbay paymān kunēd kū ka tō Mihrēn xwāhē Mihrēn ō tō abespārom ēnyā 200 be dahom ud pas Ādurfarrbay Mihrēn az Farrox xwāhēd ud Farrox Mihrēn nē abespārēd ud agar Farrox pad abespard ī Mihrēn a-tuwānīg ud pad ān a-tuwānīgīh a-wināh ka-iz pas ō tuwānīgīh rasēd tan nē abespārišn ud 200-iz nē. agar-iš guft kū-m padīrift ka-iz pad ān ēwēnag a-tuwānīg be bawēd ēg-iš čiyōn ō tuwānīg(īh) rasēd tan abāz abespārišn.* 'When Farrox makes a contract with Ādurfarrbay: "When you request Mihrēn I will deliver Mihrēn to you, otherwise I will pay 200 (st./dr.)", and afterwards Ādurfarrbay requests Mihrēn from Farrox and Farrox does not deliver Mihrēn and if Farrox is incapable of delivering Mihrēn and is guiltless with regard to that incapability: even if he (= Farrox) later acquires the capability, he does not have to deliver the person (*tan*), nor to pay the 200 (st./dr.). If he (= Ādurfarrbay) says: "I have accepted", then even if he (= Farrox) is incapable/insolvent in that manner, when he reaches capability/solvency, then the person (*tan*) has to be returned.' The concise wording of this sentence is by no means easy to understand, but the main point is that the obligations of the surety (Farrox) and the creditor (Ādurfarrbay) are contrasted with each other in the specific case of non-performance of contract: (1) if the surety is through no fault of his own unable to deliver the principal debtor (or another person provided as security, called Mihrēn) on the date requested by the creditor, he is not obliged to do so later, nor to pay the debt (since, as we may add, the surety himself would be taken into debt bondage by the creditor in lieu of the principal debtor); (2) on the other hand, if the creditor has agreed to the terms of the contract with the words 'I have accepted' (*kū-m padīrift*), and the person (*tan*) (*i. e*, the debtor or another pledged person, Mihrēn) has been delivered to him, the obligation to release (*abāz abespārišn*) the latter from debt bondage remains in force, when the debt is paid. See also commentary to the whole

be gained from this passage is that Sasanian law still knew an ancient type of personal security, already attested in cuneiform law as Paul Koschaker has elucidated in his work on suretyship in the Babylonian-Assyrian cuneiform legal texts. The surety did not initially accept liability for the debt of the borrower, but promised to deliver the latter to the creditor on non-fulfilment of contract or to ensure that the debtor would not leave his original location. Koschaker distinguishes these two elementary types of suretyship in the cuneiform texts as 'Stillesitzbürgschaft' (suretyship of location) and 'Gestellungsbürgschaft' (suretyship of delivery).[367] In the first type the surety guarantees that the principal debtor will remain accessible to the creditor and not escape payment (by hiding or fleeing); in the second type he promises to seize and hand over the debtor to the creditor. In the statement we have cited above, the surety commits himself to transfer a person named Mihrēn (who is either the debtor himself or another person the debtor has provided as security, see the variant of this type of suretyship discussed as the next type below) to the creditor. If he fails to do so, he will repay the debt (or a sum of money, not necessarily identical with the debt). In other words, the surety promises to ensure performance of contract by two means: (1) by delivering the debtor (or another person provided as security) to the creditor (this would usually lead to debt bondage and later enslavement of the debtor or the security if the debtor remained insolvent), or (2) by repaying the debt (with or without an additional compensation).

A modified or extended form of this ancient type of suretyship seems to be a combination of real and personal security. This variant is indirectly attested in several short sentences of the same chapter, in which the term *tan* (lit. 'body, person'), specifically in the phrase *pad tan* (lit. 'as a person/body'), refers either to the principal debtor himself or to another person, who is provided as security by the debtor. This seems to be the background of several cases, in which the creditor gives his consent to accept a person 'as a body' (*pad tan*) using the formal words:

MHD 57.12–13; 57.15
kū-m Farrox (Mihrēn) pad tan az tō padīrift

'I have accepted Farrox/Mihrēn "as a body" from you.'[368]

MHD 57.17–58.1
kū-m Farrox pad tan az Ādurfarrbay padīrift

'I have accepted Farrox "as a body" from Ādurfarrbay.'[369]

---

chapter in Macuch 1993, pp. 396–407 (especially no. 11 on the terminology used in this section): *padīriftan* 'to receive, accept' refers to the consent of the creditor with the guarantee provided by the surety, whereas *abespārdan* 'to commit, entrust, consign, deliver' denotes the actual transfer of the principal debtor (or of another person as security) to the creditor; *abāz abespārdan* 'to consign back, return' denotes the release of the debtor (or of another person) from debt bondage.

367 Koschaker 1911, p. 75.

368 Macuch 1993, pp. 388, 393.

369 Macuch 1993, pp. 389, 394.

In some of the earliest loan contracts (*e. g.*, the Roman *nexum* 'bond') the borrower bound himself by pledging his body as security for the payment of a debt.[370] The Iranian phrase *pad tan* could have a similar provenance, denoting a form of pledge in which either the debtor pledged his own 'body' or that of another person as security for a loan. The phrase is, however, not attested in the sections on pledge (*graw*), but in the chapter on suretyship (*pāyandānīh*, the title of which we have already quoted above), presumably due to a combination of these two forms of security. It seems that a debtor (who had no property or not enough property at his disposal) could offer himself or provide another person, *e. g.*, a member of his family, one (or several) of his children, as security to the creditor (the names used in the formulae cited above are interchangeable and stand for "such-and-such a person", N.N.). The creditor gave his consent to this type of security with the formula *kū-m ... pad tan ... padīrift* 'I have accepted (so-and-so) as a body (from so-and-so)' (which does not imply that the pledged person has already been transferred, but only that the creditor agrees to the security; the term denoting the actual transfer is *abespārdan* 'to hand over, deliver').[371] If the debtor failed to repay the loan on the contracted date, he himself or the person (family member) provided as security was obliged to place his work capacity at the disposal of the creditor either until the debt was paid or for a certain limited period recorded in the contract (*e. g.*, one year).[372] The consequences of debt bondage are not elucidated in the sources, but we can reasonably infer that the *tan* could be released from bondage on fulfilment of contract, but would be finally enslaved if the total sum of the debt was not returned by a specified period. It seems that in Iranian law the delivery of the *tan* (that is, of the debtor himself or one of his family members) was guaranteed by a third party, a surety, with whom the creditor(s) reached (a separate or additional) agreement. Unfortunately none of the sentences using this technical term are conclusive, but in the context of the chapter on suretyship they imply that a third party (besides the debtor and creditor) was involved, who accepted responsibility for handing over the pledged person to the creditor, as can be concluded not only from the title of the chapter, but also from the following passage:

> MHD 57.14–16:
> *ka Ohrmazd rūz Farrox ud Wahman rūz {...} az pusag andar Ādurfarrbay kard kū-m Mihrēn pad tan az tō padīrift pāyandānīh har dō xūb.*
>
> 'If Farrox on day Ohrmazd and {...} on day Wahman have agreed with Ādurfarrbay regarding the son: "I have accepted Mihrēn as a body from you", (then) both suretyships (*pāyandānīh*) (are) proper.'[373]

370 On *nexum* see du Plessis/Borkowski 2010, p. 297; dalla Massara 2017, p. 154; Kaser 1986, p. 182f.
371 On the terminology employed in the formulae of this chapter of the Law-book see fn. 366 above.
372 As in MHD 57.16–58.3 (Macuch 1993, pp. 389, 394).
373 Macuch 1993, pp. 388, 393.

If my understanding of this sentence is correct, two creditors (Farrox and another person whose name is missing in the manuscript due to a lacuna) reach an agreement to accept one and the same person as security for two subsequent loans, contracted on the first and second days (*Ohrmazd rūz* and *Wahman rūz*) of a certain (unnamed) month. For both loans the same person, the debtor's (or the surety's) son (*pusag*, lit. 'little son', 'younger son'?), called Mihrēn, is provided as security. The creditors enter a contract with the surety, named Ādurfarrbay, who guarantees that the son will be delivered to the two creditors. By speaking the formel words *kū-m Mihrēn pad tan az tō padīrift* 'I have accepted Mihrēn "as a body" from you' the creditors consent to the procedure (on the terminology see fn. 366 above). Both suretyships (*pāyandānīh*) are 'good, proper, impeccable, (legally) correct' (*xūb*).

To be sure, the sentence postulates knowledge of this branch of law, is hence short and does not reveal all the details we would like to know, but if this is the correct interpretation, this type of suretyship is an extended variant of the first type described above and combines two forms of security, the pledge (of a 'body') and a warranty (*pāyandānīh*) vouchsafing for the actual transfer of the pledge to the creditor(s) on default of the debtor. The surety was only obliged to hand over the pledged person to the creditor, but could not be held liable for payment if he fulfilled this commitment according to the terms of the contract.[374]

Another type of suretyship, comparable to the guarantee, was created by two other formulae, spoken either by the principal debtor or by the surety himself. The principal debtor could declare:

> MHD 56.5–6
> *kū-m pad ēn xwāstag* ⟨NKSY'⟩ *wāhmān mard pāyandān kard.*
> 'I have made such-and-such a man surety for this money (= loan).'[375]

The implications of this wording are explained precisely: the surety is only liable for payment when the principal debtor is insolvent or inaccessible (*rāh ō pāyēndān ān zamān bawēd ka mērag an-ādān ayāb nē mad ēstēd.* 'a claim against the guarantor is effective at the time when the man [= debtor] is insolvent or has not come'). The duties generated by this formula are those of the 'guarantee', a secondary obligation that can only be enforced, when the principal debtor is in default. As long as the debtor—being primarily responsible for repaying the debt—can be held liable and be sued by the creditor, the surety or guarantor cannot be compelled to make payment. Our passage clearly states that payment could only be extracted from the surety if the principal debtor was insolvent (*an-ādān*) or did not show up (*nē mad ēstēd*) to pay back the loan at the stipulated time (or in court, if a lawsuit was initiated by the creditor).

374 This type of security is indirectly confirmed by a passage of the Babylonian Talmud which discusses suretyship in 'Persian law'. See Chapter VII, pp. 606–608, and Macuch 2016b.

375 Macuch 1993, pp. 387, 392.

Another formula, spoken by the surety (or several sureties) has exactly the same consequences:

MHD 57.1–2
pad ēn xwāstag ⟨NKSY'⟩ *wāhmān mard pāyandān hēm.*
'I am (we are) a surety (sureties) of such-and-such a man for this money (= loan).'[376]

With this wording the surety (sureties) took on a secondary obligation to compensate the loss of the creditor only if the principal debtor (*mādagwar*) was insolvent (the implications are stated clearly: *ka mādagwar ādān rāh ō pāyandān nēst* 'there is no claim against the surety if the principal debtor is solvent'). As in the preceding case, payment could only be extracted from the guarantor after the principal debtor had been found insolvent and incapable of repaying the loan.

Another form of surety, comparable to the indemnity, is obviously represented in another passage. A primary obligation could be created by the use of another wording in the contract, giving the creditor—in contrast to the guarantee—direct access to payment by the surety. In this case the surety used another formula:

MHD 56.15–17
man pāyandānīh ī wāhmān rāy xwāstag ⟨NKSY'⟩ *and ō tō dahom.*
'Because of suretyship for such-and-such a man I will pay you this much money.'[377]

This phrasing in the contract generated a primary obligation. The creditor could claim the debt directly from the surety without suing the principal debtor first (*rāh ō pāyandān u-š abāz ō bun nē bawēd* 'a claim against the surety [is in effect] and does not return to the origin [= principal debtor]'). We are informed that if there was no time limit in the agreement on suretyship, the contract was not conditional on default of the debtor. The creditor was hence permitted to demand payment from the surety directly *without* first suing the principal debtor.

Two or several debtors in a partnership (*hambāyīh*) could agree to act at the same time as co-sureties (*ham-pāyandān*), *i. e*, they could warrant for the debt together, using the following formulae:

MHD 56.1
ham-pāyandān hēm.
'We are co-sureties.'[378]

MHD 56.8–9
kū-mān xwāstag ⟨NKSY'⟩ *abām stad ham-pāyandān hēm.*
'We have taken money as a loan (and) are co-sureties.'[379]

376 Macuch 1993, pp. 388, 393.
377 Macuch 1993, pp. 387, 393.
378 Macuch 1993, pp. 386, 391f.
379 Macuch 1993, pp. 387, 392.

MHD 56.9–10
pad ān xwāstag ⟨NKSYʾ⟩ *ēk ōy ī did ham-pāyandān hēm.*
'For this money (loan) we are co-sureties, one for the other.'[380]

In all these cases the co-sureties were jointly liable for the debt and the creditor could demand full payment of the whole sum from any one of the persons under contract (*az har kē kāmēd pādixšāy xwāst* 'he [= the creditor] is authorized to claim it [= the debt] from any one he wishes to'). The co-sureties were, to use Sasanian legal terminology, *hamāg-tōzišn* 'joint and several debtors', *i. e*, every debtor could be sued for the total amount. The partner who paid back the whole debt had the right to demand regress from the other joint debtors.[381] The implications were completely different if the co-debtors were *not* at the same time co-sureties. If the partners were only joint debtors, but did not take on co-suretyship, the creditor could only sue each debtor at a time for the amount he himself had taken as a loan (they were, to use the technical term, *xwāstag-tōzišn* 'part debtors'). Even if the contract explicitly allowed the creditor to claim the whole sum from one of the co-debtors, the debtor who paid the total amount had no right to demand regress from the others.[382] The reason for this distinction between co-debtors and co-sureties is not conveyed, but the Law-book makes it quite clear that in the case of co-debtors, who are *not* co-sureties, each of the joint debtors is only liable for his own share of the debt, but can be sued for the whole sum by the creditor in accordance with the contract or if the other partners are insolvent. On the other hand, if joint debtors are at the same time co-sureties each debtor is liable in a dual function, as debtor for himself and as surety for the other(s), giving the creditor the option to sue any one of the partners for the whole sum. This distinction between co-debtors and co-sureties seems to have been very similar in Jewish law.[383]

Table 30. Overview of terminology: personal security (*pāyandān*, *pāyandānīh*)

abāz abespārdan[384]	'to consign back, return, release' (action of the creditor, who releases the pledged person/surety from debt bondage)
abāz padīriftan[385]	'to take back, redeem' (action of the debtor, who redeems the pledged person/surety from debt bondage)

380 Macuch 1993, pp. 387, 392.
381 MHD 55.17–56.5 (Macuch 1993, pp. 386, 391–392).
382 MHD 56.3–5 (Macuch 1993, pp. 387, 392).
383 See Herzog 1939, pp. 215–216.
384 For attestations see Macuch 1993, index p. 687; on the specific use of the verb in this context see *ibid.* pp. 402–403 (no. 11).
385 For attestations see Macuch 1993, index, p. 724; on the specific use of the verb see *ibid.*, p. 404 (no. 13).

abespārdan (*ō* ... *abespārdan*)[386]	'to commit, entrust, consign, deliver (to)' (the actual transfer of the principal debtor or pledged person to the creditor)
ēk ōy ī dīd pāyandān (*ham-pāyandān*) *hēm*[387]	'We are sureties (co-sureties), one for the other'
ham-pāyandān hēm[388]	'We are co-sureties'
kū-m pad ēn xwāstag ⟨NKSY'⟩ (*wahmān mard*) *pāyandān kard*[389]	'I have made for this money (such-and-such a man) surety'
kū-m... pad tan az ... padīrift[390]	'I have accepted (so-and-so) as personal security (lit.: body) from (so-and-so)'
pad ēn xwāstag ⟨NKSY'⟩ *wahmān mard pāyandān hom/hēm*[391]	'For this money I am (we are) surety (sureties) for such-and-such a man'
padīriftan (*az* ... *padīriftan*)[392]	'to receive, accept (from)' (consent of the creditor to the suretyship)
pāyandānīh nēst[393]	'there is no suretyship; suretyship is not in effect'
pāyandānīh xūb[394]	'the suretyship is proper; in force'
rāh ō pāyandān ... nē bawēd/nēst[395]	'the surety is not liable; cannot be made liable' (lit.: 'there is no way to the surety')

Our sources admittedly leave many questions unanswered, but they reveal clearly that Sasanian law knew a great variety of different types of suretyship, permitting a creditor to look to a third party for satisfaction in various ways. A surety could promise to deliver the debtor (or another person provided as pawn) to the creditor on a specified date, with no further obligation to pay the debt if he performed accordingly. On the other hand, the surety could accept a secondary obligation to make payment on default of the principal debtor (in accordance with a contract comparable to the guarantee), or he could take a primary obligation to pay the debt irrespective of the possibility of suing the debtor (in a contract comparable to the indemnity). Co-debtors could at the same time act as co-sureties, each one of the debtors accepting liability for the other partners.

386 For attestations see MACUCH 1993, index, p. 687.
387 MHD 59.3,6 (MACUCH 1993, pp. 390, 395).
388 MHD 56.1,9,10 (MACUCH 1993, pp. 386f., 390f.).
389 MHD 56.5 (MACUCH 1993, pp. 387, 392).
390 MHD 57.13,15; 57.17–58.1 (MACUCH 1993, pp. 388f.; 393f.); 89.2 (*ibid*., pp. 569, 572).
391 MHD 57.2,8 (MACUCH 1993, pp. 388, 393).
392 For attestations see MACUCH 1993, index, p. 724; on the specific use of the verb see *ibid*., p. 404 (no. 13).
393 MHD 89.2 (MACUCH 1993, pp. 569, 572).
394 MHD 57.15 (MACUCH 1993, pp. 388, 393).
395 MHD 56.17; 57.2,6 (MACUCH 1993, pp. 387f., 392f.).

It would not be too far-fetched to assume that these different forms of suretyship, although they are all attested as variants alongside each other, also reflect to a certain degree the historical development of Sasanian credit law. The first type described above (suretyship of performance), by which the surety ensures that the debtor will be accessible to the creditor when the loan is due, was presumably a very ancient form of personal security, already attested in cuneiform law, which survived alongside other more recent forms. Originally the surety only guaranteed that the debtor would stay at a certain place (suretyship of location) or that he would deliver him to the creditor (suretyship of delivery), but he was not initially held responsible for repaying the debt. The second type (suretyship of the body/person) could have well been a further development of this first type by extending the possible group of persons against whom the creditor had recourse. The surety would agree to deliver a specific person (a child or another family member of either the debtor or the surety) to the creditor should the debtor himself fail to do so or be inaccessible (due to flight, hiding, escape from the claims of several creditors etc.). The pledged child would be kept in debt bondage until the loan was paid or the creditor satisfied in some other manner. Both forms are presumably precursors of accessory suretyship, permitting the creditor to exact payment from the surety if the debtor is insolvent.

Originally the surety in the first type (suretyship of performance) and the second variant (suretyship of the person/body) is liable not only with his property, but with his *whole person* if the debtor fails to perform (corresponding with the liability of the debtor, who has pledged his own 'body', *tan*, or that of a family member, to the creditor). If he cannot deliver the debtor (or the person agreed upon as *tan*) to the creditor, the surety takes upon himself the consequences: he is forced in lieu of the debtor or the pledged person into debt bondage, but can free himself by satisfying the creditor and paying back the debt. In the course of the further historical development of credit law this 'detour', leading the surety first into debt bondage, from which he could release himself by paying, was at some point abandoned. The surety no longer pledged himself entirely, with his whole person, but restricted his commitment to satisfying the creditor on default of the debtor. This minimal, but important change presumably led to the most common form of suretyship, known today as the 'guarantee' or 'accessory suretyship', by which a secondary obligation is generated: the promise of the surety to answer for the debt of another person takes effect only when the principal debtor is insolvent or inaccessible.[396] The 'indemnity' as a primary obligation could be a later development or simplification, permitting the creditor—in contrast to the 'guarantee'—to extract payment from the surety without having to sue the principal debtor first and irrespective of the latter's capacity to repay the loan. Joint suretyship of co-debtors and the distinction between co-debtors and co-sureties are presumably further differentiations, which are to be expected in

396 On the development of Sasanian suretyship see also Macuch 1981, pp. 225–227.

an economy gradually increasing in complexity over the centuries.[397] That these different forms of suretyship were all operative in the Sasanian period is not only confirmed by the passages of the Law-book discussed above, but also indirectly in the Babylonian Talmud, causing apparently some confusion in rabbinic discussions due to the many different forms suretyship could assume.[398]

Table 31. Historical development and types of suretyship

Stages	Type of suretyship	Legal implications
I	suretyship of performance	The surety guarantees that the principal debtor will either 1) stay at the location or place of performance (suretyship of location), or 2) he guarantees to deliver the debtor to the creditor (suretyship of delivery).
II	suretyship 'of the body/person' (*pad tan*)	The surety guarantees that he will deliver a specific person (*tan*), agreed upon as security with the debtor, to the creditor if the principal debtor is in default (variant of I, 2).
III	accessory suretyship, guarantee	The surety accepts a secondary obligation to pay the debt. He is only liable for payment if the principal debtor is insolvent or inaccessible.
IV	indemnity	The surety accepts a primary obligation to pay the debt. The creditor can demand payment directly from the surety without first addressing or suing the debtor.
V	joint suretyship of co-debtors	Co-debtors who are co-sureties have joint liability. The creditor can demand full payment of the whole sum from any one of the persons under contract.

397 A fascinating, completely unique sentence in the whole Law-book is transmitted in the chapter on suretyship, MHD 57.2–12, which I have discussed extensively in Macuch 2009b. The passage involves a number of women (presumably originally three; five in the ms.) 'sitting on the way' who interrogate a jurisconsult named Ādurfrazgar on his way to the 'place of the oath' (*xwūrestān*). The women are very well informed on legal matters and ask three questions regarding the liability of sureties, the last of which the jurisconsult cannot answer. I have argued that this passage represents a literary topos, that of the 'three Fates', who are represented in a variety of forms not only in a large number of Indoeuropean fables and myths, but also in another Pahlavi source (the *Kārnāmag of Ardaxšēr ī Pābagān*), in which three women 'sitting on the way' tell Ardaxšēr, the future king, his fortune. As several significant elements of this topos can also be recognized here, this passage of the Law-book (most unfortunately) cannot be taken as any kind of proof for women's knowledge of jurisprudence in the Sasanian period or their education in this field (beyond the religious, moral and ritual instructions also given to women).

398 See Macuch 2016b and Chapter VII, pp. 606–608 below.

4.1.3 Liabilities and claims of the family

Among the subjects discussed to a somewhat larger extent (maybe due to its importance for the survival of noble families) in the fragmentary material on credit law are claims and liabilities of succession after the demise of a *kadag-xwadāy*. Besides a whole chapter dedicated to this topic (with the title *dar ī tōzišn ī az dūdag kunišn ud ēd čē ō dūdag xwāhišn* 'Chapter on payments to be made by the family and those which are to be requested for the family'),[399] scattered entries in other sections of the Law-book address these and similar problems, which were evidently so significant that even women were permitted in certain cases to appear in court as one of the parties (or as witnesses). As we have already noted above, usually the eldest legitimate son, who was of age or reached maturity after the death of the *paterfamilias* became 'guardian of the family' (*dūdag-sālār*) and took over (as *sālār ī būdag* 'natural guardian', and *xwāstagdār* 'possessor of property, heir') responsibility for the management of family property (*xwāstag-sālārīh* 'guardianship of the property'). One of the main duties of the son as guardian after succeeding the father was to protect the proprietary interests of the family, to collect debts owed to the family, but also to assume liability for debts of the father. If the *pādixšāy* son was established by testament alone as *abarmānd-xwāstagdār* ('possessor/heir of the total estate'), he assumed sole responsibility among the heirs for the 'liabilities of the forefathers' (*tōzišn ī pidarān*) and had no right of recourse against the other co-heirs (*hambāyān* 'partners, shareholders').[400] If several sons were installed by testament as heirs (*xwāstagdār*), they took joint responsibility for liabilities of the family as *hamāg-tōzišn* 'joint and several debtor(s)', no matter when the property was assigned to them, whether at different periods (*pēš ud pas* 'before and after') or at the same time (*pad ēwbār* 'at once').[401] As we have already elucidated above, joint debtors (*hamāg-tōzišn*) in a partnership or association have joint liability and can be charged either together or individually to repay the entire debt. The sons as heirs (*xwāstagdār*) took on full responsibility for all the liabilities of the father as joint debtors, that is, the creditor could charge each of them for the whole debt. In contrast, other beneficiaries and legatees (*mard ī šahr*, lit. 'men of the land') were *xwāstag-tōzišn* ('part-debtors'), who could be charged only in proportion to their individual shares (*bahr-marīhā*) of the whole sum, but not for the entire debt.[402]

The son who took over as 'natural guardian' (*sālār ī būdag*) represented the family in litigation alone, if a debt was claimed, as we are informed only indirectly: the widow of the deceased, the *kadag-bānūg*, was *not* summoned to

399 MHD 15.2–3 (Macuch 1993, pp. 139, 142).

400 MHD 2.4–5 (Macuch 1993, pp. 40, 42). On the obligation of the son as successor and heir (*xwāstagdār*) to pay for liabilities of the father see Chapter III, pp. 207–209.

401 MHD 60.5–7 (Macuch 1993, pp. 409, 414).

402 See above, pp. 208–209.

appear in court in this case (a woman would normally be represented by her husband or legal guardian in all legal matters).[403] If a legal guardian had already been appointed before the son reached maturity, the latter replaced him on his coming of age and immediately took over all legal responsibilities, including lawsuits against the family and those that had been initiated by the previous guardian.[404] After accepting guardianship the son could even dispute an alleged debt that had been already recognized by the previous guardian (together with the mistress of the house) and for which property had been handed over in repayment of the debt and as compensation.[405]

The situation was different if the legal guardian of a family was not the legitimate son (or *sālār ī būdag* 'natural guardian'), but recruited from one of the other types of guardianship (*kardag* or *gumārdag*).[406] As we have seen, restrictions were placed on all transactions of the legal guardian in those cases, which could cause damage to family property or in some manner diminish it. In contrast to usual legal practice, the widow or widows of a deceased *paterfamilias* were included in legal proceedings involving liabilities of the family presumably in order to avoid decisions detrimental to the interests of a *dūdag*. In a large number of cases the *kadag-bānūg* plays a prominent role in these disputes alongside the guardian, both as plaintiff and as defendant.[407] She can take legal action and also be sued (together with the legal guardian); her statement is heard in court; she can be obliged to take an oath and both statement and oath can effect the outcome of the trial.[408] In the case of contradictory statements, if the mistress of the house declines a payment claim, but the legal guardian recognizes it, the acceptance of the guardian is documented and another guardian is specifically appointed to continue the lawsuit together with the mistress.[409] If the deceased master of the house has several wives (all in the *pādixšāy* status, as only a *pādixšāy*-wife is at the same time *kadag-bānūg*), a claim against the family involving a liability has to be forwarded against all of them.[410]

403 MHD 15.10–11 (Macuch 1993, pp. 139, 143).
404 MHDA 32.9–13 (Macuch 1981, pp. 57f., 215).
405 MHD 15.12–14 (Macuch 1993, pp. 140, 143); see also below.
406 On these different categories of guardianship see Chapter II, pp. 179–181.
407 One of these cases mentioning the name of a woman as one of the claimants, possibly a *kadag-bānūg*, is documented in an original court record from Tabarestān (Tab. 1A; see Macuch 2016a, p. 159). The document notes that a 'complaint' (*garzišn*) has been filed by 'the clan (or house, lit. 'men') called Yazd' (*mardān ī Yazd nām*) and 'a woman called Duxtxwašīh' (*ud zan-ēw Duxtxwašīh nām*). Unfortunately she does not appear again in the document, but she is explicitly listed as one of the plaintiffs in a dispute regarding proprietary rights.
408 MHD 13.6–13; 15.3–7; 16.1–2, 5–10 (Macuch 1993, pp. 127, 130f.; 139, 142; 140, 143f. respectively).
409 MHD 16.14–17 (Macuch 1993, pp. 141, 144).
410 According to MHD 15.8–9 (Macuch 1993, pp. 137, 142) if payment is demanded from a family (*az dūdag tōzišn be kunišn*) and there are three women (= wives, *zan*), then the claim is only permitted if the plaintiff sues all three women (*har sē hamēmālīh be kunēd*).

These regulations only make sense if we assume, first, that women in the position of *kadag-bānūg* were conceded (limited) legal capacity to a specific purpose, that of preserving the material interests of the family in absence of a *kadag-xwadāy* or his direct male successor, and, second, that in the described cases no incontestable debt contract (bearing the seal of an official authority) was in existence that could serve as evidence for the legality of the claim. We have seen that even if the mistress of the house and the legal guardian both recognized a debt (*pad tōzišn ī kadag-xwadāy xwastūg hēnd* 'they recognize the payment obligation of the *paterfamilias*'), the son could contradict their statements on reaching maturity and take renewed legal action against the claimant. In this case the burden of proof was reversed and lay on the latter: the claimant was obliged to provide evidence: *abām būd paydāg kunišn* 'he (= the creditor) must prove that there was a debt'. Under specific circumstances, if the property that was claimed for the debt was of fundamental importance for the maintenance of the family (*ka dārišn āsn pad dudag* 'if the possession [is] substantial for the family'), the evidence provided by the creditor had to be 'reliable, certain, binding' (*ēwar*), *i. e*, no doubt should be left as to the legality of the claim.[411]

Forms of evidence considered as *ēwar* 'reliable, (legally) binding' (as opposed to *warōmand* 'uncertain, unreliable, not binding') are transmitted as: (1) a 'reliable document' (*wizīr ī ēwar*), referring to a contract sealed by a legal authority; (2) the testimony of three witnesses or the highest legal authority, the *mowbedān mowbed*; (3) the oath (*war*).[412] The last type of 'reliable' evidence, the ordeal or oath, seems to have been one of the main means of providing proof for the existence or non-existence of a liability in absence of a legal contract or of witnesses. As we will see in Chapter VI, the oath could take on different forms, depending on the statement of the person under oath. The court decided which one of the litigants should take the oath according to the key criterion of *wehdādestāntar*, lit. 'better suited to good justice', a technical term referring to the person, whose oath would lead to 'better judgement', *i. e*, a judgement exceeding the minimum requirements of justice (*wehdādestānīh*).[413] In most cases the defendant(s) (or: alleged debtors) are called to take the oath if they deny the loan (*nagīrā[y] hēnd*) (but see the cases described above).[414] In the context of the 'liabilities of the forefathers/parents' (*tōzišn ī pidarān*) three types of oath are mentioned, depending on the statement the defendant is requested to confirm under oath:

411 MHD 15.12–16.1 (Macuch 1993, pp. 139f., 143).

412 MHD 15.12–16.1 (Macuch 1993, pp. 139f., 143); on this passage and its legal terminology see also commentary, Macuch 1993, pp. 147–148 (no. 6 and 7), with further attestations.

413 On this technical term see Macuch 2019a and pp. 554–555 below. The term is used in the context of liabilities of succession in MHD 13.7 (Macuch 1993, pp. 125, 130).

414 MHD 13.6–13 and 13.13–15 (Macuch 1993, pp. 127f., 130f.).

1. The defendant (alleged debtor) claims to have 'no knowledge' (*nē dānist*) of a debt. The court can prescribe the *war ī dēnīg* (or: *dēnīg war*) 'religious oath' by which the defendant refutes the claim of his opponent (the alleged creditor) with the words *nē ēdōnīh* 'it (is) not so' (lit. 'not-thusness').[415]
2. The defendant neither refutes the claim, nor accepts it, but only declares that he/she is not informed of any liabilities of the family or of the *paterfamilias*. The court can prescribe the *war ī pāy-nišān* 'oath of binding the feet' by which the defendant (alleged debtor) speaks the words *nē dānom* 'I do not know', stating that he or she has no knowledge of a debt. The plaintiff (alleged creditor) is obliged to provide 'reliable' evidence that a debt does indeed exist.[416]
3. The defendants, in this case the legal guardian and the *kadag-bānūg*, both declare that they have 'no knowledge' (*nē dānist*) of a debt. They can both be obliged to take the *war ī pad sōgand* 'sulphurous water oath'.[417] A similar case, presumably requiring the same type of oath, is transmitted RivAF 66: the son of the *paterfamilias* denies knowledge of a debt of the deceased father with the words: 'I have no knowledge of it' (*kū-š man āgāhīh nēst*) and proposes to take a corresponding oath.[418]

Another problem discussed at some length in the Law-book is the question, whether a 'prepayment, advance payment' (*pēš-tōzišnīh*) for liabilities of the *paterfamilias* has to be made before a testament or donation takes effect.[419] As we have already noted above, this word is used of an obligation of the *kadag-xwadāy* (due to a debt or a pious gift or a *margarzān* offence) that had to be settled *before* other dispositions came into force and the heirs and beneficiaries took possession of the estate.[420] In the context of debt, this technical term seems to have referred to a kind of 'charge', a form of security protecting the creditor (chargee) by giving him the right to payment from the sale of mortgaged property in priority to any rights resulting from inheritance (or claims any other creditors might have against the debtor). The passages are not very clear, but the general rule seems to have been: in three cases obligations of the deceased had to be fulfilled by effecting advance payment (*peš-tōzišnīh*) before the heirs or beneficiaries received access to the inheritance: (1) for a debt (*abām*) that had been taken out by the testator/donor prior to the testament or donation, (2) for

415 MHD 13.1–2 (Macuch 1993, pp, 125, 130).
416 MHD 13.2–3 (Macuch 1993, pp, 125, 130).
417 MHD 13.6–13 (Macuch 1993, pp. 127, 130f.). The sentence implies that the same litigants could be obliged by the court to take subsequently two different oaths, see commentary *ibid.* pp. 135f. (no. 3). On these and other types of oaths see Chapter VI, pp. 551–560.
418 This passage is discussed in the context of the oath (Chapter VI, pp. 556–557). Anklesaria 1969 (vol. I, p. 35, 120; II, p. 77) has a misleading reading and translation of this *Pursišn*. The whole text is in Appendix IX, pp. 696–697.
419 MHD 29.12–32.10 (Macuch 1993, pp. 220–227).
420 See pp. 339–340 above.

a pious gift (*ahlawdād*) to be financed from the property of the deceased; (3) for a penalty in the case of a *margarzān* ('deserving death') offence.[421]

Table 32. Overview: technical terms and phrases in the context of liabilities

abām būd paydāg kardan[422]	to prove the existence of a debt
hamāg-tōzišn hēnd[423]	'they are joint and several debtors'
(*pad abām/tōzišn*) ... *nagīrā(y) hēnd*[424]	'they deny (the debt/payment obligation)'
pad tōzišn (*abām*) ... *xwastūg hēnd*[425]	'they recognize the payment obligation (debt)'
pad war ... *wehdādestāntar*[426]	'better suited for taking the oath'
tōzišn ... *az dūdag kardan*[427]	to effect a payment from the family (property)
(*tōzišn*) ... *ō dūdag* (*andar*) *xwāstan*[428]	to request (a payment) for the family
xwāstag-tōzišn hēnd[429]	'they are part debtors'

4.1.4 Debt cancellation

A creditor could waive his claim to repayment by cancelling the debt. The implications of debt relief are discussed particularly in the context of joint debtors, who are partners (*hambāyān*) or co-proprietors (*hamxwāstagān*) or co-sureties (*hampāyandān*), due to the questions involved in determining the exact proportions attributable to each of the partners.[430] In one instance three men take up

421 See specifically MHD 31.2–3 (Macuch 1993, pp. 222, 226). See also pp. 339–340 and fn. 327 above.

422 MHD 15.15 (Macuch 1993, pp. 140, 143).

423 MHD 60.6 (Macuch 1993, pp. 409, 414).

424 MHD 13.14 (Macuch 1993, pp. 128, 131). Compare: *ka tōzišn pad nagīrā(y)īh wizārēnd* 'if they make the payment whilst denying the debt' (MHD 102.13; *ibid.* pp. 616, 624). On *nagīrā(y)* see Buyaner 2015.

425 MHD 15.12 (Macuch 1993, pp. 140, 143).

426 On this term see below Chapter VI, pp. 554–555.

427 MHD 15.2–3 (Macuch 1993, pp. 139, 142). Variants: *az dūdag tōzišn be kunišn* 'on the part of the family a payment must be made' (MHD16.14, *ibid.* pp. 141, 144); *tōzišn dahišn* 'a payment must be given' (MHD 76.4, 6; *ibid.* pp. 510, 512).

428 MHD 15.3, 16.5 (Macuch 1993, pp. 139, 142 and 140, 143 respectively). Variants: *ka tōzišn az dūdag xwāst* 'if he has demanded a payment from the family' (MHD 15.4; 63.3; *ibid.* pp. 139, 142); *ka tōzišn ō dūdag xwāhēd* 'if she claims a payment for the family' (MHD 15.9,10; *ibid.* pp. 139, 142).

429 MHD 60.7 (Macuch1993, pp. 409, 414).

430 Particularly chapter two of the Law-book, MHD 2.1–17 (Macuch 1993, pp. 40–43). On co-proprietors (*hamxwāstagān*) and partners (*hambāyān*) see Chapter III, pp. 245–253; on co-sureties (*hampāyandān*) see above pp. 349–359.

a money-loan together (*abām stānēnd*) and seal a document (*wizīr āwāšēnd*). Afterwards the creditor conveys property[431] worth the sum of the loan (or: money corresponding to the amount of the loan?) in ownership (*pad xwēšīh*) to one of the three joint debtors. In compliance with the general rule in partnerships (of the *āgenēn xwēš* 'co-ownership [with equal shares]' category) every acquisition of one of the associates belongs jointly to all the partners.[432] Hence the partners are all released from debt and the co-debtor who has received the whole donation/money from the creditor is not authorized to claim from his associates a larger share of the money than the portion to which he is individually entitled in the partnership.[433]

Interestingly, the Law-book also transmits a diametrically opposed decision (based on the statements of the jurisconsults Farroxzurwān and Wehohrmazd) in a very similar case: three men (who are partners) take out a loan of 100 (drachms/staters) from a moneylender (called Farrox). The creditor (Farrox) later releases one of the debtors from debt with respect to the whole amount of the loan (*i. e*, 100 drachms/staters). According to the quoted jurisconsults the shares of the debtor who has been released from debt and those of the other two debtors are separate (*ǰuttar*). Hence (as we may surmise) the two other co-debtors are not released from debt and the creditor can demand payment from them in proportion to their shares.[434]

The difference between these two described cases seems to lie in the assessment of the type of partnership of the co-debtors: in the former case, presumably of the *āgenēn xwēš* 'co-ownership' type, the partners have *equal* shares (and are possibly 'joint and several debtors', *hamāg-tōzišn*, that is every one of the joint debtors is obliged to take full responsibility for satisfying the claims of the creditor and can be sued for the whole amount). If the creditor waives his claim to repayment, it is to the benefit of all the partners. In the second case the partners do *not* necessarily have equal shares and are, moreover, 'part-debtors' (*xwāstag-tōzišn*), that is, the associates are responsible in proportion to their individual shares of the whole debt for repaying the creditor. Complete release from debt of one of the partners would not imply cancellation of the whole debt for the others.[435]

This interpretation seems to be confirmed by another sentence dealing with suretyship. Two men take out a loan together (*pad āgenēn*) as joint debtors with equal shares.[436] The moneylender later waives his claim to a part of the loan (*ān*

431 The term *xwastag* is written here (MHD 2.2) ⟨hw'stk'⟩ 'property, thing, object, res', whereas the heterogram ⟨NKSY'⟩ *xwāstag* for 'money', is explicitly used in lines 1 and 3 of this sentence (MHD 2.1–4); on this differentiation see Chapter III, p. 190.

432 See Chapter III, p. 248.

433 MHD 2.1–4 (Macuch 1993, pp. 40, 42). On the phrase *frāy az ān ī-š xwad niyābēd* 'more than that to which he is entitled himself' see *ibid.*, p. 45, no. 2.

434 MHD 2.14–16 (Macuch 1993, pp. 41, 43).

435 On these terms and their implications see p. 360 above.

436 On the terminology (*pad āgenēn*) see Chapter III, pp. 247–248.

abām ast ī be hilēnd 'a part of that debt is cancelled'). Having equal shares, both borrowers benefit from the abatement to exactly the same proportion. One of the co-debtors pays back his own share of the loan (*bahr ī xwēš wizārēd*). The cancelled portion of the debt is deducted from the amount he is still liable to pay as surety (*pāyandān*) for his associate.[437] This is not said explicitly in this passage, but the co-debtors are in fact treated as co-sureties (*hampāyandān*). Each debtor is liable in a dual function, as debtor for himself and as surety for the other, which enables the creditor to sue any one of the debtors for the whole sum (the partners are in fact *hamāg-tōzišn* 'joint and several debtors').[438] Consequently, if one of the co-debtors pays back his share of the debt he is still liable as surety for the share of his partner, albeit with the reduction conceded by the creditor to the same amount.

Another passage refers to the cancellation of a debt after the creditor has sued the debtor for fulfilment of contract. The court sets a fixed date (*brīn zamān*) for repayment of the debt. If the creditor waives his claim (*ka tōzišn be hilēnd* 'if the debt is cancelled') *before* the date specified by the court, the debtor is released from his obligation. If the fixed deadline has passed and the borrower is in default, the surety can be obliged to pay. Hence if the debt is cancelled *after* the specified date the surety (*pāyandān*) is released from liability.[439] The creditor can explicitly release a surety from suretyship (*kū-m az pāyandānīh hišt hē* 'I have released you from suretyship') with the 'three words' (*pad sē gōwišn*).[440] But if he releases the surety *before* the payment deadline (*brīn zamān*) fixed by the court this does not mean that he waives his claim to the debt, but only that he foregoes his right to make the surety liable if the debtor is insolvent.[441]

One of the most interesting (but far too concise) entries in the context of debt relief is in a chapter concerned with a completely different topic, that of substitute succession (*stūrīh*, or in specific cases: trusteeship of a fire). As we have elucidated in the context of fire foundations, the institutions taking care of sacred fires could obviously increase the property at their disposal (*xīr ī ātaxšān*) by giving out loans and taking interest.[442] Our passage informs us, that there can be 'no release from a loan granted by the fire foundations' (*pad abām ī ādurān ātaxšān hišt dād būd nē šāyēd*), hence the property of a deceased man who has taken out a loan from the 'fire foundations' (*abām az ādurān ud ātaxšān*) is to be used to redeem his financial liabilities instead of appointing a *stūr* for his succession. No explanation is given, but we can surmise that this is one of the exceptions noted in the sections on the *stūrīh*-institution above, forcing the heirs and

437 MHD 2.6–8 (Macuch 1993, pp. 40, 42). On *ast ī* 'part of, portion of' see *ibid.* p. 47, no. 5, with further references.

438 On suretyship see pp. 349–359 above.

439 MHD 2.8–10 (Macuch 1993, pp. 40, 43). On *brīn zamān* see *ibid.* p. 49.

440 On the 'three words' see Macuch 1993, pp. 49–51 (no. 8), and Chapter VI, p. 538.

441 MHD 2.11–13 (Macuch 1993, pp. 41, 43). See also commentary *ibid.* p. 51 (no. 9).

442 See Chapter III, p. 228.

legatees to use the property necessary for the upkeep of the *stŭrīh*-institution to another purpose deemed more important, namely that of amortizing a loan granted by the administration of fire foundations.[443] We can only speculate on the reasons why no debt relief was possible in these cases, but it seems most likely that keeping the property of sacred fires intact was regarded as a very important religious duty and that the diminishment of a fire's assets could not be risked.

Table 33. Overview: technical terms and phrases relating to debt cancellation

abām ast ī hištan	to cancel part of a debt
abām az ādurān ud ātaxšān	loan from the fire foundations
bahr ī xwēš wizārdan	to pay one's own share
brīn zamān	fixed (payment) date, deadline
pad abām hišt dādan	to grant a debt relief, to cancel a debt
tōzišn hištan	to cancel the obligation/debt

4.2 Lease (*tāg*)

A landlord (or leasor) could grant property (usually an immovable object yielding income, *e. g.*, farming land, an orchard, vineyard, etc.) for use in the form of a lease (*tāg*)[444] to a tenant (or leasee/leaseholder) for a specified term in return for the payment of a fixed sum or a periodic rent, reckoned in cash or in kind. In the Law-book the property under lease is generally designated by the abstract expression *xwāstag* 'property, object, thing, *res*', but two of the Tabarestān documents explicitly refer to agricultural land yielding wheat (*gandum*) in one case and a vineyard (*razestān*) yielding grapes, in another (to which we will return

443 MHD 50.3–4 (Macuch 1993, pp. 310, 326). On *stŭrīh* see Chapters II, pp. 169–174, and III pp. 213–219.

444 The term *tāg* 'lease, leasehold, rent' is spelled ⟨t'k'⟩ in Pahlavi legal literature as well as in the Tabarestān documents. It has been wrongly corrected to **task*/**tasak* by Perikhanian 1997 (p. 390), who relates the expression to the Aramaic loanword *tasqā*/*ṭasqā* in the Babylonian Talmud, a connection which might seem intriguing on first sight, but is nevertheless rather unlikely. Besides the divergent meaning (*ṭasqā*/*ṭaqsā* denotes the Persian land tax; Sokoloff 2002, p. 508), *tāg* is always written with ⟨'⟩, never with ⟨ε⟩, both in the Book Pahlavi and cursive scripts, and seems to have still been in use in the Islamic period (with a shortening of the vowel, in *tah bāzārī* 'ground rent of a stall in the market', Steingass 1892, p. 338). The specific meaning of 'lease, leasehold, rent' is amply attested in Pahlavi legal texts and even a whole chapter in the Sasanian Law-book is dedicated to this topic, but has unfortunately only survived in a very short fragment (*dar ī tāg* 'chapter on leasehold', MHD 72.13–17; Macuch 1993, pp. 485, 486); for examples see also Macuch 2017c, p. 170.

presently).[445] The leased object could be conveyed to the tenant for a limited time or in perpetuity (possibly comparable to the long-term Roman agricultural lease called *emphyteusis*, but we are not very well informed on the Sasanian lease).[446] The latter variant seems to be referred to in a lease contract (*paymān*) in which the 'payment of a yearly rent' (*sāl sāl tāg wizārdan*) has been fixed. The right of the leasor to take back the leased property (*abāz grift pādixšāy-būd rāy*) is explicitly restricted by the following words in the contract (addressed to the proprietor):

MHDA 25.10
bē ka ān tāg nē wizārd ēnyā ān xwāstag ma stān.

'Except when the rent (*tāg*) is not paid, do not take (back) that property!'[447]

As long as the yearly rent is paid, the proprietor is not allowed to end the lease and take back his property (*be stad nē šāyēd*). This formulation in the lease contract implies that the tenant holds the leased property in perpetuity as long as he pays the yearly rent agreed upon, restricting the right of the leasor to retrieve his property on other grounds except non-fulfilment of contract.

We can furthermore surmise from the only sentence surviving in the (otherwise lost) chapter on leasehold in the Law-book that the contractors could arrange for the rent to be paid in either one of two possible forms for the period of the lease. Again, the exact type of payment was determined by the wording of the contract. A statement of the leaseholder to this effect: 'For this property I give you a rent of 300 (drachms)' (*ēn xwāstag rāy tāg 300 ō tō dahom*) implies that a fixed (yearly) sum has been agreed upon, which must be paid 'in full' (*pad bowandag*) irrespective of the actual harvest or increase (*waxt*) attained within this period. On the other hand, if the contract states 'From this property I give you a rent of 100 (drachms)' (*⁺az ēn xwāstag tāg 100 ō tō dahom*), then the tenant has only agreed to pay a rent corresponding to the increase (*waxt*) he will obtain from the leased property during the contracted period. If this income is effectively less than the settled sum (of 100 drachms), then the amount actually gained should be discharged (*and dahišn čand waxt* 'as much as the amount of the income must be given').[448] This sentence suggests that two types of payment for a lease could be arranged:

1. The rent could be a fixed sum independent of the amount of income (*waxt*) achieved by the leaseholder.
2. It could be a fee based on the amount of income (or harvest) brought in by the leaseholder.

445 Tab. 13 and 23, on both documents see Macuch 2017c, pp. 167–172 and 173–176 respectively (see also Appendix XI).
446 On the Roman *emphyteusis* see Nicholas 1962, pp. 148–149.
447 Macuch 1981, pp. 49, 172.
448 MHD 72.14–16 (Macuch 1993, pp. 485, 486).

A basic sum was fixed in both cases, also in the second type of leasehold (100 drachms in our sentence), but the second variant also took the possibility of crop shortfall into consideration, whereas in the first type the leaseholder was obliged to pay the fixed sum even in the case of crop failure without reduction.

The documents on leasehold in the Tabarestān collection illustrate a few of the problems that could arise in these cases. In both texts the leased land was part of the collective property (*bun*) of the village referred to repeatedly in the documents called *Asp-gurd (previously read as *Haspīn-raz). The land was leased (in parcels?) by the co-proprietors, consisting of several *dehgān*[449] families, to tenants who cultivated it, harvested the crops and paid a specific amount of the crops as rent (*tāg*) in kind.[450] In Tab. 13 (dated to the year 73 PYE = 724/725 CE) the leased property consists of a vineyard (*razestān*) yielding grapes, which are processed into wine by the harvester(s), who were presumably the tenants of this property (although this is not explicitly said in the document). A dispute breaks out regarding the exact amount of rent (*tāg*) to be paid in kind, leading to the question: how much of the produce should be delivered as rent by the tenant (or tenants) of the vineyard? In order to settle the dispute, an official authority (not named in the document) in charge of investigating tillage (*kišwānīh wizōstan*) gives order (*framān*) to dispatch a scribe (called Ādurōy) to evaluate the land (*zamīg ayārd*) of the said vineyard. The scribe summons in situ several men who represent four *dehgān* families. Their names are listed in the document, but they are unfortunately not further identified. They could be either co-proprietors of the leased 'vineyard' or co-tenants or—most likely—co-proprietors of village land, who were collectively in charge of determining the payments to be made, mediating conflicts and dealing with cases like this one (this at least seems to be the task of a committee of *dehgāns* in Tab. 23, see below). Although these details are not elucidated, we have good reason to assume that the statements of the men representing the four *dehgān* families summoned by the scribe were necessary in order to

449 This well-known title (< *dahigān* 'pertaining to the land') for a new class of landed magnates apparently emerged after the land reform of Husraw I in the 6th century. In a large range of Persian and Arabic sources the *dehgānān*/*dahāqīn* are described as the local gentry, who assumed the main task of collecting taxes in the Sasanian period and became central political and social figures in their districts and villages after the gradual decline of the grand Iranian nobility after the Muslim conquest (the word is used with a large range of meanings, see CHRISTENSEN 1944, p. 112; ALTHEIM/STIEHL 1954, p. 134; TAFAZZOLI 2000, pp. 38–59; it is also attested in the fragment of a sentence in the Sasanian Law-book, MHD 1.1, MACUCH 1993, pp. 22, 24). In the Tabarestān texts several *dehgān* families are named, but it is difficult to assess their exact rank and social position due to the lack of information in the documents. However, it seems likely that these *dehgāns* were not simply landless farmers having cultivation rights, but co-proprietors of village land, who enjoyed a collective right to a share in the produce of this land, which was not necessarily cultivated by themselves, but could be leased to other peasants and farmers for cultivation.

450 The whole text of the two documents is in Appendix XI.

determine the amount of rent (*tāg*) to be paid by the tenant (or tenants) of the vineyard. The scribe (Ādurōy) then records the settlement (*wirāyišn*) reached by the parties involved in the dispute: the rent in kind for the leased vineyard is fixed as follows: for each yield of grapes weighing 6 *kabīz* (a *kabīz* is one-tenth of a *grīw*, the measure for solid matters) one-third of a *dēg* ('cauldron', the measure for liquids) of wine should be delivered as rent. All the involved persons, including the scribe, seal the document (called *wizōstan-nāmag* 'transcript of investigation'), thereby recording their consent with the terms of the settlement.[451]

The second document (Tab. 23, dated to the year 104 PYE = 755/756 CE) is concerned with agricultural land, on which wheat (*gandum*) is produced. The co-proprietors (or co-leasors) are four *dehgāns* (called Dēl-āzād, Wazurgnimād, Xwāst-Dēlān and Dēn-abzūd) from the village of *Asp-gurd, who grant the use of this land to tenants (or: co-tenants) in return for the payment of a rent in kind. Interestingly, they also agree to an abatement (*āsānīh*) on the rent. This could point to a variant of the second type of lease contract elucidated above, based on an average calculation of crop yieldings, but taking the actual amount of harvest into consideration. The abatement seems to provide a margin between the sum calculated as rent and the effective amount of wheat produced in one year. A scribe (called Yōdmardān, son of Dēlzād), who himself has leased a parcel (*pārag*) in the village, undertakes an 'evaluation of the farmers' (*ayārd ī dehgānān*). The expression is not explained, but seems to denote a procedure by which the amount of rent the co-leasors are entitled to is assessed. The four *dehgāns* (co-leasors) do not agree with the evaluation of this scribe and file a complaint (*garzišnīg būd*) which they, interestingly, address to some kind of collective body or committee of *dehgāns* in charge of settling arguments and mediating disputes in matters of the village. The complaint concerns the amount of wheat the tenants (or: co-tenants) are obliged to deliver as rent in the year 104 PYE (= 724/725 CE). The complainants request three measures:

1. a revision of the calculation of the amount of wheat (*gandum ayārd*) produced by the tenants in the year 104;
2. the establishment of a price (*be āzardan*) for the surplus to be discharged as rent (*tāg*);
3. adjustment of the abatement (*āsānīh*, which had been already agreed upon) on the rent.

A new calculation of the expected crop yields (*gandum ayārd*) is undertaken by this committee of *dehgāns*, who base their assessment on an investigation in situ,

451 For a full discussion of the technical terminology and the contextual problems of this document see MACUCH 2017c, pp. 167–172.

taking both the costs for the upkeep (*ǰadārīh*) of the leased property and the income (*mad*) from past harvests into consideration. The document then lists the exact amount of rent in kind calculated by the committee as follows:

Table 34. Amount of rent

Cultivators/ tenants	Amount of rent (*tāg*)
Yōdmardān (on the parcel of Dēlxwašīh)	4 *grīw* (of wheat)
Xwāst-Dēlān	1 *grīw* (of wheat)
Windād-Ohrmazd	1 *grīw* (of wheat)
Yazdfarrox	1 *grīw* (of wheat)
Juxt	1 *grīw* (of wheat)
Farroxzād from *Brāzasp	1 *grīw* (of wheat)
Total sum	9 *grīw*

The abatement (*āsānīh*) granted by the co-leasors is also adjusted (*āsūd kard*) in accordance with the new evaluation:

Table 35. Amount of abatement

Land of the *dehgāns*	Amount of abatement (*āsānīh*)
Farroxgušnasp	5 *grīw* of wheat
Dēl-āzād	1 *grīw* of wheat
Wazurgnimād	6 *kabīz* of wheat
Farroxzād	7 *kabīz* of wheat
joint land of Xwāst-Dēlān and Dēn-abzūd	5 *kabīz* of wheat
Dēlxwašīh	5 *kabīz* of wheat
Total sum	6 *grīw*, 23 *kabīz* = 8 *grīw*, 3 *kabīz*

The total sum of the rent due for the year 104 PYE (= 724/725 CE) is established at 9 *grīw* of wheat (first list); the arranged abatement (or: margin) is then adjusted to the new calculation at a total of 8 *grīw*, 3 *kabīz* of wheat (10 *kabīz*= 1 *grīw*; second list). This document (called *zastbūd-nāmag* 'transcript of interrogation') is sealed by all the persons named in the text, including the scribe (called Dērā) and a legal authority (called Wīrgušnasp, the Elder).[452]

452 For a full discussion of the technical terminology and the contextual problems of this document see MACUCH 2017c, pp. 173–176.

Table 36. Overview: technical terms and phrases relating to leasehold

āsānīh	abatement, reduction, lowering of the price
āsūd kardan	to adjust (lit.: 'make easier)
ayārdan (*gandum*; *zamīg*)	to take measure; evaluate; calculate (wheat; land)
ayārd ī dehgānān	evaluation of the farmers
āzardan	to establish a value, price
dehgān	farmer, local gentry, landlord
ǰadārīh	maintenance, preservation, upkeep, support
kišwānīh wizōstan	to investigate tillage
mad	income; surplus
tāg	lease, leasehold, rent
tāg wizārdan	to pay the rent
wirāyišn	arrangement, settlement, agreement, deal
wizōstan-nāmag	transcript of investigation
zastbūd-nāmag	transcript of interrogation

4.3 Sale (*frōxš*) and barter (*guharēn*)

Commerce and trade were well developed in the Sasanian Empire, as we may conclude from several observations, although the economy of Ērānšahr was based—in this period as in later centuries—mainly on agriculture. Despite their importance for the economy of the State, the main producers of sustenance for the whole community, the peasants, farmers and cultivators (*wāstaryōšān*) and the manufacturers of wares that could be sold or bartered, the artisans (*hutuxšān*), are given the lowest rank in the social hierarchy of Ērānšahr according to all our available sources.[453] The letter of Tansar also includes 'merchants' (NP *bāzargānān*) and 'dealers, traders' (Arab. *tuǧǧār*) in the lowest estate of this 'imagined order'. Although this classification certainly reflects ideal power structures, it might not necessarily describe realistically the wealth, position or acclaim talented artisans or particularly skilful merchants and traders may have attained in the Sasanian period. But belonging to the lowest estate of commoners definitely had legal consequences regarding the ability to enact specific transactions with the higher strata of Sasanian society, since the former were not allowed to buy land and estates from the nobility, as we have already noted.[454] Artisans and craftsmen (*kirrōg* < OP *kṛnavaka-*) were organized in guilds (*pēšag*) in the towns under the supervision of the *pēšag-sālār* 'head of

453 See Chapter II, pp. 95–101.
454 See Chapter II, pp. 111–112.

the guild', titled *kirrōgbed* 'chief of the craftsmen', the *qārugbed* of Syriac texts,[455] or *hutuxšbed* 'chief of the artisans' according to Masʿūdī.[456] They also worked in specialized workshops, and we may assume that most of them mainly produced goods for barter or sale, besides being engaged to satisfy specific needs and demands of the higher classes of society.[457] Surplus agricultural products, such as grain, olives, wine, fruits and nuts, could also be turned over to the market, particularly in the vicinity of large towns.[458]

Besides the exchange of goods within the Iranian Empire, mercantile activities spread across the Central Asian trade routes between East and West. It is well known that Iranians, notably Sogdians, were engaged as merchants and traders along the famous land trade routes known since the 19th century as the 'Silk Roads', and that maritime trade also flourished along the sea routes to the Far East and China. The important strategic geographical position of Iran between East and West led to competition with Byzantium, the other great Empire of late antiquity, in trading valuable goods (particularly silk and silken products) imported from China.[459] The immense impact of Iranian traders is adequately reflected by the survival of commercial expressions brought by merchants from East to West, which are still—as has been perceptively observed—in common usage today, such as 'bazaar' (MP *wāzār* 'market'), 'caravan' (MP *kārwān* 'troupe of travelling merchants'), 'caravanserai' (MP *kārwān-sarāy*; 'hospice for travellers').[460] To these we can now add the term *čak* 'cheque, check', originally a written 'document', which recorded a certain amount of money paid for goods and could be transported safely across long distances to be cashed by the traders at their final destination. A 'cheque' had the advantage that it was useless to highwaymen or robbers who might attack the caravans and could only be turned into cash by the merchants themselves. The corresponding term MP *čak*, a loanword from Chinese *tsʾə* (Middle Chinese *tṣak* 'writing tablet, list, document, diploma'), is attested not only in the Law-book (as 'document' and 'note/

455 Ciancaglini 2008, p 251.

456 On trades and crafts in the Sasanian period see Tafazzoli 1974 with further references.

457 One of the Tabarestān documents (Tab. 15) describes a case, in which a scribe, *dibīr*, sues a shield-maker, *spargar*, for not delivering on time a shield that the latter had taken in order to mount on it an 'image of the sun' (*rōy ī dēnxwar[r]*; presumably of the winged solar disk or *xwarənah-*; Tab. 15.6); see Weber 2017a, pp. 115–119, and Macuch 2017c, pp. 180–182.

458 On commerce and economy see Pigulevskaya 1956.

459 The central role of the Sogdians as merchants and traders in Central Asia is attested by a large number of original sources, bearing witness to their impact not only on the exchange of merchandise, but also on the dissemination of ideas and religions, including Buddhism, Zoroastrianism, Christianity and Manichaeism, along the trade routes, where they built colonies and Sogdian became a kind of *lingua franca*. On the sources (with further references) see Chapter I, pp. 41–43. On economy and trade see Daryaee/Rezakhani 2016, pp. 57–61; for a comprehensive general history of the Silk Roads see Hansen 2012 and Frankopan 2015.

460 See Daryaee/Rezakhani 2016, p. xv.

entry in a transcript)' in the context of procedural law (see Chapter VI, p. 537), but also in a large number of documents written in the Pahlavi cursive script with the meaning of 'payment entitlement, check' (see Chapter IV, pp. 279–281). The route of transmission from the Chinese to European languages cannot be reconstructed exactly, but it is most likely that Sogdian merchants, whose far-reaching mercantile (and other) activities along the Silk Roads have been recorded in several impressive documents (beginning with the Ancient Letters from the 4th century), brought the term with them from Central Asia.[461]

4.3.1 The sale contract

Despite the economic impact of commerce the legal material in this field is sparse, presumably due to the late compilation of the Law-book at a period, when the Sasanian Empire was in decline, or—if this work was compiled in the Islamic period—when trade on this large scale was no longer relevant to the Zoroastrian communities.[462] Simple cash sales, in which the object of sale and the price are exchanged simultaneously and no further problems arise from the transfer are, unsurprisingly, not a matter of discussion in the legal texts. We can reasonably infer that—as in other systems—the basic requirements consisted of an agreement between seller and buyer regarding the thing sold and the price. Without consent between the two parties no sale would take effect. But for anything more than a straightforward immediate exchange of goods for money, if the transfer of the goods or the money was delayed and payment or delivery were to take place at a later period, exact regulations were necessary.

A (presumably verbal) contract of sale came into being by the procedure of offer and acceptance described in section 3 (pp. 301–305) above: the seller declares his will to sell a thing and names the price: 'I will sell (this) for 30 (drachms) to Mihrēn (= the buyer)' (*30 ō Mihrēn frōxšēm*); the buyer (Mihrēn) declares his will to buy with the formulaic words 'it is needed' (*andar abāyēd*), by which the deal takes effect.[463] In this specific case the buyer does not declare his wish to purchase the thing offered to him by the seller immediately, but after a reflection period of three nights (*se šabag*). Although this is not explained directly in this passage, the context implies that the vendor could withdraw his offer during the three nights conceded to the purchaser to reconsider the deal, but was bound to his offer *after* the buyer had accepted.[464] Was granting a period of reflection a standard procedure (at least in larger undertakings)? This is not explicitly said, but the timespan of 'three nights' to consider or reconsider a bargain is also one of the main components of barter, as will be seen below.

461 For an attestation of the term in Sogdian see p. 280, fn. 110 above.

462 The Law-book of Īšōʿbōxt, based on Sasanian law, is somewhat more detailed and will be used to supplement the fragmentary Iranian texts. On this source see Chapter I, p. 48.

463 On this procedure see pp. 301–305 above.

464 MHDA 11.17–12.2 (Macuch 1981, pp. 33f., 125).

According to Īšōʿbōxt a sale based on a written and sealed contract was subject to a different set of rules (in the Christian community) than the verbal contract,[465] but given the religious importance attached to keeping word in Zoroastrianism, we may doubt that this also applied as a general rule in Sasanian law. It stands to reason, however, that it was far easier to prove the terms of a sale if a deal was recorded and confirmed by the seals of the contractors or of an official authority (on the evaluation of seals see pp. 296–301 above). In a written contract the conditions of a sale could be minutely documented, the vendor could expressly accept responsibility for the quality of the goods and for keeping them intact and undamaged up to delivery and would consequently be liable for defects (this was not necessarily the case if the deal was verbal and the seller refused to accept liability for damages). The text of a (presumably) written sale contract concluded with two vendors is transmitted in the Sasanian Law-book:

> If two men sell together an item to a man and make a (written) contract (*pašt/nibišt*): 'we will keep it intact/undamaged (*drust dārēm*)', (then) Wahrām said that he (= the buyer) (is) authorized to request warranty (*drust dārišnīh*) from any one (of the two sellers) he wishes to.[466]

The text quotes the jurist Wahrām, a recognized legal authority of the Sasanian period, on a problem which might have caused legal disputes, namely the question, whether two (or more) vendors, who guarantee in a written contract together for the quality of the sold goods, are jointly liable or only partly liable in proportion to their individual shares. Wahrām's statement settles the (implicit) question: the buyer can demand warranty from any one of the two vendors, *i. e*, they are jointly liable, every one of the sellers is obliged to take full responsibility for satisfying possible reclamations of the purchaser. The formula used in sale contracts stating the willingness of the seller to guarantee for the soundness of his goods—up to delivery, as in the last example—is *drust dāštan* 'to keep intact, undamaged'. Another passage using this formula describes a somewhat more complicated case: the seller guarantees in the contract (*paymān*) with the buyer to take good care of the thing he has sold until delivery and to recompense the buyer with something else if he acts otherwise (*ka drust nē dāram* 'if I do not keep it intact'). In this case the vendor promises as compensation a specific slave (*anšahrīg*), who does not belong to him, but for whom he has a mandate or letter of attorney from the slave-owner allowing the vendor to assign the slave in ownership to a person of his choice. Consequently the guarantee takes effect if the seller fails to keep the goods undamaged (*ka*

465 Īšōʿbōxt, Book V, Chapter XI, § 1c (Sachau 1914, pp. 172–173).

466 MHD 6.13–14: *ka mard dō āgenēn xwāstag ē(w) ō mard frōxšēnd ud pašt* (or: *nibišt*) *kunēnd kū drust dārēm Wahrām guft kū drust dārišnīh az har kē kāmēd xwāst pādixšāy* (Macuch 1993, pp. 88, 93; both readings ⟨W pšt'⟩ *ud pašt* 'and a contract' or ⟨npšt'⟩ *nibišt* 'written record' are possible in this sentence; see also p. 265, fn. 24 above).

xwāstag drust nē dārēd 'if he does not keep the [sold] thing intact') and the slave is transferred to the purchaser.[467]

Sales of immobiles, land and buildings, were presumably documented on a regular basis in a title deed (*wizīr*) or document proving a person's ownership and the terms on which he bought and owned the immovable property.[468] As we have already elucidated, transactions of all kinds involving land and estates, including sales, were prohibited between aristocrats and commoners (according to the Tansar letter, see pp. 111–112 above), but there is no information whatsoever on the legality of selling immovable property to adherents of other creeds (among the nobility or among affluent commoners, merchants, traders etc.). To judge by the sparse entries in the Sasanian Law-book immovables were rather bequeathed (by intestate succession or by testament, donation or gift) than sold, but the passages quoted in the last chapter on the transfer of landed estates (*dastgird*), land (*zamīg*, *gil*) and houses (*xānag*, *kadag*) to the next generation could have well been the model for all other kinds of business transactions, including sales.[469] Nota bene, this important compilation does not explicitly differentiate between sale and other types of transactions (it employs the neutral verb *dādan* 'to give, hand over, deliver, transfer, bequeath' in almost all instances, including donations, gifts, inheritance, barter and sale), but it distinguishes between these transactions *implicitly*—and this is an important point—by the use of the ergative/agential construction *kū-m … dād* ('I gave, I have given'). This wording implies that the undertaking referred to should take effect *after* the death of the donor/testator and was hence employed in the will, testamentary contract or donation in contemplation of death (*donatio mortis causa*), as elucidated above.[470]

This said, we can reasonably assume that the rules on the devolution of landed property in the context of inheritance were similar to those involving the sale of immovable property. If we transpose these rules to sale, then the purchase of an immovable presumably took effect by transferring the title deed (*wizīr*) to the buyer, an official act which put not only the document, but the landed property itself under the control of the recipient, as we are told in the following sentence:

467 MHD 64.10–15 (Macuch 1993, pp. 434, 437). The main problem in this sentence is the formulation of the guarantee, which is transmitted in two variants (one in which the name of the slave-owner is given, the other only referring to the slave) both of which, however, have the same implications, at least according to the opinion of the jurist Rādohrmazd; the legal authority Wahrām seems to doubt this, as he cautions (unfortunately with no further explanations): 'this (matter) must be particularly reflected upon' (*wēš uskārdan abāyēd*); on this sentence see also commentary Macuch 1993, p. 442 (no. 6).

468 This can be deduced from MHD 18.11 and 18.15 (*ibid.* pp. 153, 159), which refer, however, to the devolution of immovable property by will, donation or testamentary contract, not explicitly to sale.

469 See Chapter III, pp. 240–244.

470 See Chapters I, pp. 83–85, and III, pp. 238–239 and the extensive discussion of these forms in Macuch 2015c.

'if he states: "I gave this title deed (*wizīr*) to you, then (both) the land (*gil*, lit. 'soil') and the (sealed) document ⟨MGLT'⟩ have been transferred."'[471] The sale of a building or house (*xānag*, *kadag*) would have included any fixtures (columns, doors, windows), additional assets (a storehouse, a well) and accessories (keys). An estate (*dastgird*) was presumably sold together with the slaves and animals residing and working on the property and the sale contract would also include the use of a water canal (*kahas*) running through another plot of land.[472]

4.3.2 Earnest money

If there were no witnesses to a sale contract and no written contract had been drawn up, the question could arise, whether a verbal agreement of sale (or credit sale) could be proved in any manner. In several legal systems of this period the buyer gave the seller a pawn or earnest money (or part-payment) as a token of good faith and proof of serious intent to confirm the deal. The term used in this context in Greek and Roman law, ἀρραβών and *arrabo*, (shortened to) *arr(h)a*, is presumably a Phoenician loanword from Semitic *ʿarab*, *ʿerabon*, meaning 'security, pawn, pledge', which underwent several changes in the course of legal history, but originally referred to an item of value, usually a ring, given by the purchaser to the vendor as security.[473] The buyer could redeem the *arra*, if he fulfilled the contract, but forfeited it in case of default. The *arra* could also consist of money, of an advance payment or 'earnest money', a kind of token sum or deposit the buyer lost if he defaulted, but would be set off against the price, if he performed his obligations. In the reverse case that the seller failed to keep the sale contract or wished to withdraw his offer, Greek practice (and possibly also Roman law) provided that he would have to return the double sum of the *arra*,

471 MHDA 34.2–3: *ka gōwēd kū-m ēn wizīr ō tō dād ēg-iš gil ud nāmag* ⟨MGLT'⟩ *dād bawēd* (Macuch 1981, pp. 59f., 217). The Pahlavi reading given for ⟨MGLT'⟩ in the FīO is ⟨mwlwt'⟩ (FīO 15.2 in Junker 1911, p. 56; XV.4 in Nyberg 1988, p. 12) *mōrūt* (according to Junker 1911, p. 114, who equates it with ⟨KTYḆ⟩ *nāmag*, p. 113), or *mūrvat* < *muhr-gat* 'sealed document' (according to Nyberg 1988, p. 85, who derives the word from *muhr* 'seal' and *gat* 'deed'). The latter expression (referred to by Nyberg as *gat*) is ⟨GTk; gtk⟩ to be read either (as a heterogram for) *nāmag* or (as a loan-word from the Semitic as) *gitt(ag)*, see above pp. 275–279. The reading of ⟨MGLT'⟩ as *nāmag* remains uncertain, but the term definitely designates a written (and presumably sealed) document, since it is specified as *wizīr* 'title deed' in the text.

472 On the transfer of immovables in the context of inheritance (with corresponding examples) see Chapter III, pp. 238–239.

473 On the transformations of *arra* in Greek and Roman law see Platschek 2017, pp. 73–74, with further references. The term is widespread, as *ʿerabon* 'earnest-money' in Jewish law (Herzog 1939, vol. II, p. 71); Babylonian Aramaic ⟨ʿrbʾ/ʿrʾbʾ⟩ 'guarantor, surety' (Sokoloff 2002, p. 880); Arabic *ʿurbūn*, *ʿarubūn* 'down payment, advance payment, earnest money, pledge, pawn' (Wehr 1956, p. 542); NP *ʿurbān* 'earnest money' (Steingass 1892, p. 842); *rabūn* 'money advanced on goods which is returned if they should be damaged; earnest; drink-money …' (Steingass 1892, p. 569).

i. e, the pledge (ring) itself and its equivalent in value, or twice the deposited token sum to the purchaser.

The practice of conveying a pawn or earnest money to the seller was also known in Iran, as we may conclude both from Pahlavi sources and from Īšōʿbōxt's Law-book, based (in the parts not dominated by Zoroastrian precepts) essentially on Sasanian law. The procedure described in the Chapter on 'Sale and Purchase' in Īšōʿbōxt corresponds roughly to the one in Greek and Roman law (and other legal systems): a seller cannot withdraw the sold object, if he has already received payment and the sale has taken effect, but if the price has not yet been paid and the buyer has only deposited an *arra* or 'earnest money' (Syr. *rāh̆būnā*),[474] the seller can undo the sale (on grounds of fraud and if the thing is a movable, a tool or an animal) and take back the sold thing from the buyer by paying back twice the sum of the deposit. The buyer, on the other hand, can cancel his purchase by foregoing the *arra*.[475] The text stresses that renouncement of a sale in this manner is only possible, when the agreement is verbal and no written contract has been sealed.

Unfortunately the entries in the Sasanian Law-book are not as easy to understand as Īšōʿbōxt, but a payment that was possibly treated *as if* it were an advance payment on a sale could be meant in a passage of the Law-book, although there is no direct reference here to earnest money. An important prerequisite of sale (besides the consent of the involved parties) is that there must be a thing to be sold, otherwise there is no sale. But what if one person (the potential buyer) gives money in advance to a potential seller for something the latter does not have (yet or any more) and therefore cannot sell? The Sasanian Law-book mentions a disputed case, in which a person pays a man for sheep (or small livestock, *gōspand*) using the words: 'give me sheep against payment' (*kū-m gōspand pad wahāg dah*), although the potential seller 'has no sheep' (*gōspand nēst*). The exact circumstances of the case are not explained, but we can infer that the potential seller accepts the money, hereby concluding a contract with the potential buyer, without being able to deliver the goods (because the sheep either no longer exist or have not yet been acquired or due to any another reason why he 'has no sheep'). Two contradictory decisions are transmitted: (1) the potential buyer loses his money (*appār bawēd*) and it is not returned to him; (2) he does not lose his money (*appār nē bawēd*), since he has not committed an offence/sin (*wināh-ē nē kard*).[476] Unfortunately the passage is short and to the point, as most entries in this text, and the arguments for the two contradictory decisions are not transmitted, but if we take all that has been said on the sale contract up till now into consideration, we can assume the following: (1) the first decision

474 Sachau 1914, p. 172, lines 24 and 29; on Syriac ⟨rhbwn'⟩ see Payne Smith 1903, p. 531: 'ἀρραβών, arles, earnest-money, a pledge, earnest'; Maclean 1901, p. 289: 'a pledge, an earnest'.

475 Īšōʿbōxt, Book V, Chapter XI, § 1 (Sachau 1914, pp. 172–173).

476 MHD 104. 6–8 (Macuch 1993, pp. 618, 626).

is based on the simple surmise that the contract between buyer and seller is null and void, as there is no object of sale at the time of the agreement, hence no obligation to deliver, therefore the money paid by the potential buyer is lost to him. (2) The second decision is somewhat more complex and could be based on the practice of giving a token sum as instalment in advance. The justification for this decision has a religious undertone (the potential buyer has 'committed no offence/sin') and could reflect the Sasanian practice of *wehdādestānīh* (or *mehdādestānīh*) 'good, greater justice', *i. e*, doing more or going beyond the basic requirements of law, in order to reach a just decision.[477] The potential buyer does *not* lose his money, since one could treat the case *as if* he had given a kind of pre-payment (or earnest money) to the vendor that reverts to the buyer, if the vendor fails to perform (as in our case, in which there is no object of sale). This explanation is of course pure conjecture (and would, moreover, apply *stricto iure* only in the case of a valid contract), but the passage only makes sense in a legal context if we assume that the second decision was based on some kind of analogy (based on the *arra* procedure, following the principle of *wehdādestānīh*) which was understood in this context by jurists and needed no further explanations.

Besides this problematic passage another hitherto largely ignored Pahlavi source refers unmistakably to an advance payment (or instalment or *arra*) and even employs the same technical term *rabŭn*/*rabŭna* (corresponding to *răhḇūnā* in Īšōʿbōxt) for the token sum paid by the buyer to the seller to seal a bargain.[478] The word occurs in three lines of the 51st *Pursišn* of the *Dādestān ī dēnīg*, but has not been recognized or read correctly in previous editions due to the unusual spelling. This must have also puzzled copyists who were obviously not acquainted with the expression, as they have continuously misspelt the term in most manuscripts (fortunately it is still discernable as ⟨rbn'⟩ and ⟨rbn⟩ in the oldest ms. K 35, fol. 171v., lines 5 and 7; line 16 has ⟨bwn⟩, presumably from an original ⟨*rbwn⟩, for the same word).[479] In this *Pursišn* the author of this text, the ninth century high-priest Manuščihr, records his answer to a legal problem regarding the sale of grain, for which a payment has been made in advance as deposit or instalment for the goods that will be delivered later. The buyer pays the sum of one drachm in advance as *arra* or, to use the form employed here, *rabŭna*, for one load of 5 *kabīz* (a grain measure corresponding to one-tenth of a *grīw*) with the words: 'to the end of the month I give to you this as prepayment/

477 On this term see Chapter VI, p. 569, and Macuch 2019a.

478 The whole text is transcribed and translated (with notes) in Appendix II, pp. 659–661; for an extensive discussion of this remarkable *Pursišn* and its legal implications see Macuch 2022c.

479 West 1882, p. 181, reads *'vaban'* in fn. 1 and has corrected the term to '*bôn-ae*' in his translation. In Anklesaria's critical edition of the Dd-manuscripts in his (unpublished) thesis submitted to the University of London 1958 (p. 109, lines 4, 6) the word has completely disappeared; only the letter ⟨b⟩ has survived.

earnest money (*rabŭna*) for one (load of grain) of 5 *kabīz'* (*kū māh ō sar ēn 5 kabīz ē[w] pad rabŭna ō tō dahom*) and concludes a contract (*pašt*) with the seller. At the end of the month, however, the price of grain for one load of 5 *kabīz* has increased to five times worth the sum the parties had agreed upon. The question is, whether the buyer is entitled (*dastwarīhā*) to take this load for the original price according to the terms of the contract or not.

Manuščihr's answer emphasizes the importance of taking the exact circumstances of the case into consideration (which might again reflect legal practice based on the principle of *wehdādestānīh* 'good justice', in the second part of his response): (1) If the contract was concluded without duress, without pressure on the seller to agree to its terms, and the seller acts 'without fear' (*abēbīmīhā*), according to his own will (*pad xwēš kām*) and consciously (*āgāhīhā*) and, moreover, transfers the load of grain to the buyer for the agreed price, then the latter is entitled to take it despite the large increase in value. (2) If, on the other hand, the seller closed the deal due to extreme poverty and want (*abēr garān niyāzīhā*), he would not be 'a person who could grant favours freely according to his own will' (+*wasasəyāna nē*). The latter term, written here as ⟨wss'y'⟩, is attested correctly as ⟨w's'sy''n'⟩ *wasasəyāna* in the Law-book, a Pahlavi rendering of the Avestan term **vasasə.yāna-* 'who grants favours at will', with an obviously religious connotation.[480] In this case the buyer is admonished to refrain from insisting on the terms of the contract and taking excess profit (*sūd frehbūd*) from the seller (in correspondence with the principle of *wehdādestānīh*, as we may add). The reason given for the second part of the response is notable: this is better for the soul of the buyer. If the buyer—contrary to the admonition of the high-priest—insists that the seller keep to the terms of the contract, he would set a precedence for later generations (*pasēnīgān*), who in turn would fear making a loss should the value of their crops rise before delivery. They would hence demand higher sums as earnest money or advance payment than one could reasonably calculate on the basis of the average crop-yields of the region. In short: the buyer is asked to voluntarily forego his right according to contract, to renounce excess gain for the welfare not only of the seller, who is destitute (*a-čār*), but of the whole community, including later generations of Zoroastrians.

4.3.3 Sales in public and private

A sale became 'perfect' when a consensual contract based on the consent of the parties consisting of offer and acceptance—usually verbal, but presumably documented and sealed in the case of larger dealings—came into being, as we have seen, but what were the legal consequences if the sale was fraudulent or there was a misunderstanding between seller and buyer or the object of sale was damaged? Interestingly, Īšōʿbōxt distinguishes between things (animals, specifically

480 MHD 62.14; on *wasasəyāna* see Appendix II, fn. 69, and Macuch 2022c, pp. 315–317.

beasts of burden, and inedible wares) sold 'in the markets' (*bᵊ-šūqē*) and those sold 'in houses' (*mn bātē*).[481] Although no explanation or reason whatsoever is given, the context implies that this distinction actually refers to deals closed in a public place (= market) and those made in private (= building, house) with divergent legal consequences (possibly due to the difficulty of proving a deal in the latter case if there were no witnesses), but the information is wanting. The divergent rules applying to sales in 'markets' (= public) and 'houses' (= private) might be based on the ancient Zoroastrian distinction, which we have already elucidated (and to which we will return presently). According to Īšōʿbōxt, in the former case (purchase in public) the buyer can give back the animal or (inedible) object he has bought to the seller and reclaim his money before the market begins, but not after the market has begun; edibles cannot be returned, once they have been bought. Apart from the rule on edibles, the passage leaves several questions open: why is the right of the purchaser to make reclamations restricted to the time *outside* market hours? And does this rule only apply to the same day or can the buyer return the purchased animal or object on another day? The particulars on purchases made in private (houses) are just as incomplete and limited to the sale of beasts of burden (which might have been the most disputed cases): the buyer can give back the animal within the timespan of forty days if he notices a defect which he had not seen at the time of purchase and had not been mentioned by the seller and receive his money back after delivering the profit made by the animal during this period to the seller and paying for its wear and tear. But if the animal goes lame within the timespan of forty days or is injured in another manner, it cannot be returned to the vendor.[482] (How were all these details determined? We are not told, but it seems that the outcome would depend on the bargaining skills of the parties and only lead in insoluble cases to arbitration or litigation.) Another paragraph mentions fraud, when vendor or purchaser declare that they have been cheated. In this case reclamations by the buyer only take effect if the deception consists of a mix-up of substances, for example, when glass is passed off as a precious stone (hyacinth or emerald) or brass is passed off as gold.[483] This seems to point to a general rule similar to the Roman *caveat emptor* 'let the buyer beware': the seller is not liable for obvious defects the buyer should have been aware of on making the deal, but only in cases of explicit dishonesty, which would be inconsistent with the requirement of good faith in the sale contract.[484]

This division between deals in the market and those in houses might be based on the ancient Zoroastrian distinction between offences committed in public (in the open) and those committed in private (in seclusion), which were connoted

481 Īšōʿbōxt, Book V, Chapter XI, §2 (Sachau 1914, pp. 172–175).
482 Īšōʿbōxt, Book V, Chapter XI, §3 (Sachau 1914, pp. 174–175).
483 Īšōʿbōxt, Book V, Chapter XI, §4 (Sachau 1914, pp. 174–175).
484 See du Plessis/Borkowski 2010, pp. 269f.

with the Avestan terms for 'robber' (*hazaŋhan-*)[485] and 'thief' (*tāiiu-*)[486] respectively, the former being defined as a person, who steals openly, and the latter as a person, who steals secretly. The corresponding Pahlavi terms, *appar* or *apparag* 'robber' and *duz(d)* 'thief' and the abstracts *apparīh* 'robbery' and *duz(d)īh* 'theft' are defined in exactly the same manner. These terms were employed not only literally in the context of criminal law to designate the act of stealing openly or secretly, but were transferred to other legal fields and used in a figurative sense to designate contractors who did not keep their contractual obligations.[487] It is very likely that this was the background for the distinction transmitted by Īšōʿbōxt regarding sales in the market (= public) and in houses (= private). But there is another good reason for assuming that this author had precise knowledge of this Zoroastrian model. The next paragraph unmistakeably confirms that this was exactly the scheme according to which offences against contract law involving a criminal act were punished in the Christian community, as we my conclude from the following entry: a man sells (or donates) a thing that is not his property to another man, who knows that the seller (or donor) is not the owner. If the buyer (or recipient) holds this thing secretly, in private, then he is judged as if he were a 'thief' (*ganāḇā*); if he shows it openly, in public, he is judged as if he were a 'plunderer, ravisher' (*ḥāṭōpā*).[488] Needless to say, the Syriac terms *ganāḇā* and *ḥāṭōpā* correspond exactly to *duz(d)* and *appar(ag)* in the Middle Persian texts (these were presumably the exact expressions which stood in the original Pahlavi version of Īšōʿbōxt's Codex), and the procedure is not only similar, but has been obviously adapted from Zoroastrian law. Moreover, this passage reveals that the division of transgressions into two categories (those committed openly and those committed secretly) with the corresponding punishments was not just a scholastic remnant from the past, but was actually transposed into legal practice in both the Zoroastrian and Christian communities.

4.3.4 Prohibited sales

That both contractors, seller and buyer, could be treated as thieves and penalized according to the punishment for theft (*drōš*)[489] is confirmed in several Pahlavi texts in the context of prohibited deals involving slaves. It was strictly forbidden to sell a 'Zoroastrian slave' (*bandag ī hu-dēn*, according to

485 Bartholomae 1904, col. 1799 (with references to the sources).

486 Bartholomae 1904, col. 647 (with references to the sources).

487 Vd 4.1, for a translation and discussion of this passage see above pp. 312–315 (Moazami 2014, p. 99, has a different translation).

488 Īšōʿbōxt, Book V, Chapter XI, §5a (Sachau 1914, pp. 174–175); on *ḥāṭōpā* see Payne Smith 1903, p. 138: 'an extortioner, plunderer, ravisher'; Maclean 1901, p. 97: 'ravenous, rapacious; a spoiler'.

489 Av. *draoša-* (Bartholomae 1904, col. 770), the punishment for theft, MP *drōš*, was presumably (at least originally) a 'mark, branding' or some kind of incision or cut (in the face or hands) that stigmatized the thief visibly.

the *Hērbedestān*)[490] or any 'slave' (*anšahrīg*, according to the Law-book and the PRDd, with no mention of any religious affiliation)[491] to the adherents of another religion (*ag-dēnān*). If a sale takes place, both seller and buyer are to be treated as thieves and receive the punishment for theft (*drōš*).[492] The slave is lost to both and is transferred to the *radān*, the religious authorities in charge of judgement in mercantile affairs.[493] But it seems (at least according to the rudimentary commentary in the *Hērbedestān*) that the judges were obliged to determine the *intent* of the (Zoroastrian) seller before returning a verdict: only if the latter was fully aware that he was dealing with a non-Zoroastrian would the sale be unlawful and the vendor classified as thief: *agar ān dānēd ud a-dastwarīhā frōxt* 'if he (= the seller) knows that and has (nevertheless) sold (the slave) without authorization'.[494] Another transaction that is null and void is the sale of a slave who has a physical defect (*rēš*) that is noticed later: the slave is returned to the original owner (interestingly, the same applies to marriage with a divorced woman, who has a physical defect: she is returned to the original husband).[495]

Late Pahlavi texts mention other prohibited deals with non-Zoroastrians (referring in the Islamic era mainly to Muslims, besides Jews and Christians), but it seems that decisions regarding the legality of many of these undertakings depended on the material needs of the Zoroastrians involved in these transactions or to other practical considerations, which could lead to judgements even contradicting Zoroastrian legal norms. It is, however, important to bear in mind that these post-Sasanian texts were written under drastically changed conditions. These may have encouraged new rules which might not have been in effect in the Sasanian Empire with its wide-reaching trade relationships across the Silk Roads and its large Christian and Jewish communities with which transactions of different kinds took place (an important passage of the Sasanian Law-book in fact expressly states that the same laws applied to Zoroastrians and non-Zoroastrians alike, apart from three exceptions: the latter were not allowed to install a 'proxy'; they could

490 Hēr. 11.7 (for a translation of this passage see Macuch 1993, p. 38; Kotwal/Kreyenbroek 1992, pp. 60–63, have a divergent translation.)

491 MHD 1.13–15 (Macuch 1993, pp. 23, 25); PRDd 30.1–3 (Williams 1990, pt. I, pp. 134–135; pt. II, p. 56).

492 According to MHD 1.13–15 and PRDd 30.1–3.

493 My reading and interpretation of *bandag o radan appār*, lit. 'the slave is lost to the *radān*' (Hēr. 11.7) is based on attestations of the phrase *ō radān appār* 'lost to the *radān*' in the Sasanian Law-book (MHD 38.10 and 89.4), which refers to a thing (or a right) that is transferred to the legal authorities, since the owner (or holder) has lost his entitlement to the thing (or right) due to some kind of offence. Kotwal/Kreyenbroek 1992, p. 61, correct ms. (TD) *bandag* to **bunīgīh* and translate 'the responsibility (for dealing with this) is transferred to the (religious) authorities', which is in fact a superfluous statement (it must have been well known that the *radān* were in charge of dealing with business matters), besides the strange translation 'responsibility' for **bunīgīh*.

494 See commentary Macuch 1993, pp. 35–39, where these passages are cited.

495 MHD 105.16–106.1 (Macuch 1993, pp. 641, 648).

only be held liable as part debtors and their right to inherit was restricted).[496] The 49th *Pursišn* of the *Dādestān ī dēnīg* takes up one of these problems involving trade with infidels and poses the question, whether it is lawful for Zoroastrians to sell wine to non-Zoroastrians.[497] The response of the high-priest Manuščihr—as in *Pursišn* 51 discussed above—again involves two parts: a decision on principle and an exception based on *mehdādestānīh* 'greater justice':[498] (1) Selling wine to non-Iranians (*an-ērān*), infidels (*ag-dēnān*) and those who drink immoderately is an 'evil profession' (*wad pēšagīhā*), 'very sinful' (*was wināhīhā*) and 'not authorized' (*nē dastwarīhā*), *i. e*, it is prohibited on principle. (2) If, however, the seller contributes to the well-being of the Zoroastrian community by selling wine to infidels, hereby restraining immoderate drinkers among his fellow-believers from drinking excessively (by creating a shortage of wine), and promotes the material and spiritual welfare of Zoroastrians (keeping them 'solvent', *tuwān*, and free from sin), then this corresponds to the principle of *mehdādestānīh* 'greater justice', *i. e*, going beyond the basic requirements of law. These beneficial effects neutralise the negative ones, turning trade with infidels under these specific conditions even into one of the 'reliably' (*ēwarīg*) virtuous deeds (*kirbag*).

Another *Pursišn* (number 52) discusses the sale of small livestock or sheep (*gōspand*) by Zoroastrians to traders of a different religion (*ǰud-dēnān windakkarān*, using the rare term *windakkar* 'trader', lit. 'a person, who acquires, obtains something, who makes a gain').[499] The high-priest Manuščihr replies again in the well-tried manner of giving two judgements, one based on principle, the other on 'greater justice' (although the term is not explicitly used here): (1) Selling sheep to non-Iranians (Muslims) is a 'very severe sin' (*abēr garān wināhīhā*) and this is an 'evil profession' (*wad +pēšagīhā*) which is 'not authorized' (*nē dastwarīhā*) if it is done for profit (*sūd*); *i. e*, it is forbidden on principle. (2) If, however, the livelihood of the Zoroastrian seller and persons under his guardianship depends on this profession and there are no solvent Zoroastrians who would buy his goods, then he is authorized (*pādixšāy*) to take a partner or collaborator (*hamkār*) and to sell his sheep for slaughter to non-Iranians. The text does not explain the term *hamkār* 'collaborator, partner, fellow-worker' and the question is, whether it refers to a business partner, in this case an infidel purchaser, or to a Zoroastrian associate, maybe a priest who would sanction the deal (an equivalent could be the *hambāy ī dēnīg* 'religious partner, associate', mentioned

496 MHD 60.16–61.1 (Macuch 1993, pp. 409, 415). On this passage see also Macuch 2014b and Chapter VI, pp. 527–528.

497 For the whole text see Appendix II, pp. 657–659; for an extensive discussion see Macuch 2024a.

498 This term, which (besides *wehdādestānīh*) designates a procedure extending or going beyond the basic requirements of law, is in fact expressly used in this context (K35, fol. 170v., l. 2; see Appendix II, pp. 658–659).

499 The whole text is transcribed and translated in Appendix II, pp. 661–663; on *ǰud-dēnān windakkarān* see there (p. 662) also fn. 101.

in the Law-book).[500] Be it as it may, the main reasons for these two judgements are given in a concise manner at the end of the response, leading to two conclusions: (1) The decision on principle (forbidding the sale) is based on the notion that the number of sheep left for the maintenance of Zoroastrians (*ērān* 'Iranians') would be decreased by selling to non-Zoroastrians for profit. (2) The exception (allowing the sale) takes the concrete living conditions of Zoroastrians into account: it is a 'lesser, smaller (sin)' (*xwārtar*) to seek a bargain with non-Zoroastrians (Muslims), than to risk the life of a 'righteous man' (*mard ī ahlaw*) and all persons in his guardianship (*sālārīh*) because he would be unable to make a living and to support them. These two late passages demonstrate quite well, how the high-priest applied the method of *mehdādestānīh* (or *wehdādestānīh*), developed in Sasanian law, to circumvent legal decisions detrimental to the well-being of the Zoroastrian community. But the legal problems discussed in this text definitely reflect the radically changed living conditions of Zoroastrians in the Muslim period. New solutions had to be found due to the gradual decline of the Zoroastrian communities and conversion to Islam in increasingly large numbers. Similar problems with converts might have emerged in the Sasanian period (since conversions to other religions did in fact occur, as in the case of Mār Abā, p. 47), but they would not have had the same relevance and were possibly dealt with in a different manner.

4.3.5 Lawsuits

If another person contested the sale and claimed to be the rightful owner of the sold object, then he could take legal measures. The alleged rightful owner could sue the buyer, who in turn could name his 'legal predecessor' (*dastwar*, Lat. *auctor*), *i. e*, the vendor, from whom he had bought the property, as proof for the legality of the purchase. Interestingly, the burden of proof lay on the purchaser, who was obliged to reveal how the object of dispute had come into his ownership (or, to use the appropriate legal phrase, 'which kind of ownership', *čē ēwēnag xwēšīh*, he enjoyed)[501] and to arrange for his 'legal predecessor', the seller, to appear in court personally in order to give testimony on his behalf.[502]

500 The latter term occurs in two passages of the Law-book, MHD 23.15 and 24.2 (Macuch 1993, pp. 173, 178f.). See Chapter III, p. 246. Among the Pārsīs of Navsari the expression *hamkār* assumed a technical meaning as the designation for a qualified priest (according to Modi 1937, p. 455, and Boyce 1968, p. 285). This meaning would fit in well with the context of our *Pursišn*, especially since Manuščihr himself employs the plural forms *hamkārān* (Dd 47.13) and *hamkārīhā* (Dd 47.23) in this specific sense, referring to priests, who assist or work together with the chief officiating priest (*zōt*) during the performance of the liturgy. On the term and these passages see Macuch 2024a, pp. 292–295.

501 MHD 9.15, 10.7, 95.11 (Macuch 1993, pp. 102–103; 106–107; 608 respectively); DkM 707.22; see also Chapter III, p. 197.

502 This procedure, mentioned in the Law-book, is now confirmed by the Tabarestān documents, see Chapter VI, pp. 542–544, and Macuch 2016a. On *dastwar* (= Roman *auctor*) see also Chapter III, pp. 195–196.

He could submit a request at the preliminary hearing that a special court date be fixed for this purpose (*zamān ō dastwar xwāhēd* 'he requests a date for [bringing] the *auctor*/legal predecessor').[503] The court complied with this request, taking only into account that the buyer (defendant) applied to involve a third party (*xwāhišn ī tan* 'request regarding a person') in his defence; the value of the object of dispute (*mādag*) was not decisive: even if it was worth less than *virō.mazō* (*i. e*, 500 drachms) a special date had to be set within a year. In legal practice (*pad kardag*), however, the hearing was not scheduled until the *dastwar* was able to appear in court (which might have been important for bargains with traders, who travelled over long distances and needed more time to arrive at the venue).[504] A date for bringing the *dastwar* was also granted to the buyer (defendant) if the alleged true owner (plaintiff) laid claim to the fruits of the sold thing, *e. g.*, the earnings (*windišn*) of a slave (*anšahrīg*) or to a child born of this slave.[505] If the seller (*dastwar*) himself made a request to be heard in the lawsuit, the court had to fix a special date for his statement.[506] According to another entry, however, the court did not necessarily always have to set a separate date for hearing the *dastwar*, but made this decision in accordance with the statement of the buyer (defendant). Moreover, the different legal schools of Mēdōmāh and Abarag (representing restrictive and extensive interpretations of law respectively) followed different criteria in their decisions.[507]

If the court decided to schedule a special session, the seller (*dastwar*) was obliged to follow summons and—ideally—to defend the title of the buyer by confirming that he had previously indeed been the rightful owner and the sale had been undertaken legally (a procedure comparable to the *legis actio sacramento in rem* and the *actio auctoritatis* of Roman law).[508] If there were two vendors who were at the same time witnesses in the trial, they could be both classified either as 'legal predecessors' (*dastwar*) or as 'witnesses' (*gugāy*) by the court, but—despite the difference between these two categories—either of these two categorizations would lead to a verdict based on the legal entitlement of the two sellers to undertake the sale, that is (as we may add) a verdict in favour of the buyer (defendant).[509] But if the buyer (defendant) named two legal predecessors and

503 MHD 5.11 (Macuch 1993, pp. 87, 91).

504 MHD 8.11–13 (Macuch 1993, pp. 90, 95). On *virō.mazō*, ⟨wyrwk' mzy⟩, from Av. *vīrō. maza-*, lit. 'the size of a man', the equivalent of 500 drachms see p. 262 and fn. 12.

505 MHD 7.4–6 (Macuch 1993, pp. 89, 93); for a discussion of this passage see also Macuch 1988b, p. 183.

506 MHD 8.10–11 (Macuch 1993, pp. 90, 95).

507 See MHD 5.9–16 (Macuch 1993, pp. 87f., 91f.) and Chapter VI, pp. 542–544; on the legal schools see Chapter I, pp. 64–66.

508 On the procedure in ancient Roman law see Liebs 1982, pp. 228–229, and Kaser 1986, pp. 104f., 124f., 194f.

509 MHD 7.6–8 (Macuch 1993, pp. 89, 93f.). The last part of this sentence is a fine example of legal jargon: *dō dastwarīhā dārišnīh rāy wizīr kunišn* 'the verdict is to be reached on the basis of (proof of) possession by double entitlement'.

only one of the two appeared in court, the latter could not enter *auctor*-ship for the whole lawsuit (further implications are not noted).[510] The *dastwar* also had the right to refuse testimony if the object in dispute was not shown in court and he was uncertain, whether he was in fact the vendor.[511] On the other hand, if the seller (*dastwar*) admitted in the hearing that he was *not* the rightful owner of the object he had sold to the buyer (defendant), then the true owner (plaintiff) could demand restitution of the property and, moreover, a compensation (*wināhgārīh*; *guharīg*) from the seller, which the latter was obliged to grant. On receiving both the property back and an adequate compensation, the rightful owner (plaintiff) could no longer pursue the lawsuit against the buyer (defendant).[512] However, the buyer (defendant), did not necessarily have to accept a verdict against his 'legal predecessor', but could continue the lawsuit after confirming in written form that he would attend the date scheduled for the *dastwar* himself.[513]

Our sources reveal that it was in practice by no means easy to prove rightful ownership by summoning the *dastwar*. In a case documented in the Tabarestān texts the defendant (buyer) fails to bring his 'legal predecessor' to court on the fixed date on three occasions and loses the lawsuit.[514] The place of jurisdiction or legal venue seems to have caused another problem, if sale and lawsuit took place in different regions. Two contrasting opinions are recorded in the Law-book: (1) If the buyer is sued in another region or city (*pad any šahr*) than the place where he had made the purchase, the vendor is nevertheless obliged to act as *dastwar*, *i. e*, to defend the buyer's title in court, by travelling to the venue and covering the costs of the journey himself (*nē pādixšāy bē ka šawēd u-š uzēnag az xwēš* 'he is obliged to go and [to bear] the costs from his own').[515] For example, if the vendor is from Gōr and he sells a thing to a buyer from Kāzrōn and the legality of the sale is contested in Kāzrōn, then—according to the opinion of the jurist Wayayyar—the seller has the duty to go to Kazrōn in order to give testimony on behalf of the buyer.[516] (2) The second opinion states exactly the opposite: the seller does not have to go to Kāzrōn, *i. e*, the *dastwar* is *not* obliged to give testimony in another place of jurisdiction than the region or city in which the sale took place.[517] Reasons for these contradictory decisions are not transmitted, but we can speculate that a restrictive handling of the (rather expensive and time-consuming) juristic duties of the 'legal predecessor', often a merchant or trader, would have caused a serious obstacle to long-distance commercial activities on the long run

510 MHD 6.9–11 (Macuch 1993, pp. 88, 92).
511 MHD 7.3–4 (Macuch 1993, pp. 89, 93).
512 MHD 7.15–8.2 (Macuch 1993, pp. 90, 94).
513 MHD 7.8–11 (Macuch 1993, pp. 89, 94).
514 See Macuch 2016a, pp. 159–162, and Chapter VI, p. 543 below.
515 MHD 6.6–9 (Macuch 1993, pp. 88, 92 (*nē pādixšāy bē ka šawēd*, lit. 'he is not authorized, but to go', *i. e*, 'he is obliged to go').
516 MHD 5.5–7 (Macuch 1993, pp. 87, 91). On the geographical names see de Menasce 1964b (1985), pp. 85–87, with further references.
517 MHD 5.8 (Macuch 1993, pp. 87, 91).

4.3.6 Barter

Many of the regulations regarding sale presumably also applied to barter (*guharēn*) which must have been rather common in a predominantly rural society. Besides several general statements, the sparse entries in the Law-book mainly discuss the exchange of animals and the problem of overreaching that could have applied to sale as well (when the price paid exceeded the market value by far). In contrast to sale, in which money constitutes at least part of the price, barter is defined as an exchange of goods (including animals and slaves), which are more or less (but not necessarily exactly) equivalent in value. A difference of up to one-fourth of the total value of the bartered object is permitted in Sasanian law (but we are not informed, how the relative worth of the exchanged objects was calculated). Any profit exceeding one-fourth of the total value was considered as overreaching and classified as theft.[518] This at least is implied in a case in which the husband authorizes his wife to 'undertake barter' (*guharēn kunēd*), by which he entitled her to exchange one thing for another equivalent one (*guharēn rāst* 'equal barter; exchange on a par'). But the wife was also allowed to make a barter deal without explicit authorization of the husband if the bargain was to his advantage and drew a profit of one-fourth of the total value (*pad čahar bahr ē[w] bahr*) of the exchanged goods. A profit of more than one-fourth was treated as theft with respect to the surplus amount, *i. e*, the quota exceeding one-fourth (*pad ān ī az wēš duz* 'regarding this surplus amount she [is] a thief').[519] We can moreover infer from two further entries that a reflection period of three nights (*se šabag*) was conceded to both barterers involved in the exchange, during which they could withdraw from the deal (this also applied to sale at least in certain cases, see above).[520] An exception to this general rule is also noted: the wife who has a mandate from the husband to undertake barter cannot withdraw from the deal within 'three nights' in contrast to her business partner, who can reconsider the exchange during this timespan and cancel the deal. Whether the husband could reject the deal under these circumstances seems to have been controversial and a 'matter to be reflected upon' (*abāyēd uskārdan*).[521]

A lawsuit involving the barter of a donkey (*xar*) and an ox or cow (*gāw*) is also noted, illustrating how disputes in these cases were handled. The plaintiff has traded his ox (or cow) for a donkey from the defendant and files a complaint 'because of the damage he has suffered from the defendant' (*pad zyānag ī az pasēmāl*). Two possible verdicts with different implications are transmitted: (1) The court explicitly confirms the claim of the plaintiff that he has suffered a

518 On this classification see pp. 313–314 above and section 4.1 on loans and credit law, pp. 310–359.

519 MHD 37.2–10 (Macuch 1993, pp. 273, 274).

520 MHDA 12.3–5; 12.5–7 (Macuch 1981, pp. 34, 125).

521 MHD 37.5–10 (Macuch 1993, pp. 273, 274).

damage by the exchange, but this does not imply that the defendant is culpable or has acted with fraudulent intent or even is the original owner of the donkey (if he denies that this is in fact the animal he has traded). In this case the barter is reversed: the plaintiff takes back his ox (or cow) from the defendant and the defendant receives his donkey back (even if he first refuses to accept the decision, denying that the donkey is his, but later requests the return of the animal). (2) The court decides that the defendant is guilty of damaging the plaintiff. In this event the defendant has to pay a fine (*tāwān*) for the donkey, the barter is reversed and the ox (or cow) remains in the possession of the plaintiff.[522] Although the specifics of this case are not transmitted very clearly, the mere possibility of initiating a lawsuit indicates that barter was recognized as an enforceable contract, which could also include a warranty on both sides and compensation (*tāwān*) for defective goods. Moreover, it seems that the intention of the business partners was a decisive element in judging these cases: trading with the will to deceive or to make a profit beyond the allowed margin (however this intent might have been determined by the court) was punished by means of a fine.

4.3.7 Gifts and donations (*dād*)

The noun *dād* (besides the seldom *dāšn* 'gift, donation')[523] designates the gift or donation, a voluntary and gratuitous transfer of property made with the intention of transmitting ownership of a corporeal thing, a title or a real right from one person (the donor, *rād*) to a recipient (the donee, ⟨ḤSN̠ʾ⟩ **dārāg/dārīg*? lit. 'possessor, holder'?).[524] In contrast, the verb *dādan* 'to give, transfer, convey,

522 MHD 102.3–9 (Macuch 1993, pp. 615, 623; see also commentary pp. 634–635, no. 17). There is an unfortunate mistake in my German translation of this passage, p. 623, third line from below, first word, where I have written 'ox' ('Rind') instead of 'donkey' ('Esel'), but the transliteration, p. 615, has the correct ⟨HMRʾ⟩ *xar* (instead of ⟨TWRʾ⟩ *gāw*). Perikhanian 1997, pp. 228–229, has a completely different translation of the whole passage due to superfluous emendations of the text.

523 The term *dāšn* does not occur in the Law-book, but it is attested in the *Dēnkard* (DkD 109.7–13; DkM 143.20–144.6) in this sense (besides other texts), particularly in the context of religious donations in the expression *dāšn ī ēzišn* 'donation(s) for worship', see Chapter II, p. 111.

524 For a discussion of these two terms see Macuch 1993, pp. 234–237 (no. 21), and 457–460 (no. 11) respectively: *rād* 'donor' (presumably < **rātā*, nom. sg. of an agent noun **rātār-* from √*rā* 'to give, grant'; Bartholomae 1904, col. 1518; Kellens 1995, p. 57) and ⟨HSNʾ⟩ 'donee, recipient (of a gift)' (presumably an act.part., status emphaticus from the Aramaic root ḤSN, haf'el 'to possess, to take possession [of]'; for attestations of ḤSN in the Elephantine papyri see Cowley 1923, index p. 288; in the Aršama letters Driver 1954, index p. 101; in the Babylonian Talmud Sokoloff 2002, p. 475). The Pahlavi reading of ⟨ḤSN̠ʾ⟩ (if this is indeed the correct interpretation of the word) is uncertain, but the heterogram for *dāštan*, *dār-* ⟨YḤSNN⟩ 'to have, possess' is derived from the same root (*yaḥsen* [*yaḥsenan*?] impf. 3d. pl. of haf'el *haḥsen* 'to take possession [of a thing]'; see Nyberg 1974, p. 6, and 1988, p. 95 [Ch. XXI, 3]). A possible, but questionable reading (!), could be either the corresponding present participle *dārāg* (< *dār-*+-*āg*, attested

transmit, bestow, grant, deliver' from the same root, is used generally of any kind of transfer and does not necessarily refer to gifts and donations, but to any one of the various types of transactions discussed above (including bequests, loans, transfer of a security, sale, barter etc.), depending on the context. The specific act of granting or conveying a gift is denoted by *pad dād dādan* 'to give as a gift'[525] and, in the context of transfer of ownership, by the phrase *tō xwēš* 'it (is) your own' or *tō xwēš ē bawēd* 'it shall be your own', spoken by the transferor. The latter two phrases can refer to a gift (see examples below), but also to the conveyance of ownership due to the fulfilment of an obligation (*e.g.*, the transfer of a security, a pawn or pledge, to the ownership of the pledgee instead of repayment of a debt).[526] Given the concise character of most of the entries in the Law-book and the lack of explanations, it is at times difficult to decide which kind of undertaking is exactly meant (particularly if only the verb *dādan* or the phrase *tō xwēš [ē bawēd]* are used with no further explanations). It seems that Sasanian jurists were more interested in discussing the general problems of conveyance, which were presumably the same in different types of transactions. In this context the compiler of the Law-book included a large range of case studies involving the gratuitous transfer of property in the sense noted above, as several passages on both donations made in contemplation of death (*donatio mortis causa* in Roman law), which only took effect after the demise of the donor (testator), as well as gifts that were fully operative in the donor's lifetime (*donatio inter vivos*) are brought together in this source.[527] But here again the entries are more concerned with interpreting the wording of the donor's will or stipulation and its consequences than explaining the exact circumstances of the transfer or formulating general rules. As in other legal fields, however, the language of these passages is an important clue to the exact legal background of the cases.

As we have noted above, the precise use of legal phrases and formulae was an important prerequisite of any legal agreement.[528] Jurists (and the compiler of the Law-book) could forego lengthy explanations of the quoted case studies, since

in MMP, see Durkin-Meisterernst 2004, p. 135; on the ending see Durkin-Meisterernst 2014, p. 249f., §502) or *dārīg*, lit. 'possessor, holder' (< *dār-+-īg*, on the suffix see Durkin-Meisterernst 2014, p. 174, §344). The original reading *dārīg* for a term attested in the documents of the 'Pahlavi Archive' (Weber 2008, pp. 29–30; attestations see *ibid.* index, p. 268, under ⟨d'lyk⟩) has now been revised by Weber 2022b (p. 326) to ⟨g'lyk⟩ *gālīg* 'member of the household; belonging to the household' (< OP **garda-* + suffix *-īg*).

525 See MHD 30.10 (Macuch 1993, pp. 221, 225): *pad dād be dahēd* (written ⟨pt̲ YHBWNt BR̲' YHBWNyt⟩) 'he gives as a gift'.

526 MHD 17.5,6,17; 18.2 (Macuch 1993, pp. 151f., 157f.) and other examples below. For the use of this phrase in the context of a pledge to be transferred to the creditor in lieu of debt payment see MHD 89.11–15 (Macuch 1993, pp. 570, 573).

527 Particularly in Chapter 10 of the Law-book, which is fragmentary and has no title (MHD 17.1–21.3; Macuch 1993, pp. 151–169).

528 See Chapter I, pp. 72–85.

the language of the stipulation itself would reveal the exact context to a legal expert. We have already elucidated the significance of the agential/ergative form in the will, donation or testamentary contract: by employing the words *kū-m … (ō tō) dād*, lit. 'I gave, I have given (such-and-such a thing to you/or name of the recipient)' the donor or testator explicitly reveals his intent of transferring something *after his death* to the recipient. The donor 'speaks from death' (reflected in the use of the preterite) and the transaction can only take place after his demise. In contrast, by using the present tense (*dahom* 'I give, bestow, transmit, convey' or, in transfers of ownership, *tō xwēš* 'it [is] your own', or the optative *tō xwēš ē bawēd* 'it shall be your own') the transferor expresses his wish to convey a proprietary right or a gift to the transferee either immediately (*pad gyāg*) or at some specifically fixed time (*e. g., pas az dah sāl* 'after ten years') during his lifetime.[529]

This fundamental distinction enables us to differentiate at least between donations made in contemplation of death (*mortis causa*) and those that took effect during the donor's lifetime (*inter vivos*), but in certain cases, if only the verb *dādan* is employed, it still remains difficult to determine whether the statement of the stipulator refers to some kind of voluntary gratuity or to a transaction in fulfilment of an obligation. In either case, however, the same formalities of conveyance applied as in all legal agreements (which we have already discussed above): the donor made an offer, which only took effect if it was explicitly accepted by the donee (*pad dād … padīrišn paydāgēnīd* 'he has revealed consent to the transfer/gratuity').[530] With these basic rules in mind, we can distinguish between these two types of donations, which seem to have been subject to rather detailed regulations depending on the formulation of the stipulation. As we have already discussed donations in contemplation of death (including those to pious institutions and fire foundations in Chapter III), we will restrict the following scrutiny of the sources to gifts fully operative in the donor's lifetime (*inter vivos*).

The following case seems to be an example for a general donation of ownership rights during the lifetime of the donor:

529 See particularly Chapter III, pp. 238–239; on *pas az dah sāl* see MHD 17.4 (Macuch 1993, pp. 151, 157; quoted below).

530 MHD 17.8 (Macuch 1993, pp. 151, 157). In this procedure called *padīrišn paydāgēnīdan* 'to reveal acceptance' the transferor or donor declared his will (*kāmag*) to transfer something to the recipient using the words: *an ī tō sahēd* 'that which you approve of' or *ān ī tō kāmēd* 'that which you desire' or *ān ī tō passandē* 'that which you approve of' or *ān ī tō (andar) abayed* 'that which you have need of'. The recipient gave his consent with the prescribed formulae: *dōšīd* 'it is sanctioned' or *kāmag dōšīd* 'the will (of the transferor) is sanctioned' or *andar abāyēd* 'it is necessary'. He could refuse the offer with the words *andar nē abāyēd* 'it is not necessary; there is no need'. See above pp. 301–305.

MHD 17.4–5
ka gōwēd kū pas az dah sāl xwāstag ī man xwēš tō xwēš ān dād bawēd ī pas az dah sāl xwēš.

'If he (= the transferor/donor) says: "After ten years the property that (is) my own (is) your own", (then) that is given which is his (= the transferor/donor's) own after ten years.'[531]

If we are correct in our assessment of the legal language, the donor stipulates to transfer property in his ownership during his lifetime after a specific timespan to the recipient with the words 'after ten years the property that (is) my own (is) your own' (*pas az dah sāl xwāstag ī man xwēš tō xwēš*). This wording implies that the recipient is not entitled to the property existent at the time of the stipulation, but only to that which is still in the ownership of the transferor after ten years, that is, the gains and losses in the interim period between offer and acceptance, on the one hand, and implementation, on the other, must be taken into consideration.

Many of the case studies discuss the conveyance of ownership of the surplus of property, that is, income that did not initially belong to the category of property inherited from the ancestors (*abarmānd*). As we have elucidated above, this surplus (comparable to the Roman *bona adventicia*) was called *xwāstag ī mad ud rasēd* (or simply: *mad ud rasēd*) '(property that) has been gained (lit.: has come) and will be acquired (lit.: will arrive)'. These two categories of income could be separated into *mad*, denoting the surplus that had been acquired in the past (before the stipulation), and *rasēd*, the increase expected to be obtained in the future (after the stipulation).[532] In one instance the transferor (Farrox) expresses his will to transfer the surplus of his property to the transferee (Mihrēn) with the words: 'The property which will arrive into my ownership (is) your own' (*xwāstag ī ō xwēšīh ī man rasēd tō xwēš*). The transferee (Mihrēn) has generally accepted the offer (*padīrišn paydāgēnīd* 'he has revealed consent'), but then refuses to accept a 'thing' (*xwāstag*) conveyed afterwards by a third party to the transferor (Farrox) by 'declaring that he has no need' (*andar nē abāyidan gōwēd*). Having already consented to the general offer of the transferor (Farrox) this second statement of the transferee (Mihrēn) is null and void.[533]

Different formulations, stipulating the surplus of property consisting of silver and gold (money/objects) as a gift are elucidated in another passage:

1. 'The silver that has come (*mad*) into my ownership and the gold that will arrive (*rasēd*) into my ownership: a sum amounting to the worth of 200

531 Macuch 1993, pp. 151, 157).
532 On these terms see Chapters I, p. 78, and III, pp. 192–193.
533 Lit. 'the thing does not remain with Farrox' (*xwāstag pad Farrox be nē ēstēd*), that is, the surplus of property ('thing', *xwāstag*) given to the transferor, Farrox, is passed on to the transferee, Mihrēn, due to the latter's previous general acceptance of the transfer. MHD 17.5–9 (Macuch 1993, pp. 151, 157).

(drachms) shall be your own' (*asēm ī ō xwēšīh ī man mad ud zarr ī ō xwēšīh ī man rasēd čand arz 200 wahāg arzēd tō xwēš ē bawēd*). If the donor acquires no further income in gold after the offer then only the income in silver in the donor's ownership at the time of the stipulation is transferred to the donee to half of the total amount of the gift (in this case ⁺100 drachms).[534]

2. 'The silver that has come (*mad*) into my ownership and the silver that will arrive (*rasēd*) into my ownership: a sum amounting to the worth of 200 (drachms) (is) your own' (*asēm ī ō xwēšīh ī man mad ud asēm ī ō xwēšīh ī man rasēd čand arz 200 wahāg arzēd tō xwēš*). In contrast to the first statement, the donor offers only the income in silver in his ownership as a gift, including future gains in silver up to a specified amount (200 drachms). The donee is entitled to the whole sum (200 drachms) in silver, even if there is no further gain after the stipulation.[535]
3. 'The gold, on the one hand, and the silver, on the other ...' (*ēk zarr ud ēk asēm* ...) or: 'the gold and the silver that has come (*mad*) into my ownership: a sum amounting to the worth of 200 (drachms) (is) your own' (*zarr ud asēm ī ō xwēšīh ī man mad čand arz 200 wahāg arzēd tō xwēš*). Both formulations (with *ēk* ... *ēk* in the former and *ud* in the latter case) refer only to the surplus (*mad*) already in the ownership of the donor and have the same implications: the donee is entitled to half the amount of 200 (drachms) in silver and half the amount in gold.[536]

We can conclude from these case studies that gifts of income classified as *mad* and as *rasēd* were treated differently. A deed of gift conveying the income of property gained *before* the stipulation (of the *mad* category) took effect without deduction on acceptance of the donee. On the other hand, a gratuity of the *rasēd* category depended on the increase of the donor's property *after* the stipulation. It was hence conditional and only became effective to the extent to which a surplus of property was actually realized.

The transfer of the future income (*rasēd*) of the same property could be restricted to a fixed period of time and bestowed to two recipients, as we can conclude from another passage of the Law-book. Here again the formulation of the stipulation is decisive. The donor (Farrox) conveys ownership of the income of the same 'thing/property' successively to two men, to the first recipient (Mihrēn) for one year and to the second one (Kērēn) for five years. The wordings of the two stipulations differ slightly, but crucially. The contract (*pašt*) of the donor with the first donee (Mihrēn) for one year states: 'the property that is my own: that which will indeed arrive (*rasēd*) into my ownership (is) your own' (*xwāstag ī man xwēš ēd-iz o xwēšīh ī man rasēd tō xwēš*). This wording implies that the first recipient (Mihrēn) receives ownership of the income produced in

534 MHD 17.16–17 (Macuch 1993, pp. 152, 158).
535 MHD 18.1–2 (Macuch 1993, pp. 152, 158).
536 MHD 18.3–6 (Macuch 1993, pp. 152, 158).

one year (as *bar-xwēš* 'owner of the fruits'), but not of the property itself. The agreement with the second recipient (Kērēn) for five years, on the other hand, states: 'the property that is my own and that which will arrive (*rasēd*) into my ownership (is) your own' (*xwāstag ī man xwēš ud ēd čē ō xwēšīh ī man rasēd tō xwēš*). By this statement the donor transfers the property itself as well as the income of five years into the ownership of the second recipient (Kērēn).[537] If our interpretation of this difficult passage is correct, the distinction between these two (otherwise similar) stipulations lies in the conjunction 'and' (*ud*), which is only used in the second statement, explicitly conveying both the specified property *and* its surplus of five years to the donee (as both *bun-xwēš* 'owner of the substance' and *bar-xwēš* 'owner of the fruits', as we may add).

A gift could be made subject to a specific limitation (until a certain event takes place, but not necessarily for an exactly fixed period of time) under the condition that it be returned afterwards. A remarkable passage in the Law-book reveals the difficulties Sasanian jurists were confronted with in these cases, besides being an impressive example of their sophistry in interpreting the formulation of a contract.[538] A man transfers a thing/property into the ownership of another person before undertaking a journey to Babylonia with the words: 'until I return from Babylonia, this thing/property (is) your own' (*tā az Sūrestān abāz āyam ēn xwāstag tō xwēš*). What happens to the property, if the donor dies in Babylonia during this voyage? The stipulation evidently conveys a gift, but contains at the same time a limitation, which can be understood in various ways. The opinions of two jurists are recorded, transmitting a restrictive and an extensive interpretation: (1) According to Pusānweh ī Burzādur-Farrbayān 'the property is not returned to him' (*ā-š xwāstag abāz nē rasēd*), that is, the gift is not given back to the family of the donor (who himself has died), but remains in the ownership of the donee. Obviously this jurist interprets the limitation stated in the stipulation ('until I return') literally. (2) According to Dādfarrox ī Mardbūdān the literal meaning of the stipulation is not decisive, but rather the intention of the donor. The contract should be interpreted as if the donor had stipulated: 'possess it until I return to the base' (*tā abāz ō bun āyam tō dār*). If

537 MHD 20.16–21.3 (Macuch 1993, pp. 156, 161; the erroneous 'und' in my German translation of the first stipulation is wrong and should be deleted). Compare MHD 55.3–7 (Macuch 1993, pp. 375, 378).

538 MHD 72.5–10 (Macuch 1993, pp. 478, 480): *abāg ān ī Pusānweh ī Burzādur-Farrbayān guft kū ka gōwēd kū tā az Sūrestān abāz āyam ēn xwāstag tō xwēš ud andar Asūrestān be mīrēd ā-š xwāstag abāz nē rasēd ud Dādfarrox ī Mardbūdān guft kū-š abāz rasēd čē ōwōn bawēd čiyōn ka ān gōwēd kū tā abāz ō bun āyam tō dār ka mīrēd pad āmad ī ō bun dārišn.* 'Together with the statement of Pusānweh ī Burzādur-Farrbayān: if he (= the donor) declares: "until I return from Babylonia, this thing/property (is) your own" and he (= the donor) dies in Babylonia, then the thing/property is not returned to him. And Dādfarrox ī Mardbūdān said: it is returned to him, since it is as if he had said: "possess it until I return to the base", (then) if he (= the donor) dies, it should be considered as if he (= the donor) had returned to the base.'

the donor dies in a foreign country, this 'should be considered as if he had returned to the base' (*pad āmad ī ō bun dārišn*), hence 'the property is returned to him' (*kū-š abāz rasēd*), *i. e*, it reverts to the family of the donor. This second extensive interpretation of the stipulation presumably connotes *bun* 'base, foundation, origin' with the hereafter (to which all mortals return, when they die), but it also has a completely different understanding of the donor's intent. This jurist infers that (contrary to the wording of the stipulation) the said property has *not* been transferred as a temporary gift in ownership (*tō xwēš* 'it [is] your own'), but only as a possession (*tō dār* 'possess it') for a limited period.

Taking the evidence of these (and other) passages into consideration, it seems that, in contrast to classical Roman law, Sasanian law accepted temporary and returnable gifts, but discussed the legal consequences controversially, as in the last example. Temporary gifts could have been a means of conveying full proprietary rights for a limited period (*e. g.*, as long as a proprietor was absent by journeying to another country, or until a male successor came of age), after which the gratuity or a part of it (the 'substance') was returned to the original owner.[539] In classical Roman law this type of *donatio* for a limited period of time was not allowed, being incompatible with the Roman concept of ownership as an absolute right (temporary gifts were, however, evidently later permitted under Justinian).[540] Sasanian law had a divergent concept of ownership, as we have seen in Chapter III above, and could, moreover, be more flexible due to the option of splitting ownership rights into a title to the 'substance' (*bun*), on one hand, and to the 'fruits' (*bar*) of a 'thing', on the other.

Other entries confirm that it was possible to limit a gift temporarily from the outset by binding its duration to the approval of the donor or to a specific condition or event. The donor could stipulate: 'as long as it pleases me this thing/property (is) your own' (*ta man sahēd ēn xwāstag tō xwēš*). An exact time limit is not mentioned in the stipulation, but the duration of the gift is tied to the approval of the donor, can be terminated according to the latter's wish and ends with his death, is hence not transferred to the donee's heirs, but returned to the family of the donor.[541] Another case reveals another possible background for the existence of temporary and returnable gifts. The donor can stipulate: 'until

539 See MHD 64.15–17 (Macuch 1993, pp. 434, 437); 69.3–5 (*ibid.* pp. 463, 467); 72.6–16 (*ibid.* pp. 478, 480); MHDA 2.11–12 (Macuch 1981, pp. 22f., 70f.); 32.13–15, 15–17 (*ibid.* pp. 58, 215).

540 According to Buckland 1963 on Roman law (p. 256; *apud* Elman 2008, p. 182): 'Donatio commonly contemplates transfer of property. As there could be no temporary ownership, this excludes, for classical law, any donatio for a time or to be returnable on any event. The alienation accompanied by a provisio was void. But, under Justinian, such gifts were allowed, and it seems that the ownership reverted on arrival of the time or condition.' On ownership in Sasanian law see Chapter III, pp. 193–197.

541 MHDA 32. 13–15 (Macuch 1981, pp. 58, 215): *pad wēšistīh tā zīndagīh ud pad kamistīh tā sāhēd dād bawēd* 'it (= the gift) is conveyed at most for the duration of his (= the donor's) life and at least as long as it pleases him (= the donor).'

the lad comes of age it (is) your own' (*tā rēdag purnāy bawēd tō xwēš*) restricting the duration of the gift to the period in which a boy (presumably the male successor in the family of the donor) is still underage. On reaching maturity at the age of 15 years the gift reverts from the donee to (the family of) the donor. On the other hand, if the boy does not reach maturity and dies underage, the conveyed property remains with the donee and is never returned to the donor (or his family).[542] The sentence suggests that one of the reasons for limiting the timespan of a gift was to enable the use of a certain property (*e. g.*, land, which would otherwise remain uncultivated) in the interim period until a male heir would reach maturity and take over.

The donor (or testator) could make over a share in his estate, for example one-half, one-third or one-fourth of his property.[543] Most of the passages treating shares in property rights deal with gifts in contemplation of death (*mortis causa*) and address one of the main problems discussed in this context: is the share (*bahr*) bequeathed as a gift granted to the beneficiary as an 'undivided' (*a-baxt*) share, that is an 'ideal' portion of the whole estate to be shared jointly as common property with the other heirs and legatees, or should it be separated from the rest of the inheritance?[544] Among these cases one of them discusses a gift that presumably took effect during the lifetime of the donor, to judge by the phrasing of the stipulation (and the use of the term *rād* 'donor'). The sentence is not understood easily, as it treats the matter in the (by now well-know) concise manner of the Law-book, offering no explanations, but the problem is the same.[545] The donor declares: 'one-third of this thing/property shall be Mihrēn's own' (*ēn xwāstag se bahr ē bahr Mihrēn xwēš ē bawēd*), but does not specify whether the granted portion should be given as an 'undivided' (*a-baxt*) share. The question is: has the donor granted an ideal share of the whole estate to be held by all shareholders as common property or should a quota of one-third

542 MHDA 32.15–17 (Macuch 1981, pp. 58, 215): *pad wēšistīh tā 15 sāl guft bawēd ud Pērōz ī guft kū ka rēdag andar ⁺aburnāyīh mīrēd xwāstag hagriz abāz nē āyēd* 'It (= the gift) is stipulated at most for 15 years. And Pērōz said: "if the lad dies underage, it (= the gift) never comes back."'

543 MHD 53.12–13, 13–15; 53.15–54.2; 54.15–17; 65.1–2, 7–9 (Macuch 1993, pp. 373f., 376f.; 435, 438 respectively). All these sentences refer to gifts in contemplation of death (*mortis causa*), as we can infer from the use of the agential/ergative construction in the quoted stipulations (on these gifts see Chapter III, pp. 238–239).

544 See particularly MHD 53.15–54.2 (Macuch 1993, pp. 373, 376).

545 MHD 54.2–5 (Macuch 1993, pp. 374, 377): *pad guft ī Wayayyār nibišt kū ka gōwēd kū ēn xwāstag sē bahr ē bahr Mihrēn xwēš ē bawēd u-š a-baxt abāg nē gōwēd ēdōn bawēd čiyōn ka-š nēm-ē gōwē ud kāmag pad rād ud any gyāg-ē nibišt kū ka-š pad bahr dahēd a-baxt dād bawēd.* 'According to the statement of Wayayyār it is written: If he says: "One-third of this thing/property shall be Mihrēn's own" and does not formulate (the statement) with *a-baxt* ("undivided"), (then) it is considered as if he had assigned one-half (of the property) and the deed of gift (remains) with the donor. In another passage it is written: If he (= the donor) gives (something) as a share, then it is considered to have been given as an "undivided" (*a-baxt*) (share).'

be separated from the rest of the property? Two contradictory decisions are transmitted: (1) According to the jurisconsult Wayayyār, the case should be considered *as if* the donor had stipulated one-half of his property. This implies that the donated portion consisting of one-third should be separated from the rest of the estate; the donor (*rād*) receives the original copy of the deed of gift (*kāmag*, lit. '[statement of] will; volition'). This enigmatic decision of Wayayyār can only be understood correctly, if we take another passage into account, supplying the necessary information: the person with the larger share of a property receives the original document of transfer (or deed of gift), the one with the smaller share receives a copy.[546] Applied to our case Wayayyār's decision implies (a) that the shares are to be separated; (b) the donor (*rād*) retaining the larger portion (two-thirds), keeps the original deed; the beneficiary, receiving one-third, is given a copy of the deed of gift (*kāmag*). (2) A diametrically opposed opinion is transmitted subsequently in the same passage: the donated share is an 'undivided' (*a-baxt*) share, *i. e*, it is a gift of an ideal portion to be held jointly with others and not to be separated from the rest of the property of the donor.

Other frequently discussed cases interpolate a third person, to whom the donor assigns the right to grant a specified property in the donor's ownership to a person of his or her choice. In one example the *kadag-xwadāy* seals a document (*wizīr*) for his *pādixšāy*-wife, conveying to her the right to designate a beneficiary with the phrase: 'this thing/property shall be in the ownership of the one whom you designate as owner' (*ēn xwāstag ōy kē tō xwēš būd rāy gōwē xwēš ē bawēd*).[547] By this document the husband entitles his *pādixšāy*-wife to allocate a specified property to a person of her choice. The formula *xwēš būd rāy guftan* 'to designate (a person) as owner', occurs in several variations, in which a third person is always inserted between the donor and the donee and given the sole right to determine the recipient of the assigned property.[548] This interpolated person is only allowed to choose the beneficiary, but is not granted an individual ownership title to the property, if this is not explicitly stated in the stipulation.[549]

546 MHDA 33.15–34.1 (Macuch 1981, pp. 59, 216) states that the original copy (*mādagwar*) of a document (*wizīr*) conveying one-third of a property to Mihrēn and two-thirds to Farrox goes to Farrox, the copy (*hampaččēn*) to Mihrēn. According to MHDA 33.17–34.1 *kāmag*, lit.'will, wish', designates the document in which the gift is registered; *rād* the 'donor' (see fn. 524 above).

547 MHD 64.3 (Macuch 1993, pp. 434, 437).

548 Particularly in chapter 24 of the Law-book, titled *dar ī xwēš būd guft* 'Chapter on the assignment of (a thing) as (someone's) own' (MHD 63.6–65.17, Macuch 1993, pp. 433–439).

549 The consequences are diametrically opposed in one instance using this phrase. If the donor states: 'this (thing) shall be your own until you assign it to (another) person in ownership' (*ēn ta tō kas xwēš būd rāy gōwē tō xwēš ē bawēd*), the implications are of course completely different. According to this stipulation the recipient of the gift only retains ownership as long as he/she does not pass it on in ownership to a third person. The donee retains the property as long as he lives, but it cannot be bequeathed to his heirs. On the donee's demise it is returned to the donor or his family (lit. it reverts to its 'base, origin', bun) (MHD 64.15–17; Macuch 1993, pp. 434, 437).

Gifts to persons under guardianship (*sālārīh*) with limited or no legal capacity (*alieni iuris*), notably women and underage children, were as a rule subject to the consent of the guardian (but see below). As their legal representative the guardian expressed his agreement to the gift or refused it, following the procedure described above as *padīrišn paydāgēnīdan* 'to reveal consent'. By choosing the words 'I give my consent to the gift that man has made' (*pad ān ī ōy mard dād kard hunsand hom*) a husband could agree to a gift (*mortis causa* in this case) to his wife and at the same time retain a claim to the donated property himself. But if he declared 'I give my consent that that man give it *in ownership*' (*pad ān ī ōy mard pad xwēšīh be dād hunsand hom*), only the beneficiary who was granted ownership rights, *i. e*, his wife, was entitled to the gratuity.[550] Gifts to underage children were the father's own until the former reached maturity.[551] The legal guardian of an underage child and the husband could explicitly refuse a donation to their wards with the formula 'we have no need of it' (*kūmān andar nē abāyēd*), but the transaction nevertheless took place despite the rejection (to the underage child after reaching maturity).[552] The background of this ruling is the basic idea that transactions benefiting family members and the family as a whole cannot be rejected. Limiting the capacity of a legal guardian or head of a household to refuse gifts and donations to his wards was one of the means of curbing losses and avoiding the diminishment of family property by mismanagement.[553]

A gift could be granted by verbal contract or stipulation (*guft*), by a sealed document (*āwišt*) or by testament (*handarz*). In contrast to an informal arrangement, a formal agreement by stipulation following the general rules of offer and acceptance described above was enforceable and could as a rule not be revoked, but this did not necessarily apply to the testament or written contract. The different implications of an oral contract, which has *not* been recorded in a sealed document (*guft ī nē pad āwišt*), on the one hand, and the testament (*handarz*) or sealed document (*āwišt*), on the other, are explained in a longer passage.[554] The donor can revoke a gift made by testamentary disposition, as he is entitled to change his last will. This also applies to the written contract as long as the document has not yet been sealed. On the other hand, he cannot revoke an oral stipulation (*guft*), since it has to be endorsed by at least three witnesses (*sē gugāy*) making it absolutely legally binding (*was az-iš ēwarīh*) or—in presumably seldom cases—by the Chief Mobed (*mowbedān mowbed*) alone (whose testimony and judgment were final and could not be contested).

550 MHDA 4.5–10 (Macuch 1981, pp. 24f., 72).
551 MHD 20.2–5 (Macuch 1993, pp. 155, 160).
552 MHD 19.7–10 (Macuch 1993, pp. 154, 160).
553 See also Chapter II, pp. 177–183 on guardianship.
554 MHDA 10.2–13 (Macuch 1981, pp. 31f., 123f.).

Table 37. Overview: terminology relating to gifts and donations

Persons involved	
rād	donor (person who grants a gift)
⟨ḤSN̠ʾ⟩ (**dārāg/dārīg?*)	donee (recipient of a gift)
Modes of transfer and contract types	
guft (*guft ī nē pad āwišt*)	verbal contract or stipulation (not recorded in a sealed document)
āwišt	sealed document
handarz	testament, last will
Wordings in stipulations	
ēn xwāstag ōy kē tō xwēš būd rāy gōwē xwēš ē bawēd	'This thing/property shall be in the ownership of the one whom you designate as owner'
kū-m … (*ō tō*) *dād*	'I gave, I have given (such-and-such a thing to you/or name of the recipient)' (*donatio mortis causa*)
pad dād dādan	to give as a gift
pad dād … padīrišn paydāgēnīd	'he has revealed consent to the gratuity'
tō xwēš (*ē bawēd*)	'it (is/shall be) your own' (*donatio inter vivos*)
xwēš būd rāy guftan	to designate (a person) as owner

Chapter V

Sins and Offences

Introductory: The religious dimension of penal law

Pahlavi religious sources list a myriad of sins and offences (*wināh*) consisting of violations of ritual precepts, purity laws and moral values as well as all kinds of illegal acts, reaching from smaller infringements of another person's rights to grievous criminal acts such as theft, robbery, assault, physical injury and homicide.[1] As we have seen, Zoroastrian law distinguished between two types of transgressions, 'offences regarding opponents' (*wināh ī hamēmālān*), *i.e.* disputes between men, comprising all kinds of illegal acts by which another member of the Zoroastrian community is damaged or injured (both civil and criminal cases), and 'sins pertaining to the soul' (*wināh ī ruwānīg*), encompassing all offences endangering the delinquent's own soul, both criminal acts and sins committed against ritual and moral norms.[2] This differentiation does not necessarily mean that transgressions were separated into two distinct categories, since every offence of the *hamēmālān* type was also considered as a sin damaging to the soul of the perpetrator, but it creates a means of distinguishing between the two main forms of punishment and compensation. A sin of the *ruwānīg* type is atoned for by repentance and confession, by accepting the penalty imposed by one's spiritual mentors, by performing pious deeds and paying a fine to religious authorities (the *rad* as recipient of the fine is regularly mentioned in this context),[3] whereas a *wināh ī hamēmālān* can be atoned for solely by compensating the opponent directly, not by performing any other righteous deeds.[4] This, however, does not necessarily exclude the need to confess and repent the sin or to pay an additional fine or part of the fine to the

1 Sins and offences are mentioned in almost all sources. The main ones, referred to in this chapter, are: the *Wīdēwdād*; different sections of the *Nērangestān* and *Hērbedestān*; the penitential sections of the *Xorde Avesta* (*patits*); *Dēnkard* 8; *Šāyist-nē-šāyist*; Supplementary texts to the *Šāyist-nē-šāyist*; *Riwāyat* of *Ādurfarrbay*; on these sources see Chapter I.

2 These distinctions have already been discussed in Chapter I, pp. 62–63.

3 The specific authority of the Av. *ratu-* to discipline those under his authority, the *ratunaiia-*, and to impose fines is already implied in the Avesta, particularly in the *Āfrīnagān* prayer for the *Gāhāmbār* festivals, see Kreyenbroek 1994, pp. 3–5.

4 This is explicitly said in DkD (M) 89.14–90.1; DkM 696.16–18 (see Appendix VI, p. 682): a sin regarding opponents (*wināh ī hamēmālān*) cannot be atoned for by any other good deed (*kirbag*) except towards the adversary himself (who receives the compensation); see also Šnš 8.1, cited in Chapter I, pp. 62–63.

rad in order to redeem one's soul (as indicated, for example, in the Pahlavi commentary to Vd. 13.12).[5] No matter how the offence is penalized and to whom a compensation has to be paid, every transgression of Zoroastrian law in its different facets is considered as damaging to the soul in various degrees.

We have hence every reason to conclude that Sasanian penal law has a very important religious dimension that distinguishes it basically from all non-religious, secular legal systems. Besides protecting individuals and society by punishing offenders and enforcing moral values the foremost purpose of Zoroastrian penal law is to save the souls, or better, 'eschatological souls' (*ruwān*) of the delinquents from the dire consequences of their sins in the afterlife and after the Restoration (*frašgird*).[6] As we have seen above, law (*dād*) was perceived in Zoroastrian doctrine as having three dimensions: (1) the law of the corporal world (*gētīy*) which is in force as long as a person is 'in a corporal state' (*pad tanōmandīh*); (2) the law of the spiritual world (*mēnōy*) that prevails after the soul has left the body; and (3) the law which is finally fulfilled by the Restoration (*frašgird*).[7]

When a person dies, the good and evil deeds he has committed in his lifetime are judged in the course of three nights before the soul leaves the body.[8] A triad of three divinities (or *mēnōy* judges)[9] pass judgement over the soul: these are Mithra (MP Mihr), lord of the covenant, who presides over the proceedings, Sraoša (MP Srōš), protector of prayer, and Rašnu (MP Rašn), the hypostasis of judging.[10] It is Rašn who holds the scales upon which the sins and virtues of the deceased are impartially judged.[11] While the soul of the deceased is still in

5 See the translation and commentary to this passage by Buyaner 2016, pp. 355–356 (Moazami 2014, p. 325, has not understood the sentence).

6 The *ruwān*, the 'interior soul liberated by death' or 'eschatological soul', incorporates the principle of immortality and is distinguished from the 'vital soul', *gyan*, which disappears with the death of the body (*tan*); see Gignoux 2001, pp. 20–21, with further references; see also fn. 42 below.

7 See Introduction, pp. 6–7, according to *Dēnkard* 3.78 (DkD 51.7–11; DkM 69.18–70.2); for the whole text see Appendix III, pp. 665–667.

8 The revered number three is reminiscent of the sacred Zoroastrian triad, encompassing the main moral teachings of Mazdaism (*humat*, *hūxt*, *huwaršt*), and recurs not only in the context of rituals, but also in a legal context. The extent of time conceded to business partners to reconsider legal transactions consists of three nights (*sē šabag*); litigants make their statements at a distance of three steps (*sē gām*) from the judge; there are three different types of guardianship and *stūr*-ship, etc. The Zoroastrian triad also corresponds to the three stations preceding Paradise and the threefold scheme of repentance of sins, consisting of three steps: 'contrition—confession—redemption' (see Buyaner 2016, pp. 26–30).

9 See Dk. 3.302 (Appendix III, pp. 667–668) and Introduction, pp. 7–8.

10 See Boyce 1975c, pp. 240–241, and recently König 2022, pp. 353–355, and (on Mithra) 401–431, with references to the sources; the ceremonies performed for the soul after death are described Vd. 8.22 (Moazami 2014, pp. 232–235); Dd 27 (Jaafari Dehaghi 1998, pp. 88–89) and Šnš XVII (Kotwal 1969, pp. 70–75); see also Modi 1937, pp. 75–82. On Mithra, lord of the covenant, see also Chapter IV above, pp. 260–263.

11 On Rašnu see the edition of *Rašn Yašt* by Goldman 2015.

the body Rašn evaluates it by weighing the good and evil thoughts, speech and deeds of the individual during his lifetime on his 'yellow golden scales' (*tarāzūg ī zard zarrēn*).[12] On the fourth morning Rašn reaches a verdict regarding the abode of the deceased's soul either in heaven or hell until the time of Restoration and the soul advances to the *Činwad* Bridge (Av. *cinuuatō.pərətu-*), the crossing to the afterlife, where it encounters its image or manifestation *(dēn*; Av. *daēnā-* 'vision') in the form of a beautiful maiden or a hideous hag.[13] The souls of those individuals whose meritorious and evil deeds are on a par are kept in an intermediate place between heaven and hell (**hamiyastagān*), a kind of purgatory, until their destiny is resolved and they are given their final form (*tan ī pasēn*) in the future Universe.[14]

In this setting the foremost task of Zoroastrian priestly authorities was to minimize the amount of sins that would pile up during the lifetime of an individual and determine his or her destiny after death. The technical phrase used in this context to designate the accumulation of sins and merits forming the soul of the individual is *ō bun* (*būdan*) '(to accrue) to (one's) stock/account'.[15] Interestingly, the phrase contains exactly the same legal term we have already discussed in the context of property law, namely *bun* 'substance, capital, principal, stock, core assets', *i. e.* the more or less permanent part of every physical 'thing' (a parcel of land, a house, etc.) as opposed to the 'fruits' of this 'thing', called *bar* 'increase, produce, income, profit' (*i. e.* crops, rent, revenue, etc.).[16] The 'capital, substance, stock' of a lineage usually consisted of property accumulated across several generations, as we have seen in Chapter III. The parallel idea in a religious context seems to be that sins and merits accumulate in the course of time, forming the 'capital' or 'stock' of a person's soul as it appears at his/her demise and finally passes to the afterlife. One category of offences, called 'sins

12 The cited passage is from the *Ardā Wirāz Nāmag* 5.5 *apud* Goldman 2015, p. 30.

13 See Goldman 2015, pp. 26–32, with numerous references to the sources. Rašn reaches his verdict on the fourth morning, which incidentally corresponds to the instructions given to Zoroastrian judges to pronounce judgment 'until noon' (*tā nēmrōz*) or 'in the morning' *(andar frayar*; see Macuch 1981, p. 155, no. 25, and Chapter VI, p. 569 below). In the Pahlavi text *Wizīdagīhā ī Zādspram* from the ninth century the author distinguishes between three different manifestations of the soul: (1) the *ruwān ī andar tan* (or: *ruwān ī tanīg*), the 'soul that is in the body' or 'corporeal soul'; (2) the *ruwān ī bērōn* or *ruwān ī andar rāh*, the 'external soul' or 'soul that is on the way', *i. e.* the soul that leaves the body (during sleep) and meets its manifestation (Av. *daēnā-*; MP *dēn*) at the *Činwad* Bridge (after death); (3) the *ruwān ī pad mēnōyān axwān*, the 'soul in the world of the *mēnōy*' or heavenly soul (see Sohn 1996, pp. 1, 21–26; Gignoux 2001, pp. 20–23). On Av. *daēnā-*; MP *dēn* 'vision' see the articles by Cantera 2013, pp. 127–131, Hintze 2017 and Panaino 2019, with further references.

14 According to the *Ardā Wirāz Nāmag* 6.3, see Gignoux 1984, pp. 52–53, 160. On Av. *hāməmiiāsaitē*, MP ⟨hmystk'n⟩ **hamiyastagān* see Klingenschmitt 1972.

15 On this phrase see also Buyaner 2016, pp. 221–225, with references to and quotations from the sources.

16 See Chapter III, pp. 197–202.

which go to the Bridge' (*winâh ī ō puhl šawēd*), can in fact only be atoned for after the death of the perpetrator at the Činwad Bridge.[17] The basic notion is obviously—in full accordance with Zoroastrian teaching—that every Mazdean moulds the essence of his or her own soul and can increase its valuable assets by performing meritorious deeds (*kirbag*) and reduce (or remove completely) its liabilities by atoning for sins in the manner prescribed by religious authorities. The sum of all good or evil thoughts, words and deeds forms the 'substance, stock' (*bun*) of the soul of the deceased, which is then evaluated by Rašn on the threshold to the hereafter.

Needless to say, the whole concept indirectly endows the priesthood with enormous power, besides a constant flow of income due to the fines that were imposed on the sinners. Particularly those priests engaged in jurisdiction in the Sasanian period (the *rad ī xwēš* 'one's own *rad*', the individual's chosen spiritual leader, the *rad*, a local priest, and the *mowbed* up to the Chief Mobed) could act as judges and impose penalties (to their own advantage or to the advantage of the Zoroastrian Church) with the higher goal of saving the souls of the sinners.[18] Sins and offences were punished in Zoroastrian law according to an ingenious system, which took both the type of sin and its frequency into consideration (see pp. 468–486 below). But before describing this rather abstract scheme (which does not differentiate between *ruwānīg* and *hamēmālān* sins) we will first attempt to reconstruct the emergence of Mazdean penal law based on a short synopsis describing this process in *Dēnkard* 8. In the subsequent section we will address the important question, whether Zoroastrian law developed some kind of recognizable theory with regard to the constitutive elements of a crime. We will then try to determine as closely as possible the most important transgressions and criminal acts belonging to the *winâh ī hamēmālān* category, *i.e.* offences involving another person (an 'opponent' or 'adversary'), which could be tried both by priests and in State courts. It would go beyond the scope of this study to discuss the countless sins of the purely *ruwānīg* type, notably violations of ritual and moral precepts and purity laws, which were sanctioned alone by religious authorities (the bulk of the Av. *dāta- vīdaēuua-*; MP *dād ī ǰud-dēw*).[19] The following survey hence excludes offences pertaining exclusively to the *ruwānīg* category and focuses on transgressions of the *hamēmālān* type, which explicitly infringe the rights of another party (or of third parties) and can only be atoned for by compensating the opponent or victim directly.

17 These involve sins which occur when a person fails to celebrate religious rites and ceremonies at the fixed times of the year; see BUYANER 2016, pp. 357–363.

18 The concept could be ancient, as the Av. *ratu-* seems to have had a similar function, see KREYENBROEK 1994, pp. 3–5.

19 A large number of violations of purity laws and ritual doctrines are mentioned in Zoroastrian texts, which have already been discussed in text editions and other studies. For those sins noted in the penitential texts (*patit*) see the recent edition of BUYANER 2016; for those in the *Šāyist-nē-šāyist* see TAVADIA 1930; on the *Nērangestān* see KOTWAL/

1 Historical development: from the private feud to legal proceedings

In the eighth book of the *Dēnkard*, right at the beginning of the synopsis of the Avestan legal *nasks* (the first part of the *Nīgādom*), a truly remarkable text has survived in the—unfortunately far too short—survey of the compiler, which enables us to reconstruct crucial stages in the development of Zoroastrian penal law.[20] Although this section contains several strata from different historical periods (as all parts of the *Dēnkard*)[21] and later additions cannot be excluded, it seems to have preserved to a large extent the intention of the ancient text: a description of the transition from an early (presumably pre-Zoroastrian) state of affairs, in which the law of vendetta and the private execution of justice prevailed, to the formation of legal institutions in charge of settling disputes and imposing penalties. It permits us to reconstruct the different stages leading from self-help to legal action according to the rules established in the Zoroastrian community, besides enabling us to form a hypothesis regarding the relation between the judicial powers of religious authorities in the Sasanian period, on the one hand, and the judicial institutions of the State, on the other (the latter will be discussed in Chapter VI).

The legal section (*dād bun* 'the beginning of the legal [*nasks*]') starts with exactly this juxtaposition of self-help versus taking legal action according to the rules of the Zoroastrian community in a section called *pahikār-radestān* 'Division on Judicial Dispute', an expression that has been regularly misinterpreted in the past, although both elements of the compound are well known: *pahikār* (< OIr. **patikāra-*; 'struggle, dispute, argument, quarrel, litigation, process, trial') + *rad* (< Av. *ratu-*; 'spiritual chief, master, judge, magistrate') + suffix *-stān* (denoting a location or section/chapter). As I have already elucidated elsewhere, this compound and other corresponding derivatives are *technical terms*, which cannot be translated literally: *pahikār-rad* denotes a 'person (involved) in a judicial dispute', that is, a litigant who proceeds against his opponent according

---

KREYENBROEK 1995–2009; for the explanations in the *Frahang ī ōīm* see KLINGENSCHMITT 1968; for the Pahlavi version of the *Wīdēwdād* see MOAZAMI 2014. For comparisons of the ritual doctrines and practices in Zoroastrianism and Rabbinic Judaism see particularly the numerous contributions of YAAKOV ELMAN (in the list of his publications in the Festschrift in his honour, ed. by SECUNDA/FINE 2012); furthermore the studies of KIEL 2008, 2011, 2013, 2014a and 2014b; SECUNDA 2007; SKJÆRVØ/ELMAN 2014 (on the *Zand ī fragard ī juddēwdād*).

20 The whole text is in Appendix V.

21 As we have described above (Chapter I, pp. 24–26) the synopsis of Avestan texts in *Dēnkard* 8, following the Pahlavi version of the Avestan original, contains at least three intertwined strata, consisting of (1) elements from the Avestan text (albeit taken from the Pahlavi translation); (2) components from the commentary (*zand*) of Sasanian exegetes; (3) interpretations of the text according to the understanding of the author at the time of the composition of the *Dēnkard* in the 9th century.

to legal prescriptions; its opposite *a-pahikār-rad* 'who does not dispute before a judge', 'who is not (involved) in a judicial dispute', is a person who practices self justice and takes the law into his own hands. The abstract forms *pahikār-radīh* 'judicial dispute' and *a-pahikār-radīh* 'non-judicial dispute' (or: private feud) designate the corresponding procedures.[22]

The intention of the section on 'Judicial Dispute' is made clear from the very outset: danger and illness (*sēǰ ud xīndagīh*) in the world are not only a result of the onslaught of the Evil Spirit (*ēbgat*), but ensue from the sinful actions of humans, when they 'assault/injure one another unlawfully' (*az a-dādestānīhā zanišn ī ēk abar did*). The word *zanišn* 'assault, injury' (lit. 'blow, smiting, beating')[23] in this context is used as a technical term for five different kinds of aggressive acts, including the threat of force and actual bodily injuries, reaching from battery to homicide, which are listed minutely in a later passage (see below). Nota bene, not the act of *zanišn* in itself is sinful, but threatening, assaulting, injuring or killing 'unlawfully' (*a-dādestānīhā*), taking measures against an opponent *without* the sanction of legal instances.

The text continues to state four admonitions (*handarz*) to humankind: (1) people should abstain from retaliating, when they are threatened or injured, but should take resort to 'measuring injury according to the law' (*dādestānīg zanišn handāzišn*); (2) they should aim at 'injuring slightly or not injuring at all' (*kam zanišnīh ud* ⁺*a-zanišnīh*); (3) they should proceed against those who are 'involved in a non-judicial dispute' (*a-pahikār-radān*), *i. e.* who take the law into their own hands, 'according to (the procedure in) a judicial dispute' (*pahikār-radīhā*), hereby preventing harm to their relatives and damage to their property; (4) they should refrain from pre-emptively injuring (*pēštom zanišn*) a 'person in a non-judicial dispute' (*a-pahikār-rad*), *i. e.* in a private feud.[24]

The content of this passage obviously reaches back to the beginnings of Zoroastrian penal law in a period of transition from self-help to the formation of legal instances in the Zoroastrian community, observed from the perspective of Avesta commentators of later generations. The aggressive acts referred to collectively by the term *zanišn* are crimes usually prosecuted and punished

22 I have discussed this section and its technical terminology in Macuch 2002a.

23 A verbal noun (expressing the 'result or output of an action', Josephson 1998, p. 88) from *zadan*, *zan-* 'to beat, strike, smite', from the well attested root Ir. √**jan* 'to kill, slay, strike' (Cheung 2007, p. 224–225), OP √*ja*(*n*) 'to strike, smite, defeat (enemy in battle); mould (brick)'; Av. √*jan* (*γn*) 'to kill, slay' (Bartholomae 1904, col. 490; Kellens 1995, p. 23). On the suffix *-išn* see also Durkin-Meisterernst 2014, p. 170 (§ 338)

24 DkD (M) 83.4–11 (DkM 693.6–11; Appendix V, pp. 674–675). The terms *pahikār-rad* and *a-pahikār-rad* also occur in the late RivAF, *Pursišn* LVIII. The *Pursišn* discusses the categorization of a combat between two persons as a duel (*ardīg* ⁺*tazišnīh*) placing the duel within the legal framework of combatants in a judicial dispute (*pahikar-rad*). On *ardīg tazišnīh* and this passage see below p. 425, fn. 103. B.T. Anklesaria 1969 (vol. I, pp. 30–31, 117–118; vol. II, p. 73) in his edition of the text has completely misunderstood this passage.

by the state today, but in the very early stages of community-building prior to the formation of a state, particularly in segmented societies with no clear hierarchical structure, an injured person had to take measures against offences on his own. According to the material collected by social anthropologists and the information available on the genesis of legal systems, the oldest reaction to an aggression was the personal revenge of the offended or his next-of-kin by retaliating against the person who had committed the offence. Individuals practised self-help on their own authority, usually by force. Retaliation was often the only means to compensate an injustice, if no agreement could be reached between the combatting parties. In most cases the individual did not act alone, but with the help of his nearest relatives or clan, seeking justice by attacking the offender, his family and relatives, or taking his possessions (a reaction designated generally as *a-pahikār-radīh* 'non-judicial dispute' in our text). Vengeance did not have to be immoderate, as it is sometimes assumed, but followed specific (unwritten) norms in most communities, in order to prevent the emergence of the most dangerous form of retaliation, the vendetta or blood revenge, which could lead to a feud. If an injustice was answered immoderately, a series of mutual injuries or killings could evolve, resulting in a long blood feud between two kinship groups. As the outcome of a feud could be disastrous for both groups as well as for the community as a whole, the opposing parties usually sought to settle the quarrel after a while, particularly if they were members of the same community. Mediators and arbitrators could be engaged to conciliate the parties following specific rules, which would later lead to the formation of legal norms.[25] After the emergence of legal systems certain transgressions continued to be considered as private offences, which could still be avenged by the injured party or his family or friends (private justice was practised in Europe up to the end of the 19th century, usually to avenge an insult, in the highly ritualized form of the duel between gentlemen following specific rules that had to be kept meticulously). Despite the development of a complex judiciary, Sasanian law continued to file most crimes against another individual as private offences to be prosecuted by the injured person himself, albeit within the framework of Zoroastrian law according to the norms set down by religious authorities (as offences of the *hamēmālān* category). This latter form of taking action against an aggressor is denoted in our text as *pahikār-radīh* 'judicial dispute'.

There can be no doubt that this is exactly the context of our text, as we can conclude from the fairly precise definitions of these two terms in the following sentences: *a-pahikār-radīh* 'non-judicial dispute', occurs, when someone performs an aggressive act against another person (either initially or in retaliation) 'unlawfully' (*a-dādestānīhā*). There are five types of aggressive acts (for which the general term *zanišn* is used at the beginning of this section): (1) 'threatening'

25 Wesel 1984, pp. 21–30, and 1985, pp. 324–331; Rouland 1988, pp. 291–335, with further references.

(*andar nimūd*), (2) 'tearing off' (*kanišn*), (3) 'wounding' (*zaxm*), (4) 'injuring (grievously)' (*rēš kardan*) and (5) 'killing' (*ōzad[an]*).[26] This passage is especially valuable, since it transmits not only a list of criminal acts denoted as *zanišn* (as they were presumably still differentiated in the Sasanian period), but offers a retrospective view of private justice in pre-Zoroastrian times seen from the viewpoint of later Zoroastrian exegetes, who explicitly denote these violent acts in retaliation as 'unlawful'. From the perspective of these religious authorities a 'lawful' (*dādestānōmandīhā*) reaction to an aggression is to proceed against the opponent by initiating a 'judicial dispute' (*pahikār-radīh*).[27] The text then informs us that there are two possibilities of taking legal action in this manner: the initiator or litigant can present his case by 'speaking' (*gōwišnīg*), *i. e.* by making an oral statement, or by 'demonstrating' (*nimāyišnīg*), *i. e.* by showing the injuries he has suffered or acting out the transgression before a group of persons acting as mediators and arbitrators or before a judge. These two forms of taking legal action can be combined with each other and are again differentiated into several categories based on the capacity of the litigants to participate in the hearings (to which we will return later).[28]

The most important information of this text is to be gained from the next part: disputes of the 'speaking' (*gōwišnīg*) type, in which oral statements are made, can be carried out within the framework of four kinds of proceedings (*pahikārišn*):

1. in a judicial dispute (*pahikār-radīh*);
2. in the presence of one's own spiritual master (*rad ī xwēš*);
3. in the presence of at least three pious men (= Zoroastrians; *weh mard* 'good men');
4. in front of witnesses (*⁺gugāyān*).[29]

This remarkable passage informs us that there were several different means of reacting to a transgression without having to practice self-justice. Moreover, it enables us to reconstruct several earlier stages of Zoroastrian law prior to the establishment of legal courts, besides suggesting how different religious and legal instances might have continued to operate side by side in the Sasanian period. In the case of assault, we are told, taking legal action against the perpetrator is not restricted to the procedure described as the 'judicial dispute' (*pahikār-radīh*), that is, suing one's opponent before a judge. The case could also be brought before 'one's own spiritual master' (*rad ī xwēš*) or negotiated in the presence of other persons acting as arbitrators and mediators. It is known that the *rad*, besides being an important religious authority, administered justice in commercial

26 DkD (M) 84.7–12 (DkM 693.20–694.1; Appendix V, p. 676).
27 DkD (M) 83.11–13 (DkM 693.11–13; Appendix V, p. 675).
28 DkD (M) 83.14–84.2 (DkM 693.12–16; Appendix V, p. 675).
29 DkD (M) 84.3–7 (DkM 693.16–20; Appendix V, p. 675).

matters in the Sasanian period and had judicial competences comparable to those of the *mowbed* (see Chapter VI, pp. 505–506). The *rad ī xwēš* was most likely the religious expert chosen by the injured person as his spiritual leader or personal instructor in religious matters, who had judicial power in the community, in which the assault took place.[30] As one of the community's influential men 'a person's own *rad*' might have been initially engaged as an arbitrator, whose first duty would be to find a settlement acceptable to both sides, but who could also act as judge and return a verdict if the combatting parties could not reach a compromise.[31]

Besides the *rad ī xwēš* other individuals could be engaged as mediators or arbitrators to settle a conflict according to our text: at least three good (or pious) men (*weh mard*), *i.e.* Zoroastrians, or other witnesses (*+gugāyān*). These two additional options probably represent the two earliest stages of legal history, prior to the engagement of a religious authority as umpire or judge. Given that the members of a settled community were strongly dependent on each other, it was in the best interest of the whole community to avoid strife and violence over a longer period of time. It was crucial to find a way out by replacing the social obligation of avenging oneself or one's next-of-kin by some kind of 'face-saving' agreement with the opponent. The simplest solution would be to negotiate directly, but if the parties in dispute became so entangled in their differences that they could find no solution on their own, arbitrators or mediators could be engaged with the task of reconciling the opponents. The three 'pious men' and 'witnesses' in our passage are most likely persons acting as go-betweens or mediators put in charge (by the community or the parties themselves) of conducting negotiations between the opponents and helping them reach a consensus. The offended or injured party would abstain from taking revenge in exchange

30 On the *rad* (Av. *ratu-*) as a personal spiritual leader see Kreyenbroek 1994, pp. 3–5, who has convincingly argued that the *ratu-* 'must have been the religious leader of a local community, who knew his followers personally and had considerable power over them (…)' (*ibid.*, p. 4). Cantera 2003, pp. 28–29, has shown that the MP term *xwaddōšagīh* 'Eigenwilligkeit' ('wilfulness') has a pejorative meaning and was used of individuals, who refused to follow the teachings of a recognized religious authority, who had no *dastwar* or *rad ī xwēš*, personal spiritual master. The term is also attested in *Dēnkard* 8 in the following passage (DkM 699.13–16): *abar pad čē paymānag pādixšāyīh ī rad ī xwēš wināh ī any kas andar hāwišt ī ōy-iz ān-iz ī hāwišt ī ōy ruwānīg kunēd hišt.* 'on the extent of the authority of one's own spiritual master (*rad ī xwēš*) to pardon the sin, which another person (15) commits against a disciple of his (= of the *rad*), and also (to pardon) the sin, which a disciple of his commits against the soul.' (The notion that the laity cannot interpret and practise religion on its own, but has to be instructed by learned religious authorities is very similar in Shīʿite Islam; on the role of the *mujtahid* see Halm 1994, pp. 117–120).

31 Disputes could still be submitted to arbitration in the Sasanian period, as we can conclude from the two technical terms *dādwar ī pēšēmāl* 'judge of the plaintiff', and *dādwar ī pasēmāl* 'judge of the defendant'. The construction of these terms indicates that the litigants themselves chose these judges as arbitrators (see Chapter VI, pp. 497–498).

for an amendment from his opponent (usually in form of some kind of property, cattle or other possessions, later also in form of a monetary compensation or fine).[32] If the mediators had authority and social standing in the community the agreement would almost have the quality of an arbitration award (or ruling given by the arbitrators) and be accepted as binding by the parties.[33]

This list of options advising Mazdeans how to deal with an assault of the *zanišn* kind enables us to reconstruct several sequential stages in the development of Zoroastrian criminal law, besides illuminating the various measures that could be taken in these cases instead of engaging State courts. If we read the list in reverse (beginning with number 4) the first step from self-help to the emergence of legal institutions is the dispute in presence of witnesses (+*gugāyān*), *i. e.* persons who were either actually present, when the transgression took place, or were picked out later by the opponents to act as mediators with the goal of negotiating a voluntary settlement. The second stage involves the mediation of three pious Mazdeans (*weh mard*) chosen by one or both parties with the task of conducting negotiations and conciliating between the parties. If these men had authority and a good standing in the community they would be more likely to reach a consensus. The third stage is the hearing in the presence of a *rad ī xwēš*, the personal spiritual leader of the injured or of both parties, who has judicial powers in the community and can act as an arbitrator, but also serve as judge due to his authority as a legal expert, whose ruling would be binding for all Mazdeans. The fourth and last stage is finally the procedure called *pahikār-radīh*, the 'judicial dispute' or trial in the presence of a judge or several judges, who were more than mere arbitrators and could return a verdict regardless of the attitude of the parties towards reaching a settlement. As the decision of the court was binding on both sides, the parties were not allowed to use violence with a single exception; if one of the opponents did not accept the verdict and continued to cause harm, the other party was permitted to act in self-defence and to restrain the delinquent by force.[34]

One of the notable aspects of this text is the inclusion of disabled men in the list of litigants who can take legal action. As we have seen above, a litigant could present his case either by making an oral statement (*gōwišnīg*) or by demonstration (*nimāyišnīg*) or by combining these two means of communicating with the legal authorities.[35] Men who have no disability that might impede them

32 This procedure is in fact confirmed by another entry (DkM 705.21–22), stating that persons involved in a private feud (*a-pahikār-radān*) and their helpers (*ayar*) are liable to pay a fine (*tōzišnōmandīh*) to those who carry out a dispute according to law (*pahikār-radān*) and their helpers (*ayār*). For a translation of this passage see Macuch 2002a, pp. 86–87.

33 On this development in early communities see Wesel 1985, pp. 329–331.

34 DkD (M) 85.4–10 (DkM 694.6–11; Appendix V, pp. 676–677).

35 The following conclusions are based on a combination of two passages of this text: DkD (M) 83.14–84.2 and 84.13–85.4 (DkM 693.14–16 and 694.1–6). The latter sentence is unfortunately incomplete; a whole line is missing (see Appendix V, pp. 675, 676).

as litigants, who 'hear and see' (*āšnawāg ī wēnag*),[36] can make their statement by both verbal declaration and by showing (their injuries, how they were attacked, etc.) in a trial based on both 'speaking and demonstrating' (*gōwišnīg nimāyišnīg*).[37] Litigants who hear, but are blind (**āšnawāg ī nē wēnag*) present their case only by an oral statement, with no demonstration (*gōwišnīg ī nē nimāyišnīg*).[38] Those who 'see, but are deaf' (*wēnag ī nē āšnawāg*)[39] make their statement by demonstration alone, without a verbal declaration (*nimāyišnīg nē gōwišnīg*).[40]

Despite the inclusion of men with a disablement, not all members of a community were permitted to take legal action: men who are both deaf and blind (*an-āšnawāg ī a-wēnag-iz*), women (*zan*) and minors (*aburnāyīg*) are generally excluded from jurisdiction (*pahikār-radīh abāg-šān nēst* 'there is no judicial dispute with them'). A person from one of these three groups, who is attacked, cannot take legal action against the perpetrator, but a judgment (*wizīr*) should be pronounced, urging the delinquent to cease causing harm, unless he is acting in self-defence.[41] Other individuals who are not liable to jurisdiction are foreigners (*an-ēr* 'non-Iranians'), persons who 'deserve death' (*margarzān*) and highwaymen (*rāhdār*). Killing the 'vital soul' (*gyān*) of a person from one of these groups is regarded as a virtuous deed (*kirbag*).[42] Three other groups of persons can be killed without retribution (one does not become 'sinful', *wināhgār*, by the act): individuals who have no permanent place of residence, who occupy ruins, and those who are not responsive, when submitted to interrogation, but are not foreigners.[43] (Were these precepts actually followed in the Sasanian period? Given the more or less rigid hierarchy of the State, the division of society into estates and the dominance of descent groups, this could well have been the case, since a person outside the community would not necessarily have had any actionable legal rights. On the other hand, the 'non-Iranian' citizens of Ērānšahr, *i. e.* the religious minorities, were not outlawed, but definitely had certain rights, as we have seen in Chapter II (see also Chapter VI, pp. 526–532).

The last sentence of the *pahikār-radestān* chapter refers to the well-known rule of *ius talionis*, the ancient principle of equal retribution, submitting the culprit to exactly the same harm that he has caused his victim ('an eye for an eye,

36 DkD (M) 84.14 (DkM 694.3; Appendix V, p. 676).
37 DkD (M) 83.14–84.1 (DkM 693.14; Appendix V, p. 675).
38 DkD (M) 84.1 (DkM 693.14–15; Appendix V, p. 675).
39 DkD (M) 85.2 (DkM 694.4; Appendix V, p. 676).
40 DkD (M) 84.2 and 85.3 (DkM 693.15 and 694.5; Appendix V, pp. 675, 676).
41 DkD (M) 85.10–14 (DkM 694.11–14; Appendix V, p. 677).
42 DkD (M) 85.14–86.7 (DkM 694.14–19; Appendix V, p. 677). On the *gyān*, the 'principle of animation, the vital breath, which naturally disappears with the death of the body (*tan*)' see Gignoux 2001, p. 21. Sohn 1996, pp. 1–2, 18–20 (in his edition of the medical chapters of Zādspram) translates 'vital fire' ('Lebensfeuer') due to the analogy between *gyān* and the fire in a fire temple in this text.
43 DkD (M) 86.7–13 (DkM 694.19–695.2; Appendix V, pp. 677–678).

a tooth for a tooth').[44] Answering an injury by a corresponding one (*abāz zaxm* 'a wound in retribution')[45] was originally not an extremely severe form of retaliation, if we take into account that vengeance in a private feud often consisted of taking the life of the opponent or of a member of his family. On the contrary, the *ius talionis* was a barrier restraining the avenger from taking excessive measures against his opponent. This type of retaliation as a moderate form of taking the law into one's own hands is explicitly allowed in the final passage, which leads us back to one of the earliest historical stages of Zoroastrian law.

Table 38. Overview: terminology relating to the private feud versus the judicial dispute

pahikār-rad	person (involved) in a judicial dispute
a-pahikār-rad	person in a private feud (lit. 'who is not [involved] in a judicial dispute')
pahikar-radīh	judicial dispute
a-pahikar-radīh	private feud (lit. 'non-judicial dispute')
Presentation of the case	
gōwišnīg	by making an oral statement
nimāyišnīg	by demonstration, acting out
gōwišnīg nimāyišnīg	by speaking and demonstrating
Categories of *zanišn* 'assault, injury'	
andar nimūd	threatening
kanišn	tearing off, pulling apart, splitting
zaxm (kardan)	wounding
rēš kardan	injuring physically
ōzad(an)	killing, homicide

2 Constitutive elements of a crime

Despite the myriad of sins listed in the available sources, no surviving text describes or discusses the fundamental theoretical elements constituting an offence or actionable crime according to Zoroastrian norms. But although the material at our disposal is extremely fragmentary, we can attempt to reconstruct

44 DkD (M) 86.13–87.2 (DkM 695.2–5; Appendix V, p. 678). On the *ius talionis* in Roman law see Kaser 1986, pp. 148–149, and Liebs 1982, p. 287; in Mosaic law see *Exodus* 21.23–25.

45 The term *abāz zaxm* is also attested DkM 699.10: *ud* ⁺*abar mard kē bīm ī abāz zaxm rāy wirēzēd.* 'And ⁺on the man who flees for fear of (10) retaliation (*abāz zaxm*).'

a few basic ideas by contextualizing the legal terms employed in this context in the Law-book and other sources, which will be discussed in more detail in the following sections. To be sure, one can hardly claim that these scattered entries form a general theory, but they suggest that Sasanian jurists distinguished precisely between various levels or grades of offences according to specific criteria.

Taken together, several legal terms and short entries in the available texts suggest that Zoroastrian law—at least in the form it had reached by the Middle Iranian period—distinguished between two basic components of an offence, no matter whether it was a transgression of the *ruwānīg* or *hamēmālān* type:

1. the mental element (*mens rea*), involving the intention (*menišn*) or will (*kām*) to commit a sin or criminal act; and
2. the physical element (*actus reus*), the actual execution (*kunišn*) of the sin or criminal act (including omissions, *i. e.* the failure to perform a duty).

With the exception of certain cases of strict liability (see under *adwadād*, pp. 463–468,) these two elements together seem to constitute most of the actionable offences and crimes alluded to in the sources. Criminal intent *alone* was not liable to punishment even in certain *ruwānīg* cases (one example is contemplating to commit adultery without actually performing the act, see pp. 452–460), whereas the offence or criminal act itself, committed unintentionally (accidentally) or, to use the Pahlavi term, 'unconsciously' (*a-bōyīhā*), did *not* constitute guilt. Furthermore, a distinction was made between at least three types of offences involving damage and physical injury:

1. 'intentional offence' (*wināh ī nigerišnīg*; *bōdōwaršt*) and 'intentional injury' (*pad nigerišnīg zanišnīh*; *bōdōzed*);
2. 'injury by carelessness; negligence' (*sūdagīhā zanišn*; *kādōzed*);
3. 'unintentional' or 'unconscious offence' (*wināh … andar a-bōyīh*).[46]

46 On the technical terms *bōdōwaršt*, *bōdōzed* and *kādōzed*, derived from the Avestan, see below pp. 417–422. The readings adapted here for *bōdōzed* and *kādōzed* follow the single attestation of these two terms in the Law-book, MHDA 15.3: ⟨bwtwkẕt'⟩ and ⟨k'twkẕt'⟩ respectively (on this passage see also p. 444 below; for an overview of the various spellings of these words see Macuch 2003a, p. 181, fn. 67 and 70). According to DkD 83.4–11; 84.7–12 (DkM 693.4–11; 693.20–694.1) the general term *zanišn/zanišnīh*, lit. 'blow, smiting' (as in *pad nigerišnīg zanišnīh* 'intentional smiting', and *sūdagīhā zanišn* 'unintentional smiting'), encompasses five kinds of offences: 'threatening' (*andar nimūd*); 'tearing off' (*kanišn*); 'wounding' (*zaxm*); 'injuring grievously' (*rēš kardan*) and 'killing' (*ōzad[an]*); see Appendix V, p. 676, and the section on assault, physical injury and homicide, pp. 423–434 below. The literal meaning of *nigerišnīg* 'intentional, deliberate', seems to be '(something) that is looked at, observed; manifest, evident' (from *nigerīdan*, *nigēr-* 'look, observe; MacKenzie 1971, p. 59); *sūdagīhā* 'unintentionally, negligently' may have been derived from a literal 'being at rest' (implying the opposite in the sense of 'not being observant; not being aware'); *sūdag* 'slack', from a cognate form of the verb *āsāy-/āsūd* 'to rest' (see Skjærvø 2010, pp. 204–205, also fn. 49 below); Ir. √**saiH* 'to lie down, go to sleep' (Cheung 2007, p. 328).

In short: the intention of the offender was in some manner taken into consideration in the verdict, reminiscent of the Latin maxim *actus non facit reum nisi mens sit rea* (the act itself does not constitute guilt unless done with a guilty mind). This maxim corresponds in fact very well with the famous Zoroastrian triad of practising *humat* or *hu-menišn* 'good thought', which leads to good speech (*hūxt*) and good deeds (*huwaršt*), whereas an evil act always begins with *duš-menišn* 'evil thought', or to use the term employed in the context of assault, *kēn-menišn* 'malicious intent' (besides other terms quoted below).[47] The central significance of the Zoroastrian triad in the context of sins is reflected in the act of repentance and penitence, consisting of three steps: 'contrition—confession—redemption'. The soul of the sinner is redeemed (with the help of a 'soul physician', *ruwān bizešk*, appointed by religious authorities) by 'regretting in thought' (*pašēmānīh ī menišnīg*), 'repentance by speech' (*abaxšīh ī gōwišnīg-iz*; *i. e.* confessing the sin) and 'redemption from sins by action' (*az wināh patit ī kunišnīg*).[48] The notion of offences committed intentionally (with 'evil thought') or unintentionally (without 'evil thought', *i. e.* without malice aforethought) seems to be already inherent in this well-known religious precept and might even be ancient (see Vd. 4.17 below). The idea of 'negligence', on the other hand, is generally a late development in legal history. It is well attested in MP *sūdag(īh)/sūdagīhā*,[49] but was presumably superimposed on the term *kādōzed*, (from an unattested Av. **kāiδiiō.jaiti-*) which originally designated an offence of a completely different nature, as we will see below (pp. 417–422; and fn. 71).

The texts we will discuss later in more detail confirm this assumption by their use of the corresponding legal terms and definitions of the criminal acts. In the context of theft (*duzīh*) and robbery (*apparīh*), these two methods of appropriating property are distinguished both by the mental element and the physical act: the 'will of the robber' (*appar-kām*)[50] or 'intent of the robber' (*appar-menišnīgīh*)[51] differs from 'the intent of thieves' (*duzagān-menišn*)[52] or 'intent of the thief' (*duz-menišnīh*; *duz-menišnīgīh*).[53] The physical element of robbery also differs from that of theft in that the thief steals stealthily, whereas the robber steals openly, in view of the public, using force or threatening to use force (see section 3.2 below on theft and robbery, pp. 434–451).

That these two elements together, the intent and the act itself, constituted a crime, seems to be confirmed in the context of assault and other violent acts. The

47 Vd. 4.17 (Moazami 2014, pp. 108–109 [C]).
48 See Buyaner 2016, pp. 27–30.
49 A large number of text-passages confirming this meaning for *sūdag(īh)* have been discussed by Dhabhar 1955, pp. 136–145, and Klingenschmitt 1968, no. 684. See also Skjærvø 2010, pp. 204–205 (also fn. 46 above).
50 DkD 236.11 (DkM 309.9); see Appendix III, pp. 667–668.
51 Her. 6.6 §3–5 (= 6.11–21); see Appendix VIII, pp. 691–692.
52 DkD 236.11 (DkM 309.9), see Appendix III, pp. 667–668.
53 Hēr. 6.6 §3–5 (= 6.11–21); see Appendix VIII, pp. 691–692; DkD 548.18 (DkM 721.22); Appendix VII, p. 688.

original meaning of the first item in the list of 'core' degrees or levels (*pāyag*) of sin (on these see below, pp. 468–486), *āgrift* (< Av. *āgərəpta-*), is explained in the penitential texts as the act of taking a weapon in one's hands with the 'intent to smite' (*pad menišn zadan*) another person.[54] The same two basic components are present in the explanation of the next technical term in the list of degrees of sin, *awōirišt/ōirišt* (< Av. *auuaoirišta-*), originally in its Pahlavi context the act of brandishing (or: revolving over one's head) a weapon with the 'intent to smite' (*pad menišn zadan*).[55] The third degree of sin, *arduš* (< Av. *araduš-*), refers, according to Vd. 4.17, to a person, who approaches someone with the 'intention of mistreating' (Av. *aēnō.manaŋhan-*)[56] that person. Interestingly, the Pahlavi version of this passage not only translates Av. *aēnō.manaŋhan-* by MP *kēn-menišn* 'malicious intent', but adds in the gloss: 'he lays hands upon him (= the victim)' (*kū-š dast abar nihēd*). I take the gloss to mean that the intention of the delinquent alone would not constitute an *arduš* offence without the act itself. By the time of the emergence of the Pahlavi exegesis it became necessary to clarify the Avestan text by adding this gloss, which in fact spells out that the malicious intent of the perpetrator must produce a concrete criminal act of assault in order to be assessed as an offence of the *arduš* level.[57]

The mental element of an offence is also taken into account in the context of sexual abuses involving illicit intercourse with the wife of another man. Interestingly, the sexual sins in this context are treated as crimes involving theft and robbery (similar to transgressions in the fields of credit law and sale, as we have seen above): the intent of the offender to cohabit (*gādan menišnīg*; *gād pad uzkārišn*) with another man's wife is assessed as the 'intent of the thief' (*duz-menišnīgīh*), if the perpetrator decides to actually perform the act after a certain timespan, or as the 'intent of the robber' (*appar-menišnīgīh*), if he uses force (*pad rēš*); illicit sexual intercourse is *gād-duzīh* 'theft of intercourse'[58] and *tan-duzīh* 'body-theft'.[59] Another important information to be gained from this source is that the premeditated intent to commit adultery is only punishable in conjunction with the sexual act itself, that is, both elements constituting the offence have to be fulfilled (as in the case of assault noted above). The intent alone, if one restrains oneself, does not even form a punishable offence according to the *ruwānīg* assessment of sins (see discussion of this text in section 4.1, pp. 454–458 below).[60]

54 Pp II Phl. A/B 4.1.7 (Buyaner 2016, p. 281), see also pp. 471–472 below.
55 Pp II Phl. A/B 4.1.8 (Buyaner 2016, pp. 282–283); see also p. 472 below.
56 Bartholomae 1904, col. 22: 'who intends to violate, to mistreat' ['der die Absicht der Vergewaltigung, Misshandlung hegt'].
57 For the whole text see Buyaner 2016, p. 286; Moazami 2014, pp. 108–109, has the Pahlavi version. On the degrees or levels of sins see section 5, pp. 468–486 below.
58 Hēr. 6.7 §3 (Appendix VIII, p. 694).
59 Hēr. 6.7 §1 and §3 (Appendix VIII, pp. 692–693, 694 respectively).
60 Hēr. 6.7 §2 (Appendix VIII, pp. 693–694).

Moreover, in the context of bodily harm and physical injury (*zaxm*, *zanišn*, *rēš*) wounds inflicted by a perpetrator consciously (intentionally) are distinguished from those inflicted 'in a state of unconsciousness' (*andar a-bōyīh*), *i. e.* unintentionally or with diminished responsibility, which were in turn differentiated into 'seven symptoms of unconsciousness' (*haft ēwēnag ī daxšag ī a-bōyīh*).[61] Pleading 'unconsciousness' (*a-bōyīh*) was presumably a means of defending oneself in Zoroastrian law in accordance with the maxim, that the act alone does not constitute guilt unless performed with a guilty mind. This legally important issue is in fact indirectly confirmed by a short entry in the Law-book regarding a case of bodily injury (*zaxm*):

> MHD 10.9–11
> *ud pad-iz zaxm ka gōwēd kū-m nē zad hē ud pas gōwēd kū-m andar a-bōyīh-ē(w) zad hē ēg-iz ēraxt.*
>
> 'And if he (= the defendant/accused) says with regard to a wound (*zaxm*): "I have not struck you" and later says: "I have struck (you) in a state of unconsciousness (*a-bōyīh*)", then he is (nevertheless) guilty.'[62]

The sentence is clear enough: in a concrete case an individual accused of wounding another person first denies having caused the injury, and later pleads 'unconsciousness' (*a-bōyīh*). He is nevertheless deemed guilty (*ēraxt*) of the offence. The passage only makes sense if we assume that pleading 'unconsciousness', or lack of conscious intent, on the part of the accused would be a means of avoiding or diminishing punishment due to the maxim noted above. In our concrete case, however—and contrary to the rule—the accused is *not* acquitted, since (as we may conclude) the modification of his statement in court is not convincing: he first completely denies the act, then alters the strategy of his defence to pleading *a-bōyīh*, lack of conscious intent, a claim which the court obviously considers as an implausible pretext (possibly assessing it as an offence of 'twisting, turning, distorting' one's statement in court, *waštagīh*, see Chapter VI, pp. 561–562 below).

The attitude of an accused was not only a significant factor in a criminal trial, involving theft, robbery or physical injury, but also in civil cases, as we may conclude from an interesting sentence in the Law-book, in which a litigant requests the court to convict his opponent for 'having evil intent; ill-will' (*wad xwāh*).[63] As we have noted in the section on guardianship, a family guardian (*dūdag-sālār*), who is involved as a plaintiff in a lawsuit regarding a matter of the family, is not allowed to continue proceedings if a son in the family comes of age during the trial and automatically replaces the former as family guardian. The background of this specific case is not described, but most of the lawsuits in this context were filed in order to exact payment for a liability, to retrieve a loan

61 DkD (M) 87.4–7 (DkM 695.7–9); Appendix VI, pp. 679–680.
62 Macuch 1993, pp. 104, 107.
63 MHDA 32.9–13 (Macuch 1981, pp. 57–58, 215).

or enforce the fulfilment of some other kind of contractual obligation.[64] Our passage states: If the former guardian does not refrain from pursuing the lawsuit (*az rāyēnišn be nē hilēd*), although he has been dismissed from his duties, then the defendant can withdraw his legal documents (*hampaččēn stānēd*) and can 'request a verdict against the (former) family guardian on the grounds of "evil intent"' (*pad wad-xwāh andar dūdag-sālār wizīr xwāhēd*). That is, a litigant in a civil case could request a verdict, which would take the attitude of his opponent (or: the mental element of the offence) into account (on offences during a trial see Chapter VI, pp. 561–569).

The term *wad-xwāh* is also attested as the opposite of *rāst-xwāh* 'with good intent; good-willed' in a late Pahlavi religious text in a reference to legal proceedings:

> PRDd 4.2
> *čē mard ī* ***rāst-xwāh*** *ka-š dādestān rāyēnēd ud andar dādestān rāyēnīdan guft-ē* *⁺mustīh* ⟨mw st'h⟩ *garzēd ud dādestān ī āhōgēnīhā rāyēnēd ā-š ān ⁺a-dādestānōmandtar* ⟨'DYNmndtr⟩ *čiyōn mardōm (ī)* ***⁺wad-xwāh*** ⟨wt'hw'h⟩ *ka dādestān xūb rāyēnēd ud a-dādīh andar ō kār dārēd čē ān ī* ***drō-xwāhāg*** *wināh az* ***⁺wad-xwāhān*** ⟨wthw'hn'⟩ *(ī) kas bēd ōy az har dō ⁺ōh* ⟨'L⟩ *bawēd ēk az xwāstag ⁺appar* ⟨w'pl⟩ *būdan ēk az* ***wad-axw*** *(ī) kas.*
>
> 'For if a man of good-will (*rāst-xwāh*) conducts legal proceedings and during the conduct of these proceedings files an appeal (*⁺mustīh garzēd*) and conducts a faulty trial, then that is more illegal (*⁺a-dādestānōmandtar*) than when people of ill-will (*⁺wad-xwāh*) conduct proceedings correctly, but are involved in an unlawful (*a-dādīh*) issue. For the sin of a person with a deceitful will (*drō-xwāhāg*) stems from being ill-willed (*⁺wad-xwāhān*) towards someone. He is (sinful) due to both: (on) one (hand) from the appropriation of property; (on) the other by having an evil mind (*wad-axw*) towards someone.'[65]

This is not a legal text, but it elucidates the significance attached to *both* a person's inner attitude *and* his outward actions in the course of a legal dispute. The text compares the action of a 'man of good-will' (*mard ī rāst-xwāh*), who conducts legal proceedings faultily (*āhōgēnīhā rāyēnēd*) by (hastily) filing an appeal (*⁺mustīh garzēd*)[66], with the behaviour of 'men of evil will' (*mardōm [ī] wad-xwāh*), who conduct proceedings correctly (*dādestān xūb rāyēnēd*), but have an illegal issue in mind (*a-dādīh ō kār dārēd*). In the religious context of our text the behaviour of a 'man of good-will', which does not correspond to his inner attitude, is even 'more illegal' (*⁺a-dādestānōmandtar*) than that of

64 See Chapter IV, section 4.1.3 on liabilities and claims of the family, pp. 360–364 above.

65 Pahlavi-text in Dhabhar 1913, pp. 5–6 (reprinted in Williams 1990, pt. II, pp. 274–275). I have a slightly different understanding of this passage than in Macuch 2019b, p. 120. On *⁺mustīh garzīdan* 'to file an appeal' see Chapter VI, pp. 524–525 (Williams 1990, pt. I, p. 45; pt. II, p. 7f., has an entirely different translation of the whole section; he reads and translates: **mustīhā garzēd* 'complains bitterly').

66 On this term see Chapter VI, pp. 524–525.

ill-willed persons, who conduct legal proceedings correctly (possibly, as we may add, because one expects impeccable behaviour from the former, but not from the latter). The text then gives a definition of an 'ill-willed' (*wad-xwāh*) person, who 'seeks deceit' (*drō-xwāhāg*): his sin (*winā*h) arises both from the action of (illegally) appropriating property (*az xwāstag* +*appar*) as well as having an 'evil mind' (*wad-axw*) towards others. I take this explanation to mean: these two elements together, the intent and the act itself, constitute the offence. The sin of *wad-xwāhīh* 'evil intention; malevolence' is even listed in the *Dēnkard* among the offences 'deserving death' (*margarzān*, see the first list in Appendix XVI, p. 738).[67]

The three ancient terms from Avestan noted above have been discussed by KLINGENSCHMITT in his edition of the *Frahang ī Ōīm* as well as the present author in the specific context of sins against animals and extensively in BUYANER's recent edition of the penitential texts:[68] *bōdōwaršt* (< Av. *baoδō.varšta-* 'conscious, intentional, wilful act');[69] *bōdōzed* (< Av. *baoδō.jaiti-* 'conscious, wilful, intentional blow')[70] and *kadōzed* (< **kāiδiiō.jaiti-* 'injury inflicted by means of magic').[71] These expressions refer in the Pahlavi texts to a wide (and confusing)

67 A similar notion is transmitted in the *Dēnkard* regarding litigation with 'harmful (intent)' (*pad bēšīdārīh*): DkD 229.13–16; DkM 300.17–20 (Dk 3.290.2; DE MENASCE 1971, p. 286–287): *hād dādestān (14) hangirdīgīh pēšēmālīh pad bēšīdārīh ō gyān-iz nē raft(an). ud kē (15) pēšēmālīg pad bēšīdārīh a-dād abar āyēd pēš az dādīg* +*pahikārdan ī (16) awiš pad čār [ud] tuwān nē bēšīdan.* 'That is: The summary of justice (is): not to take legal action (*pēšēmālīh … nē raftan*) against (another) soul with harmful (intent) (*pad bēšīdārīh*). And the one, against whom the complainant (*pēšēmālīg*) proceeds illegally (*a-dād abar āyēd*) with harmful (intent) (*pad bēšīdārīh*), is not allowed to harm (his opponent) before complaining against him legally (*dādīg*) for a remedy (*čār*).'

68 KLINGENSCHMITT 1968, no. 680–685; MACUCH 2003a, pp. 180–182; 187–188; BUYANER 2016, pp. 259–280 (§26 and §27).

69 BARTHOLOMAE 1904, col. 920: 'mit Erkenntnis, Einsicht (in die Folgen) getan … insbes. Körperverletzung, vorsätzliche Körperverletzung' ['done with awareness, insight (in the consequences) … especially bodily harm; intentional bodily harm']; KLINGENSCHMITT 1968, no. 681: 'vorsätzlich Getanes' ['done deliberately; premeditated action'].

70 BARTHOLOMAE 1904, col. 919–920: 'Schlagen, Ertöten des Wahrnehmungsvermögens, Bezeichnung eines Delikts' ['striking, killing perceptiveness', designation of a delict], but according to the definition given in the FīO 25a (REICHELT 1900, p. 206; KLINGENSCHMITT 1968, no. 685) the correct translation of the Avestan compound is 'striking with consciousness, intentional blow' ['Schlagen mit Bewußtsein, vorsätzliches Schlagen'; KLINGENSCHMITT, *ibid.*]. Other unsustainable translations have been previously suggested for the term (on these see BUYANER 2016, p. 260). TAVADIA 1930, p. 45 (fn. 5 to Šnš 2.39), has the correct 'consciously striking'.

71 KLINGENSCHMITT 1968, no. 684, explains Av. *kaiδua-* (Y. 57.15; 61.3; not translated by BARTHOLOMAE 1904, col. 463) as 'Gleichgültigkeit' ['indifference'] and the reconstructed Av. **kāiδiiō.jaiti-* (in accordance with the definition in the Pahlavi text of the FīO) as 'Schlagen bzw. Verletzung oder Beschädigung durch Gleichgültigkeit, Nachlässigkeit, Fahrlässigkeit' ['Beating or harming or damaging by indifference, carelessness, negligence']. BUYANER 2016, pp. 267–280, rejects his explanation of the term and suggests a completely different derivation. In his extensive discussion of **kāiδiiō.*

variety of offences, including transgressions against animate beings (neglecting and tormenting humans; harming beneficent animals) and damage to inanimate objects (sullying fire, water and the *drōn* offering; spoiling food; destroying walls, clothing and other property), but the only definitions of these words as technical terms, as they were understood in the Middle Iranian period, are to be found in the *Frahang ī Ōīm*.[72] It will be useful to repeat the whole (extremely corrupt) passage with these three terms, as I have a completely different understanding of a crucial part of this text than both authors referred to above:

FīŌ XXVa (680–685; K20, fol. 84v.13–85r.2; M51, fol. 125v.6–16)
(680) ***baoδajaṯ***[73] *bōdōzed* (681) ***baoδō.varštahe*** *bōdōwaršt* (682) *čiyōn wēnāgīhā zad bawēd ud abar zaxm*[74] *ud*[75] *tabāh*[76] *kardan ī čīš-ē nigerišnīg wēš gōwēd* (683) *pad drō abārīg wināh ī nigerišnīg* (684) *⁺kādōzed*[77] *kastārīhā zad čiyōn zaxm*[78] *tabāh*[79] *kardan ī čīš-ē pad sūdagīh* (685) *⁺keh*[80] *wināh kādōzed wināh ī pad mardōmān ⁺az*[81] *bōdōzed pasā*[82] *⁺keh ēdōn-iz ⁺kādōzed*[83] *az bōdōwaršt frahist bōdōzed ān ī gōspandān pad nigerišn bōdōzed pad sūdagīh kādōzed.*

---

jaiti- (> MP *kāyδyōzet*) he analyses *kāiδiia-* as an abstract noun derived from *kaiiaδa-*, the designation of 'a conscious enemy of Faith and the pious' (p. 272), 'soothsayer, magician (?)' (p. 273), to be taken together with two other synonymous terms, *kaxvarəδa-* and *kaxužī-*, as designations for 'different species of wizards or magicians' (p. 274), and MP *kundāg* (< OI *kundāka-*) 'wise; soothsayer', to which he connects the Avestan names of demons *kuṇda-*, *kuṇdižā-* and *kauuaṇda-* (p. 275). He hence reconstructs the original meaning of *kāiδiia-* as 'a kind of magic' (p. 280) and of Av. **kāiδiiō.jaiti-* as 'injury inflicted by means of magic' (p. 279). As this derivation does not correspond with the explanation of *kāyδyōzet* in the FīŌ (*kastārīhā zad*; FīŌ 684), he assumes that the original meaning of Av. *kāiδiia-* had been lost and the word was identified (by means of its Pahlavi translation *xwarrah kāstārīh* 'diminishing of divine grace, devilling') 'with the vṛddhicized form of the etymon of Phl. *kēh* "less, minor", *i.e.* OP **kaϑyah-* ...' (p. 280). He hence suggests the translation of Phl. *kāyδyōzet* by 'the minor injury', instead of 'injury caused by negligence' (p. 280). Whatever the original meaning of the Avestan term might have been, however, the Middle Persian explanation of the term as *sūdagīhā zanišn* 'injury by negligence, carelessness' leaves no doubt that the word was later understood as a technical term in exactly this sense.

72 For attestations see Klingenschmitt 1968, no. 680–685; Buyaner 2016, pp. 259–280, and Macuch 2003a, pp. 180–182; 187–188.

73 K20: ⟨baōzaja⟩.

74 Both K20 and M51: ⟨ztwm⟩.

75 K20: om. ⟨W⟩.

76 Mss.: ⟨twpʾh⟩.

77 Mss.: ⟨tkʾyt ywdt⟩.

78 Mss.: ⟨ztwm⟩.

79 Mss.: ⟨twpʾh⟩.

80 M51: ⟨kyk⟩.

81 Mss.: ⟨MNW⟩.

82 Mss.: written in Pāzand script.

83 Mss.: ⟨yst ywk ywdt⟩. Buyaner 2016, p. 279, fn. 190, reads the sequence together with the preceding /c/ as ⟨cyst ywk ywyt⟩ *⁺kāyδyōzet* and explains the 'initial /c/' in the distorted spelling by an interference of the Pāzand and Pahlavi scripts. But the letter he takes as 'initial /c/ (= Pāz. /δ/)' in fact simply belongs to the preceding *ēdōn*, to be read

> '(680) (Avestan) ***baoδaǰaṯ*** (Pahlavi) *bōdōzed* (681) (Avestan) ***baoδō.varštahe*** (Pahlavi) *bōdōwaršt* (682) corresponds to "struck in the manner of someone who sees" (*wēnāgīhā zad*) and it is mostly said of wounding and destroying something deliberately (*nigerišnīg*), (683) regarding the lie (and) other deliberate sins (*wināh ī nigerišnīg*). (684) +*kādōzed* (means) "struck in the manner of someone who diminishes" (*kastārīhā zad*), such as wounding and destroying something by carelessness (*pad sūdagīh*). (685) The lesser sin (is) *kādōzed*, (as) sin (committed) against people, than *bōdōzed*. The lesser (sin committed) against animals (is) thus likewise (*ēdōn-iz*) +*kādōzed*. Among the intentional offences (*bōdōwaršt*) the foremost (is called) *bōdōzed*. Those (sins committed) against small cattle (*gōspandān*) deliberately (*pad nigerišn*) (are called) *bōdōzed*; (those committed) negligently (*pad sūdagīh*) (are called) *kādōzed*.'[84]

Despite the shortness of the text and its numerous distorted spellings, we can reasonably infer that it is an attempt, first, to translate and explain the Avestan words and their Pahlavi correspondences, second, to define the use of these expressions as technical terms in the period, when the *Frahang ī Ōīm* was put to writing. Following this scheme, Av. *baoδaǰaṯ* (corrupted from *baoδō.jaiti-*) is rendered by Phl. *bodōzed* and explained as 'struck in the manner of someone who sees' (*wēnāgīhā zad*) (Av. *baoδō.varštahe* and its Phl. derivative *bōdōwaršt* are interpolated between *bōdōzed* and its explanation, disclosing that *bōdōzed* belongs to the *bōdōwaršt* 'deliberate', category of offences).[85] The technical term *bōdōzed* is then explicitly defined as 'wounding and destroying something deliberately' (*nigerišnīg*). The same sequence can be observed in the case of *kādōzed* with the difference that the Avestan term (reconstructed as **kāiδiiō.jaiti-*) is missing: first, *kādōzed* is explained as 'struck in the manner of someone who diminishes, destroys' (*kastārīhā zad*)[86], then it is defined as a technical

⟨'ytwnc⟩: *ēdōn-iz* (*i.e. edōn-iz* +*kādōzed*) (Klingenschmitt 1968, no. 685, completely ignores ⟨'ytwnc⟩ *ēdōn-iz* and adds these letters to the corrupt spelling of +k'ytywkzyt). This reading (together with +*az* for the following heterogram ⟨MNW⟩ *kē*, which is occasionally confused with the similarly written ⟨MN⟩ *az*; see fn. 81) is decisive for understanding the text, which in my version differs considerably from both Klingenschmitt's and Buyaner's translations.

84 Reichelt 1900, p. 206; differently Klingenschmitt 1968, no. 680–685; Buyaner 2016, pp. 261; 279–280. On the manuscripts see Reichelt 1900, pp. 177–179, and Klingenschmitt 1968, pp. I-V.

85 MP *wēnāgīhā* ('in the manner of someone who sees, as an observer') is an agent noun from the present stem of *dīdan*, *wēn-* 'to see' (MacKenzie 1971, p. 26) + suffixes -*āg* (forming agent nouns) and– *īhā* (forming adverbs; on the suffixes see Durkin-Meisterernst 2014, p. 162, § 311, and p. 217, § 442, respectively). On the interpolation of Av. *baoδō.varštahe* and its Phl. derivative *bōdowaršt* after *bōdōzed* see also Klingenschmitt 1968, no. 681.

86 MP *kastārīhā* ('in the manner of someone who diminishes; as a diminisher') is an agent noun with the adverbial suffix -*īhā* (*kastār* 'diminisher, destroyer, wrongdoer'; MacKenzie 1971, p. 50; on the suffixes -*tār* and -*īhā* see Durkin-Meisterernst 2014, pp. 179–180, § 357, and p. 217, § 442, respectively). Likewise, Av. *kāiδiia-* is rendered in the Pahlavi version of Y 57.15 (*kāiδiiehe*) by *kastārān* 'diminishers, destroyers,

term: 'wounding and destroying something by carelessness, negligence' (*pad sūdagīh*). The parallel scheme in FĪŌ 680–684 in both cases is:

Table 39. Deliberate injury and injury by negligence in the FĪŌ

Avestan word	Pahlavi derivative	Explanation	Definition of the technical term
baoδajat̰ (*baoδō.jaiti-*)	*bōdōzed*	a *bōdōwaršt* offence, meaning *wēnāgīhā zad* ('struck in the manner of someone who sees; as an observer')	Deliberate, wilful, intentional (*nigerišnīg*) damage and injury.
(missing in the text) (**kāiδiiō.jaiti-*)	*kādōzed*	*kastārīhā zad* ('struck in the manner of someone who diminishes; as a diminisher')	Damage and injury by negligence (*pad sūdagīh*).

The immediately following section (FĪŌ 685) reveals how these two offences were assessed: the authors of the Pahlavi text understood *kādōzed* as the 'lesser sin ... than *bōdōzed*' (*⁺keh wināh kādōzed ...⁺az bōdōzed*), both with respect to humans (*mardōmān*) as well as (*ēdōn-iz*) with respect to animals (*pasā*).[87] It is in fact to be expected that an offence caused by negligence or carelessness (*pad sūdagīh*), *i. e. kādōzed*, according to its definition as a technical term, would be qualified as a 'lesser sin/offence' (*⁺keh wināh*) than a 'deliberate, wilful' (*nigerišnīg*) one, *i. e. bōdōzed*. In contrast to the wilful offence, which involves the full or specific intention of the perpetrator to harm or injure, negligence is the culpable breach of a duty by carelessness, the failure to act appropriately towards persons and animals under one's guardianship or care. It would therefore indeed be evaluated as the 'lesser sin' in comparison to the more serious offence of intentional injury. Moreover, the final sentence in this text informs us explicitly that sins committed against small cattle (*gōspandān*) deliberately (*pad*

wrongdoers'; in Y 61.3 (*kāiδiiąsca*) by *kāstārīh* 'diminishing' (Bartholomae 1904, col. 463; MacKenzie 1971, p. 50; *kāstan, kāh-* 'to diminish, decrease, lessen'; √**kas* 'to be small, diminish, lessen'; Cheung 2007, p. 247.

87 See fn. 83 above. The translations of this passage by Klingenschmitt and Buyaner are not conclusive. Klingenschmitt 1968, no. 685, has: 'Das kleinere Vergehen ist kʾtytywzyt; das Vergehen, welches gegenüber Menschen kleiner ist, ist bwtwkzyt; (das Vergehen, welches) gegenüber Tieren kleiner ist, ist kʾytywkzyt.' ['The smaller offence is kʾtytywzyt; the offence, which is smaller with regard to humans is bwtwkzyt; (the offence, which) is smaller with regard to animals is kʾytywkzyt']. Buyaner 2016, p. 280, translates: 'The minor sin (is) *kāyδyōzet*; the (same) sin which (is considered) *bōδōzet* (if committed) against people, (is qualified as) minor, *i. e. kāyδyōzet* (if committed) ⟨against⟩ cattle.' In both translations the two offences are evaluated differently depending on whether humans or animals are affected, but, besides contradicting other statements on the treatment of animals (see the final part of this passage and Macuch 2003a), neither translation fits in with the definition of these words as technical terms.

nigerišn) are called *bōdōzed* and those committed negligently (*pad sūdagīh*) are called *kādōzed*. We can hence conclude that these two definitions applied to both humans and beneficent animals alike (and were then transposed to inanimate objects under guardianship, such as a sacred fire). A corresponding idea with regard to animals is expressed in the *Dēnkard*:

> DkD 554.10–13 (DkM 728.20–23)
> *āmār ī andar nigerišnīg ud sūdagīhā zanišn [ī sūdagīhā zanišn] ī gōspandān abar čē ēwēnagīhā dādestān ī jud jud sūdagīhā zanišn ī pad nigerišnīg zanišnīh dārišn was dādestān ī čē andar im dar.*
>
> '(About) taking into account (*āmār*) the intentional (*andar nigerišnīg*) and negligent (*sūdagīhā*) striking of cattle. About the separate forms of judgements for striking (animals) negligently (*sūdagīhā*) (and those) which have to be considered as striking them intentionally (*pad nigerišnīg*), (and) many (other) judgements on matters on this subject.'

This passage is the final part of a longer text (which I have commented elsewhere)[88] describing injuries to animals, and informs us unequivocally that there were 'separate forms of judgements' (*dādestān ī jud jud*) for striking small cattle negligently (*sūdagīhā zanišn … ī gōspandān*) and striking them intentionally (*pad nigerišnīg zanišnīh*).

The terms *bōdōzed* and *kādōzed* are also attested in the context of theft (*duzīh*) in both the Law-book and the *Dēnkard*. Although the terms are not explained in either of these texts, the context suggests that they were further removed from their original designation of injuries and came to denote *different levels of intention*, which had to be qualified by the court: deliberate theft (stealing property with the intention of appropriating it), on the one hand, or theft by carelessness (e. g. failing to return a loan; not paying for a purchased object or not paying enough, etc.), on the other. In either case a fine or compensation in money (*guharīg ī mādag*) had to be paid to the victims of the theft (the *bun-xwēšān* 'owners of the substance' of the stolen object) as a part of the penalty.[89]

Although fragmentary, these details suggest that transgressions against humans and beneficent animals were evaluated not only according to the gravity of the actual harm or injury, but divided into further general categories according to the intention of the delinquent, as we have seen above. We can reasonably infer that assessing the mental element of a crime was a significant ingredient of the decision-making process by the Sasanian period, both with regard to *ruwānīg* and *hamēmālān* offences, and that it was based on the important Zoroastrian moral precept of *humat* or *hu-menišn*, the violation of which would be the first step to actually committing an illicit act or criminal offence and being found guilty.

88 Macuch 2003a, pp. 179–180.
89 MHDA 15.2–4 (Macuch 1981, pp. 37, 144); DkD 548.17 (DkM 721.21); Appendix VII, p. 688; see also section 3.2 on theft and robbery below, pp. 434–451.

Table 40. The mental element of an offence

Three levels of intention		
1	*wināh ī nigerišnīg*; *bōdōwaršt*	'intentional, wilful, deliberate offence';
	pad nigerišnīg zanišnīh; *bōdōzed*	'intentional, wilful, deliberate injury'
2	*sūdagīhā zanišn*; *kādōzed*	'injury by carelessness; negligence'
3	*wināh andar a-bōyīh*	'unintentional offence' (lit. 'offence in a state of unconsciousness')
The mental element of an offence		
appar-kām; *appar-menišnīgīh*		'will of the robber'; 'intent of the robber'
drō-xwāhāg		'seeking deceit; having a deceitful will'
duzagān-menišn; *duz-menišnīh*; *duz-menišnīgīh*		'intent of the thief (thieves)'
gādan menišnīg; *gād pad uzkārišn*		'intent to cohabit'; 'cohabitation with aforethought'
kēn-menišn		'malicious intent'
pad menišn zadan		'with the intent to smite'
wad-axw		'having an evil mind'
wad-xwāh (opposite: rāst-xwāh)		'having bad, evil intention; ill-willed' (opposite: 'having honest intentions; good-willed')
wad-xwāhīh		'evil intention; malevolence'

3 Criminal offences

Although the transgressions we will discuss in the two following sections were assessed as grievous crimes, they were not necessarily prosecuted by the State. They could be brought to court (as offences of the *hamēmālān* type) either by the infringed party or a representative of the infringed party, with the goal of attaining justice and receiving a compensation for the injury or damage inflicted by the perpetrator. High crimes and misdemeanours prosecuted by the judiciary of the State (such as heresy, apostasy, rebellion, treason, possibly also sorcery and magic) will be addressed separately in Chapter VI, pp. 489–494.

3.1 Assault, physical injury and homicide

There is very little material on crimes involving physical injury in the Sasanian Law-book, as the compiler was obviously more interested in collecting intruiging civil cases. But some of the sources mentioned above[90] register not only various criminal acts involving physical injury, but also offer (to a limited degree) explanations of the technical terms used in this context, allowing us—together with the information in the Law-book—to form a few assumptions on the most important concepts of criminal law. Particularly two sections from the synopsis of the *nasks* in *Dēnkard* 8 (the *zaxmestān* 'section on wounding' and the *rēšestān* 'section on bodily harm', both in Appendix VI), despite being only short surveys, convey the impression that offences of this kind were defined exactly and punished according to precise criteria in Zoroastrian law. The problem with this source is (as noted above) that it is often difficult to distinguish between the different strata, to determine, which parts are taken from the (older) Avestan text in its Pahlavi version, which from the (more recent Sasanian) Pahlavi commentary or were formed in the Islamic period.[91] Other problems are the shortness of the entries, the ambiguity of the content due to too little context and the lack of a discernable systematic approach. Despite all these difficulties it is an indispensible source containing many details, which can enhance our understanding of how these criminal acts were dealt with in a Zoroastrian context.

As we have already noted, five kinds of aggressive acts are listed in the section on 'Judicial dispute' (discussed in section 1, pp. 406–407 above) for which the general term *zanišn*, lit. 'blow, smiting', is used: (1) 'threatening' (*andar nimūd*), (2) 'tearing off' (*kanišn*), (3) 'wounding' (*zaxm*), (4) 'injuring (grievously)' (*rēš kardan*) and (5) 'killing' (*ōzad[an]*).[92] The list seems to advance from the lesser offence of 'threatening', *i. e.* intimidating or bullying another person by signalling to harm, injure or kill that person (or one of his next-of-kin), up to the most grievous crime of homicide ('killing'). Two of these terms, *zaxm* and *rēš*, listed in this sequence, are defined more exactly in the following sub-sections of the *nask*: *zaxm* 'wound', denotes an 'aperture' (⁺*wišāyišn*) or 'opening, cut' in the skin, causing pain (*dard*), the (visible) flow of blood (*xōn*) and unconsciousness (*a-bōyīh*).[93] But the term also seems to denote (invisible) internal injuries, which can be detected only by observing various symptoms of an injured person, as we are informed in the next section, the *rēšestān* (see below).

A distinction was made between wounds inflicted by a perpetrator consciously (intentionally) or 'in a state of unconsciousness' (*andar a-bōyīh*), *i. e.* unintentionally or with diminished responsibility (see above pp. 411–422).[94]

90 See footnote 19 in this Chapter.
91 See Chapter I, pp. 24–26.
92 DkD (M) 84.7–12 (DkM 693.20–694.1); Appendix V, p. 676.
93 DkD (M) 87.2–4 and 87.5–8 (DkM 695.6–11); Appendix VI, pp. 679; 679–680.
94 DkD (M) 87.4–7 (DkM 695.7–9); Appendix VI, pp. 679–680.

Seven symptoms (*daxšag*) of 'unconsciousness' were differentiated (which are unfortunately not described in the synopsis). If I have understood the passage correctly, it seems that an adult perpetrator could plead to have acted without intent if he had wounded a minor in a painful manner causing the flow of blood (*dard [ud] xōn ōh rawēd*). Moreover—if there is a connection to the following sentence (which is by no means certain)—a problem would arise if a person with a 'violent temper' (*xēšm xōg*) repeatedly pleaded to have unintentionally caused 'pain and bloodshed' (*dard ud xōn*) over a longer period of time.[95]

Although the text is not very clear, it indicates that a distinction was made between intentional and unintentional injury (particularly in cases involving minors or violent repeat offenders) and that the intent of the offender was in some manner taken into consideration in the verdict. That the mental element (*mens rea*) or intention of the perpetrator played in important role in assessing the degree and the severity of an offence, is also evident in the context of theft and robbery and sexual abuses (as we have noted in the preceding section): the sources distinguish between the 'intent of the thief' (*duz-menišnīh/duz-menišnīgīh*) and the 'intent of the robber' (*appar-menišnīgīh/appar-kām*).[96] Similarly, as we have elucidated above, Zoroastrian law in an advanced phase distinguished between injury caused intentionally (*pad nigerišnīg zanišnīh*; *bōdōzed*) and injury caused by negligence (*sūdagīhā zanišn*; *kādōzed*).[97]

The section on *zaxm* also introduces two other terms for specific acts, which could result in wounding or injuring in another manner: *xwēhišn* 'pursuit' and *ardīg tazišnīh* 'engaging in battle/conflict'. The first term is defined in the *Frahang ī ōīm*: 'Pursuit is when someone chases a person in order to sin against him' (*xwēhišn ān bawēd ka pad wināhgārīh az pas ī kas dawēd*).[98] In our text, remarkably, seven types of 'pursuit' are listed, each of which involves warriors (foot-soldiers, *payg*, and horsemen, *aswār*) chasing other warriors in different constellations.[99] The synopsis is unfortunately incomplete. We are neither informed, why these seven specific combinations were differentiated, nor how injuries resulting from *xwēhišn* were assessed.

The second term, *ardīg tazišnīh* 'engaging in conflict', is a general expression, encompassing six different aggressive or harmful acts, including *xwēhišn* and *zaxm*:

1. wounding (*zaxm*);
2. pursuit/chase (*xwēhišn*);
3. false teaching (*miϑōsāst*);
4. abandonment; withholding sustenance (*adwadād*);

95 DkD (M) 87.6–8 (DkM 695.8–11; Appendix VI, pp. 679–680.
96 See p. 413 above and pp. 455–458 below.
97 See pp. 412–422 above.
98 Klingenschmitt 1968, no. 691. On this term see also Appendix VI, fn. 4.
99 DkD (M) 87.8–88.5 (DkM 695.11–19); Appendix VI, p. 680.

5. speaking in the manner of sorcerers (*gōwišn ī jādūg gōwišnīhā*); and
6. speaking in a threatening manner (*gōwišn ī +sahm nimāyišnīhā*).[100]

Moreover, *ardīg tazišnīh* is explicitly used of conflicts or confrontations between opponents who battle against each other simultaneously in a kind of duel, that is, a confrontation following specific rules, in which the opponent is not injured beforehand (*zaxm kard ēk az ōy ī did nē pēš*).[101] It furthermore designates a form of conflict in which like was paired with like obviously in a attempt to implement an equal balance of adversaries: an adult engages in conflict against another adult; a childless woman against a childless woman, a pregnant woman against a pregnant woman; a minor of seven years against a child of his own age under the supervision of the parents. Interestingly, the text informs us that in this form of duel every offence committed by one party against the other is punished by a fine to be paid to the *radān*.[102] We can hence conclude that duels could take place under the supervision of elders or religious authorities, following specific rules and that a violation of these rules was an offence liable to punishment by a fine.[103]

The term *rēš* 'physical injury, harm, bodily harm',[104] following *zaxm* in the sequence of *zanišn*-offences we have mentioned above, seems to be the general expression for all kinds of physical injury, including *zaxm*, but it also encompasses other means of causing grievous bodily harm besides wounding with or without a weapon. As we are informed immediately at the beginning of the *rēšestān* section of the *Dēnkard*, the term encompasses injuries caused by: (1) cutting (*brīn*) (2) splitting/tearing (*+darrišn*), (3) ripping (*oškāfišn*), (4) pulling out (*frāz-rūdag*), (5) piercing (*sumbišn*), (6) treading (*xwāhišn*), (7) rupturing (*škenišn*), (8) crushing (*xwurd kardan*), (9) mutilating (*tāšīdan*), and (10) causing (a limb) to wither

100 Two of these terms, *miϑosāst* and *adwadād*, will be discussed below pp. 462–468.
101 DkD (M) 88.12–89.3 (DkM 696.4–8); Appendix VI, pp. 680–681.
102 DkD (M) 89.4–11 (DkM 696.8–14); Appendix VI, p. 681.
103 The term *ardīg tazišnīh* also occurs in the *pāsox* to RivAF, *Pursišn* LVIII (misspelled here as ⟨twcšnyh⟩) which we have mentioned above (p. 405, fn. 24). This passage discusses the categorization of a combat (*jang*) between two persons as a duel (*ardīg +tazišnīh*), following the rules in a judicial dispute (*pahikār-rad*): RivAF LVIII.2: (*pāsox*): *čiyōn dānom pahikār nigerišn ud kā [kū] a-pahikār rad warōmand ud andar warōmandīh ēd har kē pad gyāg ī xweš ēstēd pad pahikār-rad dārišn ka ēk zaxm kunēd ān-iz ī dudīgar kunēd ardīg +tazišnīh* [mss: ⟨twcšnyh⟩] *ēk pad dīd be šawēd*. '(Answer): As far as I know, this (= the fight; *jang*) should be considered as a (legal) dispute (*pahikār*). And if it (is) doubtful (*warōmand*), which one (of the combatants is) in a non-judicial dispute (*a-pahikār-rad*), due to this doubtfulness (*warōmandīh*), each one (of the combatants) who stands in his place should be considered as taking part in a judicial dispute (*pahikār-rad*). If one wounds the other (and) the other (retaliates), then it becomes a duel (*ardīg +tazišnīh*), one against the other.' B.T. Anklesaria 1969 (vol. I, pp. 30–31 117–118; vol. II, p. 73) in his edition of the text has completely misunderstood this passage. The other terms occurring in this list will be discussed further below.
104 < Av. *raēša-* 'damage, physical injury' (Bartholomae 1904, col. 1486 'Schädigung; körperliche Schädigung überhaupt').

(+*huškēnīdan*).[105] The term also denotes internal injuries or wounds (*zaxm*), which are only visible by observing various symptoms an injured person might show, reaching from 'stupefaction' (*stardīh*) and weakness (*nizārīh*) to a change in appearance and eating habits, amnesia (+*a-šnās[ag]īh* 'not recognizing'), the diminishment of a person's ability to speak, see and hear (*gōwišn ud wēnišn āšnawišn*) or of his/her intelligence and strength (*xrad ud ōz*) or fertility (*šusr ud šīr ud ābusīh* '[production of] semen and milk and pregnancy').[106]

An instrument causing physical injury is named explicitly in the second sentence: the *mārgan*, the 'whip' (lit. 'serpent-scourge'), which, when 'slashed over (a person's) body' causes the 'flow of blood' (*xōn tazišnīh*).[107] The next part of this entry is far from being clear, but it seems that the original text (of which we only have an incomprehensible synopsis) contained a description of how injuries caused by the whip were judged differently depending on which organ (*hannām* 'limb' or 'member') of the body was harmed. If I have understood the sentence correctly, the human body was divided into seventy-six (!) sections, 'limb by limb' (*hannām hannām*), consisting of two principal forms (*2 ēwēnag mādayāntar*), building eight principal parts (*8 mādagwar*) each with a different 'substance' (*ēk az did ǰud mādag*). Injuries to different organs of the body were hence subject to different judgements (*ǰud wizīr hēnd*).[108] This would imply that a verdict regarding physical injury was passed after determining the 'substance, essence' (*mādag, i. e.* quality, texture, place, importance?) of the organs that were damaged according to a specific scheme (not elucidated here, but see pp. 468–486 below).

The question, whether a weapon or several weapons (*sneh*) were used to cause bodily harm, also seems to have had an impact on the verdict: which kind of devices can be 'completely' considered as weapons (*pad sneh uspurrīg*), that is, as instruments that were explicitly constructed for use as weapons? Which objects cannot be considered as weapons and which ones can be considered as weapons (*pad sneh mehmān*),[109] even if they were not conceived originally as arms, for example, a stone (*sang*) that is used to injure a person?[110] We can only speculate on the reasons for these distinctions: the use of an instrument conceived as a weapon might point to a pre-meditated act, whereas the use of another object (a stone) could be the result of an action in the heat of the moment or even an accident with different consequences for the perpetrator. Another presumably important distinction (since Avestan words are used) was made between wounds

105 DkD (M) 90.7–10 (DkM 697.3–5); Appendix VI, pp. 682–683 (on +*huškēnīdan* see p. 682, fn. 11).

106 DkD (M) 91.6–92.3 (DkM 697.13–22); Appendix VI, p. 683.

107 DkD (M) 90.11–12 (DkM 697.6–7); Appendix VI, p. 683.

108 DkD (M) 90.11–91.5 (DkM 697.7–13); Appendix VI, p. 683. On the organs of the body and their functions according to Zādspram see Sohn 1996, particularly pp. 1–18.

109 DkD (M) 88.6–7 (DkM 695.20–21); Appendix VI, pp. 680–681.

110 DkD (M) 92.11 (DkM 698.6); Appendix VI, p. 684.

inflicted by one weapon (*sneh*) or by several weapons at once or on separate occasions.[111] Unfortunately the consequences are not elucidated, but we can assume that determining the *exact cause* of an injury or several different injuries would have had an impact on deciding which persons to punish and the type of punishment. Exactly this seems to be meant in several passages of the Law-book dealing with imprecise testimonies, as we will see below.

Injuries could be caused by other means than using a weapon. If a person is thrown into a 'cavity' (*gabrag*), the environment of the cavity (*e.g.* the walls and surroundings of a well belonging to a house) and the type of injuries caused by the fall are investigated: is the body 'crushed' (*xwurd kard*) or 'torn apart' (*ōškāft*) or 'cut' (*tāšīd*) or 'besmeared all over with blood (and) moisture' (*abāg xōn +xwēdāg mālūn*)?[112] Interestingly, the extent, breadth and depth (*drahnāy ud zahā*) of the injuries caused by the fall are examined, which could point to the punishment of the perpetrator according to the scheme discussed below in section 5, even though this is not mentioned here.

One of the rare passages on physical injury in the Law-book not only uses *zaxm* and *rēš* in a similar context, but seems to refer indirectly to the details we have noted above on procuring evidence in these cases:

> MHDA 14.13–15.1
> *gugāyīh ī pad zaxm ēn and was ka gōwēd kū-š and zaxm kard ud tōzišn be kunišn. spurrīgīh ī sneh ud čandīh rēš ud nāmčištīgīh ī gyāg-ē(w) guftan nē abāyēd. pad zaxm hamāg pad rēš ud +mārgan*[113] *ud wars-rūnišnīh ud kirb-abganišnīh ud dard ud xōn-tazišnīh ud pad-iz zaxm sardag čiyōn zaxm sardag āhanjišn ud āspōzišn ud kešišn ud miϑōsāst tā nē drō(g) rāh nimūd +hangārdan*[114] *adwadād bawēd.*
>
> 'The testimony on a wound (*zaxm*) (is) sufficient, when he (= the witness) says: "He/she has inflicted a wound to this extent". a fine (*tōzišn*) has to be imposed. It is not necessary for him (= the witness) to give a statement on the completeness of the weapon (*spurrīgīh ī sneh*) and the extent of the injury (*čandīh rēš*) and the specifics of the site (of the injury) (*nāmčištīgīh ī gyāg-ē*). Every (harm caused) by physical injury (*rēš*), (by) the whip (+*mārgan*), (by) tearing out hair (*wars-rūnišnīh*), (by) throwing a body (*kirb-abganišnīh*), (causing) pain (*dard*) and the flow of blood (*xōn-tazišnīh*) (is considered) as a wound (*zaxm*). And for (every) type of wound (there is a penalty) corresponding to the type of wound: extracting (*āhanjišn*) and thrusting (*āspōzišn*) and drawing (*kešišn*). And considering "false teaching" (*miϑōsāst*)—so that deceit is not shown a way—counts as a "withdrawal of sustenance" (*adwadād*).'[115]

111 DkD (M) 91.3–7 (DkM 697.22–698.2); Appendix VI, p. 683; on the Avestan words see Appendix VI, p. 684, fn. 22.

112 DkD (M) 92.7–11 (DkM 698.2–6); Appendix VI, p. 684.

113 Ms. ⟨m'lwk'⟩. The term is emended here in accordance with DkD (M) 90.11–12 (DkM 697.6–7), where the 'serpent-scourge' (*mārgan*) is explicitly named as one of the weapons causing injury (see above and Appendix VI, p. 683).

114 Ms. ⟨hngltn'⟩.

115 Macuch 1981, pp. 37, 143f. (with a slightly different translation).

The text is unfortunately far too concise and not very clear, but in the light of the (more or less theoretical) details conveyed in the *Dēnkard* we may draw a few conclusions on how criminal offences involving injuries were dealt with in legal practice. Three main issues are addressed:

1. the extent to which a witness has to give testimony on physical injury ('wounding', *zaxm*) for the alleged perpetrator to be punished by means of a fine (*tōzišn*);
2. different types of physical injury (*rēš*), which are assessed as *zaxm* and penalties corresponding exactly to the type of wound;
3. the categorization of 'false teaching' (*miϑōsāst*) as an *adwadād* offence.

In the context of the first issue, that of testimony, we are informed that it is sufficient for a witness to confirm that a person has actually caused bodily harm with the words 'He/she has inflicted a wound to this extent' (*kū-š and zaxm kard*). This testimony alone will lead to the imposition of a fine (*tōzišn*) on the perpetrator. It is not necessary for the witness to make a statement on the 'completeness of the weapon' (*spurrīgīh ī sneh*). This last expression corresponds obviously to *pad sneh uspurrīg* 'complete as a weapon', in the *Dēnkard* passage discussed above, addressing the question, whether the instrument employed by the perpetrator to injure the victim was explicitly constructed for use as a weapon (such as arms used in warfare in contrast to other items, *e. g.* a stone). As we have already noted, the use of a device conceived as a weapon might point to a voluntary or pre-meditated act, whereas an injury caused by another object could be assessed in a completely different manner. Moreover, according to our text, the witness is neither obliged to give details on the extent of the injury (*čandīh rēš*), nor any specifics on the site of the injury (*nāmčištīgīh ī gyāg-ē*). The last expression is not explained, but it could be an allusion to the details transmitted in the *Dēnkard* on the evaluation of injuries regarding different organs of the body (divided into 76 parts), which were subject to different judgements (*ǰud wizīr*).[116] Our passage of the Law-book explicitly states that neither of these issues (which might have been theoretically important according to the *Dēnkard* passages discussed above) has to be included in the testimony of a witness in order for a fine to be imposed by legal instances.

The passage then continues to explain which kinds of physical injury (*rēš*) are to be assessed as *zaxm*. As we have seen, the latter term designates in the *Dēnkard* a 'wound' in the literal sense of the word, *i. e.* an aperture, cut or break in the skin, leading to pain (*dard*), the flow of blood (*xōn*) and unconsciousness (*a-bōyīh*). Similarly our text states that all kinds of injuries (*rēš*) are considered as *zaxm*, which cause pain (*dard*) and the flow of blood (*xōn-tazišnīh*), including those caused by the use of a whip (⁺*mārgan*) or by tearing out the hair of the victim (*wars-rūnišnīh*) or throwing the victim's body (*kirb-abganišnīh*). The

116 DkD (M) 90.12–91.5 (DkM 697.7–13); Appendix VI, p. 689. On this passage see above p. 426.

next part of the sentence is enigmatic, but it seems—if my understanding of the text is correct—that injuries produced by these acts were liable to corresponding forms of corporal punishment, which possibly consisted of three torturous methods, denoted (not very clearly) as 'extracting' (*āhanǰišn*), 'thrusting' (*āspōzišn*) and 'drawing' (*kešišn*). Do these three forms of penalties (if penalties are meant!) correspond to the three types of injuries noted explicitly in the text? Was 'tearing out the hair' (*wars-rūnišnīh*) punished by 'extracting/pulling' (*āhanǰišn*); throwing the victim's body (*kirb-abganišnīh*) by 'thrusting/throwing' (*āspōzišn*); injuries caused by the whip (*+mārgan*) by 'drawing/cracking' (*kešišn*)? These methods would in fact correspond with some of the corporal punishments mentioned in the sources.[117]

The third part of our text alludes to another type of injury which is not caused directly, but by an omission, by not fulfilling a duty where there is an obligation to act. The term *adwadād* is used for various offences caused by a failure to comply with the important duty of maintaining individuals as well as beneficent animals and sacred fires under one's custody by abandonment or withdrawal of sustenance. Another remarkable aspect of *adwadād* is that it also denotes the offence of withdrawing *spiritual* sustenance, for example, when a teacher refuses to instruct his student in religious matters or does not instruct him fully or correctly. The term 'false teaching' (*miϑōsāst*) is not defined in our text, but in the context of *adwadād* the sin of *miϑōsāst* most likely refers to this kind of defective behaviour of a teacher towards his student (an offence explicitly noted in *Hērbedestān* 15.1; it is definitely *not* 'false testimony', which is called *zur-gugāyīh*). Our passage requires that 'false teaching' be considered and punished as an offence of the *adwadād* type, by which injury is caused indirectly by omission, by failing to fulfil the religious duty of instructing a pupil correctly in religious matters.[118]

The Law-book also mentions a few cases, in which injuries lead to the death of the victim. In general homicide is considered as one of the capital crimes, as an act 'deserving death' (*margarzān*), which could have dire consequences for the perpetrator, including the death sentence. The latter could, however, avoid an indictment on the basis of a *margarzān* if he voluntarily came forward and confessed the crime to the judge (*dādwar*) with the words 'I have killed a man in this manner' (*kū-m mard-ē ī ēdōn ōzad*). If the perpetrator has not been arrested by a *frēzwān* (a guard, policeman or inspector responsible for detaining suspects, see Chapter VI, pp. 518–519) and there are no witnesses to the homicide, the crime is *not* assessed as a *margarzān* in the 'bill of indictment' (*nibištag*, lit. 'written record'). On the other hand, the same act of homicide is considered as a *margarzān* in the 'bill of indictment' (*nibištag*), if the perpetrator has *not*

117 On punishments see Chapter VI, pp. 580–585.

118 On the *adwadād* offence see Macuch 2012a and 2012b; Chapter I, pp. 75–76 above and pp. 463–468 below.

come forward on his own, but has been arrested by the *frēzwān*, even if he confesses (*xwastūg bawēd*) to the crime and there are no witnesses.[119]

Other short entries in the Law-book take up the problem of imprecise testimonies in cases of physical injury causing the death of the victim. It seems that care was taken to avoid indicting persons accused of homicide, whose guilt could not be sufficiently proved, even if there was reason to believe that they were possibly not completely innocent of the crime. Following cases are discussed:

1. A witness declares: 'A man, whom I do not know particularly (and) Mihrēn have beaten Pusag. Pusag died as a result of the beating by either Mihrēn or the beating by the man, of whom I have declared that I do not particularly know him.'[120] In this case the witness cannot name or identify one of the parties. The court hence rules that the accused Mihrēn is not a suspect (*nē warōmand*, lit. 'not liable to the oath'). A reason is not transmitted, but we can assume that this kind of incomplete testimony, naming only one of two assailants, did not sufficiently prove that the known and named suspect was guilty of homicide.
2. The witness states: 'Farrox and Mihrēn have beaten Pusag and Pusag has died as a result of either the beating by Farrox or the beating by Mihrēn and I do not know, which one of the beatings by whom resulted in his death.'[121] Again, the testimony of the witness is incomplete, as he has named two suspects, but cannot specify the principal offender, the person guilty of killing the victim. Even if the witness later changes his statement and makes one of the named persons responsible for the victim's death, the suspects have to be acquitted *(kam nē bōxtišn*, lit. 'they have to be acquitted nevertheless').
3. The witness declares: 'In the first year {(this person)} has beaten him {...}. As a result of this beating in the first year and the beating (of another person) in the second year (he died).'[122] The accused persons are not considered as suspects (*nē warōmand*) on the basis of this testimony (since the individual shares of the perpetrators leading to the death of the victim remains unclear, as we may deduce). On the other hand, the case is assessed differently, if

119 MHD 92.2–6 (Macuch 1993, pp. 580, 585 with a slightly different translation). On the consequences of *margarzān* offences see Chapter VI, pp. 581–585.

120 MHD 92.7–9: *ka gōwēd kū mard ī nāmčišt nē dānom (ud) Mihrēn Pusag zad Pusag az zad ī Mihrēn ayāb az zad ī ān mard ī-m guft kū-š nāmčišt nē dānom bahr murd* (Macuch 1993, pp. 580, 585). The names Farrox, Mihrēn and Pusag in these sentences are used to designate fictive persons involved in a lawsuit (similar to the use of Aulus Agerius [A. A.] and Numerius Negidius [N. N.] in Roman law to denote the plaintiff and defendant).

121 MHD 92.10–12: *ka gōwēd kū Farrox ud Mihrēn Pusag zad ud Pusag az ān zad ī Farrox ayāb az ān zad ī Mihrēn bahr murd ud ēn kū az ān zad az ān ī kē bahr murd nē dānom...* (Macuch 1993, pp. 581, 585).

122 MHD 92.14–15: *ka gōwēd kū sāl ēk {(ōy)} zad ī {...} az ān zad ī sāl ēk ān ī zad ī sāl 2 bahr (murd)...* (Macuch 1993, pp. 581, 585).

the witness states: 'They have beaten him together (*āgenēn*) and he has died as the result of the beating of the one or the other.'[123] On the basis of this testimony both accused persons are considered as principal offenders and suspects (*har dō warōmand hēnd*). Again, no reason is transmitted, but if we take the legal use of the term *āgenēn* (lit. 'together') into consideration (as we have elucidated above in the section on 'Joint property and partnership', Chapter III, pp. 245–253), the testimony of the witness implies that both accused persons had an *exactly equal share* in injuring the victim and can hence both be prosecuted as principal offenders for homicide.

4. The witness states: 'Farrox and Ādurfarrbay have wounded Mihrēn separately (*ǰud ǰud*) and I do not know, who wounded him first, but I do know that they wounded him separately'.[124] The passage continues to reason that both assailants are considered as principal offenders and suspects (*har dō warōmand hēnd*), if the victim Mihrēn was wounded by both of them to a similar degree and died after receiving the second wound and the second wound (*ān ī dudīgar*) was not less serious (*nē xwārtar būd*) than the first one.

Despite the shortness of these passages, they suggest that suspects in cases of injuries leading to the death of the victim were only prosecuted for homicide on the basis of reasonably reliable evidence. In all the cases described above two persons are accused of causing injuries which finally result in the death of the victim. Are they both principal offenders and responsible for the victim's death? The main task of the court is to find out, whether the fatal blows were caused by only one or by both of the assailants, whether they had a joint purpose and to which degree each of them injured the victim. In this context the testimony of the witness is crucial and assessed precisely by the court: if it is incomplete, imprecise or untrustworthy and does not explicitly name the person guilty of killing the victim or blame both assailants to the same degree, the accused persons are not considered as suspects (*warōmand*, lit. 'liable to the oath'), that is, they are not prosecuted for homicide (but they might be nevertheless prosecuted or punished for injuring the victim, if not for homicide, although this is not said in the text).

As one of the many capital crimes belonging to the *margarzān* ('deserving death') category, homicide in theory deserved the death penalty, but an indictment against the accused person(s) depended on the reliability of the evidence brought forward in the individual cases, as we have seen. Did Sasanian law differentiate between manslaughter and murder, *i. e.* killing with malice aforethought, a premeditated act? The sources are too meagre to permit any conclusions, but,

123 MHD 92.15–16: *ka gōwēd kū-šān āgenēn zad az an ī ōy ayāb az ān ī (ōy) bahr {(murd)}...* (Macuch 1993, pp. 581, 585f.).

124 MHD 92.16-(continued)97.2: *ka gōwēd ku Farrox ud Ādurfarrbay ǰud ǰud pad Mihrēn zaxm kard ud ēn kū zaxm kē pēš kard nē bē ēn dānom kū ān zaxm pad ǰud bahr kard...* (Macuch 1993, pp. 581, 586).

as we have noted above, a distinction was obviously made between killing consciously, on the one hand, and without intent or responsibility (*a-bōyīh*), on the other, which can be interpreted as an equivalent to voluntary and involuntary manslaughter, or, in the language of the texts, acting with 'evil thought' (*duš-menišn*) or as a person who has 'evil intent' (*wad-xwāhīh*)[125] or 'unconsciously/without intent' (*a-bōyīh*). Moreover, it seems that Sasanian criminal law also distinguished other offences in the context of homicide, such as participation in the crime or incitement, the act of encouraging, suggesting or persuading another person to commit a crime, which can include threats or pressure used to influence that person. A noteworthy (but, again, far too concise) passage in the Law-book notes a concrete case of homicide, involving a master and his slave, which could point to one (or both) of these offences:

MHD 97.3–7
ka anšahrīg guft kū šawam ud Karēn be ōzanam ud xwadāy guft kū čim gōwē ka-t kardan nē tuwān ud anšahrīg šud u-š ān mard ōzad gyāg-ē(w) nibišt kū pad mowbedīh ī Burzag mad u-šān nibištag pad-iš kard ud pas Zurwāndād guft kū nē warōmand u-šān az ān nibištag be hišt.

'When the slave has declared: "I will go and kill Karēn", and the master has said: "You will state the reason, if you cannot do it", and the slave has gone and killed that man: in one place it is written: (the case) came to Burzag in his capacity as *mowbed* and they drew up a "bill of indictment" (*nibištag*) for it. And later Zurwāndād said: "He (= the master) is not a suspect (*nē warōmand*)" and they removed (his name) from that "bill of indictment".'[126]

This is indeed a strange description, which I understand as follows: In a case of homicide a witness (or witnesses) hear two remarks made by a slave and his master: the slave declares that he will kill a certain person called Karēn; the master replies: 'You will state the reason, if you cannot do it' (*čim gōwē ka-t kardan nē tuwān*). The slave kills the man as he has announced and the case is brought to court. The question arises: how should the testified words of the master be assessed? Do they imply that he is an accessory to the homicide in some manner (by counselling, instigating, inciting or encouraging his slave to perform the killing or procuring the act by taking appropriate steps to see that the crime is accomplished)? The words of the master are evidently so ambiguous that two diametrically opposed positions can be taken: Burzag, the *mowbed*, obviously decides that the master is an accessory to the crime, hence a suspect and arranges that a 'bill of indictment' (*nibištag*) be written. Another official named Zurwāndād (a jurisconsult often cited in the Law-book),[127] on the other hand, decides 'later' (*pas*; in a later stage of the trial or in an appellate court) that the master is 'not a suspect' (*nē warōmand*) and lets his name be removed from the 'bill of indictment'.

125 On this term see above pp. 415–417.
126 Macuch 1993, pp. 581, 586.
127 See the list of jurisconsults and commentators in Appendix XVII, pp. 745–747.

Table 41. Overview: assault, physical injury and homicide

<table>
<tr><th colspan="2">Criminal acts</th><th>Definitions</th></tr>
<tr><th colspan="3">zaxm 'wound'</th></tr>
<tr><td>⁺wišāyišn</td><td>'aperture, opening'</td><td rowspan="4">1. a (visible) opening or cut in the skin, caused with or without a weapon (sneh), leading to pain (dard), flow of blood (xōn; xōn-tazišnīh), unconsciousness (a-bōyīh)
2. wounds caused by other means than cutting (listed in the first row)
3. internal injuries (see under rēš)</td></tr>
<tr><td>mārgan</td><td>(injuries caused by) the 'whip'</td></tr>
<tr><td>wars-rūnišnīh</td><td>'tearing out hair'</td></tr>
<tr><td>kirb-abganišnīh</td><td>'throwing the body'</td></tr>
<tr><th colspan="3">rēš 'physical injury, harm, bodily harm'</th></tr>
<tr><td>brīn</td><td>'cutting'</td><td rowspan="10">1. injuries caused by inflicting physical harm by different means (listed in the first row)
2. internal injuries leading to 'stupefaction' (stardīh), 'weakness' (nizārīh), a change in appearance and eating habits, 'amnesia' (⁺a-šnās[ag]īh), and a diminishment of a person's abilities with regard to:
(a) speech, seeing and hearing (gōwišn ud wēnišn āšnawišn)
(b) intelligence and strength (xrad ud ōz)
(c) fertility (šusr ud šīr ud ābusīh)</td></tr>
<tr><td>⁺darrišn</td><td>'splitting/tearing'</td></tr>
<tr><td>oškāfišn</td><td>'ripping'</td></tr>
<tr><td>fraz-rūdag</td><td>'pulling out'</td></tr>
<tr><td>sumbišn</td><td>'piercing'</td></tr>
<tr><td>xwāhišn</td><td>'treading'</td></tr>
<tr><td>škenišn</td><td>'rupturing'</td></tr>
<tr><td>xwurd kardan</td><td>'crushing'</td></tr>
<tr><td>tāšīdan</td><td>'mutilating'</td></tr>
<tr><td>⁺huškēnīdan</td><td>'causing (a limb) to wither'</td></tr>
<tr><th colspan="3">ardīg tazišnīh 'engaging in conflict'</th></tr>
<tr><td>zaxm</td><td>'wound(ing)'</td><td rowspan="6">1. a conflict carried out by the means of various aggressive or harmful acts (listed in the first row of this table)
2. a duel which takes place simultaneously between equal opponents, following specific rules</td></tr>
<tr><td>xwēhišn</td><td>'pursuit/chase'</td></tr>
<tr><td>miϑōsāst</td><td>'false teaching'</td></tr>
<tr><td>adwadād</td><td>'abandonment; withholding sustenance'</td></tr>
<tr><td>gōwišn ī jādūg gōwišnīha</td><td>'speaking in the manner of sorcerers'</td></tr>
<tr><td>gōwišn ī ⁺sahm nimāyišnīhā</td><td>'speaking in a threatening manner'</td></tr>
</table>

Pahlavi sources mention a large number of sins designated as capital crimes (*margarzān*), which include offences from both *ruwānīg* and *hamēmālān* categories. An assessment of all the sins of this category would go beyond the scope of this work, as many of the transgressions mentioned in this context belong solely to the *ruwānīg* group, which were not tried by judicial officials or in State courts, but evaluated and punished by religious authorities in the communities of the perpetrators. Capital crimes prosecuted by the State will be treated in Chapter VI, section 1.[128]

3.2 Theft and robbery

Zoroastrian law distinguished precisely between the criminal acts of theft and robbery, as we have already elucidated in the context of credit law and sale.[129] In criminal law the Avestan technical terms for 'robber' (*hazaŋhan-*) and 'thief' (*tāiiu-*) and the corresponding Pahlavi terms *appar(ag)* 'robber', *duz(d)* 'thief' designate perpetrators, who appropriate property unlawfully in a different manner: the 'robber' steals openly, in public; the 'thief' stealthily, in secret.[130] One example will suffice to illustrate the point, as this basic distinction is well known and expressed in several Avestan texts as well as in their corresponding Pahlavi translations:

> Nēr. 45.4
> *aniiō kascit̰ aŋhāuš astuuatō para.baraiti akå̄ hazaŋha anākå̄sə tāiiuš.*
>
> 'Anyone else in the material world who takes it away openly is a robber, (if) stealthily, (he is) a thief.'

The Pahlavi translation has:

> *any kadar-iz-ē axw ī astōmand be barēd [mard ī šahr] ka āškārag apparag kā nihān duz.*
>
> 'Anyone else who takes away (part of) material existence [(if he is) a man of (this) country] is a robber if (he takes it) openly, and a thief if secretly.'[131]

By the Sasanian period these definitions had been transposed to the legal field of contract law and the terms were used in a figurative sense to designate contractors who did not keep their contractual obligations, who committed the offence of *mihrōdrujīh* 'breach of contract'. If a person failed to honour a contract, which had been agreed upon in the presence of witnesses (in public), this offence was assessed and punished according to the offence of 'robbery' or stealing 'manifestly, openly' (*āškārag*); if the deal had been closed in private, without witnesses, its breach was assessed according to 'theft', or stealing in 'secret'

128 See pp. 489–494. For an overview of the most frequently named *margarzān* sins see Appendix XVI.
129 See Chapter IV, pp. 312–315 and 381–382.
130 On these terms and definitions see already Bartholomae 1904, col. 1799 and 647 respectively (with references to the sources).
131 Kotwal/Kreyenbroek 2009, pp. 196–197.

(*nihān*), and punished accordingly. As we have seen in Chapter IV, the same expressions were also used in a figurative sense in the context of sale not only in Zoroastrian law, but also in the law of the East Christians, adapted from the former, as confirmed in a corresponding passage of the Corpus Iuris of Īšōʿbōxt using the Syriac translations *ḥāṭōpā* 'robber' (lit. 'extortioner, plunderer, ravisher') and *ganāḇā* 'thief' for the original Pahlavi terms *appar* and *duz* respectively in an identical context.[132]

The translation of Pahlavi *appar* as *ḥāṭōpā* in the Syriac version of Īšōʿbōxt's Corpus is also significant from another point of view for determining the precise difference between 'robbery' and 'theft' in criminal law. The Syriac translator of the Pahlavi original seems to have been well aware of another aspect of robbery, besides the definition given above of 'stealing manifestly'. The Syriac root ḤṬP 'to take by force, violate, snatch away, seize, rob, carry off', from which the term is derived, stresses another important feature of 'robbery' (in contrast to 'theft'): the use of force.[133] This significant difference is not explicitly stated in the texts, but can be derived from a number of observations. The Pahlavi exegetes of the Avesta seem to have been aware that the Avestan term *hazaŋhan-* 'robber' is derived from *hazah-* 'force, violence',[134] since the usual Pahlavi translation for this term, MP *appar(ag)*, in certain *zand* texts (*Wīdēwdād*, *Hērbedestān* and *Nērangestān*) is replaced in other texts (*Yasna* and *Niyāyišn*) by the MP term *stahmag*, designating a 'violent person' or 'oppressor'.[135] In the latter texts the second translation is chosen, notwithstanding the pairing of *hazaŋhan-* with *tāiiu-*, as in *paitištātəe tāiiunąmca hazasnąmca* 'to withstand the thieves and the robbers', translated by: *pad abāz-ēstišnīh ī duzān ud stahmagān* 'in order to restrain the thieves and oppressors' (*Nyāyišn* 1.14).[136] Or in: *hamistayaēca … tāiianąmca hazasnąmca* 'to suppress … the thieves and robbers', which is rendered as: *pad hamēstārīh … duzān ud stahmagān* 'in opposition … to thieves and oppressors' (*Yasna* 61.3).[137] Similarly, the term *stahmag* 'oppressor' is paired with *duz* 'thief' in a passage of the *Dēnkard*: *abar dādwar ī rāst ī hanǰamanīg pad hamēstārīh ī duzān stahmagān ahlaw-ga(n)ān dād(an)*. 'On the appointment of a true judge who is a (notable) member of the community in opposition (*pad hamēstārīh*) to thieves (*duzān*) (and) oppressors (*stahmagān*) (and) killers of righteous men' (DkD 283.9–10/DkM 720.8–9).

132 Īšōʿbōxt, Book V, Chapter XI, §5a (Sachau 1914, pp. 174–175); on this passage see above Chapter IV, pp. 381–382.
133 Payne Smith 1903, p. 138, translates Syriac ḤṬP as 'to take by force, do violence, violate; to seize, snatch, catch at'; compare Mandaic HṬP, HTP 'to snatch away, seize by force, rob, carry off' (Drower/Macuch 1963, p. 140).
134 Bartholomae 1904, col. 1799: *hazah-* 'Gewalt, Macht; Gewalttat'.
135 On this distribution of translations see Cantera 2004, p. 312.
136 Taraf 1981, pp. 44–45.
137 Taraf 1981, p. 129.

That these two means of unlawfully taking possession of property were distinguished in this manner seems to be indicated in another (unfortunately far too concise and difficult) passage in the long Pahlavi commentary to *Hērbedestān* 12, in which theft and robbery are contrasted.[138] In this specific context the passage treats the question, whether it is allowed to appropriate property belonging to an infidel woman (*zan ī ag-dēn*), who has converted to Zoroastrianism (*ō wehdenīh* ⁺*mad ēstēd*), but has died in the same year as a person 'deserving death' (*margarzān*). The question is: who will inherit her property? One of the general instructions against this background is that 'it is permitted to steal (*duzīdan*) from the infidels (*ag-dēnān*) in order to convert them, but not to rob (*appurdan*) them. (But) if (the convert) reverses conversion, it is also permitted to rob him/her' (*az ag-dēnān mardōm hāxtan rāy duzīdan pādixšāy appurdan nē pādixšāy. ka hāxtan abāz šawēd appurdan-iz pādixšāy*) (TD 13v.15–14r.1).[139] This is of course a ruling in a specific setting with regard to property left as inheritance by a convert, who has been assessed as a *margarzān* sinner by Zoroastrian authorities, but there can be no doubt that an important distinction was made between *duzīdan* 'to steal' and *appurdan* 'to rob': the quoted passage sanctions taking property from adherents of another religion (*ag-dēnān*) by 'stealing' in order to enforce conversion to Zoroastrianism, but it does *not* allow 'robbing' property by using force, unless the new convert has returned to her former faith (and is hence a *margarzān*, as in this specific case of the converted woman). The passage in fact fits in well with other entries regarding the property of *margarzān* sinners, which was usually confiscated (by religious authorities or the State), and it corresponds to the different rules regarding infidels (*ag-dēnān*) in the field of inheritance.[140] But it is strange that verbs designating two obviously unlawful criminal acts, are used in the context of measures deemed as 'permitted, authorized' (*pādixšāy*). Although this source is, strictly speaking, a theological commentary, not a legal text, this use of words could in fact reflect the precarious position of infidels from the viewpoint of Zoroastrian legal theory: it was perfectly lawful to 'steal' their property under certain circumstances, particularly in order to enforce their conversion to Zoroastrianism, but not to use force. In Sasanian legal practice, however, these questions might have been handled differently, specifically when dealing with the larger religious minorities of Ērānšahr.

To sum up, the provenance of the Avestan term for 'robber' (from *hazah*- 'force, violence'), its rendering into Pahlavi by both *appar* 'robber' and *stahmag* 'violent (person), oppressor' in the quoted passages and the translation into

138 I have discussed the first part of this long legal commentary, which discusses questions regarding the inheritance of a convert to Zoroastrianism, in MACUCH 2009f.

139 Both editions have different translations of this passage; HUMBACH/ELFENBEIN 1990 (Hēr. 12.23–27), pp. 88–91; KOTWAL/KREYENBROEK 1992 (Hēr. 12.4), pp. 64–65.

140 For lists of *margarzān* sins see Appendix XVI, pp. 738–740; on religious minorities Chapter VI, pp. 526–533.

Syriac as *ḥāṭōpā* 'extortioner, plunderer, ravisher, robber' make it rather likely that the idea of 'robbery' was connoted with violence, with the use of force in some manner to deprive another individual of property. This is, unsurprisingly, another basic difference between theft and robbery apart from the notion of stealing openly or secretly.

Both of these components that define 'robbery', stealing in full view of the public and using force, are indirectly confirmed by one of the Tabarestān documents.[141] Tab. 22 is a letter (dated to the year 104 PYE = 755/756 CE) from the *rad* of Parišwārgar[142] (named Windād-Xwaršēd) to an official (named Xradzād) in charge of judicial affairs in the 'residence' (*dar-espās*) of the King of Parišwārgar in *Halīg.[143] In his letter the *rad* reports that a complaint (*garzišn*) has been filed in the presence of the said *rad* regarding an alleged act of robbery and he requests the official Xradzād to undertake a thorough investigation of the case in situ. The complainant in this case is a scribe whose name occurs frequently in the Tabarestān documents (Burzēn-Pērōz, son of Farroxgušnasp, resident in the village of *Asp-gurd, from the house of Dēl-Dēlān). He is accompanied by another person, called the '*painter of adornments' (*payr(ā)[s]tag-nigār*) from the guild (*pēšag*) of artisans, who is not introduced, but is presumably either the manufacturer of the appropriated objects, consisting of ornaments or jewels (*payrāyag*) and chalices (*ǰāmag*), or the representative of the guild that produced these items. By filing his suit the complainant makes two requests:

1. He asks the court to grant him a delay or 'postponement' (*pādrōzag*) (we are not told the reason, but can assume that payment had to be made to the manufacturer[s] of the robbed goods for which the claimant requests a postponement).
2. He demands 'satisfaction' (*hušnūdīh*), *i.e.* restitution and compensation, by a verdict that is 'legally binding' (*ēwēn-būd*) for an occurrence, which he describes as an act of robbery.

The accused persons are four men from the village of *Asp-gurd, who are named by the complainant (Dādgušnasp, son of *Ātars; Yazd, his brother; Rāstdād, son of Wištāsp; Yazdsar, son of Dēlāzād). They have violently seized from the *pādixšāy*-wife (named Sazā) of the complainant 'ornaments/jewels' (*payrāyag*) and 'chalices/vessels' (*ǰāmag*), worth altogether the sum of 500 stater, by an

141 For an extensive study of Tab. 22 see WEBER 2019b, pp. 97–101, and MACUCH 2019b, pp. 125–132. A transcription and translation of the whole document is in Appendix XIII, pp. 723–725, with several recent readings and changes as compared to the earlier versions in the cited studies.

142 On the location of Parišwārgar see GYSELEN 2019b, pp. 129, 172–173, with maps illustrating the assumed location of the region, corresponding roughly to Mazandarān today.

143 On the reading **Halīg* and the possible location of the residence of the King between Āmol and Sarī (NP Halī [Bāγ], Bābolsar County, in the province of Māzandarān) see WEBER 2016b, p. 190.

act of coercion and force ('by violence and shouting' *pad stahm ud xrōst*). The accused persons have taken these items from a skin bag (*mašk*), which, in the words of the complaint, 'they tear away (*abar wišāyēnd*) and tie up (*bandēnd*)'.

The *rad* asks the official Xradzād to check the registers (*ayāragīhā*) of the persons accused of this violent act, to summon these men to a hearing and to reach a verdict that will satisfy the complainant and restrain him from proceeding to the next instance. Should the latter uphold his complaint, the *rad* gives order (*framān*) that the case be brought before him. He then gives concrete instructions to the recipient of the letter, the official *Xradzād*, to undertake the following measures:

1. to examine the circumstances of Burzēn-Pērōz's complaint by hearing the statements of the men accused of robbery (Dādgušnasp and the other three men);
2. to give judgement (*wizīr ud dādwarīh*) if the circumstances of the case correspond to the description of the complainant;
3. to register proof (*čim*) 'explicitly and clearly' (*gōwizār ud rōšn*) so that the complainant may reach satisfaction (be 'made uncomplaining', *abēmustīh rasād*)[144] by 'judicial means' (*pad rāh ī dādestān*);
4. to order the accused Dādgušnasp to name the men involved in the case and to dispatch them back (*abāz wisē kardan*) together with the complainant Burzēn-Pērōz so that legal action may be taken (*pahikārdan*).

The letter does not give a reason for the last instruction, but we may assume that the circumstances of the case would require further inquiries, and also the punishment of the delinquents, if this was in fact a criminal act of robbery and no other conclusive reasons are put forward for forcefully seizing the items from the complainant's wife.

Both features of robbery are visible in this remarkable document: the four perpetrators take possession of the objects in public, they are even known by name, and they use force or put the victim in fear of being subjected to force (*pad stahm ud xrōst* 'by violence and shouting'). Unfortunately we have no knowledge whatsoever of the background of this case, but it is obviously not one of the usual crimes of anonymous highway robbery, since the perpetrators could be easily identified and were known to the complainant and his wife. We even have good reason to assume that the four men had some plausible reason to appropriate the objects, possibly because of some kind of unfulfilled obligation on part of the complainant Burzēn-Pērōz (as compensation for a liability; for not keeping a contract or failing to return a loan, etc.) or because they laid claim to the items—or to a part of them—in the skin bag. The motivation would have an impact on the verdict (although resorting to self-help would be nevertheless an unlawful act).

144 On the technical terms *abēmustīh* 'uncomplaining, content, satisfied' and *abēmust kardan* 'to satisfy, make content, uncomplaining', specifically: to satisfy a claimant by a decision that will not lead to an appeal in the next instance', see Macuch 2019b, p. 127, and Chapter VI, pp. 522–526.

It is most fortunate that another document (Tab. 22bis) in form of a formal letter referring explicitly to this case has survived, which was recorded only two years later.[145] It shows that this was indeed not a simple act of highway robbery, although the objects were seized in the manner described by the complainant, but had another background. The complaint went through several legal instances during the period of two years that separates the two documents. The first man accused of robbery, Dādgušnasp, obviously laid claim to the items in the skin bag (due to reasons not revealed). The main problem at this stage still seems to be the question, whether the seized items (or at least some of them) belonged to the complainant, Burzēn-Pērōz (and his wife, Sazā) or to the accused Dādgušnasp. The letter (Tab. 22bis) discloses that the complainant and his wife are attempting to prove their entitlement to the items taken by Dādgušnasp by presenting documents, which show that specific objects in the bag were part of the dower of the wife. These items are listed in a (separate) document (*wizīr*) and in the (marriage) contract (*paymān*). The letter is (presumably) from a higher legal official to the *keeper of archives (*zaydār*) and the Elder (*mahistag*) of the village of **Asp-gurd* instructing them to hear the statement of the wife regarding these items and to treat it as 'final evidence' (*čim ī abdom*) bringing this case to a close. The outcome of the proceedings is not recorded.

Theft (*duzīh*) is the subject of a whole section of *Dēnkard* 8, disclosing several significant details on the treatment of thieves and their accomplices in the typically short and ambiguous style of this source.[146] If my reading of this truly challenging text is correct, we can at least draw a few conclusions on how Zoroastrian communities dealt with thieves (although the most intriguing questions are not answered in this far too concise synopsis of the *nask*). According to this summary of matters pertaining to the thief (*duz*) and his accomplice (*abāg*),[147] the atonement for theft involved three measures:[148]

1. First, the degree or grade of the sin was determined (*ān ī-š trift passazag wināh* 'the suitable [degree of] sin for the theft' or *pāyag ī duzīh* 'degree of theft'); presumably following the Zoroastrian categorization of sins and offences described below pp. 468–486, which took both the severity of the offence and the number of repetitions into consideration.
2. Corporal punishment was executed in the form of fettering the thief and mutilating or branding him (*band ud drōš*).[149]

145 The whole text is in Appendix XIII, pp. 725–727; for an extensive study of this document see Weber 2022a, pp. 115–118, and Macuch 2022a, pp. 144–149.
146 DkD 548.1–549.8 (DkM 721.1–722.15). A tentative reading and translation of the whole first section of the *nask* is in Appendix VII, pp. 685–689, (the recent Persian edition of Fārsānī 2018, pp. 106–109, differs considerably from the interpretation proposed here).
147 On this reading see Appendix VII, pp. 685–686, fn. 3 and 8.
148 DkD 548.2–5 (DkM 721.2–5); Appendix VII, pp. 685–686.
149 On *band ud drōš*, the punishment for theft, see below pp. 441–447.

3. A compensation was fixed as redemption for the sin (*wizārišn ī wināh*) according to the apportioned punishment (*baxtīg pādofrāh*). The recompense could be in kind, such as an animal from the livestock, or it could be a money fine to be paid to the victims ('litigants', *hamēmālān*, see below).[150]

The last element in this list, redemption by delivering a compensation in kind, was apparently one of the main means of satisfying the victim (both at the time of the composition of the Avestan text and in the Sasanian period), as it is discussed in detail in the *nask* and is also mentioned in the Law-book. We are informed that an animal from the livestock was to be submitted as 'cattle-atonement' (**fšŭ-ciϑā-*; reminiscent of the pastoral communities, in which these texts took form) and that the compensation involved different types of animals according to the measure of the crime: these were discussed one by one in the original text (*čandīh ī ǰud ǰud andar ēk ēk pāk kadāmīh* '[on] the extent of every separate [atonement], one by one, which one of the young animals [should be submitted]').[151] Interestingly, the same form of compensation in kind is mentioned in the Law-book as ⟨p'k pswc'š'⟩ **pāk(a) fšŭ-ciϑā-* 'atonement in kind by (submitting) a young animal', albeit in another context, that of *azišmānd* offences (obstruction of justice), as an alternative to paying a money fine:

MHDA 15.2
*pad azišmānd har ān kē mādag hast mādag ud ān kē nēst *pāk(a) fšŭ-ciϑā-.*

'For an obstruction (of justice) (*azišmānd*) every one who has money (pays a fine) in money (*mādag*), who has none, atones in kind (**pāk(a) fšŭ-ciϑā-* "by [submitting] a young animal from the livestock as atonement").'[152]

150 As we have already noted above, the term *wizārišn* 'atonement, payment' is also employed as a legal term in Sasanian law: *wizārdan*, lit. 'to atone, expiate' has usually the very concrete meaning of 'to pay, reimburse, remunerate' (besides *tōxtan*, lit. 'to fulfil, redeem', which is used in the same concrete sense of 'to pay, reimburse, remunerate') in the context of loans, debts and compensations to be paid for a damage, see p. 63 (for attestations of these terms see Macuch 1993, index pp. 738 and 734 respectively). The compensation for theft is also mentioned in DkM 710.11–12: *ud abar čandīh tōzišn ī band ud drōš ud pādofrāh ī asparōn anumē ud stōr ī duzīdag čē andar ham dar.* 'And on the amount of atonement/payment as penalty for theft *(band ud drōš* "fetters and mutilation") and the punishment (worth) an *asparōn* and a sheep and large cattle that has been stolen, and that, which (is) in the same chapter.' The term *asparōn*, Av. *aspərəna-* (Bartholomae 1904, col. 218, 'Name einer Münze') in Vd. 4.48 and 5.60 seems to designate an object (or animal) worth as much as a drachm or, as Andrés-Toledo 2022, p. 27, argues, 10 drachms (according to other Vd. mss.). In his extensive discussion of Avestan *aspərəna-* he concludes that the term originally designated a 'he-goat' and that the cited passage refers to the exact price for a goat, which would fit in very well with the other animals named in this context. On the Pahlavi versions of the *Wīdēwdād* Passages see Moazami 2014, pp. 116–117; 162–163.

151 DkD 548.4–5 (DkM 721.4–5); Appendix VII, pp. 685–686.

152 Macuch 1981, pp. 37, 144, with a correct translation, but inaccurate reading; see also Appendix VII, fn. 6. On *azišmānd* offences see Chapter VI, pp. 561–569.

This remarkable passage allows the conclusion that offering compensation for an offence in kind was still an option in the Sasanian period, but the Avestan **pāk(a) fšŭ-ciϑā-* might have been already used as a general technical term designating any type of payment in kind, not only cattle and other livestock animals, in contrast to 'money' (*mādag*). The *Dēnkard* passage states later that the victims of the theft (here: *hamēmālān* 'litigants', that is, the persons who take legal action against the thief) are entitled to the compensation in ownership *(band ud band ī šahr hamēmālān xwēš arz ī ān ī guharīgōmand*, lit. 'fetters and fetters of the State: the litigants (receive) in ownership the value of the thing that is to be compensated').[153] This statement discloses unequivocally that theft belonged to the offences of the *hamēmālān* category, which could only be atoned for by compensating the victim(s), not by performing any other virtuous deeds, as we have seen above.[154]

The text continues with details on the second measure, that of corporal punishment, which was apparently executed in a specific place, called *kār gyāg ī pādofrāh* 'venue of execution of punishment'. Interestingly, our source differentiates between perpetrators and accessories, that is, between the thief himself and his accomplice (*abāg*). The two are separated at the outset of proceedings and the question, which of the two has initial responsibility for the theft, has to be addressed: who is the principal perpetrator and what kind of accomplice does he have (*čē tan ud ēwēnag ī abāg*); are both equally responsible or did one of the perpetrators initially commit the theft (*padisārīg kadām pēš kardan kard*)?[155] The problem of assessing the exact degree of responsibility of a thief and his accomplice seems to have been important and is taken up again later in this text (see below).[156]

The corporal punishment for theft consisted of two elements called consistently *band ud drōš* 'fetters and mutilation/branding' in the sources. Our text suggests that the punishment of *band* 'fetters' consisted of tying the limbs (*band hannām*) of the perpetrator in a tormenting (*+bēšišn*) manner and that both the degree of 'tightness' (*tangīh*) and the 'duration of the binding' (*drang ī bastag*) were determined by the degree of the offence committed by the thief. The term 'fetters/binding of the land' (*band ī šahr*) is not explained in this context, but could refer to some kind of additional confinement of the thief provided by the State, such as imprisonment (which was definitely part of the punishment in the Sasanian era, at least after the fourth theft, as we may conclude from a passage of the Law-book, see below).[157]

153 DkD 548.8–9 (DkM 721.9–10); Appendix VII, pp. 686–687. On *hamēmālān xwēš* see below p. 447.
154 DkD (M) 89.14–90.1 (DkM 696.16–18); see Appendix VI, p. 682: a sin regarding opponents (*wināh ī hamemālān*) cannot be atoned for by any other virtuous deed (*kirbag*) except towards the adversary himself (who receives the compensation). On *hamēmālān xwēš* compare MHD 73.2 (see below, p. 447).
155 DkD 548.5–6 (DkM 721.6–7); Appendix VII, p. 686.
156 DkD 548.17–549.1 (DkM 721.20–722.5); Appendix VII, p. 688.
157 DkD 548.7–8 (DkM 721.7–9); Appendix VII, pp. 686–687. On MHD 73.1–2 see p. 447.

The *drōš* punishment consisted originally of a visible mark cut or burnt in the skin of the perpetrator, stigmatizing him as a thief or robber.[158] Our source indicates that the extent of the mutilation or branding and the exact type of cut or brand was determined precisely according to the degree of the theft (*pāyag ī duzīh*), following the requirements of the penal law of the land/State (*drōz ī šahr*; *drōšīh ī šahr*). It was considered as an offence or sin (*wināh*) to impose an extreme penalty, to mutilate/brand the thief in an excessive or different way (*wēš ǰud ēwēnag drōšišnīh*) than in the prescribed manner, but it was likewise sinful to dispense altogether with the penalty required by the State (*hišt drōšīh ī šahr*). However, the passage also suggests that this type of corporal punishment could be replaced by a 'compensation for mutilation/branding' (*drōšīh guharīg*) in kind or in money that was conveyed to the victims of the theft (lit. 'litigants') in ownership (*hamēmālān xwēš*).[159]

These are more or less fragmentary entries, which, however, make perfect sense if we assess them in the light of another important source, the so-called letter of Tansar (either from the reign of Ardašīr, the founder of the Sasanian dynasty, or Husraw I, if we prefer to explain this text as propaganda for the

158 The term *drōš* < Av. *draoša-* (Bartholomae 1904, col. 770) has been discussed extensively by Bartholomae 1911–1918 (here: III, 1913, pp. 352–353); Bailey 1930–32b, pp. 594–595; Pagliaro 1951, 52–56; and Buyaner 2016, pp. 448–453. Cheung 2007, p. 80, tentatively derives *draoša-* from the Ir. root **drau(H)š* 'to make a mark, brand?' and treats it as an 'ingressive s-formation of a root **dreuH-*'. Buyaner (*ibid.*) has a divergent etymological explanation, which takes the parallel MP form *drōz* (besides *drōš*) into consideration, reconstructing the Iranian prototype of *drōz* <**drau̯ź-a-* and *drōš* < *drau̯š-a-* from a primary root **dhrau̯-* (< IE **dhreu̯-*) with the abstract meaning 'to harm', 'which was subsequently specified by means of different amplifications' (*ibid.*, p. 453). The use of MP *drōš* has been already established by Bartholomae (*ibid.*), who concluded correctly that the word designated a punishment for theft, and Bailey (*ibid.*) who determined its meaning as 'a mark cut or burnt in' by comparison with the Armenian loanword *drošm* used in the same sense (compare also NP *darūš* 'the wound or impression made by a cautery or surgical instrument'; Steingass 1892, p. 515). That besides mutilation also branding must have been designated by the term, is evident in the *Dēnkard* passage cited by Bailey: *abar drōšīdan ī* +*gōspandān* 'On the branding of sheep' (DkM 763.3; Bailey, *ibid.*, p. 595). Buyaner (*ibid.*, p. 451, fn. 646) seems to doubt that *drōš* designated the punishment for theft due to the attestations of the term in the context of credit law, but he has not perceived that the notions of 'robbery' and 'theft' as well as the corresponding punishments were transposed to other fields of law (particularly credit law and sale!) by the Sasanian period, using the same terms, as we have elucidated above (see pp. 312–315). His translation of *drōš* as 'torturing' in *band ud drōš* 'fetters and torturing' follows the Neo-Pahlavi gloss *šekanje ud rēš* 'tortures and wounds', but does not take the explicit description of punishments for theft, notably in the letter of Tansar, into consideration, which do not refer to torture in this context, but rather confirm the meaning 'a mark cut or burnt in', in any case a visible mutilation (by cutting off the ears and the nose) or branding inflicted to stigmatize the offender (see the following).

159 DkD 548.9–14 (DkM 721.11–17); Appendix VII, p. 687.

reforms of the latter king transposed into the reign of the former).[160] Two passages are relevant for our topic:

> *siyum ānki bi-rūzgār-i sābiqa sunnat ān būd ki zananda rā bāz zanand-u ḫasta kunanda rā ḫasta kunand wa ġāṣib-u sāriq rā muṯla kunand wa zānī rā hamčenīn … sunnat farmūd ki ǧarāḥat-u ġarāmat [har dō ṣudūr yābad] muṯla čēnānki ẓālim az ān bi-ranǧ āyad wa maẓlūm rā manfaʿat rasad na čenānki duzd rā čūn dast bi-burrand hīč kas rā manfaʿat na-buwad wa nuqṣān fāḥiš dar miyān-i ḫalq ẓāhir āyad. wa ġāṣib rā [ġarāmat] čahār čandān ki duzd rā wa zānī rā bīnī bi-burrand wa dīgar hīč ʿużwī ki quwwat nāqiṣ šawad ǧudā na-kunand tā ham īšān rā ʿār-u šanar bāšad wa ham bi-kār-u ʿamal nuqṣān nayuftad wa īn aḥkām dar kitāb-i sunūn bi-farmūd niwištand.*[161]

> 'Third, in former times the norm was that the one who dealt a blow (*zananda*) received a blow in return and the one who inflicted a wound (*ḫasta kunanda*) received a wound (in retaliation) and the robber (*ġāṣib*) and the thief (*sāriq*) were mutilated (*muṯla kunand*) and the adulterer (*zānī*) likewise. He (= the king) ordered a law by which the wound (*ǧarāḥat*) and the fine (*ġarāmat*) (for it) both be fixed (and) mutilation (*muṯla*) be executed in a manner that the perpetrator (*ẓālim*) be afflicted (*bi-ranǧ āyad*) and the victim (*maẓlūm*) receive a benefit, (but) not in this manner: when the hand of a thief is cut off, no one benefits hereof and disproportionate wastage is caused among people. And the compensation (extracted from) the robber (*ġāṣib*) (is) four times as much as that (taken) from the thief (*duzd*) and the nose of the adulterer is cut off. And no member may be severed, by which diminished capacity would arise (*quwwat nāqiṣ šawad*), so that they (= the perpetrators) may suffer both shame and disgrace (*ʿār-u šanar*), but their work and activity be not diminished. And he ordered these decrees to be written in a book of laws.'

> *qużāt rā amr kardīm ki agar īn ǧamāʿat-i muǧrimān ki ġarāmāt-i īšān muʿayyan ast pas az īn ġarāmāt nubatī dīgar bā gunahā muʿāwadat kunand gūš-u bīnī bi-burrand wa dīgar ʿużw rā taʿrīż na-rasānand.*[162]

> 'We have ordered the judges that if this group of culprits (*muǧrimān*), whose compensations (*ġarāmāt*) are fixed, after (paying) the compensations repeat their offences a second time, their ears and noses be cut off, but not to extend (the punishment) to another limb.'

This important source, written by the alleged dispatcher of the letter, Tansar/Tōsar, the prime minister of Ardašīr, reveals that the punishments for theft and robbery (besides adultery) were reformed by the founder of the Sasanian dynasty (or by Husraw I in the 6th century) in a remarkable manner: all measures mentioned in the Avestan *nask*, are retained, but obviously modified to comply with the changed necessities of the times. The text informs us that in 'former

160 On this source see Chapter I, p. 52.

161 Persian text in Darmesteter 1894, p. 220, lines 6–17; compare Boyce 1968a, pp. 42–43. The preceding sentences of this important text are translated below in Chapter VI, pp. 490–491.

162 Persian text in Darmesteter 221, lines 11–15; compare Boyce 1968a, p. 43.

times' assault and physical injury were dealt with by the law of retaliation, *ius talionis*, and that the robber (*ġāṣib*) and the thief (*sāriq*) were punished by mutilation (*muṯla*; presumably the equivalent of *drōš* in the Pahlavi original of the letter); the adulterer (*zānī*) received a similar punishment.[163] Corporal punishment for theft involved cutting off the hand of the perpetrator, hereby disabling him and hindering him in his tasks. This type of mutilation is henceforth explicitly forbidden by the King in order to retain the working capacity of the offenders. His reform involves three measures, which were written down in a 'book of laws' (*kitāb-i sunūn*):

1. For every type of physical injury (*ǧarāḥat*) he fixes a fine (*ġarāmat*) in a manner profitable to the victims; the compensation paid by the robber (*ġāṣib*) is four times more than the one paid by the thief (*duzd*).
2. He orders mutilation (*muṯla*) of the offender in a manner that afflicts the perpetrator and stigmatizes him visibly, making him 'suffer shame and disgrace' (*ʿār-u šanar bāšad*) by cutting off the nose and ears (according to the second quoted passage), but does not hinder him in his work.
3. He orders judges to punish repeat offenders, who have paid a fine for the first offence, by cutting off their ears and noses (*gūš-u bīnī bi-burrand*) the second time, but not to mutilate another limb.

Are these details a reliable account of how robbers and thieves were punished in the early (or late) Sasanian period? Apart from the parallels to the *Dēnkard* text discussed above, several similarities can be detected in the Law-book regarding the punishment of thieves and robbers:

> MHDA 15.2–4
> *pad duz drōš ī šahr mādag 10 bāy pad appar mādag čahār bāy pad bōdōzed ud kādōzed guharīg ī mādag ō bun-xwēšān ud rēš ō wināhgārān dād rāy wizīr kardan.*
>
> 'Judgement is to be given (*wizīr kardan*) with regard to a thief (*duz*) the punishment ("mutilation/branding") of the State (*drōš ī šahr*): ten times the amount of the (stolen) money (*mādag 10 bāy*); with regard to the robber (*appar*): four times the amount of the (stolen) money (*mādag čahār bāy*); with regard to intentional injury (*bōdōzed*) and injury by negligence (*kādōzed*): a compensation in money (= a fine; *guharīg ī mādag*) to the owners of the substance (*bun-xwēšān*) and (judgement is to be given) regarding the submission of the offenders to physical injury (*rēš*) (= corporal punishment).'[164]

The different components of the penalty for theft and robbery subsumed under *drōš ī šahr* in this text suggest that the term was not only used in its literal sense

163 For *muṯla*, a form of punishment which was obviously retained in the Islamic period, Steingass 1892, 1172–1173, has: 'making an example of (a homicide) by mutilating (him) in the nose, ears, lips, or extremities, and leading (him) about the streets mounted on an ass.'

164 Macuch 1981, pp. 37, 144.

('mutilation/branding of the land/State'), but as a technical term for the whole complex of measures taken by the State to punish the thief and the robber, including both corporal punishment (*rēš*) and compensation in money *(guharīg ī mādag)* to be paid to the victims of the criminal act, the 'owners of the (stolen) substance' (*bun-xwēšān*). According to this passage the verdict (*wizīr*) against a thief and a robber has to contain the following elements:

1. The thief has to recompense the victim by paying him the tenfold equivalent (*mādag 10 bāy*) of the stolen object; the robber by paying him the fourfold amount (*mādag čahar bāy*).[165]
2. Injury caused willfully (*bōdōzed*) or by negligence (*kādōzed*) is to be recompensed by a fine (*guharīg ī mādag*).[166]
3. The offenders are subjected to corporal punishment (*rēš*).

The two main elements of the penalty, compensation and corporal punishment, correspond to those described in the letter of Tansar (albeit with less details), but there is a divergence regarding the amount of compensation to be paid by the thief and the robber: according to the letter of Tansar four times more recompense is to be extracted from the robber than from the thief, whereas the Law-book requires a larger amount from the thief (tenfold) than from the robber (fourfold). Interestingly, the second element of the verdict, the additional compensation to be paid for injuries caused willfully (*bōdōzed*) or negligently (*kādōzed*), is also mentioned in the *Dēnkard* in its summary of the treatment of thieves and their accomplices (without further explanation).[167] Despite the shortness of the entries, we can surmise that the particularities of a theft were examined according to certain criteria, which may have had an impact on the verdict: first, the question of willful or negligent injury (*bōdōzed ud kādōzed*) on part of the thief and his accomplice (*duz [ud] abāg*); second, the question, whether other offences were committed by the thief before being joined by his accessory, and which offences were committed afterwards, which ones together with the accomplice (*wināh pad pēšīh ud pasīh hiδih*). In this context the criminal intent of the thief (*duz-menišnīh*) seems to have been of importance: did he carry out the theft alone, without the accomplice (*nē ham*), or together with an accomplice, sharing the stolen goods (*ham-bahr duzīh*), or did the thief and his accomplice divide the stolen goods into separate shares *(ǰud-bahr duzīh)*? That both the 'intent of the thief' (*duz menišnīh/menišnīgīh*) and the 'intent of the robber' (*appar-menišnīgīh*) were taken into account by judicial instances is confirmed in a passage of the *Hērbedestān*, which will be discussed below.[168]

165 On *bāy* < Av. *baga-*, *baγa-*; *bāga-* 'portion, lot' see Bartholomae 1904, col. 921, 951 ['Anteil, Los']; Parthian *bg*, Durkin-Meisterernst 2004, p. 106, 'portion, present'; MP *hambāy* 'shareholder, partner'.
166 On the technical terms *bōdozed* and *kādōzed* see pp. 417–422.
167 DkD 548.17–549.1 (DkM 721.20–722.5); Appendix VII, p. 688.
168 Hēr. 6.6–6.7; see pp. 454–458; the whole passage is in Appendix VIII.

Other questions were addressed in the original Pahlavi text of the *nask* with respect to the verdict, regarding the sentence against a perpetrator whose crime is 'obvious' (+*āškārag*), but who denies having committed it (*nagīrāygar*), and the opposite case of a sentence, by which the accused is found to be innocent, the claim dismissed and the accused acquitted (*hišt ud bōxt wizīr*). Three groups of perpetrators are finally named in this section, for whom special regulations seem to have existed: underage children (*aburnāyīg*), childless women (*zan ī starwan*) and pregnant women (*ābestan*). We are only informed that their 'possessions (and) earnings' (*dārišn windišn*) are to be retained as atonement (*tōzišnīg kār*) for the theft. Providing evidence for the theft is another problem discussed in the next passage: how to proceed, when the thief is caught red-handed with the stolen goods (*pad dast* 'in his hands'), how, when the stolen goods are not in his possession (*nē pad dast* 'not in his hands') and the question, whether the testimony of a thief against another thief is acceptable as evidence.[169]

The answers to these questions are not transmitted, but the concise summary of the *nask* suggests that the judge was obliged to investigate a large number of issues, besides taking the particular circumstances of a theft or robbery into consideration, before reaching a verdict. That the concrete circumstances of a theft were important and taken into account, is confirmed in one of the noteworthy cases transmitted in the Law-book:

> MHDA 35.6–9
> *zan kē šōy pad adwadād dāštānmāh wizārdan wināhgār ka duz kunēd duz nē zan bē šōy bawēd. ud pas ka-š gīrēnd ēwēn ī šahr rāy be drōšišn.*
>
> 'If a woman, whose husband is guilty of "abandonment/withdrawal of sustenance" (*adwadād*), commits a theft (during the observance of her) monthly (menstrual) cycle, (then) not the wife, but the husband is considered as a thief. And afterwards, when he is arrested, he is to be punished/mutilated (*be drōšišn*) according to the law of the State (*ēwēn ī šahr*).'[170]

The background of this ruling is of course the legal obligation of the husband as the guardian of his wife to maintain her and to sustain her particularly during the period of menstruation, when a woman is in enclosure and not allowed to take part in any social or religious activities (including the preparation of food). In our passage a husband commits the offence of *adwadād*, that is, he abandons his wife by failing to sustain her.[171] If she then commits a theft (in a state of emergency in order to sustain herself, as we may add) during menstruation, then not she is guilty of theft, but the husband, who has caused the criminal act (willfully or by negligence). He is hence sentenced to punishment (by fine/mutilation) according to the 'law of the State' (*ēwēn ī šahr*).

169 DkD 549.1–5 (DkM 722.6–10); Appendix VII, p. 688.
170 Macuch 1981, pp. 61, 218. On *ēwēn ī šahr* see Colditz 2023.
171 On the offence of *adwadād* see Macuch 2012a; 2012b and pp. 463–468.

We have already noted that by the Sasanian period the term *drōš* (particularly in *drōš ī šahr*) was used as a technical expression to designate both elements of the punishment for theft (and robbery), consisting of corporal punishment as well as the payment of a compensation or fine to the victims. But the term could also be used as a technical term for the compensation alone, as we can deduce from the phrase *drōš hamēmālān xwēš*, lit. 'the *drōš* (is) the litigants' own', which can mean nothing else than that the victims, or claimants *(hamēmālān)* in a lawsuit regarding theft, are entitled as owners to the recompense paid by the thief. This is somewhat more clearly expressed in connection with the other term referring to the penalty for theft, *band*, in the phrase *band ud band ī šahr hamēmālān xwēš arz ī ān ī guharīgōmand* 'fetters and fetters of the State: the litigants (receive) in ownership the value of the (stolen) thing that is to be compensated'.[172] The following passage of the Law-book also uses this abbreviated phrase:

> MHD 73.1–2
> *ka 4 bār drōš kard ud pas-iz any wināh ī pad ān ēwēnag kunēd hagriz az zēndān be nē hilišn ud drōš hamēmālān xwēš.*
>
> 'When he (= the thief) has received the punishment for theft (*drōš*) four times and afterwards commits another offence of that kind, (then) he is never to be released from prison. And the *drōš* (= the penalty/compensation for theft) is the litigants' own.'[173]

The passage is clear enough: a thief who repeats his offence a fifth time, after having been already punished four times with the penalty for theft (*drōš*), is sentenced to a lifetime in prison; the victims receive in ownership the compensation paid by the thief as an element of the penalty (*drōš hamēmālān xwēš*). We can hence conclude that both *band* and *drōš* were employed not only in their concrete sense of 'fetters' and 'mutilation/branding' respectively, but as *technical terms for the whole punishment for theft*, including the compensation (*guharīg*), and could even refer primarily (as in the shortened phrases quoted above) to the compensation alone.

This curtailed use of terms and phrases is not unique, but fits in well with the abridged style of theologians and jurists writing for their schooled colleagues, who understood what was meant and needed no explanations. Elliptical sentences are typical for the jargon of the Pahlavi commentaries to the Avestan texts. These have repeatedly caused curious misunderstandings and wrong translations in the past and even in recent years, but this is in fact a style well known from other exegetical texts and is very similar to that of rabbinic discussions in the Babylonian Talmud. In chapter 6 of the *Hērbedestān*, for example, the long Pahlavi commentary discusses offences arising in a specific context,

172 DkD 548.8–9 (DkM 721.9–10); Appendix VII, p. 687.

173 Macuch 1993, pp. 489, 492. On *hamēmālān xwēš* in a corresponding context compare DkD 548.11 (DkM 721.9–10), Appendix VII, p. 687.

that of a woman, who seeks to pursue religious studies, with or without the authorization of her husband, and is accompanied by a man who is not her husband (possibly another male member of the woman's family, a brother, uncle etc., as an escort to protect the woman, but this is not said in the text). If this male companion injures the woman, he has to pay a recompense for the offence to the husband, or, in the condensed words of the passage, *ka rēšēd ā šōy xwēš* 'When he (= the companion) hurts her, then it (is) the husband's own', which can mean nothing else than that the husband is entitled to the compensation paid by the male escort for the offence of causing physical injury to his wife (in full compliance with the regulations noted on *rēš* in the preceding section above).[174] The immediately following part of this text discusses in a long Pahlavi commentary the offence of illicit sexual intercourse with the wife of another man in the same context.[175] Interestingly, the whole Pahlavi commentary, following the Avestan text, transposes the sexual offences committed in this setting into criminal law and treats them legally as theft or robbery with the same consequences (at least with regard to the compensation) for the perpetrator. Illicit intercourse with the wife of another person is called *tan-duzīh* 'body-theft' (not necessarily involving the offence of abduction) and was evidently punished accordingly. The text continues to explain to whom the compensation for this type of 'body-theft' has to be paid with the curtailed phrase:

> *čagar gāyēd duzīh čagar xwēš abārīg dūdag xwēš*
>
> '(If) he copulates with a *čagar*-wife, (then the compensation for) theft is the *čagar*-wife's own; (if it is) another (type of wife), it (= the compensation for theft) is the family's own.'[176]

This kind of abridged formulation was perfectly comprehensible to theologians and jurists, well acquainted with legal language: *čagar xwēš* can mean nothing else than '(it is) the *čagar*-wife's own'; *dūdag xwēš* '(it is) the family's own'. The content also corresponds perfectly with the details we have discussed above in the context of Sasanian family law: due to her specific status in an 'auxiliary

174 Hēr. 6.5 (according to KOTWAL/KREYENBROEK 1992, pp. 42–43); 6.9 (according to HUMBACH/ELFENBEIN 1990, pp. 46–47). The abridged content of this passage has not been understood correctly in any of the editions. HUMBACH/ELFENBEIN (*ibid.*) have: '... if he injures her then (he injures) her own husband'; KOTWAL/KREYENBROEK (*ibid.*): '... if he does harm her, then (the injury) is for the husband (to deal with)'.

175 This part of the text (Hēr. 6.6–6.7) is in Appendix VIII. See also section 4.1 on sexual offences, pp. 452–460.

176 Hēr. 6.7 § 3 (= 6.30); Appendix VIII, p. 694. None of the editions have the correct translation. HUMBACH/ELFENBEIN 1990, p. 53, read '*čagar gāyēd duzīh* [*cager xwēš abārīg dūdag ī xwēš ī pēšag*]' and render the phrase by '(When) he cohabits with the co-wife (of someone else he is guilty of) theft (of a body) [(*i. e.* when he cohabits with) the co-wife of another (member) of a family of his own class].' KOTWAL/KREYENBROEK 1992, p. 45, translate: '(If) he has intercourse with a *čagar*-wife, the theft concerns the *čagar*-wife (only); in other cases, it concerns the family.'

marriage', the *čagar*-wife does *not* belong to the family of the *čagar*-husband and is *not* under his guardianship, hence the recompense for 'body-theft' goes to her personally, not to the family of the husband. In contrast, other wives (of *pādixšāy* status, as we may add) are members of the husband's lineage and family (*dūdag*), hence it is the family that receives the compensation for 'body-theft' in these cases. Corporal punishment is not mentioned in this context or in the Law-book (but according to the Tansar letter cited above, the nose of the adulterer was cut off; see also section 4.1 on sexual offences, pp. 452–460).

To conclude, Sasanian law, following the Avesta, distinguishes between the thief and the robber. The former steals stealthily, in secret, the latter in full view of the public, using force or threatening to use force in some manner. The expressions 'thief' and 'robber' and the corresponding penalties are transposed to offences in other fields of law, particularly credit law and other transactions, such as sale and barter. Sexual offences infringing on the rights of another man are also treated as theft or robbery and differentiated according to the criteria named above, distinguishing between the '(criminal) intent of the thief' (*duz menišnīh/menišnīgīh*) and the '(criminal) intent of the robber' (*appar-menišnīgīh*).[177] The two basic punishments for theft are *band ud drōš*, lit. 'fetters and mutilation/branding'; *band* designates originally the 'fetters' (bands and chains) with which the limbs of the perpetrator are tied in a painful manner for a fixed period of time in compliance with the degree (*pāyag*) of the offence; *band ī šahr*, lit. 'fetters/binding of the land/State', refers, moreover, to some kind of additional confinement provided by the State, such as imprisonment. Lifetime imprisonment in gaol (*zēndān*) was imposed if the perpetrator repeated the offence after the fourth theft. The term *drōš* designates originally a 'cut or brand', with which the thief was stigmatized visibly. The letter of Tansar reports that originally this punishment in an early period involved severing the hand of the thief, but that the King (Ardašīr or Husraw I) in the course of his legal reforms forbade the mutilation of a limb that was crucial for working and ordered instead to cut off the ears or noses of the offenders in order to shame them, retaining at the same time their working capacity. Both the *band* and the *drōš* penalties provided for a compensation (*guharīg*) either in money (*mādag*) or in kind (**fšu-ciϑā-*; an animal from the livestock) to be extracted from the offenders and transmitted to the victims (= litigants) in ownership (*hamemālān xwēš*). Moreover, both expressions, *band ud drōš*, were used as technical terms to designate the whole penalty for theft, encompassing two elements, recompense and corporal punishment, but the terms could also be individually employed to refer to the compensation alone.

177 On these terms see pp. 452–460.

Table 42. Overview: terminology relating to theft and robbery

Perpetrators		Definitions
abāg	'accessory, accomplice'	person who aids or supports the thief in some manner before or during the theft or after the offence has been committed (*wināh pad pēšīh ud pasīh hiδih* 'the offence committed before, after and together')[178]
appar; *apparag*	'robber'	person who steals manifestly (*āškārag* 'openly'), using force or threatening to use force (Av. *hazaŋhan-* 'robber'; Syriac translation: *ḥāṭōpā* 'robber'; lit. 'extortioner, plunderer, ravisher')
duz	'thief'	person who steals stealthily (*nihān* 'secretly') (Av. *tāiiu-* 'thief'; Syriac translation: *ganāḇā* 'thief')
stahmag	'robber' (lit. 'violent person'; 'oppressor')	person who steals manifestly (*āškārag* 'openly'), using force or threatening to use force (Av. *hazaŋhan-* 'robber')
Criminal Acts		Definitions
apparīh	'robbery'	appropriation of property in public, using force or threatening to use force
duzīh	'theft'	appropriation of property in secret
ham-bahr duzīh	'theft with common shares'	stealing property with an accomplice (*abāg*) and sharing the stolen goods
ǰud-bahr duzīh	'theft with separate shares'	stealing property with an accomplice (*abāg*) and dividing the stolen goods into separate shares
Punishments		Definitions
band	'fetters; binding'	tying the limbs of the perpetrator in compliance with the degree (*pāyag*) of the offence (by which the tightness, *tangīh*, of the fetters and the duration of the binding, *drang ī bastag*, are determined)
band ī šahr	'fetters; binding of the State'	Penalty of the State consisting of tethering the culprit (see *band*) and imprisonment (or some other form of confinement)

178 DkD 547.18 (Appendix VII, p. 688).

Punishments		Definitions
drōš	1. 'mutilation; branding; a mark cut or burnt in' 2. penalty for theft	1. a visible cut or brand stigmatizing the perpetrator as a thief or robber 2. technical term for the whole complex of measures taken to punish the offender, consisting of corporal punishment (*rēš*) and compensation in money (*guharīg ī mādag*) or in kind (**fšŭ-ciϑā-* 'cattle-atonement'). The latter is specifically referred to in *drōš hamēmālān xwēš* 'the penalty (= compensation) is the litigants' own'
drōš ī šahr; *drōšīh ī šahr*; *drōz ī šahr*	1. 'mutilation, branding of the State' 2. Penalty of the State for theft	1. Penalty of the State consisting of two measures, corporal punishment and compensation in money or in kind (see *drōš*) 2. technical term for the punishment for theft prescribed by the State
The Verdict		**Definitions**
appar-menišnīgīh	'criminal intent of the robber'	mental element (*mens rea*) of the crime: intention of the robber to appropriate property openly, using force
duz-menišnīh; *duz-menišnīgīh*	'criminal intent of the thief'	mental element (*mens rea*) of the crime: intention of the thief to appropriate property in secret
nagīrāygar	'person denying the crime'	the accused party pleading not guilty
hišt ud bōxt wizīr	'judgement dismissing (the claim) and acquitting (the accused)'	verdict of not guilty

4 Other transgressions

Not all of the countless sins listed in the penitential texts and other Pahlavi sources were subject to litigation as *hamemālān* sins, *i. e.* as transgressions involving an opponent, who was harmed or damaged in some manner and could hence take action against the offender by appealing to religious authorities or suing the perpetrator in a State court. Most of the noted offences consist of violations of moral and religious precepts, of purity laws and other sins damaging to the soul of the offender, but not necessarily infringing the rights of another party. There are among these, however, several offences that can be subject to punishment in both the *ruwānīg* and *hamēmālān* categories and will be taken into consideration in the following overview.

4.1 Sexual offences

We have seen in the context of family law how sexual alliances were regulated in a manner favourable to the uppermost echelons of Sasanian society by combining patrilineal descent with a flexible system of marriages, permitting aristocratic women to generate legitimate children for different men in the course of their lives. Seen from this perspective, the precise regulation of lawful sexual practises with the goal of producing numerous children was one of the central concerns, whereas, generally speaking, sexual acts that took place outside the framework of legal marriage and those that impeded the procreation of children were all strictly prohibited in Zoroastrianism. The penitential texts list the following sexual taboos:

1. *ǰehi-marz wināh* 'sin of copulation with a whore';[179]
2. *daštān-marz wināh* 'sin of copulation with a menstruating woman';[180]
3. *kūn-marz wināh* 'sin of anal intercourse (sodomy)';[181]
4. *abārōn-marzišnīh* 'unlawful sexual intercourse'.[182]

179 Buyaner 2016, pp. 337–343 (§37). For a thorough discussion of Av. *jahī-* and *jahikā-* 'bad female, witch, crone, meretrix', the general daēvic term for women (*i. e.* women who are sterile, use contraceptive methods and commit adultery, in sharp contrast to the Mazdean wife, *nāirikā-*, according to König 2010, p. 132,) and the Pahlavi *ǰeh* or *ǰahi/ǰehi* (as Buyaner 2016, p. 341, reads the word) 'whore, prostitute', see also de Jong 1995 and König 2010, pp. 121–132. According to Buyaner 2016 (p. 343) the background of the semantic development of the word from the general term for a 'bad woman' in Avestan to 'whore, prostitute' in Pahlavi and the prohibition against cohabiting with a whore in Pahlavi texts is the 'habitude of the "bad woman", particularly the prostitute (*i. e.* Phl. *jeh*, *jehi*), to mix the semen of different men, *i. e.* engage in promiscuity'.

180 Buyaner 2016, pp. 343–345 (§38). The taboos in the context of menstruation have been studied by König 2010, pp. 141–150, who interestingly concludes that the prohibition of cohabiting with a menstruating woman was due not only to the defiling effect of the act, but to its connotation with infanticide, since it was known that a bleeding which was artificially provoked after conception would cause a miscarriage (*ibid.*, p. 146). Buyaner 2016 (p. 345) furthermore infers that 'the underlying concept was obviously that a coition during the menses leads to immediate evacuation (*i. e.* killing) of the conceived embryo'

181 Buyaner 2016, pp. 345–346 (§39). König 2010 in his extensive study of sexuality (especially pp. 284–353; 402–431) concludes that the terms *kūn-marz* 'sodomite, sodomy, anal intercourse' (denoting both the perpetrator and the sin) and *kūn-marzīh* 'anal intercourse; sodomy', did not particularly refer to male homosexuality, but were used with respect to both genders and irrespective of the passive or active role of the involved individuals (p. 301). The bulk of the Pahlavi texts describe *kūn-marz* in drastic words, stressing the abhorrence and revulsion provoked by anal intercourse, which was

Unsurprisingly all these prohibitions involve sexual activities which, from the viewpoint of Zoroastrian doctrine, diametrically oppose the crucial Mazdean precept of reproducing, maintaining and propagating the creation of Ohrmazd, the religious foundation upon which family law was built in the form it assumed by the Sasanian period. As we have seen in Chapter II, sexuality and the procreation of offspring were regulated within the legal framework of matrimony, which involved the promotion of polygyny and the prohibition of polyandry, based on the concept of patrilineal descent, allowing a woman to be married to only one husband at a time and to generate children for this one man alone (despite legal strategies designed to circumvent the rule, such as time-limited marriage). The basic notion of keeping the seed of the man 'pure' whilst ensuring patrilineal descent is incompatible with the first sin in the list, cohabitation with a whore (*ǰeh/ǰehi*), who engages in promiscuity and mixes the semen of different men. The second sin in the list, sexual intercourse with a menstruating woman (*daštān-marz*), was not only conceived as defiling, but connoted with infanticide due to the observation of the similarity between the symptoms of miscarriage, abortion and menstrual bleeding. The most grievous sexual sin from the perspective of Zoroastrianism, anal-intercourse (*kūn-marz*, used with respect to both genders), was perceived as a horrifying, repulsive act, which involved the mingling of excrements, particularly faeces, with life-spending sperm, resulting, according to the ninth century theologian Manuščihr, in the 'destruction of offspring' (*zahag murnǰēnāg*) or, according to a presumably older idea, in the formation of noxious creatures and demons, in any case

obviously perceived by Zoroastrians not just as another offense, but as one of the gravest sins, if not the most grievous (König 2010, p. 353; see also Buyaner 2016, p. 346). As König has convincingly shown, the main background of this negative assessment seems to be the horror and nausea aroused by excrements, particularly faeces, in Zoroastrianism, which were perceived as a breeding ground for the emergence of evil and had to be neutralized and disposed of by specific ritual measures. The anus as their source was regarded as a place where 'offspring was destroyed' (*zahag murnǰēnāg*) and connoted with *dušox* 'hell', a place full of 'stench and burning' (*gand ud sōzag*), as its microcosmic equivalent. The notion that *kūn-marz* led to the destruction of life-giving sperm (according to Manuščihr) was juxtaposed against another, possibly older idea, that its practice led to the insemination of excrements and the formation of noxious creatures and demons by the mixture of faeces and sperm (König 2010, pp. 339; 352–353).

182 Buyaner 2016, pp. 347–354 (§ 40), according to whom 'unlawful sexual intercourse' covers, besides the sexual offences already mentioned (*ǰehi-marz*; *daštān-marz*; *kūn-marz*), the following sins: (1) seduction of another person's wife (*zan ī bēgānag*); (2) sexual intercourse with a woman of foreign faith (*zan ī anēr*); (3) cohabitation of a man with his own wife during pregnancy and within a specific period after delivery (forty days after childbirth; another forty days to avoid the interruption of lactation by a new pregnancy); (4) waste of semen (*šuδr winābišnīh*; Pāz. *šoiϑra.gunāh.sašnī*), which encompasses masturbation and unfruitful ejaculation (also unconsciously, during sleep); sex with a barren woman (*zan ī anāzāy gayēd*) or a woman incapable of lactation (*zan ī … pēm-judāg*); generally all sexual activities that 'render semen ineffective' (*kē šuδr a-kār be kunēd*).

contrary to the purpose of reproduction in Mazdaism. Similarly, the sexual taboos subsumed under *abārōn-marzišnīh* 'unlawful sexual intercourse' encompass, besides the sins noted above, all activities involving (1) the 'waste of semen' (*šuδr-wināhišnīh*), such as masturbation and unfruitful ejaculation (also unconsciously, during sleep) or sex with a barren woman (*zan ī anāzāy*) or a woman incapable of lactation (*zan ī … pēm-ǰudāg*) and (2) acts endangering the life of an embryo or infant, such as sex with one's own pregnant wife or within a prohibited period after childbirth (altogether 80 days). Besides these practices which 'render semen ineffective' (*kē šuδr a-kār be kunēd*), the prohibitions include sexual intercourse with an 'un-Iranian woman' (*zan ī anēr*), *i.e.* a foreigner or adherent of another faith, and with the wife of another man (*zan ī bēgānag*; lit. 'strange woman').[183]

We can reasonably infer that all these sexual offences were liable to punishment according to the *ruwānīg* category of sins. As far as I can see, the only sexual transgression actionable according to the *hamēmālān* category (involving the infringement of the rights of another individual) is the last one mentioned above, that of adultery, unlawfully seducing and cohabiting with the wife of another man (*zan ī bēgānag*). A long passage in the *Hērbedestān* addresses this offence in a specific context, that of a woman who requests religious knowledge and is accompanied by a man, who is not her husband.[184] The background is not elucidated, but we can assume from the scattered information in the same text and in other sources that not only priests, but also lay persons, both men and women, were directed to seek religious instruction by a priestly teacher, the *hērbed*, a priest well-versed in the Avesta and Zand and authorized to instruct disciples (*hāwišt*), in a type of priestly circle or school or according to a specific curriculum, called *hērbedestān*.[185] Women seeking religious education were obviously accompanied by a male for the purpose of ensuring their safety, besides other persons needed for domestic chores (such as the maidservant, *paristār*, mentioned in Hēr. 6.7, §4–6, who could also be a member of the family). The

183 See the preceding footnotes. Buyaner 2016 (p. 354) suggests that the underlying conception of the sinfulness of unfruitful ejaculation is the notion that 'the waste of semen results in a multiplication of demons' and divides the sexual taboos into three principle groups: '(1) defilement (*kun-marz*, *daštān-marz*, sexual intercourse with one's own wife before the expiry of the first 40-days period after delivery); (2) the mixing of semen (*jahi-marz*); (3) the injury inflicted upon one's offspring, whether born or unborn (*daštān-marz*, sexual intercourse with one's own wife before the expiry of the second 40-days period after delivery).'

184 Hēr. 6.6–6.7; see Appendix VIII. On this text see also p. 414 above.

185 The term *hērbedestān* has been understood as referring either to a specific place or to a specific course of religious studies. Kotwal/Kreyenbroek 1992, pp. 15, cite the following authors: 'Dhabhar (1949: gloss. 57) translates: "course of priestly studies, priestly duties, priestly college, theological seminary"; MacKenzie (1971: 43): "priestly school"; Shaked (1979: 330): "house of learning"; Humbach (1990, *passim*): "religious studies".' After discussing several sources in which the term appears, they conclude, that 'the type of study known as *hērbedestān* was open to priesthood and laity alike.' (p. 18).

passage relevant to our subject matter discusses sexual offences, which might occur in this context, if the man accompanying the woman is not her husband, but another male. The whole setting is not as strange as it might seem at first glance, if we assume that a husband could entrust his wife to another allegedly trustworthy male, such as her father, brother, uncle, or another relative from his own family, or the wife could place herself under the protection of one of these relatives. In fact Hēr. 6.7 §3 and §4–6 seem to indicate that this indeed was the background the exegetes had in mind and that several members of a family could form a troupe seeking religious knowledge (maybe similar to later religious pilgrimages in the Islamic period). The text (citing the exegete Sōšāns) uses the term *xwēdōdah* ('next-of-kin marriage') to designate the legitimate form of practising intercourse in this context (in contrast to the illegitimate form, called *tan-duzīh* 'body-theft') with specific reference to an (unmarried) maidservant accompanying the wife and her escort.

As we have already mentioned in the section on theft, the text treats the sexual offences committed under these conditions as theft or robbery with apparently similar consequences for the perpetrator. The problems addressed in the Pahlavi commentary deal with the transgressions of *gād-duzīh* 'theft of intercourse'[186] and *tan-duzīh* 'body-theft',[187] which in fact both designate illicit sexual intercourse (but obviously *not*, as the second term seems to suggest, in concurrence with abduction). The Avestan text treats this offence in a very elementary manner as theft or robbery, according to the definitions of these terms stated above (*i. e.* cohabiting secretly is dealt with as theft; cohabiting openly as robbery), but the Sasanian exegetes, operating under changed circumstances, evidently had a more complex approach and distinguished between several important issues, as we may conclude from their (partly controversial) discussion of the following questions:

1. Does the treatment of illicit sexual intercourse as theft or robbery apply in both cases, when the husband has authorized (Av. *haxta-*) an escort to accompany his wife, and likewise, when he has *not* authorized (Av. *anahaxta-*) a specific person for this task? That illicit intercourse should be treated as theft or robbery in both instances seems to be the opinion of most commentators, but one exegete maintains that this *only* applies in the latter case, when the husband has *not* explicitly authorized (Av. *anahaxta-*) a specific person as escort[188]
2. Does the escort accompany the woman with the intention of cohabiting with her (*pad gādan menišnīg*)? When does this intent become manifest: within the distance of a *hās*^{u}*r* or later? Does the perpetrator act with the 'intent of the thief' (*duz-menišnīgīh*) or with the 'intent of the robber'

186 Hēr. 6.7 §3 (Appendix VIII, p. 694).
187 Hēr. 6.7 §1 and §3 (Appendix VIII, pp. 692–693; 694 respectively).
188 Hēr. 6.1 (Appendix VIII, fn. 7) and 6.6 §1–2 (Appendix VIII, pp. 690–691).

(*appar-menišnīgīh*)? Unfortunately the text is far too concise and defective, but three factors seem to have been of importance in the assessment of the offence: (a) the intent to cohabit with the woman; (b) the distance at which the perpetrator commits the offence (within a *hās*ᵃ*r* or later); and (c) the use of force (*pad rēš*), which turns theft immediately into robbery. We are informed that the intention alone is not to be considered as theft or robbery, if the illicit act is not actually performed (see also 4 below). But if the perpetrator does carry out his specific intention (*gād pad uzkārišn* 'sexual intercourse with reflection'), then the assessment of the sin as theft or robbery depends on the outset (*az bunīh*) of the offence: if it begins with the escort accompanying the woman openly (but the cohabitation takes place secretly) the offender is assessed as a robber; if it begins with him leading her forth secretly (but the offence is manifest) the offender is a thief. This last part seems to be a very scholastic interpretation of the Avestan text, Hēr. 6. § 1–2, which is in fact ambiguous and had to be put into practice somehow.[189]

3. Who takes responsibility for the act of 'body-theft' (*tan-duzīh*), the perpetrator alone or both the perpetrator (= escort) and the guardian (*sālār*) of the woman? The answer is very clear: both persons are held responsible for the offence of 'body-theft' (*tan-duzīh*) every time it is committed. No matter under which circumstances the offence has taken place, the sin accruing 'to the stock is one (and the same)' (*pad ē[w] bun-ē*). Interestingly, the term used here is not 'husband', but 'guardian' (*sālār*), which need not necessarily refer to the husband, but could designate any another man engaged as guardian of the woman (father, brother, uncle etc.). In any case, the offence is a *ruwānīg* sin, which accrues to the stock (or account of sins) of both men involved directly and indirectly, since a guardian is obliged to protect his wards (that this sin is also treated as a *hamēmālān* offence becomes apparent later; see 5 below).[190]
4. Is the intent of cohabitation (*gād-menišnīg*) itself punishable, even if the escort abstains (*pādīrānēnīdan*) from sexual intercourse, or only the act itself? This question has already been dealt with rudimentarily at the beginning of this section (see 2 above). Two famous exegetes are cited: Sōšāns maintains that if the perpetrator only restrains himself for the (very small distance) of a *frārāst*, but then performs the act (as we may add), then he is considered as a thief. Kay-ādur-bōzēd contends that the man is only sinless if he practises refrainment. If he commits the act, the sin accrues to his stock (⁺*ō bun*) and goes to his account (*ō mar āyēd*).[191]

189 Hēr. 6.6 § 3–5 (Appendix VIII, pp. 691–692). A *hās*ᵃ*r* is a measure of time, an unequal hour (one-twelfth of daylight); or a measure of length, corresponding to a *frasang* or one-fourth of a *frasang*, approx. one mile (MacKenzie 1971, p. 43); Av. *hāϑra-* (Bartholomae 1904, col. 1802–1803).

190 Hēr. 6.7 § 1 (Appendix VIII, pp. 692–693).

191 Hēr. 6.7 § 2 (Appendix VIII, pp. 693–694).

5. Who receives the compensation for the offence of cohabiting with a woman under the guardianship of another man and who takes legal action? Up to this section of the text the sin of illicit sexual intercourse is treated as a *ruwānīg* sin, which accrues to the account of sins committed by the perpetrators if they do not follow the threefold scheme of contrition, confession and redemption.[192] This part, however, reveals that illicit sexual intercourse was also treated as an actionable *hamēmālān* offence, for which a compensation had to be paid to the victim(s). We are informed (in the typically elliptical style of the commentators) that the degree (*pāyag*) of the sin of 'body-theft' (*tan-duzīh*) was assessed according to the degree of 'theft of sexual intercourse' (*gād-duzīh*; unfortunately not explained) and that a man (= guardian?) takes legal action (*mard rāyēnēd*), except when he is 'far away' (*bē dūrīh*). The compensation paid for theft (*duzīh*) goes to the ownership of the family (*dūdag xwēš*). But in the case of illicit cohabitation with someone's *čagar*-wife, it is the woman herself who receives the compensation for the '(body-)theft' in ownership (*duzīh čagar xwēš*), since (as we may add) she is not under the guardianship of the *čagar*-husband and does not belong legally to his family.[193]
6. How is illicit sexual intercourse with a maidservant (*paristār*) accompanying the woman and her escort assessed? When is it permitted to enter a *xwēdōdah* (next-of-kin) marriage in this context? The final section of this text evidently discusses a completely different matter, copulation with a maidservant, who in this specific case is a member of the family of the perpetrator and is not married. This sin is assessed as a minor one (corresponding to the 'theft of goat-milk', *šīr ī buz duzīh*). Again Sōšāns is cited, according to whom a *xwēdōdah*-marriage can (or should) be arranged in order to enable legitimate intercourse, when the girl has reached the age of nine years and menstruates. Sexual intercourse before the onset of menstruation is prohibited, as it would cause physical injury (*rēš*).[194]

The text allows us to draw several general conclusions on the assessment of sexual abuses involving the wife of another man, apart from the specific context of this source. Adultery was obviously a sexual offence liable to punishment according to both *ruwānīg* and *hamēmālān* categories and was evaluated by religious authorities according to the following criteria: First, the mental element (*mens rea*) of the offence, *i. e.* the intent of the perpetrator to cohabit (*gādan menišnīg*) with the wife of another man, was assessed, either as the 'intent of the thief' (*duz-menišnīgīh*), if the act took place secretly within a certain timespan after deciding on it, or the 'intent of the robber' (*appar-menišnīgīh*), if the

192 On this scheme see Buyaner 2016, pp. 27, 30, and pp. 400–403 above.
193 Hēr. 6.7 § 3 (Appendix VIII, p. 694). On the phrasing and terminology of this section see especially pp. 447–449 above.
194 Hēr. 6.7 § 4–6 (Appendix VIII, pp. 694–695).

perpetrator used force (*pad rēš*). The intent is only punishable in conjunction with the sexual act itself: both accrue (as *ruwānīg* sins) to the stock or account (*ō bun*) of the perpetrator.[195] Second, sexual intercourse with a woman under the guardianship of another man (*andar sālārīh ī mērag*) is evaluated as an offence of 'body-theft' (*tan-duzīh*), which accrues to the stock of sins of both men to the same amount (*pad ē[w] bun-ē*). Third, the offence of 'body-theft' is rated according to the degree (*pāyag*) in which 'theft of sexual intercourse' (*gād-duzīh*) takes place (a criterion, which is unfortunately not explained, but refers to the violation of the husband's exclusive right to intercourse with his wife; on the degrees of sin see section 5 below).[196] A male (the guardian or another male relative of the woman) can take legal action (*rāyēnēd*) against the perpetrator in the matter of 'body-theft' and request compensation, which goes in ownership to the family of the woman (*dūdag xwēš*) or, if a *čagar*-wife has been abused, to the woman herself (*čagar xwēš*). We can furthermore conclude that illicit sexual intercourse with an unmarried woman or girl, who has reached sexual maturity (beginning with nine years, if her menses have set in, up to the fifteenth year) and is a member of the family, is a minor sin, which can be expurgated by entering a *xwēdōdah* marriage.

The compensation for adultery is also mentioned in several passages of the Law-book. According to one entry, the highest rate of recompense was fixed at some period by a decision (of general principle?), requesting judges (*dādwarān*) not to impose a financial penalty (*tāwān*) higher than 300 (staters).[197] This corresponds with another passage, stating very concisely that the fine (*tāwān*) for cohabiting with the wife of another person 'without authorization' (of the husband) amounts to 300 staters.[198] The immediately following sentence transmits a different amount: the fine for abducting and cohabiting with the wife of another man 'without authorization' amounts to 700 drachms for the sexual offence and 500 drachms for the abduction.[199] The phrase 'cohabiting without authorization' (*a-bādixšāyīhā gādan*) in both sentences is an important addition, since,

195 On *ō bun* (*bawēd*) see p. 402 above.

196 REA 24.2 (Tarapore 1962, p. 97) the term *zan apparīh* 'wife robbery/abduction' is employed in the context of a man, who obstructs the *xwēdōdah*-marriage of siblings and marries the woman himself. The 'degree, level' (*pāyag*) of this sin is assessed as that of a *margarzān*-offence: *zan apparīh andar pāyag ī margarzānīh u-š ēn-iz andar kū girān wināh ī xwēdōdah škenīh padiš* 'abducting a woman/wife (is) on the level of a sin deserving death and this (is) also added that (in this case) it includes the grievous sin of breaking *xwēdōdah*' (compare Safa-Isfehani 1980, pp. 177–178).

197 MHDA 15.4–5 (Macuch 1981, pp. 37; 144): *pad gād tāwān pad ēd wizīr kard ī dādwarān frāy kū 300 wizārdan nē kard* 'with regard to the fine for (illicit) cohabitation a decision was reached that the judges should not impose a larger payment than 300 (staters)'.

198 MHD 73.7 (Macuch 1993, pp. 489, 492): *zan ī kasān a-bādixšāyīhā gādan tāwān 300 stēr* 'the fine (*tāwān*) for unauthorizedly cohabiting with the wife of another person (is) 300 stater'.

199 MHD 73.8–9 (Macuch 1993, pp. 489; 492): *ka zan ī mard-ē(w) duzēd ud a-bādixšāyīhā gāyēd 700 gād tāwān 500 drahm duz rāy be dahišn* 'if he abducts the wife of a man and

as we have seen in Chapter II, a man could officially lend his wife to a fellow Zoroastrian who had no children for a specific period for the purpose of generating offspring within the framework of a time-limited marriage. Enabling sexual intercourse in this context was considered as a virtuous deed (*kirbag*), was 'authorized' legally and would of course not be assessed as adultery.[200] That the compensation for adultery was to be paid to the victim(s) of the offence (in compliance with the procedure regarding offences of the *hamēmālān* category), is indirectly confirmed by the following entry:

MHDA 14.4–5
pad gād tāwān ka šōy ayāb zan ayāb gādār murd ud ō xwāhišn ne kard ēstād wizīr nē kard.

'Regarding the compensation (= payment) for (illicit) sexual intercourse (*gād tāwān*): if the husband or the wife or the fornicator has died and no request has been filed, (then) a judgement is not passed.'[201]

We can draw two conclusions from this passage: first, that legal action was taken (usually by the husband as guardian of his wife) against the perpetrator and a request (*xwāhišn*) regarding compensation for the offence (*gād tāwān* 'fine for cohabiting') had to be filed; second, that judgement (*wizīr*) was only passed, when the complainant filed his request during the lifetime of the three persons involved, the husband, the wife and the adulterer (*gādār*). A request brought forward after the death of one of these parties was ineffective. Neither the *Hērbedestān* nor the Law-book mention corporal punishment in the context of adultery, but we cannot exclude the possibility that in certain cases some kind of visible mutilation was carried out in accordance with the penalty for theft or, in this case, 'body-theft' (*tan-duzīh*). According to the testimony of the Tansar letter, the nose of the adulterer was cut off (see section 3.2 on theft and robbery, p. 443).

Table 43. Overview: terminology relating to sexual offences

Perpetrators		Definitions
gādār	'fornicator; adulterer'	person who practices illicit sexual intercourse with the wife of another man[202]
tan-duz	'body thief'	person who cohabits illegally and secretly with the wife of another man; adulterer

cohabits with her without authorization, (then) a fine (*tāwān*) of 700 (drachms) have to be paid for cohabitation, 500 drachms for abduction'.

200 See Chapter II, pp. 160–161.

201 Macuch 1981, pp. 36, 143.

202 Not to be confused with *gādār* as technical term for the husband in a consensus-marriage, see Chapter II, pp. 145–148.

Sexual offences		Definitions
a-bādixšāyīhā gādan	'cohabiting without authorization'	practicing sexual intercourse without the explicit entitlement of the husband
gād-duzīh	'theft of sexual intercourse'	appropriating the exclusive right of another man to sexual intercourse
tan-duzīh	'body-theft'	secret, illicit sexual intercourse with the wife of another man; adultery
The verdict		**Definitions**
gādan menišnīg; *gād-menišnīg*; *gād pad uzkārišn*	'intention of cohabiting; cohabitation with reflection'	mental element (*mens rea*) of the offence: decision of the perpetrator to cohabit with the wife of another man
gād tāwān	'compensation for (illicit) sexual intercourse'	financial penalty or fine to be paid by the adulterer to the victim(s)
ō xwāhišn kardan	'to file a request' (for compensation)'	the infringed party files a request for compensation
duzīh čagar xwēš	'(the compensation) for (body-) theft (is) the *čagar*-wife's own'[203]	the *čagar*-wife herself is entitled to ownership of the compensation paid by the adulterer
(duzīh) dūdag xwēš	'(the compensation) for (body-) theft (is) the family's own'[204]	the family of the abused (*pādixšāy-*)wife is entitled to ownership of the compensation paid by the adulterer

4.2 Offences against family law

Given the importance of reproduction for the preservation of the lineage within a legal framework and the general significance of procreation in Zoroastrianism, it comes as no surprise that transgressions of family law were counted among the grievous offences. Although the information on their treatment is rudimentary, we may assume that they could be subject to punishment according to both the *ruwānīg* and *hamēmālān* categories, as we have noted above in the case of adultery. It would not be too far-fetched to assume that a family member could take legal action against the perpetrator and sue him for compensation,

203 On the phrasing see also pp. 447–449, 457 above.
204 On the phrasing see pp. 447–449, 457 above.

although this is not explicitly stated in the short entries relating to these sins. In the penitential texts three major offences are mentioned:

1. *stŭ̄r-škenišnīh* 'breaking *stŭ̄r*-ship';[205]
2. *xwēdōdah-wišōbišnīh* 'destroying next-of-kin marriage';[206]
3. *dūdag ī wehān wišōbišnīh* 'destroying the family of the pious'.[207]

The first of these offences, *stŭ̄r-škenišnīh*, is the failure to establish or maintain properly the important institution of 'substitute succession' by proxy, called *stŭ̄rīh*, which we have discussed extensively in Chapter II.[208] The description of this sin in the penitential texts is rather short as a violation committed by relatives (*xwēšān*), who take the "goods and property (*xīr-ē [ud] xwāstag*) of the deceased, but do not install for him a proxy (*stŭ̄r*) of the *kardag* type (*i. e.* a person designated by the deceased in his will as his 'substitute successor') and also remove a proxy provided by someone else.[209]

There is a longer passage in the *Dādestān ī dēnīg* with more details on the assessment of this sin, but we should keep in mind, that the author Manuščihr was a conservative priest, writing in the post-Sasanian period, at a time, when continuing the lineages of affluent notables was presumably less important than preserving the Zoroastrian communities and keeping the priesthood from financial ruin. In this line of thought, according to Dd 59.2, a man is entitled to give away his whole property (*xwāstag hamāg*) as a pious gift (*pad ahlawdād*). If no more property is left, his relatives are not obliged to arrange a *stŭ̄rīh* for him.[210] (Although the last statement corresponds with entries in the Law-book regarding the minimum amount of property needed for a *stŭ̄rīh*, in the latter text *stŭ̄rīh*-property and *ruwān*-property, reserved for pious gifts, constitute two separate categories of a wealthy family's total property and are used for different purposes.) However, once a *stŭ̄rīh* has been established and a proxy installed, the latter is obliged to carry out the task of providing an heir for the deceased, for which he or she has been engaged. The sins the proxy commits, when (s)he 'breaks substitute succession' (*stŭ̄rīh be škenēd*) are:

1. not exercising *stŭ̄r*-ship (*stŭ̄rīh nē rāyēnēd*);
2. destroying a part of the substance of the property (*bun kardag-⁺e ⁺wišōb[ēd]*);
3. throwing away the 'cult of the name' (*nāmagānīh be abganēd*);
4. ruining the property (*xwāstag be abesīhēnēd*).

205 Pp I 10.1 (Buyaner 2016, pp. 74–75); Pp II 10.1.1 (Buyaner 2016, pp. 142–143; 393–396).
206 Pp I 10.1 (Buyaner 2016, pp. 74–75); Pp II 10.1.2 (Buyaner 2016, pp. 143; 396).
207 Pp I 10.1 (Buyaner 2016, pp. 74–75); Pp II 10.1.3 (Buyaner 2016, pp. 143; 397–398).
208 See pp. 169–174.
209 For the whole text see Buyaner 2016, pp. 142–143; 393. On the *stŭ̄r ī kardag* 'designated proxy' see Chapter II, p. 170.
210 See the whole text of Dd 59 in Appendix I, pp. 652–653.

The sin of *stŭr-škenišnīh* is assessed as a offence 'deserving death' (*margarzān*), but the author states very clearly that this does not lead to the death-sentence, but can be atoned for by the means of paying a corresponding fine for 'every single drachm' (*abar drahm-ē*) that has been misused.[211] We are not informed as to whom the fine goes, but it would not be too far-fetched to assume that *stŭr-škenišnīh*, as the other sins listed in this context, could be treated as both *ruwānīg* and *hamēmālān* offences, and the relatives of the deceased, who had installed the proxy, could request a compensation for the mismanagement of *stŭrīh*-property.

The same may be assumed for the second sin in this context, *xwēdōdah-wišōbišnīh* 'destroying next-of-kin marriage', which was, given the importance attached to endogamy in Zoroastrianism, certainly a *ruwānīg* sin, but could also have been assessed, *e.g.* in the context of adultery, as an infringement of another man's exclusive sexual rights (*gād-duzīh*; *tan-duzīh*), resulting in a fine to be paid to the victim, as we have seen above.[212]

The third sin of 'destroying the family of the pious' (*dūdag ī wehān wišōbišnīh*) is described in the penitential texts as an offence by which the families of priests and religious authorities (*dastwarān ud mowbedān*) and of 'righteous, pious, god-fearing and religiously devout children' (*frazandān [ī] ahlawān ud tarskārān ud xwadāy-tars ud dēn-dōstān*) are ruined out of 'envy' (*arešk*) and 'enmity' (*dušmenīh*).[213] Buyaner cites in this context Dk.6.235, which distinguishes between two acts leading to the disruption of families (*wišōbišn ī dūdag*): (1) 'adversity' (*petyārag*), and (2) 'oath-breaking' (*mihr-drōzīh*), both offences liable to prosecution according to the *hamēmālān* category.[214]

4.3 Violation of legal responsibilities

Among the numerous sins listed in the religious sources, several offences, which are also mentioned *en passant* in the legal texts, were presumably punishable according to the *hamēmālān* principle. We have already discussed one of the most serious violations of a legal responsibility, *miϑrōdrūǰīh* (*mihr-drōzīh*) 'contract breaking; breach of contract', in Chapter IV.[215] Honouring agreements and contracts was not only a legal requirement similar to the Roman *pacta sunt servanda*, but an important religious duty, safeguarded by the Lord of the Covenant, Mithra/Mihr. The expression is mainly attested in a religious context (including *zand*-literature), but a noteworthy passage of the Law-book lists *miϑrōdrūǰīh* among the offences subject to criminal litigation, which, following

211 Dd 59.3; Appendix I, pp. 652–653.
212 On next-of-kin marriage see Chapter II, pp. 151–157.
213 See the discussion of this sin in Buyaner 2016, pp. 397–398.
214 Buyaner 2016, p. 397.
215 See Introductory to Contracts and Obligations, pp. 260–263 above.

the statement of the Chief Mobed (*mowbedān mowbed*), were recorded in a *pursišn-nāmag* ('transcript/protocol of interrogation') and could also be prosecuted by the State (see Chapter VI, p. 574).[216]

One of the most frequently mentioned offences is the tort called *adwadād*, derived from Av. *aδβadāitī-* 'act of placing on the way, leaving on the road'[217] (or from a possible variant **aδβadāta-* 'placed in the road, left on the way'). As a MP technical term it denotes primarily (but not exclusively) the violation of a legal responsibility by omission, *i. e.* by not acting, where there is a duty to act (the failure of a guardian to maintain his wards and animals under his protection; refusal of teachers to instruct their pupils; negligence in taking proper care of a fire; withholding bought goods, etc). As I have discussed the attestations of this term in a large range of texts elsewhere, the following is restricted to a summary of the results of this scrutiny.[218]

The original meaning of the Avestan *aδβadāitī* 'abandonment', reflects the initial offence of a parent or a guardian leaving a child (or another person under custody) to its fate by literally placing it 'on the road' (as we may deduce from the context of Hēr. 9.8, which discusses the transgressions against a child that is accompanied by an escort on its way to receive religious instruction).[219] The initial sin designated by this expression was obviously that of forsaking a minor (or another helpless person) for whose wellbeing one is morally and legally responsible, by abandonment. In the course of its evolvement into a technical term, its Pahlavi derivative *adwadād* took on a range of specific meanings, which are elucidated in the exegetical discussions using this word. In the Pahlavi commentary to Hēr. 9.8 the exegete Abarag connotes *adwadād* with the legal expression, *a-dādīhā sālārīh* 'unlawful' or 'illegal guardianship', in order to stress that *adwadād* designates a tort in this passage, for which a specific guardian is held personally responsible, and not a state of emergency due to the shortage of food (also called *adwadād*, as we will see below).

In other exegetical sources the Avestan expression *tarō.piϑβa-* 'shortage' or 'lack of food' is translated by MP *tar-pih(īh)* and explained in the glosses to the Avestan text by MP *adwadād*, disclosing that the latter term was linked to a specific form of 'abandonment', that of forsaking a person or beneficent animal by withholding nourishment.[220] Moreover, the Pahlavi glosses reveal that *adwadād* designated a delict of the *tanāpuhr* grade, the highest possible offence according to the

216 MHDA 34.10–13 (Macuch 1981, pp. 60, 217).

217 Bartholomae 1904, col. 61: '„Setzen an den Weg", im Strafgesetz „Aussetzung", Verbringen in hilflose Lage und Verlassen in solcher'; from *aδβan-* 'way, road' + √*da* 'to set, put, place' (Bartholomae 1904, 62; Kellens 1995, p. 29; Ir. √**daH2* 'to place, put', Cheung 2007, pp. 45–46).

218 See Macuch 2012a and 2012b; also Chapter I, pp. 43–44..

219 Hēr. 9.8; translated and discussed in Macuch 2012a, pp. 249–251.

220 Hēr. 17.4; Vd. 13.20; Vd. 13.24; translated and discussed in Macuch 2012b, pp. 525–527.

Zoroastrian degrees of sins.[221] In the *Dēnkard* the sin of 'committing *adwadād*' (*adwadād kardan*) is counted among the sins 'deserving death' (*az margarzānān*).[222] That the Pahlavi expression became a technical term for the offence of 'withholding provisions, withdrawing maintenance, depriving (a person, animal, sacred fire) of nourishment' is confirmed by the definition given in the Avestan-Pahlavi glossary *Frahang ī Ōīm*.[223] The text explains *adwadād* explicitly as the act of a person who 'keeps back (*abāz dārēd*) food and drink (*xwarišn ud xwārišn*) from the one who has hunger and thirst (*kē suy ud tišn*)'. It also states the exact amount of food and fuel needed to nourish 'righteous men' (*mard ī ahlaw*)[224] and a sacred fire (*ātaxš ī Ohrmazd*): three meals in the summer and two meals in the winter. A person who has missed four meals in unbroken succession is to be considered as 'unconscious' (*a-bōy*), that is, he is no longer consciously responsible for his actions. This corresponds to another entry in the *Dēnkard*: a man who has suffered from 'lack of food' or 'withdrawal of sustenance' (*adwadād*) three times in unbroken succession, acts 'unconsciously' (*a-bōyīhā*) if he misses a fourth meal.[225] The reference to sacred fires in the *Frahang ī Ōīm* suggests that by the Sasanian period *adwadād* comprised far more than the original offence of abandonment (in the literal sense of leaving a person on the road) and had become a technical term. Other text passages reveal that the proper distribution of food was established legally (*dādīhā*), that the amount of sustenance to be given to 'worthy' (*arzānīg*) or 'righteous' (*ahlaw*) men and to 'inferior' (*niyuruzd*) persons, as well as to women, minors, sheepdogs and sacred fires was regulated according to specific criteria (these are not named here, but see the section on the remuneration of the *stūr* and the guardian).[226] In this context *adwadād* designates the offence of failing to comply with these rules of food distribution by the deliberate act of 'withholding sustenance' with far-reaching consequences for the delinquent.[227]

Besides this specific use of the word, there can be no doubt that *adwadād* was also employed in a far more general sense, denoting not only an offence liable to punishment, but also a state of emergency caused by a shortage of supplies, for which no specific individual could be held responsible. Two passages of the Lawbook dealing with questions of maintenance discuss the conditions under which the head of a household was allowed to sell persons under his guardianship.[228] We

221 On these see section 5 below.
222 DkM 715.7–8; see Macuch 2012a, p. 255.
223 FīO XXVb (Reichelt 1901, p. 209,1–7; Klingenschmitt 1968, no. 711). The passage is discussed in Macuch 2012b, pp. 528–529.
224 On the term *mard ī ahlaw* see König 2005 and Shaked 2022.
225 DkM 756.13–15; see Macuch 2012b, p. 529.
226 Chapter II, pp. 173–174, 182; see also Macuch 1990.
227 DkM 727.10–13; 750.12–19; MHDA 35.7–9 (discussed in Macuch 2012a, pp. 254–258). One of the major sins of the Mazdakites from an orthodox Zoroastrian perspective consisted in not complying with these rules of food distribution; see Appendix IV and Macuch 2015b, pp. 159–164.
228 MHD 33.6–9; 33.13–17; see Macuch 2012a, pp. 258–260.

are informed that as a rule the guardian/father is 'not entitled to sell' (*nē … frōxt pādixšāy*) his wives, underage children, adopted sons and daughters or women he has married, who serve as proxy (*stūr*) for another man. But there is one exception: a state of affairs called *adwadād*, caused by a shortage of supplies, which forces the *paterfamilias* to sell one of the persons under his guardianship in order to be able to sustain the others. The father is only allowed to sell his child into slavery under two conditions: (1) if the child would otherwise suffer death or significant harm (*margīh ud rēštagīh* 'death and injury'), and (2) in the case of an emergency, called *adwadād* 'shortage of supplies; lack of food; inability to maintain'. The legal terminology of these sentences is precise, distinguishing between a situation in which only the minor might be injured, on the one hand, and a crisis, which could also cause harm to other members of the family, on the other. In the case of impending 'death and injury' (*margīh ud rēštagīh*) the father is only allowed to sell his child for the sake of the child itself (*pad ān ī ōy*), *i. e.* in order to save the minor from being harmed seriously or losing its life (not in order to gain from the bargain or to save himself or another member of the family from some kind of loss, as we may add). In an emergency caused by a shortage of food (*adwadād*), on the other hand, the father is authorized to sell the child both for 'his own (= the father's) sake' (*pad ān ī xwēš*) and the child's sake (*pad ān ī ōy*), as well as for the sake of the mother (*ud mād*) and other persons affected by food shortage (*pad ān ī ōy kē abar mad ēstēd*), *i. e.* the father may sell the minor into bondage not only in order to save the child, but also himself and the rest of the family from starvation. Other guardians (*abārīg sālār*) of the family, apart from the father, have the same right. Later Pahlavi texts indicate that every Zoroastrian was obliged to support at least one other needy member of the community, as long as his own family did not suffer itself from *adwadād* 'food shortage; lack of supplies'.[229]

These examples indicate that, besides the original meaning of 'leaving on the road; abandonment', *adwadād* designated both an offence resulting from the deliberate act of withholding maintenance, as well as a state of emergency arising from a shortage of food, for which no specific person could be held accountable. Despite these two different connotations of the term, the phraseology is precise: *adwadād* in the neutral sense of 'lack of food, shortage of supplies, inability to maintain' is employed with the verbs *abar madan* or *fraz madan* 'to appear, to affect, to befall' or *budan* (with a preceding personal pronoun in the sense of 'to have').[230] In addition to these three meanings, *adwadād* is also attested in a

229 Particularly PRDd 39b3 and 42.6; Macuch 2012a, pp. 261–262.

230 Examples: *adwadād … ōy kē abar mad ēstēd* 'he who has been affected by the lack of food; whom lack of food has befallen' (MHD 33.16–17; corrected accordingly in MHD 33.9; see Macuch 2012a, pp. 258–260); *adwadād mad ēstēd* '(they) have been affected by lack of food'; *adwadād nē mad ēstēd* '(they) have not been affected by lack of food' (both phrases in PRDd 42.5; Macuch 2012, p. 261) *kē adwadād … frāz mad* 'whom lack of food … has befallen' (DkM 756.13–15); *u-š adwadād bawēd* 'he has lack of food; lack of food affects him' (PRDd 39b3; Macuch 2012a, pp. 261–262).

fourth figurative sense in at least one example involving a priestly teacher who refuses to teach his pupil. In this setting *adwadād* refers to the act of forsaking a person in a *metaphorical* sense, *i. e.* withdrawing religious sustenance, not giving a student spiritual maintenance by refusing to instruct him or, as we have seen above, by conveying false doctrines (*miθōsāst*).[231]

These various attestations of the technical term may well reflect consecutive stages of legal development. The notion of 'absolute' or 'strict liability', *i. e.* liability without proof of fault or intention (meaning that even if the circumstances of a case are beyond a person's control, that person may nevertheless be held liable for the ensuing damage) and the idea of personal responsibility are both inherent in *adwadād*. The term's ambiguity of meaning could be a survival from an early stage of law, in which the intent of the offender was not necessarily one of the main elements in determining legal accountability. In this context a guardian/custodian/teacher may have been imposed with strict liability for an *adwadād*-offence, even if there was no proof that he personally neglected his duties and if his wards were harmed by circumstances which were unavoidable or in any case beyond his control, such as food shortage. The interesting attestations of the term in the Law-book noted above, seem to list *exceptions* to this rule: a father/guardian is *not* strictly liable for a state of emergency involving food shortage (*adwadād*) and is allowed to sell a member of his family under specific circumstances to avoid starvation. Be it as it may, holding back victuals or other necessities of daily life (clothing), whether wilfully or due to circumstances beyond the control of the offender, definitely counted as an *adwadād*-offence liable to punishment, as we may conclude from the short synopsis in the *Dēnkard*:

> DkD 575.9–15 (DkM 769.8–15)
> *ud abar kē-š pih abar kas [ayāb] be xrīd ud frōxtār* +*az*[232] *frēzwānīg dādār*[233] *ōh pādīrānēnēd kū ān ī pādīrāngar čand pad rōz ī hāmīnīg ud čand pad ān ī* +*zamestānīg*[234] *adwadād pad bun dādīhā pihīh ī mardōm ud ātaxš pad ēk rōzag šabān hāmīnīg ān ī zamestānīg abar wastarag ka kē az dahišn pādīrānēnēd. abar tāwān ī fradom adwadād ud waxš ī-š tāwān ān ī dudīgar ud sidīgar tā dahom.*

231 Hēr. 15.1; discussed in Macuch 2012b, pp. 534–535. On *miθōsāst* (from an unattested Av. **miθō.sāsta-*) as an *adwadād*-offence see MHDA 14.15–15.1 (Macuch 1981, pp. 37, 144). According to the definitions in FīŌ XXVa (Reichelt 1901, p. 207, 5–7; Klingenschmitt 1968, no. 693) and the penitential texts (Pp I 4.1; Pp II Pāz. 4.1.3; Buyaner 2016, pp. 255–256), *miθōsāst* denotes the offence of 'teaching lies' (*drō-hammōzišnīh*) and disseminating unorthodox ideas by committing the following sins: (1) teaching 'the way of the lie' (*rāh ī drō*); (2) teaching 'truthfully' (*rāstīhā*), but 'unlawfully' (*an-ēwēnīhā*); (3) giving 'bad and false advice' (*pand [ī] wad ud drō*); (4) showing a 'bad way' (*rāh [ī] wad*); (5) showing 'a right way' (*rāh-ē [ī] rāst*), but having 'doubt in the heart' (*andar dil gumān*).

232 DKD 575.10 (DkM 769.9): ⟨W⟩.

233 DkD 575.10 (DkM 769.10): ⟨d''t'r⟩.

234 DkD 575.11 (DkM 769.1): ⟨dmcyk⟩.

'And on the one who has bought food for (from?) somebody and the seller (*frōxtār*) holds it back (*pādīrānēnēd*) from the person to whom he is obliged to give it (*frēzwānīg dādār*): how many *adwadād*(-offences) (accrue) to the substance (*bun*) of the one, who holds it back on a summer day, and how many on a winter (day)? (On) the legally (*dādīhā*) (allocated) food of people and the fire on a summer and a winter day. On clothing (*wastarag*): when one holds back its transfer. On the penalty (*tāwān*) for the first *adwadād*(-offence) and the increase of its penalty for the second and third (offence) up to the tenth.'

This short passage allows several important conclusions: *adwadād* denotes here the specific offence of a vendor (*frōxtār*), who fails to deliver victuals (*pih*; later in the text 'clothing', *wastarag*, is also mentioned) to the person who has acquired a right to them (the buyer or another individual to whom the goods are to be delivered). The person, who illegally holds back (*pādīrāngar*) these goods, whether deliberately or due to other circumstances, is strictly liable for the ensuing harm and pays a penalty (*tāwān*) for the *adwadād*-offence. According to our synopsis, which probably relied on the Pahlavi commentary to this *nask*, the penalty was increased after the first offence for every recurrence up to the tenth (is it pure coincidence that the Zoroastrian degrees, *pāyag*, of sin consist altogether of ten levels? See below section 5). We can hence reasonably assume that the tort of 'withholding sustenance', besides being a *ruwānīg* sin, accruing to the substance (*bun*) of the sinner's soul, was also treated as a *hamēmālān* offence, particularly in the context of sale, for which the damaged party could demand compensation in form of a fine (see also section on sale above).[235]

Table 44. Overview: four uses of the term *adwadād*

Meanings		Definitions	Phraseology
1	'abandonment' (Av. *aδβadāitī-*)	deserting, forsaking or leaving someone in a helpless situation (lit. 'placing on the way')	
2	'withholding maintenance; withdrawal of sustenance; failure to maintain'	depriving a person, a sheepdog or a fire of nourishment; not supplying a person or dog with food or a sacred fire with fuel (offence of the *tanāpuhr* or *margarzān* type)	

235 Chapter IV, pp. 372–388.

	Meanings	Definitions	Phraseology
3	'lack of food; food shortage; inability to maintain'	a state of emergency resulting from a shortage of supplies; not being able to provide sustenance to one's wards and animals under guardianship	*adwadād … ōy kē abar mad ēstēd* 'he who has been affected by the lack of food'; *adwadād mad ēstēd* '(they) have been affected by lack of food'; *kē adwadād … frāz mad* 'whom famine … has befallen'; *u-š adwadād bawēd* 'lack of food affects him'[236]
4	'withdrawing spiritual nourishment'	failing to instruct a pupil with religious knowledge; not teaching a disciple willing to learn; conveying 'false teaching' (*miϑōsāst*)	

5 Degrees (*pāyag*) of sins in Zoroastrian law

One of the characteristic features of Zoroastrian penal law is the evaluation of sins and offences according to an ancient scale of crimes and misdemeanours, the core of which was derived from Avestan terms originally designating concrete acts of threatening, assault and physical injury. This gradation of sins is mentioned in several Pahlavi sources with four major variants in ascending order (in some cases together with the corresponding corporal punishments and monetary penalties), consisting of a basic core of six offences derived from the Avesta (the first list below). This list is expanded in several texts by the addition of further elements to eight, nine and ten levels or degrees (*pāyag*) of sin:

1. the six 'basic' degrees: *āgrift*, *awōirišt*, *arduš*, *xwar*, *bāzā*, *yāt*;[237]
2. the 'classical' list of eight degrees (*i. e.* the core of six basic degrees framed by *framān* and *tanāpuhr*): *framān*, *āgrift*, *awōirišt*, *arduš*, *xwar*, *bāzā*, *yāt*, *tanāpuhr*;[238]
3. an extended list of nine degrees (the 'classical' list of eight degrees with the further addition of *srōšōčaranām*): *framān*, *srōšōčaranām*, *āgrift*, *awōirišt*, *arduš*, *xwar*, *bāzā*, *yāt*, *tanāpuhr*;[239]

236 For attestations see fn. 230 above.
237 *Xwad patit* 4.1 (Buyaner 2016, pp. 50, 178); FīŌ XXVb (Reichelt 1900, p. 208; Klingenschmitt 1968, no. 705; Buyaner 2016, p. 52).
238 Šnš 1.1–2 (Tavadia 1930, pp. 27–28; Buyaner 2016, p. 50).

4. a further extended version of ten degrees (by the addition of *margarzān*): *framān*, *srōšōčaranām*, *āgrift*, *awōirišt*, *arduš*, *xwar*, *bāzā*, *yāt*, *tanāpuhr*, *margarzān*.[240]

The historical development of these terms, particularly the basic core of six expressions, from concrete offences to abstract degrees can be retraced to a certain extent by scrutinizing their use in the Avestan and Pahlavi versions of the *Wīdēwdād* (Vd. 4.17–42) and *Nērangestān* (Nēr. 24.15–27.4) and their manifold attestations in later Pahlavi texts. As Buyaner has shown in his extensive study of the relevant terms, their interpretation in the *Nērangestān* (together with the *Hērbedestān*) represents an intermediary stage between our oldest source, the *Wīdēwdād*, and Pahlavi literature.[241] The *Nērangestān* passages reflect the process of transformation of the basic sins from concrete acts of assault and physical injury to grades of sin, by which the *gravity* of an offence is evaluated, independent of the concrete type of sinful action. In the Avestan sources, however, the expressions are not yet employed as technical terms for abstract levels of sin (as in the Pahlavi texts noted above), but continue to function in their original sense, with the difference that they designate in the *Nērangestān* different kinds of corporal punishment, not the various concrete acts of assault or physical injury listed in the *Wīdēwdād* from which they were derived.[242] In the Pahlavi sources he detects two trends: (1) one group of texts mentions the terms in this scale (either together or omitting some of them) in a mixture with other names of sins;[243] (2) another group (encompassing the texts cited above) continues the tradition of the *Nērangestān*, reinterpreting it in accordance with the replacement of corporal punishment by monetary penalties.[244]

This second group of Pahlavi texts suggests that by the Middle Iranian period the 'core' of six sins (the first list above) was crystallized in a fixed sequence and the corresponding Pahlavi derivatives of the Avestan terms became abstract designations for different levels or degrees (*pāyag*) of offences. These six basic levels were extended by adding other degrees to the scale (as in lists two to four above), due possibly to the amalgamation of two systems of degrees and the need of further differentiating the system. The completely abstract nature of this gradation becomes evident, when at some (not datable) period not only sins (*wināh*), but also various levels of virtuous deeds (*kirbag*) are assessed according

239 Šnš Suppl. 11.1–2 (Kotwal 1969, pp. 22–23; Buyaner 2016, p. 51).
240 RivAF, *Pursišn* 72 (Anklesaria 1969, pt. I, pp. 39–40; 122; pt. II, p. 81, who has eleven terms, although the text explicitly states that there are 'ten degrees of sin' (*pāyag ī wināh dah*); but on this passage see Buyaner 2016, p. 52, particularly fn. 90).
241 Buyaner 2016, pp. 49–62 and 281–295; on the subsequent stages of development see particularly pp. 60–62.
242 Buyaner 2016, pp. 53–62.
243 DkM 698.10–17; FīO XXVa-b (680–720); Pp I 4.1; Pp II 4.1.1–4.1.25; Pm 4.1 (see Buyaner 2016, p. 61).
244 Šnš 1.1–2; Šnš suppl. 11.1–2; 16.5; RivĀF 72; *Xwad patit* 4.1 (Buyaner 2016, p. 62).

to the same scale, using the same technical terms, which originally designated forbidden violent acts.[245] The sources referring to this scheme make no distinction between offences of the *ruwānīg* and *hamēmālān* type and we are not informed, whether this method of classifying and evaluating offences was used exclusively by priestly authorities or also in State courts. But before addressing this question, it will be useful to reconsider first the six basic components (list one above, p. 468), then the additions to this scale of degrees, based to a large extent on BUYANER's meticulous work:[246]

1. *āgrift* (< Av. *āgərəpta-*, lit. 'seizure'):[247]
Our oldest source, the Avestan text of Vd. 4.17, explains *āgərəpta-* as the sin of a man, who 'rises' (*usəhištaiti*) 'violently' (*snaϑəm*) against another man. The Pahlavi exegetes of this text seem to have been uncertain, whether to translate this passage by rendering Av. *snaϑa-* 'blow' by MP *snāh* (written ⟨sn'h⟩) 'blow, strike, violence' (the correct translation) or *sneh* (written ⟨snyh⟩) 'weapon, arms, sword' from Av. *snaiϑiš-* 'weapon'.[248] Both spellings are attested in the Pahlavi translations of this source, but the latter version with *sneh* 'weapon' obviously agreed better with the exegetes' understanding of the content of the Avestan text and their own usage of the term *āgrift*, as it corresponds to the explanation of this term in other texts. The *Frahang ī Ōīm* has the following definition: '*āgrift*—"taking" (*grift*) is this: when he/she seizes (*abar gīrēd*) a weapon (*sneh*) in order to smite an innocent (person)'.[249] The intention of the perpetrator (as an important element of the offence, see above section 2) is part of the definition of this term in the penitential texts: '(if) someone with the intent to smite (*pad menišn zadan*) takes a weapon (*sneh*) in (his/her) hand(s), that sin is called *āgrift*'.[250] The exact circumstances of this specific manner of threatening are described in the

245 FīŌ XXVb (705–706) (REICHELT 1900, p. 208; KLINGENSCHMITT 1968, no. 705–706; BUYANER 2016, p. 52); see also TAVADIA 1930, p. 14, with further references to the sources.

246 BUYANER 2016, pp. 281–295.

247 Ir. √*grabH* 'to grab, seize, take'; Av. √*grab* 'to grab, seize, take' + *ā-* 'to grab (to)' (CHEUNG 2007, pp. 119–121); BARTHOLOMAE 1904, col. 310: 'im Strafgesetz „Bedrohung" mit bewaffneter Hand' ['in penal law "threatening" armed with a weapon']; KLINGENSCHMITT 1968, no. 699: 'Ergreifen (der Waffe)' ['seizure (of a weapon)']; BUYANER 2016, pp. 108, 281 (§28; *āgrift wināh*): 'the sin of menace'.

248 Vd.4.17: (Av.) *yō narš snaϑəm usəhištaiti aētaṯ hē āgərəptəm* (MP) *kē pad [ān] mard snāh/sneh ul ēstēd [pad zanišn ī mard-ē] ēdōn ōy [kē-š] āgrift [andar +ō bun bawēd]* "(Av.) He who rises violently against a man, this (is) an *āgərəpta-* (sin) by him. (MP) He who rises against a man violently/(with) a weapon [to smite a man] thus he (has committed) an *āgrift* [it (accrues) to (his) account/stock]." (CANTERA 1998, pp. 207–208; BUYANER 2016, pp. 281–282); on Av. *snaϑa-* and *snaiϑiš-* see BARTHOLOMAE 1904, col. 1627; MOAZAMI 2014, pp. 108–109, has a slightly different translation of the Pahlavi text.

249 FīŌ XXVb (699): *āgrift grift ān bawēd ka zad ī a-wināh rāy sneh abar gīrēd* (REICHELT 1900, p. 208; KLINGENSCHMITT 1968, no. 699; BUYANER 2016, p. 281).

250 Pp II Phl. A 4.1.7: *kas-ē pad menišn zadan sneh andar dast gīrēd ān wināh rāy āgrift gōwēd* (BUYANER 2016, p. 281; similarly Pp II Phl. B. 4.1.7: *agar kas-ē pad menišnīh zadan sneh dar dast gīrēd ān rāy āgrift gōwēd*, see BUYANER *ibid.*).

Šayast nē šāyast as holding any kind of weapon (*sneh*), with which one can attack another person, and lifting it four fingerbreadths from the ground (*4 angušt az zamīg abar grift*).[251] Moreover, a short entry in the *Dēnkard* indicates that this sin consisted of a threat, but did not include actually using the weapon to inflict physical injury: 'which (is) the *āgrift*(-sin) that does not turn down (the weapon)?' (*kadār āgrift ī a-frōd-wardišn*).[252] Based on these attestations we can conclude that Avestan *āgərəpta-* originally denoted some kind of (unspecified) menace or threat, whereas Pahlavi *āgrift* was understood as a threat to use violence by taking hold of a weapon and raising it to a certain level (four fingerbreadths) above the ground. The expression became the abstract technical term for the smallest degree (*pāyag*) in the 'core' scale of sins and offences (and at some point of the exact opposite, namely virtues) and was at some period pushed further down the list of degrees by the addition of two further levels: *framān* and *srōšōčaranam*.

2. *awōirišt/ōirišt* (< Av. *auuaoirišta-*, lit. 'turning [up, down, away]'):[253]
Vd. 14.17 explains *auuaoirišta-* as the sin of a man who 'advances' (*frašusaiti*) (against another person), which in turn is translated by MP *frāz rawēd* 'he advances, proceeds forward' and elucidated in the gloss as: 'driving him (= the victim) away' (*kū be rawēnēd*).[254] As in the case of *āgərəpta-*, the Avestan text does not mention any use of a weapon: *auuaoirišta-* is defined as the sin of threatening another person in some manner, making him turn away or retreat. The basic meaning of the term as 'turning' is conveyed in the definition of the Pahlavi derivation *awōirišt* in FīŌ XXVb, albeit with respect to the use of a weapon: '*awōirišt*—"turning" (*wardišn*) is this: when someone turns upwards (*abar wardēd*) the weapon against an innocent (person).'[255] According

251 Šnš Suppl. 16.2: *āgrift-ē bud čē andar gehan mardōm padiš zanēnd sneh u-š 4 angust az zamīg abar grift ā-š āgrift-ē ō bun* 'an *āgrift* (involves holding) any weapon with which one can strike people and lifting it four fingerbreadths from the ground: then this (is) an *āgrift* (accruing) to the account/stock (*ō bun*)' (Klingenschmitt 1968, no. 699; Kotwal 1969, pp. 68–69; Buyaner 2016, pp. 281–282).
252 DkM 712.10 (Klingenschmitt 1968, no. 699).
253 Ir. √**u̯rais* 'to turn, spin'; Av. √*uruuaēs* 'to twist, turn' + *auua-* 'to turn down' (Cheung 2007, p. 437); Bartholomae 1904, col. 168–169: 'im Strafgesetz „Angriff" mit bewaffneter Hand' ['in penal law "assault" armed with a weapon']; Klingenschmitt 1968, no. 700: 'Hinwenden, Richten (der Waffe)' ['pointing, focusing (the weapon)']; Buyaner 2016, pp. 108, 282–285 (§ 29; *awōirišt wināh*): 'the sin of making (one) retreat (lit.: "turning back")'; on the diverse spellings of the word see Buyaner, *ibid.*, p. 283.
254 Vd. 4.17: (Av.) *yat̰ frašusaiti aetat̰ he auuaoirištəm* (MP) *ka frāz rawēd [kū be rawēnēd] ēdōn ōy awōirišt [kū-š awōirišt ō bun bawēd u-š āgrift andar šawēd ast kē ēdōn gōwēd ay nēst]*. '(Av.) If he advances, it is for him an *auuaoirišta-* (sin). (MP) If he advances [that is, drives (the victim) away] thus it (is) for him an *awōirišt* [that is, it accrues as *awōirišt* to (his) account/stock, and the *āgrift* (sin) is included in it; there is one (commentator) who says thus: "it (= the *āgrift*) is not (included in the *awōirišt*)"].' (Cantera 1998, pp. 207–208; Moazami 2014, pp. 108–109; slightly different Buyaner 2016, p. 284).
255 FīŌ XXVb: *awōirišt wardišn ān bawēd ka a-wināh rāy sneh abar wardēd* (Klingenschmitt 1968, no. 700, with a slightly different translation).

to ŠnŠ 16.3 this sin takes place, 'when he turns the weapon downwards (*frōd wardēd*).'[256] Both texts qualify the action of 'turning' a weapon as 'turning (it) upwards or downwards' (*abar wardēd/frōd wardēd*), which in the definition of the penitential texts is replaced by *abar sar be gardānēd* 'he lets it turn (= brandishes it; lets it revolve) above (his) head': 'If someone with the intent to smite (*pad menišn zadan*) another (person), having taken a weapon in his hand, brandishes it over his head, this sin is called *awāwaršt*.'[257] These definitions imply that the Avestan word originally designated some kind of (unspecified) threat by advancing (in a menacing manner) in the direction of the victim, forcing the latter to retreat, whereas Pahlavi *awōirišt/ōirišt* was understood as a threat to use violence by brandishing, swinging, whirling or revolving a weapon and later became the abstract technical term for the second level of sin (virtue) in the list of six 'core' degrees and the fourth level after the addition of *framān* and *srōšōčaranām*.[258]

3. *arduš* (< Av. *arəduš-*, lit. 'blow, injury'):[259]
The Avestan text of Vd. 4.17 defines the offence as approaching a person with 'the intention of mistreating' (*aēnō.manaŋha*), which is translated in the Pahlavi version as 'malicious intent' (*kēn-menišn*) and complemented by the gloss 'he lays hands upon him (= the victim)' (*kū-š dast abar nihēd*).[260] As in the case of

256 ŠnŠ Suppl. 16.3: *ka ān sneh frōd wardēd ā-š awōirišt-ē ō bun* 'when (s)he turns down the weapon, then an *awōirišt* (accrues) to his account/stock' (Kotwal 1969, pp. 68–69).

257 Pp II Phl. A.4.1.8: *agar kas-ē pad menišn zadan sneh andar dast griftag abar sar be gardēnēd ān wināh rāy awāwaršt gōwēd* (slightly different Buyaner 2016, pp. 282–283).

258 See Buyaner 2016, pp. 282–285; on the possibly magic origin of this gesture see *ibid.*, p. 285. His rendering of *awōirišt wināh* as 'the sin of making (one) retreat (lit.: "turning back")' is based on the Avestan attestations of *auuaoirišta-*, not on the definitions of *awōirišt* provided in the Pahlavi texts, which obviously had a specific understanding of the term, as Buyaner himself elucidates.

259 On the etymological connection with OInd. *árdati* 1. 'flows'; 2. 'disturbs'; *ardáyati* 1. 'makes one flow'; 2. 'oppresses, tortures, kills', see Buyaner 2016, p. 288, and Bartholomae 1904, col. 194. The latter has the following definition: '„Verletzung, Hieb", im Strafgesetzbuch vorsätzliche Körperverletzung mittelst einer Waffe ohne sichtbare Folge, nur mit Schmerzgefühl verbunden' ['"injury, blow", in the penal code deliberate bodily harm by the means of a weapon without visible effect, only connected with the sensation of pain']; followed by Klingenschmitt 1968, no. 701: 'Berühren mit der Waffe, ohne daß eine schwere Verwundung zugefügt wird' ['touching with a weapon, without causing a serious wound']; Buyaner 2016, pp. 108–109; 285–288 (§30; *arduš wināh*): 'the sin of assault'.

260 Vd. 4.17: (Av.) *yat̰ dim aēnō.manaŋha paiti.aṣ̌naōiti aētat̰ hē arəduš.* (MP) *ka andar ō ōy kēn-menišn be rasēd [kū-š dast abar nihēd] ēdōn ōy arduš [kū-š arduš andar ō bun bawēd u-š awōirišt andar šawēd ast kē ēdōn gōwēd ay nēst.* '(Av.) If he approaches him with the intent of mistreating, this (is) an *arəduš*-(sin) for him. (MP) If he approaches him with malicious intent [that is, lays hands on him], thus it (is) for him an *arduš* (sin) [that is, it accrues as *arduš* to (his) account/stock, and the *awōirišt* (sin) is included in it; there is one (commentator) who says thus: "it (= the *awōirišt*) is not (included in the

the two preceding sins, neither the quoted passage, nor the attestation of the term in Vd. 4.26 refers to arms. The Pahlavi exegetes render Av. *snaϑa-* 'blow' in this second passage ambiguously by ⟨sn'h/snyh⟩ *snāh/sneh* ('blow, strike, violence'; 'weapon, arms, sword', respectively; see also *āgrift* above), but they obviously had the latter meaning in mind, as they describe the extent of the wound inflicted on the victim as one-fifth (*rēš ī panǰūdag*) of a span.[261] Other Pahlavi sources define the term similarly as an armed assault causing an injury extending to one-fifth of a span. FīŌ XXVb has: 'when one sinfully lays a weapon upon the sinner (*sneh abar wināhgār nihēd*) (this is) called *arduš*'.[262] Šnš 16.4: 'If he lays that weapon upon him (*abar be dahēd*) (it is) an *arduš* to (his) stock (…). If he inflicts on him an injury of one-fifth of a span (*panǰ ēk-ē ī dišt*), then one *arduš* (accrues) to his stock (…)',[263] and the penitential texts: 'If he inflicts an injury of one-fifth (of a span) (*rēš ī panǰūdag*) on someone, causing pain up to three days or strikes someone in the manner of that injury, so that that injury causes a wound up to (the width of) two fingers (*tā dō angušt zaxm*), that sin is called *arduš*.'[264] These definitions suggest that Avestan *arəduš-* denoted an assault with the malicious intent of mistreating the victim in some (unspecified) manner, whereas Pahlavi *arduš* is defined as an armed assault with the malicious intent of occasioning actual bodily harm, resulting in a wound reaching up to the extent of one-fifth of a 'span' (*dišt*, a measure equal to the breadth of ten fingers) or, in other words, a wound extending to the breadth of 'two fingers' (*dō angušt*). It became the third level of sin (virtue) in the list of six 'core' degrees; the fifth degree after the addition of *framān* and *srōšōčaranām*.[265]

---

arduš)"].' (Cantera 1998, pp. 207–208; Moazami 2014, pp. 108–109; slightly different Buyaner 2016, p. 286).

261 Vd. 4.26: (Av.) *dātarə … yō narəm arəduša snaϑa jainti kā.hē asti ciϑa* (MP) *dādār … kē ō mard arduš snāh/sneh zanēd* [*rēš ī panǰūdag*] *kadār ōy ast tōzišn*. '(Av.) O Creator … he who strikes a man with an *arəduš-* blow, what is the atonement for him? (MP) O Creator … he who strikes a man an *arduš*-blow/(with) a weapon [a wound of one-fifth (of a span)], what is the atonement for him?' (Cantera 1998, p. 216; Moazami 2014, pp. 110–111; Buyaner 2016, p. 286).

262 FīŌ XXVb: *ka pad wināhgārīh sneh abar wināhgār nihēd arduš nām* (Reichelt 1900, p. 208; different Klingenschmitt 1968, no. 701; for this version see Buyaner 2016, p. 292).

263 Šnš Suppl. 16.4: *ka-š sneh abar be dahēd arduš-ē ō bun* (…) *agar-iš rēš panǰ ēk-ē ī dišt padiš kard ā-š arduš ēw* (…) (according to Buyaner 2016, p. 287; Kotwal 1969, pp. 68–69 erroneously has *xwar* instead of *arduš*, see Buyaner *ibid.*, fn. 208).

264 Pp II Phl. A. 4.1.9: *agar kas-ē rāy rēš* (*ī*) *panǰūdag zadag tā se rōz dard kunēd ayāb kas-e rāy čiyōn ān rēš zanēd kē ān rēš tā dō angušt zaxm rasēd ān wināh rāy arduš gōwēd* (Buyaner 2016, p. 285; compare Pp II Phl. B. 4.1.9, *ibid.*).

265 On *dišt* (< Av. *dišti-*) 'span', a measure equal to the width of ten fingers, see Klingenschmitt 1968, no. 701 and 733, and Buyaner 2016, p. 287, fn. 210. As both authors elucidate, an injury of one-fifth (*rēš ī panǰūdag*) of a *dišt* (= the breadth of ten fingers) corresponds to a wound up to the breadth of two fingers (*tā dō angušt zaxm*), the extent given in the penitential texts.

4. *xwar* (< Av. x^{v}*ara-*, lit. 'wound, sore'):[266]

The preceding three Pahlavi terms in the scale of sins can be easily traced back to their Avestan prototypes in the *Wīdēwdād*, despite all divergences in detail. Pahlavi *xwar* in the list of degrees, on the other hand, does not correspond with the whole range of sins designated as x^{v}*ara-*, lit. 'wound, sore', in this Avestan text. Moreover, discrepancies can be detected between this source and the degrees of sins in the *Nērangestān*. The *Wīdēwdād* differentiates between three types of x^{v}*ara-*: (1) Av. *vīxrūmant-* x^{v}*ara-* (MP *guxrūnōmand xwar*) 'contused (?) wound'[267] (2) *tacaṯ.vohunī-* x^{v}*ara-* (MP *tazāg xōn xwar*) 'bleeding wound';[268] (3) *astō.bid-* x^{v}*ara-* (MP *ast-šken xwar*) 'bone-breaking wound/injury'.[269] The *Nērangestān*, representing an intermediary stage between the *Wīdēwdād* and Pahlavi literature, on the other hand, distinguishes between three grades,

266 Ir. √*hu̯ar4 'to have a sore, scratch, itch'; Av. x^{v}*ara-* 'wound, sore' (Cheung 2007, p. 150). Bartholomae 1904, col. 1867: 'Wunde, Verwundung (...) im Strafgesetz vorsätzliche Körperverletzung mittelst einer Waffe mit sichtbaren Folgen (...) a) insbes. Term. techn. für die leichteste Art solcher Körperverletzungen (...)' ['wound (...) in penal law deliberate bodily harm using a weapon with visible consequences (...) especially a technical term for the lightest form of this kind of physical injury (...)']. For an extensive discussion and critique of Bartholomae's explanation of the three forms of x^{v}*ara-* see Buyaner 2016, pp. 288–292; Buyaner *ibid.*, p. 288 (§31; *xwar winā h*): 'the sin of injury(-infliction)'.

267 Vd. 4.30: (Av.) *dātarə (...) yō narəm vīxrūmąṇtəm* x^{v}*arəm jaiṇti kā.hē asti ciϑa* (MP) *dādār (...) kē ō mard guxrūnōmand xwar zanēd [rēš ī čahrušūdag] kadār ōy ast tōzišn.* '(Av.) O Creator (...) who inflicts on a man a contused (?) wound, what is the atonement for him? (MP) O Creator (...) who inflicts on a man a contused (?) wound [injury of one-fourth (of a span)], what is his atonement?', following Buyaner's translation (2016, p. 290) of *vīxrūmant-* x^{v}*ara-* as 'contused wound', which is definitely better than Bartholomae's inherently contradictory translations of the term as: (1904, col. 1436–1437) '1) über und über blutig ... 2) unblutig' ['1) bleeding all over; 2) unbleeding']. Buyaner's interpretation still does not agree with the Pahlavi gloss 'injury of one-fourth (of a span)' (*rēš ī čahrušūdag*), which rather presupposes a wound, from which blood flows, than a contused wound, but the discrepancy between the Avestan and Pahlavi version could be due to the fusion of the two different types of wounds, distinguished as *vīxrūmant-* x^{v}*ara-* and *tacaṯ.vohunī-* x^{v}*ara-* ('bleeding wound'), to one and the same degree of sin in x^{v}*ara-* in the *Nērangestān* and Pahlavi *xwar.*

268 Vd. 4.34: (Av.) *dātarə (...) yō narəm tacaṯ.vohunīm* x^{v}*arəm jaiṇti kā.hē asti ciϑa* (MP) *dādār (...) kē ō mard ān ī tazāg xōn xwar zanēd [rēš ī srīšūdag] kadār ōy ast tōzišn.* '(Av.) O Creator (...) who inflicts on a man a bleeding wound, what is the atonement for him? (MP) O Creator (...) who inflicts on a man a bleeding wound [injury of one-third (of a span)], what is his atonement?' (Cantera 1998, pp. 222–223; Moazami 2014, pp. 112–113; Buyaner 2016, p. 291).

269 Vd. 4.37: (Av.) *dātarə (...) yō narəm astō.biδəm* x^{v}*arəm jaiṇti kā.hē asti ciϑa* (MP) *dādār (...) kē ō mard ān ī ast-šken xwar zanēd [rēš ī nēm dišt] kadār ōy ast tōzišn.* '(Av.) O Creator (...) who inflicts on a man a bone-breaking wound, what is the atonement for him? (MP) O Creator (...) who inflicts on a man a bone-breaking wound [injury of half a span], what is his atonement?' (Cantera 1998, pp. 224–225; Moazami 2014, pp. 112–113; Buyaner 2016, p. 293); compare also Vd. 4.39.

corresponding to the three final core degrees in Pahlavi texts, only the first of which is called *x^vara-*: (1) *x^vara-* (MP *xwar*) 'wound, sore'; (2) *bazūjata-* (MP *bāzā-zanišnīh*) 'arm-striking/breaking'; (3) *yāta-* (MP *yāt*) 'leg(-striking/breaking)'.[270] BARTHOLOMAE identifies these two Avestan lists one to one, concluding that the three types of *x^vara-* in the former source correspond to the three degrees of sin in the latter, despite all obvious divergences with respect to both the terms and their definitions.[271] BUYANER, who rejects BARTHOLOMAE's equation, has a far more convincing explanation of the evolution of these degrees. He assumes that *vīxrūmant- x^vara-* ('contused wound') and *tacat̰.vohunī- x^vara-* ('bleeding wound'), both designations of different types of wounds, were united in the degree of *x^vara-* ('wound') > Pahlavi *xwar*; whereas *astō.bid- x^vara-* ('bone-breaking wound/injury'), the designation for a more grievous kind of bodily harm resulting in bone-fracture, was splitted into two separate degrees: (a) *bāzu.jata-* ('arm-striking/breaking') > Pahlavi *bāzā*; and (b) *yāta-* ('leg[-striking/breaking]') > Pahlavi *yāt* (see grades 5 and 6 below).[272] In the Pahlavi texts *xwar* is explained as: (FīO 697) '*x^varahe*—"wound" (*xwar*) (is) like *rēš* ("injury"); one should take into account, whether blood flows from it, then up to which measure (*tā-š kū*), how (*čiyōn*) and how often (*čand*) and with which (object) it (= the wound) was inflicted (*pad čē zad*)'.[273] (Pp II Phl. A.4.1.10): 'he who inflicts on someone an injury (*rēš*), a cut (*burrīdag*) reaching up to two and a half fingers (*tā dō ud nēm angušt*), that sin is called *xwar*.'[274] To sum up, three types of wounds were originally designated by Avestan *x^vara-*, two of which (the 'contused wound' and the 'bleeding wound') were amalgamated already in the Avestan period to one category, resulting later in the Pahlavi degree of *xwar*. The third type of *x^vara-* (the 'bone-breaking injury') in turn was split into two categories, out of which the Pahlavi degrees of *bāzā* (< *bāzā-zanišnīh*; Av. *bazū.jata-* 'arm breaking') and *yāt* (< Av. *yāta-* 'leg-[breaking']) evolved. Pahlavi *xwar* originally refers to an armed assault occasioning actual bodily harm, causing an 'injury' (*rēš*) or a 'cut' (*burrīdag*) reaching up to the extent of 'two and a half finger(breadths)' (*tā dō ud nēm angušt*), or, according to the Pahlavi gloss to Vd. 4.30, an injury of one-fourth of a span (*rēš ī čahrušūdag*).[275] It became the fourth level of sin (virtue) in the list of six 'core' degrees; the sixth degree after the addition of *framān* and *srōšočaranām*.

270 Particularly Nēr. 24.19 (KOTWAL/KREYENBROEK 2003, pp. 54–55; BUYANER 2016, p. 54).
271 BARTHOLOMAE 1904, col. 1867.
272 For a comprehensive overview see particularly the diagram in BUYANER 2016, p. 295
273 FīŌ XXVa (697): *x^varahe xwar čiyōn rēš ān āmār ⁺kū* (mss.:⟨MNW⟩) *xōn az-iš āyēd pas tā-š kū čiyōn ud čand pad čē zad*. (REICHELT 1900, p. 207; slightly different KLINGENSCHMITT 1968, no. 697; BUYANER 2016, p. 291)
274 Pp II Phl. A.4.1.10: *kē kas ray rēš kunēd kē ān rēš tā dō ud nēm angušt burrīdag bawēd ān wināh rāy xwar gōwēd*. (BUYANER 2016, p. 289).
275 See fn. 266 above.

5. *bāzā* (< *bāzā-zanišnīh*; Av. *bazū.jata-*, lit. 'arm-striking/breaking').[276]
On the provenance of this degree see the preceding expression. The penitential texts have the following definition of the original injury: 'if one inflicts an injury (*rēš*) on someone's hand (*dast*), that it breaks (*be škenēd*): (if) the injury (*rēš*) is a cut (*burrīdag*) reaching up to three finger(breadths) (*tā sē angušt*), that sin is called *bāzā*.'[277] Although this is not a very exact definition, it suggests that Pahlavi *bāzā* originally involved inflicting grievous bodily harm by fracturing the hand (*dast*) or arm (*bāzā*) of another person, causing an 'injury' (*rēš*), consisting of a 'cut' (*burrīdag*) reaching up to the extent of 'three finger(breadths)' (*tā sē angušt*). It is the fifth level of sin (virtue) in the list of 'core' degrees; the seventh degree after the additions mentioned above.

6. *yāt* (< Av. *yāta-*, lit. 'leg[-striking/breaking]').[278]
On the provenance of this degree see *xwar* above. The entry in FīŌ XXVb (704) has: '*yāt* is explained as 'going/movement' (*rawišn*); the movement (*⁺rawišn*) of people is possible because of legs (*padištān*); one *yāt* (is) the atonement (*tōzišn*) for striking the leg (*⁺padištān zanišnīh*).'[279] The penitential texts explain: '(if someone) inflicts an injury (*rēš*) on the leg (*pāy rāy rēš kunēd*) that breaks it (*be škenēd*), causing a wound that reaches from three finger(breadths) to five finger(breadths), that sin is called *yāt*.'[280] Based on these definitions we can conclude that *yāt* originally designated the sin of inflicting grievous bodily harm by fracturing the leg (*padištān*; *pāy*) of another person, causing a wound extending from three fingerbreadths to five fingerbreadths (*az se angušt tā panǰ angušt*) or one-half of a span (*rēš ī nēm dišt*, according to Vd. 4.37[281]). It is the sixth level of sin (virtue) in the list of 'core' degrees; the eighth degree after the additions mentioned above.

As we have noted above, several Pahlavi texts frame this core of six degrees by one to two further smaller sins, *framān* (or *handarz-framān*) and *srōšōčaranām*,

276 Pahlavi *bāzā* is a curtailed form of *bāzā-zanišnīh* < Av. *bāzu.jata-*; Bartholomae 1904, col. 956, has as literal translation 'mit dem Arm geschlagen(?)' ['struck with the arm']; Klingenschmitt 1968, no. 703: 'Schlagen auf den Arm' ['striking on the arm']. Buyaner 2016, p. 293: 'struck in the arm'; for *bāzā winăh*: 'the sin of arm(-breaking)', *ibid.* p. 292.

277 Pp II Phl. A.4.1.11: *agar kas-ē rāy dast rāy rēš kunēd kū be škenēd ān rēš tā se angušt burrīdag bawēd ān wināh rāy bāzā gōwēd.* (Klingenschmitt 1968, no. 703; slightly different Buyaner 2016, p. 292).

278 Possibly an elliptical expression (in analogy to *bāzā.jata-* one would expect **yāta.jata-*); Ir. √**Hai* 'to go' (Cheung 2007, pp. 154–157); Av. √*yā* 'to go' (Klingenschmitt 1968, no. 704; but see also Buyaner 2016, p. 294); Buyaner, *ibid.*, p. 293 (*yāt wināh*) 'the sin of leg(-breaking)'.

279 FīŌ XXVb (704): *yāt rawišn wizārēd ⁺rawišn ī mardōm padištān šāyēd būdan padišt(ān) zanišnīh yāt-ē tōzišn.* (Reichelt 1900, p. 208; slightly different Klingenschmitt 1968, no. 704, and Buyaner 2016, p. 294).

280 Pp II Phl. A.4.1.12: *pāy rāy rēš kunēd kū be škenēd kū az se angušt tā panǰ angušt rēs kunēd ān wināh rāy yāt gōwēd* (slightly different Buyaner 2016, pp. 293–294).

281 See above fn. 269; on *dišt* 'span', the width of ten fingers, see fn. 265 above.

at the beginning of the sequence, and one to two grievous sins, *tanāpuhr* and *margarzān*, at the end. BUYANER assumes that the elements of two originally separate systems of degrees were combined by incorporating an older system (consisting of a threefold gradation: three *srōšōčaranām—tanāpuhr—margarzān*) into the scheme of the six core elements described above.[282] The minor sin called *srōšōčaranām* (< Av. *sraošō.čaranā-* '[whip] making obedient')[283] is derived from the designation of the 'whip, lash, bastinado' with which corporal penalties were originally carried out. The *Wīdēwdād* lists drastic punishments for sins, which were executed with this instrument (besides the 'horsewhip', Av. *aspahe aštrā-*, MP *asp aštar*)[284] and were at some period replaced by fines calculated on the basis of the number of lashes envisaged for the specific offence. The minor sin called *framān* (or *handarz-framān*), is explained in the penitential texts as the offence of violating a man's last will and testament (based on *handarz* 'advice, instruction, testament' and *framān* 'order, judicial decision, will/testament'), but this seems to be a reinterpretation of an expression whose provenance had been completely lost by the Middle Iranian period. BUYANER derives *framān* 'minor degree of sin' from a hypothetical Av. **framāna-* 'drawing near, impending' (OI $\sqrt{}^{3}$*man* 'protrude') and *handarz* in this context from the Avestan hapax *handarəzan-* 'grasping, seizing' (Vd. 8.76), reconstructing the original term as **handarəza.framānō*, the sin of 'approaching (too) closely', which, although unattested, in fact fits in well with the sins consisting of threats at the beginning of the sequence of the 'core' degrees.[285]

The scale of degrees is completed in several Pahlavi texts by the major offences of *tanāpuhr*, a loan word from the Avesta,[286] and *margarzān*, the highest possible degree of crime. CANTERA has pointed out that the former term corresponds neither in form, nor in meaning exactly to its attested Avestan equivalents, *tanu.pərəϑa-* (besides *parətō.tanū-*) and *pəšō.tanū-*'whose body is forfeited; surrendered to justice'.[287] He contends that both Avestan terms designate the person who has committed the sin (*i. e.* the offender whose body/person is forfeit/surrendered),

282 BUYANER 2016, pp. 62; 234–236 (§ 18); 257.
283 BARTHOLOMAE 1904, col. 1636–1637.
284 BARTHOLOMAE 1904, col. 263.
285 BUYANER 2016, pp. 257–259 (§ 25).
286 That the term is a loan word to be read *tanāpuhr* (not **tanāpuhl*, as in MACKENZIE 1971, p. 81) is confirmed by its Persian pronunciation (written in Arabic script) as *tanafūr*, numerously attested (besides the more seldom *tanawīr*) in the New Persian Riwāyats, see *e. g.* UNVALA 1922, pt. I, p. 89 (line 1); 121 (line 11), 122 (line 15); etc.; (*tanāwīr*), *ibid.*, I, p. 95 (line 7); for numerous further references see DHABHAR 1932, p. 654; see also STEINGASS 1892, p. 326.
287 BARTHOLOMAE 1904, col. 636 and 897: 'des Leib verwirkt, dem Gericht verfallen ist', KOTWAL/KREYENBROEK 2003, pp. 288 and 289: '(one), whose body is forfeit'; according to BUYANER 2016, pp. 298, 344: 'surrender by oneself; surrendering oneself'. CANTERA 2004, pp. 57–58, derives the loan word *tanāpuhr* from a reconstructed **tanu.āpərəϑa-* to account for the long /ā/; but see also BUYANER *ibid.*, p. 296.

whereas Pahlavi *tanāpuhr* designates the sin itself. This is certainly true of the attestations of the word in the *Wīdēwdād* (and perhaps in two penitential texts),[288] but as far as I can see, apart from these texts Pahlavi sources employ the term (just as *margarzān*) quite ambiguously to designate both the offence as well as the perpetrator. KLINGENSCHMITT hence assumes both meanings for *tanāpuhr* 'one, who atones with the body' (= the perpetrator) as well as 'sin, for which one atones with the body' (= the capital crime deserving the death penalty).[289] Unfortunately the definition of this word in the *Frahang ī Ōīm* is far from illuminating and the central part of this text (no. 709) has too little context to be conclusive. It will nevertheless be useful to cite the whole passage as I have come to a somewhat different understanding of the content than both authors, KLINGENSCHMITT and BUYANER, who have hitherto attempted to make sense of this enervatingly elusive text:[290]

> FīŌ XXVb
> (708) (Av.) *pəṣ̌ōtanuš* *+tanūm*[291] *+piriiete*[292] (MP) *zand tanāpuhr čiyōn 300 kirbag 300 hamgōnag ham-andāzagīhā rāy tanāpuhr xwānēnd ēnyā čim ī nām tanāpuhr pad wināh andar āyēd.*
>
> (709) *ud az tanāpuhr ast ī ǰau ast ī frāzōštān +kē*[293] *frāz az gyān wizārēd pad ēn kū-š az gyān ǰudāg abāyēd guftan.*
>
> (710) *bē har čē tanāpuhr-masā nē saxwan ī pādifrāh nē-iz ham pādāšn čē az kirbagīhā hāwandīh ī ān (ī) dīd wēš-mizdtar gōwēd.*

"(708) (Av.) A *pəṣ̌ōtanuš* atones with his body/surrenders himself; (MP) the translation-cum-exegesis (*zand*) (is) *tanāpuhr*, corresponding to (the penalty of) 300 (stater). Virtuous deeds (*kirbag*) of 300 (stater) are likewise called *tanāpuhr* due to the same measure of calculation. Despite this (*ēnyā*), the reason for the designation *tanāpuhr* derives from the sin (*wināh*).

(709) And among the *tanāpuhr*(-sinners/benefactors) a part (*ast ī*) is 'alive' (*ǰau*), a part is 'out of life' (*frāzōštān*), which is explained as 'beyond the vital soul' (*frāz az gyān*), in this (sense) that he (= the sinner/benefactor) must be said to be separate from the vital soul (*kū-š az gyān ǰudāg abāyēd guftan*).[294]

288 In the Pahlavi version of the *Wīdēwdād tanāpuhr* denotes the sin, whereas the perpetrator is designated by the extended forms *tanāpuhrīg/tanāpuhrag* 'who has committed a *tanāpuhr* (sin)' (see *e.g. tanāpuhrīgān/tanāpuhragān* Vd. 5.4,7,14; 12.1,3,5 etc.); for all attestations see MOAZAMI 2014, p. 547. This form also occurs as *tanāpuhragān wināh* 'the sin of *tanāpuhr*-perpetrators' in the penitential texts (Pp I 4.1 /m/ and Pm 4.1 /m/; BUYANER 2016, pp. 66, 84, 295; rendered by the latter as 'the sin worth self-surrender').

289 KLINGENSCHMITT 1968, no. 709: 'einer, der mit dem Leib büßt'; 'Sünde, für die man mit dem Leib büßt'.

290 KLINGENSCHMITT 1968, no. 708–710; BUYANER 2016, p. 297; REICHELT 1900, pp. 208–209.

291 Mss.: *tanum.*

292 Mss.: *piriete.*

293 Mss.: ⟨MN⟩.

294 On the Avestan terms see KLINGENSCHMITT 1968, no. 709: *ǰau* stands for Av. *jauua-* 'alive'; *frāzōštān* for an unattested Av. **frazaoštāna-* < **frazā-uštāna-* 'das Leben als weggehendes (oder verlassendes) habend, das Leben verlierend' ['departing from (or leaving) life; losing life']; on *ast ī* in the sense of 'partly, partially, in part' see BARTHOLOMAE 1911–1918, III, p. 359, fn. 4, and 1918–1923, I, p. 23; also MACUCH 1993, p. 47 (n. 5)

(710) But not every matter of *tanāpuhr* size is subject to punishment, nor to reward, since of the virtuous deeds (*kirbag*) it is said that if they are on a par (*hāwandīh*) with the others (= the sins) the reward for them (= the virtues) is higher."

The exposition consists of three connected parts. As other entries in this 'glossary', it begins (no. 708) with a definition of Av. *pəṣ̌ō.tanū-*, giving the Pahlavi equivalent of this term as *tanāpuhr*. It then clarifies the use of the word as a technical term: *tanāpuhr* denotes not only a specific level of sin (*wināh*), but a corresponding degree of virtue (*kirbag*), both worth (a penalty or a reward of) 300 stater (this corresponds exactly to the constant monetary value of a *tanāpuhr* given in a large number of Pahlavi sources as 300 *stēr*).[295] The passage continues: despite (*ēnyā*) this use of the word as a technical term in the context of both sins and virtues, *tanāpuhr* originally designates a sin (*wināh*). The second, most interesting (and difficult) part of this exposition (no. 709) maintains that there are two types of *tanāpuhr*(-sinners/benefactors): (1) a part which is 'alive' (*az tanāpuhr ast ī ǰau*); (2) a part which is 'out of life; lifeless' (*ast ī frāzōštān*), which in turn is explained in the text as 'beyond the vital soul' (*frāz az gyān*) and further elucidated by 'it must be said that he (is) separate from the vital soul' (*kū-š az gyān ǰudāg abāyēd guftan*). Klingenschmitt concludes from this passage that part of the *tanāpuhr* perpetrators were penalized by corporal punishment, another part by receiving the death sentence. Buyaner, on the other hand, interprets the *tanāpuhr* offenders who are 'alive, living' versus those who are 'lifeless' as sinners 'who had atoned for the *tanāpuhl* sin before death vs. those who had not'.[296] Both authors obviously assume that *tanāpuhr* is used here in its original sense, denoting sinners whose life is forfeit, not as a technical term, referring to the highest grade of both sins and virtues. But if we reconsider this passage in the light of the third part of this text (no 710), another interpretation is possible. This section unequivocally refers to the judgement of both sins and virtues of the *tanāpuhr* level in the afterlife: not every *tanāpuhr* is subject to punishment or to a reward. The sins and virtues are weighed up against each other and if the latter are of equal measure (*hāwandīh*) to the former, the reward for the virtues is higher than the punishment for the sins. Seen in this context the central passage of our text (no. 709) seems to suggest the following idea: *tanāpuhr* sinners/benefactors are divided into two categories: those who are punished/rewarded as long as they are alive; those who are judged in the afterlife.[297]

and p. 165 (n. 13). On *gyān* 'the vital soul', the principle of animation which disappears, when the body dies, in contrast to *ruwān* 'the eschatological soul', see Gignoux 2001, pp. 20–21, with further references.

295 See the table of sins and their money-values in Kotwal 1969, p. 115.

296 Klingenschmitt 1968, no. 709; Buyaner 2016, p. 298.

297 Moreover, the verb *wizārdan* (in *frāz az gyān wizārēd*) has a large range of meanings, which need not be translated as 'to explain, elucidate, interpret' (although this is the translation chosen here), but could refer to the act of redeeming oneself, expiating for a *tanāpuhr* sin after death: *frāz az gyān wizārēd* could mean: 'it (= the sin) is expiated in the afterlife (lit.: beyond the vital soul)'.

As we have noted above, Zoroastrian penal law has a very significant religious dimension, which seems to be voiced in this passage: a person's 'eschatological soul' (*ruwān*)—in contrast to the 'vital soul' (*gyān*) which disappears when the individual dies—cannot escape judgement; *tanāpuhr* (sins/virtues) that are not assessed during the life of a person, will be evaluated after that person's demise, but the virtues outweigh the corresponding sins.[298]

The only other definition to be found is in the penitential texts, which classify this sin as if it were the immediately next level of physical injury after *yāt*:

> He who inflicts an injury (*rēš*) on someone, so that he (= the victim) becomes lame from that injury or is unable to work or when that injury is from five to ten finger(breadths) (*az panǰ angušt tā dah … angušt*), that sin is called the sin of *tanawir*-perpetrators (*tanawiragān wināh*). Who does not perform expiation (*wizārišn*) of this sin, becomes purulent (*rēman*) and death-deserving (*margarzān*).[299]

The form *tanawir/tanāwīr* is possibly chosen here as a variant of *tanāpuhr* to distinguish the concrete physical injury (consisting of a wound from five to ten fingerbreadths) from the technical term, designating both sins and virtues. The description of this sin interestingly corresponds to the offence of Av. *frazā.baoδah-* 'taking away perceptiveness, consciousness' in Vd. 4.40, as Cantera has perceptively recognized.[300] The word is translated into Pahlavi as *frāz az bōy* 'forth from consciousness' and elucidated in the gloss as an injury of a span (*dišt*), which in turn agrees with the wound of 'up to ten fingerbreadths' (*tā dah … angušt*) stated in the penitential text quoted above.[301] This observation is significant in the context of determining punishments and reconstructing the underlying structure of the religious penal system, to which we will return below.

The most serious crime of all, *margarzān* 'deserving death', is presumably a late addition to the degrees of offences, possibly adapted from the legal

298 See p. 479 above.

299 Pp II Phl. B. 4.1.13: *kas-ē rāy rēš kunēd kē ōy az ān rēš lang šawēd ayāb az kār kardan abāz mānēd ayāb ān rēš az panǰ angušt tā dah [kū 10] angušt bawēd ān wināh rāy tanawiragān* ⟨tn'wlg'n'⟩ *wināh gōwēd kē wizārišn (ī) ēn wināh nē kunēd ōy rēman ud margarzān šawēd* (compare Buyaner 2016, p. 295). On *tanawirag/tanāwīrag*, besides *tanāpuhrag* '*tanāpuhr*-sinner' see fn. 286 and 288 above. The form *tanāwīr* is the most common, after *tanāfūr*, in the New Persian *Riwāyats*, see attestations in Dhabhar 1932, p. 654. On *dišt* 'span', a measure equal to the width of ten fingers, see fn. 265 above.

300 Cantera 1998, p. 227, fn. 4. Bartholomae 1904, col. 1005: 'das Wahrnehmungsvermögen wegnehmend, mit *snaϑa-* … im Strafgesetzbuch Term techn. für die vorsätzliche Körperverletzung mit tötlichem Ausgang' ['taking away consciousness, with *snaϑa-* in penal law technical term for intentional bodily injury with fatal outcome.'].

301 Vd. 4.40: (Av.) *dātarə … yō narəm frazābaoδəm snaϑəm jaiṇti kā.hē asti ciϑa* (MP) *dādār … kē ō mard ān ī frāz az bōy snāh zanēd [rēš ī dišt] kadar ōy ast tōzišn.* '(Av.) O Creator (…) who inflicts on a man a blow taking away consciousness, what is the atonement for him? (MP) O Creator (…) who inflicts on a man a blow causing unconsciousness [an injury of a span)], what is his atonement?' (Cantera 1998, p. 227; for the Pahlavi version see also Moazami 2014, pp. 112–113).

vocabulary of State courts, as it is missing in the list of terms taken from the Avesta, but is employed—in contrast to the other terms—in the Sasanian Lawbook. In the bulk of the late Pahlavi texts it is the final level of sin that is reached, when a *tanāpuhr* offence is not atoned for in the course of a year.[302]

The system by which offences were assessed following this scale was rather complex (see Table 45). As we have seen, the 'core' six degrees (perhaps also the first lowest degree of *framān* or *handarz framān*) originated in violent acts, leading from the mere threat or attempt to cause injury (hereby taking the attitude or intent of the delinquent into consideration) to concrete acts of assault and grievous bodily harm and, finally, to the most severe offence, deserving the death penalty. By the Middle Iranian period the designations of violent acts had become abstract technical terms, by which religious authorities evaluated the severity or grade of an offence (or, as it were, of a virtue). This scheme seems to have been applied not only to offences involving force or the threat of force, but to all kinds of sins, including both *ruwanīg* and *hamēmālān* categories, which did not necessarily have to involve assault or bodily injury at all (such as disregard of Zoroastrian rituals or purity rules, sullying water and fire, having intercourse with a menstruating woman, not feeding beneficent animals, etc.).[303] The evaluation of a sin took not only the gravity of the transgression into consideration, but also the frequency with which it was committed: if someone perpetrated a sin of *āgrift* level, then failed to repent, confess and atone for it and later repeated a sin of the same level, it was no longer assessed as an *āgrift*, but as a sin of the the next higher degree, as *awōirišt*. Every time an offence of a certain degree was repeated (and not atoned for) it was considered as the next higher one in the scale, no matter of its nature: that is, an offence of *āgrift* level, when repeated, became an *awōirišt*, which in turn became an *arduš*, etc. if the same sin or a qualitatively similar one was replicated. This at least seems to be the procedure indicated indirectly in the sources, as Darmesteter already perceived more than a century

302 Numerous sins of both *ruwānīg* and *hamēmālān* quality are listed as *margarzān* in the penitential texts (Buyaner 2016, pp. 299–335; §35) and other sources (see Appendix XIII). On *margarzān* offences prosecuted by the State see Chapter VI, pp. 489–494 below.

303 See generally Tavadia 1930, pp. 13–16. An example for the degree of *awōirišt* applied to a *ruwānīg* sin is transmitted in PRDd 15a13: *kē gāhānbār ē sāl nē yazēd ā-š har ēk-ē rāy awōirišt-ē ō bun ud ān wināh be ō puhl šawēd tā-š pādifrāh be kard ā-š puhl andar šudan nē tuwān* 'he who does not celebrate the *gāhānbār* (festivals during) one year, then for every single one (of the uncelebrated festivals) it is one *awōirišt* to his stock/account (*ō bun*), and those sins go to the Bridge; until he has atoned for them, he cannot step on the Bridge' (compare Williams 1990, I, pp. 82–82; II, p. 29). On the phrase *wināh ī ō puhl šawēd* 'sins which go to the Bridge' see Buyaner 2016, pp. 357–363. Sins of this category encompassed omissions, such as failing to celebrate religious ceremonies at the fixed times of the year. They cannot be atoned for in the physical state, but only after a person's death at the Činwad Bridge (on the judgement of the soul after death see introductory above, pp. 402–403). Other examples for the degree of *yāt* (besides *framān* and *tanāpuhr*) applied to a *ruwānīg* sin are transmitted in PRDd 2.5, 6 (Williams 1990, I, pp. 42–43; II, p. 6).

Table 45. Overview: degrees or levels (*pāyag*) of sins in ascending order

Degrees of sin		Avestan terms	Pahlavi terms	Provenance	Type of offence
1	Lowest degrees	**framāna-*; **handarəza. framānō*	*framān*; *handarz-framān*	sin of 'approaching (too) closely' > violation of a man's last will and testament	minor sin
2	Lowest degrees	*sraošō.čaranā-*	*srōšōčaranām*	'whip, bastinado' with which corporal punishment was carried out > monetary penalty	minor sin
3	Six core degrees	*āgərəpta-*	*āgrift*	(unspecified) threat > threat to use force by 'seizure' of a weapon (taking hold of a weapon and lifting it to the extent of four finger-breadths from the ground)	threat
4	Six core degrees	*auuaoirišta-*	*awōirišt/ ōirišt*	(unspecified) threat enforcing retreat > threat to use force by 'turning' a weapon (brandishing, whirling it, making it revolve)	threat
5	Six core degrees	*arəduš-*	*arduš*	(unspecified) assault with malicious intent > armed assault with malicious intent occasioning actual bodily harm (a wound up to the extent of one-fifth of a span or two fingerbreadths)	assault
6	Six core degrees	*x^{v}ara-*	*xwar*	(unspecified) assault causing three types of wounds > armed assault occasioning actual bodily harm (injury or cut up to the extent of one-fourth of a span or two and a half fingerbreadths)	assault
7	Six core degrees	*bazū.jata-*	*bāzā* (< *bāzā-zanišnīh*)	fracturing the hand or arm of another person > grievous bodily harm (injury or cut up to the extent of three fingerbreadths)	grievous bodily harm
8	Six core degrees	*yāta-*	*yāt*	fracturing the foot or leg of another person > grievous bodily harm (injury reaching from three fingerbreadths to five fingerbreadths = one-half of a span)	grievous bodily harm
9	Highest degrees	*tanu.pərəϑa-*; *pəṣ̌ō.tanū-*	*tanāpuhr*	whose body/self is forfeit/surrendered (injury of five to ten finger-breadths = one span) > major offence	capital crime
10	Highest degrees		*margarzān*	person deserving the death penalty; major offence	capital crime

ago in the introduction to his translation of the *Wīdēwdād*.[304] As we have noted above, the Pahlavi version of Vd. 4.17 discloses that the sins denoted by these terms accrue to the stock/account (*ō bun*) of offences committed by the perpetrator: the first offence as a *āgrift* sin; the second one as an *awōirišt* including the *āgrift*; the third one as an *arduš*, including the *awōirišt*, etc.[305] Although one exegete is mentioned, who obviously does not agree with this type of inclusion of sins, the Pahlavi commentary generally maintains that every unexpiated sin becomes a sin of the next higher degree if it is repeated.

There is another indicator that offences were indeed assessed according to this method. The Avestan text reveals that originally the penalty for all these sins consisted of corporal punishment by executing a fixed amount of lashes with the 'whip, bastinado' (Av. *sraošō.čaranā-*, MP *srōšōčaranām*) or the 'horsewhip, thong' (Av. *aspahe aštrā-*, MP *asp aštar*), both instruments with which the punishments were carried out (possibly two different designations for the same instrument, as Darmesteter already assumed).[306] According to Vd. 4.18–42 the lowest penalty for an *āgərəpta-* consisted of five lashes (with the 'whip' or the 'horsewhip'), the penalty for an *auuaoirišta-* of ten lashes, for an *arəduš-* of fifteen lashes, for a *vīxrūmant- xᵛara-* thirty lashes, and so on, in ascending order. The amount of lashes allocated to each of these transgressions describes a pattern, by which each sin, when repeated, becomes the next immediately higher one and is punished accordingly, if it is not atoned for within a specific timespan. Cantera has elucidated the system very well by placing the punishments in a comprehensive chart, which I have adapted from his edition in the following overview:[307]

Table 46. Sins according to the Avesta (Vd. 4.18–42)

	Punishment: number of lashes							
	āgərəpta-	*auuaoirišta-*	*arəduš-*	*vīxrūmant-xᵛara-*	*tacat̰.vohunī-xᵛara-*	*aštō.bid-xᵛara-*	*frazā.baoδah-xᵛara-*	**tanāpuhr*
1×	5	10	15	30	50	70	90	200
2×	10	15	30	50	70	90	200	
3×	15	30	50	70	90	200		
4×	30	50	70	90	200			
5×	50	70	90	200				
6×	70	90	200					
7×	90	200						
8×	200							

304 Darmesteter 1880, p. xcvi.
305 See fn. 248, 254, 260 above.
306 Darmesteter 1880, p. xcvi, fn. 3.
307 Cantera 1998, p. 209, fn. 3. The *tanāpuhr* sin is not explicitly stated in the Avestan text, but the term used for the sinner who deserves 200 lashes is the corresponding Avestan *pəṣ̌ō.tanū-* 'whose body is forfeited; surrendered to justice'; Cantera, *ibid.*

We have good reason to assume that by the Sasanian period two developments took place. First, the six 'core' sins described above became abstract terms, denoting the grade or degree (*pāyag*) of a sin, independent of the exact nature of the transgression; to these other offences of lesser and higher degrees were added. Second, corporal punishment was largely—if not completely, in the case of severe crimes—replaced by monetary fines (*tōzišn*) calculated on the basis of the grade of the offence. An elaborate system of fines was construed, which is transmitted with several variations in the texts (due presumably to differences in the value of currency in various regions of the country and changes across time). But despite striking discrepancies in the calculations for the lesser sins (*i. e. framān*, *srōšōčaranām*, *āgrift* and *awōirišt*, which may have been the more frequent ones, hence subject to change more easily) the monetary equivalents for the higher (and presumably more seldom) levels have remained surprisingly constant across the centuries. According to Kotwal, exactly the same fines are transmitted for the following degrees in Pahlavi, New Persian and Gujarati sources:[308]

Table 47. Fines

Degrees of sin	Fines	Sources
1 *arduš*	30 stater (*stēr*)	Šnš 1.2; 11.2; 16,5; *Saddar Bundahiš*, Ch. 13; *Hormazyār Framarz Riwāyats* (Dhabhar 1932, p. 288); F96 (Gujarati ms.)
1 *xwar*	60 stater	
1 *bāzā*	90 stater	
1 *yāt*	180 stater	
1 *tanāpuhr*	300 stater	

We can reasonably infer that this system of degrees and corresponding fines (together with corporal punishment for grievous crimes) was already established in the Sasanian period and that religious authorities passed judgement on the basis of this scheme after evaluating the gravity and frequency of a sin. No distinction seems to have been made between sins committed against Zoroastrian moral and ritual precepts, on the one hand, and civil and criminal offences, on the other, apart from the manner of atonement for *ruwānīg* and *hamēmālān* offences, as we have seen above (by repentence, confession and payment of a fine to religious authorities in the former case; by establishing a compensation to be paid to the victim directly in the latter).

We are not informed, whether the Zoroastrian system of offences and fines was in some manner taken into account in the civil and criminal courts of the Sasanian State. In the context of legal proceedings the question arises, whether

308 Following the table of sins and their monetary values in Kotwal 1969, p. 115.

this method of qualifying transgressions and imposing penalties was generally integrated into legal practice or remained the prerogative of religious authorities. Besides at least four types of State judges (*dādwar*), Zoroastrian dignitaries (*rad*, *mowbed*, *mowbedān mowbed*, perhaps also the *hērbed*) were also engaged in the jurisdiction of the State in the higher instances. Hence we cannot completely rule out that this scale (or a corresponding one) was also employed in Sasanian courts, if presided over by one of the religious authorities (as the evaluation of sins based on this ancient system presumably required the qualifications of an expert trained in religion or theology, rather than than those of a *dādwar*). On the other hand, we have reason to conclude from the available material that courts passed judgement on the basis of specific criteria, following established rules of procedure, which point to different methods of attaining justice altogether. Moreover, the Sasanian Law-book does not employ the technical terms for the degrees of sin derived from the Avesta and there is no mention whatsoever of the scale discussed above. The only technical term designating a capital crime is the more recent *margarzān*, never *tanāpuhr*. Although the former term is incorporated into the framework of degrees of sins in late Pahlavi texts, its inclusion might be an attempt to bring two systems of jurisdiction together: in these post-Sasanian sources a *margarzān* occurs, when a *tanāpuhr* is not atoned for in the course of a year. But in the Law-book a *margarzān* is dealt with as a criminal act in its own right, not as one derived from an original *tanāpuhr*. Two passages mention a *xwar ī šahr*, lit. 'wound(ing) of the State' and *xwar ud dād ī šahr*, lit. 'wound(ing) and the law of the State', with no further explanations. Although this expression could be translated as '(offence of) *xwar*(-degree) of the State' and might be a reference to (or a derivation from) the fourth grade of sin (*xwar*) in the list of 'core' sins, it seems more likely that it designates the penal law of the State (or corporal punishment inflicted by official instances) with no specific connection to the technical term denoting the Zoroastrian degree.[309]

All these observations make it far more plausible to assume that two separate, but overlapping areas of jurisdiction existed in the Sasanian period, which allowed for a flexible system. Alongside the State courts, religious authorities (*hērbed*, *rad* and *mowbed*) were engaged in jurisdiction on a large scale, particularly in small towns and rural communities, with the right to impose sanctions

309 MHDA 35.5–6; 35.10 (Macuch 1981, pp. 61, 218); *xwar* is written in both attestations ⟨hwr⟩ (not ⟨hwl⟩, as in MacKenzie 1971, p. 226). As we have noted in the context of theft above, according to MHD 73.1–2 (Macuch 1993, pp. 489, 492) a thief was kept in confinement or imprisoned for life if he committed theft a fifth time, after having already been punished for the same offence with the penalty for theft (*drōš*) four times. The *xwar*-offence is the fourth level of sin according to the 'core' scale of sins. This is the only correspondence I can find between the Zoroastrian degree of sin and the term *xwar ī šahr*, but it could be purely coincidental.

and punish offences of both the *ruwānīg* and *hamēmālān* type, following the rules described above (these functions continued after the downfall of the Sasanian State in the Zoroastrian communities far into the Islamic period, as we can conclude from the evidence of the Persian Riwāyats). In addition, the State had its own legal officials and courts (possibly in the larger cities of the counties), to which a person could take resort, if he sought revision of a judgement passed in his own community or a binding (*ēwar*), enforceable verdict in a *hamēmālān* case. Certain disputes regarding, for example, business transactions with persons outside the community, foreigners or non-Zoroastrians, might have been tried as a rule in a State court. It seems that this double system of jurisdiction was also practised successfully in the communities of the religious minorities of Ērānšahr, which we will discuss in Chapter VI, section 2.3.[310]

310 JANY 2007, discussing the system of Zoroastrian degrees, reaches a different conclusion, but he has not taken all the evidence into consideration.

Chapter VI

Civil and Criminal Proceedings

Introductory: religious norms and the jurisdiction of the State

One of the characteristic elements of Sasanian law, as we have seen, is the close bond between religious norms and legal prescriptions, many of which reflect Zoroastrian ideals and values of this period, which could not have been realized in this specific form or combination in any other legal system (particularly in the fields of family law and succession, besides penal law). On the other hand, the legal material from the Sasanian period in the Law-book bears witness to an advanced legal system, largely detached from theology, with its own jurisdiction, based on the work of experts, who discussed legal matters in the specific jargon of jurisprudence with hardly any mention of religious issues. Although many of the quoted jurisconsults are also named as religious authorities in the commentaries to the Avesta (*zand*) and other Pahlavi texts, the overall impression is that by the late Sasanian period theology and jurisprudence had developed into two connected, yet separate fields, distinguishable not only by their content, but specifically by their technical languages. Religious authorities remained engaged in jurisprudence both as commentators and judges, as we have elucidated above, and their theoretical works (*čāštag*) are cited as guidelines in several instances, but the rather elementary laws of the Avestan texts regulating social life in a pastoral community were evidently no longer sufficient to cope with the multi-layered legal problems of a complex society in a huge empire.

The need to distinguish between these two fields seems to have been felt at an early stage. A differentiation between jurisprudence proper and other religious norms is already discernable in the Avesta in the distinction between *dāta- zaraϑuštri-* 'the law of Zoroaster' and *dāta- vīdaēuua-* 'law keeping the demons away'. The arrangement of the legal *nasks* in *Dēnkard* 8, separating ritual precepts from legal matters, and the further differentiation between the two categories of 'sins pertaining to the soul' (*wināh ī ruwānīg*) and 'offences regarding opponents' (*wināh ī hamēmālān*) seem to reflect this ancient divide. We have already noted that the latter division is a *theoretical* construct with overlapping categories, as in fact *every* offence against a fellow Zoroastrian is at the same time a transgression of religious prescriptions and ethical rules.

This classification of offences into two main groups is only mentioned in the religious sources, not in the available legal material, but it suggests that at least two separate, albeit overlapping areas of jurisdiction, existed in the Sasanian period. It seems that the judicial system of the State with its clear hierarchies and appellate courts dealt exclusively with the category of offences involving disputes between opponents (although the term *wināh ī hamēmālān* is not used in the Law-book), whereas Zoroastrian religious authorities were engaged in *both* areas, but had the *exclusive right* to impose sanctions and punish offences of the *ruwānīg* type. How did this division function in practice, why was it upheld and how do the religious minorities of Ērānšahr, particularly the Jews and the Christians, fit into this scheme? These questions are not easily answered, but we will attempt a few suggestions based on a scrutiny of the—rather meagre—material on the relation between courts that were active in the latter communities and the jurisdictional powers of the Sasanian State.

These two areas of jurisdiction do *not* correspond by any stretch of the imagination to the two categories of private law and public law, but both these fields seem to have existed rudimentarily in the Sasanian period. A *theoretical* distinction between civil cases, dealing with disputes between individuals or the infringement of a person's rights, on the one hand, and criminal acts, threatening the security or order of the State, on the other, is not transmitted, but we can definitely ascertain that Sasanian law distinguished *in legal practice* between criminal and civil proceedings. However, individual crimes of the *hamēmālān* category involving assault, physical injuries of different degrees and homicide, seem to have been prosecuted to a far lesser extent by the State than in contemporary legal systems. We have good reason to assume that an injured person or his next-of-kin were expected to take action against the perpetrator on their own, not by retaliation, but by calling in Zoroastrian mediators, arbitrators or religious authorities (here again the *rad* is often named) in charge of dealing with these matters in the vicinity of the persons involved. Taking action in a civil court could well have been a last resort, when other means of attaining justice had not been successful. On the other hand, crimes endangering the religious and social order of Ērānšahr or the security of the king and his subjects were prosecuted by the State, as we can conclude from general descriptions and several case studies. On the whole, we have reason to assume that both civil disputes and criminal acts could be tried according to two overlapping systems, which seem to have existed side by side:

1. The jurisdiction of religious authorities, following an ancient Zoroastrian classification of sins (described in Chapter V, section 5) and exact prescriptions regarding their atonement and punishment. These included offences of both the *rūwānīg* and *hamēmālān* categories, consisting of violations of the moral and ritual order as well as torts and criminal acts.
2. The jurisdiction of the State, following a different procedure altogether, which distinguished between civil cases brought forward by individuals (albeit restricted to the *hamēmālān* category of offences) and criminal

offences, consisting of acts which threatened the order or security of the Sasanian State and the Zoroastrian Church.

The first (and presumably more ancient) method of dealing with offences is already described in the Avesta, but was subject to significant changes across the centuries, as we have seen in Chapter V. Likewise, the second area of Iranian jurisdiction was presumably old and not necessarily an innovation of the Sasanian period, for State courts already existed in the previous empires of the Achaemenids and the Parthians. Cuneiform sources from the former period testify to courts separated into two major divisions, secular courts and temple courts, with different jurisdictional powers in the Achaemenid empire. The Babylonian Talmud indirectly confirms the existence of State courts in the Parthian period.[1] We can assume that these in turn interacted with other legal systems of the Near and Middle East (*e.g.* with the rabbinic courts of Babylonia), hence the notion of several separate, but intertwined, systems of jurisdiction must have been well known by the time the Sasanians took over.

1 Criminal offences prosecuted by the State

Despite the lack of a theoretical justification, Sasanian law distinguished in legal practice exactly between criminal and civil proceedings, as we may conclude from a few descriptions of divergent procedures and different technical terms for court transcripts and protocols. In contrast to contemporary legal systems, however, individual crimes, involving theft, robbery, assault, physical injuries of different degrees and homicide, which are prosecuted in criminal law by the State today (sometimes initiated by a private party), seem to have been put on trial to a far lesser extent directly by official instances in the Sasanian period. The victims of a criminal act or, in the case of homicide, the victim's relations were expected to take action against the perpetrator themselves by requesting mediation (*e.g.* in the case of a feud) or by applying to the Zoroastrian authority in charge in the immediate vicinity of the injured party (the *rad ī xwēš*), or by taking action in a State court as prosecutors. Specific individual crimes of the *hamēmālān* category, however, which were classified as capital crimes (*margarzān*), were brought to trial directly by governmental or judicial authorities, particularly those criminal acts endangering the religious and social order of Ērānšahr or the security of the king and his subjects. Transgressions prosecuted immediately by the State presumably included violent acts threatening individuals or whole communities, such as armed attacks, theft, robbery and sorcery, but we are not very well informed on the procedure in these specific

1 On the Achaemenid period see MAGDALENE 2009, p. 175, and DANDAMAEV/LUKONIN 1989, p. 122, with further references. On the testimony of the Talmud regarding the Parthian period see pp. 526–533.

cases, nor on public law in general.[2] Only a few conclusions can be drawn from a few rudimentary entries in the Law-book in comparison with other sources.

A noteworthy passage in the letter of Tansar conveys information on 'three (kinds of) offences' (*se gunāh*), for which new punishments were established by the king (referring either to the founder of the Sasanian dynasty, Ardašīr I, 3rd century, or to Husraw I, 6th century):

> *bi-dān ki ʿuqūbāt bar se gunāh ast yekī miyān-i bande-u ḫudāy ʿazza ismu-hu ki az dīn bar-gardad-u bidʿatī iḥdāṯ kunad dar šarīʿat wa yekī miyān-i raʿīyat-u pādišāh ki tamarrud-u ʿiṣyān-u ḫiyānat-u ṭuġyān nimāyad wa yekī miyān-i barādarān-i dunyā ki bar yek dīgar ẓulm kunand. dar īn se šāhanšāh sunnatī padīd kard bisyār bihtar az sunan-i pīšīnagān či dar rūzgār-i pīšīn har ki az dīn bar-gaštī ḥālā-u ʿāǧilan qatl-u siyāsat farmūdandī šāhanšāh farmūd ki čenīn kas-rā bi-ḥabs bāz-dārand-u ʿulamā muddat-i yek sāl bi-har waqt ū-rā bi-ḫwānand-u naṣīḥat kunand-u adilla bar-ū ʿarż dārand-u šubha-ra zāʾil gardānand. agar bi-touba-u ināba bāz-āyad ḫalāṣ dahand wa agar iṣrār-u istikbār ū-rā istidbār bāz-dārad baʿd az ān qatl farmāyad. duwum ānki har ki bā mulūk ʿiṣyān kardī yā az zaḥf bi-guriḫtī hīč kudām-rā bi-ǧān amān na-būdī. šāhanšāh sunnatī padīd kard az ān ṭāʾifa baʿżī-rā barāye rahbat bi-kušand tā dīgarān ʿibrat gīrand-u baʿżī-rā zinda guzārand tā umīdwār bāšand bi-ʿafw miyān-i ḫauf-u raǧāʾ qarār gīrand wa īn-rāy šāmiltar-ast mar ṣalāḥ-i ǧahāndārīh-rā.*

'You should know that punishments (*ʿuqūbāt*) are for three (kinds) of offences (*gunāh*). One (type is) the (transgression) of a creature/servant (*bande*) against the Lord (*ḫudāy*) (may his name be glorified!), when he turns from the religion (*dīn*) and introduces a heresy (*bidʿatī*) into divine law (*šarīʿat*). And one (type is) the (transgression) of a subject (*raʿīyat*) against the king (*pādišāh*), when he is disobedient (*tamarrud*) and rebellious (*ʿiṣyān*) and practises treason and treachery (*ḫiyānat-u ṭuġyān*). And one (type is) (offences) between worldly brethren (*barādarān-i dunyā*), when they commit injustices (*ẓulm*) against each other. For these three (types of offences) the King of Kings has created a law that is far better than the laws of the ancients (*pīšīnagān*). For in former times every person who turned from religion (*dīn*) was ordered to be put to death and punished immediately and hastily. The King of Kings has ordered that such a person be confined to prison (*ḥabs*) and that learned men (*ʿulamā*) summon him frequently during the course of a year and advice him and present him with arguments (*adilla*) and destroy his doubts (*šubha*). If he repents and returns to the true faith, he is released. And if obstinacy and pride keep him from renouncing, then it is ordered that he be put to death. Secondly, no one, who (in former times) rebelled against the king or fled from an army marching against an enemy (*zaḥf*), was pardoned. The King of Kings has established a law, by which a part of this troop are put to death to instil fear, so that others may take warning (*ʿibrat gīrand*), and others among them are left alive, so that they may hope for pardon (*ʿafw*), suspended

2 A few passages on sorcery (*ǰādūgīh*) and heresy (*zandīkīh*) are included in the Law-book (MHDA 15.15–17; 38.12–16; 38.16–39.1; Macuch 1981, pp. 38, 145; 65, 222 respectively), which will be discussed below pp. 583–584.

between fear and hope (*miyān-i ḫauf-u raǧā'*). And this is a more comprehensive measure for good governance (*ṣalāḥ-i ǧahāndārī*).'[3]

This short text conveys several important details on criminal acts prosecuted and punished by governmental authorities: first, we are informed that a distinction was made between three main types of offences, for which specific penalties had been established since ancient times. These are:

1. the transgression of a creature/servant against the Lord (*miyān-i bande-u ḫudāy*) by introducing a heresy (*bidʿatī*);
2. the transgression of a subject against the king (*miyān-i raʿīyat-u pādišāh*) by acts of disobedience, rebellion, treachery and treason;
3. offences between 'worldly brethren' (*miyān-i barādarān-i dunyā*), *i. e.* fellowmen, by committing injustices against one another.

The text then explains that the king has introduced reforms in all three areas 'far better than the laws of the ancients' (*bihtar az sunan-i pīšīnagān*; we will return to these reforms below).

Interestingly, the first two of these offences correspond exactly to two major *margarzān*-sins, called in the Law-book *yazdān-dušmenīh* (lit. 'enmity towards the gods'; 'blasphemy, apostasy'), and *xwadāy-dušmenīh* (lit. 'enmity towards the sovereign'; 'rebellion, treason'), to which a third category, that of 'heresy' (*ahlomōγīh*), is added.[4] The passage in the Law-book mentioning these crimes is immediately followed by a sentence referring to the specific case of a man accused of all three capital crimes (apostasy, rebellion, heresy), to which other offences of the *margarzān* category (such as *mihrōdrujīhā* 'breaches of contract', lies and falsehoods) are added. These capital crimes were noted in a memoir (*ayādgār*) and included in the transcript of interrogation (*pursišn-nāmag*), which was always written in criminal cases, following the instructions of the Chief Mobed.[5] Both sentences, in which these terms occur, are embedded in a series of loosely connected entries (MHDA 34.6–35.11) on the question of how to deal with *margarzān* offences, what to include in the transcript of interrogation (*pursišn-nāmag*) and how to assess the special circumstances of a case. The overall impression is that the bulk of the capital crimes mentioned in this context were prosecuted by the State, following the rules set down by the highest judicial (and religious) dignitary, the Chief Mobed (*mowbedān mowbed*). We can hence surmise that the two *margarzān* crimes (corresponding to the first

3 Persian text in Darmesteter 1894, pp. 219, line 6–220, line 6; Boyce 1968a, p. 42, has a slightly different translation. The immediately following part of this text has been translated and discussed in Chapter V, p. 443.

4 MHDA 34.9–10: *pad yazdān-dušmenīh ud xwadāy-dušmenīh ud ahlomōγīh pursišn-nāmag ōh kunišn* 'in (cases of) blasphemy/apostasy (*yazdān dušmenīh*) and rebellion against the sovereign (*xwadāy-dušmenīh*) and heresy (*ahlomōγīh*) a transcript of interrogation (*pursišn-nāmag*) has to be made' (Macuch 1981, pp. 60, 217).

5 MHDA 34.10–13 (Macuch 1981, pp. 60, 217).

two categories of transgressions named in the Tansar-letter), *yazdān-dušmenīh* and *xwadāy-dušmenīh*, denote public wrongs punishable by the State in criminal proceedings, presided by judges and religious authorities, or in tribunals which could include members of the Sasanian nobility (as in the specific case of the Catholicos Mār Abā).[6] The third type of transgression in the letter of Tansar, involving disputes between fellow-men, refers unmistakably to the category of offences described as *wināh ī hamēmālān* in the Pahlavi texts, which could be brought to court either by the victims (and their relatives) or were prosecuted by the State, if these were criminal acts endangering the religious and social order of the community or the security of the king and his subjects.

These sources suggest that Sasanian law distinguished between four (or possibly three) categories of capital crimes, which were directly prosecuted by State authorities (in the fourth case if a capital crime was involved):

1. *yazdān-dušmenīh* 'blasphemy; apostasy' (lit. 'enmity towards the gods'); defined in the letter of Tansar as: 'the (transgression) of a creature/servant (*bande*) against the Lord (*ḫudāy*) ..., when he turns from the religion (*dīn*) and introduces a heresy (*bidʿatī*) into divine law (*šarīʿat*)';
2. *xwadāy-dušmenīh* 'insubordination; rebellion; high treason' (lit. 'enmity towards the sovereign'); according to the Tansar-letter: 'the (transgression) of a subject (*raʿīyat*) against the king (*pādišāh*), when he (= the subject) is disobedient (*tamarrud*) and rebellious (*ʿiṣyān*) and practises treason and treachery (*ḫiyānat-u ṭuġyān*)';
3. *ahlomōyīh* 'heresy' (which seems to have been—at least according to MHDA 34.9–10—a separate category from *yazdān-dušmenīh*, but is evidently subsumed under 'blasphemy, apostasy' in the Tansar-letter);
4. *wināh ī hamēmālān* 'offences regarding adversaries'; according to the Tansar-letter: '(offences) between worldly brethren (*barādarān-i dunyā*), when they commit injustices (*ẓulm*) against each other'.

The second part of the quoted passage from the letter of Tansar describes the measures taken by the king to improve the norms set down in the 'laws of the ancients' (*sunan-i pīšīnagān*). These relate to the three areas of law mentioned in the text, which we have reconstructed as (1) *yazdān-dušmenīh*, (2) *xwadāy dušmenīh* and (3) *wināh ī hamēmālān* (reforms are also introduced by the king in this final category, which we have already discussed in the section on theft and robbery above).[7] Interestingly, the changes enacted by the king regarding the first category of 'blasphemy, apostasy' correspond well with the details conveyed in Syriac sources on the treatment of the Catholicos Mār Abā, a Christian convert from Zoroastrianism (whose case we will discuss in section 3.2 below).

6 On the trial against Mār Abā, a Christian convert from Zoroastrianism, see MACUCH 2014c and below pp. 575–581.

7 See Chapter V, pp. 443–444.

The Tansar-letter states: in ancient times the apostate/heretic (*har ki az dīn bargaštī* 'whoever turns from religion') was quickly put to death, but the king orders that he be imprisoned for a year, in the course of which religious authorities (*ʿulamā* 'learned men') should summon him from time to time to their presence to present arguments and destroy his doubts. If the apostate/heretic repents and re-converts he is to be set free, if not, he is executed. The second measure of the king, concerning 'crimes against the sovereign, rebellion', consists of disseminating uncertainty and fear among the traitors: in earlier times rebellion and insubordination (desertion during a campaign) was invariably punished with the death penalty, but the king orders that a part of the men be killed, another part be kept alive, oscillating 'between hope and fear' (*miyān-i ḫauf-u rağāʾ*), hoping for pardon (*ʿafw*). According to the prime minister Tansar, this Machiavellian reform is an important means of achieving 'good governance' (*ṣalāḥ-i ğahāndārī*). Although this statement might sound strange from the viewpoint of justice on first sight, the power of granting a pardon for a capital crime is in fact one of the important rights of the sovereign in many legal systems. The case of Mār Abā, however, demonstrates well, how far the king's (theoretically unlimited) power to reprieve a condemned person was limited in practice by the interests of other power-groups in the Empire.[8]

To sum up, we can conclude that specific 'death deserving' crimes, imperilling the stability of the Empire and its religious and social hierarchies, were prosecuted directly by the State. These include, as we have indicated above: (1) refuting the official religion of the State and converting to another faith (*yazdān-dušmenīh* 'blasphemy, apostasy'); (2) breaching the alliance owed to the sovereign and his government (*xwadāy-dušmenīh* 'treason, rebellion'); (3) refuting the orthodox version of Zoroastrianism upheld by religious authorities by a divergent exegesis of the sacred texts (*ahlomōγīh* 'heresy');[9] (4) endangering the inhabitants of Ērānšahr and disrupting public order (a part of the criminal acts pertaining to the category of *wināh ī hamēmālān*, such as robbery, theft, sorcery, armed attacks). Unsurprisingly, the category of 'sins pertaining to the soul' (*wināh ī ruwānīg*) is missing in this typology of criminal acts prosecuted by the State, as offences of this type obviously did not fall within the responsibility and legal competence of governmental instances, but were subject to the rulings of religious authorities alone.

Interestingly, the exact opposites of these four groups of capital crimes are listed in *Dēnkard* 5 (9.13)[10] as virtues (*kirbag*) of the highest order, indirectly confirming the information in the Letter of Tansar on criminal acts prosecuted

8 See p. 581 below and Macuch 2014c.

9 The Mazdakites were evidently accused of this type of heresy, among other transgressions, see Macuch 2015b and 2021 with further references.

10 DkM 443.9–13. I have translated this passage in Macuch 2019a, p. 90; Amouzegar/Tafazzoli 2000 (9.13) pp. 44–45, have a slightly different rendering; compare Cantera 2003, p. 26, n. 26.

by the State and the categories named in the Law-book, which we have listed above:

Table 48. Overview: Capital crimes versus highest virtues

Capital crimes	Highest virtues (Dk 5.9.13)
yazdān-dušmenīh 'blasphemy, apostasy'	*yazdān-dōstīh* 'love of the gods'
xwadāy-dušmenīh 'treason, rebellion' against the sovereign	*xwadāy-dōstīh* 'love of the sovereign' *xwadāy-dārīh*, *xwadāy-paristīh* 'keeping the sovereign, serving the sovereign'
ahlomōγīh 'heresy'	*ērīh ud hudēnīh* 'being Iranian and Zoroastrian'
wināh ī hamēmālān 'sins regarding adversaries' (criminal acts such as robbery, theft, sorcery, armed attacks, etc.)	*weh-dōstīh*, *dām-dōstīh* 'love of good (beings), love of creation'

2 The judiciary

As we have noted above, two overlapping areas of jurisdiction may be detected in the sources. One was based on religious law and can be traced back to the ancient norms set down in the Avesta; the other may have been more or less a continuation of older judicial systems of the Achaemenid and Parthian periods, which were in turn adapted to some extent from the ancient legal systems of the Near East, known from a large number of surviving cuneiform sources. These two areas of religious law and jurisdiction of the State (encompassing civil and criminal courts) continued to exist side by side in the Sasanian period, as we may conclude from the observation that both religious authorities and State officials were engaged as judges. This double structure seems to have enabled not only a quick and efficient treatment of disputes among Zoroastrians and the punishment of criminal acts, but it presumably also facilitated the integration of other religious communities, notably the Jews and Christians, into the judicial system of the State.

According to the *Dēnkard* passage discussed above (Chapter V, p. 407), four different methods of taking legal action 'by speaking' (*gōwišnīh*; *i.e.* by making verbal statements in the presence of an impartial third party, a mediator or judge) were known, which seem to have survived from the very beginnings of Zoroastrian law.[11] This source allows us to distinguish between four methods of carrying out disputes (in the reverse sequence of their occurrence in the passage):

11 DkD 84.3–7; DkM 693.16–20; for the whole text see Appendix V, pp. 674–678.

1. The dispute in the presence of witnesses (+*gugāyān*), who act as mediators and arbitrators. The task of the witnesses is to conduct negotiations between the opponents and help them reach a consensus.
2. The dispute carried out before at least three 'good' or righteous men (*weh mard*), that is, Mazdeans, who act as arbitrators or mediators with the goal of reaching a settlement between the opponents.
3. The dispute in the presence of an individual's 'own *rad*' (*rad ī xwēš*). The *rad ī xwēš* is a religious and spiritual master chosen by the individual as his personal moral guide, who has authority and jurisdiction in the community, in which the parties in conflict live. The *rad ī xwēš* can be engaged as an arbitrator, chosen by one or both of the opponents, or act as judge.[12]
4. The 'judicial dispute' (*pahikār-radīh*), that is, legal proceedings against an opponent in the presence of a judge, corresponding in the Sasanian period to litigation in a State court.

The three first methods of solving conflicts describe proceedings, which were not carried out in State courts, but on a lower level in the communities, in which the parties in conflict lived. As we have argued above, these are ancient means of solving disputes, which were also known in other societies. It was crucial for a settled community, whose members were dependant on each other, to avoid strife and violence over a long period of time. The simplest solution was for the opponents to negotiate with one another in the presence of witnesses in order to reach a convenient agreement for all parties (no. 1 above). In the case of a vehement dispute or feud, which could not be resolved easily, impartial mediators or umpires could be engaged, consisting of 'three righteous men' (no. 2 above). Instead of these, or if the mediators were not successful in ending the strife, the 'personal *rad*' or moral guide of the opponents in the community could be engaged as arbitrator or judge (no. 3). If none of these measures were successful, the dispute could be taken to a higher instance (no. 4), to an official judge of the State, a *dādwar*, and beyond the *dādwar*, to the highest possible courts of appeal, involving the *rad* and *mowbed* up to the Chief Judge (*dādwarān dādwar*) or Chief Mobed (*mowbedān mowbed*), whose judgement was final (with one exception: when it was incompatible with an 'order, command', *framān*, of the *dahibedān* 'rulers of the land', see pp. 522–526).

In short, the Sasanian judicial system left enough room for different forms of arbitration and jurisdiction in the dispersed communities of the empire. The laws of the East Christians (Nestorians) and the vast material on the legal work of the rabbis and Jewish courts in the Babylonian Talmud seem to confirm the assumption that religious minorities were integrated into this lucid system. The State obviously permitted them to uphold their own judicial authorities among the rabbis and the clergy. These in turn had autonomy to implement the norms

12 See Kreyenbroek 1994; Macuch 2002a, p. 84; and Cantera 2003, p. 28.

and customs of their own religion in the Jewish and Christian communities to a comparatively large extent in certain legal areas (with the exception of norms undermining significant Zoroastrian customs and criminal law), as long as they did not interfere with the work of the State courts and disturb the stability of the empire (see below section 2.3).

2.1 Judicial and public officials

One of the striking features of the judicial system of the State lies in the combination of courts presided by civil judges in the first two instances and those presided by religious dignitaries in the higher instances of appeal. On a lower level in the Zoroastrian communities informal mediators could be engaged to negotiate settlements and members of the priestly class (notably the *rad ī xwēš*, an individual's personal spiritual guide) were active as umpires and judges in conflicts with the authority to punish offences ranging from smaller transgressions to grievous criminal acts. But as soon as a lawsuit was brought to trial in a State court, an authority appointed by the sovereign, the *dādwar*, took over. This points to a court system in which public officials, who had no function in the religious hierarchy, were active as judges in the bulk of the lawsuits initially brought to trial in a civil or criminal court. Although religious authorities, the *rad* and *mowbed*, again occupied the important positions in the appellate courts, it might be significant that they were not engaged in jurisdiction in the civil courts of the lower instances. We have furthermore reason to assume that even the verdict of the most powerful religious dignitary, the Supreme Judge or Chief Mobed, was not considered as more binding than a decree or command (*framān*) of the worldly rulers or high officials of the State (*dahibedān*) appointed by the King. It was certainly not in the best interest of the sovereign (and possibly of other powerful descent groups belonging to the nobility) to leave the entire judicial power in the hands of the Zoroastrian priesthood. Moreover, it may have been easier for non-Mazdeans (foreign business partners or members of the large religious minorities of Jews and Christians) to apply to a court presided by a 'worldly' judge of the State than by a Zoroastrian religious professional. The whole structure of the judiciary suggests an organization based on the distribution and balance of power between the Sasanian State and the Mazdean clergy, permitting these two important constituents of the Iranian empire to control and check each other, whilst preventing the accumulation of judicial power in a single hand.

2.1.1 The judge (*dādwar*)

The information on the judiciary is as fragmentary as in all other areas of Sasanian law, although even a whole chapter of the Law-book is dedicated to describing the competences (*ēwarīh* 'certainty, reliability, qualification, binding power') of public officials (*kārdārān*).[13] We may conclude from this far too concise text, that the *dādwar* was the central figure of State jurisdiction with extensive competences in the first two instances. He was supported by other officials acting as informants and witnesses, the *war-sālār* 'supervisor of the oath', the *frēzwān* 'policeman, inspector' (see below) as well as scribes (*dibīr*), who recorded the minutes of the sessions. According to a short entry in the *Dēnkard*, there were four different kinds of judges, which, interestingly, corresponds well with the information to be gained from the Law-book.[14] Two judges with the title *dādwar* were engaged in State courts: the 'Junior Judge' (*dādwar ī keh*) and the 'Senior Judge' (*dādwar ī meh*), representing different stages of appeal, the former presiding over the court of the first instance, whose judgment could be overruled by the 'Senior Judge' if one of the parties in a civil case did not agree with the decision of the first court and gave notice of appeal.[15] The designations of two further judges, *dādwar ī pēšēmāl* 'Judge of the Plaintiff', and *dādwar ī pasēmāl* 'Judge of the Defendant' suggest that (at least in certain cases) each of the parties in conflict could appoint a *dādwar* of their own choice as arbitrator. This seems to be meant by the following entry:

> MHDA 13.15–16
> *ka pēšēmāl abāyēd ēranǰēnīdan dādwar ī pasēmāl be ēranǰēnēd u-šān zamān be ō dādwar ī pēšēmālān kard.*
>
> 'If the plaintiff (*pēšēmāl*) has to be sentenced (and) the "Judge of the Defendant" (*dādwar ī pasēmāl*) sentences him, then a date is to be scheduled before the "Judge of the Plaintiff" (*dādwar ī pēšēmāl*).'[16]

That is, if a party (the plaintiff/claimant) brings charges against another party (the defendant) and it turns out that the claimant is in some manner guilty and is sentenced by the 'Judge of the Defendant', then—in order to maintain impartiality (as we may add)—a date should be scheduled before the 'Judge of the Plaintiff'. Unfortunately, this is the only attestation of the two unexplained terms *dādwar ī pēšēmāl* and *dādwar ī pasēmāl*, but the context suggests that these officials were rather arbitrators than judges in the strict sense of the word (that is, independent officials of the State with the power to adjudicate on disputes and other matters, who were *not* chosen by the litigants). In contrast, arbitrators were appointed directly by the claimant and the defendant or by both litigants together with the task of negotiating an agreement regarding the matter

13 MHDA 25.15–30.5: *dar ī ēwarīh ī kārdārān* 'Chapter on the competences of (public) officials' (Macuch 1981, pp. 49–50; 188–193).

14 DkD 550.16–17 (DkM 724.7–9): *ud abar čahār ēwēnag dādwar ud wizīr ī padiš ēk kē wizīr dānēd kardan kunēd ud ēk kē dānēd nē kunēd* 'and on the four types of judges (*dādwar*) and (on) the judgement regarding the one, who knows how to reach a verdict and reaches it, and the one, who knows (how to reach a verdict), but does not reach it'.

15 The judges in the context of appellate courts are mentioned MHD 3.6–8 (Macuch 1993, pp. 54–55; 56–57); see also below section 2.2.

16 Macuch 1981, pp. 35, 142.

in dispute. The procedure might be a continuation of the age-old method of solving conflicts by mediation and arbitration discussed in Chapter V (pp. 404–411), for which each of the parties in conflict could select witnesses, righteous men or their 'own spiritual master' (*rad ī xwēš*) with the goal of reaching a compromise and settling the dispute. Arbitrators chosen by the litigants from among the public judges (*dādwar*) would be juristic experts and legally bound to applying the law accurately, but may have had more freedom to choose their approach and not be bound to the same extent to the formalities of procedure as a regular judge. Our sentence suggests that both arbitrators had to be consulted in the interest of impartiality if one party was condemned for an offence by the arbitrator chosen by the opposing party.

A similar idea is possibly expressed by another term derived from the Avesta in a passage enumerating different kinds of judges in the *Dēnkard*: *dādwar ī vaiiōzušt* 'the judge agreeable to both' (from *vaiiō* [+*uuaiiō*] *zuštō* 'agreeable to both'; written in the Avestan script) and its opposite: *ān ī nē vaiiōzušt* 'one who is not agreeable to both':

> DkD 550.14–16 (DkM 724.5–7)
> *ud abar dādwar ī vaiiōzušt ān ī nē vaiiōzušt zamān ī az dādwar ī nē vaiiōzušt ō ān ī vaiiōzušt.*
>
> 'And about the judge who is agreeable to both (litigants) (and) the one who is not agreeable to both; (on) the date (of the hearing), which (leads) from the one who is not agreeable to both (litigants) to the one who is agreeable to both.'

The only explanation of the Avestan term in the *Frahang ī Ōīm* is hardly helpful: *vaiiō zuštō* is explained as a judge (*dādwar*) who is 'a seeker of that which is doubtful (*warōmand*) and a hearer of that which is certain (*ēwarīh*)'.[17] This definition is not more than a general description of the qualities expected of a competent judge. But taken together these sources suggest that Avestan *vaiiō zuštō* was used of a judge, who investigated a case impartially, distinguishing between doubtful (*warōmand*) and reliable evidence (*ēwarīh*), and whose decision or judgement was acceptable to both parties, who was thus 'agreeable' to both the claimant and the defendant. The notion of a judge who is approved of by both parties, whose judgement satisfies both opponents, again points to a form of settling conflicts by means of arbitration, as we have seen. The *dādwar ī vaiiōzušt* might have been a precursor or a variant of *dādwar ī pēšēmāl* and *dādwar ī pasēmāl*, but whereas the former expression seems to designate an arbitrator or umpire with judicial capacity, who is trusted and selected by *both* parties, the two latter terms refer to arbitrators appointed *separately* by the opponents.

17 FiŌ XXVIIb (no. 764): *vaiiō* (+*uuaiiō*) *zuštō ī dādwar ēn wizārēd kū xwāstār ī warōmand niyōšītār ī ēwarīh ast* 'The (Avestan term) *vaiiō zuštō*—"agreeable to both" (is) a judge (*dādwar*). It is explained thus: he is a seeker of that which is doubtful and a hearer of that which is certain.' (Reichelt 1900, p. 213; Klingenschmitt 1968, no. 764).

A longer passage of the Law-book contains a detailed list of the specific duties and competences of the *dādwar*, albeit in the typically unsystematic and far too concise manner of this source without explanations. If we attempt to group these loosely connected entries, we can reconstruct the following responsibilities and areas of activity of the judge:[18]

1. The *dādwar* has the general duty to preside over court proceedings and to examine the specifics of a case 'for the sake of reaching judgement' (*padisāy dādestān anayīhēd*).
2. It is his task to initiate proceedings (*hamēmālīh kardan*), to schedule court sessions (*zamān kard*),[19] to admit witnesses (*gugāy padīrift*), to have them brought to court (*āwurd*) and to order their detention (*dāšt*).
3. In a dispute regarding ownership (*xwēšīh*) he examines the object of the dispute to find out how much (*čand*) it is worth, how (*čiyōn*) it came into the ownership of a litigant and to which type of ownership (*čē ēwēnag xwēšīh*) it belongs.[20]
4. He ascertains, whether a litigant has waited for his opponent to appear in court or has not waited (*pād ud nē pād*),[21] and whether a litigant takes legal action or fails to take legal action (*kār rāyēnēd ud kār nē rāyēnēd*). He determines, whether a party has committed an obstruction of justice (*azišmānd*), and ensures that a corresponding entry (*čak*) is made in the record of court proceedings.[22]
5. It is his duty to discern offences committed during the trial (*winąh ī andar dādestān*). He should strive to reveal: (a) concealed facts or evidence (*nihān būd*, lit. 'that, which is concealed'); (b) a false claim to entitlement (*mihpaitim/miϑōpaitim* < Av. **miϑō.paiϑimna-?*);[23] (c) the distortion of a statement in court (*waštagīh*).[24]

18 MHDA 25.16–26.11 (Macuch 1981, pp. 49–50; 188–189). The following list of duties and competences of the *dādwar* tries to retain the (somewhat jumbled) sequence in this passage, but it does not follow it slavishly.

19 On *zamān kardan* ' to set a date (for a hearing)' see Macuch 2016a, p. 158. See also p. 536 on civil proceedings.

20 On the various types of ownership see Chapter III, pp. 193–202.

21 On *pādan* 'to stay, wait (in court)' in the specific context of legal proceedings, see Macuch 2016a, pp. 154–155.

22 On *kār rāyēnīdan* 'to take legal action; to conduct legal proceedings' and *čak* 'note, entry (in the transcript of proceedings)' see MHD 73.13–74.5 (Macuch 1993, pp. 489–490; 493) and *ibid.* pp. 497–498 (n. 7); also Macuch 1981, p. 153 (n. 153); also above Chapter IV, p. 279; on *azišmand* 'obstruction of justice' see MHD 10.2–12.17 (Macuch 1993, pp. 115–121) and section 3.1.5, pp. 561–569.

23 As far as I can see, *mihpaitim/miϑōpaitim* < Av. **miϑō.paiϑimna-* is a hapax legomenon, possibly from **miϑō* 'false' + *paiϑimna-* 'having false entitlement, false possession'; Bartholomae 1904, col. 844: '*paiϑya-* „potiri" (1) in Besitz sein von – (Akk.) teilhaftig sein ["to have possession of; having part of"]'.

24 On *waštagīh* and *waštag-saxwanīh* 'changing, twisting, distorting' a statement in court, see MHD 8.15–10.11 (Macuch 1993, pp. 102–108) and below, pp. 561–569.

6. He is responsible for identifying the individuals (parties and witnesses) who take part in the proceedings. The following details have to be established: (a) a person's age (*syā ud spēdīh*, lit. 'blackness and whiteness [of the hair]'); (b) a person's gender (*narīh ud mādagīh*, lit. 'maleness and femaleness'); (c) the identity of a person and the conformity of person, name and seal (*hamtanīh ud hamnāmīh ud hammuhrīh*), that is, the judge has to ascertain the name and descent of the individual and make sure, that he is entitled to the seal he uses (*e.g.* on contracts, other documents presented as evidence, transcripts of legal proceedings, etc.).[25]
7. He registers the acknowledgement of a liability (or: the confession of guilt; *xwastūgīh*) on the part of one of the litigants, and takes interim possession (*dārišn ī pad nidāšt?*) of the object of dispute.[26]
8. It is his duty to listen to the claim of the plaintiff and the answer of the defendant, when they file a complaint/appeal (*saxwan ud passox garzīdan ī must*) at a distance of three steps (*andar sē gām*).[27]
9. After having passed judgement, the judge has the following responsibilities: (a) he hears the statements of the ligitants regarding consent (*hunsandīh*) or disagreement (*a-hunsandīh*) with the verdict; (b) he ensures that the scribe who has taken down the court transcripts and noted the verdict (*dib ud wizīr*) also records his own name (*kū kē kard*); (c) he makes sure that the witnesses who have confirmed the identities of the involved individuals and their seals (*tan ud muhr kū kē pad āšnāg guft*) are recorded in the transcript; (d) he sees to it that the transcripts of the case and the verdict (*nāmag ud wizīr*) are conveyed to the archivars (*dīwānbān*); (e) he arranges for the person sentenced to gaol to be transferred to the gaoler (*zēndānbān*) and the wardens (*gizīrān*).[28]

25 On this phrase and the function of seals see Chapter IV, 2, p. 288. See also MHDA 29.9–30.5, where *hamtanīh* is elucidated by an example (Macuch 1981, pp. 54–55; 192–193).

26 On *xwastūgīh* 'acknowledgement, recognition of a liability, debt; confession of guilt' see Chapter IV, pp. 360–364. The reading and meaning of the word read tentatively here as *nidāšt* (in *dārišn ī pad nidāšt*), written ⟨nd'št'; nyš'ť; nyyd'št'⟩ (MHDA 26.3; 26.10; 28.4 respectively; variant reading: *widāšt*) is uncertain (from *nī-* + √^{3}*dar* ; Bartholomae 1904, col. 691, 'nieder-, festhalten' ['hold down; hold, retain']?; Ir. √**dar*^{1}, Cheung 2007, pp. 57–59). I take *dārišn ī pad nidāšt*, lit. 'holding in retainment', to designate a thing held only temporarily and provisionally in possession (*dārišn*). The judge may have had the right to keep an object of dispute 'in retainment' (*pad nidāšt*) until he reached a verdict; a variant of this term might be *dārišn ī uzīdag* 'provisional possession' (MHDA 26.11), see below.

27 The phrase *saxwan ud passox garzīdan ī must* is literally: 'statement and answer in filing a complaint'. On the terminology of legal proceedings see Macuch 2016a, on the quoted phrase particularly pp. 152–153; the 'three steps' are an interesting detail, which is repeated several times in the sources, see below p. 538.

28 The Tabarestān documents enable us to understand to a large extent the procedure described so concisely in this passage, using the same technical terminology, see particularly Macuch 2016a and 2017c. On *gizīr* 'warden, policeman'; Syriac *gzīrāyā* 'lictor'; Talmudic Aramaic *gzyrpṭ'* 'collector, lictor' see Hübschmann 1895, p. 105 (no. 1084) and p. 272, and Ciancaglini 2008, p. 143.

The first section of this long passage on the judge ends with the statement, that if a case does not fall within the competence of the *dādwar*, legal proceedings (*rāyēnišn ī saxwan*) are suspended (*pādīrān*).[29] But the text continues to add other competences to the list, which were possibly disputed among the jurists and legal schools, as they were conceded to the *dādwar* only within the framework of legal practice (*pad kardag*). In the specific context of the daily work of the courts, where unforeseeable problems were bound to arise, the judge is considered to be entitled and competent (*pad ēwar dārēnd*) to carry out the following necessary tasks in the course of a trial:[30]

1. to investigate under which circumstances (*čē*) and to which amount (*čand*) a pledge (*ǰāmag*) or object of dispute (*čīš*), held in deposit by the wardens (*gizīrān*), has been stolen and taken away (*duzīd ud burd*);
2. to break and mark a seal (on a document) that has to be broken and marked (*muhr-iz ī škastan ud nišān kardan abāyēd*);
3. to keep the object of dispute 'in retainment' (*pad nidāšt?*) (according to one unnamed jurisconsult) or to take temporary possession (*dārišn ī uzīdag*) of it (according to the legal school of Pēšagsīr).[31]

In short, our text transmits a long list of specific competences and responsibilities of the *dādwar* in all phases of the trial: it is his task to preside over proceedings (keeping a distance of three steps from the litigants), to summon the parties, to hear their initial statements, to identify the litigants and witnesses and their seals, to schedule the sessions, to collect the preliminary information necessary for taking legal action, to evaluate and take provisional possession of the object of dispute, to assess the evidence and to pass judgement. After the verdict is delivered and the litigants have stated their consent or disagreement with the judge's decision (a request can be filed to an appellate court in the latter case), the judge makes sure that the transcripts of the trial have been recorded correctly (including the name of the scribe and the witnesses who have identified the parties and their seals). It is furthermore his responsibility to arrange for the transfer of the court records to the archival and to ensure that a litigant, who has been sentenced to gaol, is delivered to the wardens and the gaoler.[32]

These duties suggest that the judge was actively involved in all phases of the trial by inquiring into the facts and circumstances of a case, examining the evidence, interrogating the witnesses, supervising the correct documentation of the

29 MHDA 26.7 (Macuch 1981, pp. 50; 188).

30 MHDA 26.7–11 (Macuch 1981, pp. 50; 189; Perikhanian 1997, pp. 292–293, has divergent readings and a completely different understanding of the whole passage).

31 On this last task see also the first list on the competences of the *dādwar* (under 7).

32 The seal of a *dādwar* of the province of *Māh-kust ī Wastān* in the North-West of Iran has survived; see Gyselen 2019, pp. 262–263. On anonymous administrative seals with the inscription *driyōšān ǰādag-gōw ud dādwar* or *ǰādag-gōw dādwar ī driyōšān* 'Advocate of the Poor and Judge' see Chapter IV, pp. 293–295, with further references.

case and the implementation of the verdict. The Sasanian legal system was hence obviously an inquisitorial system of adjudication (prevalent today in continental Europe) as opposed to an adversarial or accusatorial system (found today in Anglo-American jurisdiction). The main difference between the two systems is to be found in the role of the presiding official, usually a judge, who in an inquisitorial trial participates directly in questioning the parties and witnesses and developing the evidence. By contrast, the judge in an accusatorial procedure acts as an impartial umpire, whose task it is to secure a fair trial, while the process of finding evidence is conducted by the prosecutor and the defense, competing with each other to advocate their respective viewpoints within the constraints of the existing rules of evidence and procedure. But we cannot completely exclude the possibility that some variant of the accusatorial procedure was also known in Sasanian law. As we have seen above, the judges titled *dādwar ī pēšēmāl/pasēmāl* and *dādwar ī vaiiōzušt*, seem to have acted as arbitrators or umpires, but the entries on these officials are far too brief for any reliable conclusions.

The head of the judges employed by the State, the *šahr dādwarān dādwar* 'Chief Judge of the State', is mentioned *en passant* in a single passage of the Law-book in a context that transmits no details or explanations whatsoever on this presumably important official. The compiler of the Law-book cites from the endowment document of a Wahrām fire founded by a certain Farroxgyān ī Zarduxštān, who held this title at an unknown time, possibly in the late Sasanian period.[33] Another attestation of this title may have originally been in the late Pahlavi text called *sūr saxwan* 'banquet speech', but the passage has not been transmitted correctly: ⟨štr' Y d'twl'n⟩ *šahr ī dādwarān* does not make sense as a title and has been corrected in the editions of Tavadia and Daryaee to *šahr(-dādwar) ī dādwarān* and *šahr dādwarān* respectively.[34] The context in which the term appears makes it very likely that the misrepresented title is not the common *šahr dādwar* 'judge of the State' (also attested as loanword in Syriac *šahrdawer*),[35] but that of a significant, high-ranking official, presumably the *šahr dādwarān dādwar*. In the ranking of State officials he is placed in this text between men of high standing: in the fourth position after the King of Kings, between the powerful Generals (*Ērān-spāhbed*) of the (four) climes and the *mowān handarzbed* 'Chief Counsellor of the Magi'.[36] If this is in fact a garbled form of the same title, we can reasonably infer that the *šahr dādwarān dādwar* was an important government official, probably the superior of judges (*dādwar*) employed by the State, but his exact position in the judicial hierarchy, especially in comparison to the

33 MHD 110.5–11 (Macuch 1993, pp. 645, 652).

34 For the Pahlavi text see Jamasp-Asana 1897–1913, p. 107 (l. 13–14); these readings and other variant readings in more recent Persian editions of the text have been noted by Daryaee 2007, p. 68 (§ 13), no. 27.

35 On the Syriac loanword see Ciancaglini 2008, pp. 260–261, with further references.

36 On this ranking see Daryaee 2007; one of the four climes is missing in the Pahlavi text, see *ibid.* fn. 7.

mowbedān mowbed 'Chief Mobed', is difficult to determine on the basis of this sparse material. Both high officials may have been on a par in the hierarchy, the former as the superior of the judges employed by the State, the latter as the head of priests, who were active in jurisdiction (besides other areas of priestly work). However, only the *mowbedān mowbed* is explicitly designated in the Law-book as the highest judicial authority, whose judgement is infallible and cannot be contested (with presumably one exception: if there is a deviating royal decree, *framān*, of the sovereign or his representatives, see pp. 510–511). This would rather suggest a more important position in the judicial hierarchy, but we cannot exclude the possibility that the compiler of the Law-book, being a priest or theologian himself, was interested in selecting for his compilation those sources, which underlined the immense power of Zoroastrian religious dignitaries in the Sasanian period. This line of thought would fit in well with the content of the passage, in which the *šahr dādwarān dādwar* is mentioned, namely as a founder of a Wahrām fire: the context stresses this official's devotion to religious matters rather than his high position as Chief Judge of the State.

Table 49. Overview: State judges (*dādwar*)

Type of judge	Translation	Definition
dādwar ī keh	Junior Judge	judge in the court of the first instance
dādwar ī meh	Senior Judge	judge in the court of the second instance
dādwar ī vaiiōzušt	Judge who (is) agreeable to both	arbitrator or umpire with judicial capacity, selected by both parties to the conflict
dādwar ī pēšēmāl	Judge of the plaintiff	arbitrator or umpire with judicial capacity chosen by the claimant
dādwar ī pasēmāl	Judge of the defendant	arbitrator or umpire with judicial capacity chosen by the defendant
šahr dādwarān dādwar	Chief Judge of the State	head of the judges appointed by the State

2.1.2 Religious authorities in the judiciary

After listing the tasks and working areas of the *dādwar*, the 'Chapter on the competences of officials' (*dar ī ēwarīh ī kārdārān*)[37] elucidates the duties of the two religious authorities, who were engaged in the judiciary in the higher instances, the *mowbed* and the *rad*. Interestingly, the compiler of the Law-book refers to a 'Book on the specific duties of the *mowbeds*' (*xwēškārīh nāmag ī mowbedān*), from which he has excerpted the details in this section. Although the entries are

37 MHDA 25.15–30.5 (Macuch 1981, pp. 49–50; 188–193).

once again far too short and leave a large number of unresolved questions, they certainly convey an impression of the *mowbed*'s vast area of responsibility:[38]

1. The *mowbed* has all the judicial competences, which have been already mentioned above with regard to the *dādwar* (*pad-iz ān kē dādwar pad-iš ēwar* 'he is also qualified with regard to that, for which the judge is qualified').
2. In addition to these areas of judicial competence, he is responsible for nominating (*gumārdan*) a person as 'substitute successor, proxy' (*stūr*) and as guardian (*sālār*) of a family, when a request has been made (that is, when there is no *būdag* 'natural', or *kardag* 'appointed', proxy or guardian in a family and a suitable person has to be chosen by religious authorities for one of these institutions).[39]
3. The statement (*saxwan*) of the *mowbeds* is necessary (*abāyēd*) in order to detain and to levy taxes (*pad abāz grift ud sāk/nisāk abar nihād*) on property (*xwāstag*), which goes 'back to the fire' (*abāz ō ātaxš*).[40] This phrase is far from lucid, but seems to mean that the *mowbedān* had to be consulted in matters concerning tax assessment and collection from property dedicated to the upkeep of fire foundations (the *rad* and the *āmārgar* are also mentioned in this context, see below). This property consisted of fertile land, orchards, vineyards, etc., which were subject to taxation, but for which obviously specific rules were in force, when the proceeds went to a sacred fire (on fire foundations see Chapter III, pp. 213–229).
4. The *mowbed* is authorized to 'remove a disturbance' (*wizāy hišt*) and to seal the 'document (containing the verdict?)' (*fragār brīd*) in a criminal trial. The first phrase is used in the context of disturbances caused by one of the litigants during a trial, which were assessed as *azišmānd* offences, *i. e.* obstructions of justice. The first obstruction was reprimanded with the phrase: *tā dādestān sar bawēd mā wizāy* 'Until the trial has come to an end, do not disturb (proceedings)', for the second obstruction the offender had to submit a pledge, the third obstruction led to the loss of the case (see pp. 561–569 below).[41]
5. He is obliged to suspend (*pādīrān*) proceedings, if he cannot reach a reliable (*ēwar*) verdict.

38 MHDA 25.11–16 (Macuch 1981, pp. 50–51; 189).

39 On these institutions and technical terms see Chapter II, sections 4.4 and 6.

40 The term misspelled as ⟨nkd'k'⟩ (MHDA 26.13; 27.12); ⟨nd'k'⟩ (MHDA 26.17); ⟨kd'k'⟩ (MHDA 28.5) is presumably ⟨s'k'⟩ or ⟨ns'k'⟩ *sāk/nisāk* 'tax, duty, toll, tribute, revenue'; compare *sāk ud bāj* 'tribute and tax' (*Wizārišn ī čatrang* 3, 7, 36; Daryaee 2010b, pp. 23, 24, 26); Armenian loanword *sak* 'tribute' (Hübschmann 1897, p. 234, no. 563); NP *sā*, *sāw* 'tribute, revenue' (Steingass 1892, pp. 637; 644). The term *abāz griftan* ⟨L'WHL 'HDWNtn⟩ is attested in several passages of the Law-book always with the meaning 'to hold back, detain, confiscate', as in: *abāz grift pādixšāy hēd* 'you are authorized to detain it' (MHD 67.5–6); *pādixšāy ka … guharīg ī parwarišn rāy abāz gīrēd* 'he is authorized to confiscate it … as a compensation for fostering (a child)' (MHD 33.4–5).

41 On *wizāy hištan* 'to remove harm, damage' see Macuch 1981, p. 197 (n. 31; Durkin-Meisterernst 2004, p. 360, ⟨wyz'y⟩ *wizāy-* 'to impair, harm'). The term *fragār*

The competences of the *rad* correspond to a certain degree to those of the *mowbed* (see numbers 1 and 5 below) and the *āmārgar* (see pp. 512–514), but he is not mentioned in the Law-book in the context of nominating a proxy or family guardian. In two of the Tabarestān documents, however, the *rad* of the region of Parišwārgar (*Parišwārgar rad*) called Windād-Xwaršēd, is explicitly named in connection with legal disputes regarding inheritance and the instalment of a *stūrīh*, areas in which the *rad* might also have acted as judge in the Sasanian period. The documents moreover suggest that the *Parišwārgar rad* was one of the high Zoroastrian dignitaries presiding over jurisdiction in the whole region (*kustag*) of Parišwārgar, which encompassed several provinces, among these the province (*ōstān*) of Tabarestān.[42] In the Law-book the specific areas of jurisdiction of the *rad* relate particularly to commercial issues and to the administration of fire foundations:[43]

1. It is the task of the *rad* to detain and to levy taxes (*pad abāz grift ud sāk/nisāk abar nihād*) on the property dedicated to the fires (*xīr ī ātaxšān*).[44]
2. He adjudicates matters regarding sale (*froxt*) and compensation (*guharīg*).
3. He ascertains the worth (*arz*) and the value (*wahāg*) of things pertaining to the property of the fires (*xīr ī ātaxšān*).
4. He records entries (*adēn*) on the amount of surplus that has been taken in (*čand mad*) and also on the lack of surplus (*pad-iz nē mad ī čīš*) of property belonging to a specific group of sacred fires, namely those fires, whose core assets (*bun*) and holdings (*handraxt*) are registered in the *dīwān ī kardagān* ('archive of pious institutions').[45]

'document (containing the verdict?)' in *fragār brīdan* 'to seal a document' (MHD 78.4,7; MHDA 26.14, 27.2; on this phrase see also Macuch 1981, pp. 198–199, n. 32) or *fragār kardan* 'to make/record a document' (MHD 92.2;) is not explained, but occurs together with *pursišn-nāmag* 'transcript of interrogation', which was written in criminal cases. The word possibly designates a document containing the sentence from a criminal trial (the etymology is not conclusive: < *fra* + √[1]*kar* 'to do, make; Kellens 1995, pp. 14–15; Cheung 2007, pp. 236–238; MMP ⟨prg'r⟩ *fragār* 'defeat', Durkin-Meisterernst 2004, p. 278). The verdict was also noted at the end of the *pursišn-nāmag*.

42 Tab. 11 (Macuch 2020b, pp. 191–199) and Tab. 28 (Macuch 2020b, pp. 199–209); the documents are in Appendix XIV. For a discussion of legal proceedings in the Tabarestān documents and the position of the *Parišwārgar rad* see Macuch 2024c.

43 MHDA 26.17–27.4 (Macuch 1981, pp. 51, 189).

44 On this phrase see the competences of the *mowbed* under number 3.

45 The *dīwān ī kardagān* was an archive in which pious endowments and fire foundations were registered, see Chapter III, p. 227. The meaning 'holdings' assumed here for *handraxt* is hypothetical, as this is the only attestation of the term in this specific context (< Av. √*dranj* [*dranž*] 'to fix, fasten, hold' + *ham-* 'to encompass'; Kellens 1995, p. 32; OIr. √**dra(n)ǰ*; Cheung 2007, p. 76; Bartholomae 1904, col. 772: √[1]*drang* 'firmare'; 'festigen, kräftigen, bestärken' ['strengthen, consolidate, solidify']). I take the term to refer to possessions, which were not part of the *bun* ('substance, core assets') of property belonging to a sacred fire, but whose income was dedicated to its upkeep.

5. He is authorized to 'remove a disturbance' (*wizāy hišt*) and to seal the 'document (containing the verdict?)' (*fragār brīd*) in a criminal trial and everything else pertaining to these issues (*har ān ī pad ān ēwēnag*).
6. He is considered as competent (*pad ēwar dārend*) in every matter regarding the property of the sacred fires (*pad har xīr ī ātaxšān*), just as the *āmārgar* is competent with respect to all issues regarding sacred fires pertaining to the crown (*šāhīgān*).[46]

Despite its shortness, the passage conveys quite clearly that, apart from various tasks in the judiciary, one of the specific duties of the *rad* was to administer the (presumably vast) properties dedicated to sacred fires registered in the *dīwān ī kardagān*, which obviously encompassed all larger pious institutions with the exception of those, which were established on land belonging to the crown (*šāhīgān*). The latter were administered by the *āmārgar*, to whom we will return below.

The *hērbed* is not mentioned in this chapter of the Law-book, but a few short remarks in our sources suggest that religious dignitaries in this position were also engaged in jurisdiction, possibly restricted to a specific area, and on a lower level of the hierarchy than the *mowbed* and *rad*. Only a single sentence of the Law-book mentions the *hērbed* en passant in the context of claims involving property issues. In the chapter on the *dastwar* ('predecessor in title'; *auctor*) a longer passage discusses the question, how to proceed on the question of scheduling a date for summoning the *dastwar* of the defendant, that is, the 'legal predecessor' who can testify for the defendant, providing proof that the object in dispute has been transferred legitimately to the latter. The sentence ends with the statement: 'proceedings are to be conducted according to the instruction of the *hērbeds*' (*dādestān be rāyēnīdan čiyōn hērbedān gōwēnd*).[47] This is not a

46 This at least seems to be meant by MHDA 27.3–4, which states literally: 'he (= the *rad*) is considered as competent for every matter pertaining to the sacred fires, for which the *āmārgar* would be regarded as competent, if they (= the fires) belonged to the crown' (*pad har xīr ī ātaxšān ka pad šāhīgān hē āmārgar pad-iš ēwar hē pad ēwar dārēnd*).

47 MHD 5.9–13: *ka pēšēmāl pad ēn kū xwāstag man xwēš ud abadaxšāyīhā pasēmāl dārēd pasēmāl hamēmāl pasēmāl nē xwēšīh ī pēšēmāl pad tāšt gōwēd pas ō zamān ō dastwar xwāhēd Pusānweh ī Āzādmardān guft kū ka ēdōn gōwēd ēg-iš zamān ōh dahišn bē ka gōwēd kū tō nē xwēš čē man xwēš zamān ī ō dastwar nē dahišn čē dādestān be rāyēnīdan čiyōn hērbedān gōwēnd* 'When the plaintiff because of this (statement): "the property (is) my own (*man xwēš*) and the defendant holds it without entitlement (*abadaxšāyīhā pasēmāl dārēd*)", (is) an opponent of the defendant (and) the defendant states with certainty that the plaintiff has no ownership (title) (*nē xwēšīh ī pēšēmāl*), then afterwards requests a date for (calling his) "predecessor in title" (*dastwar*), Pusānweh ī Āzādmardān said: If he (= the defendant) speaks thus, then a date should be scheduled. But if he (= the defendant) says: "It is not your own, since it (is) my own" (*tō nē xwēš čē man xwēš*), (then) no date should be scheduled for the "predecessor in title" (*dastwar*), since proceedings are to be conducted according to the instruction of the *hērbeds*.' On the term *dastwar* see Chapter IV, pp. 385–387, and below pp. 542–544.

very informative statement on its own, but taken together with the information to be gained from the Tabarestān court records we have good reason to assume that the office of *hērbed* involved duties in the judiciary in the specific area of lawsuits on property rights. The title appears in two almost identical documents (Tab. 1A and Tab. 8B) with regard to an official called Farroxabzūd, who is addressed as *hērbed* and was evidently engaged as judge in the canton (*tasūg*) of Dēl ī Dēlān in the province of Tabarestān. He deals with complaints of residents from the villages of this canton (to which the village of *Asp-gurd belongs) and presides over a civil case involving a dispute regarding an ownership title.[48] This can be deduced only indirectly by the measures taken in preparation of the trial. One of these in a preliminary hearing requests the defendant to summon his *dastwar* to testify for him in court. Taken together these details allow two conclusions: (1) that legal proceedings on ownership issues operated on the basis of instructions given by the *hērbeds* and (2) that the *hērbed* acted as judge in disputes regarding a claim to ownership requiring the testimony of a *dastwar*. Although the information is sparse, we can confidently surmise that the *hērbed* was engaged as judge (presumably already in the Sasanian period) in lawsuits regarding property issues, specifically in cases demanding the testimony of the defendant's 'legal predecessor' due to a more or less recent transfer of ownership rights (by sale, barter, gift).

It might be significant that the next judicial authority in the sequence of officials in the quoted chapter of the Law-book after the *mowbed* and the *rad*, is the *mowbedān mowbed*. He is the last religious expert to be named before the compiler of the Law-book enumerates the responsibilities of public officials of the State, who had no religious duties and did not belong to the priesthood. The Chief Mobed is depicted as the highest judicial authority in the final instance, whose judgement is 'certain, reliable, competent, binding' (*ēwar*) in contrast to the 'uncertain, unreliable, not binding' (*warōmand*) sentences of all other persons (*kas*).[49] There are two means of attaining 'reliability' (*xwastūgīh*) in a verdict: either by the oath (*war*) or by the judgement of the *mowbedān mowbed*, but the verdict of the Chief Mobed is to be considered—according to the jurisconsult Dibīr—as even 'more binding' (*ēwartar*) than the oath.[50] The same idea is expressed concisely in the *Dēnkard*:

> DkD 534.9–15 (DkM 705.12–17)
> *ud abar abē-niyāzīh ī pēšēmālān (ud) pasēmalān az tan ī dādestān guftan ka gugāy ud dadwar mowbedān mowbed ud wāwarīh ī wizīr ī mowbedan mowbed az xwēš dānišn gugāyīh kunēd ka-iz pad tan nē wizurd ud a-wāwarīh ī abārīg*

48 On the Tabarestān court records see Macuch 2016a; on the *hērbed* in this context see specifically Macuch 2024c, pp. 279–282; the documents are transcribed and translated in Appendix XII. On the *herbed* in a legal context see also Azarnouche 2019.
49 MHDA 27.4–7 (Macuch 1981, pp. 51; 190); translated below p. 510.
50 MHDA 28.5–7 (Macuch 1981, pp. 52–53; 191; translated below p. 545, fn. 161).

dādwar ka-iz pad tan wizurd niyāzōmandīh ī pēšēmālān (ud) pasēmālān ō tan ī dādestān guftan ka-iz dādwar az dādestān āgāh.

'And on (this, that) there is no need (*abē-niyāzīh*) for the plaintiffs and the defendants to make statements before the personnel of the court (*tan ī dādestān*), when the Chief Mobed (*mowbedān mowbed*) is (both) witness (*gugāy*) and judge (*dādwar*). And on the validity (*wāwarīh*) of the verdict (*wizīr*), which the Chief Mobed passes due to his own knowledge (of the case) as witness, even if it is not confirmed by the personnel (*ka-iz pad tan nē wizurd*), and (on) the invalidity (*a-wāwarīh*) of the (verdict of) other judges (*dādwar*), even if it is confirmed by the personnel (*ka-iz pad tan wizurd*). (On) the need of the plaintiff and the defendant to make statements before the personnel of the court (*tan ī dādestān*), even if the judge (*dādwar*) has (personal) knowledge (of the case).'

The phrase *tan ī dādestān*, lit. 'body of the court', *i. e.* 'members, personnel of the court', designates the assembly of officials, who take part in a trial (the judge, the scribes, the *war-sālār*, the *frēzwān*, to be described below, and other public officials) and whose statements in their specific areas of competence (*xwēškārīh*) contribute to finding a verdict. Our passage highlights in this context the significance of the Chief Mobed as judge: there is no need for the litigants to present their case before the assembled personnel of the court, when the highest judicial authority functions both as witness (*gugāy*) and judge (*dādwar*) and can hence pass judgement based on his personal knowledge of the case. His verdict is final and decisive, it has 'validity' (*wāwarīh*), and there is no need for it to be upheld or confirmed (*wizurd*) by the other members of the court. In sharp contrast, all other verdicts can be questioned and considered as invalid, even if they are confirmed by all court members; the litigants are moreover obliged to make their statements, even if the judge (*dādwar*) presiding over the proceedings has personal knowledge of the case.[51] The notion of the infallibility of the Chief Mobed is the theoretical position to be found in most attestations. In practice, however, we have reason to assume that in specific matters, apart from issues pertaining to the priesthood, the judgement of the Chief Mobed was *not* considered as more binding than a decree or command (*framān*) of high public officials and governors (*dahibedān*, lit. 'rulers of the land') appointed by the sovereign, as we will argue in the next section.

Besides the Chief Mobed the title *mowān handarzbed* 'Chief Counsellor of the Magi' is recorded in several sentences of the Law-book. This official seems to have been one of the higher religious authorities in the judicial hierarchy (maybe on a par with the *mowbedān mowbed* and the *šahr dādwarān dādwar*), but, strangely, he neither appears in the abovementioned chapter on the competences of State

51 According to MHDA 10.10–13 the testimony of the Chief Mobed is equivalent to that of three other witnesses, that is, it is decisive (Macuch 1981, pp. 32; 123–124). Compare DkD 540.3–5 (DKM 711.18–20); see below p. 545, fn. 163.

Table 50. Overview: religious authorities in the judiciary

Authorities	Areas of competence
hērbed	adjudication of lawsuits on property issues, particularly disputes on ownership requiring the testimony of a *dastwar* (*auctor*)
mowbed	– judicial competences equivalent to those of a *dādwar* – nomination (*gumārdan*) of a 'proxy' (*stŭr*) or a guardian (*sālār*) for a family – matters involving the taxation of property dedicated to the upkeep of fire foundations – confirmation of obstructions of justice and of documents from a criminal trial by sealing them (*fragār brīd*)
rad	– matters involving the taxation of property dedicated to the upkeep of fire foundations – adjudication of commercial disputes – administration of the property of the fires (*xīr ī ātaxšān*) registered in the *dīwān ī kardagān* – confirmation of obstructions of justice and of documents from a criminal trial by sealing them (*fragār brīd*)
mowān handarzbed	– supervision of disputed measures taken in lower judicial instances – confirmation or revision of problematic decisions in civil and criminal cases
mowbedān mowbed	Head of the Priesthood and Supreme Judge

officials (*kārdārān*), nor are his judicial competences elucidated in any of the other available sources. Although the short passages of the Law-book only mention the *mowān handarzbed* en passant, they leave no doubt that this official was engaged in jurisdiction in several areas as a kind of supervisor in a higher instance:

1. In matters of family law and inheritance: a *kadagbānūg* passes on *stŭrīh* to a person who is less suitable for this task without authorization to do so. The issue is brought before the *mowān handarzbed*, but he does not change the new *stŭr*.[52] In another passage the *mowān handarzbed* determines guardianship (*sālārīh*) of a sacred fire, for which no provisions have been made in the founder's testament.[53]
2. In disputes relating to suretyship: The *mowān handarzbed* adjudicates complex cases regarding the liability of co-sureties (*hampāyandān*).[54]

52 MHDA 15.14–15 (Macuch 1981, pp. 37–38; 145); on *stŭrīh* see Chapter II, pp. 169–174.
53 MHDA 37.11–15 (Macuch 1981, pp. 64, 221); on *sālārīh* see Chapter II, pp. 177–183.
54 MHD 57.2–12 (Macuch 1993, pp. 388, 393; on the narrative components in this unique passage of the Law-book see Macuch 2009b and Chapter IV, p. 359, fn. 397); MHD 59.6–10 (Macuch 1993, pp. 390, 395).

3. In criminal law: The *mowān handarzbed* confirms the decision of the *mowbed* of Staxr allowing the testimony of two women in preparation of a bill of indictment (*nibištag*).[55]

These concrete cases suggest that the *mowān handarzbed* was called upon to control unorthodox decisions of lower instances, to adjudicate problematic legal issues, to confirm or revise disputed measures taken by lower officials (such as the *mowbed* of Staxr, see 3 above). In short, his task was to supervise the work of lower judicial instances in both civil and criminal cases and to reach decisions on unresolved problematic issues. But the information is far too concise to draw any further conclusions.

2.1.3 Public officials with judicial power

In the chapter on judicial and public officials of the Law-book, the sentence following the competences of the Chief Mobed is truly remarkable, as it seems to reduce the power of the latter—immediately after stressing his absolute authority as Supreme Judge—in comparison to that of other high government officers and the King himself (*dahibedān*, lit. 'rulers of the land'). As we have noted above, the organisation of the judiciary seems to have been based in the interest of *Realpolitik* on a balance of power between officials appointed by the State in the first two instances and religious authorities acting as arbitrators and judges on a lower level in the communities and in the appellate courts. In this context the question may have emerged, whether the infallible verdict of the Chief Mobed as Supreme Judge was to be implemented in all cases and under all circumstances or whether the *dahibedān* (presumably a collective term denoting the King and governors, vice-regents, princes etc. appointed by the sovereign) could follow a different procedure (under the pressure of reasons of State, *e.g.* to avoid uprisings, or on other grounds). It will be worthwhile to quote the whole passage:

> MHDA 27.4–7
> *mowbedān mowbed pad har ān ī ka abārīg kas gōwēd warōmand ka mowbedān mowbed gōwēd ēwar. ud az abar framān ī dahibedān būd nē šāyistan ī čīš-iz ēwarīh rāy pad ān čīš ī nē andar pēšag ī āsrōnān ud pad framān ī dahibedān ud ǰād-gēhān kār-framān padiš.*
>
> 'The Chief Mobed is competent for every (statement/judgement), which, when pronounced by another person, (is considered as) uncertain (*warōmand*): when the Chief Mobed pronounces (judgement), it (is) binding (*ēwar*). And there is a decree on this (issue) (*kār-framān padiš*), that the legal force (*ēwarīh*) of no (judgement) can be above the command (*framān*) of the *dahibedān* regarding a case, which (is) not a matter of the guild of priests (*pēšag ī āsrōnān*), and (is) under the command (*framān*) of the *dahibedān* and (regards) their share of property (*ǰād-gēhān*).'[56]

55 MHD 98.1–3 (Macuch 1993, pp. 582, 587).
56 Macuch 1981, pp. 51, 190.

This is admittedly a syntactically twisted text, but in my opinion there can be no doubt that the second sentence qualifies the first statement on the legal force or binding power (*ēwarīh*) of the Chief Mobed's judgement. We are first informed that the verdict of the *mowbedān mowbed* is 'reliable, qualified, competent, certain, binding' (*ēwar*), whereas, in contrast, other judgements are considered as 'unreliable, doubtful' (*warōmand*). There is, however, an official decree (*kār-framān*)[57] (of the sovereign?) which puts this statement into perspective: the verdict of the Chief Mobed is absolutely binding with respect to matters pertaining to the guild of priests (*pēšag ī āsrōnān*), but apart from these issues, no judgement has more legal force than a 'command, order, decree' (*framān*) of the 'rulers of the land' (*dahibedān*), particularly with respect to matters under their administration and property under their control. I take this to mean that the various interests of the priesthood and of the worldly rulers (the King and his governors, vice-regents, etc.) are put into balance and weighed against each other: the 'command' (*framān*) of the latter is given preference over the judgement of the Chief Mobed in matters regarding the immediate interests of the State and its property. As the case against the Catholicos Mār Abā (alongside other Acts of Christian martyrs) demonstrates, it is in fact the King who has the last word in passing judgement and also the option of pardoning the convicted criminal, albeit not without taking the decision and the interests of the Chief Mobed into consideration.[58]

Outside the priesthood several officials of the State with judicial power in their specific areas of responsibility are mentioned in the same chapter (who might have been included in the general term *dahibedān*). The *ōstāndār* or 'governor of a province (*ōstān*)' is one of the omnipresent officials not only in the original documents of the 'Pahlavi Archive', but also on seals and seal imprints, which, however, do not convey information on the specific competences of this public official.[59] The information in the Law-book is limited, but it is, as far as I can see,

57 The technical term *kār-framān* is used with two meanings in the Law-book: (1) 'instruction, decree, edict, directive, command, order, instruction in a will', as in *muhr ī pad kār-framān dāštan* lit. 'seal(s) for exercising command', the designation for anonymous administrative seals on which only the name and place of the administration issuing or confirming an instruction were engraved (MHD 93.3; 100.6,10,14; see Chapter IV, section 2.3 above); (2) 'manager, overseer, steward, functionary, official', the general designation for a public official, who exercises command in a specific area and is entitled to pass judgement in this field, as in *pad wizīr ī radān ud any {kār}framānān* 'according to the verdict of the *radān* and other *kār-framānān* ("officials exercising command")' (MHD 78.2–3; the word is also attested in this sense in the Pahlavi papyri and other original documents, see Gignoux 2004, pp. 45–46). On this term see also Macuch 1993, p. 357, with further references.

58 See p. 581 below

59 On this official see Weber's 2015 edition of two original documents referring to an *ōstāndār*, and Gyselen 2019a, pp. 4–6, also index, p. 364.

the only description of the *ōstāndār*'s operational range, whose household must have been enormous, as WEBER has pointed out.[60] The terms and phrases used in the Law-book to describe his competences are similar or even identical to those employed with regard to the *rad* (and the *āmārgar* below), indicating overlapping areas of responsibility in certain fields (such as commercial issues). We have reason, however, to assume that in the areas of tax assessment and collection the competences of the *rad* and the *mowbed* were restricted to the property of fire foundations, whereas the *ōstāndār* and the *āmārgar* had far larger areas of operation. The Law-book lists the following tasks:[61]

1. The *ōstāndār* detains and levies taxes (*pad abāz grift ud sāk/nisāk abar nihād*).
2. He is concerned with matters pertaining to sale (*frōxt*) and the acceptance and transfer of a value (*wahāg padīrift ud dād*).
3. He is in charge of registering (*paydāg kard*) the entry of property into the royal treasury (*ō šāhīgān madan ī xwāstag*).

The competences of the *ōstāndār* overlap to a certain degree with those of the next official, the high-ranking *āmārgar*, lit. 'calculator, accountant', a title which was already in use under the Achaemenids and designated in the Sasanian period one of the significant officials of the State in charge of administering the finances of the crown.[62] His long list of competences are summarized as follows:[63]

1. The *āmārgar* is responsible for registering the worth (*arz*) and value (*wahāg*) of property and the entry of assets into the royal treasury (*ō šāhīgān madan*) and expenditures from the royal treasury (*az šāhīgān be madan ī xwāstag*).
2. He provides evidence that a property belongs lawfully to the crown, as in the following case: a property, which was formerly in the possession of a

60 WEBER 2015, p. 31.

61 MHDA 27.12–13 (MACUCH 1981, pp. 52; 190). The *ōstāndār* as the governor of a province presumably had far more responsibilities than those listed in this passage, including military competences. For example, in Ṭabarī's account of the battle of Iṣfahān the title of the general commanding the army is given as *ustāndār* (= *ōstāndār*); see POURSHARIATI 2008, p. 247.

62 The word is written *hmrkrʾ* in 5th century BCE Aramaic documents, indicating an original pronunciation of the title with initial *h*- (Persepolis Fortification Tablet no. 281 *apud* GREENFIELD 1977, p. 115; Elephantine papyri, COWLEY 1923 [1967], no. 26, and Aršama letters, DRIVER 1957, p. 17), which also corresponds to the Armenian loanword *hamarakar* (< OP **hamāra* < *ham-hmāra-*, HÜBSCHMANN 1895, p. 105, no. 1101, or **hammāra-* < *ham* + √*mar* + *-kāra-*, MACKENZIE 1985, p. 925). Babylonian Jewish Aramaic, on the other hand, has *ʾmrkl* (< **ahmār-kāra-*, SHAKED 1987, p. 260, or < **hammārgar*, MACKENZIE 1985, p. 925), corresponding to the MP title *āmārgar*, which is attested in Sasanian inscriptions (GIGNOUX 1972, p. 15) and on numerous seals, see *e.g.* GIGNOUX 1973, p. 139; GYSELEN 1989, p. 112, 2002a, pp. 39–43, 214–219, and 2019a, pp. 6–8, with numerous attestations, see index, p. 363. For an extensive discussion of the different attestations of the word see also CHAUMONT 1985 and GIPPERT 1993, pp. 77–83.

63 MHDA 27.13–28.5 (MACUCH 1981, pp. 52; 190–191).

'recipient of a payment' (**abasēgōmand*), is returned to the royal treasury (*abāz ō šāhīgān kard*). A potential heir (or another person) takes legal action regarding ownership of that property (*kas pad xwēšīh abar pahikārd*). It is the task of the *āmārgar* to prove that the litigant (the 'recipient of a payment') is not the owner of that property (*pad nē xwēšīh ī *abasēgōmand*).[64]

3. He procures documents (*nāmag*) on request of the provincial governor (*ōstāndār*), which he imprints with his seal (*kē āwišt padiš*) regarding, for example, the amount of remuneration a 'proxy' receives (*mizd ī stŭr*), and other matters of this kind (*abārīg-iz ān ī pad ān ēwēnag*).
4. He provides documents (*nāmag*) on expenditures and outgoing payments (*dād ud uzīd*) and also on refraining from expending money and from making any outgoing payments (*pad-iz nē dād ud nē uzīd ī xwāstag* ⟨NKSY'⟩).
5. He is responsible for drawing up a document (*dib*) on the damage (*ziyān*) a person has caused to the property of the crown (*xīr ī šāhīgān*) and for fixing a fine or compensation (*tāwān*) to be paid by the one who has caused the damage.
6. He is in charge of drawing up documents (*dib*) and fixing fines (*tāwān*) in similar cases (*pad-iz ān ī pad ān ēwēnag*).
7. It is the task of both *āmārgar* and *rad* to keep accounts of the amount (*čand*) of property pertaining to the crown (*pad xīr ī šāhīgān*); to keep it undamaged (*kū nē wizīdan*) and to determine among whom (*abar kē*) and how

64 The background of this passage is the following: the sovereign could bestow a grant consisting usually of land belonging to the crown on 'recipients of a payment' (**abasēgōmand*), *i.e.* subjects who received payment in kind for their services to the crown. In MHD 77.6–9, for example, some kind of grant (not specified in the text) consisting probably of land in ownership of the crown was given to horsemen (*aswār*) for them to finance their military equipment (*pad ēmōzan hangārišn* 'to be taken into account for the equipment'). The context of this passage implies that the horseman had lifetime possession of the grant, but that he was only the holder, not the owner, and that the property allotted to him was returned to the royal treasury (*šāhīgān*) after his death (Macuch 1993, pp. 516; 519; see also Macuch 2005c, pp. 96–98). Both the reading and translation of ⟨'psyg'wmnd⟩ **abasēgōmand*, lit. 'endowed with payment/rent', are tentative. The term ⟨'psyg⟩; ⟨'psyk⟩ **abasēg* occurs in another passage of the Lawbook in the phrase **abasēg ī pidarān* 'payment/rent/pension of the parents' (MHDA 38.3,4; Macuch 1981, pp. 64, 221). It is presumably the Middle Persian equivalent to Parthian *'wpsyk* 'payment; additional payment' and *pt(y)syk* 'rent payment, payment' in the Nisā documents (see Weber 2010, pp. 502–504). Hinz 1973, p. 90, reconstructs for Parthian *ptsyk* OP **pati-θaika-* or **pati-θaičana-* 'Vergütung, Zahlung' ['remuneration, payment'], the equivalent of elam. *bat-ti-še-kaš* with the same meaning; Weber, *ibid.*, p. 502 (with reference to Bader 1996, p. 260) has OP *pati-sāwa-* 'taxable' 'in a general sense…more probably "rent payment", less probably "tax"'; Parth. *'wpsyk* (with preverb **upa-*) is presumably built with the same etymon *-syk* ('payment'?) and could mean 'extra payment, additional payment' ('*Zuzahlung, *Draufzahlung', Weber, *ibid.*, p. 504). See also Perikhanian 1997, p. 337 (**apasēk*), who has, however, another understanding of the term as 'liability, debt'.

(*čiyōn*) shares should be distributed (*baxtan*) or kept back (*nidāštan?*) by decree (**pāymār*).[65]

8. The *āmārgarān* are authorized to calculate and to take in taxes (*pad hangārd ud ūl stad ī sāk*)

65 (MHDA 28.4–5): … *abar kē čiyōn baxtan ud nidāštan* (?) *rāy pad *pāymār* ⟨PKDWN⟩ *kunēnd ēwar* '… they are competent to determine among whom (and) how shares are to be distributed and kept back by decree' (differently MACUCH 1981, pp. 52; 191, see below). According to the *Frahang ī Pahlawīg* the Iranian equivalent of the heterogram ⟨PKDWN⟩ is ⟨ptym'l⟩ (NYBERG 1988, Ch. XVII, no. 4, p. 48: *pātēmār*) *pādimār* or **pāymār* 'appointment, assignment' (MACKENZIE 1971, p. 67). NYBERG 1988 explains the heterogram as Aramaic *piqdōn* 'official decree, testament, deposition' and translates the Iranian equivalent, following PERIKHANIAN, as 'legal procedure, judgement, decree' (*ibid.*, p. 87), from the Aramaic root PQD 'to retain, command, deposit' (SOKOLOFF 2002, pp. 924–925); compare also Syriac *puqdānā* 'command, commandment, decree' and 'authority, rule, dominion, domination' (PAYNE SMITH 1903, p. 438); 'a commandment, command, order' (MACLEAN 1901, p. 248) and Mandaic *puqdana* 'command, order, injunction, charge, appointment' (DROWER/MACUCH 1963, p. 368). In the Syriac version of Īšōʿbōxt *puqdānā* designates a 'disposition, provision' in a person's oral last will (see *e.g.* SACHAU 1914, p. 127, § 1, who renders the word as 'Verfügung'). The Iranian word is also attested in MMP ⟨p'dyhm'r⟩ *pādihmār*, *pādihammār* 'entrusted, an obligation' (DURKIN-MEISTERERNST 2004, p. 258). Although the meaning 'decree, disposition, provision' fits in well with the context of this far too short description, the Pahlavi equivalent *pādimār/*pāymār* in the Law-book does not always seem to have this meaning, but rather designates a person 'entrusted with' a specific duty, that is, an officer, delegate or representative. This is presumably the reason why PERIKHANIAN 1997 (pp. 348–349; 380) assumes that one and the same heterogram ⟨PKDWN⟩ stood for two different Middle Persian terms, *pātīmār (ibid.*, p. 380) and *dastaβar (ibid.*, pp. 348–349), which, however, in my opinion is very unlikely. Her interpretation of the latter term, following BARTHOLOMAE, is in any case untenable, according to the unequivocal testimony of the Tabarestān documents (on *dastwar* in the context of legal proceedings in these texts see MACUCH 2016a, pp. 150–151, and Chapter IV, pp. 385–387, in the present work). If ⟨PKDWN⟩ **pāymār* could also designate a person, one could think of the title *pqyd* 'officer' in Imperial Aramaic, from the same root PQD. In the Aršama letters from the Achaemenid period (fifth century BCE) *pqyd* 'denotes a high, possibly the highest, officer under the satrap in the administration of Egypt' (DRIVER 1957, pp. 15–16): it is the title given (in letter IV) to Psamšek, the officer of Aršama (DRIVER, *ibid.*, pp. 24–25). In cuneiform texts from the same period late Babylonian *paq-du* is mentioned as the 'representative, delegate' of the 'house' of the royal prince ([lú]*paq-du šá bīt mār šarri*), 'Beauftragter des „Hauses" des königlichen Prinzen' (EILERS 1940, pp. 64–65). The title might have survived as an ideogram in Middle Persian, but it may have taken on a different shade of meaning and designated another type of official or person entrusted with a specific duty. Unfortunately none of the attestations are conclusive. The earliest MP attestation of ⟨PKDWN⟩ (in ⟨PKDWN 'BYDWN⟩ **pāymār kard*) is to be found in two controversially discussed parallel passages in the inscriptions of Kirdīr from the 3rd century (Kaʿba-ye Zardušt, line 3; Naqš-ī Rustam, line 6; BACK 1978, pp. 390–391; HENNING 1957; GIGNOUX 1972a; p. 31, and 1972b, p. 182; for a discussion of the various interpretations of the passage see also HUMBACH 1974). In the Law-book the technical term, always written ⟨PKDWN⟩, appears in altogether five sentences (MHD 100.15; MHDA15.7; 28.4; 36.1,5). A translation in the sense of 'representative, delegate' makes more sense in the following cases: MHD 100.14–15: … *ēn dib ud dib-iz ī did pad muhr*

Besides these authorities other public officials were evidently engaged in jurisdiction, but the sources convey even less information on their specific responsibilities and their position in the judicial hierarchy. In the context of criminal law the Law-book mentions two groups of notables, the *čašmagān* (lit. 'renowned ones') and *šahrīgān* (lit. 'men of the state/land'),[66] who at the time of Husraw I (531–579 CE) formed an assembly (*hanǰaman*) with the task of consulting (*pad hampursagīh*) and verifying documents (containing the verdict? *fragār*) and checking transcripts of criminal cases (*pursišn-nāmag*). These documents obviously had to be confirmed in this assembly by the seals of these two groups of notables (*pad muhr ī čašmagān ud šahrīgān*) according to certain criteria, which

---

*ī Xūnābagān mānān pad kār-framān dāštan ud Anōšzād kē tasūg ī Xūnābagān pad mānāgīh *pāymār* ⟨PKDWN⟩ *āwišt.* '... this document and also this other document were sealed by the seal of the places (of jurisdiction) of Xūnābagān with the seal "for executing command" (*pad kār-framān dāštan*) and Anōšzād, who in the canton (*tasūg*) of Xūnābagān (is) the representative/delegate (**pāymār*) for the (legal) venue, sealed (them)' (MACUCH 1993, pp. 614, 622). Here ⟨PKDWN⟩ **pāymār* seems to refer to the official called Anōšzād in the canton (*tasūg*) of Xūnābagān in his function as a representative of this specific legal venue. This translation also makes sense in another attestation: *ātaxš rāy nibišt kū az frazandān ī man ōy *pāymār kē mard pahlōm had* 'with respect to the (sacred) fire he wrote: "From among my children he shall be the representative (of the fire) who (is) the foremost (= most worthy) man"' (MHDA 36.4–5, MACUCH 1981, pp. 62, 219). In other passage **pāymār kardan* is ambiguous and could be both 'to designate as delegate/representative' or 'to make a disposition/provision/decree', as in: *Mihr-Narseh ī wuzurg-framadār ātaxš dō rāy guft kū-m pad sālārīh ēk mērag ud ēk mērag *pāymār kard* 'Mihr-Narseh, the Prime Minister, stated with respect to two sacred fires: "I have designated for guardianship this man and this man as representatives (of the fires)" [or: "I have made for this man and this man a provision regarding guardianship"]' (MHDA 35.17–36.1; MACUCH 1981, pp. 62, 219). This is also true of **pāymār kard* in the two Kirdīr inscriptions mentioned above: *ud ēn and ādur ud kirdagān čē pad nibišt ān-am ōh gōnagtar Šābuhr šāhān šāh pad wāspuhragān *pāymār* ⟨PKDWN⟩ *kard kū-t bun-xānag ēn ēw bawēd.* 'And these numerous fires and pious institutions which (are) in the inscription: over these in a special manner Šābuhr, King of Kings, made me the representative of the hereditary property (*pad wāspuhragān*) [or: Šābuhr ... made me a disposition regarding the hereditary property] thus: "This one foundation-house shall be yours"' (on the wording of the last part and the much discussed *bun-xānag* from the perspective of legal texts see MACUCH 2008b, pp. 255–257, with further references; on *wāspuhragān* [lit. 'pertaining to the *wāspuhr/wispuhr*'] 'hereditary property, inheritance', and *pēšīgān-wāspuhragān* [lit. 'advance-hereditary share'] 'dowry' of the daughter, see MACUCH 1981, p. 85, n. 17). In one of the papyri edited by DIETER WEBER, P. 141, (2003, p. 26) the term *paymār-baxtag* occurs, which he translates as 'Einstellungsanteil' (or 'share of transfer' in WEBER 2007, p. 737). Unfortunately the context of the papyrus is not conclusive, but the term refers obviously to the portion of a high-ranking 'horseman' (*aswār ī az gund ī aswārān-sālārān* 'a horseman from the troup of the leaders of the horsemen', *ibid.* 737) and could designate the share ('portion of the delegate') to which this military official is entitled.

66 On the *šahrīg*, a derivative from *šahr* 'land, country, region, state, empire; city', see also GYSELEN 1989, p. 28 (not to be confused with the high-ranking title *šahrab* or with the term *šahrīg* 'subject, citizen'); on the loanword in Syriac, *šahrīgān* 'landed proprietors', see CIANCAGLINI 2008, p. 261, with further references.

will be discussed below (see section 3.2 on criminal proceedings).[67] The term *čašmag* is also attested in one of the most significant Tabarestān documents concerned with the replacement of a *stūr* (Tab. 28.13,16,17) together with the designation of another group of notables, called *stēndag*, lit. 'upright one(s)'. These two groups of *čašmag ud stēndag* (lit.) 'renowned and upright ones' are listed among other nobles, high dignitaries and legal authorities who come together to evaluate a claim to the institution of *stūrīh*, a difficult procedure, especially when large income-producing property was involved, as we may assume in this specific case.[68]

Following Masʿūdī and the Syriac source Barbahlūl, we can assume that the term *šahrīgān* denoted the eldest and most esteemed men among the landed magnates of a region from the rank of the aristocracy (*āzādān*), who were chosen as local representatives, and ranked one level higher in the hierarchy than the *dehgānān*, the local gentry.[69] The *šahrīg* was hence both a landed proprietor and an official of the State, who may have had judicial competences similar to the *dādwar*, if we follow the short entry in the *Dēnkard*:

> DkD 550.8–11 (DkM 723.21–724.2)
> *ud abar xwēškārīh (ī) gumārdag dādwarān az ān ī nidom ān ī abardom ēk azabar ēk wizīr ī abar dādestān ān ī šahrīg dō āgenēn ān ī šahrīg abāg dādwar ud dō dādwar āgenēn čē andar im dar.*
>
> 'And on the duties of the appointed judges (*dādwarān*), from the lowest up to the highest, one above the other. (On) the judgement (*wizīr*) from the trial (*dādestān*): that, which two *šahrīgs* (pass) together, that which a *šahrīg* (passes) together with a *dādwar*, and that which two *dādwars* (pass) together, and (other) matters in this chapter.'

This synopsis (which evidently relies on the Pahlavi commentary of the *nask* rather than on the translation of the Avestan original) confirms that there were several levels of judges (*dādwar*), who held different positions in the judicial hierarchy (see above pp. 496–503). Both the *dādwar* and the *šahrīg* were obviously entitled to pass judgement (*wizīr*). The competences of two *dādwars* and two *šahrīgs* or of a *dādwar* and a *šahrīg* could be combined to reach a joint verdict. The passage confirms that the *šahrīg* had jurisdictional power (maybe to the same extent as the *dādwar*), but it seems far more likely that the *šahrīg* was a distinguished layman from the ranks of the nobility rather than a legal expert. As both the *dādwar* and the *šahrīg* could be involved in jurisdiction in three possible combinations, we can assume that, besides the officials appointed by the king and judges from among the Zoroastrian clergy, the nobility also had a

67 MHD 78.2–11 (Macuch 1993, pp. 517, 520).

68 For an extensive discussion of Tab. 28 see Macuch 2020b, pp. 199–208; the whole document is in Appendix XIV, pp. 728–734. On *stūrīh* see Chapter II, pp. 169–174.

69 For references see Macuch 1993, p. 525; the Syriac source Barbahlūl is cited in Hoffmann 1880, p. 239; on the extensively discussed *dehgān* see Macuch 2017c, p. 169, with further references.

Table 51. Overview: public officials with judicial power

Authorities	Translation	Areas of competence
dahibed	'ruler of the land'	issuance of a decree or command (*framān*) by which a legal act or sentence takes effect
ōstāndār	'governor of a province'	– detainment and levying of taxes – adjudication of commercial issues – registration of financial matters pertaining to royal property (*šāhīgān*)
āmārgar	'calculator, accountant'	– registration of property receipts and disbursements from the royal treasury (*šāhīgān*) – providing evidence that a property belongs lawfully to the crown – procuring documents on expenditures and outgoing payments from the royal treasury, also on request of the *ōstāndār* – drawing up documents on damage caused to royal property and fixing fines (*tāwān*) to be paid by the offender – keeping accounts on the property of the crown and on the distribution of shares to subjects for their services to the crown – calculating and taking in taxes (*sāk*)
čašmag	'renowned (person)'	– verification of documents (*fragār*) and transcripts of criminal cases in an assembly (*hanǰaman*) together with the *šahrīgān* – evaluation of a claim to *stūrīh* together with the *stēndag*, other dignitaries and legal authorities.
stēndag	'upright (person)'	evaluation of a claim to *stūrīh* together with the *čašmag*, other dignitaries and legal authorities.
šahrīg	'man of the State/land'	– jurisdictional power (to the extent of the *dādwar*?). – verification of documents (*fragār*) and transcripts of criminal cases in an assembly (*hanǰaman*) together with the *čašmagān*.
pēšag-sālār	'head of a guild'	limited power of jurisdiction in matters pertaining to the guild.

say in passing and confirming a verdict (at least in criminal cases, as the material from the Law-book cited above suggests, and in conflicts involving the transfer of large property via *stūrīh*, as in Tab. 28).

Another group involved in the judiciary are the *pēšag-sālārān* 'Heads of the Guilds' (the chiefs of the organisations of priests, artisans, traders, scribes, etc.), who were obviously engaged in jurisdiction in matters pertaining to their particular guild, as we can conclude indirectly from the Law-book. We have already seen above that the verdict of the Chief Mobed was binding (*ēwar*) with respect to issues regarding the 'guild of priests' (*pēšag ī āsrōnān*), although other decisions of this Supreme Judge could under certain circumstances be held back by a decree/command (*framān*) of the 'rulers of the land' (*dahibedān*). In contrast, all judgements of the other Heads of the Guilds could only become effective on confirmation by the *dahibedān*, as a short passage of the Law-book implies: 'Executing the verdict of the "Heads of the Guilds" is not permitted except on the basis of a command (*framān*) by the rulers of the land' (*wizīr ī pēšag-sālārān kardan bē pad framān ī dahibedān nē šāyēd*).[70]

2.1.4 Lower officials and members of the court

Besides the indispensible scribes (*dibīr*), who took down the minutes of the proceedings, several other lower officials supported the work of the judge (*dādwar*) as members of the court or informants, supervisors and witnesses. Judgement could be reached by several means, one of which was, especially if no other evidence was available, the act of taking the oath (*war*), a procedure derived from the ancient ritual of the ordeal, originally an important method of finding out the truth by submitting the case to divine judgement. The oath took place in a special venue, called *xwārestān* 'swearing place' or *war gāh* 'place of the oath' under the supervison of the *war-sālār* 'supervisor of the oath', whose competences are listed as follows:[71]

1. The *war-sālār* is in charge of matters pertaining to the oath: of suspending the oath (*pādīrān ī war*) and of (letting the litigant) take the oath (*warzīdan ī war*).
2. He supervises the recitation during oath taking (*yazišn ī pad war*).
3. He seals (*āwišt*) the transcript or protocol of oath taking (*yazišn-nāmag*).
4. He is also qualified in those matters for which the judge is qualified (*pad-iz ān čīš kē dādwar padiš ēwar*).

Although the last point is far from clear, we can at least conclude that a special executive apart from the judge, the *war-sālār*, was in charge of all the proceedings connected with oath taking, who decided, when the oath should be taken, recorded the whole act in a separate transcript (*yazišn-nāmag*) and was held responsible for this important part of the trial (on the different forms of oaths see below pp. 551–560).

Another executive who is mentioned in the context of the trial is the *frēzwān* (lit. 'fulfiller of duty'), a kind of 'policeman, inspector' whose responsibilities

70 MHD 2.17 (Macuch 1993, pp. 54, 56).
71 MHDA 27.7–9 (Macuch 1981, pp. 51, 190, with a slightly different understanding of this passage).

can be reconstructed to a limited degree by bringing together a few dispersed entries in the Law-book:[72]

1. The *frēzwān* is qualified in those matters for which the judge is qualified (*pad-iz ān čīš kē dādwar padiš ēwar*).
2. He provides the judge with (information/evidence), which the latter needs in order to conduct legal proceedings (*pad hamēmālīh kardan andar abāyēd*).
3. He is authorized to identify a person (*tan āšnāg kardan*) and to accept a seal (*muhr padīriftan*), but can be held responsible (*griftār*) if 'other circumstances become evident' (*any ēwēnag paydāg*), that is, when his investigation into these matters turns out to be faulty.
4. He gives testimony against a thief (*duz*) in whose possession he has found a stolen object (*jāmag ī … pad ān duz būd*).
5. He arrests persons who are suspected of having committed a 'death-deserving' (*margarzān*) crime, such as homicide.

This rather rudimentary information suggests that the *frēzwān* was some kind of policeman or inspector who had the duty to provide the judge with the necessary evidence for conducting legal proceedings by identifying persons involved in litigation and their seals, but also to arrest alleged criminals (thieves, *margarzān* suspects), to identify them and to give testimony in court on the persons he has taken into custody.

Another public official one would not necessarily expect to find in this list, but whose testimony was obviously needed in order to identify imprisoned criminals under specific circumstances (presumably when no other records were kept or could be found), is the warden of a prison or 'gaoler' (*zēndānbān*), whose area of responsibility is discussed controversially. According to one jurist, the gaoler has no other competence than to keep the prisoners in custody (*ēwāz dārišn ī pad zēndan ēwar* 'he is only qualified for keeping in gaol'), but another jurist concedes to him a more extensive role: he considers the testimony of the gaoler as 'certain, binding' (*ēwar*) in three areas, called *hamtanīh*, *hamnāmīh* and *hamwināhīh*:[73]

1. Identification of the person (*hamtanīh*), which is explained by the following example: If a person has been imprisoned (*zēndān kard ēstēd*) on the first day of the month (day *Ohrmazd*) for theft and another person on the second day of the month (day *Wahman*) for a *margarzān* offence and it is not obvious (*nē paydāg*), on which date which one of these two persons has been imprisoned, the gaoler reliably identifies the prisoners by declaring: 'This (person) has been imprisoned on day *Ohrmazd* because of theft; this (person) on day *Wahman* because of a "death-deserving" offence' (*ēn Ohrmazd rūz pad duz ud ēn Wahman rūz pad margarzān ō zēndān kard ēstēd*).

72 MHDA 27.9–12; 30.3–5 (Macuch 1981, pp. 51–52, 190; 55, 193 respectively); MHD 92.2–6 (Macuch 1993, pp. 580, 585). On the *frēzwān* see also Macuch 1981, pp. 202–204 (n. 48).
73 MHDA 28.11–29.5 (Macuch 1981, pp. 53–54; 191–192).

2. Identification of the name (*hamnāmīh*). If a person named Mihr-Ādurfarrbay is under arrest because of theft and another person named Kay-Ādurfarrbay because of a *margarzān* offence, and it is not obvious (*nē paydāg*), which one is the thief, which one the *margarzān*-offender, the gaoler gives reliable testimony on their names by declaring: 'This (is) Mihr-Ādurfarrbay, who has been imprisoned because of theft; this (one) Kay-Ādurfarrbay, imprisoned because of a *margarzān*-offence' (*ēn Mihr-Ādurfarrbay ī pad duz ud ēn Kay-Ādurfarrbay pad margarzān ō zēndān kard ēstēd*).
3. Identification of the criminal act (*hamwināhīh*). If someone is under arrest due to theft, another person due to a *margarzān*-offence, and it is not obvious, which person has committed which crime, the gaoler gives reliable testimony regarding the prisoner and the crime by declaring: 'This one has been imprisoned because of theft and this one because of a *margarzān*-offence' (*ēn pad duz ud ēn pad margarzān ō zēndān kard ēstēd*).

In short, according to the opinion of one legal commentator, the *zēndānbān* is not only responsible for keeping criminal offenders in gaol, but for providing the court with exact information on the identity of the prisoners, their names and the offences they were imprisoned for. This would imply that a prisoners' archive was kept with the details listed above that could be consulted if it became necessary to revise a case or to provide information for another trial.

In contrast to this comparatively extensive and comprehensible passage on the responsibilities of the *zēndānbān*, the next short entry on a hitherto unnamed and unknown official does not transmit any of the necessary details, which might enable us to decipher the title or reconstruct the duties of this office holder with any certainty. How is the title (ending on the suffix *-bān* 'keeper, guard, protector') to be read and what exactly does the passage describe? The whole sentence reads:

MHDA 29.6–7
**kōybān* ⟨*kwdp'n⟩? *pad ēn kū-m ō tō guft u-t ašnūd ud pad-iz ēn kū guharīg ō tō mad ēstēd ēwar.*

'The **kōybān* (?) is qualified for (confirming/testifying/proclaiming) the following: "I have spoken to you and you have heard it" and also: "The compensation (*guharīg*) has come to you" '.[74]

The only other attestation of this officer in the *Dēnkard* is unfortunately not helpful, but if we follow West's translation the title could tentatively be read ⟨*kwdp'n⟩ **kōybān* 'keeper of a town, village, street, district', *i. e.* a person in charge of controlling a certain street, district or section of a village or town.[75]

74 Macuch 1981, pp. 54; 192.

75 DkM 733.10–11: *ud abar ānayēd ī māzdēsn *kōybān xwēškārīh ī *kōybān u-š čē andar im dar* 'and on bringing a Mazdean **kōybān*; (on) the duty of the **kōybān* and what is in this chapter'. West 1892, p. 91 (no. 9) reads *kûpânŏ* and translates 'street-keeper'; MP *kōy* 'street, lane' (MacKenzie 1971, p. 52); NP *kūy* 'a town, village; a side, quarter, district ...' (Steingass 1892, p. 1065); see also Perikhanian 1997, p. 371.

Table 52. Overview: lower officials and members of the court

Authorities	Translation	Areas of competence
war-sālār	'supervisor of the oath'	– determines both suspension and performance of the oath – supervises the recitation during oath taking – seals the transcript of oath taking (*yazišn-nāmag*) – his qualifications correspond to those of the judge (*dādwar*)
frēzwān	'fulfiller of duty' (policeman, inspector)	– provides the judge with information/evidence – identifies persons and their seals – arrests suspects and gives testimony in court – his qualifications correspond to those of the judge (*dādwar*)
zēndānbān	'gaoler; warden of a prison'	identifies prisoners and their crimes in three areas: – *hamtanīh* (identification of the person) – *hamnāmīh* (identification of the name) – *hamwināhīh* (identification of the crime)
**kōybān* (?)	*'keeper/ protector of a district, street' (?)	(tentative) inspector in charge of a specific district or section of a village or town; trustworthy witness in court for his area of responsibility (?)

The phrases quoted in our passage can be interpreted as examples for the testimony of this official as a witness in court. But the vague content of the sentence does not necessarily imply this understanding of the title and other interpretations can be taken into consideration, which remain, however, without further material, highly speculative.[76]

76 A completely different explanation—on the lines I have considered previously—is possible, if we assume that the title refers to a member of the court and the quotations transmitted in the passage cited above are the words spoken, confirmed or repeated by this official (Macuch 1981, pp. 206–207, n. 67). This executive might have been a kind of clerk in charge of noting and repeating loudly and audibly certain formulaic phrases spoken by the litigants in a trial. The quoted phrases 'I have spoken to you and you have heard it' and 'the compensation has come to you' could be examples of these announcements, by which perhaps the first phase of a trial (filing a complaint against an opponent in the latter's presence) and last phase of a trial (transfer of a compensation to the infringed party) were formally confirmed and concluded. This is of course very speculative, but given the importance attached to the spoken word in legal matters and its binding effect, it is not unlikely that a type of official or clerk acting as 'proclaimer, announcer', was engaged in courts of the Sasanian period. If our Pahlavi word designates a clerk with this duty, one could think of reading the term as a heterogram ⟨*KRYp'n⟩ from the Semitic root QR'/QRY 'to call, summon, designate, read, recite, name, call forth' (Sokoloff 2002, pp. 1039–1042; Drower/Macuch 1963, pp. 414–415) + the Iranian suffix *-bān*

2.2 Instances and appellate courts

The Sasanian judiciary developed a system of appellate courts with a clear structure, allowing a litigant dissatisfied with the verdict in a civil lawsuit to bring an appeal to the next higher instance. The material is scant and does not allow more than a superficial sketch of the procedure, but there can be no doubt that at least certain appeals were permitted and could be taken through a hierarchy of courts if the appellant had the financial means to do so. It seems that conflicts that were not solved on a lower level in the communities of the opponents (by negotiation, arbitration, mediation, decision of the individual's spiritual guide, the *rad ī xwēš*)[77] could be brought to a State court presided by a judge (*dādwar*), who was appointed directly by the King or indirectly by the King's representatives.

The Junior Judge (*dādwar ī keh*) was the competent authority of the first instance, whose judgement could be accepted or disputed by one of the litigants or by both parties. A litigant, who initially accepted the verdict *(ka pad wizīr hunsand būd* 'if he was satisfied by the verdict') could not subsequently contest it effectively *(a-hunsandīh ī pad wizīr nē padīrišn* '[his] dissatisfaction with the verdict should not be accepted'), with one exception: if it later somehow became evident that the verdict must be altered due to new evidence or other circumstances.[78] On the other hand, if a litigant contested the decision of the Junior Judge (*dādwar ī keh*) immediately, an appeal could be brought to the next higher instance, presided by the Senior Judge (*dādwar ī meh*), with the exception of interlocutory judgements regarding obstructions of justice (*azišmānd*) during the first trial, as we are explicitly informed by the following sentence:

> MHD 3.6–8
> *bē pad wizīr kard ī pad azišmānd abārīg wizīr ī dādwar (ī) keh kunēd a-hunsandīh ī pasēmāl [kunēd] ōh [ō] padīrišn zamān-ē(w) ō dādwar ī meh ōh dahišn.*
>
> 'Apart from judgements passed on obstructions of justice (*azišmānd*), the dissatisfaction (*a-hunsandīh*) of the defendant with the other judgements that the Junior Judge (*dādwar ī keh*) passes should be accepted (and) a date should be fixed (for the trial) before the Senior Judge (*dādwar ī meh*).'[79]

That the judgement of the first instance need not be final is confirmed by a short entry in the synopsis of the *nasks* in *Dēnkard* 8, obviously based on the Pahlavi commentary, as we may conclude from the content, which gives a short

---

'keeper, guard, protector' (Durkin-Meisterernst 2014, p. 184, §367). But which Iranian term could a hypothetical ⟨*KRYp'n⟩ represent? The Semitic root is attested in Pahlavi ⟨KRYTWNtn'; KLYTWNtn'⟩ *xwandan, xwān-* 'to call, summon, proclaim, read' (*Frahang ī Pahlawīg* XXIII.5; Nyberg 1988, p. 97), which would fit in well contextually, but a derivation from this verb seems very unlikely.

77 See Chapter V, p. 407.

78 MHD 3.1–3 (Macuch 1993, pp. 54, 56; presuming that the second *kunēd* and *ō* before *padīrišn* are mistakes).

79 Macuch 1993, pp. 55, 56–57.

summary of exactly the same procedure (although only the title *dādwar* is noted here instead of the more exact *dādwar ī keh*):

> DkD 536.18–19 (DkM 708.1–2)
> *ud abar pādīrānēnīdan ī dādwar wizīr ud zamān kard-ē(w) ō dādwar ī meh.*
>
> 'On the suspension (*pādīrānēnīdan*) of the judgement of the *dādwar* and fixing a date (for the trial) before the *dādwar ī meh*'.[80]

Two similarly constructed expressions, *dādestān ī keh* 'lesser judgement' (an elliptical expression for 'judgement of the Junior Judge'?), and *dādestān ī meh* 'higher judgement' (= judgement of the Senior Judge?) might also refer to the decisions reached in these two consecutive instances.[81]

An appeal to the *dādwar ī meh* was not the last option for seeking a revision of the initial verdict, as we may deduce from three entries indicating *en passant* further stages of appeal:

> MHDA 12.10–11
> *ud abar iz dādestan nāmagīhā nibišt ēstēd az dādwarān ō war ud tā rad ud abar madan az dādwarān ud az-iš mowbedān ō xwārestān zamān nē dād.*
>
> 'And also on the judgements, (which) have been recorded in transcripts: from the judges (*dādwarān*) up to the oath (*war*) and to the *rad*. And also (on) coming from the judges (*dādwarān*) as well as from the *mowbeds* to the place of the oath (*xwārestān*), (when) no date has been fixed.'[82]
>
> MHDA 12.12–13
> *zamān ī ō dādwar ī meh tā ō mowbedān pad hamēmāl ud az ān frāz pad tan-ē(w) kard.*
>
> 'The dates for the dispute (*pad hamēmāl*) before the *dādwar ī meh* up to the *mowbeds* and beyond these (instances) are fixed separately.'[83]
>
> MHD 93.9–10
> *ka a-hunsandīh ī pasēmāl pad wizīr rāy az dādwarān ō mowbedān wisē kard …*
>
> 'When due to the dissatisfaction of the defendant with the verdict he is dispatched from the judges (*dādwarān*) to the *mowbeds* …'[84]

Despite their shortness, these passages confirm that legal proceedings, which were brought to a close in the courts of the various public judges, the *dādwars*, could be followed up by an appeal to a religious official, a *rad* or a *mowbed*.

80 Macuch 1993, p. 60.
81 DkD 546.2 (DkM 718.14).
82 Macuch 1981, pp. 34, 141. I am quoting the whole passage here, as there is a printing error on the last line of this sentence (MHDA 12.12) on p. 141 of my edition (where the beginning of the third paragraph on this page has been erroneously transposed by the printer to the end of the first sentence).
83 Macuch 1981, pp. 34, 141.
84 Macuch 1993, pp. 593, 596. On *wisē kardan* 'to dispatch, send, summon' see Macuch 2016a, p. 156 with references to the Tabarestān documents.

Could these two authorities be called upon alternatively or did they represent two further, separate instances? We are not informed on this specific question, but a notable passage of the Babylonian Talmud indirectly confirms the existence of two types of Sasanian courts, distinguished as *bei* +*dā(d)war* (written ⟨dwʾr⟩) 'court of judges' and *bei dina de-magista* 'magian court'.[85] The first expression presumably refers to a court presided by a *dādwar* (if this reading of ⟨dwʾr⟩ is correct)[86], the judge in the first two instances, whereas the second term designates a court presided by a religious authority in the next higher court of appeal (a *mowbed* or *rad*). A final appeal could be brought to the court of the *mowbedān mowbed*, whose verdict was evidently considered—at least according to one of the jurists cited in the Law-book—as even more reliable or binding (*ēwar*) than the oath (*war*). The relation to the *šahr dādwarān dādwar*, the Chief Judge of the State, however, remains unclear, and, as Syriac sources suggest, it was the King who spoke the final verdict in criminal cases. Capital punishment, it seems, was only implemented by 'command' or 'order' (*framān*) of the King and his representatives.[87]

Legal language may reflect the appeals procedure. Two different terms are attested in the context of civil litigation to designate a 'complaint': *garzišn* and *must*. As I have suggested elsewhere, *must* does not seem to be simply a synonym of *garzišn*, the term used most frequently for 'complaint' in Pahlavi legal literature and in the Tabarestān documents. Particularly the latter sources suggest that *must*, besides just meaning 'complaint', may have been employed in the specific sense of 'complaint in the next instance; appeal'. Although this use of the word is not elucidated, it could be meant in phrases, in which both terms appear, such as *saxwan ud passox garzīdan ī must*[88] 'statement and answer filing an action of appeal' or *mustōmandān garzišn*[89] 'complaint of those who appeal', or +*mustīh garzīdan*[90] 'to file an appeal'. Both terms for 'complaint' are united in the compound *mustgarzīh*, lit. 'appeal-complaint' in *abar mustgarzīh ī pēšēmālān ud pasēmālān*,[91] 'on the complaint of appeal of the plaintiffs and defendants', which most likely refers to the act of taking action in the next higher instance due to disagreement with the verdict of the first (or lower) instance. In the Tabarestān documents the phrases *abēmustīh kardan* (or *abēmust kardan*), lit. 'to make (someone) uncomplaining', and *ō abēmustīh madan* (besides *ō abēmustīh rasīdan*), lit. 'to achieve an uncomplaining (state); to reach satisfac-

85 *B. Bava Qamma* 113b–114a; quoted in Secunda 2014, p. 92. On the variant spellings of these two terms see *ibid.* p. 195, fn. 32, 34 and 35. For a discussion of this passage see below pp. 530–531.

86 Instead of an expected ⟨dʾwr⟩ (with a shift of the long vowal from the first to the second /a/). See discussion in Sokoloff 2002, p. 310, and Secunda 2014, p. 195, fn. 32 and 34.

87 See discussion above, pp. 510–511 and pp. 528–529 below (Babyl. Talmud).

88 MHDA 26.3f. (Macuch 1981, pp. 50, 188).

89 DkM 741.12f.

90 PRDd 4.2 (this passage is cited and discussed above, Chapter V, p. 416).

91 DkM 709.3; *must* + *garz-*, from *garzīdan*, *garz-* 'to complain', + abstract suffix *-īh*.

Table 53. Overview: instances and appellate courts

Stage of the lawsuit	Appellate courts
First instance	*dādwar ī keh* 'Junior Judge'
First court of appeal	*dādwar ī meh* 'Senior Judge'
Second (and third?) court of appeal	*rad*; *mowbed*
Final court of appeal	*mowbedān mowbed*; the King; (*šahr dādwarān dādwar*?)
Terminology	
abēmust/abēmustīh kardan	'to make (someone) uncomplaining' (= to end a case in a manner that satisfies the claimant and hinders an appeal to the next instance)
garzīdan ī must	'to file a complaint/appeal'
mustgarzīh	'appeal-complaint': complaint to a court of appeal
+mustīh garzīdan	'to file a complaint/appeal'
mustōmandān garzišn	'complaint of those who appeal'
ō abēmustīh madan/rasīdan	'to achieve an uncomplaining (state)' (= to end a case in a manner that satisfies the claimant and hinders an appeal to the next instance)

tion' are used in the sense of: to satisfy a claimant by a decision that will bring the lawsuit to a close. The official in charge of investigating the dispute is requested to reach a verdict that finds the approval (*hunsandīh*) of the claimant in a manner that would hinder him from continuing the lawsuit and filing an appeal to the next instance.[92]

The sources we have hitherto scrutinized suggest that a wide range of legal authorities and officials were engaged in the Sasanian judicial system, ranging from Mazdean priests who functioned as moral guides, arbiters and judges (*rad ī xwēš*; *hērbed*) on a local level in the diverse communities of the empire up to the courts of the State presided by judges installed by the king (*dādwar ī keh*; *dadwar ī meh*) and Zoroastrian religious experts engaged in jurisdiction in the higher instances (*rad*; *mowbed*, *mōwan handarzbed*; *mowbedān mowbed*). The system was obviously structured in a manner that allowed flexibility in the management of legal disputes to a certain degree. Theoretically a claimant who did not agree with the decision of a spiritual guide (*rad ī xwēš*) or *hērbed* in his own community could bring a lawsuit to a State court presided by a *dādwar* and continue to defend his interests in higher instances before a *mowbed* (or

92 Tab. 21.15–16 (see Macuch 2019b, pp. 119–120); Tab. 22.13–14, 15–16, 24–25 (*ibid.*, pp. 126–127); for the whole text of Tab. 22 see Appendix XIII, pp. 723–725.

rad) if he was not satisfied with the verdict. In practice, however, only wealthy litigants would have had the means to exhaust all the options of appeal, if allowed to, since high fees were charged for services in the judiciary.[93] The duty of a judicial authority was to conduct investigations in a manner that would, ideally, satisfy the claimant and hence impede the continuation of the lawsuit in a higher instance, or, to use legal language, he should take the appropriate measures to make the claimant 'uncomplaining by judicial means' (*pad rāh ī dādestān ō abēmustīh rasād*).[94]

2.3 The jurisdiction of religious minorities

The Sasanian judiciary did not restrict its services to Zoroastrians. Adherents of other faiths (*ag-dēnān* 'infidels'), particularly the two largest religious minorities of the Iranian Empire, the Jews and Christians, were not excluded from appealing to Sasanian courts, nor were the cases tried in these courts restricted to transactions between non-Mazdeans and Mazdeans, as we have already noted above (Chapter II, pp. 113–120). These religious minorities were largely allowed to practise their own cult and implement their own norms on the condition that these did not undermine the authority of the central government, challenge the superiority of the Good Religion or threaten the security and order of the State. The Babylonian Talmud testifies to periods of relative peace for the Jewish community, in which its law-schools could prosper and rabbis held judgement over a wide range of civil disputes among the Jewish population following the rules laid down in the Torah. The East Christians, on the other hand, gradually developed their own legal system based almost entirely on Sasanian law with a few important exceptions in the fields of family law and inheritance. It seems that Jewish rabbis and Christian legal authorities were not only generally familiar with the law of the Empire in which they lived, but had intimate knowledge of its diverse branches, made use of its technical terminology and were well acquainted with the Sasanian law of proceedings, as we may conclude from both the Talmud and Syriac legal sources.[95]

We may further assume that in criminal law the same rules applied to the followers of other religions as to Mazdeans with regard to capital crimes prosecuted by the State, that is, in the categories of *xwadāy-dušmenīh* (rebellion; treason); *yazdān-dušmenīh* (blasphemy; apostasy); *ahlomōyīh* (heresy) and specific offences of the *hamēmālān* category endangering the security and order of the State.[96] Unsurprisingly, Jews and Christians who violated the norms of peaceful co-existence by committing one of these capital crimes were just as

93 On litigation costs see below pp. 585–587.

94 Tab. 22.24–25 (see Appendix XIII, p. 725).

95 See Chapter VII on the impact of Sasanian law on other legal systems.

96 On capital crimes prosecuted by the State see above pp. 489–494.

liable to prosecution by Sasanian authorities as adherents of the Good Religion. This simple fact might account for the large number of reports on persecutions of Jews and Christians, a part of which may have taken place because an *ag-dēn* seriously violated Sasanian law rather than due to extreme religious fanaticism on the part of the Zoroastrian priesthood or general attempts of the State to eliminate other religions.[97] The well-attested case against the Catholicos Mār Abā, a convert to Christianity, in fact suggests that all the accusations of Zoroastrian dignitaries against the Catholicos were justified and legally sound from the viewpoint of Sasanian criminal law.[98] Despite comparative freedom in their communal affairs, religious minorities and their leaders were obviously expected to accept the predominance of the Iranian legal system specifically in those areas, which were separate from religious law. Acknowledging the validity of Iranian law for keeping peace in the whole Empire was a prerequisite for all other individual legal activities on a sublevel within the religious communities. This essential requirement seems to be reflected in the famous and often cited statement of the prominent Jewish authority, R. Samuel, who held office as judge in the third century: 'The law of the government is law' (*dyn*ʾ *dmlkwt*ʾ *dyn*ʾ).[99] Although the impact of this quotation has been the subject of controversial discussions among talmudists, there can be, in my opinion, no doubt that Samuel's apodictic statement alludes to the undeniable fact that Iranian law was *in force* in the Sasanian Empire and that it would be senseless, even dangerous, to ignore it. As Brody observes, this dictum 'applied primarily with regard to relations between Jews and the non-Jewish government …'.[100]

From the viewpoint of Sasanian jurisdiction we have good reason to assume that in the area of civil law generally the same laws were applied to Zoroastrians and unbelievers alike with only a few exceptions, which are easily explained from the perspective of Mazdean orthodoxy. We have already discussed above a passage of the Law-book calling our attention to three major legal distinctions between Zoroastrians and non-Zoroastrians in the specific context of inheritance:

1. Infidels (*ag-dēn*) cannot be held liable as joint debtors or co-debtors (*hamāg-*⁺*tōzišn*), but only as part-debtors (*xwāstag-tōzišn*).

97 I fully agree with Payne 2015b, pp. 44–58, who has argued that Christians were not generally prosecuted because of their religious identities, but because of 'disobeying the court or for violating mutually recognized norms in particular acts' (*ibid.*, p. 57). Brody 1990, p. 62, comes to a similar conclusion: '… both Jewish and non-Jewish sources for the Sasanian period present a picture of a Jewish community which enjoyed several centuries of security and tranquillity, a situation which must have contributed in no small measure to the development of the Babylonian Talmud and of Talmudic Judaism'.

98 See Macuch 2014c and below section 3.2.

99 For example, *Bava' Batra'* 54b, 55a; *Bava' Kamma* 113a; see also Neusner 1965–1970 (here: 1966, p. 69 and 1968, p. 44, with further references).

100 Brody 2016, p. 213.

2. A 'substitute successor' or 'proxy' (*stūr*) cannot be engaged for an infidel (*ag-dēn*).
3. Further restrictions regarding the right of infidels (*ag-dēn*) to inherit property (deleted by a lacuna in the text).[101]

The most interesting piece of information for assessing the position of religious minorities within the judicial system is gained from the last part of this passage, which explicitly states that, apart from these three exceptions (which are comprehensible from a Zoroastrian perspective), the same laws are to be applied to Mazdeans and infidels alike: *enyā-šān abārīg dādestān ōwōn čiyōn ān ī wehdēnān* 'all other decisions concerning them (*i. e.* infidels) are as those regarding adherents of the Good Religion'. It seems that Sasanian law treated adherents of other faiths—at least theoretically—according to lucid principles, setting clear-cut limits to the activities of the authorities engaged in jurisdiction in the Jewish and Christian communities (this might be the background of R. Samuel's statement quoted above).[102] The vast material on the legal work of the rabbis and Jewish courts in the Babylonian Talmud seems to confirm that Jews had autonomy to a comparatively large extent in matters pertaining to religious norms and in those areas, which were significant for securing peaceful coexistence within the Jewish community and in its relationship to the central government. According to Neusner, Jewish jurisdiction was involved in three main fields:

1. regulations concerning only the Jewish religion (matters of ritual, dietary and sexual taboos, proper observance of religious norms, etc.) which had no impact on public policy;
2. laws concerning the economic, social and political welfare of the community;
3. rules relating to the relationship between the Jews and the government (such as the collection of taxes and the regulation of land-ownership).[103]

Severe capital crimes involving transgressions against the security of the State or its religious order were not dealt with in Jewish courts, but the latter passed judgement in minor criminal acts involving injury to persons and damage to property, including petty crimes such as theft.[104] Although Jewish courts had no jurisdiction over capital crimes, the rabbis were well acquainted with the Iranian procedure in these cases, as we may conclude by the use of the Iranian

101 MHD 60.16–61.1 (Macuch 1993, pp. 409, 415). See Chapter II, pp. 118–119.

102 We have already mentioned in the context of business transactions that Zoroastrians were required to honour contracts with adherents of another faith (*ǰud-dēnān*) in the same manner as agreements with relatives (*xwēšāwandān*) and friends (*dōstān*): 'Do not break a contract with relatives, friends and those confessing another religion' (*abāg xwēšāwandān dōstān ǰud-dēnān mardōmān mihr ma drōzēd*; in: *Handarz ī dānāgān ō māzdēsnān* 6; Jamasp-Asana 1897–1913, p. 52). On the treatment of infidels and non-Iranians see also Macuch 2010a, pp. 199–203.

103 Neusner 1965–1970 (here: 1966, vol. II, pp. 117–118).

104 Neusner 1965–1970 (here: 1970, vol. V, p. 318).

technical term *pursišn-nāmag* 'transcript of investigation' in the Talmud, denoting a record or protocol taken down in criminal cases.[105]

Jewish and Syriac legal sources both testify to the existence of civil courts on a communal level, but there is only little information on the relationship between the legal activities of rabbis, clergymen and bishops, on the one hand, and the jurisdiction of Sasanian courts, on the other. Despite this deplorable lack of precise descriptions, I contend that it is possible to determine the position of Jewish and Christian jurisdiction within the Sasanian legal system to a limited degree by placing it within the framework of the overall judicial structure we have sketched above.

As we have seen, it became necessary in an early phase of Zoroastrian law to distinguish between two main categories of norms by separating religious prescriptions pertaining to ritual matters and purification rules from other laws conceived to enable social coexistence within the Zoroastrian communities. Another, presumably later distinction took place by separating sins that would harm an individual's own soul (*ruwānīg*) from offences that would cause harm to another person (*hamēmālān*) (besides one's own soul). This disconnection of ritual and moral precepts from all other laws not only paved the way for the establishment of an independent judiciary, but enabled other religious groups to practise their own norms within their communities as long as they did not interfere with the laws of the State and offend Zoroastrian precepts. We have also seen that, besides calling on public courts, other forms of settling disputes were practised in the Zoroastrian communities. Opponents involved in a conflict could ask witnesses (+*gugāyān*) or three righteous men (*weh mard*) to act as mediators or they could engage their own spiritual guide (*rad ī xwēš*) as arbiter or judge and, finally, they could initiate legal proceedings before a judge (*pahikar-radīh*). In short: there were different methods of solving conflicts, which did not all lead to a trial in a Sasanian court. The legal system left enough room for different forms of jurisdiction on a lower level in the diverse communities of the huge empire.

This multi-layered judicial system enabled the State to integrate its diverse religious communities to a certain extent despite all doctrinal controversies. The diligent activities of Jewish and, to a lesser degree, Christian courts could have easily been integrated into the structure of the Iranian judiciary due to two reasons. First, the Sasanian government was itself interested in relying on Jewish and Christian legal administrations to maintain peace and order in their communities. Second, the separation of ritual and moral issues from legal affairs involving conflicts in Zoroastrian law facilitated the development of a judicial system detached from religious issues, despite being based on Mazdean precepts. On the lowest level of jurisdiction the judgement of a rabbi, clergyman or bishop was the equivalent of that of the *rad ī xwēš* in a Zoroastrian community,

105 *Gittin* 28b; see MACUCH 1999 and Chapter VII, pp. 594–595.

whose verdict in a *hamēmālān* case (in contrast to a *ruwānīg* offence) could, however, be contested in a higher Sasanian court of law (although this might have occurred only in exceptional cases). Similarly, an aggrieved party could complain to a higher instance if he did not agree with the judgement of a rabbi or bishop, just as his Zoroastrian counterpart could bring an appeal to a higher court if he was not satisfied with the decision of his 'personal spiritual master'. The balance of power between the Zoroastrian clergy and judicial officials appointed by the State may have further eased the incorporation of Jewish and Christian jurisdiction into the judicial hierarchy.

On first sight one could doubt that Christians and Jews would have sought the revision of a verdict of their religious authorities in a Sasanian court. There was presumably considerable social pressure to solve conflicts within the religious community and to keep legal affairs on a local level. But a revealing passage of the Babylonian Talmud indirectly confirms that Jews could be involved in litigation against a 'non-Jew' and participate as witnesses in civil proceedings in a 'non-Jewish', *i.e.* Sasanian court (*bei gōīm*). Moreover, this passage discloses the existence of two types of Sasanian courts, which we have explained above as different levels of the judiciary, the lower instances involving State judges (*dādwar*) and the higher ones referring to the appellate courts presided by religious authorities (*rad*; *mowbed*; *mowbedān mowbed*):[106]

> Rava proclaimed—and others say, Rav Huna: [To] those who go up [to the land of Israel] and who come down [to Babylonia]—a Jew who knows some evidence concerning a fellow Jew about a non-Jew, and he goes and testifies about him in a non-Jewish court, we excommunicate him. What is the reason? Since non-Jews adjudicate the payment of money [even based] on the evidence of one witness, we excommunicate him. But this is the case only in a magian [court]. However in a **dā(d)war* court they too [like the rabbis] impose an oath upon every single witness [before adjudicating].[107]

Although this short text is far from lucid, it definitely distinguishes between two different types of Sasanian courts, the *bei ⁺dā(d)war* 'court of judges' and *bei dina de-magista* 'magian court', besides imparting two further significant details: (1) Jews could give testimony as witnesses regarding the payment of money (*i.e.* in a civil case) in both of these courts; and (2) the courts followed different procedures regarding oath-taking, if there was only one witness: a *⁺dā(d)war* court regularly imposed the oath on a single witness, whereas a 'magian' court did not necessarily do so (maybe due to its function as an appellate court). The means of punishing a Jew who acted as a witness in a Sasanian court was to excommunicate him from the Jewish community, but this severe penalty

106 See pp. 522–526.

107 *B. Bava Qamma* 113b–114a (translation according to Secunda 2014, p. 92, where the original text can also be found.) On the emendation of ⟨dw'r⟩ to ⟨d'wr⟩ see *ibid.* p. 195, fn. 32 and 34.

was obviously only implemented if legal action was taken in a 'magian court', not in a State court presided by a *dādwar.* If we take all that has been said on legal instances above into consideration, this statement suggests that giving testimony as a single witness in an appellate court presided by a Zoroastrian religious dignitary, in which there was no need to take an oath, was considered by the rabbis as incompatible with Jewish law. On the other hand, the procedure of applying the oath in the first instance of a trial in a State court was in agreement with the rules of Jewish procedure, hence treated differently.

Even though Jewish and Christian religious leaders may have discouraged members of their communities to bring their civil lawsuits to a Sasanian court, these cases obviously did occur, particularly when a litigant resented alleged unjust treatment by a rabbi or clergyman. Appealing to a public court seems to have been considered as a perfectly normal procedure by Sasanian jurists. A Syriac source reports that Christians who carried out legal disputes against each other could apply to a Sasanian court and be given an official 'document of acquittal' *(bwktn'mg*; MP **bōxt-nāmag*) with the seal of the *mowbedān mowbed*, which exonerated the bearers from particular charges.[108] The implications of receiving a **bōxt-nāmag* with the seal of the Supreme Judge are not elucidated, but we can reasonably infer that this important certificate, acquitting the bearer, would overrule all other judgements of lower instances, hence annul any decision of a clergyman or bishop (or rabbi) on a communal level. Moreover, as the judicial authority of Jewish (and presumably Christian) courts was reduced to certain branches of civil law, excluding the right to inflict capital punishment, we can assume that capital crimes committed by unbelievers could not be prosecuted in any other manner than in a Sasanian court. Particularly if the penalty consisted of corporal punishment, this could only be implemented by the State following a 'command' (*framān*) of the king or one of his representatives. In the Babylonian Talmud a Jew who has been lashed because of intercourse with a gentile woman complains to the (Sasanian) government that he has been condemned illegally without a *hrmn' dmlk'* 'command of the king', an expression using the Parthian term **hramān* 'command, order', corresponding to Middle Persian *framān.*[109] Again, the consequences are not explained, but the complaint of the Jew to an Iranian court only makes sense if the execution of the verdict of the Jewish court was seen as a violation of the exclusive right of the Sasanian judiciary to administer corporal punishment in the context of criminal proceedings (on illicit intercourse, *gād-duzīh*, lit. 'theft of intercourse', see above, Chapter V, pp. 452–460).

108 BEDJAN 1895, pp. 233–234; BRAUN 1915, p. 200; see also SHAKED 1987, p. 261, and CIANCAGLINI, p. 122.

109 *Berakhot* 58a; see also NEUSNER 1965–1970 (here: 1966, vol. II, pp. 32–33); on the *framān* of the king or his representatives see pp. 510–511 above.

To conclude, the Sasanians tolerated that Jews and Christians follow their own religious laws in administering justice in the interest of keeping peace and order in the communities as long as these legal activities did not endanger the security of the State or challenge the superior status of the Good Religion. The range of jurisdiction of an 'infidel' (*i. e.* Jewish or Christian) court was restricted to civil cases and minor criminal acts on a communal level. Capital crimes were prosecuted by the State, which alone had the right to implement corporal punishment on the basis of a *framān* of the king or his delegates. On a local level the jurisdiction of a rabbi or clergyman is comparable to that of the Zoroastrian *rad ī xwēš*. The judgements of these three authorities were not final, but could be challenged on the next higher level of the judiciary in a Sasanian court in several instances, from the 'courts of the *dādwars*' (*bei* ⁺*dāwar*) up to the 'magian courts' (*bei dina de-magista*) and to the final court of appeal before the Supreme Judge, the *mobedān mobed*, or, in specific cases, the King (although taking a complaint to the highest court might have only rarely occurred in practice due to social pressure and the high costs of jurisdiction). With a few significant exceptions in the areas of property law and inheritance, the same laws applied to Zoroastrians and infidels alike.

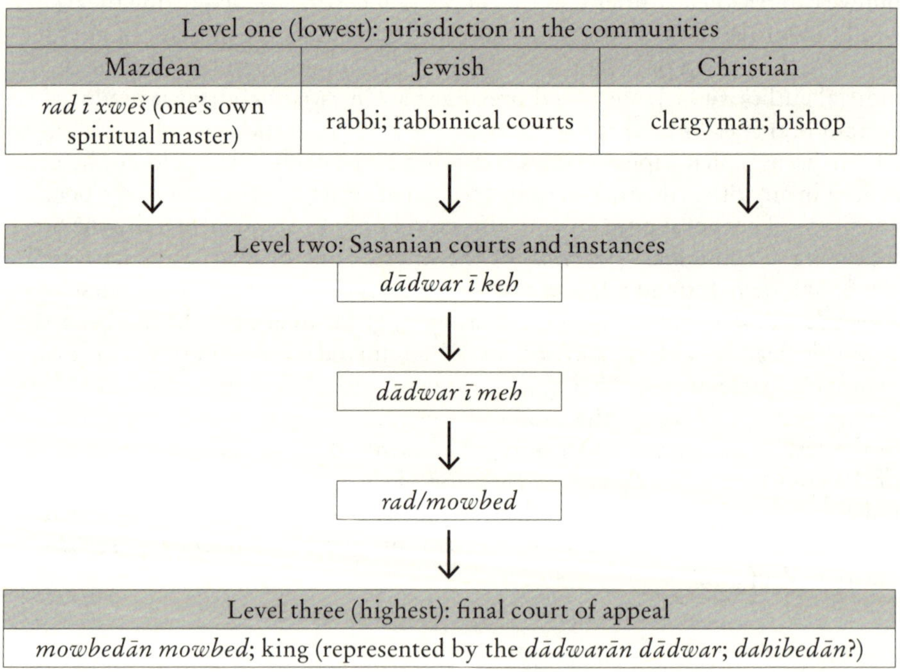

Fig. 5: Overview: hierarchy of the judiciary

3 The law of procedure

We are far better informed on civil litigation than on the criminal trial. A large number of cases discussed in the Law-book seem to have been taken directly from the practice of Sasanian law courts, but there is no coherent description of the consecutive stages of the proceedings. Fortunately the Tabarestān documents confirm many specific features of the civil trial and offer valuable additional information, but one should keep in mind that they describe cases from the *post*-Sasanian era, in which further changes might have taken place. We do not know whether different courts tried civil and criminal cases, but a distinction was definitely made between civil trials initiated by private individuals and criminal offences prosecuted by the State, as we may surmise from the different terms used for the transcripts (or protocols) recorded in these two instances. Both disputes regarding the recovery of money or property or the enforcement of a right (tried in civil courts today) and complaints regarding individual criminal acts (involving fraud, cheat, theft, robbery, bodily injury, etc.) were subject to private prosecution. In contrast, as we have already seen above, criminal acts endangering the security or order of the State and Church were prosecuted by official organs of the State, but, given the fragmentary state of the sources, we are not well informed on how these two types of criminal offences were distinguished and under which specific circumstances prosecution was initiated by State officials.

3.1 Civil proceedings

Legal action commenced with an official complaint (*garzišn*) of the plaintiff (*pēšēmāl*) against the defendant (*pasēmāl*), succeeded by a preliminary hearing, in which both parties were interrogated before they were summoned to court for the main trial. It seems that in the first session of the official trial *both* parties had to consent explicitly to the procedure by declaiming their will to enter litigation audibly with the words 'we complain' (*garzēm*).[110] The main phases of a civil trial can be divided into several stages:

1. complaint (*garzišn*) of the plaintiff;
2. preliminary investigation:
   a) interrogation of the opponents by a (subordinate?) official;
   b) request that the defendant provide evidence;
   c) summons to court;
3. official trial, phase one:
   a) consent of both parties to enter litigation;
   b) entries (*čak*) of the parties in the 'transcript of statements' (*saxwan-nāmag*);

110 According to Tab. 2B.5 (Appendix XII, p. 717); see also Macuch 2016a, pp. 152–153; 159.

   c) self-commitment of the defendant to provide 'proof and evidence' (*čim ud bōzišn*);
4. official trial, phase two: establishing evidence by:
   a) the statement of the defendant's 'predecessor in title' (*dastwar*);
   b) witnesses (*gugāy*);
   c) documents;
   d) the oath (*war*);
5. official trial, phase three: the verdict (*dādestān*; *wizīr*).

The first two phases of the official trial could consist of several sessions in order to give the defendant time to procure evidence, particularly if in a dispute over proprietary rights proof was based on the testimony of the defendant's 'predecessor in title' (*dastwar*) or other witnesses (*gugāy*), who had to be brought to court. A special date (*zamān*) was also fixed for taking the oath (*war*), which was considered as a sacral act to be performed in a special venue, the 'place of the oath' (*war gāh* or *xwārestān*).

3.1.1 Filing action

We are not informed on the formalities of lodging a claim or complaint (*garzišn*), but can deduce indirectly from the Tabarestān-documents that this was the first step to legal action, initiated by the plaintiff (*pēšēmāl*). According to the Tabarestān court records (Tab. 1A; 1B) a complaint (regarding a proprietary right) is filed with an official in charge of jurisdiction, in this instance a religious dignitary, a *hērbed* named Farroxabzūd, in the canton (*tasūg*) in which the plaintiff lives.[111] Interestingly in this case, the claimants are not only men (from the clan of Yazd), but include a woman (called Duxtxwašīh) who is also represented by the plaintiff who files the claim. Keeping in mind that these sources are from the post-Sasanian period, in which smaller changes may have taken place, the parallel procedure in the Sasanian period might have been to file a complaint with the official in charge of jurisdiction in the first instance, the 'Junior Judge' (*dādwar ī keh*). This is suggested by a passage of the Lawbook, in which a plaintiff (*pēšēmāl*) and two defendants (*pasēmāl*) are conceded 'admittance' (*dēmān*) before 'the judges' (*dādwarān*) in order to take down the 'transcript of statements' (*saxwan-nāmag*), a recording (or protocol) of civil proceedings, in which the complaint of the plaintiff and the statements of the parties were documented.[112] According to another passage the plaintiff initiates (*bun kardan rāyēnēd*) legal action (*dādestān*) by recording

111 See Appendix XII, p. 716.

112 MHD 73.13–14: *ka pad dādestān pēšēmāl ēk ud pasēmāl dō saxwan-nāmag rāy ō pēš (ī) dādwarān dēmān kunēnd …* "When because of a legal case one plaintiff and two defendants are conceded admittance before the judges (*dādwarān*) for (recording) the 'transcript of statements' (*saxwan-nāmag*) … (Macuch 1993, pp. 490, 493).

his complaint in the *saxwan-nāmag*.[113] But there is no information on the sequence of these actions. Given that the initial statements of *both* parties were recorded in this document, it seems far more likely that the *saxwan-nāmag* was taken down *after* the preliminary hearing and *not* in this very first phase of filing action.

After the complaint has been filed, the official in charge of jurisdiction orders one of his (subordinate?) officials to summon the opponents to a hearing and to undertake a preliminary investigation (*ō gōw ī pēš tō wisē ē kunēd* 'you should summon [them] to a hearing in your presence') in order to determine the 'legality of the claim' (*ēwēn ī ōy garzišn rāy*).[114] This at least is the procedure recorded in the Tabarestān documents. Although a preliminary hearing is not mentioned in the Law-book, a similar procedure seems to have been followed in criminal law, as we may conclude indirectly from Syriac sources on the trial against Mār Abā (see section 3.2.1 below). It is therefore likely that this course of action originates from the Sasanian period (despite minor changes that might have taken place in the post-Sasanian period) and that the main task of this second official was to grant permission for bringing a claim to the court of the first instance (or, in case of an appeal, to the court of the following instances) after questioning the opponents.

Table 54. Overview: filing action

dādestān bun kardan rāyēnīdan	to initiate legal action
dēmān	admittance
ēwēn ī garzišn	legality of a claim/complaint
garzišn	claim, complaint
gow	hearing, statement
ō gōw wisē kardan	to summon to a hearing
pasēmāl	defendant
pēšēmāl	plaintiff, claimant, complainant
saxwan-nāmag	transcript (protocol) of statements
wisē kardan	to summon

113 MHDA 31.17: … *pad saxwan-nāmag dādestān bun kardan rāyēnēd* 'he initiates legal action by (means) of the "transcript of statements" (*saxwan-nāmag*)' (Macuch 1981, pp. 57, 210).

114 Tab. 1A.8–12; Appendix XII, pp. 715–716; on the legal terminology in these texts see Macuch 2016a, pp. 148–158.

3.1.2 The preliminary hearing

The main purpose of this initial hearing was presumably to decide whether a claim should be permitted or averted by interrogating the opponents, maybe also to check whether the dispute could be settled out of court. According to Tab. 1B, the official in charge undertakes three measures. After questioning the parties intensely (*zāyistan-tar*), he requests the defendant (called Dēnyadān) to 'supply *auctor*-ship' (*dastwarīh … frāz xwāst*), that is, to call his 'predecessor in title' (*dastwar*), the person from whom he had acquired the object in dispute, to testify on his behalf in the lawsuit.[115] In this particular case the official obviously decides to grant permission for bringing the claim to the court and, consequently, sets a specific date for the first session of the official trial. He also summons the opponents to the court of the official in charge of jurisdiction, in our document the *hērbed* called Farroxabzūd.[116]

The official act of setting a date (*zamān*) for the trial or fixing an individual date for calling one's legal predecessor (*dastwar*) is amply attested in the Lawbook in the context of litigation with the verbs *kardan*, as in *zamān ō gōw kardan*[117] 'to set a date for the hearing', and *dādan*, as in *zamān ō dastwar ōh dahišn*[118] 'a date for (calling) the legal predecessor should be set' (or its negation: *zamān ō dastwar nē dahišn*[119] 'a date for (calling) the legal predecessor should not be set'), as we will see below (pp. 542–544). The information to be gained from Tab. 1B (and Tab. 10A) implies that, besides interrogating the opponents and examining the legality of the claim, the official in charge of the preliminary hearing was to make sure that the defendant would provide evidence, in our document by prompting his 'legal predecessor' (*dastwar*) to testify on his behalf in court.

Table 55. Overview: the preliminary hearing

dastwar	legal predecessor, predecessor in title, *auctor*
dastwarīh frāz xwāstan	to request *auctor*-ship
zamān	date (of a hearing, trial)
zamān dādan/kardan	to set a date
zamān ō dastwar dādan	to set a date for (calling) the legal predecessor
zamān ō gōw kardan	to set a date for the hearing
zāyistan	to investigate, interrogate

115 Tab. 1B. 12–13; Appendix XII, p. 716; on the term *dastwar* see Chapter IV, pp. 385–387, and below pp. 542–544.

116 Tab. 1B.9: *ō pēš hērbed wisē kardan* 'they are to be summoned to the presence of the *hērbed*'; Tab. 1B.15: *ō gōw ī pēš hērbed wisē kard* 'he (= the defendant) is summoned to the hearing before the *hērbed*'); Appendix XII, p. 716.

117 DkM 706.12.

118 MHD 5.16 (Macuch 1993, pp. 87, 92), MHD 7.6 (Macuch 1993, pp. 89, 93).

119 MHD 5.12–14 (Macuch 1993, pp. 87, 91).

3.1.3 The trial

It is not clear, whether the litigants (*hamēmālān*) or 'main claimants' (*mādagwar*) were obliged to be personally present for the initial session of the official trial on the date (*zamān*) fixed by the official in charge of the preliminary hearing or could alternatively send their legal representatives (*ǰādag-gōw*) for this first session. The procedure documented in Tab. 2B seems to demand the personal presence of the main claimants. In this document the plaintiff (*pēšēmāl*) and the defendant (*pasēmāl*) declare 'together' (*āgenēn*) their will to enter litigation by declaiming loudly: *garzēm* 'We complain!'.[120] Was this declaration a necessary part of the formal procedure implying that legal proceedings could only be initiated with the consent of *both* parties? There is no corresponding description in the Law-book of the initial session, but we are informed that the statements of both parties were put to writing in the *saxwan-nāmag* 'transcript/protocol of statements' and that the plaintiff was not permitted (*nē šāyēd*) to submit a transcript alone 'without awareness and knowledge' (*ǰud az āgāhīh ud dānišn*) of the defendant.[121] This document or its equivalent is apparently called simply *nāmag* in the Tabarestān documents, but written with the ideogram ⟨GTk⟩ to distinguish it from other documents or letters, also called *nāmag* (written ⟨n'mk'⟩).[122]

The scattered entries in the Law-book and details in other Pahlavi sources enable us to reconstruct the main stages of the procedure. In the first session of the trial the opponents were admitted before the judges to make their statements, which were taken down in the *saxwan-nāmag*. The trial was scheduled for the morning (*andar frayar*) and it seems that significant phases of the proceedings, such as making entries (*čak*) in the *saxwan-nāmag*, recording offences against the judiciary (*azišmānd*) and taking the oath (*war*) all took place in the morning.[123] According to the Bundahišn, the judge was likewise

120 Tab. 2B.5; Appendix XII, p. 717.
121 MHD 90.4–6 (Macuch 1993, pp. 570, 574).
122 But see on the reading of this word Chapter IV, pp. 275–279.
123 According to DkM 706.14: *abar … zamān ī rāyēnišn andar frayar* 'on … the date of the lawsuit in the morning'; on *frayar* < Av. *fraiiara-* 'morning'; Bartholomae 1904, col. 989 (for attestations of the word in the Nērangestān see Kotwal/Kreyenbroek 2003, pp. 290, 302); also MHDA 13.17–14.1 (Macuch 1981, pp. 35f., 143). I no longer fully agree with my own interpretation of this enervatingly short passage, which I now understand as follows: *čak ud azišmānd pad har dō war andar frayar pad dādwarān pad dib hu-frāšmōdād dabēnd* '(Making) entries (*čak*) (in the transcript) and (determining) an obstruction of justice (*azišmānd*) and (implementing) the oath (*war*) for both (litigants) should be undertaken in the morning by the judges (and) taken down in a document (*dib*) by sunset'. I take this passage to mean that three elements of the trial are to take place in the presence of the judges in the morning (*frayar*): (1) the entries (*čak*) of the parties in the *saxwan-nāmag*; (2) the verdict regarding a *contumacia* (*azišmānd*); (3) the implementation of an oath to be taken by both (or by one of) the litigants. These phases of the trial are to be protocolled in a document (*dib*) by sunset. On *hu-frāšmōdād* (Av. *frāšmō.dāti-*) 'setting (of the sun)' see Bartholomae 1904, col. 1022; for attestations in the Nērangestān see Kotwal/Kreyenbroek 2003, pp. 290, 306.

urged to pass his verdict until midday (*tā nēm-rōz*), which is explained as the best time to reach a decision due to the vigilance of the sun god (and god of contract) Mihr at this period of the day.[124] However, as the Bundahišn is not a legal text, we cannot be certain that this was the usual or prescribed procedure in the Sasanian period. A lawsuit could stretch out over several sessions, as both the Law-book and the Tabarestān documents demonstrate, and take far longer than just one forenoon, even if the judge was required to pass his final verdict in the morning.

Another noteworthy detail of the first session is that the plaintiff states his claim before the judge (*dādwar*) at a distance of 'three steps' (*sē gām*), after which the defendant gives his statement of defence, keeping the same distance. This interesting formal feature is embedded in the concise, syntactically somewhat twisted description of the competences of the *dādwar*, whose task it is to hear, literally 'within (the distance of) three steps both the statement (of claim) and the answer (of defence) in filing action of complaint' (*andar se gām ud saxwan ud pāsox garzīdan ī must*).[125] The 'three steps' are not explained, but could be a relict of the religious origins of the trial, corresponding symbolically to *se gōwišnīh* (or: *se wāzag*) 'three utterances' mentioned elsewhere, the famous threefold Zoroastrian maxim of *humat*, *hūxt*, *huwaršt* (good thought, good speech, good deeds).[126] If one of the parties did not appear in court, the litigant who was present was obliged to confirm per entry (*čak dahišn*) in the transcript that his opponent 'has not come' (*nē āmad*) and that the latter 'is not taking legal action' (*kar nē rāyēnēd*).[127] The transcript also confirmed that a party was present and consented to litigation with the words 'he is taking legal action' (*kār rāyēnēd*).[128]

The litigants could engage an 'intercessor' or 'advocate' (*ǰādag-gōw*) to represent them in court. This term specifically denotes a person, who stands in for the 'main claimant' (*mādagwar*) and could be both an advocate in the modern sense of the word, that is, a person schooled in jurisprudence, or a lay person with a mandate (*pādixšāy kard*),[129] to speak or act on behalf of one of the parties. That the *ǰādag-gōw* could be a layman is quite evident in several cases described in the Law-book, for instance, when a *materfamilias* (*kadag-bānūg*)

124 Bd. 26.76 (Pakzad 2005, p. 305): *har rōz abāg xwaršēd pad ēn kār ēd rāy dādwar pad gētīy tā nēm-rōz wizīr kunēd* 'Every day he (= Mihr) is with the sun doing this work (of vigilance). This is the reason why the judge in the material world should pass judgement (*wizīr*) by mid-day (*tā nēm-rōz*).'

125 MHDA 26.3–4 (Macuch 1981, pp. 50, 188).

126 MHD 60.8: *pad sē gōwišnīh gōwēd* 'He declares with the "three utterances"' (Macuch 1993, pp. 409, 414).

127 MHD 73.13–74.5 (Macuch 1993, pp. 490f., 493). On *čak* see also Chapter IV, pp. 279–284.

128 MHD 73.13–74.5 (Macuch 1993, pp. 490f., 493).

129 MHD 74.13–14 (Macuch 1993, pp. 500, 503).

appoints the family guardian (*dūdag-sālār*) to represent her in court[130] or in the case of a claimant, who assigns a *ǰādag-gōw* to take an oath on his behalf.[131] The legal representatives or intercessors of the 'plaintiff' and the 'defendant' are labelled *ǰādag-gōw ī pēšēmāl*[132] and *ǰādag-gōw ī pasēmāl*[133] respectively. This representative could in turn be replaced by another person in this function, the *ǰādag-gōw ǰādag-gōw ī pasēmāl*[134] 'deputy of the representative of the defendant'. The main claimant designated his legal representative with the words: *kū-m ǰādag-gōw kard*[135] 'I have appointed him as intercessor' or, if he appointed two persons, *kū-m āgenēn ǰādag-gōw kard hēd*[136] 'I have appointed you *together* as (my) intercessors'. In the latter case the wording of the mandate was important: the intercessors/advocates could only represent *jointly* (*āgenēn*) the same claimant and *both* had to be present at the proceedings. Moreover, one of these two intercessors was not allowed to act as a deputy of the other one.[137] Divergent statements of the two legal representatives were considered as an obstruction of justice (*azišmānd*) and punished accordingly.[138] If the plaintiff and the defendant appointed two men as *ǰādag-gōw* both 'together and separately' (*āgenēn ud ǰud-iz ǰud*), only *one* of them was permitted as legal representative.[139] Unfortunately this last passage is not very clear, but it seems that the wording of the mandate is not precise enough and could be taken to imply that the litigants (the plaintiff and the defendant) are appointing the same representatives to intercede for them together, which is of course not possible due to the conflict of interest that would emerge, if identical persons represented both parties. Hence, only one intercessor was eligible for each party. Be it as it may, the mandate of the intercessors (*ǰādag-gōwān*) was limited, as they were not permitted to change any of the statements of the main claimants (*mādagwarān*).[140]

130 MHD 75.13: *ka kadag-bānūg dūdag-sālār ǰādag-gōw kunēd xūb* 'When the mistress of the house appoints the family guardian as (her) legal representative, (it is) proper' (Macuch 1993, pp. 501, 504).

131 MHD 78.17: *kū-m pad war ī pad sōgand ud war ī pad nāmag passāz ǰādag-gōw kard* 'I have appointed him as legal representative for (taking) the "oath of sulphur" and the "oath of recording the transcript"' (Macuch 1993, pp. 518, 521).

132 MHD 75.6–7; 77.12, (Macuch 1993, pp. 501, 504); MHD 77.15 (Macuch 1993, pp. 516, 519).

133 MHD 75.7 (Macuch 1993, pp. 501, 504).

134 MHD 75.7 (Macuch 1993, pp. 501, 504).

135 MHD 74.12 (Macuch 1993, pp. 500, 503).

136 MHD 74.17 (Macuch 1993, pp. 500, 503).

137 MHD 74.17–75.1; 75.10–11 (Macuch 1993, 500f., 503f.). The last sentence of the first passage (MHD 75.1) is not very clear. I take *ka ēk ōy ī did ǰādag gōw kuned nē xūb* 'When one makes the other one (his) intercessor, (it is) not proper' to refer to the two men installed as *ǰādag-gōw*, who had a joint mandate and could hence only represent the main claimant jointly.

138 MHD 75.11–12 (Macuch 1993, pp. 501, 504).

139 MHD 75.9–10 (Macuch 1993, pp. 501, 504).

140 MHD 75.14–17 (Macuch 1993, pp. 501, 504). For further details on the rights and duties of the *ǰādag-gōw* see Chapter IV, pp. 289–290.

After agreeing to enter litigation, the defendant declared his will to follow summons to the next session *(ō gōw āyēm* 'I will come to the hearing') and to provide 'evidence and proof' (*čim ud bōzišn*) for his statement.[141] The official in charge of jurisdiction and the litigants subsequently fixed a date together (*u-šān āgenēn zamān kard*) for the next session of the trial and both parties committed themselves to be present in court on the date agreed upon with the words 'we shall come to the hearing' (*ō gōw āyēm*).[142]

Evidence was obviously presented in the second session of the official trial, but the Tabarestān documents only record a case in which the defendant repeatedly fails to appear in court and to provide proof. The transcript of the second session only notes that the plaintiff (*pēšēmāl*) is present with the words 'he has come to the hearing (and) waited' (*ō gōw āmad pād*)[143] and his opponent (the defendant, *pasēmāl*) has not turned up: 'neither the defendant nor his legal representative came' (*pasēmāl ud ǰādag-gōw-iz nē āmad*).[144] Failing to follow summons or disturbing jurisdiction in some other manner was considered as an 'obstruction of justice' or *contumacia* (*azišmānd*) and punished, according to the Law-book, by an interlocutory decree consisting of a fine or a pledge equivalent in value to the property in dispute to be deposited with the court until the trial was over. After the third *azišmānd* the trial came to an end and the final verdict was passed against the party that had committed *contumacia* thrice (see pp. 561–569.).

Notwithstanding the defendant's first 'obstruction of justice', the Tabarestān documents reveal that a third session was scheduled, in which both parties took part. Tab. 4A first notes that the litigants take action in the said lawsuit (*im dādestān*), then records a statement spoken by the defendant (there is a lacuna in the text, but the passage is identical to Tab. 7A), by which the latter again commits himself to providing 'evidence and proof' (*čim ud bōzišn*) for his rightful possession (*dāštan abāyistan*) of the property in dispute. In this context the defendant explicitly names the original proprietor of the disputed object (a man from the Māhōy clan) and commits himself to bringing this person, who is the 'legal predecessor of that property' (*dastwar ī ān xwāstag*), to the next session of the trial so that he may testify on the defendant's behalf.[145] However, the next document discloses that the defendant is not successful in bringing his alleged *dastwar* to court for the fourth session of the trial, but he is present himself and repeats in exactly the same manner his willingness to provide 'evidence and proof' by bringing his 'legal predecessor' to court.[146] The readiness of the judiciary to concede another court session and the repetition of the whole

141 Tab. 2B.6; 4A.6; 7A.5; Appendix XII, pp. 717, 718.
142 Tab. 5A.4–6; 6A.4–6; Appendix XII pp. 722, 721.
143 Tab. 3B.5–6 (also 7B.5; 8A.6–7); Appendix XII, pp. 717, 719, 720.
144 Tab. 3B.7–8 (also 7B.6; 8A.7–9); Appendix XII, pp. 717, 719, 720.
145 Tab. 4A.6–7; Appendix XII, p. 718.
146 Tab. 7A; Appendix XII, p. 718.

Table 56. Overview: the trial

Persons involved in litigation	
ǰādag-gōw	intercessor, advocate, (legal) representative
ǰādag-gōw ī pasēmāl	(legal) representative of the defendant
ǰādag-gōw ī pēšēmāl	(legal) representative of the plaintiff
ǰādag-gōw ǰādag-gōw ī pasēmāl	deputy of the representative of the defendant
mādagwar	main claimant
pasēmāl	defendant
pēšēmāl	plaintiff, claimant, complainant
Statements of the litigants	
garzēm	'we complain!' (statement of the plaintiff and the defendant)
kar rāyēnēd/ kar nē rāyēnēd	'he takes legal action/ does not take legal action' (entry in the *saxwan-nāmag*)
nē āmad	'he has not come' (entry in the *saxwan-nāmag*)
ō gōw āyēm	'we will come to the hearing!' (statement of the plaintiff and the defendant)
Other technical terms and phrases	
azišmānd	obstruction of justice; contempt of court; *contumacia*
čak dādan	to make an entry; to place on record (in the *saxwan-nāmag*)
čim ud hōzišn	evidence and proof
garzīdan ī must	to file action of complaint
saxwan ud pāsox	statement (of claim) and answer (of defence)
sē gām	three steps (corresponding figuratively to *sē gōwišnīh* 'three utterances', the Zoroastrian triad)

procedure shows how difficult it must have been at times to procure evidence by calling one's 'legal predecessor'. Given that the testimony of the *dastwar* seems to have been the only available proof, the court was willing to make concessions in order to enable the defendant to supply this evidence. But the following documents in turn impart that both the defendant and his representative (*ǰādag-gōw*) fail to appear in court for the fifth session and also for the final session, hence committing a second and third 'obstruction of justice'.[147] It seems that after the fifth session (and second *azišmānd*) a renewed interrogation of the litigants took

147 Tab. 7B and 8A; Appendix XII, pp. 719, 720.

place, identical to the preliminary hearing, possibly in order to make sure that the defendant still wished to continue the lawsuit or to reach a settlement between the parties.[148] We are not informed on the outcome of this dispute, but can assume that the defendant lost the case due to three obstructions of justice, which would usually lead to a verdict in favour of the plaintiff.[149]

3.1.4 Evidence

In the few civil cases recorded in the Tabarestān documents it is always the defendant who is requested to present evidence (*čim ud bōzišn*) in the preliminary hearing or commits himself to providing evidence in the first session of the official trial, but this might not have been necessarily the rule. We can reasonably infer that cases occurred in which the judge first had to decide, which one of the parties would have to carry the burden of proof (*onus probandi*). The material is sparse, but this was definitely the procedure, when evidence was based on the oath or ordeal (*war*). The judge decided in this case which one of the parties should take the oath and also on the specific form of oath taking. The technical phrase used in this context with respect to the litigant, who was considered to be the best choice for oath-taking, is: *pad war … wehdādestāntar* 'he/she (is) better/best suited to take the oath for "better justice"' (that is, for a judgement exceeding the minimum required by law, see pp. 554–555). Judicial evidence could be provided by four means: (1) by the testimony of a litigant's 'legal predecessor' (*dastwar*), (2) by witnesses (*gugāy*), (3) by written documents sealed by witnesses or officials of the State, and (4) the oath (*war*).

3.1.4.1 The legal predecessor (*dastwar*)

One of the means of providing proof in a dispute over proprietary rights was to summon the person to court, who had previously held a title to the property in dispute, the *dastwar*, lit. 'authorized, entitled (person), *auctor*', with the technical meaning of 'legal predecessor; predecessor in title'. The term denotes a person who was previously entitled to the property, from whom the defendant had acquired it by sale, barter or any other means of transaction, as we have already elucidated in previous chapters in the context of proprietary rights and legal transactions.[150] The *dastwar* guaranteed that he was entitled to the property he had transferred to the recipient and that this transfer was legal. He was, moreover, obliged to defend the title of the recipient (defendant) in court against the claims of a third party. This procedure was also known in ancient Roman law in the institution of the *auctor* 'legal predecessor, informant', the precise equivalent of the Sasanian *dastwar*, with exactly the same function in the context of

148 Tab. 10A and 8B; Appendix XII, pp. 719, 720.
149 See also Chapter IV, pp. 385–387, on lawsuits in the context of sale.
150 Chapter III, pp. 195–196.

disputes regarding property in the procedure known in ancient Roman law as the *actio auctoritatis*.

Although the *auctor* or *dastwar* testified in court as spokesman of the defendant, he was *not* a lawyer or advocate. The Sasanian technical term and its abstract form *dastwarīh*, lit. authorization, entitlement', with the technical meaning of '*auctor*-ship' (that is, the duty to testify on behalf of the recipient of the object in dispute in court) have been repeatedly misunderstood in the past, leading to inaccurate and completely misleading translations.[151] As I have explained elsewhere, there can be no doubt that *dastwar* has a specific meaning in the context of civil litigation, corresponding exactly to the *auctor* in ancient Roman law (there is even a whole chapter in the Law Book dedicated to the tasks of the *dastwar* in this specific context).[152] The *dastwar* was obliged to defend the person to whom he had transferred the property in court if he was summoned, but he definitely did *not* represent the defendant in the sense of being an advocate or another lay person with a mandate. The term used for the advocate or legal representative in this sense is always *jādag-gōw* (see section 3.1.3 above), never *dastwar.*

The evidence of the Law-book is now confirmed by the Tabarestān documents and we can reconstruct the procedure as follows: in a dispute regarding the right to a specific property the defendant was requested in the preliminary hearing to provide evidence that he was legally entitled to the property claimed by the plaintiff. The defendant could prove that he indeed had a legal title by asking the person from whom he had received the object (by sale, barter, gift etc.) to give testimony in court. This previously 'entitled person', the *dastwar* or, more precisely, *dastwar ī dārišn* 'entitled person/legal predecessor of (a property in) possession' or *dastwar ī xwēšīh ud dārišn* 'entitled person/legal predecessor of (a property in) ownership and possession',[153] was obliged to vouchsafe for the defendant and to defend him in court. According to the Law-book, a specific date could be required for calling one's legal predecessor (*ō dastwarān zamān xwāstan* or *zamān ō dastwarān xwāstan* 'to require a date for the legal predecessors').[154] This specifically scheduled date for hearing the testimony of the *dastwar* was called *zamān ī ō dastwar* 'date for (calling) the legal predecessor'.[155] The statement of the *dastwar* could be decisive for the verdict if

151 Contrary to BARTHOLOMAE's interpretation (followed by PERIKHANIAN) *dastwar* in the context of litigation is *not* a 'Vertreter einer Prozeßpartei, der beklagten ebenso wie der klagenden ... also ihr Mandatar, Stellvertreter, Anwalt' (BARTHOLOMAE 1918–1922, IV, p. 52) nor, as PERIKHANIAN writes, 'an empowered, entitled person; a legal representative (= the representative of a litigating party in a case [/trial]; a *mandatary*' (PERIKHANIAN 1997, p. 348).

152 MHD 5.3–8.13 (MACUCH 1993, pp. 87–101); for an extensive study of the technical term see MACUCH 1988b.

153 DkD 545.15–16 (DkM 718.4); DkD 537.10 (DkM 708.16) respectively.

154 MHD 8.11; 5.11 (MACUCH 1993, pp. 90, 95; 87, 91 respectively).

155 MHD 5.14f. 8.11 (MACUCH 1993, pp. 87, 91f.; 90, 95).

he was able to prove that the disputed property previously belonged to him and had been lawfully transferred to the defendant. If the testimony of the *dastwar* was accepted, the plaintiff lost the case. On the other hand, if the legal predecessor of the defendant failed to convince the court or admitted that the object he had sold was not his own (*kū-m xwāstag frōxt bē az xwēš nē būd* 'I have sold the thing, but it was not in my ownership') and the plaintiff won the case, the latter could sue the *dastwar* directly for damages. The legal predecessor was then obliged to recompense the plaintiff, who could not continue suing the defendant if he had received due compensation (*mādag guharīgān*) from the *dastwar.*[156]

The person designated as legal predecessor by the defendant could deny being the original owner and refuse to testify for the defendant in court (*dastwar az dastwarīh nagīrā[y] bawēd* 'the legal predecessor denies *auctor*-ship").[157] Agreeing to testify as *auctor* in court is expressed by *dastwarīh kardan* 'to perform as *auctor*; to do *auctor*-ship' and *pad dastwarīh andar ēstādan* 'to function as *auctor*; to enter *auctor*-ship'.[158]

Table 57. Overview: the legal predecessor (*dastwar*)

az dastwarīh nagīrā(y) būdan	to deny *auctor*-ship
dastwar ī dārišn	(lit.) '(person) entitled to possession' (= legal predecessor of a property in possession)
dastwar ī xwēšīh ud dārišn	(lit.) '(person) entitled to ownership and possession' (= legal predecessor of a property in ownership and possession)
dastwarīh kardan	to perform as *auctor*; to do *auctor*-ship
mādag guharīgān	compensation for the object of dispute
ō dastwarān zamān xwāstan	to require a date for (calling) the legal predecessors
pad dastwarīh andar ēstādan	to function as *auctor*; to enter *auctor*-ship
pad dastwar nagīrā(y) būdan	to deny (being) the legal predecessor/*auctor*
zamān ī ō dastwar	date for (calling) the legal predecessor
zamān ō dastwarān xwāstan	to require a date for (calling) the legal predecessors

156 MHD 7.15–8.2 (Macuch 1993, pp. 90, 94).
157 MHD 6.12 (Macuch 1993, pp. 88, 93). Henning 1946 (p. 732) has read **nakkīrā* as a loan-word from the Aramaic root nkr 'to repudiate, deny'. Buyaner 2015 argues convincingly that the expression is an early loan-word, derived from the Akkadian verb *nakāru(m)*, attested already in the Codex Hammurabi in the same technical sense, and should be read *nagīrā(y)*.
158 MHD 6.11; 5.7; 6.12; 7.4 (Macuch 1993, pp. 88, 92; 85–89; 91–93 respectively).

3.1.4.2 Witnesses (*gugāy*)

The judge was obliged to assess the 'reliability, certainty' (*ēwarīh*; *xwastūgīh*) of witnesses according to criteria which are only alluded to *en passant* in the texts, such as reputation and standing in the community, position in the social hierarchy, status as a free man or a slave, gender and age. That the court was obliged to evaluate the credibility of witnesses and decide whether they qualified to give evidence, is indicated in the concise summary of *Dēnkard* 8, but not elucidated (as so often in the short entries of this source).[159] In three cases decisions based on the testimony of witnesses were considered as 'reliable, binding' (*ēwar*). First, if the Chief Mobed, the *mowdedān mowbed*, was engaged as both witness (*gugāy*) and judge (*dādwar*), as we have seen above. His testimony had 'validity' (*wāwarīh*) and his verdict, as the highest judicial authority, was final and legally binding (with the possible exception of a *framān* of the 'rulers').[160] According to the Law-book two types of evidence were absolutely reliable: the testimony of the Chief Mobed and the oath (*war*), but the statement of the former was assessed as even 'more binding' (*ēwartar*) than the oath (at least according to the opinion of one jurisconsult).[161] Second, the evidence provided by the testimony of State officials (*kārdār*) or public authorities (*xwēškārīh sālārān*) in their specific areas of competence, but with the difference that a verdict based on this evidence could be contested under certain circumstances in a court of appeal. Several examples of testimonies given by public officials, such as the *war-sālār* 'supervisor of the oath', the *frēzwān* 'inspector' or the *zēndānbān* 'gaoler', are listed in the Law-book.[162] Third, the testimony of 'three witnesses' (*sē gugāy*), who, as we have reason to assume, were all adult males confessing Zoroastrianism and had been evaluated by the court as trustworthy, respected members of the community.[163]

159 DkD 535.17–19 (DkM 707.1–2): *abar sāmān ī gugāyīh [ī] ud čim ī šāyestan rāy nē šāyestan ī kas-⁺ē(w) pad gugāyīh čē andar im dar* 'On the measure of (giving) testimony and the reason for permitting or not permitting a person to (give) testimony (*gugāyīh*), which is in this chapter'.

160 Particularly DkD 534.9–15 (DkM 705.12–17); see above pp. 507–508.

161 MHDA 28.5–7: *xwastūgīh guft ī mowbedān ⁺mowbed ud war ud čiyōn az Dibīr be gōwēnd guft ī mowbedān ⁺mowbed az-iz war pad ēwartar dārišn* 'Reliable (are) the statement of the Chief Mobed and the oath. And, as reported according to Dibīr, the statement of the Chief Mobed is to be considered as more binding than the oath' (Macuch 1981, pp. 52f.; 191).

162 See sections 2.1 and 2.2 above.

163 These three groups of witnesses, whose statements are considered as reliable (*ēwarīh gōwišn*), are brought together in the précis of DkD 540.3–5 (DkM 711.18–20): *abar ēwarīh gōwišn ī čand az xwēškārīh sālāran pad ān ī-šān xwēškārīh padiš mowbedān mowbed ayāb 3 gugāy pad har dādestān* 'On the reliable statements (*ēwarīh gōwišn*) of several authorities with specific duties (*xwēškārīh sālārān*) in their areas of competence (*ān ī-šān xwēškārīh padiš*); (on the statements of) the Chief Mobed or three witnesses in every trial'. On the evaluation of witnesses see below.

A (non-legal) Pahlavi source lists three groups of people, who as a rule should *not* be accepted as witnesses: women (*zan*), underage children (*rahīg ī aburnāy*) and male slaves (*bandag ī mard*).[164] It seems, however, that in practice women and slaves were permitted or called to act as witnesses under specific circumstances. We have already seen in the context of debts and liabilities of succession that after the demise of a *paterfamilias* (*kadag-xwadāy*) lawsuits could be both initiated by and directed against the newly installed guardian of the family (*dūdag-sālār*) together with the *materfamilias* (*kadag-bānūg*). In these cases the *kadag-bānūg* could be summoned to court as one of the parties or as a witness.[165] In a criminal prosecution transmitted in the Law-book the testimony of two women is admitted by the *mowbed* of Staxr and results in the recording of a 'bill of indictment' (*nibištag*), which is in turn confirmed by a high dignitary of the State, the *mowān handarzbed.*[166] This was, however, obviously an unusual procedure, as the same passage cites the jurisconsult Zurwāndād, who apodictically declares that this is 'not done in legal practice' (*pad kardag nē kard*). The next sentence explains that a 'transcript of interrogation' (*pursišn-nāmag*) is recorded, if the witnesses are 'one woman' (*ēk zan*) and 'one man' (*ēk mard*), but not if they are a woman (*zan*) and a slave (*anšahrīg*). Unfortunately there is a lacuna in the following text, but it is quite clear by the terminology employed in this context that both entries refer to criminal cases and that the testimony of women could be used in exceptional instances to draw up a 'bill of indictment' and a 'transcript of interrogation' (on these terms see section 3.2 below).

A woman was evidently also allowed to perform as both witness and *auctor* (*dastwar*) in the seldom case of not having a legal guardian or if she was authorized by her husband to do so, according to the following entry:

> DkD 537.12–14 (DkM 708.18–20)
> *abar šāyistan ī zan pad gugāyīh ud +dastwarīh* ⟨d'twblyh⟩ *ka abar tan ī xwēš sālār pādixšāy pad-iz dastwarīh (ī) šōy nē šāyistan ī an-ēr ud margarzān pad ēk-iz čē andar im dar.*
>
> 'On the (legal) capacity of a woman to (give) testimony (*gugāyīh*) and (enter) *auctor*-ship (+*dastwarīh*), when she (is) guardian of her own person/body (*abar tan ī xwēš sālār*) (and when) she is authorized by the entitlement of the husband (*pādixšāy pad-iz dastwarīh ī šōy*) (and on) the incapacity of a non-Iranian (*an-ēr*) and a person "deserving death" (*margarzān*) (to do) either (*pad ēk-iz*), which (is) in this chapter.'

According to this précis of a longer (lost) legal text a woman, who was 'guardian of her own person/body' (*abar tan ī xwēš sālār*), *i. e.* who had no male legal

164 MX 38.37/33 (39.37 according to de Menasce 1945, p. 222, 17): *ud ēn 3 pad gugāh nē padīrišn zan ud rahīg ī aburnāy ud bandag mard* 'And these three should not be accepted as witnesses: women and underage children and slave men'.

165 See Chapter IV, pp. 360–364.

166 MHD 98.1–5 (Macuch 1993, pp. 582, 587). On *nibištag* 'bill of indictment' see pp. 573–574.

guardian, was permitted to act both as witness and *auctor* in court. A woman was also enabled to appear in court in both functions if her husband 'authorized her by entitlement' (*pādixšāy pad-iz dastwarīh*) to be involved in a lawsuit in either of both capacities. In sharp contrast the quoted *Dēnkard* passage subsequently notes that a non-Iranian (*an-ēr*) and a person found guilty of a capital crime (*margarzān*) were accepted neither as witnesses nor could enter *auctor*ship. That a woman was admitted to make a statement in court or to act as witness after being authorized (*pādixšāy*) by the men of her family is confirmed by one of the most interesting Tabarestān documents (Tab. 28), in which a woman (named Pidarōš) makes a statement regarding her own suitability to act as 'substitute successor' (*stŭr*) of a deceased man, her paternal uncle, in a claim regarding the right to this man's *stŭrīh*.[167]

A curious passage of the Law-book reveals that a woman could be sued and at the same time be the object of the suit and act as witness. In a complex case we have already discussed above two men lay claim to a woman, both presenting as evidence documents with seal imprints: one sealed with a 'reliable, valid seal' (*muhr ī ēwar*), which is still in use; the other with a 'genuine seal' (*muhr ī wizurd*), which was formerly in use (*ī pēš az ān*).[168] The second document with the older seal is evaluated by the court as an 'unreliable, doubtful document' (*wizīr ī warōmand*), in contrast to the first one, considered as a 'reliable, valid document' (*wizīr ī ēwar*). This evaluation would as a rule give priority to the claim of the man with the 'valid document' (*wizīr ī ēwar*), if the men litigate against each other. But if the two men put claim to the woman in two individual lawsuits, not against each other, but separately (*ǰud ǰud*) against the woman herself (*dādestān abāg ziyānag kunēnd*), then the testimony of the woman can be decisive. If she declares 'I am the wife of him who has the "doubtful, unreliable document"' (*ōy zan hom kē wizīr ī warōmand dārēd*), then the man with the 'doubtful document' (*wizīr ī warōmand*) is to be recognised as the husband (at least according to one jurisconsult, but the case is disputed). This ruling allows two conclusions: first, a woman could be sued directly by a man claiming her as wife and testify herself in this matter, and, second, her testimony could be conceded higher credibility than a 'valid document' (*wizīr ī ēwar*) of marriage brought forward by another litigant as evidence on the same issue in a parallel lawsuit against the same woman. Given the intricacies of Sasanian marriage law (see Chapter II) legal disputes regarding the right to a specific woman as wife might have been fairly frequent. We can hence assume that the statement of the woman regarding her marital status was significant evidence, provided that the formalities of the lawsuit permitted this procedure.

We have already mentioned the double legal status of the slave in legal practice as an object and as a legal person, capable of being sued, and testifying in

167 See Chapter II, p. 171, and Macuch 2020b; the whole document is in Appendix XIV.

168 MHD 32.4–10 (Macuch 1993, pp. 223, 227); see Chapter IV, pp. 296–301; on the technical terms designating seals and documents see also below pp. 550–551.

court in his own case.[169] A passage in the Law-book describes the lawsuit of a plaintiff (*pēšēmāl*) against a person, who he claims to be his own slave.[170] The slave is in this instance both the defendant (*pasēmāl*) and the object of the lawsuit, but he does not claim to be a freedman, since he testifies to being the slave of another master: 'the defendant declares with respect to another specific man: "I am his slave"' (*pasēmāl any mard pad nāmčišt rāy gōwēd kū-š anšahrīg hom*), hence the property of a third party. The statement of the slave regarding his own proprietary status is admitted in court, but is evidently not qualified to avert the claim of the plaintiff. The slave, however, has brought a witness with him to confirm his statement *(u-š gugāy abāg* '[there is] a witness with him'), whose testimony subsequently leads to the dismissal of the claim: 'legal action is not to be taken' (*dādestān nē rāyēnišn*). This would imply that a slave was allowed to give a statement concerning his own status in court, but that it had to be confirmed by a witness to be admissible as evidence.

The litigants were obviously obliged to bring their witnesses to court on their own, as we may infer from the formulations *gugāy abāg* '(there is) a witness with (him); (he has) a witness with (him)' or *gugāy abāg nēst* '(there) is no witness with (him)',[171] and indirectly from a passage listing offences a party might commit during a lawsuit, one of which is: 'When he (= the litigant) does not initially bring the witness he has named or completely fails to bring him (to court)' (*ka gugāy ī gōwēd fradom ayāb bowandag nē āwarēd*).[172] The summary in the *Dēnkard* uses the same wording (*gugāy abāg*) besides *dārišn abāg* 'having the property (in dispute) with (him)' in a list of diverse combinations of evidence the parties could present in court, albeit—as all the entries in this source—without elucidations:

> DkD 536.13–17 (DkM 707.18–22)
> *abar pahikārišn ī pad xwāstagīg čiš ka ēk dārišn (ud) gugāy-ē(w) abāg ēk nē dārišn abāg nē gugāy ayāb ēk dārišn abāg ēk gugāy-ē(w). ayāb ēk gugāy abāg-šān ēk-iz dārišn nē paydāg ud ka har dō ādehīg ayāb har dō uzdehīg hēnd.*
>
> 'On a dispute regarding a matter of property (*xwāstagīg čiš*): When one (of the parties) has the property (*dārišn*) and a witness with him (*gugāy-ēw abāg*) (and) one (of the parties) (has) neither the property with him (*nē dārišn abāg*) nor a witness, or one (of the parties) (has) the property with him (*dārišn abāg*), the other (party has) a witness. Or (when) one (of the parties) (has) a witness with them (*gugāy abāg-šān*) and it is not clear, whether the (other party) (has) the property, and when both (litigants) are citizens (*ādehīg*) or both are foreigners (*uzdehīg*).'

An offence committed by a party's witness, such as lying *(ka gugāy drōzan* 'when the witness [is] a liar'), is also in the list of offences mentioned above and

169 See Chapter II, pp. 108–109.

170 MHD 107.9–12 (Macuch 1993, pp. 642, 650).

171 MHD 107.11,14 and 92.4,5 respectively (Macuch 1993, pp. 642, 650, and 580, 585); also RivAF 72.1 (Anklesaria 1969 vol. I, p. 39; II, p. 81): *gugāy-ē(w) abāg ayāb dō* '(there are) one or two witnesses with (him)' (for the whole text see Appendix IX).

172 MHD 91.12 (Macuch 1993, pp. 579f., 584).

Table 58. Overview: the testimony of witnesses

abar tan ī xwēš sālār	guardian of her own person/body
drō wizīr	deceitful judgement
ēwarīh	reliability, certainty
gugāy abāg; *gugāy abāg nēst*	with a witness; without a witness
gugāy āwardan	to bring a witness (to court)
gugāyīh dādan	to give testimony
nibištag	bill of indictment
pad gugāyīh šāyēd; *pad gugāyīh nē šāyēd*	'it is admissible as testimony'; 'it is not admissible as testimony'
pad kardag nē kard	'it is not done in legal practice'
pad nīrmad ī xwēš; *nē pad nīrmad ī xwēš*	(testimony) to his own advantage; (testimony) to his own disadvantage
pādixšāy pad-iz dastwarīh	authorized by entitlement
xwastūgīh	reliability, certainty
zur-gugāyīh	false testimony

seems to have been assessed as contempt of court on the part of the litigant who introduced this witness.[173]

The court decided whether a testimony was admitted (*šāyēd*) or refused (*nē šāyēd*). A criminal case (regarding theft committed by several persons) in the Law-book discloses that if one of the accused persons makes a statement to his own disadvantage (*nē pad nīrmad ī xwēš*), hereby incriminating himself, it is admissible as testimony (*pad gugāyīh šāyēd*), but a statement he makes to his own advantage (*pad nīrmad ī xwēš*) is not admissible (*pad gugāyīh nē šāyēd*).[174] Refusal to act as witness and give testimony (*gugāyīh nē dahēd*) is compared in another source to the 'deceitful judgement' (*drō wizīr*) of a judge, hence assessed as a grievous offence.[175] False testimony (*zur-gugāyīh*) is, moreover, included as a capital crime in the long lists of offences 'deserving death' (*margarzān*) in several Pahlavi sources.[176]

173 MHD 91.11 (Macuch 1993, pp. 579, 584). On offences against the judiciary see pp. 561–569.

174 MHD 73.2–7 (Macuch 1993, pp. 489, 492). Compare DkD 535.17–19 (DkM 707.1–2) *abar sāmān ī gugāyīh [ī] ud čim ī šāyestan ud nē šāyestan ī kas-⁺ē(w) pad gugāyīh čē andar im dar* 'On the measure of giving testimony and the reason why a person is permitted or not permitted to give testimony, which (is) in this chapter'.

175 According to DkD 543.14–15 (DkM 715.18–19): *abar hāwandīh ī gugāy ke gugāyīh nē dahēd abāg dādwar (ī) drō wizīr* 'On the equivalence of a witness who does not give testimony with a judge (who passes) a deceitful verdict'.

176 For attestations see list of *margarzān* crimes in Appendix XVI.

3.1.4.3 Documentary evidence

Documents provided as evidence needed to be evaluated by the court according to specific criteria, which we have already discussed extensively in Chapter IV (section 2.4 on the function of seals).[177] In sum, the court distinguished between two main categories of documents according to the validity of the seals attached to them: (1) 'reliable, valid documents' (*wizīr ī ēwar*) and (2) 'unreliable, doubtful documents' (*wizīr ī warōmand*). Documents imprinted with the personal seal of a public official bearing his name and those with the imprint of an anonymous administrative seal (called *muhr ī pad kār-framān dāštan*, lit. 'seal for exercising command') were assessed as 'reliable, binding' (*ēwar*) and accepted in court as evidence. These two types of seals were regarded as 'valid seals' (*muhr ī wāwarīgān*) and in turn differentiated into two further categories: (1) 'reliable, legally binding seals' (*muhr ī ēwar*) and (2) 'genuine seals' (*muhr ī wizurd*). As we have already elucidated, *muhr ī ēwar* denoted a personal or administrative seal that was currently in use, whereas *muhr ī wizurd* designated an older seal of the personal or administrative type that was employed previously, but no longer utilized to certify documents. Documents with either of these two seal imprints would have been presumably admitted as evidence, but an evaluation took place if one litigant presented a document with a *muhr ī ēwar* as proof and his opponent brought forward a document with a *muhr ī wizurd* as counterevidence. Under these circumstances the court was obliged to appraise the evidential value of the two documents, giving at least in the case discussed MHD 32.4–10[178]priority to the more recent one (with the *muhr ī ēwar*). Interestingly, the older document was estimated in comparison to the more recent one as a 'doubtful document' (*wizīr ī warōmand*) despite the fact that it was sealed with a 'genuine seal' (*muhr ī wizurd*) and hence had also been certified by a State official, albeit at an earlier period.

Documents with the seals of private individuals as witnesses to a transaction, which were verified with a 'witness-seal' *(gugāy-muhr*; or the 'seal of [bearing] witness', *gugāyīh muhr*) or several 'witness-seals' (*gugāy-muhrān/muhrīhā*), were generally regarded as 'unreliable, doubtful documents' (*wizīr ī warōmand*), which had to be evaluated following specific criteria, described by Īšō'bōxt.[179] To this purpose the court carried out an investigation regarding the trustworthiness of these witnesses by appraising their reputation in the community. If they were found to be pious men, honest and esteemed in the region, the document was accepted as a 'reliable' one (*wizīr ī ēwar*), but if the result of the investigation was not convincing, it was estimated as a 'doubtful document' (*wizīr ī warōmand*). We can hence conclude that Sasanian courts accepted as evidence both documents validated with official seals as well as those confirmed with private seals, after having examined the trustworthiness of the witnesses.[180]

177 See pp. 296–301.
178 See discussion pp. 299–301.
179 On this description and the technical terms see Chapter IV, pp. 296–297.
180 See also MHD 93.11–14, discussed p. 297.

According to both the Law-book and original Pahlavi sources, documents could be verified by several seals of private persons and witnesses as well as with the personal seal of a legal authority to make them 'legally binding' (*ēwarīh rāy*).[181] A 'reliable document' (*wizīr ī ēwar*) was a document validated with a 'valid seal' (*muhr ī wāwarīgān*) or several 'valid seals' (*wāwarīgān muhrān*) of legal authorities, but it could also be a document confirmed by a 'witness-seal' (*gugāy-muhr*) or several 'witness-seals' (*gugāy-muhrān/muhrīhā*) of private individuals, whose reputation had been scrutinized in an official inquiry and approved of by the court.

Table 59. Overview: documentary evidence

Evaluation	Type of seal	Definition
wizīr ī ēwar 'reliable, valid document'	*muhr ī wāwarīgān* 'valid seal'	1. seal of a State official or anonymous administrative seal (*muhr ī pad kār-framān dāštan*) 2. seal of a trustworthy witness (*gugāy-muhr*)
	(a) *muhr ī ēwar* 'reliable, legally binding seal'	(a) official seal currently in use
	(b) *muhr ī wizurd* 'genuine seal'	(b) official seal no longer in use
wizīr ī warōmand 'unreliable, doubtful document'	(a) *gugāy-muhr* 'witness-seal'; *gugāyīh muhr* 'seal of (bearing) testimony'	(a) seal of a witness, whose trustworthiness is questionable (unless assessed as 'reliable', *ēwar*)
	(b) *muhr ī wizurd* 'genuine seal'	(b) official seal no longer in use (as counterevidence to a document with a *muhr ī ēwar*)

3.1.4.4 The oath (*war*)

No distinction is made in legal terminology between the 'ordeal' and the 'oath'. The term *war* (< Av. *varah-*) seems to refer in the legal texts to both methods of providing proof, based on the ancient belief in 'divine judgement' (*iudicium dei*) by calling on the interference of a deity to protect the truthful person and punish the perjurer.[182] But whereas the 'oath' is usually a solemn statement or promise to be truthful, invoking the presence of a divine entity as witness to the

181 For attestations see (under personal seals of officials) Chapter IV, pp. 290–291.
182 On the Iranian ordeal/oath see Bartholomae 1918–1923 (1918, vol. II, pp. 7–37); Perikhanian 1979 and Goldman 2015, pp. 50–86. On the ordeal in the Indo-Iranian cult see also Boyce 1975, pp. 34–36.

veracity of one's statement, the 'ordeal' goes beyond this assertion by including an additional test to prove the truthfulness of the statement with divine assistance. Another term, *passāxt*, explicitly designates this 'test' or 'ordeal' in a religious context (as in *passāxt ī mēnōy* '*mēnōy* ordeal'), but it is presumably an elliptical expression, derived from an original *war passāxt* 'test of the ordeal' or *war passāxtan* 'to prepare the ordeal; to test by ordeal'.[183] The ordeal in the Indo-Iranian tradition originally involved placing the oath taker in some kind of physical danger (passing through fire; being submerged in water, among numerous other methods) and took place within a ritual framework under the surveillance of a deity, in an Iranian context frequently Mithra/Mihr, the god of contract, or Rašnu/Rašn, the epitome of justice.[184]

The lack of a terminological differentiation between 'oath' and 'ordeal' suggests that legal evidence provided by the oath in a Sasanian trial involved more than a solemn statement to tell the truth and was ritually combined with a specific type of ordeal (although the term *passāxt* is not used in the Law-book). Our sources seem to point in this direction, but there is far too little description to conclude that generally all types of oaths were linked to an ordeal. An oath taken by a litigant to confirm his initial statement in the transcript of the lawsuit (*saxwan-nāmag*) might have just been a pronouncement that he is telling the truth, for which no ordeal was arranged (if this is what *war ī pad nāmag-passāz* 'oath in preparation of the transcript' means).[185] We can, however, infer from two observations that the ritual aspect of oath taking was in many cases an important element of the procedure. First, as we have seen above, the oath counted among those forms of proof considered as *ēwar* 'reliable, (legally) binding' (as opposed to *warōmand* 'uncertain, unreliable, not binding').[186] This high estimation of its evidential value makes it rather likely that the oath taker—at least in some cases in the absence of witnesses or documentary evidence—was obliged to verify his statement by undergoing an ordeal. Second, several passages imply that oath taking took place within a ritual framework in a special venue, called *xwārestān* 'place of swearing', *war gāh* 'place of the oath' or *passāxt gāh* 'place of

183 For *passāxt ī mēnōy* see DkM 927.4; compare *war passāxt ī mēnōy* 'test by *mēnōy*-ordeal' (DkM 771.17), also *pad passāxt ī abar dēn* 'in an ordeal regarding (the truth) of the religion' (DkM 664.14) and *pad gōwišn ī passāxt* 'by the statement of the ordeal' (DkM 413.5). The last two phrases refer to the famous ordeal of Ādurbād ī Māraspandān, who proved the truth of the Mazdean religion by having molten copper (*widāxtag rōy*) poured over his breast (on these expressions see also Macuch 1987 with further references). The term *mēnōy* in *passāxt ī mēnōy* is presumably an allusion to the type of judge in these ordeals, who is a 'spiritual' or *mēnōy* judge, not a 'worldly' (*gētīy*) one (the transcription of *mēnoy* and *gētīy* follows Skjærvø 2009, p. 481, fn. 12). On the difference between these two kinds of judges see *Dēnkard* 3.302 (DkD 236.8–9; DkM 309.5–6; the whole text is in Appendix III) and Introduction, pp. 7–8.

184 Boyce 1975, p. 35; Goldman 2015, pp. 50, 52, with further references.

185 MHD 78.16 (Macuch 1993, pp. 518, 521).

186 MHDA 28.5–7 (Macuch 1981, pp. 52f.; 191), see p. 545, fn. 161 above.

the ordeal', under the supervision of a special officer called *war-sālār* 'supervisor of the oath/ordeal', and that the proceedings were recorded in a special transcript called *yazišn-nāmag* 'protocol/transcript of recitation' (or, in criminal law, in the *uzdād-nāmag* 'protocol/transcript of arrangement [of the ordeal]', but the meaning of the last term is very uncertain).[187] Oath and ordeal might have been distinguished by the verbs employed together with *war*: the Lawbook prefers the phrases *war warzīdan*[188] and *war rāyēnīdan*,[189] 'to take an oath', whereas the *Dēnkard* frequently uses—besides *warzīdan*—*war passāxtan*[190] and *war sāxtan*[191] 'to prepare/implement an ordeal; to test by ordeal', which both suggest that formal preparations were made for the observance of a special ceremony in connection with taking the oath.

The ritual element of the whole procedure is visible in the descriptions of late Pahlavi texts and in the New Persian *Riwāyats*, especially the Persian *Sōgand nāma* 'Book of the oath', which contains both a short and a long description of the ordeal and quotes recitations calling on the deities to protect the truthful person.[192] A concise general description, underlining the ritual aspect, is transmitted in the summary of the *Dēnkard*:

> DkD 535–536.3 (DkM 707.3–8)
> *abar ast ī saxwan ī az war ud ō war* ⁺*gāh šud čand pād ī* ⁺*pēš-madār pas-madār rāy zamān kard [ī] ud gōwišn ud pašn ud ērāxtagīh ī padiš ud ēwēnagān ērāxtagīh [ī] ud čiyōn pahrēxtan ī [ud] hannāmān ī war padiš warzīd ēstēd ēk ēk nērang ī pahrēz abar pāyišnīh ī ō nigerīdan ī yazišn wizīr abar bōxt (ud) ēraxt.*

"On the part (or: veracity?)[193] of the statement that is (confirmed) by the oath and (when) he (= the litigant) has gone to the place of ordeal (*war* ⁺*gāh*), how long

187 For attestations of these terms see Macuch 1993, pp. 108–109 (n. 2). The *uzdad-nāmag* is mentioned MHD 78.14 (Macuch 1993, pp. 518, 521).

188 As in MHD 13.2: *war pad nē edonīh warzišn* 'he should take the oath on the "not-thusness" (= falsity) (of a claim)' (Macuch 1993, pp. 127, 130), or MHD 13.5: *ka-šān pad nē dānist war warzēd* 'when they took the oath on "not knowing"' (Macuch 1993, pp. 127, 130). For other examples see *ibid.*, index, p. 736; also DkM 707.6; 709.15; 711.7.

189 MHD 76.6: *tā ō war rāyēnišn ī pad dādestān* 'until taking the oath in a lawsuit'; MHD 76.7: *pēš az war rāyēnišn ī pad dādestān* 'before taking the oath in a lawsuit' (Macuch 1993, pp. 510, 512).

190 DkD 577.7 (DkM 771.17): *abar war passāxt ī mēnōy* 'on the test of the *mēnōy* ordeal'; DkM 743.12: *abar nērang ī war passāxt* 'on the incantations of the ordeal test' (or is *nērang* 'ritual direction', as translated by Kotwal/Kreyenbroek 2003, p. 309?) In the context of the ordeal specific incantations or charms, spells, effective formulae, seem to have been meant that were to be spoken by the oath taker during the ritual, as the expression *nērang ī pahrēz* 'incantations of protection' suggests (DkM 707.7, see the following translation of this passage); see also the next fn.

191 DkD 538.13 (DkM 709.22–710.1): *čand abzār ud nērang ī andar war sāxtan abāyišnīg* 'several instruments and incantations necessary for preparing the ordeal'; DkD 577.15 (DkM 772.5): *ud abar ēwēnag sāxtan ī garm ud sard war* 'on the methods of preparing the warm and the cold ordeal'.

192 Unvala 1922, vol. I, pp. 46–54; translation in Dhabhar 1932, pp. 39–51. For a similar passage in this text to the Sasanian *war ī pāy nišān* see Macuch 1993, p. 134.

(*čand*) he has waited (*pād*); (on) the one who comes first (+*pēš-madār*) (and) the one who comes afterwards (*pas-madār*) on the fixed date (*zamān kard*). And (on) the statement and the contract and the punishment for it and (on) the types of punishment (*ēwēnagān ērāxtagīh*). And (on) how to protect the members of the body (*hannāmān*) on which the oath has been taken (*ī war padiš warzīd ēstēd*), (listing) one by one the incantations of protection (*nērang ī pahrēz*). On the supervision up to the observation of the recitation (of the oath) (*yazišn*); (on) the verdict regarding acquittal (*bōxt*) (or) conviction (*ēraxt*).

Despite the deplorable shortness of these entries, the text suggests that oath taking consisted of a supervised recitation (*yazišn*), which took place in a special venue, the 'place of the ordeal' (*war* +*gāh*), on a specific date (*zamān kard*) in a fixed sequence of participants: there is an oath taker 'who comes first' (+*pēš-madār*) and one 'who comes afterwards' (*pas-madār*). The wording furthermore implies that in the course of taking the oath specific limbs or members (*hannāmān*) of the oath taker's body were put to the test. These could in turn be protected from harm by chanting specific 'incantations of protection' (*nērang ī pahrēz*). However, we cannot be certain that this rudimentary description truly reflects Sasanian practice, since the précis of the *Dēnkard* is based on a mixture of religious and legal texts from different periods and could contain many archaic elements, which at this period were no longer part of a civil trial.

According to the information to be gathered from the Law-book, the judge first decided, which one of the litigants was to take the oath. The technical phrase employed in this context is *pad war … wehdādestāntar*, lit. '(he/she is) better (suited) for (taking) the oath for better justice', a phrase that contains far more information, than can be transmitted by a mere literal translation. The expression *wehdādestāntar*, lit. 'better suited for better justice', is a comparative of *wehdādestān*, lit. 'good justice' (*weh* 'good, better' + *dādestān* 'decision, judgement, justice'). Its abstract *wehdādestānīh* is one of the few technical terms in Īšōʿbōxt's Corpus Iuris, which the translator has wisely refrained from rendering into Syriac (although he does add an explanation), employing the term in its original Iranian form (albeit with the pronunciation of his time: *behdādestānīh*). Although the literal meaning of the word is 'good justice', its technical meaning in Sasanian law is, according to Īšōʿbōxt 'extension of justice', referring to a procedure that *extends a certain legal right* by doing *more* than formally required by law.[194] In the context of the oath the phrase *pad war … wehdādestāntar* refers in the Law-book (and also RivAF 72)[195] to the litigant, who should take the oath, since the court has decided that his (or her) statement would lead to an 'extension of justice', that is, to a judgment

193 ⟨'YT' Y⟩ *ast ī* could be a mistake for the similarly written ⟨'ytwnyh⟩ *ēdōnīh*, lit. 'thusness', *i. e.* 'veracity' of a statement; see elucidations below.

194 See Macuch 2019a and Chapter I, pp. 71–72, also Chapter VII, p. 610.

195 See Appendix IX, p. 697, for the text.

exceeding the minimum requirements of legal procedure. The process of deciding, who should take the oath, is mentioned in several passages, using the following formulations:

- *ka dādestān pad war ud pasēmāl wehdādestāntar* lit. 'if the procedure (is) based on the oath and the defendant "fulfils justice better" ';[196]
- *pad war pēšēmāl/pasēmāl wehdādestāntar*, lit. 'the plaintiff/defendant fulfils justice better by taking the oath';[197]
- *pad war wehdādestāntar kū* … and *pad war* … *az* … *wehdādestāntar*, lit. '(he/she) fulfils justice better by taking the oath than …'.[198]

The lawsuits, in which these phrases occur, refer to disputes regarding ownership of a specific property or payment liabilities of a deceased *paterfamilias*.[199] These are complex cases taken from the daily legal practice of the courts, but they all have one thing in common: evidence is based mainly on the oath, even if other kinds of proof are available, but not decisive. We can only speculate on the reasons, why one litigant should be preferred over his opponent to take the oath (or perform the ordeal), but it seems likely that putting the burden of proof on the party, whose testimony under oath would better serve the process of decision making by *going beyond the minimum evidence* required by the law of procedure, was considered as a significant step to attaining a binding verdict.

The Law-book mentions four different kinds of oaths in the context of civil trials, three of them in combination with specific statements to be spoken by one party (usually the defendant) or both parties. These are:

1. The *war ī dēnīg* (or: *dēnīg war*) 'religious oath'.[200] This oath could be administered, if in a lawsuit regarding a 'liability of the forefathers/parents' (*tōzišn ī pidarān*) the defendant claimed to have 'no knowledge' (*nē dānist*) of the debt. The words he is obliged to speak under oath are (with respect to the claim of the plaintiff): *nē ēdōnīh* 'it (is) not so' (lit. 'not-thusness').[201] With this wording the defendant swears that there is definitely *no payment obligation*, although he has originally only declared that he is not informed on the existence of a debt. By taking this oath the defendant explicitly repudiates the debt, thus refuting the veracity of the plaintiff's claim (see also under 3). Both this passage and another longer sentence of the Law-book suggest that—notwithstanding the original statement of the litigant—the

196 MHD 6.5; 14.1 (Macuch 1993, pp. 88, 92; 128, 131 respectively); also Macuch 2019a, p. 77f.
197 MHD 14.15,16 (Macuch 1993, pp. 129, 132); also Macuch 2019a, p. 79.
198 MHD 14.12; 13.6f. (Macuch 1993, pp. 129, 132; 127, 130 respectively); also Macuch 2019a, p. 80f.
199 See Chapter IV, pp. 360–364.
200 MHD 13.1; DkM 400.2; 771.15 respectively.
201 MHD 13.1–2 (Macuch 1993, pp, 125, 130).

goal of this type of oath was to confirm the veracity (*ēdōnīh* 'thusness') or falsity *(nē ēdōnīh* 'not-thusness') of a claim. Compare also the short entry in the *Dēnkard* (DkD 311.19; DkM 400.2:) *ēdōnīh ud an-ēdōnīh paydāgīh pad dēnīg war* 'the revelation of the veracity and falsity [of a claim] by the "religious oath" '.[202]

2. The *war ī pāy-nišān* 'oath of binding the feet'.[203] This oath was administered under similar circumstances, if a defendant declared to have no knowledge of a liability. But the words spoken under oath were significantly different, corresponding to the original statement of the defendant: 'I do not know' (*nē dānom*).[204] In contrast to the *war ī dēnīg*, the person who takes this oath only states that he (or she) has *no knowledge* of a debt, but does not make any definitive statement regarding the existence of an obligation. It was, however, also possible to explicitly refute the claim of the plaintiff under this oath: in a lawsuit regarding proprietary rights the defendant denies the claimant's claim to ownership of a specific property with the words: *nē tō xwēš* 'it is not your own'.[205]
3. The *war ī pad sōgand* 'sulphurous water oath'.[206] This third type is mentioned in two passages, the first of which again involves a liability of succession. The defendants (the guardian and the mistress of the house) declare that they have 'no knowledge' (*nē dānist*) of a debt. Both can be obliged to confirm their statement of 'having no knowledge' (*nē dānist*) by taking the 'sulphurous water oath'.[207] As in the case of the *war ī pāy-nišān*, the defendants only swear that they are *not informed* on the existence of a debt. But it seems that this oath could also be imposed in a different manner, if the same type is meant RivAF 66 by the imperative *sōgand xwār* 'take a (sulphurous water) oath!'[208] In the case transmitted in this late Pahlavi text the heir of a deceased *paterfamilias* denies being informed of a debt (*kū-š man āgāhīh*

202 On *ēdōnīh* and *nē ēdōnīh* see also MHD 13.17–14.1 (Macuch 1993, pp. 128, 131). The whole *Dēnkard* passage is translated in Macuch 1993, p. 133.

203 MHD 13.3 and 14.3 (Macuch 1993, pp, 125, 130 and 128, 131 respectively). The expression *nišān* is presumably from **nišāna-* (< Ir. **hHai* 'to chain, bind'; Avestan *ni-* + √*hi* 'to chain, bind' + *-na-*; Cheung 2007, p. 135), see Macuch 1993, p. 134 with further references, and the description of this oath.

204 MHD 13.2–3 (Macuch 1993, pp. 125, 130).

205 MHD 14.2–4 (Macuch 1993, pp. 128, 131).

206 MHD 13.9; 78.16 (Macuch 1993, pp. 127, 130f. and 518; 521 respectively).

207 MHD 13.6–13 (Macuch 1993, pp. 127, 130f.).

208 The conventional explanation of *sōgand xwārdan* 'to swear; take an oath' from an original 'to drink sulphur' (< Av. *saokəṇta-* 'sulphur'; Bartholomae 1904, col. 1550, from Ir. **¹sauč* 'to burn, emit flames', Av. √*saoc* 'to burn', Cheung 2007, p. 338, and Ir **¹hu̯ar* 'to consume, eat', Cheung 2007, p. 147) has been disputed by Schwarz 1989, who argues that 'to swear an oath' is the original meaning of *sōgand xwārdan*, deriving it from **sau̯kanta-* 'declaration > oath' from the root Ir. **²sauč* 'to call' (Cheung 2007, p. 240) and the verb Ir. **²hu̯ar* 'to swear' (Cheung 2007, p. 149). See the perceptive discussion in Goldman 2015, pp. 66–69.

nēst 'I have no knowledge of it') and suggests taking an oath to confirm that he and the other heirs 'have no knowledge of the matter' (*az ēn čīš āgāhīh nēst*). But according to the answer to this *Pursišn*, the defendant cannot just swear that he and his co-heirs are ignorant of the existence of a debt, but is obliged to explicitly confirm under oath that his parents did not take a loan from the plaintiff (*ēn abām az tō mērag nē stad* '[they] did not take this debt from you, O man!') and that there is no payment obligation (*ēn abām ō tō tōxtan nē abāyēd* 'there is no obligation to pay this debt to you').[209] The second passage of the Law-book referring to this type of oath implies that a litigant could engage an 'intercessor' (*ǰādag-gōw*) to take this oath (and also the type of oath under 4).[210]

4. The *war ī pad nāmag-passāz* 'transcript-preparation oath'. This oath is mentioned together with the preceding 'sulphurous water oath' in a context suggesting that the main claimant in a lawsuit could engage an intercessor (*ǰādag-gōw*) for taking both of these oaths in his (or her) place. There are no further clues as to the *raison d'être* of this oath, apart from its designation, suggesting that it had something to do with confirming a *nāmag*, in civil procedure, possibly the *saxwan-nāmag*, the 'transcript' or 'protocol of statements', taken down in the initial session of a trial, or the *yazišn-nāmag*, the transcript of oath-taking, or the *pursišn-nāmag* 'transcript of interrogation' in a criminal case. We have already mentioned above that court transcripts in the civil cases of the Tabarestān documents are simply called *nāmag*, albeit written as a heterogram ⟨GTk⟩.[211]

We can cautiously conclude from these—admittedly sparse—entries that a distinction was made between three statements, for which a specific type of oath/ordeal could be administered:

- the confirmation of a claim as true (*ēdōnīh* 'thusness');
- the repudiation of a claim as false (*nē ēdōnīh* 'not-thusness'; *nē tō xwēš* 'it is not your own');
- the denial of having any knowledge of the veracity or falsity of a claim (*nē dānom* 'I do not know'; *nē dānist* 'having no knowledge [of the matter]'; *kū-š man āgāhīh nēst* 'I have no knowledge of it').

These statements correspond to the types of oath listed above in the following manner:

209 For the whole text of RivAF 66 see Appendix IX, pp. 696–697.
210 MHD 78.16 (Macuch 1993, pp. 518, 521).
211 See above p. 537. These four are by no means the only attested forms of the oath/ordeal, but the only ones referred to in the Law-book. According to the *Denkard* (DkD 497.14; DkM 644.16) thirty-three different forms were known (possibly a symbolic number), ten of which have been identified and discussed extensively by Goldman 2015, pp. 50–86; see also overview p. 75.

Table 60. Types of oath

Types of oath	Statements of the litigants or witnesses	Definition
war ī dēnīg; dēnīg war 'religious oath'	*ēdōnīh* 'It (is) so' (lit. 'thusness' = veracity)	confirmation of a claim (or allegation)
	nē ēdōnīh 'It (is) not so' (lit. 'not-thusness' = falsity)	repudiation of a claim (or allegation)
war ī pāy-nišān 'oath of binding the feet'	*nē dānom* 'I do not know'	denial of knowing whether a claim (or allegation) is true or false
	nē tō xwēš 'It is not your own'	repudiation of a claim to ownership
war ī pad sōgand 'sulphurous water oath'	*nē dānist* (= *nē dānom* 'I do not know') *kū-š man āgāhīh nēst* 'I have no knowledge of it'	denial of knowing whether a claim (or allegation) is true or false
	ēn abām az tō … nē stad … ēn abām ō tō tōxtan nē abāyēd 'This debt has not been taken from you … there is no obligation to pay this debt to you'	repudiation of a claim

A remarkable passage of the late RivAF, *Pursišn* 74, refers in a very long (and in parts enigmatic) text to the oath of sulphur (*war ī sōgand*) in the context of an ordeal (*passāxt*).[212] This text is particularly interesting, as it transmits three Avestan phrases to be spoken during the ceremony in the original together with their Pahlavi translations and gives exact directions as to which of the persons involved in legal proceedings should utter these statements under oath in the presence of the deity Rašn. According to the elucidations in the text, these Avestan passages or their Pahlavi equivalents were to be spoken by the following persons in the context of a *war ī sōgand*:

1. The statement of the defendant (*pad pasēmālīh*): (Av.) 'Thus is this (judicial) case' (*⁺iϑa asti auuaṯ arəϑəm*); (MP) 'Thus (is) this (judicial) case' (*ēdōn ēn dādestān*).
2. The statement of a witness (*pad gugāyīh*): (Av.) 'Or thus is my knowledge thereof' (*⁺iϑa vā mē ⁺aŋ́he asti ⁺vaēδīm*); (MP) 'Or thus is my knowledge thereof' (*ayāb ēdōn man pad ān ast āgāhīh*).
3. The statement of a litigant (*hamēmāl*): (Av.) 'Or I know not thereof' (*nōiṯ vā ⁺aŋ́he ⁺vaēδa*); (MP) 'Or that is not in my knowledge' (*ayāb nē man ān pad āgāhīh ast*), corresponding to 'I do not know' (*nē dānom*).[213]

212 For the whole text of the relevant part of this *Pursišn* see Appendix IX, pp. 697–698.

These three oaths to be taken by a defendant (*pasēmāl*), a witness (*gugāy*) or a litigant (*hamēmāl*) correspond exactly with those transmitted in the sources mentioned above. The same phrases spoken in the sacred Avestan language might have given the whole procedure more 'weight' and conveyed additional significance to the ceremony of oath taking with or without the additional proof of the ordeal.

Table 61. Statements under oath

Persons involved in legal proceedings	Statements under oath	
	Avestan	Middle Persian
Defendant (*pasēmāl*)	*⁺iϑa asti auuaṯ arəϑəm* 'Thus is this (judicial) case'	*ēdōn ēn dādestān* 'Thus (is) this (judicial) case'
Witness (*gugāy*)	*⁺iϑa vā mē ⁺aŋ́he asti ⁺vaēδīm* 'Or: thus is my knowledge thereof'	*ayāb ēdōn man pad ān ast āgāhīh* 'Or: thus is my knowledge thereof'
Litigant (*hamēmāl*)	*nōiṯ vā ⁺aŋ́he ⁺vaēδa* 'Or: I know not thereof'	*ayāb nē man ān pad āgāhīh ast* 'Or: that is not in my knowledge' *nē dānom* 'I do not know'

Defendants, who repudiate a claim or allegation (*nagīrāy hēnd*), were obliged to take the oath 'for certainty' (*pad tāšt war warzišn*); their refusal to do so was considered as an obstruction of justice (*azišmānd*).[214] An oath was also required if a litigant revised his statement (*waštagīh*) in court; a defendant who first declared with regard to a liability: '(the debt) has been paid' (*wizārd*), then alters his statement to '(the debt) has been cancelled for me' (*pad man be hišt*), is required to confirm both statements in the 'place of swearing' to attain 'reliability' (*pad xwārestān … ēwarīh xwāst*).[215] Is there a difference between administering an oath 'for certainty' (*pat tāšt*) and requiring it (*xwāst*) for 'reliability, binding force' (*ēwarīh*)? A distinction is not conveyed, but the notion of attaining a 'reliable', that is, legally 'binding' (*ēwar*) verdict, by means of the oath, is inherent in the latter term (see below section 3.1.6). No oath was administered to those who admitted the correctness of a claim or allegation or whose truthfulness was beyond doubt, according to the *Dēnkard* (DkD 536.10; DkM 707.15): *abar xwastūgān war nē būdan ēdōn-iz abar husrawagān*

213 On the Avestan passages see Klingenschmitt 1971, pp. 127–129, and Appendix IX, pp. 698–699; the phrases in the original without emendments read: (1) *iδa asti auuaṯ arəϑəm*; (2) *iδa vā mē aŋhən asti vaiδīm* (3) *nōiṯ vā ā̊ŋhe vaiδa*.

214 MHD 13.13–15 (Macuch 1993, pp. 128, 131). On *pad tāšt* 'for certainty'; *tāštīg* 'certain, sure' see Bailey 1933–1935b, pp. 280–281; MacKenzie 1971, p. 82.

215 MHD 8.15–16 (Macuch 1993, pp. 102, 105). On *waštagīh* see below pp. 561–562.

'On not administering an oath on those who admit/confess, neither on those with a good reputation'.

Table 62. Overview: terminology relating to the oath/ordeal

Types of oaths	
war ī dēnīg; dēnīg war	religious oath
war ī pad nāmag-passāz	transcript-preparation oath
war ī pad sōgand	sulphurous water oath
war ī pāy-nišān	oath of binding the feet
Venue of the oath/ordeal	
passāxt gāh	place of the ordeal
war gāh	place of the oath/ordeal
xwārestān	place of swearing
Protocols	
uzdād-nāmag	protocol/transcript of arrangement (of the ordeal) (?)
yazišn-nāmag	protocol/transcript of recitation
Procedure	
hannāmān ī war padiš warzīd ēstēd	limbs/members (of the body) on which the oath has been taken
nagīrāy hēnd	'they repudiate (the claim)'
nērang ī pahrēz	incantations of protection
pad tāšt war warzidan	to take an oath 'for certainty'
pad war... wehdādestāntar	(he/she is) better (suited) for (taking) the oath for the 'extension of justice'
pad xwārestān ... ēwarīh xwāstan	to request 'reliability' in the 'place of swearing'
war passāxt	test of the ordeal
war passāxtan	to prepare/implement an ordeal; to test by ordeal
war rāyēnīdan	to take an oath
war-sālār	supervisor of the oath/ordeal
war sāxtan	to prepare/implement an ordeal; to test by ordeal
war warzīdan	to take an oath
xwastūg	(person who) admits/confesses
yazišn	recitation (during the ordeal)

3.1.5 Offences against the judiciary and obstruction of justice

Hindering the work of the judiciary and obstructing justice (*contumacia*) were offences punished by the court either by an interlocutory judgment or conviction of the offender depending on the frequency of their occurrence and the type of obstruction. Two expressions are transmitted in the Law-book for two major kinds of obstruction, differentiated in the Sasanian law of procedure as (1) *waštagīh*, lit. 'twisting, turning, revising, modifying, distorting' or, more precisely, *waštag saxwanīh*[216] 'revision, distortion of statement', and (2) *azišmānd*,[217] the technical term for offences showing 'contempt of court' or causing generally 'obstruction of justice', which comprise various violations of procedural law committed by the litigants in the course of a trial.

The terms *waštagīh* and *waštag saxwanīh* denote obstructions of legal proceedings caused by a litigant who revises or distorts a statement he has made in court, turning it into an assertion with a different informative value. The term, however, does not apply to all alterations of an initial statement. If the change is helpful to the court and the litigant revises an obviously false statement into a trustworthy one, this is not assessed as a punishable offence, as we are informed in a very general passage of the Law-book: a litigant, who alters his (originally false or faulty) statement to a 'reliable' one (*ō ēwarīh wardēd*), is not to be convicted (*ēraxt*) for committing 'revision/distortion of statement' (*waštag saxwanīh*), but he is to be convicted, if the statement is not changed to a 'reliable' one (*nē ō ēwarīh wardēd*). The issue is, however, disputed, as the jurist Ādurohrmazd contends that even in the latter case not every revision of statement would necessarily lead to conviction.[218] The reason for this objection is not elaborated in this passage, but another longer one suggests that the precise informative value of a statement played a decisive role in assessing *waštagīh*. If a litigant modified parts of his statement *without* explicitly refuting the claim of his opponent or laying claim to the object of dispute, these changes did *not* lead to conviction. As this illuminative sentence explains, a litigant in a dispute over a proprietary right could as a rule be convicted for changing (*wardēnīdan*) three issues in his statement: (1) the timespan (*hangām*) in which he had possession of the property in question; (2) the name and identity of his 'legal predecessor' (*dastwar*); (3) the category of ownership (*čē ēwēnag xwēšīh*) to which the

216 From the Ir. root *u̯art 'to turn' (Cheung 2007, p. 423); Av. √varət 'to turn' (Kellens 1995, p. 51); NP *gaštan*.

217 The term is usually employed in the technical sense of *contumacia*, a literal translation of the compound as 'hindrance, default, failure' would hence be misleading (< *az* + *iš* + *mānd* 'that which is defect, left behind', from *māndan*, *mān-* 'to remain, stay, wait, dwell, leave behind', from Ir. *(d)mān 'to remain, dwell'; Cheung 2007, pp. 73–75; Av. √²*man* Bartholomae 1904, col. 1124; Kellens 1995, p. 42). Pagliaro 1949 has a wrong interpretation and translation of the word as *interdictum*. On this term see also Perikhanian 1974 and Shaki 1977.

218 MHD 9.1–3 (Macuch 1993, pp. 102, 105); compare MHD 102. 11–12 (*ibid.*, pp. 616, 624).

property belongs. But none of these alterations were assessed by the court as *waštag saxwanīh*, if the litigant did *not* explicitly declare that he had a title to the property in question with the words: 'I possess it by that entitlement' (*pad ān dastwarīh dāram*).[219] That is, the revision of a statement (even regarding important details such as the timespan, the legal predecessor or the type of ownership) did not lead to conviction (*nē ēraxt*), as long as the defendant did not clearly and expressly assert his legal right (*dastwarīh*) to the matter in dispute.

Other significant details in assessing *waštagīh* were the timing of the revision and the reaction of the opponent: a defendant, who alters (*waštag bawēd*) his initial statement *before* the plaintiff seals (and hereby confirms) the transcript of the lawsuit (*saxwan-nāmag*), can no longer be convicted for the offence of 'revision/distortion of statement', if the plaintiff has not queried the error beforehand (*pad ahōg čīš nē nimāyēd*).[220] The Law-book also transmits two interesting examples for offences of *waštag saxwanīh* that are assessed as obstructions of the judiciary and lead to conviction of the accused. In one case the plaintiff accuses the defendant that he has committed adultery with his, the plaintiff's, wife, to which the defendant answers: 'I did not have sexual intercourse with your wife' (*kū-m zan ī tō nē gād*), but later modifies his statement to: 'I had sexual intercourse, but I did not have it during the time she was married to you' (*kū-m gād bē-m nē andar zanīh ī tō gād*). Unfortunately neither the background of this lawsuit relating to a sexual tort, nor the reasoning behind this decision are elucidated, but it seems likely that the court assessed this modification of the original statement as a ruse of the defendant to avoid compensating the plaintiff for the offence of adultery, hence as an offence of *waštagīh*. The same can be surmised for the second example in a lawsuit involving physical injury (*zaxm*), the implications of which we have already discussed in Chapter V: the accused first states: 'I have not struck you' (*kū-m nē zad hē*) and later says: 'I have struck (you) in a state of unconsciousness' (*kū-m andar a-bōyīh-ē zad*). The revised statement, pleading 'unconsciousness' or lack of conscious intent (*a-bōyīh*), is obviously regarded by the court as a pretext of the accused to avoid or diminish the penalty for assault and the amount of compensation for the victim and is hence assessed by the court—as the inclusion of this case in the chapter on *waštagīh* implies—as a 'revision/distortion of statement' leading to the conviction of the offender.[221]

The term *azišmānd* seems to have been originally a general designation for various offences causing some kind of 'hindrance' or 'obstruction', *e.g.* of ownership or possession, such as promising to transfer a specific object to a certain recipient, but then giving it to someone else.[222] In the context of legal procedure it

219 MHD 9.14–10.7 (Macuch 1993, pp. 103f., 106f.).
220 MHD 9.6–8 (Macuch 1993, pp. 103, 106).
221 MHD 10.9–11 (Macuch 1993, pp. 104, 107). See discussion of this passage Chapter V, p. 415.
222 As in MHDA 9.3–5 (Macuch 1981, pp. 30, 122).

took on the specific meaning of *contumacia*, obstruction of justice or contempt of court, and is used in most attestations to denote different forms of disobedience to court orders and other offences of the litigants or their legal representatives (*ǰādag-gōw*) during the course of a trial. The following obstructions are mentioned in connection with this technical term in the Law-book:

- not following summons to court, *i. e.* failing to obey an official order to appear in court at a specified time and place;[223]
- interfering with the process of administering justice (*e. g.* impeding the opponent in his right to hold a specific property until judgement is passed by utilizing it, attempting to seize it, actually seizing it or in some other manner);[224]
- refusal of a party to take an oath;[225]
- withholding crucial evidence (*e. g.* not naming a significant witness who might testify in favour of the opponent);[226]
- deviating statements of two intercessors (*ǰādag-gōw*) with a joint (*āgenēn*) mandate of the same party.[227]

Not all of these *azišmānd* offences are described in detail, but we are fairly well informed on the legal consequences of an obstruction of justice in the context of lawsuits over a proprietary right. The Law-book mentions various procedures depending on which party has committed the offence (the plaintiff or the defendant), whether the dispute regards the right to ownership (*xwēšīh*) or possession (*dārišn*) of a specific property and whether the object of dispute is an inanimate 'thing' or an animate being (woman, slave, animal). These cases will have to be discussed separately.

In a lawsuit over possession (*dārišn*) the plaintiff complains with regard to his opponent: 'I possess it (= the object of dispute) in ownership and the defendant impedes me in my (right of) possession' (*man xwēš dāram u-m pasēmāl az dārišn wizāyēd*). The formulation of the complaint implies that the complainant is taking possessive action with regard to a thing that he owns (any physical object can be meant, also a piece of land, a house etc.), but which is being held by the defendant in pledge, leasehold, rent, etc., or has been seized by him unlawfully. By not returning the property the defendant impedes the plaintiff's alleged right to possession. If this conduct is assessed as an obstruction of justice (*azišmānd bawed*), judgement is immediately passed determining the plaintiff's right of possession (*dārišn*) and the trial comes to an end (*sar bawēd*).[228]

223 MHD 15.3–7; 73.10–12; 73.13–74.1 (Macuch 1993, pp. 139, 142; 490f., 492f. respectively).
224 MHD 10.12–11.7 (Macuch 1993, pp. 115, 118f.); MHDA 30.12–16 (Macuch 1981, pp. 55, 209).
225 MHD 13.13–15 (Macuch 1993, pp. 128, 131).
226 MHDA 31.15–32.2 (Macuch 1981, pp. 57, 210).
227 MHD 75.10–12 (Macuch 1993, pp. 501, 504). On the legal implications of the term *agenēn* see pp. 538–539 above on the *ǰādag-gōw* and Chapter IV, pp. 246–250.
228 MHD 10.12–14 (Macuch 1993, pp. 115, 118).

The consequences of an obstruction of justice are different in a lawsuit over ownership (*xwēšīh*). The complaint of the plaintiff can be brought forward in two variants:

1. 'I possess it (= the object of dispute) in ownership and the defendant impedes me therein' (*man xwēš dāram u-m pasēmāl az-iš wizāyēd*); or, with a more precise wording:
2. 'I possess it (= the object of dispute) in ownership and the defendant impedes me in my ownership of it' (*man xwēš dāram u-m pasēmāl az pad xwēšīh dāštan wizāyēd*).

The issue is far more complex than in the former case of possessive action, since the plaintiff asserts a claim to ownership, which is not recognized by the defendant or actively contested by him (*e.g.* by utilizing this property, seizing it from the plaintiff, not returning it, etc.). The court is therefore required to determine the far more difficult question of ownership. In this context an obstruction of justice does not lead immediately to loss of the lawsuit, but is dealt with by interlocutory judgements: the first obstruction (*ēk azišmānd*) is admonished by the court with the words: 'Until the trial comes to an end do not impede (the right of the plaintiff to ownership)' (*tā dādestān sar bawēd mā wizāy*); for the second obstruction (*azišmānd ī dudīgar*) the defendant is obliged to deposit a pledge equivalent in value to the object of dispute (*graw hāwand-ē be abespārišn*); the third (*sidīgar*) obstruction leads to the defendant's conviction (*ēraxt*). It seems, however, that there was no standardized procedure in dealing with *azišmānd* offences in ownership lawsuits, as three further variants are mentioned:

1. According to a lost 'Book of Judgements' (*Dādestān nāmag*) the court should admonish the offender (with the words quoted above) for the first two obstructions, convict him for the third one and consign the right of ownership to the plaintiff.
2. The jurist Zurwāndād opines that the defendant should only deposit a pledge (*graw*) equivalent in value to the object of dispute for the third obstruction (but not necessarily lose the lawsuit, as we may add).
3. If it is not the defendant, but the plaintiff, who commits an obstruction, judgement is to be passed that he should deposit a pledge equivalent in value to the object of dispute for each of the first two *azišmānd* offences. He loses the suit on the third obstruction and the property (*xwāstag*) is to be consigned to the defendant (*ō pasēmāl abespārišn*).[229]

To sum up, the descriptions agree—with the possible exception of the second variant—that a litigant, who commits an *azišmānd* on three occasions (*sē jār*) in a civil trial on ownership, loses the lawsuit.

229 MHD 10.14–11.7 (Macuch 1993, pp. 115, 118f.; read ⟨stygl⟩ *sidīgar* instead of (erroneously) ⟨dtygr⟩ in the transliteration of MHD 11.1,4,5; *ibid.*, p. 115).

A modified procedure is alluded to in the context of lawsuits conducted against a party accused of having committed robbery (that is, stealing openly) or of an act deemed as equivalent to robbery.[230] In one concrete case the plaintiff sues a man (= the defendant) with the words: 'Three men have robbed it (= the object of dispute); I am litigating against one of the men' (*mard 3 be appurd mard-ē hamēmāl hom*). If the defendant causes an obstruction of justice (*az pasēmāl azišmānd bawēd*), he is obliged to deposit a wager (*srāy*) and a fine (*tāwān*) of 12 (drachms) as pledge (*graw*) for each of the first two offences; the third obstruction leads to his conviction. The plaintiff is also entitled to demand 12 drachms from each of the other two accused men. If all three men are in court (*pad dādestān hēnd*), they are required to pay a sum corresponding to their share (*pad bahrag*) and the property is consigned to the plaintiff.[231] Another noteworthy case shows that the term *appar* 'robber; robbery' was not always employed with its literal meaning in jurisdiction, but far more often in a figurative sense, as we have already seen in previous chapters. In contrast to the first case described above, the plaintiff does not explicitly accuse his opponent of 'robbery', but only asserts that the defendant is holding a specific property without being entitled to it (*a-bādixšāyīhā tō dārē* 'You hold it without authorization'). The case is treated as equivalent to robbery (*appar*) with similar consequences: for each of the first two obstructions of justice the defendant has to deposit a wager (*srāy*) and an equivalent pledge (*graw*). He is convicted on the third offence and the property is consigned to the ownership of the plaintiff.

Slaves and women could be objects of a lawsuit with specific consequences for the litigant who obstructs justice. In one case the intention of the plaintiff in taking legal action is made clear, when he addresses the object of dispute, a slave, directly with the words: 'You are my slave and you have to carry out the work of my slave' (*man anšahrīg hē u-t anšahrīgīh ī man kunišn*). If the defendant commits an obstruction of justice in this context, the court is to pass judgement that the slave should 'carry out the work of the plaintiff until the trial comes to an end' (*tā dādestān sar bawēd kār ī pēšēmāl kunēd*). The same judgement is passed with regard to the woman: 'until it (= the trial) comes to an end she should act as his (= the plaintiff's) own wife' (*tā sar bawēd zanīh ōwōn čiyōn zan ī xwēš … ē kunēd*).[232] The jurist Mardag has far more precise regulations for both instances. In a lawsuit regarding a slave the first obstruction should be punished by ordering the offender to transfer the amount (*andčand*) necessary for taking legal action (*dādestān nīyūšīdan rāy*) from the daily earnings (*rūzkār*) of the slave to his legal opponent.

230 On the difference between robbery (*apparīh*) and theft (*duzīh*) and the extensive figurative use of these terms in a legal context see pp. 313–314.

231 MHD 11.8–13 (Macuch 1993, pp. 116, 119); insert ⟨grwb'⟩ *graw* (MHD 11.9 after the number 12), erroneously left out in the transliteration on p. 116. On *sray* 'wager' see Perikhanian 1974; on the similarity of this procedure to the Roman *provocatio sacramento* see Macuch 1993, pp. 124–125 (n. 4).

232 MHD 11.16–12.4 (Macuch 1993, pp. 116, 119).

For the second obstruction the offender should—if he is solvent (*ādānīh*)—deposit a pledge (*graw*) equivalent to the worth of the slave or 500 drachms if the slave's worth is not known. With the third obstruction the trial is brought to a close. In a lawsuit regarding a woman Mardag has the following remarkable instructions: as punishment for the first obstruction the court is to prescribe that the woman 'act as the wife' of the harmed party, but 'without intercourse' (*zanīh ī ǰud az gād kunēd*); for the second obstruction the offender should deposit a pledge (*graw*) worth 500 drachms; the trials ends with the third obstruction.[233]

The jurist Mardag does not state exactly, what the final verdict might be, when a woman is the object of a lawsuit. In the described cases (with one possible exception) ownership of the disputed property, including a slave, was as a rule transferred from the litigant charged with three obstructions of justice to his legal opponent, but it seems to have been far more difficult to consign a woman to a man on the same grounds. Another passage addresses this problem: the plaintiff complains: 'This woman is my wife; you hold her without authorization' (*en zan man zan tō a-bādixšāyīhā dārē*). In the course of the trial his opponent, the defendant, commits three obstructions of justice, but—in contrast to the disputes on ownership discussed above—the woman is *not* to be conveyed to the plaintiff (*zan be nē abespārišn*). The reason given for this decision is noteworthy: '(the right to) possession (is) certain and ownership of the substance (is) uncertain' (*dārišn ēwar ud bun-xwēšīh warōmand*).[234] This is a truly remarkable sentence in three respects. First, as a general statement it refers to the immense difficulty of defining 'ownership of the substance' (or 'basic ownership', *bun xwēšīh*) in contrast to mere 'possession' (*dārišn*), due to the relativity of the concept of ownership in Sasanian law (as elucidated in Chapter III, 1.2). Second, it alludes to the concrete problem a law court is confronted with, when it is called to establish ownership in the face of missing or faulty evidence. Third, it draws a parallel between a proprietary right over a thing and over a woman/wife. This does not necessarily mean that the woman was regarded or treated as a 'thing' in legal practice. On the contrary, as we have seen, if the defendant commits three obstructions of justice, the court does not simply apply the rules of procedure by consigning the woman to his opponent, but respects the existing status quo, leaving the woman with the man, who holds her (given the intricacies of matrimony, especially the existence of time-limited marriages, it is rather likely that disputes over women occurred from time to time in the absence of a valid legal marriage contract). The further procedure is not elucidated in this passage, but other cases suggest that the testimony of the woman would have been taken into consideration by the court before passing a final verdict (see the interesting lawsuit discussed in section 3.1.4.2 above).[235]

233 MHD 12.4–9 (Macuch 1993, pp. 116, 120).
234 MHD 12.13–15 (Macuch 1993, pp. 117, 120).
235 MHD 32.4–10 (Macuch 1993, pp. 223, 227); Chapter VI, p. 547; see also Chapter IV, pp. 299–301.

The Law-book transmits a long enumerated list of twenty-two offences in contempt of court in another fragmentary chapter, which might be a conglomeration of offences of the *waštagīh* and *azišmānd* types. Although these two technical terms are not attested here, they were possibly used in the missing part at the beginning of the chapter.[236] Transgressions that could be committed by the plaintiff or defendant are listed in the following sequence:

1. failing to state in a lawsuit which kind of property is under dispute (*ka xwāstag dādestān nē gōwēd kū čē*);
2. not identifying oneself (*ka nē [gōwēd] kū kē*);
3. lying (*ka drō gōwēd*);
4. making confused ('mixed') statements (*ka pad gumēzag gumēzag gōwēd*);
5. making a statement without witnesses (*ka a-gugāy gōwēd*);
6. assigning possession of a thing/property to someone who does not hold it (*ka dārišn ī xwāstag ān gōwēd ī nē dārēd*);
7. not assigning ownership of a thing/property to the one who is the owner (*ka xwēšīh ī xwāstag nē ān gōwēd ī ast*);
8. making a statement in secret (*ka saxwan nihānīg gōwēd*);
9. making a statement without a 'legal predecessor/*auctor*' (*ka a-dastwar gōwēd*);
10. making a statement first with certainty, then expressing doubt, then abandoning (the case) and departing before the trial has come to an end (*ka saxwan nazdist pad ēwarīh ud pas pad gumānīgīh gōwēd ast nē sar ud hilēd ud be šawēd*);
11. declaring: 'I think of it thus' (*ka gōwēd kū-m ēdōn mēnēd*);
12. declaring: 'It seems to me thus' (*ka gōwēd kū-m ēdōn sahēd*);
13. making a statement first with certainty (*par ēwarīh*) and then expressing doubt (*pad gumānīgīh*) (repetition of the first part of number 10);
14. not making a statement before the (other) litigants (*ka ne pēš ī hamēmālān gōwēd*);
15. becoming speechless in the middle of a statement, when catching sight of the opponent (*ka andar mayān ī saxwan ka hamēmāl wēnēd a-saxwan bawēd*);
16. not declaring: 'The judge is capable of passing just judgement' (*ka nē edōn gōwēd kū dādwar pad rāstīh wizīr tuwān kardan*);
17. when the witness is a liar (*ka gugāy drōzan*);
18. when the litigant (witness) does not appear at the specified venue on the arranged date (*ka nē gyāg kū zamān kunēd nē āyēd*);
19. when the witness the litigant has named does not come initially or does not come at all (*ka gugāy ī gōwed fradōm ayāb bowandag nē āyēd*);
20. when the litigant (witness) is not present at the specified 'place and time' with respect to which he has declared 'I will be present' (*ka pad gyag gāh ī kū gōwēd kū ēstēm nē ēstēd*);
21. when the litigant (witness) does not remain properly at the 'time and place', where he is obliged to be present (*ka pad gāh gyāg kū ēstēd abāyēd nē xub ēstēd*);

236 MHD 91.1–15 (Macuch 1993, pp. 579f., 584f.).

22. when the litigant does not deliver the 'thing and property' which is the object of a contract and the matter of dispute intact to the judges (*ka xwāstag ud xīr kē paymān ud pahikār abar drust ō pēš ī dādwarān nē āwarēd*).

Table 63. Overview: offences against the judiciary

<table>
<tr><th colspan="3">Distortion/revisal of statement</th></tr>
<tr><td colspan="2">ō ēwarīh wardēd;
nē ō ēwarīh wardēd</td><td>'he alters his (false or faulty) statement to a reliable one';
'he does not alter his statement to a reliable one'</td></tr>
<tr><td colspan="2">pad gumēzag gumēzag guftan</td><td>to make confused ('mixed') statements</td></tr>
<tr><td colspan="2">saxwan nihānīg guftan</td><td>to make a statement in secret</td></tr>
<tr><td colspan="2">saxwan pad ēwarīh guftan</td><td>to make a statement with certainty</td></tr>
<tr><td colspan="2">saxwan pad gumānīgīh guftan</td><td>to make a doubtful statement</td></tr>
<tr><td colspan="2">wardēnīdan</td><td>to twist, turn, revise, modify, change, distort</td></tr>
<tr><td colspan="2">waštagīh; waštag saxwanīh</td><td>twisting, turning, distorting; revision/distortion of statement</td></tr>
<tr><th colspan="3">Obstruction of justice</th></tr>
<tr><td colspan="2">a-bādixšāyīhā dāštan</td><td>to hold (something) without authorization</td></tr>
<tr><td colspan="2">a-dastwar guftan</td><td>to make a statement (in court) without (bringing) one's 'legal predecessor' (auctor)</td></tr>
<tr><td colspan="2">a-gugāy guftan</td><td>to make a statement (in court) without (bringing) a witness</td></tr>
<tr><td colspan="2">azišmānd</td><td>hindrance/obstruction of justice; contempt of court; contumacia</td></tr>
<tr><td colspan="2">azišmānd bawēd</td><td>an obstruction occurs/is committed</td></tr>
<tr><td colspan="2">az dārišn wizāyīdan</td><td>to impede (a person's right to) possession</td></tr>
<tr><td colspan="2">az pad xwēšīh dāštan wizāyīdan</td><td>to impede (a person's right to) ownership</td></tr>
<tr><td colspan="2">az pasēmāl azišmānd bawēd</td><td>the defendant causes an obstruction of justice</td></tr>
<tr><th colspan="3">Interlocutory judgements</th></tr>
<tr><td>1st offence</td><td>tā dādestān sar bawēd mā wizāy</td><td>'Until the lawsuit comes to an end do not impede (the opponent)'</td></tr>
<tr><td>2nd offence</td><td>graw hāwand-ē be abespārišn</td><td>'An equivalent pledge is to be consigned'</td></tr>
<tr><td>3rd offence</td><td>ēraxt</td><td>'He/she is convicted' (= loss of the lawsuit)</td></tr>
</table>

These offences obviously consist of various obstructions of justice, contempt of court and other acts and statements impeding legal proceedings. Obstructions of the *azišmānd* type were punished by an interlocutory judgement (admonishment of the offender; deposit of a pledge or wager or a specific amount of money). The litigant, who committed three *azišmānd* offences, lost as a rule the lawsuit, but exceptions were possible (*e. g.* in a dispute over a woman).

3.1.6 The verdict

The sources suggest that the presiding official, usually a judge, was actively involved in all phases of the trial. Sasanian proceedings were based on an 'inquisitorial' system of adjudication, in which the judge questions the parties and witnesses directly, views and develops the evidence and finally returns a verdict.[237] Before reaching a final decision, the judge could make use of specific devices to expand the legal options at his disposal by calling on the litigants' sense of justice. Two technical terms are used in this context: *passand* (lit. 'pleasure, liking') or 'leniency (in justice)', designating a procedure by which *less* is done than required by the 'letter of the law' in order to achieve justice. A judge could, for instance, compel a litigant to renounce a specific legal right, *e. g.* the immediate repayment of a debt with interest, in order to comply with the financial possibilities of his opponent, who did not have the resources to pay back both debt and interest.[238] The opposite principle is denoted by the terms *wehdādestānīh* and *mehdādestānīh* (lit. 'good/greater justice, law; good/greater decision, judgement') or 'extension of justice', a procedure by which *more* is done than required by law. A litigant (*hamēmāl*) could, for example, be counselled to give his opponent a higher compensation for an offence than the minimum amount prescribed by law.[239]

Both interlocutory judgements regarding obstructions of justice (*azišmānd*) and the final verdict (*dādestān*; *wizīr*) were given in the morning (*andar frayar*); the judge was urged to reach his final judgement until mid-day (*tā nēm-rōz*).[240] The dispersed data we have brought together in the preceding chapters suggest that ideally the judge was obliged to take the specific circumstances of a case into account before

237 On the inquisitorial system in contrast to the adversarial or accusatorial system see above pp. 501–502.

238 On these terms see Chapters I, pp. 71–72, and VII, pp. 610–611; also Macuch 2019a and 2017b, pp. 367–369.

239 This exactly—albeit with a religious connotation—is meant by PRDd 18g2: *ud paydāg bawēd kū wināh ī hamēmālān ka-š hamēmāl hušnud ā-š wizārd bawēd paydāg kū +yazdān iz mehdādestānīh ōh nigerēnd.* 'And it is revealed that (in the case of) an offence of opponents (*wināh ī hamēmālān*) if the opponent (is) contented, then he has been paid (a compensation). It (is) revealed that the gods will also take an "extension of justice" (*mehdādestānīh*) into consideration.' That is, acting on the principle of *mehdādestānīh*, in this case giving a larger compensation to one's opponent than legally required, is a gesture that will be likewise seen (and rewarded accordingly) by the gods. Williams 1990 has a different translation (pt. I, p. 110f.; pt. II, p. 43).

240 See above pp. 537–538.

passing his sentence. In a private trial involving a delict or criminal act (physical injury, theft, robbery etc.) the judge evaluated both the mental element (*mens rea*), the intention (*menišn*) or will (*kām*), of the accused person to commit a specific offence, and the physical element (*actus reus*), the actual performance (*kunišn*) of the offence (including an omission, *i. e.* the failure to fulfil a duty). A distinction was made between offences (*wināh*) committed intentionally (*nigerišnīg*; *bōdōwaršt*; *bōdōzed*), those brought about by carelessness, negligence (*sūdagīhā*; *kādōzed*) and unintentional offences committed 'in an unconscious state' (*andar a-bōyīh*). We have good reason to assume that the intention of the offender was in some manner taken into consideration in the verdict and that an accidental or unintentional injury was assessed in a completely different manner than an intentional act (but unfortunately none of our sources transmits the exact wording of a final verdict).[241]

The attitude of a party could also be taken into account in a civil lawsuit, which did not involve physical injury or theft. A litigant could request the court to convict his opponent for having evil intent, for being 'ill-willed' (*wad-xwāh*), a term designating a person who seeks to deceive his fellow human beings (*drō-xwāhāg* 'desiring deceit'). The judge can condemn this party for the offence of being *wad-xwāh*, which also involves the two elements constituting a delict or crime: the offender is found guilty of having actually committed an offence (in this specific case of illegally appropriating property) and of having malicious intent (acting with an 'evil mind', *wad-axw*) with the intention of misleading his opponent and the court.[242]

A remarkable example, which we have already discussed above in the context of theft, demonstrates how the particular circumstances of a case were taken into consideration in the verdict: a woman who is the victim of an *adwadād* offence by her husband (by abandoning her or failing to maintain her with food) during the time of her menstruation, commits a theft in order to sustain herself. In this specific case not the woman, who has acted out of an emergency, is found guilty of theft, but the husband, who has failed to fulfil his obligations towards his wife as her legal guardian. He is held responsible for the offence and receives the penalty (*drōš*) for theft consisting of a fine and corporal punishment.[243]

Judgements regarding trivial matters (*čiš ī keh*) could be based on a different—possibly simplified, in any case divergent—procedure called *kardag* (legal 'practice'), which deviated from the formalities of due process required in legal 'doctrine/theory' (*čāštag*). These verdicts were, however, more or less temporary solutions, as they were not considered as final or 'reliable, binding' (*ēwar*) and could be revised if one of the parties required a 'reliable, binding' procedure (*pad ēwarīh*) based on canonical law (*čāštag*) either in the lawsuit at hand or in a court of appeal. The court was hence obliged to record the procedure on which the sentence of the judge was based with either of the corresponding formulae: (a) '(the

241 See Chapter V, pp. 412–413.
242 See Chapter V, p. 416.
243 See Chapter V, p. 446.

case) is put to *kardag* (procedure)' (*ō kardag kard ēstēd*) or, in the opposite case, (b) '(the case) is not put to *kardag* (procedure)' (*ō kardag nē kard ēstēd*) or '(the case) is withdrawn from *kardag* (procedure)' (*az kardag hišt ēstēd*). Another formula was used to note individual decisions of the court, which deviated from legal doctrine, even if a specific case was not necessarily assessed as 'trivial': '*kardag* (procedure) was applied' (*pad kardag mad* or *pad kardag mad ēstēd*). Generally, all decisions of the court, which did not comply with legal doctrine, were labelled *pad kardag* ('according to legal practice'; *via administrationis*) and distinguished from those based on canonical law, called *pad čāštag* ('according to legal doctrine'; *ex lege*).[244]

After hearing the judgement of the judge, both parties had the right to either declare their consent (*hunsandīh*) or dissent (*a-hunsandīh*) with the verdict and to appeal to the next instance in the sequence of judicial authorities. The appellate courts, however, did not overrule interlocutory rulings regarding *azišmānd* offences of the first instance. Transcripts, protocols and other records of the lawsuit were kept in an archive (*dīwān*).

Table 64. Overview: the verdict

Elements forming the verdict	
pad čāštag	according to legal doctrine; *ex lege*
pad kardag	according to legal practice; *via administrationis*
passand	leniency (in justice)
wehdādestānīh; *mehdādestānīh*	extension of justice
Intention and execution of an offence	
kām; *menišn*	intention (*mens rea*)
kunišn	execution (*actus reus*)
wināh ī nigerišnīg; *bōdōwaršt*	intentional offence
bōdōzed	intentional injury
(wināh ī) sūdagīhā; *kādōzed*	(offence by) carelessness; negligence
(wināh) andar a-bōyīh	unintentional, unconscious (offence)
wad-xwāh	ill-willed (person)
wad-axw	evil-minded (person)
kardag **procedure (in trivial cases: *čīš ī keh*)**	
ō kardag kard estēd	'(the case) is put to *kardag*'
ō kardag nē kard ēstēd	'(the case) is not put to *kardag*'
az kardag hišt ēstēd	'(the case) is withdrawn from *kardag*'
pad kardag mad (ēstēd)	'*kardag* (procedure) was applied'

244 On these legal formulae see the extensive discussion in Chapter I, pp. 66–71.

3.2. Criminal proceedings

We are not very well informed on criminal proceedings, despite the extensive Syriac material describing the prosecution of Christians who were charged with a capital crime in a Sasanian court. The Syriac acts of Christan martyrs have still not been examined adequately from the perspective of Sasanian law, but they seem to generally convey less concrete details on legal matters than would be necessary to reconstruct *in extenso* the diverse phases of a criminal trial.[245] An exception are the proceedings against the Catholicos Mār Abā, which will be used as a significant source of information, but one should keep in mind that they describe an exceptional case, the tribunal against a high dignitary, the spiritual leader of the Christians, who represented a large religious minority of the State in the 6th century and was, moreover, obviously protected by the king (possibly due to political and strategic reasons).

As we have already elucidated above, Sasanian law distinguished between criminal and civil proceedings, but not all individual offences involving assault, theft, robbery, physical injuries, and homicide were prosecuted by the State. We have good reason to assume that only those crimes endangering the religious and social order of Ērānšahr or the security of the king and his subjects were brought to trial by officials of the State, but the criteria by which these offences were assessed as crimes against the public order are not transmitted, although they could obviously also include individual cases of assault, theft, robbery, sorcery etc. and especially capital crimes (*margarzān*).[246] Three major *margarzān*-offences prosecuted by the State are distinguished in the Law-book as (1) *yazdān-dušmenīh* (lit. 'enmity towards the gods'; 'blasphemy, apostasy'), (2) *xwadāy-dušmenīh* (lit. 'enmity towards the sovereign'; 'rebellion, treason') and (3) *ahlomōyīh* ('heresy'), for which a specific transcript, the *pursišn-nāmag* or 'record/protocol of interrogation', has to be taken down.[247] To these the Letter of Tansar adds a fourth category regarding criminal acts of the *wināh ī hamēmālān* category, which encompass, as we have seen, all offences involving another person and his property. Most importantly, the terminology used in the context of civil and criminal proceedings points to differences in procedure: in a civil trial the 'transcript of statements' (*saxwan-nāmag*) renders mainly the statements of private litigants in a dispute between opponents, whereas the transcript of a criminal trial, the *pursišn-nāmag*, is a document containing a minute list of accusations brought forward against the offender in a *margarzān* case by

245 See Wiessner 1967 (particularly pp. 157–178) who has examined the legal content of two groups of Syriac sources describing the prosecution of Christian martyrs at the time of Šābuhr II (309–379 CE).

246 See above p. 489.

247 MHDA 34.9–10 (Macuch 1981, pp. 60, 217); English translation in fn. 4 above. On these criminal acts see above pp. 490–494.

official authorities. At its end the verdict and the punishment for the criminal act was noted.[248]

In the following we will attempt to sketch the procedure in a Sasanian criminal trial based on the fragmentary material at our disposal, using as an important source of reference the case against Mār Abā, the Catholicos of the Christian church of the East from 540 to 552, one of the remarkable personalities of the 6th century during the reign of King Husraw I (531–579), whose life and reforms are exceptionally well documented.[249] Mār Abā was originally a Zoroastrian, probably of noble descent, well educated in Mazdaism, who was promoted because of his brilliance to the position of *arzbed/harzbed* (*'rzbd*[250] in the Syriac text) 'chief of the royal eunuchs; Chief Eunuch'. He, moreover, worked in the high administration of the secretary of the *āmārgar/hamārgar* (*hmrgrd*[251] in the Syriac text), lit. 'Calculator, Accountant', the high treasurer or fiscal administrator of the region of Bēth Ārāmāye.[252] After his conversion to Christianity he gave up his position, gained fame in the Christian community and was elected Catholicos in 540 as the successor of Mār Simon. As the head of the church he is famous both for his propagation of Christianity as well as for being the first to establish Christian marriage rules, which were explicitly opposed to Mazdean custom and Sasanian law (hereby transmitting inadvertently important information on Zoroastrian marriage practices, as we have elucidated above).[253] He seems to have had the unfailing support of King Husraw despite his conversion, possibly provoking the jealousy of the Chief Mobed and the Zoroastrian clergy. Because of Mār Abā's strict handling of these issues, besides other matters, he was prosecuted by the Mazdean clergy with a series of serious charges, which allow insight into many details of Sasanian criminal procedure, although not every criminal case may have been conducted with the same precision and caution as the one against this influential high dignitary, who was shielded by the King.

3.2.1 The accusation

In the first stage of collecting material for the prosecution two technical terms are employed in the Law-book for documents, which are recorded *before* the *pursišn-nāmag* ('transcript of interrogation'; *accusatio scripta*) is written. The expression *nibištag*, lit. 'written record', is a technical term attested in the context of homicide for 'bill of indictment', a formal written document containing

248 MHDA 34.6–9 (Macuch 1981, pp. 60; 217).

249 I have discussed Mār Abā's Vita and the particulars of his trial extensively in Macuch 2014c.

250 Bedjan 1895, p. 210.

251 Bedjan 1895, p. 215.

252 On these titles see Macuch 2014c, pp. 47–49; on the *āmārgar* see pp. 512–514, above.

253 See Chapter II, pp. 155–157.

the charges of the prosecution against the perpetrator, assessed frequently—depending on the exact circumstances of the case—as a *margarzān* or capital crime. The *nibištag* was evidently taken down in a preliminary stage of the prosecution, before the beginning of the sessions in a law court. As we have seen above in the context of sins and offences, the evaluation of homicide as a capital crime in the 'bill of indictment' depended to some extent on the attitude of the accused person and the circumstances of his arrest: a person, who voluntarily confessed to having committed homicide could avoid an indictment on the basis of a *margarzān* if he had *not* been arrested by the *frēzwān* ('guard, policeman, inspector') and there were no witnesses to the crime. But the same criminal act was noted as a *margarzān* in the 'bill of indictment', if the perpetrator had been arrested by the *frēzwān*, despite the lack of witnesses and the unwillingness of the accused person to confess.[254]

The second term for a document taken down in a preliminary stage, before writing the *pursišn-nāmag* and preceding the first session of the trial, is *ayādgār* 'memorandum', a well-known word designating a large range of different types of written records (see Chapter IV, pp. 283–284). In the context of criminal law the Law-book informs us that, according to a statement of the Chief Mobed (*pad gōwišn ī mowbedān mowbed*), an *ayādgār* should be written in the case of a person accused of the capital crimes of *yazdān-dušmenīh* ('blasphemy, apostasy') and *xwadāy-dušmenīhā* ('rebellion, treason'), noting all the offences the perpetrator is charged with. These include: *mihrōdrujīhā* ('breaches of contract'); *ahlomōyīhā* ('heresies'); *drōzanīhā* ('lies') and *a-rāst-gōwišnīhā* ('false statements'). On the basis of this 'memorandum' the *pursišn-nāmag* is to be drawn up.[255] The significance of the 'memorandum' as a preliminary to the *pursišn-nāmag* is not elucidated, but we can infer that this document brought together various offences committed by the accused, possibly also noting witnesses and other kinds of evidence, which would support the charges of the prosecution and substantiate the drafting of a *pursišn-nāmag*. Other entries in this context seem to endorse this notion: one passage confirms that it is allowed to record transgressions that are not assessed as *margarzān* in order to depict the accused

254 See Chapter V, pp. 429–430; MHD 92.2–6 (Macuch 1993, pp. 580, 585 with a slightly different translation); for *nibištag* see also MHD 97.3–7 (Macuch 1993, pp. 581, 586), quoted and discussed above p. 432. On the *frēzwān* see Chapter VI, pp. 518–519.

255 MHDA 34.10–13: *abāg ān ī abar hampaččēn ham-mard rāy pad gōwišn ī mowbedān mowbed nibišt kū yazdān-dušmenīh ud xwadāy-dušmenīhā ud mihrōdrujīhā ud ahlomōyīhā ud drōzanīhā ud a-rāst-gōwišnīhā ayādgār kard u-š ōy wināh rāy pursišn-nāmag padiš kunišn* 'Together with (the sentence) that was written in the copy (of the transcript) with regard to the same man, according to the statement of the Chief Mobed: Enmity towards the gods (*yazdān-dušmenīh*) and (acts of) enmity towards the sovereign (*xwadāy-dušmenīhā*) and the breach of contracts (*mihrōdrujīhā*) and heresies (*ahlomōyīhā*) and lies and falsehoods are to be taken down in a memoir (*ayādgār*) and because of the offences (committed) by him a transcript of interrogation (*pursišn-nāmag*) is to be recorded' (Macuch 1981, pp. 60, 217).

in the *pursišn-nāmag* as a 'greater offender/sinner' (*wināhgārtar*).[256] Another passage confirms that the *ayādgār* contains a list not only of *margarzān* crimes, but also of other offences.[257]

Obviously a *pursišn-nāmag* was not only drafted on the basis of offences of various grades, including capital crimes and other transgressions brought together in the *ayādgār*, but could also be recorded on the basis of circumstantial evidence, such as 'notoriety' (*āšnāgīh ī šahr*, lit. 'being known in the land') and being held in 'disrepute; dishonour' (*dusraw*).[258] Two corresponding entries, referring to the accused, are quoted from a *pursišn-nāmag*, transmitting the exact wording of these recordings: 'The man (is held in) disrepute and is considered in the land as an evil man' (*mērag dusraw ud andar šahr wadmardīhā raft ēstēd*)[259] and 'The man (is being held) in disrepute by the people for committing that (specific) offence' (*mērag pad kardan ī ān wināh pādram dusraw*).[260]

These details convey the impression that the prosecution was urged to bring together as many indictable offences as possible, including an assessment of the reputation of the accused, in the documents called *nibištag* and *ayādgar* before initiating criminal proceedings on this basis. At which point was the *pursišn-nāmag* taken down? We are not informed, but the case against Mār Abā suggests that this transcript was written only *after* the beginning of the official trial, not in the first stages of preparing the bill of indictment, nor in the preliminary hearings, which took place before the formal trial.

The Vita of the Catholicos also gives us insight into the concrete charges brought forward against a person accused of a severe capital crime. These are listed exactly in the initial complaint of the Chief Mobed (in the Syriac text *mwbdn mwbd*[261], *mowbedān mowbed*) Dādohrmazd and a group of the Great Mobeds to the King, holding Mār Abā responsible for the following crimes:

1. He does not honour and respect the King as his sovereign and master.
2. He refutes and destroys the Mazdean religion, which is the foundation of the empire, and converts Magians to Christianity.
3. He is, therefore, a friend of the Byzantine emperor and an enemy of the Sasanian King.[262]

256 MHDA 34.13–15 (Macuch 1981, pp. 60, 218).
257 I am citing the whole sentence, as I now have a different understanding of the text: MHDA 34.15–16: *abāg ān ī abar ayādgār jomā wināh ī margarzān any-iz wināh rāy pad ān ēwēnag nibišt ēstēd* 'Together with that which (is stated) regarding the "memorandum" (*ayādgar*) (namely, that) together with *margarzān* offences also other offences have been written down in that manner' (Macuch 1981, pp. 60, 218 with a different translation).
258 MHDA 34.17–35.3 (Macuch 1981, pp. 60–61; 218).
259 MHDA 35.2 (Macuch 1981, pp. 61; 218).
260 MHDA 35.4–5 (Macuch 1981, pp. 61; 218).
261 Bedjan 1895, p. 226.
262 Bedjan 1895, p. 226f.; Braun 1915, p. 196.

These charges fit in perfectly with the details we were able to collect on criminal offences prosecuted by the State.[263] If we compare the accusations of the Chief Mobed with the details on offences against public security noted above, it becomes evident that Mār Abā is accused of the two most severe capital crimes endangering the social and religious order of the empire: *xwadāy dušmenīh* ('insubordination, rebellion, high treason' against the sovereign; the first and third accusations) and *yazdān-dušmenīh* ('blasphemy, apostasy' against the Zoroastrian church; the second accusation). Despite these serious charges of treason and apostasy the King first hesitates to give his consent to the initiation of proceedings against the Catholicos (due presumably to strategic reasons), but later yields to the appeals of the Zoroastrian clergy and allows a preliminary investigation.[264] The text suggests that a preliminary hearing (or several preliminary hearings) took place before the initiation of the formal trial. In the case of Mār Abā these hearings were obviously used to intimidate the Catholicos and to hear witnesses, who would substantiate the general allegations of treason and apostasy brought forward by the Chief Mobed and his staff.

3.2.2 The preliminary hearing(s)

There are unfortunately no Pahlavi sources describing this part of criminal procedure, but we may again draw several conclusions from the Syriac material on Mār Abā. The next steps in the proceedings are narrated as follows: while the King is on a campaign the Chief Mobed summons the Catholicos on altogether four occasions to an assembly of clergy and judges under his chairmanship. In these sessions Mār Abā is only threatened and accused informally, a description which corresponds well with the passage on the handling of heretics in the Letter of Tansar discussed above (see pp. 490–491). The most important information in this context is that the Chief Mobed does not act as judge: he neither interrogates the Catholicos (as one would expect in a formal trial), nor gives judgement (as he would be obliged to at the end of a formal trial).[265] Moreover, no *pursišn-nāmag* is taken down; the 'transcript of interrogation' is mentioned in this account only in a later phase, after the official trial has begun. These details suggest that the text describes a preliminary hearing in several sessions with two main goals: to put pressure on the accused to renounce his beliefs and actions (corresponding exactly with the procedure against heretics described in the Letter of Tansar), but also to underline the charges by hearing witnesses, who confirm the allegations of the Chief Mobed and increase the pressure by demonstrating their willingness to provide evidence against the accused. In this context two officials, the **šahr-dādwar* (*šhrdwr* in the Syriac text)[266] and the *rad* (of the province) of Pārs, give

263 See above pp. 489–494.
264 On the possible motivation of the King see Macuch 2014c, p. 50.
265 Bedjan 1895, p. 227; Braun 1915, p. 198.
266 Bedjan 1895, p. 228. On the *šahr-dādwar* see above p. 502.

testimony in the fourth session to the charge of blasphemy/apostasy by confirming that the Catholicos has committed the following offences:

1. He converted many Magians to Christianity when he was in Pārs.
2. He banned the eating of meat of 'murmur' (meat from ritually sacrificed animals which had been consecrated with *wāz* 'grace', the recitation of specific Zoroastrian prayers in a low murmuring voice before consumption).[267]

Both testimonies definitely underline the general allegation of *yazdān-dušmenīh* and substantiate the case against Mār Abā, but the Catholicos refuses to answer to these charges in the absence of the King.[268] His refusal to comply suggests that he was well acquainted with the procedure and relied to some extent on the protection of the King, who would be—as other Syriac sources suggest—the presiding judge in a formal trial against a high dignitary such as Mār Abā, and, moreover, have the authority to grant a pardon in the event of a conviction.[269]

In the meantime the preliminary hearings continued and the assembly consisting of clerics, judges and also nobles, including Christians, sought to find a compromise with the Catholicos rather than to convict him. In the course of these sessions other witnesses against Mār Abā are heard, first the *mowbed* of Bēth Ārāmāye, then the *rad* and *mowbed* of the same province who testify to the following:

1. He induces Christians who have judicial disputes against each other to leave the court and destroys the **bōxt-nāmag* (*bwktn'mg*)[270] ('document of acquittal') with the seal of the *mowbedān mowbed*; he judges all the cases which should be judged by us.[271]
2. He expels Christians from the Church who have married their mother-in-law, daughter-in-law, wife of their uncle or two sisters.[272]

These statements have a somewhat different quality, as they charge Mār Abā with interfering in legal matters. The first testimony confirms that he undermines the judicial authority of the Zoroastrian clergy in all higher instances (*mowbed*, *rad* and *mowbedān mowbed*) by causing Christians to avoid or leave Sasanian courts and by tearing up the official document of exoneration (the **bōxt-nāmag* or 'document of acquittal') which was issued and sealed by the Chief Mobed. The second one accuses Mār Abā of opposing Sasanian marriage laws by forbidding Christians to follow Zoroastrian customs and norms of

267 Bedjan 1895, p. 228f. On *wāz/bāj dādan/griftan* 'giving/taking *wāz*' see Hutter 2003, p. 170; on animal sacrifice in Zoroastrianism see de Jong 2002 and Cantera 2022.
268 Bedjan 1895, p. 227f.; Braun 1915, p. 198.
269 Wiessner 1967, p. 158; see section 3.2.2 below.
270 Bedjan 1895, p. 234.
271 Bedjan 1895, p. 233f.; Braun 1915, p. 200.
272 Bedjan 1895, p. 234; Braun 1915, p. 200ff.

matrimony.[273] These two assertions testify not only to crimes against Mazdean authorities in their priestly functions (as the first two charges), but bear witness to Mār Abā's obstruction of their work as jurists and judges of the State. This is a grave accusation, presumably with the main purpose of underlining the general allegation of 'insubordination, treason' (*xwadāy dušmenīh*): by indicting the Catholicos for undermining the legal system and the jurisdiction of the State he is held responsible for endangering the security of Ērānšahr (according to the *Dēnkard* this is also one of the main accusations against the Mazdakites, who were, as we may recall, suppressed by the same King Husraw I).[274]

The last accusation against Mār Abā indicts him of the crime of apostasy: he was formerly a 'pagan' (which in the Syriac text refers to his Zoroastrian origin) and converted later to Christianity.[275] It seems strange that the most grievous charge of apostasy—from the viewpoint of the Mazdean prosecutors—should be the last one, but the uncompromising attitude of the Catholicos, who was unwilling to make any concessions, might have provoked this final accusation. As we learn later from the text, apostasy is the only crime that the King was not able or willing to pardon, hence it might have been used as a last resort to pressure Mār Abā. After this final indictment the council decides that the offences committed by the Catholicos are 'death deserving' or, in Sasanian legal terminology, *margarzān*, and the preliminary hearing comes to an end after several sessions, in which the Catholicos was repeatedly urged to renounce his ways. These charges (together with the testimony of the witnesses) were presumably documented in one of the records mentioned above, the *nibištag* ('bill of indictment') or *ayādgār* ('memorandum') and used as a basis for conducting the criminal trial against the accused.

3.2.3 The trial

The Syriac Acts on the prosecution of Christians under Šābuhr II (309–379 CE) distinguish, according to Wiessner, between two types of trials. The first type encompasses proceedings which were conducted under the direct control of the king as presiding judge, who either personally interrogated the accused, or let him be questioned in his, the king's, immediate presence. This procedure seems to have been the rule with regard to influential high dignitaries of the State, including the representatives of the larger religious minorities (such as, in the sixth century, Mār Abā). The second type of trial took place under the chairmanship of a deputy (or several deputies) of the king (*šarrīrā dᵊ-malkā*), representing the crown, and was applied in cases against less significant personalities.[276] Both types of proceedings consisted of four parts:

273 On Mār Abā's presumably most important achievement in the context of law, the formulation of Christian marriage rules, see pp. 155–157 above.

274 See Macuch 2015b and pp. 253–259 above.

275 Bedjan 1895, p. 237f.; Braun 1915, p. 203.

276 Wiessner 1967, pp. 158; 167–168.

1. the accusation;
2. the arrest, transfer and arrival of the accused at the legal venue;
3. the main trial, consisting of two separate sessions, ending with the death sentence;
4. transfer of the convicted person to the place of execution and implementation of the punishment.[277]

In this material no preliminary hearing is mentioned. This might be due to the fact that the Syriac texts examined by Wiessner reflect legal procedure in the 4th century, whereas the trial against Mār Abā took place in the sixth. Criminal procedure either evolved across the decades or was deliberately reformed by Husraw I in the 6th century, as we have good reason to assume according to the details conveyed in the Letter of Tansar regarding the handling of heretics and apostates (see above pp. 490–491). But generally we cannot expect to find minute descriptions of these proceedings in the Syriac material, as the main purpose of these texts was to record the religious steadfastness, faith and resilience of Christian martyrs, not to offer a precise account of the Sasanian criminal trial.[278]

The main trial against Mār Abā is unfortunately not as well documented as the preliminary hearings, but it is possible to reconstruct a few traits. It seems that the official part of the proceedings begins with the recording of the *pursišn-nāmag* 'transcript of interrogation' (*pwrššnmg* in the Syriac text[279]), in which all the accusations brought together during the preliminary hearings are written down (presumably together with the testimonies of the witnesses on the basis of the 'bill of indictment', *nibištag*, or 'memorandum', *ayādgār*).[280] The charges recorded in the *pursišn-nāmag* are not listed in Mār Abā's Vita at this point, but can be reconstructed from a later passage, in which the Catholicos asks the sovereign for a pardon. The King, addressing the Catholicos, quotes from the entries taken down in this document the following accusations:

1. You induce Magians to turn away from the *dēn* and convert to Christianity.
2. You do not allow your adherents to marry as many wives as they want to.
3. You have seized jurisdiction from the Magians.
4. You were a 'pagan' (= Mazdean) first and later became a Christian.
5. You install bishops, priests and deacons everywhere you are and order them to teach and spread Christianity as you do so yourself.[281]

In short, all the criminal offences the Catholicos was charged with during the preliminary hearings were recorded in the *pursišn-nāmag*. These are

277 Wiessner 1967, p. 158; 176–177.
278 On religious controversies regarding the interpretation of the sacred texts and priestly practice by Zoroastrian exegetists *within* the Zoroastrian community see Cantera 2020.
279 Bedjan 1895, p. 238.
280 Bedjan 1895, p. 238; Braun 1915, p. 203.
281 Bedjan 1895, p. 254; Braun 1915, p. 211; Sachau 1914, p. XXVI.

transgressions pertaining to the three major crimes of (a) *yazdān-dušmenīh* (interference in religious matters by converting Magians in Pārs, forbidding the meat of 'murmur' to Christians and spreading Christianity); (b) *xwadāy dušmenīh* (interference in legal matters by seizing jurisdiction from the Zoroastrian courts and compelling Christians to dissolve their legal marriages); and (c) *ahlomōyīh* (heresy; in this case: apostatizing from Zoroastrianism to Christianity). It seems that the court (or assembly) considered these crimes to be evident after hearing the testimonies given during the preliminary sessions. In any case, there is no mention of any further witnesses or any other type of evidence. The Catholicos is again given the choice to escape being sentenced by confirming that he will refrain from continuing the transgressions he has been charged with, and again refuses to comply.

The trial against Mār Abā as one of the high religious dignitaries, whose political influence might have had been feared by the King (and maybe also other members of the assembly acting as judges), may have diverged in certain respects from the usual procedure in *margarzān* cases prosecuted by the State. Due to the deplorable lack of case studies and other information in the Pahlavi sources, we are not in a position to reconstruct the consecutive phases of the criminal trial, apart from the very last act, which consisted of recording the verdict at the end of the *pursišn-nāmag* and sealing the document.[282]

3.2.4 The verdict and punishments

While the proceedings narrated in the Syriac Acts of Christian Martyrs under Šābuhr II regularly end with the death sentence and the execution of the martyrs, the Vita of the Catholicos recounts another outcome. After his renewed refusal to refrain from continuing his offensive actions, the *pursišn-nāmag* against Mār Abā is sealed with the sentence at its end. So far this was the regular procedure by which a criminal trial came to an end and the case was officially closed. This is confirmed indirectly by a short passage of the Babylonian Talmud, using the Iranian technical term for the 'transcript of interrogation' (written *pwrsyšnmg*; variants: *pwrsyšmng*; *pwrsy šnmg*).[283] The text quotes the statement of a rabbi (Rabbi Joseph), who explains that trying to bribe a 'worldly' (*i. e.* Sasanian) judge (in a criminal trial) would be useless after the *pursišn-nāmag* has been sealed. What the rabbi is saying is in fact that once the sentence is pronounced in a Sasanian court and the transcript of interrogation sealed, it would be completely pointless to try to bribe the judge, since with the formal act of sealing this document the case is officially closed. According to the Law-book, the *pursišn-nāmag* was (additionally?) sealed—at least under Husraw I—with an administrative seal (*muhr ī pad kār-framān dāštan*). This could imply that the

282 MHDA 34.6–9 (Macuch 1981, pp. 60, 217).

283 *Giṭṭin* 28b; on this passage see Macuch 1999, pp. 98–100, and Chapter VII, pp. 594–595.

verdict had to be confirmed by an anonymous official seal of the State, regardless of the individual judge (or judges) who had passed the sentence.[284]

Mār Aba's Vita does not impart the exact content of the verdict against the Catholicos (apart from designating his crimes as 'death deserving'), nor the role of the King in finding it, but we are informed that he escaped not only death, but even imprisonment due to the interference of influential Christians at the court of the King and was instead sent to exile in Azerbaijan. The King later grants Mār Abā a pardon for four of the charges recorded in the *pursišn-nāmag*. The only accusation he is not able or not willing to pardon is that of apostasy (number 4 quoted above p. 579), as he orders Mār Abā to justify himself before the Chief Mobed, should he demand it. It seems that the same political considerations, which induced the King to respect and follow the appeals of influential Christians at his court, would not allow him to ignore the will of the Chief Mobed in a matter of immense religious significance such as apostasy.

The main punishment for a capital crime, as the term *margarzān* itself suggests, was presumably the death sentence before fines and other lesser punishments were introduced (on these see Chapter V, pp. 484–486). In one of the rare references to the Avesta in the Law-book, it is said that a person prosecuted because of a *margarzān* is to be decapitated (*sar brīd abāyīdan*) if he is found responsible for only one 'obstruction of justice' (*azišmānd*), a statement, which—due to the use of the Middle Persian technical terms—refers to the Pahlavi exegesis (*zand*) of the sacred texts rather than the original Avestan source itself.[285] Although this concise passage is difficult to contextualize, it suggests that the accused in a *margarzān* criminal case was to be convicted to death if he committed only one *contumacia* during the trial (whereas, as we may recall, in other cases three offences of this kind led to the conviction of the transgressor).[286] The case against Mār Abā, however, demonstrates that under specific circumstances even the most grievous *margarzān* offences were not necessarily punished by executing the convict (at least in the late Sasanian period after the reforms of Husraw I). The King, it seems, was relatively free to exert the death punishment or to pardon the accused after the court (or tribunal) had found the latter guilty. The

284 MHD 100.7–11 (Macuch 1993, pp. 613f.; 621); on administrative seals see Chapter IV, pp. 293–296.

285 MHD 14.17–15.1 (Macuch 1993, pp. 129; 132); on *azišmānd* offences see above pp. 561–569.

286 Zoroastrian law might have been very similar to Roman law in this respect. Interestingly, the outcome of the—in many parts enigmatic—trial against Jesus of Nazareth before the *praefectus Judaeae* Pontius Pilate has been interpreted in this sense. Rosen 1996 (pp. 68–69) argues that in all the accounts of the trial by the Synoptics (Matthew, Mark, Luke) Jesus is reported to have said only two words at the beginning of the proceedings and then remained silent for the rest of the interrogation by Pilate, refusing to answer any of his questions. This conduct of an accused towards the presiding judge counted as insubordination or obstruction (*contumacia*) in Roman law and could be punished by the governor of a Province with the death sentence, if the accused was not a Roman citizen. This corresponds roughly with the regulation cited in the Law-book.

Letter of Tansar confirms the arbitrariness of Sasanian criminal justice in this respect and provides a general description of how the King exercised his power with regard to the subjects of his realm, citing his own words:

> *mā mardōm rā be-si ṣanf yāftīm wa rāżī-u šākir-īm az īšān be-si sīyāsat ṣanf-ī az īšān ki andak-and ḫāṣṣa-u nīkū-kārān-and sīyāsat-i īšān mawaddat-i maḥż wa ṣanf-i duwum ki bisyār-and bad-kār-u fitān-u ašrār-and siyāsat-i īšān maḫāfa-i sirf wa siyum ki aʿdād-i īšān dar taʿdād na-yāyad ʿāmma-i muḫtaliṭ siyāsat-i īšān ǧamʿ miyān-i raġbat-u rahbat na amn-ī ki dilīr šawand-u na raʿb-ī ki āwāra gardand waqthā bi-gunāh-ī ki bi-ʿafw nazdīk-u lāyiq bi-bāyad kušt-u bi-gunāh-ī ki qatl wāǧib āyad ʿafw farmāyad.*
>
> 'We have found people (divided) into three groups (*ṣanf*) and have contented ourselves (to treat them according) to three policies (*sīyāsat*). One of these groups, which is small, consists of the noble (*ḫāṣṣa*) and virtuous (*nīkū-kārān*). (Our) policy towards them (is) pure kindness (*mawaddat-i maḥż*). And the second group, encompassing many, consists of evil-doers (*bad-kār*) and seducers (*fitān*) and criminals (*ašrār*). (Our) policy towards them (is) pure terror (*maḫāfa-i sirf*). And the third (group), whose members are innumerable, consists of plebeians of unknown (genealogy) (*ʿāmma-i muḫtaliṭ*). (Our) policy towards them is generally a mixture of favour (*raġbat*) and fear (*rahbat*); neither such security that would make them audacious, nor such terror that would make them flee. At times it is necessary to kill (*bi-bāyad kušt*) for an offence, which is suitable and deserving of a pardon (*ʿafw*) and to grant a pardon (*ʿafw farmāyad*) for an offence deserving death (*qatl wāǧib āyad*).'[287]

In this noteworthy passage describing the King's policy towards his subjects, the sovereign distinguishes between his subordinates not only according to moral and ethical criteria, but also according to their rank and station in society (this distinction disappears completely in Boyce's translation of this passage due to her divergent rendering of *ḫāṣṣa* and *ʿāmma*). The first group of subjects consists not only of the 'virtuous', but of the 'noble and virtuous' (*ḫāṣṣa-u nīkū-kārān*), the morally impeccable aristocracy, worthy of being treated kindly, whereas the last group encompasses the mass of the people, the 'plebeians of unknown (genealogy)' (*ʿāmma-i muḫtaliṭ*), who are to be kept in an oscillating state of insecurity in order to ensure their subordination. Only the evil-doers of the second group are not cast into a social rank. The last sentence of this section underlines the unique power of the King to pass a death sentence arbitrarily—at least with regard to the plebeian citizens of Ērānšahr—as well as to grant a pardon for a 'death deserving' offence (*qatl wāǧib āyad*), *i. e.* a *margarzān* crime.

According to the Law-book and other Pahlavi sources, a person convicted of a *margarzān* would, even if he was not executed, lose his standing in the community, his status as *paterfamilias* (by the loss of wives and children) and

287 Persian text in Darmesteter 1894, pp. 220, l. 17- p. 221, l. 8; largely different Boyce 1968a, p. 43.

his whole property.[288] Another passage of the same source quotes from an official document (*dib/nāmag*) of the Sasanian period with the impressive title 'the authorized edict and document on the area of competence of the public official of the provinces' (*dib ī pādixšāy kard ud xwēškārīh nāmag ī kār-framān ī šahrīhā*).[289] This important sounding writ is not described, but it would not be too far-fetched to assume that it was some kind of official decree (possibly of the king himself) conveying instructions to the officials responsible for public affairs (*kār-framān*) in the regions or provinces (*šahrīhā*) of the Empire. The content of the decree is noteworthy: it gives order to transfer the property (*xwāstag*) of persons convicted of heresy (*zandīkīh*) and heretical beliefs (*zandīk wurrōyišnīh*) to the *šāhīgān* ('pertaining to the king'), the property of the crown, held by the king, suggesting that the belongings of convicted heretics could be confiscated or legally appropriated by the sovereign (if all kinds of heretics are meant by the term *zandīk*, not only the Mazdakites).[290] The immediately preceding sentence suggests that another procedure was also possible. According to this ruling the property of a heretic is to be treated as that of a person convicted by the *rad* for committing sorcery (*ǰādūgīh*): it goes to the person who has been harmed by the sorcerer (or heretic), but if no specific person is said to have been damaged, then the witnesses who have given testimony against the suspect receive the property.[291] Another remarkable passage on sorcery reports how this offence was dealt

288 MHD 97.15–98.1: *ka pad margarzān ēraxt ēg-iš xwāstag ī ast az-iš appār būd kē guft kū-š rōzīg ī zan ud frazand az-iš be gīrišn pad kardag nē kunēnd čē ka margarzān būd ēg-iš zan ud frazand gēhān az-iš appār bawēd.* 'If he (= the accused) is found guilty of a *margarzān*, then his property is removed from him. There is one (commentator) who said: "The daily maintenance of wives and children should be taken from him." In legal practice this is not done, since, if the (crime) is a *margarzān*, then wives, children and property are taken from him' (Macuch 1993, pp. 582; 587). Compare also REA 4.1–8. According to MHDA 35.9–11 (Macuch 1981, pp. 61; 218f.) a person even suspected (*warōmand*) of having committed a *margarzān* is to be excluded from the prayers uttered in *wāz* (the low and suppressed tone of 'murmur' used when reciting specific prayers; see Nyberg 1974, p. 200).

289 The term *kār-framān* designates both (1) a 'public official' of the State (who is bound by instructions in his specific area of competence) and (2) the 'official authority' of the State (as in *muhr ī pad kār-framān dāštan* 'seal for exercising official authority'). See Macuch 1993, pp. 357–358; also Chapter IV, pp. 270–271, fn. 60.

290 MHDA 38.16–39.1: *abāg ān ī pad dib ī pādixšāy kard ud xwēškārīh nāmag ī kār-framān ī šahrīhā paydag kū zandīkīh ud zandīk wurrōyišnīh rāy xwāstag xwāstag ⟨ō⟩ šāhīgān kard.* 'Together with that, which is (stated) in the "authorized edict and document on the area of competence of the public official of the provinces" it is revealed, that the property of (those convicted of) heresy and heretical beliefs is to be transferred to the "property pertaining to the king" (*šāhīgān*)' (Macuch 1981, pp. 65; 222).

291 MHDA 38.12–16: *ān ī guft kū ōy ī ǰādūg xwāstag ī-š ast ka-šān ǰādūgīh ōst pad rad ēstēd ud ka-šān marnǰēnišn kard ō ōy kē marnǰēnišn andar kard ud ka-š gugāyīh abar dahēnd ud wināh andar kē kard pad nāmčišt nē paydāg ō gugāyān appār ud zandīkīh ǰādūgīh.* 'And that which is said: (regarding) the property belonging to a sorcerer (*ǰādūg*): if (the act of) sorcery (*ǰādūgīh*) has been definitely established by the *rad* and if they (= the

with, when the evidence did not suffice to convict the accused, despite the person's 'notoriety in the community' (*pādram dusraw*) as a sorcerer: a (wooden or iron) collar (*čambar*) was placed around the neck of the suspect and a heavy weight (*duš̌xwār*) on his shoulders until the crime of sorcery was 'made doubtful' (*warōmand kard*) or the suspect was acquitted (*bōxt*). If one of these two items broke, the offence counted as 'doubtful' (*warōmand*, lit. 'liable to the oath').[292] The procedure seems to describe a method of torture to obtain a confession from the suspect in combination with an ordeal or judgment of the gods.

As to the penalties that could be administered, a large range of brutal methods of execution and extremely cruel means of torture are described in the Coptic *Homilies* and the Syriac Acts of Martyrs, which have been collected and commented by other authors.[293] We have already discussed extensively one of the punishments elucidated in somewhat more detail in the Pahlavi sources, the penalty for theft (*band ud drōš* 'fetters and mutilation/branding') in Chapter V above.[294] A large variety of different methods of execution were obviously known, among them practices labelled the 'elephant', the 'cow', the 'donkey' and the 'tree' in the Letter of Tansar: highway-robbers and heretics could be trampled to death under an elephant's hooves; a cauldron in the shape of a cow was filled with molten lead into which the convict was cast; an iron with three legs, called the 'donkey', was employed for hanging convicts by the feet until they died; the 'tree' was used to crucify sorcerers and highway-robbers.[295] Ruthless punishments were imposed on converts to Christianity, which have been brought together by Colditz, who assumes that the same penalties were also administered to converts to Manichaeism:

> Their worldly goods were plundered and they were banished from their homes. Those who had held titles or offices were dismissed. But in most cases mentioned the Christian martyrs were fettered with bonds of many kinds on their hands and feet and had to wear heavy chains or iron and collars round their necks. They were held in bondage and had to suffer hunger and thirst, cold, heat and darkness; they were sentenced to prison under the worst conditions; some of them were even walled up. They were beaten and scourged with whips of leather; they were skinned or combed with iron combs to tear their flesh to pieces. Very often they were sentenced to mutilation by the cutting-off of limbs (hands, feet, arms, legs), tongue, the ears and nose together, or the scalp. They also suffered blinding by means of knives or hot iron nails and the cauterizing of their mouths, ears and

---

sorcerers) have caused harm, (then) it (= the property goes) to the one who has been harmed. And if testimony is given and it is not clear against whom exactly the sin was committed, (then) it (= the property) is lost to the witnesses. And heresy (is treated as) sorcery.' (Macuch 1981, pp. 65; 222).

292 MHDA 15.15–17 (Macuch 1981, pp. 38, 145).

293 See especially Colditz 1998 and Jany 2007 and 2012, pp. 65–68.

294 See pp. 441–446.

295 Boyce 1968a, p. 48.

> eyes with vinegar and mustard. Most of these torments were carried out immediately before the actual execution, or they led to death directly. To kill the martyrs the authorities made use of many brutal methods of execution: cutting off their heads by the sword, chopping them in pieces, piercing them with arrows, burning and scalding them by means of fire, naphta, boiling water or molten metal. The Christians were drowned, crucified, stoned or crushed underfoot by elephants. To make things worse, these cruel methods were even used in combination. The corpses of Christians were also treated badly and desecrated by being fed to animals; the bones were scattered around.[296]

As horrific as these atrocious tortures and penalties sound, they do not differ substantially from the maltreatment and cruel punishments, which could be imposed on suspects and convicts in ancient Rome or in mediaeval Europe and the Western world up to the early modern period.[297] The question is, whether these extremely painful methods of torture and punishment were restricted to criminals found guilty of one of the three worst capital crimes (of the *xwadāy-dušmenīh*, *yazdān-dušmenīh* or *ahlomoyīh* category) or were also applied in other cases, even to Zoroastrian transgressors willing to confess, repent and atone according to the system described in Chapter V.[298] The sources are silent in this respect, but it would not be too far-fetched to assume that the Zoroastrian clergy would protect to some degree its repentant adherents from suffering the worst mistreatments, even when the death sentence was imposed in a *margarzān* case.

3.3 Litigation costs

We are not informed in detail on the overall costs of a lawsuit, but a concise passage of the Law-book mentions the expenses charged for drafting a transcript or protocol:

> MHDA 15.17–16.5
> *uzēnag ī pad nāmag passāz pad kardag pad xwāstag gyāg-ē(w) guft kū 9 drahm 2 ud gyāg-ē(w) guft kū 10 drahm 3 ud pad margarzān 95 ud ka dādestān az ān ī abēr was ēg-iz pad margarzān wēš nēst kū 95 ud pad xwāstag ōwōn paydāg čiyōn ka wēš nē hē kū 17 ud drahm 2 pad kardag uzenag ī pad nāmag-passāz andar abāyēd az ataxšān be dahēnd ud az pēšēmālān pasēmālān abāz xwāhēnd*
>
> '(On) the costs for drawing up a document (protocol/transcript): in legal practice (*pad kardag*) regarding the object of dispute (*xwāstag*) it says in one place: for 9 drachms 2 (drachms). And in (another) place it says: for 10 drachms 3 (drachms).

296 Colditz 1998, pp. 30–31, with numerous references to the sources. On flaying alive as a particularly cruel form of punishment see now Rollinger/Wiesehöfer 2023.
297 See *e.g.* van Dülmen 1988 and Arnold 2012.
298 On capital crimes prosecuted by legal authorities of the State see above pp. 489–494; on the Zoroastrian degrees of sins see Chapter V, pp. 468–486.

> And for a capital crime (*margarzān*) 95 (drachms). And if the lawsuit (*dādestān*) (costs) far more, even then for a *margarzān* (the cost of the transcript) does not exceed 95 (drachms). And with regard to the object of dispute (*xwāstag*) it is made manifest (*paydāg*) as if it were (worth) not more than 17 drachms and 2 drachms are according to legal practice (*pad kardag*) the necessary costs for drafting the document (protocol/transcript). (These) are paid out of (the funds of) the 'fires' (*ātaxšān*) and reclaimed from the plaintiffs and defendants.'[299]

The passage is unfortunately not very clear, but the phrase *uzēnag ī pad nāmag passāz* ('the costs for drawing up a document/protocol/transcript') seems to refer specifically to records taken down during a trial, not to documents in general. The following context implies that *nāmag* designates documents drawn up in the course of a lawsuit, particularly the two types of transcript mentioned above, the *saxwan-nāmag*, taken down in civil cases, and the *pursišn-nāmag*, the transcript from a criminal trial (but maybe also other transcripts, such as the *yazišn-nāmag* and the *uzdād-nāmag*, among others), although these specific terms are not used in this context. If my understanding of the sentence is correct, the costs of recording a transcript in a civil trial are calculated 'in legal practice' (*pad kardag*) on the basis of the value of the object of dispute (*xwāstag*) in the lawsuit in three ways: (1) two drachms for an object worth nine drachms, or (2) three drachms for an object worth ten drachms, or (3) the maximum value of the object of litigation (*xwāstag*) is fixed (fictively) at seventeen drachms and two drachms are taken for the recordings in 'legal practice' (*pad kardag*). In a lawsuit involving a capital crime (*margarzān*) the costs to be met for drafting the transcript are always 95 drachms, even if the overall expenses of the trial exceed this sum by far. The most interesting information is in the last passage: the costs of drafting these documents are paid in advance from the funds or property of fire foundations (*ātaxšān*) and later reclaimed from the plaintiffs and defendants (possibly with interest). This remarkable statement calls our attention to the huge impact of the larger fire foundations in Sasanian society, not only as an economic factor, but also in controlling diverse activities of daily life, particularly in the sphere of the judiciary.[300]

Another entry addresses the question of payment for carrying out an ordeal or oath. MHD 33.11–13 discloses that a master or *paterfamilias* is obliged to continue to maintain his daughter, wife or male slave (*anšahrīg ī mard*) and to carry the costs of implementing an ordeal (*pad passāxtan*) if one of these persons under his guardianship is suspected of having committed an offence (*wināh*).[301] It seems that payment for the costs of litigation could be secured by an official *framān* ('order, command' of the king or one of his officials), at least in a case of appeal, as the following passage implies:

299 Macuch 1981, pp. 38, 145 (with a slightly different translation).
300 On fire foundations see Chapter III, pp. 225–229.
301 Macuch 1993, pp. 241, 244.

MHD 93.9–11
ēk ēn kū ka a-hunsandīh ī pasēmāl pad wizīr rāy az dādwarān ō mowbedān wisē kard mowbed ān wizīr pad wizār dāštan abar ān xīr ī pad uzēnag ud pādrōz abar pasēmāl framān dād.

'One (passage) is this: When due to the dissatisfaction of the defendant with the verdict he is dispatched from the judges (*dādwarān*) to the *mowbeds*, (then) the *mowbed*, in order to examine that verdict, has issued a *framān* regarding the defendant with respect to the property (of the defendant) for the costs and (his) daily maintenance.'[302]

The background of this somewhat garbled sentence is the following: The defendant in a lawsuit is not satisfied with the verdict of the judges (the *dādwar ī keh* and the *dādwar ī meh*) in the first two instances and appeals to the next higher court, presided by a *mowbed*. The latter is requested to check the verdict (*ān wizīr pad wizār dāštan*). In order to secure the costs (*uzēnag*) of the proceedings and his own daily expenses (*pādrōz*) the *mowbed* issues a *framān* (or causes a *framān* to be issued) with respect to the property (*xīr*) of the defendant, ensuring—as we may assume—that these costs will be paid for out of this property.[303]

The information is fragmentary, but we can conclude from the cited sources that the litigants in a civil trial paid a sum equivalent to a specific percentage of the value of the object of dispute to the court for the recording of transcripts; in a criminal trial a fixed sum of 95 drachms. The costs for recording these documents could be advanced from the property or funds belonging to fire foundations (*ātaxšān* or *xīr ī ātaxš*) and be later reclaimed from the parties (possibly with a fixed rate of interest). The head of a family and the master of a slave were held responsible for paying the costs of an ordeal/oath for one of the persons under their guardianship. In an appellate court the official in charge could issue a *framān* with respect to the property of the litigant who appealed in order to ensure that the daily expenses of the official and the costs of the appeal were covered.

302 Macuch 1993, pp. 593, 596 (with a divergent translation). On *wisē kardan* 'to dispatch, send, summon' see Macuch 2016a, p. 156, with references to the Tabarestān documents.
303 On instances and appellate courts see above, pp. 522–526.

Chapter VII

Sasanian Law and other Legal Systems

Introductory: the impact of Sasanian law

Sasanian jurisprudence left its distinctive mark not only on those contemporary legal systems, which were shaped or further developed in the Christian and Jewish communities of Ērānšahr, but reached far beyond its prime to contribute to the formation of some of the most significant institutions of Islamic law in the early centuries of the new religion. Despite divergent opinions regarding the extent to which Iranian law interacted with other systems or contributed to the shaping of specific legal concepts, there can be no serious doubt that it was known in rabbinic circles and discussed in the Babylonian Talmud, that it formed the foundation of East Christian (Nestorian) law and offered templates for the development of several characteristic institutions of Islamic law, particularly in its Shīʿite (Jaʿfarite) branch, after the establishment of the Caliphate. Remarkable parallels can also be detected between Sasanian law and Roman/Byzantine law, due either to a similar, albeit independent, development in the two systems, or to some kind of interaction during the long history of contacts between the two empires (which would, however, be impossible to reconstruct with any certainty on the basis of the available sources).

It is admittedly one of the basic challenges of comparative law to demonstrate beyond reasonable doubt that close correspondences between legal systems are more than just parallel developments. Although individual similarities and striking analogies might indicate reception or a common ancestor, it is often difficult or even impossible to decide whether congruent ideas emerged independently or were transferred from one culture to the other or were the outcome of many decades of interaction between connected communities. Legal provisions are hardly ever simply adapted without re-adjustment, re-contextualisation and numerous alterations, including the deliberate *concealment* of their reception specifically in religious legal systems intent on keeping their age-old traditions undefiled. These deliberate or unconscious strategies make it extremely difficult to unravel the modalities involved in the transfer of juristic concepts and institutions. But despite all these obstacles there are a few approaches to the question of legal reception, which put us on more solid ground.[1] One of the most evident points of departure

1 The most important criteria of reception analysis are brought together in Jokisch 2019 with further references.

is the use of Iranian legal expressions either as loanwords in their original form or in an easily recognizable (often literal) translation, reflecting the use of these words or phrases in a Sasanian legal context. Iranian technical terms are employed both in the Babylonian Talmud and in East Christian law, specifically in the Syriac Law-book of Īšōʿbōxt, which is based almost entirely on Sasanian law. The use of these expressions offers a solid foundation for the further analysis of the legal and social context in which they occur, sometimes allowing conclusions regarding the impact of Iranian concepts on rabbinic discussions in the Talmud (which possibly encouraged the further development of Jewish law) and—with respect to the Syriac texts—the formation of East Christian law. It must be said, however, that the mere use of an Iranian technical term does not necessarily mean that the whole underlying legal concept was adapted in some form, but it does suggest that the legal experts using the word or phrase were acquainted with its meaning and employed it to be both precise and to avoid lengthy explanations, that they were hence familiar to some degree with Iranian law.

Another method of assessing the impact of Sasanian law on other systems may be found in what has been called the congruency of features in content and structure. This approach implies that a comparison of single isolated elements in two systems does not necessarily point to a connection between the two, but interconnectedness can be reasonably assumed, when a large number of distinctive features are in agreement within the framework of a specific institution and preserve or reflect, despite all modifications, a characteristic legal concept, not to be found in this particular form in another neighbouring system.[2] Unsurprisingly a large number of corresponding concepts can be found in both East Christian law (such as the precise distinction between theft and robbery and its transposition to other areas of the law) and in Islamic jurisprudence in some of its most prominent institutions (such as the Islamic pious foundation, the *waqf*, the Shīʿite temporary marriage and the law of inheritance). Striking similarities can also be found in complex discussions of specific ideas in the fields of property law and the law of obligations in the Babylonian Talmud that cannot even be understood properly without taking recourse to Sasanian concepts. Even in these cases—which in my opinion can only be explained in the context of Iranian law—some will argue that the congruencies are purely coincidental and that long centuries of contact between these different religious communities in the Sasanian period and during the first centuries of Islam hardly had any effect on the development of their respective legal systems. Admittedly, in many cases adaptations are difficult to prove, but many of these objections tend to forget that adapted institutions almost never appear unaltered in their original form, but are modified and re-contextualised—often extensively—to fit into a completely different legal framework in correspondence with the divergent religious

2 See Jokisch 2019, p. 109 (who refers specifically to the comparison of texts, but the same may be inferred with regard to legal institutions).

worldview on which the legal system is based. The following overview, besides bringing together my dispersed attempts to assess the impact of Sasanian law on other legal systems, will restate the main findings and arguments I have already brought forward in a number of contributions dedicated to this intriguing subject and add a few new observations, without claiming to present an exhaustive or definitive treatment of this complex field, which experts in comparative legal history might be better equipped to investigate.

1 Rabbinic law in the Babylonian Talmud

Numerous studies are dedicated to the long history of Iranian-Jewish relationships in the pre-Islamic period, reaching from Achaemenid rule to the Islamic invasion of Iran in the seventh century CE, in which the mutual impact of Zoroastrianism and Judaism after the Jews and Persians came into contact in the mid-sixth century BCE has been discussed controversially.[3] The Babylonian Talmud (or Bavli) was composed to a large extent in the Jewish community of Mesopotamia under Parthian and Sasanian dominion and completed in the fifth (or sixth century CE) under Sasanian rule. The cultural environment, in which this monumental text came into being, suggests that Iranian mores and law may have had some—or even considerable—impact on Babylonian rabbinic culture in general and legal concepts in particular, but there is no consensus on this issue among the experts in this field. Several contributions of Talmudists in recent decades, notably Yaakov Elman and Shai Secunda, who claim to have detected many significant parallels between Zoroastrian and Talmudic legal concepts (based on new findings in Iranian Studies) due to substantial cross-cultural contacts and the transfer of ideas, have been criticized for their approaches.[4] But although

3 The impact of Zoroastrianism on the so-called Abrahamic religions has been the subject of controversies ever since the discovery of the ancient Zoroastrian texts especially with regard to the similarity of apocalyptic and eschatological ideas. Descriptions of eschatological events correlating with Zoroastrian concepts only emerge in Judaism after the Jews came into contact with the Persians in the post-exilic period, but the late date of our most detailed Iranian sources on eschatology, the ninth century Pahlavi texts, has been repeatedly cited as an insurmountable obstacle to finding the origin of these concepts (*e.g.* Brody 2016, pp. 209–210; for an overview of the sources with further references see Macuch 2009a, pp. 152–160). In this context the recent research of Almut Hintze is most significant. In her scrutiny of Avestan texts, particularly the Gathas, which definitely predate the Jewish sources, she has been able to show that similarly interconnected and coherent eschatological concepts are already visible in the most ancient Zoroastrian texts, which correlate with those developed at a later period in Judaism (and subsequently Christianity and Islam). See Hintze 1995, 1999 and 2019.

4 See particularly Elman's articles listed in the Festschrift in his honour (ed. Secunda/Fine 2012, pp. xv–xxii); Secunda 2014 with further references; critique by Brody 2016; see also Chapter I, pp. 50–51, fn. 145.

individual assumptions and the general extent of Iranian influence may remain controversial, there are several remarkable debates on legal issues in the Talmud, which would remain completely enigmatic without knowledge of Sasanian juristic concepts. In these cases we can reasonably infer that, no matter whether these ideas were adapted in some form or were merely discussed, they were at least well known in rabbinic circles. As we have already noted, an important indicator is the use of an Iranian technical term, in the original or in translation, with which only the legally schooled would have been acquainted, in inner-rabbinic debates. Iranian concepts are also referred to without employing a loanword by an explicit reference to the 'law of the Persians', albeit often in a far too concise and generally confusing context with no explanations whatsoever (reminiscent of the Pahlavi glosses and commentaries of the *zand*). In the following we will attempt to assess the impact of Sasanian law in the context of those passages of the Talmud, in which either a loanword (or its translation) occurs, or in which the context unequivocally includes or refers to an Iranian legal concept.

1.1 Iranian legal terms in the Bavli

The Sasanian legal system left enough room for different forms of jurisdiction in the diverse communities of the empire, as we have argued above.[5] It seems that the State did not interfere with the religious life of the Jews, but reacted only in those fields of law involving its interests, such as the proper management of property and its transfer, the regular payment of taxes and the punishment of criminal offences, particularly those for which a *framān* ('decree, command') of the sovereign (or one of his high representatives) was necessary. Interestingly, the areas of law in which the Talmud shows traces of Sasanian jurisprudence using Iranian loanwords fit precisely into this description. As we have noted in a previous chapter, Sasanian technical terms and formulae emerged from mainly three different sources: (1) Avestan words or phrases, extracted from the sacred texts; (2) expressions taken from the common vernacular and given a specific legal meaning; (3) terms of art formed in the daily practice of the courts.[6] Unsurprisingly, the Talmud does not make use of any Iranian technical terms adapted from the Avesta or Zand, which is exactly what we would expect due to the origin of these expressions in religious law. As these words or phrases often represent age-old Mazdean notions and are obviously anchored in Zoroastrian law, they would have been inacceptable to the rabbis. But no reservations seem to have existed when it came to utilizing technical terms derived from the more or less 'secular' areas of Sasanian law, which were not necessarily linked to Zoroastrian theology or religious practice, notably in the fields of property and procedural law. In fact all the Iranian technical terms in the Bavli can be

5 See Chapter VI, pp. 526–532.
6 See Chapter I, pp. 73–80, and Macuch 2005a.

attributed to one of these two fields. Another important observation is that none of these terms needed to be explained, suggesting that Jewish legal authorities were well acquainted with the professional language of Iranian jurists and deliberately used these words to express themselves concisely and clearly. All of these loanwords represent well-defined legal concepts, which were presumably well known to the rabbis and could not have been replaced by an Aramaic equivalent or expressed with the same precision by a literal translation. Interestingly, where the literal translation of a technical term is used, the exact meaning of the original expression or phrase tends to be blurred, a tactic which Jews may have employed deliberately to their advantage in contacts with Persian officials (as we can infer from the use of the ambiguous expression *bdʾ d-nwrʾ* 'servant/slave of the fire' to avoid taxation, see below, pp. 599–602).

An example, which I have already dealt with elsewhere, may be cited from the third category of technical terms noted above, the daily practice of the courts.[7] The Iranian expression (with an Aramaic plural ending), *muhraqē wāwarīgānē* (*mwhrqy wʾbwrgny*), is attested in *ʿErubin* 62a in a longer discussion regarding the renting of a yard in which a non-Jew is involved. Among other matters the short and very concise passage addresses the problem of distinguishing between a rental, which is 'solid, firm, definite' (*skyrwt bryʾh*), *i. e.* based on a legally binding contract, and one that is 'weak, infirm, defective' (*skyrwt rʿwʿh*), based on a contract whose legal validity is doubtful. In this context the Iranian term is employed to specify the legal meaning of the word 'firm, solid': a rental is regarded as 'firm' (*bryʾh*), *i. e.* legally binding, when it is attested by *mwhrqy wʾbwrgny*, but is 'defective' (*rʿwʿh*) or doubtful, if it is *not* attested by *mwhrqy wʾbwrgny.*

The Talmudic *muhraqē wāwarīgānē* can be easily recognised as a plural rendering of Iranian **muhrag ī wāwarīgān*, an extended form of the technical term attested in the Sasanian Law-book as *muhr ī wāwarīgān* or (pl.) *wāwarīgān muhrān*, lit. 'valid seal/seals'.[8] As we have elucidated in a previous chapter, seals were used extensively to verify all kinds of documents and contracts which could be presented to a court as evidence in civil litigation.[9] Courts adjudicated conflicting claims based on documents imprinted with different types of seals, which in turn had to be evaluated by the judges (or, in our case, the rabbis) according to specific criteria. Three terms are employed in the Law-book to

7 Macuch 1999, pp. 92–98, with further references.

8 The first word was already recognized by de Lagarde 1866 (p. 29, no. 3) as MP *muhrag* 'document', which is not attested with this specific meaning in Pahlavi legal sources, but is known from the loanword in Armenian *murhak* 'document' (Hübschmann 1897, p. 197, no. 417). Geiger 1937 (pp. 52–54) supplied the correct reading of the second word as MP *wāwarīgān* 'authentic, credible, reliable', translating the whole expression *muhraqē wāwarīgānē* as 'reliable (authentic) contracts' ('glaubwürdige [authentische] Vertragsurkunden'). Geiger, however, had no knowledge of the technical use of this term in Sasanian law and even (wrongly) assumed that *wāwarīgān* is only attested in a religious context

9 See Chapter IV, pp. 286–301.

classify the most important official seals, consisting usually of the personal seal of an official or of an anonymous administrative seal used in the law-courts: *muhr ī wāwarīgān* 'valid seal', *muhr ī ēwar* 'reliable, legally binding seal' or *muhr ī wizurd* 'genuine seal'.[10] The expression *muhrag* (an *-ag* extension of *muhr*) is attested in Pahlavi, as far as I can see, only in a non-legal context with the meaning of 'bead, vertebra, piece (in backgammon etc.)'; as in NP *muhra* 'bead, etc.'),[11] but the Armenian loanword *murhak* 'document', suggests that the corresponding MP **muhrag* denoted a written record to which a bulla was attached, hence explicitly designated a *sealed* document or contract. As we have noted in the section on seals above (Chapter IV, pp. 296–298), MP *wāwarīgān* corresponds in Īšōʿbōxt's Corpus Iuris to the Syriac term *šarrīrā* 'firm, valid'; **muhrag ī wāwarīgān* to the Syriac *šṭārā men šarrīrā*, a phrase denoting documents sealed by officials of the State, which were evaluated in court as 'reliable, firm' and accepted as evidence. According to Īšōʿbōxt and the Law-book documents confirmed with the private seals of witnesses to a transaction could also be assessed as 'reliable, firm', if these witnesses were known as God-fearing men in the region and community and had an impeccable reputation.[12]

Based on this material, the exact technical meaning of the Talmudic *muhraqē wāwarīgānē* can be determined as 'documents (imprinted) with valid seals (of State officials or trustworthy witnesses)' in contrast to those confirmed only by the private seals of witnesses, whose reliability has not been assessed by official instances. If we follow the legal practice of the courts described in the Law-book and by Īšōʿbōxt, however, a court could evaluate a document as *wāwarīgān* 'reliable, firm', if it was sealed by private witnesses who had an excellent reputation and were held by the judges to be God-fearing and truthful.

Legal documents also played a prominent part in Jewish civil litigation, since the rabbis were obviously entitled to issue decrees and documents and to evaluate those written outside of court.[13] If we assume that Jewish authorities were authorized to validate documents with their seals, the question arises, whether *muhraqē wāwarīgānē* refers in the Talmud to *all* valid official documents (and those assessed as reliable), including those confirmed by Jewish authorities, or whether the technical phrase was only used of documents issued by Persian officials. Although the use of the Iranian term suggests that Jewish legal instances were well acquainted with the correct technical expression, the context, in which it appears involving a non-Jew, seems to support the second assumption. This would rather indicate that the rabbis used this phrase in their discussion to refer exclusively to documents validated by Persian authorities, which could be presented by a non-Jew to a Sasanian civil court as reliable evidence, hence

10 See pp. 296, 300.
11 MacKenzie 1971, p. 56; Steingass 1892, p. 1354
12 See p. 298.
13 See Neusner 1965–1970, vol. III (1968), pp. 315.

could not be simply ignored in conflicts (*e.g.* between a Jew and a non-Jew) brought to a rabbinic court. If this assumption is correct, the Iranian expression would rather highlight the distinction the rabbis retained between Jewish and Sasanian legal practice, although the latter, representing the law of the State, had to be taken into consideration in rabbinic rulings. To sum up, there is good reason to assume that the expression *muhraqē wạ̄warīgānē* in the Talmud denotes documents (including contracts) validated by the official seals of Persian authorities, which had to be accepted in a rabbinic court as reliable evidence especially if they were presented as proof for a claim against the evidence of other documents that had not been confirmed in this manner. Unsurprisingly, this would imply that Jewish courts were not only obliged to accept the validity of documents sealed by Persian authorities, but to base their rulings on them, being well aware that their judgement could be contested and overthrown in the next instance in one of the State courts if they simply ignored the evidence provided by these documents.[14]

Another expression taken from the daily practice of the courts is transmitted in *Giṭṭin* 28b as *pursišn-nāmag* (*pwrsyšnmg*) with the variant spellings *pwrsyšmng* and *pwrsy šnmg* (written in two words).[15] The correct reading and meaning of this word was first suggested by Telegdi, who recognized it as a rendering of the Sasanian technical term for 'accusatio scripta' or 'record of questioning/ interrogation', the designation for the official transcript or protocol taken down in criminal proceedings.[16] The term is employed in a context which leaves no doubt that the rabbis had knowledge of Sasanian criminal law and were, moreover, well acquainted with the correct procedure in a criminal trial.

The passage of the Talmud, in which this word appears, transmits an inner-rabbinic discussion on the question, whether a person, who has been sentenced to death by a 'worldly', *i.e.* Sasanian, court, should be regarded as dead (by a rabbinic court) or not. In the discussion of this question Rabbi Joseph suggests that the person in question would be executed after having received a death sentence (and should therefore, as we may conclude, be considered as dead). Abbaye objects to this conclusion with the argument that a worldly (= Sasanian) court could be liable to bribery (*šwdʾ*), in which case—as we may add—the death sentence would be suspended due to the bribe the judge had received with the result that the sentenced person would still be alive. In his answer to this argument Rabbi Joseph uses our Iranian technical term, replying that bribery would only make sense *before* the *pursišn-nāmag* had been sealed, but not *after* sealing the *pursišn-nāmag*.

14 On instances and appellate courts see Chapter VI, pp. 522–526.

15 Macuch 1999, pp. 98–100, with further references.

16 Telegdi 1935, p. 233. Various (wrong) translations have been previously suggested for this word, including 'chief judge; chairman of the court' ('Oberrichter, Vorsitzender des Gerichts'; Levy 1876 [1924] IV, p. 127); 'court sentence' ('Urteil'; Goldschmidt 1935, V, p. 443); 'oath of innocence' ('Eid der Schuldlosigkeit'; Frye 1967, p. 78).

Short as this exchange of opinions is, it demonstrates beyond doubt that Rabbi Joseph was well acquainted with the legal vocabulary of criminal proceedings. Sasanian legal terminology distinguishes precisely between different forms of court transcripts, particularly between the *saxwan-nāmag* 'transcript of statements' to be taken down in a civil case, and the *pursišn-nāmag* 'transcript of interrogation', written in a criminal trial (see Chapter VI, pp. 572–573). The *pursišn-nāmag* was apparently not just a protocol of court proceedings, but an extensive document in which all the major offences and crimes with which the accused was charged were recorded, such as blasphemy (*yazdān-dušmenīh*), treason (*xwadāy-dušmenīh*), heresy (*ahlomoyīh*), contract breaking (*mihrōdrujīh*), falsehood (*drōzanīh*), among others; in short all crimes considered as 'death-deserving' (*margarzān*).[17] Besides these criminal acts other negative traits associated with the accused, such as bad reputation (*āšnāgīh-iz ī šahr*, lit. 'being known in the realm') and notoriety (*dusrawīh*), were noted in the *pursišn-nāmag* in order to characterize the person on trial as a criminal deserving punishment.[18] The Law-book conveys two further significant details for understanding the Talmudic passage: the punishment (*pādifrāh*) of the criminal is to be recorded at the end (*pad sar*) of the *pursišn-nāmag*[19] and the document is sealed with an administrative seal (*muhr ī pad kār-framān dāštan*), not with the personal seal of a judge.[20]

These details suggest that the rabbis had exact knowledge of the procedure in a Sasanian criminal trial, otherwise Rabbi Joseph would not have employed the Iranian technical term in his short statement without adding explanations for his colleagues. Obviously they knew that a specific document was taken down in a criminal trial and were acquainted with the correct technical term, which is by no means self-evident given that different expressions were used for court records in civil and criminal cases. We may furthermore conclude that they were informed that the verdict in a criminal trial was noted at the end of the *pursišn-nāmag*. Only in this context does Rabbi Joseph's statement make sense that bribery would be senseless after the *pursišn-nāmag* had been sealed. What he is actually saying is: once a case is closed, the sentence pronounced and written down, and the transcript sealed with an official (administrative) seal, it would be useless to try to bribe the judge. These details suggest that he knew the prescriptions regarding the preparation of a *pursišn-nāmag*, that he was exactly informed on the judge's sentence being recorded at the end and also knew that a case was considered as closed once the transcript of criminal proceedings had been confirmed by an administrative seal.

17 MHDA 34.6; 34.9–13 (Macuch 1981, pp. 60; 217); on criminal proceedings see Chapter VI, pp. 572–580.

18 MHDA 34.13–35.3 (Macuch 1981, pp. 60–61; 218).

19 MHDA 34.6–9 (Macuch 1981, pp. 60; 217).

20 MHD 100.7–11 (Macuch 1993, pp. 613–614; 621).

A term taken from the daily vernacular is the well-known Iranian expression *dastwar*, employed with different meanings in Middle Persian legal and non-legal texts, and attested in two difficult passages of the Talmud, *Ārakhin* 28a and *Qiddušin* 60b, as **dastwarēn* (*dsṭwrn/dstwrn*), *i. e. dastwar* with the adjectival suffix *-ēn*, lit. '*dastwar*-like, in the manner of a *dastwar*, as a *dastwar*'.[21] In religious texts of the post-Sasanian period *dastwar* is frequently employed with the general meaning of '(person having religious) authority', often as the common title of a Zoroastrian priest (NP *dastūr*), which gradually replaced the differentiated administrative titles of religious dignitaries in the Sasanian period.[22] In Pahlavi legal texts *dastwar* designates in a general context a '(legal) authority', that is, a person regarded as competent in legal matters (a renowned jurist, a State official, a plenipotentiary, a legal commentator, etc.). This is presumably the meaning Sokoloff had in mind with the (inaccurate) translation of *dsṭwrn/dstwrn* as 'authority' in his dictionary, which, however, does not fit in with the context of the two abovementioned passages of the Talmud.[23] In the context of property law or procedural law *dastwar* is a technical term with far-reaching legal implications that are not immediately visible by a general rendering and have to be explicated.[24] As we have elucidated above in the chapters on sale and civil proceedings, *dastwar* denotes in the context of a civil trial regarding a property right the 'legal predecessor' (Lat. *auctor*) of a person to whom a certain object has been transferred (by sale, barter, gift, or in some other manner). The *dastwar* is the previous owner (or holder) of the transferred object, who was previously entitled to it and is now obliged to guarantee that the transfer of the object to the new owner (holder) is legal and to defend the new owner (holder) in court against claims of a third party (comparable to the *auctor* in ancient Roman law).[25] The abstract form *dastwarīh*, meaning 'legal authorization, entitlement,

21 For an extensive discussion of these passages see Macuch 2008a. On the frequent suffix *-ēn* see Durkin-Meisterernst 2014, § 325, pp. 166–167.

22 See Kreyenbroek 1987, p. 165.

23 Sokoloff 2002, p. 345.

24 This term has also been misunderstood in earlier translations of these sentences, since most authors have attempted to relate it in some manner to the word 'field', which occurs in both Talmud passages. Levy (1876 [1924], vol. I, p. 415), referring to Persian *dastūr*, 'venia, promissio', interprets it as 'Pachtverhältnis, Beaufsichtigung des Feldes'; Goldschmidt (1897–1935, vol. V, p. 911 and vol. IX, p. 306) has 'Pacht'; Fleischer, referring to Persian *dastwara* 'was jmd. mit seiner Hände Arbeit gewinnt', has 'Pachtsumme' (*apud* Levy 1876 [1924], vol. I, p. 443); Jastrow (1926/1950, vol. I, p. 303) ignores the Iranian provenance of the term and explains it as a Dithpe. or Dispe. of *ʾsr* ('to surround, enclose, to chain, imprison') *i. e.* 'a binding relation, the relation of a serf or peasant, a sort of tenancy'; Telegdi (1935, p. 240, number 53) correctly identifies it as an Iranian loanword, but cites the wrong (and misleading) explanation of Bartholomae ('Vertreter einer Processpartei…ihr Mandatar, Stellvertreter, Anwalt').

25 See Chapters IV, pp. 385–387, and VI, pp. 542–544. On *dastwar/dastwarīh* in this sense see also Macuch 1988 and 1993, pp. 87–101. This meaning is now spectacularly confirmed by the Tabarestān documents, see Macuch 2016a, pp. 150–151, with further references.

empowerment' in a general context, refers in this specific setting to the act of guaranteeing as 'legal predecessor' (*dastwar/auctor*) the legality of a transaction in court and is best translated by '*auctor*-ship'.

This specific meaning of the word in procedural law is presumably a further development of the technical term as it was formed in the context of property law. In the latter field *dastwar*, lit. 'entitled, empowered (person)', designates someone who has a *right* or *title* to a specific property. The exact form of 'entitlement' (*dastwarīh*) is not immediately visible by the use of this expression alone, since the *dastwar's* title could relate to the 'substance, capital, principal' (*bun*) or to the 'increase, fruit, product' (*bar*) of a specific 'thing' (*xwāstag*), and did not necessarily have to include ownership in both categories. As we have seen above, every 'thing' (*xwāstag*) was divided theoretically into the two main categories of 'substance' (*bun*) and 'fruit(s)' (*bar*) with significant implications in all areas of property law.[26] A person's 'entitlement' (*dastwarīh*) could hence pertain to the substance (*bun*) of a property or to its income (*bar*) and could also be restricted to legal possession (*dārišn*). It could also include both of these categories, giving the *dastwar* full ownership rights (*xwēšīh*) of both *bun* and *bar*. The exact nature of the entitlement was determined in controversial cases by the court.

Taking these different uses of the word into consideration, *dastwar* has three main meanings, depending on the context in which it appears:

1. in a general context: 'person having (legal or religious) authority' (*e.g.* a competent jurist or theologian, a State official, a plenipotentiary, a legal commentator, etc.);
2. in property law: 'person having an (unspecified) right or title to property' (as owner or holder of a 'thing' [*xwāstag*] with regard to its 'substance' [*bun*], or its 'fruit' [*bar*] or to both categories);
3. in procedural law: 'legal predecessor, *auctor*' (previous owner or holder of a transferred object, who is obliged to guarantee the legality of the transfer in court).

The two Talmudic passages with the Iranian expression discuss completely different cases, but they have one thing in common: the technical term is used in connection to landed property in the sense of a 'person having an (unspecified) right or title to property' (number 2 above). In the *Ārakhin* it refers to someone who is entitled to an inherited field (*śdh ʾḥwzh*); in the *Qiddušin* to a person entitled to a group of fields or an 'estate' (*bqʿh*). The *Ārakhin* passage states that a person is not allowed to consecrate his entire property for a sacred purpose, with obviously one exception: he may set apart his inherited field entirely for a pious purpose in the 'manner of an entitled person' (*b-dstwrn*, MP. **dastwarēn*).[27] In the *Qiddušin* a bridegroom shows his prospective bride his property consisting of an estate or a group of fields 'as a person entitled' to it (*b-dstwrʾ/dstwryn*, MP *dastwar/*dastwarēn*).[28]

26 See Chapter III, pp. 197–202.

In the context of Sasanian law, if a person holds land 'as a *dastwar*; in the manner of a *dastwar*' this implies that he has *some kind of title* to the land and/or its produce. This right or title could include ownership (*xwēšīh*) of the substance (*bun*), but was often restricted to ownership of the income (*bar*), particularly with regard to the joint-property of co-heirs (*xwāstagdārān*), or only possession (*dārišn*) of the income (*i. e.* usufruct) with regard to leasehold property or property held in pledge. In both passages of the Talmud the Iranian expression designates a person who has a title to a plot of land, giving him power of disposal over the produce or crops, but not over the substance, *i. e.* the land or estate, itself. In the *Ārakhin* a person is allowed in only one case to dedicate all of his landed property to a sacred purpose: if he retains the right to its income 'in the manner of a *dastwar*', that is, as a person who continues to benefit in some manner from the produce or fruits of the endowed property. In the *Qiddušin* the *dastwar* is a bridegroom who profits from the income of a group of fields or an estate either as usufructuary or as owner of the income, without being owner of the substance, the land, itself.

It is especially noteworthy that the commentators of these passages, by selecting the Iranian technical term, were able *to express all these complicated details in a single word.* We can hence conclude that they were well acquainted with the intricacies of Sasanian property law. Moreover, in these passages the term refers to Jews, not to heathens, allowing the further conclusion that the rabbis were not only fully versed in this field and knew its complex vocabulary, but adapted a term that could only be understood in a context corresponding conceptually to that of Sasanian property law. We have in fact good reason to assume that the legal notion underlying the term *dastwar* was well known, since there is another revealing discussion in the Talmud on one of the fundamental distinctions in this field, the difference between the right of usufruct, on the one hand, and ownership rights of the fruits, on the other, an important concept in Iranian property law (see below, section 1.2).

27 *Ārakhin* 28a: 'If the Merciful had only written: "*of all which is his*", then one could assume that one may not renounce (for sacred purposes) everything one has, but that one may renounce one kind (of property) entirely, thus the Merciful wrote: "*of the persons*", but not all persons. And if the Merciful had only written: "*of the persons*", (one could assume, the reason is that) it is impossible (to live) without labour, but (in the case of) a field (*śdh*) it is possible (to hold it) in the manner of a *dastwar*.' (Goldschmidt 1897–1935, vol. IX, p. 306, 20–24; cited and discussed in Macuch 2008a, p. 127).

28 *Qiddušin* 60b: '(If he says:) "under the condition that I show you land (of the size requiring a) *kor* (of seed) (*byt kwr*)", then she is betrothed to him and he should show it to her; and if he shows it to her in a group of fields (*bqʿh*), then she is not betrothed to him.' (*Gemara*): '(If he says:) "under the condition that I show you land (of the size requiring a) *kor* (of seed) (*byt kwr*) [etc.]" it is taught: she only wanted to see that belonging to him. "If he shows it to her in a group of fields, then she is not betrothed to him": is it not self-evident? In the case he holds it as a *dastwar*.' (Goldschmidt 1897–1935, vol. V, p. 910.11–12; 910.21–911.2; cited and discussed in Macuch 2008a, p. 128).

Another well-known Iranian loanword, *dastgird* 'estate', is attested in the phrase *dsqrt᾽ d-ʿbdy* 'estate of slaves' in *Giṭṭin* 40a.[29] As we have seen in Chapter III, the *dastgird* is defined exactly in a legal context as a plot of land (of any size) which is cultivated, has access to an irrigation canal and on which roads and houses are built, in contrast to plain *zamīg* 'land', the term for uncultivated land without the components defining an 'estate'.[30] The *Giṭṭin* passage is concerned with the consequences of the sale of an 'estate of slaves' (*dsqrt᾽ d-ʿbdy*), obviously belonging to a Jew, to a heathen or non-Jew. As far as I can see, the exact Middle Persian equivalent of the Talmudic expression is not attested in Pahlavi sources, but the practice of binding slaves to the estate, as suggested in the *Giṭṭin*, is mentioned in Sasanian law. According to an informative passage of the Law-book animals and slaves (*stōr-iz anšahrīg*) belonged to the estate (*dastgird*) on which they worked and were alienated together with the land.[31] These slaves obviously had the status of *glebae adscripti*, were engaged in agriculture, bound to the soil, and transferred together with the animals when the estate changed owners. This Iranian practice seems to be referred to in the Talmud in connection to the sale of a *dsqrt᾽ d-ʿbdy*, an estate to which slaves were bound, by a Jew to a non-Jew.[32] Although the phrase is not explained (as none of the abovementioned technical terms) we may conclude from the context on manumission in which it appears, that the slaves bound to the soil (and referred to here) were Jews, who were to be manumitted properly and set free when an estate was sold in order not to be transferred with the land on which they worked into the possession of a non-Jew. The use of the technical term reveals that the Iranian practice of alienating slaves together with the estate was known and that the rabbis took appropriate measures to avoid the disadvantageous legal consequences of these transactions between Jews and non-Jews.

One of the remarkable passages of the Talmud indirectly illustrates the tense relationship between Jews and Persian fiscal authorities by making use of an Iranian expression in translation, not because the precise original technical term was unknown, but in order to obscure its exact meaning. In *Nedarim* 62b the expression *ʿbd᾽ d-nwr᾽* 'servant/slave of the fire' is attested in an exceptional context, that of a ruse intended to avoid paying the poll tax to the Persians.

29 See Geiger 1935, pp. 123–128, who has the correct meaning 'Landgut' (p. 125) and quotes previous (wrong) translations of the Talmudic phrase as 'Dorf der Sklaven' (Levy), 'Sklavenmarkt', 'Marktplatz' (Krauss); 'a settlement of slaves' (Jastrow; *apud* Geiger, *ibid.*, p. 124).

30 All attestations should be taken into consideration (Macuch 1993, pp. 700 and 740), see especially MHD 19.5–7, *ibid.*, p. 159 and commentary pp. 165–166; see also Chapter III above, pp. 243–244. For a general discussion of the term (not only in a legal context) see now Panaino 2022a.

31 MHD 18.9–10 (Macuch 1993, p. 158, and 1981, p. 80).

32 Goldschmidt 1897–1935 (vol. V), p. 485.

The text discusses the question, whether it is lawful for a master (a rabbinical disciple or scholar) to use certain strategies in order to avoid paying the poll (or capitation) tax (*krgʾ*), to which the Jews were liable in fourth century Babylonia. The discussion ends in the context of a longer passage with the comment: 'A rabbinical disciple/scholar is permitted to say: "I am a servant/slave of the fire (*ʿbdʾ dnwrʾ*) and do not pay the poll tax (*krgʾ*)." '[33]

The poll or capitation tax at this period was a considerable burden that could lead to ruin and slavery, forcing people to sell their property in order to pay the demanded amount with dramatic consequences if they could not bring up the sum. If no patron accepted to pay the required amount, insolvent taxpayers were left with the choice between fleeing their homes or being enslaved.[34] Our passage describes a specific case, in which a rabbinical disciple or scholar is due to pay the poll tax during his sojourn in a place where his status is unknown and he is not registered. In his commentary Rava, a contemporary of Šābuhr II (309–379) and a master of the fourth generation of Talmudic scholars (d. 352), explicitly allows the disciple/scholar to refuse payment of the poll tax, justifying this view with reference to Ezra 7:24, according to which the personnel of a temple are exempt from paying diverse taxes, one of which is the poll tax. In this context he adds the strange sentence cited above permitting the disciple/scholar to declare that he is an *ʿbdʾ dnwrʾ* 'slave/servant of the fire', and therefore not liable to the capitation tax. This is an extraordinary statement, which has led to several curious (and highly improbable) explanations in a number of Talmudic studies, among these the notion that it designates a 'fire-worshipper', *i. e.* Zoroastrian. This is an impossible explanation, as it would imply that Rava encouraged rabbinic masters to declare that they were Zoroastrian apostates in order to avoid paying the poll tax.[35] The Iranian material, however, reveals that this was *not* what Rava had in mind, and that the ruse he proposed is far more refined.

33 For an extensive discussion of this term in the light of Sasanian law see Macuch 2002b. The whole passage runs: '(62a) Rava said: "It is permitted for a man to make himself known in a place where he is not known" … (62b) Rava said: "It is permitted for a rabbinical disciple/scholar to say: 'I will not pay the poll tax (*krgʾ*)' as it is written (Ezra 7:24): 'It shall not be lawful to impose tribute (*mndʾ*), tax (*blw*) or toll (*hlk*) on them (= the personnel of the temple).' And Rav Yehudah said: '*mndʾ* is the king's portion; *blw* is the poll tax (*ksp gwlgltʾ*) and *hlk* is the corvée.' " And Rava said: "A rabbinical disciple/scholar is permitted to say: 'I am a servant of the fire (*ʿbdʾ dnwrʾ*) and do not pay the poll tax (*krgʾ*).' " What is the reason? He only says it in order to drive away a lion from himself.' (Text and translation Goldschmidt 1897–1935, vol. IV, p. 963, and Goodblatt 1979, p. 281).

34 On the taxes and the background of the text see Goodblatt 1979. Although he discusses this passage and the term *ʿbdʾ d-nwrʾ* extensively, the results of his study cannot be upheld, since he does not take the Iranian legal material into consideration.

35 Neusner 1965–1970 (vol. IV, 1969), p. 88f. See the overview in Goodblatt 1979, pp. 282–287.

Three interpretations for *ʿbdʾ dnwrʾ* have been suggested in the vast literature on this subject:

1. 'servant of a fire-temple or a fire-priest';[36]
2. 'worshipper of the fire' (*i. e.* Zoroastrian);[37]
3. 'fire-priest' (*i. e.* Zoroastrian priest).[38]

In the light of the Iranian sources the only approximately correct definition is the first one, but although it already appears in several mediaeval commentaries to the Talmud (of Ran, Rosh and Rashbam)[39] the explanation is not precise enough and remains incomprehensible without knowledge of the Iranian legal background. The translated form *ʿbdʾ dnwrʾ* in fact renders *two* Iranian technical terms which are both attested in the context of fire foundations:

1. *bandag ī ātaxš/ātaxš-bandag/ādurān-bandag* 'servant/attendant of the fire';
2. *anšahrīg ī ātaxš* 'slave of the fire'.[40]

As we have seen in Chapter III (pp. 225–229), fire foundations could be huge institutions whose personnel encompassed not only Zoroastrian priests and guardians (*sālār*; in charge of the administration of the foundation), but included numerous other persons who worked in various positions within the foundation. In this context the technical terms *bandag ī ātaxš* (*ātaxš-bandag* or: *ādurān bandag*), on the one hand, and *anšahrīg ī ātaxš*, on the other, designate two distinct groups of laymen (not priests) engaged in the service of a fire foundation with divergent duties. The status of these two groups differed fundamentally. Whereas the *anšahrīg* was only a 'slave', that is, an unfree person, who was literally fixed to the estate on which he/she worked, the *bandag ī ātaxš* 'servant of the fire' could even be a high dignitary of the State, 'bound' only in a metaphorical sense to the fire. The slaves (*anšahrīg*) of a fire foundation cultivated the land and worked on the (often huge) estates dedicated to the sacred fire and were *not* necessarily Zoroastrians. The attendants (*bandag*), on the other hand, were Zoroastrians and free (or manumitted) persons involved in some manner in the upkeep (*dāštārīh*) of the sacred fire. That they could even be high dignitaries of the State, is demonstrated by the example of the famous prime minister Mihr-Narseh (5th century), who was subsequently engaged as 'attendant/servant' in the service (*bandagīh*) of several fires.[41] Contrary to the 'attendant/servant' (*bandag*), a 'slave' (*anšahrīg*) working on the estates of a fire foundation need not have been a Zoroastrian, but could belong

36 Newman 1932, p. 169; rejected by Goodblatt 1979, p. 283, on the grounds that 'the crucial word 'priest' or 'temple' is missing'
37 Frye 1963, p. 219, Neusner 1965–1970; vol. IV, 1969, pp. 88–89, and Goodblatt 1979, p. 284.
38 Hahn 1959, p. 158, among others.
39 Goodblatt 1979, p. 183, fn. 137, with further references.
40 For examples and attestations see Macuch 2002b.
41 See above Chapter III, pp. 226–227, and MHDA 39.11–17, 40.1–5 (Macuch 1981, p. 223).

to another religious group. Hamza Iṣfahānī in fact offers clear evidence on this matter, recounting that during the reign of Pērōz, son of Yazdegird (459–484 CE), the Jews of Isfahān were accused of having flayed two *hērbeds* alive. In retaliation half the Jewish population of Isfahān was slaughtered and the children of the Jews were transferred into the service of a fire-temple called Srōš Ādurān in the village of Harwān.[42] This short passage reveals unequivocally that Jews could be forced to work as slaves on the estates belonging to a Zoroastrian fire-temple.

The two Iranian technical terms 'slave of the fire' (*anšahrīg ī ātaxš*) and 'attendant/servant of the fire' (*bandag ī ātaxš*) are always distinguished in legal literature in the sense described above and never confused, but since *ʿbdʾ* renders both 'servant' and 'slave' the significant difference between the two Iranian terms is lost in translation. In the light of this legal background a completely different interpretation of our Talmudic passage becomes possible. A rabbinical disciple/scholar is allowed to claim, according to Rava, that he is an *ʿbdʾ dnwrʾ* 'slave/servant of the fire' in order to avoid having to pay the poll tax. By using the ambiguity of the translation, which could render either one of the two Iranian technical terms, he would circumvent an exact description of his status. He is definitely *not* declaring that he is an apostate, since the function he is referring to is not necessarily that of a *bandag ī ātaxš* (for which he must have been a Zoroastrian, therefore an apostate). He is only saying that he works on the estate of a fire foundation, hereby suggesting that he belongs to the personnel of a fire-temple (albeit only as an *anšahrīg ī ātaxš*), and is not liable to paying the poll tax. It seems that Rava explicitly allows the rabbinic disciple/scholar to use the ambiguity of the translated expression to his advantage.

In relation to the numerous Iranian loan words from daily life in the Talmud, Sasanian legal vocabulary seems to have been seldom used in the original. This is not as significant as it may initially appear. The legal material of the East (Nestorian) Christians in Syriac, especially the Law-book of Īšōʿbōxt, hardly leaves any Iranian legal terms in the original, although there can be no doubt that fundamental legal concepts are based on Sasanian law (see section 1.2 below). The passages of the Talmud utilizing Iranian terms suggest that these were employed either with explicit reference to Sasanian legal practice or when they were needed to express an *exactly defined legal concept* for which there was no equivalent or alternative expression. The technical terms taken from procedural law (such as *muhraqē wāwarīgānē* and *pursišn-nāmag*) demonstrate that the rabbis were well acquainted with the vocabulary of the Sasanian courts (and had to take their rulings into consideration), but there is no evidence that they were adapted to the practice of Jewish courts.[43] On the other hand, loan words

42 The passage is cited and discussed in MACUCH 2002b, p. 127; for the original text see GOTTWALDT 1844, text p. 56, 1–3; translation p. 41.

43 On Jewish and Sasanian courts see also Chapter VI, particularly pp. 529–532.

from Iranian property law comprising a mass of information in a single word (such as *dastwar* and *dastgird*) indicate that the underlying legal concept was not only known, but also accepted and integrated to a certain degree into Jewish property law (see also next section, 1.2). The use of these clearly defined Iranian terms in a context involving Jews would be otherwise inexplicable. The opposite effect took place, when two distinct Iranian terms (such as *anšahrīg ī ātaxš* and *bandag ī ātaxš*) were translated imprecisely as one general expression (*ʿbdʾ dnwrʾ*) obscuring the exact connotations of the original expressions in dealings with Persian officials. Interestingly, the use of an imprecise translation was evidently not considered as a misleading or false statement and was even recommended to rabbinical masters as a ruse to avoid taxation in their confrontations with Persian fiscal authorities.[44] Jewish legal authorities evidently made creative use of their knowledge of the legal background of these terms to circumvent objectionable demands of the State, without giving rise to any illegal action according to rabbinic norms.

1.2 Allusions to Sasanian institutions and concepts

The Iranian legal background shines through several lengthy discussions in the Talmud, in which Sasanian legal concepts are recognizable. Jewish legal authorities were clearly acquainted with some of the most complex institutions and theoretical distinctions, as we may infer from their controversial debates notably in the fields of property law and the law of obligations, both areas in which legal ideas very similar to Iranian juristic concepts are contemplated, if not necessarily adapted.

One of the unresolved controversies, repeatedly debated in different books of the Talmud, relates to a fundamental problem in the field of property rights.[45] Jewish legal authorities were obviously aware of the difficulties involved in assessing ownership rights, particularly if the title to a material 'thing' was restricted to its income or fruits. In this context several passages of the Talmud controversially discuss the question, whether 'ownership of the fruits' (*qinyan perōt*) of a specific property should be assessed as 'ownership of the substance' (*qinyan ha-gūf*) or whether these are two completely different categories.[46] The distinction between these two forms of 'ownership' is highly reminiscent of Iranian property law, but the similarity tends to disappear in modern scholarly treatises of the Talmudic passages. The two technical terms, *qinyan ha-gūf* 'ownership (or acquisition) of property/substance', and *qinyan perōt*, are constructed with

44 See also Macuch 2010b.
45 For an extensive discussion see Macuch 2015d.
46 *Baba Bathra* 50a, 136a–137b, 147b–148b; *Baba Mezia* 109b; *Baba Qamma* 88b, 90a; *Giṭṭin* 47b-48a.

the same word for 'ownership' (*qinyan*),[47] but the latter expression, *qinyan perōt*, is usually translated by 'usufruct'[48] or, more generally, 'the right to income'.[49] However, since the two expressions correspond exactly, the precise translation of *qinyan perōt* would in fact be '*ownership* (or acquisition) of the fruits', *not* 'usufruct'. Despite his (imprecise) translation of the term as 'usufruct', Herzog correctly observes that the Hebrew word cannot have been influenced by or derived from the Roman *ususfructus*, the source of our usufruct, since the latter means 'use of fruit' (relating to the use of an agricultural field for its crops or an orchard for its fruit, etc.).[50] There is no corresponding expression in Roman law to the Jewish legal term *qinyan perōt*, whereas the Sasanian *bar-xwēšīh* 'ownership of the fruit(s)' is a remarkable parallel, not only because of the similar construction of the term, but especially because of the underlying idea that ownership of the fruit(s) (*bar*) can be a *proprietary right in itself*, independent of ownership of the principal (*bun*).

As we have seen in Chapter III (pp. 197–202), Sasanian law divided each material 'thing; *res*' (*xwāstag*) into two categories, distinguishing theoretically between its 'substance, principal' (*bun*) and its 'fruit(s), income' (*bar*). Ownership of these two parts of a thing could be separated: the 'owner of the substance' (*bun-xwēš*) could be a different person from the one who owned the income, the 'owner of the fruit(s)' (*bar-xwēš*), with significant implications in all fields of law. The heirs of a *paterfamilias*, for example, had a permanent and inheritable right to the income (*bar*) of specific forms of family property, without being owners of the substance (*bun*). This perpetual right was defined as 'ownership of the income' (*bar-xwēšīh*) and distinguished precisely from mere *usufruct*, the right to the income of another person's property, and *antichresis*, the right to the income of a property instead of interest. In short: Sasanian jurists distinguished between *bar-xwēšīh* 'ownership of the fruit(s)' as the permanent, inheritable right to the income of a specific property, and *bar-xward* (*bar-burd*; *bar-grift*) 'use of the income, usufruct, *antichresis*', the restricted right to the fruits for a certain specified period. 'Ownership of the fruit(s)' (*bar-xwēšīh*) was regarded as a *separate form of ownership*, to be furthermore distinguished from 'ownership of the substance' (*bun-xwēšīh*), but having similar legal implications with respect to permanency and inheritability.

In the Bavli the technical term *qinyan perōt* occurs in the post-*tannaitic* period (*i.e.* after ca. 220) in a division of opinion of two leading *Amoraim* (ca.

47 The word is employed according to Herzog 1936 (vol. I, p. 72) in the Talmud in the threefold sense of '(1) mode of acquiring; (2) that which is owned, the subject-matter of the right of owning vested in someone; (3) the right of owning, or ownership'; Elon 1994 (vol. I, Glossary, p. 7) has: (1) a formal mode of acquiring or conveying property or creating an obligation; (2) ownership; (3) contract; (4) abbreviation of *kinyan sudar*".

48 Herzog 1936, vol. I, p. 74.

49 Elon 1994, vol. I, Glossary, p. 7.

50 Herzog 1936, vol. I, p. 323.

220–500 CE), R. Joḥanan and R. Simon ben Lakish (Resh Lakish), both sages of the second generation of *Amoraim* in third century Palestine.[51] These two experts differ in their legal definition of *qinyan perōt.* R. Joḥanan explains it as an exact equivalent to *qinyan ha-gūf*, that is, he holds the opinion that the right to the income of a specific object should be regarded as 'ownership', just as the fundamental right to its substance (*gūf*) constitutes 'ownership'. Resh Lakish holds the opposite opinion: *qinyan ha-gūf* and *qinyan perōt* are two different kinds of rights and the latter term does not designate 'ownership' of the income, but only the right of usufruct. These two divergent interpretations are repeated in several case studies side by side indicating that the basic problem remained unresolved in the Talmudic period and that, moreover, both opinions were held to be necessary instruments for solving difficult legal problems (this is even explicitly stated in *Giṭṭin* 47b-48a). The main question in most of these case studies (which I have discussed extensively elsewhere)[52] is: does the perpetual right to the income of a specific property constitute ownership, or, in the words of the Talmud, is *qinyan perōt* like *qinyan ha-gūf* (*qnyn pyrwt k qnyn hqwp*) 'is ownership of the income like ownership of the substance'?[53] In R. Joḥanan's opinion both proprietary rights have under specific circumstances the same quality of 'ownership', whereas Resh Lakish distinguishes between the two, apparently defining *qinyan perōt* as usufruct in the sense of a right in *re aliena.*[54]

Both options represented by the opinions of R. Joḥanan and Resh Lakish were possible in Sasanian law, in sharp contrast to Roman law where the right of usufruct is a *ius in personam* (a personal right which can be enforced or claimed) and differs fundamentally from *dominium* 'ownership', a *ius in re* (a generally respected right to a thing). In Iranian jurisprudence the right to the income could be defined, depending on the specific circumstances of a case, either as a fixed category of ownership, as a proprietary right in itself (*bar-xwēšīh*), on the one hand, *or* as a restricted right to the fruits of property belonging to another person (*bar-xward*; *bar-burd*; *bar-grift*). The discussion in the Talmud regarding the two contrasting definitions of *qinyan perōt* only makes sense if we assume that a concept very similar to that of the Sasanian *bar-xwēšīh* was contemplated among the rabbis with divergent results. The very fact that this question is debated over and over again in the abovementioned passages of the Bavli makes it very likely that these two categories remained relevant due to Iranian legal theory and practice and that it was this specific legal background that encouraged the ongoing theoretical discussion regarding the interpretation of *qinyan perōt*. According to HERZOG, the dilemma was only solved in the *post*-Talmudic period, long after the fall of the Sasanian State, by the famous

51 HERZOG 1936, vol. I, p. 319. On the literary sources of Jewish law, the tannaitic and amoraic periods see ELON 1994, vol. III, pp. 1057ff.; on the leading *Amoraim ibid.*, p. 1086.
52 See MACUCH 2015d.
53 *Giṭṭin* 47b.
54 *Baba Bathra* 136a-137a; *Baba Qamma* 88b-89a; see also HERZOG 1936, vol. I, p. 322f.

philosopher and theologian of the Middle Ages, Maimonides (1135–1204), who adopted the opinion of Resh Lakish (that *qinyan perōt* is *not* like *qinyan ha-gūf*), hereby rejecting the concept of 'ownership of the income' as it was known in Sasanian law.[55]

Another debate in *Baba Bathra* 173b relates to a problem from the law of obligations, in the course of which the text explicitly refers to the 'law of the Persians'. The passage cites controversial opinions of several Jewish legal authorities on a question of suretyship (guarantee), which seems to have caused considerable confusion both among earlier rabbinic authorities of the Talmud as well as in recent studies.[56] As we have elucidated in Chapter IV, different forms of suretyship emerged in Iranian law in the course of a long historical development of personal security, permitting a creditor (lender) to look to a third party for satisfaction if the debtor (borrower) was unable or unwilling to repay a loan he had received from the creditor.[57] In the Sasanian legal system archaic forms of personal security continued to exist side by side with fairly recent types of suretyship apparently causing confusion even among legal experts. The exact form of suretyship was determined by specific formal words in the loan contract, expanding or limiting the commitment of the surety (guarantor) and the rights of the creditor. A major difficulty emerged due to these different types of personal security in the credit law of both legal systems and is discussed in both Rabbinic and Sasanian legal texts: when exactly, under which specific circumstances, does the creditor have the right to exact payment from the surety? It is in this context that one of the rabbis in the Talmud explicitly relates one of the explanations to the 'law of the Persians'.

The discussion in the abovementioned passage of the Talmud refers to a text in the *Mishna*,[58] in which two types of suretyship are mentioned very shortly with no further explanations:[59]

1. The first type, strangely, forbids the creditor to make a claim against the surety (guarantor). This ruling creates a major problem in the ensuing rabbinic discussion, since it does *not* correspond with the obvious reason for

55 Herzog 1936, vol. I., p. 321.

56 I have discussed this passage extensively in Macuch 2016b; see also Secunda 2014, pp. 93–100, 107–109, with further references.

57 On suretyship see Chapter IV, pp. 349–359.

58 The code edited by R. Judah the Patriarch c. 200 CE, a collection of statements, discussions and Biblical interpretations of the *Tannaim*, Rabbinic sages from c. 10–220 CE.

59 The whole passage in the *Mishna* runs: 'If a man lent his fellow money through a guarantor (surety), he may not exact payment from the guarantor. If he said: "On the condition that I may exact payment from whom I wish", he may exact payment from the guarantor. R. Shimʿon b. Gamliel says: "If the borrower (debtor) has property, in either case [the creditor] may not exact payment from the guarantor."' (translation according to Secunda 2014, p. 93, where the original text of this passage may also be found.) See also Goldschmidt 1897–1935 (here 1933), vol. 6, 1401.

agreeing on suretyship in the first place (*i. e.* providing additional security for the creditor), and is hence in need of explanation.

2. The second type of suretyship is defined exactly by a precise formulation in the credit contract or stipulation: the creditor/lender gives the loan 'on the condition that I may exact payment from whom I wish'. That is, the creditor has agreed to giving a loan on the condition that he may approach either the principal debtor or the surety and is hence allowed to exact payment from both or even from the surety directly. This ruling is in turn restricted (by R. Shimʿon b. Gamliel): the creditor may make a claim against the surety in both cases *only* if the (principal) debtor is insolvent.

The allusion to Persian law appears in the ensuing rabbinic discussion in the cited Talmudic passage offering a remarkable explanation for the abovementioned first ruling, forbidding the creditor to put a claim against the guarantor.[60] Rabba and Rav Yosef relate this decision to a specific form of suretyship, in which the creditor cannot claim payment from the guarantor, since the latter can refuse to pay, speaking the words: 'You have handed over to me a man; and a man I have handed over to you'. This (rather obscure and unexplained) phrase apparently refers to a historically early type of suretyship which was still practiced in Sasanian law (beside other forms): the surety does *not* agree to make payment in lieu of the debtor, but pledges to deliver either the principal debtor or another person (*tan*) agreed upon as security to the creditor when payment is due. The obligation of the surety ends with 'handing over the man' and he cannot be called upon to repay the debt. According to these two rabbis this is the reason why the creditor in the *Mishna* cannot reclaim the debt from the guarantor in the first case noted above. As we have seen in Chapter IV the surety did not accept liability for the debt in this ancient form of personal security, but ensured that the debtor would not leave his original location ('suretyship of location') or he promised to deliver the latter (or another person offered as security) to the creditor on non-fulfilment of contract ('suretyship of delivery').[61] In the first type the surety guarantees that the principal debtor will remain accessible

60 The whole text in Baba Bathra 173b runs: 'What is the reason [that the *mishna* does not require the guarantor to pay the loan]? Both Rabba and Rav Yosef say: [Because the guarantor can say,] "You have handed over to me a man; and a man I have handed over to you." Rav Naḥman raised an objection: *This is the law of the Persians! "The law of the Persians"?! On the contrary; they pursue the guarantor!* Rather [the following is Rav Naḥman's objection]: "[Is not this ruling] like Persian law [where we find that the judges] do not give reasoning for their matters (*i. e.* rulings)!" Rather said R. Naḥman: What is [the meaning of] "he may not exact payment from the guarantor?" [That] he may not demand [payment from] the guarantor first. [...] And if he said, "On the condition that I may exact payment from whom I wish," he may demand [payment from] the guarantor first.' (The translation follows SECUNDA 2014, p. 94; the italics, emphasizing the section on Persian suretyship, are mine); see also GOLDSCHMIDT 1897–1935 (here 1933), vol. 6, 1401.

61 See Chapter IV, pp. 357–359.

to the creditor and not escape payment (by hiding or fleeing); in the second type he promises to seize the debtor (or another person agreed upon as security) and deliver him to the creditor.

The connection to Persian law is made by Rav Naḥman, one of the Babylonian Amoraim (c. 200–500 CE) depicted as a Jewish authority acculturated to Persian elite society.[62] Seeing a parallel to Iranian law, he comments this interpretation of the two rabbis with the exclamation 'This is the law of the Persians!' He obviously understood that the interpretation of the mishnaic ruling by Rabba and Rav Yosef was *very similar to or even followed Iranian law*. His comment is in fact a perfectly correct assessment of the type of suretyship in Sasanian law described above, but it caused complete confusion in later interpretative layers of this passage, leading to a different (and faulty) analysis of this phrase.[63] The main objection to Rav Naḥman's (correct) assessment is that the surety was—contrary to the latter's statement—indeed pursued in Persian law and made liable for the debt. Given the different forms of personal security in Iranian law, this objection is not wrong, but conveys an incomplete picture: besides the type referred to by Rabba and Rav Yosef, there were other forms of personal security in Sasanian law allowing the creditor to sue the surety either in the event of the debtor's insolvency (according to another comment attributed to Rav Naḥman) or even immediately under specific conditions. The rabbinic discussion in fact alludes to at least three (maybe four) different types of suretyship, all well attested in Sasanian law. Whereas Rabba and Rav Yosef seem to have had 'suretyship of performance' (subsuming 'suretyship of location'[64] and 'suretyship of delivery') in mind, a form, which Rav Naḥman correctly identified as one of the specifically Iranian variants of personal security, later layers of the text probably refer to those more recent types of guarantee, known as 'accessory suretyship' and 'indemnity' (on these see above Chapter IV, pp. 357–359). There is no reason to doubt Rav Naḥman's precise knowledge of a rather complex and sophisticated branch of Sasanian law and his correct assessment of different forms of personal security, without having to assume that his comment on Persian law was derogatory, as has been suggested in several recent studies of this passage.

These examples demonstrate that Jewish legal authorities were indeed acquainted with diverse concepts of Iranian law in the Sasanian period, even though these cases from the complex fields of property law and suretyship seem to have caused some confusion among those who were no longer well informed, notably later commentators, who were at a loss trying to understand the concise remarks of their predecessors.

62 SECUNDA 2014, p. 95.
63 See the extensive discussion of the different layers in SECUNDA 2014, pp. 95–97.
64 Called 'suretyship of place' in MACUCH 2016b; on these diverse forms of personal security see above Chapter IV, pp. 349–359.

2 East Christian (Nestorian) law

In contrast to the numerous studies on juridical issues in the Talmud, the legal literature of the East Christians has hardly received the attention it deserves in the light of Iranian jurisprudence. Apart from a few remarks in the edition of Syriac law-books by SACHAU more than 100 years ago and, most recently, the contributions of RICHARD PAYNE, who is, as far as I can see, the only researcher to take Sasanian law into account in his contributions, the numerous correspondences between the two legal systems have remained largely unnoticed.[65] Particularly important for a comparison between the two systems is the *Corpus Iuris* of Īšōʿbōxt, the archbishop of the Christians in eighth century Pars, who wrote this text in Middle Persian (either in the Pahlavi or in the Syriac script) for the use of the Christian community after the downfall of the Sasanian Empire, remarking that before him there was no *written* text on the civil law (of the Christians) in Pars.[66] With the sole exception of marriage law his Law-book is based almost completely on Sasanian customary law which continued to be practiced to a large extent in Iranian courts after the fall of the Sasanian Empire before the formation and implementation of Islamic jurisprudence.[67] A full appreciation of the rich legal material in Syriac lies beyond the scope of this study and will still have to be undertaken. The following observations are hence restricted to a few significant correspondences and adaptations detectable in the use of Iranian loanwords or the application of Sasanian legal concepts.

2.1 Iranian legal terms in the *Corpus Iuris* of Īšōʿbōxt

Īšōʿbōxt's *Corpus Iuris*, as we have already noted in Chapter I above, has only survived in a Syriac translation of the Middle Persian original, which was prepared by an anonymous translator of whom nothing is known apart from the fact that he took up this work at the instigation of the Nestorian patriarch Timotheos (780–823 in Baghdad) at a time when the author was no longer alive.[68] As the German editor of the *Corpus Iuris*, EDUARD SACHAU, has rightly remarked, the quality of this translation is truly admirable, not only due to the difficult task of rendering a complex legal text written in an Indo-European language into a Semitic one, but due to the dexterity with which the translator has managed to convey complicated trains of thought and to find precise Syriac equivalents for Pahlavi technical terms.[69] Although the Syriac version is a remarkable

65 SACHAU 2014; PAYNE 2015a; 2015b; 2016, 2017; DE MENASCE 1964c (1985) discusses very shortly a few Iranian legal terms in Īšōʿbōxt's Corpus Iuris in the original and in translation; on Iranian legal terms in Īšōʿbōxt see also MACUCH 1989 and 2019a.

66 According to SACHAU 1914, intr., p. X.

67 On Īšōʿbōxt see Chapter I, p. 48.

68 SACHAU 1914, intr., p. XV, and 289.

69 SACHAU 1914, intr., p. XV.

achievement, it is most deplorable for all those interested in Sasanian law that the translator has reduced the use of Iranian technical terms to an absolute minimum, utilizing them only as a last resort, when they were needed to express an *exactly defined legal concept* for which no appropriate Syriac equivalent could be found (comparable to the use of Iranian technical terminology in the Talmud). Due to the translator's intellectual fervour in this respect the adaptation of fundamental concepts of Sasanian law in Īšōʿbōxt's *Corpus Iuris* remains in many instances initially hidden, but emerges clearly when these basic tenets are compared with the corresponding legal material in Pahlavi texts, revealing how Zoroastrian elements were adapted to Christian law (see section 2.2 below).

In a few cases the translator retains Iranian technical terms in the original, adding Syriac explanations, which, however, do not suffice to disclose the legal meanings of the Iranian terms. But Īšōʿbōxt illustrates how these expressions were employed by including short case studies from legal practice to illuminate important Sasanian theoretical concepts that would remain unrecognized without the help of his work.[70] The original Sasanian legal terminology is retained in the two expressions *passand* (lit. 'pleasure, liking') and *behdādestānīh* (lit. 'good/better justice'; the NP form, corresponding to MP *wehdādestānīh*). The anonymous Syriac translator renders Pahlavi *passand* by Syriac *ḫasīrūt dīnā* 'decrease, reduction of justice' ('Rechtsminus' in Eduard SACHAU's German translation) and *behdādestānīh* as *yaṯīrūt dīnā* 'extension of justice' ('Rechtsplus' according to SACHAU), both in fact inadequate translations, which do not convey the technical meanings of the words, as the translator seems to have realized.[71] The two Iranian terms denote specific approaches to decision-reaching in legal practice permitting legal authorities to take exceptional circumstances into consideration in the interest of 'higher justice' instead of following legal prescriptions according to strict judicial criteria.

As we have already noted in Chapter I, Īšōʿbōxt defines the concept of *passand* as 'acquiescing to less than required by law' and exemplifies it by a case of loan and debt. A debtor owns both money and interest to another man (creditor), but cannot pay back both the principal debt and interest because of his personal situation (poverty, illness, etc.). He asks the creditor to refrain from claiming interest. Legal authorities can admonish the creditor to accept the request of the debtor and restrict his claim to the principal debt, or, in other words, to practice *passand* 'leniency (in justice)'. The concept involves the voluntary *renouncement of a legal right* given to one legal party by contract or agreement in the interest of higher justice.[72]

70 See also above Chapter I, pp. 70–72.

71 Īšōʿbōxt, Book I, Chapters V and VI (SACHAU 1914, pp. 13 and 15); Book V, Chapter VIII, §3 (SACHAU 1914, p. 167); Book V, Chapter XI, §6 (SACHAU 1914, p. 175); Book V, Chapter XIII, §7 (SACHAU 1914, p. 179).

72 SACHAU 1914, pp. 13, 15; 289–290.

The term *behdādestānīh* (*wehdādestānīh*, lit. 'good/better justice'), on the other hand, designates a legal procedure by which one is willing to go beyond the boundaries of formal prescriptions by *extending a legal right* given to another person.[73] Īšōʿbōxt exemplifies the concept by the case of a daughter who is given as inheritance the same share of property as a son, although a daughter is legally entitled to only half the share of a son.[74] By bequeathing to the daughter the share of a son so that she may marry well, the testator does more than is legally required, extending the right of the daughter to inheritance according to the notion of *behdādestānīh*.[75]

The opposite principles of *passand* and *behdādestānīh* are important instruments of law providing flexibility in legal practice by enabling the *renouncement* and *extension* of a legal right, which Īšōʿbōxt has quite obviously adapted directly from Zoroastrian law. Both terms reflect in fact the same notion that in specific cases 'better justice' *cannot* be achieved by a strict application of legal provisions, but by transcending them, by making concessions (*passand*), on the one hand, or by doing more than the minimum required by law (*behdādestānīh*), on the other. This concept of attaining a just decision in legal practice by a flexible handling of norms and regulations according to the 'spirit of the law' (instead of following the 'letter of the law') corresponds well with Christian values, but is in fact adapted from Zoroastrian jurisprudence, as the terminology shows.

Īšōʿbōxt's translator notes another technical term in the original, *abēsaxwanīh*, lit. 'renunciation, waiver (of a claim)', rendering it by Syriac *mbarayūṯā* 'renunciation, avoidance'.[76] The Iranian expression is also noted by Jean DE MENASCE in his list of Pahlavi expressions in the *Corpus Iuris*, but he wrongly adds that it is 'a word not hitherto found in Pahlavi texts'.[77] The term is, on the contrary, rather well attested in a legal context as ⟨'p'shwn'⟩ *abēsaxwan*, but the spelling has been confused in several instances with the similarly written ⟨'p'yšn'⟩ *abāyišn*, causing misunderstandings.[78] Īšōʿbōxt employs the abstract *abēsaxwanīh* in a chapter on inheritance, inducing SACHAU to translate it as 'renunciation of inheritance' ('Erbschaftsverzicht'),[79] but although the abstract form is in fact also attested in the Sasanian Law-book in a sentence involving inheritance (MHD 64.6), the term is not exclusively used in this context.

73 On this expression and its use in Pahlavi legal texts see MACUCH 2019a with further references.
74 SACHAU 1914, pp. 13,15; 290; on inheritance see above Chapter III, pp. 230–235.
75 On the phrase *pad war … wehdādestāntar*, lit. '(he/she is) better (suited) for (taking) the oath for better justice', in the context of the oath see above Chapter VI, pp. 554–555.
76 Īšōʿbōxt, Book V, Chapter VI; SACHAU 1914, pp. 150–155. I have discussed this term extensively in MACUCH 1989, albeit without reference to the corresponding Bactrian expression, which was not yet known at the time this article was published. See also Chapter III, p. 245.
77 DE MENASCE 1964c (1985), p. 122.
78 See MACUCH 1993, pp. 51–52, note 10, on *abēsaxwan*.
79 SACHAU 1914, p. 151

The literal meaning of *abēsaxwan* is 'without word/speech' (< *abē* + *saxwan*), *i. e.* 'without claim'; the abstract *abēsaxwanīh* 'waiver, renunciation' denotes the act of abandoning a claim or refraining from asserting a claim (or exercising a right) in any legal context, not only that of inheritance. It is well attested in the Sasanian Law-book in the fixed formula: *az … abēsaxwan būdan* 'to renounce, waive a claim (to something)' in the context of the following legal issues:

1. Debt remission. Case studies: Three men who are partners have taken out jointly a loan. The creditor (Farrox) waives his claim against one of the three men with regard to the whole sum: *Farrox pad ān xwāstag* ⟨NKSY'⟩ ***az mard-ē(w) abēsaxwan bawēd*** 'Farrox waives (his) claim against one man regarding that money'. According to the opinion of two legal experts the waiver does not cancel the obligation of the other two debtors to repay their shares of the loan: *bahr ī ōy ī* ***az-iš abēsaxwan bawēd*** *ud ān ī abārīg (ī) az abārīg xwāst tuwān bawēd ǰuttar* 'The share of the one (= debtor) against whom he (= the creditor) waives his claim and the (shares) of the other (debtors), from whom he (= the creditor) can claim (the loan), are separate'.[80] Compare also: *agar* ***az*** *xwāstag ī ōy kē ān xwāstag* ⟨NKSY'⟩ *tōzišn* ***abēsaxwan bawēd*** 'If he (= the creditor) waives (his) claim against him, who owes the money (= debtor)'.[81]
2. Right of lien. Case studies: A creditor who abstains from taking security in form of a pledge has not renounced his claim to repayment of the debt: *ka* ***az*** *xwāstag ī graw* ***abēsaxwan bawēd*** *ēg-iš drahm nē hišt bawēd* 'If he (= the creditor) waives (his) claim to a pledged object, then the money ("drahms" = debt) has not been remitted'.[82] Also: *Farrox xwāstag az andar Mihrēn ī* ***az-iš abēsaxwan būd*** *pad abām ī andar ān ī ka* ***abēsaxwan būd*** *Mihrēn ō Farrox abāyēd dād abāz grift nē pādixšāy* 'Farrox (= the creditor) is not entitled to take back the thing from Mihrēn (= the debtor) which he (= the creditor) had renounced for a debt that Mihrēn had to pay to Farrox at the time when he (= Farrox) had waived (his) claim'.[83]
3. Donation and inheritance. Case study: a *paterfamilias* (*kadag-xwadāy*) draws a document (*wizīr*) for his *pādixšāy*-wife, giving her the right to donate a thing (*xwāstag*) to a person of her choice, but bequeaths the thing in his last will (*handarz*) to a person of his own choice. Even if the wife consents to the will and 'has renounced the claim to that thing' (***az*** *ān xwāstag* ***abēsaxwan būd*** ***ēstēd***), she retains the right to make the donation despite her renunciation: ***abēsaxwanīh*** *rāy ǰuttar be nē bawēd* 'It is not different because of (her) waiver (of this right)'.[84]

80 MHD 2.14–16 (Macuch 1993, pp. 41,43).
81 MHD 89.9 (Macuch 1993, pp. 569, 572–573). For a discussion of this sentence see also Macuch 1989, pp. 154–155.
82 MHD 89.5–6 (Macuch 1993, pp. 569, 572).
83 MHD 99.13 (Macuch 1993, pp. 612, 621). For a discussion of this passage see also Macuch 1989, p. 155.
84 MHD 64.2–7 (Macuch 1993, pp. 434, 437; Macuch 1989, pp. 155–156).

The Syriac translation of Īšōʿbōxt renders *az … abēsaxwan būdan* 'to renounce, waive a claim' by the Paʿʿel and Eṯpaʿʿal forms of the root BRY 'to free oneself; to renounce; to desist from' in a context indicating a more extensive use of the technical term than suggested by SACHAU's translation 'renunciation of inheritance' ('Erbschaftsverzicht') in at least two instances.[85] In one of these a man renounces his right to a certain property (*gaḇrā meṯbarē men qenyānā*) and commits himself by written contract to desist from claiming a right to this property by litigation. This commitment implies that he may never conduct a lawsuit in this matter without the consent of his contractual partner.[86] The other passage (employing the exact translation of a Sasanian legal formula) states that a man is entitled to claim a right to a property that is not in his hand: *šallīṭ leh dlā neṯbarē menneh*, lit. 'he has the right not to waive (his) claim to it'. But if he has lost the right to this property in a lawsuit, then he is obliged to renounce his claim: *lā šallīṭ leh dlā neṯbarē menneh*, lit. 'he has no right except to renounce his claim to it'.[87] The Syriac translation renders almost slavishly the legal wording of the Pahlavi original, which we can easily reconstruct as **pādixšāy ka az-iš abēsaxwan nē bawēd* 'he has the right not to waive (his) claim to it' (= Syr. *šallīṭ leh dlā neṯbarē menneh*) and **nē pādixšāy bē ka az-iš abēsaxwan bawēd*, lit. 'he has no right/option except to waive (his) claim to it' (= Syr. *lā šallīṭ leh dlā neṯbarē menneh*), *i. e.* 'he is obliged to waive his claim'. The fixed formula *nē pādixšāy bē ka* 'he/she has no right than; he/she has no (other) option but', meaning 'he/she is obliged, has the duty, is compelled to (do/say/perform something)', the original of Syriac *lā šallīṭ leh dlā*, is common in Iranian legal *argot* and well attested in several passages of the Law-book, as in: *xwāstag* ⟨NKSYʾ⟩ … *nē pādixšāy bē ka stānēd* 'he has no (other) right/option than to accept the money' (= he is obliged to accept the money',[88] *nē pādixšāy hēnd bē ka-š sālārīh kunēnd* 'they have no right/option, but to perform guardianship' (= they are obliged to perform guardianship";[89] *ān stūrīh nē pādixšāy bē ka kunēd* 'she has the duty to perform as proxy'.[90]

This technical term is also attested in Bactrian sources as αβησαχοανο (F8, 9, 14'),[91] αβοσαχοανο (C15'*, aa26*, ab9)[92] and αβσαχοανο (C13f)[93] 'without claim'; also αβησαχοανιγο 'connected with the renunciation of a claim' (F2).[94] The latter

85 SACHAU 1914, p. 150. 8, 10, 18, 26; p. 152. 1, 4, 23, 30; p. 154. 1,5. For the full text of these two passages and a discussion of the context see MACUCH 1989, pp. 158–159.
86 Īšōʿbōxt, Book V, Chapter VI, § 10 (SACHAU 1914, pp. 152–153).
87 Īšōʿbōxt, Book V, Chapter VI, § 11 (SACHAU 1914, pp. 154–155).
88 MHD 40.9 (MACUCH 1993, pp. 280; 285)
89 MHD 45.16–17 (MACUCH 1993, pp. 305, 321).
90 MHD 101.2 (MACUCH 1993, pp. 614; 622), on these phrases see also Chapter I, pp. 87–88.
91 SIMS-WILLIAMS 2007, p. 184.
92 SIMS-WILLIAMS 2007, p. 186.
93 SIMS-WILLIAMS 2007, p. 186.
94 SIMS-WILLIAMS 2007, p. 184.

expression occurs in a document of manumission, called μολρογο αβησ̣α̣χοανιγο̣, lit. 'sealed document of renunciation (manumission)', recording the release of a slave named Zer, son of Bag-bandag, after his master has received full payment of the price from the slave himself.[95] In this context the master sets the slave free, obliging himself to refrain in the future from raising a claim to the manumitted slave using another fixed formula (possibly adapted from Sasanian law): αβησαχοανο οδο αβηαο̣[ι]σαρο (**F**8) and αβησα̣χοανο οδο αβηαοισαρο (**F**9) 'without claim and without argument', according to the translation by Nicholas Sims-Williams.[96] The same phrase is attested (as αβσαχοανο αβοισαρο 'without claim, without argument') in other Bactrian documents, among these a deed of gift (**C**13–14).[97] There might have been a corresponding formula in Sasanian law, but this is pure speculation, since it is not attested in any of the known Pahlavi legal sources. In this constellation the second expression αβηαοισαρο could have a far more concrete meaning, if it was indeed adapted from a Pahlavi **abēwizār* (< *abē* + *wizār* 'without payment'). The verb *wizārdan*, *wizār-* ('separate; explain, interpret; perform, fulfil, redeem'[98]) is amply (but not exclusively) attested in a legal context in the concrete sense of 'to pay, discharge', possibly a further semantic extension of 'to atone' for a sin or offence by paying a fine or compensation (as in: *pādixšāy ka drahm nē wizārēd* 'he is entitled not to pay the money [lit. drachms]';[99] *drahm be wizār* 'pay the money!';[100] *ān xwāstag* ⟨NKSY'⟩ *nē wizārd* 'the money is not paid';[101] *tā drahm wizārēnd* 'until they pay the money',[102] among numerous other attestations). In this light the most likely translation for αβηαοισαρο would be 'without payment; without compensation'. If the provenance of the Bactrian formula is indeed Sasanian, the whole phrase αβησαχοανο οδο αβηαο̣ισαρο would correspond to a Pahlavi **abēsaxwan ud abēwizār* 'without claim and without compensation', constituting a guarantee that the person using this legal formula will neither lodge a claim against his contractual partner, nor ask him for any kind of payment or compensation in this matter in the future.

Another Iranian technical term Īšōʿbōxt's translator retains in the heading of a short chapter on guardianship is *dūdag-sālārīh* 'guardianship of the family'.[103] Interestingly, § 1 of this section notes a question that is not discussed in the Pahlavi sources, but might have been handled similarly in both Sasanian and Christian law: is the oral last will of a *paterfamilias* on the day of his demise

95 For the whole text of this document see Sims-Williams 2012a, pp. 38–41.
96 Sims-Williams 2012a, pp. 38, 39.
97 See attestations in Sims-Williams 2007, p. 186.
98 MacKenzie 1971, p. 92.
99 MHD 38.9 (Macuch 1993, pp. 278; 283).
100 MHD 38.11 (Macuch 1993, pp. 278; 283).
101 MHD 38.15 (Macuch 1993, pp. 278; 283).
102 MHD 39.5 (Macuch 1993, pp. 279; 284).
103 Īšōʿbōxt, Book IV, Chapter IX (Sachau 1914, pp. 126–127); see also de Menasce 1964, p. 122.

regarding the installation of a family guardian (Syr. *rēš baytā*; MP *dūdag-sālār*) valid? The passage confirms that the will (*puqdānā* 'disposition') of the *pater-familias* (*d-mārā baytā*; MP *kadag-xwadāy*) spoken on his deathbed is considered as valid and the person he chooses should be installed as family guardian. Īšōʿbōxt's translator retains the important distinction between 'master of the house' (*mārā baytā*) for *kadag-xwadāy* and 'head of the house' (*rēš baytā*) for *dūdag-sālār*, although the latter translation is not an exact rendering of the Pahlavi original term.

Missing in JEAN DE MENASCE's list of Iranian legal loanwords is the compound **zūr-gird* 'false document', written ⟨zwlrgrd⟩ with a superfluous ⟨l⟩, which might have stood in the Pahlavi script for the original ⟨zwl⟩ *zūr* 'false, deceitful', and was erroneously retained in the Syriac script.[104] The literal meaning of the word is most likely, as PHILIPPE GIGNOUX[105] has suggested, 'fait faux', a fitting designation for a forged document, which has no legal validity and is not accepted as evidence in court according to the chapter of the *Corpus Iuris* in which it occurs. As far as I can see, the word is not attested in any of the extant Pahlavi legal texts.

2.2 Iranian concepts in East Christian law

The significant impact of Sasanian law is apparent in several distinctly Iranian concepts in the Syriac legal material, which have been partly discussed in the previous chapters. As SACHAU has already noted, Īšōʿbōxt divides law into three areas: (1) *nāmōsā*, law in its abstract form, teaching people what to do and to avoid (= the ideal law of the New Testament); (2) *dīnā*, civil or common law; law in its concrete form (based on two sources, the New Testament and tradition, a modified form of Mosaic law); (3) *terīṣūṯā* 'integrity, rectitude, truthfulness, trustworthiness, righteousness': the law which is perceived in word (*bᵊ-melṯā*), thought (*bᵊ-ḥušāḇā*) and matter (*bᵊ-ṣḇūṯā*)[106] (by following ethical norms).[107] The Iranian provenance of the third area of law (*terīṣūṯā*) can easily be identified by the well-known Zoroastrian triad *humat, hūxt, huwaršt*.[108] Moral norms and ethical behaviour, marked by this triad, played an important part not only in Zoroastrian religious practice, but also in jurisdiction, both in the *ruwānīg* and the *hamēmālān* categories of offences. The evaluation of a person's guilt and his/her amount of culpability were based on an assessment of the intention

104 Īšōʿbōxt, Book 6, Chapter III, § 2, SACHAU 1914, pp. 190–191.
105 *Apud* CIANCAGLINI 2008, p. 173.
106 On *ṣḇūṯā* 'a matter, affair, thing; a possession, property, goods' see PAYNE SMITH 1903, p. 472; 'a matter, business', MACLEAN 1901, p. 262;
107 SACHAU 1914, pp. XII-XIII; Īšōʿbōxt, Book 1, Chapter III (SACHAU 1914, pp. 10–13).
108 This correspondence has already been noticed by SACHAU 1914, pp. XIII and 290–291. The terms *se gōwišnīh* and *se wāzag* 'three utterances' refer to the Zoroastrian triad in Pahlavi legal texts; see Chapter VI, p. 538.

(*menišn*; *kām*) of the perpetrator in combination with the act, the execution of the deed *(kunišn)*.[109] Hence Īšōʿbōxt's third category of law might in fact reflect a corresponding element of Zoroastrian legal theory and be the direct Syriac rendering of a MP term (one could think of *ahlawīh/ahlāyīh* 'righteousness', *ardāyīh* 'rectitude', *rāstīh* 'truthfulness, honesty' or *frārōnīh* 'righteousness, honesty'). But even if Syriac *terīṣūṯā* is not the translation of a Pahlavi term, the idea that moral integrity in thought, word and action constitutes the 'spirit of the law' and is far more relevant than the mere 'letter of the law', is clearly discernable in Zoroastrian legal practice.[110] It is in this context that Sasanian jurisprudence developed several methods by which the strict application of legal norms could be circumvented in the interest of 'better justice' (*weh-dādestānīh*; *meh-dādestānīh*) that were adapted into East Christian law, as we have noted above (section 2.1).

Besides the devices of *passand* and *weh-dādestānīh*, Īšōʿbōxt also makes use of another important Sasanian concept involving the distinction between proceedings and decisions based on legal theory/doctrine (*pad čāštag*) and those following legal practice (*pad kardag*).[111] The latter category presumably emerged in the course of legal practice in Sasanian law courts dealing with concrete lawsuits which required a far more flexible handling of juristic norms than envisaged in legal doctrine (*čāštag*). Without mentioning the Pahlavi technical terms, Īšōʿbōxt's translator renders these expressions by Syriac *bᵊ-dīnā* (for *pad čāštag* 'according to legal doctrine') and *bᵊ-mparnsānūṯā* (for *pad kardag* 'according to legal practice').[112] They are utilized in the *Corpus Iuris* especially in the chapters on the renunciation of a right (*abēsaxwanīh*; see section 2.1 above) and on credit law and pledge, in which also other parallels to Sasanian law may be detected. Although SACHAU comments on these two terms, translating *bᵊ-dīnā* by *'ex lege'*, and *bᵊ-mparnsānūṯā* as *'via administrationis'*, he had no knowledge of the corresponding categories or technical terms in Sasanian law and the underlying concept.[113] We can reasonably infer that the two Syriac expressions rendering *pad čāštag* and *pad kardag* stand for the corresponding methods of dealing with concrete legal cases in Iranian law. These could be decided either restrictively in a procedure following the rules and tenets of 'doctrine' or canonical law (*pad čāštag/bᵊ-dīnā*) *'ex lege'*

109 See Chapter V, pp. 411–422.

110 For an example see MACUCH 2022c.

111 On *čāštag* and *kardag* see Chapter I, pp. 66–72.

112 Īšōʿbōxt, Book V, Chapter VI, §2,5,7 (SACHAU 1914, pp. 151, 153) and Chapter VII, §2 (SACHAU 1914, p. 155). On Syriac *mparnsānūṯā* 'management, administration' see PAYNE SMITH 1903, p. 292; from the root PRNS 'to take the oversight, manage, rule, administer (property)', PAYNE SMITH 1903, p. 462.

113 On *dīnā* see SACHAU 1914, introduction, p. XII, on *bᵊ-mparnsānūṯā/mparnsānūṯā* introduction, p. XIV; see also his translations of the passages noted in the preceding fn. 112.

or—particularly in problematic cases with no precedent—in a divergent procedure according to the practice established in Iranian courts (*pad kardag*/*bᵊmparnsānūṯā*) '*via administrationis*'. Rulings reached by *kardag*-procedure could be later used as guidelines for decisions in similar cases, but they could also be challenged and revised if a litigant requested a 'binding' (*ēwar*) verdict according to *čāštag*-procedure.

The section on credit law and pledge in Īšōʿbōxt's Law-book, in which the Syriac translations of these two terms appear, discusses several cases involving the claims of creditors with and without real security, which I have already studied above in the context of obligations.[114] In this section the impact of Sasanian law may also be detected in Īšōʿbōxt's distinction between movable and immovable pledges and his further differentiation between two forms of pledge: the pledge that is transferred to the creditors, which is 'in their hand' (*bʾīdayhōn*), on the one hand, and the pledge/mortgage recorded in a written document (*ktāḇā*) which is *not* transferred to the creditors, on the other. The pledge 'in their hand' (*bʾīdayhōn*) corresponds to Pahlavi *graw*, the 'pledge, pawn' transferred as security to the creditor, whereas the mortgage recorded in a document (*ktāḇā*), but not transferred to the creditor, corresponds to *āgraw* 'hypothec' in Sasanian legal terminology. These were presumably the Iranian terms that stood in Īšōʿbōxt's original Pahlavi text.

Another basic concept of Sasanian property law may be detected in the same chapter relating to real security of the *grawagānīh* (*antichresis*) type: the fundamental distinction between 'substance, principal, capital' (*bun*) and 'income, fruit(s)' (*bar*).[115] The corresponding Syriac terms are *ʿeqārā* 'root', the equivalent of MP *bun*, and *pīʾrā* 'fruit', the equivalent of MP *bar*.[116] Īšōʿbōxt discusses the question, whether the offspring of a living pledge, *i. e.* a slave or an animal, in the hand of the creditor is to be considered as *ʿeqārā* 'root' or as *pīʾrā* 'fruit'. This is a pertinent question, since a creditor who holds a slave or animal of the debtor's as security (of the *antichresis* type) for a loan would have the right to profit from the 'fruit' of their work, *i. e.* from the income their labour provides, but would the offspring of the slave or animal also count as 'fruit'? The answer is clear: the progeny of a pledged slave or a pledged animal (camel, sheep or goat) born during the period in which the pledge is in the hand of the creditor does *not* count as *pīʾra* 'fruit' (*bar*), but as *ʿeqārā* 'root' (*bun*), belongs hence to the debtor, not to the creditor. The newborn child or animal can be raised and provided for by the creditor, but remains in the ownership of the debtor, who in turn is obliged to reimburse all costs involved in its rearing and to recompense the creditor for

114 Īšōʿbōxt, Book V, Chapter VII, § 2 (Sachau 1914, pp. 154–155); on the content of these passages see above Chapter IV, pp. 341–342.

115 Īšōʿbōxt, Book V, Chapter VII, § 10 (Sachau 1914, pp. 159–161); on *grawagānīh* (*antichresis*) see Chapter IV, pp. 343–349.

116 On *pīʾrā* 'fruit', see Payne Smith, p. 433; *ʿeqārā* 'root' (*ibid.* p. 426); on the distinction between *bun* and *bar* and its implications see above Chapter III, pp. 197–202.

any losses he might have endured in this context.[117] Īšōʿbōxt was evidently well acquainted with the basic distinction between *bun* and *bar* in Iranian property law, but whether he also adapted the concept of *bar-xwēšīh* 'ownership of the fruit' (as opposed to *bar-xward* 'use of the fruits, *usufruct*') which distinguishes Sasanian law from Roman law, is an open question that still has to be studied.[118]

A characteristic feature of Zoroastrian law discussed extensively in previous chapters, reappears in Īšōʿbōxt's work: the precise distinction between theft and robbery *not* only in criminal law, but by transposition also *in various other fields* of civil law.[119] In criminal law the Pahlavi terms *appar(ag)* 'robber' (Av. *hazaŋhan-*) and *duz(d)* 'thief' (Av. *tāiiu-*) designate originally offenders who appropriate property illegally, but in a different manner: the 'robber' steals openly, in public; the 'thief' stealthily, in secret.[120] By the Sasanian period these expressions had been adapted to other legal fields, particularly contract law and sale, and utilized in a figurative sense to denote contractors who did not keep their contractual obligations, that is, who committed the offence of *mihrōdrujīh* 'breach of contract', or who sold or gave away purloined property. In this context the basic distinction between robbery (= stealing openly) and theft (= stealing stealthily) remained significant: if a contract had been concluded *in the presence* of witnesses (in public) its breach was assessed and punished according to the offence of 'robbery' (*appar*) or stealing 'manifestly, openly' (*āškārag*); if the deal had been closed *without* witnesses (in private) its breach was assessed and punished according to the offence of 'theft' (*duz[d]īh*) or stealing 'secretly' (*nihān*). Īšōʿbōxt uses the same expressions (transmitted unfortunately only in Syriac translation) in this precise figurative sense in the context of sale, distinguishing in a similar manner between *ḥāṭōpā* 'robber' (lit. 'extortioner, plunderer, ravisher') and *ganāḇā* 'thief' (for the original Pahlavi terms *appar* and *duz* respectively): a man sells (or donates) a thing that is not his property to another man, who knows that the seller (or donor) is not the owner. If the buyer (or recipient) holds this thing secretly, in private, then he is judged as if he were a 'thief' (*ganāḇā*); if he shows it openly, in public, he is judged as if he were a 'plunderer, ravisher' (*ḥāṭōpā*).[121] There can be no doubt that this ruling is based on the distinction between robbery and theft in Zoroastrian law in the figurative sense it

117 On this passage see also Chapter IV, pp. 343–344.

118 On the distinction between *bar-xwēšīh* 'ownership of the fruit(s)' and *bar-xward* '*usufruct*' see Chapter III, pp. 197–202; on the discussion regarding this problem in the Babylonian Talmud see above pp. 603–606.

119 See Chapter IV, pp. 312–315, 381–382.

120 See already Bartholomae 1904, col. 1799 and 647 respectively (with further references to the sources).

121 Īšōʿbōxt, Book V, Chapter XI, §5a (Sachau 1914, pp. 174–175); on *ḥāṭōpā* see Payne Smith 1903, p. 138: 'an extortioner, plunderer, ravisher'; Maclean 1901, p. 97: 'ravenous, rapacious; a spoiler' (ḤṬP 'to take by force, do violence, violate'; compare Mandaic HṬP, HTP 'to snatch away, seize by force, rob, carry off', Drower/Macuch 1963, p. 140).

had assumed by the Sasanian period. The Syriac translation *ḥāṭōpā* (from the root ḤṬP 'to take by force, do violence, violate; to seize, snatch, catch at') for MP *appar(ag)* also clarifies another aspect of the Iranian term: besides designating a person who 'steals manifestly', the Syriac word stresses another important feature of 'robbery': the use of force.[122] This could be another significant aspect of the criminal offence called *appar*, which, being committed openly, could involve violence in contrast to 'theft', which might have been considered basically by definition as a non-violent criminal act.

In the context of sale the use of 'earnest money' is another correspondence between Christian and Zoroastrian law, but in contrast to the abovementioned feature, the transfer of a pledge or a specific sum as pre-payment to seal a bargain is by no means a unique trait of these two legal systems. The term employed in commercial dealings in Iranian law, ⟨rbn'/rbn⟩ *rabŭn/rabŭna* 'security, pawn, pledge, earnest money', is a loanword from the Semitic *ʿarab*, *ʿerabon* 'security, pawn, pledge', and, unsurprisingly, the same expression attested in Īšōʿbōxt's *Corpus Iuris* as *răhbunā*.[123] This widely used technical term of originally Phoenician providence is also known in Greek and Roman law as *ἀρραβών* and *arrabo*, often shortened to *arrha/arra*. In the context of an oral contract involving the sale of goods that would be delivered at a later period, the word originally designated an item of value, often a ring, which the buyer gave to the seller as a token of good faith and proof of serious intent to keep the deal. The *arra* could also consist of money instead of a pledge or 'earnest money', a part-payment, advance payment or deposit given to the vendor to seal the bargain. The procedure in cases of default on the part of the buyer or seller in both Zoroastrian and Christian law seems to correspond—despite possible divergences in detail—roughly to the one known in Greek and Roman law and has been already described above.[124]

Further similarities can be observed in almost all legal fields. In the context of slavery both Zoroastrian and East Christian law allows for a slave to belong as joint property to different masters simultaneously. The latter were co-proprietors who held the slave with ideal shares, which could consist of one-half, one-third or even one-tenth of the slave.[125] A common feature of both systems is that the slave could be manumitted to the extent of the share of one (or several) of the masters (to one-half, one-third or one-tenth) and subsequently be free to this specific extent, but have the status of a slave to the proportion of the other shares, resulting in the curious situation that—in contrast to Roman law—a slave could be partly manumitted and partly enslaved at the same time.[126]

122 On this aspect of the Pahlavi term see above Chapter V, pp. 434–435.
123 Īšōʿbōxt, Book V, Chapter XI, § 1 (Sachau 1914, pp. 172–173).
124 See Chapter IV, pp. 377–380; on MP ⟨rbn'/rbn⟩ *rabŭn/rabŭna* see also Macuch 2022c.
125 MHD 1.6–7 (Macuch 1993, p. 24); 48.13–15 (Macuch 1993, p. 324); 101.11–15 (Macuch 1993, p. 623); Īšōʿbōxt, Book V, Chapter XIII, § 5, 7 (Sachau 1914, p. 179).
126 See above Chapter II, pp. 108–109.

Significant information can also be gained in the context of legal administration on the evaluation of documents and the validity of seals, corresponding to the details on their trustworthiness (*wāwarīgānīh*) or reliability *(ēwarīh)* in the Pahlavi sources. According to Īšōʿbōxt, documents were divided into 'valid' and 'doubtful' ones (*šṭārā šarrīra wa-d-bᵊ-pušākā*).[127] A valid document (*šṭārā men šarrīrā*) is one that is sealed by officials of the State, whereas a doubtful one (*d-bᵊ-pušākā*) is only sealed by the (private) witnesses of a transaction, a description corresponding to the distinction made in Sasanian law between seals and documents assessed as *ēwar* 'reliable, binding' or *wāwarīgān* 'valid, true, trustworthy' (= Syr. *šarrīrā* 'firm, valid'), on the one hand, and as *warōmand* 'doubtful, untrustworthy, unreliable" (= Syr. *pušākā* 'doubtful'), on the other. The procedure undertaken to distinguish between the two types of seals and documents described by Īšōʿbōxt seems to correspond exactly with Sasanian practice as far as it can be reconstructed from the available Pahlavi material.[128]

Interestingly, even in a context least expected to agree with Zoroastrian law, that of marriage and inheritance, both Mār Abā and Īšōʿbōxt confirm unwittingly in their refutation of Mazdean norms that Christians in Iran did in fact practice one of the characteristic Zoroastrian institutions called *stūrīh* ('substitute succession'), albeit in the disguise of the levirate.[129] Eduard Sachau already remarked in the commentary to his edition of the *Corpus Iuris* that Īšōʿbōxt's description of the levirate among Christians in Iran does *not* correspond with the Jewish institution.[130] The latter only permits the marriage of the widow of a deceased sonless man with his brother in order to continue the lineage. In contrast, Īšōʿbōxt lists as marriage partners suited to continue the lineage not only the brother of the deceased as a potential husband for the widow, but as alternatives also his uncle (brother of the father) or his nephew (son of the uncle) or any other blood relative.[131] Obviously this custom among Christians, criticized by Īšōʿbōxt, does not correspond with the levirate, but with the Zoroastrian *stūrīh*. At the time of the publication of Sachau's edition more than one-hundred years ago this Iranian institution was still completely unknown, it is hence all the more remarkable that he perceived the significant discrepancy between the Jewish levirate and legal practice among Christians in Iran despite being unacquainted with the Zoroastrian institution. As Richard Payne has recently shown, the marriage practices described by Mār Abā and Īšōʿbōxt as levirate (Syr. *yabmuta*) correspond in fact exactly to the Sasanian *stūrīh* in a simplified form. Although both Christian authors sought to suppress the custom in their

127 Īšōʿbōxt, Book VI, Chapter II, § 1 (Sachau 1914, pp. 187–189).

128 On the evaluation of seals and documents see above Chapter IV, pp. 296–301.

129 Īšōʿbōxt, Book IV, Chapter I, § 5 (Sachau 1914, pp. 97–101); on Mār Abā see Payne 2017, 58–60; on *stūrīh* see above Chapter II, pp. 169–174.

130 Sachau 1914, pp. 309–310.

131 Īšōʿbōxt, Book IV, Chapter I, § 5, second paragraph (Sachau 1914, p. 97).

marriage treatises, they in fact testify to its existence among Christians and reveal the manner in which it was readjusted to fit in with Christian religious discourse by linking it to an alleged precedent in Mosaic law, the levirate.[132] The adaption of *stūrīh* in the Christian community is a remarkable example for the process of legitimizing a legal norm obviously taken from another religious system by concealing its provenance and re-contextualizing it to fit in with the tradition of Mosaic law, one of the important elements constituting *dīnā*, the civil law of the East Christians in its concrete form.[133]

3 Islamic law

Sasanian law had a significant impact on the formation of several basic institutions of Islamic law in the formative period of Islamic jurisprudence (7th to 9th centuries), particularly of the Jaʿfarite (Shīʿite) school, which stands out in several important aspects from the four Sunnite schools of law. This has long been assumed in early Western studies on the history of Islamic law, but remained a general, unproven hypothesis in most analyses for a very long time due to the inaccessibility of the Middle Persian legal sources. As is well known, Islamic law is not encoded in a single uniform doctrine, despite being based on divine revelation in the Qur'ān and on the precedents (*sunna*) set by the Prophet Muḥammad. Diverse doctrines emerged in the first centuries of Islam due to the necessity of defining and interpreting divine revelation and of formulating concrete laws to be implemented in the growing Islamic communities. We have good reason to assume that legal provisions were not only formed by divergent theological approaches to Qur'ān and *sunna*, but also by external factors, particularly various local traditions and customary laws, many of which were based on ancient legal systems practiced across many centuries in the numerous localities of the Caliphate. Islamic jurisprudence seems to have been strongly guided in the development of several of its more complex institutions by the three widespread legal systems operating in the lands of the Caliphate before the Muslim conquest: Roman (Byzantine), Jewish (Talmudic) and Sasanian (Zoroastrian) law. We can reasonably infer that many existing customary laws of the conquered countries and legal administrations were left intact during the first two centuries of Islam and were only gradually replaced by Islamic institutions. In Iran the continuing impact of Zoroastrian law is not only evident in Book-Pahlavi sources of the ninth century from Pārs, but, more significantly, in the original legal documents from eighth century Tabarestān, bearing witness to the perseverance of Sasanian law and administrative structures in the Caspian region of northern Iran, and in the documents of the 'Pahlavi Archive'

132 Payne 2017.
133 According to Īšōʿbōxt, see above, p. 615.

from the environment of Qom.[134] It has been rightly said that Islamic law is an amalgam of multiple ingredients that will ideally all have to be taken into consideration in discussing the emergence of Islamic legal institutions, a truly Herculean task given that many imported ideas have been re-interpreted and re-contextualized almost beyond recognition. But it is also true that within the framework of this admittedly complex configuration the visible impact of several well-established Sasanian concepts has been largely ignored in recent studies on Islamic legal history. Although the four main Sunnite schools of law, emerging in different regions of the Caliphate, are not uniform, it is remarkable that they all recognize certain basic principles, which are in turn completely disregarded in Twelver Shīʿite law. As COULSEN has astutely remarked, Twelver Shīʿite legal doctrine entertains several fundamental ideas, which stand in sharp contrast to the Sunnite system as a whole and cannot be explained merely by a divergent theological approach to legal issues.[135] The following is a survey of presumably Iranian elements in three institutions of Islamic law, which I have discussed extensively in earlier contributions: the pious foundation in Zoroastrianism and Islam, temporary marriage and the law of succession in Twelver Shīʿite jurisprudence.

3.1 The pious foundation (*waqf*)

All three advanced legal systems operating in the Near East before the advent of Islam, Byzantine, Jewish and Sasanian law, knew pious foundations and developed elaborate regulations regarding their establishment and management. The models set up in these legal systems, and in pre-Islamic Arabia, have been discussed as possible forerunners of the *waqf* in the vast literature on the formation of the Islamic pious foundation.[136] Despite the attempts of Muslim jurists to link the emergence of Islamic foundations, which are not mentioned in the Qur'ān, solely to the environment of the Prophet and the first Caliphs, it is far more likely that the foundations in the conquered lands offered templates for the Islamic institution in interaction with other possible local influences. Several early studies have identified the large charitable foundations of Byzantine law, the so-called *piae causae*, as the precursors of the *waqf*, arguing that the rules governing the establishment and administration of an Islamic pious foundation are similar to the regulations known from the Byzantine institution.[137] CLAUDE CAHEN, on the other hand, has argued that according to the

134 On these sources see Chapter I, pp. 17–20.
135 COULSEN 1964, pp. 109–119.
136 KÖPRÜLÜ 1942 still offers in my opinion the best overview of early studies on the provenance of the *waqf*. More recently HENNIGAN 2004, pp. 50–70, explains the emergence of the Islamic institution from different local traditions based in turn on Byzantine, Sasanian, Jewish or pre-Islamic Arabic models.
137 See overview in KÖPRÜLÜ 1942 on the studies of BECKER, MORAND and HEFFENING.

oldest Islamic legal sources the origin of the *waqf* should be rather sought in the smaller family foundation (*waqf ahlī* in Islamic law), than in the comparatively large foundation of public character (*waqf ḫairī*) comparable to the *piae causae*.[138] But both CAHEN and, more recently, PETER CHARLES HENNIGAN confirm that the terminology of the oldest sources of the two Ḥanafīs, Hilāl ar-Raʾy[139] and al-Ḫaṣṣāf,[140] in fact does not allow any differentiation between the two forms of the Islamic pious foundation, the *waqf ahlī* and the *waqf ḫairī*, although both types are mentioned.[141] It seems that the distinction between these two forms in legal doctrine is a later development in Islamic legal theory, although both types of endowments were known in practice and established at an early period. Contrary to CAHEN's assumption, JOHN PHILIP THOMAS in his work on Byzantine pious foundations provides evidence that the smaller family foundation was not only known in Byzantine law, but even widespread in the Near East.[142] Interestingly, the rules determining the establishment and administration of pious foundations in Byzantine and Sasanian law display many remarkable parallels, as I have tried to show elsewhere.[143] These are perhaps not purely coincidental, but might be the result of the mutual impact of two legal systems that existed for a very long time side by side.[144]

As we have seen above, in Sasanian law the total patrimonial (residuary) estate (*abarmānd*) of a wealthy family group was divided into four separate categories subject to different legal regulations.[145] One of these categories consisted of property reserved for pious and religious purposes 'for the soul' (*pad ruwān* or *ruwān rāy*) or 'for keeping the soul' (*pad ruwān dāštan*). Wealthy lineages set apart a considerable portion of their property, called *xwāstag ī ruwān* ('property of the soul'), for preserving the souls of the deceased in accordance with the importance attached in Zoroastrianism to taking care of the well-being of the souls of the departed. This could be achieved by different means, by financing rites and ceremonies (*yazišn*) for the soul, by performing charitable acts (*ahlawdād*), by establishing a pious foundation (*ruwānagān*) or a sacred fire (*ādur/ātaxš*) equipped with property in the name of the departed. As we may deduce from the list of Sasanian *dīwāns* transmitted in al-Ḫwārezmī's *Mafātīhu'l-ʿulūm*, the general term for the Iranian pious foundation was *ruwānagān*, lit. 'relating to the soul', a term which is otherwise only attested in Manichaean Middle Persian texts, albeit in a different religious context.[146] In Zoroastrian legal literature,

138 CAHEN 1961 (1977), p. 302 (according to 1977).
139 Hilāl b. Yaḥyā, called Hilāl ar-Raʾy, from Basra (died 247h.): *Aḥkām al-waqf*.
140 Abū Bakr Aḥmad b. ʿAmr aš-Šaybānī, called al-Ḫaṣṣāf, the *qāḍī* of Baghdad (died 261h.): *Aḥkām al-auqāf*.
141 CAHEN 1961 (1977), p. 297 (according to 1977); HENNIGAN 2004, p. 224.
142 THOMAS 1987.
143 MACUCH 2004.
144 See below p. 640.
145 See Chapter III, pp. 202–206.
146 See Chapter III, p. 221, fn. 151.

however, corresponding formulae are attested: *pad ruwān* or *ruwān rāy* 'for the soul' are the words employed in the context of the (written or oral) endowment act expressing the will of the founder to establish a pious foundation for the sake of his or another person's soul. It seems that al-Ḫwārezmī was aware of the striking similarities between the Sasanian and the Islamic pious foundation, since he translates *rūwānakān dafīra* (= MP *ruwānagān *dibīrag*) 'register of religious foundations' by *kitābat al-awqāf*, using the Arabic plural form of *waqf* to render *ruwānagān*.[147] Since I have already dedicated several articles to this topic (to which I would like to refer the reader)[148] and Chapter III above contains an extensive description of the Sasanian institution, the following general comparison between the Iranian *ruwānagān* and the Islamic *waqf* is restricted to the most significant legal correspondences (and a few divergences) in the two legal systems as far as they can be reconstructed from Pahlavi juristic sources.

According to the main doctrines of Islamic jurisprudence (*fiqh*) a *waqf* is established, when a free, adult person, sound of mind, having contractual and legal capacity relinquishes a precisely defined part of his/her lawful property and dedicates its income to an exactly designated charitable purpose. Since the donated property *(mauqūf*, pl. *mauqūfāt)* has to be permanent and generate income (*manfaʿa*), as a rule immovable property is endowed (such as agriculturally or commercially utilized land or real estate, rented buildings, shops, madrasas, hospitals, mills, baths, etc.) and immediately excluded from commercial transactions after the foundation act. Whether movable property may be established as *waqf* is discussed controversially in the diverse legal schools, but is usually permitted if the property can be the subject of a contract according to *šarīʿa* law and is profitable (animals due to their produce, *e. g.* milk and wool, trees due to their fruits, slaves due to their work force, books for studying), whereas property whose substance can be used up (*e. g.* victuals or money due to the prohibition of interest in Islam) can only be donated as a pious gift, a *ṣadaqa*. The final purpose of the endowment is a God-pleasing work (*qurba*) in the widest sense of the word (such as the performance of cultic acts, the dissemination of the faith, the promotion of religious learning, alleviation of poverty and need) by which the donor hopes to receive a reward in the hereafter.

As we have elucidated above,[149] at least two types of pious donations 'for the soul' (*pad ruwān*; *ruwān rāy*) were known in Sasanian law, first, those consisting only of a principal (*bun*), yielding no profit (*a-bar*), comparable to the Islamic *ṣadaqa* (which in turn corresponds to the Zoroastrian *ahlawdād* 'pious gift'), and, second, permanent endowments consisting of surplus-producing

147 See the list of *dīwāns* in Chapter II, p. 99.

148 On the Sasanian pious foundation in comparison to the *waqf* see MACUCH 1991b; 1994a; 2009d with further references regarding the sources and secondary literature.

149 See Chapter III, pp. 220–229.

(*barōmand*) property (agricultural land, villages, vineyards, orchards, also cattle and slaves) subject to specific regulations comparable to the Islamic *waqf*. Profit-yielding pious endowments dedicated to a sacred fire consisted of immovable property (real estate, agricultural land, villages, orchards, date palms), but could also include income-producing movables, such as slaves, cattle and money (no prohibition of interest in Zoroastrianism!). As in Islamic law, the principal (MP *bun*; Arab. *mauqūf*) of the endowment was considered as inalienable, only the profit (MP *bar*; Arab. *manfaʿa*) was used for the purposes specified in the foundation deed by the founder.

The will of the founder to establish a *waqf* had to be expressed unequivocally with the words *waqaftu*, *habbastu* or another clear formulation with the additional clause that the endowed object is inalienable, cannot be donated or bequeathed. In Sasanian law the specific purpose to which the funds were dedicated could be specified in a person's will by using different formulae: if he determined *ruwān yazišn rāy* 'for religious services for the soul' the funds were mainly used to perform rites and ceremonies (*yazišn*) after his demise. But if he specified that they should be spent *ruwān rāy* 'for the soul' (with the formula: *kū-m xwāstag ruwān rāy paydāg kard* 'I have established property for the soul')[150], they were set apart for other pious acts and used to establish a permanent endowment for the benefit of the founder's soul, or that of his relations and friends, according to the disposition of the founder. As in Islamic law, the statement of the founder also contained a provision forbidding the alienation of the endowed property dedicated to the soul: *ruwān* property could neither be sold, nor given away *(ān xwāstag frōxt ud be dād nē pādixšāy* 'one is not authorized to sell or give away that property')[151] nor inherited as personal property in ownership (*pad xwēšīh*). Hence in both systems the beneficiaries named in the foundation deed had *no right of ownership of the substance* (MP *bun*; Arab. *mauqūf*; also *aṣl*, *raqaba*[152]), nor the right to change the legal status of the endowment (with the exception of the Hanbalīs, who maintain that the beneficiaries are owners of both substance and fruits, albeit without the right to alienate the substance, which in fact reveals that the right of ownership of the substance is only a theoretical construction).[153]

According to both Sasanian and Islamic regulations a guardian, custodian or administrator (MP *sālār*; Arab. *nāẓir*, *walī* or *mutawallī*) manages the pious endowment, who is usually appointed by the founder and remunerated out of the income of the foundation. In both systems the founder had the right to assign custodianship of the endowment to a person of his choice and could also nominate himself (except in Mālikī law) as the first custodian. In Sasanian law

150 See Chapter III, p. 216.
151 MHD 35.5 (Macuch 1993, pp. 253, 256.
152 Jokisch 2017, p. 50.
153 Jokisch 2017, p. 51.

guardianship (*sālārīh*) of the *ruwānagān* went to one of the sons of the founder or to another family member, if the founder did not explicitly designate a specific person as *sālār*. Under specific circumstances women could also be appointed as custodians, if they were nominated by the founder or had themselves established the pious foundation.

After meeting the expenses of the custodian and other costs specified in the foundation deed, both legal systems agree that the income (*bar*; *manfaʿa*) of the pious foundation goes to the beneficiaries (MP *ōy kē awiš dād*; Arab. *mauqūf ʿalaihi*) designated by the founder in his deed. Another part of the surplus is spent for the charitable and pious purposes (MP *ahlawdād*; Arab. *qurba*) specified by the founder, but it has been remarked with reference to the Islamic foundation that in many cases the only recognizable charitable purpose is the support of the beneficiaries, usually relatives and descendants of the founder. This is also true of the Sasanian foundation.

Classical Islamic jurisprudence distinguishes between two forms of pious foundations, the endowment of a public character (*waqf ḫairī*) for the common benefit of the community (such as mosques and other sacred establishments, madrasas, caravanserais, hostels, streets, bridges, water canals) and the usually smaller family foundation (*waqf ahlī*), established by the founder for himself, his family and later generations of beneficiaries. Both types are attested in Sasanian law, albeit without the classification into two separate categories. It seems that in many cases the endowed property (*xwāstag ī ruwān*) remained a distinct part of the total property (*abarmānd*) of a descent group and was transferred as such to the founder's heirs and descendants, who were not authorized to change its legal status and had no right of ownership (*xwēšīh*) of the substance (*bun*). However, the distinction between two types of foundations in Islamic law is evidently a later construction, since the oldest treatises of the Ḥanafīs Hilāl ar-Ra'y and al-Ḫaṣṣāf (9th century) do not differentiate between the two, although both types are mentioned, as we have already noted above. The evidence suggests that both in Sasanian Iran and in the Islamic period one of the main reasons for establishing a pious foundation—apart from religious piety—was to secure a *permanent income* for one's own children and descendants or those of other family members and relations, particularly since the foundation would have been safe from confiscation by government authorities and may have also offered some protection against other calamities (armed conflicts, bankruptcy, etc.) that might befall a family or lineage leading to a massive loss of property.

This last point is significant for assessing the impact of Sasanian law on the legislation of the *waqf*. As we have elucidated above, in Iranian property law the theoretical possibility of securing a permanent income for one's descendants is based on the concept of *bar-xwēšīh* 'ownership of the fruit(s)', that is, the *permanent, inheritable right to the income* of a specific property, independent of ownership of its substance (*bun-xwēšīh*), a concept unknown in Roman law (to be distinguished from 'usufruct', *bar-xward*, the restricted right to the fruits for a specified period).[154] In a fairly recent comparative study BENJAMIN JOKISCH has shown that there is a significant congruity between Sasanian and Islamic law regarding this separate form of *ownership of the fruits* specifically in the context of the pious foundation.[155] In his minute comparison of the legal terminology of property law in four legal systems (Roman, Rabbinic, Sasanian and Islamic) he comes to the remarkable conclusion that Islamic law as a rule does *not* recognize a separate form of ownership of the fruits (*ṯamar*), but that Muslim jurists made *significant exceptions* in two instances: in the context of the bequest (*waṣiya*), by permitting a person's heirs to partake of, for example, the fruits of a garden or a tree in perpetuity, and particularly in the context of the *waqf*, by enabling the beneficiaries to enjoy the income of the foundation on a permanent basis. This specific correlation between Sasanian and Islamic law, he maintains, is an additional argument supporting the hypothesis that the Islamic foundation has been inspired by the Iranian institution.[156] It is particularly striking that Islamic jurists were compelled to adapt a position similar to that of Sasanian law regarding the right of ownership of the fruits in order to enable permanent access to the income of a pious foundation, although this is a concept not generally accepted in Islamic law. This in fact substantially supports the hypothesis that the first Islamic pious foundations were established according to the guidelines of prevailing (Sasanian, Byzantine and other) models and that legal doctrine was later adapted to fit in with the requirements necessary to sustain the existing institutions and to promote the formation of further foundations.

Table 65. Overview: the pious foundation

	Sasanian law	Islamic law
designation	*ruwānagān*	*waqf*
donated property, principal	*xwāstag ī ruwān*; *bun*	*mauqūf* (*aṣl*, *raqaba*)
donation formulae	*kū-m xwāstag ruwān rāy paydāg kard*	*waqaftu*; *habbastu*
profit, income	*bar*	*manfaʿa*
guardian, custodian	*sālār*	*nāẓir*; *walī*; *mutawallī*
beneficiaries	*ōy kē awiš dād*	*mauqūfʿalaihi*
surplus spent for charitable purposes	*ahlawdād*	*qurba*

154 See Chapter III, pp. 197–202; in comparison to Rabbinic law, see pp. 603–606 above.
155 JOKISCH 2017.
156 JOKISCH, 2017, pp. 52–53. A useful table of legal terms in Sasanian, Roman and Islamic property law is on p. 53.

3.2 Temporary marriage (*mutʿa/ṣīġe*)

In his exemplary overview of the history of Islamic law, N. J. Coulson remarks that Twelver-Shīʿite legal doctrine 'assumes in several fundamental respects a unique character sharply opposed to that of the Sunnite (and the Khārijite) systems as a whole'.[157] Two of these distinctive features, he maintains, are temporary marriage and the Shīʿite law of inheritance, which both demonstrate a legal approach to marriage and succession completely alien to Sunnite concepts of matrimony and the descent group.[158] As I have argued elsewhere, the only satisfactory explanation for the emergence of these two unique features of Twelver-Shīʿite legal doctrine is to assume that they were continuations of age-old Iranian concepts, albeit in a re-adjusted form adapted to the changed requirements of a society no longer based on Zoroastrian precepts.[159]

Temporary marriage, called *mutʿa* ('enjoyment marriage'; Arab. *matāʿ* 'enjoyment') in the Arabic sources or usually *ṣīġe* in Persian (according to the designation of the wife), is a legal form of matrimony in Twelver-Shīʿite jurisprudence, in which none of the principal rights and duties of the regular Islamic marriage, conceived as a permanent bond, apply. In contrast to the life-long conjugal alliance (*nikāḥ*), temporary marriage is contracted from the outset for a specific, limited period of time, reaching from a certain part of the day to several days, months or years (from 'one hour up to ninety-nine years'). The maximum limitation to four wives does not apply to temporary marriage: a man may enter an unrestricted number of *mutʿa* marriages simultaneously with Muslim women or women belonging to 'people of the book' (*i. e.* Christians, Jews, by analogy also Zoroastrians), whereas a woman may only contract a temporary marriage with one Muslim man at a time. The wife (*ṣīġe*) is entitled to a remuneration or consideration (*uǧra*; *aǧr* 'payment, consideration')[160] that has to be specified exactly in the marriage contract. Failure to state the amount of consideration due to the wife or the exact length of the marriage renders the contract invalid. In contrast to the regular marriage, the *ṣīġe* has no right to maintenance and the partners have no rights of mutual inheritance, but, significantly, as in the *nikāḥ*, children born of the *mutʿa* are considered as legitimate children of the father and heirs of both

157 Coulson 1964, p. 109.

158 Coulson 1964, pp. 110–119.

159 On temporary marriage within the framework of Sasanian family law see Macuch 2006 and Chapter II, pp. 157–162 above.

160 Coulson 1964, p. 110; Haeri 1989, p. 53; Denffer 1978, p. 301, has *mahr* 'brideprice', the term employed in a contract of permanent marriage; *mahr* might have been used in *mutʿa* contracts (instead of *uǧra/aǧr*) in order to avoid the impression that temporary marriage was considered as a kind of hire or lease (*iǧāra*), although it is in fact categorized in Islamic jurisprudence as a type of hire or lease in contrast to the regular marriage (*nikāḥ*), which is classified as a type of sale (*bayʾ*), see Coulson 1964, p. 111, and Haeri 1989, pp. 53–54.

father and mother. The marriage ends immediately with the expiration of the contract, without divorce proceedings.[161]

Taking these distinctive legal regulations into consideration, COULSON remarks: '*Mutʿa*, then, is not simply a *nikāḥ* with an accompanying condition of a time-limit, but is a distinct and individual legal institution.' And: 'Such a concept of marriage is utterly alien to general Muslim jurisprudence …'[162] Other studies on the inner-Islamic debate regarding the legality of the *mutʿa* support this view, maintaining that this type of marriage is rejected by Sunnite *ʿulamā*, who consider it as a relict surviving from Iran's pre-Islamic past, and, due to the time limitation, even as another form of prostitution amounting in strict legal theory to the forbidden act of fornication (*zinā*ʾ).[163] Outside Iran its legality is even questioned by certain Shīʿite authorities, who remark that this type of marriage is not practised among the Shīʿites of Syria, Lebanon and Iraq, but only in Iran.[164] These are significant assessments substantiating the impression that temporary marriage is viewed not only as a problematic institution in learned Muslim circles outside Iran, but as a foreign custom altogether, disguised in an Islamic garb.

Although several in-depth studies have been published in the past decades on various aspects of the *mutʿa*, none of these offer a convincing explanation of the provenance of this striking institution.[165] Most of them either repeat the assumption that *mutʿa* is the result of a divergent Shīʿite interpretation of Sura 4:24 or that it has survived as an ancient Arabian custom into Islam. Neither of these explanations is convincing, given that an interpretation of Sura 4:24 as a reference to temporary marriage in the sense assumed in Shīʿite jurisprudence has been repeatedly refuted by Sunnite *ʿulamā* and that the Arabian custom of time-limited marriage has almost nothing in common with the Shīʿite *mutʿa*. As DENFFER has elucidated, one of the most striking regulations of the Shīʿite temporary marriage has *no parallel* in the old Arabian institution: children born during the *mutʿa* are considered as legitimate offspring of their father and his heirs, whereas temporary marriage in pre-Islamic Arabia does not recognize the children as legitimate heirs of their father.[166]

161 For a more detailed account of the legal implications of the *mutʿa* see DENFFER 1978, pp. 300–303; MADELUNG 1985; HAERI 1989, pp. 51–60; HEFFENING 1993.

162 COULSON 1964, p. 111.

163 DENFFER 1978, pp. 318–325; ENDE 1980, pp. 15–17; COULSON 1964, p. 111.

164 ENDE 1980, pp. 15–17. The situation in Iraq and Syria might have changed by now, given the increased influence of Iranian politics in both countries in the past two decades.

165 Due to the revival of the Sharīʿa in Iran after the revolution of 1979 and the encouragement of temporary marriages on a large scale a significant number of Western publications have been dedicated to studying mainly three aspects of the *mutʿa*: (1) its genesis with references to Qurʾān and tradition (*ḥadīṯ*) (DENFFER 1978; Ferdows 1985; HAERI 1989, p. 7; HEFFENING 1993; MADELUNG 1985); (2) the inner Muslim discussion on the question of its legality (ENDE 1980 with numerous further references); (3) its legal and social consequences in modern Iranian society and its impact on the status of women (HAERI 1989 and 1994; MIR-HOSSEINI 1993, 1998 and 2000).

Circumstantial evidence corroborates the view that temporary marriage was *not* a new concept based on Sura 4:24, although the verse is used by Shīʿite *ʿulamā* to legitimize its existence. Apparently in Iran not only Shīʿite Muslims contracted temporary marriages, but also Christians and—in the Sasanian era—Jews resident in Babylonia (which was part of the Sasanian empire, Ērānšahr). Europeans travelling in Iran in the past centuries have described the practice of *ṣīġe* marriages both between Muslim women and Europeans, who were obviously not Muslims, and between (Nestorian) Christian women and European residents in Iran.[167] One of the longest descriptions is that of Dr. MORITZ WAGNER who visited Iran in the 1850s and was shocked to discover that Iranian Christians entered temporary marriages with European residents (Greeks and Russians) on a regular basis, noting: 'The Christian sect of the Nestorians, which is even more numerous than the Gregorian-Armenian in Azerbaijan, has a remarkable partiality for Europeans, and its members have not the least scruple, on religious, national, or ethical grounds, to give their daughters in marriage to Europeans, for a limited period, (be it six years or six months,) and for a stipulated sum.'[168] Most remarkable is a passage in the Babylonian Talmud revealing that at a far earlier period two of the major rabbinic authorities, the renowned Talmudic sages Rav (3rd century CE) and R. Nahman (4th century CE), would contract temporary marriages whilst travelling in Babylonia by taking a wife for a day: 'Whenever Rav came to Darshis [that is, Weh Ardashir, known to the Jews as Mahoza], he would announce: Who would be mine for a day? Whenever R. Nahman would come to Shekhunzib [on the eastern bank of the Tigris] he would have it announced: Who will be mine for a day?'[169] YAAKOV ELMAN maintains that the acceptance of temporary marriage by these famous rabbis is an indicator of the high degree of acculturation to Iranian norms and customs the Babylonian Jewry had reached by the Sasanian period.[170]

These striking accounts together with the well-attested cases of temporary marriage in Sasanian law make it very likely that this form of matrimony was *not* a Shīʿite invention, but one of the age-old traditions of the Iranians that continued to be practiced in customary law in the early Islamic period not only by Zoroastrians, but also in other religious communities of Iran, and was adapted into Twelver Shīʿite jurisprudence with the necessary changes. Temporary marriage in Sasanian law is a significant, even indispensible, ingredient of a complex, well-conceived system of marriage and inheritance, whereas in the context of Muslim family law it is not only alien to the concept of marriage, as COULSON

166 DENFFER 1978, pp. 318–325.

167 Brown 1893, pp. 505–506; Polak 1861; WAGNER *apud* MABRO 1991, pp. 229–230; see also ENDE 1980, pp. 14–15.

168 For the whole text see MABRO 1991, pp. 229–230; WAGNER's long description is also partly quoted in MACUCH 2006, p. 586.

169 Yoma 18b; for the whole text see ELMAN 2019, p. 92.

170 ELMAN 2019, p. 91.

has perceptively remarked, but has absolutely no discernable function except as a legal outlet for sexual needs. Even in Iran where *ṣīġe* marriages are legal and have increased considerably due to their promotion by the Muslim leaders since the 1979 revolution (especially after the Iraq war) they are socially seldom accepted as being equivalent to the permanent marriage and women concluding them are often regarded as economically and socially inferior.[171]

As we have elucidated above, marriage for a precisely limited period of time was one of the characteristic features of the Sasanian law of matrimony as an inherent part of the system, *not* as a separate institution.[172] Each one of the three types of marriage with divergent functions (*pādixšāy*, *čagar* and *xwasrāyēn/gādār*) could be contracted either as a permanent marriage (*az ān ī hamēīg*) or as a temporary alliance (*nē az ān ī hamēīg*) within an exactly determined period of time (one, two, three, four and ten years are attested in the Pahlavi sources; that marriages for one day were also possible is suggested by the Talmudic passage quoted above). In contrast to the Shīʿite *mutʿa*, temporary marriage was not a distinct form of marriage, but was fully integrated in the overall Sasanian concept of matrimony, albeit as a strategy with a specific purpose rather than an individual marriage form. This seems to be in fact the reason why no special technical term is transmitted for time-limited marriage: each one of the three legal forms of matrimony could be concluded temporarily and confined to a precisely specified period.

If we recall that the main objective of matrimony in the Sasanian patrilineal system is the procreation of legitimate children, that a man's legal rights over the wife and children have to be exactly defined, that polygyny (several wives) is permitted, whereas polyandry (several husbands) is forbidden and that it is vitally important to continue the lineages of Zoroastrian noble families, the existence of time-limited matrimony makes perfect sense.[173] According to an unwritten rule in every patrilineal system a woman can only be married to one man at a time to ensure that the children born from this alliance are the husband's. Hence in a permanent marriage a wife can generate legitimate children for only one man or lineage in the course of her lifetime (if there is no divorce and re-marriage). Sasanian law obviously found a way to circumvent this restriction by creating the legal possibility of limiting the duration of a legal marriage from the very outset: a fertile woman could generate offspring for several different men or lineages by contracting time-limited marriages *in different phases of her life*. For example, a woman could conclude a *pādixšāy*-marriage on a temporary basis in an exogamous alliance, entering the lineage of the husband with all the rights and duties of a *pādixšāy*-wife for the stipulated period of time. After expiration of the marriage contract she could re-enter her native lineage and put her reproductive

171 See especially the interviews with *ṣīġes* in Haeri 1989, pp. 105–152, and Haeri 1994.
172 On temporary marriage in Sasanian law see Chapter II, pp. 157–162, and Macuch 2006.
173 On kinship and descent groups see Chapter II, pp. 126–133.

faculties at the disposal of her original family (as *ayōgēn* or *stūr*) by concluding a *čagar*-marriage and generating offspring for her native lineage. The reversed sequence was also possible: a woman could be first married in *xwēdōdah* wedlock to a man from her native lineage (her own father, brother, uncle, grandfather, etc.)[174] for a limited period in order to procreate children and later enter an exogamous alliance after expiration of the first marriage. By using the device of time limitation the reproductive faculties of the fertile females of a lineage could be used to the advantage of several men or lineages to the fullest possible degree without having to give up the patrilineal concept of succession.

Hence, in contrast to the *mutʿa*, the Sasanian temporary marriage has its indispensible place in family law and fulfils a crucial function in both a legal and religious context. In Shīʿite law, on the other hand, time-limited marriage remains a strange annex, inconsistent with the Muslim concept of matrimony and an issue controversially debated up to this day between Shīʿite and Sunnite legal authorities. It seems very likely that temporary marriage, as one of the important ancient institutions of Iranian law in the pre-Islamic period, continued to be practiced by Zoroastrians and, maybe to a lesser degree, also by Christians and Jews in the diverse provinces of the Sasanian empire after the Muslim conquest and gradually found its place in Shīʿite jurisprudence as one of the elements of customary law. Notably, although temporary marriage is no longer embedded in Zoroastrian concepts, its main *raison d'être* in the Sasanian period, the procreation of legitimate offspring (for different lineages), has survived as one of the important ingredients of the Shīʿite institution in the recognition of the children from this union as legitimate heirs of the father.

3.3 The Twelver Shīʿite law of inheritance

All advanced legal systems develop exact rules regarding the devolution of inheritance to the heirs and beneficiaries on the death of the proprietor. The laws and procedures under which the beneficiaries become entitled to the property and the question of legal entitlement itself can vary considerably from system to system. These legal variations are never developed in isolation, but reflect basic tenets, social values and ancient mores of the society, in which they are implemented. In this light it seems most significant that one of the most distinctive features of the Twelver Shīʿite legal system in comparison with Sunnite law is its completely divergent law of succession.[175] Whereas the Sunnī concept, upheld by all four legal schools, concedes a privileged position to agnate relatives, the Twelver Shīʿī (*iṯnā-ʿašarī*) law of inheritance explicitly repudiates this basic

174 A remarkable original document from Tabarestān (Tab. 11) mentions the incestuous marriage between a grandfather and his granddaughter, see Macuch 2020b, pp. 191–199, and App. XIV below.

175 See Coulson 1964, pp. 113–119, and 1971, pp. 108–134.

principle. This is a major and even irreconcilable divergence between Shīʿite and Sunnite law, which is by no means coincidental, but based on a *principally different concept* of the family and descent group.

On the other hand, the Sasanian law of inheritance and succession, designed to support the specific needs of aristocratic lineages, displays a basic conception of family ties and descent groups very similar to the one demonstrated in the corresponding Twelver Shīʿite regulations. As Coulson has shown, the Sunnite law of inheritance did not emerge exclusively on the basis of Qurʾānic prescriptions, but relies to a large extent on pre-Islamic tribal law in Arabia (see below). We have good reason to assume that, in a parallel development, the Twelver Shīʿite law of inheritance, was inspired by the Iranian concept of the family and descent group and formed its own distinct laws on the basis of age-old Iranian social values and traditional norms.[176]

It will be best to first outline the major divergences between the Sunnite and Twelver Shīʿī concepts of inheritance, following Coulson's extensive work on Islamic succession,[177] then discuss the topic in its Zoroastrian-Sasanian context. According to the cited author the Sunnite law of inheritance evolved as an amalgam of two basic legal elements:

1. the customary law of pre-Islamic Arabia;
2. new Islamic standards specified in the Qur'ān.

In the patriarchal and patrilineal pre-Islamic Arabian tribe women played a subordinate role and descent from a common ancestor was exclusively defined through male links. Thus only the male agnate relatives, the *ʿaṣaba*, were entitled to inherit, whereas all the females, even the wives and daughters of the deceased, as well as all other non-agnate relatives were completely excluded from succession. The changes made by the Prophet introduced a new category of heirs by establishing the right of inheritance between the spouses (husband and wife) and by including close female blood relatives (the mother, the daughter, the sisters) as well as certain other non-agnate relatives of the deceased (such as the uterine brother) in the group of beneficiaries. Although these new Qur'ānic heirs, called *ahl* (or *aṣḥāb*) *al-farā'iḍ* ('persons entitled to prescribed portions'), now had a legal claim to fixed fractional shares (*farā'iḍ*) of the deceased's estate, the old tribal system of inheritance by male agnates remained intact in Sunnī law. Muslim jurists of the formative period maintained the older prescriptions by superimposing the new heirs upon the pre-Islamic customary system of succession: the male agnates remained entitled to inheritance, but only after the relatives named in the Qur'ān had taken their allotted shares. Thus the Sunnite law of inheritance recognizes two distinct groups of legal beneficiaries:

176 On succession and inheritance in Shīʿite and Sasanian law see Macuch 2017d; the following text is a shortened version of this contribution.
177 Particularly Coulson 1971; see also Coulson 1964, pp. 113–119.

1. the *ahl al-farā'iḍ*, or Qur'ānic heirs;
2. the *ʿaṣaba*, or male agnates of the deceased.

The latter succeed alone to the residue of the estate after the former have received their prescribed portions. In the unusual case that no blood relative of these two categories should survive, a third group of heirs, consisting of other female and cognate relatives of the deceased, may inherit.[178] COULSON divides these three groups of relatives into two categories, the 'inner family', encompassing the Qur'ānic heirs and the male agnates, and the 'outer' family, consisting of all other relatives who are only called to succession in the absence of blood relatives of the inner family.[179]

This is not the place to discuss the intricacies of the complex Sunnī law of inheritance, but it is important for our comparison to note two significant points: First of all, the system of priorities basically remained those of customary tribal law, based on agnatic succession, since the Qur'ān did not formulate an entirely new law of inheritance, but only modified existing rules by including a number of next-of-kin, especially women, who would formerly have had no rights of inheritance at all. Second, the Qur'ānic heirs do not *de jure* exclude other relatives of the inner family from succession, although they take their allotted portions first and reduce the *quantum* of inheritance available for the male agnates. It remains the prerogative of the *ʿaṣaba* to exclude other relatives from succession according to certain criteria of class, degree and strength of blood-tie determining priority. All male agnates are divided in the order of priority into five classes, relatives of a higher class totally excluding those of a lower class:

1. the son and his descendants,
2. the father and his descendants,
3. the descendants of the father (the brothers and nephews of the deceased and their issue),
4. the descendants of the paternal grandfather (uncles, cousins),
5. the descendants of the great paternal grandfather and higher grandfathers in ascending order.

In sharp contrast to the Sunnī system, outlined here very briefly, the Twelver Shīʿite law of inheritance assigns no distinctive position to agnate relatives. This is a striking divergence from the Sunnī law of inheritance and is adequately illustrated by a famous quotation attributed to the sixth Shīʿite Imam Jaʿfar aṣ-ṣādiq (d. 765), the alleged founder of the Jaʿfarite, or Shīʿite school of law. He dismisses the claims of the agnates with the words 'Dust in the teeth of the *ʿaṣaba*', meaning that the male agnates of a deceased proprietor should receive nothing more than a mouthful of dust, a derogatory form of declaring that they

178 COULSON 1971, pp. 29–30.
179 COULSON 1971, p. 31.

should receive absolutely nothing. The sole standard accepted in Twelver Shīʿite law is that of 'relationship' (*qarāba*) with the deceased, the nature and quality of which is determined by the further criteria of class, degree and strength of blood. With the exception of the spouse relict, who always takes his or her Qur'ānic share and stands outside the system of priorities, all blood relatives of the deceased are divided into three classes:

1. lineal descendants (sons and daughters; grandchildren) and parents;
2. brothers and sisters with their issue and grandparents;
3. uncles and aunts and their issue.

Members of the first class completely exclude those of a lower class and entitlement depends solely upon the position of the claimant heir in this order. Although the same rules mentioned above are applied to the Qur'ānic heirs and a male takes twice the share of a female relative of the same class and degree (according to Sura 4,11), the system differs fundamentally from that of Sunnī law by giving no special place to the male agnates. Thus not only a male member, but *also a female member of the first class, a daughter, granddaughter or mother*, excludes an agnatic brother or nephew, belonging to the lower classes, from succession; male agnates of a lower class take nothing in competition with females belonging to a higher class.[180] This is not only a completely different concept, but also a far simpler one than the complex Sunnī model based on the claims of the *ʿaṣaba*, described by COULSON picturesquely as a troublesome 'Gordon knot' being 'severed, at one clean stroke' by the Shīʿite system.[181]

To sum up, the Sunnite and Twelver Shīʿite systems reflect fundamentally *different ideas of descent and family*, which cannot be explained merely in the context of the radical political conflict between these two religious groups or their divergent theological ideas of Islam. COULSON is certainly right in describing the Sunnī law of succession as an amalgam of Qur'ānic rules and ancient custom in pre-Islamic Arabia, but his attempt to derive the Shīʿite system solely from Qur'ānic provisions, excluding any criteria derived from pre-Islamic legal practice, is not convincing.[182] It not only contradicts his own statement regarding the rudimentary nature of the regulations in the Qur'ān, but completely ignores the fact that other age-old legal systems existed in the diverse regions of the Caliphate, which were still practised well into the formative period of Islamic jurisprudence and could have served as a model for the development of a law of succession based on other priorities than those prevailing in ancient Arabia.

As we have elucidated in Chapter II above, the minute attention given to problems of succession in Sasanian law reveals the immense significance of this branch of law in forming and upholding Sasanian society. Exact regulations

180 COULSON 1971, pp. 109–110.
181 COULSON 1971, p. 110.
182 COULSON 1971, pp. 127–134, and 1964, pp. 117–119.

were especially important for maintaining the material interests of powerful descent groups belonging to the two foremost estates of society, the Zoroastrian clergy and the Sasanian nobility, whose wealth had been accumulated across many generations. It was vital to these influential families to keep their vast property together and to transfer it intact from one generation to the next. Hence it became crucial to secure the continuity of a man's lineage by all means.[183] Although succession in Sasanian law was patrilineal or agnatic and the members of a descent group were related through males, in contrast to pre-Islamic Arabia, patrilineal descent was combined with cognatic elements. The women of a family could play an important part in preserving the lineage as 'intermediary successors' (*ayōgēn*) and 'subsidiary successors' (*stūr*) and were thus also entitled to a portion of the property of their natal lineage, as we have seen above. A large number of unique institutions of family law and inheritance emerged with the same goal: to uphold the lineage under all circumstances, using both real and fictive legal alliances and various other options to achieve this purpose. Hence in the Zoroastrian concept of succession children of both genders were entitled to inheritance and not only sons, but also *daughters and wives* (in the *pādixšāy* status) as well as *sisters* had the right to an individual portion of the family estate.

Why should women be given these privileges in a patrilineal society, which conceded the right to replace the head of a family or descent group only to a male? Should we not rather expect a concept similar to the one in pre-Islamic Arabian customary law, restricting the right of inheritance to male agnates? Let us recall that usually in patrilineal systems the women of a lineage, daughters and sisters, are not 'useful' for purposes of reproduction and continuity of their *natal* lineage, since they join the descent groups of their husbands after marriage and their children count as members of the husband's lineage. Although this is also the rule for exogamous alliances in the Sasanian system, the law of succession nevertheless differs fundamentally from that of other patrilineal communities. The females of a lineage did not become 'useless' to their own descent group as far as reproduction is concerned because of three reasons:

1. the lack of an incest taboo forbidding inter-generational marriages and marriages between siblings (marriages between siblings, between mother and son as well as father and daughter were not only allowed, but regarded as especially meritorious religious acts);[184]
2. the possibility of contracting a time-limited marriage, allowing women to conceive for various men in different phases of their lives;[185]

183 On the political and social implications of this branch of law see Macuch 1995.

184 On the significance of endogamy and incestuous marriages (*xwēdōdah*) in family law see Macuch 2010c and Chapter II above, pp. 151–157.

185 On the use of temporary marriage within the framework of family law see Macuch 2006 and Chapter II above, pp. 157–162.

3. the development of elaborate laws engaging the women (wives, daughters, sisters) of a lineage to reproduce for the head of a household if he died sonless.

The use of females to continue the line of the family reveals that kinship was defined by *both* male and female links, although the final successor had to be a male. The institution of 'intermediary succession' (*ayōgēn[īh]*) by which the lineage is preserved and continued by a *female* would be completely impossible in a purely agnatic system.[186] The general term employed in Sasanian law for 'successor', *yōhē pasčaēta*, lit. 'who (succeeds) him afterwards', is used of both male and female descendants, but Sasanian jurists differentiated between two forms of succession:

1. *direct succession* by a legitimate son (*dādestān-pus*);
2. *intermediary succession* by a legitimate daughter (*dādestān-duxt*).

As we have elucidated above, if the head of a household left only a daughter (or several daughters) at his demise, but no son, then this daughter (or the eldest one if there were several) was obliged to function as 'intermediary successor' (*ayōgēn*) of the father with the obligation of generating a male successor. Besides the daughters, also the wives in the *pādixšāy* status and the sisters of the deceased were obliged to act as 'intermediary successors' in these cases. These women were committed to generating a male successor for the *paterfamilias* by entering a *čagar-zanīh* or 'auxiliary marriage', with a man from their own lineage or from another household in order to conceive. This form of matrimony was specifically concluded to the purpose of engendering offspring for the deceased man and could be time-limited from the outset. The children from the *čagar*-marriage of the wife, daughter or sister never belonged to their natural father, but were counted as offspring of their legal father, who had left no son. If only daughters were born of the 'intermediary successor', one of these continued to serve as *ayōgēn*. The son, who was finally installed as legal successor, could even be separated from the deceased *paterfamilias* by several generations.[187] In this manner *the descent group was in fact continued by the female line*, which often constituted the only 'blood link' to the lineage of the deceased *paterfamilias*.

It is admittedly extremely difficult to demonstrate, let alone prove, that correspondences between Zoroastrian and Islamic law are in any form connected to each other. But it is not too far-fetched to assume that the diverse social, political and traditional backgrounds of the jurists who formulated Islamic law played a decisive role in their interpretation of Islamic rules and that these led

186 The idea of cognatic descent is also present in the diverse legends transmitted in epic literature on the genealogy of Ardašīr, the founder of the Sasanian Empire, see MACUCH 2014a.

187 On the *ayōgēn*-daughter as a link between the father and his male successor in epic literature see MACUCH 2020a

to principally different concepts of the family and descent groups in the Sunnite and Shīʿite systems of succession. The basic ingredient of Sasanian law that *a daughter can and must continue the lineal issue of a man* in the absence of a son is completely incompatible with the Sunnite concept of succession by male agnates (despite the provision in the Qur'ān that specific shares are to be given to the females). On the other hand, it corresponds perfectly with the Shīʿite idea of hereditary succession, determining that lineal descendants of the deceased, particularly the daughter and her children (both male and female) have complete priority over all agnate collaterals. It is also fully consistent with the Shīʿite view that the only legitimate successors of the Prophet are the sons of his daughter Fāṭima from her marriage to ʿAlī, his cousin and son-in-law, the first Imam, and their descendants. Although the intricacies of Sasanian succession described above no longer apply, the underlying notion of family ties and blood links is the same and clearly recognizable in the Shīʿite law of succession. In short: the Shīʿite doctrine of priority by *qarāba* agrees astonishingly well with the concept of the family in Sasanian law and its cognatic elements.

4 Roman (Byzantine) law

An in-depth study of the legal systems of the two most powerful empires of late antiquity, Sasanian Iran and Imperial Rome/Byzantium, still has to be undertaken.[188] This arduous task, requiring minute expertise in both disciplines, lies clearly beyond the scope of this work. But it will be useful to repeat very concisely a few random observations on similar concepts in Sasanian and Roman law that we were able to detect in the course of this study. The congruencies could be purely coincidental and due to a parallel, albeit independent evolution of law in the two systems, but they demonstrate at the very least an astonishingly similar theoretical approach to specific legal issues. Although Iranian law originated from sacred law and Roman law was, as CORCORAN emphasizes, 're-lentlessly secular',[189] it seems that by the Sasanian period Iranian jurisprudence had developed into an individual discipline and became as differentiated and precision orientated as its Roman/Byzantine counterpart.

In previous chapters we have discussed a few examples of precise legal terminology and the concepts underlying this meticulous use of legal language. One example is in the context of property law the use of the MP term *xwāstag*

188 A few attempts have been made by CORCORAN 2011 in his article on the Sasanian Lawbook in the light of Roman legal writing and FOREST 2020 in his dissertation on the Sasanian law of succession. On Sasanian rank titles in comparison with Roman rank titles see PURWINS 2019; for a preliminary attempt to compare Byzantine and Sasanian pious foundations see MACUCH 2004. On comparable administrative structures see PURWINS (forthcoming).

189 CORCORAN 2011, p. 107, citing ALAN WATSON.

in a threefold sense[190] corresponding almost exactly to the Roman *res*. Both terms have the primary meaning of 'thing', the designation of a concrete physical object (chair, table, house, estate, etc.), but are also used in an abstract sense of 'thing' (*e. g.* a loan or a specific right) and came to denote any asset that had economic value.[191] A comparison of the two terms demonstrates astonishing conformity:

Table 66. Uses of *res* and *xwāstag*

res[192]	*xwāstag*
'thing': an individual, limited, legally independent corporeal thing or physical object	'thing, object': any corporeal object, encompassing both movable and immovable property
'legal object': anything that can be the object of a (private) right or of civil litigation	'object of dispute; matter in dispute': anything that can be the subject-matter of civil litigation
property as a whole (*patrimonium*, *bona*)	property as a whole (including the complete mass of inheritable family property, *abarmānd*)

Unsurprisingly, both Roman and Sasanian law distinguish precisely between 'ownership' (Lat. *dominium*, *proprietas*; MP *xwēšīh*) and 'possession' (Lat. *possessio*; MP *dārišn*),[193] a necessary distinction in all advanced legal systems. As we have elucidated above, we have good reason to assume that the concept of 'ownership' was identical in both systems at an early period of Roman law before the latter developed the idea of ownership as an 'absolute right' or 'real right', conceding the owner a legally protected title to a 'thing' that could be defended on this ground against other contenders. But this was apparently a late development, still unknown in *ancient* Roman law. In contrast to *classical* Roman law Sasanian law obviously considered 'ownership' as a 'relative right', a concept that corresponds roughly to *pre-classical* Roman law, as we may conclude from the procedure in the lawsuit concerning property, known as the *legis actio sacramento in rem*. These lawsuits were *not* decided on the basis of a party's absolute right of ownership, but because one of the litigants proved to have a 'better right' to the object of dispute, often a purchased (or bartered) item that was claimed by another party. The procedure, involving the testimony of the original owner of the object, the legal predecessor of the defendant, called

190 The fourth sense of *xwāstag* 'money', is meticulously distinguished from the other three by its spelling as an ideogram ⟨NKSY'⟩ in a legal context to distinguish it from *xwāstag* = *res*; see Chapter III, p. 190.

191 See Chapter III, pp. 189–190.

192 According to Kaser 1986, p. 90.

193 See Chapter III, pp. 191–197.

auctor, corresponds exactly with that of the Sasanian lawsuit, in which the legal predecessor (*dastwar*) of the defendant was called upon to defend the latter's title to the acquired item against claims of the plaintiff or another party. The judge decided which one of the opponents could present *better* proof of ownership, based on the testimony of the *auctor/dastwar*.[194] Despite the striking similarity, there is no proof of influence and this type of lawsuit could have evolved in both systems independently.

The pious foundation is another example for a wide spread institution in both empires governed by similar rules. These foundations, which were established from the time of Justinian across the Byzantine empire in close vicinity of the Sasanian State, were subject to meticulous regulations, almost identical to those in Sasanian law. Since I have already discussed this topic with regard to Byzantine and Sasanian law extensively elsewhere, the following is restricted to a very concise summary of the results of this comparison.[195] The phrase *piae causae* 'pious motives, objects, purposes', designating Byzantine charitable foundations, was apparently not yet employed at the time of Justinian, but is the general expression used in later treatises of all kinds of endowments in Byzantine law, showing major similarities to the Sasanian *ruwānagān*.[196] Both systems knew the two major types of pious endowments, the foundation of public utility established for the benefit of the community (churches, monasteries, other philanthropic institutions, *e. g.* hospitals, old-age homes, etc. in Byzantium; fire-temples, roads, bridges, etc. in Sasanian Iran) and endowments founded by private benefactors, who appointed either themselves or members of their own families as trustees and administrators, hereby ensuring an income for their families and heirs. In both legal systems the substance or principal of the foundation was unalienable and assets assigned to it were considered as property of the foundation itself. The managers and trustees had no right of ownership, but only a right to a specified part of the income. Moreover, the majority of family foundations remained in both systems in the hands of the family and descendants of the founders. We have good reason to assume that providing a permanent income for one's relatives was one of the main reasons for establishing a private foundation in both Sasanian Iran and the Byzantine empire. These wide-spread foundations in the lands conquered by the Muslims in the 7th century obviously served as templates for the later Islamic *waqf*.[197]

194 On this procedure see Chapters IV, pp. 385–387, and VI, pp. 542–544.

195 See Macuch 2004 with further references.

196 On the *ruwānagān* see Chapter III, pp. 220–229.

197 See above pp. 622–627.

Appendix I

Dādestān ī dēnīg: On Inheritance and Family Law (*Pursišn* 53–61)

The following sections on inheritance and family law are not included in the edition of Jaafari-Dehaghi 1998, which has only the first part of the Dd (up to *Pursišn* 40). P.K. Anklesaria 1958 has edited the second part of the Dd (*Pursišn* 41–92) in his thesis submitted to the University of London in 1958, but this work consists only of a hand-written Pahlavi text with no transliteration, transcription or translation and has never been published. Moreover, he does not take all important manuscript variants into consideration in the apparatus. The following transcription hence does *not* follow his reconstructed Pahlavi text, but is based on a collation of the two oldest Iranian manuscripts, K35 and TD4a; references to page numbers in Anklesaria's edition follow the manuscript of the thesis. The translation by West 1882 (pp. 183–196) is by now completely antiquated. De Menasce 1964a (pp. 33–35) has translated questions 55–58 (with no transliteration or transcription). For a description of the surviving manuscripts of the Dd see West 1882, pp. xv–xix, P.K. Anklesaria 1958, pp. 7–37, and Jaafari-Dehaghi 1998, pp. 26–28.

***Pursišn* 53** (K35, fol. 172r.16–173v.13; TD4a, pp. 324.16–328.6)[1]:

1. *panǰāh-seyom pursišn pāsox. ān ī pursēd kū mard-ē(w)*[2] *kē-š zan ud duxtar ud xwahar ud xwēšāwand*[3] *čand u-š xwāstag ī was ast mērag dardōmand bawēd*[4] *andar dardōmandīh*[5] *xwāstag ēwkard be ō duxt-ē(w)*[6] *dād.*
2. *u-š az*[7] *xwaharān ud duxtarān ī*[8] *abārīg padiš nē*[9] *ham-dādestān hēnd gōwēnd kū ēn xwāstag andar tan-drustīh*[10] *ud ōšyārīh ahāyist dād nē andar*

1 West 1882, pp. 183–187, Anklesaria 1958, pp. 111–113.
2 K35: ⟨GBR' Y⟩; TD4a: ⟨GBR'-1 Y⟩.
3 Both K35 and TD4a: ⟨hwyšwnd⟩.
4 K35: ⟨YHWWNyt⟩; TD4: om.
5 TD4a: ins. ⟨YHHWNyt⟩.
6 K35: ⟨BRTH̱ Y⟩; TD4a: ⟨BRTH̱-1⟩.
7 K35: ⟨MNW⟩; TD4a: ⟨MN⟩.
8 K35: ⟨Y⟩; TD4a: om.
9 K35: ⟨L'⟩; TD4a: om.
10 K35: ⟨tn'drwstyh⟩; TD4a: ⟨tn' Y drwystyh⟩.

dardōmandīh ud nūn nē pādixšāy hē andar dardōmandīh čiš-iz be[11] *ō kas dād čē agar čiš-ē dād*[12] *xwāstag hamāg abāz ō mayān baxšišn āyēd.*

3. *ān xwāstag andar dardōmandīh čiš-iz ō kas dād pādixšāy ayāb nē?*
4. *zan duxtar*[13] *ud xwahar har*[14] *ēk čand rasēd az ān xwāstag? ān mard rāy*[15] *stūr abāyēd gumārdan ayāb nē?*
5. *zan ud duxtar ud xwahar kē-šān xwāstag bahr stānēnd hāmōyēn dēnīgīhā andar gardan ast u-šān ān mard rāy*[16] *pad rōzag sālag yazišn ī sālwār*[17] *abāyēd framūdan*[18] *ayāb nē?*
6. *pasōx ēn kū ka-š čiš andar nēst ān rāy ǰuttar ōwōn sahom kū mard*[19] *andar dardōmandīh tā*[20] *be widerišnīh bē ka-š abām padiš ayāb-iš zan aburnāyīg ayāb zarmān ayāb pid ī andar sālārīh kē frēzwān abāyēd dāštan [čiyōn ayāb pid ī čand andar sālārīh az]*[21] *čiyōn and*[22] *čand pad*[23] *tōzišn ī*[24] *abām ayāb xwarišn*[25] *(ud) dārišn pānagīh ī awēšān čiyōn-am nibišt a-wizīrišnīg andar abāyēd be dād nē*[26] *pādixšāy. ēnyā az ān ī nibišt*[27] *bērōn čandīh xwēš andar ōšyārīh be dād pādixšāy.*
7. *andar abārīg dardōmandīh nē pad*[28] *widerišnīh har čē-š xwad be dād andar ōšyārīh pādixšāy ka nē ōšyār*[29] *nē pādixšāy.*
8. *ud ān ī nē andar ōšyārīh gōwēd padiš nē awestwār ud nē wāwar ud ān ī andar ōšyārīh ud ān-iz ī im mard be ō duxt dād agar-iš*[30] *ōšyārīhā dād ka wēmār būd ēg-iz rawāgān*[31] *dahišn. agar-iš nē andar ōšyārīh dād ēdōn bawēd čiyōn ka an-handarz*[32] *murd*[33].

11 TD4a: ⟨BR'⟩ *super lin.*
12 K35: ⟨YHWWNyt W⟩; TD4a: ⟨YHBWNt⟩.
13 K35: ⟨BRTH̱l⟩; TD4a: ⟨BRTH̱⟩.
14 K35: om.; TD4a: ⟨KR'⟩.
15 K35 : ⟨L'⟩; TD4a: ⟨l'd⟩.
16 K35: ⟨L'⟩; TD4a: ⟨l'd⟩.
17 K35: ⟨s'lw'l⟩; TD4a: ⟨s'l'lw'l⟩.
18 K35:⟨plmwtn'⟩; TD4a: ⟨plmwt'⟩;
19 K35:⟨GBR'⟩; TD4a: ⟨GBR'-1⟩.
20 K35: ⟨wndk⟩; TD4a: ⟨'D⟩.
21 K35: in brackets: a copyist's mistake, deleted by dots in the ms.
22 K35: ⟨'ywp⟩; TD4a: ⟨'nd⟩.
23 K35: ⟨pṯ⟩; TD4a: ⟨BR'⟩.
24 K35: om.; TD4a: ⟨Y⟩.
25 Thus K35; TD4a omits the whole following passage after *xwārišn* (TD4a: ⟨hwlšn'yk⟩) until *andar abāyēd* (*i. e. dārišn pānagīh ī awēšān čiyōn-am nibišt a-wizīrišnīg* is missing in the ms.).
26 K35: ⟨L'⟩; TD4a: ⟨l'd⟩.
27 K35: ⟨npšt'⟩; TD4a: ⟨npšt''n⟩.
28 K35: ⟨pṯ⟩; TD4a: ⟨pṯ BR'⟩.
29 K35: ⟨'wšd'lyh⟩; TD4a: ⟨'wšyh⟩.
30 K35: ⟨HT-š⟩; TD4a: ⟨'P-š⟩.
31 K35: ⟨lwb'k'n⟩; TD4a: ⟨lwb'k⟩.
32 K35: ⟨'n'ndpylwc⟩; TD4a: ⟨'nhndlc'⟩.
33 K35: ⟨YMYTNt'⟩; TD4a: ⟨YMYTWNyt⟩.

9. *xwāstag [abāg]*[34]*abē-handarz mānd har duxt ēk*[35] *kē-š šōy nē kard ēk bahr ō zan (ī) pādixšāyīhā 2 bahr niyābag tā ka zan zīndag čiyōn dūdag kadag-bānūg ast be ō stūr gumārdan nē niyābag čē stūrīh abar ōy ēstēd. az xwēšāwandān*[36] *mard-ē(w) nazdīk paywandtar pad dūdag-sālārīh xwāstan rāyēnēd.*
10. *az bahr*[37] *ī xwarišn ud dārišn (ī) xwāstag*[38] *(ī) zan duxtarān tā šōy kunēnd ān-iz frēzwānīgīh andar sālārīh parwarišn ī ān mard dād. yazišn kirbag (ī) pad dūdag nihādag*[39] *padiš frēzwānīg būd rawāg dāšt xwad sēnag masāy ud bāzā masāy az bar stad.*
11. *xwaharān (ī) ān mard bē agar ān mard handarz jud ayāb-šān*[40] *šōy nē kard nēst xīrīh rāy andar sālārīh ī ān mard būd hēnd ayāb any čiš ān rāy juttar tā-šān az xīr*[41] *(ī) ōy mard čis-iz nē niyābag ud agar frēzwānīg pad-iz parwarišn andar sālārīh ī ōy būd hēnd u-šān az any rāh xīr*[42] *nēst az bar ī xwāstag xwarišn-iz ud dārišn ī awēšān* ⁺*dādan*[43] *niyābag.*
12. *ān ī duxtarān šōy pad dastwarīh dūdag-sālār ud hamdādestānīh ī dūdag-kadagbānūg ud ēdōn ka kunišn [ī] nē kard u-š pus nē zād widerān bawēd duxt šōy nē kard an ēk kē-š šōy nē kard* ***aeuuō kaē*** *xīr iz*[44] *ī dūdag-kadagbānūg dāštan*[45] *ōy padiš*[46] *stūrīhā niyābag.*
13. *ka andar stūrīh šōy kunēd ēg-iš xwāstag pad xwēšīh abar rasēd. ka dūdag-kadagbānūg widērēd ud duxtarān šōy kard stūrīh gumārišn.*

1. The fifty-third question (and) answer. That which you ask: A man who has a wife and daughters and sisters and several (other) relatives and who has a large property (*xwāstag ī was*), becomes ill (*dardōmand*) and during (this) illness has given (= bestowed/bequeathed) his (whole) property in one piece (*ēwkard*)[47] to one of (his) daughters.
2. And his sisters and other daughters do not agree with him (and) say: 'He should have given (= bestowed/bequeathed) this property in health and full

34 K35: ⟨LWTH̱⟩, *super lin.*: ⟨'pyy⟩; TD4a: ⟨'pyy hndlc'⟩.
35 K35: ⟨'ywk'⟩; TD4a: ⟨-1⟩.
36 TD4a: repeats ⟨hwyš'wnd'n⟩.
37 KD35: ⟨b'hl⟩; TD4a: ⟨bl Y hw'stk⟩.
38 TD4a: ⟨hw'stk⟩; K35: om.
39 K35: ⟨n'htk'⟩; TD4a: ⟨'htk'⟩.
40 K35: ⟨š'n⟩, *super lin.*: ⟨dhšn'⟩; TD4a: ⟨'ywp-š'n⟩.
41 K35: ⟨SBW'⟩; TD4a: ⟨bwn⟩.
42 K35: ⟨SBW'⟩; TD4a: ⟨bwn⟩.
43 K35: ⟨YHWWNtn'⟩; TD4a: ⟨YHWWNyt'⟩.
44 TD4a: inserts after ***aeuuō kaē***: ⟨ZK GBR' GBR' W⟩ before ⟨hyl-c⟩.
45 K35: ⟨d'štn'⟩; TD4a: ⟨d'št'lyẖ'⟩
46 K35.⟨'LH pt-š⟩; TD4a: ⟨'-š⟩.
47 The technical terms ⟨'yklt'⟩ *ēwkard* and *ewkardag* 'in one piece' refer to property (usually land) that is not divided or partitioned into shares; *ēwkardagīhā* 'in one piece; undivided' in the Law book is contrasted with *pad bahr* 'in shares'; for a definition of *ēwkardagīhā* (with reference to land) see MHD 19.3–7 (Macuch 1993, pp. 154; 159) and Chapter III, p. 243.

consciousness (*andar tan-drustīh ud ōšyārīh*)[48], not during illness (*andar dardōmandīh*). And now he should not be authorized (*nē pādixšāy hē*)[49] to give (= bestow/bequeath) something (*čiš-iz*) to someone during illness. Since if he gives something (*čiš-ē*), the whole property (*xwāstag hamāg*) will return to be partitioned among (us) (*abāz ō mayān baxšišn āyēd*).'[50]

3. Is he authorized (*pādixšāy*) to give something from that property to someone during (his) illness or not?
4. How much of that property goes to every wife, daughter and sister? Is it necessary to appoint a 'substitute successor' (*stūr*) for that man or not?
5. Are the wives, daughters and sisters, who take a share (*bahr*), all responsible[51] for the religious rites (*dēnīgīhā*) and must they order the annual ceremonies (*yazišn ī sālwār*)[52] at the daily and yearly (periods) or not?
6. The answer (is): If there is nothing (in this case) that would require another (decision), (then) it seems to me (as follows): A man who has a fatal illness[53], unless he has a debt (*abām*) or a wife or an underage child or an aged person (*zarmān*) or a father, who is under his guardianship (*sālārīh*), whom he has the duty to maintain, he is not authorized to give away (*be dād nē pādixšāy*) (more than) the (sum) corresponding (*čiyōn*) or amounting to (*čand*) that which (is) unavoidably necessary for the payment of the debt (*tōzišn ī abām*) or for food and maintenance and shelter of those (persons) I have noted above. Otherwise, with the exception of the (cases) noted (above), he is authorized to give away (= bequeath) (*be dād pādixšāy*) in full consciousness (*andar ōšyārīh*) the amount that (is) his own (*čandīh xwēš*).
7. During another (type of) illness that (is) not fatal, everything he has given away (= bestowed/bequeathed) himself in full consciousness (*andar ōšyārīh*)

48 The term *ōšyārīh* 'consciousness' designates in a legal context 'accountability' and 'saneness'; *ōšyār* a person who is of sound mind, hence accountable for his actions.

49 On *hē*, written ⟨HWḤ-'h⟩, 3rd sg. opt. of *h-* 'to be', see Skjærvø 2018, pp. 164–166; on the verbal ending ⟨-yyh⟩ *-ē* see Cantera 1999, pp 179–180.

50 The sisters and daughters who are entitled to inheritance argue that the testator should not be authorized to bequeath any part of family property (*čiš-iz*) during a fatal illness. If he bequeaths 'something' (*čiš-ē*), *i.e.* a part of the inheritance, then the property is not transmitted as a whole to the heirs as shareholders with ideal shares (*pad abarmānd*), but in individual shares (*pad bahr*), and should hence be returned to be partitioned (*baxšišn*) among the heirs. On these two different forms of bequeathing family property see Chapter III, p. 204.

51 Tentative translation of the phrase *hāmōyēn dēnīgīhā andar gardan ast* 'are all the religious rites on (their) necks?', which could be an idiomatic expression for 'are they all responsible for arranging the performance of religious rites?' (see also West 1882, p. 184).

52 The ceremonies to be performed after the death of a Zoroastrian are listed in the Pahlavi commentary of Vd. 8.22 (Moazami 2014, pp. 232–237) and Šnš (suppl.) XVII, 3–5 (Kotwal 1969, pp. 70–72. Specific rites are to be held (1) on three days after the death of the person and on the fourth day; (2) on the tenth day and month-day; (3) after thirty days (*sīrōzag*); (4) after a year (*yazišn ī sālwār*). On the rituals performed in modern times see Boyce 1977, pp. 160–163.

53 Lit. 'in an illness until death' (*andar dardōmandīh tā be widerišnīh*).

is authorized (*pādixšāy*); if he (is) not conscious (*nē ōšyār*), (then) it (is) not authorized (*nē pādixšāy*).

8. And that which he says in an unconscious state (*nē andar ōšyārīh*) (is) unreliable (*nē awestwār*) and invalid (*nē wāwar*).[54] Moreover, (as to) that which this man has given away (= bestowed/bequeathed) to the daughter, if he gave it in full consciousness (*andar ōšyārīhā*) during his illness, then it is to be bequeathed in continuous succession (*rawāgān dahišn*). If he did not give it in full consciousness (*nē andar ōšyārīh*), (then) this is considered as if he had died without a testament (*an-handarz*).
9. Property which has remained without testament (*abē-handarz*): for every daughter who has not married, one share (*ēk bahr*), for the *pādixšāy*-wife two shares (*dō bahr*) (are) needed (*niyābag*). As long as the wife is alive, there is no need to appoint a 'substitute successor' (*stŭ̄r*), since she is the family mistress of the house (*dūdag kadag-bānūg*) (and) the (duty) of 'substitute succession' (*stŭ̄rīh*) is incumbent on her (*abar ōy ēstēd*). From among the relatives she conducts a request for a man who (is) most closely related (to her) (*nazdīk paywandtar*) for family guardianship (*dūdag-sālārīh*).
10. That which (is) necessary for the maintenance (*parwarišn*) of that man in his position as guardian (*andar sālārīh*) is given from the share of property (set aside) for the nourishment and maintenance of the wife and the daughters until they marry. Religious ceremonies (*yazišn*) and virtuous deeds (*kirbag*) imposed on the family, which have to be carried out on a regular basis (*rawāg dāšt*), are taken (= financed) from the increase (of property) (*az bar stad*); the remuneration (*sēnag masāy ud bāzā masāy*)[55] for him (= the guardian) himself is (also) taken from the increase (of property).
11. (As to) the sisters of that man (= the deceased), unless that man (has) different (dispositions) in (his) testament (*handarz*) or they (= the sisters) have not married due to the lack of property (*nēst xīrīh rāy*), (and therefore) were under the guardianship (*andar sālārīh*) of that man (= the deceased) or (if) there (is) another matter, which would (require) another (decision): until they have no more need (of support) from the property of that man and if they were under his guardianship out of necessity and they have no property from another source (*az any rāh*), it is necessary that nourishment and maintenance be given to them from the increase of the property (*az bar ī xwāstag*).
12. The husband of the daughters (is) family guardian (*dudag-sālār*) by entitlement (*pad dastwarīh*) and with the consent (*hamdādestānīh*) of the family

54 In a legal context *wāwar* is a technical term meaning 'valid, lawful, legal, (absolutely) reliable', the opposite is *nē wāwar* 'invalid'; compare *muhr ī wāwarīgān* 'valid seal' (see Chapter IV, p. 300); *abar wāwarīgānīh ī mowbedan mowbed pad wizīr kardan* 'On the (absolute) reliability of the Chief Mobed with regard to passing judgement' (DkM 711.12).

55 On the meaning and provenance of the phrase *srēnag/sēnag masāy ud bāzā masāy*, lit. 'the size of a buttock and size of a forefoot', designating the remuneration of the guardian (*sālār*) and the *stŭ̄r* see Chapter I, pp. 76–77; on the monetary equivalent see Chapter II, pp. 173–174.

mistress of the house (*dūdag kadag-bānūg*). And (it is) as follows: if she (= the mistress of the house) has not performed the task and dies without having born a son, (then) the daughter, who has not married, the one who has not taken a husband, (is) the 'intermediary successor' (*aeuuō kaē*).[56] It is necessary that she take possession of the property of the family mistress of the house (*dūdag kadag-bānūg*), that (which is) in it for 'substitute succession' (*ōy padiš stŭrīhā*).

13. When she (= the daughter) takes a husband during *stŭr*-ship, then the property goes to her in ownership (*pad xwēšīh*). If the family mistress of the house dies and the daughters have married, (then the position of) 'substitute succession' (*stŭrīh*) has to be officially appointed (*gumārišn*).

Pursišn **54** (K35, fol. 173v.14–174r.1; TD4a, p. 328, 6–11)[57]:

1. *panǰāh-čahārom pursišn pāsox ān ī*[58] *pursēd kū awēšān kē-šān pad stōš dāštan ī*[59] *kas xwēškārīh ud griftārīh kē ast kē bawēd?*
2. *pāsox ēd kū mard pad stōš ī zan (ī) pādixšāyīhā*[60] *pid ān ī frazand xwadāy ān ī*[61] *bandag dāštan frēzwānīg guft ēstēd.*

1. The fifty-fourth question (and) answer: That which you ask: Whose duty (*xwēškārīh*) and responsibility (*griftārīh*) is it and shall it be (*kē ast kē bawēd*) to keep/protect (the deceased's soul) by (performing) *stōš* (*pad stōš dāštan*)?[62]
2. The answer (is) this: it is said that a man is obliged to keep/protect (the soul) of (his) *pādixšāy*-wife by (performing) the *stōš* (prayers), the father (the soul) of (his) child, the master (the soul) of (his) servant/slave (*bandag*).

56 On *ayōgēn*, written here *aeuuō kaē* in *pāzand*, see Chapter II, pp. 163–168.
57 West 1882, p. 187; Anklesaria 1958, p. 114.
58 K35: om.; TD4a: ⟨Y⟩.
59 K35: om.; TD4a: ⟨Y⟩.
60 TD4a: ⟨W⟩; K35: om.
61 K35: ⟨Y⟩; TD4a: om.
62 The *stōš/sidōš* (MacKenzie 1971, p. 77) are the prayers said by relatives for the soul of the departed in the interval of three nights (and the fourth morning) after death, when Rašn evaluates the person's sins and virtues and passes judgement (*āmār ī stōš* 'reckoning of *stōš*'; WīZ 30.43; Gignoux/Tafazzoli 1993, pp. 106–107; Sohn 1996, pp. 80–81; see also Chapter V, pp. 401–402). The term also designates the commemoration ceremonies for dead relatives held on their monthly and yearly anniversaries: *pad stōš dāštan*, lit. 'to keep/protect (the soul) by (performing) the *stōš* (prayers/ceremonies)' refers to the obligation of the relatives to attend to the soul of the deceased by praying on his/her decease and ordering the proper ceremonies to be held in commemoration of the person's soul, which are described in Vd 8.22, (Moazami 2014, pp. 232–235); Dd 27 (Jaafari-Dehaghi 1998, pp. 88–89); Šnš XVII (Kotwal 1969, pp. 70–75). See also Williams 1990, pt. II, p. 150, n. 5. This *Pursišn* names the specific individuals held responsible for performing, ordering (and financing) these vast religious rites.

***Pursišn* 55** (K35, fol. 174r.1–174v.14; TD4a, pp. 328.11–330.11)[63]:

1. *panǰāh-panǰom pursišn ud pāsox ān ī pursēd kū ēn stūrīh ud*[64] *dūdag-sālārīh*[65] *čē ast ud čē bawēd*[66] *čē ēwēnag abāyēd gumārdan u-š*[67] *xwarišn ud wastarag az kū abāyēd kardan u-š čiyōn abāyēd būd*[68]*?*
2. *pāsox ēd kū stūrīh ēdōn bawēd ka kū mard ī wehdēn* ⁺*āzād*[69] *ī*[70] *šāhān šāh*[71] *bandag kē-š zan ud frazand ī pādixšāyīhā ud padīriftag ud brād ī hambāy ud stūr ī*[72] *kardag nēst u-š xwāstag šast stēr ast ī barōmand*[73] *widerān bawēd ud ān*[74] *xwāstag ōdāyēnd ān widardag*[75] *guharīg paydāg kunišn ud xwānīhēd stūr*[76].
3. *u-š padiš*[77] *gumārišn ān ī nazdīktar az ham-nāfān*[78] *kē pad ān ī ōy nāmagānīh rāyēnēd ud paywand dārēd.*
4. *xwāstag dūdag-sālārīh ān bawēd ka*[79] *mard pad ān ēwēnag kē-š zan ayāb duxt ayāb pus (ī) aburnāyag pad xwēš sālārīh nē šāyēnd abar [abar]*[80] *dūdag-sālār gumārišn.*
5. *ēdōn abāyēd gumārdan ud stūr dūdag sālārīh čiyon-šān ast sazāgīh pad hangām abayēd gumārdan ud ka widerēd mard ī čiyōn nibišt pad ān*[81] *gāh ī čiyōn nibišt abāyēd gumārdan ud zamānīg nē dastwarīhā spōxtan abar*[82] *sāl dra(h)nāy.*
6. *pad stūrīh xwah ī purnāy kē pad any dūdag nē stūr pas duxt ī brād ud pas pus ī brād pas abārīg paywand ī nazdīktar pad dūdag-sālārīh fradom pid ī čagar pas brād pas* ⁺*pus*[83] *ud pas abārīg paywand ī nazdīktar andar brādarān andar ān ē meh sazāgtar.*

63 West 1882, pp. 188–190; Anklesaria 1958, pp. 115–116; de Menasce 1964, pp. 33–34.
64 TD4a: ⟨W⟩; K35: om.
65 K35: ⟨dwtk' srd'lyh⟩; TD4a: ⟨dwtk Y srd'lyh⟩.
66 Thus K35; TD4a: om. ⟨MH̱ 'YT W MH̱ YHWWNyt⟩ *čē ast ud čē bawēd*.
67 K35: deleted ⟨'p'yt'⟩; *super lin.*: ⟨'P-š⟩; TD4a: ⟨'P-š⟩.
68 K35: ⟨YHWWNt'⟩; TD4a: ⟨YHWWNyt⟩.
69 Both K35 and TD4a: ⟨'p'yt'⟩.
70 K35: ⟨'D⟩; TD4a: ⟨Y⟩.
71 K35: ⟨MLK''nyh'⟩; TD4a: ⟨MLK''n MLK'⟩.
72 K35: ⟨stwlyh⟩ *super.lin.* ⟨Y⟩; TD4a: ⟨stwl W krk'⟩.
73 Thus K35; TD4a: ins. ⟨W⟩.
74 Thus K35; TD4a: ⟨ZK Y⟩.
75 K35: ⟨wtwltk'⟩; TD4a: ⟨wtltk'⟩.
76 K35: ⟨stwlyh⟩; TD4a: ⟨stwl⟩.
77 K35: ⟨'P-š pt-š⟩; TD4a: om.
78 K35: ⟨hm'p'n⟩; TD4a: ⟨hmn'p'n⟩.
79 Thus K35; TD4a: ins. ⟨'MT YHWWNyt⟩.
80 K35: *super lin.* ⟨MDM⟩.
81 Thus K35; TD4a: ⟨ZK Y⟩.
82 K35: ⟨MDM⟩; TD4a: ⟨MN⟩.
83 K35: ⟨'HL BRTH̱⟩; TD4a: ⟨'H BRTH̱⟩, both mss. have ⟨BRTH̱⟩ *duxt*; in this context most likely a mistake for the similarly written ⟨BRH̱⟩ *pus*.

7. *ud zan (ī) pādaxšāyīhā kē dūdag kadag-bānūg ayōgēn-stūr ast zīndag pus ī aburnāy tā purnāy bawēd duxt ī dūdag tā pad sālārīh*[84] *bawēd ī dūdag-sālārān*[85] *tā*[86] *andar kār bawēd xwarišn wastarg az xīr ī dūdag ēwēnag būd dūdag-sālār*[87] *sēnag masāy bāzā masāy har māh-ē(w)*[88] *4 stēr ī ast 16 (drahm ī) purr.*
8. *zan ka šāyēd ēdōn čiyōn kadag-bānūg hammis ēdōn čiyōn-šān adwadād*[89] *brahnagīhā ud a-dādīhā abar nē rasēd az bar ayāb az bun ī xwāstag ī pad dūdag ēstēd ud xwarišn ud wastarg darmān pānagīh handāzišn*[90].

1. The fifty-fifth question and answer: That which you ask: What is 'substitute succession' (*stūrīh*) and guardianship (*sālārīh*) and how is it considered (*čē ast ud čē bawēd*)? In which manner should they (= proxy and guardian) be officially appointed (*gumārdan*) and from whence should they receive food and clothing and how must it be?
2. The answer (is) this: 'substitute succession' (*stūrīh*) is considered as this: when a man of the Good Religion has passed away, (who is born) free, a subject of the King of Kings, who has no *pādixšāy*-wife and children nor adopted ones, nor a shareholding brother (*brād ī hambāy*), nor an appointed proxy by testament (*stūr ī kardag*), but has income producing (*barōmand*) property worth 60 stater, and they take care (*ōdāyēnd*)[91] of the property of the deceased, (then) a substitute (*guharīg*) must be established and (he/she) is called *stūr.*
3. And for him (= the deceased) the closest of his relatives (*ham-⁺nāfān*) should be appointed (*gumārišn*) who will procure the cult of his (= the deceased's) name (*nāmagānīh*) and (his) offspring (*paywand*).
4. Guardianship of the property (and) the family (*xwāstag dūdag-sālārīh*) is considered as this: If the circumstances of a man are such that his wife or his daughter or his underage son cannot exercise guardianship over their own (persons), (then) a family-guardian (*dūdag-sālār*) has to be appointed (*gumārišn*) over them.
5. They should be appointed (*abāyēd gumārdan*) in this manner: the proxy (*stūr*) and the guardian (*sālār*) must be appointed according to their suitabil-

84 Thus K35; TD4a: ⟨'D srd'l⟩.
85 TD4a: *super lin.* ⟨dwtk'⟩.
86 K35: *super lin.* ⟨'D⟩.
87 Thus K35; TD4a: ⟨dwtk' dwtk srd'l⟩.
88 K35: ⟨BYRH-1⟩; TD4a: ⟨GBR'-1⟩.
89 TD4a: *super lin.* ⟨'tpd't⟩.
90 K35: ⟨hnd'čšn'⟩; TD4a: ⟨hnd'čšnyk⟩.
91 MMP ⟨'wd'y⟩ *udāy-* 'to help, save' (Durkin-Meisterernst 2004, p. 66); Skjærvø (by personal communication) reads MP ⟨'wt'y-⟩ *ōdāy-* 'to take care of', from the Iranian stem √**daH⁵* 'nourish, suck, suckle' (Cheung 2007, p. 47); comparing MP *dāyag* '(wet-) nurse'. The meaning established by Skjærvø fits in very well with this passage and the attestations of the word in MMP texts.

ity (*sazāgīh*) within a (prescribed) period (*pad hangām*). And when a man passes away in the manner described (above), (then) they must be appointed within the timespan (*gāh*) as written (above). And one is not entitled to delay (the matter) more than a year.

6. For 'substitute succession' (*stūrīh*) the mature sister, who is not a proxy (*stūr*) in another family, then the daughter of the brother and then the son of the brother, then another relative, who is closest (to the deceased), (is) most suitable (*sazāgtar*). For family guardianship (*dūdag-sālārīh*) first the *čagar*-father, then the brother, then the +son and then another relative who is closest (to the deceased) (is) most suitable. Among the brothers the one who is the oldest (is) most suitable.
7. And the *pādixšāy*-wife, who is the family mistress of the house (*dūdag kadag-bānūg*) (and) 'intermediary successor and proxy' (*ayōgēn-stūr*) has a legal right (*ēwēnag būd*) as long as she lives (*zīndag*) to food and clothing from the property of the family (*az xīr ī dūdag*), the underage son until he reaches maturity, the daughter of the family as long as she is under guardianship, the family-guardians (*dūdag-sālāran*) as long as they are in office (*andar kār*). The guardian (receives remuneration) 'the size of a buttock and size of a forefoot' (*sēnag masāy ud bāzā masāy*)[92] every month four stater, that is 16 full (drachms).
8. (Other) wives, if it is possible, should be apportioned (*handāzišn*) together with the mistress of the house (*kadag-bānūg*), from the increase (*bar*) or the substance (*bun*) of the property, which is at the disposal of the family, both food and clothing, remedy (*darmān*) and shelter (*pānagīh*), so that they are not subject to 'abandonment/withdrawal of sustenance' (*adwadād*)[93] and nakedness (*brahnagīhā*) and lawlessness (*adādīhā*).

***Pursišn* 56** (K35, fol. 174v.14–175r.6; TD4a, pp. 330.11–331.5)[94]:

1. *panǰāh-šešom pursišn*[95] *ān ī pursēd kū kē stūrīh šāyēd kē*[96] *nē šāyēd.*
2. *pāsox ēd kū mard ī purnāy ī hudēn ī ōšyārag*[97] *ī šāhān-šāh bandag ī*[98] *frazand-ēmēdag nē margarzān pad stūrīh šāyēd ayāb ka-iz stūrīh-ē(w) ayāb was stūrīh padīrift ēstēd pas-iz pad any stūrīh šāyēd.*
3. *ud zan ī purnāy ud aburnāyag-iz pad ēk stūrīh šāyēd ka pad dūdag-ē(w)*[99] *stūr-ē(w) pad any stūrīh nē šāyēd mard šāyēd.*

92 On this phrase see fn. 55 above.
93 On this technical term see Macuch 2012a, 2012b, and Chapter I, pp. 75–76; Chapter V, pp. 463–468.
94 West 1882, pp. 190–191; Anklesaria 1958, p. 117; de Menasce 1964, pp. 34–35.
95 K35: ⟨pwrsšn' p'shw⟩, TD4a: ⟨pwrsšn'⟩.
96 K35: ⟨MN⟩; TD4a: ⟨MNW⟩.
97 K35: ⟨'wšy'lk⟩; TD4a: ⟨'wšy'l⟩.
98 TD4a: ⟨Y⟩; K35: om.
99 TD4a: repeats ⟨'MT pt̲ dwtk-1⟩

4. *zan*[100] *ka*[101] *bandag paristār ayāb* ⁺*an-ēr*[102] *ayāb ag-dēn ayāb margarzān hēnd pad stūrīh a-sazāg ēdōn-iz ān ī šābestān ud ān ī (a-)šusᵃr zan (ī) rōspīg ān ī daštān-sazāg.*

1. The fifty sixth question: That which you ask: Who is suitable for 'substitute succession' (*stūrīh*), who is not suitable?
2. The answer (is) this: A mature man, (adherent) of the Good Religion (*hudēn*), who is sane (*ōšyārag*), a subject of the King of Kings (*šāhān šāh bandag*), procreative (*frazand-ēmēdag*), not death-deserving (*nē margarzān*) is suitable for 'substitute sucession' (*stūrīh*). Or if he has already (accepted) a *stūrīh* or many *stūrīh*s (and) is later (requested) for another *stūrīh*, he is suitable.
3. And the mature woman and also the underage one is suitable for one *stūrīh*. If she is proxy (*stūr*) in one family, she is not suitable for another *stūrīh*. The man is suitable.
4. Women, who are slaves (*bandag*), servants (*paristār*) or foreigners (⁺*an-ēr*) or adherents of an evil religion (*ag-dēn*) or death-deserving (*margarzān*) are not suitable for *stūrīh*. The same applies to eunuchs (*šābestān*) and (men) who have no semen (*[a-]šusar*), (to) prostitutes (*zan ī rōzpīg*) and (women) in menopause (*daštān-sazāg*).[103]

***Pursišn* 57** (K35, fol. 175r.7–17; TD4a, p. 331.5–332.1)[104]:

1. *panǰāh-haftom pursišn ān ī pursēd kū čand ēwēnag bawēd dūdag-sālārīh ud stūrīh.*
2. *pāsox ēd kū 3 ēwēnag bawēd guft ēstēd ī ast*[105] *būdag ud kardag ud gumārdag.*
3. *ud stūr (ī) būdag ēdōn čiyōn zan ī pādixšāyīhā duxt ī ayōgēn az pad xwad ēstišnīh stūr*[106] *čiyōn ān bawēd*[107] *ka zan nēst duxt kē-š šōy nēst nē kard ēstēd ān ēk*[108] *mānd ēstēd.*
4. *stūr ī kardag ēdōn pus ī padīriftag kē-š xwad padīrift ud az gumārdan*[109] *abē-niyāz.*[110]

100 K35: after ⟨NYŠH̱⟩ the first three letters of the heterogram ⟨NYŠ⟩ are mistakenly repeated.
101 K35: *super lin.*: ⟨'MT'⟩.
102 K35: ⟨'n'wyl⟩; TD4a: ⟨'n'w''nyl⟩.
103 Tentative translation, lit. 'whose menstruation is passing'; in this specific context *sazāg* cannot mean 'suitable' (MacKenzie 1971, p. 74; √*sač¹ 'to fit, be suitable, be able, be in command of'; Cheung 2007, pp. 323–324) as in the preceding passages, but is probably a pres.pt. of the verb *sazistan*, *saz-* 'to pass' (MacKenzie *ibid.*, p. 74); √*sač² 'to pass' (Cheung *ibid.*, pp. 324–325). On the ending *-āg* see Durkin-Meisterernst 2014, p. 162 (§ 311) and pp. 249–250 (§ 502).
104 West 1882, pp. 191–192; Anklesaria 1958, p. 118; de Menasce 1964, p. 35.
105 K35: ⟨Y 'YT'⟩; TD4a: ⟨'YT' Y⟩.
106 K35: ⟨stwl⟩; TD4a: ⟨stwlyh⟩.
107 K35: ⟨YHWWNyt'⟩; TD4a: ⟨YHWWNytk'⟩.
108 K35: ⟨ZK 'ywk⟩; TD4a: ⟨ZK Y 'ywk⟩.
109 K35: ⟨gwm'lt'⟩; TD4a: ⟨gwm'ltn'⟩.

5. *ud stŭr ī gumārdag ān ī andar paywandān ī pad stŭrīh šāyēd ud* ⁺*ōy* [111] *ān kē stŭr gumārišn nazdīktar ud* [112] *padān ī dēn gumārišn.*
6. *ud* [113] *dūdag-sālārīh būdag pus*[114] *ān ī gumārdag*[115] *ān ī kē-š*[116] *mardān nabānazdištān nazdīktarīh* ⁺*rāy*[117] *gumārīhēd.*

1. The fifty-seventh question. That which you ask: How many types of family-guardianship (*dūdag-sālārīh*) and 'substitute succession/proxy-ship' (*stŭrīh*) are there?
2. The answer (is) this: It is said that there are three types, which are: 'natural' (*būdag*), 'appointed' (*kardag*) and 'nominated' (*gumārdag*).
3. And the 'natural proxy' (*stŭr [ī] būdag*), such as the *pādixšāy*-wife (and) the *ayōgēn*-daughter, are proxies (*stŭr*) due to their very existence (*pad xwad ēstišnīh*). The (latter) is in force when there is no wife, (but) a daughter, who has no husband, has not married, that one (daughter) remains (as 'intermediary successor'; *ayōgēn).*
4. The 'appointed proxy' (*stŭr ī kardag*) (is) thus: (he is) the adopted son, whom he (= the *paterfamilias)* himself has adopted and there is no need to nominate (another proxy).
5. And the 'nominated proxy' (*stŭr ī gumārdag*) (is) the one who is suitable among the family members for *stŭr*-ship. And (it should be) the one closest to the one for whom a proxy (*stŭr*) has to be nominated and religious authorities (*padān ī dēn*) should nominate him.
6. And (regarding) family-guardianship (*dūdag-sālārīh*): the 'natural' (*būdag*) (is) the son; the nominated (*gumārdag*) (is) the one who has been nominated due to his proximity (to the deceased) among the male relatives.[118]

***Pursišn* 58** (K35, fol. 175r.17–175v.8; TD4a, p. 332.1–9)[119]:

1. *panjah-haštom pursišn pāsox*[120] *ān ī pursēd kū pad čand xwāstag ēg-iš stŭr-ē(w) padiš abāyēd gumārdan.*

110 K35: ⟨'ywb nyy'c⟩; TD4a: ⟨'pynyy'c⟩.
111 K35: ⟨š'yt' W 'L⟩; TD4a: ⟨'št' 'L 'L⟩.
112 K35: ⟨W⟩; TD4a: om.
113 K35: ⟨W⟩; TD4a: ⟨Y⟩.
114 K35: ⟨k'l 'BYDWNyt⟩; TD4a: ⟨bwtk' BRH̱⟩.
115 K35: ⟨gwm'ltk'⟩; TD4a: ⟨krtk'⟩.
116 K35: ⟨MN⟩; TD4a: ⟨MNW š⟩.
117 Both mss.: ⟨r's⟩.
118 In this list of persons suited for family guardianship TD4a mentions the *būdag* and *kardag* types (both missing in K35), but not the *gumārdag* variant. The definition in this ms. for *kardag* guardianship, however, is wrong and refers obviously to the *gumārdag* type. K35 only notes the *gumārdag* variant, but gives the correct definition. It seems very likely that different parts of the original text are missing in both mss. On *dūdag-sālārīh* see Chapter II, pp. 177–183.
119 West 1882, pp. 192; Anklesaria 1958, p. 119; de Menasce 1964, p. 35.
120 Thus K35; Td4a: om. ⟨p'shw'⟩.

2. *pāsox ēd kū ka xwāstag kē ōy mānd kē-š stŭ̆r abāyēd gumārdan*[121] *čand 60 stēr ī barōmand ast ēg-iš stŭ̆r padiš gumārdan*[122] *frēzwānīg ud ka-iz kam ast ōy kē-š stŭ̆rīh*[123] *niyābag ast stŭ̆rīh* *+rāyēnīdan*[124] *padīrēnd* *+homānag*[125] *+stŭ̆r-ē(w)*[126] *padiš gumārišn ka nē pad xwēšīh be*[127] *ō ōy rasēd kē pad stŭ̆rīh*[128] *sazāgtar.*

1. The fifty-eighth question (and) answer. That which you ask: For how much property must a proxy (*stŭ̆r*) be nominated for him (= the deceased)?
2. The answer (is) this: If the property left by the one for whom a proxy (*stŭ̆r*) should be nominated is (worth) sixty income-producing (*barōmand)* stater, then it is obligatory (*frēzwānīg*) to nominate a proxy for him (*padiš gumārdan*). And even if it is less (and) establishing 'substitute succession' (*stŭ̆rīh*) for the one who is in need of a *stŭ̆rīh* is accepted, (then) a proxy should likewise be nominated for him, if it (= the property) does not go in ownership (*pad xwēšīh*) to the one, who is most suited (*sazāgtar*) for (practising) *stŭ̆rīh.*

***Pursišn* 59** (K35, fol. 175v.8–176r.1; TD4a, pp. 332.9–333.5)[129]:

1. *panǰāh-nohom pursišn pāsox*[130] *ān ī pursēd kū az nē gumārdan wināh čē.*
2. *pāsox ēd kū xwad pādixšāy ka xwāstag hamāg pad ahlawdād be dahēd ka-š xīr nēst stŭ̆rīh ī awiš nē kard ōy-š*[131] *paywandān padiš a-wināh*[132] *hēnd.*
3. *bē ōy kē-š*[133] *stŭ̆rīh ī widardag padīrift*[134] *ayāb-iš* *+gāh*[135] *ī stŭ̆rīh padīrift ēstēd ud xwāstag ī pad stŭ̆rīh stad ēstēd stŭ̆rgar gumārd ud stŭ̆rīh nē rāyēnēd bun kardag-+ē*[136] *+wišōb(ēd)*[137] *ud nāmagānīh be abganēd ud xwāstag be abesīhēnēd ud stŭ̆rīh be škenēd ka-š a-bōyīh*[138] *rāy guft ēstēd margarzān abar drahm-ē(w)*[139] *wināh be ōzad*[140] *nē guft ēstēd.*

121 TD4a: ins. ⟨Y⟩. K35: om.
122 K35: ⟨gwm'ltn'⟩; TD4a: ⟨gwm'lt⟩.
123 K35: ⟨'LH̱ MNW-š stwlyh⟩; TD4a: ⟨'DYN-š stwl⟩.
124 Both mss.: ⟨l'dynyt'⟩
125 Both mss.: ⟨hm'nwk'⟩.
126 K35: ⟨stwlyh⟩; TD4a: ⟨pṯ stwlyh⟩.
127 K35: ⟨BR'⟩; TD4a: ⟨pṯ⟩.
128 K35: ⟨stwlyh⟩; TD4a: ⟨stwl⟩.
129 West 1882, pp. 192–193; Anklesaria 1958, p. 120.
130 K35: ⟨p'shw'⟩; TD4a: om.
131 K35: ⟨'LH̱-š⟩; TD4a: ⟨'LH̱ wyš⟩.
132 K35: ⟨'-wn's⟩; TD4a: ⟨wn's⟩.
133 K35: ⟨BR' 'LH̱ MNW-š⟩; TD4a: ⟨BR' MNW-š⟩.
134 K35: ⟨MKBYLWNṯ⟩; TD4a: ⟨MKBLWNṯ⟩.
135 Both mss.: ⟨g'y⟩.
136 K35: ⟨Y⟩; TD4a: om.
137 Both mss.: ⟨wšwp'⟩.
138 K35: ⟨'bwdyh⟩; TD4a: ⟨'bwd nsy⟩.
139 K35: ⟨ZWZN'-1⟩; TD4a: ⟨'wgwn'⟩.
140 K35: ⟨YKTLWNt⟩; TD4a:⟨YKTLWNyt⟩.

1. The fifty-ninth question (and) answer. That which you ask: What is the sin of not nominating (a proxy)?
2. The answer (is) this: He (= the deceased) himself is authorized to give his whole property (*xwāstag hamāg*) as a pious gift (*pad ahlawdād*). If he has no (more) property (and) no 'substitute succession' (*stūrīh*) is established for him, his relatives are without sin.
3. But (if) someone has accepted the *stūr*-ship of the deceased or the position (+*gāh*) of *stūr*-ship has been accepted and a proxy (*stūrgar*)[141] is nominated for the property that has been taken for *stūrīh* and he/she does not exercise *stūrīh* (and) destroys (*wišōb[ēd]*) a part of the substance (*bun kardag*-+*ē*) and throws away (*be abganēd*) the 'cult of the name' (*nāmagānīh*) and ruins (*be abesīhēnēd*) the property and breaks (*be škenēd*) *stūrīh*: (even) if it is said that he/she (acted) unconsciously (*a-bōyīh*), it (is) a *margarzān*-sin regarding (every) single drachm. It is not said that (the offender) is killed outright.

***Pursišn* 60** (K35, fol. 176r.2–11; TD4a, p. 333.5–15)[142]:

1. *šastom pursišn pāsox*[143] *ān ī pursēd kū* +*šāyist*[144] *nē* +*šāyist*[145] *xūbīh nē xūbīh (ī) dūdag-sālārīh čē bawēd*[146].
2. *pāsox ēd kū xūbīh gumārišn padīrišn ud ān kē sazāgtar xūbtarīh frazāmēnēd.*
3. *nē xūbīh ān ī a-sazāg ayāb ān kē-š sazāgīh nē gumārd*[147] *nē xūbtarīh spōxtan wiškīdan ī* +*sazāgān*[148] *stūrīh dūdag-sālārīh.*
4. *kē pad stūrīh šāyēd kē nē šāyēd purnāy*[149] *ī weh-dēn ī xwēškārīh ī andar paywand ī pidarān* +*ōy*[150] *kē dūdag-sālār gumārišn*[151] *nazdīktar xwurdag ōšmārišn ī 5 fragard ī huspārom ud griftagīhā ī andar nask*[152] *nask uskār(išn) ī andar was dādestān*-+*nāmag*[153].

1. The sixtieth question (and) answer. That which you ask: What is allowed (and) not allowed, (what) is proper (and) improper with regard to family-guardianship (*dūdag-sālārīh*)?

141 On the suffix *-gar* forming agent nouns see Durkin-Meisterernst 2014, p. 167, §§ 326 and 327.
142 West 1882, pp. 193–194; Anklesaria 1958, p. 121.
143 K35: ⟨p'shw'⟩; TD4a: om.
144 K 35: ⟨šy'yst'⟩; TD4a: ⟨š'yyt'⟩.
145 K 35: ⟨šy'yst'⟩; TD4a: ⟨š'yyt'⟩.
146 K35: ⟨YIIWWNyt⟩; TD4a: ⟨'YT'⟩.
147 K35: ⟨gwm'lt'⟩; TD4a: ⟨gwm'lytn'⟩.
148 K35. ⟨sc'n⟩; TD4a: ⟨sc'k⟩.
149 K35: ⟨'pwln'y⟩; TD4a: ⟨pwln'y⟩.
150 Both mss: ⟨'L⟩.
151 TD4a: ins. ⟨Y⟩; K35: om.
152 K35: ins. ⟨W⟩; TD4a: om.
153 K35: ⟨d'tst'n 'mk⟩; TD4a: ⟨d'tsp'n'⟩.

2. The answer (is) this: it (is) proper to accept the nomination (*gumārišn padīrišn*)[154] and the one who is most suitable (*sazāgtar*) accomplishes it (= guardianship) in the most proper manner.
3. It (is) not proper, (when) an unsuitable (*a-sazāg*) (person is nominated) or the one, who is suitable (*kē-š sazāgīh*), has not been nominated; (moreover,) disobeying (*spōxtan*) in a most improper manner (and) separating (*wiškīdan*) *stūrīh* (and) family-guardianship (*dūdag-sālārīh*) of those who are suitable (for both tasks, is not proper).
4. (On the question) who is allowed for *stūrīh*, who is not allowed; (on) the person of age[155] of the Good Religion, who has a duty (*xwēškārīh*) in the family of the forefathers (*paywand [ī] pidarān*), who is the closest (relative) of the one nominated as family-guardian, (many) details are enumerated in five sections (*fragard*) of the Huspārom (Nask) and the problems (*griftagīhā*) discussed in each *nask* (*nask nask uskār[išn]*) (are) in numerous Law-books (*dādestān-⁺nāmag*).

***Pursišn* 61** (K35, fol. 176r.11–177r.1; TD4a, pp. 333.15–335.9)[156]:

1. *šast-ēkom pursišn pāsox*[157] *ān ī pursēd kū baxšišn ī mayān wehdēnān pad xwāstag mīrāṯ*[158] *čiyōn ēstēd u-šān čiyōn padiš abāyēd ēstād.*
2. *pāsox ēd kū xwāstag pad xwāstagdārīh azabar azēr ēdōn rasēd čiyōn āb ka pad jōy pad šēb šawēd bē ka ō frōd widarag bandīhēd*[159] *pad *ping-āb*[160] *abāz šawēd ēnyā ō pas nē šawēd.*
3. *ka handarz ud any*[161] *čīš andar nēst xwāstag be ō zan duxt ī pādixšāy ud agar-iš pad handarz čīš-ē(w) dahēd ēnyā-iš awiš nē ⁺niyāzēd.*[162]
4. *ān kē-š nē kard bahr-ē(w) pus rāy har ēk hāwand ud zan ī pādixšāyīhā dō hāwand ud pusarān zan-iz ī pus-ē(w) ān kē pad har dō čašm kūr ayāb pad*

154 Lit. 'the propriety (lies in) accepting the nomination'.
155 The two manuscripts differ fundamentally: according to K35 this passage refers to the *aburnāy*, the underage child, whereas TD4a has *purnāy*, the adult or person of age. Although K35 is on the whole more reliable, it does seem rather unlikely that the whole Huspārom *nask* would only be concerned with the suitability of an underage child, who, according to other attestations, was not regarded as a candidate for either of the two institutions discussed here.
156 West 1882, pp. 194–196; Anklesaria 1958, pp. 122–123.
157 K35: ⟨p'shw'⟩; TD4a: om.
158 K35: ⟨myl't'⟩; TD4a: ⟨myl'yt'⟩. This is not an Iranian term, but presumably an Arabic loan-word in this late Pahlavi text from the 9th century: *mīrāṯ* 'heritage, succession, patrimony' (Steingass 1892, p. 1361). Arabic loan-words can already be found in documents written in the Pahlavi cursive script from the late 7th and 8th centuries (see *e.g.* Weber 2014b).
159 K35: ⟨'SLNx2yhyt'⟩; TD4a: ⟨BR' 'SLWNx2yhyt'⟩.
160 K35: ⟨png'p'⟩; TD4a: ⟨png'p⟩; (tentative reading **ping-āb*); see below fn. 171.
161 K35: ⟨WW 'HRN⟩; TD4a: ⟨W 'HRN⟩.
162 K35: ⟨yy'cyt'⟩; TD4a: ⟨''tyt'⟩.

har dō pāy armēšt ayāb-(6)iš har dō dast +*abēkār*[163] *dō and čand ān ī drust bahr niyābag.*

5. *ān kē andar* +*sālārīh ī pid*[164] *andar sālārīh ēstēd čiyōn ka pid ayāb mād zarmān* +*wizīrēnd*[165] *ayāb parwarišn ī jud az ōy ī sālār*[166] *ayāb-iš brād ayāb xwāh ī aburnāy ayāb pid ayāb a-parwarišn jud az ōy a-sālār mard (ī) tuwān passazag sālārīh ud pānag*[167] *parwarišn frēzwānīg būd.*
6. *frāz az ōy xwāstagdārān ī ōy kē xwāstag kard ēdōn frēzwānīg čiyōn ōy frēzwānīg būd.*
7. *agar az ān pus*[168] *nē bē-š duxt ayāb zan ast ud agar az ān mard čiyōn zan pad sālārīh nē šāyēnd dūdag-sālār*[169] *abāyēd gumārd.*
8. *agar-iš zan-iz duxtar nēst*[170] *stūr abāyēd gumārdan ēd kū ka dūdag-sālār abāyēd gumārdan kē sazāgtar ka stūr abāyēd gumārdan čē sazāgtar pad dar ī pursišn nibišt.*

1. The sixty-first question (and) answer. That which you ask: How is the partitioning (*baxšišn*) of the inherited property to be undertaken among the adherents of the Good Religion and how should they (= the heirs and beneficiaries) react to it?
2. The answer (is) this: Property in inheritance (*pad xwāstagdārīh*) is transmitted from above (to) below in the manner of water, when it flows in a stream on a declivity: unless its downward passage is closed (and) it flows back, (as) in the water clock (**ping-āb*), otherwise it does not flow back.[171]

163 K35: ⟨ʾpkʾl⟩; TD4a: ⟨ʾpydʾl⟩.
164 K35: ⟨BYN ʾB' Y srdʾlyh⟩ (*super lin.* ⟨ʾB' Y⟩); TD4a: ⟨ZK Y MNW ʾB' Y srdʾlyh⟩.
165 K35: ⟨wcylyn⟩; TD4a: ⟨wcyl⟩.
166 K35: ⟨ʿLH̱ Y srdʾl⟩; TD4a: ⟨ʿLH̱ ʾ-srdʾl⟩.
167 K35: ⟨pʾnk'⟩; TD4a: ⟨pʾnkyh⟩
168 K35: ⟨MN ZK BRH̱⟩ ; TD4a: ⟨ZK Y GBRʾ BRH̱⟩.
169 K35: ⟨dwtk' srdʾl⟩; TD4a: ⟨dwtk dʾl⟩.
170 K35: ⟨BRTH̱l LʿYT'⟩; TD4a: ⟨BRTH̱l pṯ⟩.
171 The expression read here tentatively as **ping-āb* seems to denote an instrument used for measuring time with water (clepsydra); see Steingass 1892, p. 258, NP *ping*: 'a copper basin with a small hole in the bottom, for water in which it is placed to flow through, used for measuring time; a clepsydra'. This sentence is of course a metaphor referring to the principle that inheritance is transmitted as a rule to the descendants (offspring, children) of a man, not to his ascendants (parents, grandparents) (= water flows from 'above [to] below', *azabar azēr*). The latter only inherit if there are no descendants. The image of the well-known water clock explains the *exception* to this rule: if the flow of water is blocked (= there are no descendants), then it rises, as in the water clock (= the inheritance goes to the ascendants). Water clocks belong to the oldest devices for time measuring in antiquity and were known in two forms involving the inflow or outflow of water. Our author obviously had the former type in mind: a container or bowl with markings and a small hole in the centre is placed in another larger basin full of water. The bowl sinks gradually into the basin as it is filled with rising water through the small hole and the observer can tell how much time has passed by reading the markings on the bowl (for further details on water clocks in antiquity, specifically Persia, and images of the instruments see Wikipedia, English).

3. If there is no last will (*handarz*) or any other issue (= disposition) in this (matter), (then) the property (*xwāstag*) (goes) to the *pādixšāy*-wife (and) daughter(s). If he (= the deceased) gives her (= the wife or daughter) something (else) in (his) last will, (it goes to her), otherwise she has no need of it.
4. He who has made no (will): the share (*bahr-ē*) of each son (is) exactly the same (*hāwand*). And the *pādixšāy*-wife (receives) twice as much. And it is fitting that the sons and also the wife of a son, who is blind in both eyes or crippled in both legs or whose both arms are inactive (receive) twice the share of a healthy one.
5. Those (persons) who (were) under the guardianship of the father, stay under guardianship (*sālārīh*). If an aged father or mother are dispensed with, or (when) their sustenance (*parwarišn*) (is) separate from (that of) the one who (is) guardian, or (when) he (has) an underage brother or sister or a father, or (when the persons concerned are) without sustenance (*a-parwarišn*), (are) separate from him (and have) no guardian (*a-sālār*), a suitable, legally capable man (*mard [ī] tuwān passazag*) is obliged to (provide) guardianship (*sālārīh*) and shelter (*pānag*) and nourishment (*parwarišn*) (for them).
6. After his death (*frāz az ōy*) his heirs (*xwāstagdārān*), to whom the property has been bequeathed, are (just) as obliged (to provide for them) as he (= the deceased) was obliged to.
7. If he (= the deceased) has no son, but a daughter or a wife, and if no-one among the (relatives) of the man or woman is suitable, a family-guardian (*dūdag-sālār*) must be nominated (*abāyēd gumārd*).
8. If he (= the deceased) has neither wife nor daughter, a 'proxy' (*stūr*) must be nominated. As to the (questions), who is most suitable, when a family-guardian (*dūdag-sālār*) has to be nominated, (and) who is most suitable, when a 'proxy' (*stūr*) has to be nominated, these have been recorded in the (corresponding) *Pursišn*-chapters (above).

Appendix II

Dādestān ī dēnīg: On Sale (*Pursišn* 49, 51, 52)

The following passages on sale are not included in the edition of Jaafari-Dehaghi 1998, which only has the first part of the Dd (up to *Pursišn* 40). P. K. Anklesaria's 1958 Pahlavi edition of the second part of the Dd (*Pursišn* 41–92) has no transliteration, transcription or translation of the text, has not been published and contains numerous misreadings. The following transcription therefore does *not* rely on his edition, but is based on a collation of the two oldest manuscripts, K35 and TD4a. References to page numbers in Anklesaria's edition follow the above mentioned manuscript of the thesis submitted to the University of London in 1958. The only translation by West 1882 (pp. 176–183) is by now completely antiquated. All three *Pursišns* have been discussed extensively elsewhere by the present author (*Pursišn* 51 in Macuch 2022c; *Pursišn* 49 and 52 in Macuch 2024a). For a description of the surviving manuscripts of the Dd see West 1882, pp. xv–xix, P. K. Anklesaria 1958, pp. 7–37, and Jaafari-Dehaghi 1998, pp. 26–28.

***Pursišn* 49** (K35, fol. 170r, l. 4–170v., l. 5; TD4a, pp. 318.7–319.11)[1]

1. *čehel-nohom pursišn pāsox*[2] *ān (ī) pursēd kū kē*[3] *may* ⟨HS⟩ *frōšēd*[4] *be ō an-ērān ag-dēnān frōšēd*[5] *ēg-iš dādestān čē.*
2. *pāsox ēd kū aber saxt garān wināh bīm ud wad pēšagīhā.*
3. *bē agar kardan*[6] *ī-š ān may-frōšīh rāy may az awēšān kē may a-paymān xwarēnd*[7] *may xward*[8] *rāy wattar bawēnd*[9] *wēš abāz dārīhēd ō awēšān kē may pad paymān*[10] *xwarēnd may xwardan rāy weh bawānd*[11] *wēš rasēd kū ān ī ka ōy*[12] *ān may-frōšīh nē kard ēg-iš ān may*[13]*-frōšīh rāy tuwān ī pad*

1 Anklesaria 1958, p. 106; West 1882, pp. 176–177; Macuch 2024a.
2 K35: om., TD4a: ⟨p'shw Y⟩.
3 K35: om.; TD4a: ⟨MNW⟩.
4 K35: om.; TD4a: ⟨MZB̲NW-x2⟩;
5 K35: ⟨MZB̲NW-x2⟩ *super-lin.* ⟨-yym⟩; TD4a: ⟨MZB̲NW-x1⟩.
6 K35: ⟨krtn'⟩; TD4a: ⟨krt'⟩.
7 K35: om.; TD4a: ⟨'ŠTH̲nd⟩.
8 K35: only ⟨ŠTH̲t'⟩; TD4a: ⟨HS 'ŠT' 'ŠTH̲' t'⟩.
9 K35: ins. ⟨W⟩; TD4a: om.
10 K35: ⟨ptm'n'⟩; TD4a: ⟨ptm'n' Y⟩.
11 K35: ⟨YHWWNynnd⟩; TD4a: ⟨YHWWN'nd⟩.
12 K35: ⟨'LH̲'⟩; TD4a: ⟨'L⟩.
13 K35: om.; TD4a: ⟨HS⟩.

xwāstag[14] *kē-šān abāz dāštan mardōm pad wehdēnīh* *+pattāyēnēd*[15] *ud*[16] *az šudan*[17] *ī ō ag-dēnīh*[18] *wardēnēd rawāgīh ī*[19] *wināh bast*[20] *kirbag rawāgēnēd*[21] *ān*[22] *bawēd wehān ayārīh ud dēn-pānagīh wināh hamēmālīh ud*[23] *kirbag ayārīh ī ka nē kunēd ān may-frōšīh nē bawēd ī wēš frāy az wināh*[24] *wināh ud +wadīh*[25] *ī a-dādīhā xwarišnīh ī may rawāgīhēd ayāb-iš any meh-dādestānīh ud meh kirbag ī*[26] *ēwarīg.*

4. *andar ēdōn ōy kē may*[27] *ō*[28] *an-ērān ud ag-dēnān abārīg-iz kē*[29] *mastīh*[30] *rāy a-dādīh az-iš bawēd frōšēd*[31] *was wināhīhā nē dastwarīhā.*

1. Forty-ninth question (and) answer. That (which) you ask: One who sells wine (*may*), (if) he sells it to non-Iranians (*an-ērān*), infidels (*ag-dēnān*), then what is the judgment (*dādestān*)?
2. The answer (is) this: (There is) concern (*bīm*) that it (is) a very grievous sin (*saxt garān wināh*) and an evil profession (*wad pēšagīhā*).
3. But if by practicing wine-selling (to non-Iranians and infidels) the wine is kept away more *(wēš abāz dārīhēd)* from those who drink wine immoderately (*a-paymān* 'without measure') and become worse due to drinking wine and (if) more accrues (*wēš rasēd*) to those who may become better by drinking wine moderately (*pad paymān*) than if he (= the seller) had not sold the wine (to non-Iranians and infidels), then because of that sale they (= the Zoroastrians) (stay) solvent (*tuwān*) with regard to property (*xwāstag*), due to his restraining them, (and) the people are induced to remain in the Good Religion and to refrain from converting to the Evil Religion (and) the dissemination (*rawāgīh*) of sin is impeded (and) virtuous deeds are disseminated: this means aiding the righteous and guarding the Religion (and) opposing sin (and) promoting virtuous deeds. If he (= the seller) does not do (this), (if) no wine-selling (to infidels) takes place, (then there is) a large

14 K35: ⟨hw'stk' Y⟩; TD4a: om. ⟨Y⟩.
15 Both K35 and TD4a: ⟨ptyynyd'⟩.
16 K35: ⟨W⟩; TD4a: om.
17 K35: ⟨'ZLWNt'⟩; TD4a: ⟨'ZLWNytn'⟩.
18 K35: ⟨'kdyn' yh⟩; TD4a: ⟨'k 'dyn' yh⟩.
19 K35: ⟨Y⟩; TD4a: om.
20 K35: ⟨bst'⟩; TD4a: ⟨bstk'⟩.
21 K35: ⟨rwb'kynyt⟩; TD4a: ⟨rwb'ynytn'⟩.
22 K35: om.; TD4a: ins. ⟨Y⟩.
23 K35: ins. ⟨W⟩; TD4a: om.
24 K35: ⟨wn's⟩; TD4a: ⟨wn's⟩, super. lin. ⟨HS⟩.
25 K35: ⟨wt' Y⟩; TD4a: ⟨wyn'⟩.
26 K35: ⟨krpk' yh⟩, super lin.: ⟨Y⟩ (above ⟨–yh⟩); TD4a: ⟨krpk' Y⟩.
27 K35: ⟨wn's⟩; TD4a: ⟨HS⟩.
28 K35: ⟨'L⟩; TD4a: ⟨'LH̱⟩.
29 K35: ⟨MNW⟩; TD4a: ⟨Y⟩.
30 K35: ⟨mst' yh⟩; TD4a: ⟨mst' Y⟩.
31 K35: om.; TD4a: ins. ⟨W⟩.

increase in sin (and) sin and evil are disseminated because of the unlawful (*a-dādīhā*) drinking of wine. Or he (acts) otherwise (*ayāb-iš any)*: (this is) *meh-dādestānīh* ('greater justice') and a great(er) virtuous deed (*meh kirbag)*, which is binding (*ēwarīg*).

4. This (answer) implies (lit.: 'in this thus'): He who sells to non-Iranians and infidels and others, to whom (sale of wine) is unlawful due to drunkenness (*mastīh*), (is) very sinful (*was wināhīhā*); (it is) not authorized (*nē dastwarīhā*).

***Pursišn* 51** (K 35, fol. 171v., 3–16; TD4a, pp. 322.17–323.12)[32]

1. *panǰāh-ēkom pursišn pāsox*[33]. *ān ī*[34] *pursēd ēd*[35] *kū mard-ē(w) kē drahm-ē(w)*[36] *pad ē(w) 5 kabīz frāz dahēd kū māh ō sar ēn 5*[37] *kabīz ē(w) pad rabŭ̆na*[38] *ō tō dahom*[39] *ud*[40] *pad māh ō sar*[41] *ud ān ē(w) 5 kabīz 5*[42] *wahāg bawēd pad ān rabŭ̆n*[43] *ī-š frāz dād u-š pašt*[44] *kard ē(w) 5 kabīz stad dastwarīhā ayāb nē.*
2. *pāsox ēd kū ka ān*[45] *kē-š drahm stad abēbīmīhā pad xwēš kām ē(w) 5*[46] *kabīz abespārdan pašt*[47] *kard ud ōwōn čiyōn-aš agāhīhā abēbīmīhā pašt ōwōn čiyōn*[48] *pašt kard dād dastwarīhā wizīr*[49]
3. *bē ka-š ān †pašt*[50] *kard*[51] *abēr garān niyāzīhā ī ō +wasasəyāna*[52] *nē ōy*[53] *xwāstag* ⟨NKSY'⟩ *dādār*[54] *ī xrīdēnīdār*[55] *az*[56] *ōy ī ačār sūd ī*[57] *frehbūd nē*[58]

32 Anklesaria 1958, p. 109; West 1882, pp. 180–182; Macuch 2022c.
33 K35: ⟨p'shw⟩; TD4a: om.
34 K35: om.; TD4a: ⟨Y⟩.
35 K35: ⟨'y⟩; TD4a: om.
36 K35: ⟨Z̲WZ̲N⟩; TD4a: ⟨Z̲WZ̲N-1⟩.
37 K35: ⟨5⟩; TD4a: om.
38 K35: ⟨rbn'⟩; TD4a: ⟨b⟩.
39 K35: ⟨YHBWNm⟩; TD4a: ⟨YHBWNyt⟩ and super lin. ⟨-m⟩ (above ⟨-yt⟩).
40 K35: ⟨W⟩; TD4a: om.
41 K35: ⟨L'YŠH̲⟩; TD4a: ⟨sl⟩.
42 K35: ⟨5⟩; TD4a: ⟨6⟩.
43 K35: ⟨rbn⟩; TD4a: omits the whole passage ⟨pt̲' ZK rbn⟩ *pad ān rabŭ̆n*.
44 K35: ⟨pšt'⟩; TD4a: ⟨npšt'⟩.
45 K35: ⟨ZK⟩; TD4a: ⟨ZK Y⟩.
46 K35: ⟨5⟩; TD4a: om.
47 K35: ⟨pšt'⟩; TD4a: ⟨ypšt'⟩ super lin. ⟨p⟩ (above ⟨yp-⟩).
48 According to K35: ⟨'k'syh' 'pybymyhyh' pšt' 'wgwn čygwn'⟩; this whole passage beginning with *āgāhīhā* (*āgāhīhā abēbīmīhā pašt ōwōn čiyōn*) is omitted in TD4a.
49 K35: ⟨wcl⟩; TD4a: ⟨wcyl⟩.
50 Both K35 and TD4a: ⟨pwšt'⟩.
51 K35: ⟨krt'⟩; TD4a: om.
52 K35: ⟨wss'y'⟩; TD4a: om.
53 K35: ⟨L' 'LH̲⟩; TD4a: om.
54 K35: ⟨d't'l⟩; TD4a: ⟨d't'lyh 'y⟩.
55 K35: ⟨ZB̲NNyyn't'l⟩; TD4a: ⟨ZB̲NN-x1 't'l⟩.
56 K35: ⟨MN⟩; TD4a: ⟨MNW⟩.
57 K35: om.; TD4a: ⟨Y⟩.
58 K35: ⟨l'd⟩; TD4a: ⟨L'⟩.

xwāst[59] *ō ruwān sāzišnīgtar čē pasēnīgān*[60] *sūd*[61] *pad xwāstag* ⟨NKSYʾ⟩ *andar gyāg andar*[62] *sāl wēš čē hāwand* ⁺*rabŭn*[63] *xwāst*[64] *nē pad šahrag barišn*[65] *dāštan*[66].

1. Fifty-first question (and) answer. That which you ask: A man (= the buyer) who hands over one drachm for one (load of grain) of 5 *kabīz*[67] thus: 'To the end of the month I give to you this as prepayment (*rabŭna*)[68] for one (load of grain) of 5 *kabīz*' and the month comes to an end and that one (load of grain) of 5 *kabīz* is worth five times as much, is he (= the buyer) due to the prepayment (*rabŭn*) he has made and the contract he has concluded (*pašt kard*) entitled (*dastwarīhā*) to take this one (load of grain) of 5 *kabīz* or not?
2. The answer (is) this: If the one who took the drachm (= the seller) has concluded the contract (*pašt kard*) without duress (*abēbīmīhā* 'without fear') according to his own will (*pad xwēš kām*) to hand over one (load of grain) of 5 *kabīz* and has transferred it in accordance with the contract he has concluded consciously (*āgāhīhā*) and without duress (*abēbīmīhā*) in correspondence with the terms of the contract (*ōwōn čiyōn pašt kard*), (then) the verdict (*wizīr*) (is): he (= the buyer) (is) entitled (to take the load).
3. But if that contract was concluded under (conditions of) severe penury (*abēr garān niyāzīhā*), which do not (fit in) with a person granting favours

59 K35: ⟨BʿYHWNst'⟩; TD4a: ⟨BʿYHWNyt'⟩.
60 K35: ⟨psynykʾn'⟩; TD4a: ⟨psʾynykʾn⟩.
61 K35: om.; TD4a: ⟨Y⟩.
62 K35: ⟨B̲YN⟩; TD4a: om.
63 K35: ⟨bwn⟩; TD4a: om.
64 K35: ⟨BʿYHWNst'⟩; TD4a: ⟨BʿʿYHWNstn'⟩.
65 K35: ⟨blšn⟩; TD4a: ⟨bgʾn'⟩.
66 K35: ⟨dʾštn'⟩; TD4a: ⟨dʾšt'⟩.
67 The *kabīz* is a grain measure, corresponding to one-tenth of a *grīw*. On these measurements see also the Tabarestān documents, particularly Tab. 18 and 23 (Macuch 2017c, pp. 183–188 and 173–176 respectively).
68 The correct reading of the technical term written in K35, fol. 171v., line 5, as ⟨rbnʾ⟩, line 7 ⟨rbn⟩, and line 16 ⟨bwn⟩ is *rabŭn/rabŭna*, the equivalent of Syriac *răhb̲ūnā* (Sachau 1914, p. 172, l. 24; Payne Smith 1903, p. 531: 'ἀρραβών, arles, earnest-money, a pledge, earnest') and NP *rabūn* (Steingass p. 569, 'money advanced on goods which is returned if they should be damaged; earnest'), corresponding to the terms *ἀρραβών* in Greek law and *arrabo*, (shortened to) *arr(h)a*, in Roman law (a Phoenician loanword from the Semitic *ʿarab*, *ʿerabon* 'security, pawn, pledge'; on the widespread attestations of this technical expression in different languages see Chapter IV, fn. 473). This word was obviously completely unknown to the copyist of TD4a, as the manuscript has only ⟨b⟩ in the first attestation (p. 322, line 17) and omits it entirely in the rest of the *Pursišn*. Neither West, nor Anklesaria have recognized it. West 1882, p. 181, corrects it to '*bôn-ae*' based on the last attestation (with the reading '*vaban*' in fn. 1 for the first two variants). In Anklesaria's critical edition of 1958 only the letter ⟨b⟩ has remained of the original word in the first two attestations (p. 109, lines 4, 6) and ⟨bwn⟩ in the third one (line 17). Neither of these readings makes sense in this context. On *rabŭn/rabŭna* see also Macuch 2022c, pp. 313–315.

according to his (own) will (⁺*wasasəyāna* < **vasasə.yāna-*)[69], (then) the conveyor of the money, the buyer (*xwāstag dādār ī xrīdēnīdār*), should not request from him who is without means (*ačār*) (= the seller) profit in excess (*sūd ī frehbūd*). It is better for the preparation of his (= the buyer's) soul, since following (generations) (*pasēnīgān*) will request as profit for the money given at once (= as advance payment) for a year more than the equivalent of the prepayment (⁺*rabŭn*), without regard to the crop-yields of the region.

***Pursišn* 52** (K35, fol. 171v.,16–172r.,15; TD4a, pp. 323.13–324.15)[70]

1. *panǰāh-dōwom pursišn pāsox*[71] *ān ī*[72] *pursēd kū andar šahr bē šahr mardōm ī*[73] *wehdēn xrīd frōxt ī pad gōspand*[74] *abāg ǰud-dēnān windakkarān*[75] *kunēnd ud ō awēšān frō(x)šēnd*[76] *ēg-iš dādestān čē ud*[77]
2. *ka wehdēn ka nē mad ēstēnd pad*[78] *arz nē xrīnēnd*[79] *bē ō windakkarān*[80] *ǰud-dēnān frōxšēnd*[81] *ēg-iš*[82] *dādestān čē*
3. *ān kē-š*[83] *zīwišn*[84] *čiš ēg-iš dādestān čē*

69 This expression, written ⟨wss'y'⟩ (misspelled presumably from an original ⟨w's'sy''n'⟩, see below), is most likely a loan-word from an Avestan **vasasə.yāna-* 'who grants favours at will' (< *vasah-* 'wish, will'; adv. 'at will' + *yāna-* 'favour, grant'; from Ir. √**u̯as*; Av. √*vas* 'to want, wish'; Cheung 2007, p. 427); compare Av. *vasō.yāna-* 'who grants favours at will' (Bartholomae 1904, col. 1384: 'der nach Wunsch Gefallen, Gunst empfängt oder erweist'); *vasō.xšaϑra-* 'who commands at will, exercises power at will' (Bartholomae 1904, col. 1384: 'nach Gefallen schaltend sva. unbeschränkte Selbständigkeit, Freiheit geniessend, frei, unabhängig') and *vasasə.xšaϑra-* 'who commands at will, exercises power at will, rules at will' (Bartholomae 1904, col. 1383: 'Herrschaft, Reich nach Gefallen sva. das unumschränkte Reich [im Jenseits]'). As ⟨w's'sy''n'⟩ (in Pahlavi script) it is also attested in the Sasanian Law-book, MHD 62.14, in the context of a daughter who can no longer dispose freely over her work income after she has married: *ud ka-š šōy kard ā-š* **vasasə.yāna-* ⟨w's'sy''n'⟩ *pad kār-windišn nē bawēd* 'And when she has married, she no longer has free disposition over her work-income' (Macuch 1993, pp. 411, 417). For an extensive discussion of this word see Macuch 2022c, pp. 315–317.
70 Anklesaria 1958, p. 110; West 1882, pp. 182–183; Macuch 2024a.
71 K35: ⟨p'shw⟩; TD4a: om.
72 K35: ⟨Y⟩; TD4a: om.
73 K35: ⟨Y⟩; TD4a: om.
74 K35: ⟨gwspnd⟩; TD4a: ⟨gwspnd'n⟩.
75 K35: ⟨wndkgl'n'⟩; TD4a: ⟨wndkl'n⟩.
76 K35: ⟨MZB̲N⟩; *super lin.* ⟨MZB̲NNnd⟩; TD4a: ⟨MZBNNx₂⟩.
77 K35: om.; TD4a: ⟨W⟩.
78 K35: om.; TD4a: ⟨pṯ'⟩.
79 Both mss.: ⟨ZB̲NNx₂⟩.
80 K35: ⟨wndk gl'n'⟩; TD4a: ⟨wndkl'n⟩.
81 K35: ⟨MZB̲NNx₂⟩; TD4a: ⟨MZB̲NNx₁⟩.
82 K35: ⟨'DN' -š⟩; TD4a: om.
83 K35: written twice: ⟨ZK MNW-š ZK MNW-š⟩; TD4a: ⟨ZK MNW-š⟩.
84 K35: ⟨zywšn'⟩; TD4a: ⟨ZB̲NNx₁ zywšn'⟩.

4. *pāsox ēd kū ōwōn kār kardan*[85] *abēr garān wināhīhā ud*[86] *wad* ⁺*pēšagīhā*[87] *pad wizār ud tuwān*[88] *an-hangār kardan pad ōwōn sūd xwāstan nē dastwarīhā*
5. *bē*[89] *agar ān wehdēn kē nibišt kū*[90] *zīwišn čiš*[91] *ud pad any-iz ēč kār ī frārōn pēšag ī čiš kam wināhtar zīwišn xwāstan*[92] *nē tuwān purr xrīdār ī*[93] *wehdēn ayāft be ō wehdēnān*[94] *frōxšēd*[95] *čiyōn-iš kam wināhtar tuwān kē*[96] *hamkār zīwišn xwāstan pādixšāy čē ēk-iz mard ī ahlaw abāg ahlawān ī-š andar sālārīh zīwistan ēdōn*[97] *tuwān ka gōspandān be ō ōzanišn an-ērān*[98] *xwarišnīh frōxšēd was gōspand be-iz ō* ⁺*kāhēnišn*[99] *ērān dārišn mad xwārtar kū mard ī ahlaw pad an-ayābišnīh ī zīwišn marg bīm ōzad.*[100]

1. Fifty-second question (and) answer. That which you ask: (When) adherents of the Good Religion practice buying (and) selling small livestock (= sheep; *gōspand)* in the country (and) outside the country with traders of another religion (*ǰud-dēnān windakkarān*),[101] and sell to them, what is the decision?
2. If adherents of the Good Religion (*wehdēn*) are not present[102] (or) do not buy (according to) value (and) they (= the Zoroastrian vendors) sell (the sheep) to traders of another religion (*windakkarān ǰud-dēnān*), what is the decision?

85 K35: ⟨'wgwn' k'l krtn'⟩; TD4a: om. the whole passage beginning with ⟨'wgwn'⟩.
86 K35: ⟨W⟩; TD4a: om.
87 Both mss.: ⟨pyšyh'⟩. The correct form ⟨pyškyh'⟩ (in *wad pēšagīhā*) is attested in a parallel context Dd. *Pursišn* 49 (see above).
88 K35: ⟨tb'n⟩; TD4a: ⟨twb'n⟩.
89 K35: ⟨BR'⟩; TD4a: ⟨BR' W⟩.
90 K35: om.; TD4a: ⟨'YK⟩.
91 TD4a: ins. ⟨k'l⟩; K35: om.
92 K35: ⟨BʿYHWNst'⟩; TD4a: ⟨BʿYHWNstn'⟩.
93 K35: ⟨Y⟩; TD4a: om.
94 K35: ⟨wyhdyn' 'n⟩; TD4a: ⟨ŠPYLdyn' 'n⟩.
95 K35: ⟨MZB̲NNx2⟩; TD4a: ⟨MZB̲NNx1⟩.
96 K35: ⟨MNW⟩; TD4a: ⟨MN⟩.
97 TD4a: ins. ⟨Y⟩; K35: om.
98 TD4a: ins. ⟨Y⟩; K35: om.
99 K35: ⟨ksyn' šn⟩; TD4a: ⟨ks'nšn'⟩.
100 K35: ⟨YKTLWYN' t'⟩; TD4a: ⟨YKTLWNt'⟩.
101 This rare expression ⟨wndkl/wndkgl⟩ *windakkar*, lit. 'a person, who acquires, obtains something, who makes a gain' designates presumably the 'trader' or 'merchant', from *windag* + *-gar/-kar* (*windādan*, *wind-* 'to find, obtain, acquire, get, gain, win'; MacKenzie 1971, p. 91; Nyberg 1974, p. 213; Ir. √*u̯aid*² 'to find', Cheung 2007, pp. 409–410; Av.√²*vaēd* 'to find', Bartholomae 1904, col. 1318;; on the suffix *-gar/-kar* see Durkin-Meisterernst 2014, pp. 167–169, §§326, 333). Is *windakkar* simply a synonym for *wāzāragān* 'merchant' (MacKenzie 1971, p. 89; Durkin-Meisterernst 2004, p. 334) or does it have a specific technical meaning? Was it used in a pejorative sense in connection with infidels? The construction is reminiscent of Sogd. *γwʾʾkr*; *whʾkr*; *xwʾqr* 'merchant, trader' (Gharib 1995, num. 4295, 10045, 10688 respectively); compare MP *wahāg* 'trading' (MacKenzie 1971, p. 86), but a corresponding MP **wahākkar* does not seem to be attested. West 1882, p. 182, reads '*vanîkgarān*' with no further explanation.
102 Lit. 'have not come' (*nē mad ēstēnd*).

3. Regarding the (person), whose living (*zīwišn čiš*) is made (by trade), what is the decision?
4. The answer (is): practising this (is) a very severe sin (*abēr garān wināhīhā*) and it is an evil profession (*wad* ⁺*pēšagīhā*); it is not authorized (*nē dastwarīhā*) to do this inconsiderately (*an-hangār*) for payment (*pad wizār*) and being solvent (*tuwān*), in order to seek profit (*sūd*).
5. But if that adherent of the Good Religion, who (you) have written about, makes a living (*zīwišn čiš*) (by trade) and he cannot seek a living by any other righteous profession (*kār ī frārōn pēšag*), which is less sinful, by obtaining fully (solvent) buyers of the Good Religion, and selling to the adherents of the Good Religion, as this is less sinful, he is authorized (*pādixšāy*) to seek a collaborator (*hamkār*)[103] in making a living, since this one righteous man together with the righteous, who are under his guardianship, can live thus, when he sells sheep for slaughtering to be eaten by non-Iranians. Even (if) the number of sheep for maintaining Iranians is decreased (*be-iz o* ⁺*kāhēnišn ... mad*), this is a smaller (sin) than (when) a righteous man (has) fear of death (and) is killed due to not being able to obtain a living.

103 The term *hamkār* 'collaborator, partner, fellow-worker, associate, assistant' could refer to a fellow-trader or business partner of the Zoroastrian trader, but Manuščihr might have had his own profession in mind: *hamkār* could refer to a member of the priestly class, who would control and sanction the deal between the Zoroastrian vendor and the infidel purchaser. In any case, Manuščihr uses *hamkār* in this technical sense of 'assistant' or 'associate' priest in the context of the ritual in Dd 47.13 (*hamkārān*) and 47.23 (*hamkārīhā*) referring to those persons who assist the chief officiating priest (*zōt*) in the performance of the liturgy (*yazišn*). See Macuch 2024a, pp. 292–295.

Appendix III

Dēnkard 3: Excerpts on Law and Justice

Pages and lines in the following transcription and translation are numbered according to DkD (manuscript B; the pages in DkM are noted). The numbering of the paragraphs follows DE MENASCE 1973.

Dk. 3.52 (DE MENASCE 1973, pp. 62–63)

DkD 32.19 (DkM 44.9)
abar rāyēnišn (ī) dādestān abāg dēn

On taking legal action with the *dēn*

DkD 32.20–33.1 (DkM 44.10–13)
hād dādestān pad zahagīh ī āsn-xrad abāg weh-dēn ēk radagīg brādarīh-iz (21) *padiš wāwarīgānīgīh ud padīrišn ud rawāgīh ud pad ān ī dādestān āsn-xrad* (DkD 33.1) *āsn-xrad pad mardōm ī hamāg ān ī ham-wispag mardōm padiš wāspuhragānagīh.*

That is (lit: 'so be it'):[1] Justice (*dādestān*) (exists) as the offspring of innate wisdom (*āsn-xrad*) with the Good Religion in one rank and brotherhood; in it (is) trustworthiness and acceptance and dissemination and by the innate wisdom (*āsn-xrad*) of justice (*dādestān*) innate wisdom (is) in all people; people altogether (have) a share in its inheritance (*wāspuhragānagīh*).

DkD 33.1–4 (DkM 44.14–16)
ud ān-iz ī (2) *ag-dēnān pad fragānīh ud nihumbīh ud rōyīh ud rawāg ī-šān ag-dēn ī zyānīgīh* (3) *ōwōn barēnd čiyōn *paygālgar pad zarr ō srub hamīh srub pad zarr nām* (4) *rawāgēnēd.*

And the harm (*zyānīgīh*) which the infidels (*ag-dēnān*) bring about by founding and concealing and making grow and disseminating their evil religion (is) like the cup-maker (**paygālgar*), (who) by mixing gold with lead (*srub*) propagates lead under the name of gold.

1 According to SKJÆRVØ 2010, pp. 182–190, the particle *hād* (originally the 3rd sg. Subjunctive of 'to be': 'so be it; be it as it may') is used in the *Dēnkard* primarily to introduce citations from the Avesta in Pahlavi.

DkD 33.4–7 (DkM 44.16–21)
az ham bun ka andar handāzišn ī šnāsagān ag-dēnīh āzāristagīh (5) *pad-iz tarāzūg ī ham-dādestān wānīdārīh bawēd ān ī āzāristagīh ān ī pad* (6) *handāzišn ī weh-dēn ristag ō dādestān wēnīhēd ast ham-zahag pad* (7) *āgenēn zahagīh ī-šān āsn-xrad ī Ohrmazd.*

Because of (having) the same substance/origin (*bun*), when in the assessment (*handāzišn*) of the experts (*šnāsagān*) (the matter of) causing injury (*āzāristagīh*) by adherence to an evil religion (*ag-dēnīh)* will also be vanquished on the scale (*tarāzūg*) of consistent judgement (*ham-dādestān*), (then) the (issue) of causing injury by assessment (*handāzišn*) in the manner of the Good Religion will manifest itself in justice (*dādestān*); it is of the same offspring together with the offspring, from which (stems) the innate wisdom (*āsn-xrad)* of Ohrmazd.

Dk. 3.78 (DE MENASCE 1973, pp. 83–84)

DkD 51.7–8 (DkM 69.17)
abar dād xwābar rāstagīh (8) *ī māzdēsn dēn*

On the beneficent truth of the law of the Mazdean religion.

DkD 51.7–11 (DkM 69.18–70.2)
hād čiyōn hučihrag rōšnīh abar wuzurg rōšnīh wihānag (9) *ud dānāgīh rāst abar hamāg dānāgīh ud rāstīh čiyōn nimūdār ōwōn dād xwābar rāstagīh ī* (10) *dēn māzdēsnīh ham* ⁺*nimūnag*[2] *ī ēn 3 wāzag ī wehdēn dād ēk ī nūn andar* (DkM 70.1) *tanōmandīh* (DkD 51.11) *pad gētīy ud ēk ī pas az tanōmandīh pad* (2) *mēnōy ud ēk ī abdom pad frašgird.*

That is (lit: 'so be it'): as the beautiful light (is) the reason for the great light and true knowledge (is) above all knowledge and truth (is) like a guide, likewise the law (is) the beneficent truth of the Mazdean religion following the muster of the three utterances of the Good Religion: (1) one law (*dād*) (is) that which (is in) a corporal state (*tanōmandīh*) in the corporal world (*gētīy*), and (2) one (law is) that which after the corporal state (*tanōmandīh*) (is) in the spiritual world (*mēnōy*), and (3) one (law is) that which (prevails) finally in the Restoration (*frašgird*).

DkD 51.12–16 (DkM 70.2–9)
(12) *dād ān ī nūn pad gētīy dād (ī) pahrēz ī (az) margīh ud bēš ī kas čār ud yaštar* (13) *a-bēšīdār ī pad dād kunišn hāwand pahrēz ī az rēš ud bēš ī xwēš tan wisp [āgāhīh]*[3] (14) *āsānīh ud šnāyišn dādārīh ī ō kadār-iz-ē(w) kē-š āsānīh*

2 B has ⟨hm MNW kry⟩ which does not make any sense. By adding a stroke ⟨n⟩ after ⟨hm⟩ we can read ⟨nmwnk'⟩ ⁺*nimūnag* 'sample, example, specimen, type, form, pattern; a muster; like, resembling' (NP *nimūna/namūna*, STEINGASS 1892, p. 1427), as DE MENASCE (1973, p. 83) has already perceptively observed.

3 B ⟨'k'syh⟩ after ⟨wsp⟩ is presumably a mistake (due to the frequent compound *wisp-āgāhīh* 'omniscient').

ud šnāyišn dādārīh (15) *ō ī šnāyišn ag-dēnīh*[4] *arzānīg dād kunišn ast pad dādestānōmandīh ī* (16) *dāštan ī druwandīh-iz jōmā ahlaw nē druxtan ī mihr abāg kas-iz.*

The law that (is) now in the world (*gētīy*) (is) the law of abstaining from (causing) death and harming a person, (that of) giving remedy (*čār*) and making the worshipper free from harm by means of the law; likewise (it is the law of) avoiding physical injury and harm (*rēš ud bēš*) to one's own person (*xwēš tan*); (that of) giving full ease (*āsānīh*) and satisfaction (*šnāyišn*) to whoever is worthy of being given satisfaction and ease, (including) the one worthy of satisfaction (from an) evil religion (*ag-dēnīh*); it is (the law of) keeping legally (*pad dādestānōmandīh*) (contracts) with the unrighteous (*druwandīh)* together with the righteous (*ahlaw*), of not breaking (*druxtan*) a contract (*mihr*) with any person.

DkD 51.16–19 (DkM 70.9–13)
ud ān ī pas (17) *az tanōmandīh pad mēnōy dād āmār ī abar kadār-iz-ē(w) ruwān kām ud dānišn tuwān ī-š* (18) *andar tanōmandīh būd sāmān frōxtan ī abar kirbag passazagīhā pad darrēnīdan ī* (19) *abar wināh bizeškīh.*

And the (law prevailing) after the corporal state (*tanōmandīh*) in the spiritual world (*mēnōy*) (is) the law of giving account (*āmār*) regarding the intent (*kām*) and knowledge (and) power of the soul (*ruwān*) of all those, who were in a corporal state (*andar tanōmandīh būd*); (it is) the measure to sell virtuous deeds (*kirbag*) in a suitable manner as a remedy (*biziškīh*) to cause the splitting of sins (*wināh*).

DkD 51.19–52.3 (DkM 70.13–20)
ān ī abdom pad frašgird dād dādār frazānīhā handāzišn (20) *ī-š hu-frazānagīh ō xūb frazāmīh ī xēm dahišn passazag wānīdan bē burd ī* (21) *pad dahišnān abzārīh ēbgat ī wināh-iz druwandīh ud any druwandān ruwān az dušox* (DkD 52.1) *ābādēnīdan u-šān az wināh arwand bowandag*[5] *yojdahrēnīdan awēšān-iz abāg harwisp ahlawān* (2) *ruwān rast wirāst pad tanōmandīh jāwēdān a-marg ud purr šēdā winnārdan ud ēč* (3) *az xwēš dahišn* +*abēdān*[6] *pad xāk nē*[7] *hišt.*

The law that (prevails) finally in the Restoration (*frašgird*) (is that of) the wise judgement of the Creator, whose good wisdom (is) suitable to bring to a good end the nature of the creation, to destroy with the means of (his) creations the

4 B ⟨'kdyn'yh⟩ *ag-dēnīh* (with *šnāyišn*) could be a mistake for *āsānīh* (if we follow DE MENASCE 1973, p. 83; see *āsānīh ud šnāyišn* in this passage), but I prefer to keep *ag-dēnīh*, since the following context explicitly refers to how Zoroastrians should keep contracts (*mihr*) with both the just and the unjust.

5 B ⟨bndk⟩, a frequent mistake for ⟨bwndk'⟩.

6 B ⟨'pyt'⟩.

7 The heterogram for *xāk* ⟨'PL'⟩ ends with ⟨L'⟩, which is the heterogram for *nē*. The original manuscript, from which B is copied, presumably had ⟨'PL' L'⟩, from which the second ⟨L'⟩ was later deleted. This difficult passage is, however, far from being very clear and other readings could also be taken into consideration.

Adversary (*ēbgat*)[8] of sinful unrighteousness and to clear out hell from other sinful souls and to purify them swiftly completely from sin, to arrange for them together with all the righteous souls, restored to a corporal form, (to exist) without death and full of bliss, and nothing of his own wanted creation is dismissed into dust (?).

Dk 3.292 (DE MENASCE 1973, p. 288)

DkD 230.14 (DkM 302.1)
abar jud-bunīh ī dād must az nigēz ī weh-dēn

On the different substances/origins of law (and) violence from the exposition of the Good Religion

DkD 230.15–17 (DkM 302.2–5)
(15) *hād čiyōn dād bun dānāgīh dānāgīh bun āsn-xrad āsn-xrad āfurišn ast ī* (16) *dādār andar dahišnān. ud must bun duš-āgāhīh bun waran ud waran ī duš-āgāhīh* (17) *ud must bun dādār dādār andar dahišn kardan nē bē az any sazēd.*

That is: Just as the substance/origin (*bun*) of law (is) knowledge (*dānāgīh*), the substance of knowledge (is) innate wisdom (*āsn-xrad*). Innate wisdom is inherent in the creation of the Creator. And the substance/origin of violence (is) ignorance (*duš-āgāhīh*). Its substance (is) lust (*waran*); it is not fitting (to assume) that the Creator created the lust of ignorance (*waran ī duš-āgāhīh*) and the substance of violence (*must bun*) whilst shaping creation, but (that they) stem from another (source).

Dk. 3.302 (DE MENASCE 1973, p. 294)

DkD 236.8–9 (DkM 309.5–6)
abar wizīr handāzišn ī mēnōy dādwar ud ān ī gētīy dādwar az nigēz ī (9) *weh-dēn*

On passing judgement by the *mēnōy* judge and by the *gētīy* judge from the exposition of the Good Religion.

DkD 236.9–12 (DkM 309.7–9)
hād mēnōy dādwar (10) *wizīr handāzišn ō ān ī pad xwadīh bōzišn ērang ēwar čē-š ō* (11) *wēnišn rōšn kē xwēš čiš ud kē appar-kām kē +duzagān-menišn* (12) *ud kē rāst kē drōzan.*

That is (lit. 'so be it'): Judgement passed by the *mēnōy* judge (leads) to an acquittal (or) a conviction, which (is) implicitly (= by itself) reliable (binding), since it is clear to the (judge's) vision, to whom a thing belongs in own(ership) and who

8 On *ebgat* < Av. **aibi-gaiti-*, the approach, attack of Evil, see KLINGENSCHMITT 2000, p. 219 (§ 5.2.7).

(has) the will to rob (and) who (has) the intention of a thief, and who (is) truthful (and) who (is) deceiving.

DkD 236.12–16 (DkM 309.10–15)
gētīy dādwar wizīr handāzišn ō ān ī pad saxwan (13) *bōzišn ud ērang pad ēwar dārišn čē ān ī mēnōy dādwar pad mēnōy*(14)*-wēnišnīh ō wēnišn rōšn ud gētīy dādwar nē harw ō wēnišn* (15) *a-xuftag u-š az pēšēmāl ud pasēmāl ud gugāyīhān saxwan ān ī pad ēwar* (16) *dārišnīh ī bōzišnīg ud ērangīg dādīg ud hādīg*[9] *wizīr kardan ēwēn.*

Judgement passed by the *gētīy* judge (leads) to an acquittal (or) a conviction (*bōzišn ud ērang*)[10] on the grounds of statements, which he (= the judge) takes to be reliable (*pad ēwar dārišn*), since the *mēnōy* judge (receives) clarity on the grounds of *mēnōy*-vision and not every *gētīy* judge (has access) to an alert (*a-xuftag* 'unsleeping') vision. And the norm (*ēwēn*) for him (= the *gētīy* judge) (is) to pass judgement regarding acquittal or conviction on the grounds of the statements of the plaintiff and the defendant and the witnesses, which he takes to be reliable (*pad ēwar darišnīh*), (following) legal and ritual (?) norms.

9 This word seems to be a shortened form of *hādamāns*^{a}*rīg* 'pertaining to ritual matters' (reading it as $^{+}$*a-dādīg* does not make sense to me), as de Menasce 1973, p. 294, has already assumed: *hādīg* < *hād(amānsar)īg*? This abbreviation—if it is one—is strange, but certainly makes sense in this context. According to Dk. 8 not only the legal *nasks* (*dādīg*) are concerned with juristic matters, but also the *nasks* on the ritual (*hādamānsarīg*).

10 In this semi-legal, semi-religious context, comparing the two types of judges, the most likely translation for *bōzišn ud ērang* is 'acquittal and conviction' (compare: *bōxt ud ēraxt* 'acquitted and convicted'; 'redeemed/saved and damned/condemned' in a religious context). Whereas *čim ud bōzišn* 'evidence and proof' in the Tabarestān documents (Macuch 2016a, pp 149–150) is a hendiadys used for emphasis, *bōzišn ud ērang* is a pair of opposites. The original meaning of *bōzišn*, from *bōxtan* 'save, redeem', is most likely 'salvation'; the technical term 'proof, evidence' is most likely a further semantic development: '(that which leads to) acquittal' > 'evidence, proof'.

Appendix IV

Dēnkard 3 and 7: Excerpts on the Mazdakite Movement

The following passages in *Dēnkard* 3.5.1–2 and 7.7.22–25 contain a concise summary of the legal and social aspects of Zarduxšti/Mazdakite social doctrine from an orthodox point of view. The texts have been already excerpted and translated by MOLÉ[1], SHAKI[2] and SUNDERMANN[3], but neither of these renderings are reliable due to too many amendments and wrong readings. For an extensive commentary on these passages see MACUCH 2015b and 2021.

Dk 3.5.1–2

The Zarduxšti/Mazdakite doctrine of avoiding strife and hate by distributing property and women equally is refuted (from an orthodox viewpoint) in this text. Unfortunately the manuscript is torn at one side, leaving several lacunae. The legible parts run as follows:[4]

DkD 5.12–6.13; DkM 6.9–7.16
haftom pursišn
pursēd any ahlomōγ kū ka āz ud waran [ud nang(?)][5] *ud arešk ud abārīg winah-āyōz druz wānīdan weh-dēn meh handarz awēšān [...] wināh-āyōzīh ī mardōm frayistīhā pad* *⁺wihān*[6] *ī xwāstag ud zan zan [ud xwāstag (?)]*[7] *ō hamīh ī amaragān dād kē padiš āz ud warun ud arešk ud nang ud any-iz was [...] az*

1 Dk 3.5.1–2 in MOLÉ 1961 (partly translated), pp. 24–25; Dk 7.7.22–25 in MOLÉ 1967, p. 75 (nr. 22–25).
2 Both texts in SHAKI 1978, pp. 290–293 and 293–295.
3 SUNDERMANN 1988, p. 184.
4 SHAKI 1978, pp. 290–293, translates the whole text, but his version is far too speculative to be convincing. MOLÉ 1961, pp. 42–25, wisely abstains from translating the whole text.
5 The missing word could be *nang* in correspondance with the list of sins given a few lines later in the same text DkD 5.15 (= DkM 6.11): *āz ud waran ud arešk ud nang*. Thus also SHAKI 1978, 290.
6 Thus SHAKI 1978, *ibid.*; MOLÉ 1961, 24 reads *pat šūn*; another possible reading for ms. pwryšn could be ⁺*pursišn*.
7 The missing words were probably *ud xwāstag* in accordance with the content of DkM 653.10–654.8 (= DkD 326[505].11–325[506].7), cited above. Thus both MOLÉ 1961, *ibid.* and SHAKI 1978, *ibid.*

winādh-ayōzīh ī mardōm stō bawēnd ud gannāg-mēnōy nērōg [...] čiyōn amāh pad paywand dastwarīh (ī) Zarduxšt čāštag kardag čim.

pāsox
hād hamīh ī ašmāh pad xwāstag ud zan az Zarduxšt [...] ī-šān Xrōsagān[8]*-iz xwand ī az Fasāy būd frēftārīhā [...]*

Seventh question
'Another heretic asked: 'If destroying lust and desire [and disgrace(?)] and envy and the other sin-inciting *druz* (is) the greatest injunction of the Good Religion, (and if) people mostly succumb to sins because of property and women (*xwāstag ud zan*), (then) women [and property (?)] (should be) given jointly to the communality, so that by this (act) lust and desire and envy and disgrace and also many other [vices (?)] be powerless to make people sin and the power of the Evil Spirit [be destroyed (?)]—as we (practice) in accordance with the authorization of Zarduxšt.' What is the reason (for this according to) doctrine (*čāštag*) (and) practice (*kardag*)?'

Answer
"Be it as it may.[9] Your joint possession of property and women based on [the authorization of (?)][10] Zarduxšt, also called Xrōsagān (=son of Xrōsag), who was from Fasā, (is) deceiving (*frēftārīhā*) [...]."

(There are too many lacunae in the following lines to attempt a reliable translation. The most interesting part of the text continues with a description of Zarduxšti/Mazdakite practices:)

ud pad apaydāg paywandīh ī ǰud ǰud mardōm [...] pad āmextag zanīh abāg šutr[11] *pad gumēzagīh wanīgarīh nāmagānīh*[12] *ud stŭrīh ī ēk ēk az mardōm wišuftārīhā ud pad wāspuhragān xwēšīh [...] kardag xwādāyīh gāh ud pāyag ī mardōm agārēnīdan gēhān nirfsēnīdārīhā [...] kas* ⁺*mādag*[13] *kastārīhā ud pad xwēšīh ud dārišn ōftārīhā [...] dādwarīh ānābīhā.*

'And by obscuring the descent of very single person, [...] by mingling (the institution of) marriage with sperm, by mixture destroying (the institution of) 'name-preservation' (*nāmagānīh*) and demolishing (the institution of) 'substitute succession' (*stŭrīh*) of each individual, and by [removing?] ownership of hereditary property (*wāspuhragān xwēšīh*), by abolishing the rank of sovereignty and the station of the people he caused the decrease of property (*gēhān*) (and)

8 Thus Molé 1961, *ibid.*; Shaki 1978, *ibid.* emends to **drisden.*
9 On the different uses of *hād* see Skjærvø 2010, pp. 182–190.
10 The missing word could be *dastwarīh* in accordance with the preceding sentence. Thus Shaki 1978, *ibid.*
11 šwtl *šutr* (which Shaki 1978, *ibid.*, emends to **šusr)* is most probably a transcribed term from Av. *xšuδra-* 'liquid, fluid, semen'.
12 Written n'mknnyh (instead of n'mk'nyh) in the *Dēnkard*, see also DkM 718.17.
13 B: m't Y *mād ī.*

diminution of the (material) substance (+*mādag*) of relations (*kas*); and by removing ownership (*xwēšīh*) and possession (*dārišn*) (he caused) the rejection of jurisdiction (*dādwarīh*).'

Dk 7.7.22–25

This passage is embedded in the legendary history of the Mazda-worshipping religion at the time of its revelation to Zarathustra by Ohrmazd.[14] It refers to the Mazdakites, 'the most heretical of heretics' (*ahlomōyān ahlomōy*), in the context of heretical teachings which will emerge according to a prophecy ascribed to Ohrmazd himself.

DkD 505.11–18; DkM 653.10–18
az dēn petyāragān ahlomōyān ahlomōy ī-šān Mazdakīg-iz xwand hēnd čiyōnšān ēn-iz abar gōwēd kū ēn ī man dēn pad any[15] *menišn* +*nagīrā(y)*[16] *was be nigerē*[17] *Zarduxšt ka was ahlomōy āgāh ahlāyīh kardārīh ud āsrōgīh-iz gōwēnd awināhīh*[18] *ud kam āškār(ag) warzīdār hēnd. pad dēn ī māzdēsnān ēd kū pad dēn be niger u-šān čārag xwāh ud kē*[19] *awēšan čegām-iz-ēw* +*petyāragtar*[20] *būd ēstēnd andar axw ī astōmand ud agriftār āsnōmand*[21] *ahlāyīh kē az hastān pahlom.*

14 The 'Legend of Zoroaster' (Dk 7) has been translated by Molé 1967. On the quotations see also Sundermann 1988, p. 184. On the text's 'Sitz im Leben' see Josephson 2003.

15 Molé 1967, pp. 74–75 (nr. 22) has *axw* (in *axw-menišn* 'énergie'); Shaki 1978, pp. 293–294, reads the same word as *anē* (*anē menišn* 'other conception'). Both readings are possible (as 'hw' or as the heterogram AHRN respectively).

16 Molé 1967, *ibid.*: *nikīrēh* 'regarde' (nkylyb); Shaki 1978, *ibid.*, corrects to *ud sraw* 'and Word' (W slyb). In ms. B (DkD 326.13) the word occurs twice written identically in the same line nkylyb. With a very slight correction of the second y to ' it can be read as nkyl'ȳ *nagīrā(y)*, a technical term well known from legal texts, signifying 'refusal, rejection, repudiation, non-recognition' (read previously as **nakkīrā*; on the technical term see Macuch 1993, p. 63–65, no. 5). The slight mistake could have been caused by the second, identically written expression in the same line, which is transmitted correctly here and should be read nkylyb *nigerē* (as Molé has it; curiously Shaki has corrected this second attestation to +*nakkīrā* instead of the first. His translation of the whole passage is grammatically impossible). Henning 1946 (p. 732) has read **nakkīrā* as a loanword from the Aramaic root nkr 'to repudiate'. Recently Buyaner 2015 has argued that the expression is an early loan-word, derived from the Akkadian verb *nakāru(m)*, attested already in the Codex Hammurabi in the same technical sense, and should be read *nagīrā(y)*.

17 Molé 1967, *ibid.*: *nikīrēh*; Shaki 1978, *ibid.*: +*nakkīrā*.

18 Shaki 1978, *ibid.*, changes the sequence of the words, reading *awināhīh ud āsrōgīh iz gōwēnd*.

19 Shaki 1978, *ibid.*, corrects to *az*.

20 Ms. B (DkD 326.16) pytyd'lt'l; Molé 1967, *ibid.*, reads *pityārtar*; Shaki 1978, *ibid.*, has **petyāragtar*.

21 Molé 1968, *ibid.* reads *adak hend.*

'Among the adversaries of the Religion (there are) the most heretical of heretics (*ahlomōyān ahlomōy*), who have also been called Mazdakites, with regard to whom also this is said: 'This, my Religion, (will) often (experience) repudiation by other conceptions. Observe it (= the Religion), O Zarathustra, when many heretics will say that they perform with knowledge religious duties (*ahlāyīh kardārīh*) and even the priesthood (*āsrōgīh*), but (only) few will fulfil the (Religious) Duty (*āškār[ag] warzīdār*) without sin.' In the Mazda-worshipping Religion this (is said:) 'Observe the Religion and seek a means against them (= the heretics) (*u-šān čārag xwāh*) and those among them who were the worst adversaries in the material world and inapprehensive of the primordial righteousness, which is the highest of existences.''

(The text then continues with a precise summary of Mazdakite practices contrary to orthodox teachings:)

DkD 505.18–506.7; DkM 653.18–654.8
ud ēdōn dēn ī māzdēsnān pad tōhmag ⁺*bazišnīh*[22] *baxšēnd*[23] *kardārīh*[24] *xwēšān rāy gōwēnd ud bahr ō xwēšān dahēnd xwarišn fšōnēnēnd*[25] *kū xwarišn suy paymān gōwēnd ud zahagīh gōwēnd gōwēnd kū paywand pad mādarān gōwēnd ud gurgīh hunēnd*[26] *kū čiš gurgīhā kunēnd awēšān sāxtan ī pad kāmag rawišnīh čiyōn ān ī gurg zahag pas mādar awēšān-iz paywand pad mādarān kunēnd awēšān nārīg*[27] *ī gōspand xrīnēnd ān-iz ī zahag pus brād*[28] *be barēnd ō bar kū-šān ašmāh ō hamīh dād hēm nē pādixšāy hēd bē pad hamīh ēstād awēšān nē-iz* ⁺*wurrōyēnd*[29] *war nē ka āškārag abar dahēd*[30] *kū be bōxtēd*[31] *awēšān pad-iz frazandān druzēnd kū-šān mihrōdruj abar rasišn ud pad-iz ān ī xwēštan.*

22 B. bwcšnyh *bōzišnīh*, which in the *Dēnkard* is very often written mistakenly for bcšnyh *bazišnīh* (thus also Molé 1967, *ibid.*); Shaki 1978, *ibid.*: *bōzišnīh*.

23 Shaki 1978, *ibid.*, emends to **baxšišn*.

24 *kardār* is the technical term for a person who performs religious rites and duties, lit. 'fulfiller, performer' (of religious duties).

25 *fšōnēnīdan* 'to fatten', here used as a technical expression, referring to Yasna XI.1f. (see Macuch 2015b, pp. 160–161). It is the Pahlavi translation of Av. *fšaoniia-* 'to fatten' (Bartholomae 1904, col. 1027, *fšaonaya-* 'vermästen, als Mast brauchen für –'; on the form *fšaoniia-* see Kellens 1984, p. 131). Molé 1967, *ibid.*, has *pihān vēnend*; Shaki 1978, *ibid*, reads *pih*^{w} *gōwēnd*; Sundermann 1988, p. 185, emends the first letters to *pašn* 'Vertrag'.

26 The verb is *hunīdan* 'to bring forth; procreate, give birth' with respect to daēvic creatures (Av. ^{2}HŪ, Kellens 1995, p. 73 'engendrer'; Bartholomae 1904, col. 1782, ^{3}*hav-* 'gebären, von *daēv*ischen Wesen'); Molé 1967, *ibid.*: *havend*; Shaki 1978, *ibid.*, emends to *gōwēnd*.

27 Shaki 1978, *ibid.*, emends to **šīr* 'milk'.

28 B: AH, *brād*, is also easily confused with 'š, *ā-š* (thus Molé 1967, *ibid.*); Shaki 1978, *ibid.*, has *brād* (with a completely different translation).

29 B has the second pl. HMYTWNyt *wurrōyēd*; also Molé 1967, *ibid.*: *virravend*; Shaki 1978, *ibid.* emends to *wirrōyīdār*.

30 Shaki 1978, *ibid.* emends to *dahēnd*.

31 Shaki 1978, *ibid.* emends to *bōxtēnd*.

'And thus the Mazda-worshipping Religion (states): "In the family (*tōhmag*) they (= the arch-heretics/Mazdakites) distribute shares (*bazišnīh baxšēnd*); they say their own (people/relatives/followers; *xwēšān*) perform (religious) duties (*kardārīh*) and they give shares (*bahr*) to their own (people/relatives/followers; *xwēšān*). They use food for fattening (*xwarišn fšōnēnēnd*) {*i. e.* they allot food according to the measure of one's hunger}. And they propagate matrilineal descent (*zahagīh*), *i. e.* they recognize lineage (*paywand*) through the mother. And they procreate (*hunēnd*) as wolves {*i. e.* they perform in a wolfish manner in relieving their (sexual) desire}; as the offspring of a wolf is afterwards the mother('s), they also recognize lineage through the mother. The females, which they buy (as?) small cattle, and also that which belongs to the offspring, sons (and) brothers, they take as profit (*bar*): 'We have given them (= the profit/females) to you all jointly (*hamīh*). You are only permitted to keep them jointly (*pad hamīh ēstād*)'. They do not believe in the oath (*war*), not even when it is obvious, that (the person) for whom one gives it, will be acquitted. They lie through their children {*i. e.* (the sin of) the contract-breaker (*mihrōdruj*) must come upon them and upon their kindred (*xweštan*)!}." '

Appendix V

Dēnkard 8: On Judicial Dispute (*pahikār-radestān*)

DkD 83.1–87.2 (ms. M: Meherji Rana copy of B); DkM 693.3–695.5. There is a gap in ms. B: 8 folios are missing, corresponding to DkM 682.17–701.11 (see Dresden 1966, p. 300). The missing folios are extant in the Meherji Rana copy (M) of manuscript B (see Dresden 1966, p. 16). The pages and lines in the following transcription and translation are numbered according to M (Dresden 1966, pp. 102–104); the corresponding pages in DkM are noted. The translation of West 1892, pp. 35–39, is rather speculative and by now completely antiquated. A Persian translation has been published by Fārsānī 1397/2018 in his edition of *Dēnkard* 8. The main terminology of this section has been discussed in Macuch 2002a.

Nīgādom. Pahikār-radestān 'Division on Judicial Dispute'

M 83.1; DkM 693.3
dād bun Nīgādom 30 fragard brīnag pahikār-radestān (2) *abar ēn kū ǰud-iz az mēnōy rasišnīg sēǰ (ud) xīndagīh ī* (3) *az ēbgat ō mardōm ud gōspand mardōm-iz pad wināhgārīh* (4) *dastag bawēnd.*

'The beginning of the legal (*nasks*) (is) the *Nīgādom* (consisting of) 30 *fragards*. The section *pahikār-radestān* ("Division on Judicial Dispute") (is) (2) on this: apart from the spiritual existence (*mēnoy*) (because of) the danger and illness (3) that befall mankind and animals by the (onslaught of) Evil (*ēbgat*) people (4) also generate sinfulness.'[1]

rawāgīh [ud] (ī) sēǰ ud xīndagīh andar gēhān (5) *az a-dādestānīhā zanišn ī ēk abar did ud handarz ī* (6) *ō mardōm abar pahrēz [ī] az-iš ud dādestānīg* (7) *zanišn handāzišn abāz ō kam zanišnīh ud ⁺a-zanišnīh*[2] (8) *ud padīrag-iz a-pahikār-radān pahikār-radīhā* (9) (*andar*) *ēstādan pad a-rēšagīh ud ⁺a-ziyānīh*[3] *ī xwēš* (10) *az-iz ēd pēštom*[4] *zanišn ī abar-iz a-pahikār-rad be* (11) *pahrēxtan.*

1 The phrase *pad wināhgārīh dastag bawēnd*, lit. 'they have a hand in sinfulness' seems to be idiomatic for 'they participate in sinfulness, generate sinfulness' (if ⟨YHWWNd⟩ *bawēnd* is not a mistake for ⟨YHBWNd⟩ *dahēnd*). In any case this is exactly the message of the following sentence. On *ēbgat* < Av. **aibi-gaiti-*, the approach, attack of Evil, see Klingenschmitt 2000, p. 219 (§ 5.2.7).

2 M 83.7: ⟨2 znšnyh⟩ *dō-zanišīh.*

3 M 83.9: ⟨2 zyd'nyh⟩ *dō-ziyānīh.*

4 M 83.10: written in one word ⟨HN'L'YN''twm⟩.

'Danger and illness (are) current in the world (5) as a result of assaulting one another unlawfully. And the advice (given) (6) to mankind (is) to abstain from it and to measure (7) assault according to the law, to aim at injuring slightly or not injuring (at all) (8) and also to proceed against those who are involved in a non-judicial dispute (*a-pahikār-radān*) according to (the procedure in) a judicial dispute (*pahikār-radīhā*), (9) without injury and without damage to one's own and to abstain (10) also from preemptively injuring (a person) in a non-judicial dispute (*a-pahikār-rad*) (11).'

hamāg pahikār-radīh kē ka ēk [ī] (12) *ast dādestānōmandīhā (andar) ēstād u-š stī* (13) *saxwan [ī] 2 ī hēnd gōwišnīg ud nimāyišnīg ī pad ǰud* (14) *brahm nihišnīh bawēnd 4 ēwēnag gōwišnīg* (M 84.1) *nimāyišnīg gōwišnīg ī nē nimāyišnīg nimāyišnīg* (2) *nē gōwišnīg nē gōwišnīg nē-iz nimāyišnīg.*

"Every (dispute is) a judicial dispute (*pahikār-radīh*) when someone has proceeded (against another person) according (12) to the law. And two (kinds of) statements are in existence (13) which are: the spoken (word) (*gōwišnīg*) und (the statement) by demonstration (*nimāyišnīg*), which are arranged in different (14) forms, (consisting of) four categories:

i) the verbal (declaration together with) (M 84.1) the (statement based on) demonstration (*gōwišnīg nimāyišnīg*);
ii) the verbal (declaration alone), without the (statement based on) demonstration (*gōwišnīgīh nē nimāyišnīg*);
iii) the (statement based on) demonstration (alone), (2) without a verbal (declaration) (*nimāyišnīg nē gōwišnīg*);
iv) the (statement based) neither on speech, nor on demonstration (*nē gōwišnīg nē-iz nimāyišnīg*)."

(3) *andar sāmān ī gōwišnīg* ⁺*nihād*[5] *4 ēwēnag pahikārišn ī* (4) *ǰud sāmān ud ǰud ēwāz ī ast ō pahikār-*(5)*radīh*[6] *ō rad ī xwēš ō any weh mard čiyōn* (6) *az-iš 3 abāyišnīg hēnd ō-iz ō* ⁺*gugāyān*[7] (7) *ud andar ān ī nimāyišnīg* ⁺*nihād*[8] *6 ēwēnag.*

"(3) Within the framework (of legal action) taken by speech (*gōwišnīh*) (there are) four forms of dispute (4) with various settings and different utterances (*certa verba*) which are:

i) the judicial dispute (*pahikār-radīh*) (5);
ii) (the dispute in the presence of) one's own spiritual master (*rad ī xwēš*);
iii) (the dispute before) other righteous men (= Zoroastrians, *weh mard)* (6) of whom three are necessary;
iv) (the dispute in front of) witnesses (⁺*gugāyān*).

5 M 84.3: ⟨nht'⟩.
6 M 84.4: ⟨'ptk'l⟩.
7 M 84.6: ⟨gwk'yyh⟩ *gugāyīh*.
8 M 84.7: ⟨nht'⟩.

(7) And within the framework (of legal action) taken by (means of) demonstration (*nimāyišnīg*) there are six categories (of legal disputes)."

ud ō (8) *a-pahikār-rad ēwāz čiyōn hammis ēwēnagān ī andar* (9) *ham dar bawēnd 12. ud hamāg a-pahikār-radīh kē* (10) *ka ēk ast a-dādestānīhā abar raftan u-š* (11) *ēwēnagān 5 ī hēnd* (DkM 694.1) *andar nimūd ud kanišn zaxm* (12) *ud rēš kardan ōzad(an).*

"And for (8) the person (involved) in a non-judicial dispute (*a-pahikār-rad*), the utterances (*certa verba*) together with the categories given in (9) the same chapter (are) twelve. And every (dispute is) a non-judicial dispute (*a-pahikār-radīh*) (or: private feud) (10) when someone proceeds (against another person) unlawfully. And there are five forms which (DKM 694.1) are:

i) threatening (*andar nimūd*);
ii) tearing off (*kanišn*);
iii) wounding (*zaxm*) (12);
iv) injuring grievously (*rēš kardan*) and
v) killing (*ōzad[an]*).

ud pahikār-rad hēnd (13) *12 ēwēnag baxt ēstēnd pad 4 brīnag ī 3 +and*[9] (14) *brīnag ī hēnd āšnawāg ī wēnāg ēd ī* (M 85.1) *pahikārišn ī awiš {......}*[10] *gōwišnīg nē nimāyišnīg.* (2) *ud wēnāg ī nē āšnawāg ēd ī pahikārišn ī +awiš*[11] (3) *nimāyišnīg nē gōwišnīg. ud ēn 3 ī andar ēk brīnag* (4) *pahikār-radīh abāg-šān hast.*

"And persons involved in a judicial dispute (*pahikār-rad*) (13) are divided into twelve categories in four sections, (consisting) of as much as three parts. (14) The sections are (concerned with persons):

i) who hear and see (*āšnawāg ī wēnag*); (M 85.1) the dispute with them {uses language as well as statement by means of demonstration};
ii) {who hear, but do not see; the dispute with them uses} language, (but) not statement by (means of) demonstration (*gōwišnīg nē nimāyišnīg*); (2)
iii) who see, but do not hear (*wēnag ī nē āšnawāg*); the dispute with them (uses) statement (by means of) (3) demonstration, but not language (*nimāyišnīg nē gōwišnīg*).

And with these three (categories of persons) who are in one section (4) judicial dispute (*pahikār-radīh*) is (possible)."

ud pahikār-rad (5) *bē agar bīm ī pad tan ēwar ēnyā +abē-pahikārišn*[12] *ī* (6) *čiyōn guft ēstēd pad rēš abāz dāštan* (7) *nē pādixšāy ud wizīr ī pad-iš ēn kū ka pad*

9 M 84.13: 〈'nk'〉.
10 Corresponding to DkM 694.3–4. A whole line has been presumably already left out in ms. B to judge by the content of this passage.
11 M 85.2: 〈'wbšn'〉.
12 M 85.5: 〈'p' ptk'lšn'〉.

(8) *dādīg pahikārišn nē wardēnd ud* +*āzāriš(n)īhā*[13] (9) *abāz dāštan nē šāyēnd pad-iz rēš abāz* (10) *pādixšāy dāštan.*

"The person involved in a judicial dispute (*pahikār-rad*) (5) is not allowed to restrain (another person) by injuring (him) without taking action (6) in the manner described (above), unless it is certain that he must fear bodily harm (7). And the judgment in this case is (as follows): if they (= the opponents) do not revert (from injuring) by (the judgment) (8) in a legal dispute (*dādīg pahikārišn*) and (9) it is not possible to keep them from doing harm, then it is allowed to restrain them by force (10).[14]"

brīnag-ē an-āšnawāg ī (11) *a-wēnag-iz ud zan ud aburnāyīg ēn 3 ī andar ēk* (12) *brīnag pahikār-radīh abāg-šān nēst. ud wizīr ī* (13) *tan pad-iš ēn kū bē agar-iš az be waštan* (14) *bīm ī pad tan ēwar ēnyā be wardišn.*

'A section (is) on (persons) who neither hear (11) nor see and women and underage children. With these three (persons) who are (discussed) in one (12) section no judicial dispute (*pahikār-rad*) is (possible). And the judgement (pronounced) (13) with respect to the (assailing) person is (as follows): unless it is certain that by retraining (from injury) (14) he must fear bodily harm, he should refrain from (injuring them).'

brīnag ī (M 86.1) *ān-ēr ud margarzān ēwar az dādwarān pad ōzad wizīr* (2) *pad-iš kardan. rāhdār ka andar rāh ēstēd* (3) *u-š zanišn paydāgēnīd ēstēd grift nē* (4) *šāyēd. ud ēn-iz 3 ī andar ēk brīnag pahikār-*(5)*radīh abāg nēst bē [ud] wizīr ī pad-iš ēn-iz kū* (6) *ka-š gyān be ōzanišn hēnd pad-iš kirbag* (7) *hēnd.*

'A section (is) (M 86.1) on foreigners (*an-ēr*) and persons worthy of death (*margarzān*) certain of receiving the death penalty (*pad ōzad wizīr*) by the judges (2). (On the) highway robber, when he is on the road (3) and the (necessity) of slaying him has been proclaimed, but he cannot be caught (4). And with these three (persons) who are (discussed) in one section there is no judicial dispute (*pahikār-radīh*) (5). But the judgement in this case is: (6) when their vital soul (*gyān*) has been destroyed, (then) a good deed (*kirbag*) has been done thereby (7).'

brīnag-ē(w) ēd ī abē-gāh raftan ahar madan (8) *pad škastag gyāg* +*burdēnīd* +*bar-iš*[15] *ka-šān pad* (9) *gōwišnīh pursēnd passox nē kardan nē pad* (10) *an-ērīh warōmand hēnd. ēn-iz 3 ī andar ēk* (DkM 695.1, M 86.11) *brīnag pahikār-radīh nēst ud wizīr pad-iš* (12) *ēn kū ka-šān be ōzanēd pad-iš wināhgār* (13) *nē bawēd.*

'A section (is) on (persons, who) roam about without a place (to live), (persons, who) seize (8) a ruined place letting its income be taken (?), (persons, who) when they are (9) spoken to, do not answer, (but) are not suspected of being (10)

13 M 85.8: ⟨ʾcʾlyšyhʾ⟩.
14 Lit. 'by injury' (*pad-iz rēš*).
15 M 86.8: ⟨bltynytʾ blʾh⟩.

foreigners. With these three (categories of people) who (are discussed) in one (DkM 695.1; M 86.11) section there is also no judicial dispute. And the judgement in this case is: (12) if (someone) slays them, (then) he does not become a sinner thereby (13).'

čē andar ham dar andar āwarēd was (14) *dādestān. ud ēn-iz kū abāz zaxm ān ī zaxm ud rēš* (M 87.1) *bawēd ōwōn kunišn ka pad har čiš ī rāst* (2) *abāz kardan šāyēd.*

'The (matters) expounded in the same chapter consist of many (14) judgments. And also this: in retaliation of a wound (*abāz zaxm*), the one who is wounded and injured (M 87.1), should act in the same manner. If every thing (= injury) (2) is returned justly, (then) it is allowed.'

Appendix VI

Dēnkard 8: On Assault, Wounding and Bodily Harm (*zaxmestān/rēšestān*)

DkD 87.2–93.1 (ms. M: Meherji Rana copy of B); DkM 695.6–698.9. There is a gap in ms. B: 8 folios are missing, corresponding to DkM 682.17–701.11 (see Dresden 1966, p. 300). The missing folios are extant in the Meherji Rana copy (M) of the B manuscript (see Dresden 1966, p. 16). The pages and lines in the following transcription and translation are numbered according to M (in Dresden 1966, pp. 99–104); the corresponding pages in DkM are noted. The translation of West 1892, pp. 39–43, is rather speculative and by now completely antiquated. A recent Persian translation is to be found in the edition of *Dēnkard* 8 by Fārsānī 1397/2018.

Nīgādom 1.2. *Zaxmestān* 'Section on Wounding'
(M 87.2–90.6; DkM 695.6–697.2)

(DkD [M] 87.2; DkM 695.6) *dudīgar brīnag zaxmestān* (3) *mādayān abar zaxm ud* ⁺*wišāyišn*[1] *az zaxm čiyōn dard* (4) *ud xōn a-bōyīh wināh ī mard andar a-bōyīh ē kunēd.*

'The second section, the *Zaxmestan* ('section on wounding') (is) (3) a treatise on wounds (*zaxm*) and the ⁺aperture (⁺*wišāyišn*) from the wound when (causing) (4) pain and blood (and) unconsciousness. And (on) the sin a man should commit in the state of unconsciousness (*a-bōyīh*).'

(5) *ud abar 7 ēwēnag ī daxšag ī a-bōyīh ud ǰud* (6) *wizīrīh ī abar zaxm ī purnāyān andar ān ī aburnāyīgān* (7) *kunēnd ud andar-iz zaxm kē dard (ud) xōn ōh rawēd. ud andar* (8) *ān kē xēšm xōg dra(h)nāy dard ud xōn nišanēd.*

'(5) And on the seven symptoms of unconsciousness and (on) the (6) different decisions concerning the wounds that persons of age inflict on underage (children)

1 M 87.3: ⟨w'hdšn⟩, presumably a slight misspelling of ⟨wyšdšn⟩ ⁺*wišāyišn* 'opening, gap, aperture', from *wišādan*, *wišāy-* 'to open, loose, free' (MacKenzie 1971, p. 92); Ir. √**hHai* 'to chain, bind', Av. √*hi* 'to chain, bind'+ *vi-* (Cheung 2007, p. 135–136; Kellens 1995, p. 72); NP *gušādan*, *gušāy-* 'to open, disclose, detect' (Steingass 1892, p. 1031 and 1090), *gušāyiš* 'aperture, opening, unloosing' (Steingass 1892, p. 1031). The meaning 'aperture' fits in perfectly with the exact definition of a 'wound' (*zaxm*), see discussion of this text in Chapter V, pp. 423–429.

(7). And also concerning the wound from which pain (ensues and) blood flows. And concerning (8) the (person) who due to a violent temper (*xēšm xōg*) causes pain and blood(shed) over a length (of time).'

ud abar (9) *xwāhišn (ud?) xwēhišn čiyōn ān ī pad mādagwarīh* (10) *gōwēd 4 ēwēnag ka aswār payg xwēhēd* (11) *ud ka payg* +*aswār*[2] *xwēhēd ud ka aswār* (12) *aswār xwēhēd (ud) ka payg [ud] payg xwēhēd. ud any* (13) *3 ēwēnag ī az ēn 2 pad āgenēn hampursagīh zāyēd* (14) *ka aswār ud payg [ud] aswār ud payg xwēhēnd* (M 88.1) *ud ka aswār ud payg [ud] aswār xwēhēnd. ud ka* (2) *aswār ud payg [ud] payg xwēhēnd ī bawēnd hammis 7* (3) *ēwēnag any-iz čand abāz ō ēn handāzīhēd ud abar-iz* (4) *kastār dahm ud dahm kastār xwēstan čē* (5) *andar ham dar.*

"And on (9) trampling (*xwāhišn*)[3] (and) pursuit (*xwēhišn*)[4], like those which are said (to consist of) essentially (10) four types:

i) when a horseman pursues a foot-soldier; (11)
ii) and when a foot-soldier pursues a +horseman;
iii) and when a horseman (12) pursues a horseman;
iv) when a foot-soldier pursues a foot-soldier."

And three (13) other forms (of pursuit), which come into being by these two (= horseman and foot-soldier) taking counsel together (14):

v) when a horseman and a foot-soldier pursue a horseman and a foot-soldier;
vi) (M 88.1) and when a horseman and a foot-soldier pursue a horseman;
vii) and when (2) a horseman and a foot-soldier pursue a foot-soldier.

These are together seven (3) types (of pursuit). Several other (types) are judged by analogy (*abāz handāzīhēd*) to these. Also on (4) a wrongdoer pursuing a pious man and a pious man (pursuing) a wrongdoer, which (5) belong to the same subject.

abar +*sneh*[5] *gīrišnīg ud sneh apparēd* (6) *ēd kū čē ān čiš ī pad sneh uspurrīg ud* (7) *čē ān ī nē. ud čē ān ī pad sneh mehmān.* (8) *ud čē ān ī ka kas pad sneh abāz* (DkM 696. 1) *ō kas* (M 88.9) *kunēd ā-š xwad čiš apparag. ud čē ān* (10) *ī-š guharīg appār ud čē ī-š dādag ān* (11) *xwāstag tōzišn ud ǰud(āg)īh ī wizīr ī abar mard 2* (12) *sneh barēnd az sneh 2 be burdan.*

2 M 87.11: ⟨pšyt⟩ is a mistake for ⟨PRŠY'⟩ *aswār* (Nyberg 1988, XIV.1, pp. 47, 83) 'horseman, knight, equestrian'.

3 On *xwāhišn* 'trampling, trashing, treading', from *xwastan*, *¹xwāh-* 'to tread, trample, trash' (MacKenzie 1971, p. 96) see Bartholomae 1926–1925, II, p. 30 (who reads *xwahišn* with a short *a*); NP *ẖwast*, *ẖost* designates 'a beaten road, rubbed (...)' (Steingass 1892, p. 485).

4 The term *xwēhišn* 'chasing, hunting, pursuit' (from *xwēstan*, *xwēh-* 'to chase, hunt, pursue') translates in FīO XXVa (Reichelt 1900–1901, p. 207, line 2) Av. *vāiti* 'pursuit' (Ir. √**u̯aiH* 'to hunt, chase'; Av. √*vaii* ‚to hunt, chase', Cheung 2007, p. 411; Bartholomae 1904, col. 1409); the reading *xwēstan*, *xwēh-* is based on the Pāzand form *xᵛə̄šīṯ* (Antia 1909, p. 349, *apud* Klingenschmitt 1968, num. 61).

5 M 87.5: ⟨sn'h⟩.

'On seizing a weapon and robbing (with) a weapon. (6) (On the question) which thing (is considered) completely as a weapon (7) and which is not. And which (thing) (is) acceptable as a weapon. (8) And what (happens in the following case): when someone brings back (DkM 696.1) (something) to (another) person (M 88.9) with (the use of) a weapon, then (is afterwards) himself a robber of the thing. And what (is) the (10) compensation for (something being) taken away (*guharīg appār*), and what (is) the transfer (*dādag*) (as a) (11) fine for that thing (*xwāstag tōzišn*). On the difference of the verdict regarding two men (12) carrying weapons from the (verdict) on carrying two weapons.'

ud abar (13) *6 ēwēnag ardīg tazišnīh pat zaxm xwēhišn* (14) *miϑōsāst adwadād gōwišn ī jādūg gōwišnīhā* (M 89.1) *ud gōwišn ī +sahm*[6] *nimāyišnīhā ud kū ardīg tazišnīh* (2) *ēg bawēd ka pad andar ēstādan be ēstād* (3) *ud zaxm kard ēk az ōy ī did nē pēš.*

"And on (13) the six forms of engaging in battle/conflict (*ardīg tazišnīh*) by:

i) wounding (*zaxm*);
ii) pursuit/chase (*xwēhišn*); (14)
iii) false teaching (*miϑōsāst*);
iv) abandonment; withholding maintenance (*adwadād*);
v) speaking in the manner of sorcerers (*gōwišn ī jādūg gōwišnīhā*) (M 89.1) and
vi) speaking in a threatening manner (*gōwišn ī +sahm nimāyišnīhā*).

And (on this), that engagement in battle/conflict (*ardīg tazišnīh*) (2) takes place when (the adversaries) are involved in it (at the same time) (3) and one is not wounded by the other beforehand."

(4) *ud ēn-iz kū purnāy abāg purnāy ud zan ī sturwan abāg* (5) *zan ī sturwan ud zan ī ābestan abāg zan ī* (6) *ābestan ud aburnāyīg ī 7 sālag abāg aburnāyīg ī* (7) *7 sālag ardīg tazišnīh bawēd aburnāyīg ī* (8) *7 sālag rāy pad wēnišn ī pidarān [pidarān]* (9) *ardīg tazišnīh bawēd u-š dādestān ēd kū* (10) *har wināh ī ardīg tazišnīhā kunē andar tōzišn* (11) *ō radān šawēd.*

(4) And also this: (on the following persons) engaging in battle/conflict (*ardīg tazišnīh*): a person of age with (another) person of age and a childless woman (5) with a childless woman and a pregnant woman with (6) a pregnant woman and a minor of seven years with a minor of (7) seven years. Regarding minors of (8) seven years, their engagement in conflict/battle (*ardīg tazišnīh*) takes place under supervision of the parents (9). And the decision (is) this: (10) (for) every offence which might be committed by engaging in battle/conflict (*ardīg tazišnīhā*) a fine (*tōzišn*) (11) goes to the spiritual authorities (*radān*).

abar appārīh xwadāy pāk ī (12) *kas andar bowandag a-bun būd ēstēd wēnēd ka* (13) *bowandag hamē xwāhēd war (ī) xwēšīh nē pahikārēd.*

6 M 89.1: ⟨sm⟩ for ⟨shm⟩ *sahm* throughout the manuscript.

"On the removal of a young animal (*pāk*)[7] on the part of the master which (12) (another) person regards as not belonging to any stock (*bowandag a-bun*) whatsoever: when he (= the other person) (13) claims it totally, (but) does not litigate by giving an oath on ownership (*war [ī] xwēšīh*)."

(14) *abar wināh ī hamēmālān bē andar xwad-iz hamēmāl pad* (M 90.1) *any ēč kirbag nē* ⁺*tōzīhistan*[8] *[ī] abar koštan ī [ud]* ⁺*bandag*[9] *abāg xwadāy-iz čē andar ham dar.*

"(14) On the offence regarding opponents (*wināh ī hamēmālān*): except towards the opponent himself, it (= the offence) cannot be atoned for by (M 90.1) any (other) good deed. (18) Also on killing a slave together with (his) master, (and) what (belongs) to the same subject.

abar koštan ī (3) *7 sālag aburnāyīg ī a-hammōxt 8 sālag-iz* (4) *pad wēnišn ī pidarān wināhgārīh ī pidarān* (DkM 697.1) *padiš* (M 90.5) *ka-šān abāz dāštan tuwān abāz nē* (6) *dārēnd ud ān ī ka-šān abāz dāštan nē tuwān.*

'On (the offence of) homicide (lit.: killing) by (3) uninstructed underage (children) of seven years (and) also (of) eight years (4) under the observance (*wēnišn*) of the parents. (On) the sinfulness of the parents (DkM 697.1) therein, (M 90.5) if they are able to prevent it, (but) do not (6) prevent it, and in the case that they are not able to prevent it.'

Nīgādom 1.3. *Rēšestān* 'Section on Bodily Harm' (M 90.7–93.1; DKM 697.3–698.9)

(M 90.7; DkM 697.3) *sidīgar brīnag rēšestān mādayān abar brīn* (8) *ud* ⁺*darrišn*[10] *oškāfišn frāz-rūdag ud sumbišn* (9) *ud xwāhišn škenišn ud xwurd kardan ud tāšīdan* (10) *ud* ⁺*huškēnīdan*[11] *čiyōn hamāg rēš xwānīhēd.*

7 This word, written ⟨p'k⟩, is confused with ⟨np'k⟩ *nabāg/nibāg* 'living pawn, pledge, hostage' in several passages of *Dēnkard* 8 (the only difference in spelling being the initial ⟨n⟩; *e.g.* DkM 699.18; 717.3), but in this sentence the spelling seems to be correct, since *pāk* 'young animal' (? < *pāka-*?; Skr. *pā̆kaḥ* 'young animal, cub'; Mayrhofer 1956–1980, vol. II, pp. 243–244; Perikhanian 1997, p. 413) is also attested in DkD 548.4 (DkM 721.5) in the context of ⟨pšwcws'⟩ **fšū̆-ciϑā-* or **fšū̆-ciϑiia-* 'atonement by (submitting) cattle', and MHDA 15.2 in ⟨p'k pswc'š'⟩, **pāk(a) fšū̆-ciϑā-* 'atonement (in kind) by (submitting) cattle: young animal'. On these expressions see Appendix VII, fn. 6). The syntax of the whole sentence is strange and seems to have been taken from the Pahlavi translation of the Avestan original (usually a slavish one-to-one rendering), not from the commentary.

8 M 90.1: ⟨tn'cyhstn'⟩.

9 M 90.2: ⟨bwndk⟩.

10 M 90.8: ⟨dyyyrršn'⟩.

11 M 90.10 ⟨hwšynytn'⟩ and DkM 697.5 ⟨hwyšynytn'⟩ suggest *xwēšēnīdan* 'to make (something) one's own', which would be perfectly acceptable in another legal context. In a list of physical injuries, however, this meaning seems completely out of place. I have hence assumed that it is a misspelling of an original ⁺*huškēnīdan* 'to cause to wither'.

"The third division, *Rēšestān* ("section on bodily harm"), (is) especially on (injuries by): cutting (*brīn*) (8) and splitting/tearing (*⁺darrišn*), ripping (*oškāfišn*), pulling out (*frāz-rūdag*), piercing (*sumbišn*), (9) treading (*xwāhišn*), rupturing (*škenišn*), crushing (*xwurd kardan*), mutilating (*tāšīdan*) (10) and causing (a limb) to wither (*⁺huškēnīdan*), since all these (actions) are called *rēš*."

(11) *wāhmān mārgan dard rawišnīh ī abar [abgan] kirb* (12) *abganišnīh ud xōn tazišnīh az mardōmān tan čiyōn* (13) *hannām hannām baxt ēstēd ō 76 ī* (14) *mādagwar ī parwastag andar 2 ēwēnag mādayāntar* (M 91.1) *xwānīhēd ay ⁺2 ī*[12] *wistarag hēnd ī ēk az did* (2) *jud mādag ud az darūnišnīh ī az 8 mādagwar ī* (3) *parwastag andar 2 ēwēnag hannām ī andar ān 76 ī* (4) *ham-gōnag ēk az did jud mādag ud ēk az did jud* (5) *čim ud jud wizīr hēnd.*

'(11) (On) causing someone pain by the whip (*mārgan*, "serpent-scourge") being slashed over the body and (12) (causing) the flow of blood from the bodies of people; how they (= the bodies) (13) are divided limb by limb into seventy-six (14) principal (parts), consisting of two principal forms, (M 91.1) which are called the most essential: that is, two (forms), which are covered and are different from each other (2) in (their) substance and inner (structure), which consists of eight principal (parts) (3) in two forms. The limbs belonging to the seventy-six (4) similar ones are different from each other as to (their) substance and different (5) in (their) purpose and are (subject to) different judgments.'

ēn-iz kū ka kas ō (6) *kas pad ⁺*zaxm[13] *stardīh ayāb stabrīh* (7) *ayāb nizārīh ayāb syāhīh ayāb spēdīh* (8) *ayāb gišnagīh ayāb bulandīh ayāb ⁺a-šnās(ag)īh*[14] (9) *ayāb frāy-xwārišnīh ayāb kam-xwarišnīh ayāb* (10) *a-paymān-xwarišnīh*[15] *ayāb ajgahānīh ayāb* (11) *tuxšāgīh ayāb enyā tēzīh dahēd ayāb* (12) *saxwan kāmēd guftan u-š abāz zanēnd* (13) *ayāb-iš gōwišn ud wēnišn āšnawišn ayāb xrad* (14) *ud ōz ud šusr ud šīr ud ābusīh be kāhēnīd ka* (M 92.1) *⁺spul*[16] *ayāb šīr ī mādagān abēsīhēnīd ayāb andar* (2) *⁺spul*[17] *pus be ōzanēd ka rēš rēš* (3) *kunēd u-š ⁺xwēdāg*[18] *ud xōn rawēd.*

'And also (on) this: when someone produces (the following symptoms) (6) in another person by wounding (him): stupefaction or coarseness (7) or weakness or blackness or whiteness (8) or shortness or tallness or amnesia (lit.: not

12 M 91.1: ⟨ynd⟩.
13 M 91.6: ⟨zt mn⟩.
14 M 91.8: ⟨ʾnšnʾsyh⟩.
15 M 91.10 seems to have the correct *a-paymān-xwārišnīh*, although the ⟨ʾ⟩ at the beginning of line 10 is smeared. DkM 697.16 has *paymān-xwārišnīh*, which does not make sense in this context.
16 M 92.1: ⟨spl⟩.
17 M 92.2: ⟨spl⟩.
18 M 92.3: ⟨hwtʾk⟩ instead of ⟨hwytʾk⟩ *xwēdāg* 'moisture' (presumably a noun formed from the adj. *xwēd* 'moist'+ *-āg*; compare *sardāg* 'coldness'; *garmāg* 'warmth'); on the suffix see DURKIN-MEISTERERNST 2014, p. 162 (§ 311).

recognizing) (9) or gluttony or too little eating or (10) immoderate eating or indolence or (11) diligence or some other kind of pungency. Or (a person) (12) wishes to speak and is beaten in return. (13) Or (a person's ability of) speech and sight and hearing or intelligence (14) and strength and (production of) semen and milk and pregnancy are diminished. (Or) when (M 92.1) (a person's) spleen or the milk of females is destroyed. Or (when someone) by (damaging) (2) the spleen kills a son; when he adds injury to injury (3) and from it moisture and blood flow.'

ud abar-iz (4) *zaxm ī pad ēk ayāb* (DKM 698.1) *2 ayāb 3 sneh ayāb* (M 92.5) *frāy pad ēwkardagīh ayāb* ***+ōiϑrih***[19] *ayāb* (6) ***hiδih*** *ayāb* ***apauuarāuuarštih*** (7) *kunēnd. ud abar +paymān*[20] *ī rēš ka gabrag frōd* (8) *abganēd srāy ud dīwār ud pērāmōn ud kirb ī abgand* (9) *ān xwurd kard ayāb ōškāft ayāb tāšīd* (10) *ayāb abāg xōn +xwēdāg*[21] *a-sāmān mālūn wimand ud dra(h)nāy* (11) *ud zahā ud sang ī sneh.*

"And on the (4) wound (*zaxm*) which is inflicted by one, (DkM 698.1) two or three weapons or (M 92.5) more all at once (= in conjunction, *pad ēwkardagīh)* or separately (*+ōiϑrih)* or (6) together (*hiδih*) or later (*apauuarāuuarštih*).[22] (7) On the measure of injury (*rēš*), when (someone) throws (a body) down into a cavity; (8) the house and the walls and surroundings (of the cavity) and (on) the body which has been thrown: (9) whether it has been crushed (*xwurd kard*) or torn apart (*ōškāft*) or cut (*tāšīd*) (10) or besmeared all over ('unlimitedly') with blood (and) moisture (*abāg xōn +xwēdāg mālūn*). (On) the extent (lit. limit/ boundary) and the breadth (11) and depth (of the injuries); (on) a stone, which (is used as) a weapon."

nērang ī rēš rawišnīh (12) *ud dard rawišnīh ud 3 šabag sāl drahnāy abar* (13) *pāyišnīh ud xwārtarīh ud a-xwārtarīh ud spurrīgīh* (14) *ud an-uspurrīgīh ud čē andar ham dar. xwardīg* (M 93.1) *ud āmārēnīdārīhā ud wizīr ī abar ǰud ǰud.*

'On the incantation for healing an injury (*rēš*) (12) and healing pain and (on) watching over (the injured) for three nights in the course of a year (13) and (on) the lightness or graveness (of the injury) and its completeness (14) and incompleteness and (other) matters belonging to the same subject. Details (M 93.1) and enumerations and judgments, which are (listed) one by one separately.'

19 M 92.5: ⟨'L *iϑrih⟩*; *iϑrih* written in the Avestan script.

20 M 92.7: ⟨ptmd'n'⟩.

21 M 92.10: ⟨hwt'k'⟩ (on this word see fn. 18 above).

22 On the three terms written in the Avestan script see Klingenschmitt 2000, pp. 220–222 (and fn. 96) with examples from the texts: *+ōiϑrih*, from the Av. adverb *ōiϑra* + MP abstract suffix *-īh* 'separately' ('getrennt', translated by MP *ǰūdāgīh* 'in separate form'); *hiδih* (besides *haδīh)* from Av. *haδa* 'together' ('Zusammen-sein, zusammen'); *apauuarāuuarštih* from Av. **aparāuuaršta-* 'done later; committed later (than another sin)' ('später getan; später begangen [als eine andere Sünde']).

Appendix VII

Dēnkard 8: On the Thief (and his) Accomplice (*abar duz abāg*)

DkD 548.1–549.8 (ms. B); DkM 721.1–722.15 (pages and lines in the following transcription and translation are numbered according to DkD; the pages in DkM are noted; West 1892, pp. 74–77, is by now completely antiquated; the recent Persian edition by Fārsānī 1397/2018, pp. 106–109, has a different interpretation of the text in many respects).

Duz(d)-sar-nizad/ōzad 18**. 'The Head of the Thief Severed: eighteen (sections)'**

Variant readings of the title:
duz(d) ī druz +*tan* 'the *druz*-embodied thief';
duz(d) ī +*drōzan* 'the lying/false thief'[1]

(DkD 548.2; DkM 721.2) *fradom brīnag mādayān abar duz abāg griftārīh ī-š pad mādag* (3) +*duz*[2] *ān ī-š trift passazag wināh ud band ud drōš ud wizārišn ī wināh* (4) *rāy baxtīg pādofrāh ud kār warzišnīh ud *fšŭ-ciϑā- ud čandīh ī ǰud ǰud* (5) *andar ēk ēk pāk kadāmīh.*

"(2) The first section (is) essentially on the thief (and his) accomplice (*duz abag*);[3] (on) the seizure (*griftārīh*) of the stolen goods; (3) (on) the suitable (degree) of

1 The diverse possible readings of the curious title of this *nask* as ⟨GNB'slnct'⟩; ⟨GNB'slwct'⟩; ⟨GNB' Y dlwc +tn'⟩; ⟨GNB' Y +dlwcn'⟩ are all problematic. On the different suggestions see Chapter I, p. 25, fn. 39.

2 B: ⟨GNB'y⟩.

3 The difficulties of understanding the text begin immediately in the first line with the words ⟨MDM dwc' LWTH̱ glpt'lyh ZY-š pt m'tk GNB'y⟩ *abar duz abag griftārīh ī-š pad mādag duz*. The third word is the heterogram ⟨LWTH̱⟩ for the prep./adv. *abāg* 'with, together, together with', which, however, does not make sense in this context, nor fits in with the rest of the text (literal translation: 'on the thief together with the seizure of the stolen goods'). My assumption is that a copyist replaced an original noun ⟨'p'k⟩ *abāg* 'helper, assistant, accomplice' by the heterogram ⟨LWTH̱⟩ for the homonymous prep./adv. *abāg*. Both readings *duz abāg* and *duz ud abāg* are possible here, as the final stroke in ⟨dwc'⟩ can also be read as ⟨W⟩ *ud* 'and' according to ms. B (where there is an empty space between ⟨dwc⟩ and ⟨W⟩). In my opinion only the noun *abāg* 'helper, assistant, accomplice' can be meant here and on the same page, lines 6 ⟨'p'k⟩ and 17 ⟨LWTH̱⟩ in *duz abāg* 'accomplice of the thief' or *duz ud abāg* 'the thief and [his] accomplice'. On the

sin for the theft (*trift*)[4] and 'fetters and brand/mutilation' (*band ud drōš*)[5] and redemption (*wizārišn*) for the sin (4) by the apportioned punishment. And (on) the execution (of the punishment) and atonement by (submitting) an animal from the livestock (**fšū̆-ciϑā-* 'cattle-atonement')[6] and (on) the extent of every separate (atonement), (5) (determining) one by one which of the young animals (*pāk*)[7] (should be submitted)."

ud kār gyāg ī pādofrāh čē tan ud ēwēnag ī (6) *abāg*[8] *čiyōn ān ī padiš abāg wizīhīd +padisārīg*[9] *kadām pēš kardan kard.*

'And (on) the venue of execution (*kār gyāg*) of the punishment, which person (is the thief) and in which manner (6) (is there) an accomplice (*abāg*); how the one who (is) an accomplice to him (= the thief) is separated at the beginning; which one has initially committed (the theft).'

(7) *ud abar tan ī band hannām ī +bēšišn*[10] *ud paymān ī tangīh ī band ud drōš ud drang ī bastag ī* (8) *wināh ī duz abar band ud band ī šahr hamēmālān xwēš arz ī ān ī guharīg*(9)*ōmand ud čē andar im dar.*

---

noun see Nyberg 1974, p. 21, who cites the cas. obl. plural form *abāgān* 'helpers, assistants'; on the abstract *abāgīh* 'company, assistance', see MacKenzie 1971, p. 1. See also fn. 8 below and Chapter V, pp. 439, 441.

4 B: ⟨tlpt'⟩ *trift*, from the root Ir. √**tarp* 'to steal', Av. √*trəp* 'to steal' (Cheung 2007, p. 383; Bartholomae 1904, col. 643; Kellens 1995, p. 25); MP ⟨tlwptk'⟩ *truftag* 'stolen' (MacKenzie 1971, p. 84); ⟨tlpt'⟩ *trift* 'theft'; *triftagīh* 'stealing'; *triftēnīdan* 'to commit theft' (Nyberg 1974, p. 195).

5 On *band ud drōš*, the punishment for theft, see Chapter V, pp. 441–445.

6 B: ⟨pšwcws'⟩ renders Av. **fšū̆-ciϑā-* or **fšū̆-ciϑiia-* 'atonement by (submitting) cattle' (see Klingenschmitt 2000, p. 224, 5.9–5.9.1 'Vieh-Buße, Buße, die man in Form einer Abgabe von Vieh leistet'). See also MHDA 15.2 ⟨p'k pswc'š'⟩, **pāk(a) fšū̆-ciϑā-* 'a young animal': atonement (in kind) by (submitting) cattle/livestock': *pad azišmānd har ān kē mādag hast mādag ud ān kē nēst *pāk(a) fšū̆-ciϑā-* 'For an obstruction (of justice) (*azišmānd*) every one who has money (pays a fine) in money, who has none, atones in kind (= by submitting a young animal from the livestock).' I had no idea how to read the term in Macuch 1981 (pp. 37, 144) but could explain its technical meaning correctly as 'Naturalien', '(fine paid) in kind' (p. 159, no. 49) due to the context of the sentence in which it occurs. The first word ⟨p'k⟩ *pāk* 'young animal' (? <**pāka-?*; Skr. *pākaḥ* 'young animal, cub') is also attested in our *Dēnkard* passage in line 5, confirming this interpretation (Mayrhofer 1956–1980, vol. II, pp. 243–244; Perikhanian 1997, p. 413; the meaning 'young animal, cub' ['Tierjunges'] is, however, later questioned in Mayrhofer 1992–2001, vol. II, p. 115). On *pāk* see also Appendix VI, fn. 7.

7 On *pāk* (in **pāk[a] fšū̆-ciϑā-* see fn. 6 above).

8 B: ⟨'p'k⟩. Due to the ambiguity of the Pahlavi script this word can be read both *abāg* and *a-pāk*. The thief's 'accomplice, helper', *abāg*, (written both ⟨'p'k⟩ and as the prep./adv. ⟨LWTH̱⟩ in this text) is mentioned not only in lines 2 and 6, but again later in line 17 (⟨dwc' LWTH̱⟩ *duz abāg*) in the context of accompliceship to theft, hence the preference for the former reading (which is, moreover, the only possible reading and interpretation that makes sense right at the beginning of this section in line 2, see fn. 3 above).

9 B: ⟨pts'lyk⟩.

"(7) And on the person whose limbs are bound (*band hannām*), (causing) torment, and (on) the degree of the tightness of the fetters (*band*) and (on) the brand/mutilation (*drōš*) and the duration of the binding (corresponding to) (8) the sin of the thief; on the fetters (*band*) and the fetters of the land/state (*band ī šahr*): the litigants (receive) in ownership (*hamēmālān xwēš*) the value of the (stolen) thing that (9) is compensated (*guharīgōmand*); and (on) that, which (is) in the same section.

ud čandīh ī gyāg ī drōš ud ǰud ǰud ān ī (10) *kadām duz dārēd. ud čand čiyōn pad čē drōšišnīh duz drōz*[11] *(ī) šahr* (11) *ān hamēmālān xwēš arz ī ān ī guharīgōmand ud gyāg ī abāyist* (12) *drōšīh guharīg wināh ī az wēš ǰud ēwēnag drōšišnīh ud ān ī az hišt* (13) *drōšīh ī šahr sāmān ī az wēš drōš-arzānīgīh ud čandīh pāyag ī duzīh* (14) *az sāmān ī drōš-arzānīgīh frāz ān-iz ī frōd az sāmān ī drōš-arzānīgīh.*

'And (on) the amount of places of brand/mutilation (*gyāg ī drōš*) and (enumerating) one by one separately: (10) which thief has which (brand/mutilation). And (on) the extent, the manner, the type of branding/mutilating (*drōšišnīh*) of the thief (according) to the brand/mutilation of the land (*drōz ī šahr*); (11) (on) the litigants (receiving) in ownership (*hamēmālān xwēš*) the value of the (stolen) thing that is compensated (*guharīgōmand)* and the place where the compensation for the brand/mutilation (*drōšīh guharīg*) (is) due; the sin which ensues on excessively (or) differently branding/mutilating (*drōšišnīh*) and the (sin) that ensues by remitting (the punishment) (13); (on) the branding/mutilation of the land (*drōšīh ī šahr*): the measure (*sāmān*) which ensues from (a thief) deserving extensive punishment by brand/mutilation (*drōš-arzānīgīh*) and (on) the amount of degrees (*pāyag*) of theft; (14) on the measure of (a thief) deserving more punishment by brand/mutilation (*drōš-arzānīgīh*) and also on (a thief) deserving less punishment by brand/mutilation (*drōš-arzānīgīh*).'[12]

(15) *abar ēwēnagān ī duzīh ud abzōnīg wināhīh ī duz ud pad tan ǰūdan ud rēšīdan* (16) *ud a-paydāgēnīdan ī mādag ī pad duz ī pad hās*^{a}*r ud ān ī pad ān gyāg ud ān ī pad* (17) *ēk gām bawēd.*

"(15) On the forms of theft and the increasing sinfulness of the thief; and (on) chewing and injuring the body (16) and not revealing the (stolen) object which is with a thief, who is at a distance of a *hās*^{a}*r* (measure of length) and of (the thief), who (is) in that place and the one, who (17) (is only) a pace away.

10 B: ⟨byšn'⟩ for ⟨byššn'⟩ *bēšišn* 'harm, torment', noun from *bistan*, *bēš-* 'to hurt, torment' (MacKenzie 1971, p. 18).

11 On the parallel form ⟨dlwc'⟩ *drōz*, semantically identical with *drōš*, see Buyaner 2016, p. 451.

12 I had a different understanding of parts of this difficult passage in Macuch 1993, p. 495.

ud duz abāg abar +bōdōzed[13] *ud +kādōzed*[14] *any-iz* (18) *winā̆h pad pēšīh ud pasīh* ***hiδih*** *abar duz-menišnīh ī* (19) *duzīh ī nē ham ud ham-bahr* (DkM 722.1) *duzīh ud ǰud-bahr duzīh [ī] abar winā̆h ī duz* (DkD 548.20) *+āškārag*[15] *ud nagīrāygar ud hišt ud bōxt wizīr ud bastār ī duz ān ī* (21) *ayārīh dādār ī duz pad duzīh ud wirēg ud wizīr ī abar duzīh ī aburnāyīg* (22) *ud zan ī starwan ān ī ābestan u-šān dārišn windišn ī andar tōzišnīg* (DkD 549.1) *kār ud kār ī ābestan duz.*

"And (on) the thief (and his) accomplice (*duz abāg*); on intentional injury (*+bōdōzed)* and injury by negligence (*+kādōzed)*; (on) other (18) offences (committed) before (and) after (and) together (*hiδih*);[16] on the intention of the thief (*duz-menišnīh*) of (19) stealing alone *(nē ham*, lit.: 'not together') and (on) stealing with joint shares (*ham-bahr duzīh*) (DkM 722.1) and stealing with separate shares (*ǰud-bahr duzīh*); on the sin of the thief (being) (DkD 548.20) obvious (*+āškārag)* and his denying it (*nagīrāygar*); and (on) the verdict regarding dismissal and acquittal (*hišt ud bōxt wizīr*); and (on) the person who confines the thief, the one who (21) helps (him) steal and escape. And on the verdict regarding the theft of an underage (child) (22) and a childless/barren woman (and) a pregnant (woman) and (on retaining) their possessions (and) earnings as atonement for the (DkD 549.1) deed and (on) the deed of a pregnant thief."

ud abar xwāstag ī āmēxtag amaragān ī az (2) *duzān abāz dārānd ud duz pad dast ud ān ī duz nē pad dast abar gugāyīh (ī)* (3) *duz kū pad čē padīrišnīg kē pad duz frāz rasēd čiyōn ān ī ka* (4) *griftan bastan ud čiyōn ān ī ka +wāxtan*[17] *ud frēftan abāyēd tā ō kām*(5)*gārīh padiš rasēd.*

'And on the property of the mixed commonalty (*āmēxtag amaragān*), which should be safeguarded from thieves. And on (that) which a thief (has) in his hands and that which a thief does not (have) in (his) hands; on the testimony of (3) the thief, (namely) under which circumstances it can be accepted, when it extends to (another) thief; how it is, (4) when it is necessary to seize and fetter (the thief) and how it is, when it is necessary to speak and deceive (him) until (5) he is subdued (*ō kāmgārīh padiš rasēd*).'

ud abar pašn ī abāg duzān. abar ǰuttarīh (6) *ī duz az appar abar xwāstag ī burd abāz ō xwēšān* (7) *rasēnīdan čiyōn ān ī az anērān marzānān ud ān ī az duzān dādwar ud bahr ī* (8) *az* ***+āstərəϑβąŋ***[18] *az duzān be grift.*

13 B: ⟨b'ynwkzyt'⟩. On this term see Chapter V, pp. 417–422.

14 B: ⟨k'ytynkyt⟩. On this term see Chapter V, pp. 417–422.

15 B: ⟨'š'lk⟩.

16 On *hiδih*, written in the Avestan script, from Av. *haδa* 'together' see KLINGENSCHMITT 2000, pp. 220–222, ('Zusammen-sein, zusammen'); see Appendix VI, fn. 22.

17 B: ⟨ww'htn'⟩.

18 Written in the Avesta script: *astərəϑβąŋ*; a form not attested in the extant Avestan texts as far as I can see; from Av. √*star* 'to sin' + *ā-* (BARTHOLOMAE 1904, col. 1597–1598,

'And on the contract with thieves. On the difference between the thief and the robber (*appar*). On returning the taken property to their owners (7). How (one proceeds with) that which is taken from non-Iranians (*anērān*), border residents (*marzānān*) and that which the judge has taken from thieves and the share (8) taken from sinners (⁺*āstərəϑβąŋ*) by thieves.'

ud abar pānāgān (9) *pāsbānān ī duz ud any-iz was dādestānīh andar duzīh.*

'And on the protectors (9) (and) guardians of the thief and many other judgments regarding theft.'

'sündigen, sich versündigen, in den Zustand der Sündigkeit geraten; sündig sein, sich im Zustand der Sündigkeit befinden'; see also BARTHOLOMAE 1904, col. 340); Ir. √*star 'to sweep, throw down; to sin' (CHEUNG 2007, pp. 363–364); MP *āstār* 'sin' (MACKENZIE 1971, p. 12; NYBERG 1974, p. 32); *āstārēnīdan*, *āstārēn-* 'cause to sin' (MACKENZIE 1971, p. 12).

Appendix VIII

Hērbedestān 6.6–7: On Illicit Sexual Intercourse

Hēr. 6.6 (§ 1–5)-6.7 (§ 1–6); according to the edition of Kotwal/Kreyenbroek 1992, pp. 42–47; 6.10–6.37 (according to the edition of Humbach/Elfenbein 1990, pp. 46–53); Mss: TD 6v.3–7v.8 (Kotwal/Boyd 1980); HJ 6v.3–8r.14 (Sanjana 1894); both editions have divergent readings and a largely different understanding of the long Pahlavi commentary to this passage, for which I am suggesting a new (in parts tentative) translation. This section of chapter 6 discusses sexual offences occurring in the specific context of a woman, who seeks to pursue religious studies (with or without the authorization of her guardian) and is accompanied by a man who is not her husband (see discussion of the text in Chapter V, pp. 454–458).

6.6 § 1–2 (= 6.10–11) (Av.) *frōit̰.varə̄*[1] *+paraŋhacāiti*[2] *ākå̄ hazaŋ^{v}ha +anākå̄sə*[3] *tāiiuš*

'(If he) accompanies her forth with the intention of having sexual intercourse: (if he does it) openly (he is a) robber, (if) stealthily, a thief.'

(MP) *ka gādan*[4] *dužāmul*[5] *rāy abāgēnēd ka āškārag apparag ka nihān duz. [abāz* haxtō ud anahaxtō *gōwēd ast kē abāz ō* anahaxtō *gōwēd]*[6]

1 Bartholomae 1904, col. 1024, does not translate *frōit̰.varə̄* ('[wenn einer eines andern Frau] zum Zweck von –?– mit sich wegführt'), but refers to the preverb *frōit̰* 'forth' *(ibid.)* and the root √^{4}*var* 'make pregnant, become pregnant' (Bartholomae 1904, col. 1363: 'schwanger machen, werden'); the Pahlavi translation has *gādan* 'to copulate, have sexual intercourse'; on the Avestan passage see also König 2010, p. 291, with elucidations and further references.

2 TD 6v.3: *paraŋhacaitē*; HJ 6v.3f.: *paraŋhacāiti* (misprinted as **paracaŋhaiti* in Kotwal/Kreyenbroek 1992, p. 42); Ir. √**hač* 'to follow' (Cheung 2007, p. 124); Av. √*hac* 'suivre' (Kellens 1995, pp. 70–71) + *para-* 'to follow forth' (Cheung, *ibid.*; Bartholomae 1904, col. 1741–1742: '(1) etwas (Akk.) mit sich fortnehmen… (2) mit Jemandem (Instr.) weggehen … (a) Jemanden (Instr.) mit sich, in seiner Begleitung wegführen … mit Akk. des Ziels [Zwecks]').

3 Both mss. (TD 6v.4; HJ 6v.5): *anākå̄se*; (*an-ākāh-* 'invisible, hidden', n.sg. *+anākå̄sə*; Bartholomae 1904, col. 122, 'unsichtbar; der sich [dabei] nicht sehen last, es heimlich tut'; opposite of *ākå̄*, n.sg.; *ā-kā-* 'visible, manifest'; Bartholomae 1904, col. 310 'manifestus; der sehen läßt, was er tut, sich bei dem was er tut sehen läßt, es offenkundig tut').

4 TD 6v.5: ⟨SLYTWNtn'⟩; HJ 6v.5: ⟨SLYTWN⟩.

5 Both mss. (TD 6v.5; HJ 6v.6): ⟨dwšʾml⟩ *dužāmul*, according to Bartholomae 1904, col. 1024, 'fornication' ('Unzucht'). This could also be a twisted spelling for ⟨dwšʾlm⟩ *+dōšāram* 'love, desire' (with ⟨ml⟩ instead of ⟨lm⟩), as Kotwal/Kreyenbroek 1992, p. 42, read the word.

'(if he) accompanies her with (the intention) of copulating [fornication]: if (he does it) openly (he is a) robber, (if) stealthily, a thief. [(This) refers to (Av.) *haxtō* "authorized" and *anahaxtō* "not authorized"; there is one (commentator) who says: "It refers to *anahaxtō* 'not authorized'."]'[7]

6.6 § 3–5 (= 6.11–21) *ēn az abestāg paydāg*[8] +*any*[9] *bawēd ka-š pad gādan menišnīg nayēd u-š ǰāmag abar nē dārēd u-š andar hās*^{a}*r nē gāyēd. ka pad hās*^{a}*r ka āškārag apparag*[10] *ud ka nihān duz. ka-š ǰāmag*[11] *abar dārēd u-š*[12] *rānēnēd duz pad gyāg gyāg ud appar pad*[13] *hās*^{a}*r čē duz-menišnīgīh ǰud ⟨abar pad hāsar-iz ī duz-menišnīgīh ǰud⟩*[14] *appar-menišnīgīh. hād*[15] *appar pad rēš nē bawād ka-š ēd duz*[16] *appar pad ⟨ē⟩*[17] *gyāg bawēd ay har ān (ē)*[18] *ka-š gād nē bawēd ā-š hagriz*

6 According to HJ 6v.7–9; TD 6v.6v.6–7 has only '*abāz* haxtō *ud* anahaxtō *gōwēd*', omitting '*ast kē abāz ō* anahaxtō *gōwēd*'. According to Kotwal/Kreyenbroek 1992, p. 42, no. 168, the facsimilie of TD (om. in Kotwal/Boyd 1980) has *ā-š *hagriz nē būdan* written in pencil on the margin of this passage, which they translate as '*i. e.* it is never (permissible) for him.'

7 The part in square brackets is a Pahlavi gloss referring to the Avestan text with which this section begins, Hēr. 6.1: *yō aniiehe nāirika anahaxtō aϑaurunəm paraŋhacāiti* 'One who accompanies the wife of another person to pursue religious studies without authorization (*anahaxtō*)'. The Pahlavi translation of this passage has for Av. *anahaxtō* MP *anāfrāh* 'without instruction', which is explained in the gloss by *abēdastwar* 'without authorization', but the following Pahlavi commentary elucidates that the exegetes understood the text as referring to a husband who indeed allows his wife to pursue religious studies, but does not explicitly authorize a specific man to be her escort: *hād guft-iš ēstēd kū ō hērbedestān kardan šaw bē-š nē guft ēstēd kū abāg kē šaw* 'That is, he (= the husband) has told her: 'Go to pursue religious studies', but has not said with whom she should go' (Kotwal/Kreyenbroek 1992, pp. 40–41; Humbach/Elfenbein 1990, pp. 44–45). The following problem arises in this context for the exegetes: is the offence of illicit sexual intercourse treated as theft and robbery, (1) when the escort of the woman is authorized (*haxtō*) as well as when he is not authorized (*anahaxtō*) to accompany her, or (2) *only* if the escort has *not* been authorized (*anahaxtō*) by the husband? Both opinions are transmitted in this gloss.

8 TD 6v.7: om. *paydāg*.

9 Both mss. (TD 6v.7; HJ 6v. 10): ⟨ZK⟩, which makes no sense here; see also Kotwal/Kreyenbroek 1992, p. 42.

10 HJ 6v.13: om. *apparag* (gap in the ms.).

11 TD 6v.10: ⟨yymk'⟩; HJ 6v.14: ⟨YDH̱⟩.

12 HJ 6v.15: om. *u-š* (gap in the ms.).

13 HJ 7r.1: om. *pad* (gap in the ms.).

14 Both mss. (TD 6v.12–13; HJ 7r.2–3) have mistakenly repeated (after *jud*): *abar pad hās*^{a}*r-iz ī duz menišnīgīh jud* (correctly deleted in the edition of Kotwal/Kreyenbroek 1992, p. 44).

15 HJ 7r.3: om. *hād* (gap in the ms.).

16 TD 6v.14: ⟨dwcʾn⟩; HJ 7r.4f.: ⟨dwcʾ⟩

17 The ⟨ʾy⟩ is superfluous (see fn. 18); *pad gyāg* in legal texts has a temporal meaning: 'immediately, on the spot' and is probably also used in this sense here.

18 The superfluous ⟨ʾy⟩ *ē* between *pad* and *gyāg* could belong here: *har ān ē* 'every time'; compare *andar ān ē* 'at the (specified) time' in juristic texts; *e. g. agar andar ān ē tōzišn*

nē bawēd. gād pad uskārišn ēdōn bawēd čiyōn-iš ⟨ēdōn bawēd čiyōn⟩[19] *az bunīh ka-š āškāragīhā be*[20] *nayēd ka-š nihānag gād appar*[21] *bawēd ka čē-š nihānag be nayēd u-š āškārag gāyēd duz bawēd.*

"This is revealed in the Avesta: This is different, when he (= the escort) leads her forth with the intent of having sexual intercourse (*pad gādan menišnīg*) and he does not remove her garment and does not copulate with her within (the distance/timespan of a) *hāsᵃr*.[22] If he (does copulate with her) within a *hāsᵃr*, if he does it openly (*āškārag*), he (is a) robber, if stealthily (*nihān*) he (is a) thief. If he removes her garment and flings it aside (*u-š rānēnēd*)(?),[23] he (is considered as) a thief from place to place and a robber within (the distance/timespan of) a *hāsᵃr*, since the intent of the thief (*duz-menišnīgīh*) is different from the intent of a robber (*appar-menišnīgīh*). That is, he should not be considered as a robber using force (*pad rēš*): when he (is) a thief, he is considered as a robber immediately, that is, the moment when he has copulated with her (using force). If he has not (copulated with her), then this does not apply to him by any means. (The offence of) sexual intercourse with reflection (= intention; *gād pad uzkārišn)* is assessed according to the outset (*az bunīh*): if he (= the escort) leads her forth openly and has copulated with her secretly, (then) he is considered as a robber (*appar*); when he leads her forth secretly and copulates with her openly, then he is considered as a thief (*duz*)."

6.7 §1 (= 6.22–24) *ka andar sālārīh ī mērag gāyēd har ēk bār tan-duz bawēd u-šān tan-duzišnīh*[24]*⟨ī⟩ andar ēstēd pas ka-iz-iš andar sālārīh ī mērag gāyēd*

---

xwāhēnd 'when the payment is requested at the (specified) time' (MHD 60.11–12; Macuch 1993, pp. 409, 414); also *pēš az ān ē* 'before the (specified) time' (*e.g.* MHD 106.1–4); on *ē* (as in *ham-ē* 'always') < IE **ai̯u* 'time, duration' see Bartholomae 1918–1923; here: part III, 1920, pp. 26–28.

19 Both mss. (TD 6v.17; HJ 7r.8–19) mistakenly repeat ⟨*ēdōn bawēd čiyōn*⟩ (deleted in both editions).

20 TD 7r.1: inserts ⟨cgwn⟩ after ⟨BR'⟩.

21 TD 7r.2: ⟨hcpl⟩; HJ 7r.10: ⟨hc'pl⟩.

22 A *hāsᵃr* (Av. *hāϑra-*; Bartholomae 1904, col. 1802–1803) is according to MacKenzie 1971, p. 43 'a measure of time (unequal hour, 1/12 of daylight); a measure of length (= *frasang*, or 1/4 *frasang*, 1 mile)'.

23 The verb *rānēnīdan* is derived from *rāndan* (on the suffix *-ēn* see Durkin-Meisterernst 2014, p. 229, §465), Ir. √**ran(H)?* 'to fight, enjoy (to fight)' (Cheung 2007, p. 313); NP 'to drive, drive away; to banish, expel; to purge, to force; to pursue; to incline (to a colour); to move off' (Steingass 1892, p. 565). Nyberg 1974, p. 166, translates *rānēnīdan* as 'to throw, fling aside', which I have tentatively adapted. The translations in both editions (Humbach/Elfenbein 1990, p. 49: 'If he lifts her garment and forces her'; Kotwal/Kreyenbroek 1992, p. 45: 'if he takes off her clothes and assaults [?] her') imply the use of force on the part of the escort, which would, however, lead to an assessment of the offence as robbery, not theft.

24 TD 7r.5: ⟨tn' dwcšnyh⟩; HJ 7r.14f.: ⟨'D tn' Y dwcšnyh⟩.

+ā-z[25] *+tan-duzīh*[26] *ān ham ēk bār har čiyōn-iš gāyēd pad +tan-duzīh*[27] *ō bawēd. ēn ka čiyōn bawēd ka-š andar sālārīh (ī) mērag gāyēd (ciyōn) bawēd ka andar gyāg-ē(w) ī framān ī +ōy*[28] *ī +azabar*[29] *pad framān ī +ōy*[30] *(ī) nē andar ān gyāg ud +ōy*[31] *ī +az-iš*[32] *pad ē(w) bun-ē.*

"If he (= the escort) copulates with her while she is under the guardianship (*sālārīh*) of a man (*mērag*), then he is (considered) on each occasion (as) a 'body-thief' (*tan-duz*) and they (= escort and guardian) take responsibility (*u-šān … andar ēstēd*)[33] for the 'body-theft' (*tan-duzišnīh*), then, if he (= the escort) copulates with her, while she is under the guardianship (*sālārīh*) of the man (*mērag*), then he (= the guardian) is likewise (guilty) of body-theft (*+tan-duzīh*) once, every time he (= the escort) copulates with her. How is this assessed, when he copulates with her while she is under the guardianship of the man, (how) when he (= the escort) is in a place under the command (*framān*) of the above named (guardian) (or) he (= the escort) is under the command (*pad framān*) of him, who is not in that place and of him, who is from that (place)? (The offence accruing) to the stock is one (and the same) (*pad ē[w] bun-ē*)."

6.7 §2 (= 6.26–29) *ka-š gād-menišnīg*[34] *ē(w) hās*^{a}*r az kār ī +pādīrānēnīdan*[35] *pad čāštag ī Sōšāns frārāst*[36] *kū pad duz ī +ōy*[37] *bawēd pad-iz ān ī Kay-ādur-bōzēd ēd-iz*[38] *ō*[39] *bun hād mā agar-iš pādīrānēnīdan ō mar āyēd.*

"When he (leads her forth the distance of) one *hās*^{a}*r* with the intent of sexual intercourse (*gād-menišnīg*): on the matter of restraining (*+pādīrānēnīdan*) oneself (it is said) in the doctrine (*čāštag*) of Sōšāns: (at the distance of a) *frārāst*,[40] he

25 Both mss. (TD 7r.6; HJ 7v.1): ⟨'py⟩.
26 Both mss. (TD 7r.6; HJ 7v.1): ⟨tn' Y dwcyh⟩.
27 TD 7r.7: ⟨tn' dwc'y⟩; HJ 7v.3: ⟨tn' Y dwcy⟩.
28 Both mss. (TD 7r.9; HJ 7v.5): ⟨'L⟩. The whole following section is extremely corrupt and the readings are only tentative.
29 Both mss. (TD 7r.9; HJ 7v.5): ⟨hcpr⟩.
30 Both mss. (TD 7r.10; HJ 7v.6): ⟨'L⟩.
31 Both mss. (TD 7r.10; HJ 7v.6): ⟨'L⟩.
32 Both mss. (TD 7r.10; HJ 7v.6): ⟨hcy⟩.
33 On *andar ēstādan* 'to take responsibility (for something); to take on (an issue)' see Bartholomae 1918–1923; here: part II, 1918, pp. 45–47.
34 TD 7r.10f.: ⟨SLYTWNt' mynšn⟩, HJ 7v.7: ⟨SLYTWN' mynšnyk⟩.
35 Both mss. (TD 7r.11; HJ 7v.8): ⟨p't'l'nynytn'⟩
36 TD 7r.12: ⟨pl'l'st'⟩; HJ 7v.9: ⟨pl'y l'st'⟩.
37 Both mss. (TD 7r.12: HJ 7v.10): ⟨'L Y⟩.
38 Both mss. (TD 7r.12: HJ 7v.11): ⟨'yc⟩.
39 Both mss. (TD 7r.12: HJ 7v.11): ⟨'y⟩.
40 Humbach/Elfenbein 1990, pp. 50–52, read *frāy rāst* 'more correct'; Kotwal/Kreyenbroek 1992, pp. 44–45, have the measure of length *frārāst*, the equivalent of 'cubit' or 24 *angust*, one foot, six inches, according to MacKenzie 1971, p. 143. Both readings are possible (see fn. 36 above), but the latter seems to fit in better into the context.

is considered as her thief; according to the (doctrine) of Kay-ādur-bōzēd this (sin) also (accrues) to the stock (*bun*), that is, unless he (practises) refrainment (*pādīrānēnīdan*), it goes to (his) account."

6.7 §3 (= 6.30) *čagar gāyēd duzīh čagar xwēš abārīg*[41] *dūdag*[42] *xwēš. pāyag (ī) tan-duzīh*[43] *andar ōh gād-duzīh šawēd ud bē dūrīh mard rāyēnēd.*[44]

'(If) he copulates with a *čagar*-wife, (then the compensation for) theft is the *čagar*-wife's own; (if it is) another (type of wife), it (= the compensation for theft) is the family's own (*dūdag xwēš*). The degree (*pāyag*) of "body-theft" (*tan-duzīh*) depends on the (degree of) "theft of sexual intercourse" (*gād-duzīh*) and the man (= guardian?) takes legal action (*mard rāyēnēd*), except (when he is) far away (*bē dūrīh*).'[45]

6.7 §4–6 (= 6.31–37) *paristār ī abāg ēd kū pad ⁺arzān*[46] *ī duz(īh) bawēd pas ka pad gādan gādan bawēd duzīh*[47] *pad šīr ī buz*[48] *duzīh*[49] *bawēd. Sōšāns guft andar 9 sālag ka (āb) pad tan mad ēstēd ā-š pad zan ī ōy*[50] *u-š xwēdōdah*[51] *ī ōy*[52] *u-š ham-iz dādestānīh*[53] *(ī) ōy*[54] *abāyēd*[55] *u-š gādan kunišn*[56]*. ka pad tan āb*[57] *nē mad ēstēd ā-š nē gāyēd nē kunišn čē-š rēš kunišn. daštān-māh tā 15 sālag pādixšāy ka nē wizarēd.* paṇcadasaiiā[58] sarəide[59] *daštān hamē ⁺dagr*[60] *ud hamē rēman*[61].

41 Both mss. (TD 7r.15; HJ 7v.13) insert ⟨Y⟩ after *abārīg*.
42 Both mss. (TD 7r.15; HJ 7v.13) insert ⟨Y⟩ after *dūdag*.
43 TD 7r.15: ⟨tn' Y dwcyh⟩; HJ 7v.14: ⟨tn' Y dwc⟩.
44 TD 7r.16: ⟨l'yn''yt⟩; HJ 7v.15: ⟨L' YHWWNyt⟩. The original form (changed to *nē bawēd* in HJ) is transmitted almost correctly in TD; on *rāyēnīdan* (and *kār rāyēnīdan)* 'to take legal action' see glossary.
45 Both editions have completely different readings and translations of this passage and the next one.
46 Both mss. (TD 7v.1; HJ 8r.1): ⟨'lcyn'⟩.
47 TD 7v.2: ⟨dwc⟩; HJ 8r.3: ⟨dwcy⟩.
48 In both mss. (TD 7v.2; HJ 8r.3) *šīr ī buz* is written together: ⟨šyly'Z⟩. On ⟨'Z⟩, the ideogram for *buz* 'goat' see NYBERG 1988, Chapter VII, 11 (pp. 5, 43, 70).
49 Both mss. (TD 7v.2; HJ 8r.4): ⟨dwcy⟩.
50 Both mss. (TD 7v.4; HJ 8r.6): ⟨'L⟩.
51 TD 7v.4: ⟨hwytwdwdy'⟩; HJ 8r.6: ⟨hwytwdwkdy'⟩.
52 Both mss. (TD 7v.5; HJ 8r.6): ⟨'L⟩.
53 Both mss. (TD 7v.5; HJ 8r.7): ⟨hmc DYNN'yh⟩. (Compare HUMBACH/ELFENBEIN 1990, p. 52; KOTWAL/KREYENBROEK 1992, p. 44, read *ham-ciyōn *ī-š.*)
54 Both mss. (TD 7v.5; HJ 8r.7): ⟨'L Y⟩.
55 TD 7v.5: ⟨'p'yt'⟩; HJ 8r.7: ⟨'p't' 'YT'⟩.
56 TD 7v.5f.: ⟨SLYTWNytn' 'B̲YDWNšn⟩; HJ 8r.8: ⟨SLYTWNyt 'L 'B̲YDWNšn'⟩.
57 TD 7v.6: ⟨'p⟩; HJ 8r.9: ⟨Y⟩.
58 TD 7v.9: *paṇdaiiasaiia*; HJ 8r.13: *paṇcadaiiasiia.*
59 TD 7v.9: *sarəidən*; HJ 8r.13: *sarəidə.*
60 TD 7v.10: ⟨d'l⟩; HJ 8r.14: ⟨g'l⟩.
61 TD 7v.10: om.; HJ 8r.14: ⟨lymn'⟩.

"As to (sexual intercourse with) the maidservant, who (is) with (them), this (applies): (the offence) is worth less than (the penalty for) theft; then, if it (= the penalty) is for repeated sexual intercourse, the theft is considered (worth as much) as the theft of goat-milk (*šīr ī buz duzīh*). Sōšāns said: 'With nine years, when (water) has come to her body, then, as his wife and in a next-of-kin marriage (*xwēdōdah*) with him, for which her consent is also necessary, he may have intercourse with her. If water[62] has not yet come to her body, then he shall not copulate with her. He must not do it, as it would cause her physical injury (*rēš*). Menstruation (sets in) until (she is) 15 years; (until then) it is permitted for her not to perform (the prescribed rites). *In her fifteenth year* (she is subject to) menstruation, always long(-lasting) and always defiling.'"

62 The word *āb* 'water' obviously denotes the liquid form of menstruation: *ka pad tan āb nō mad ēstēd* 'if the menses have not yet begun'; compare MP *šōyēnīg* 'menstruating' < Ir. **xšaud*- 'to become liquid'; Av. *xšaoδah*- 'gush, flush of water' (Cheung 2007, p. 455); *apud* Buyaner 2016, p. 347, who cites Dk.8.31.7: *abar xōn ī pad zan ī šōyēnīg* 'On the blood which (is) in a menstruating woman'.

Appendix IX

Riwāyat ī Ādurfarrbay ud Farrbay-Srōš: On the Oath (*Pursišn* 66, 72, 74)

The following passages diverge from Anklesaria's 1969 edition in many respects, particularly with regard to the legal terminology in this text. The important excerpt from RivAF 74 is not based on his edition, but on a collation of mss. TD2 and G (the latter following Anklesaria's notes).

RivAF, *Pursišn* 66 (Anklesaria 1969, vol. I, p. 35, 120; II, p. 77)

pursišn. (1) *mard-ē(w) kē abām be mard- ē(w) dahēd mard az gētīy be šawēd u-š zan ud frazand pad ham dūdag ziyānag az mērag abām stad abāz nē tōzēd. ka az gētīy be šawēd ud pus ud duxt pad dūdag hēnd ud mērag az pus abām abāz xwāhēd ud pus nagīrā(y) bawēd ud gōwēd kū-š man āgāhīh nēst mērag ī ham abāmdār gōwēd kū sōgand xwār kū pid (ī) tō ēn abām az man be nē stad ud man abārīg xwāstagdārān ī pid ī man ēn xwāstag* ⟨NKSY'⟩ *ō tō nē tōzišn ud nē dahišn u-šān tōxtan ud dādan nē ēwēn. mērag kē abām stad gōwēd kū man*[1] *war ēdōn warzēm kū man ud abārīg xwāstagdārān ī pid ī man az ēn čīš āgāhīh nēst pad dādestān čiyōn bawēd.*

pāsox. (2) *čiyōn man dānom ēg-iš war ō warzēd kū pid ud mād ī man ēn abām az tō mērag nē stad ud amā kē xwāstagdār ī pidar ud mādar hēm ēn abām ō tō tōxtan nē abāyēd.*

Question. A man who gives a loan to (another) man (and) the (latter) man leaves the material existence and (there are) a wife and children in the same family (and) the woman does not pay back the loan taken from the man (= the moneylender): if she leaves the material existence and (there are) a son and daughter in the same family (and) the man (= the moneylender) requests the money back from the son and the son denies (the loan) and says: 'I have no knowledge of it' (*kū-š man āgāhīh nēst*) (and) the same creditor (*mērag ī ham abāmdār*) says: 'take an oath (*sōgand xwār*) that your father did not take this

1 According to G: ⟨L⟩ *man*; Anklesaria 1969, vol. I, p. 35, reads ⟨LK⟩ *tō*, which makes absolutely no sense in this context. His transliteration (vol. I, p. 120) and translation (vol. II, p. 77) are both misleading.

loan from me' and: 'I and the other heirs of my father do not owe this money to you and do not have to give it and for them to pay it and transmit it (is) not legal (*nē ēwēn*)' (and if) the man who (allegedly) took the loan (*mērag kē abām stad*) says: 'I will take the oath as follows: "I and the other heirs of my father have no knowledge of this matter" (*az ēn čīš āgāhīh nēst*)', (then) what is the judgement in this case?

Answer. As far as I know, he (= the son) should take the oath: 'My father and mother did not take this loan from you, O man, and we, who are the heirs of our father and mother, do not have to pay this loan (back) to you.'

RivAF, *Pursišn* 72 (Anklesaria 1969, vol. I, p. 39–40; II, p. 81). In the following text only the first sentence in the 'answer' (2) refers to the oath; the following section (3) consists of a list of the 'degrees of sins' (*pāyag ī winābh*) and is left out here. On these see Chapter V, pp. 468–486.

pursišn. (1) *ka pēšēmāl pad tōzišnōmandīh gugāy-+ē(w)*[2] *abag ayāb dō ud pasēmāl nagīrā(y) war kē warzišn. ud ka az kustag-+ē(w) gugāy-+ē(w) az kustag-+ē(w) dārišn war kē warzišn.*

pāsox. (2) *čiyōn man dānom war pāyēnišn pad har dō dādestān pēšēmāl wehdādestāntar ud ham ān kē nagīrā(y) ud ham ān kē dārišn abāg ham xwad pad war warzišn ud ham pad war abāz ō pasēmāl dāštan.*

Question. (1) If the plaintiff (*pēšēmāl*) in the matter of a financial obligation (*pad tōzišnōmandīh*) has one or two witnesses with (him) and the defendant (*pasēmāl*) denies (the obligation) (*nagīrāy*), who has to take the oath? And if one party (lit.: 'side') (has) a witness (*gugāy*), the other party (lit.: 'side') (has) the property (*dārišn*), who has to take the oath?

Answer. (2) As far as I know, the plaintiff (*pēšēmāl*) 'fulfils justice better' (*wehdādestāntar*) in both (cases): both (in the case) of the one (= the defendant), who denies (the obligation) (*nagīrāy*) as well as of the one, who (has) the property with him (*dārišn abāg*). Both he himself (= the plaintiff) should take the oath (*ham xwad pad war warzišn*) and it is also to be considered to revert the oath to the defendant (*ham pad war abāz ō pasēmāl dāštan*).

Excerpt from RivAF, *Pursišn* 74[3] (Anklesaria 1969, vol. I, pp. 41–44, 123–124; vol. II, pp. 82–85; the excerpt from the long 'answer' to this *Pursišn* is in. Anklesaria 1969, vol. I, pp. 43, line 3, to p. 44, line 1; TD2, p. 364.3–15)

2 Both mss.: ⟨HN'⟩ *ēd* for -*ē(w)* throughout the whole text in the mss. according to Anklesaria.

3 The following transcription is based on a collation of mss. TD2 (*Pahlavi Codices and Iranian Researches* 1978, vol. 54, pp. 362.10–13 and 364.3–365.1) and G (according to Anklesaria 1969, vol. I, pp. 41–44).

pursišn. (1) *kē sōgand ēd be xwarēd pad ēn ēwēnag ēwāz kū har kār ud kirbag ī az ēn rōz frāz kunēm*[4] *ēg-am*[5] *ō*[6] *wāhmān kas dād*[7] *ud ēn kū-š dād bawēd ayāb nē dādestān ī abar*[8] *ēn dar čiyōn.*

pāsox. (2) *(………) ēdōn bawēd čiyōn kē pad jud az mizd ud nīrmad (ī) gētīy ruwān ī kasān rāy yašt-⁺ē(w)*[9] *kunēd ēg-iš andar ⁺ušt*[10] *ōšmurišnīh*[11] *ī pad war ī sōgand ī*[12] *passāxt ī pad ēn ēwēnag kam āwarēd ēg-iš ī rašn saxwan ān gōwišn abestāg nimūd ēstēd ayāb ān ī ō hangāštan*[13] *šāyēd čiyōn ān ī gōwēd kū* ***iδa asti auuaṯ arəϑəm***[14] *ēdōn ēn dādestān pad pasēmālīh*[15] ***iδa vā mē aŋhən asti vaiδīm*** *ayāb ēdōn man*[16] *pad ān ast āgāhīh pad gugāyīh* ***nōiṯ vā åŋhe vaiδa*** *ayāb nē man ān pad āgāhīh ast ka-š pad a-srāyišnīh abar hamēmāl hom ēg-iš ān saxwan ī-š nē dastwarīhā bawēd guftan pad kārīgīh ō mar kard*[17] *ud wizīr abar kard nērang-ē(w) nē dānom.*

Question. (1) (If) someone takes an oath speaking words in this manner: 'I have donated every act (*kār*) and good deed (*kirbag*) that I perform from this day on to such-and-such a person': does the donation take effect or not? What is the decision (*dādestān*) regarding this case?

Answer. (2) (………) It is like the one who, without worldly reward and profit, performs worship for the soul of others, then during the recitation of the *uštauuaiti* (*Gāthā*) during the oath of sulphur (*pad war ī sōgand*) of the ordeal (*passāxt*) in this manner misses (a word/line), then he should speak the words of Rašn, (which) the Avesta has shown, or he should take (them) into consideration, like the one who declares: (Av.) 'Thus is this (judicial) case' (*iδa asti auuaṯ arəϑəm*),[18] (MP) 'Thus (is) this (judicial) case' (*ēdōn ēn dādestān*)*:* (the statement of the) defence (*pad pasēmālīh*); (Av.) 'Or thus is my knowledge thereof' (*iδa vā*

4 TD2: ⟨'ḆYDWNym⟩; G: torn.
5 TD2: ⟨'DYN'm⟩; G: torn.
6 Both mss: ⟨KN⟩ (instead of 'L throughout the *Pursišn).*
7 TD2: ⟨YHBWNtn'⟩; G: ⟨YHBWNt⟩.
8 TD2: ⟨MDM⟩; G: torn.
9 Both mss.: ⟨HN'⟩ *ēd* for *-ē(w)* throughout the mss., see fn. 2 above.
10 TD2: ⟨'wz't'⟩ and super lin.: ⟨zšt⟩; G: ⟨'wzšt⟩. (Corr.: ⁺*ušt* 'the *uštauuaiti Gāthā*'; Nērangestān 13.11; Kotwal/Kreyenbroek 1995, pp. 88–89 (besides *uštwad*, Nēr. 28.5, Kotwal/Kreyenbroek 2003, pp. 66–67; Nēr. 84.5,8; Kotwal/Kreyenbroek 2009, pp. 78–79).
11 TD2: ⟨'wšmlšnyh⟩; G: ⟨'wšmwlšnyh⟩.
12 TD2: ⟨Y⟩; G: ⟨W⟩.
13 TD2: ⟨hng'štn'⟩; G: torn.
14 TD2: *warəϑəm*; G: *arəϑəm.*
15 Both mss.: ⟨ps''m'lyh⟩.
16 TD2: ⟨wl⟩; G: ⟨L⟩.
17 TD2: ⟨'ḆYDW…tn⟩; G: ⟨'ḆYDWNt' W⟩.
18 The Avestan passages have been discussed extensively by Klingenschmitt 1971, pp. 127–129. All mss. have *iδa* 'here' (and in the following Avestan passage) instead of *iϑa* 'thus', corresponding to *ēdōn* 'thus' in the Pahlavi translation, hence ⁺*iϑa asti auuaṯ arəϑəm (ibid.* pp. 127–128).

mē aŋhən asti vaiδīm);[19] (MP) 'Or thus is my knowledge thereof' (*ayāb ēdōn man pad ān ast āgāhīh*): (the statement of) the witness (*pad gugāyīh*); (Av.) 'Or I know not thereof' (*nōit̰ vā ā̊ŋhe vaiδa*);[20] (MP) 'Or that is not in my knowledge' (*ayāb nē man ān pad āgāhīh ast*): (this) is when without reciting (he says): 'I am an opponent against (him)' (*abar hamēmāl hom*), then that statement, which he is not entitled to declare, is effectively taken into account and the judgement regarding this act (corresponds to) the short formula (*nērang*)[21]: 'I do not know' (*nē dānom*).

19 With *aŋhən ...vaiδīm* instead of +*aŋ́he* (gen sg. of the pronoun *a-*)... +*vaēδīm* 'knowledge thereof', nom. sg. of *vaēδiia-* 'knowledge', hence: +*iϑa vā mē* +*aŋ́he asti* +*vaēδīm* (Klingenschmitt 1971, p. 128).

20 With *vaiδa* instead of +*vaēδa* 'I know' (1st person sg. √*vid* 'to know'; Kellens 1995, p. 54) and *ā̊ŋhe* instead of +*aŋ́he*, hence: *nōit̰ va* +*aŋ́he* +*vaēδa* (Klingenschmitt 1971, pp. 128–129).

21 On *nērang* 'short formula' see Kotwal/Kreyenbroek 2003, pp. 184–185 (N. 43.2), 309.

Appendix X

Tabarestān 17, 18 and 24: Loan Contracts

The original documents with an edition and extensive philological and contextual commentary have been published in the series *Res Orientales* XXVI (Tab. 17 and 18: Weber 2017a; Macuch 2017c) and XXVII (Tab. 24: Weber 2019b; Macuch 2019b). The following transcription includes revised readings since our publications of the texts in 2017 and 2019 (*e.g.* the reading of the village name as *Asp-gurd instead of *Haspīn-raz).

Tabarestān 17[1]

(1) *māh Hordād abar sāl 77 rōz Xwar mardān ī*	(1) Month *Hordād* in the year 77, day *Xwar*: the men called
(2) *Xwāst-Dēlān nām Hormizd pus ī az ān *Asp-gurd deh*	(2) *Xwast-Dēlān*, son of *Hormizd* from the village of *Asp-gurd,
(3) *ī pad xānag ī Dēl-Dēlān pad darspās ī yazdān-bānag*	(3) in the house of *Dēl-Dēlān* in the service of the protector of the gods,
(4) *Xorāsān-spāhbed ī pad *Halīg pēš kē xwēškārīhā*	(4) the *spāhbed* of the East, who (is) in **Halīg*, before whom he spoke (line 5) regarding his area of responsibility (*xwēškārīhā*)
(5) *guft kū man xwāstag* (NKSY') *arz s(atēr) 4 ī sazēd*	(5) thus: "I have an obligation regarding money, a sum worth 4 staters,
(6) *ī pēš mehtarān az mardān ī Farrox-Xusrō*	(6) which I take (*stānēm*, line 8) before the Elders (*mehtarān*) from the men called *Farrox-Xusrō*,
(7) *nām ī andar ān *Asp-gurd deh mānēd ān ham*	(7) who live in the village of *Asp-gurd, from the said (persons).
(8) *stānēm man ān xwāstag* (NKSY') *rōz Ardwahišt ī māh*	(8) I will give back (*abāz … dahēm*, line 10–11) that money on day *Ardwahišt* of the month
(9) *Tīr ī ham sāl 77 pad ān marag ī*	(9) *Tīr* of the same year 77 to that sum
(10) *azabar nibišt sazēd ī pēš mehtarān abāz ō*	(10) written above before the Elders to

1 Weber 2017a, pp. 155–157; Macuch 2017c, pp. 189–191.

(11) *Farrox-Xusrō dahēm agar ǰuttar kunēm uzīd*	(11) *Farrox-Xusrō*. If I act otherwise, after
(12) *ān māh ud rōz ī azabar nibišt harw 1 māh pad*	(12) the month and day written above have passed (line 11),
(13) *harw xwāstag* (NKSY') *s(tatēr) 2 drahm 2 abzōn drahm 1 ān-iz ī bun āb*	(13) I will give back (line 14) for the whole sum of money, 2 staters, 2 drachms (and) one additional drachm for the water of the *bun* (= substance)
(14) *abāz ō Farrox-Xusrō dahēm agar ǰuttar kunēm*	(14) to *Farrox-Xusrō*. If I act otherwise,
(15) *tāwān-iz arz s(tatēr) 4 ō Farrox-Xusrō dādan*	(15) I have made a contract (*paymān kard*, line 16) to pay a compensation (*tāwān*) of 4 staters to *Farrox-Xusrō*."
(16) *paymān kard ēn paymān-nāmag pad āšnāg*	(16) This document of contract (*paymān-nāmag*) was sealed (*āwišt*, line 18) according to the identification (*pad āšnāg*)
(17) *ī Dērā ī ganǰwar ī az ān *Asp-gurd deh*	(17) of *Dērā*, the treasurer, from the village of **Asp-gurd*
(18) *pad muhr ī ham Xwāst-Dēlān āwišt*	(18) with the seal of the same *Xwāst-Dēlān*.
(19) *ēwarīh rāy* (////////// *muhr abar nihād*)	(19) To make it legally binding (//// / placed his seal upon it).

Tabarestān 18[2]

(1) *māh Ādur ahar sāl 101 ud rōz Aštād Dēlgušnasp ī*	(1) Month *Ādur* in the year 101 and day *Aštād*: *Dēlgušnasp*
(2) *spargar Dērā pus az ān *Asp-gurd deh ī*	(2) the shield-maker, son of *Dērā* from the village of *Asp-gurd, who
(3) *pad xānag ī Dēl-Dēlān pad dar-spās ī yazdān-bānag*	(3) (is) in the house of *Dēl-Dēlān* in the service of the residence of the god-protecting
(4) *Parišwārgar šāh ī pad *Halīg pēš kē xwēškār[īhā]*	(4) King of *Parišwārgar* in **Halīg*, before whom he spoke (*guft*, line 5) regarding his area of responsibility (*xwēškār[īhā]*)
(5) *guft kū man xwāstag* (NKSY') *arz sazēd s(atēr) 6 [drahm 1]*	(5) thus: "It is my obligation to give (*dādan*, line 7) (back) money, a sum worth 6 staters [and one drachm]

2 Weber 2017a, pp. 150–154; Macuch 2017c, pp. 183–188.

(6) *ō Farroxgušnasp ī dibīr ī az *Asp-gurd deh abām*	(6) to *Farroxgušnasp*, the scribe from the village of *Asp-gurd, for a loan (*abām*).
(7) *dādan ān xwāstag* (NKSY') *ǰādag pad bun ī az ān *Asp-gurd deh*	(7) That money (is) a share in the *bun* (= substance) from the village *Asp-gurd.
(8) *az ān man xwēš zamīg ī kišwzār ēw-kardag taxlīh*	(8) From the cultivated land (*zamīg ī kišwzār*) of my own in one piece (*ēw-kardag*) called (line 9) *Taxlīh* a measure (*sāmān*, line 12) of the
(9) *xwānēnd k(abīz) 9 āhang kē az ēw zayt ī darrag az ēw*	(9) crop yields (consisting) of 9 *kabīz*, which (are) from one olive-tree of the 'canyon', from one
(10) *zayt ī zamīg ī xwāstagdārān ī mardān ī a-ǰomāyīg ī andar*	(10) olive-tree on the land of the heirs of men, who are not together (= shareholders),
(11) *būd az ēw zayt ī zamīg ī ham Farroxgušnasp az ēw zayt ī*	(11) from one olive-tree on the land of the same *Farroxgušnasp*, from one olive-tree on
(12) *zamīg ī mardān ī Windāspagān nām sāmān pas zamīg ēw-kardag*	(12) the land of the men called *Windāspagān*. Then (from) the land in one piece (*ēw-kardag*)
(13) *Dašt-sag-kam-ī-ul xwānēnd k(abīz) 8 āhang kē az ēw zayt ī*	(13) called *Dašt-sag-kam-ī-ul* a measure (*sāmān*, line 16) of the crop yields (consisting) of 8 *kabīz*, which (are) from one olive-tree on
(14) *zamīg ī mardān ī xwāstagdārān ī mardan ī Dērā nām būd*	(14) the land of the men, who are heirs of the men called *Dērā*,
(15) *az ēw zayt ī zamīg ī Dēlxwašīh nām būd any mard*	(15) from one olive-tree on the land of (those) called *Dēlxwašīh* (and) another man,
(15[bis])*az ēw zayt ī zamīg ī mardān ī Āzādmard nām any mard*	(15[bis]) from one olive-tree on the land of the men called *Āzādmard* (and) another man,
(16) *sāmān az ēw zayt ī zamīg ī mardān ī Dadōy nām būd sāmān pas*	(16) a measure (*sāmān*) from one olive-tree on the land of the men called *Dadōy*. Then
(17) *zamīg ēw-kardag ēwēn pid xwānēnd k(abīz) 3 āhang kē az ēw zayt ī*	(17) (from) the land in one piece (*ēw-kardag*) called lawfully *Pid* a measure (*sāmān*, line 20) of the crop yields (consisting) of 3 *kabīz*, which (are) from one olive-tree on

(18) *zamīg ī mardān ī Windāspagān nām az ēw zayt ī zamīg ī mardān ī Yazdāngird*	(18) the land of the men called *Windāspagān*; from one olive-tree on the land of the men called *Yazdāngird*
(19) *nām būd az ēw zayt ī zamīg ī mardān ī Gōr (nām az) ēw zayt ī zamīg*	(19) from one olive-tree on the land of the men called *Gōr*, (from) one olive-tree on the land
(20) *ī mardān ī Xwaršēd nām sāmān tā ān xwāstag* (NKSY') *s(atēr) 6 drahm 1 abāz dādan*	(20) of the men called *Xwaršēd*. Until that sum of 6 staters, one drachm, is given back,
(21) *pad Farroxgušnasp grawagān ud grawagānīh pad Farroxgušnasp drust[īh] harw kē*	(21) the usufruct is mortgaged (*grawagān*) to *Farroxgušnasp*. And the *antichresis* (*grawagānīh*) (is kept) intact (*drustīh*) by *Farroxgušnasp*. Anyone
(22) *pad-iš pahikārēd az Farroxgušnasp abēzār ud Farroxgušnasp pad ān xīr*	(22) who disputes this, (is) without expedient (*abēzār*) against *Farroxgušnasp*. And (if) *Farroxgušnasp* by that property
(23) *zyān sazēd jud (az) ān-iz xwāstag* (NKSY') *hamē ka Farroxgušnasp xwāhēd*	(23) suffers a loss, I will give back that money to *Farroxgušnasp* (line 24) any time when *Farroxgušnasp* requests it.
(24) *abāz ō Farroxgušnasp dahēm agar čiš-iz juttar kunēm ān xwāstag* (NKSY')	(24) If I act otherwise, that money
(25) *ēk rāy dō ē bawēd s(atēr) 12 drahm 2 ō Farroxgušnasp dahēm*	(25) shall be doubled. I will give 12 staters, 2 drachms, to *Farroxgušnasp*."
(26) ⟨*ēn*⟩ *paymān-nāmag pad āšnag guft ī *Wangird ī dibīr ī Dērā pus*	(26) ⟨This⟩ document of contract (*paymān-nāmag*) was sealed (line 27) according to the identification (*pad āšnāg guft*) of **Wangird*, the scribe, son of *Dērā*
(27) *ī az ēn *Asp-gurd deh ī pad xānag ī Dēl-Dēlān pad muhr ī ham Dēlgušnasp āwišt*	(27) from this village of *Asp-gurd, who (is) from the house of *Dēl-Dēlān*, with the seal of the same *Dēlgušnasp*.
(28) *ēwarīh rāy Farroxzād muhr abar nihād abarag tāg ī az ēw zayt ī*	(28) To make it legally binding (*ēwarīh rāy*) *Farroxzād* placed his seal upon it. Above the rent (*tāg*) from one olive-tree
(29) *zamīg ī mardān ī (Āzād)mard nām any mard*	(29) on the land of the men called *(Āzād)mard* (and) another man (is added).

Tabarestān 24[3]

(1) *māh Day abar sāl 103 ī pas az ōy bay Yazdegird šāhān šāh ī nab ī ōy bay Husraw ī Ohrmazdān ud rōz Rašn ka Wanandpanāh kē tasūg ī*

(1) Month *Day* (10th month) in the year 103 after his late majesty *Yazdegird*, King of Kings, grandson of his late majesty *Husraw*, son of *Ohrmazd*, and day *Rašn* (18th day), when *Wanandpanāh*, who (in) the district of

(2) *Dēl ī Dēlān ī abar Taburestān dādestān čiyōnīh tasūg ī *Sūrīgān ī abar Taburestān dādestān pad dehīhā (!) pad-iš framān sāxtan pad dehīhā pūdag ham tasūg ī*

(2) *Dēl ī Dēlān* presided over judgement in *Taburestān*, likewise over judgement in the 'Syrian quarter' (**Sūrīgān*) of *Taburestān* in the villages, (and) was in charge of preparing orders relating to foul (crops) in the villages of the same district of

(3) *Dēl ī Dēlān būd mardān ī Bōxt nām ō Wanandpanāh guft kū mardān ī Frawardīn nām būd mardān ī Ātaxšbōyag nām būd kardērīh pus wispān ham tasūg ī Dēl ī Dēlān az*

(3) *Dēl ī Dēlān*. The men called *Bōxt* spoke to *Wanandpanāh* thus: "The men called *Frawardīn*, the men called *Ātaxšbōyag*, all (of them of) authoritative progeny of the same district of *Dēl ī Dēlān* from

(4) *⟨ān⟩ *Asp-gurd deh būd hēnd ud mardān ī Yazdfarrox nām Dēlānfarrox pus mardān ī Windād-Yazd nām mardān ī Windād-Ohrmazd nām Zādānfarrox pus mardān ī Farrox-Xusrōyān nām Farrox-Xusrō*

(4) the village of *Asp-gurd were present. And the men called *Yazdfarrox*, son(s) of *Dēlānfarrox*, the men called *Windād-Yazd*, the men called *Windād-Ohrmazd*, son(s) of *Zādānfarrox*, the men called *Farrox-Xusrōyān*, son(s) (line 5) of *Farrox-Xusrō*,

(5) *pus az ān *Asp-gurd deh Farrox-Xusrōyān ōy Frawardīn duxt Rašnweh ud Windād-Yazd ud Windād-Ohrmazd ud Yazdfarrox ōy Ātaxšbōyag pusarāwandān ud xwāstagdārān ud pad bun ī ān *Asp-gurd*

(5) from the village of *Asp-gurd. The sons of *Farrox-Xusrō*, the daughter of the late *Frawardīn*, (named) *Rašnweh*, and *Windād-Yazd* and *Windād-Ohrmazd* and *Yazdfarrox*, the descendants and heirs of the late *Ātaxšbōyag*. [A] And in the substance (*bun*) of the village (line 6) of *Asp-gurd

(6) *deh kišwzār zamīg ī kōfag xār-wanīgān xwānēnd g(rīw) 1 āhang kē az ēw zayt ī zamīg ī xwāstagdārān ī mardān ī Yazdegird nām būd ud*

(6) (from) the cultivated land (*kišwzār zamīg*) on a mountain saddle (*kōfag*) called *Xār-wanīgān* ('Thorn Groves'): a measure (*sāmān*, line 7) of 1 *grīw* of

3 Weber 2019b, pp. 102–110 Macuch 2019b, pp. 132–146.

any mard ud az ēw zayt ī zamīg ī xwāstagdārān ī

the crop yields (*āhang*) from one olive tree on the land of the heirs of the men called *Yazdegird* and another man; and from one olive tree on the land of the heirs (*xwāstagdārān*) of

(7) *mardān ī Zādānfarrox nām būd ud az ēw zayt ī zamīg ī [[xwāstag paymāyagān]] ī Māhōy nām būd ud az ēw zayt ī zamīg ī xwāstagdārān ī mardān ī Māhanōš* (?) *nām būd sāmān ud zamīg ī [[kōfag]] ǰadārīh xwānēnd*

(7) the men called *Zādānfarrox*; and from one olive tree on the land of [[the measurers of property?]] called *Māhōy*; and from one olive tree on the land of the heirs of the men called *Māhanōš* (?). [B] And (from) the land on the [[mountain saddle]] called *Jadārīh* ('Maintenance'):

(8) *g(rīw) 2 āhang kē az ēw zayt ī zand ud az ēw zayt ī zamīg ī xwāstagdārān ī Dērā nām būd ud az ēw zayt ī zamīg ī xwāstagdārān ī mardan ī Farroxzād nām būd*

(8) a measure (*sāmān*, line 9) of 2 *grīw* of the crop yields which (are) from one olive tree of the community; and one olive tree on the land of the heirs of the men called *Dērā* and from one olive tree on the land of the heirs of the men called *Farroxzād*;

(9) *ud az ēw zayt ī zamīg ī xwāstagdārān ī ōy Māhōš ud any mard sāmān ud zamīg ī kōfag wanīgarīh xwand g(rīw) 1 āhang kē az ēw zayt ī zamīg ī mardān ī Farroxān nām ud az ēw zayt ī*

(9) and from one olive tree on the land of the heirs of the late *Māhōš* and another man. [C] And (from) the land on the mountain saddle called *Wanīgarīh* ('Waste'): a measure (*sāmān*, line 10) of 1 *grīw* of the crop yields which (are) from one olive tree on the land of the men called *Farroxān*; and from one olive tree on

(10) *zamīg ī mardān ī Farroxgušnasp nām ud az ēw zayt ī zamīg ī xwāstagdārān ī ōy Dērā ud az ēw zayt ī zamīg ī ham Farrox-Xusrōyān sāmān zamīg ī*

(10) the land of the men called *Farroxgušnasp*; and from one olive tree on the land of the heirs of the late *Dērā*; and from one olive tree on the land of the same *Farrox-Xusrōyān*. [D] (From) the land

(11) *ī kōfag g(rīw) 1 k(abīz) 8 āhang kē az ēw zayt ī zamīg ud xānag ī xwāstagdārān ī mardān ī Yazdōy nām būd ud any mard ud az ēw zayt ī zamīg ud xānag ī xwāstagdārān ī mardān ī ōy Dērā*

(11) on the mountain saddle a measure (*sāman*, line 12) of 1 *grīw*, 8 *kabīz* of crop yields which (are) from one olive tree from land and house of the heirs of the man called *Yazdōy* and another man; and from one olive tree from land and house of the heirs of the men of the late *Dērā*

(12) *ud any mard ud az dō zayt ī čand ud rawišn ī zamānag drahm ī az ān *Asp-gurd deh sāmān ud xānag ud spinǰānagīh ud čīš enyā abar ⟨nimāyēd ud⟩ wizandag kard rāy zyān ēwēn sĕ-ǰādag az 6*

(12) and another man; and from two olive trees as much (in yields) according to the current value of drachms from the village of *Asp-gurd. And (the costs of) house and hospitality and other matters you shall take into account and because of the damage due to the earthquake (*wizandag*) according to the norm three shares (*sĕ-ǰādag*) from 6

(13) *bārag-bār ud ham tasūg ī Dēl ī Dēlān pad bun ī frōd deh razist zamīg ī kōfag g(rīw) 1 k(abīz) 5 āhang kē az ēw zayt ī razist zamīg ī xwāstagdārān ī mardān ī Wahištān nām*

(13) mount loads (*bārag-bār*). [E] And (in) the same district of *Dēl ī Dēlān* in the substance (*bun*) of the 'Lower Village' (*Frōd Deh*), (on) forest land on the mountain saddle a measure *(sāmān*, line 14) of 1 *grīw*, 5 *kabīz* of the crop yields, which (are) from one olive tree on the forest land of the heirs of the men called *Wahištān*;

(14) *būd ud az ēw zayt ī zamīg ī xwāstagdārān ī mardān ī ōy Ātaxšbōyag ud az ēw zayt ī zamīg ī xwāstagdārān ī az ān frōd deh ud az ēw zayt ī pēš sāmān ud raz ud sarw ud čīš enyā*

(14) and from one olive tree on the land of the heirs of the men of the late *Ātaxšbōyag*; and from one olive tree on the land of the heirs from the 'Lower Village'; and from one olive tree which (is) before (the latter one). And vines and cypresses and other things

(15) *abar nimāyēd ud ēd kard rāy zyān ēwēn sĕ-ǰādag az sĕ-bār dō-bār ud kišwānzār zamīg ī kōfag ī ān-iz pad bun ī ān *Asp-gurd deh ud mayg-rist xwānēnd g(rīw) 3 āhang kē az zayt ī*

(15) you shall take into account and because of the damage (by the earthquake) according to the norm of three shares (*sĕ-ǰādag*): from three loads two loads. [F] And (from) the cultivated land on the mountain saddle which (is) also in the substance (*bun*) of the village of *Asp-gurd and is called *Mayg-rist* ('Dead as a Locust') a measure *(sāmān*, line 16) of 3 *grīw* of crop yields, which are from a damaged (line 16) olive tree;

(16) *rēš ud az ⟨ēw⟩ zayt ī zamīg ī mardān ī Wahmandād nām xwāstagdārān ī mardān ī Wahmanpanāh nām būd ud az dō zayt ī zamīg ī Anagrān sāmān ud zamīg ī kōfag asp-tāzān xwānēnd g(rīw) 4 āhang kē az ēw*

(16) and from one olive tree on the land of men called *Wahmandād*, the heirs of the men called *Wahmanpanāh*; and from two olive trees on the land of *Anagrān*. [G] And (from) the land on the mountain saddle called *Asp-tāzān*

('Horse Paddock') a measure (*sāmān*, line 17) of 4 *grīw* of crop yields, which (are) from one

(17) *zayt ī rēš ud az ēw zayt ī zamīg ī xwāstagdārān ī mardān ī Ērāzād nām būd ud az ēw zayt ī zamīg ī mardān ī Āzad-Xusrō nām {ud az ēw zayt ī zamīg ī mardān ī Āzad-Xusrō nām sāmān ud zamīg*

(17) damaged olive tree; and from one olive tree on the land of the heirs of the men called *Ērāzād*; and from one olive tree on the land of the men called *Āzad-Xusrō* {and from one olive tree on the land of men called *Āzad-Xusrō*}. [H] And (from) land

(18) *ī [[kōfag]] damēnag ul-(ā)mad ī kišw ī g(rīw) 1 āhang kē az ēw zayt ī škihist ud az ēw zayt ī zamīg ī xwāstagdārān ī ōy Dēlānfarrox ud az ēw zayt ī zamīg ī Anagrān ud az ēw zayt ī zamīg ī mardān ī*

(18) on [[the mountain saddle]] in a fan, with rising tillage: a measure (*sāmān*, line 19) of 1 *grīw* of crop yieldings which (are) from one broken olive tree and from one olive tree on the land of heirs of the late *Dēlānfarrox*; and from one olive tree on the land of *Anagrān*; and from one olive tree on the land of the men

(19) *Dābōy nām ud any mard sāmān ud zamīg ī kōfag hurām xwānēnd zayt g(rīw) 6 āhang kē az dō zayt ī zamīg ī mardān ī Dābōy nām ud any mard ud az zayt ī zamīg ī mardān ī *Wangird nām ud az ēw zayt ī*

(19) called *Dābōy* and another man. [I] And (from) land on the mountain saddle called *Hurām* ('Blissful'): a measure (*sāmān*, line 20) of 6 *grīw* of crop yields, which (are) from two olive trees on the land of the men called *Dābōy* and another man; and from one olive tree on

(20) *zamīg ī mardān ī Frawardīndād nām sāmān ud xānag ud spinǰānagīh ud kunǰid ud sarw ud čīš enyā abar nimāyēd ud gannāg kard rāy zyān ēwēn ōy Frawardīn xwēš ǰādag ud tan ī Frawardīn*

(20) the land of men called *Frawardīndād*. And you shall take (the costs of) house and hospitality and the (number of) sesame plants and cypresses and other things into consideration and decaying (crops) due to the damage (by the earthquake) according to the construct that the late *Frawardīn* made legally (*ēwēn … sāxt kard rāy*, line 21) regarding his own share (*xwēš ǰādag*) and that of the pool members (*tan*) of *Frawardīn*.

(21) *ēwēn pad ān Frawardīn sāxt kard rāy Frawardīn pad paymān ī Frawardīn kard dastwarīh ō xwēšīh ud dārišn ī Farrox-Xusrōyān madan*

(21) *Frawardīn*, in the contract that *Frawardīn* made, (provided that) the right of disposal (*dastwarīh*) should pass to the ownership (*xwēšīh*) and

Yazdfarrox ud Windād-Ohrmazd ud Windād-Yazd

possession (*dārišn*) of *Farrox-Xusrōyān*. *Yazdfarrox* and *Windād-Ohrmazd* and *Windād-Yazd*

(22) *ōy xwāstag nē būd čē abāg Farrox-Xusrōyān guftan abar pahikārdan nē čīš rāst ud ka ēd xīr ōwōn čiyōn man guft būd ēstād Windād-Ohrmazd ud Windād-Yazd*

(23) do not have (the right of disposal of) that property, hence (it is) not proper (*nē čīš rāst*) (that) they proceed against (*abāg ... guftan*) *Farrox-Xusrōyān* taking legal action (*pahikārdan*). And if this matter has been as I have explained it, *Windād-Ohrmazd* and *Windād-Yazd*

(23) *ud Yazdfarrox ōy xwāstag kē tō sāmān pad nāmagīhā ud ō xwēšīh ud dārišn ī Farrox-Xusrōyān madan guft nē az im rōz Rašn frāz pad čīš-iz ēwēnag abar ud abāg*

(23) and *Yazdfarrox* from this day *Rašn* on, have no kind (of disposal) (*čīš-iz ēwēnag*) over that property, which you have decreed to put according to proportion (*sāmān*) into the records (*nāmagīhā*) and to pass into the ownership and possession of *Farrox-Xusrōyān*. And against

(24) *Farrox-Xusrōyān ud Windād-Ohrmazdān ud Windād-Yazd ud Yazdfarrox āgenēn ōwōn čiyōn nē pahikārdan harw kē pad dastwarīh ī Windād-Ohrmazd ud Windād-Yazd ud Yazdfarrox āgenēn*

(24) *Farrox-Xusrōyān* and *Windād-Ohrmazdān* and *Windād-Yazd* and *Yazdfarrox* jointly in this manner there will be no litigating. Every person who lays claim (*pahikafēd*, line 25) in *auctor*ship (*pad dastwarīh*) of *Windād-Ohrmazd* and *Windād-Yazd* and *Yazdfarrox* jointly—

(25) *ud tasūg-iz ǰud pahikafēd az Farrox-Xusrōyān abēzār ud Farrox-Xusrōyān pad ān xīr arz 101 abāyistan ud agar čīš-iz ǰuttar kunēd arz 202 drahm ō Farrox-Xusrōyān*

(25) also in another district—is without expedient (*abēzār*) against *Farrox-Xusrōyān* and must pay (*abāyistan ... dād*, line 26) *Farrox-Xusrōyān* because of that matter the value of 101 (drachmas) and if he acts otherwise, he must pay the value of 202 drachmas to *Farrox-Xusrōyān*.

(26) *dād ud grawagān kē abāg Farrox-Xusrōyān paymān kard kū amā rāst handāxt rāst frēzān ī tō kāstan čīš pad ān ēwēnag čē rāy pahikārd paymān kardan nē koxšīd*

(26) And (regarding) the mortgage of the usufruct (*grawagān*), for which they made a contract with *Farrox-Xusrōyān*, thus: 'We allotted it equally (*rāst*). We did not strive to make a contract to diminish your equal dues (*rāst frēzān*) by that kind (of disposal) regarding which we litigated.

(27) *ud rāst wizārišnīh ī amā ān čē az paymān kard nē āmad nē ēwar nē paččēn ham ud Windād-Ohrmazd ud Windād-Yazd ud Yazdfarrox āgenēn ud ēd az ham az ērmānīh ī*

(27) And our equal payment (*rāst wizārišnīh*) (regarding) that (part) which has not been acquired by concluding the contract, (is) not legally binding (*nē ēwar*) (and) not (noted) in a copy (*paččēn*).' And *Windād-Ohrmazd* and *Windād-Yazd* and *Yazdfarrox* jointly and together with my (line 28) humble (self)

(28) *man pad-iz muhr ī tō wizīr āwišt ud pēš tō az-išān pad dīd čiyōn zaytēn wizīr ī 1 nīd ∅ ud ān-iz Windād-Ohrmazd ud Windād-Yazd ud Yazdfarrox ī *Bōxt guft pēš Wanandpanāh*

(28) also sealed the document (*wizīr*) (bearing) your seal. And in your presence under inspection (*pad dīd*) they drew up one 'olive (tree) document' (*zaytēn wizīr*)." ∅ And *Windād-Ohrmazd* and *Windād Yazd* and *Yazdfarrox* confirmed and promised (line 29) what **Bōxt* said in the presence of *Wanandpanāh*.

(29) *būd ud padist ⟨ād⟩ ∅ ud Windād-Ohrmazd ud Windād-Yazd ud Yazdfarrox guft kū im rōz Rašn amā ōwōn čiyōn Bōxt guft paymān kard ud ǰadišnīg-iz ān čē Bōxt guft*

(29) ∅ *Windād-Ohrmazd* and *Windād-Yazd* and *Yazdfarrox* stated: "On this day *Rašn* we have made a contract in accordance with what *Bōxt* said, and also the imponderabilities (*ǰadišnīg-iz*), which *Bōxt* stated,

(30) *ōwōn čiyōn Bōxt pattūg ast ∅ ud abar ēn nāmag didom sāxt ēstād čihrān ī ayārīh ī tō ud nibišt ∅ ud ēn nāmag pad muhr ī ham tasūg ī*

(30) are, as *Bōxt* (said). It is permanent (*pattūg*)." ∅ And from this document (*namag*) a second one was made in the same form (*čihrān*) with your help, and was recorded. ∅ And this document was sealed (*āwišt*, line 33) with the seal of the same district of

(31) *Dēl ī Dēlān čiyōnīh ham tasūg ī *Sūrīgān pad dehīhā pad-iš framān sāxtan deh pad kār-framān zāyistan ud Wanandpanāh*

(31) *Dēl ī Dēlān*, likewise of the same 'Syrian quarter' in order to prepare an order for the villages, to investigate them by the overseer (*kar-framān*), and *Wanandpanāh*

(32) *ud Dērzamān ī dibīr ud muhr ī dehbedān kē kard ud az mardān ī Dād-Burz-Mihr nām Mihrpanāh pus mardān ī Yazdfarrox nām Yazdpanāh*

(32) and *Dērzamān*, the scribe, and by the seals of the landlords (*dehbedān*), who made (the document), and among the men called *Dād-Burz-Mihr*, the son of *Mihrpanāh*, (among) the men called *Yazdfarrox*, the son (line 33) of *Yazdpanāh*,

(33) *pus az ān *Asp-gurd deh ud abar ēwāzīh guft ud Windād-Ohrmazd ud Windād-Yazd [[ud Wanandpanāh]] ud Yazdfarrox āwišt* ∅

(33) from the village of **Asp-gurd*, and they declared (consent) unanimously, and *Windād-Ohrmazd* and *Windād-Yazd* and *Wanandpanāh* and *Yazdfarrox* sealed it. ∅

Appendix XI

Tabarestān 13 and 23: Documents on Leasehold

These original documents with an edition and extensive philological and contextual commentary have been both published in the series Res Orientales XXVI (Weber 2017a; Macuch 2017c). The following transcription includes revised readings since our publications of the texts in 2017 (*e.g.* the reading of the village name as **Asp-gurd* instead of **Haspīn-raz*).

Tabarestān 13[1]

(1) *ēn māh Amurdād abar sāl 73 rōz Ādur Ādurōy ī dibīr*	(1) This month *Amurdād* in the year 73, day *Ādur*: *Ādurōy* the scribe
(2) *pad framān ī kē kišwānīh wizōstan be dānistan ī*	(2) by order of the one, who is in charge of investigating tillage (*kišwānīh wizōstan*), in order to find out about
(3) *xīr xwand razestān zamīg ayārd ī pad bun ī *Asp-gurd deh*	(3) the property (*xīr*) called 'the vineyard' (*razestān*) evaluated the land (*zamīg ayārd*) which (is) in the *bun* ('substance') of the village of **Asp-gurd*.
(4) *Farroxohrmazd abāg *Hormizd pahikar rāy abar ō ān *Asp-gurd deh*	(4) Because of the dispute between *Farroxohrmazd* and **Hormizd*, he (= *Ādurōy*, line 1) went (line 5) to the village of **Asp-gurd*
(5) *šud dehgānān wēnišnīh ī az ān *Asp-gurd deh frāz*	(5) (for) an inspection of the farmers (*dehgānān*) from the village of **Asp-gurd*.
(6) *xwāst mardān ī Dērā nām *Tagōy pus mardān ī*	(6) He summoned (*frāz xwāst*) the men called *Dērā*, son of **Tagōy*; the men
(7) *Dērā nām Gušnasp pus mardān ī Farroxgušnasp nām*	(7) called *Dērā*, son of *Gušnasp*; the men called *Farroxgušnasp*,
(8) *Dēlgušnasp* ⟨*pus*⟩ *mardan ī Mihrōhrmazd nām Dēr pus*	(8) ⟨son⟩ of *Dēlgušnasp*; the men called *Mihrōhrmazd*, son of *Dēr*.

1 Weber 2017a, pp. 133–135; Macuch 2017c, pp. 167–172.

(9) _ud wirāyišn ī dibīr ān zamīg ī Farroxohrmazd ud Hormizd_	(9) And the settlement (_wirāyišn_) of the scribe (is): that land, with regard to which _Farroxohrmazd_ and _*Hormizd_
(10) _pahikār ka be *tarāzēnēd k(abīz) 6 *sišw dēg dahād_	(10) (have) a dispute: when (the crops) attain a weight of 6 _kabīz_, (then) one third of a _dēg_ (‘cauldron’) should be given.
(11) _ēn wizōstan-nāmag pad muhr ī awēšān ī_	(11) This transcript of investigation (_wizōstan-nāmag_) with the seal of those
(12) _azabar nibišt nām ud Ādurōy āwišt_	(12) named above and (with that of) _Ādurōy_ was sealed.
(13) _tāg ī razestān zamīg ayārd pad spār nibištag_	(13) The (amount of) rent (_tāg_) for the land of the vineyard (_razestān zamīg_) he evaluated (_ayārd_) (was) written down by appointment (_pad spār_).

Tabarestān 23[2]

(1) _māh Spandarmad abar sāl 104 rōz Ādur Farroxgušnasp_	(1) Month _Spandarmad_ in the year 104, day _Ādur_: _Farroxgušnasp_,
(2) _Dēl-āzād Wazurgnimād Xwāst-Dēlān ud Dēn-abzūd ī az *Asp-gurd deh_	(2) _Dēl-āzād_, _Wazurgnimād_, _Xwāst-Dēlān_ and _Dēn-abzūd_, who (are) from the village of _*Asp-gurd_,
(3) _andar ēn ēw tan ī ayārd ī dehgānān ī az ān *Asp-gurd pad pārag ī_	(3) concerning this one person, who made an evaluation of the farmers (_ayārd ī dehgānān_) from the (village of) _*Asp-gurd_ in the parcel of
(4) _Dēlxwašīh ī dibīr Yōdmardān ī Dēlzād pus andar ō gandum ayārd ī_	(4) _Dēlxwašīh_, (that is) the scribe, _Yōdmardān_, son of _Dēlzād_, with regard to the evaluation of wheat (_gandum ayārd_),
(5) _awēšān ī im sāl 104 zād pad frāx ēstēd šawišn_	(5) produced by them in this year 104, because of the transfer of the surplus,
(6) _be āzardan ud āsānīh kard ēstādan rāy pēš dehgānān garzišnīg_	(6) in order to establish the price (_be āzardan_) and because of having made an abatement (_āsānīh kard ēstādan_) filed a complaint with the farmers (_pēš dehgānān_).
(7) _būd awēšān dehgānān be dānistan ī ān asazišn rāy ǰadārīh mad_	(7) The farmers (_dehgānān_) in order to find out the permanent (rate) of upkeep (_ǰadārīh_) (and) income (_mad_)

2 Weber 2017a, pp. 136–140; Macuch 2017c, pp. 173–176.

(8) *ī pad ān *Asp-gurd *zaydār widard dō-māhag +saxt ud dastgīr abar*	(8) in the (village of) of **Asp-gurd*, (since) the *keeper of the archives* (**zaydār*) died two months ago, they (themselves) and a helper
(9) *ō ēdar āmad āsānīh ī kard ēstēd be āsūd kard*	(9) came here. The abatement (*āsānīh*) that had been made, was adjusted (*āsūd kard*) (and)
(10) *nāmčišt nibišt ∅ rōz Hordād pad pārag ī ham Dēlxwašīh*	(10) explicitly recorded. ∅ Day *Hordād* for the parcel (*pārag*) of the same *Dēlxwašīh*
(11) *Yōdmardān pad g(rīw) 4 tāg ān ī raγ pad pārag Xwāst-Dēlān*	(11) *Yōdmardān* a rent (*tāg*) of 4 *grīw* because of the meadow in the parcel; *Xwāst-Dēlān*
(12) *pad g(rīw) 1 tāg Windād-Ohrmazd pad g(rīw) 1 tāg Yazdfarrox pad g(rīw) 1 tāg*	(12) a rent of 1 *grīw*; *Windād-Ohrmazd* a rent of 1 *grīw*; *Yazdfarrox* a rent of 1 *grīw*;
(13) *Juxt pad g(rīw) 1 tāg Farroxzād ī az *Brazasp pad g(rīw) 1 tāg*	(13) *Juxt* a rent of 1 *grīw*; *Farroxzād* from **Brāzasp* a rent of 1 *grīw*,
(14) *āzard ud āsānīh kard ēstād pad zamīg ī Farroxgušnasp*	(14) was established as value (*āzard*) and the price had been lowered (*āsānīh kard ēstād*) for the land of *Farroxgušnasp*
(15) *pad gandum g(rīw) 5 pad zamīg ī Dēl-āzād gandum g(rīw) 1 pad zamīg ī*	(15) of 5 *grīw* of wheat; for the land of *Dēl-āzād* 1 *grīw* of wheat; for the land of
(16) *Wazurgnimād gandum k(abīz) 6 pad zamīg ī Farroxzād gandum k(abīz) 7*	(16) *Wazurgnimād* 6 *kabīz* of wheat; for the land of *Farroxzād* 7 *kabīz* of wheat;
(17) *pad zamīg ī Xwāst-Dēlān ud Dēn-abzūd āgenēn gandum k(abīz) 5 pad zamīg ī*	(17) for the joint land of *Xwāst-Dēlān* and *Dēn-abzūd* 5 *kabīz* of wheat; for the land of
(18) *Dēlxwašīh gandum k(abīz) 5 ∅ hāmist pad g(rīw) 9 tāg āgenēn āzard*	(18) *Dēlxwašīh* 5 *kabīz* of wheat. ∅ Together they established a rent of 9 *grīw*
(19) *ud āsānīh kard ēstēd gandum g(rīw) 8 k(abīz) 3 ∅ ham Dēlxwašīh*	(19) and the price has been lowered to 8 *grīw* 3 *kabīz* of wheat. ∅ Regarding that same *Dēlxwašīh*
(20) *Yōdmardān ān pad g(rīw) 4 tāg ī pad pārag ī awēšān ān-iz rāγ pad pārag*	(20) *Yōdmardan* the rent of 4 *grīw* for their parcel as well as the meadow in the parcel,
(21) *be āzardan ud āsānīh kardan *dānbed bawišn guft ∅ ēn*	(21) establishing the price and making an abatement was implemented by the *master of grain supplies* (**dānbed*). ∅ This

(22) *zastbūd {āwišt} nāmag pad muhr ī ham awēšān [[ud Wīrgušnasp ī mahistag]] āwišt Dērā*	(22) transcript of interrogation (*zastbūd-nāmag*) was sealed by the seal of all those [[and *Wīrgušnasp* the Elder]]. *Dērā*
(23) *(ān) harwisp nibišt muhr abar nihād ham frāz Wīrgušnasp ī mahistag abarag*	(23) recorded everything; the same *Wīrgušnasp* the Elder placed (his) seal upon it.

Appendix XII

Tabarestān 1–8; 10: Records of Civil Proceedings

The original documents with an edition and extensive philological and contextual commentary have been published in the series *Res Orientales* XXIV (Weber 2016a; Macuch 2016a). The first group of legal documents from the legal archive in Tabarestān (Tab. 1–8 and 10; no. 9 is missing) consists of recordings of three different (incomplete) civil cases, which were brought to trial in the years 86 and 87 (=737/738 CE) of the post-Yazdegird era (PYE; beginning in 651). The following transcription includes revised readings since our publications of the texts in 2016 (*e. g.* the reading of the village name as **Asp-gurd* instead of **Haspīn-raz)*.

Case 1

(Sequence of the documents: Tab. 1A; 1B; 2B; 3B; 4A; 7A; 7B; 10A; 8B; 8A)

Tabarestān 1A

1. *ō anōšayād Āzād-Xusrō namāz*	1. To the ever-remembered *Āzad-Xusrō*, reverence!
2. *Farroxabzūd drōd was az garzišn ī*	2. (From) *Farroxabzūd* many greetings! Regarding the complaint of
3. *mardān ī Yazd nām ud zan-ēw*	3. the men of (the house) named *Yazd* and a woman, named
4. *Duxtxwašīh nām tasūg ī Dēl ī Dēlān*	4. *Duxtxwašīh*, (in) the quarter of *Dēl ī Dēlān*
5. *az *Asp-gurd deh ast čiš kē*	5. from the village of **Asp-gurd*, there is a matter,
6. *rāy mardān ī Denyadān nām az ān *Asp-gurd*	6. with regard to which the men of *Denyadān* from the village of **Asp-gurd*
7. *deh pēš tō andar abayed xwadāy*	7. are needed in your presence. Sir,
8. *ka-š ēn nāmag ēwēn ī ōy*	8. when you (will have received) this note regarding the legality of that
9. *garzišn rāy Denyadān abāg*	9. claim you should summon (line 11–12) *Dēnyadān* together

10. *awēšān ī garzēd pad māh ud rōz ī*	10. with those who complain, on a specific month and day
11. *nāmčišt ō gōw ī pēš tō wisē*	11. to a hearing in your presence.
12. *ē kunēd ēn nāmag māh Day*	12. This note was written in the month *Day* (10th month),
13. *abar sāl 86 und rōz Māh kard*	13. in the year 86, on day *Māh* (12th day).

Tabarestān 1B

1. *ō hērbed ī xwadāy Farroxabzūd*	1. To the *hērbed*, lord *Farroxabzūd*,
2. *namāz Āzād-Xusrō drōd was. nāmag ī*	2. reverence! *Āzād-Xosrō* (sends) many greetings. (Regarding) the note
3. *hērbed az garzišn ī mardān ī Yazd nām*	3. the *hērbed* (sent) on the complaint of the men called *Yazd*
4. *⟨ud⟩ zan-ēw Duxtxwašīh nām tasūg ī*	4. (and) the woman named *Duxtxwašīh* (in) the quarter of
5. *Dēl-Dēlān az *Asp-gurd deh ast čīš*	5. *Dēl-Dēlān* from the village of **Asp-gurd* regarding the matter
6. *ke rāy mardān ī Dēnyadān nām az ān *Asp-gurd*	6. for which the men named *Dēnyadān* from the village of **Asp-gurd*
7. *deh pēš hērbed andar abāyistan ōy*	7. are needed before the *hērbed*
8. *garzišn rāy Dēnyadān abāg awesān ī*	8. because of the complaint. *Dēnyadān* together with those who
9. *garzēd ō pēš hērbed wisē kardan*	9. complain are to be summoned to the presence of the *hērbed*.
10. *abārīg-iz ān xīr ō man framūd kardan*	10. Another thing he also ordered me to do:
11. *zāyistan-tar pad nāmag ī hērbed framūd*	11. to question intensively according to the instructions in the *hērbed's* letter;
12. *kardan dastwarīh Dēnyadān frāz*	12. to request *auctor*-ship (*dastwarīh*) from *Dēnyadān*
13. *xwāst ān pahikār rāy ēn māh*	13. for that dispute. This month
14. *Day abar sāl 86 rōz Tīr*	14. *Day* (10th month), in the year 86, day *Tīr* (13th day)
15. *ō gōw ī pēš hērbed wisē kard.*	15. he was summoned to the hearing before the *hērbed*.

Tabarestān 2B

1. *ēn māh] Day abar sāl 86 ud rōz Tīr*	1. [This month] *Day* (10th month) of the year 86 and day *Tīr* (13th day)

2.	*Yazd] ī pēšēmāl Dēnyadān ī pasēmāl*	2.	*Yazd*] the plaintiff, *Dēnyadān*, the defendant,
3.	*pēš] Farroxabzūd kē tasūg ī Dēl ī Dēlān*	3.	were present (line 4) before *Farroxabzūd*, (in) whose quarter of *Dēl ī Dēlān* the village (of **Asp-gurd* is located),
4.	*deh] būd hēnd u-šān āgenēn wāng*	4.	and they declaimed together:
5.	*kar]d kū garz(ē)m Dēnyadān guft*	5.	'We complain!'. *Dēnyadān* said:
6.	*k]ū man az čim [ud] bōzišn hammis rōz*	6.	"I will come together with evidence and proof on day
7.	*Rā]m ī māh Day pēš Farroxabzūd*	7.	*Rām* (21st day) of the month *Day* (10th month) before *Farroxabzūd*
8.	*]ō gōw āyēm* ∅	8.	to the hearing" ∅
	Farroxbudān		*Farroxbudān* (signature of the scribe)

Tabarestān 3B

1.	*ēn māh Day abar sāl*	1.	This month *Day* (10th month) in the year
2.	*86 rōz Rašn*	2.	86, day *Rašn* (18th day)
3.	*Yazd ī pēšēmāl pēš*	3.	*Yazd*, the plaintiff, came before
4.	*Farroxabzūd ī tasūg-iz*	4.	*Farroxabzūd*, (in) whose quarter
5.	*ī Dēl ī Dēlān deh ō*	5.	of *Dēl ī Dēlān* the village (of **Asp-gurd* is located), to
6.	*gōw āmad pād*	6.	the hearing (and) waited.
7.	*ud Dēnyadān ī pasēmāl*	7.	Neither *Dēnyadān*, the defendant,
8.	*ud jadag-gōw iz nē āmad*	8.	nor his legal representative came.
	(Vertically)		(Vertically)
	1. *Wahman Ard*		1. Until *Wahman* (11th month), day *Ard* (25th day)
	2. *kē ō pād* ∅		2. he waited ∅
	Tīrgušnasp ∅		*Tīrgušnasp* ∅ (signature of the scribe)

Tabarestān 4A

1.	*ēn māh Wahman abar sāl 86 rōz[*	1.	This month *Wahman* (11th month) in the year 86, day
2.	*Day pad Dēn Yazd ī pēšēmāl Dēnyadān[*	2.	*Day* (23rd day), *Yazd*, the plaintiff, *Dēnyadān*,
3.	*ī pasēmāl im dādestān rāy pēš*	3.	the defendant, because of this legal case were present (line 5) before

4. *Farroxabzūd ī tasūg-iz ī [Dēl ī Dēlān]*
5. *deh būd hēnd...[*
6. *guft kū man az čim ud bōzišn [*
7. *dāštan abāyistan ān xwāstag ī mardān [ī*
8. *Māhōy nām būd ud ēg-iz a[z*
9. *dastwar ī ān xwāstag hammis rōz*
10. *Māh ī māh Spandarmad ī im s[āl*
11. *86 pēš Farroxabzūd ō gōw āy[ēm*

(Vertically)
Tīrgušnasp

4. *Farroxabzūd*, (in) whose quarter of [*Dēl ī Dēlān*]
5. the village (of **Asp-gurd* is located).
6. He said: "As evidence and proof [...]
7. for (rightfully) holding that property of the men [...]
8. called *Māhōy* and also together with
9. the legal predecessor (*dastwar*) of that property on day
10. *Māh* (12th day) of the month *Spandarmad* (12th month) of this year
11. 86 I will come to the hearing before *Farroxabzūd*".

(Vertically)
Tīrgušnasp (signature of the scribe)

Tabarestān 7A

1. *māh Spandarmad abar sāl 86 ud rōz Māh*
2. *Yazd ī pēšēmāl Dēnyadān ī pasēmāl im*
3. *dādestān rāy pēš Farroxabzūd kē tasūg ī*
4. *Dēl ī Dēlān deh būd hēnd Dēnyadān ī*
5. *pasēmāl guft kū man *ēwēn az čim ud bōzišn*
6. *dāštan (abāyist)an ān xwāstag ī mardān ī Māhōy*
7. *nām būd ēg-iš az dastwar ī ān xwāstag*
8. *hammis rōz Xwār ī māh Frawardīn ī nazdist*
9. *im sāl 87 pēš Farroxabzūd ō gōw*
10. *āyēm.*

(vertically)
Farroxbudān

1. Month *Spandarmad* (12th month) of the year 86 and day *Māh* (12th day)
2. *Yazd*, the plaintiff, *Dēnyadān*, the defendant,
3. were present (line 4) because of this case before *Farroxabzūd*, (in) whose quarter of
4. *Dēl ī Dēlān* the village (of **Asp-gurd* is located). *Dēnyadān*,
5. the defendant, said: "I will come (line 10) with evidence and proof
6. for (my) lawful possession (of) that property, which belonged to the men called *Māhōy*,
7. and also together with the legal predecessor (*dastwar*) of that property
8. on day *Xwar* (11th day) of the next month *Frawardīn* (1st month)
9. of this year 87 to the hearing before *Farroxabzūd*".

(vertically)
Farroxbudān
(signature of the scribe)

Tabarestān 7B

1. *māh Frawardīn abar sāl 87*	1. Month *Frawardīn* (1st month) in the year 87,
2. *ud rōz Xwar Yazd ī pēšēmāl*	2. and day *Xwar* (11th day) *Yazd*, the plaintiff,
3. *ī abar ēn nāmag nibišt pēš*	3. who is recorded in this note, came (line 5) before
4. *Farroxabzūd kē tasūg-iz ī Dēl ī Dēlān*	4. *Farroxabzūd*, (in) whose quarter of *Dēl ī Dēlān* the village (of **Asp-gurd* is located),
5. *deh ō gōw āmad pād Dēnyadān*	5. to the hearing (and) waited. Neither *Dēnyadān*,
6. *ī pasēmāl ud ǰādag-gōw-iz nē āmad*	6. the defendant, nor his legal representative came.

Tabarestān 10A

1. *o anōšayād [......] namāz Farroxabzūd drōd was*	1. To the ever-remembered [......], reverence! (From) *Farroxabzūd* many greetings!
2. *az garzišn ī Yazd ī dibīr ī tasūg ī*	2. Regarding the complaint of *Yazd*, the scribe of the quarter of
3. *Dēl ī Dēlān az *Asp-gurd deh ast čiš*	3. *Dēl ī Dēlān*, from the village of **Asp-gurd*, there is a matter,
4. *kē rāy būdan Dēnyadān nām az ān *Asp-gurd deh*	4. with regard to which (the men) named *Dēnyadān* from that village of **Asp-gurd*
5. *pēš man andar abāyēd ∅ xwadāy ka-š ēn*	5. are needed in my presence ∅. Sir, when you (will have received) this
6. *nāmag ēwēn ī ōy garzišn rāy Dēnyadān*	6. note regarding the legality of that claim, you should summon (line 8) *Dēnyadān*
7. *abāg Yazd pad māh ud rōz ī nāmčišt ō*	7. together with *Yazd* on a specific month and day to
8. *gōw ī pēš man wisē ē kunēd ēn nāmag*	8. a hearing in my presence. This note was ordered to be written (line 10) in the
9. *māh Frawardīn abar sāl 87*	9. month *Frawardīn* (1st month) of the year 87,
10. *rōz Rām framūd kardan* ∅∅	10. day *Rām* (21st day) ∅∅.

Tabarestān 8B

1. *ō hērbed ī xwadāy Farroxabzūd*	1. To the *hērbed*, lord *Farroxabzūd*,
2. *namāz Yazdāngird drōd was ∅ az*	2. reverence! *Yazdāngird* (sends) many greetings ∅ On
3. *garzišn ī mardān ī Yazd nām tasūg ī*	3. the complaint of the men named *Yazd*, (from) the quarter of
4. *Dēl-Dēlān az *Asp-gurd deh ast čīš*	4. *Dēl-Dēlān*, from the village of **Asp-gurd*, there is a matter,
5. *ke rāy Dēnyadān nām ī az ān *Asp-gurd*	5. regarding which (the men) named *Dēnyadān* from that village of **Asp-gurd*
6. *deh pēš hērbed andar abāyistan*	6. are needed before the *hērbed*.
7. *ōy garzišn rāy Dēnyadān abāg*	7. Regarding that complaint *Dēnyadān* together with
8. *[Yazd] pad māh ud rōz ī nāmčišt*	8. [*Yazd*] are to be summoned (line 9) on a specific month and day
9. *ō pēš hērbed wisē kardan abārīg-iz*	9. to the presence of the *hērbed*. Another
10. *ān xīr ō man kard zāyistan-tar pad*	10. matter also he ordered me (to do): to question intensively for
11. *nāmag ī hērbed kard dastwarīh*	11. the transcript the *hērbed* has made; he requested *auctor*-ship (*dastwarīh*)
12. *Dēnyadān frāz xw[ā]st ān pahikār*	12. from *Dēnyadān* for that dispute.
13. *rāy ēn māh Frawardīn abar sāl*	13. This month *Frawardīn* (1st month) in the year
14. *87 rōz Wād ō gōw ī*	14. 87, day *Wād* (22nd day) (he was summoned) to the hearing
15. *(pēš hērbed wisē) kard.*	15. (before) the *hērbed*.

Tabarestān 8A

1. *māh Frawardīn abar sāl*	1. Month *Frawardīn* (1st month) of the year
2. *87 ud rōz Wād Yazd*	2. 87 and day *Wād* (22nd day) *Yazd*,
3. *ī pēšēmāl ī abar ēn*	3. the plaintiff, who has been recorded in this
4. *nāmag nibišt ēstēd pēš*	4. transcript, came (line 7) before
5. *Farroxabzūd kē tasūg-iz ī*	5. *Farroxabzūd*, (in) whose quarter
6. *Dēl ī Dēlān deh ō gōw*	6. of *Dēl ī Dēlān* the village (of **Asp-gurd* is located), to the hearing
7. *āmad pād Dēnyadān ī*	7. (and) waited. Neither *Dēnyadān*,
8. *pasēmāl ǰādag-gōw-iz nē*	8. the defendant, nor his legal representative
9. *āmad ∅*	9. came ∅

Case 2

(Tab. 6A and 6B)

Tabarestān 6A

1. *māh Spandarmad abar sāl 86 rōz Māh*	1. Month *Spandarmad* (12th month) in the year 86, day *Māh* (12th day)
2. *Šedrēš ī pēšēmāl Āzādōg ī pasēmāl*	2. *Šedrēš*, the plaintiff, *Āzādōg*, the defendant were present (line 4)
3. *pēš Farroxabzūd ī tasūg-iz ī Dēl-Dēlān deh*	3. before *Farroxabzūd*, (in) whose quarter of *Dēl-Dēlān* the village (of **Asp-gurd* is located),
4. *būd hēnd u-šān āgenēn zamān kard* (super.lin.) *ī nazdist*	4. and they fixed together a date:
5. *kū rōz Xwar ī māh Frawardīn im sal 87*	5. "On day *Xwar* (11th day) of the first month *Frawardīn* (1st month) of this year 87
6. *pēš Farroxabzūd o gōw āyēm.*	6. we will come to the hearing before *Farroxabzūd*."
(vertically) *Šīrzād*	(vertically) *Šīrzād* (name of the scribe)

Tabarestān 6B

1. *māh Frawardīn abar sāl 87 ud rōz Xwar*	1. Month *Frawardīn* (1st month) of the year 87 and day *Xwar* (11th day)
2. *[Šedrēš] ī pēšēmāl pēš Farroxabzūd kē*	2. [*Šedrēš*], the plaintiff, came (line 3) before *Farroxabzūd*, (in) whose
3. *tasūg-iz ī Dēl-Dēlān deh ō gōw āmad*	3. quarter of *Dēl-Dēlān* the village (of **Asp-gurd* is located), to the hearing (and)
4. *pād Āzādōg ī pasēmāl ī abar ēn nāmag*	4. waited. *Āzādōg*, the defendant, who has been recorded in this transcript,
5. *nibišt ēstēd ǰādag-gōw iz nē āmad*	5. and his legal representative did not come.
(vertically) *Dēnohrmazd*	(vertically) *Dēnohrmazd* (name of the scribe)

Case 3

(Tab. 5A)

Tabarestān 5A

1. *ēn māh Wahman abar sāl 86 rōz Day pad*	1. This month *Wahman* (11th month) of the year 86, *Day pad*
2. *Dēn Yazd ī pēšēmāl Āzādōg ī pasēmāl pēš*	2. *Dēn* (23rd day) *Yazd*, the plaintiff, (and) *Āzādōg*, the defendant, were present (line 4) before
3. *Farroxabzūd ī tasūg-iz ī Dēl ī Dēlān deh*	3. *Farroxabzūd*, (in) whose quarter of *Dēl ī Dēlān* the village (of **Asp-gurd* is located),
4. *būd hēnd u-šān āgenēn zamān kar[d* (super lin.) *ī māh Spandarmad*	4. and they fixed together a date:
5. *kū rōz Māh ī im sāl 86 [pēš*	5. On day *Māh* (12th day) of the month *Spandarmad* (12th month) of this year 86 we will
6. *Farroxabzūd ō gōw āyēm tāg ī band.[*	6. come to the hearing before *Farrox-abzūd*. An item of this obligation
7. *pad abarag nibišt.*	7. is written above (the line).
(vertically) *Tīrgušnasp*	(vertically) *Tīrgušnasp* (name of the scribe)

Appendix XIII

Tabarestān 22 and 22bis: A Criminal Act

These two original documents with an edition and extensive philological and contextual commentary have been published in the series *Res Orientales* XXVII (Tab. 22: Weber 2019b; Macuch 2019b) and XXIX (Tab. 22bis: Weber 2022a; Macuch 2022a). The following transcription of Tab. 22 has the following *revised readings* since our publication of the document in 2019 (see Weber 2022a, p. 116): line 4: the village name **Asp-gurd* (instead of **Haspīn-raz)*; line 9: the name of the wife *Sazā* (instead of **Dēzā*); line 11: ⟨hw'sṭk'⟩ *xwāstag* (instead of *duzīdag)*; line 12: ⟨'SLWN*tny*⟩ *bandēnd* (instead of ⟨YHNCLWN*tny*⟩ *apparēnd)*. The following translation is altered according to these revised readings.

Tabarestān 22[1]

(1) *ō hazār-anōšayād āzarmīgtom brād Xradzād namāz*	(1) To the thousand-fold remembered, greatly honoured brother *Xradzād*, reverence!
(2) *Windād-Xwaršēd ī Parišwārgar rad drōd ud harw farroxīh pad*	(2) *Windād-Xwaršēd*, the *rad* of *Parišwārgar*: greetings and complete felicity shall be (*bawād*, line 3) for (you),
(3) *xwadāy bawad ⊘ Burzēn Pērōz [ī] dibīr ī Farroxgušnasp pus*	(3) Sir! ⊘ *Burzēn-Pērōz*, the scribe, son of *Farroxgušnasp*
(4) *ī az *Asp-gurd deh ī pad xānag ī Dēl-Dēlān ī pad tan*	(4) from the village of **Asp-gurd*, in the house of *Dēl-Dēlān*, who came (line 5) personally (*pad tan*)
(5) *abāg payr(ā)[s]tag-nigār pad garzišn pēš man āmad Burzēn-Pērōz*	(5) together with the *painter of adornments* because of a complaint (*garzišn*) to my presence: *Burzēn-Pērōz* (came)
(6) *pādrōzag pad ān pēšag ud hušnūdīh xwāstan ku ēwēn-būd*	(6) to request a postponement (*pādrōzag*) regarding that guild (*pēšag*) and satisfaction (*hušnūdīh*) that (is) legally binding (*ēwēn-būd*)
(7) *andar ēn ēw Dādgušnasp nām-ēw *Ātars pus abāg Yazd nām-ēw*	(7) regarding this (occurrence): a (person) named *Dādgušnasp*, son of **Ātars*, together with a (person) named *Yazd*,

1 Weber 2019, pp. 97–101; Macuch 2019b, pp. 125–132.

(8) *brād ud Rāstdād nām-ēw Wištāsp pus ud Yazdsar nām-ēw Dēlāzād pus ī*	(8) (his) brother, and a (person) named *Rāstdād*, son of *Wištāsp*, and a (person) named *Yazdsar*, son of *Dēlāzād*,
(9) *az ān *Asp-gurd deh pad stahm ud xrōst zan ēw Sazā*	(9) from the village of **Asp-gurd*: by (an act of) violence (*stahm*) and shouting (*xrōst*) from the person *(az tan*, line 10) of the woman named *Sazā*,
(10) *nām ī pādixšāyīhā Burzēn-Pērōz zan az tan payrāyag ud ǰāmag*	(10) the 'privileged' (*pādixšāy-*)wife of *Burzēn-Pērōz*, they tear away *(abar wišāyēnd*, line 11) and tie up (*bandēnd*, line 12) ornaments (*payrāyag*) and chalices (*ǰāmag*)
(11) *ud xwāstag ī pad mašk arz s(atēr) 500 hămist abar wišāyēnd* (ŠRYṬWN*tny*)	(11) and the property (*xwāstag*) in a skin bag (*mašk)*, worth altogether 500 Stater.
(12) *ud bandēnd* ('SLWN*tny*) *gyāg gyāg ud ān ayāragīhā pad ēk ī kas kas zāyistan*	(12) To ask in every place (*gyāg gyāg*) and to check the registers (*ayāragīhā*) of every single person
(13) *bē agar abar ān xīr framūd mard mard xwāstan ud pad*	(13)—unless this has (already) been ordered for that property (*xīr*)—to summon every single man and to
(14) *abēmustīh ī Burzēn-Pērōz wizīr ud dādwarīh kardan az man ō xwadāy*	(14) give a verdict and judgement in favour of making *Burzēn-Pērōz* uncomplaining, is (the purpose of this) letter *(nāmag*, line 15) from me to (you), Sir.
(15) *nāmag bawēd enyā Burzēn-Pērōz ō abēmustīh madan nē*	(15) Otherwise it will not be possible to make *Burzēn-Pērōz* uncomplaining (*abēmustīh*)
(16) *sāxtan ud must būd ud pad ān čiš framān dād pēš man (pa)ssox*	(16) and the complaint will be upheld (*must būd*) and with regard to that case order is given, (that) an answer (be given) in my presence.
(17) *agar ast ēn čiš ēdōn čiyōn Burzēn-Pērōz garzēd pad ān*	(17) If this matter (*čiš*) is as *Burzēn-Pērōz* complains (*garzēd*), (then)
(18) *ud awēšān mard ēdōn frāz frēstādan nē sazēd ∅ xwadāy*	(18) it does not seem fitting to send him and the (other) men forth. ∅ Sir,
(19) *čiyōn Burzēn-Pērōz pad ēwēnag garzēd ēd xīr rāy Dādgušnasp*	(19) the circumstances (*čiyōn … be būdan*, line 20) of *Burzēn-Pērōz's* complaint concerning this property (*ēd xīr rāy*) regarding *Dādgušnasp*
(20) *ud awēšān mard be būdan ud saxwān az-iš āšnūd ēstād čiš gōwizār*	(20) and the (other) men (are to be examined) and (if after) his statement has been heard, the matter (is made) explicit (*gōwizār*)

(21) *awēšān ud pad-iš ō gōšān rasīd agar pad ēwēnag ī*	(21) to them and by this (statement) has reached (their) ears, if (the circumstances) become evident *(paydāg bawēd*, line 22) in the manner that
(22) *Burzēn-Pērōz guft paydāg bawēd čē ān xīr pad Dādgušnasp*	(22) *Burzēn-Pērōz* has stated, that that property (*xīr*) (is) with *Dādgušnasp*
(23) *ud awēšān mard saxt-iš Wahrām abar nihēnd wizīr ud dādwarīh ēdōn *kunēnd*	(23) and those men, (then) after (day) *Wahrām* has passed, a verdict should be reached and an appropriate judgement should be given.
(24) *ān pad Burzēn-Pērōz abēčimīh rāy ud pad rāh ī dādestān ō*	(24) Due to *Burzēn-Pērōz*'s lack of proof (*abēčimīh rāy*), and (so) that he may by judicial means (*pad rāh ī dādestān*)
(25) *abēmustīh rasād agar čim ān andar ī framān ayār ēwēnag abzāyīg*	(25) be made uncomplaining (*abēmustīh rasād*), if proof (*čim*) (emerges), the order implies (*andar ī framān*) that it be registered (*ayār … dad*) in an additional manner (*ēwēnag abzāyīg*).
(26) *dād pad čim ī čiš gōwizār ud rōšn pad passox nibēs Dādgušnasp-iz*	(26) Record (*nibēs*) the proof (*čim*) of this case explicitly and clearly (*gōwizār ud rōšn*) in (your) answer, also order *(framāyēd*, line 27) *Dādgušnasp*
(27) *framāyēd mard guftan ud pahikārdan ī abar ān xīr [[rāy]] abāg Burzēn-Pērōz ō ān mard*	(27) to name the men and (in order) to take legal action with regard to that property (*xīr*) to dispatch them back *(abāz wisē kardan*, line 28) together with *Burzēn-Pērōz* to that man.
(28) *abāz wisē kardan nāmag māh Wahman abar sāl 104 ud rōz Wahrām*	(28) (This) letter in the month of *Wahman*, in the year 104 and on day *Wahrām*
(29) *framūd kardan*	(29) was ordered to be made.
(30) *ō hazār-anōšyād āzarmīgtom brād Xradzād namāz*	(30) To the thousand-fold remembered, greatly honoured brother *Xradzād*, reverence!
(31) *Windād Xwaršēd ī Pariswārgar rad*	(31) *Windād-Xwaršēd*, the *rad* of *Parišwārgar*.

Tabarestān 22bis[2]

(vertically) *az Dādburzmihr*	(vertically) From *Dādburzmihr*
(1) *zaydār ud mahistag ī pad *Asp-gurd deh*	(1) (To the) *keeper of archives (*zaydār*) and the Elder (*mahistag*) in the village of **Asp-gurd*

2 Weber 2022a, pp. 115–118; Macuch 2022a, pp. 144–149.

(2) *rōz Ardwahišt* ∅ *Burzēn-Pērōz ī pādixšāy az ēd*	(2) day *Ardwahišt* (3rd day) ∅ *Burzēn-Pērōz*, the *pādixšāy*(-husband) from the
(3) **Asp-gurd deh pēš man āmad zan ī Sazā nām ī*	(3) village of **Asp-gurd* came before me, (his) *pādixšāy*(line 4)-wife, named *Sazā*,
(4) *pādixšāy mardān ī Xwāst-Dēlān nām ud ān *Asp-gurd deh*	(4) (from) the lineage called *Xwāst-Dēlān*, who resides *(mānēd*, line 5) in the village of **Asp-gurd*,
(5) *mānēd duxt ī az būd ud dastwarīh ud wizīr ud paymān*	(5) the natural daughter *(duxt ī az būd)* (?). And the entitlement (*dastwarīh*) and the document (*wizīr*) and the contract (*paymān*)
(6) *ī Xwāst-Dēlān andar Burzēn-Pērōz kard ud āwišt paydāg ō*	(6) that *Xwāst-Dēlān* had made and sealed for *Burzēn-Pērōz* (is) revealed (*paydāg*) for
(7) *zanīh ī Burzēn-Pērōz madan ud Sazā pad ān wizīr*	(7) entering marriage with *Burzēn-Pērōz*, recording *(nibištan*, line 8) the amount *(ēw-čand*, line 8) to which *Sazā* (has) entitlement *(dastwarīh*, line 8) by that document (*wizīr*)
(8) *dastwarīh ēw-čand tā pad zanīh ī Burzēn-Pērōz nibištan*	(8) as long as she is in matrimony with *Burzēn-Pērōz*.
(9) *Dādgušnasp ī dibīr ī az *Asp-gurd deh Sazā rāy*	(9) *Dādgušnasp*, the scribe, from the village of **Asp-gurd*, because of *Sazā*
(10) *az zanīh ī Burzēn-Pērōz zāyendag pahrēxtan ud az ǰāmag*	(10) is to abstain (*pahrēxtan*) from investigating *(zāyendag)* the marriage to *Burzēn-Pērōz*. And (this is) because of (the case of) the chalices (*ǰāmag)*
(11) *ud xwāstag ī pad mašk ī čand ud payrāyag ī abāg ǰahist hămist*	(11) and the amount of property (*xwāstag*) in the skin bag (*mašk*) and the ornaments/jewellery *(payrāyag)* (she had) with (her) which happened to be
(12) *be bastan ud Burzēn-Pērōz abar ān xīr pēš rad wēš rēxt *paymānag*	(12) tied up together. And *Burzēn-Pērōz* regarding that matter (*xīr*) was to complain *(garzīdan*, line 13) in a far too extensive measure (*wēš rēxt *paymānag?*) before the *rad* (according to)
(13) *garzīdan nāmag ī awēšān ud kardan-iz ī Dādgušnasp ān abēčimīh*	(13) their transcript (*nāmag*) (of investigation) and the (legal) action (*kardan-iz*) of *Dādgušnasp*. He had with him (*abāg dāšt*, line 15)

(14) *ud adādīh pad Burzēn-Pērōz rēš wizōst-nāmag ī pad muhr*	(14) a transcript of investigation (*wizōst-nāmag)* bearing a legally binding seal (*muhr ī ēwar*, line 15) (to prove) the groundlessness *(abēčimīh*, line 13) and illegality (*adādīh*) of the (allegation of) injury (*rēš*) inflicted on *Burzēn-Pērōz*.
(15) *ī ēwar abāg dāšt ud abar ān xīr must bawišn guft*	(15) And he confirmed that a complaint existed in this matter (*ān xīr must bawišn*):
(16) *tō wēm čiyōn Burzēn-Pērōz pad ān ēwēnag garzēd ud [ēd] xīr rāy*	(16) 'You (are) obstinate *(wēm*; lit:. a rock).' When *Burzēn-Pērōz* complains in that manner (*ān ēwēnag*) and because of this matter (*xīr rāy*),
(17) *dehgān ud mādag ī ēd deh ud Sazā-iz pōhišn xwāhēd ud az ān saxwan*	(17) (then) he requests corruption (*pōhišn)* from the *dehgān* and the women (*mādag*) of this village and also of *Sazā*." And from that statement
(18) *ašnawēd čim ī ān čiš be dānēd enyā čiyōn čim*	(18) (that) you will hear you will learn of the evidence (*čim*) in this matter, moreover it (is to be treated) as the
(19) *(ī abdo)m ud saxwan ī Sazā čē ēwēnag pad passox*	(19) final evidence. And you shall write down *(nibēsēd*, line 20) the statement of *Sazā* (regarding) the circumstances (*čē ēwēnag*) (of the case), according to (her) answer (*pad passox*).
(20) *(ī …) nibēsēd ud Sazā-iz abāg mašk xwāstagān čand (būd)*	(20) And *Sazā* also will declare *(gōwēd*, line 21), how many things/items of property (*xwāstagān*)
(21) *ī Burzēn-Pērōz ham pad nāmčišt gōwēd ud man pēš tō āyēm*	(21) of *Burzēn-Pērōz* were with the skin bag *(mašk*, line 20) (and) will also list them individually (*pad nāmčišt*). And I will come before you
(22) *ud pašt-iz druxt ī abāyēd niyāz* (*čim*) *māh*	(22) and also (give), if necessary, evidence (*čim*) on the breach of contract (*pašt-iz druxt*) (?). Month
(23) *Frawardīn ī sāl*	(23) *Frawardīn* (1st month) of the year
(24) 106	(24) 106
(25) *rōz*	(25) day
(26) *(Ardwahišt)*	(26) (*Ardwahišt*) (3rd day)

Appendix XIV

Tabarestān 11 and 28: Two Cases of *stŭrīh*

These original documents with an edition and extensive philological and contextual commentary have been both published in the series *Res Orientales* XXVIII (Tab. 11 and 28: Weber 2020a; Macuch 2020b).

Tabarestān 11[1]

(1) *ō anōšyād Farroxabzūd namāz. Windā[d-Xwaršēd ī Parišwārgar rad drōd*	(1) To the ever remembered *Farroxabzūd*, reverence! (From) *Windād-Xwaršēd*, the *rad* of *Parišwārgar*, many greetings! ∅
(2) *was ∅ čīš xwēšēnišn ī ān wahištag [Rahāg] zan ī [……]*	(2) (In) the matter of taking in ownership (*xwēšēnišn*) of that paradise-dwelling [*Rahāg*] the woman/wife of [……]
(3) *[……] ī pursišn ud dādestān ī *Asp-gurd deh mānēd pad garzišn pēš man*	(3) [……] inquiry and judgement (?), who resides in the village of **Asp-gurd*, came (line 4) before me with a complaint (*garzišn*),
(4) *āmad ud mard 2 āšnāg guft kū ašō Rahāg ī xwarrah xānag sar-tanīg*	(4) and two identified men declared: “The righteous *Rahāg*, whose abode (is) in the Divine Splendour (*xwarrah*), was sound in mind and body (*sar-tanīg andar būd*).
(5) *andar būd ī az ān *Asp-gurd būd ud Dērwīndād Duxtxwašī[h]*	(5) He was from **Asp-gurd*, and *Dērwīndād*, (was) the father (line 6) of *Duxtxwašīh*,
(6) *pid ud Rahāg ī Duxtxwašīh mādar-pid būd Rahāg ī xwāstag*	(6) and *Rahāg* was the maternal grandfather (‘father of the mother’, *mādar-pid)* of *Duxtxwašīh*: (this) *Rahāg*, who had property
(7) *ī-š xwēš būd pus ī zan-1 Anōšīzag nām būd ī*	(7) that was his own (*xwāstag ī-š xwēš būd*), was the son of a woman called *Anōšīzag*;

1 Weber 2020a, pp. 172–175; Macuch 2020b, pp. 191–199.

(8) *Duxtxwašīh nām andar zanīh waxšēndagīh ī Rahāg ī zāyēd ud purnāy*	(8) he (held the woman) called *Duxtxwašīh* in matrimony (*andar zanīh*) (for the) increase (of the progeny) of *Rahāg*, so that she give birth (to children) and (they) reach maturity.
(9) *bawēd ud agar Anōšīzag pus nē bē duxt zāyēd ud duxt ī*	(9) And if *Anōšīzag* does not bear (another) son, but a daughter, and the daughter that
(10) *Anōšīzag zāyēd 10 brād ō purr-xwadīh rasēd pad stūrīh*	(10) *Anōšīzag* bears, (brings forth) 10 brothers, (who) reach full maturity, (then) for the 'substitute succession' (*stūrīh*)
(11) *ī Rahāg ī xwēš būd nē paymān kardan ud wizīr āwištan*	(11) of *Rahāg* regarding (the property) that was his own (*ī xwēš būd*) no contract (*paymān*) should be made and no document (*wizīr*) sealed.
(12) *ud Anōšīzag bē Duxtxwašīh ēč frazand ī nē zād*	(12) And (if) *Anōšīzag*, apart from *Duxtxwašīh*, does not give birth to any children, (then) it is deemed legal (*ēwēn būdan*, line 15)
(13) *xwāstag ī ōy Rahāg ī xwēš būd pad ān dastwarīh*	(13) for the property that was the late *Rahāg*'s own (*ī xwēš būd)*, to be transferred (*madan*, line 14) by that entitlement (*dastwarīh*)
(14) *ō xwēšīh ī Duxtxwašīh madan ud Duxtxwašīh dāštan*	(14) into the ownership (*xwēšīh*) of *Duxtxwašīh* and for *Duxtxwašīh* to possess it (*dāštan*)."
(15) *ēwēn būdan mardān-iz ī-š guft kū Farroxohrmazd nām ī*	(15) The men also said: "(The man) called *Farroxohrmazd*, who
(16) *az ān *Asp-gurd deh Duxtxwašīh juttar Rahāg [.........]*	(16) (is) from the (same) village of **Asp-gurd*, *Duxtxwašīh* otherwise *Rahāg* [.........]
(17) *Farroxohrmazd ān [.........] pad*	(17) *Farroxohrmazd* [.........] in
(18) *zanīh ud sālārīh (kār?) mardān [...] az ān *Asp-gurd*	(18) matrimony and guardianship. The men [...] who were from the village of **Asp-gurd*
(19) *deh būd ud ham-gōnag [.........]*	(19) and in the same manner [.........]
(20) *pad ān dastwarīh* (?) *Duxtxwašīh [.........]*	(20) by that entitlement (?) *Duxtxwašīh* [.........]
(21) *pēš man guft ∅ xwadāy čiyōn Duxtxwašīh pad ān ēwēnag*	(21) spoke before me. ∅ Sir, as *Duxtxwašīh* complains (*garzēd*, line 22) in that manner

(22) *garzēd ēd xīr rāy awēšān mard frāz ē xwāhēd ud paymān*	(22) with regard to this matter (*ēd xīr rāy*), (then) you shall summon those men (*frāz ē xwāhēd*) and lay down (*ē nišāyēd*, line 23) a contract (*paymān*),
(23) *ī-š guft ē nišāyēd andak rāyēnišn bē dānišn ī*	(23) according to her statement, (for a) part of the litigation (*rāyēnišn*), but without letting (them) know of
(24) *xwēš kardan agar pad ān ēwēnag ī Duxtxwašīh guft pad ān*	(24) the transfer of ownership. If this is the case in the manner (*pad ān ēwēnag*) that *Duxtxwašīh* has declared,
(25) *bawēd pad ān xīr dādestān ud wizīr ud dādwarīh ēdōn ē*	(25) (then) you shall administer justice (*dādestān*) in this matter and pass a verdict (*wizīr*) and reach a judicial decision (*dādwarīh*) in an appropriate manner,
(26) *kunēd ī Duxtxwašīh andar dādestān must rāy nē*	(26) so that *Duxtxwašīh* no (longer) in this lawsuit has a complaint (= reason to appeal; *must*),
(27) *būd ī wizīr ī pad dādestān rāy (h) āwand abar ēn gōw*	(27) (so) that there is no need for her to file a complaint (*pad garzišn āmad nē abāyēd*, line 28) because of the verdict (*wizīr*) in this lawsuit (*dādestān*) similar to this statement (*gōw*).
(28) *pad garzišn āmad nē abāyēd ud agar juttar čim ī*	(28) And if (the case) is different, (then) you shall write (*ē nibēsēd*, line 30) the reason (*čim*)
(29) *a-sazišn ī ān rāyēnišn drust ud rōšn pad passox ō man*	(29) for the impropriety (*a-sazišn*) of that lawsuit correctly and clearly (*drust ud rōšn*) in your answer to me.
(30) *ē nibēsēd ud awēšān mard ān pahikār rōšn kardan rāy*	(30) And you shall summon (*wisē ē kunēd*, line 32) those men in order to clarify that judicial dispute (*pahikār*)
(31) *abāg Duxtxwašīh pad māh Wahman ī nāmčišt ō gōw*	(31) together with *Duxtxwašīh* in the month of *Wahman* specifically to a hearing (*gōw*)
(32) *ī pēš man wisē ē kunēd. nāmag m[āh Ā]dur abar*	(32) before me. The letter was written (*kard*, line 33) in Month *[Ā]dur*
(33) *sāl 81 ud rōz Aštād kard*	(33) of the year 81, on day *Aštād*.
(34) *ō anōš-ayād Farroxabzūd namāz. Parišwārgar rad*	(34) To the ever remembered *Farroxabzūd*, reverence! (From) the *rad* of *Parišwārgar*.

Tabarestān 28[2]

(1) *ō xwadāy Windād-Xwaršēd namāz. Windād-Ohrmazd drōd was. māh Mihr abar sāl 107 ī pas az bay Yazdegird šāhān šāh ī nab ī ōy bay*

(1) To the lord *Windād-Xwaršēd*, reverence! (From) *Windād-Ohrmazd* many greetings! (In) the month *Mihr* in the year 107 after (the reign of his) majesty *Yazdegird*, King of Kings, grandson of (his) late majesty

(2) *Xusrō ī Ohrmazdān ka ēn tasūg ī Dēl ī Dēlān ī abar Taburestān dādestān būd hēm zan ī Pidarōš nām ī mardān pādixšāy*

(2) *Xusrō*, son of *Ohrmazd*, when I was (in) this quarter of *Dēl ī Dēlān* in charge of jurisdiction (*dādestān*) in *Taburestān*, a woman called *Pidarōš*, who (is) authorized (*pādixšāy*) by the men,

(3) *mardān ī *Zāzā nām Dērā pus ham tasūg ī Dēl ī Dēlān az *Asp-gurd deh zan an *Asp-gurd deh mānēd ō man guft kū mardān ī Zadōy nām*

(3) (that is) the men called **Zāzā*, son of *Dērā*, (from) the same quarter of *Dēl ī Dēlān*, from the village of **Asp-gurd*: the woman, (who) dwells in the (same) village of **Asp-gurd*, said to me: "(Of) the men called *Zādōy*,

(4) *būd Aštād pus būd az ān *Asp-gurd deh būd man pidar-brād būd duxtag any ōy Zādōy xwēš būd ud ān Zādōy xīndag*

(4) son of *Aštād*, from the village of **Asp-gurd*: he (= *Zādōy)* was my paternal uncle *(pidar-brād* 'brother of my father'). The late *Zādōy* had another daughter of his own (*xwēš būd*). And that *Zādōy* was ill;

(5) *būd Zādōy saxt Zādōy handarz nē kard ka ān baxt šawed zan ud frazand ud ham-duxtag nē būd duxtag ī ōy Zādōy xwēš būd*

(5) (when) *Zādōy* (was) strong, *Zādōy* made no last will (*handarz*). When that fortune befalls him (= when he dies) and he has no wife and child, nor a daughter from the same line (*ham-duxtag*), (and that) daughter who is *Zādōy*'s own,

(6) *andar pasīh ka Zādōy ān baxt šawēd pad ēw stŭ̆rīh bowandag nē būd kas pad stŭ̆rīh ī Zādōy sāxtan ī duxtag ī pad*

(6) afterwards, when *Zādōy*'s fortune befalls him (= when he dies), is not satisfactory (*bowandag nē būd*) for (undertaking) a 'substitute succession' (*stŭ̆rīh*), (then) someone (is needed) to generate (offspring) in the *stŭ̆rīh* of *Zādōy*; a daughter (*duxtag*) who (is) from

2 Weber 2020a, pp. 176–181; Macuch 2020b, pp. 199–209.

(7) *dūdag ī Zādōy dārišn man andar nē ēstād ud andar nē ēstēd ud paywand ī pad xwēšāwandīh ī ō dūdag ī Zādōy andar-iz ān ēw ka*

(7) the family (*dūdag*) of *Zādōy* should hold it (= his *stū̆rīh*). I (= *Pidarōš*) have not undertaken (a request/complaint) (*andar nē ēstād*) and shall not undertake (a request/complaint) (*andar nē ēstēd*). But the lineage (*paywand*) who is related (*pad xwēšāwandīh*) to that family (*dūdag*) of *Zādōy* has undertaken (a request) in that one respect: When

(8) *Zādōy ān baxt šawēd man wehsazāgtar būd ud nūn-iz ēn wehsazāgtar ēn čiš man wehsazāgtar kas nēst duxtag ī ōy Zādōy xwēš būd pad*

(8) *Zādōy*'s fortune befalls him (= when he dies), I (= *Pidarōš*) am the most suitable (*wehsazāgtar*) and now too (I am) most suitable (for) this matter (of *stū̆rīh*); no person is more suitable (*wehsazāgtar*) than I am. The daughter, who is the late *Zādōy's* own,

(9) *ān čiyōn-am guft dastwarīh ō dōšīh ī man mad ēstēd ud ō ēwēn sāxtan ud ast ī ēn ahōg-am pad ān čē man guft ka abāz* ~~*xwāst*~~

(9) (and has) an entitlement (*dastwarīh*) to it (= the *stū̆rīh*), as I have stated, has come to support me (*ō dōšīh ī man mad ēstēd*) and to make it legal (*ō ēwēn sāxtan*). And (if) there is a fault in what I have said, when it (= the *stū̆rīh*) is

(10) *xwāst ud wizōst ōwōn čiyōn man guft paydāg bawēd ud agar tō čār sahēd pad ēn čē man guft kū ka abāz xwāst ud wizōst*

(10) requested back and investigated (and) it becomes evident (*paydāg bawēd*) as I have stated, and if it seems to you (*i. e. Windād-Ohrmazd*) to be a proper remedy (*tō čār sahēd*), (then), on the basis of what I have said, that when it has been requested back and investigated and

(11) *ōwōn čiyōn man guft paydāg bawēd abāz xwāh ud wizōy ud čiyōn passazag ud ēdōn framān dah* ∅ *ud ka mardān ī Farroxdēl nām Farroxān pus*

(11) what I have stated becomes evident, request it (= the *stū̆rīh*) back (*abāz xwāh*) and investigate (the case), as it (is) fitting (*čiyōn passazag*), and issue a corresponding order (*ēdōn framān dah*)." ∅ And when the men called *Farroxdēl*, son of *Farroxān*,

(12) *mardān ī Yazdānfarrox nām Yazdānpanāh pus mardān ī Gušnaspōy nām Māhgušnasp pus mardān ī Wazurgummēd nām Wahištwar pus mardān ī Yōdmardān nām Māhgušnasp pus*

(12) the men called *Yazdānfarrox*, son of *Yazdānpanāh*, the men called *Gušnaspōy*, son of *Māhgušnasp*, the men called *Wazurgummēd*, son of *Wahištwar*, the men called *Yōdmardān*, son of *Māhgušnasp*,

(13) *mardān ī Dērā nām Yazdōy pus mardān ī Dādgušnasp nām Dādrāst pus mardān ī Rāstdād nām Wištāsp pus az ān *Asp-gurd deh ud any-iz wēzag ud čašmag ud stēndag*

(13) the men called *Dērā*, son of *Yazdōy*, the men called *Dādgušnasp*, son of *Dādrāst*, the men called *Rāstdād*, son of *Wištāsp* from the village of **Asp-gurd*, and also other chosen (*wēzag*) (dignitaries), the *čašmags* ('renowned ones') and *stēndags* ('upright ones'),

(14) *ī ham čim ī dahigānān ī Dēl ī Dēlān abāg man būd hēnd pad ān čē Pidarōš guft kū ka abāz xwāst ud wizōst ōwōn čiyōn man guft paydāg*

(14) following the same cause of the *dehgāns* of *Dēl ī Dēlān* were with me (= *Windād-Ohrmazd*), (then) regarding the statement of *Pidarōš*, (namely) that 'when it is requested back and investigated, it will be evident (*paydāg bawēd*) that it (is) as I (= *Pidarōš*) have stated',

(15) *bawēd man az xwēšāwandān ud nabānazdistān ī ōy Zādōy ud kē ēwēn saxwan āšnūd. Farroxdēl ud Yazdānfarrox ud Gušnaspōy ⟨ud⟩ Wazurgummēd ud Yōdmardān ud Dērā*

(15) I (= *Windād-Ohrmazd*) heard the statements of the relatives and next-of-kin of the late *Zādōy* and of those legally (affiliated). *Farroxdēl* and *Yazdānfarrox* and *Gušnaspōy* ⟨and⟩ *Wazurgummēd* and *Yōdmardān* and *Dērā*

(16) *ud Dādgušnasp ud Rāstdād ud čašmag ud stēndag ī abāg man būd hēnd pad gōwizār gōwizār abāz xwāst ud wizōst ōwōn čiyōn Pidarōš guft.*

(16) and *Dādgušnasp* and *Rāstdād* and the *čašmags* ('renowned ones') and the *stēndag* ('upright ones'), who were with me, explicitly (and) precisely (*pad gōwizār gōwizar*) requested it (= the *stūrīh*) back (*abāz xwāst*) and investigated (the case) according to the statement of *Pidarōš*.

(17) *Farroxdēl ud Yazdānfarrox ud Gušnaspōy ud Wuzurgummēd ud Yōdmardān ud Dērā ud Dādgušnasp ud Rāstdād ud čašmag ud stēndag ī abāg man būd hēnd pēš man guft (ēwarīh)*

(17) And *Farroxdēl* and *Yazdānfarrox* and *Gušnaspōy* ⟨and⟩ *Wazurgummēd* and *Yōdmardān* and *Dērā* and *Dādgušnasp* and *Rastdād* and the *čašmags* ('renowned ones') and the *stēndags* ('upright ones'), who were with me, made their binding (*ēwarīh*) statements before me

(18) *ud Pidarōš gugāyīh dād. ∅ ud xwēšāwandīh ī Pidarōš ōy Zādōy ud abāgīh ī Pidarōš sāxtan ī duxtag ī pad xwēšāwandīh guftag ī*

(18) and gave testimony for *Pidarōš*. ∅ And the relationship of *Pidarōš* with the late *Zādōy* and the (readiness) to assist (*abāgīh...saxtan*) *Pidarōš* on the part of the daughter, who, as stated, (is) in the relationship

(19) *ōy Zādōy dārišn rāy pad-iz wizōst ī pēš ī man abar āmad paydāg būd* ∅ *ud man az ham ān čim xwāstag ī Pidarōš pad xwēš būd*

(19) of the late *Zādōy*, with regard to possession (*dārišn*) (of *stūrīh* property), came up (*abar āmad*) during the investigation before me (= *Windād-Ohrmazd)* (and it) was evident (*paydāg būd*). ∅ And I (= *Windād-Ohrmazd)* because of the same reasons, gave order *(framān dād*, line 21) that the property (*xwāstag*) that *Pidarōš* declared (to be) in the ownership (*pad xwēš būd*)

(20) *ī ōy Zādōy guft ēw čiyōn Farroxdēl ud Yazdānfarrox ud Gušnaspōy ud Wazurgummēd ud Yōdmardān ud Dērā ud Dādgušnasp ud Rāstdād ud čašmag ud stēndag ī abāg man*

(20) of the late *Zādōy*, as *Farroxdēl* and *Yazdānfarrox* and *Gušnaspōy* ⟨and⟩ *Wazurgummēd* and *Yōdmardān* and *Dērā* and *Dādgušnasp* and *Rāstdād* and the *čašmags* ('renowned ones') and the *stēndag* ('upright ones'), who were with me,

(21) *būd hēnd pad ān ēwēnag guft pad ān dastwarīh pad xwēšāwandīh kardan ud sāxtan rāy Pidarōš framān dād* ∅ *wizīd Pidarōš*

(21) declared it to be in that manner (*pad ān ēwēnag*) in that entitlement (*pad ān dastwarīh*), be transferred to *Pidarōš* for the purpose of producing and generating offspring (*xwēšāwandīh kardan ud sāxtan rāy*). ∅ The chosen *Pidarōš*

(22) *ō man guft zūd-ōm framāyišn nibištan* ∅ *ud im axw Dād-Burz-Mihr ud Windād-Ohrmazd kē kard Farroxdēl-iz Yazdānfarrox ud Gušnaspōy ud Wazurgummēd*

(22) asked me to write the court order (*framāyišn*) immediately. ∅ And these lords *Dād-Burz-Mihr* and *Windād-Ohrmazd*, who issued (the order), as well as *Farroxdēl* and *Yazdānfarrox* and *Gušnaspōy* and *Wazurgummēd*

(23) *ud Yōdmardān ud Dērā ud Dādgušnasp ud Rāstdād muhr abar nihād* ∅
(Vertically:) *dīd* ∅

(23) and *Yōdmardān* and *Dērā* and *Dādgušnasp* and *Rāstdād* placed their seals upon it. ∅
(Vertically:) seen ∅

(24) *ō xwadāy Windād-Xwaršēd ī Parišwārgar rad namāz. Windād-Ohrmazd (tasūg-iz) Dēl ī Dēlān ī abar Taburestān ud dādestān čiyōnīh tasūg ī*

(24) To the lord *Windād-Xwaršēd*, the *rad* of *Parišwārgar*, reverence! (From) *Windād-Ohrmazd*, (the quarter of) *Dēl ī Dēlān*, in *Taburestān* and (in charge of) jurisdiction (*dādestān*) as well as the quarter of

(25) **Sūrīgān ī abar Taburestān ud dādestān čiyōnīh [........] ud dehīhā āgenēn.*

(25) **Sūrīgān*, in *Taburestān* and (in charge of) jurisdiction (*dādestān*) as well as [........] and the villages altogether.

Appendix XV

Tabarestān 20 and 26: Payment Entitlements (*čak*)

These original documents with an edition and extensive philological and contextual commentary have been published in the series *Res Orientales* XXIV and XXVIII (Tab. 20: Weber 2022a; Macuch 2022a); (Tab 26: Weber 2016b; Macuch 2022b).

Tabarestān 20[1]

(Margin vertically:) *az kē-t Kurrag*	(Margin vertically:) From your *Kurrag*
(1) *hazār-anōšayād āzarmīgtom brād Dādēnbōxt*	(1) With thousand-fold immortal remembrance, most honoured brother *Dādēnbōxt*!
(2) *drōd ud harw farroxīh pad xwadāy bawād*	(2) Greetings and every good fortune may there be for (you), Sir!
(3) ∅ *xwadāy az ān ī ātaxš ī ēr-draxt*	(3) ∅ Sir, because of the undergrowth fire
(4) *ud ān xar pad asp a-kard ī ān rust*	(4) and (because of tillage with a) donkey, not with a horse, of that hard ground/fallow land (*rust*)
(5) *ān ī pēš Pērōzohrmazd ī abarmagān-iz*	(5) the (following) has been requested (*xwāst*, line 6) before *Pērōzohrmazd*, (one) of the superiors,
(6) *xwāst ī sāl 103 ō gird-windād ān nāmag* (GṬk')	(6) for the (following) year 103: in order to collect gain (*gird-windād*) according to the document (*nāmag… rāy*, line 8)
(7) *warzīdan ī pad a-ganǰ aspwarz ī xwēš*	(7) for tilling without profit (*pad a-ganǰ*) by ploughing with (his) own horse (*aspwarz ī xwēš*)
(8) *rāy zamīg g(rīw) 10 ō Farroxgušnasp ī dibīr*	(8) 10 *grīw* (of the produce) of the land is given (*dād*, line 9) to *Farroxgušnasp*, the scribe,

1 Weber 2022a, pp. 112–114; Macuch 2022a, pp. 141–143.

(9) *dād kē abāyēd framān dah čak*	(9) who has need (of it) (*kē abāyēd*). Issue the order (*framān dah*)! The *čak* was made (line 11)
(10) *māh Day abar sāl 102 rōz*	(10) month *Day* (10th month) of the year 102 (753/754 CE), day
(11) *Dēn kard*	(11) *Dēn* (24th day)

Tabarestān 26[2]

(1) *māh Hordād abar sāl 107 rōz Dēn garzišn ī (Farroxgušnasp ī dibīr)*	(1) Month *Hordād* (3rd month) in the year 107 (PYE = 758/759 CE), day *Dēn* (24th day). Complaint (*garzišn*) of the (scribe *Farroxgušnasp*),
(2) *Dādgušnasp pus ī az *Harwahišt deh ī pad xānag ī Dēl-Dēlān pad*	(2) son of *Dādgušnasp*, from the village of **Harwahišt* in the house of *Dēl-Dēlān* in
(3) *dar-espās ī yazdānbānag Pariš-wārgar šāh ī pad *Halīg pēš kē xwēškārīhā*	(3) the residence of the King of *Parišwārgar*, protected by the gods, in **Halīg*, who spoke (*guft*, line 4) before the one, who has this area of responsibility (*xwēškārīhā*) (thus):
(4) *guft kū man xwāstag* (NKSYʾ) *ī sazēd s(atēr) ēw az Farroxgušnasp ī dibīr ī Hor(m)izd ī*	(4) "I am taking out a loan (*abām stānēm*, line 5) of money, (a sum) worth one stater, from *Farroxgušnasp*, the scribe of *Hor(m)izd*,
(5) *mard ī az *Asp-gurd deh ī frāz ān xānag abām stānēm šabān-rōz*	(5) a man from the village of **Asp-gurd*, from that house. Day and night,
(6) *tā rōz Rām ī māh Amurdād ī ham sāl 107 čārag ī*	(6) until day *Rām* (21st day) of the month *Amurdād* (5th month) of the same year 107 by means (*čārag*) of
(7) *čak sazišn ān ī andar sāl 106 ō man ān ī frāz ēstēd*	(7) a cheque (*čak*) that is due for the year 106, that will be forwarded to me (*ān ī frāz ēstēd*),
(8) *ān xwāstag* (NKSYʾ) *s(atēr) ēw sazāg ō Farroxgušnasp dahēm ēwēn-tar kunēm*	(8) I will give that money, worth one stater, to *Farroxgušnasp*. I will do more than legally required (*ēwēn-tar kunēm*):
(9) *tāwān-iz arz s(atēr) ēw ō Farroxgušnasp dahēm* ∅ *ēn paymān-nāmag*	(9) I will give as compensation (*tāwān*) the worth of one stater to *Farroxgušnasp*." ∅ This written contract (*paymān-nāmag*)

2 WEBER 2016b, pp. 188–190; MACUCH 2022b, pp. 167–172.

(10) *pad āšnāg guft ī Dēlxwašīh nām-ēw *Dērā pus ī az *Asp-gurd*	(10) has been sealed (*āwišt*, line 11) according to the identification (*pad āšnāg guft*) of *Dēlxwašīh*, son of *Dērā*, from the village (line 11) of **Asp-gurd*
(11) *deh pad muhr ī ham Dādgušnasp āwišt ēwarīh rāy*	(11) with the seal of the same *Dādgušnasp*. To make it legally binding (*ēwarīh rāy*)
(12) *Farrox-[...] muhr abar nihād spār tāg ī harwisp dehbedān frēstādag*	(12) *Farrox-[...]* placed his seal upon it. (By) delegation (*spār*) the rent (*tāg*) of all the landlords (*dehbedān*) (is) dispatched (*frēstādag*).

Appendix XVI

Overview: Capital Crimes (*margarzān*)

A long list of *margarzān* sins with short explanations can be found in the *Patit (ī) pašēmānīh* II, see the extensive discussion in Buyaner 2016, 4.1.14, pp. 111–118, in his edition of all the penitential texts of the *Xorde Avesta*, specifically § 35, pp. 299–335. There is hence no need to repeat the list here. Shorter lists of *margarzān* sins are transmitted in two passages of *Dēnkard* 5 and in the *Pahlavi Riwāyat accompanying the Dādestān ī dēnīg*. The following overview retains the sequence of sins in these texts.

***Dēnkard* 5.9.9–10** (DkD 345.15–20; DkM 442.21–443.4)[1]

dēw-yazagīh	'demon worshipping'
ahlaw-ganīh	'killing a righteous man'
ahlomōγīh	'heresy, apostasy'
kūn-marz	'anal intercourse'
ǰādūgīh	'sorcery, witchcraft'
rāh-dārīh	'brigandage, highway robbery'
zan-⁺rōbīh[2]	'robbing, kidnapping women' (?)
dūdag-apparīh	'robbing the family'
sālārīh appurdārīh	'robbing guardianship'
drō dādwarīh	'(giving) false judgement'
drō-čāšīh	'(giving) false instruction'
stŭ̄r-škenīh	'destroying substitute succession'
dūdag a-sālārēnīdārīh	'causing the family to be without a guardian'
wad-xwāhīh	'malevolence'
zur-gugāyīh	'bearing false witness'
zur-panahīh ī pad margarzān	'wrongly giving refuge to a person who deserves death'
ātaxš ī Wahrām ōzad(an)	'extinguishing a Wahrām fire'

1 Transcription and translation of the whole text: Amouzgar/Tafazzoli 2000, pp. 42–45.

2 DkD (B) 345.16 and DkM 442.3: ⟨lyp'h⟩. Amouzgar/Tafazzoli 2000, p. 42–43, read *zan-*rēbīh* and translate 'le rapt (?) des femmes'. The tentative reading *zan-⁺rōbīh* suggested here is derived from Ir. √**raup* 'to take away, up, rob, *cueillir*' (Cheung 2007, p. 319), MP *rōb*, *rōbag* 'pillage, plundering' (Cheung, *ibid.*); *rōb* 'robbery' (MacKenzie 1971, p. 72). On a possible allusion here to Dahāg, who kidnapped the sisters of Yima, Arənauuācī- and Saŋhauuācī-, see König 2010a, p. 419, fn. 143.

nasā-ǰōyīh	'chewing, devouring dead matter'
nasā ō ātaxš ud āb burdan	'bringing dead matter to fire and water'
a-dādīhā pahrēxtan ī tanīhā ud andar zamīg nigān kardan	'taking care of (dead) bodies in an unlawful manner and burying them in the earth'
a-petītīg marg-puhlīh	'not repenting sins punishable by death'

Dēnkard 5.10.3 (DkD 346.13–15; DkM 443.23–444.5)[3]

framān-spōzīh ī dahibedān ud abārīg an-ērīh	'disobedience to the commands of the rulers and other (types of) insubordination'[4]
abāz stāyīdan ī az weh-dēn ud stāyīdan ī nōg ag-dēnīh	'withholding praise of the Good Religion and praising a new bad religion'
a-dādīhā ōzad ī mardōm	'killing people unlawfully'
kūn-marz	'anal intercourse'
ǰādūgīh	'sorcery, witchcraft'
rāh-dārīh	'brigandage, highway robbery'
nasā-pazīh	'cooking dead matter'[5]

Pahlavi *Riwāyat* accompanying the *Dādestān ī dēnīg* 41.1 (Dhabhar 1913, pp. 122–123)[6]

mard ōzadan	'killing a man'
ǰādūgīh +framūdan[7]	'ordering sorcery, witchcraft'

3 Transcription and translation of the whole text: Amouzgar/Tafazzoli 2000, pp. 46–47; Buyaner 2016, pp. 300–301.

4 Amouzgar/Tafazzoli 2000, p. 47, translate *abārīg an-ērīh* by 'd'autres défauts (appartenant) aux non-iraniens', but it is also possible to understand the word as a derivative of ¹*ēr* 'down, below; low, under' (MacKenzie 1971, p. 30; see also *ēr-tan* 'humble', *ibid.* p. 31). The translation 'insubordination' for *an-ērīh* (lit. 'not being humble, subordinate' instead of 'being non-Iranian') follows Buyaner 2016, p. 300 (fn. 247), who convincingly refers to Dk. 5.9.4 (in which various kinds of insubordination to authorities are called *an-ērīh*) to confirm this interpretation, derived from OI **adari* (Av. *aδairi*) 'under'.

5 Amouzgar/Tafazzoli 2000, p. 47, have a longer list, as they interpret the part following *abarīg margarzān* (DkD 346.15; DkM 444.3–4) as a continuation of the enumeration of *margarzān* sins. However, König 2010, p. 419 (also fn. 145) has shown—in my opinion correctly—that the passage beginning with *puhl marg ud appārīh (ī) hamāg xwāstag* 'the punishment (is) death and loss of the entire property' in fact describes the consequences of committing a *margarzān* sin, an interpretation which corresponds well with the information on capital crimes in the Law-book (see Chapter V, pp. 468–486).

6 Transliteration, transcription and translation of the whole text: Williams 1990, pt. I, pp. 156–157; pt. II, p. 69. See also Buyaner 2016, p. 301 (with divergent readings and interpretations of several terms).

7 According to Dhabhar 1913, p. 122 (and fn. 15), the mss. have: BK: ⟨PL'NWNtn'⟩, the ideogram for *xwastan*, *xwāh-* 'tread, trample; thresh' (MacKenzie 1971, p. 96); MR_1 and J: ⟨plm'nwtn'⟩, presumably a misspelling for *+framūdan*, *framāy-* 'order, command'

nasā be ō āb ud ātaxš burdan	'bringing dead matter to water and fire'
nasā pad wināhgārīh xwārdan	'sinfully eating dead matter'
nasā ī sag nē dīd pad wināhgārīh pad tan-ē ǰumbēnīdan	'sinfully moving dead matter (a corpse) alone which has not been seen by a dog'
nasā nigān kardan pad dah sāl	'burying dead matter (a corpse) for ten years'
kūn-marz	'anal intercourse'
rāh dāštan	'highway robbery, brigandage'
stūr-škenišnīh	'destroying substitute succession'[8]
zan ī kasān stad pad sāl drahnāy	'taking the wife of another for the duration of a year'
ātaxš ī Wahrām ōzadan	'extinguishing a Wahrām fire'
wad-⁺āhang-ē(w)[9]	'one, who (is) malicious'
zur-gugāh[10]	'false witness'
drō-čāš	'false teacher'[11]
⁺nagīrāyīgar[12]	'repudiator (of obligations)'
asrūdār[13]	'who does not recite (religious texts)'

(MacKenzie 1971, p. 32). Williams 1990, pt. II, p. 157, emends the word to **hammōxtan* ⟨'LPWNtn'⟩ and translates *ǰādūgīh *hammōxtan* 'to learn sorcery' *(ibid.* pt. I, p. 69). Buyaner 2016, p. 301, seeks to take both variants into consideration: he reads *⁺xwāstan*, assuming an erroneous use of the ideogram (instead of ⟨BʿYHWNtn⟩ *xwāstan*, *xwāh-* 'seek, want, desire'), but then translates 'ordering sorcery' due to the variant in MR_1 (and J) which 'indicates a contamination with *framān* 'order, command' or with *framūdan* 'to order'' (*ibid*, fn. 256).

8 Williams 1990, pt. II, p. 69: 'to break adoption' is by now completely antiquated, see Chapter II, pp. 169–174, on the institution of *stūrīh*.

9 BK: ⟨wt'hng'⟩; MR_1 and J: ⟨'hw'y⟩ (Dhabhar 1913, p. 123, and fn. 2). Williams 1990, pt. I, p. 157, reads *wad-axwīh* and translates 'bad faith' (*ibid.* pt. II, p. 69). Buyaner 2016, p. 301, reads *wad-⁺āhang-ē* ⟨wt'hnHD⟩ 'malicious (individual)'. In fn. 257 he compares the list of *nomina agentis* beginning with this word to the corresponding list in MHDA 15.10–11, in which indeed the same sequence occurs. However, the first corresponding term is in MHDA 15.10 ⟨wt'hngyh⟩ *wad-āhangīh*, an abstract, not an agent noun, which I translated by 'maliciousness' ('schlechte Gesinnung'; Macuch 1981, p. 37, and 145). His version of the sentence (with an emendation to *wad-⁺āhang-ē* instead of *wad-āhangīh)* nevertheless makes sense in the light of the PRDd passage and the two corresponding text passages have to be assessed together, see Chapter V, pp. 411–422, on criminal intent.

10 Williams 1990, pt. I, p. 157, emends to *zūr-gugāyīh* 'false testimony' *(ibid.*, pt. II, p. 69).

11 Williams 1990, pt. II, p. 69: 'false-teaching'.

12 Following Buyaner 2016, p. 301–302. On the reading of this word see Buyaner 2015 and 2016, §61, pp. 418–422; on the use of *nagīrāy* in a legal context see Macuch 1993, pp. 63–65 (no. 5; read at that time as **nakkīrā*, **nakkīrāyīh).*

13 BK: ⟨wn'slynt'l⟩; MR_1 and J: ⟨'slwt'l⟩. The version in the two latter manuscripts corresponds exactly to the similar list in MHDA 15.10: ⟨'slwt'l⟩ (see fn. 9 above) and should most likely be read *asrūdār*, as Buyaner 2016, pp. 301–302 (see also fn. 259), has already perceived. Williams 1990 (pt. I, pp. 156–157, pt. II, p. 69) has a completely different reading and interpretation of this last part of the text: *ān man wināh ī garāntar (sahēd)* 'And these sins seem to me to be very grave sins'.

Appendix XVII

Sources Cited by the Compiler of the Law-book

The compiler of the Law-book, Farroxmard ī Wahrāmān cites and refers to a large range of sources from which he has excerpted the material for his legal compilation, the *Hazār dādestān*, in several passages of this important text.[1] The following list offers an overview of these sources in their immediate context with references.

The Avesta:[2]

az ***abestāg*** *paydāg* 'it is revealed in the Avesta' MHD 15.1
az wāhmān ***abestāg*** *ōwōn paydāg* 'it is thus revealed in the Avesta of so-and-so' (or: the Avesta of +Wahman) MHD 48.15

Archives:

dīwān *ī mowbedān (ī) Ardaxšēr-Xwarrah* "**register** of the *mowbeds* of Ardaxšēr-Xwarrah" MHDA 40.11
nāmag-niyān *ī ātaxš ī Hurām-Ardaxšēr ī Ardaxšēr-Xwarrah nahang Xabr Hurām-Ardaxšēr deh* '**archive** of the fires of Hurām-Ardaxšēr of the province of Ardaxšēr-Xwarrah, (in) Xabr, village in Huram-Ardaxšēr' MHD 78.12–13

Documents and edicts:

abarmad *ī radān pad xīr ī ādur ī Farrbay* '**disposition** of the *rads* regarding the property of the Farrbay fire'[3] MHD 103.9
ayādgār hampaččēn-ē(w) *pad-iz muhr ī Wehšābuhr ī mowbedān mowbed būd āwišt* '**copy of a memorandum** sealed with the seal of Wehšābuhr who was Chief *mowbed*' MHDA 34.7–8
ayādgār hampaččēn *ī pad muhr (ī) mowbedān mowbed pad gōwišn ī šāhān šāh nibišt* '**copy of a memorandum** sealed with the seal of the Chief *mowbed*, recorded according to the statement of the King of Kings' MHDA 38.7–8

1 On the *Hazār dādestān* see Chapter I, pp. 20–22.
2 Both passages actually refer to the *zand*, see Chapter III, p. 236, fn. 227.
3 On *abarmad* 'record, settlement, disposition, deed' see Macuch 2007b, p. 201.

dib ī pādixšāy kard ud xwēškārīh nāmag ī kār-framān ī šahrīhā 'authorized **edict** and treatise on the competences of the public official (*kār-framān*) of the provinces' MHDA 38.16–17

framān ī Kawād ī Pērōzān '(royal) **edict** of Kawād, son of Pērōz'; ***framān*** *ī Husraw ī Kawādān* '(royal) **edict** of Husraw, son of Kawād' MHD 93.6–7

frawardag hampaččēn *... rāyēnišn ī Zardušt Bīšābuhr mowbed pad xīr ī ātaxš* '**copy of an epistle** ... on the procedure of Zardušt, the *mowbed* of Bīšābuhr, regarding the property of the fire' MHD 93.3–4

abar ***gitt(ag) (/nāmag)***[4] *ī Farroxgyān ī Zarduxštān [būd] ī šahr dādwarān dādwar būd dō-wardān āwišt ēstēd ōwōn nibišt ...* "in the **foundation deed** of Farroxgyān, son of Zardušt, who was *šahr dādwarān dādwar*, that was sealed on both sides, it is written thus ... MHD 110.5–6

pad muhr ī Warangohrmazd ādur ī Ērān-Xwarrah Husraw ī čāšān būd ***gitt(ag) (/nāmag)*** *āwišt ud framān-iz ī Ādurbād pad ōšagān ō* ***gitt(ag) (/nāmag)*** *burd* 'Husraw, who was *čāšān*, sealed with the seal of Warangohrmazd the **foundation deed** (for) the fire of Ērān-Xwarrah and also inserted the disposition (*framān*) of Ādurbād on the occasion of (his) demise into the **foundation deed**.' MHDA 36.10–12

pad ***gitt(ag) (/nāmag)*** *ī Dādgušnasp ī Šahr ī Zādaragān kard ud pad muhr ī Wehšābuhr mowbedān mowbed āwišt pad gōwišn ī Dādgušnasp ōwōn nibišt ...* 'in the **foundation deed**, made by Dādgušnasp from the province/city of Zādaragān and sealed with the seal of the Chief *mowbed* Wehšābuhr, it is written thus ...' MHDA 39.3–5

hampaččēn *... pad gōwišn ī mowbedān mowbed nibišt* '**copy** (of a document) ... recorded according to the statement of the Chief *mowbed*' MHDA 35.11

Records from legal proceedings:

dib ī Gōr dādwar ō Ardaxšēr-Xwarrah mowbed kard '**protocol** transferred by the judge of Gōr to the *mowbed* of Ardaxšēr-Xwarrah' MHD 100.12

čand dādestān kē paydāgīh az ***nibišt āwišt*** *(ī) pēšēnīg* 'several judgements which are evident from earlier **sealed documents**' MHD 77.4

čiyōn(-m) pad ***nibištag***[5] *dīd Māraspand ī rad būd pad tōzišn... be hišt* 'as (I have) seen in the **bill of indictment,** Māraspand, who was *rad*, cancelled the liability' MHD 13.4–5

abar ēn wāzag čiyōn-am pad ***nibištag*** *dīd Wehpanāh-iz ī mowān handarzbed bawēd wizīr hamgōnag kard* 'regarding this statement—as I have seen in the **bill of indictment**—Wehpanāh, who is *mowān handarzbed*, gave a similar verdict.' MHD 59.9–10

4 On this technical term, to be read either as ⟨gtk⟩ *gitt(ag)* or as an ideogram ⟨GTk⟩ *nāmag* 'foundation deed', the name of an official document, often referring of a fire foundation, see Chapter IV, pp. 275–279.

5 On the technical term *nibištag* 'bill of indictment' see Chapter VI, pp. 573–574.

Wahrām az Pusānweh (ī) Āzādmardān be guft kū ***nibištag****-ē(w) az gugāyīh ī zan dō pad mowbedīh ī Staxr ī mowbed kard ēstēd ud mowān handarzbed frāz padīrift* … 'Wahrām reported from Pusānweh ī Āzādmardān that he had made a **bill of indictment** following the (statement) of two women witnesses in his position as *mowbed* of Staxr and the *mowān handarzbed* accepted it.' MHD 98.1–3

pursišn-nāmag-ē(w) *ī sāl 26 (ī) Husraw ī Ohrmazdān rāyēnīd ud andar Ardaxšēr-Xwarrah pad-iz ōstīgānīh ī Māhādur-Frāyzarduxšt ī Ohrmazd-Ardaxšēr mowbed nāmag pad-iš pad sāxt ud andar Gōr ī Ardaxšēr-Xwarrah pad-iz muhr (ī) Ohrmazd-Ardaxšēr mowbed pad kār-framān dāštan āwišt* 'a **transcript of interrogation** made in the year 26 of Husraw, son of Ohrmazd: in Ardaxšēr-Xwarrah under (the administration of) the *ōstīgān* Māhādur-Frāyzarduxšt, the *mowbed* of Ohrmazd-Ardaxšēr, the document was made and sealed in Gōr of Ardaxšēr-Xwarrah with the 'seal for exercising command' of the *mowbed* of Ohrmazd-Ardaxšēr'[6] MHD 100.7–10

wizīr *ī radān ud (kār)framānān abar Ardaxšēr-Xwarrah nahang* '**verdict** of the *rads* and *(kār)framāns* of the province of Ardaxšēr-Xwarrah'[7] MHD 78.2–3

Burzag ī Ardaxšēr-Xwarrah mowbed būd ***wizīr*** *kard* 'Burzag, who was *mowbed* of Ardaxšēr-Xwarrah, gave the **verdict**' MHD 100.4–5

*Burzag ī Ardaxšēr-Xwarrah mowbed būd pad ēn …*___wizīr___ 'Burzag, who was *mowbed* of Ardaxšēr-Xwarrah, (gave) the following … **verdict**' MHDA 37.9–11

Māraspand ī rad būd ***(wizī)r*** *kard* 'Māraspand, who was *rad*, gave the **verdict**' MHDA 36.1

Wādayyār ***wizīr*** *kard Dādfarrox ī Dādohrmazd mowan handarzbed būd* 'Wādayyār gave the **verdict** (when) Dādfarrox ī Dādohrmazd was *mowān handarzbed*' MHDA 37.11–12

Testaments:

abar ***handarz*** *ī ham Wehšābuhr pad gōwišn ī Wehšābuhr nibišt ēstēd* … 'in the **testament** of the same Wehšābuhr was written according to the statement of Wehšābuhr …' MHDA 35.14–15

abar ***handarz*** *ī Ādurbād ī Zarduxštān … ī mowbedan mowbed būd pad gōwišn ī Ādurbād ātaxš rāy nibišt* … 'in the **testament** of Ādurbād ī Zarduxštān … who was Chief *mowbed*, was written according to the statement of Ādurbād regarding the fire …' MHDA 36.3–4

6 On the *muhr ī pad kār-framān dāštan* 'seal for exercising command' see Chapter IV, pp. 293–296.

7 With explicit reference to the time of King Husraw, son of Kawād (*abar ōy bay Husraw ī Kawādān*).

Legal treatises and commentaries:

pad ***čāštag*** *ī Abarag* 'in the **Commentary (Doctrine)** of Abarag' MHD 22.5; 52.3

pad ***čāštag*** *ī Mēdōmāh* 'in the **Commentary (Doctrine)** of Mēdōmāh' MHD 22.5; 51.9; 52.3

pad (/abar) ***dādestān-nāmag*** *ōwōn nibišt (ēstēd)* ... 'in the ***Dādestān-nāmag***[8] it is written thus ...' MHD 11.2; 36.2; 44.14; 62.10

az ***dādestān-nāmag*** *ī pad Gurgān kardag sahist kū paydāg* ... 'from the ***Dādestān-nāmag*** that is (used) in legal practice in Gurgān, it seems evident that...' MHD 44.3

pursišn *(ī) Dādfarrox ī Ādurzandān pad* ***pursišn*** *ī Dādfarrox ōwōn nibišt* ... '***Pursišn*** of Dādfarrox ī Ādurzandān: in the **Questions** of Dādfarrox it is written thus ...' MHD 4.15

ōwōn čiyōn abar ***xwēškārīh nāmag*** *ī mowbedān nibišt* ... 'as it is recorded in the **Treatise on the competences** of the *mowbeds* ...' MHD 26.25

xwēškārīh nāmag *ī kār-framān ī šahrīhā* '**Treatise on the competences** of the public official (*kār-framān*) of the provinces' MHDA 38.16–17

čiyōn pad ***mustbahrnāmag*** *nibišt ēstēd* 'as it is recorded in the ***Mustbahrnāmag*** ...'[9] MHDA 5.11

Legal schools:

Abarīg *gōwēnd* ... '**adherents of** (the school of) **Abarīg** declare ...' MHD 50.13

Mēdōmāhīg *ēn wāzag pad uskārišn gōwēnd* '**adherents of** (the school of) **Mēdōmāh** put this statement up for discussion ...' MHD 17.14

Mēdōmāhīg *gōwēnd kū Mēdōmāh guft kū* ... '**adherents of** (the school of) **Mēdōmāh** declare that Mēdōmāh said ...' MHD 50.15

Mēdōmāhīgān *hamgōnag gōwēnd* '**adherents of** (the school of) **Mēdōmāh** declare the same ...' MHD 52.15

Pēšagsīr *gōwēnd* '**adherents of** (the school of) **Pēšagsīr** declare ...' MHD 61.9

8 The treatise called *Dādestān-nāmag* is not described, but the reference to 'legal practice' (*kardag*) in MHD 44.3 makes it rather likely that it was a collection of legal decisions or case studies. Due to the large range of meanings of *dādestān* ('law court, lawsuit, legal proceedings, verdict, judicial decision, jurisdiction, judiciary, judgement, law, justice', see Introduction, pp. 4–6), it is impossible to decide what kind of work is meant without further explanations.

9 There are no further explanations of the *mustbahrnāmag*, lit. 'treatise on the portioning of violence', but as the title is attested in a chapter on the insubordination (*a-tarsagāhīh*) of dependant persons (women, children, slaves), it could refer to a collection of instructions on how to punish insubordination or to some kind of penal code.

Legal practice in specific regions:

Ardaxšēr-Xwarrah and **Darabgird** (regarding *stūrīh*) MHD 42.7
Darabgird (on the entitlement of the wife to inherit, when the status of a *čagar*-wife is changed into that of a *pādixšāy*-wife) MHD 70.12

Legal authorities:

Abarag jurisconsult; author of a legal commentary (*čāštag*); founder of a legal school MHD 5.14; 22.5; 52.3; MHDA 30.3
Ādurbād ī Mardbūdān donor of a fire foundation; (official function?) MHDA 36.6,7,8,11
Ādurbād ī Zarduxštān *mowbedān mowbed* under Yazdegird I (?) (399–421 CE) MHDA 36.3–4; 38.10
Ādurbōzēd *mowbedān mowbed* under Yazdegird I (?) (399–421 CE) MHDA 38.10
Ādurfrazgar *mowān handarzbed* (?) MHD 57.3
Ādurohrmazd jurisconsult, commentator MHD 9.1
Anōšzād legal official; representative of a legal venue in the canton (*tasūg*) of Xūnābagān[10] MHD 100.15
Bōzišn jurisconsult, commentator MHD 40.3; 42.13; 49.10; 76.8
Burzag *mowbed* in Ardaxšēr-Xwarrah MHD 97.6; 100.4; MHDA 37.9
Dādfarrox *mowān handarzbed* (probably identical with Dādfarrox ī Dādohrmazdān in MHDA 37.11) MHDA 15.14–15
Dādfarrox jurisconsult, commentator MHD 29.6; 35.9; 101.5
Dādfarrox ī Ādurzandān jurisconsult, commentator MHDA 4.15; 5.2
Dādfarrox ī Dādohrmazdān *mowān handarzbed* (probably identical with Dādfarrox in MHDA 15.14–15) MHDA 37.11
Dādfarrox ī Farroxzurwān jurisconsult, commentator MHDA 1.8–12; 12.3
Dādfarrox ī Mardbūdān jurisconsult, commentator MHD 72.8
Dādfarrox ī Sīrgān jurisconsult, commentator MHDA 16.15–17
Dādgušnasp ī Šahr ī Zādaragān 'Dādgušnasp from the province/city of Zādaragān'; donor of a foundation; (legal function?) MHDA 39.3–5
Dibīr jurisconsult, commentator MHD 65.3; MHDA 28.6
Farrhay authority under Yazdegird I (399–421 CE) (?) MHDA 38.10
Farroxgyān (identical with the next person?) MHDA 36.10
Farroxgyān ī Zarduxštān *šahr dādwarān dādwar* 'Chief judge of the State' MHD 110.5
Farroxmard ī Wahrāmān compiler of the *Hazār dādestān* MHD 80.17
Farroxzurwān jurisconsult, commentator MHD 2.15; 14.5; MHDA 29.12
Frāyzarduxšt *mowbed* in Ohrmazd Ardaxšēr MHD 100.8
Hudād authority under Yazdegird I (399–421 CE) (?) MHDA 38.10

10 On this representative and the terminology in this passage see Chapter VI, p. 514, fn. 65.

Juwān-ǰam jurisconsult, commentator MHD 89.8; MHDA 10.5; 11.16; 12.14; 31.9; 36.2
Māhādur *ōstīgān* in Ardaxšēr-Xwarrah MHD 100.8
Māhādur-Frāy-Gušnasp *mowbed* in Ardaxšēr-Xwarrah MHD 95.17; 96.1; 99.7
Māhdād-Gušnasp ī Yazdān-afzūd jurisconsult, commentator MHD 70.9–10
Māhweh jurisconsult, commentator MHDA 31.10
Māhwindād jurisconsult, commentator MHD 24.4; 59.1
Māhwindād ī Wuzurgbūdān jurisconsult, commentator MHD 65.14
Manuščihr jurisconsult, commentator MHD 24.2
Māraspand *rad* MHDA 36.1; 39.7
Mardag jurisconsult, commentator MHD 4.7; 12.4; 19.15; 41.8; 71.4; 72.3
Mardag Pusānweh jurisconsult, commentator MHD 31.7; 42.7
Mardbūd *mowbedān mowbed* under Pērōz (459–484 CE) MHDA 39.16
Mēdōmāh jurisconsult; author of a legal commentary (*čāštag*); founder of a legal school MHD 5.13; 22.5; 50.15; 51.9; 52.3, 4, 9
Menōymardān jurisconsult, commentator MHD 13.2
Mihr-Narseh *wuzurg framādār* under Yazdegird I (399–421 CE), Wahrām V (421–439 CE) and Yazdegird II (439–457 CE) MHDA 35.17; 39.11; 40.3
Nēw-Gušnasp jurisconsult, commentator MHDA 31.9
Pērōz jurisconsult, commentator MHD 95.9; MHDA 32.16; 36.5
Pērōz ī Weh-Ohrmazdān jurisconsult, commentator MHD 108.10
Pēšagsīr jurisconsult; author of a legal commentary (*čāštag*); founder of a legal school MHD 42.17; 50.17; 52.17; MHDA 11.10; 26.11
Pusānūz jurisconsult, commentator MHD 4.7, 8
Pusānweh jurisconsult, commentator MHD 41.5; 51.3; 94.3; 95.10, 12, 15; MHDA 7.11
Pusānweh ī Āzādmardān jurisconsult, commentator MHD 5.11; 14.4, 6; 19.4; 43.6; 52.12; 56.17; 90.15; 95.9, 10, 12, 15; 98.1; 99.3, 8; 100.1; MHDA 4.2; 16.14; 29.14, 17
Pusānweh ī Burzādurfarrbay(ān) jurisconsult, commentator MHD 16.13; 28.3; 69.11; 72.6; 100.16; 108.10; MHDA 40.12
Rādohrmazd jurisconsult, commentator MHD 20.10; 32.1; 42.9; 49.15; 64.9; 67.8; 69.13; 70.13, 16; MHDA 4.4; 9.5
Siyāwaxš jurisconsult, commentator MHD 20.9, 11; 31.17; 38.7–9, 16; 41.5; 54.10; 67.8; 69.16; 89.6; 96.3, 9, 10, 13, 16; 101.5; MHDA 11.10
Sōšāns jurisconsult, commentator MHD 1.3; 21.8
Wādayyār jurisconsult, commentator MHDA 37.11
Wahrām jurisconsult, commentator MHD 4.17; 6.2,14; 7.11; 8.8; 17.13; 20.7; 21.14; 31.8; 51.15; 57.3; 61.16; 64.14; 65.9,12,17; 70.4; 98.1,4; MHDA 3.16; 9.5; 10.13; 11.12; 16.14; 19.1, 5; 29.16
Wahrāmšād jurisconsult, commentator MHD 69.13; MHDA 9.5; 11.16
Warangohrmazd jurisconsult, commentator MHDA 30.2

Wayayyār jurisconsult, commentator MHD 5.4; 16.14; 23.1; 27.7; 31.4; 42.2, 6, 12; 45.1; 46.4; 47.7; 54.2; 62.2–4; MHDA 7.8; 18.4
Wehohrmazd jurisconsult, commentator MHD 2.15; 41.5; 50.16; MHDA 10.4; 29.9, 17; 30.2
Wehpanāh *mowān handarzbed* MHD 59.10
Wehšābuhr *mowbedān mowbed* under Husraw I (531–579) MHDA 14.13; 34.7; 36.17
Xwadāybūd ī Dibīr jurisconsult, commentator MHD 2.5
Žāmāsp jurisconsult, commentator MHD 32.1
Zarduxšt *mowbed* in Bīšābuhr MHD 93.4
Zurwāndād jurisconsult, commentator MHD 11.5; 15.7; 28.16; 97.6; 98.3; 99.7; MHDA 10.5
Zurwāndād ī Juwān-ǰam jurisconsult, commentator MHD 36.9

Glossary of Legal Terms and Phrases

The glossary is restricted to the legal terms and phrases discussed in the present study. References call attention to the main passages; for a list of all references see Index. Relevant etymological discussions of technical terms are found in the body of this work. All entries are conventionally alphabetized ignoring accents and diacritics (*e. g.*, š is treated like s).

āb abzūdan 'to increase the water'; to expand the construction of a water channel (*ǰōy-kahas*) 251
a-bādixšāyīhā without authorization, without entitlement 458, 460, 565–566, 568
  a-bādixšāyīhā dāštan to hold without authorization; *a-bādixšāyīhā tō dārē* 'you hold it without authorization' 460
  a-bādixšāyīhā gādan to cohabit without authorization; to practice sexual intercourse with someone else's wife without the explicit authorization of the husband 458, 460
abāg helper, accomplice, accessory (of a thief); *čē tan ud ēwēnag ī abāg* 'who is the principal perpetrator (= thief) and what kind of accomplice does he have?' 439, 441, 445, 450
abāg xōn ⁺xwēdāg mālūn 'besmeared all over with blood (and) moisture'; description of an injury liable to punishment 427, 684
abām loan, debt, credit 316–319
  see also ***abāmdān*** and ***tōzišn***
  abām abaz dādan to pay back a loan; to repay a debt 318
  abām az ādurān ud ātaxšān loan from (the property of) the fires 366–367
  abām būd paydāg kardan to prove the existence of a debt; obligation of a litigant to provide evidence that a loan had been taken out 323, 362, 364
  abām dādan to give/pay (back) a loan 318, 346
  abām-dādār lender, moneylender, creditor (lit. 'loan giver') 318
  abām hišt release from debt; debt relief 319
  abām hištan to release from debt, grant a debt relief, remit/cancel a debt; *abām ast ī hištan* 'to cancel a part of a debt' 366–367
  abām ī pidarān liabilities of the forefathers/parents 308, 318–319
    see also ***tōzišn ī pidarān***
  abām stadan to take out a loan 318
  abām tōxtan to repay a debt 318
  abam tōzišnīh payment of a debt 308, 318
    see also ***tōzisn***
  abām ud tōzišn debt and liability 308, 310, 318
  abām xwastan to demand (payment of) a debt 319
  abām-xwēš lender, creditor (lit. 'loan-owner') 318

abāmdān loan, debt (lit. 'containing, holding, involving, comprising a loan'); possibly a (money) loan granted in exchange for some kind of real security, a pawn or pledge (*graw*) 316–320
abāmdān ī ēwar legally binding loan 318
abāmdān wizīr loan contract, document of debt (= *wizīr ī abāmdān)* 317–318
see also ***xwāstag ī abāmdān***
abāmōmand borrower, debtor 318
a-bar non-profitable (property); property that does not produce income 223–224, 624
abarmad ⟨'plmt'; MDMmt'⟩ official document containing an order, disposition, injunction or decree which is sanctioned and sealed by high religious authorities (*pahlom dēn burdārān*), judges (*dādwarān*) or other legal/religious dignitaries (*radān*); *abarmad kardan* to draw an order/decree 273–275
abarmānd total (unpartitioned) patrimonial/residuary estate, encompassing several distinct categories of property (see below); the complete mass of a family's collective property, consisting of different elements transferred from the forefathers to the present generation as a unity, to be handed down as an unpartitioned whole to the heirs as shareholders (*hambāy*) after the payment of debts, liabilities and other expenses. The categories constituting the *abarmānd* of a family/lineage consist of property (1) *pad xwāstagdārīh* 'in (hereditary) possession'; (2) *pad xwēšīh* 'in ownership'; (3) *pad stūrīh* 'in trust; for substitute succession'; (4) *pad ruwān / ruwān rāy* 'for the soul' and *pad ruwān dāštan* 'for keeping the soul' 202–206
abarmānd ī pidar/pidarān total (patrimonial/residuary) estate of the father/forefathers; the estate of a lineage consisting of several different categories (*see* under ***abarmānd)***, passed down from the ancestors as an unpartitioned whole
see also ***xwāstag ī pidar/pidarān*** 'estate of the father/ancestors' 192–193
abarmānd-xwāstagdār heir of the total (patrimonial/residuary) estate 206–210
see also ***xwāstagdār***
abar māndan to remain, be left (as inheritance/residue); *az pidarān abar mānd* 'left (as inheritance/residue) from the forefathers; inherited from the ancestors' 203
abārōn-marzišnīh unlawful sexual intercourse 452, 454
abar tan ī xwēš sālār 'guardian over one's own person'; woman who is her own guardian and not subject to the *manus* of a man 116, 546–547
abasēg ī pidarān* payment, rent, pension of the parents 513 (fn. 64)
abasēgōmand* recipient of a payment; person who receives payment in kind for services to the crown 513
abaxšīh ī gōwišnīg repentance by speech, confessing the sin; second step in redeeming a sin 413
a-baxt undivided, not partitioned; in the context of succession the designation of an 'ideal' (= unpartitioned) share in the inheritance 229, 234, 305
abāyēd uskārdan '(the matter) has to be reflected upon'; phrase referring to problematic legal issues that are not finally resolved, but discussed controversially among jurisconsults 376, 388
abāz back, again, re- (prev.)
abāz abespārdan to consign back, return, release; in the context of credit law: action of the creditor (pledgee), who releases the pledged person/surety from debt bondage 335, 352, 356

abāz padīriftan to take back, redeem; in the context of credit law: action of the debtor (pledgor), who redeems the pledged person/surety from debt bondage352, 356
abāz wisē kardan to dispatch back, to send back 438
abāz zaxm a wound in retribution; retaliation 411
abē-āhōgīhā unspoilt 140
abēčim groundless; without proof 252
see also **čim ud bōzišn**
abē-dastwarīhā without entitlement, unauthorized (= *a-dastwarīhā*; *nē dastwarīhā*) 149–150
abēmustīh uncomplaining, content, satisfied 438, 524–526
abēmust/abēmustīh kardan to make (someone) uncomplaining; to satisfy, make content; specifically: to satisfy a claimant by a decision that will not lead to an appeal in the next instance 524–525
see also **ō abēmustīh madan**; **ō abēmustīh rasīdan**
abē-nām nameless; a *paterfamilias* who leaves no son as his heir and successor becomes 'nameless' 130, 174
abēr garān niyāzīhā extreme poverty and want 380
abēsaxwan without claim (lit. 'without word/speech'); in the formula *az … abēsaxwan būdan* 'to renounce, waive a claim (to something)'. Bactrian αβησαχοανο, αβοσαχοανο, αβσαχοανο 245, 611–614
***abēsaxwan ud abēwizār** 'without claim and without compensation'; formulaic phrase in a document or contract, attested in Bactrian αβησαχοανο οδο αβηαοισαρο, constituting a guarantee that the contractual partner employing this legal formula will neither lodge a claim against his contractual partner, nor ask him for any kind of payment or compensation in this matter in the future 613–614
abēsaxwanīh waiver, renunciation (of a claim); the act of abandoning a claim or refraining from asserting a claim or exercising a right. Syr. translation *mbarayūṯā* 'renunciation, avoidance' 245, 611–612
abespārdan to commit, entrust, consign, deliver (to); in the context of credit law: the actual transfer of the principal debtor or pledged person to the creditor 335, 352–353
abestāg Avesta, referring not to the Old Iranian original text, but to its Pahlavi translation-cum-exegesis (*zand*) 236 (fn. 227)
ābestan pregnant woman 446
***abēwizār** without compensation (< *abē* + *wizār* 'without payment'; *see* *wizārdan*, *wizār-*). Bactrian αβηαοισαρο, αβοισαρο 613–614
abēzār without expedient 347
a-bōy unconscious (person); person who cannot be held responsible for his actions 464
a-bōyīh unconsciousness; *wināh … andar a-bōyīh* 'unintentional/unconscious offence'; *daxšag ī a-bōyīh* 'symptoms of unconsciousness' 412, 415, 570
aburnāy minor, underage, immature; as opposed to *purnāy* 103, 126, 546
abzōn (total) income, surplus, growth, increase; specifically the income of a *pādixšāy* wife, consisting of five elements: (1) *rōzīg* (daily) ration, (2) *padēxīh* extra allocation (lit. 'prosperity'), (3) *kār-wahāg* work-based/related income (lit. 'work-value'), (4) *paymōzan* clothing, (5) *abzūd* surplus 252–253
abzōn bahr share of the income 251

abzūd surplus; designation of one type of income among five categories of income due to a *pādixšāy*-wife (*see* ***abzōn***) 253

a-čār/a-čārag without means, poor, destitute 112, 380

a-dādestānīhā unlawfully, illegitimately 405–406

a-dādīhā unlawfully, illegitimately 91–92, 463

ādānīh solvency; financial capability 566

a-dastwar guftan to make a statement (in court) without an *auctor* (legal predecessor) 568

a-dastwarīhā without entitlement, unauthorized (= *nē dastwarīhā*; *abē-dastwarīhā*) 383

ādehīg inhabitant of the realm, citizen; as opposed to ***uzdehīg*** foreigner 114–115

adēn entry (in a register) 505

ādur (sacred) fire 623

ādurān ātaxšān (sacred) fires; collective designation for consecrated fires and fire foundations 220, 225

ādurān-bandag servant of the fires; a free individual, not necessarily a priest, but a layperson, often of high social standing engaged in the service of a sacred fire (not to be confused with *anšahrīg ī ātaxš* slave of the fire) 105, 107

see also ***ātaxš-bandag***

adwadād lit. 'act of placing on the way, leaving on the road' (< Av. *aδβadāitī-*; or possible variant: **aδβadāta-* 'placed in the road, left on the way'); technical term for four types of offences involving abandonment: (1) deserting a person, animal or sacred fire, for whom one has legal responsibility; (2) withholding nourishment/fuel from a person/animal/fire under guardianship; (3) inability to maintain a person/animal/fire under guardianship due to food shortage (a state of emergency; *see* ***adwadād mad ēstēd***); (4) withdrawing spiritual nourishment from a pupil willing to learn, refusing to give religious instruction 74–76, 463–468

adwadād kardan to commit an *adwadād* offence 464

adwadād mad ēstēd 'affected by an *adwadād* (= lack of food, famine)'; formulaic phrase denoting a state of emergency caused by food shortage 465, 468

āgāhīhā consciously, in full consciousness 380

ag-dēn evil religion; adherent of an evil religion; infidel 118–119, 526–528

ag-dēnīg dād law of an evil religion 114

āgenēn dārišn joint possession with equal shares 249–250

āgenēn hamwindišn persons having joint income with exactly equal shares 251–252

āgenēn xwēš joint owner(ship) with exactly equal shares; shareholder(ship) in a *societas* of owners with equivalent shares (contrasted with *ǰud ǰud xwēš* '[having] separate ownership') 247–249

āgraw/āgrawīh hypothec; mortgage of the substance (*bun*) of a specified property of the debtor (mortgagor) as security for a loan entitling the creditor (mortgagee) to take possession in the event of a default; comparable to the Roman *hypotheca* 336–342

āgraw kardan to hypothecate the substance (*bun*) of property 229

āgrift (Av. *āgərəpta-*, lit. 'seizure') degree of sin in Zoroastrian law 468–471

a-gugāy guftan to make a statement (in court) without (bringing) a witness 567–568

āhang crop yields 346–348

āhanǰišn extracting, drawing out, pulling up (penalty for a corresponding injury) 429
ahlawdād righteous/pious gift, charitable deed 220, 222
ahlomōγīh heresy; capital crime (*margarzān*) prosecuted by the State 492–494
a-hunsandīh dissatisfaction, disagreement, dissent; *a-hunsandīh ī pad wizīr* 'dissatisfaction with the verdict'; in the context of legal proceedings rejection of the verdict of the judge by a litigant 522–523
āmārgar calculator, accountant; a treasurer or fiscal administrator appointed by the king 512–514
ān that, he (dem.pron.)
ān ī tō abāyēd (or: *ān ī tō andar abāyēd*), 'that which you have need of', formulaic words spoken by a person offering a transaction (the transferor/offeror) to the potential recipient (offeree); variants: *ān ī tō kāmēd*; *ān ī tō passandē*; *ān ī tō sahēd* 303–305
ān ī tō kāmēd 'that which you desire', formulaic words spoken by the offeror (transferor) offering a transaction to the potential recipient (offeree); variants *see* ***ān ī tō abāyēd*** 303, 305
ān ī tō passandē 'that which you approve of', formulaic words spoken by the offeror (transferor) offering a transaction to the potential recipient (offeree); variants *see* ***ān ī tō abāyēd*** 303, 305
ān ī tō sahēd 'that which you approve of', formulaic words spoken by the offeror (transferor) offering a transaction to the potential recipient (offeree); variants *see* ***ān ī tō abāyēd*** 303, 305
ān kē abām be dād lender, creditor (lit. '[person] who granted the loan') 318
ān kē abām stad/stānēd borrower, debtor (lit. '[person] who took/takes out a loan') 318
an-āšnawāg ī a-wēnag-iz 'who is both deaf and blind'; disabled person who cannot take legal action 410
andar in, within, among (prep., prev.)
andar abāyēd 'it is necessary', formulaic words spoken by the recipient of a transaction accepting the offer of the transferor; variants: *dōšīd* 'it is sanctioned'; *kāmag dōšīd* 'the will (of the transferor/offeror) is sanctioned'; opposite: *andar nē abāyēd* 'it is not necessary; there is no need' 303, 305
andar dūdag zād 'born in the family'; child generated within the lineage in one of the institutions of intermediary or substitute succession (*ayōgēnīh*; *stūrīh*) 176
andar nē abāyēd 'it is not necessary; there is no need', formulaic statement of the recipient of a transaction refusing the offer of the transferor 304–305
andar nimūd threatening; criminal act, categorized as *zanišn* 407, 411, 423
an-ēr non-Iranian; foreigner, non Zoroastrian; as opposed to *ēr* 'Iranian, Zoroastrian' 102–103, 115–116
an-ērīg xēm un Iranian character; temperament, mentality of a non-Iranian 114
anšahrīg 'outlander, foreigner'; slave; person with no legal capacity or with limited legal capacity (if partly manumitted) working in three major areas: (1) household, (2) agriculture (as *glebae adscripti*, persons 'bound to the soil'); (3) fire foundations 104–110, 126, 599
anšahrīg ī ātaxš slave of the fire; fire-slave; person with no legal capacity, working on the property dedicated to a fire foundation (not to be confused with

ātaxš-bandag or *ādurān-bandag)*; *ʿbdʾ d-nwrʾ* 'slaves/servants of the fire' in the Babylonian Talmud 105, 226, 601–603

anšahrīg pad grawagān slave whose work force is mortgaged 349

a-pahikār-rad '(who does) not dispute before a judge, (who is) not in a judicial dispute'; person who practices self justice and takes the law into his own hands instead of calling on legal instances; opposite: *pahikār-rad* 404–411

a-pahikār-radīh non-judicial dispute; private feud; opposite: *pahikār-radīh* 405, 411

apēdag lost (prominently of animals), also referring to a pledge or pawn, *graw apēdag bawēd* 'the pledge is lost' 316 (fn. 254), 329

appār taken away, removed, lost; *xwāstag ō radān appār* 'the thing (is) lost to the *radān*' 328–329, 378

appar/apparag robber; person who steals manifestly (*āškārag* 'openly'), in public using force or threatening to use force; often used in a figurative sense to designate any offence committed openly, *see* ***apparīh***; Syriac rendering: *ḥāṭōpā* 313–314, 434–439

apparīh robbery; appropriation of property in public manifestly, using force or threatening to use force; transposed to other offences committed openly, *e.g.* the visible breach of a contract (*mihrōdrujīh*) which had been concluded in the presence of witnesses 67–68, 382, 434–439, 450

see also ***duz(d)īh***

appar-kām criminal intent/will of the robber; mental element (*mens rea*) of the crime 413, 422, 424

appar-menišnīgīh criminal intent of the robber; mental element (*mens rea*) of the crime 413–414, 422, 424, 451

see also ***appar-kām***

appurdan to rob; to appropriate something openly, manifestly, using force 436

a-rāst-gōwišnīh (making a) false statement 574

ardīg tazišnīh 'engaging in conflict'; (1) a conflict carried out by the means of various aggressive or harmful acts (*e.g.* wounding, pursuing, threatening, practising magic, among others); (2) a duel between equal opponents following specific rules in the presence of a legal authority 424–425, 433

arduš (Av. *arəduš-*, lit. 'blow, injury') degree of sin in Zoroastrian law 472–473

arteštār (Av. *raθaēštā-*) warrior; *arteštārān* '(estate of) warriors' (Arab translation *al-muqātila*) 95, 98

arzānīg worthy, valuable; person on the highest level in the hierarchy of those deserving sustenance; opposite: *niyuruzd* 464

a-sālār without guardian 125

āsānīh abatement, reduction, lowering of the price/rent 370–372

āškārag manifestly, openly (referring to the offence of the robber, who steals openly, using force) 446, 450, 618

āšnāgīh ī šahr 'being known in the land'; notoriety, bad reputation, negative trait of a delinquent that is noted in the *pursišn-nāmag* 575, 595

+a-šnās(ag)īh 'not recognizing'; amnesia caused by an injury 426, 433

****āšnawāg ī nē wēnag*** 'who can hear, but not see'; disabled person who can hear, but is blind, and can take legal action by presenting his case orally, without demonstrating (*gōwišnīg ī nē nimāyišnīg*) 410

āšnawāg ī wēnag 'who can hear and see'; litigant who presents his case by 'speaking and demonstrating' (*gōwišnīg nimāyišnīg*) 410

āsn-xrad innate wisdom 8

asp aštar (Av. *aspahe aštrā-*) horsewhip, thong; instrument of punishment 477, 483

āspōzišn thrusting, shoving, pushing (penalty for a corresponding injury) 429

āsrōn priest (Av. *aϑauruuan-*); *āsrōnān* '(estate of) priests' (Pers. translation *aṣḥāb-i dīn*) 95, 98, 511

āsūd kardan 'to make easier', to adjust 371–372

aswār horseman, knight, equestrian 209, 513

aswār-nibēg horseman's document; legal certificate recording a grant bestowed on an *aswār* 'equestrian, horseman, knight', by the king for military services 271, 285
 see also ***nibēg*** and ***dast-nibēg***

a-tarsag disobedient, unruly; insubordinate behaviour of a person under guardianship 123

a-tarsagāhīh disobedience; undutiful, insubordinate behaviour of persons under guardianship (underage children, women, slaves) 123–124, 138

ātaxš (sacred) fire 225–228, 250, 277, 464
 ātaxš-bandag servant of the fire; a free individual, often of high social standing, not necessarily a priest, engaged in the service of a sacred fire (not to be confused with *anšahrīg ī ātaxš*) 105
 see also ***ādurān-bandag*** and ***bandag ī ātaxš***
 ātaxš hamār *dibīrag 'register of the accounts of fire foundations'; one of the main *dīwāns* of the Sasanian State according to al-Ḫwārezmī (Arab. translation: *kitābat ḥusbānāt an-nīrān*) 99, 228, 270
 ātaxš-madār 'fire-comer'; warden of a (sacred) fire 181

ātaxšān (sacred) fires; collective designation for fire foundations 225–228, 366, 586–587
 see also ***ādurān ātaxšān*** and ***xīr ī ātaxš(ān)***

a-tuwān(īg) (1) powerless, legally incapable; (2) insolvent, financially incapable; opposite: *tuwān(īg)* 351

a-tuwānīgīh (1) powerlessness, lack of legal capacity; (2) insolvency, lack of financial capacity 89, 266, 351

a-wāwarīgān invalid, null and void; opposite: *wāwarīgān* 289

a-wāwarīh invalidity, without binding force; opposite: *wāwarīh* 508

āwišt sealed document; document confirmed with a seal imprint 398–399

awōirišt/ōirišt (Av. *auuaoirišta-* lit. 'turning [up, down, away]') degree of sin in Zoroastrian law 471–472

āxur hamār *dibīrag 'register of the accounts of the (royal) stables'; one of the main *dīwāns* of the Sasanian State according to al-Ḫwārezmī (Arab. translation: *kitābat al-iṣṭablāt*) 99

ayādgār memorandum, memoir (1) a separate or additional register of undertakings, often (but not always) based on transactions noted in the documents called *čak* (cheque, payment entitlement) and *pădīrāy* (receipt); (2) record of capital offences in a criminal case to be included in the transcript of interrogation (*pursišn-nāmag*); (3) decree, edict or memorandum of the *mowbedān mowbed* 283–284, 291, 574–575

ayārag register 438

ayārd evaluation, assessment, calculation; *ayārd ī dehgānān* 'evaluation of the farmers/ landlords' 369–370
ayārdan to take measure, evaluate, calculate (land, crop-yields, produce) 372
  see also ***zamīg ayārdan***
ayōgēn/ayōkēn intermediary successor; used exclusively of women, who formed a real or constructed 'blood' link between a man and his prospective male legal successor. The *ayōgēn* was obliged to generate a male heir for a deceased, sonless man (husband, father or brother) possessing property. Three groups of women in the family or lineage of the deceased man are named in this context: (1) the wives (in both *pādixšāy* and *čagar* forms of marriage); (2) daughters (from both of these types of marriage); (3) the sisters. These women were categorized in the Sasanian law of succession as 'natural proxies' (*stūr ī būdag*) of the men they were serving in this function (*see* ***stūr***). For a discussion of the diverse readings of *ayōgēn* and the suggested etymologies 164 (fn. 223), 165
  on the institution 163–168
ayōgēnīh/ayōgānīh intermediary succession
  on diverse readings of this word and the suggested etymologies 164 (fn. 223), 165
  on the institution 163–168
ayōgēn-stūr intermediary succession by proxy 167, 172
az from, of (prep.)
  az abāmdān ud grawīh nagīrā(y) 'he refutes the debt and the pledge' 317
  az … abēsaxwan budan to renounce, forego, cancel (a right) 245, 612–613
  az dārišn wizāyīdan to impede (a person's right to) possession 564, 568
  az dastwarīh nagīrā(y) būdan to deny *auctor*-ship 544
  az graw abāz wēxtan to redeem the pledge (always referring to an action performed by the debtor/pledgor) 330,335
  az grawīh hištan to release from pledge (always referring to an action performed by the creditor/pledgee) 329, 335
  az kār guharīg kardan to replace (an official), to assign a replacement (for an official)296
  az pad xwēšīh dāštan wizāyīdan to impede (a person's right to) ownership 564, 568
  az pasēmāl (pēšēmāl) azišmānd bawēd 'the defendant (plaintiff) causes an obstruction of justice' 565, 568
    see also ***azišmānd***
  az rāyēnišn hištan to refrain from pursuing a lawsuit 416
  az wināh patit ī kunišnīg 'redemption from sin by action'; third step in redeeming a sin 413
  az xwāstag ī graw abēsaxwān būdan to forego, renounce the pledged property (action performed by the creditor) 335, 338–339
āzād noble, freeborn, free; a prerequisite for having legal capacity 102–103, 125
āzādān freeborn (men); rank of the nobility 111, 516
āzardan to evaluate, assess, establish the value, price 370, 372
azišmānd obstruction of justice, *contumacia*; technical term for various offences causing some kind of obstruction during a lawsuit (such as failing to appear in court on the scheduled date of a hearing; interfering with the process of administering

justice; refusing to take an oath; withholding crucial evidence; giving a joint mandate to two intercessors whose statements deviate); *azišmānd bawēd* 'an obstruction occurs/is committed'; *az pasēmāl (pēšēmāl) azišmānd bawēd* 'the defendant (plaintiff) causes an obstruction of justice' 561–568

bahr share, portion (in the inheritance, in a partnership) 139, 142, 204, 231–232, 237, 258
bahr ī duxt/duxtīh share of the daughter (in the inheritance) 153, 232
bahr ī kadag-bānūg/banūgīh share of the *materfamilias* (in the inheritance) 123–124, 140, 232
see also ***bahr ī zanīh***
bahr ī pus/pusīh share of the son (in the inheritance) 140, 232
bahr ī stūrīh portion of the inheritance reserved for substitute succession 145
bahr ī xwēš wizārdan to pay one's own share 366–367
bahr ī zanīh share of the wife (in the inheritance) 153, 232
see also ***bahr ī kadag-bānūg/banūgīh***
bahr-marīhā 'in proportion to one's share'; obligation to repay a liability in proportion to one's individual share in a partnership 208, 309, 360
bahr-xwēš co-proprietor, shareholder 108
band fetters, binding; penalty for theft; bands and chains with which the limbs of the perpetrator are tied in a painful manner in correspondence with the degree (*pāyag*) of the offence, determining the tightness (*tangīh*) of the fetters and the duration of the binding (*drang ī bastag*) 441, 447, 449–450
band ī šahr fetters, binding of the State; penalty of the State for theft consisting of tethering the culprit (*see* ***band***) and imprisonment or some other form of confinement 441, 447, 449–450
see also ***drōš/drōšīh ī šahr***; ***drōz ī šahr***
band ud drōš 'fetters and mutilation'; basic punishments for theft; technical term for the whole penalty for theft, encompassing the corporal punishment (fettering and mutilating) and the compensation (*guharīg*) to be paid to the victims 439, 441, 449
bandag slave; servant; subject; *šāhān šāh bandag* subject of the King of Kings; *ātaxš-bandag*; *bandag ī ātaxš* servant of the fire; *ādurān-bandag* servant of the fires (not to be confused with *anšahrīg ī ātaxš* slave of the fire) 102–103, 105
bar fruit(s), income, increase, product, profit, revenue of a *xwāstag* (*res*, thing, physical or legal object), which could be owned separately from its *bun* (substance, capital, principal); Syriac rendering: *pīʾrā* 197–202
bar burd/grift use of the fruit(s); usufructuary (to be distinguished from *bar-xwēš*) 201
see also ***bar-xward***
bar-xward use of the fruit(s), usufruct; usufructuary (to be distinguished from *bar-xwēš*) 200–202, 214, 216, 338, 343, 604–605
see also ***bar burd/grift***
bar-xwēš owner of the fruit(s); person, who has permanent ownership of the income/produce of a 'thing' (*xwāstag*) (to be distinguished from *bar-xward*, *bar burd/grift* usufructuary and *bun-xwēš* owner of the substance) 198–199, 216, 218, 224, 604

bar-xwēšīh ownership of the fruit(s), income; permanent ownership of the fruits of a 'thing' (*xwāstag*) (to be distinguished from *bar-xward*, *bar burd* or *bar grift* and *bun-xwēšīh*) 198, 200–202, 229–230, 336, 604–605

barōmand surplus producing; capable of bearing fruits, of generating income 202, 213, 217, 223–224, 343, 624

baxtan to distribute 514

baxtīgīh kardan to partition (family property, inheritance), to separate into individual shares 129, 225, 234, 255

bayǎspān exogamy, marriage outside the natal lineage (as opposed to *xwēdōdah*, endogamy, marriage within the natal lineage) 148–150, 183–184

bāzā (< *bāzā-zanišnīh*; Av. *bazū.jata-*, lit. 'arm-striking/breaking') degree of sin in Zoroastrian law 468, 476

bērōn dašt outside the borders of the field, on which a water channel is dug 250
see also ***nindār dašt***

bēšīdārīh harmful (intent) 417

bōdōwaršt (Av. *baoδō.varšta-*) conscious, intentional wilful act/offence 412, 417–420, 422
see also ***bōdōzed*** and ***winīh ī nigerišnīg***

bōdōzed (Av. *baoδō.jaiti-*) conscious, wilful, intentional blow/injury; explained as *wēnāgīhā zad* 'struck in the manner of someone who sees' 412, 417–422
see also ***bōdōwaršt***, ***nigerišnīg*** and ***pad nigerišnīg zanišnīh***

****bōxt-nāmag*** (Syr. bwktn'mg) document of acquittal; official document of exoneration (bearing the seal of the *mowbedān mowbed*) 531, 577

bōzišn (1) acquittal, verdict of not guilty; opposite: *ērang*; (2) evidence; *čim ud bōzišn* proof and evidence 7, 80, 534, 540

brād ī hambāy shareholding brother, associate brother; partner within the family group (distinguished from *hambāy ī dēnīg*) 129, 170, 179, 234, 245–246, 252
see also ***hambāy*** and ***mērag***

brīn (injury caused by) cutting 425, 433

brīn zamān fixed date; (1) official date appointed by the court for a session of a trial or a hearing; (2) deadline for a payment 366–367

bun (1) in legal theory: substance, capital, principal, parent thing, core assets; the permanent part of a *xwāstag* (*res*, thing, corporal thing, legal object), which can be owned separately from its *bar* (fruit, income, product); (2) in a concrete sense (in Pahlavi documents in cursive script): base, storehouse; the central repository or inventory of a village, in which specific products were collected to be apportioned among shareholders or used for some other purpose. Shareholders and partners had specific accounts (*mar*) in the *bun* from which payments and other transactions were undertaken under the supervision of an official called *bunbān* 'custodian of the *bun*'; (3) in religious doctrine: stock, substance of the soul, whose essence is formed by the accumulation of virtues and sins during a person's lifetime. Syriac rendering: *ʿeqārā* 197–202, 204–205, 224–225, 338–339, 342
see also ***ō bun (budan)***

bun āb water of the 'substance'; water of irrigation canals leading through several plots of land belonging to the collective property (*bun*) of the village 321

bun-xānag foundation building, ground building 243
bun-xwēš owner of the substance/principal (to be distinguished from *bar-xwēš* owner of the fruit) 198, 202, 218, 302
bun-xwēšīh ownership of the substance (to be distinguished from *bar-xwēšīh* ownership of the fruit) 200–201, 229–230
bunbān custodian of the *bun* ('base'); official responsible for the central repository of a village 200 (fn. 62)
see also **bun** (2)
burdār 'bearer'; natural mother, *genetrix* 152

čagar (or: *zan ī čagar*) wife in an auxiliary marriage 142–145
čagar-zanīh auxiliary marriage; a form of matrimony *sine manu mariti* concluded with the purpose of procreating children for another man 131–133, 142–145
čak (1) document, cheque, receipt, payment entitlement; a written document specifying the amount of payment (either in kind or in money) to be given to a person for a specific item, product, service or performance; (2) note, entry in a transcript of legal proceedings; statement of a litigant in a legal transcript or protocol 279–284, 373–374, 537
čak dādan 'to make an entry, to place on record'; in procedural law: the act of taking down a statement of a litigant in a legal transcript or protocol 279, 538, 541
čambar (wooden or iron) collar (placed around the neck of a person suspected of sorcery) 584
čāšān title of an official or dignitary 277
čašmag 'renowned one(s)'; notables named together with the *stēndag* ('upright ones') in the context of evaluating the claim to a *stŭrīh*, and together with the *šahrīgān* ('men of the state/land') in an assembly with the task of consulting, verifying documents and checking the transcripts of criminal cases 515–517
čāštag (1) teaching, theory, legal doctrine; canonical law; *pad čāštag* according to legal doctrine; *ex lege* (as opposed to *pad kardag* according to legal practice; *via administrationis*); (2) legal or religious treatise (commentary) written by a theologian or jurisconsult 66–72, 342, 570–571
čē for, because, since, as; what, which? (interrog.pron.)
čē dārišn ēwar ud bun-xwēšīh warōmand 'since possession is certain, whereas ownership of the substance is uncertain' 200, 566
čē ēwēnag xwēšīh '(which) kind of ownership'; formula referring to the provenance of an ownership right. Participants in a transaction and litigants were required to bring proof of ownership by revealing how they had acquired an object (by inheritance, sale, barter, gift, donation, etc.) 212, 302, 385, 499, 561
čim proof, evidence 80, 438, 534
see also **čim ud bozišn**
čim ī abdom final evidence 439
čim ud bōzišn 'evidence and proof'; fixed hendiadys designating the evidence a litigant has to provide in a lawsuit (corresponding to *bōzišn u ḥujjat* 'evidence and proof' in two early Judaeo-Persian texts) 80, 540–542
čīš ī keh negligible, trivial matter; petty case that can be adjudicated on the basis of *kardag* procedure 67, 72, 570–571

[1]***dād*** law, legal order, legislation; body of normative rules constituting the legal order of the State (*dād ī šahr*) 4–6, 8, 114
see also ēwēn
dād *dibīrag 'register of laws, decrees, judgements'; one of the main *dīwāns* of the Sasanian State according to al-Ḫwārezmī (Arab. translation *kitābat al-aḥkām*) 99
dād ī šahr law of the State 4
see also ēwēn ī šahr

[2]***dād*** gift, donation, transmitted property; used of all kinds of gifts, both *inter vivos*, which were fully operative during the donor's lifetime and gifts in contemplation of death (*donatio mortis causa*) which took effect after the demise of the donor/testator 193, 235–236, 389–399
see also ***pad dād dādan*** 'to give as a gift'
dād pašt xwēš 'the transferred contract (is her/his) own; the contract of transfer (is her/his) own'; formula implying that there is *no time limit* to the validity of a contract of transfer of ownership rights. The contract using this formula does not expire with the death of the recipient, but is transferred to the heirs and beneficiaries. The formula *pašt dād xwēš* has diametrically opposed legal consequences 82
dād ud uzīd expenditures and outgoing payments 513

dādan to give, transfer, convey, transmit, bestow, grant, deliver; generally any kind of transfer in the context of bequests, loans, security, sale, barter, gifts, donations, etc. 389–390

dādestān law court, lawsuit, legal proceedings, jurisdiction, judiciary, judgement, verdict, judicial decision, law, justice 4–6
dādestān az rāyēnišn mānēd 'the verdict from (ongoing) proceedings has yet to be passed' 5
dādestān-brād brother according to the law; legitimate brother 5, 175
dādestān bun kardan rāyēnīdan to initiate legal action 534–535
dādestān-duxt daughter according to the law, legitimate daughter 5, 123, 137, 175, 231, 637
dādestān ī keh 'lesser judgement' (elliptical expression for 'judgement of the *dādwar ī keh*', the Junior Judge?) 523
dādestān ī meh 'higher judgement' (elliptical expression for 'judgement of the *dādwar ī meh*', Senior Judge?) 523
dādestān kardan to administer justice 5
dādestān-nāmag recordings/book of judicial decisions; Law-book 5
dādestān-pus son according to the law, legitimate son 5, 123, 137, 175, 231, 637
dādestān rāyēnīdan to take legal action, to conduct legal proceedings; *dādestān nē rāyēnišn* 'legal action is not to be taken' 416, 506, 548, 565
dādestān sar bawēd 'the lawsuit comes to an end' 565
dādestān-xwāh sister according to the law, legitimate sister 5, 175

dādestānīg pertaining to law, legal 5, 405
dādestānīg zanišn handāzišn 'measuring injury according to the law'; the process of assessing the grade or degree of an injury according to the directives in Zoroastrian law 405

dādestānōmandīhā according to law, lawfully 5, 407
dādgāh place, sanctuary of a consecrated fire
dādwar judge
  dādwar ī keh 'minor judge'; Junior Judge; lower judge in the hierarchy of judges employed by the State, who presides in the first instance of a trial 65, 497, 522–523, 525, 532
  dādwar ī meh 'major judge'; Senior Judge; higher judge in the hierarchy of judges employed by the State, who presides in the first court of appeal 65, 497, 522–523, 525, 532
  dādwar ī nē vaiiōzušt 'judge who is not agreeable to both (litigants)'; judge whose judgement is *not* acceptable to both parties, the claimant and the defendant 498
  dādwar ī pasēmāl 'Judge of the Defendant'; official of the State chosen as an arbitrator by the defendant 497–498
  dādwar ī pēšēmāl 'Judge of the Plaintiff'; official of the State chosen as an arbitrator by the plaintiff/claimant 497–498
  dādwar ī vaiiōzušt 'judge who is agreeable to both (litigants)'; judge whose judgement is acceptable to both parties, the claimant and the defendant 498
  dādwar pad rāstīh wizīr tuwān kardan 'the judge is capable of passing just judgement' 567
dādwarīh jurisdiction 61, 258, 438
dahibed ruler of the land; worldly ruler; delegate of the king 495, 510–511, 517–518
****dārāg/dārīg*** (?) ⟨ḤSN̲'⟩ donee, recipient of a gift, donation (lit. 'possessor, holder') 389, 399
dard ud xōn pain and bloodshed; symptom calling attention to an offence of *zaxm* injury, wound or *rēš* bodily harm 424
dārišn possession; physical or actual control of a thing, corresponding roughly to *possessio* in Roman law. The *de facto* possession of a property can, but does not necessarily include ownership (*e.g.* leased property, tenancy, goods in pledge) and might even be unlawful (possession of a stolen object). *dārišn ī xwāstag / xwāstag dārišn* possession of property; *pad dārišn dāštan* to possess, hold (lit. 'to hold in possession') 193–195, 200–202
  dārišn āgenēn persons having exactly equal proprietary shares 86, 247, 249–250, 252
    see also ***āgenēn***
  dārišn ēwar ud bun-xwēšīh warōmand '(the right to) possession (is) certain and ownership of the substance (is) uncertain' 200, 566
  dārišn ī pad nidāšt (?) interim possession, holding in retainment; temporal and provisional retainment of the object of dispute by the judge/court 500–501
    see also ***dārišn ī uzīdag***
  dārišn ī uzīdag temporary possession 500–501
dāšn gift, donation 114, 278, 301, 389
dāštan to hold, possess; *kū m ... dāštan ray framān dād* 'I have willed it (to such-and-such a person) to be held', formula bestowing guardianship (*sālārīh*) or trusteeship (*dāštārīh*; *stūrīh*) of a sacred fire, fire foundation or pious endowment to a specific person 195, 205, 217, 220, 223–224, 242

dāštan abāyistan rightful possession 540

dāštan rāy framān nē bawēd 'the right of possession is not determined' 250

daštān-marz wināh sin of copulation with a menstruating woman 452

dāštārīh keeping, preserving; trusteeship, tutorship of a sacred fire, a fire foundation or pious endowment 187, 223, 248, 254, 601

dastgird landed estate, consisting of cultivated, agricultural land with fixed borders, water canals, roads and buildings (in contrast to *zamīg*, uncultivated land) 241–244, 327, 377, 599

+*darrišn* (injury caused by) splitting, tearing apart 425, 433

dast-mušt (contract) by handshake (renders Av. *zasta.maršta-*) 262

dast-nibēg handwritten record, template of a document/text (as opposed to a 'copy', *paččēn*) with the signature of the scribe 271–272, 285

see also ***nibēg***

dastwar (1) person having (legal or religious) authority; (2) authorized, empowered, entitled (person); person who has a right or title to a specific property with regard to its substance (*bun*) or its fruits (*bar*) or to both elements of a 'corporal thing' (*xwāstag*); (3) legal predecessor, predecessor in title, *auctor* 88–89, 196–197, 385–387, 542–544

dastwar az dastwarīh nagīrā(y) bawēd 'the legal predecessor denies *auctor*-ship'544

dastwar ī dārišn '(person) entitled to possession' 543–544

dastwar ī xwēšīh ud dārišn '(person) entitled to ownership and possession' 543–544

**dastwarēn* *dastwar*-like, in the manner of a *dastwar*, as a *dastwar* 596–597

dastwarīh (1) entitlement, authorization, empowerment, right of disposal; in property law: the title (or right) to ownership of the substance (*bun*) or fruits (*bar*) or of both elements of a corporal 'thing' (*xwāstag*); (2) *auctor*-ship; in procedural law: the act of defending the right of a litigant to a specific property and confirming that it has been transferred legally to the latter against the claims of a third party 88–89, 196–197, 536, 543–544

dastwarīh frāz xwāstan to request *auctor*-ship 536

dastwarīh kardan to act as *auctor;* to perform *auctor*-ship 544

daxšag symptom (of an injury or wound) 415, 424

dēg 'cauldron'; a measure for liquids 370

dehgān farmer, local gentry, landlord 369–372

dehgānān small nobility; minor rank of the nobility 111, 516

deh-masāy 'the size of a piece of land' (renders Av. *daŋhu.maza-*); contract defined by its worth in land; the equivalent of more than five-hundred drachms 262

dēmān admittance (before the judges to file a claim) 534–535

dēnīg war religious oath (= *war ī dēnīg*) 363, 555–556, 558, 560

dib writ, document, transcript, protocol; any kind of written and sealed document, specifically: (1) transcript or protocol from legal proceedings; (2) recorded sentence of a judge/State official; (3) edict of public officials/judicial authorities; *dib ī pādixšāy kard ud xwēškārīh nāmag ī kār-framān ī šahrīhā* 'authorized edict and document on the area of competence of the public official of the provinces' 270, 277, 284, 500, 513, 583

dibīr scribe, secretary; *dibīrān* '(estate of) scribes, secretaries' (Arab. translation *kuttāb*) 96–100

dīwān ī kardag(ān) archive of religious institutions, in which fire foundations and endowments 'for the soul' were registered 227, 270, 505–506, 509
dīwānbān archivar 500
dō dastwarīhā dārišnīh rāy wizīr kunišn 'The verdict is to be reached on the basis of (proof of) possession by double entitlement' 386 (fn. 509)
dōšīd 'it is sanctioned', formulaic statement of the recipient of a transaction accepting the offer of the transferor; variants: *kāmag dōšīd* 'the will (of the transferor/offeror) is sanctioned'; *andar abāyēd* 'it is necessary' 139, 302–303, 305
drahnāy ud zahā breadth and depth (of an injury) 427
driyōšān the poor, needy
 driyōšān ǰādag-gōw Advocate of the Poor; title on administrative seals, replacing the title *mowbed* 293–295, 300
 see also ***driyōšān ǰādag-gōw ud dādwar***
 driyōšān ǰādag-gōw ud dādwar Advocate of the Poor and Judge; title on administrative seals 294, 300
 see also ***driyōšān ǰādag-gōw*** and ***ǰādag-gōw dādwar ī driyōšān***
drō lie, deceit
 drō guftan to make a deceitful statement; to lie (in court) 567
 drō wizīr deceitful judgement 549
drōš cut, brand, mark; penalty for theft; a kind of incision or cut (in the face or hands) or a brand stigmatizing the thief visibly 108, 382–383, 439–442, 444, 447, 451
 drōš hamēmālān xwēš 'the penalty (= compensation) for theft is the litigants' own'; the compensation to be paid by the thief as part of the penalty for theft is conveyed in ownership to the victims of the theft (= litigants) 441–442, 447, 451
 drōš/drōšīh ī šahr penalty of the State for theft consisting of two measures: corporal punishment and compensation in money or in kind 442, 451
 see also ***band ī šahr*** and ***drōz ī šahr***
drōšīh guharīg compensation for mutilation/branding; compensation replacing (?) the corporal penalty for theft in kind or money conveyed to the victims 442
drō-xwāhāg (having a) deceitful will; seeking deceit; mental element (*mens rea*) of a crime 416–417, 422, 570
drōzan lie, deceit 7, 25, 548, 567, 574
 see also ***a-rāst-gōwišnīh***
drōzanīh falsehood; offence noted in the *pursišn-nāmag* 595
drōz ī šahr penal law of the State for theft 442, 451
 see also ***drōš/drōšīh ī šahr***
drust/drustīh intact, undamaged 265, 266, 345, 347
 drust dārišnīh warranty, guarantee to keep something intact, undamaged 265
 drust dāštan to keep intact, undamaged; in the context of sale: guarantee of the seller to keep good care of the sold object/goods until delivery 375–376
dūdag family, household 107, 128, 176, 181, 449, 457, 460
 dūdag ī wehān wišōbišnīh destroying the family of the pious; grievous offence 461–462
 dūdag-sālār family guardian; person installed as guardian over the family after the demise of the *paterfamilias* (*kadag-xwadāy*); on the three different types of

guardians *see* ***sālār***; on the difference between *dūdag-sālār* and *xwāstag-sālār* *see* ***dūdag-sālārīh*** 121–122, 135, 173, 215, 231, 302, 415–416, 546, 614–615

dūdag-sālārīh family guardianship. Guardianship could be separated into guardianship over dependant members of the family (*dūdag-sālārīh*) and guardianship over family property (*xwāstag-sālārīh*) 125, 178–179

see also ***sālārīh*** and ***xwāstag-sālārīh***

dūdag tōzišn liabilities of the family 309–310, 319, 360

duš-menišn evil thought; mental element (*mens rea*) of a crime 413, 432

see also ***kēn-menišn***

dusraw disrepute, dishonour; character trait of a delinquent noted in the *pursišn-nāmag* 575, 584

dusrawīh notoriety, bad reputation; character trait of a delinquent noted in the *pursišn-nāmag* 595

dušxwār heavy weight (placed on the shoulders of a person suspected of the crime of sorcery) 584

duxt daughter

duxt-dād child born of the daughter in one of the institutions of substitute succession (*ayōgēnīh; stūrīh*) 176

duxt ī padīriftag adopted daughter 176

duxtagānīh (legal status/position of a) daughter 136

duzagān-menišn intention of a thief/of thieves 7, 413, 422

duz(d) thief; person who steals stealthily (*nihān* 'secretly'), in seclusion. Syriac rendering: *ganāḇā* 25, 313, 382, 434–435, 445, 450

duz(d)īh theft; stealing secretly, stealthily; transposed to other offences committed secretly, *e.g.* breach of a contract (*mihrōdrujīh*) concluded without any witnesses. 68, 382, 413, 439, 450, 618

see also ***apparīh***

duzīdan to steal; appropriate something stealthily, secretly 436

duz-menišnīh; duz-menišnīgīh criminal intent of the thief; mental element (*mens rea*) of a crime 413, 424, 445

ēdōn thus, so, in this way

ēdōn ēn dādestān (Av. *⁺iϑa asti auuaṯ arəϑəm*) 'thus (is) this (judicial) case'; formula spoken under oath 558–559

ēdōn man pad ān ast āgāhīh (Av. *⁺iϑa [vā] mē ⁺aŋhe asti ⁺vaēδīm*) 'thus is my knowledge thereof'; formula spoken under oath 558–559

ēdōnīh 'it (is) so; thusness'; statement or formula confirming the veracity of a claim; opposite: *nē-ēdōnīh* 363, 556–558

ēk ōy ī dīd pāyandān (*ham-pāyandān*) ***hēm*** 'we are sureties (co-sureties), one for the other'; formula establishing co-suretyship of debtors in a loan contract. Co-sureties guarantee for each other as *hamāg-tōzišn* 'joint and several debtors', i.e. the creditor can request payment of the total amount of the loan from each one of the debtors 356–357

ēr Iranian; Zoroastrian; as opposed to *an-ēr* non-Iranian; non-Zoroastrian 103, 115–117

ērang conviction; opposite: *bōzišn* 7

ēraxt guilty, convicted; opposite: *bōxt* 415, 554, 561–562, 564, 568
ērīh being Iranian, status of an Iranian, Zoroastrian 138, 494
ērīg xēm Iranian character, specific traits of the Iranian 114
ēwar reliable, trustworthy, (legally) binding (judgement, procedure, seal). opposite: *warōmand* 7, 69–70, 200, 269, 287–288, 291, 296, 299, 323, 362, 504, 507, 551
ēwarīh reliability, trustworthiness, qualification, competence; legal force; binding power (judgement, procedure, seal); *pad ēwarīh* 'by a binding (procedure); by a valid (seal)' 282, 288, 298, 498, 503, 549
  ēwarīh rāy 'to make it legally binding'; *ēwarīh rāy … muhr abar nihād* lit. 'in order to make it legally binding, (NN) placed his seal upon it (= the document)'; formulaic statement in a document authorizing the document by naming the responsible legal authority who seals it 267, 290–291, 298, 300–301, 320–322
  ēwarīh xwāstan to request reliability, trustworthiness; *pad xwārestān … ēwarīh xwāstan* 'to request reliability in the place of swearing' 559–560
ēwēn manner, custom, law 4–5, 88
  ēwēn-būd legally binding, legality (of a transaction) 88, 437
    see also ***pādixšāy būd***
  ēwēn ī garzišn legality of a claim/complaint 535
  ewēn ī šahr law of the State; body of normative rules constituting the legal order of the State 4, 446
    see also ***dād ī šahr***
ēw-kardag in one piece; land that is not partitioned or parcelled 345, 347–348
ēw-kardagīhā in one piece, as a whole, referring to land that is not partitioned or parcelled, but transferred as an undivided unit 243

fragār document, transcript (from a criminal trial?) 515, 517.
  fragār brīdan to seal the document (from a criminal trial?) 504–506, 509
framān (1) order, decree, command, edict of a legal or State authority (*see also* ***hār framan***), (2) payment order on the basis of a *čak* (payment entitlement), (3) minor degree of sin (*see also* ***handarz-framān***) 87, 223, 250, 281, 369, 438, 476–482, 495–496, 510–511, 517–518, 532, 587
framānburdārīh observance of instructions, taking orders; duty of a subordinate towards his superior; obligation of the wife towards the husband 138
frayar (Av. *fraiiara-*) morning; the prescribed time to conduct judicial proceedings, to give interlocutory judgements and the final verdict 402 (fn. 13), 537, 569
frazand child
  frazand ī nām-burdār name-bearing child; successor of a *paterfamilias* bearing his name and continuing his lineage 174
  frazand ī tanī(g)zād natural issue (lit. 'child born from the body') 175
frazandēmēdag potent, fertile (lit. 'hopeful of engendering children') 172
frāz-rūdag (injury caused by) pulling out (hair, entrails, etc.) 425, 433
frezwān 'duty fulfiller'; policeman or commissioner responsible for the detention and identification of persons involved in legal proceedings (among other duties and competences) 288, 429–430, 518–521, 574
frōd az dādīhā 'beneath entitlement by law'; in the context of food distribution: a person who is not entitled to maintenance by law 258

frōxš/frōxt sale 301, 372, 505, 512
frōxtār seller, vendor 466–467
**fšŭ-ciϑā-* animal from the livestock as compensation in kind; cattle-atonement 440–441, 449, 451, 682 (fn. 7)
  see also **pāk(a) fšŭ-ciϑā-*

gabrag (injuries caused by throwing a person into a) cavity 427
gād sexual intercourse, cohabitation
  gād-duzīh theft of sexual intercourse; appropriating the exclusive right of another man to sexual intercourse 414, 455–458, 460
  gād/gādan menišnīg intent of cohabitation; considering fornication; mental element (*mens rea*) of the offence: decision of the perpetrator to commit adultery, to cohabit with the wife of another man 414, 422, 455–457, 460, 462
    see also ***gād pad uzkārišn***
  gād pad uzkārišn 'sexual intercourse with reflection'; intent of cohabitation; considering illicit fornication with the wife of another man 414, 422, 456, 460
    see also ***gād/gādan menišnīg***
  gād tāwān fine for cohabiting; compensation for illicit sexual intercourse to be paid to the victim(s) 459–460
gādār (1) designation of the husband (lit. 'fornicator, lover') in the *xwasrāyēn/ūn*-marriage, a form of matrimony based on the consensus of the spouses 78–79, 132–133, 145–147, 160–161; (2) (illicit) fornicator, adulterer 459
  gādār kardan to take a husband (*gādār*) in the consensus marriage; to enter a consensus marriage (*xwasrāyēn/ūn*) 78–79, 145–146, 150, 160
gāh rank, station; a person's position in the social hierarchy 102, 110, 120–121
  gāh-nāmag charter/book of rank; catalogue of dignitaries classified according to their rank and station in Sasanian society 110
  gāh ud pāyag ī mardōm ranks and stations of people 258
gāh gyāg 'place and time' (= *gyāg gāh*); scheduled date, time and venue of a hearing/lawsuit/ordeal 567
*ganǰ hamār *dibīrag* 'register of the accounts of the treasury'; one of the main *dīwāns* of the Sasanian State according to al-Ḫwārezmī (Arab. translation *kitābat al-ḫazāʿin*) 99
ganǰwar treasurer 321–322
garān wināhīh grave sin, offence 117, 334, 384
garzēm 'we complain!'; joint statement of the plaintiff and the defendant emphatically declaring their will to enter litigation at the beginning of a lawsuit 533, 537, 541
garzīdan ī must to file action of complaint 500, 524–525, 538, 541
garzišn complaint, claim 524–525, 533–534–535
  see also ***must***
gētīy dādwar judge in the *gētīy* (corporal) existence 7
  see also ***mēnōy dādwar***
gitt/gittag ⟨gt/gtk⟩ (or ⟨GT-y/GTk⟩ *nāmag*?) foundation deed of a pious foundation 222, 227, 272, 275–279, 284
  see also ***nāmag***

gittag ī nēk ⟨gṭk'/GṬk' Y nywk'⟩ 'good (= proper, faultless, valid?) document'; transfer list of various agricultural products and livestock; document listing expenses, investments and transactions involving the collective property in the central repository (*bun*) of a village 275, 278–279, 284

see also ***nāmag ī nēk***

gizīr warden, policeman 500–501

gōš-bālāy 'the height of an ear'; designates the height or depth of a water channel (*ǰōy-kahas*) 250

gōwišn speech, statement

gōwišn ī ǰādūg gōwišnīhā 'speaking in the manner of sorcerers'; one of the six aggressive or harmful acts listed under the heading *ardīg tazišnīh* 'engaging in conflict' 425, 433

gōwišn ī ⁺sahm nimāyišnīhā 'speaking in a threatening manner'; one of the six aggressive or harmful acts listed under the heading *ardīg tazišnīh* 'engaging in conflict' 425, 433

gōwišn ud wēnišn āšnawišn (injury diminishing the ability to) speak, see and hear 426, 433

gowišnīg '(statement) by speaking'; making an oral statement (in a trial/dispute), as opposed to *nimāyišnīg* '(making a statement) by demonstrating' 407, 409–411

gōwišnīg ī nē nimāyišnīg 'speaking and not demonstrating'; trial/dispute in which the litigants present their case only orally without demonstration 410

gōwišnīg nimāyišnīg 'speaking and demonstrating'; trial/dispute in which the litigants present their case both orally and by demonstration 407, 409–411

gōwizār ud rōšn explicitly and clearly 438

graw/grawīh pledge, pawn; an item of movable or immovable property, also an animal or a slave, transferred by the debtor/borrower (pledgor) to the lender (pledgee/pledge-holder) as security for the payment of a debt or performance of an obligation; *pignus* in Roman law 117, 324–326, 326–336, 341, 344–345

graw abāz rasēnīdan to bring back a pledge/pawn 335

graw abāz stadan to take back a pledge/pawn 335

graw abespārdan to transfer a pledge/pawn 335

graw apēdag bawēd 'the pledge/pawn is lost' 329

graw kardan to pledge, pawn 332, 335

grawagān/grawagānīh mortgage of the fruits; type of mortgage giving the creditor (mortgagee, *grawagāndār*) only access to the fruits (*bar*) of the mortgaged property; corresponding to the Roman *antichresis* 87, 311, 325–326, 343–349, 617

grawagānīh ī xwāstag mortgaging the fruits of a property 349

grawagān kardan to mortgage the fruits of a property, to establish an *antichresis* 349

grawagāndār pledge-holder, pledgee, mortgagee; creditor who holds an *antichresis* (*grawagān/grawagānīh*) as security 325–327, 344–345, 349

grawdār pledgee, pawnee, pledge-holder; person entitled to hold a pledge/pawn (*graw*) of the debtor (pledgor) in his possession until return of the loan or performance of contract 324, 326, 331, 344–345

grawīh wišuft (nē wišuft) bawēd 'the (right to) the pledge has expired (not expired)' 336

griftār responsible (for an action, assessment or decision) 519

grīw a measure for solid matters (1 *grīw* = 10 *kabīz*) 347 (fn. 352), 370–371, 379

guft (in: *guft ī nē pad āwišt*) verbal contract or stipulation (not recorded in a sealed document) 398–399

gugāy witness; *gugāy abāg* '(there is) a witness with (him); (he has) a witness with (him)'; *gugāy abāg nēst* '(there) is no witness with (him)' 116, 386, 398, 407–409, 495, 534, 545–549

gugāy āwardan to bring a witness (to court) 548–549

gugāy-muhr witness-seal, the private seal of a witness, who is not an official of the State, but whose trustworthiness has been confirmed by official administrative or legal instances 282–283, 285, 298, 550–551

see also ***gugāyīh muhr***

gugāy padīriftan to admit a witness/witnesses (for a testimony in court) 499

gugāyīh testimony

gugāyīh dādan to give testimony 549

gugāyīh muhr witness seal, testimonial seal 298, 300, 550–551

see also ***gugāy-muhr***

guharēn barter; *guharēn rāst* equal barter; exchange on a par 388–389

guharēn kardan to practice barter; to exchange one thing for another 388

guharīg substitute, replacement, compensation, remuneration 139, 169, 249, 329, 345, 387, 442, 449, 505

guharīg ī mādag compensation in money, fine 421, 445, 451

guharīgōmand liable to compensation; *arz ī ān ī guharīgōmand* 'value of the thing that has to be compensated' 441, 447

gumārdan to nominate (a guardian, *sālār*, or proxy, *stūr*); this verb is used exclusively when official instances (legal or religious authorities) determine a guardian or proxy (*sālār* or *stūr ī gumārdag*) 118, 504, 509

gyāg gāh 'time and place' (= *gāh gyāg*); scheduled date, time and venue of a hearing/lawsuit/ordeal 567

hamāg-tōzišn joint and several debtor, co-debtor; person in a partnership assuming the obligation to satisfy the claims of potential creditors with all the property at his disposal, who can be charged either separately or jointly with his co-partners for the whole debt (in contrast to *xwāstag-tōzišn* 'part-debtor') 207, 209, 253, 308–310, 356, 360, 364, 366, 527

ham-bahr duzīh 'theft with common shares'; stealing property with an accomplice (*abāg*) and sharing the stolen goods; in contrast to *jud-bahr duzīh* 445, 450

hambarag co-partner/shareholder of the fruit(s); joint partner of the income 218, 244, 247, 250, 252

see also ***zamīg ī hambaragān***

hambāy partner, companion, associate, shareholder 204–205, 208, 229–230, 245–252, 360, 464

see also ***brād ī hambāy***, ***hambāy ī dēnīg*** and ***mērag***

hambāy ī dēnīg religious partner, associate; any adherent of the Good Religion with whom one has formed a *societas* or partnership (distinguished from *brād ī hambāy*) 246, 252, 384

hambāyīh partnership, companionship, *societas*; any type of associate partnership, of heirs and legatees, other co-proprietors and persons involved in joint ventures 129, 166, 234, 245–252, 351, 355

hamdādestānīh consensus, consent; in the context of the *pādixšāy* marriage contract: consent of the prospective bride to enter matrimony with the prospective bridegroom 135

hamdādestānīh ī wehān consensus of the Righteous 65

hamēmāl opponent, adversary, litigant, dispute 441, 523, 537, 558–559, 565–567, 569

see also ***winăh ī hamēmālān***

hamēmālān xwēš '(it is) the litigants' own'; referring to a compensation which is conveyed to the victims of theft (= litigants who proceed legally against the thief), replacing the corporal punishment for theft (*drōšīh guharīg*) 441–442, 447, 449, 451

hamēmālīh kardan to litigate; to initiate legal proceedings 499, 519

hamēwēn xwēš ownership to the same extent, with equal shares 239

hamkār (1) partner, collaborator, fellow-worker, associate, assistant; (2) (technical term) associate, assistant priest; qualified priest who assists the chief officiating priest (*zōt*) during the performance of the liturgy 384, 385

hamnāmīh '(having the) same name'; identification of a person's name; *see* ***hamtanīh ud hamnāmīh ud hammuhrīh***

hampaččēn (identical) copy of a document (as opposed to the original document, *mādagwar*) 270, 283, 291–292, 301, 416

hampāyandān co-surety, joint surety, co-warrantor, co-guarantor; debtor who has taken up a loan together with others, accepting liability for the other partners; co-sureties provide suretyship for each other as security for the loan and are 'joint and several debtors' (*hamāg-tōzišn*), i.e. every debtor is liable for the total amount of the debt 247, 252–253, 364, 366, 509

hampāyandānīh co-suretyship, joint suretyship, co-warranty, co-guarantee; two or several debtors acting as sureties for each other 253

hamtanīh '(being the) same person'; identification of a person

hamtanīh ud hamnāmīh ud hammuhrīh 'same person and same name and same seal'; process of ascertaining a person's identity and the conformity of his name and seal in court (duty of the *frēzwān*, the *dādwar* and, in specific circumstances, the *zēndānbān*) 288, 300, 500, 519–521

hamwaxš (having) joint interest, income; shareholder of the increase 247–248, 251–252

hamwināhīh '(having committed the) same offence'; identification of the criminal act 519–521

hamwindišn (having) joint earnings; shareholder of the income (with divergent shares); opposite: *jud windišn* 247, 251–252

see also ***āgenēn hamwindišn***

hamxwastag joint proprietor, business associate; variants: (1) co-owners with exactly equal shares (*pad āgenēn xwēš* 'in joint ownership'); (2) co-owners with divergent shares (*az any mard hammis xwēš* 'ownership together with other men'); (3) co-possessors with equal shares of the fruits (*pad āgenēn dārišn* 'in joint possession') 245–247, 249, 252, 364

hamxwāstagīh joint property, business association 245–252
ham-zahag of the same offspring 8
handarz last will, testament 235–236, 241, 245, 398–399
handarz-framān minor degree of sin in Zoroastrian law 476–477, 481–482
see also ***framān***
handōxt ī xwēš 'one's own acquisitions', property acquired by a person during his/her lifetime 192–193, 211
handōzišn ud windišn earnings/acquisitions and revenue 78, 192–193
handraxt holdings (of a sacred fire); possessions which were not part of the *bun* ('substance, core assets') of property belonging to a sacred fire, but whose income was dedicated to its upkeep 505
hangārdan, hangar- to consider, to take into account; *see* ***pad bahr hangārišn az bahr hangārišn*** and ***pad ēmōzan hangārišn***
hanǰaman assembly 515, 517
hannām limb, member (of the body); *hannāmān ī war padiš warzīd ēstēd* 'limbs/members (of the body) on which the oath has been taken' 426, 441, 553–554, 560
harg bār taxes (and) duties 224
hērbed religious authority engaged as judge in lawsuits regarding property issues 506–507, 509
hišt-nāmag certificate of divorce; document recording the legal separation of (*pādixšāy-*) spouses 273, 285
hišt ud bōxt wizīr judgement dismissing (the claim), acquitting (the accused); verdict of not guilty 446, 451
⟨ḤSN̲'⟩ (**dārāg/dārīg*?) donee (lit. 'possessor, holder'); recipient of a gift or a donation of a *rād* 'donor' 389, 399
hudēn Zoroastrian, adherent of the Good Religion 35, 114, 115, 172, 382
hudēnīg dād Zoroastrian law 114
humat (Av. *humata-*) good thought 6, 136, 401, 413, 421, 538, 615
hu-menišn good thought; opposite: *duš-menišn*; *kēn-menišn* 413, 421
hunsandīh approval, consent; in the context of the *pādixšāy* marriage contract: the approval of the prospective bride to enter matrimony with the prospective bridegroom; in the context of legal proceedings: consent of the litigants with the verdict; opposite: *a-hunsandīh* 135, 268, 500, 525, 571
+***huškēnīdan*** (injury by) causing a limb to wither 425–426, 433
hušnūdīh 'satisfaction', restitution and compensation 437
hutuxš artisan (Av. *hūiti-*); ***hutuxšān*** (estate of) artisans (Arab/Pers. translation *mihna*) 95, 98, 372
hutuxšbed chief of the artisans 373
huwaršt (Av. *huuaršta-*) virtue, good deed 6, 136, 401, 413, 538, 615
hūxt (Av. *hūxta-*) good speech 6, 136, 401, 413, 538, 615

ǰādag portion, share 140, 345
ǰādag-gōw advocate, intercessor, legal representative, delegate; person representing the plaintiff or defendant in a trial, who could be an advocate, a person schooled in jurisprudence, or just a layman with a mandate (*pādixšāy kard*) 289, 537–538, 540–541, 543, 557, 563

ǰādag-gōw dādwar ī driyōšān Advocate-+ (and) Judge of the Poor; title on administrative seals 294
see also driyōšān ǰādag-gōw ud dādwar
ǰādag-gōw ǰādag-gōw ī pasēmāl 'deputy of the representative of the defendant'; person acting as a delegate or substitute for the official legal representative (*ǰādag-gōw*) of the defendant 539
ǰādag-gōw kardan to appoint as legal representative/intercessor; *kū-m āgenēn ǰādag-gōw kard hēd* 'I have appointed you jointly as (my) intercessors', statement of a litigant authorizing two persons together as his legal representatives with the implication that these two persons could represent the litigant only jointly in legal proceedings 539

ǰadārīh upkeep, maintenance, support, preservation, conservation (of property) 371–372

ǰādūgīh sorcery, witchcraft 583

ǰām ⟨M'NH⟩; ⟨yy'm⟩ movable pledge/pawn or deposit (lit. 'vessel, goblet, chalice') 324, 326, 331–332, 335
see also ***ǰāmag***

ǰāmag ⟨y'mk⟩ movable pledge/pawn or deposit (lit. 'vessel, goblet, chalice') 324, 326, 331, 501, 519
see also ***ǰām***

ǰāmdār pawnee, pledgee, pledge-holder (lit. 'vessel-holder', alongside *grawdār*), creditor who holds a movable pawn 326, 331–332

ǰāmdārīh holding a movable pledge/pawn or deposit (lit. 'holding a vessel') 334, 335

ǰār-ē(w) 'once and for all', relating to a decision of general principle of the highest legal authority, the *mowbedān mobed*, on a controversial subject 248

ǰāwēdānīg perpetually, without time limitation 242

ǰehi-marz wināh sin of copulation with a whore 452

ǰōy-kahas water channel 250
see also ***kahas***

ǰud separate, different
ǰud az āgāhīh ud dānišn 'without awareness and knowledge' (of the opponent) 537
ǰud az windišn 'without (title to) the income'; formula in the marriage contract preventing the husband from taking control over the earnings of the wife122, 139
ǰud-bahr duzīh 'theft with separate shares'; stealing property with an accomplice (*abāg*) and dividing the stolen goods into separate shares 445, 450
see also ***ham-bahr duzīh***
ǰud-dēn adherent of another religion, infidel 119, 384
ǰud ǰud xwēš '(having) separate ownership' (contrasted with *pad āgenēn xwēš* 'in joint ownership') 247
ǰud-kēš adherent of another creed, infidel 112
ǰud-ristag heretic 112
ǰud windišn (having) separate incomes; opposite: *hamwindišn* 251
ǰud wizīr hēnd 'they are subject to different judgements' 426

kābēn dower; gift or settlement given by the husband to the bride (*donatio propter nuptias* in Roman law); NP *kābīn*, synonym of Arab. *mahr* 140, 274

kabīz a measure for solid matters (10 *kabīz* = 1 *grīw*) 347–348, 370–371, 379–380

kadag house, lineage, descent group 128, 242–244, 277–278, 376–377
see also ***xānag*** 'house' in the same figurative sense of 'lineage'
kadag-bānūg mistress of the household, *materfamilias*; position of the wife in a *pādixšāy-* marriage 122–124, 137, 142, 181–182, 234, 361–363, 509
kadag hamār *dibīrag 'register of the accounts of the (royal) house'; one of the main *dīwāns* of the Sasanian State according to al-Ḫwārezmī (Arab. translation *kitābat ḥisāb dār al-mulk*) 99
kadag-xwadāy master of the house, *paterfamilias* 120–121, 130, 132, 142, 175–176, 205–206, 229, 397, 615
kadag-xwadāyān 'householders'; rank of the nobility 111
kādōzed (Av. **kāiδiiō.jaiti-*) negligence, injury by carelessness; explained as *kastārīhā zad* 'struck in the manner of someone who diminishes, destroys' 412–413, 417–422, 424, 445, 570–571
see also ***sūdagīhā zanišn***
kahas water canal, *qanāt* 240–242, 249–250, 377
see also ***ǰōy-kahas***
kām will, desire, purpose, intention, intent; the mental element of a crime (*mens rea*) 7, 412, 570–571, 616
kāmag (1) will, wish, intention (of a transferor to convey a specific object to the recipient); (2) deed of gift (lit. '[statement of] will; volition') 211, 303, 397
kāmag dōšīd 'the will (of the transferor/offeror) is sanctioned', formulaic words spoken by the recipient of a transaction accepting an offer of the transferor; variants: *andar abāyēd* 'it is necessary'; *dōšīd* 'it is sanctioned' 302, 305
kanišn tearing off, pulling apart, splitting; criminal act categorized as *zanišn* 407, 411, 423
kār work, act, deed, matter, case
kār-framān (1) instruction, decree, edict, directive, command, order, instruction in a will; (2) manager, overseer, steward, functionary, official; general designation of a public official, who exercises command in a specific area and is entitled to pass judgement in this field 293, 295, 300, 510–511, 550–551, 580, 595
kār gyāg ī pādofrāh 'venue of execution of punishment' (in the context of theft) 441
kār rāyēnīdan to take legal action, to litigate, to enter legal proceedings; formulaic statements in the *saxwan-nāmag* with regard to the legal opponent in a lawsuit: *kār rāyēnēd* 'he (= the opponent) is taking legal action'; *kar nē rāyēnēd* 'he (=the opponent) is not taking legal action' 499, 535
kār-windišn work income, earnings 86
kardag legal practice; specifically: (1) a *judicial procedure* conducted at the free discretion of the court, diverging from the procedure in canonical law; (2) the *guideline or norm* resulting from judgements reached in these cases. Legal formulae: *az kardag hišt ēstēd* '(the case) is withdrawn from *kardag* (procedure)'; *pad kardag* 'according to legal practice, *via administrationis*'; *pad kardag mad (ēstēd)* '*kardag* (procedure) was applied'; *ō kardag nē kard ēstēd* '(the case) is not put to *kardag* (procedure)'; *ō kardag kard ēstēd* '(the case) is put to *kardag* (procedure)' 66–72, 207, 342, 386, 501, 546, 549, 570–571, 586, 616–617
kārdār public official of the State 497, 503, 509, 545
kardārīh performance of religious rites 258

kas kē čiš awiš tōzišn dahišn 'person to whom a payment must be given'; creditor 88, 310
  see also ***mard kē ō kas tōzišn dahišn***
kastārīhā zad 'struck in the manner of someone who diminishes; as a diminisher'; explanation of the technical term *kādōzed*, injury by negligence (*pad sūdagīh*)418–420
kēn-menišn malicious intent; opposite: *hu-menišn* 413, 422, 472
  see also ***duš-menišn***
kešišn drawing, pulling (penalty for a corresponding injury) 427, 429
kirb-abganišnīh (injury caused by) throwing a body 427–429, 433
kirbag virtue, virtuous deed 7, 9, 90, 220, 384, 403, 410, 459, 469, 493
kirrōg artisan, craftsman 372
kirrōgbed chief of the craftsmen (Syr. *qārugbed*) 373
kišwānīh wizōstan to investigate tillage 369, 372
****kōybān*** 'keeper of a town, village, street, district' (?); person in charge of controlling a street, district or section of a village or town (tentative reading and translation) 520–521
kū-m ... (ō tō) dād 'I gave, I have given (to you)'; agential/ergative construction in a will (*handarz*) or *donatio mortis causa* or testamentary contract (*paymān*) implying that the transfer of property specified in the will is 'ambulatory', taking effect not from when it was made, but only *after* the demise of the testator/donor (in contrast to the optative *ē dahēd* 'shall be given' or the present *dahom* 'I give, will give' with no such restriction) 83–85, 238–239, 391, 399
kū-m pad ēn xwāstag **⟨NKSY'⟩** ***(wahmān mard) pāyandān kard*** 'I have made for this money (such-and-such a man) surety'; in credit law: formulaic statement of the debtor offering a personal surety to the creditor for a money loan. The formulation implies that the surety is only liable for payment when the principal debtor is insolvent or inaccessible 354, 357
kū-m... pad tan az ... padīrift 'I have accepted (so-and-so) "as a body" (= as personal security) from (so-and-so)'; in credit law: formulaic statement of the creditor accepting a person as personal security from the debtor for a loan 352–354, 357
kū-mān xwāstag **⟨NKSY'⟩** ***abām stad ham-pāyandān hēm*** 'We have taken money as a loan (and) are co-sureties'; in credit law: formulaic statement of co-debtors who are at the same time co-sureties with joint liability as *hamāg-tōzišn* 'joint and several debtors'. The creditor can demand full payment of the whole sum from any one of the persons under contract 355–356
kū-š man āgāhīh nest 'I have no knowledge of it'; in credit law: statement of the alleged debtor/heir denying knowledge of any liabilities of the deceased *paterfamilias* 363
kun-marz wināh sin of anal intercourse (sodomy) 452–453, 738
kunišn action, deed, execution; the physical element of a crime (*actus reus*) 412, 570–571

mad income, surplus; income that has already been attained (in contrast to income that is expected for the future, called *rasēd*)
  mad ud rasēd '(income) that has come and shall be attained', the surplus income of family property, which is not originally part of the *patrimonium*,

corresponding roughly to *bona adventitia* in Roman law 74, 78, 139, 192–193, 211, 392–393

mādag (1) object of dispute, matter in dispute, subject-matter of a lawsuit; the object of civil litigation; (2) money 386, 421, 440–441, 444–445

mādag guharīgān compensation for the object of dispute in a lawsuit 544

mādagwar (1) original version, template of a document (as opposed to its copy, *hampaččēn*); (2) principal party, main claimant (in legal proceedings; in credit law); (3) principal organ of the body (in criminal law) 270, 355, 426, 537–539, 541

mādayān foundation deed of a sacred fire or pious endowment 276, 278, 285

mahistag (village) Elder; authoritative representative of a settlement or village 439

mar account of shareholders and partners in the *bun* ('base'; the central repository or inventory holding of a village) 200 (fn. 62)

see also ***bun*** (2)

mard man

mard ī ahlaw righteous man 217, 385, 464

mard ī āsrōn hāwišt student of a Mazdean priest 181

mard ī nihišnōmand lender, creditor (translates Av. *nəmaŋhant-* adj. 'giving a loan') 312, 319

see also ***nihišn***

mard ī šahr man of the realm, citizen of Iran (Ērānšahr) 103, 114–117, 120, 125, 207, 245, 360

mard kē ō kas tōzišn dahišn 'man who owes a payment to someone'; debtor 310

see also ***kas kē čiš awiš tōzišn dahišn*** 'creditor'

mārgan 'serpent-scourge'; whip 426–429, 433

margarzān 'death deserving' (1) capital crime deserving the death penalty; (2) person who has committed a capital crime deserving the death penalty; (3) highest degree of sin in Zoroastrian law 480–482, 485, 489, 491, 572, 574–575, 581–583, 586, 738–740

margīh ud rēštagīh death and injury 465

marīhā čand 'a corresponding equivalent' (of the loan repaid in instalments to be released from pledge) 329

marzānān border peoples; inhabitants of the borders of Ērānšahr 117, 333

mehdādestānīh 'great/greater justice'; extension of a legal right or claim; going beyond the minimal requirements of law; doing more than legally required 72–73, 379, 384, 569, 571

see also ***wehdādestānīh***

mehtarān the Elders; authoritative representatives of a settlement or village 321–322

menišn thought, disposition, intention, intent; the mental element of a crime (*mens rea*) 7, 312–313, 315, 412–414, 422, 470, 472, 570–571, 616

see also ***kām***

mēnōy dādwar judge in the *mēnōy* (spiritual) existence 7

see also ***gētīy dādwar***

mērag (1) young husband (counterpart to *ziyānag* 'young woman, wife'); (2) business partner, associate, *socius* 246, 252

mihōxt false accusation 252

mihpaitim/miϑōpaitim (Av. **miϑō.paiϑimna-*? 'having false entitlement, false possession') false claim to an entitlement 499

mihr contract, binding agreement 7, 119, 260, 262–263

mihr-drōzīh oath-breaking, contract breaking (= *mihrōdrujīh*) 462

mihrōdruǰ (Av. *miϑrō.druj-*) contract breaker 258

mihrōdrujīh breach of contract, contract breaking (= *mihr-drōzīh*); offence considered as a *margarzān* and noted in the *pursišn-nāmag* 68, 262, 313, 434, 491, 574, 595, 618

mizd reward, pay, remuneration

mizd ī stūr remuneration of a 'proxy' 513

mizd ud rōzīg remuneration and (daily) payment 224

miϑōsāst (Av. **miϑō.sāsta-*) false teaching; teaching lies; considered as an *adwadād* offence 424, 427–429, 433, 466, 468

mowān handarzbed Chief Counsellor of the Magi; title of a religious authority with judicial competences 508–510

mowbed mobed; title of a religious dignitary; judge presiding over a court of appeal 503–504, 509

mowbedān mowbed Chief Mobed; highest religious and legal official, whose judgement cannot be contested 507–511

muhr seal

muhr brīdan to engrave a document with one's seal; to seal 289, 300

muhr-dād (document of) seal transfer; document assigning a particular (administrative?) seal to another official 296

muhr ī ēwar reliable, legally binding seal; personal or administrative seal that is currently in use and effective 296, 299, 300, 547, 550–551, 593

see also ***muhr ī wāwarīgān*** and ***muhr ī wizurd***

muhr ī padiš āwišt 'the seal with which it (= the document) is sealed' 287, 300

muhr ī pad kār-framān dāštan 'seal for exercising command', anonymous administrative seal on which the name and place of the administration were engraved 293, 295–296, 300, 511 (fn. 57), 550–551

muhr ī pad wāwarīgānīh padīrift ēstēd 'seal which has been accepted as a valid one'; private seal of a witness to a transaction that has been assessed by legal instances as valid 297–298

muhr ī wāwarīgān valid seal; official seal conferring validity to a document 288, 296–298, 300, 593

see also ***wāwarīgān muhrān***, ***muhr ī ēwar*** and ***muhr ī wizurd***

muhr ī wizurd genuine seal; personal or administrative seal, which is valid, but no longer in use 296, 299, 300, 547, 550–551

see also ***muhr ī ēwar*** and ***muhr ī wāwargān***

muhr (…) pad āšnāg guftan to identify, vouchsafe for the authenticity of a (private or witness) seal 288, 300

muhr padīriftan to accept a seal (as valid) 288, 519

muhr škastan ud nišān kardan 'to break a seal and mark it'; one of the competences of the *dādwar* 501

****muhrag ī wāwarīgān*** valid document; document sealed with the valid seal (*muhr ī wāwarīgān*) of a State official or of trustworthy witnesses (in contrast to those confirmed only by the private seals of witnesses, whose reliability has not been assessed by official instances); Syr. translation *šṭārā men šarrīrā* 592–593

must violence (originating from *duš-āgāhīh* 'ignorance'; opposite of *dād* 'law') 8

mustgarzīh complaint of appeal; *abar mustgarzīh ī pēšēmālān ud pasēmālān* 'on the complaint of appeal of the plaintiffs and defendants' 524–525

+***mustīh garzīdan*** to file an appeal 416, 524–525

mustōmandān garzišn complaint of those who appeal (to the next instance) 524–525

nabāg/nibāg hostage; person transferred as a 'living' pawn for a loan 117, 326–327, 332–335

nabānazdištān relations, relatives 152, 155

nāf family 121

see also ***dūdag***

nagīrā(y) (būdan) to deny, refute, repudiate 317, 362, 364, 544, 559–560

nagīrāygar (person) who refutes, denies an accusation; pleading not guilty 446, 451

nahang province 218

nām name

nām-burdār name-bearer, name-carrier, successor of a *paterfamilias* (*kadag-xwadāy*) 120, 138, 174

nām-burdārīh process of name-bearing, of continuing the lineage 121, 131

nāmag **⟨n'mk'⟩** writ, record, document, letter; general expression any kind of *written* record 181, 270–273, 285, 287, 297–298, 500, 513, 586

as the second part of a compound a technical term referring to various types of court transcripts or protocols: *see* ***saxwan-nāmag***, ***pāymān-nāmag***, ***pursišn-nāmag***, ***uzdād-nāmag***, ***yazišn-nāmag***, ***wizōst(an)-nāmag***, ***zastbūd-nāmag***

nāmag-niyān archive, repository, deposit of documents; specifically an archive of documents of registered fire-foundations 218, 270

nāmag **⟨GT-y/GTk⟩** (or: ⟨gt/gtk⟩ *gitt*, *gittag*?) foundation deed of a pious foundation 222, 227, 275–278, 284, 293

see also ***gitt/gittag***

nāmag ī nēk, ⟨GṬk'/*gṭk*' Y nywk'⟩, lit. 'good (= proper, faultless, valid?) document', transfer list of various agricultural products and livestock; document listing expenses, investments and transactions involving the collective property in the central repository (*bun*) of a village 278–279, 284

see also ***gittag ī nēk***

nāmagānīh cult of the souls of the ancestors; name-preservation of the forefathers 121, 131, 140, 178, 220, 231, 254, 258, 461

narīh ud mādagīh 'maleness and femaleness'; process of establishing a person's gender in court (duty of the *dādwar*) 500

nazdpaywandān close relations 152

nazdpaywandtar nearest relations, members of the nuclear family 152

nē no, not, un-

nē awestwār ud nē wāwar unreliable and invalid; null and void 244

nē dānist '(having) no knowledge'; formula spoken by the alleged debtor(s)/heir(s) under oath denying knowledge of any liabilities of the deceased *paterfamilias* 363, 555–556, 558

nē dānom 'I do not know'; formula spoken by the alleged debtor(s)/heir(s) under oath denying knowledge of any liabilities of the family or the deceased *paterfamilias* 556–559

nē dastwarīhā not entitled, unauthorized (= *a-dastwarīhā*; *abē-dastwarīhā*) 384

nē ēdōnīh 'it (is) not so; not-thusness', falsity; formula spoken under oath refuting the claim of an opponent 556–558

nē man ān pad āgāhīh ast (Av. *nōiṯ [vā] ⁺aŋhe ⁺vaēδa*) 'that is not in my knowledge'; formula spoken under oath 559

nē pādixšāy bē ka he/she is obliged, has the duty, is compelled to (do/say/perform something) (lit. 'he/she is not authorized except; he/she has no right than, no [other] option but ...') 87–88

nērang incantation (during an oath/ordeal); *abar nērang ī war passāxt* 'on the incantations of the ordeal test'; *nērang ī pahrēz* 'incantations of protection' (from harm during an ordeal) 553 (fn. 190); 554, 560

nibāg *see* ***nabāg***

nibēg template, original record, on which a document of conveyance (*nāmag*) is based 271–272, 285

see also ***aswār-nibēg*** 'horseman's document' and ***dast-nibēg*** 'handwritten record'

nibišt any written document (to be distinguished from *nibištag*) 265, 285, 375

nibištag bill of indictment; formal document accusing a person of commiting a specified offence or several offences (criminal law; to be distinguished from *nibišt*) 74, 79, 285, 429, 510, 546, 549, 573–575, 578–579

nigerišnīg intentional, deliberate; *pad nigerišnīg zanišnīh* 'intentional injury' 92, 412 (fn. 46), 419–422, 424, 570

see also ***wināh ī nigerišnīg*** 'intentional offence'

nihādag 'set down, founded'; foundation, establishment, endowment, deposit 221 (fn. 153), 222, 312 (fn. 244)

nihān (in) secret, concealment, secretly (referring to the offence of the thief, who steals secretly) 434–435, 450, 618

nihān būd concealed (fact or evidence) 499

nihišn loan, debt, credit (translates Av. ²*nəmah-* 'loan, credit'), employed either only in Pahlavi translations of the Avesta or for a specific type of loan (gratuitous loan, deposit, bailment?) to be distinguished from the general *abām* 312, 315–316, 319

see also ***mard ī nihišnōmand*** and ***nihišn ⁺kē barišn***

nihišn ⁺kē barišn lender, creditor (translates Av. *nəmō.bara-* adj. 'who gives a loan, creditor') 312, 319

nimāyišnīg (statement) by demonstration (in a dispute/trial) 407, 409–411

see also ***gōwišnīg***

nimāyišnīg nē gōwišnīg (statement) by demonstration (in a dispute/trial), without a verbal declaration

nindar dašt 'within the borders of the field', on which a water channel is dug 250

see also ***hērōn dašt***

⁺niyuruzd inferior person; in the context of food distribution: a person ranking low in the hierarchy of recipients of sustenance; opposite: *arzānig* 258

nizārīh weakness (caused by an injury) 426, 433

ō to, at (prep.)

ō abēmustīh madan/rasīdan 'to achieve an uncomplaining (state); to reach satisfaction'; to satisfy a claimant by a decision that will bring the lawsuit to a close 524–526

ō bun (būdan) '(to accrue) to (one's) stock/account'; sins and virtues that accumulate during a person's lifetime and form the stock or substance (*bun*) of that person's soul 9, 402

see also ***bun*** (3)

ō dastwarān zamān xwāstan *see* ***zamān xwāstan***

ō ēwarīh wardīdan to change (a false statement in court) into a reliable one 561, 568

ō gōw āmadan to come to a hearing; to attend the trial; formal words confirming that the litigant(s) will attend the trial: *ō gōw āyēm* 'I/we will come to the hearing' 540–541

ō gōw āmad pād 'he has come to the hearing (and) waited'; formulaic entry in the protocol confirming the arrival and presence of a litigant in court 540

ō gōw ī pēš tō wisē ē kunēd 'You should summon (the litigants) to a hearing in your presence'; formula ordering an official to summon the litigants to a preliminary hearing 535

ō radān appār 'it (is) lost to the *radān*'; a specific thing/property is conveyed to the *radān* due to a prohibited transaction or an offence on part of one of the litigants 328–329

see also ***xwāstag ō radān appār***

ō tōzišn madan/rasīdan to be due for payment 309–310

oškāfišn (injury caused by) ripping 425, 433

ōstāndār governor of a province (*ōstān*); satrap 511–513

ōšyār(ag) mentally sound, healthy, conscious; one of the prerequisites for being considered as a subject of legal rights; opposite: *nē ōšyār* 'mentally unsound' 120, 125, 172, 178, 244

ōšyārīh mental health, full consciousness; one of the prerequisites for making a valid will, besides *tan-drustīh* 'good health, physical intactness'; *andar ōšyārīh* 'in full consciousness' 237, 244

ōy he, she, it (pers.pron. 3rd sg.)

ōy kē grawagān andar nihēd 'he who holds an *antichresis*' pledge-holder, pledgee, mortgagee (of the fruits) 349

ōy kē xwāstag tōzišn 'he who must pay the money', debtor 310, 338

see also ***mard kē ō kas tōzišn dahišn*** 'debtor'

ōy kē xwāstag xwēš owner of a (pledged) property, pledgor 328

ōzadan to kill, killing, homicide (criminal act categorized as *zanišn*) 407, 411, 423, 429, 432, 739

pad in, on, upon, at, for, by, with, with regard to, according to (prep.)

pad abām hišt dādan to grant a debt relief, to cancel a debt 366–367

pad abām/tōzišn ... nagīrā(y) hēnd 'they deny the debt (payment obligation)' 362, 364

pad abām/tōzišn ... xwastūg hēnd 'they recognize the debt (payment obligation)' 362, 364

pad abarmānd total (patrimonial/residuary) estate bequeathed as a whole; inheritance that is not partitioned among the heirs and legatees, in contrast to *pad bahr* or *pad ǰud bahr* 'in (separate) shares' 204
see also ***abarmānd***

pad abāz grift ud sāk/nisāk abar nihād 'for detaining and levying taxes'; responsibility of the *mowbed* and the *rad* 504–505, 512

pad āgenēn dārišn in joint possession with equal shares 247, 249–250, 252

pad āgenēn xwēš in joint ownership; co-ownership with equal shares (contrasted with *ǰud ǰud xwēš* '[having] separate ownership') 246, 252

pad ahlawdād in (fulfilment of) a pious act; as a pious gift 135–136, 210–211, 237, 254, 461

pad ān dastwarīh dāram 'I possess it by that entitlement'; formulaic statement by which a person declares that he is legally entitled to hold a specific property 562

pad ān xwāstag* (NKSY') *ēk ōy ī did ham-pāyandān hēm 'for this money (loan) we are co-sureties, one for the other'; in credit law: formulaic statement of co-debtors who are at the same time co-sureties with joint liability as *hamāg-tōzišn* 'joint and several debtors'; the creditor could demand full payment of the whole sum from any one of the persons under contract 356 357

pad āšnāg guftan to declare as known, to identify; to establish the identity of a person and his seal 288, 300

pad āšnāg guft ī … āwištan 'to seal (a document) according to the identification of (NN)' ; formulaic phrase in documents naming a witness (NN) who has identified a person and his seal 288, 300

pad āwišt ī pēšēmāl/pasēmāl sealed by the plaintiff/defendant 300

pad bahr in shares; inheritance of a *paterfamilias* partitioned into individual shares (in contrast to *pad abarmānd*) 204

pad bahr hangārišn az bahr hangārišn 'to be taken into account regarding the share; to be deducted from the share'; formulaic phrase in a testator's last will, by which he determines that a gift transferred to a beneficiary during his (= the testator's) lifetime should be deducted from this beneficiary's share at the time of the distribution of the residuary estate among the heirs and legatees in order to avoid disadvantaging the other recipients 237

pad čahar bahr ē(w) bahr one-fourth (of the total value of a thing); in the context of barter (*guharēn*): the maximal extent of profit allowed by exchanging one thing for another 388

pad čāštag according to legal doctrine; *ex lege*; Syr. rendering: *bᵊ-dīna* 70–71, 571, 616
see also ***čāštag***

pad dād by conveyance; transfer of proprietary rights in a formal procedure consisting of an offer made by the person willing to transfer an object or enter a contract (offeror/transferor), which could be accepted or refused by the recipient (offeree/transferee) 301

pad dād dādan to give as a gift; to convey in form of a gift 390, 399

pad dād … padīrišn paydāgēnīd 'he has revealed consent to the transfer/gratuity' 391, 399

pad dastwarīh andar ēstādan to function as *auctor*; to enter *auctor*-ship 544

pad dastwar nagīrā(y) būdan to deny (being) the legal predecessor/*auctor* 544

pad dīd ud wēnišn 'under surveillance and observation' (of the *sālār*); offence committed with knowledge of the legal guardian against one of his wards 182

pad do bahr ē bahr one half (lit. 'one share of two shares') 181

pad dūdag sūdōmandīhātar 'in the best interests of the family'; obligation of the nominated guardian (*sālār ī gumārdag*) regarding the proper management of family property according to the document (*nāmag*) by which he is installed 181

pad ēmōzan hangārišn '(it is) to be taken into account for the equipment'; formulaic phrase determining that a grant is to be given to a horseman or knight (*aswār*) for his military equipment 271, 513 (fn. 64)

pad ēn xwāstag* ⟨NKSY'⟩ *wahmān mard pāyandān hom/hēm 'For this money I am (we are) surety (sureties) for such-and-such a man'; in credit law: formula spoken by the surety (sureties) creating a secondary obligation to compensate the loss of the creditor only if the principal debtor was insolvent, hence unable to satisfy the creditor 355, 357

pad ēwar dāštan to consider as reliable, competent 7, 501, 519

pad ēwarīh kār az-iš kardan to treat (a document) as binding; to assess a document as trustworthy and legally binding 298

pad gōwišn (contract) by speech; verbal contract (renders Av. *vača.hina-*) 262, 264

pad graw abāz griftan to hold back as pledge/pawn 336

pad grawagānīh dāštan to hold as *antichresis* 330, 349

pad graw/grawīh dāštan to keep as pledge/pawn 330, 336

pad graw/grawīh griftan to take as pledge 336

pad graw nihādan to deposit as pledge 312 (fn. 24), 336

pad graw stadan to take as pledge 336

pad gugāyīh šāyēd 'it is admissible as testimony'; opposite: *pad gugāyīh nē šāyēd* 'it is not admissible as testimony' 549

pad gumēzag gumēzag guftan to make confused ('mixed') statements (in court) 568

pad gyāg immediately, on the spot, without delay 239, 313, 331, 391

pad kardag in legal practice, *via administrationis*; *pad kardag nē kard* 'it is not done in legal practice'; Syr. rendering: *bə-mparnsānūṯā* 70–71, 207, 342, 386, 501, 546, 549, 571, 586, 616–617

see also ***kardag***

pad menišn zadan with the intent to smite 414, 422, 470, 472

pad nigerišnīg wilfully, intentionally, deliberately'; *pad nigerišnīg zanišnīh* 'intentional injury' 92, 412, 421, 422, 424

pad rāh ī āgrawīh by means of hypothecating the substance (*bun*) of property 208, 342

pad rāh ī a-kasīh; due to having no relations (lit. 'by means of having no relations') 208

pad rāh ī dādestān by means of the judiciary, by judicial means 5, 438, 526

pad rāh ī dādestān ō abēmustīh rasād to make (a claimant) uncomplaining by judicial means; to impede the continuation of a lawsuit in a higher instance by satisfying the claimant 438, 526

pad rāh ī zahagīh ud paywand by means of offspring and descent 118–119

pad ruwān (property) for the soul; formula by which property is assigned to pious and charitable purposes; identical with *ruwān rāy* 'for the soul, on behalf of the soul' (to be distinguished from *ruwān yazišn rāy* and *pad ruwān yazišn*) 178, 200, 202, 205–206, 220, 222–223, 225, 229–231, 623–624

pad ruwān dāštan for keeping the soul 205, 220, 623

pad ruwān ī xwēš ud Mihrēn dāštan rāy 'for preserving my own soul and the soul of Mihrēn' (*i. e.* such-and-such a person, N.N.); formula with which property is reserved for pious and charitable purposes for the founder's own soul and that of another person 223

pad ruwān yazišn 'for ceremonies for the soul', formula by which funds or a specific property is assigned to financing the performance of post-mortem rites and ceremonies for the soul of the deceased (identical with *ruwān yazišn rāy*; to be distinguished from *pad ruwān* and *ruwān rāy*) 220, 254

pad sālārīh under guardianship 126

pad sē gōwišn(īh) 'by the triple formula'; confirming an agreement, contract or testimony by uttering the Zoroastrian maxim *humat, hūxt, huwaršt* ('good thought, good speech, good deeds') 136, 366, 538

pad stahm ud xrōst 'by violence and shouting'; act of coercion and force 438

pad stŭrīh (property) in trust, for substitute/subsidiary succession 173, 197, 200, 205–206, 213–219, 229–230

pad tan as personal security (lit. 'as a body; physically'); formula with which a person is pledged as personal security: *kū-m … pad tan az tō padīrift* 'I (= the creditor) have accepted N.N. (name of the security) 'as a body' (= as personal security) from you (= the debtor)' 106, 352–354

pad tāšt for certainty; *pad tāšt war warzidan* 'to take an oath for certainty' 559–560

pad tōzišn ī kadag-xwadāy xwastūg hēnd 'they recognize the payment obligation of the *paterfamilias*'; formula expressing that the heirs and legatees accept the liabilities of the deceased head of a household 362

pad war … wehdādestāntar '(he/she is) better/best suited to take the oath for better justice'; person, who is the best choice for taking the oath 364, 555, 560

pad wināh warōmand (person) suspected of having committed an offence 182

pad windišn pādixšāy(īhā) kard '(he/she has been) given entitlement to the income' 108, 139, 251, 305

pad wizīr hunsand (būdan) (to be) satisfied with the verdict; to accept the verdict 268, 522–523, 587

pad xwāst ud dād 'by request (of the groom) and acceptance (of the prospective bride's father; lit. "giving away")'; the formal act of 'giving away' (*dād*) the bride by the father is accomplished in fulfilment of a 'pious act' (*pad ahlawdād*) whilst uttering the 'triple formula' (*pad sē gōwišnīh*) 135–136

pad xwāstag … anbasān 'in disagreement regarding the matter of dispute' 191

pad xwāstag pahikārdan to enter litigation with regard to the object of dispute 191

pad xwāstag saxwan guftan to make a statement (in court) regarding the matter of dispute 191

pad xwastagdārīh (property) in hereditary possession (of the heirs and legatees) 202, 205–211, 229–230

pad xwēšīh (property) in ownership 195, 204–206, 210–212, 229–230
pad xwēšīh ī xwēš 'in my own ownership', formula by which the (alleged) owner declares that he has an ancient, vested right to an object (as heir or legatee) and that it has *not* been recently acquired (by barter, sale, donation, etc.) 195, 212
pad xwēš kām 'according to his own will' 380
pādan to stay, wait (in court); *pād ud nē pād* 'he has waited; he has not waited': entry in the court transcript recording whether a litigant has waited for his opponent to appear in court or not 499
padān ī dēn religious authorities; in charge of selecting an appropriate guardian (*sālār*) or 'proxy' (*stūr*) 171, 181, 254
pādifrāh punishment 595
pādimār *see* ****pāymār***
pādīrān suspension; *pādīrān ī war* 'suspension of the oath' 501, 504, 518
pādīrānēnidan to hold back, restrain, suspend 456, 467, 523
pādīrāngar person (vendor), who holds something back, suspends something 467
pădīrāy receipt, receipt confirmation, acknowledgement of receipt; document confirming the receipt of a payment of a specified amount of money or a certain item or product 281–282, 298
padīrišn paydāgēnīdan to declare acceptance; formula with which the recipient (transferee) of an offer officially accepts an offer (of transfer), creating a binding contract between offeror (transferor) and offeree (transferee/recipient) 304, 391–392, 398–399
see also ***pad dād ... padīrišn paydāgēnīd***
pādixšāy authorized, empowered, entitled, privileged, allowed; in the threefold sense of: (1) having a just claim; (2) being entitled to a special right or privilege/liberty (the jural correlative of 'no-right'); (3) being empowered, authorized; *pādixšāy būdan* 'to be entitled, authorized'; *pādixšāy kardan* 'to authorize, entitle; give a mandate/power of attorney'; *nē pādixšāy bē ka* (lit. 'he/she has no [other] right than; he/she has no [other] option but') 'he/she is obliged, has the duty, is compelled to (do/say/perform something)' 85–89
pādixšāy-būd authorization, entitlement 88
see also ***ēwēn-būd***
pādixšāy pad-iz dastwarīh authorized by entitlement 546–547, 549
pādixšāy(īhā)-zanīh marriage of the privileged kind; marriage with full matrimonial rights 121–124, 126, 129–130, 132, 134–145, 159–161, 183–185
pādixšāyīh authorization, empowerment, entitlement 85
pādixšīr foundation deed (of a fire foundation or pious endowment) 222, 225, 227, 276, 278, 285
pādram dusraw notoriety in the community 575, 584
pādrōz daily expenses 587
pādrōzag delay, postponement 437
pahikār dispute, judicial dispute
pahikār-rad person (involved) in a judicial dispute (following Zoroastrian law); litigant; opposite: *a-pahikār-rad* 404–411, 425 (fn. 103)
pahikār-radestān 'division on judicial dispute'; beginning of the legal nasks (*dād bun*) of *Dēnkard* 8 404, 410, 674–678

pahikār-radīh judicial dispute, litigation (following Zoroastrian law); opposite: *a-pahikār-radīh* 405–411, 495

pahikār-radīh abāg-šān nēst 'there is no judicial dispute with them'; referring to persons who are excluded from jurisdiction 410

pahikārdan to litigate, to take legal action 191, 438

pah-masāy the size of small livestock (sheep or goat) (renders Av. *pasu.maza-*); contract defined by its worth in small livestock; the equivalent of three stater 262

****pāk(a) fšū̆-ciϑā-*** ⟨p'k pswc'š'⟩ atonement in kind by (submitting) a young animal; compensation in kind for an offence 440–441

pārag parcel, piece of land 370

pasēmāl defendant; *pēšēmāl pad xwāstag … ud pasēmāl anbasān* 'the plaintiff … and defendant (are) in disagreement regarding the matter in dispute' 191, 275, 287, 290, 300, 388, 497–498, 502–503, 533–535, 537, 539, 540–541, 555, 558–559

pašēmānīh ī menišnīg 'regretting in thought'; first step in redeeming a sin 413

pasēnīgān later, following generations 380

pas-madār (person) who comes afterwards; in the context of oath taking: litigant who is not the first person to take the oath 553–554

pašn contract, bond 117, 261, 264, 285, 333

passand leniency (in justice); renouncement of a legal right or claim; Syr. translation: *ḥasīrūt dīnā* 'decrease of justice' 70–73, 569, 571, 610–611

passandārīh pawn or deposit chosen by the creditor 324, 326, 334–335

passāxt ordeal; elliptical expression, possibly derived from an original *war passāxt* 'test of the ordeal' or *war passāxtan* 'to prepare the ordeal; to test by ordeal'; *passāxt ī mēnōy* '*mēnōy* ordeal'; *war passāxt ī mēnōy* 'test by *mēnōy*-ordeal' 552, 558, 560

passāxt gāh place of the oath

passāxtan to arrange, prepare an ordeal; *pad passāxtan* 'for arranging an ordeal' 182, 552–553, 586, 560, 586

pašt contract, binding agreement; initially 'verbal agreement/contract', corresponding to the *stipulatio* in Roman law and the simple 'parol contract' in English law; but also 'written contract' due to its use in connection with the (testamentary) contract (*paymān*) and its frequent confusion with *nibišt* 'written record/document'; specifically: (1) verbal agreement; (2) sale contract; (3) testamentary contract, (4) document of conveyance; promissory note 264–268, 285

pašt dād xwēš 'the contract (is) conveyed (as her/his) own'; formulaic statement implying that a contract transferring ownership of a specific object has legal effect only with respect to the recipient named in the agreement, *excluding the heirs* from any claims 82

see also the formula ***dād pašt xwēš*** with diametrically opposed legal consequences

pāyag degree or level of sin in Zoroastrian law 414, 439, 442, 449 450, 457–458, 468–484

pāyag ī duzīh degree of theft 439, 442

pāyandān surety, warrantor, guarantor, person provided as personal security for a loan by the debtor 325–326, 350, 354–357, 366

pāyandānīh suretyship, guarantee 326, 349–359

pāyandānīh nēst there is no suretyship; suretyship is not in effect 357

pāyandānīh xūb suretyship is proper, in force 357

paydāg manifest, clear, self-evident; referring to a case, document, statement or action that has no need of proof 288, 296, 519–520

paydāg kardan to reveal, make visible, obvious (1) to establish, settle, found; legal formula for establishing a *stǔrīh* or a foundation 'for the soul' (*pad ruwān / ruwān rāy*); (2) to register (expenditures and revenues); (3) to prove 216, 221, 223, 323, 362, 364, 512, 625

see also ***paydāgēnīdan***

paydāgēnīdan to reveal, to establish, settle, found; technical term used for establishing a *stǔrīh* or a foundation 'for the soul' (*pad ruwān / ruwān rāy*) 216

see also ***paydāg kardan***

payg foot soldier 424

paymān(-nāmag) contract, binding agreement; most frequent term for all kinds of contracts, specifically: (1) loan, sale, marriage contract; (2) letter of attorney or mandate; (3) testamentary contract; (4) document of conveyance, promissory note 235, 251, 261, 265–268, 273, 285–286, 320

****pāymār*** ⟨PKDWN⟩ (1) decree, command, order, injunction, disposition, provision; (2) delegate, representative 514–515 (fn. 65)

****pāymār kardan*** (1) to make a disposition, provision, decree; (2) to designate as delegate, representative 514–515 (fn. 65)

paywand descent group, lineage, family, relations, descendants 118–119, 121, 128, 180

paywand pad mādarān matrilineal descent 258

pēšag estate, class, guild 95, 98, 120, 138, 372, 437

pēšag-sālār head of the guild 268, 372

pēšēmāl plaintiff, claimant, complainant; *pēšēmāl pad xwāstag ... ud pasēmāl anbasān* 'the plaintiff ... and defendant (are) in disagreement regarding the matter of dispute' 191, 275, 289, 300, 497–498, 502–503, 524, 533–535, 537, 539–541, 555

pēšgāhīh front rank, superior rank 112

pēšīgān-wāspuhragān dowry; property brought into the marriage by the wife (*dos* in Roman law) 140–141, 232, 274

+***pēš-madār*** '(person) who comes first'; in the context of oath-taking: litigant who takes the oath first 554

see also ***pas-madār***

pēštom zanišn pre-emptive strike, pre-emptive injury 405

pēš-tōzišnīh advance payment, prepayment; presumably in the sense of a 'charge', a type of security protecting the creditor (chargee) by giving him the right to payment from the sale of mortgaged property in priority to any rights resulting from inheritance or claims any other creditors might have against the debtor, including heirs and beneficiaries 325–326, 339–340, 363

pih victuals, food 466–467

purnāy of major age; mature, adult, as opposed to *aburnāy* 103, 120, 125, 238–239, 396

pursišn-nāmag, record of interrogation, *accusatio scripta*; transcript or protocol in a criminal trial 272, 284–285, 291, 295, 491, 515, 546, 557, 572–576, 579–581, 595

pus ī padīriftag adopted son 170, 176, 179

rabŭn/rabŭna earnest money, down payment, advance payment, pledge, pawn, *arra*; Syr. *răhḇūnā* 379, 619, 660 (fn. 68)

rad title of a religious dignitary, *ratu*; judge presiding over a court of appeal 62–63, 227, 273, 284, 328–329, 383, 404, 425, 437–438, 505–506, 509, 513, 525–526

rad ī xwēš 'one's own *rad*', a person's individual spiritual master, who could be engaged in a dispute as arbitrator, mediator or judge 403, 407–409, 489, 495, 498, 522, 532

rād donor, person who donates a gift; recipient of the gift: ⟨ḤSN'⟩ (**dārāg/dārīg*?) 'donee' 389, 396–397, 399

rāh ō pāyandān ... nē bawēd/nēst 'there is no way to the surety'; the surety/guarantor is not liable, cannot be made liable for the debt 355, 357

rāhdār highwayman 410

rasēd (expected) income, increase, profit; *see* ***mad ud rasēd***

rāst-xwāh with good intent; good-willed; opposite: *wad-xwāh*; *wad-axw* 416, 422

rāyēnišn ī saxwan legal proceedings 501

rēš physical defect; harm; grievous bodily harm; general expression for all kinds of physical injury 425–429, 433

rēšestān 'section on bodily harm' in *Dēnkard* 8 682–684

rōzīg general term for 'ration, sustenance', not only employed in its literal sense of 'daily ration' 224, 252–253, 583 (fn. 288)

ruwān soul

ruwān bizešk soul physician; religious authority who helps the sinner redeem his sins 413

ruwān ī xwēš ud anī-z kas rāy 'for (my) own soul and another person's'; formula with which property is reserved for pious and charitable purpose for the founder's own soul and that of another beneficiary 223

ruwān rāy 'for the soul', formula by which property is assigned to pious and charitable purposes (identical with *pad ruwān;* to be distinguished from *ruwan yazišn rāy*) 205, 216, 222–224

ruwān yazišn religious services and post-mortem rites for the soul(s) (of the deceased) 121, 140, 220

ruwān yazišn rāy 'for religious services for the soul'; formula by which funds or a specific property is assigned to financing the performance of post-mortem rites for the soul of the deceased (identical with *pad ruwān yazišn*; to be distinguished from *pad ruwān* and *ruwān rāy*) 222

ruwānagān pious foundation, charitable endowment (lit. 'pertaining to the soul') 77, 220–222, 254, 623–625, 627

ruwānagān *dibīrag 'register of pious foundations'; one of the main *dīwāns* of the Sasanian State according to al-Ḫwārezmī (Arab. translation *kitābat al-awqāf*) 99, 221

rūzkār daily earnings 565

šāhān šāh bandag subject of the King of Kings 103, 105, 109, 115, 125

šāhīgān property of the crown, royal property, royal treasury 209, 228, 270–271, 506, 512–513, 517

sahišn approval (of a transaction by the recipient)

sahišn ud kāmag dōšīd 'approval and compliance with the will (of the conveyor)'; acceptance by the recipient (donee) of an offer of the conveyor (donor) to enact a transaction 302–303

šahr land, empire, state

šahr hamār *dibīrag 'register of the accounts of the empire/lands'; one of the main *dīwāns* of the Sasanian State according to al-Ḫwārezmī (Arab. translation: *kitābat al-bilad li-l-ḫarāǧ*) 99

****šahr-dādwar*** (Syr. *šhrdwr*) Judge of the State 502

šahr dādwarān dādwar Chief Judge of the State 502–503

šahrīg man of the state/land; man from the nobility, landed proprietor and official of the State with the entitlement to pass judgement in the rank of a *dādwar* 516–517

šahrīgān men of the state/land; group of notables, distinguished magnates of a region from the rank of the aristocracy (*āzādān*), chosen as local representatives; grouped together with the *čašmagān* in an assembly verifying documents and transcripts of criminal cases 515–517

šahryārān local dynasties; rank of the nobility 111

sāk/nisāk taxes, obligatory payments to the State; *pad abāz grift ud sāk/nisāk abar nihād* 'regarding the detainment and levying of taxes' (description of the competences of the *rad, mowbed, ōstāndār); pad hangārd ud ūl stad ī sāk* 'for calculating and taking in taxes' (description of the competences of the *āmārgar*) 227, 504–505, 512, 514

sālār guardian; person who has legal responsibility for the dependant members of a family without legal capacity and for managing family property. Three types of guardians are distinguished: (1) *sālār ī būdag* 'natural guardian': the *padixšāy*-son of the deceased; the adopted son (*pus ī padīriftag*); the 'appointed proxy' (*stŭ̄r ī kardag*); a share-holding brother (*brād ī hambāy*); (2) *sālār ī kardag* 'appointed guardian': person designated as guardian by the deceased *paterfamilias* in his will; (3) *sālār ī gumārdag* 'nominated guardian': person chosen by legal authorities deemed 'most suitable' (*sazāgtar*; *weh-sazāgtar*) for guardianship 177–183

sālārīh guardianship, *manus*, *potestas*, *tutela*, *cura*. The institution of guardianship could be separated into guardianship over dependant members of the family (*dūdag-sālārīh*) and guardianship over family property (*xwāstag-sālārīh*) 177–183

see also ***dūdag-sālārīh*** and ***xwāstag-sālārīh***

sāmān measure 7, 345

sar head; summit; end, beginning

sar bawēd 'it comes to an end'; *dādestān sar bawēd* 'the trial comes to an end' 5, 504, 564, 568

sar brīdan to decapitate (punishment for a capital crime, *margarzān*) 236 (fn. 227)

saxwan word, speech, statement

saxwan-nāmag record of statements; transcript or protocol in a civil lawsuit 272, 279, 285, 289, 295, 534–535, 537, 541, 572

saxwan nihānīg guftan to make a statement in secret 567–568

saxwan pad ēwarīh guftan to make a statement with certainty 567–568

saxwan pad gumānīgīh guftan to make a doubtful statement 567–568
saxwan ud passox garzīdan ī must 'statement and answer filing a complaint/an appeal'; statement/claim of the claimant and answer of the defendant before the judge at a distance of three steps, initiating legal proceedings 500, 524
sazāgīh suitability for being engaged as proxy (*stūr*) or guardian (*sālārīh*) 179
sazāgtar more/most worthy, most suitable, most fitting; person who is most suitable for practicing *stūrīh* or guardianship (*sālārīh*) 169–171, 180, 254
see also ***weh-sazāgtar*** with the same technical meaning (in Tab. 28.8, p. 732)
se three
se gām three steps; distance to be kept from the judge (corresponding symbolically to *se gōwišnīh/se wāzag* 'three utterances'); *andar sē gām ud saxwan ud pāsox garzīdan ī must* 'within (the distance of) three steps both the statement (of claim) and the answer (of defence) in filing an action of complaint' 500, 538
se gōwišn(īh) three utterances; the Zoroastrian triad *humat, hūxt, huwaršt*; *pad se gōwišnīh gōwēd* 'he declares with the three utterances'136, 366, 538
see also ***se wāzag***
se šabag three nights; reflection period conceded to a contract partner in the context of a transaction (sale, barter) 374, 388, 401 (fn. 8)
se wāzag three utterances; the Zoroastrian triad *humat, hūxt, huwaršt* (good thoughts, good speech, good acts) 6, 538
see also ***se gōwišn(īh)***
škenišn (offence caused by) rupturing 425, 433
sneh weapon 426–428, 433, 470–471, 473
šōy ī pādixšāy(īhā) husband in a privileged marriage with full matrimonial rights 86, 136, 142
šōywarīh sālārīh 'husbandly *manus*', guardianship of the husband over his *pādixšāy*-wife 138
spōz-iz ud wastārīh delay and obstinacy; prohibited behaviour of a contractual partner regarding a contractual obligation 140
spurrīgīh ī sneh 'completeness of a weapon'; instrument constructed explicitly as a weapon (in contrast to an object only used as a weapon, such as a stone, *sang*) 427–428
see also ***pad sneh uspurrīg*** 'complete as a weapon'
srāy wager 565
srēnag/sēnag masāy ud bāzā masāy, lit. 'the size of a buttock and size of a forefoot'. The phrase designates the remuneration of a mature man serving as guardian (*sālār*) or as proxy (*stūr*). It originally refers to meat rations from the front and hind part of a slaughtered animal, on the basis of which the daily ration of the guardian or proxy were calculated; derived from Av. *sraoni.masah-* 'the size of a buttock' and **bāzu.masah-* 'the size of a forefoot' (the alternative form with *sēnag* 'breast' is a variant of the original *srēnag* 'forefoot') 76, 173, 182, 214
srōšōčaranām (< Av. *sraošō.čaranā-* '[whip] making obedient') (1) whip, lash, bastinado; instrument of punishment; (2) minor degree of sin in Zoroastrian law 476–477, 482–484
stahm cruel treatment, violence 108, 438

stahmag violent person, oppressor; person who steals manifestly (*āškārag* 'openly'), using force or threatening to use force; synonymous with *appar(ag)* 'robber' 435–436, 450

stardīh stupefaction (caused by an injury) 426, 433

stēndag 'upright one(s)'; notables named together with the *čašmag* ('renowned ones') in the context of evaluating a claim to a *stūrīh* 516–517

stōr-masāy 'the size of large livestock/cattle (cow, ox, horse or another beast of burden)' (renders Av. *staorō.maza-*); contract defined by its worth in large livestock, the equivalent of twelve stater 262

stūr substitute successor, proxy; person obliged to engender an heir for a deceased man who has left no son. The *stūr* is explained as a 'proxy, substitute' (*guhārīg*) for a Zoroastrian (*weh-dēn*) noble man (*āzād*) who is a subject of the King of Kings (*šāhān šāh bandag*) and dies without a male heir, leaving a property worth at least 60 'profit-earning' (*barōmand*) stater (*stēr*). Three types of proxies are distinguished: (1) *stūr ī būdag* 'natural proxy': the *ayōgēn*-women; (2) *stūr ī kardag* 'appointed proxy': person designated as proxy by the testator; (3) *stūr ī gumārdag* 'nominated proxy': person nominated as proxy by legal authorities167–174

see also ***tan-stūr*** and ***zindag-stūr***

stūr-škenišnīh breaking *stūr*-ship; destroying substitute succession; deliberately hindering or ending the institution of *stūrīh;* listed among the capital crimes (*margarzān*) 173, 461–462, 740

stūrīg-pus son born of a proxy 215 (fn. 129)

stūrīh substitute succession, subsidiary succession, succession by proxy 167–174, 205–206, 213–219, 230

stūrīh nē pad raft dārišn '*stūrīh* should not be held in succession'; formula explicitly restricting the duration of the *stūrīh* institution or the sequence of beneficiaries, determining that the heirs of the founder should not inherit *stūrīh*-property in the regular sequence of succession 215, 219

sūd frehbūd excess profit 380

sūdagīhā negligence; unintentionally, negligently, carelessly; *sūdagīhā zanišn* 'injury by negligence' 92, 412–413, 421–422, 570–571

see also ***kādōzed***

sumbišn (injury caused by) piercing 425, 433

šusr ud šīr ud ābusīh (offence regarding) semen and milk and pregnancy; injury causing the diminishment of fertility 426, 433

syā ud spēdīh 'blackness and whiteness (of the hair)'; process of establishing a person's age in court 500

tā dādestān sar bawēd 'until the lawsuit comes to an end' 5, 504, 564–565, 568

tāg lease, leasehold, rent 209, 367–372

tāg wizārdan to pay the rent; *sāl sāl tāg wizārdan* 'payment of a yearly rent' 368, 372

tan person, body; as a technical term: (1) person who is pledged as security for a debt; *see* ***pad tan***; (2) personnel (of the court); *see* ***tan ī dādestān***

tan āšnāg kardan to identify a person (task of the *frēzwān*) 288, 519

tan ī dādestān body of the court; members, personnel of the court; assembly of officials, who take part in a trial (judge, scribes, other public officials) 507–508

tan-drustīh good health, physical intactness; one of the prerequisites for making a valid will, besides *ōšyārīh*, full consciousness 237

tan-duz body-thief; person who cohabits illegally and secretly with the wife of another man; adulterer 459

tan-duzīh body-theft; secret, illicit sexual intercourse with the wife of another man; adultery 414, 448, 455–460

see also ***gād-duzīh***

tan-stūr physical proxy; woman acting as *stūr* for a limited period of time (whose 'body', *tan*, is engaged for procreating a male heir) 171, 185

see also ***zīndag-stūr***

tan ud muhr kū kē pad āšnāg guft 'person and seal: (the one) who identified (them)', person who confirms the identification of a litigant or a witness and his seal 288, 500

see also ***pad āšnāg guftan***

tanāpuhr (1) 'sin for which one atones with the body': highest degree of sin in Zoroastrian law; (2) 'one, who atones with the body': the perpetrator; person who commits a *tanāpuhr* 468–469, 477–485

tarāzug scales (of justice), on which Rašn weighs the sins and merits of a deceased soul 8–10, 402

tar-pih(īh) (Av. *tarō.piϑβa-*) shortage of food, lack of food; an *adwadād* offence: forsaking a person or beneficent animal by withholding nourishment 463

tarsagāh/tarsagāy obedient, dutiful; behaviour expected of persons under guardianship (wives, children, other members of the family, slaves); *tarsagāh warzīdārīh* behaving dutifully 138, 144

tarsagāhīh obedience, submissiveness, dutifulness 123–124, 138, 142, 144

tāšīdan (injury caused by) mutilating, cutting 425, 433

tāšt certainty, confirmation; *pad tāšt war warzišn* 'the oath is to be taken for certainty' 559–560

tasūg 'quarter'; canton 507, 534

tāwān fine, penalty, compensation 108, 182, 308, 321–322, 458–460, 467, 513, 517, 565

tōhmag lineage, descent group, seed 121, 128, 138

tō xwēš 'it (is) your own'; words spoken by the transferor/donor in the context of transfer of ownership during his lifetime (*donatio inter vivos*) 390, 392–396, 399

tō xwēš ē bawēd 'it shall be your own'; words spoken by the transferor/donor in the context of transfer of ownership during his lifetime (*donatio inter vivos*) 390, 393, 396, 399

tōzišn atonement, monetary fine, financial obligation, liability, payment; debt, compensation; both the obligation arising from contract as that arising from a wrongdoing, a sin, injury or offence to be atoned for in form of a pecuniary penalty 307–310, 484

tōzišn dādan to effect a payment (= *tōzišn kardan*, *tōzišn wizārdan*) 88, 310

tōzišn hištan to remit, abate, cancel an obligation 310, 366–367

tōzišn ī pid/pidar liabilities of the father 310

tōzišn ī pidarān debts, liabilities of the ancestors/forefathers 121, 140, 310, 318, 360, 555

see also ***abām ī pidarān***

tōzišn kardan to effect a payment (= *tōzišn dādan*, *tōzišn wizārdan*) 310
tōzišn wizārdan to pay a fine/compensation; effect a payment for a liability/debt (= *tōzišn dādan*, *tōzišn kardan*) 310
tōzišn xwāstan to request, claim, demand a payment 310
tōzišn-xwēš creditor (lit. 'owner of the payment') 310
tōzišnīg kār atonement (for theft) 446
tōzišnōmand debtor (lit. 'liable for payment') 310
tuwān (1) powerful, capable, legally capable; person who has legal capacity; (2) solvent, able to pay; *tuwān-sāmānagīhā* 'according to (one's) financial capacity'; opposite: *a-tuwān* 89, 138, 384
tuwānīgīh (1) powerfulness, capability, contractual capability, legal capacity; (2) solvency, ability to pay; opposite: *a-tuwānīgīh* 89, 103, 120, 125

uštānōmand living being; animal, slave or person deposited as pawn (*ǰām*) or taken as hostage (*nibāg/nabāg*) 327, 332
uzdād-nāmag transcript of proceedings; document accompanying the *pursišn-nāmag* 272, 285, 553, 560
uzdehīg foreigner, as opposed to *ādehīg*, inhabitant of the realm 102, 114–115
uzēnag costs, expenses; *uzēnag ī pad bun*, costs for the maintenance of the substance; *uzēnag ī pad nāmag passāz* 'costs for drawing up a document/protocol/transcript' 224, 249, 387, 585–587

waččag pid xwēš 'the child is the father's own'; proprietary right of the father over the child 105, 200
wad bad, evil
wad pēšagīhā evil profession 384
wad-axw of evil mind; evil-minded person; opposite: *rāst-xwāh* 416–417, 422, 570–571
see also **wad-xwāh**
wad-xwāh (having) evil intent, ill-will; evil-willed person; opposite: *rāst-xwāh* 416–417, 422, 570–571
wad-xwāhīh evil intention; malevolence; sin listed as a *margarzān* 432, 738
wahāg value, worth, remuneration; *wahāg padīrift ud dād* 'acceptance and transfer of a value' 345, 378, 393, 512
war ordal, oath 363, 518, 551–560
see also **passāxt**
war gāh place of the oath, swearing place; venue where the ordeal or oath (*war*) takes place 518, 534, 552, 554, 560
see also **passāxt gāh** and **xwārestān**
war ī dēnīg (dēnīg war) religious oath; this oath is prescribed in the context of credit law, when the alleged debtor claims to have 'no knowledge' (*nē dānist*) of a debt 555–556, 558, 560
war ī pad nāmag-passāz oath in preparation of the transcript 552, 557, 560
war ī pad sōgand sulphurous water oath 556–558, 560
war ī pāy-nišān oath of binding the feet 556, 558, 560
war passāxt test of the ordeal; *abar war passāxt ī mēnōy* 'on the test of the *mēnōy* ordeal' 552, 560

war passāxtan to prepare/implement an ordeal; to test by ordeal 552, 560
war rāyēnīdan to take an oath 553, 560
war-sālār supervisor of the oath/ordeal 518, 553, 560
war sāxtan to prepare/implement an ordeal; to test by ordeal 553, 560
war warzīdan to take an oath 553, 560

wardēnīdan to twist, turn, revise, modify, change, distort (a statement in court) 561, 568

warōmand 'liable to the oath' (1) doubtful, untrustworthy, unreliable (document, seal, procedure); opposite: *ēwar*; (2) suspect; person suspected of having committed an offence; *har dō warōmand hēnd* 'both (persons) are suspects'; opposite: *nē warōmand* 182, 200, 269, 287, 299, 300–301, 362, 430–432, 498, 507, 511, 547, 550–551, 566, 584

wars-rūnišnīh (injury caused by) tearing out hair 427–429, 433

warzīdan ī war to take an oath 518
see also ***war warzīdan***

was wināhīhā very sinful 384

wasasəyāna ⟨w'sʾsy''n'⟩ 'person who could grant favours freely according to his own will'; Pahlavi rendering of the Avestan term **vasasə.yana-* 'who grants favours at will' (MHD 62.14); misspelled as ⟨wss'y'⟩ in Dd. 51.3 (Appendix II, p. 661, fn. 69) 380

wāspuhragān (1) noble families, princes; rank of the nobility (Arab. translation *ahl-al-buyūtāt*); (2) hereditary property; property due to the heirs of a *paterfamilias* 99, 111
see also ***pēšīgān-wāspuhragān***
wāspuhragān xwēšīh ownership of hereditary property 258

waštag saxwanīh revision, distortion of statement (in court); major obstruction of justice in the course of a trial 561–562, 568
see also ***waštagīh***

waštagīh twisting, turning, distorting, modifying, revising; offence of revising or distorting one's statement in court 499, 561–562, 568

wastarag clothing 466–467

wāstaryōš cultivator (Av. *vāstriiō.fšuiiaṇt-*); *wāstaryōšān*, (estate of) cultivators (Arab./Pers. translations *ḥurrāṯ*; *kištārwarzān*; *pēšawarān*) 95, 98, 372

wattar-dādestāntar 'worst justice'; person who fulfils justice worst, who is not suited for taking the oath or as a witness in a judicial procedure; opposite *wehdādestāntar* 'who fulfils justice better/best' 70, 72–73

wāwar valid, in force, in effect (seal, document) 244, 287

wāwarīgān muhrān valid seals 592
see also ***muhr ī wāwarīgān***

wawarīh validity; opposite: *a-wāwarīh* 507–508, 545

waxš interest; payment for the use of a loan by the borrower calculated as a percentage of the principal sum of the loan; identical with *waxt* 78, 192, 197, 266, 319
see also ***hamwaxš***

waxt interest, increase, income; *and dahišn čand waxt* 'as much as the amount of the income must be given' (relating to the amount of rent/lease to be paid by a tenant/leaseholder based on the amount of income achieved by the leaseholder) (= *waxš*) 78, 192, 197

weh good, better

weh-dēn the Good Religion (Zoroastrianism); adherent of the Good Religion 103, 115, 118, 120, 125, 181

weh-dēn dādestānīhātar '(according to) the highest values/laws of the Good Religion'; obligation of the nominated guardian (*sālār ī gumārdag*) to manage family property according to the values named in the document (*nāmag*) issued by religious authorities installing him as guardian 181

weh-mard good, pious man; Zoroastrian, who could act as mediator or arbitrator in disputes between Zoroastrians 407–408, 495, 529

weh sahist dōšīd 'it (is) well approved of (and) sanctioned'; formulaic words spoken by the recipient in consent of a transaction 139, 305

weh-sazāgtar more/most worthy, most suitable; person who is deemed most suitable for practicing *stŭrīh* 732

see also ***sazāgtar*** with the same technical meaning

wehdādestānīh 'good justice, law; good decision, judgement'; extension of a legal right or claim; doing more than legally required; Syr. translation *yaṯīrūt dīnā* 'extension of justice' 70–73, 379–380, 385, 554, 571, 610–611

see also ***mehdādestānīh***

wehdādestāntar 'who fulfils justice better/best'; *pad war … wehdādestāntar* '(person) who is best suited for taking the oath; opposite: *wattar-dādestāntar* 'who fulfils justice worst' 70, 72–73, 362, 364, 542, 555, 560

wēnag ī nē āšnawāg 'who sees, but is deaf'; disabled person, who can take legal action by demonstrating (e.g. showing his injuries or how an assault occurred, etc.) without making an oral statement 410

see also ***nimāyišnīg nē gōwišnīg***

wēnāgīhā zad 'struck in the manner of someone who sees; as an observer'; explanation of the technical term *bōdōzed* as an intentional, deliberate (*nigerišnīg*) injury 418–420

wēnišn inner vision (of the *mēnōy* judge) 7

wināh sin, offence

wināh andar a-bōyīh unintentional/unconscious offence 412, 422, 570–571

see also ***a-bōyīh***

wināh ī hamēmālān sins/offences regarding opponents; offences by which another person is damaged or injured, encompassing both civil cases and criminal acts 3, 9, 62–63, 306, 400, 403, 487–488, 492–494

wināh ī nigerišnīg intentional, wilful, deliberate offence 412, 418–420, 422, 570–571

see also ***bōdōwaršt*** and ***bōdōzed***

wināh ī ō puhl šawēd 'sins which go to the Bridge'; sins that can only be atoned for after the death of the perpetrator at the Činwad Bridge 403, 481

wināh ī ruwānīg sins pertaining to the soul; acts endangering the delinquent's own soul; transgressions against Zoroastrian ritual and ethical norms 3, 9, 62–63, 90, 306, 400, 412, 452, 454, 481, 488

wināhgār offender, sinner; *wināhgārtar* 'greater offender/sinner' 150, 410, 473, 575

wināhgārīh compensation, remuneration 387, 424, 446

windakkar person, who acquires, obtains something, who makes a gain; trader 384

windišn income, earnings 78, 87, 108, 122, 124, 139, 142, 193, 197, 305, 386, 446
see also ***hamwindišn***
wirāyišn arrangement, settlement, agreement, deal 370, 372
wīr-masāy 'the size of a man' (renders Av. *vīrō.maza-*); contract defined by its worth in humans, the equivalent of five-hundred drachms 262–263
+***wišāyišn*** aperture, opening, cut in the skin 423, 433
wisē kardan to summon (to a preliminary hearing, to court) 80, 438, 523, 535
wišōbišn ī dūdag disruption of the family (grievous offence) 461–462
wizārdan to separate, explain, interpret, perform, fulfil, redeem; to atone for; pay, recompense, reimburse; *pādixšāy ka drahm nē wizārēd* 'he is entitled not to pay the money (lit. drachms)'; *drahm be wizār* 'pay the money!'; *ān xwāstag* ⟨NKSY'⟩ *nē wizārd* 'the money is not paid'; *tā drahm wizārēnd* 'until they pay the money' 63, 308–310, 329–330, 367, 368, 372, 614
see also ****abēwizār*** and ****abēsaxwan ud abēwizār***
wizāy hištan to remove harm, damage, a disturbance 504
wizāyīdan to disturb, impede (someone in his/her right to something); *u-m pasēmāl az dārišn wizāyēd* 'the defendant impedes me in my (right of) possession'; *u-m pasēmāl az pad xwēšīh dāštan wizāyēd* 'and the defendant impedes me in my ownership (right)'; *tā dādestān sar bawēd mā wizāy* 'until the trial comes to an end do not impede (your opponent in his right to ownership/possession)' 504, 563–564, 568
wizīdan to damage 513
wizīr (1) judgement, sentence, decision; (2) '(written and sealed) document, contract', specifically: (a) loan contract, (b) marriage contract, (c) title deed, (d) document of conveyance, (e) letter of attorney, mandate 61, 241–242, 268–270, 286, 349, 365, 376–377, 397, 410, 416, 426, 428, 445–446, 451, 508, 518, 549
wizīr ī abāmdān loan contract, document of debt (= *abāmdān wizīr*) 317–318, 320
wizīr ī ēwar valid, authentic, reliable, legally binding document; document that is assessed by legal authorities as authentic and accepted as legal evidence in a lawsuit; opposite: *wizir ī warōmand* 299–300, 362, 547, 550–551
wizīr ī warōmand uncertain, disputable, doubtful document; document whose authenticity is doubted by legal authorities, hence not necessarily accepted as evidence in a lawsuit; opposite: *wizīr ī ēwar* 300, 547, 550
wizīr kardan to pass judgement 444, 459, 567
wizīr pad wizār dāštan to check the verdict (in a court of appeal) 587
wizīr ud dādwarīh verdict and judgement 138
wizōst(an)-nāmag protocol, transcript of investigation 272, 285
wizurd genuine (seal); *see* ***muhr ī wizurd***
wizurdan to uphold, confirm 507–508
wuzurg grandee, noble, aristocrat 103, 322
wuzurgān grandees; rank of the nobility (Arab. translation: *al ʿuẓamāʾ*) 99, 111–112

xānag house, lineage, descent group; *see also* ***kadag*** 'house' with the same figurative sense of 'lineage' 121, 128, 149–150, 321, 345
xēšm xōg violent temper 424

xīr thing, object, matter (in dispute), property; *xīr ud xwāstag* 'goods and property' designates the whole range of a person's property; *xīr ud xwāstag ī xwēš* 'one's own goods and property' 189, 191, 193, 461, 568, 587

see also ***xwāstag***

xīr ī ātaxš/ātaxšān property of the fire(s) 191, 220–222, 225–228, 366, 505–506, 509

xīr ī dūdag property of the family 191

xīr ī duxt, pus, zan ī pādixšāyīhā property of the daughter, son, *pādixšāy*-wife 191

xīr ī šāhīgān property of the crown 513

xīr ī xwēš one's own property 191

xōn tazišnīh (injury causing) flow of blood 426–427, 433

xrad ud ōz (injury causing diminishment of) intelligence and strength 426, 433

xwadāy lord, sovereign

xwadāy-dārīh keeping, preserving the sovereign; one of the highest virtues (*kirbag*); opposite: *xwadāy-dušmenīh* 494

xwadāy-dōstīh love of the sovereign; one of the highest virtues *(kirbag)*; Opposite: *xwadāy-dušmenīh* 494

xwadāy-dušmenīh enmity towards the sovereign; insubordination, rebellion, high treason'; capital crime (*margarzān*) prosecuted by the State; opposite: *xwadāy-dōstīh*; *xwadāy-dārīh*; *xwadāy-paristīh* 491–494

xwadāy-paristīh serving the sovereign; one of the highest virtues (*kirbag*); opposite: *xwadāy-dušmenīh* 494

[1]***xwāhišn*** (injury caused by) treading, trampling, threshing 425, 433

[2]***xwāhišn*** request, appeal, application 161, 360, 459–460

xwāhišn ī tan 'request regarding a person'; request of a litigant to involve another person (as witness or *dastwar*) in the legal proceedings 386

xwar (Av. *x*^{v}*ara-*, lit. 'wound, sore') degree of sin in Zoroastrian law 4, 468–469, 474–475, 482, 484

xwar ī šahr 'penalty of the State' 485

xwar ud dād ī šahr 'penalty and law of the State'; criminal or penal code of the State, containing corporal penalties (*xwar*) 4, 485

xwārestān swearing place; venue where the ordeal or oath (*war*) takes place 518, 552, 559–560

see also ***passāxt gāh*** and ***war gāh***

xwārišn ud dārišn nourishment and maintenance; means by which persons under guardianship are maintained 123–124, 138, 142, 144, 147

xwārtar lesser, smaller (sin/offence) 385, 431

xwasrāyēn/ūn '(having) one's own *manus;* being one's own guardian' (1) designation of the wife in a consensus marriage (the term for the husband is *gādār*); (2) a form of matrimony based on the consensus of the spouses 78–79, 145–147, 160–161

xwāst request, proposal of marriage (of the *pādixšāy* type); *see* ***pad xwāst ud dād*** 'by request (of the groom) and acceptance (of the prospective bride's father)'

xwāstag ⟨hw'stk'⟩ thing, object, *res;* property (distinguished from ***xwāstag*** ⟨NKSY'⟩ by its eteographical spelling); (1) (legal or physical) 'thing', comprising corporeal objects of a completely different nature, encompassing immovable and movable property; (2) object of dispute; matter in dispute; subject-matter of a dispute; any 'thing' that could be the object of civil litigation; (3) property, wealth, object of value, including the complete mass of inheritable family property (*abarmānd*) 189–197

see also ***xīr***

xwāstag frōxt ud be dād nē pādixšāy 'he is not authorized to sell or give away that property'; formula determining that property reserved 'for the soul' could not be alienated and used with another purpose than that specified by the donor/founder 223

xwāstag ī āgraw hypothecated property; mortgage of the substance (*bun*) of property 190, 337–339, 342

xwāstag ī grawagān property whose fruits are mortgaged, *antichresis* 349

xwāstag ī kasān property/thing belonging to a (third) party 190

xwāstag ī mad ud rasēd 'property that has come and shall be attained'; *see* ***mad ud rasēd***

xwāstag ī man handōzam 'property that I acquire'; formula designating a person's individual acquisitions that are not part of inherited property (*abarmānd*) 204

xwāstag ī man xwēš 'thing/property that is my own'; formula by which a person lays claim to ownership of a specific thing/property 190

xwāstag ī pad kas graw object/property pledged to a person (= creditor) 336–337

xwāstag ī pad xwēšīh ī xwēš 'thing/property in one's own ownership'; formula by which a person lays claim to ownership of a specific thing/property due to its having been in his/her possession or in family possession over a longer period or as part of the *abarmānd* 195, 212

xwāstag ī pidar/pidarān estate of the father/ancestors 190

see also ***abarmānd ī pidar/pidarān*** 'total (patrimonial/residuary) estate of the father/forefathers'

xwāstag ī ruwān property of the soul; property reserved for the establishment of a pious endowment or a fire foundation 223

xwāstag ō radān appar 'the thing is lost to the *radān*'; a (pledged/stolen) object is transferred to legal authorities in charge of adjudicating theft 328–329

xwāstag pad abām āgraw 'the property (is) a hypothec for the debt' 342

xwāstag ruwān rāy yazišn nē paydāg kard '(this) property is founded "for the soul", *not* for religious ceremonies'; formula providing that property dedicated to the soul should not be utilized for religious ceremonies, but is reserved for another type of religious act (*e. g.* establishing a pious foundation or a sacred fire) 223

xwāstag-sālārīh guardianship of family property; to be distinguished from *dūdag-sālārīh* 'guardianship of the family' 122, 178–179, 360

see also ***sālārīh***

xwāstag tōzišn part-debtor; person in a partnership who can be charged by a creditor only in proportion to his individual share of a debt, not for the whole debt (as opposed to *hamāg-tōzišn* 'joint and several debtor') 208–209, 308

xwāstag ⟨NKSY'⟩ money (distinguished from ***xwastag*** ⟨hw'stk'⟩ by its spelling as an ideogram) 190, 268–269, 276, 354–357

xwāstag ī abāmdan loaned money, money debt 317, 319

xwāstag ī grawagānīh money paid for mortgaged property 349

xwāstagdār 'possessor/holder of property'; heir to family property; legatee. Family property was bequeathed to the heirs of a *paterfamilias* in the form of collective possessions and 'ideal' shares. In the ideal case the total estate (*abarmānd*) of a family was not partitioned. The basic notion that the heirs were 'possessors' of the total estate of a family, not 'owners', is visible in the construction of the term 206–210
  see also ***abarmānd-xwāstagdār***
xwāstagdārīh (hereditary) possession; *pad xwāstagdārīh* '(property) in (hereditary) possession': a category of a family's collective property, encompassing real estate, movables and immovables, held by the heirs in joint possession 206–210
xwāstārīh kardan to put in a claim, to request (something) 140
xwastūg būdan/h- to confess (a guilt); to acknowledge (a liability, debt) 362, 364, 430, 560
xwastūgīh (1) acknowledgement, recognition of a liability, debt; confession of a guilt; (2) trustworthiness, reliability (of a statement, verdict, witness) 500, 507, 545, 549
xwēdōdah next-of-kin marriage, endogamy; marriage within the natal lineage, including the nuclear family (as opposed to *bayăspān*, exogamy, marriage outside the natal lineage) 151–157, 162, 183–185
  xwēdōdah-wišōbišnīh destroying next-of-kin marriage; grievous offence 461–462
xwēhišn chase, pursuit (with the intention to harm someone) 424–433
xwēš būd rāy guftan 'to designate (a person) as owner' 397, 399
xwēšīh ownership, *dominium*; full title or right of dominion over property, corresponding to *dominium* (or *proprietas*) in Roman classical law, with one important exception: *xwēšīh* is *not* an 'absolute right' as in classical Roman law, but a 'relative right', allowing claimants to contest a person's title to a thing, particularly when ownership is derivative, *i. e.* when the owner has acquired the property from a previous owner (by sale, barter, gift); *pad xwēšīh dāštan* lit. 'to possess in ownership', to own 193–202, 210–212
  xwēšīh ī ātaxš (property in) ownership of the fire 217, 222, 225–226
  xwēšīh ī xwāstag ownership of property 195
  xwēšīh ī xwēš one's own ownership 195
xwēškārīh duty, field of responsibility, area of competence 96, 272, 274, 508
  xwēškārīh nāmag document on the area of competence, on specific duties; treatise or decree specifying the field of expertise or area of competence (*xwēškārīh*) of judicial authorities 272, 285, 503, 583
  xwēškārīh sālār public authority with a specific area of competence 545
xwurd kardan (injury caused by) crushing 425, 433
xwurdag 'small, little' person; commoner, plebeian; person who does not belong to the nobility 103, 112

yāt (< Av. *yāta-*, lit. 'leg[-striking/breaking]') degree of sin in Zoroastrian law 468–469, 475–476, 482, 484
yazdān gods, deities
  yazdān-dōstīh 'love of the gods'; one of the highest virtues (*kirbag*); opposite: *yazdān-dušmenīh* 494

yazdān-dušmenīh 'enmity towards the gods'; blasphemy, apostasy; capital crime (*margarzān*) prosecuted by the State; opposite: *yazdān-dōstīh* 491–494

yazišn recitations, religious services; recitation of specific formulae in the context of oath taking; *see* ***yazišn ī pad war*** and ***yazišn-nāmag***

yazišn ī pad ruwān ī mard 'religious services for the soul of (another) man'; formula in the will establishing religious services for another person, apart from the testator 222

yazišn ī pad war recitation during oath taking 518

yazišn-nāmag record of recitation; transcript or protocol documenting the procedure of taking an oath (*war*) 79, 285, 553–554, 557

yōhē pasčaēta 'who (succeeds) him afterwards'; technical term for 'legal successor', either in direct succession of the *paterfamilias* (in the case of a son) or indirect succession (in the case of a daughter), derived from a (lost) Avestan context 74, 123, 130, 137, 142, 144, 163, 176, 207, 231, 637

****yō xᵛa-daēnā-*** 'who (follows his) own creed'; technical term derived from a (lost) Avestan context for the follower of an un-orthodox creed (= heretic?) or a non-Zoroastrian 68–69

zamān date (of a hearing, trial) 536.

zamān dādan to schedule a court session; to set a date (for a hearing); *zamān ō dastwar dādan* to set a date for (calling) the legal predecessor 506 (fn. 47), 536

see also ***zamān kardan***

zamān ī ō dastwar date for (calling) the legal predecessor 543

zamān kard fixed date; scheduled date (for a court hearing; for taking the oath) 554

zamān kardan to schedule a court session; to set a date (for a hearing; for taking the oath); *u-šān āgenēn zamān kard* 'they fixed together a date (for the hearing)' 497, 499, 536, 540

see also ***zamān dādan***

zamān xwāstan to request a date (for a court hearing); *zamān ō dastwar xwāstan* 'to request a date for (bringing) the *auctor*/legal predecessor (to court)'; *ō dastwarān zamān xwāstan* 'to request a date for (bringing) the legal predecessors (to court)' 386, 543–544

zamīg (uncultivated) land; contrasted with *dastgird* landed estate 209–210, 243–244, 327, 599

zamīg ayārdan to evaluate land 369, 372

zamīg ī ēwkardagīhā land in one piece; land that is not partitioned or parcelled (contrasted with *zamīg ī hambaragān*) 250

zamīg ī hambaragān land of co-partners/shareholders of the fruits (contrasted with *zamīg ī ēwkardagīhā*) 250

zamīg ī kišwzār cultivated land 243, 345

zan woman

zan ī anēr un-Iranian woman, foreign woman 454

zan ī bēgānag strange woman; wife of another man 454

zan ī čagarīhā wife in an auxiliary marriage 143

see also ***čagar***

zan ī pādixšāy(īha) wife in a privileged marriage with full matrimonial rights 136, 142, 191
see also ***pādixšāy-zanīh***
zan ī starwan childless woman 446
zandīk wurrōyišnīh heretical beliefs 583
zandīkīh heresy 583
zanīh marriage; *zanīh ī jud az gād kunēd* 'the marriage is to be conducted without intercourse' (with regard to a woman who is the object of a lawsuit) 566
see also ***čagar-zanīh*** and ***pādixšāy(īhā)-zanīh***
zanišn assault, injury ('blow, smiting, beating'); criminal act encompassing according to the Dēnkard five kinds of aggressions: (1) threatening (*andar nimūd*), (2) tearing off (*kanišn*), (3) wounding (*zaxm*), (4) injuring (grievously) (*rēš kardan*), (5) killing (*ōzad[an]*) 405–407, 409, 411, 415, 423–425
zastbūd-nāmag protocol, transcript of interrogation 272, 285, 371–372
zaxm bodily abuse, physical injury, wound (criminal act categorized as *zanišn*) 108, 407, 411, 415, 423–428, 433
zaxmestān 'section on wounding/injuring' (*Dēnkard* 8) 679–682
zaydār *keeper of archives 439
zāyistan to investigate, interrogate 536
zaytēn wizīr olive (or: olive tree) document 269 (fn. 48), 320, 349
see also ***wizīr***
zēndān prison, gaol 447, 449
zēndānbān gaoler, warden of a prison 519–521
zīndag-stūr proxy for life; woman engaged as a 'proxy' for as long as she lives; contrasted with *tan-stūr* 171–172, 185
****zūr-gird*** false document 615
zur-gugāyīh false testimony 429, 549, 738

Abbreviations

General abbreviations

adj.	adjective	OInd.	Old Indian
adv.	adverb	OIr.	Old Iranian
Akk.	Akkadian	OP	Old Persian
Arab.	Arabic	opt.	optative
Aram.	Aramaic	Osset.	Ossetian
Arm.	Armenian	Pahl.	Pahlavi
Av.	Avestan	Parth.	Parthian
Bactr.	Bactrian	pers.pron.	personal pronoun
BSogd.	Buddhist Sogdian	pl.	plural
dem.pron.	demonstrative pronoun	prep.	preposition
fol.	folio	pres.	present tense
Heb.	Hebrew	pret.	preterite
IE	Indo-European	prev.	preverb
interrog.pron.	interrogative pronoun	pron.	pronoun
Ir.	Iranian	pt.	participle
Khwar.	Khwarezmian	PYE	post-Yazdegird era
Lat.	Latin	r.	recto (of a folio)
lit.	literally	sg.	singular
Mand.	Mandaic	Skr.	Sanskrit
MIr.	Middle Iranian	Sogd.	Sogdian
MMP	Manichean Middle Persian	suff.	Suffix
MP	Middle Persian	Syr.	Syriac
ms(s).	manuscript(s)	v.	verso (of a folio)
NP	New Persian	YE	Yazdegird era

Texts

AWN	*Ardā Wirāz nāmag*	GrBd	*Greater Bundahišn*
Bd	*Bundahišn*	Hēr.	*Hērbedestān*
Berk.	Berkeley documents	HKR	*Husraw ī Kawādān ud rēdag-ē(w)*
Dd	*Dādestān ī dēnīg*	KKZ	Kirdīr on the Kaʿba-ye Zardušt
Dk	*Dēnkard*	KNRb	Kirdīr in Naqš-e Rağab
DkD	*Dēnkard* (DRESDEN 1966)	KNRm	Kirdīr in Naqš-e Rostam
DkM	*Denkard* (MADAN 1911)		
FīO	*Frahang ī ōīm*		

KSM Kirdīr in Sar Mašhad
MHD *(Madayān ī) hazār dādestān*
MHDA *(Madayān ī) hazār dādestān* (T. D. Anklesaria 1912)
MīX *Mēnōy ī xrad*
Nēr. *Nērangestān*
NPi Narseh at Paikūlī
PRDd Pahlavi *Riwāyat* accompanying the *Dādestān ī dēnīg*
REA *Riwāyat ī Ēmēd ī Ašawahištān*
RAF *Riwāyat ī Ādur-Farrōbay ī Farroxzādān*
ŠH Šābuhr I at Hājjiābād
ŠGW *Škand gumānīg wizār*
ŠKZ Šābuhr I on the Kaʿba-ye Zardušt in Naqš-e Rostam
Šnš *Šāyist nē šāyist*
ŠTBq Šābuhr I at Tang-e Borāq
Tab. Tabarestān records
Vd *Vīdēvdād/Wīdēwdād*
WīZ *Wizīdagīhā ī Zādspram*
Y *Yasna*
Yt *Yašt*
ZWY *Zand ī Wahman Yasn*

Journals and editions

AAASH *Acta Antiqua Academiae Scientiarum Hungariae*
AcIr Acta Iranica
AcOr *Acta Orientalia*
ADA Avestan Digital Archive: https://ada.geschkult.fu-berlin.de/
AiW *Altiranisches Wörterbuch* (= Bartholomae 1904)
AKM Abhandlungen für die Kunde des Morgenlandes
AMI *Archäologische Mitteilungen aus Iran*
AoF *Altorientalische Forschungen*
ArOr *Archiv Orientální*
APAW Abhandlungen der Preußischen Akademie der Wissenschaften, Philosophisch-historische Klasse
BAI *Bulletin of the Asia Institute*
BSOAS *Bulletin of the School of Oriental and African Studies*
BSOS *Bulletin of the School of Oriental Studies*
CII Corpus Inscriptionum Iranicarum
CHI *Cambridge History of Iran*. Ed. by E. Yarshater
CII Corpus Inscriptionum Iranicarum
CRAIBL *Comptes rendus de l'Académie des Inscriptions et Belles-Lettres*
EIr *Encyclopædia Iranica*. Ed. by E. Yarshater
HdO *Handbuch der Orientalistik*
JA *Journal Asiatique*
JESHO *Journal of the Economic and Social History of the Orient*
JAOS *Journal of the American Oriental Society*
JCOI *Journal of the K. R. Cama Oriental Institute*
JQR *The Jewish Quarterly Review*
JRAS *Journal of the Royal Asiatic Society*
JSAI *Jerusalem Studies in Arabic and Islam*
MSB Münchener Studien zur Sprachwissenschaft – Beihefte
MSS *Münchener Studien zur Sprachwissenschaft*

OLZ	*Orientalistische Literaturzeitung*
PTS	Pahlavi Text Series
PCIR	*Pahlavi Codices and Iranian Researches*
RSO	*Rivista degli Studi Orientali*
SBE	*Sacred Books of the East*. Ed. by F. M. MÜLLER. Oxford 1879–1910 [Reprint Delhi 1965–1981]
SHAW	Sitzungsberichte der Heidelberger Akademie der Wissenschaften. Philosophisch-historische Klasse
SI	*Studia Islamica*
SOR	Serie Orientale Roma
StIr	*Studia Iranica*
WZKM	*Wiener Zeitschrift für die Kunde des Morgenlandes*
ZDMG	*Zeitschrift der Deutschen Morgenländischen Gesellschaft*
ZII	*Zeitschrift für Indologie und Iranistik*

Bibliography

Agostini, D./E. Kiesele/Sh. Secunda 2014: "Ohrmazd's Better Judgement (*meh-dādestānīh*): A Middle Persian Legal and Theological Discourse." In: StIr 43, pp. 177–202.

Altheim, F./R. Stiehl 1954: *Ein asiatischer Staat. Feudalismus unter den Sasaniden und ihren Nachbarn.* Wiesbaden.

Amouzgar, J./A. Tafazzoli 2000: *Le cinquième livre du Dēnkard.* Paris (StIr, Cahier 23).

Andrés-Toledo, M.Á. 2016: *The Zoroastrian Law to Expel the Demons: Wīdēwdād 10–15. Critical Edition, Translation and Glossary of the Avestan and Pahlavi Texts.* Wiesbaden (Iranica 23).

— 2019: "Ritual Competence and Liability of Minors in Ancient Zoroastrianism. On Avestan *dahmō.kərəta-* and *š́iiaoϑnāuuarəz-*." In: Hintze/Durkin-Meisterernst/Naumann 2019, pp. 1–12.

— 2022: "Valued and Invaluable: Avestan aspərəna-." In: Cantera/Macuch/Sims-Williams 2022, pp. 13–30.

Andrés-Toledo, M.Á./A. Cantera 2012: "Manuscripts of the *Wīdēwdād.*" In: Cantera 2012, pp. 207–243.

Anklesaria, B.T. 1949: *Pahlavi Vendidad (Zand-î Jvît-Dêv-Dât). Transliteration and Translation into English.* Bombay [repr. 2002].

— 1956: *Zand-Ākāsīh: Iranian or Greater Bundahišn. Transliteration and Translation in English.* Bombay.

— (ed.) 1962: *Rivayat-î Hêmît-î Ašavahištân.* Vol. I. Bombay.

— 1969: *The Pahlavi Rivāyat of Ādurfarnbag and Farnbag-Srōš.* Vol. I: *Text and Transcription.* Vol. II: *Translation.* Bombay.

Anklesaria, P.K. 1958: *A Critical Edition of the Unedited Portion of the Dādestān-i Dīnīk.* Doctoral dissertation. School of Oriental and African Studies, University of London [unpublished].

Anklesaria, T.D. 1911: *The Datistan-i-Dinik.* Part I: *Pursishn I–XL.* Bombay.

— (ed.) 1912: *The Social Code of the Parsees in Sasanian Times or the Madigân-i-Hazâr Dâdistân.* Part II. Bombay.

Antia, E.K. (ed.) 1909: *Pāzend Texts. Collected and Collated.* Bombay.

Arnold, C. 2012: *Underworld London. Crime and Punishment in the Capital City.* London/New York/Sydney/Toronto/New Delhi.

Asmussen, J.P. 1965–1966: "Judaeo-Persica II." In: AcOr 29, pp. 49–60.

Assemani, S.E. 1748: *Acta sanctorum martyrum orientalium et occidentalium.* 2 vols. Rome.

Avenarius, H. 1985: *Kleines Rechtswörterbuch.* Freiburg i.Br.

Avestan Digital Archive: https://ada.geschkult.fu-berlin.de/

AZAD, A. 2016: "Living happily ever after: fraternal polyandry, taxes and 'the house' in early Islamic Bactria." In: BSOAS 79.1, pp. 33–56.

AZARNOUCHE, S. 2013: *Husraw ī Kawādān ud Rēdag-ē. Khosrow fils de Kawād et un page. Texte pehlevi édité et traduit.* Paris (StIr, Cahier 49).

— 2019: "Les fonctions religieuses et la loi zoroastrienne: le cas du hērbed." In: HINTZE/DURKIN-MEISTERERNST/NAUMANN 2019, pp. 13–23.

BACK, M. 1978: *Die sassanidischen Staatsinschriften.* Leiden (AcIr 18).

BAHĀR, M.T./M.P. GUNĀBĀDĪ (eds.) 1962: (Balʿamī) *Tārīḫ-i Balʿamī.* Tehran.

BAILEY, H.W. 1930–1932a: "To the Zamasp-Namak I." In: BSOS 6, pp. 55–85.

— 1930–1932b: "To the Zamasp-Namak II." In: BSOS 6, pp. 581–600.

— 1930–1932c: "Iranian Studies I." In: BSOS 6, pp. 945–955.

— 1933–1935a: "Iranian Studies II." In: BSOS 7, pp. 69–86.

— 1933–1935b: "Iranian Studies III." In: BSOS 7, pp. 275–298.

— 1933–1935c: "Iranian Studies IV." In: BSOS 7, pp. 755–778.

— 1935–1937: "Iranian Studies V." In: BSOS 8, pp. 117–142.

— 1943: Zoroastrian Problems in the Ninth-Century Books. Oxford (Ratanbai Katrak Lectures) [repr. London 1971].

BAKHOS, C./R.M. SHAYEGAN (eds.) 2010: *The Talmud in its Iranian Context.* Tübingen (Text and Studies in Ancient Judaism 135).

BARTHOLOMAE, CH. 1904: *Altiranisches Wörterbuch.* Straßburg [repr. Berlin 1979].

— 1910: *Über ein sasanidisches Rechtsbuch.* Heidelberg (SHAW 1904,11).

— 1911–1918: "Mitteliranische Studien." Parts. I–VI. I: WZKM 25 (1911), pp. 245–262; II: WZKM 25 (1911), pp. 389–409; III: WZKM 27 (1913), pp. 19–24; IV: WZKM 27 (1913), pp. 347–374; V: WZKM 29 (1915), pp. 1–47; VI: WZKM 30 (1917–1918), pp. 1–36.

— 1916–1925: "Zur Kenntnis der mitteliranischen Mundarten." Parts I–VI. I: 1916 (SHAW 1916,9); II: 1917 (SHAW 1917, 11); III: 1920 (SHAW 1920, 2); IV: 1922 (SHAW 1922, 6); V: 1923 (SHAW 1923, 3); VI: 1925 (SHAW 1924/1925, 6). Heidelberg.

— 1918–1923: "Zum sasanidischen Recht." Parts I–V. I–II: 1918 (SHAW 1918,5); III: 1920 (SHAW 1920,18); IV: 1922 (SHAW 1922,5); V: 1923 (SHAW 1923,9). Heidelberg.

BAUMGARTNER, M.P. 1996. "The sociology of law." In: D. PATTERSON (ed.): *A Companion to Philosophy of Law and Legal Theory.* Oxford, pp. 406–420.

BEARD, M. 2008: *Pompeii. The Life of a Roman Town.* London.

BEDJAN, P. (ed.) 1890–1897: *Acta Martyrum et Sanctorum Syriace.* Paris/Leipzig [repr. Hildesheim 1968].

— (ed.) 1895: *Histoire de Mar Jabalaha, de trois autres patriarches, d'un prêtre et de deux laïque nestoriens.* Paris.

BENKATO, A. 2017: *Āzandnāmē. An Edition and Literary-Critical Study of the Manichaean-Sogdian Parable-Book.* Wiesbaden (Beiträge zur Iranistik 42).

BENVENISTE, É. 1932: "Les classes sociales dans la tradition Avestique." In: JA 221, pp. 117–134.

— 1934: "Termes et noms Achéménides en Araméen." In: JA 225, pp. 177–193.

— 1938: "Traditions indo-iraniennes sur les classes sociales." In: JA 230, pp. 529–549.

– 1969: *Le vocabulaire des institutions indo-européennes.* Vol. I: *Économie, parenté, societé.* Vol. II: *Pouvoir, droit, religion.* Paris.
– 1970: "Que signifie ‹ Vidēvdāt › ?" In: BOYCE/GERSHEVITCH 1970, pp. 37–42.
BLOCKLEY, R.C. 1987: "The Division of Armenia between the Romans and the Persians at the End of the Fourth Century." In: *Historia* 36, pp. 222–234.
BLOIS, F. DE 1985: "'Freemen' and 'Nobles' in Iranian and Semitic Languages." In: JRAS 1, pp. 5–15.
– 2006: "Du nouveau sur la chronologie bactrienne post-hellénistique: l'ère de 233 ap. J.-C." In: CRAIBL II, pp. 991–997.
– 2012: "A New Look at Mazdak." In: T. BERNHEIMER/A. SILVERSTEIN (eds.): *Late Antiquity: Eastern Perspectives.* Cambridge, pp. 1–24.
– 2015: "Mazdak the Ancient and Mazdak the Last. Further Remarks on the History and Religious Typology of Mazdakism." In: JULLIEN 2015, pp. 141–154.
BOGOLJUBOV, M.N./V.A. LIVSHITS/O.I. SMIRNOVA (eds.) 1963: *Sogdijskie dokumenty s gory Mug* [Sogdian Dokuments from Mount Mug]. Vol. III: *Hozjajstvennye dokumenty* [Economic Documents]. Moscow (CII, Part II, Vol. III, I).
BOSWORTH, C.E. 1969: "Abū ʿAbdallāh al-Khwārazmī on the Technical Terms of the Secretary's Art." In: JESHO 12, pp. 113–164.
BOYCE, M. 1966: "*Ātaš-zōhr* and *āb-zōhr.*" In: JRAS 3/4, pp. 100–118.
– 1968a: *The Letter of Tansar.* Rome (SOR 38).
– 1968b: "On the Sacred Fires of the Zoroastrians." In: BSOAS 31.1, pp. 52–68.
– 1968c: "The Pious Foundations of the Zoroastrians." In: BSOAS 31.2, pp. 270–289.
– 1969: "On Mithra's Part in Zoroastrianism." In: BSOAS 32.1, pp. 10–34.
– 1975a: "On the Zoroastrian Cult of Fire." In: JAOS 95, pp. 454–465.
– 1975b: "Iconoclasm among the Zoroastrians." In: J. NEUSNER (ed.): *Christianity, Judaism and Other Greco-Roman Cults: Studies for Morton Smith at Sixty.* Leiden, pp. 93–111.
– 1975c: *A History of Zoroastrianism.* Vol. I: *The Early Period.* Leiden/Cologne.
– 1977: *A Stronghold of Zoroastrianism.* Oxford [repr. Lanham 1989].
– 1979: *Zoroastrians. Their Religious Beliefs and Practices.* London/New York.
BOYCE, M./I. GERSHEVITCH (eds.) 1970: *W.B. Henning Memorial Volume.* London.
BRAUN, O. 1915: *Ausgewählte Akten persischer Märtyrer.* Kempten/Munich (Bibliothek der Kirchenväter 22).
BRODY, R. 1990: "Judaism in the Sasanian Empire: A Case Study in Religious Coexistence." In: SH. SHAKED/A. NETZER (eds.): *Irano-Judaica II: Studies Relating to Jewish Contacts with Persian Culture Throughout the Ages.* Jerusalem, pp. 52–62.
– 2016: "Irano-Talmudica: The New Parallelomania?" In: JQR 106.2, pp. 209–232.
BROMBERG, C.A./N. SIMS-WILLIAMS/U. SIMS-WILLIAMS (eds.) 2009: *Iranian and Zoroastrian Studies in Honor of Prods Oktor Skjærvø.* Bloomfield Hills, Mich. (BAI 19 [2005]).
BROWN, E.G. 1893: *A Year amongst the Persians.* London [repr. London 1984].
BRUNS, K.G. 1880: *Syrisch-römisches Rechtsbuch aus dem fünften Jahrhundert.* Leipzig [repr. Aalen 1985].
BUCKLAND, W.W. 1963: *A Text-book of Roman Law from Augustus to Justinian.* 3rd ed. rev. by P. STEIN. Cambridge.

Buckley, J.J. (ed.) 2012: *Lady E.S. Drower's Scholarly Correspondence. An Intrepid English Autodidact in Iraq.* Leiden/Boston.

Bulsara, S.J. 1937: *The Laws of the Ancient Persians as Found in the 'Mātikān ē hazār Dātistān' or 'The Digest of a Thousand Points of Law'.* Bombay.

Burnyeat, M.F. 1994: "Did the Ancient Greeks have the Concept of Human Rights?" In: *Polis* 13, pp. 10–11.

Buyaner, D. 2014: "Zur etymologischen Beurteilung des Pahlavi-Rechtsbegriffs <stwl>. Beiträge zur Erklärung der mittelpersischen Rechts- und Religionsterminologie. I." In: ZDMG 164, pp. 699–718.

— 2015: "Zur semantischen und etymologischen Erklärung von Pahlavi <nkyl'y> und der verwandten Begriffe. Beiträge zur Erklärung der mittelpersischen Rechts- und Religionsterminologie. II." In: ZDMG 165, pp. 351–368.

— 2016: *Penitential Sections of the* Xorde Avesta (patits). *Critical Edition with Commentary and Glossary.* Wiesbaden (Iranica 22).

Cahen, C. 1961: "Reflections sur le *waqf* ancien." In: SI 14, pp. 37–56 [repr. in: *Les peuples musulmans dans l'histoire médiévale.* Damascus 1977, pp. 287–306].

Cancik-Kirschbaum, E./A. Traninger (eds.) 2015: *Wissen in Bewegung. Institution – Iteration – Transfer.* Wiesbaden (Episteme in Bewegung. Beiträge zu einer transdisziplinären Wissensgeschichte 1).

Cannuyer, Ch. (ed.) 2016: *Entre orient et occident. Circulation des hommes, porosité des heritages: Rika Gyselen in honorem.* Brussels.

Cantera, A. 1998. *Estudios sobre la traducción Páhlavi del Avesta: Las versiones Avéstica y Páhlavi de los cuatro primeros capítulos de Videvdad.* Inaugural-Diss. Universidad de Salamanca [unpublished].

— 1999: "Die Stellung der Sprache der Pahlavi-Übersetzung des Avesta innerhalb des Mittelpersischen." In: StIr 28, pp. 173–204.

— 2003: "Phl. *xwaddōšagīh* und die Unterwerfung unter die Autorität im (nach)sasanidischen Zoroastrismus." In: Cereti/Maggi/Provasi 2003, pp. 17–30.

— 2004: *Studien zur Pahlavi-Übersetzung des Avesta.* Wiesbaden (Iranica 7).

— 2006: "Was ist av. *dāta- vīdāeuua-*?" In: Panaino/Piras 2006, pp. 53–64.

— 2010: "Legal Implications of Conversion in Zoroastrianism." In: Cereti 2010, pp. 53–66.

— (ed.) 2012: *The Transmission of the Avesta.* Wiesbaden (Iranica 20).

— 2013: "Talking with God: the Zoroastrian *ham.parsti* or Intercalation Ceremonies." In: JA 301, pp. 85–138.

— 2015: "Ethics." In: Stausberg/Vevaina 2015, pp. 315–332.

— 2020: "*Ast kē ēdōn gōwēd*: les opinions divergentes et la prise des decisions doctrinales dans le zoroastrisme sassanide et post-sassanide." In: F. Ruani/M. Timuş (eds.): *Quand les dualistes polémiquaient. Zoroastriens et manichéens.* Leuven/Paris/Bristol, pp. 31–64.

— 2021: "The *sraōšāuuarəza*-priest and the usage of the *srōš-barišnīh* in the greater Long Liturgy." In: JRAS 31.3, pp. 479–514.

— 2022: "The Offering to Satisfy the *ratu* (*miiazda ratufrī*): the Dual System of the Animal Sacrifice in Zoroastrian Rituals." In: Cantera/Macuch/Sims-Williams 2022, pp. 39–96.

Cantera, A. / M. Macuch / N. Sims-Williams (eds.) 2022: *The Reward of the Righteous. Festschrift in Honour of Almut Hintze.* Wiesbaden (Iranica 30).

Carlsen, B.H. 1984: "Who is the *bayāspān* Daughter?" In: W. Skalmowski / A. Tongerloo (eds.): *Middle Iranian Studies. Proceedings of the International Symposium Organized by the Katholieke Universiteit Leuven from the 17th to the 20th of May 1982.* Leuven, pp. 115–121.

Carra de Vaux, B. 1896: *Le livre de l'avertissement et de la revision.* Paris.

Cereti, C.G. 1995: *The Zand ī Wahman Yasn. A Zoroastrian Apocalypse.* Rome (SOR 75).

— (ed.) 2010: *Iranian Identity in the Course of History. Proceedings of the Conference Held in Rome, 21–24 September 2005.* Rome (SOR 105. Orientalia Romana 9).

— 2017: "A Short Note on MHDA 38." In: Morano/Provasi/Rossi 2017, pp. 23–29.

Cereti, C.G. / M. Maggi / E. Provasi (eds.) 2003: *Religious themes and texts of pre-Islamic Iran and Central Asia: Studies in Honour of Professor Gherardo Gnoli on the Occasion of his 65th Birthday on 6th December 2002.* Wiesbaden (Beiträge zur Iranistik 24).

Chaumont, M.-L. 1985: "Āmārgar. ii. The post." In: EIr I, pp. 925–926.

Cheung, J. 2007: *Etymological Dictionary of the Iranian Verb.* Leiden/Boston.

Christensen, A. 1925: *Le règne du roi Kawadh I et le communisme mazdakite.* Copenhagen.

— 1944: *L'Iran sous les Sassanides. Deuxième édition revue et augmentée.* Copenhagen [repr. Osnabrück 1971].

Ciancaglini, C.A. 2008: *Iranian Loanwords in Syriac.* Wiesbaden (Beiträge zur Iranistik 28).

Codices Hafniensis 1934 = *The Pahlavi Codex K35. First part containing the Pahlavi Rivāyat I, Dādhastān ē Dēnīgh and the Pahlavi Rivāyat II.* With an introduction by A. Christensen. Copenhagen (Codices Avestici et Pahlavici Universitatis Hafniensis III).

Colditz, I. 1998: "Notes on the Problem of Punishment and Conversion in Manichaeism." In: N. Sims-Williams (ed.): *Proceedings of the Third European Conference of Iranian Studies held in Cambridge, 11th to 15th September 1995.* Pt I: *Old and Middle Iranian Studies.* Wiesbaden, pp. 27–37.

— 2000: *Zur Sozialterminologie der iranischen Manichäer.* Wiesbaden (Iranica 5).

— 2015: "Iteration im zoroastrischen Recht. Rechtsfindung zwischen kanonischer Norm und Rechtspraxis." In: Cancik-Kirschbaum/Traninger 2015, pp. 223–239.

— 2017: "Pahlavi *bahr* ‚Anteil' oder ‚Brautgabe'. Zum Verständnis einer terminologischen Unschärfe in den *Pahlavi Riwāyats zum Dādestān ī dēnīg.*" In: Colditz/Jokisch/Macuch 2017, pp. 7–28.

— 2019: "Women without Guardianship." In: P.B. Lurje (ed.): *Proceedings of the Eighth European Conference of Iranian Studies.* Vol. I: *Studies on Pre-Islamic Iran and Historical Linguistics.* Saint Petersburg, pp. 106–116.

— 2023: "Landesrecht vs. lokales Recht? Fragen an das sasanidische Rechtsbuch Hazār dādestān." In: *Sasanian Studies. Late Antique Iranian World. Sasanidische Studien. Spätantike iranische Welt* 2, pp. 27–40.

Colditz, I. / B. Jokisch / M. Macuch (eds.) 2017: *Transferprozesse in spätantiken Rechtssystemen. Rezeption, Transformation und Rekontextualisierung von*

Rechtsbegriffen. Wiesbaden (Episteme in Bewegung. Beiträge zu einer transdisziplinären Wissensgeschichte 10).

Corcoran, S. 2011: "Observations on the Sasanian Law-Book in the light of Roman legal writing." In: A. Rio (ed.): *Law, Custom, and Justice in Late Antiquity and the Early Middle Ages: Proceedings of the 2008 Byzantine Colloqium.* London, pp. 77–113.

Coulson, N.J. 1964: *A History of Islamic Law.* Edinburgh [repr. 1978].

– 1971: *Succession in the Muslim Family.* Cambridge.

Cowley, A.E. 1923: *Aramaic Papyri of the Fifth Century B.C.* Oxford [repr. Osnabrück 1967].

Crone, P. 1991: "Kavād's Heresy and Mazdak's Revolt." In: *Iran* 29, pp. 21–42.

– 2012: *The Nativist Prophets of Early Islamic Iran.* Cambridge.

Dālvand, H.R. 1394 (2015): "Riwāyat-e fārsī-ye Zardoštī." In: *Ǧašn-nāme-ye Doktor Moḥammad Taqī Rāšīd Moḥaṣṣal.* Tehran, pp. 1–65.

Dandamaev, M.A. / V.G. Lukonin 1989: *The Culture and Social Institutions of Ancient Iran.* English edition by Ph.L. Kohl with the assistance of D.J. Dadson. Cambridge.

Dandamayev, M.A. 1988: "Barda and Bardadārīh. i. In the Achaemenid Period." In: EIr III/7, pp. 762–763.

Darmesteter, J. 1880: *The Zend-Avesta.* Pt. I: *The Vendidad.* Oxford (SBE IV).

– 1894: "Lettre de Tansar au roi de Tabaristan." In: JA 9.3, pp. 180–250, 502–555.

Daryaee, T. 2007: "The Middle Persian Text *sūr ī saxwan* and the Late Sasanian Court." In: R. Gyselen (ed.): *Des Indo-Grecs aux Sassanides: données pour l'histoire et la géographie historique.* Bures-sur-Yvette (Res Orientales XVII), pp. 65–72.

– 2009: *Sasanian Persia. The Rise and Fall of an Empire.* London.

– 2010a: "The Idea of Ērānšahr: Jewish, Christian and Manichaean Views in Late Antiquity." In: Cereti 2010, pp. 91–108.

– 2010b: *On the Explanation of Chess and Backgammon. Abar Wīzārišn ī Čatrang ud Nihišn Nēw-Ardaxsīr.* Irvine, Calif. (Persian Text Series of Late Antiquity 1).

– 2011: "Bazaars, Merchants, and Trade in Late Antique Iran." In: *Comparative Studies of South Asia, Africa and the Middle East* 30.3 (2010 [2011]), pp. 401–409.

Daryaee, T. / Kh. Rezakhani 2016: *From Oxus to Euphrates. The World of Late Antique Iran.* Irvine, Calif. (UCI Jordan Center for Persian Studies, Ancient Iran Series 1).

von Denffer, D. 1978: "*Mutʿa*-Ehe oder Prostitution? Ein Beitrag zur Untersuchung einer Institution des šīʿītischen Islam." In: ZDMG 128, pp. 299–325.

Dhabhar, B.N. (ed.) 1913: *The Pahlavi Rivāyat Accompanying the Dādistān-ī Dīnīk.* Bombay (PTS 2).

– (ed.) 1927: *Zand-i Khūrtak Avistāk.* Bombay (PTS 3).

– 1932: *The Persian Rivāyats of Hormazyar Framarz and Others. Their Version with Introduction and Notes.* Bombay [repr. 1999].

– 1949: *Pahlavi Yasna and Visperad.* Bombay (PTS 8).

– 1955: *Essays on Iranian Subjects.* Bombay.

– 1963: *Translation of the Zand-i Khūrtak Avistāk.* Bombay [repr. 2005].

Dresden, M.J. 1966: *Dēnkart. A Pahlavi Text. Facsimile Edition of the Manuscript B of the K.R. Cama Oriental Institute Bombay.* Wiesbaden.

Driver, G.R. 1957: *Aramaic Documents of the Fifth Century B.C.* Oxford.
Drower, E.S./R. Macuch 1963: *A Mandaic Dictionary.* Oxford.
van Dülmen, R. 1988: *Theater des Schreckens. Gerichtspraxis und Strafrituale in der frühen Neuzeit.* Munich.
Duchesne-Guillemin, J. (ed.) 1975: *Monumentum H.S. Nyberg.* Vol. II. Leiden/Tehran (AcIr 5).
Durkin-Meisterernst, D. 2004: *Dictionary of Manichaean Middle Persian and Parthian Texts.* Vol. III.1: *Dictionary of Manichaean Texts. Texts from Central Asia and China.* Turnhout (Corpus Fontium Manichaeorum).
— 2014: Grammatik des Westmitteliranischen (Parthisch und Mittelpersisch). Vienna (Veröffentlichungen zur Iranistik 73).
Eilers, W. 1940: *Iranische Beamtennamen in der keilschriftlichen Überlieferung.* Teil I. Leipzig (AKM XXV, 5).
Elman, Y. 2007: "Middle Persian Culture and Babylonian Sages: Accomodation and Resistance in the Shaping of the Rabbinic Legal Tradition." In: C.E. Fonrobert/M.S. Jaffe (eds.): *Cambridge Companion to Rabbinic Literature.* Cambridge, Mass., pp. 165–197.
— 2008: "Returnable Gifts in Rabbinic and Sasanian Law." In: Shaked/Netzer 2008, pp. 139–184.
— 2019a: "The Torah of Temporary Marriage. A Study in Cultural History." In: Hintze/Durkin-Meisterernst/Naumann 2019, pp. 83–108.
— 2019b: "Samuel's Scythe-handle: Sasanian Mortgage Law in the Bavli." In: Rubanovich/Herman 2019, pp. 129–143.
Elon, M. 1994: *Jewish Law. History, Sources, Principles.* Vols. I–IV. Philadelphia/Jerusalem.
Emmerick, R.E./M. Macuch (eds.) 2009: *The Literature of Pre-Islamic Iran. Companion Volume I to A History of Persian Literature.* London (History of Persian Literature XVII).
Ende, W. 1980: "Ehe auf Zeit *(mutʿa)* in der innerislamischen Diskussion der Gegenwart." In: *Die Welt des Islams* 20, pp. 1–43.
Erhart, V. 2001: "The Development of Syriac Christian Canon Law in the Sasanian Empire." In: R.W. Mathisen (ed.): *Law, Society, and Authority in Late Antiquity.* Oxford/New York, pp. 117–129.
Farridnejad, Sh./T. Daryaee (eds.) 2022: *Sasanian Studies. Late Antique Iranian World / Sasanidische Studien. Spätantike iranische Welt.* Vol. I. Wiesbaden.
Farridnejad, Sh./A. Zeini 2024: "Who Will Protect the Cattle? On Dogs and the Sin of Meat Consumption in Zoroastrianism." In: Macuch/Zeini 2024, pp. 97–110.
Fārsānī, M.N. 1397/2018: *Ketāb-e haštom-e Dēnkard.* Tehran.
Ferdows, A.K. 1985: "The Status and Rights of Women in *itha ʿashari* Shiʿi Islam." In: A. Fathi (ed.). *Women and the Family in Iran.* Leiden, pp. 13–35.
Forest, N. 2020: *Successions et libéralités dans l'Iran mazdéen. Droit zoroastrien de la famille.* Paris.
Fouchécour, C.-H. de/Ph. Gignoux (eds.) 1989: *Études irano-aryennes offertes à Gilbert Lazard.* Paris (StIr, Cahier 7).
Fox, R. 1967: *Kinship and Marriage. An Anthropological Perspective.* Harmondsworth, Middlesex.

Fragner, B. 1999: *Die „Persophonie". Regionalität, Identität und Sprachkontakt in der Geschichte Asiens.* Berlin.

Frandsen, P.J. 2009: *Incestuous and Close-kin Marriage in Ancient Egypt and Persia.* Copenhagen.

Frankopan, P. 2015: *The Silk Roads. A New History of the World.* London/New York.

Frye, R.N. 1963: *The Heritage of Persia.* Cleveland/New York.

— 1967: "Iran und Israel." In: G. Wiessner (ed.): *Festschrift für Wilhelm Eilers.* Wiesbaden, pp. 74–84.

— 1985: "Zoroastrian Incest." In: Gh. Gnoli / L. Lanciotti (eds.): Orientalia Iosephi Tucci Memoriae Dicata. Rome (SOR 56), pp. 445–455.

Gabbay, U. / Sh. Secunda (eds.) 2014: *Encounters by the Rivers of Babylon: Scholarly Conversations between Jews, Iranians and Babylonians in Antiquity.* Tübingen.

Gabrieli, F. 1931–1932: "L'opera di Ibn al-Muqaffaʿ." In: RSO 13, pp. 197–247.

Gariboldi, A. 2015: "The Great 'Restoration' of Husraw I." In: Jullien 2015, pp. 47–84.

Garsoïan, N.G. 1981: "Sur le titre de protecteur des pauvres." In: *Revue des Études Arméniennes* 15 [NS], pp. 21–32.

— 1985: *Armenia between Byzantium and the Sasanians.* London.

— 1999: "The Problem of Armenian Integration into the Byzantine Empire." In: H. Ahrweiler / A.E. Laiou (eds.): *Studies on the Internal Diaspora of the Byzantine Empire.* Washington, DC, pp. 53–124.

— 2009: "Armenian Sources on Sasanian Administration." In: Gyselen 2009, pp. 90–114.

Geiger, B. 1935: "Mittelpersische Wörter und Sachen." In: WZKM 42, pp. 114–128.

— 1937: "Mittelpersische Wörter und Sachen." In: WZKM 44, pp. 51–64.

Gershevitch, I. 1959: *The Avestan Hymn to Mithra.* Cambridge.

Gharib, B. 1995: *Sogdian Dictionary: Sogdian – Persian – English.* Tehran.

Gignoux, Ph. 1972a: *Glossaire des Inscriptions Pehlevies et Parthes.* London (CII, Supplementary Series I).

— 1972b: "L'inscription de Kirdīr a Naqš-i Rustam." In: StIr 1, pp. 177–205.

— 1973: "Problèmes d'interpretation des bulles sassanides." In: StIr 2, pp. 137–142.

— 1976: "Problèmes d'interpretation historique et philologique des titres et noms propres Sasanides." In: AAASH 24, pp. 104–106.

— 1984: *Le livre d'Ardā Vīrāz. Translittération, transcription et traduction du texte pehlevi.* Paris.

— 1995: "La controverse dans le mazdéisme tardif." In: A. de Boulluec (ed.): *La controverse religieuse et ses formes.* Paris, pp. 127–149.

— 1995–1998: "Pour une evaluation de la contribution des sources arméniennes à l'histoire sassanide." In: AAASH 31, pp. 53–65.

— 2001: *Man and Cosmos in Ancient Iran.* Rome (SOR 91).

— 2004: "Aspects de la vie administrative et sociale en Iran du 7ème siècle." In: R. Gyselen (ed.): *Contributions à l'histoire et la géographie historique de l'empire Sassanide.* Bures-sur-Yvette (Res Orientales XVI), pp. 37–48.

— 2009: "Les comptes de monsieur Friyag: quelques documents économiques en Pehlevi." In: Gyselen 2009, pp. 115–142.

— 2010: "La collection de textes attribuables à Dādēn-vindād dans l'archive Pehlevi de Berkeley." In: R. Gyselen (ed.): *Sources for the History of Sasanian and Post-Sasanian Iran. Bures-sur-Yvette* (Res Orientales XIX), pp. 11–134.

— 2012: "Une archive post-sassanide du Tabaristān (I)." In: Gyselen 2012c, pp. 29–96.
— 2014: "Une archive post-sassanide du Tabaristān (II)." In: Gyselen 2014, pp. 29–71.
— 2016: "Une archive post-sassanide du Tabaristān (III)." In: Gyselen 2016, pp. 171–184.
— 2019: "Les ‹ Mémoires › dans l'archive pehlevi de Berkeley/Berlin." In: Hintze/Durkin-Meisterernst/Naumann 2019, pp. 127–140.
Gignoux, Ph. / R. Gyselen 1982: *Sceaux Sasanides de diverses colocctions privées.* Paris (StIr, Cahier 1).
Gignoux, Ph. / A. Tafazzoli (eds.) 1974: *Mémorial Jean de Menasce.* Louvain.
— 1993: *Anthologie de Zādspram.* Paris (StIr, Cahier 13).
Gimaret, D. / G. Monnot 1986: *Shahrastani. Livre des religions et des sectes I. Traduction avec introduction et notes par Daniel Gimaret et Guy Monnot.* Leuven.
Gippert, J. 1993: *Iranica Armeno-Iberica. Studien zu den iranischen Lehnwörtern im Armenischen und Georgischen.* Vienna.
Gnoli, Gh. (ed.) 2004: *La Persia e Bisanzio. Convegno internazionale, Roma, 14–18 ottobre 2002.* Rome (Atti dei convegni Lincei 201).
Goeje, M.J. de (ed.) 1879–1901: *Annales quos scripsit Abu Djafar Mohammed Ibn Djarir at-Tabari: Taʾrīḫ ar-rusul waʾl-mulūk.* 16 vols. Leiden.
— (ed.) 1894: *ʿAlī Ibn-al-Ḥusain al- Masʿūdī: Kitāb at-tanbīh waʾl-išrāf.* Leiden.
Goldman, L. 2015: *Rašn Yašt. The Avestan Hymn to "Justice".* Wiesbaden (Beiträge zur Iranistik 39).
Goldschmidt, L. 1897–1935: *Der babylonische Talmud. Text und Übersetzung. Nach der ersten zensurfreien Ausgabe unter Berücksichtigung der neueren Ausgaben und handschriftlichen Materials.* 9 vols. Berlin [repr. 2002].
Goodblatt, D.M. 1979: "The Poll Tax in Sasanian Babylonia. The Talmudic Evidence." In: JESHO 22, pp. 233–295.
Goodenough, W.H. 1949: "Comments on the Question of Incestuous Marriages in Old Iran." In: *American Anthropologist* 51, pp. 326–328.
Gordon, M.S. *et al.* (eds.) 2018: *The Works of Ibn Wāḍiḥ al-Yaʿqūbī. An English Translation.* 3 vols. Leiden.
Gottwaldt, J.M.E. (ed.) 1844: *Hamzae Isphahanensis Annalium libri X.* Leipzig.
Greenfield, J.C. 1977: "On some Iranian Terms in the Elephantine Papyri." In: AAASH 25, pp. 8–118.
Greenwood, T. 2017: "A Contested Jurisdiction: Armenia in Late Antiquity." In: E.W. Sauer (ed.): *Sasanian Persia: Between Rome and the Steppes of Eurasia.* Edinburgh, pp. 199–220.
Grenet, F. 2023: "Remarks on the historical interpretation of the Ancient Letters." In: Sims-Williams 2023, pp. 63–69
Grenet, F. / N. Sims-Williams 1987: "The historical context of the Sogdian Ancient Letters." In: *Transitional Periods in Iranian History. Actes du symposium de Fribourg-en-Brisgau (22–24 Mai 1985).* Paris (StIr, Cahier 5), pp. 101–122.
Grenet, F. / N. Sims-Williams / É. de La Vassière 2001: "The Sogdian Ancient Letter V." In: BAI 12 (1998 [2001]), pp. 91–104.
Grignaschi, M. 1966: "Quelques spécimens de la littérature sassanide conservés dans les bibliothèques d'Istanbul." In: JA 254, pp. 1–142.
Guirgass, V. (ed.) 1888: *Aḥmad ibn-Dāwūd Abū-Ḥanīfa ad-Dīnawarī: Kitāb al-Akhbār al-ṭiwāl.* Leiden.

GYSELEN, R. 1989: *La géographie administrative de l'empire sassanide. Les témoignages sigillographiques.* Paris (Res Orientales I).
— (ed.) 1995: *Au carrefour des religions. Mélanges offerts à Philippe Gignoux.* Bures-sur-Yvette (Res Orientales VII).
— 2001: *The Four Generals of the Sasanian Empire: Some Sigillographic Evidence.* Rome.
— 2002a: Nouveaux matériaux pour la géographie historique de l'empire sassanide: Sceaux administratifs de la collection Ahmad Saeedi. Paris (StIr, Cahier 24).
— 2002b: "Le *kadag-xwadāy* sassanide. Quelques réflections à partir de nouvelles données sigillographiques." In: StIr 31, pp. 61–69.
— 2007: *Sasanian Seals and Sealings in the A. Saeedi Collection.* Louvain (AcIr 44).
— 2008: "The Great Families in the Sasanian Empire: Some Silgillographic Evidence." In: D. KENNET/P. LUFT (eds): *Current Research in Sasanian Archaeology, Art and History. Proceedings of a Conference held at Durham University, November 3rd and 4th, 2001, organized by the Centre for Iranian Studies, IMEIS, and the Department of Archaeology of Durham University.* Oxford, pp. 107–113.
— (ed.) 2009: *Sources pour l'histoire et la géographie du monde iranien (224–710).* Bures-sur-Yvette (Res Orientales XVIII).
— 2012a: "Scellements dans l'archive post-sassanide du Tabarestān (I)." In: GYSELEN 2012c, pp. 97–108.
— 2012b: "Le Tabaristān: lieu de mémoire Sassanide." In: GYSELEN 2012c, pp. 109–122.
— (ed.) 2012c: *Objects et documents inscrits en pārsīg.* Bures-sur-Yvette (Res Orientales XXI).
— (ed.) 2014: *Documents, argenterie et monnaies de tradition sassanide.* Bures-sur-Yvette (Res Orientales XXII).
— (ed.) 2016: *Words and Symbols: Sasanian Objects and the Tabarestān Archive.* Bures-sur-Yvette (Res Orientales XXIV).
— (ed.) 2017: *Sasanian Coins, Middle-Persian Etymology and the Tabarestān Archive.* Bures-sur-Yvette (Res Orientales XXVI).
— 2019a: *La géographie administrative de l'empire Sassanide. Les témoignages épigraphiques en moyen-perse.* Bures-sur-Yvette (Res Orientales XXV).
— 2019b: "Les données de géographie administrative sassanide dans le Šahrestānīhā-ī Ērānšahr: une réévaluation." In: HINTZE/DURKIN-MEISTERERNST/NAUMANN 2019, pp. 161–174.
— 2019c: "Les bulles de l'Archive du Tabarestān: quelques aspects matériels des scellements." In: GYSELEN 2019d, pp. 151–174.
— (ed.) 2019d: *Sasanian Persia and the Tabarestān Archive.* Bures-sur-Yvette (Res Orientales XXVII).
— (ed.) 2020: *Persia (552 BCE–758 CE): Primary Sources, Old and New.* Bures-sur-Yvette (Res Orientales XXVIII).
— (ed.) 2022: *Sometimes Sasanian, always* Ēr. Bures-sur-Yvette (Res Orientales XXIX).
— 2023: "L'‹ Archive du Tabarestān ›: bulles, sceaux et manuscrits." In: R. GYSELEN (ed.): *Reflets d'époques sassanide et post-sassanide (224–760 A.D.).* Bures-sur-Yvette (Res Orientales XXX), pp. 83–134.
— 2024a. "La géographie administrative de l'empire sassanide: données sigillographiques. Addenda et corrigenda." In: GYSELEN 2024d, pp. 11–74.

— 2024b. "Abrévations administratives et sigles monétaires sassanide." In: Gyselen 2024d, pp. 75–98.
— 2024c. "Sceaux de mages sassanides à critère chronologique." In: Gyselen 2024d, pp. 99–120.
— 2024d: *Administrations et préposés d'époque sassanide. Nouvelles données à la mémoire de Philippe Gignoux*. Paris (StIr, Cahier 66).
— Gyselen, R. / E. Khurshidian 2024: "The Sasanian *dibīr*." In: Gyselen 2024d, pp. 121–186.
Haeri, Sh. 1989: *The Law of Desire. Temporary Marriage in Iran*. London.
— 1994: "Temporary Marriage: An Islamic Discourse on Female Sexuality in Iran." In: M. Afkhami / E. Friedl (eds.): *The Eye of the Storm: Women in Post-Revolutionary Iran*. Syracuse, pp. 98–114.
Hahn, I. 1959: "Sassanidische und spätrömische Besteuerung." In: *Acta Antiqua* 7, pp. 149–160.
Halm, H. 1994: *Der schiitische Islam. Von der Religion zur Revolution*. Munich.
Heffening, W. 1993: "Mutʿa." In: *Encyclopaedia of Islam* VII, pp. 757–759.
Hansen, O. 1938: *Die mittelpersischen Papyri der Papyrussammlung der Staatlichen Museen zu Berlin*. Berlin (APAW 9).
Hansen, V. 2012: *The Silk Road. A New History*. Oxford.
Hennigan, P. Ch. 2004: *The Birth of a Legal Institution. The Formation of the Waqf in Third-Century A.H. Ḥanafī Legal Discourse*. Leiden (Studies in Islamic Law and Society 18).
Henning, W. B. 1933: "Das Verbum des Mittelpersischen der Turfanfragmente." In: ZII, pp. 158–253 [= Henning 1977, I, pp. 65–160].
— 1946: "The Sogdian Texts of Paris." In BSOAS 11, pp. 713–740 (= Henning 1977, II, pp. 231–258).
— 1948: "The Date of the Sogdian Ancient Letters." In: BSOAS 12, pp. 601–615 [= Henning 1977, II, pp. 315–330].
— 1954a: "The Inscription of Firuzabad." In: *Asia Major* 4, pp. 98–102 [= Henning 1977, II, pp. 431–436].
— 1954b: "Notes on the Great Inscription of Šāpūr I." In: *Prof. Jackson Memorial Volume*. Bombay, pp. 40–54 [= Henning 1977, II, pp. 415–430].
— 1957: *The Inscription of Naqš-i Rustam*. London (CII, Part III, Vol. II, II).
— 1958: "Mitteliranisch." In: HdO 1.4.1, pp. 20–130.
— 1965: "A Sogdian God." In: BSOAS 28, pp. 242–254.
— 1977: *W. B. Henning Selected Papers*. 2 vols. Téhéran / Liège (AcIr 14–15).
Herman, G. 2010: "Persia in the Light of the Babylonian Talmud. Echoes of Contemporary Society and Politics: *hargbed* and *bidaxš*." In: Bakhos/Shayegan 2010, pp. 58–82.
Herrenschmidt, C. 1994: "Le *xwêtôdas* ou mariage ‹ incestueux › en Iran ancient." In: P. Bonte (ed.): *Épouser au plus proche. Inceste, prohibitions et stratégies matrimoniales autour de la Méditerranée*. Paris, pp. 113–125.
Herzog, I. 1936: *The Main Institutions of Jewish Law*. Vol. I: *The Law of Property*. Colchester/London [repr. 1980].
— 1939: *The Main Institutions of Jewish Law*. Vol. II: *The Law of Obligations*. Colchester/London [repr. 1980].

Hintze, A. 1994: *Der Zamyād-Yašt. Edition, Übersetzung, Kommentar.* Wiesbaden (Beiträge zur Iranistik 15).
— 1995: "The Rise of the Saviour in the Avesta." In: Reck/Zieme 1995, pp. 77–97.
— 1999: "The Saviour and the Dragon in Iranian and Jewish/Christian Eschatology." In: Shaked/Netzer 1999, pp. 72–90.
— 2007: "On the Compositional Structure of the Avestan Gāhs." In: Vahman/Pedersen 2007, pp. 29–43.
— 2009a: "Avestan Literature." In: Emmerick/Macuch 2009, pp. 1–71.
— 2009b: "Disseminating the Mazdayasnian Religion: An Edition of the Avestan Hērbedestān Chapter 5." In: Sundermann/Hintze/de Blois 2009, pp. 171–190.
— 2017a: "The Advance of the Daēnā: The Vištāsp Yašt and an obscure word in the Hāδōxt Nask." In: Morano/Provasi/Rossi 2017, pp. 165–178.
— 2017b: "Avestan Research 1991–2017, Part 2: Morphology, Syntax, Lexicon (nos. 32–79)." In: *Kratylos* 62, pp. 1–126.
— 2019: "Defeating Death: Eschatology in Zoroastrianism, Judaism and Christianity." In: Rubanovich/Herman 2019, pp. 23–72.
Hintze, A./D. Durkin-Meisterernst/C. Naumann (eds.) 2019: *A Thousand Judgements. Festschrift for Maria Macuch.* Wiesbaden.
Hinz, W. 1973: *Neue Wege im Altpersischen.* Wiesbaden.
— 1975: *Altiranisches Sprachgut der Nebenüberlieferung.* Wiesbaden.
Hjerrild, B. 2003a: *Studies in Zoroastrian Family Law. A Comparative Analysis.* Copenhagen.
— 2003b: "The Institution of *stūrīh* in the Pahlavi Rivāyat of Āturfarnbag. Trust Settled Property." In: van Tongerloo 2003, pp. 91–107.
— 2007: "Some Aspects of the Institution of *stūrīh*." In: Vahman/Pedersen 2007, pp. 165–174.
Hoffmann, G. 1880: *Auszüge aus syrischen Akten persischer Märtyrer.* Leipzig.
Hohfeld, W.N. 1919: *Fundamental Legal Conceptions as Applied in Judicial Reasoning and other Legal Essays.* New Haven.
Houtsma, M.T. (ed.) 1883: *Ibn-Wādhih qui dicitur al-Jaʿqubī historiae.* 2 vols. Leiden.
Hübschmann, H. 1889: "Über die persische Verwandtenheirath." In: ZDMG 43, pp. 308–312.
— 1895: *Persische Studien.* Straßburg.
— 1897: *Armenische Grammatik. Erster Teil: Armenische Etymologie.* Darmstadt [repr. 1962].
Huebner, S.R. 2017: "A Mediterranean Family? A Comparative Approach to the Ancient World." In: S.R. Huebner/G. Nathan (eds.): *Mediterranean Families in Antiquity: Households, Extended Families, and Domestic Space.* Oxford, pp. 3–26.
Humbach, H. 1974: "*Bun-xānag* et *Kaʿba-ye Zardušt*." In: AcIr 3, pp. 203–208.
— 1991: The Gāthās of Zarathushtra and the Other Old Avestan Texts. Part I: Introduction – Text and Translation; Part II: Commentary. In collaboration with J. Elfenbein and P.O. Skjærvø. Heidelberg.
Humbach, H./J. Elfenbein 1990: *Ērbedestān. An Avesta-Pahlavi Text.* Munich.
Humbach, H./P.O. Skjærvø 1978–1983: *The Sassanian Inscription of Paikuli.* 3 vols. Wiesbaden.

Hutter, M. 2003: "Mār Abā and the Impact of Zoroastrianism on Christianity in the 6th Century." In: Cereti/Maggi/Provasi 2003, pp. 167–173.

Huyse, Ph. 1998: "Kerdīr and the First Sasanians." In: *Proceedings of the the Third European Conference of Iranian Studies Held in Cambridge, 11th to 15th September 1995*. Part 1: *Old and Middle Iranian Studies.* Wiesbaden (Beiträge zur Iranistik 17), pp. 109–120.

— 1999: *Die dreisprachige Inschrift Šābuhrs I an der Kaʿba-i Zardušt (ŠKZ).* 2 vols. London (CII, Part III, Vol. I. Texts I).

— 2009: "Inscriptional Literature in Old and Middle Iranian Languages." In: Emmerick/Macuch 2009, pp. 72–115.

— 2015: "Le règne de Husraw Ier aux yeux des historiographes protobyzantins." In: Jullien 2015, pp. 195–216.

Jaafari-Dehaghi, M. 1998: *Dādestān ī Dēnīg.* Part I: *Transcription, Translation and Commentary.* Paris (StIr, Cahier 20).

Jam, P. 2016 (1397): "Pāyandāni be tan wa żamāneh bi-l-nafs." In: *Pažuhešhā-ye īrānšenāsī* 5, pp. 39–73.

Jamasp, H. 1907: *Vendidâd. Avesta Text with Pahlavi Translation and Commentary and Glossarial Index.* Vol. I: *The Texts*; Vol. II: *Glossarial Index.* Bombay.

JamaspAsa, K.M./Y.M. Nawabi/M. Tavousi (eds.) 1978: *Manuscript TD4a. The Pahlavi Rivāyat, Dātistān-i Dīnīk, Nāmakīhā-i Manushchihr and Vichītakīhā-i Zātasparam etc.* Shiraz (PCIR 52).

Jamasp-Asana, J.M. (ed.) 1897–1913: *Pahlavi Texts.* Vol. I (1897); Vol. II (1913): *Contained in the Codex MK.* Bombay [repr. Tehran 1969].

Jany, J. 2005: "The Four Sources of Law in Zoroastrian and Islamic Jurisprudence." In: *Islamic Law and Society* 12, pp. 291–332.

— 2007: "Criminal Justice in Sasanian Persia." In: *Iranica Antiqua* 42, pp. 347–386.

— 2010: "Private Litigation in Sasanian Law." In: *Iranica Antiqua* 45, pp. 395–418.

— 2012: *Judging in the Islamic, Jewish and Zoroastrian Legal Traditions. A Comparison of Theory and Practice.* Surrey.

— 2017: "Übermittler von Rechtswissen in der zoroastrischen, jüdischen und islamischen Rechtskultur: *Dādestān, Responsa, Fatwā.*" In: Colditz/Jokisch/Macuch 2017, pp. 31–42.

Jastrow, M. 1926/1950: *A Dictionary of the Targumim, the Talmud Babli and Yerushalmi, and the Midrashic Literature.* 2 vols. New York/Berlin/London [repr. New York 1958].

Jokisch, B. 2017: "Sachenrechtliche Terminologie im islamischen und sasanidischen Recht. Zur Frage von Muttersache, Früchten, Eigentum und Besitz." In: Colditz/Jokisch/Macuch 2017, pp. 41–54.

— 2019: "Cultural Intertwinedness and the Problem of Proving Reception. A Case Study on Late Antique Foundations: *ruwanagān, heqdēsh, piae causae* and *waqf.*" In: Rubanovich/Herman 2019, pp. 103–128.

Jolly, J. 1896: *Recht und Sitte (einschließlich der einheimischen Litteratur.* Straßburg (Grundriß der indo-arischen Philologie und Altertumskunde II, 8).

Jong, A. de 1995: "Jeh the Primal Whore?" In: R. Kloppenborg/W.J. Hanegraaff (eds.): *Female Sterotypes in Religious Traditions.* Leiden (Studies in the History of Religions 66), pp. 15–41.

— 2002. "Animal Sacrifice in Ancient Zoroastrianism: A Ritual and its Interpretations." In: A.I. Baumgarten (ed.): *Sacrifice in Religious Experience.* Leiden/ Boston/Köln, pp. 127–148.

— 2003: "Women and Ritual in Mediaeval Zoroastrianism." In: C.G. Cereti / F. Vajifar (eds.): *Ātaš-e Dorun: the Fire Within. Jamshid Soroush Soroushian Memorial Volume II.* Bloomingdale, Ind., pp. 147–161.

Josephson, J. 1997: *The Pahlavi Translation Technique as Illustrated by Hōm Yašt.* Uppsala (Acta Universitatis Upsaliensis; Studia Iranica Upsaliensia 2).

— 1998: "The Middle Persian Nouns in *-išn* and *-išnīh*." In: *Orientalia Suecana* 47, pp. 87–104.

— 2012: "The Evolution and Transmission of the Third Book of the Dēnkard." In: Cantera 2012, pp. 541–552.

— 2019: "Aristotle's Theory of the Elements and Zoroastrian Dualism." In: Hintze/ Durkin-Meisterernst/Naumann 2019, pp. 225–235.

Jullien, Ch. (ed.) 2015: *Husraw Ier Reconstructions d'un Règne. Sources et Documents.* Paris (StIr, Cahier 53).

Junker, H.J. 1911: *The Frahang i Pahlavīk. First Part: Prolegomena.* Heidelberg.

Kapadia, D.D. 1953: *Glossary of Pahlavi Vendidad.* Bombay.

Kaser, M. 1986: *Römisches Privatrecht.* Munich.

Katrak, J.C. 1965: *Marriage in Ancient Iran.* Bombay.

Keenan, J.G./U. Yiftach-Firanko/J.G. Manning (eds.) 2014: *Law and Legal Practice in Egypt from Alexander to the Arab Conquest: A Selection of Papyrological Sources in Translation, with Introduction and Commentary.* Cambridge.

Kellens, J. 1989: "Avesta." In: EIr III, pp. 35–44.

— 1984: *Le verb avestique.* Wiesbaden.

— 1995: *Liste du verbe avestique.* Wiesbaden.

Kellens, J./E. Pirart 1988: *Les textes vieil-avestiques.* Vol. I: *Introduction, texte et traduction.* Wiesbaden.

— 1990: *Les textes vieil-avestiques.* Vol. II: *Répertoires grammaticaux et lexique.* Wiesbaden.

Khaleghi-Motlagh, D. (ed.) 1988–2008: *Abu'l-Qasem Ferdowsi, The Shahnameh. The Book of Kings.* Vols. 1–5. New York.

Kiel, Y. 2008: "The Systematization of Penitance in Zoroastrianism in Light of Rabbinic and Islamic Literature." In: BAI 22 (2008 [2012]), pp. 119–135.

— 2011: *Selected Topics in Laws of Ritual Defilement: Between the Babylonian Talmud and Pahlavi Literature.* Doctoral dissertation, Hebrew University of Jerusalem.

— 2013: "Cognizance of Sin and Punishment in the Babylonian Talmud and Pahlavi Literature: A Comparative Analysis." In: *Oqimta: Studies in the Talmudic and Rabbinic Literature* 1, pp. 1–49.

— 2014a: "Shaking Impurity: Scriptural Exegesis and Legal Innovation in the Babylonian Talmud and Pahlavi Literature." In: Gabbay/Secunda 2014, pp. 413–434.

— 2014b: "Penitential Theology in East Late Antiquity: Talmudic, Zoroastrian and East Christian Reflections." In: *Journal for the Study of Judaism* 45, pp. 551–583.

Kiel, Y./P.O. Skjærvø 2019: "Normative and Theological Dissent in Early Zoroastrian Law; Pahlavi *Nīrangestān* 23." In: Hintze/Durkin-Meisterernst/Naumann 2019, pp. 237–262.

Klíma, O. 1957: *Mazdak. Geschichte einer sozialen Bewegung im sasanidischen Persien.* Prague.
— 1966: "Zur Problematik der Ehe-Institution im alten Iran." In: *ArOr* 34, pp. 554–569.
— 1977: *Beiträge zur Geschichte des Mazdakismus.* Praha.
Klingenschmitt, G. 1968: *Frahang-ī oīm. Edition und Kommentar.* Inaugural-Diss. Erlangen.
— 1971: "Neue Avesta-Fragmente." In: MSS 29, pp. 111–175.
— 1972: "Avestisch *hąmąmiiāsaitē* and Pahlavi hmystkʾnʾ." In: MSS 30, pp. 79–92.
— 2000: "Mittelpersisch." In: B. Forssman/R. Plath (eds.): *Indoarisch, Iranisch und die Indogermanistik. Arbeitstagung der Indogermanischen Gesellschaft vom 2.–5.10.1997 in Erlangen.* Wiesbaden, pp. 191–229.
König, G. 2005: "Zur Figur des ‚Wahrhaftigen Menschen' *(mard ī ahlaw)* in der zoroastrischen Literatur." In: ZDMG 155, pp. 161–188.
— 2010a: *Geschlechtsmoral und Gleichgeschlechtlichkeit im Zoroastrismus.* Wiesbaden (Iranica 18).
— 2010b: "Der Pahlavi-Text *Zand ī Fragard ī Juddēvdād.*" In: Macuch/Weber/Durkin-Meisterernst 2010, pp. 115–131.
— 2012: "Das Nask *Bayān* und das *Xorde Awesta.*" In: Cantera 2012, pp. 355–394.
— 2018: *Studien zur Rationalitätsgeschichte im älteren Iran. Ein Beitrag zur Achsenzeitdiskussion.* Wiesbaden (Iranica 26).
— 2019: "Die Pahlavi-Literatur des 9./10. Jahrhunderts und ihre frühe Kodex-Überlieferung (I)." In: Hintze/Durkin-Meisterernst/Naumann 2019, pp. 263–286.
— 2022a: "Überlegungen zur Avesta-Transmission in der Sasanidenzeit." In: Farridnejad/Daryaee 2022, pp. 127–156.
— 2022b: *Studien zur Rationalitätsgeschichte im älteren Iran II.* Wiesbaden (Iranica 28).
Köprülü, F. 1942: "L'institution du Vakouf. Sa nature juridique et son évolution historique." In: *Vakiflar Dergisi* 2, pp. 3–48.
Koschaker, P. 1911: *Babylonisch-assyrisches Bürgschaftsrecht. Ein Beitrag zur Lehre von Schuld und Haftung.* Leipzig [repr. Aalen 1966].
Kotwal, F. M. P. 1969: *The Supplementary Texts to the Šāyest nē-šāyest.* Copenhagen.
Kotwal, F. M./J. W. Boyd 1980: *Ērbadīstān ud Nirangistān. Facsimile Edition of the Manuscript TD.* Cambridge, MA.
Kotwal, F. M./Ph. G. Kreyenbroek, with contributions by J. R. Russell 1992: *The Hērbedestān and Nērangestān.* Vol. I: *Hērbedestān.* Paris (StIr, Cahier 10).
— 1995: *The Hērbedestān and Nērangestān.* Vol. II: *Nērangestān, Fragard 1.* Paris (StIr, Cahier 16).
— 2003: *The Hērbedestān and Nērangestān.* Vol. III: *Nērangestān, Fragard 2.* Paris (StIr, Cahier 30).
— 2009: *The Hērbedestān and Nērangestān.* Vol. IV: *Nērangestān, Fragard 3.* Paris (StIr, Cahier 38).
Kraeling, E. G. 1953: *The Brooklyn Museum Aramaic Papyri.* New Haven.
— 1956: *The Synagoge. The Excavations at Dura-Europos. Final Report VIII, Part I.* New Haven.
Kreyenbroek, Ph. G. 1987: "The Zoroastrian Priesthood after the Fall of the Sasanian Empire." In: Ph. Gignoux (ed.): *Transition Periods in Iranian History.* Paris (StIr, Cahier 5), pp. 151–166.

— 1994: "On the Concept of Spiritual Authority in Zoroastrianism." In: JSAI 17, pp. 1–15.

— 2015: "Religious Knowledge in Oral and Written Traditions: the Case of Zoroastrianism." In: Cancik-Kirschbaum/Traninger 2015, pp. 93–104.

de Lagarde, P. 1866: *Gesammelte Abhandlungen*. Leipzig.

Lambton, A. K. S. 1953: *Landlord and Peasant in Persia*. Oxford [repr. 1969].

Lerner, J. / P. O. Skjærvø 2006: "The Seal of a Eunuch in the Sasanian Court." In: *Journal of Inner Asian Art and Archaeology* 1, pp. 113–118.

Le Strange, G. / R. A. Nicholson (eds.) 1921: *The Fārsnāma of Ibnu'l-Balkhī*. London [repr. 1962].

Levy, J. 1876 [1924]: *Neuhebräisches und chaldäisches Wörterbuch über die Talmudim und Midraschim*. Vols. I–IV. Berlin [first published Leipzig 1876].

Liebs, D. ^{2}1982: *Römisches Recht*. Göttingen.

Livshits, V. A. 1962: *Juridičeskie dokumenty i pis'ma* [Legal Documents and Letters]. Moscow (Sogdijskie dokumenty s gory Mug [Sogdian Dokuments from Mount Mug] 2).

— 2007: "The Leader of the People of Chach in the Sogdian Inscriptions and Coin-Legends." In: Macuch/Maggi/Sundermann 2007, pp. 173–181.

— 2008: *Sogdijskaja Èpigrafika Srednej Azii i Semirech'ja* [Sogdian Epigraphy of Central Asia and Semirech'e]. St. Petersburg.

— 2015: *Sogdian Epigraphy of Central Asia and Semirech'e*. Translated from the Russian by T. Stableford; edited by N. Sims-Williams. London (CII, Part II, Vol. III, IV).

Mabro, J. 1991: *Veiled Half-Truths. Western Travellers' Perceptions of Middle Eastern Women*. London/New York.

MacKenzie, D. N. 1966: "Ad Judaeo-Persica II Hafniensia." In: JRAS 1966, p. 69.

— 1968: "An Early Jewish-Persian Argument." In: BSOAS 31, pp. 249–269.

— 1971: *A Concise Pahlavi Dictionary*. London.

— 1974: "Finding's Keeping." In: Gignoux/Tafazzoli 1974, pp. 273–280.

— 1983: "Khwarezmian Language and Literature." In: CHI 3/2, pp. 1244–1249.

— 1985: "Āmārgar. i. Etymology." In: EIr I, p. 925.

— 1989: "Khwarezmian in the law books." In: de Fouchécour/Gignoux 1989, pp. 265–276.

— 1990: *The Khwarezmian Element in the Qunyat al-Munya*. London.

MacKenzie, D. N. / A. Perikhanian 1969: "The Model Marriage Contract in Pahlavi." In: N. D. Minochehr-Homji / M. F. Kanga (eds.): *K. R. Cama Oriental Institute Golden Jubilee Volume*. Bombay, pp. 103–112.

Maclean, A. J. 1901: *A Dictionary of the Dialects of Vernacular Syriac*. Oxford.

Macuch, M. 1981: *Das sasanidische Rechtsbuch Mātakdān i hazār Dātistān (Teil II)*. Wiesbaden (AKM XLV, 1).

— 1985: "Die Zeitehe im sasanidischen Recht – ein Vorläufer der šīʿitischen *mutʿa*-Ehe in Iran?" In: AMI 18, pp. 187–203.

— 1988a: "Barda and Bardadārīh. ii. In the Sasanian Period." In: EIr III, pp. 763–766.

— 1988b: "Der *dastwar*, ‚auctor', im sasanidischen Zivilprozeß." In: AMI 21, pp. 181–192.

— 1989: "Ein mittelpersischer *terminus technicus* im syrischen Rechtskodex des Īšōʿbōḫt und im sasanidischen Rechtsbuch." In: Ch. Müller / M. Macuch / B. Fragner

(eds.): *Studia Semitica necnon Iranica Rudolpho Macuch septuagenario ab amicis et discipulis dedicata.* Wiesbaden, pp. 149–160.
— 1990: "Eine alte Bemessungsgrundlage für die ‚Tagesration' in den Pahlavi-Schriften." In: R Gyselen (ed.): *Salaires, prix, poids et mesures.* Paris (Res Orientales II), pp. 139–142.
— 1991a: "Inzest im vorislamischen Iran." In: AMI 24, pp. 141–154.
— 1991b: "Charitable Foundations. i. In the Sasanian Period." In: EIr V, pp. 380–382.
— 1993: *Rechtskasuistik und Gerichtspraxis zu Beginn des siebenten Jahrhunderts in Iran: Die Rechtssammlung des Farroḫmard i Wahrāmān.* Wiesbaden (Iranica 1).
— 1994a: "Die sasanidische Stiftung ‚für die Seele' – Vorbild für den islamischen *waqf*?" In: P. Vavroušek (ed.): *Iranian and Indo-European Studies. Memorial Volume of Otakar Klíma.* Prague, pp. 163–180.
— 1994b: Review of Weber 1992. In: OLZ 89, nos. 5/6, pp. 576–581.
— 1995: "Herrschaftskonsolidierung und sasanidisches Familienrecht: zum Verhältnis von Kirche und Staat unter den Sasaniden." In: Reck/Zieme 1995, pp. 149–167.
— 1997: "The Use of Seals in Sasanian Jurisprudence." In: R. Gyselen (ed.): *Sceaux d'orient et leur emploi.* Bures sur-Yvette (Res Orientales X), pp. 79–87.
— 1999: "Iranian Legal Terminology in the Babylonian Talmud in the Light of Sasanian Jurisprudence." In: Shaked/Netzer 1999, pp. 91–101.
— 2002a: "A Zoroastrian Legal Term in the Dēnkard: *pahikār-rad.*" In: Ph. Huyse (ed.): *Iran: Questions et connaissances.* Vol. I: *La période ancienne.* Paris (StIr, Cahier 25), pp. 77–90.
— 2002b: "The Talmudic Expression 'Servant of the Fire' in the Light of Pahlavi Legal Sources." In: JSAI 26 [= *Volume in Honour of Shaul Shaked*], pp. 109–129.
— 2003a: "On the Treatment of Animals in Zoroastrian Law." In: van Tongerloo 2003, pp. 167–190.
— 2003b: "Zoroastrian Principles and the Structure of Kinship in Sasanian Iran." In: Cereti/Maggi/Provasi 2003, pp. 231–246.
— 2004: "Pious Foundations in Byzantine and Sasanian Law." In: Gnoli 2004, pp. 181–196.
— 2005a: "On Middle Persian Legal Terminology." In: C.G. Cereti/M. Maggi (eds.): Middle Iranian Lexicography: Proceedings of the Conference held in Rome, 9–11 April 2001. Rome (Orientalia Romana 8), pp. 375–386.
— 2005b: "Inheritance. i. Sasanian Period." In: EIr XIII, pp. 125–131.
— 2005c: "Language and Law: Linguistic Pecularities in Sasanian Jurisprudence." In: Weber 2005, pp. 95–108.
— 2006: "The Function of Temporary Marriage in the Context of Sasanian Family Law." In: Panaino/Piras 2006, pp. 585–597.
— 2007a: "On the Legal Nasks of the Dēnkard." In: Vahman/Pedersen 2007, pp. 151–164.
— 2007b: "The Pahlavi Marriage Contract in the Light of Sasanian Family Law." In: Macuch/Maggi/Sundermann 2007, pp. 183–204.
— 2008a: "An Iranian Legal Term in the Babylonian Talmud and in Sasanian Jurisprudence: *dastwar.*" In: Shaked/Netzer 2008, pp. 126–138.
— 2008b: "Zur juristischen Terminologie der Berliner Pahlavi-Dokumente." In: Weber 2008, pp. 249–266.

– 2008c: "Rudolf Macuch." In: R. Voigt (ed.): *Und das Leben ist siegreich! / And Life is Victorious. Mandäische und samaritanische Literatur / Mandean and Samaritan Literature. Im Gedenken an Rudolf Macuch / In Memory of Rudolf Macuch (1919–1993).* Wiesbaden (Mandäistische Forschungen 1), pp. 9–16.
– 2009a: "Pahlavi Literature." In: Emmerick/Macuch 2009, pp. 116–190.
– 2009b: "Gelehrte Frauen: ein ungewöhnliches Motiv in der Pahlavi-Literatur." In: D. Durkin-Meisterernst / Ch. Reck / D. Weber (eds.): *Literarische Stoffe und ihre Gestaltung in mitteliranischer Zeit. Colloquium anlässlich des 70. Geburtstags von Werner Sundermann.* Wiesbaden (Beiträge zur Iranistik 31), pp. 135–151.
– 2009c: "Disseminating the Mazdayasnian Religion: An Edition of the Pahlavi Hērbedestān Chapter 5." In: Sundermann/Hintze/de Blois 2009, pp. 251–277.
– 2009d: "Die sasanidische fromme Stiftung und der islamische *waqf*: Eine Gegenüberstellung." In: A. Meier / J. Pahlitzsch / L. Reinfandt (eds.): *Islamische Stiftungen zwischen juristischer Norm und sozialer Praxis.* Berlin, pp. 19–38.
– 2009e: "Judicial and Legal System. iii. Sasanian Legal System." In: EIr XV, pp. 181–196.
– 2009f: "The Hērbedestān as a Legal Source: A Section on the Inheritance of a Convert to Zoroastrianism." In: Bromberg/Sims-Williams/Sims-Williams 2009, pp. 91–102.
– 2010a: "Legal Constructions of Identity in the Sasanian Period." In: Cereti 2010, pp. 193–212.
– 2010b: "Allusions to Sasanian Law in the Babylonian Talmud." In: Bakhos/Shayegan 2010, pp. 100–111.
– 2010c: "Incestuous Marriage in the Context of Sasanian Family Law." In: Macuch/Weber/Durkin-Meisterernst 2010, pp. 133–148.
– 2012a: "The *adwadād* Offence in Zoroastrian Law." In: Sh. Secunda / S. Fine (eds.): *Shoshannat Yaakov. Jewish and Iranian Studies in Honor of Yaakov Elman.* Leiden/Boston (The Brill Reference Library of Judaism 35), pp. 247–269.
– 2012b: "Editing Pahlavi Legal Texts." In: Cantera 2012, pp. 519–540.
– 2013: "Vorislamisches iranisches Recht." In: L. Paul (ed.): *Handbuch der Iranistik.* Wiesbaden, pp. 123–132.
– 2014a: "Ardashir's Genealogy Revisited." In: P. Pourshariati / M. Tavakoli (eds.): *Iran Nameh* 29.2 (*A Special Issue Honoring Jaleh Amouzgar*), pp. 80–94.
– 2014b: "Jewish Jurisdiction within the Framework of the Sasanian Legal System." In: Gabbay/Secunda 2014, pp. 147–160.
– 2014c: "The Case against Mār Abā, the Catholicos, in the Light of Sasanian Law." In: ARAM 26.1–2 [= *Zoroastrianism in the Levant and the Amorites*], pp. 47–58.
– 2014d: "‚Behalte den Flug in Erinnerung …' – Leben und Werk von Rudolf Macuch." In: Ján Juráš / Daniela Kodajová (eds.): *Sláva Šláchetným III (Glory for the Noble).* Liptovský Mikuláš, pp. 61–88.
– 2014e: "Rudolf Macuch." In: Predrag Bukovec (ed.): *Christlicher Orient im Porträt – Wissenschaftsgeschichte des Christlichen Orients.* II. Hamburg, pp. 1035–1054.
– 2015a: "Law in Pre-modern Zoroastrianism." In: Stausberg/Vevaina 2015, pp. 289–298.
– 2015b: "Legal Implications of Mazdakite Teaching According to the Dēnkard." In: Jullien 2015, pp. 155–174.

— 2015c: "Precision Orientated Legal Terminology in the Sasanian Law of Inheritance." In: I. Szántó (ed.): *From Aṣl to Zā'id: Essays in Honour of Éva M. Jeremiás.* Piliscsaba, pp. 129–146.

— 2015d: "Substance and Fruit in the Sasanian Law of Property and the Babylonian Talmud." In: M.J. Geller (ed.): *The Archaeology and Material Culture of the Babylonian Talmud.* Leiden/Boston, pp. 245–259.

— 2016a: "The Legal Context of the Tabarestān Court Records (Tab. 1–8, 10)." In: Gyselen 2016, pp. 145–170.

— 2016b: "'This is the Law of the Persians'—An Allusion to the Sasanian Law of Surety in the Babylonian Talmud." In: *Iran Namag* [NS] 1.2 [= *Memorial Volume in Honour of Professor Amnon Netzer*], pp. XVIII–XXVIII.

— 2016c: "Türken in der zoroastrischen Literatur." In: I. Hauenschild/M. Kappler/B. Kellner-Heinkele (eds.): *Eine hundertblättrige Tulpe – Bir ṣadbarg lāla. Festgabe für Claus Schönig.* Berlin, pp. 308–331.

— 2017a: "A Legal Controversy from the Sasanian Period in a Late Pahlavi Rivāyat Text." In: Morano/Provasi/Rossi 2017, pp. 257–272.

— 2017b: "A Case of Loan and Mortgage in a Late Pahlavi Text." In: Team "Turfanforschung" (ed.): *Zur Lichten Heimat. Studien zu Manichäismus, Iranistik und Zentralasienkunde im Gedenken an Werner Sundermann.* Wiesbaden (Iranica 25), pp. 355–370.

— 2017c: "Pahlavi Legal Documents from Tabarestān on Lease, Loan and Compensation: The Juristic Context (Tab. 13,14, 15, 17, 18, 23)." In: Gyselen 2017, pp. 165–195.

— 2017d: "Descent and Inheritance in Zoroastrian and Shiite Law: a Preliminary Study." In: *Der Islam* 94.2, pp. 322–335.

— 2019a: "A Pahlavi Legal Term in Jesubōxt's Corpus Iuris." In: Rubanovich/Herman 2019, pp. 73–102.

— 2019b: "Pahlavi legal Documents from Tabarestān. Two Claims and a Re-evaluation of Crop Yields: The Juristic Context of Tab. 21, 22 and 24." In: Gyselen 2019d, pp. 117–150.

— 2020a: "Descent in Frēdōn's Line: An Epic Narrative in the Light of Zoroastrian Law." In: Sh. Farridnejad (ed.): *Zaraϑuštrōtəma. Zoroastrian and Iranian Studies in Honour of Philip G. Kreyenbroek.* Irvine, Calif. (Ancient Iran Series 10), pp. 253–272.

— 2020b: "Pahlavi Legal Documents from Tabarestān: Two Claims Involving 'Substitute Succession' and a Payment Commitment. The Juristic Context of Tab. 11, 28 and 27." In: Gyselen 2020, pp. 189–216

— 2021: "Mazdakite Heresy and Esotericism in the late Zoroastrian Tradition." In: A. Shayeste Doust (ed.): *Dādestān ī Denīg. Festschrift for Mahmoud Jaafari Dehaghi.* Tehran, pp. 215–264.

— 2022a: "Pahlavi Legal Documents from Tabarestān: The Juristic Content of Tab. 16, 19, 20, 22 bis and 25." In: Gyselen 2022, pp. 131–160.

— 2022b: "Pahlavi Legal Documents from Tabarestān: The Juristic Content of Tab. 12 and 26." In: Gyselen 2022, pp. 161–172.

— 2022c: "A Legal Transaction in the Zoroastrian Community and its Social Consequences." In: Cantera/Macuch/Sims-Williams 2022, pp. 307–320.

— 2024a: "Trading with Infidels: A Balancing Act in Zoroastrian Legal Reasoning." In: MACUCH/ZEINI 2024, pp. 277–299.

— 2024b: "Dieter Weber—A Scholarly Profile." In: MACUCH/ZEINI 2024, pp. XIII–XXXIII.

— 2024c: "The Tabarestān Documents on Legal Proceedings." In: G. BARBERA/M. DE CHIARA/A. DEL TOMBA/B. DHAMMADINNĀ/F. DRAGONI/P. ORSATTI (eds.): *Siddham. Studies in Iranian Philology in honour of Mauro Maggi.* Wiesbaden (Beiträge zur Iranistik 52), pp. 275–296.

— [forthcoming a]: "Sasanian Law: Society, Family and Legal Institutions." In: R. SHAYEGAN/T. DARYAEE (eds.): *Wiley Blackwell Companion to the Sasanian Empire.* Chapter 32.

— [forthcoming b]: "Sasanian Law." In: C. ANDO/M. CANEVARO/B. STRAUMANN (eds.): *The Cambridge History of Rights.*

MACUCH, M./M. MAGGI/W. SUNDERMANN (eds.) 2007: *Iranian Languages and Texts from Iran and Turan. Ronald E. Emmerick Memorial Volume.* Wiesbaden (Iranica 13).

MACUCH, M./D. WEBER/D. DURKIN-MEISTERERNST (eds.) 2010: *Ancient and Middle Iranian Studies. Proceedings of the 6th European Conference of Iranian Studies, held in Vienna, 18–22 September 2007.* Wiesbaden (Iranica 19).

MACUCH, M./A. ZEINI (eds.) 2024: *Deciphering the Illegible. Festschrift in Honour of Dieter Weber.* Wiesbaden (Iranica 33).

MADAN, D.M. 1911: *The Complete Text of the Pahlavi Dinkard.* Vols. I–II. Bombay.

MADELUNG, W. 1985: "Shiʿi Attitudes toward Women as Reflected in Figh." In: *Religious Schools and Sects in Medieval Islam.* London, pp. 69–79.

MAGDALENE, F.R. 2007: *On the Scales of Righteousness: Neo-Babylonian Trial Law and the Book of Job.* Providence, RI (Brown Judaic Studies 348).

— 2009: "Judicial and Legal System. i. Achaemenid Judicial and Legal Systems." In: EIr XV, pp. 174–177.

MANTHE, U. 2000: *Geschichte des römischen Rechts.* Munich.

MASSARA, T. DALLA 2017: "Roman Legal Tradition as an Identity-Factor towards a New Europe: Five Pillars or the Future?" In: L. GAROFALO/L. ZHANG (eds.): *Diritto Romano fra Tradizione e Modernità. Atti del Convegno internazionale di Shanghai.* Pisa. pp. 147–160.

MAYRHOFER, M. 1956–1980: *Kurzgefaßtes etymologisches Wörterbuch des Altindischen. A Concise Etymological Sanskrit Dictionary.* Vols. I–IV. Heidelberg.

— 1979: *Iranisches Personennamenbuch.* Vol. I: *Die altiranischen Namen.* Vienna.

— 1992–2001: *Etymologisches Wörterbuch des Altindoarischen.* Vols. I–III. Heidelberg.

MEILLET, A. 1907: "Le dieu indo-iranien Mitra." In: JA 1907, pp. 143–159.

MENASCE, J. DE 1945: *Škand-gumānīk Vičār. La solution décisive des doutes.* Fribourg (Collectanea Friburgensia, Publications de l'université de Fribourg en suisse, Nouvelle série, fascicule 30).

— 1962: "La ‹ Rivāyat d'Ēmēt i Ašavahištān ›." In: *Revue de l'histoire des religions* 162, pp. 69–88.

— 1963: "Le protecteur des pauvres dans l'Iran sassanide." In: *Mélanges d'orientalisme offerts à Henri Massé. A l'occasion de son 75e anniversaire.* Tehran, pp. 282–287.

— 1964a: *Feux et fondations pieuses dans le droit Sassanide.* Paris.

— 1964b: "Les données géographiques dans le Mātigān i Hazār Dātistān." In: *Irano-Indica. Mélanges presents à Georg Morgenstierne à l'occasion de son soixante-dixième anniversaire.* Wiesbaden, pp. 149–154 [= DE MENASCE 1985, pp. 83–88].

— 1964c: "Some Pahlavi Words in the Original and in the Syriac Translation of Išōbōxt's Corpus Juris." In: *D.J.M. Unvala Memorial Volume.* Bombay, pp. 6–11 [= DE MENASCE 1985, pp. 119–124].

— 1969: "Formules juridiques et syntaxe Pehlevi." In: *Bulletin of the Iranian Culture Foundation* 1, pp. 11–20 [= DE MENASCE 1985, pp. 109–119].

— 1973: *Le troisième livre du Dēnkart.* Paris (Bibliothèque des œuvres classiques persanes 4).

— 1985: *Études iraniennes.* Paris (StIr, Cahier 3).

MEYNARD, B. DE / P. DE COURTEILLE (eds.) 1861–1877: *Les prairies d'or (Murūj al-ḏhahab).* 9 vols. Paris.

MICHEL, J. 1962: *Gratuité en droit romain: Études d'histoire et d'ethnologie juridiques.* Bruxelles.

MILLER, F.D. Jr. [2]2015: "Prologue—Near Eastern Antecedents of Western Legal Thought." In: F.D. MILLER, Jr. / C.-A. BIONDI (eds.). *A History of the Philosophy of Law from the Ancient Greeks to the Scholastics.* Heidelberg/New York/London, pp. 1–6 [1st ed. 2007].

MINOVI, M. 1932: *Nāme-ye Tansar* [The Letter of Tansar]. Tehran [repr. 1975].

MIR-HOSSEINI, Z. 1993: *Marriage on Trial: A Study of Islamic Family Law in Iran and Morocco Compared.* London.

— 1998: "A Response to Shahla Haeri's Review of Marriage on Trial." In: *International Journal of Middle East Studies* 30, pp. 469–471.

— 2000: *Islam and Gender. The Religious Debate in Contemporary Iran.* London/New York.

MOAZAMI, M. 2014: *Wrestling with the Demons of the Pahlavi Widēwdēd. Transcription, Translation and Commentary.* Leiden/Boston (Iran Studies 9).

— 2021: *Laws of Ritual Purity. Zand ī Fragard ī Jud Dēw-Dād. A Commentary on the Chapters of the Widēwdād.* Leiden/Boston (Iran Studies 19).

MODI, J.J. (ed.) 1901: *Mādigān-i-Hazār Dādistān. A Photozincographed Facsimile of a Ms. Belonging to the Mānockji Limji Hoshang Hātariā Library in the Zarthoshti Anjuman Ātashbeharām.* Poona.

— 1937: *The Religious Ceremonies and Customs of the Parsees.* Bombay.

MOHL, J. 1838–1878: *Le livre des rois. Publié, traduit et commenté.* Vols. I–VII. Paris.

MOLÉ, M. 1961: "Le problème des sectes Zoroastriennes dans les livres Pehlevis." In: *Oriens* 13–14, pp. 1–28.

— 1967: *La légende de Zoroastre selon les textes pahlevis.* Paris.

MORANO, E. / E. PROVASI / A.V. ROSSI (eds.) 2017: *Studia Philologica Iranica. Gherardo Gnoli Memorial Volume.* Rome (SOR [NS] 5).

NAVEH, J. / SH. SHAKED 2012: *Aramaic Documents from Ancient Bactria. From the Khalili Collections (Fourth Century BCE).* London.

NEUSNER, J. 1965–1970: *A History of the Jews in Babylonia.* Vol. I: *The Parthian Period* (1965); vol. II: *The Early Sasanian Period* (1966); vol. III: *From Shapur I to Shapur II* (1968); vol. IV: *The Age of Shapur II* (1969); vol. V: *Later Sasanian Times* (1970). Leiden.

NEWMAN, J. 1932: *The Agricultural Life of the Jews in Babylonia between the Years 200 and 500 C.E.* London.

NICHOLAS, B. 1962: *An Introduction to Roman Law.* Oxford [repr. 2010].

NÖLDEKE, TH. 1879: *Geschichte der Perser und Araber zur Zeit der Sasaniden aus der arabischen Chronik des Ṭabarī.* Leiden [repr. 1973].

NYBERG, H.S. 1974: *A Manual of Pahlavi.* Part II: *Glossary.* Wiesbaden.

— 1988: *Frahang i Pahlavīk.* Edited with transliteration, transcription and commentary from the posthumous papers of H.S. NYBERG by B. UTAS with the collaboration of CH. TOLL. Wiesbaden.

PAGLIARO, A. 1948: "Note di lessicografia pahlavica. VIII. *pat kartak*: una formula della terminologia giuridica del MhD." In: RSO 23, pp. 52–68.

1949: "Aspetti del diritto Sāsānidico: Hačašmānd 'interdictum'." In: RSO 24, pp. 120–135.

— 1951: "Note di lessicografia pahlavica. IX. *xvaran* 'riunione, assamblea, festa'; X. *drōš* 'mutilazione, scepio, marchio'." In: RSO 26, pp. 47–56.

PAKZAD, F. 2005: *Bundahišn. Zoroastrische Kosmogonie und Kosmologie.* Vol. I: *Kritische Edition.* Tehran.

PANAINO, A. 2003a: "Short Remarks about Ohrmazd between Limited and Unlimited Time." In: VAN TONGERLOO 2003, pp. 195–200.

— 2003b: "Divine and Human Time in the Zoroastrian Cosmology." In: N. COLAFRANCESCO / G. GIOBBI (eds.): *Cosmology through Time. Ancient and Modern Cosmologies in the Mediterranean Area. Conference Proceedings, Astronomical Observatory of Rome, Monteporzio Catone, June 17–20, 2001.* Milano, pp. 15–24.

— 2006: "La sfera della sessualità nel mondo iranico-preislamico." In: *Comportamenti e immaginario della sessualità nell'alto medioevo, 31 marzo–5 aprile 2005.* Spoleto (Settimane di studio della Fondazione Centro italiano di studi sull'alto medioevo 53), pp. 223–260.

— 2007: "Ahura Mazdā and the Darkness: About the Meaning of *Y.* 44.5b." In: MACUCH/MAGGI/SUNDERMANN 2007, pp. 271–283.

— 2010: "The Astronomical Conference of the year 556 and the Politics of Xusraw Anōšag-ruwān." In: H. BÖRM / J. WIESEHÖFER (eds.): *Commutatio et Contentio. Studies in the Late Roman, Sasanian, and Early Islamic Near East. In Memory of Zeev Rubin.* Düsseldorf (Reihe Geschichte 3), pp. 293–306.

— 2015: "Cosmologies and Astrology." In: STAUSBERG/VEVAINA 2015, pp. 235–257.

— 2019: "The Liturgical Daēnā. Speculative Aspects of the Next-of-kin Unions." In: HINTZE/DURKIN-MEISTERERNST/NAUMANN 2019, pp. 331–344.

— 2022a: "Between Semantics and Pragmatics: Origins and Developments in the Meaning of *dastgerd.* A New Approach to the Problem." In: FARRIDNEJAD/DARYAEE 2022, pp. 215–242.

— 2022b: *Abēbīm "Fearless". Who was Afraid of the End of the Millennium? New Approaches to the Interpretation of the Traditional Date of Zoroaster.* With contributions by D. AGOSTINO, J. KOTYK, P. OGNIBENE and A. ZUBANI. A research volume edited by A. ZUBANI. Milano (Indo-Iranica et Orientalia 22).

PANAINO, A. / A. PIRAS (eds.) 2006: *Proceedings of the 5th Conference of the Societas Iranologica Europæa held in Ravenna, 6–11 October 2003.* Vol. I: *Ancient and Middle Iranian Studies.* Milan.

Payne, R.E. 2015a: "East Syrian Bishops, Elite Households, and Iranian Law after the Muslim Conquest." In: *Iranian Studies* 48, pp. 5–32.

— 2015b: *A State of Mixture. Christians, Zoroastrians, and Iranian Political Culture in Late Antiquity.* Oakland, Calif.

— 2016: "Sex, Death, and Aristocratic Empire: Iranian Jurisprudence in Late Antiquity." In: *Comparative Studies in Society and History* 58.2, pp. 519–549.

— 2017: "Die Christianisierung des *Stūrīh*: Recht, Fortpflanzung und Elitenbildung im Sasanidischen Reich." In: Colditz/Jokisch/Macuch 2017, pp. 57–72.

Payne Smith, R. 1903: *A Compendious Syriac Dictionary. Founded Upon the Thesaurus Syriacus of R. Payne Smith.* Oxford.

Peeters, P. 1951: „Observations sur la vie syriaques de Mar Aba, catholicos de l'église persse (540–552)." In: *Recherches d'histoire et de philologie orientales.* Vol. II. Bruxelles, pp. 117–163.

Pellat, Ch. (ed.) 1962–1997: *Masʿūdī (mort en 345/956): Les prairies d'or.* Traduction française de B. de Meynard et P. de Courteille, revue et corrigée par Ch. Pellat. 5 vols. Paris.

Perikhanian, A.G. 1970: "On Some Pahlavi Legal Terms." In: Boyce/Gershevitch 1970, pp. 349–357.

1973: *Sasanidskij Sudebnik. Kniga tysjači sudebnych rešenij (Mātakdān i hazār dātastān).* Yerevan.

— 1974: "Le contumace dans la procédure iranienne et les termes pehlevis *hačašmānd* et *srad*." In: Gignoux/Tafazzoli 1974, pp. 305–318.

— 1979: "Ordalija i kljatva v sudoproizvodstve do-islamskogo Irana." In: M.A. Dandamaev (red.): *Peredneaziatskij sbornik.* Vol. 3: *Istorija i filologija stran drevnego vostoka.* Moscow, pp. 182–191.

— 1983a: "Iranian Society and Law." In: CHI 3.2, pp. 627–680.

— 1983b: *Obščestvo i pravo Irana v parfjanskij i sasanidskij periody.* Moscow.

— 1997: *Farraxvmart ī Vahrāmān. The Book of a Thousand Judgements (A Sasanian Law-book). Introduction, Transcription and Translation of the Pahlavi Text, Notes, Glossary and Indexes.* Translated from Russian by N. Garsoïan. Costa Mesa/New York (Persian Heritage Series 39).

Pigulevskaya, N.V. 1956: "Economic Relations in Iran during the IV–VI Centuries A.D." [Translated by W. Ivanow.] In: JCOI 38, pp. 60–81.

— 1963: "Mar Aba I: Une page de l'histoire de la civilisation au VIe siècle de l'ère nouvelle." In: *Mélanges d'orientalisme offerts à Henri Massé … à l'occasion de son 75ème anniversaire.* Tehran, pp. 327–336.

Platschek, J. 2017: "*Arra* in den römischen Rechtstexten und in den *leges Barbarorum.*" In: Colditz/Jokisch/Macuch 2017, pp. 73–92.

Plessis, P. du / A. Borkowski 2010: *Borkowski's Textbook on Roman Law.* Oxford.

Polak, J.E. 1861: "Die Prostitution in Persien." In: *Wiener medizinische Wochenschrift* 35 (11. Jahrgang), cols. 563–565.

Porten, B. 1980: *Jews of Elephantine and Arameans of Syene (Fifth Century B.C.E.). Fifty Aramaic Texts with Hebrew and English Translations.* In collaboration with J.C. Greenfield. Jerusalem.

Purwins, N. 2019: "The Noble Ones of Erānšahr: Rank Titles and a Comparison with the *Imperium Romanum.*" In: Gyselen 2019d, pp. 29–88.

— forthcoming: *Der Aufbau des Sasanidenstaates. Administration und Eliten im Vergleich zum Römischen Reich.*

Pourshariati, P. 2008: *Decline and Fall of the Sasanian Empire. The Sasanian-Parthian Confederacy and the Arab Conquest of Iran.* London/New York.

Raffaelli, E.G. 2014: *The Sīh-rōzag in Zoroastrianism. A Textual and Historico-Religious Analysis.* London.

Reck, Ch./P. Zieme (eds.) 1995: *Iran und Turfan. Beiträge Berliner Wissenschaftler, Werner Sundermann zum 60. Geburtstag gewidmet.* Wiesbaden (Iranica 2).

Reichelt, H. 1900–1901: "Der *Frahang i oīm.*" In: WZKM 14 (1900), pp. 177–213; WZKM 15 (1901), pp. 117–186.

— 1928–1931: *Die soghdischen Handschriftenreste des Britischen Museums in Umschrift und mit Übersetzung.* I. Teil (1928): *Die buddhistischen Texte.* II. Teil (1931): *Die nicht-buddhistischen Texte.* Heidelberg.

Reis, L. 2012: "Zum sasanidischen Privatrecht." In: V. Sadovski/D. Stifter (eds.): *Iranistische und indogermanistische Beiträge in Memoriam Jochem Schindler (1944–1994).* Vienna (Österreichische Akademie der Wissenschaften. Veröffentlichungen zur Iranistik 51), pp. 291–310.

Rezakhani, Kh. 2010: "Balkh and the Sasanians. The Economy and Society of Northern Afghanistan as Reflected in the Bactrian Economic Documents." In: Macuch/Weber/Durkin-Meisterernst 2010, pp. 191–204.

Rezania, K. 2010: *Die zoroastrische Zeitvorstellung. Eine Untersuchung über Zeit- und Ewigkeitskonzepte und die Frage des Zurvanismus.* Wiesbaden (Göttinger Orientforschungen; Iranica [NF] 7).

— 2017: "The *Dēnkard* Against its Islamic Discourse." In: *Der Islam* 94, pp. 336–362.

Rollinger, R./J. Wiesehöfer 2023: "Emperor Valerian and Ilu-bi'dī of Hamath. Persian Cruelty and the Persistence of Ancient Near Eastern Traditions." In: *Sasanian Studies: Late Antique Iranian World / Sasanidische Studien: Spätantike iranische Welt* 2, pp. 253–272.

Rosen, K. 1996: "Rom und die Juden im Prozeß Jesu (um 30 n. Chr.)." In: A. Demandt (ed.): *Macht und Recht. Große Prozesse in der Geschichte.* Munich, pp. 47–73.

Rouland, N. 1988: *Anthropologie juridique.* Paris.

Rubanovich, J./G. Herman (eds.) 2019: *Irano-Judaica. Studies Relating to Jewish Contacts with Persian Culture Throughout the Ages.* Vol. 7. Jerusalem.

Russell, J.R. 1987: *Zoroastrianism in Armenia.* Cambridge, Mass. (Harvard Iranian Series 5).

Sachau, E. 1914: *Syrische Rechtsbücher.* Vol. III: *Corpus juris des persischen Erzbischofs Jesubocht. Erbrecht oder Canones des persischen Erzbischofs Simeon. Eherecht des Patriarchen Mâr Abhâ.* Berlin.

Safa-Isfehani, N. 1980: *Rivāyat-ī Hēmīt-ī Ašawahištān. A Study in Zoroastrian Law.* Cambridge, Mass. (Harvard Iranian Series 2).

Sahner, Ch.C. 2021: "Zoroastrian law and the spread of Islam in Iranian society (ninth–tenth century)." In: BSOAS 84.1, pp. 1–27.

Sanjana, D.P. 1848: *Vajarkard Dīnī.* Mumbai.

— 1888: *Next-of-kin Marriages in Old Iran. An Address Delivered Before the Bombay Branch Royal Asiatic Society, on the 15th and 22nd April, 1887.* London.

— 1894: *Nirangistan. A Photozincographed Facsimile of a Ms. Belonging to Shams-ul-Ulama Dastur Dr. Hoshangjee Jamaspjee of Poona.* Mumbai.

— 1916: *The Dînkard.* Vol. 15: *Book VIII: Contents of the Avesta Nasks, Part I.* London.

AŠ-ŠAYĀL, ABD AL-MUNʿIM ʾAMĪR JAMAL AD-DĪN (ed.) 1960: *Dīnawarī: Aḫbār aṭ-ṭiwāl.* Cairo.

SCHACHT, J. 1950: *The Origins of Muhammadan Jurisprudence.* Oxford.

SCHMIDT, M. G./W. BISANG (eds.) 2001: *Philologica et Linguistica. Historia, Pluralitas, Universitas. Festschrift für Helmut Humbach zum 80. Geburtstag.* Trier.

SCHMITT, R. 2004: "Byzantinoiranica: Zum Beispiel Prokop." In: GNOLI 2004, pp. 665–677.

SCHWARZ, M. 1974: "Sogdian Fragments of the *Book of Psalms.*" In: AoF 1, pp. 257–261.

— 1989: "Pers. *saugand xurdan*, etc. 'To take an oath' (Not *'to drink sulphur')." In: DE FOUCHÉCOUR/GIGNOUX 1989, pp. 293–295.

SECUNDA, SH. 2007: *'Dashtana—Ki derekh nashim li': A Study of the Babylonian Rabbinic Laws of Menstruation in Relation to Corresponding Zoroastrian Texts.* Doctoral dissertation, Yeshiva University, New York.

— 2012: "On the Age of the Zoroastrian Sages of the Zand." In: *Iranica Antiqua* 47, pp. 317–349.

— 2014: *The Iranian Talmud. Reading the Bavli in its Sasanian Context.* Philadelphia, Pa.

SECUNDA, SH./S. FINE (eds.) 2012: *Shoshannat Yaakov. Jewish and Iranian Studies in Honor of Yaakov Elman.* Leiden/Boston (The Brill Reference Library of Ancient Judaism 35).

SELB, W./H. KAUFHOLD 2002: *Das syrisch-römische Rechtsbuch.* Vol. I: *Einleitung.* Vol. II: *Texte und Übersetzungen.* Vol. III: *Kommentar.* Vienna (Veröffentlichungen der Kommission für Antike Rechtsgeschichte 9. Denkschriften der phil.-hist. Klasse 295).

SHAKED, SH. 1975: "Some Legal and Administrative Terms of the Sasanian Period." In: DUCHESNE-GUILLEMIN 1975, pp. 213–225.

— 1979: *The Wisdom of the Sasanian Sages (Dēnkard VI).* Boulder, Colo. (Persian Heritage Series 34).

— 1980: "Mihr the Judge." In: JSAI 2, pp. 1–31.

— 1987: "Iranian Loanwords in Middle Aramaic." In: EIr II, pp. 259–261.

— 2022: "Piety in Pahlavi Literature. Notes on *mard ī ahlaw* and Other Themes." In: CANTERA/MACUCH/SIMS-WILLIAMS 2022, pp. 467–480.

SHAKED, SH./A. NETZER (eds.) 1999: *Irano-Judaica IV. Studies Relating to Jewish Contacts with Persian Culture Throughout the Ages.* Jerusalem.

— (eds.) 2008: *Irano-Judaica VI. Studies Relating to Jewish Contacts with Persian Culture Throughout the Ages.* Jerusalem.

SHAKI, M. 1971: "The Sasanian Matrimonial Relations." In: ArOr 39, pp. 322–345.

— 1975: "The Concept of Obligated Successorship in the Mādiyān ī Hazār Dādistān." In: DUCHESNE-GUILLEMIN 1975, pp. 227–242.

— 1977: "The Obstruction of Justice." In: ArOr 45, pp. 48–53.

— 1978: "The Social Doctrine of Mazdak in the Light of Middle Persian Evidence." In: ArOr 46, pp. 289–306.

— 1981: "The Dēnkart Account of the History of the Zoroastrian Scriptures." In: ArOr 49, pp. 114–125.

Sheffield, D.J. 2009: "The *Wizirgerd ī Dēnīg* and the Evil Spirit: Questions of Authenticity in Post-Classical Zoroastrianism." In: Bromberg/Sims-Williams/Sims-Williams 2009, pp. 181–189.

Sheikh, H. 2022: "Aramaic Legal Terminology in the Sasanian Law-Book *Mādayān ī Hazār Dādestān*: Some Remarks on Late Antique *termini technici*." In: Farridnejad/Daryaee 2022, pp. 277–290.

— 2023: *Studies of Bactrian Legal Documents.* Leiden/Boston 2023 (Ancient Iran Series 15).

Shepher, J. 1983: *Incest. A Biosocial View.* London.

Sidler, N. 1971: *Zur Universalität des Inzesttabu. Eine kritische Untersuchung der These und der Einwände.* Stuttgart (Soziologische Gegenwartsfragen N.F. 36).

Sims-Williams, N. 1985: "Ancient Letters." In: EIr II, pp. 7–9.

— 1997: *New Light on Ancient Afghanistan. The Decipherment of Bactrian.* London.

— 2000: *Bactrian Documents from Northern Afghanistan. I: Legal and Economic Documents.* Oxford (Studies in the Khalili Collection 3. CII, Part II, Vol. VI).

— 2001a: "The Sogdian Ancient Letter II." In: Schmidt/Bisang 2001, pp. 267–280.

— 2001b: "The Sogdian Ancient Letter V. Part I." In: BAI 12 (1998 [2001]), pp. 91–98.

— 2002: "Ancient Afghanistan and its Invaders: Linguistic Evidence from the Bactrian Documents and Inscriptions." In: N. Sims-Williams (ed.): *Indo-Iranian Languages and Peoples.* Oxford (Proceedings of the British Academy 116), pp. 225–242.

— 2005a: "Towards a new edition of the Sogdian Ancient Letters: Ancient Letter I." In: É. de la Vassière/É. Trombert (eds.): *Les Sogdiens en Chine.* Paris, pp. 181–193.

— 2005b: "Bactrian Legal Documents from 7th- and 8th-Century Guzgan." In: BAI 15 (2001 [2005]), pp. 9–29.

— 2007: *Bactrian Documents from Northern Afghanistan. II: Letters and Buddhist Texts.* London (Studies in the Khalili Collection 3.2. CII, Part II, Vol. VI).

— 2009: "Before the Quarrel: A Bactrian Purchase Contract." In: Bromberg/Sims-Williams/Sims-Williams 2009, pp. 191–198.

— 2012a: *Bactrian Documents from Northern Afghanistan. I: Legal and Economic Documents.* Revised edition. London (Studies in the Khalili Collection 3. CII, Part II, Vol. VI).

— 2012b: *Bactrian Documents from Northern Afghanistan. III: Plates.* London (Studies in the Khalili Collection 3. CII, Part II, Vol. VI).

— 2017: "The Sogdian Ancient Letter No. 4 and the personal name Manavaghichk." In: *Estudios Iranios y Turanios* 3, pp. 171–178.

— 2023: *The "Ancient Letters" and other Early Sogdian Documents and Inscriptions.* With contributions by F. Grenet. London (CII, Part II, Vol. III, V).

Sims-Williams, N./F. de Blois 1998: "The Bactrian Calender." In: BAI 10 (1996 [1998]), pp. 149–165.

— 2005: "The Bactrian Calendar: New Material and New Suggestions." In: Weber 2005, pp. 185–196.

Sims-Williams, N./J. Cribb 1996: "A New Bactrian Inscription of Kanishka the Great." In: *Silk Road Art and Archaeology* 4, pp. 75–142.

Sindawi, Kh. 2013: *Temporary Marriage in Sunni and Shiʿite Islam.* Wiesbaden (Arabisch-Islamische Welt in Tradition und Moderne 9).

Skjærvø, P.O. 1983a: *The Sassanian Inscription of Paikuli.* Part 3.1: *Restored Text and Translation.* Wiesbaden.
— 1983b: *The Sassanian Inscription of Paikuli.* Part 3.2: *Commentary.* Wiesbaden.
— 1995: "Aramaic in Iran." In: ARAM 7 [= *Palmyra and the Aramaeans*], pp. 283–318.
— 2009: "OL' News: ODs and Ends." In: Sundermann/Hintze/de Blois 2009, pp. 479–495.
— 2010: "On the Terminology and Style of the Pahlavi Scholastic Literature." In: Bakhos/Shayegan 2010, pp. 178–205.
— 2013: "Marriage. ii. Next-of-Kin Marriage in Zoroastrianism." In: EIr online edition: http://www.iranicaonline.org/articles/marriage-next-of-kin.
— 2017: "Khotanese Land Purchase Deeds." In: Morano/Provasi/Rossi 2017, pp. 155–467.
— 2018: "The Pahlavi Optative and Some Feminine Forms in *-īy.*" In: BAI 28 (2014 [2018]), pp. 149–194.
Skjærvø, P.O./Y. Elman 2014: "Concepts of Pollution in Late Sasanian Iran. Does Pollution Need Stairs, and Does it Fill Space?" In: *ARAM* 26.1 [= *Zoroastrianism in the Levant*], pp. 21–45.
Slotkin, J.S. 1947: "On a Possible Lack of Incest Regulations in Old Iran." In: *American Anthropologist* 49.4, pp. 612–617.
Sohn, P. 1996: *Die Medizin des Zādsparam. Anatomie, Physiologie und Psychologie in den Wizīdagīhā ī Zādsparam, einer zoroastrisch-mittelpersischen Anthologie aus dem frühislamischen Iran des neunten Jahrhunderts.* Wiesbaden (Iranica 3).
Sokoloff, M. 2002: *A Dictionary of Jewish Babylonian Aramaic of the Talmudic and Geonic Periods.* Ramat-Gan.
Spooner, B. 1966: "Iranian Kinship and Marriage." In: *Iran* 4, pp. 51–59.
Stausberg, M. 1998: "The Invention of a Canon: the Case of Zoroastrianism." In: A. van der Kooij/K. van der Toorn (eds.): *Canonization and Decanonization. Papers Presented to the International Conference of the Leiden Institute for the Study of Religions (LISOR), held at Leiden 9–10 January 1997.* Leiden (Studies in the History of Religions 82), pp. 257–278.
Stausberg, M./R.P. Karanjia 2015: "Rituals." In: Stausberg/Vevaina 2015, pp. 363–377.
Stausberg, M./Y.D. Vevaina (eds.) 2015: *The Wiley Blackwell Companion to Zoroastrianism.* With A. Tessmann. Chichester.
Steingass, F. 1892: *Persian-English Dictionary.* London [repr. 1957].
Sundermann, W. 1976: "Commendatio pauperum. Eine Angabe der sassanidischen politisch-didaktischen Literatur zur gesellschaftlichen Struktur Irans." In: AoF 4, pp. 167–194.
— 1977: "Mazdak und die mazdakitischen Volksaufstände." In: *Das Altertum* 23, pp. 245–249.
— 1988: "Neue Erkenntnisse über die mazdakitische Soziallehre." In: *Das Altertum* 34, pp. 183–188.
— 1998: "On a Middle Persian Legal Term and its Forgotten Origin." In: N. Sims-Williams (ed.): *Proceedings of the Third European Conference of Iranian Studies, held in Cambridge, 11th to 15th September 1995.* Part 1: *Old and Middle Iranian Studies.* Wiesbaden, pp. 121–130.

— 2001: "Avesta und Neues Testament." In: Schmidt/Bisang 2001, pp. 258–266.

Sundermann, W./A. Hintze/F. de Blois (eds.) 2009: *Exegisti monumenta. Festschrift in Honour of Nicholas Sims-Williams.* Wiesbaden (Iranica 17).

Szemerényi, O. 1970: "Iranica III (Nos. 32–43)." In: Boyce/Gershevitch 1970, pp. 417–426.

— 1980: *Four Old Iranian Ethnic Names: Scythian—Skudra—Sogdian—Saka.* Vienna (Österreichische Akademie der Wissenschaften. Veröffentlichungen der Iranischen Kommission 9).

Tafazzoli, A. 1974: "A List of Trades and Crafts in the Sassanian Period." In: AMI 7, pp. 192–196.

— 1975 (1354): *Mīnū-ye ḫerad.* Tehran.

— 2000: *Sasanian Society: I. Warriors II. Scribes III. Dehqāns.* New York.

Taraf, Z. 1981: *Der Awesta-Text Niyāyīš mit Pahlavi- und Sanskritübersetzung.* Munich (MSB 10).

Tarapore, J.C. 1962: *Rivāyet-ī Hēmīt-ī Asavahistān.* Bombay.

Taubenschlag, R. 1955: *The Law of Greco-Roman Egypt in the Light of the Papyri, 332 B.C.–640 A.D.* Warszawa (2nd edition).

Tavadia, J.C. 1930: *Šāyast-nē-Šāyast. A Pahlavi Text on Religious Customs.* Hamburg.

— 1935: "Sûr Saxwan or a Dinner Speech in Middle Persian." In: JCOI 29, pp. 1–99.

— 1956: *Die mittelpersische Sprache und Literatur der Zarathustrier.* Leipzig (Iranische Texte und Hilfsbücher 2).

Telegdi, S. 1935: "Essai sur la phonétique des emprunts iraniens en araméen talmudique." In: JA 226, pp. 177–255.

Thomas, J.Ph. 1987: *Private Religious Foundations in the Byzantine Empire.* Washington D.C.

Timuş, M. 2019: "Les raisonnements taxinomiques dans le *Dēnkard* 3." In: Rubanovich/Herman 2019, pp. 221–249.

van Tongerloo, A. (ed.) 2003: *Iranica Selecta. Studies in honour of Professor Wojciech Skalmowski on the occasion of his seventieth birthday.* Turnhout (Silk Road Studies 8).

Tuplin, Ch.J./J. Ma (eds.) 2020: *Aršama and his World: The Bodlean Letters in Context.* Vols. I–III. Oxford.

Unvala, J.M. 1928: "The Translation of an Extract from Mâfâtîh al-ʿUlûm of Al-Khwârazmî." In: JCOI 11, pp. 76–110.

Unvala, M.R. 1922: *Dârâb Hormazyâr's Rivâyat.* Vols. I–II. Bombay.

Utas, B. 1968: "The Jewish-Persian Fragment from Dandān-Uiliq." In: *Orientalia Suecana* 17, pp. 123–136.

Vahman, F./C.V. Pedersen (eds.) 2007: *Religious Texts in Iranian Languages. Symposium held in Copenhagen May 2002.* Copenhagen.

van Vloten, G. (ed.) 1895: *Liber Mafâtîh al-olûm.* Lugduni-Bavatorum [repr. 1968].

Vevaina, Y.S.D. 2010: "Enumerating the *Dēn:* Textual Taxonomies, *Cosmological Deixis*, and Numerological Speculations in Zoroastrianism." In: *History of Religions* 50, pp. 111–143.

— 2023: *The* Sūdgar Nask *of* Dēnkard *Book 9. Text, Translation and Critical Apparatus.* Wiesbaden (Iranica 31).

— 2024: *Zoroastrian Hermeneutics in Late Antiquity. Commentary on the* Sūdgar Nask *of* Dēnkard *Book 9.* Wiesbaden (Iranica 32).

Vitalone, M. 1987: *The Persian Revayats: A Bibliographic Reconnaissance.* Naples.

Weber, D. 1991: "Ein bisher unbekannter Titel aus spätsassanidischer Zeit?" In: R. E. Emmerick / D. Weber (eds.): *Corolla Iranica. Papers in Honour of Prof. Dr. D. N. MacKenzie.* Frankfurt a. M., pp. 228–236.

— 1992: Ostraca, Papyri und Pergamente. Textband. London (CII, Part III, Vols. IV–V).

— 2002: "Eine spätsassanidische Rechtsurkunde aus Ägypten." In: *TYCHE. Beiträge zur Alten Geschichte, Papyrologie und Epigraphik* 17, pp. 185–192.

— 2003: *Berliner Papyri, Pergamente und Leinenfragmente in mittelpersischer Sprache.* London (CII, Part III, Vols. IV–V, Texts 2).

— (ed.) 2005: *Languages of Iran: Past and Present. Iranian Studies in memoriam David Neil MacKenzie.* Wiesbaden (Iranica 8).

— 2007: "The Vienna Collection of Pahlavi Papyri." In: B. Palme (ed.): *Akten des 23. Internationalen Papyrologenkongresses, Wien 22.–28. Juli 2001.* Vienna, pp. 725–738.

— 2008a: "Sasanidische Briefe aus Ägypten." In: *Asiatische Studien / Études Asiatiques* 62.3, pp. 803–826.

— 2008b: *Berliner Pahlavi-Dokumente. Zeugnisse spätsassanidischer Brief- und Rechtskultur aus frühislamischer Zeit.* Mit Beiträgen von M. Krutzsch und M. Macuch. Wiesbaden (Iranica 15).

— 2009: "A Pahlavi Letter from Egypt Re-visited (P. 44)." In: Sundermann/Hintze/de Blois 2009, pp. 537–550.

— 2010: "Parthische Texte." In: U. Hackl / B. Jacobs / D. Weber (eds.): *Quellen zur Geschichte des Partherreiches.* Vol. II: *Griechische und lateinische Texte, Parthische Texte, Numismatische Evidenz.* Göttingen, pp. 492–588.

— 2011: "An Interesting Pahlavi Letter from Early Islamic Times [Berk. 245]." In: ZDMG 161, pp. 91–98.

— 2012: "New Arguments for Dating the Documents from the 'Pahlavi Archive'." In: BAI 22 (2008 [2012]), pp. 215–222.

— 2013a: "Die persische Besetzung Ägyptens 619–629 n. Chr. Fakten und Spekulationen." In: F. Feder / A. Lohwasser (eds.): *Ägypten und sein Umfeld in der Spätantike.* Wiesbaden (Philippika; Altertumswissenschaftliche Abhandlungen 61), pp. 221–246.

— 2013b: "Taxation in Pahlavi Documents from Early Islamic times (late 7th century CE)." In: S. Tokhtasjev / P. Lurje (eds.): *Commentationes Iranicae: Sbornik statej k 90-letiju V. A. Livšica.* St.-Petersburg, pp. 171–181.

— 2014a: "Villages and Estates in the Documents from the Pahlavi Archive: The Geographical Background." In: BAI 24 (2008 [2014]), pp. 39–67.

— 2014b: "Arabic Activities Reflected in the Documents of the 'Pahlavi Archive' (late 7th and early 8th centuries)." In: Gyselen 2014, pp. 1–10.

— 2015: "Testing Food and Garment for the Ōstandār: Two Unpublished Documents from the 'Pahlavi Archive' in Berkeley, CA." In: BAI 25 (2011 [2015]), pp. 31–37.

— 2016a: "Court Records of Lawsuits in Tabarestān in the Year 86/7 PYE (737 CE): A Philological Examination." In: Gyselen 2016, pp. 121–144.

— 2016b: "Two Documents from Tabarestān Reconsidered (Tab. 12 and 26)." In: Gyselen 2016, pp. 185–192.
— 2016c: "Studies in Some Documents from the 'Pahlavi Archive'." In: BAI 24 (2012 [2016]), pp. 61–95.
— 2017a: "Pahlavi Legal Documents from Tabarestān on Lease, Loan and Compensation: A Philological Study (Tab. 13, 14, 15, 17, 18, 23)." In: Gyselen 2017, pp. 131–163.
— 2017b: "Accountancy of a Zoroastrian Craftsman in Early Islamic Times (662–664 CE)." In: BAI 27 (2013 [2017]), pp. 129–141.
— 2019a: "The Story of Windād-Burzmihr. A Zoroastrian Entrepreneur in Early Islamic Times." In: Hintze/Durkin-Meisterernst/Naumann 2019, pp. 373–384.
— 2019b: "Pahlavi Legal Documents from Tabarestān. Two Claims and a Re-evaluation of Crop Yields: A Philological Study of Tab. 21, 22 and 24." In: Gyselen 2019d, pp. 91–116.
— 2019c: "Studies in Some Documents from the 'Pahlavi Archive' (2)." In: BAI 29 (2015 [2019]), pp. 79–116.
— 2020a: "Pahlavi Legal Documents from Tabarestān: the Documents Tab. 11, 28 and 27: A Philological Approach." In: Gyselen 2020, pp. 171–188.
— 2020b: "Living together in Changing Iran. Pahlavi Documents on Arabs and Christians in Early Islamic Times." In: *Annales islamologiques* 54, pp. 139–164.
— 2020–2021: "Studies in Some Documents from the 'Pahlavi Archive' (3)." In: BAI 30, pp. 29–65.
— 2022a: "Pahlavi Legal Documents from Tabarestān: The Documents Tab. 16, 19, 20, 22bis and 25. A Philological Approach." In: Gyselen 2022, pp. 105–123.
— 2022b: "Sasanian Festivals in the Documents from the 'Pahlavi Archive'." In: Farridnejad/Daryaee 2022, pp. 323–345.
— 2022c: "On the Formal Structure of Checks in Pahlavi Documents." In: Cantera/Macuch/Sims-Williams 2022, pp. 515–548.
— 2023 (in cooperation with Kh. Roodani and S. Foroozanpour): "A Recently Found Pahlavi Document from Fars from the Time of Xusrō II." In: R. Gyselen (ed.): *Reflets d'époques sassanide et post-sassanide (224–760 A.D.).* Bures-sur-Yvette (Res Orientales XXX), pp. 177–192.
Wehr, H. 1956: *Arabisches Wörterbuch für die Schriftsprache der Gegenwart.* Leipzig.
Wesel, U. 1984: *Juristische Weltkunde.* Frankfurt a. M.
— 1985: *Frühformen des Rechts in vorstaatlichen Gesellschaften.* Frankfurt a. M.
— 1997: *Geschichte des Rechts. Von den Frühformen bis zum Vertrag von Maastrich.* Munich.
West, E. W. 1880: *Pahlavi Texts.* Part I: *The Bundahis, Bahman Yast, and Shâyast lā-Shâyast.* Oxford (SBE 5) [repr. 1965].
— 1882: *Pahlavi Texts.* Part II: *The Dâdistân-î Dînîk and the Epistles of Mânûskîhar.* Oxford (SBE 18) [repr. 1965].
— 1885: *Pahlavi Texts.* Part III: *Dînâ-î Maînôg-î Khirad, Sikand-Gûmânîk Vigâr, Sad Dar.* Oxford (SBE 24) [repr. 1965].
— 1892: *Pahlavi Texts.* Part IV: *Contents of the Nasks.* Oxford (SBE 37) [repr. 1965].
Wieacker, F. 1961: *Vom römischen Recht.* Stuttgart.

Wiessner, G. 1967: *Zur Märtyrerüberlieferung aus der Christenverfolgung Schapurs II.* Göttingen.
Williams, A.V. 1990: *The Pahlavi Rivāyat Accompanying the Dādestān ī Dēnīg.* Part I: *Transliteration, Transcription and Glossary.* Part II: *Translation, Commentary and Pahlavi Text.* Copenhagen.
Wolff, F. 1910: *Avesta. Die heiligen Bücher der Parsen.* Strassburg.
Yakubovich, I. 2002: "Mugh 1.I. Revisited." In: StIr 31, pp. 231–253.
— 2005: "Marriage i. The Marriage Contract in the Pre-Islamic Period." In: EIr online edition: http://www.iranicaonline.org/articles/marriage-contract-in-the-pre-islamic-period.
— 2006: "Marriage Sogdian Style." In: B.G. Fragner/V. Sadovski/R. Schmitt (eds.): *Iranistik in Europa – gestern, heute, morgen.* Vienna, pp. 307–344.
Yarshater, E. 1983: "Mazdakism." In: CHI 3(2), pp. 991–1024.
Yoshida, Y. 2019: "Some New Interpretations of the Two Judeo-Persian Letters." In: Hintze/Durkin-Meisterernst/Naumann 2019, pp. 385–394.
Yoshida, Y./T. Moriyasu 1988: "A Sogdian Sale Contract of a Female Slave from the Period of the Gaochang [in Japanese]." In: *Studies on the Inner Asian Languages* IV, pp. 1–50.
Zaehner, R.Ch. 1940: "Aparmānd." In: JRAS 1940, pp. 35–128.
— 1955: *Zurvan. A Zoroastrian dilemma.* Oxford.
Zeini, A. 2018: *Middle Persian Papyri, Ostraca and Parchments: An Introduction.* Irvine, Calif. (Sasanika Papyrological Studies 1).
— 2022: *Zoroastrian Scholasticism in Late Antiquity. The Pahlavi Version of the Yasna Haptaŋhāiti.* Edinburgh (Edinburgh Studies in Ancient Persia).
— 2024: "The Covenant that Binds: Ownership of Life in Late Antique Zoroastrianism." In: Macuch/Zeini 2024, pp. 461–480.
Zotenberg, H. (ed.) 1900: *(Ṯaʿalibī) Ġurar aḫbār mulūk al-furs wa sīyarihim.* Paris.

List of Figures and Tables

Figures

Fig. 1. Family structure: basic model . . . 130
Fig. 2. Family structure: extended model . . . 132
Fig. 3. Potential cross-combinations in marriage law . . . 184
Fig. 4. Overview: components of a family's 'total (patrimonial/residuary) estate' . . . 206
Fig. 5: Overview: hierarchy of the judiciary . . . 532

Tables

Table 1. Overview of terminology: legal theory and practice . . . 71
Table 2. Overview of terminology: leniency in justice and extension of justice . . . 73
Table 3. Representations of the social estates . . . 98
Table 4. List of *dīwān*s according to al-Ḫwārezmī . . . 99
Table 5. Overview: constituent elements forming an individual's legal status . . . 103
Table 6. Inhabitants of the Empire: basic terms . . . 115
Table 7. Overview: rights and duties of the *kadag-xwadāy* (*paterfamilias*) . . . 121
Table 8. Overview: rights and duties of the *kadag-bānūg* (*materfamilias*) . . . 124
Table 9. Legal implications of *pādixšāy*-marriage . . . 142
Table 10. Comparison of *pādixšāy*- and *čagar*-matrimony . . . 144
Table 11. Comparison of *čagar*- and *xwasrāyēn/gādār*-matrimony . . . 147
Table 12. Overview: matrimonial options . . . 183
Table 13. Strategies enabling versatility within the framework of patrilineal descent . . . 185
Table 14. Overview: basic division of property (*xwāstag, xīr*) . . . 193
Table 15. Basic proprietary rights . . . 201
Table 16. Substance and fruit: fundamental distinctions . . . 202
Table 17. Overview: proprietary rights of the heirs . . . 230
Table 18. Overview: terminology of partnership and shareholding (*hambāyīh*) . . . 252
Table 19. Overview: contracts and documents . . . 284
Table 20. Overview: terminology relating to seals . . . 300
Table 21. Transfer of property: legal formulae . . . 305
Table 22. Overview of terminology: *tōzišn* . . . 310
Table 23. Overview of terminology: *abām, abāmdān, nihišn* . . . 318
Table 24. Loan contract without security . . . 322
Table 25. Overview of terminology: real and personal security . . . 326
Table 26. Overview of terminology: *graw, grawīh* . . . 335
Table 27. Overview of terminology: *āgraw, āgrawīh*) . . . 342
Table 28. Loan contract with *grawagān* security . . . 346
Table 29. Overview of terminology: *grawagān, grawaganīh* . . . 349

Table 30. Overview of terminology: personal security (*pāyandān*, *pāyandānīh*) 356
Table 31. Historical development and types of suretyship 359
Table 32. Overview: technical terms and phrases in the context of liabilities. . . 364
Table 33. Overview: technical terms and phrases relating to debt cancellation. . 367
Table 34. Amount of rent 371
Table 35. Amount of abatement. 371
Table 36. Overview: technical terms and phrases relating to leasehold 372
Table 37. Overview: terminology relating to gifts and donations 399
Table 38. Overview: terminology relating to the private feud versus the judicial dispute 411
Table 39. Deliberate injury and injury by negligence in the FīŌ. 420
Table 40. The mental element of an offence 422
Table 41. Overview: assault, physical injury and homicide. 433
Table 42. Overview: terminology relating to theft and robbery 450
Table 43. Overview: terminology relating to sexual offences. 459
Table 44. Overview: four uses of the term *adwadād* 467
Table 45. Overview: degrees or levels (*pāyag*) of sins in ascending order 482
Table 46. Sins according to the Avesta (Vd. 4.18–42) 483
Table 47. Fines. 484
Table 48. Overview: Capital crimes versus highest virtues. 494
Table 49. Overview: State judges (*dādwar*). 503
Table 50. Overview: religious authorities in the judiciary 509
Table 51. Overview: public officials with judicial power 517
Table 52. Overview: lower officials and members of the court. 521
Table 53. Overview: instances and appellate courts. 525
Table 54. Overview: filing action 535
Table 55. Overview: the preliminary hearing 536
Table 56. Overview: the trial 541
Table 57. Overview: the legal predecessor (*dastwar*) 544
Table 58. Overview: the testimony of witnesses. 549
Table 59. Overview: documentary evidence 551
Table 60. Types of oath. 558
Table 61. Statements under oath. 559
Table 62. Overview: terminology relating to the oath/ordeal 560
Table 63. Overview: offences against the judiciary 568
Table 64. Overview: the verdict. 571
Table 65. Overview: the pious foundation 627
Table 66. Uses of *res* and *xwāstag*. 639

Index

All references are to page numbers with principal references in bold type; Iranian technical terms referred to in the following are explicated in the Glossary (pp. 749–803). All entries are conventionally alphabetized ignoring accents and diacritics (*e. g.*, š is treated like s).

Abālīš 35
abām (loan, debt) 86, 228, 230, 244, 266, 268–269, 308, 310, **316–319**, 323, 327, 335, 338, 340, 342, 346, 355, 362–367, 557–558, 612, 642, 644, 696–697, 702, 736, 749, 795
see also abām ud tōzišn; *abāmdān*; credit law; debt
abām az ādurān ud ātaxšān (loan from fire foundations) 228, 366–367, 749
abām ī pidarān (liabilities of the forefathers) 86, 230, 308, 318–319, 362, 749, 789
see also tōzišn ī pidarān
abām ud tōzišn (debt and liability) 308, 310, 318, 749
see also abām and *tozišn*
abāmdān (loan, debt) 268–269, 310, **316–320**, 338, 750
see also abām
abandonment **75**, 424, 429, 433, 446, **463–465**, 467, 649, 681
see also adwadād
Abarag (jurisconsult; founder of a legal school) 29, 32–33, 64, 386, 463, 714–745
abarmad (document) 267, **273–275**, 284, 741, 750
abarmānd (total patrimonial/residuary estate) 78, 107, 123, 129, 131, 140, 160, 190, 192–193, 199, **201–209**, 211, 213–215, 217, 219, 221, 223, 225, 227, 229–231, 234, 245, 254, 301, 308, 392, 623, 626, 639, 644, 750, 779, 782, 795–796
see also inheritance
abarmānd ī pidar/pidarān (total patrimonial/residuary estate of the forefathers) 78, **192–193**, 750, 795
abarmānd-xwāstagdār (heir to the total estate) 206, 208, 360, 750, 796
see also xwāstagdār
Abaršahr (administrative district) 294
abastāg see abestāg and Avesta/Avestan
a-baxt (undivided; ideal share of property) 129, 139, 140, 142, 207, 229, 234, 245, 305, 396–397, 750
Abdīh ud sahīgīh ī Sīstān 167
Abbasid period 35
Abbaye (rabbi) 594
abduction 448, 455, 458–459
abēsaxwan/abēsaxwanīh (without claim) 48, 245, 335, 338–339, **611–614**, 616, 751, 756, 793
abestāg 23–24, 30–31, **236** (fn. 227), 313, 691, 698, 741, 751
see also Avesta/Avestan
abestāg ud zand 24, 236
abortion 453
a-bōyīh (unconsciousness) 412, **415**, 422–423, 428, 432–433, 464, 562, 570–571, 652–653, 679, **751**, 792
Abrahamic religions 590
Abruwan (birthplace of Mihr-Narseh) 227

abuse 108, 173
sexual 414, 424, **457–460**
abzōn (income) 251, **252–253**, 344, 701, 751
accessory suretyship 350, 358–359, 608
see also pāyandānīh and suretyship
accomplice (of a thief; *abāg*) 439, 441, **445**, 450, **685–686**, 688
accountant 97, 228, 512
see also āmārgar
accusatio scripta 573, 594, 784
see also pursišn-nāmag
accusation (criminal trial) 47, 251–252, 258, 527, **572–573**, 576, 578–579, 581
accusatorial system of adjudication 502, 569
Achaemenid 1–2, 15, 95, 104, 167, 489, 494, 512, 514, 590
acquisition of property 88, 124, 192–193, 204, 211, 246, 248–249, **301–305**, 314, 334, 365, 603–604
acquittal 7, 531, 554, 577, 667–668, 688
actio auctoritatis 304, 386, 543
Acts of the Christian martyrs **49**, 511, 580, 584
ādehīg (inhabitant of the land) 102, **114–115**, 548, 752, 790
adoptio minus plena 177
adoptio plena 177
adoption 106, 127, 176–177, 266, 285, 647; of *čagar*-children 32, 132, 172–173, 233–234; of a son 168, 179–180, 651
see also duxt ī padīriftag and *pus ī padīriftag*
adultery 3, 34, 39, 62, 412, 414, 443–444, 449, 452, 454, **458–460**, 462, 562, 766, 789
ādurān ātaxšān / ādurān ud ātaxšān (fire foundations) **220**, 225, 228, 366–367, 749, 752, 755
see also ātaxš; *ātaxšān*
ādurān-bandag (servant of the fires) 105, 226, 601, 752, 754, 757
see also ātaxš-bandag and *bandag(īh) ī ātaxš*
Āduranāhīd (daughter and wife of Šabuhr I) 225
Ādurbadagān (administrative district) 294
Ādurbād ī Māraspandān, ordeal of 552
Ādurbād ī Mardbūdān (son of Mardbūd) 277, 292, 745
Ādurbād ī Zarduxštān (*mowbedān mowbed*) 743, 745
Ādurbōzēd (*mowbedān mowbed)* 292, 745
Ādurfarrbay 84, 102, 266, 271, 343, 351–354, 400, 431, 520, 696–697, 699
Ādurfarrbay ī Farroxzādān 34–36
Ādurfrazgar 359, 745
Ādurgušāsp ī Mihrātaxš ī Ādurgušnasp 36
ādurōg (simple sacred fire) 220, 225, 269
Ādurohrmazd (jurisconsult) 561, 745
Āduroy 369–370, 711–712
Ādurzandān 744, 745
advance payment *see pēš-tōzišnīh*
advocate 289, 290, 301, 538–539, 541, 543, 770
see also jādag-gōw and Advocate of the Poor (and Judge)
Advocate of the Poor (and Judge) **293–295**, 300, 501, 763, 771
see also driyōšān jādag-gōw (ud dādwar)
adwadād (offence) **74–76**, 107, 177, 217, 412, 424–425, 427–429, 446, **463–468**, 570, 648–649, 681, 752
Afghan Geniza 39
Afghanistan 39–41, 43
Āfrīnagān 400
āfrīngān 30
afterlife 10, 401–402, 479
Agathias 57
ag-dēn/ag-dēnīh (infidel/evil religion) 7–8, 10, 69, 118, 172, 208, 384, 436, 526–527, 657–658, 664–666, 752
āgenēn dārišn (joint possession with equal shares) 86, 247, **249–250**, 252, 375, 752, 769, 779
āgenēn hamwindišn (joint income with equal shares) 247, **251–252**, 752, 769

āgenēn xwēš (joint owner[ship] with equal shares) 246, **247–249,** 252, 365, 752, 769, 779
agnatic system **127–128**, 632–636, 638
āgraw/āgrawīh (hypothec) 190, 208, 229, 301, 324–326, 331, **336–342**, 617, 752
agreement *see* contract
āgrift (degree of sin) 414, **468–471**, 473, 481–484, 752
āhang (crop yields) 346–348, 702, 704–707, 740, 752
ʿAhd Ardašīr b. Bābak ʾilā man yaḫlifuhu bi-ʿuqbihi min mulūk Fārs 53
ahl al-farāʾiḍ 633, 634
ahlawdād (pious act/gift) 135–136, 205, 208, 210–211, 220, 222, 237, 254, 266, 340, 364, 461, 623–624, 626–627, 652–653, 753, 779, 781
see also property for pious purposes
ahlomōy/ahlomōyīh (heretic/heresy) 258, **491–494**, 526, 572, 574, 580, 585, 595, 669, 671–672, 738, 753
Ahriman 37, 261
ahuna vairiia (prayer) 25
ahunwar (prayer) 25
Ahura Mazdā 28, 260–261
Ahwāz 40
Alexander 15
ʿAlī 638
alieni iuris persons 124, 126, 398
Ałuank 56
āmārgar (official) 228, 293, 504–506, **512–514**, 517, 573, 753, 786
amnesia 426, 433, 683
Āmol 437
Amoraim 50, 604–605, 608
Amu-daryā 41
an-ēr (non-Iranian) 35, **102–103**, 114–115, 124–125, 453–454, 657, 662, 688–689, 753
animal rights 90–92
animals 107, 173, 182, 187, 190, 202, 212–213, 240–241, 243, 278, 280, 287, 315–316, 377, 380–381, 563, 585, 599, 624, 674; as compensation 440–441, 449, 682, 686, 766, 783; as pledge 332, 327, 329, 337, 617, 754, 767, 790; as security 338, 343–344; barter of 388–389; beneficent (*spəṇta*) 3, 29, 62, 65, 76, 90–92, 418, 421, 429, 463, 481, 789; guardianship of 75, 91–92, 177; noxious (*xrafstar*) 90; offences against 62, 92, 417–421, 429, 463–464, 468, 481, 752, 789; sacrifice of 28, 220, 577; slaughter of 32, 34, 220, 787
see also animal rights; cattle; sheep; sheepdog
anšahrīg ī ātaxš (slave of the fire) 105, 107, 226, **601–603**, 752–755, **757**
antichresis 87, 198, 201–202, 209, 266, 269, 301, 303, 311, 320, 325–326, 328, 330–331, 334, 336, 338, **343–349**, 604, 617, 703
see also grawagān/grawagānīh
Anōšzād (legal official) 296, 515, 745
Anūšīrwān 54, 111, 256, 291, 294
see also Husraw I
a-pahikār-rad/radīh (person practising self justice/self justice); opposite: *pahikār-rad/radīh* 64, **404–411**, 674–678, 751, 782 783
apostasy 28, 422, **491–494**, 526, 572, 574, 576–578, 581, 738
apostate 35, 493, 579, 600, 602
appar/apparag (robber) 313–314, 382, 416, **434–439,** 444–445, 450, 565, 618–619, 688–692, 755, 788
see also following entries
apparīh (robbery) 67–68, 382, 413, 450, 458, 565, 738, 754
see also robber and following entries
appar-kām (intent of the robber) 7, **413**, 422, 424, 667, 754
see also appar-menišnīgīh
appar-menišnīgīh (intent of the robber) **413–414**, 422, 424, 445, 449, 451, 456–457, 691–692, 754
see also appar-kām

appeal 65, 69, 416, 438, 495–497, 500, **522–526**, 530, 532, 535, 545, 570–571, 576, 581, 586–587, 730
appellate courts 65, 69, 496, 497, **522–526**, 532, 545, 570, 761, 775, 785, 793
Arabic sources 45, **51–54**, 58, 95–101, 271, 280, 369
Arabia 141, 622, 629, 633, 635–636
Ārāmāye 573, 577
arbitration 381, 408–409, 495, 498, 522
arbitrator 406–409, 488, 495, 497–498, 502–503, 510
archives 17, 20–21, 29, 42, 53, 55–56, 98, 100, 110, 199, 218, 227, 270–271, 273, 285, 321, 345, 439, 505, 520, 571, 713, 715, 725, 741
see also dīwān ī kardagān; *nāmag-niyān* and registers
Ardaxšēr (Ardašīr) ī Pābagān, I (224–239/240 CE) 44, 52–53, 97, 110, 120, 126, 167, 218, 226, 273–275, 288, 294–296, 359, 442–444, 449, 490, 637
Ardaxšēr-Xwarrah (province, *nahang*) 218, 233, 273, 288, 294–296, 741–743, 745–746
ardīg tazišnīh (engaging in conflict; duel) 405, 424–425, 433, 681, 754, 767
arduš (degree of sin) 414, 468, 469, **472–473**, 481–484, 754
Arənauuācī 738
aristocracy 11, 16, 53, 94–95, 786; legal privileges 101, **110–113**, 124, 126, 143, 186–187, 255–257, 259, 516, 582
see also nobility
Armenia/Armenian 55–56, 58, 74, 104, 148, 168, 275, 326, 343, 347, 442, 504, 512, 592–593, 630
arra/arrabo/arrha (pawn; earnest money) **377–380**, 619, 660
see also earnest money and *rabŭn/rabŭna*
Aršama 15, 389, 512, 514
arteštārān (warriors; social estate) 95, 98–99, 754
artisans 95–96, 98, 310–311, 315, 372–373, 437, 517
arzbed/harzbed (eunuch, title) 573
ʿaṣaba 633–635
a-sālār (without guardian) 125, 655–656, 754
see also sālār; *sālārīh*
ascendants 177, 655
Asia 41, 43, 280, 373–374
āsn-xrad (innate wisdom) 8, 664–665, 667, 755
Āsōristān 49
Aspbād 283
*Asp-gurd (village in the canton of Dēl ī Dēlān, province Tabarestān) 199, 321, 322, 345, 346–347, 369–370, 437, 439, 507, 700–704, 706, 710–713, 715–721, 723–726, 728–729, 731, 733, 736–737
āsrōnān (priests; social estate) 95, 97–98, 510–511, 518, 755
assault 62, 400, 405, 407–409, 411–414, **423–434**, 444, 468–469, 471–473, 475, 481–483, 488–489, 562, 572, 675, 679, 683, 692
see also rēš; *zanišn* and *zaxm*
associates 86, 148, 229, **245–253**, 261, 267, 309, 365–366, 384, 663
see also hambāy and *hamxwastag(ān)*
Assyrian 352
Aštād 346, 701, 730–731
aswār (knight, equestrian) 81, 209, 271, 285, 424, 513, 515, 680, 755
*Ātars 437, 723
a-tarsagāhīh (insubordination); opposite: *tarsagāhīh* 138, 251, 744, 755
ātaxš (sacred fire) 105, 107, 109, 181, 191, 205, 213, 217–218, 220–222, 224–226, 228, 248, 250, 270, 273, 277, 464, 466, 504, 515, 587, 601–603, 623, 735, 738–743, 755
see also ādurān ātaxšān and fire foundations
ātaxš-bandag (servant of the fire) 105, 107, 601, 753–754, 755, 757

see also āduran-bandag and *bandag(īh) ī ātaxš*
*ātaxš hamār *dibīrag* (register) 99, 228, 755
ātaxšān (fire foundation) 220, 222, **225–228**, 366–367, 505–506, 509, 585–587, 755
see also āduran ātaxšān and fire foundations
Ātaxšbōyag 704, 706
Ātaxšbōyān 349
atonement 3, 9, 32–33, 62–63, 307–308, 439–440, 446, 451, 473–474, 476, 480, 484, 488, 682, 686, 688
attorney 88, 267, 269, 286, 289, 375
auctor 57, 80, 89, 116, 196, 304, 385–387, 506, 509, 536, 542–544, 546–547, 567–568, 596–597, 640, 716, 720
see also dastwar
auctor-ship 547, 708
see also dastwarīh
Aulus Agerius (A.A.) 223, 430
Avesta/Avestan 1–3, 5, 13, 23–31, 32, 34–35, 37, 41, 58, 60–61, 64–66, 68–69, 73, 91, 94, 113, 151, 404–405, 423, 426, 440, 457, 448, 454, 487, 489, 494, 516, 581, 590, 664, 692, 698, 741, 751; canon 274–275, 284, 291, contracts 260–264; degrees of sins 468–483; derivation of the word 236 (fn. 227); loans 312–316; social groups 95–97, 100; technical terms **74–77**, 137, 163–164, 168, 207, 308, 380, 382, 412, 414, **417–420, 434–437,** 441, 449, 452, 455, 463–468, 498, **558–560,** 591, 661, 682, 684, 688, 690–691, 777, 791, 797
*see also nask*s
awōirišt/ōirišt (degree of sin) 414, 468–469, **471–472**, 481–484, 755
Awrōmān 15
*āxur hamār *dibīrag* (register) 99, 755
ayādgār (memorandum; document) 279, **283–284**, 291–292, 298, 301, 491, 574–575, 578–579, 741, 755
ayōgēn/ayōgēnīh/ayōgānīh (intermediary successor/succession) 35–36, 38, 79, 111, 123–124, 129–134, 136–138, 140, 142–147, 154–156, 159, 161–162, **163–168,** 170, 172–173, 175–176, 179, 184–185, 207–208, 214, 231, 234–235, 256, 632, 636–637, 646, 648–651, 756
see also inheritance
āzād (freeborn, noble) 102–103, 120, 125, 169, 331, 370–371, 647, 712–713, 756
āzādān (rank of the nobility) 111, 516, 756
Āzādmard 242, 348, 506, 702, 743, 746
Āzādōg 721–722
Āzad-Xusrō 707, 715–716
Azerbaijan 581, 630
azišmānd (obstruction of justice) 236, 270, 289, 440, 499, 504, 522, 537, 539–541, 559, **561–565**, 567–569, 571, 581, 686, 756–757
see also contumacia and obstruction of justice

Bābolsar 437
Babylonia 40, 49, 51, 69, 394, 489, 530, 600, 630
Babylonian Talmud 1, 10, **49–51**, 69, 79, 89, 106–107, 120, 158–159, 161, 202, 221, 226, 297, 354, 359, 367, 389, 447, 489, 495, 524, 526–528, 530–532, 588–589, **590–608**, 618, 630–631, 753–754
see also Bavli
Bactria 15, 41, 43–44, 142
Bactrian legal documents 4, 13, 41, **43–45**, 48, 71, **141–142**, 169, 200, 243, 245, 274, 332, 611, 613–614
Baghdad 48, 609, 623
bahr (share of property/inheritance) 139, 142, 204, 218, 229, 231, 237, 248, 251, 258, 265, 305, 309, 360, 366–367, 388, 396, 430, 445, 450, 612, 642–645, 654–656, 672–673, 688, 752, 757, 779–780; in *stūrīh*

84, 145, 213; of the daughter 140, 153, 232, 237, 757; of the *kadag-bānūg*/wife 123–124, 140, 153, 232, 757; of a slave 108; of the son 140, 232, 757
Bahrām Gōr 226
bailment 315–316, 319
Balʿamī 54, 97–98
band (fetters) 20, 283, 298, 313, 439–442, 447, 449–450, 584, 685–687, 757
 see also band ud drōš and *drōš*
band ud drōš (penalty for theft) 313, 439–442, 447, 449, 584, 685–687, 757
 see also band and *drōš*
bandag (servant, slave, subject) 102–103, 105, 107, 109, 114–117, 120, 124–126, 169, 172, 226, 382–383, 546, 601–603, 614, 646–647, 649–650, 682, 757
 see also ādurān-bandag; *ātaxš-bandag* and *šāhān šāh bandag*
bandagīh ī ātaxš (service of the fire) 109, 112, 224, 227, 601
 see also ādurān-bandag and *ātaxš-bandag*
bar (fruit) 9, 89, 139, 173, 192, 195, **197–202**, 210, 224, 254, 258, 325–327, 337–338, 343–344, 395, 402, 597–598, 617–618, 625–627, 643, 645, 649, 673, 757, 762, 767
 see also barōmand
 bar-xward (usufruct) 198, **200–202**, 214, 216, 218, 247, 338, 343, 604–605, 618, 626, 657, 757
 bar-xwēš/bar-xwēšīh (owner/ownership of the fruits) 175, **197–202**, 210, 212, 214, 216, 218, 221, 229, 230, 247–248, 250, 254, 302, 336, 338, 394, 604–605, 618, 757–759
Barbahlūl 516
barōmand (fruitful; income producing) 169, 202, 213, 217, 220, 222–224, 343, 624, 647–648, 652, 758
 see also bar; *bar-xward* and *bar-xwēš/bar-xwēšīh*
barren 169, 453–454, 688
barter 89, 116, 192–193, 196, 211–212, 223, 240, 264, 266–267, 287, 297, 301, 304, 313, 372–374, 376, **388–390**, 449, 507, 542–543, 596, 639, 760, 768, 779, 782, 787, 796
 see also guharēn
Bavli 50–51, 590, 591, 604, 605
 see also Babylonian Talmud
bayăspān (exogamy) **148–150**, 183–184, 758
 see also exogamy
bāzā (degree of sin) 468–469, **475–476**, 482–484, 643, 645, 648, 758
bazaar 43, 373
bāzargān (merchant) 97, 372
bāzārī 99, 367
behdādestānīh (extension of justice) 71, 554, 610–611
 see also mehdādestānīh and *wehdādestānīh*
Behistūn inscription 1
bill of indictment 74, 79, 285, 429–432, 510, 546, 549, **573–575**, 578–579, 742–743
 see also nibištag
al-Bīrūnī 52
Bīšābuhr 294, 742, 747
blasphemy 291, **491–494**, 526, 572, 574, 576–577, 595, 797
 see also yazdān-dušmenīh
bōdōwaršt (wilful offence) 412, **417–422**, 570–571, 758, 792
bōdōzed (wilful injury) 412, **417–422**, 424, 444–445, 570–571, 688, 758, 792
body-theft 414, 449, **455–460**; 693–694, 789
 see also tan-duzīh
body-thief 459, 693, 789
 see also tan-duz
bona adventitia 74, 78, 139–140, 773–774, 795
 see also mad ud rasēd

bonorum possessio 210
**bōxt-nāmag* (document of acquittal) 531, 577, 758
Bōzišn (jurisconsult) 745
bōzišn (acquittal) 7, 667–668, 758
  see also čim ud bōzišn
brād ī hambāy (shareholding brother) 129, 170, 179, 229, **234**, 245, 252, 647–648, 758, 768, 786
Brāzasp 371, 713
breach of contract 29, 117, 136, 262, 287, 291, 306, 315, 334, **462–463**, 491, 574, 595, 727, 775; punishment as theft or robbery 67–68, 313, 434, 618, 755, 766
  see also mihrodrujīh
bribe 580, 594–595
bribery 594–595
bride 78, 135–136, 139–142, 148–151, 161, 265, 285, 303, 305, 597
bridegroom 135, 148–149, 265, 285, 303, 305, 597–598
bun (substance, principal) 8–9, 89, 173, 191, 195, **197–202**, 204–208, 210–211, 214, 216, 223–225, 229–231, 234, 242–243, 246, 254, 279, 321–322, 324–326, 337–339, 342–346, 355, 369, 394–395, 397, 402–403, 456, 458, 461, 466–467, 470–473, 481–483, 505, 515, 534–535, 597–598, 604, 617–618, 624–627, 648–649, 652–653, 665, 667, 674, 681–682, 693–694, 701–702, 704, 706, 711, 758, 762, 770
  bun-kadag 243
  bun-xānag 243, 515, 759
  bun-xwēš/bun-xwēšīh (owner/ownership of the substance) 198, 200–202, 212, 218, 223, 230, 302, 330, 336, 343, 394, 421, 444–445, 566, 757–759
Bundahišn 167, 292, 537–538
burdār (natural mother) 120, 138, 152, 174, 759
  see also genetrix
Burzādur 394
Burzādurfarrbay 233, 394, 746
Burzag (*mowbed*) 432, 743, 745
Burzēn-Pērōz 437–439, 723–727
Byzantine 55, 57–58, 575, 588, 621–623, 627, 638–640
Byzantium 55, 57–58, 373, 638, 640

čagar-children 32–33, 132, 170, 172, 233, 237
čagar-father 173, 180, 647, 649
čagar-husband 126, 131, 144–145, 166, 457
čagar-marriage 78, 88, 121, 123–124, 126, 131–132, 137, **142–145**, 146–147, 150, 154–155, 157, 159–162, 166, 171–172, 175–176, 183–185, 234 (fn. 217), 299, 631–632, 637, 756, 759
čagar-wife 133, 137, 138, 143, 166, 183, 185, 233, 448–449, 457–458, 460, 694, 745, 759, 797
Cairo Geniza 39
čak (document; entry in the *saxwan-nāmag*) **279–281**, 283–284, 373, 499, 533, 537–538, 541, 735–736, 755, 759, 765
calculator *see āmārgar*
Caliph 35, 622
Caliphate 14, 588, 621–622, 635
canal 190–191, 222–223, 240–243, 269, 321, 377, 599, 626
canonical law *see čāštag*
capital crimes, prosecuted by the State 489–494
  see also margarzān
caravan 42, 373
caravanserai 373, 626
carelessness *see* negligence
čāšān (official) 277, 292–293, 742, 760
čašmag (title) 515–517, 733–734, 759, 786, 788
čāštag (legal doctrine; commentary) 2, 6, 20, 32, 65, **66–72**, 79, 207, 342, 487, 570–571, **616–617**, 670, 693, 744–746, 759, 779

Catholicos 47, 155, 157, 492, 511, 527, 572–573, 575–581
  see also Mār Abā
cattle 90–92, 190, 222–223, 258, 262, 409, 419–421, 440–441, 451, 625, 673, 682, 686
  see also animal rights and animals
  cattle-atonement (**fšū̆-ciϑā-*) 440, 451, 682, 686, 766
ceremonies for the soul *see ruwān yazišn*
certa verba 309, 675–676
  see also formulaic expressions and legal formulae
charge *see pēš-tōzišnīh*
charitable deed *see ahlawdād*
charitable foundations 16, 65, 102, **220–225**, 229, 254, 622–624, 626–627, 640
  see also ruwānagān
cheque *see čak*
chattels 109, 190, 324, 337, 341
Chief Counsellor of the Magi *see mowān handarzbed*
Chief Eunuch *see arzbed/harzbed*
Chief Judge of the State *see šahr dādwarān dādwar*
Chief Mobed *see mowbedān mowbed*
children (*frazand*), categorization of 175–177
  see also čagar-children; *pādixšāy*-children
Christians *see* East Christians (Nestorians)
čim ud bōzišn (evidence and proof) 80, 534, 540–542, 717–718, 751, 758–759
Činwad Bridge 402–403, 481, 792
citizen 11, 99, 101–105, 107, 114–117, 120–121, 124–125, 131, 166, 169–170, 207–210, 245, 261, 410, 515, 548, 581–582
  see also mard ī šahr
citizenship 102–103, 115
civil proceedings 63–64, 79, 272, 279, 284, 289–290, 295, 301, 415–416, 484, 488–500, 504, 506–508, 522, 524, 529–530, 532, **533–571**, 586, 595–596, 715–722, 774, 786
clepsydra 655
co-debtors 356, 365
  see also hamāg-tōzišn
Code of Ardašīr 53
Codex Iustinianus 57
cognatic descent/succession **128–129**, 133, 166–167, 184, 210, 636–638
cohabitation 422, 453–460
combat 261, 405, 425
commentary, legal, theological *see čāštag*
commerce 310, 373–374, 542
  see also sale
commoners 53, 99–103, 106, **110–113**, 125–126, 163, 255, 257–258, 372, 376
  see also plebeians
compensation *see guharīg*, *tāwān* and *tōzišn*
complaint *see garzišn* and *mustgarzīh*
confession 126, 400–401, 413, 457, 484, 500, 584
consanguinity 127, 130–131, 133, 144, 154, 186, 253
consciousness 237, 244, 417, 480, 644–645
consensus marriage 78, 79, 122, 125, 132–133, **145–147,** 149–150, 157, 159–161, 175–176, 183, 233, 459 (fn. 202), 766, 794
  see also gādār and *xwasrāyēn/ūn*
Constantine 57
contract 7, 19–21, 29, 42–44, 63, 72, 80–82, 97, 117, 263–264, 284–286; Avestan terms 262; between Ohrmazd and Ahriman 261; breach of *see mihrōdrujīh*; conveyance by 88, 266, 267, 269, 301–305; lease 367–372; loan 87, 209, 247, 248, 266, 268, 311–315, 317–319, 323–326, 345–346, 349, 350–359; obligations arising from 306–310; partnership with the wife 251, 252; sale 265, 266, 374–377; testamentary (*paymān*) 235, 238–240, 265, 267, 277–278; verbal 264, 265, 399; with infidels and

foreigners 119; technical terms *see* *mihr*, *pašn*, *pašt*, *paymān*, *paymān-nāmag* and *wizīr*
see also marriage contract and obligations
contumacia 289, 537, 540–541, 561, 563, 568, 581
see also azišmānd and obstruction of justice
conveyance, document of 264, 266–267, 269–271, 285–286, 777, 783–784, 793; formulae **302–305**, 334, 390, 391, 392; mandate/power of attorney 88; procedure **301–305**, 391, 779
see also contract
conveyance of property *see* acquisition of property
co-ownership with equal shares **246–249**, 252, 365, 752, 769–770
see also āgenēn xwēš
co-partners (shareholders) of the income 218, 244, 247–248, 250–252, 752, 768–769, 771, 797
see also hambaragān, *hamwindišn* and *hamwaxš*
co-proprietors **246–249**, 370, 364; *see also hamxwastagān*
Corpus Iuris Civilis 57
Corpus Iuris of Īšōʿbōxt 48, 63–64, 70–71, 105, 109, 176, 232–233, 245, 296–297, 329–331, 339–344, 374–375, **378–382**, 435, 514, 550, 554, 589, 593, 602, **609–621**
see also East Christians (Nestorians)
co-sureties 247, 252, 364, 366, 509, 769
see also hampāyandān
co-suretyship 253, 769
see also hampāyandānīh
credit law 19, **35**, 86, 87, 117–119, 198, 207–208, 308, **310–367**, 414, 434, 442, 449, 606–608, 610, 612, 616–617, 719, 751, 753, 773–774, 777, 779–781, 784, 790
see also abām, *abāmdān*, *tōzišn* and debt
crime 67, 236, 291, 403, 405–406, 411–422, 429–434, 438, 440, 446, 451, 468, 477–478, 480, 482–485, 488–489, 491–494, 519–521, 526, 528, 531–532, 547, 549, 570, 572, 574–576, 578, 580–586, 595, 739–740; constitutive elements **411–422**
see also adwadād, *margarzān*, *rēš*, *zanišn*, *zaxm* and capital crimes, degrees of sins/offences, homicide, robbery, theft
criminal proceedings 572–585; crimes prosecuted by the State 489–494; offences 422–468
see also crime with further references
crown property 209, 228, 270–271, 506, 512–513, 517, 583, 785, 794
see also šāhīgān
Ctesiphon 50
cult of (the souls of) the ancestors *see* *nāmagānīh*
cum manu mariti 121, 124, 135, 144, 149 (fn. 176), 150, 154, 159–160, 166
see also sālārīh
custody 75, 315, 429, 463, 519

Dābōy 707
dād (law) 4, 6, 64, 91–92, 99, 114, 258, 404, 665–667, 760, 770, 794–795
see also dādīg
*dād *dibīrag* (register of laws) 99, 760
dād ī jud-dēw (law keeping away the demons) 61, 403
dād ī šahr (law of the State) 4, 794
see also ēwēn ī šahr
dād ī Zardušt (the law of Zoroaster) 61, 64
Dādburzmihr 725
Dādēnbōxt 281, 735
Dādēn-Windād 282
dādestān (range of meanings) **4–5**, 760; decision, sentence, verdict 118, 528, 534, 569, 681, 698; judgement 10, 20, 33–34, 36, 68, 96, 218, 268, 421, 499, 523, 678, 696–697, 728, 742;

judicial, judicial case 81, 438, 526, 558–559, 717–718, 725, 764, 780; jurisdiction 704, 731, 734; justice 6, 8, 730; law court 507–508; legal action 534–535, 548, 664–665; legal procedure 71, 555; legal proceedings, lawsuit, trial 416–417, 504, 506, 516, 540, 545, 547, 553, 564–565, 567–568, 585–586, 788
see also following entries and *mehdādestān*, *wehdādestān*
dādestān-brād (legitimate brother) 5, 175, 760
dādestān-duxt (legitimate daughter) 5, 123, 130, 137, 163, 175–176, 231, 637, 760
dādestān-nāmag (lawbook) 5, 653, 744, 760
dādestān-pus (legitimate son) 5, 123, 130, 137, 163, 175–176, 231, 637, 760
dādestān-xwāh (legitimate sister) 5, 175, 760
Dādestān ī dēnīg **33–34**, 36, 232, 262, 379, 384, 461, 641–663, 738
Dādfarrox 64, 394, 743–745
Dādfarrox ī Ādurzandān (jurisconsult) 744–745
Dādfarrox ī Dādohrmazdān (*mowān-handarzbed*) 743, 745
Dādfarrox ī Farroxzurwān (jurisconsult) 745
Dādfarrox ī Mardbūdān (jurisconsult) 394, 745
Dādfarrox ī Sīrkān (jurisconsult) 745
dādgāh (proper place of a sacred fire) 217–218, 225, 277, 761
Dādgušnasp ī Šahr ī Zādaragān 217, 278, 742, 745
Dādgušnasp, son of *Ātars 437–439, 723–726
Dādgušnasp, son of Dādrāst 733–734
dādīg (pertaining to the law) 2, 5, 8, 25, 27, 60, 417, 668, 677
see also dād and *nasks*
Dādohrmazd 575, 743
Dadōy 348, 702
Dādrāst 733
dādwar (judge) 7, 65, 171, 180, 273, 276–277, 284, 288–289, 293–296, 300, 329, 408, 429, 435, 458, 485, 495, **496–503**, 507–509, 516–519, 521–525, 530–532, 534, 537–538, 545, 549, 567–568, 576, 587, 667–668, 688, 742, 745
dadwarān dādwar (Chief Judge) 495, **502–503**, 524–525, 532, 742, 745, 786
see also šahr dadwarān dādwar
dādwar ī keh (Junior Judge) 65, 180, **497**, 522–523, 525, 532, 534, 587, 761
dādwar ī meh (Senior Judge) 65, 180, **497**, 522–523, 525, 532, 587, 761
dādwar ī pasēmāl ('judge of the defendant; arbitrator') 408, **497**, 502–503, 761
dādwar ī pēšēmāl ('judge of the plaintiff; arbitrator') 408, **497**, 502–503, 761
dādwar ī vaiiōzušt ('judge agreeable to both; arbitrator') **498**, 502–503, 761
Dādxwaš 277
Dahāg 738
dahibed (ruler) 495–496, 508, 510–511, 518, 532, 739, 761
dahigān (landlord) 369, 733; *see also dehgān*
daily ration 224, 252, 253, 583, 751, 775, 785
see also rōzīg
Dandān-Uiliq 40
Darabgird 233, 745
dārišn (maintenance) 123–124, 138, 142, 144, 147, 642–643, 662, 794; (possession) 74, 77, 86, 139, **193–197**, 200–202, 211, 215, 219, 230, 246–247, 249–250, 252, 258, 277–278, 327, 330, 340, 362, 386, 446, 500–501, 543–544, 548, 563, 566–568, 597–598, 639, 643,

670–671, 688, 697, 707–708, 732, 734, 756, 759, 761–762, 769, 779, 793
see also possession
Darius 1, 2, 167
Darshis 630
dāšn (gift) 114, 278, 301, 389, 761
dāštārīh (trusteeship) 94, 187, 223, 248, 254, 601
dastgird (landed estate) 107, 199, 240, **241–244**, 266, 268–269, 327–328, 376–377, 599, 603
dastwar (authorized, entitled person; *auctor*) 51, 57, 79–80, **88–89**, 116, 181, 196, 212, 274, 304, **385–387**, 408, 506–507, 509, 514, 534, 536, 540–541, **542–544**, 546, 561, 567–568, **596–598**, 603, 640, 718; *see also auctor*
dastwarīh (entitlement; *auctor*-ship) **88–89**, 116, 196, 265, 274, 536, **542–544**, 546–547, 549, 562, **596–597**, 643, 645, 670, 707–708, 716, 720, 726, 729, 732, 734, 762; *a-dastwarīhā* 383, 752; *abē-dastwarīhā* 149–150; *dastwarīhā* 380, 660; *dō dastwarīhā* 386, 763; *nē dastwarīhā* 384, 647, 658–659, 662–663, 698, 777
see also auctor-ship
data- (law) 2, 4, 5, 26
see also dād
dāta- vīdaēuua- (law keeping the demons away) 61, 403, 487
dāta- vīdaēuua- zaraϑuštri (the law of Zoroaster keeping the demons away) 61
dāta- zaraϑuštri (the law of Zoroaster) 61, 487
debt 62, 70, 85–86, 88, 118–119, 121, 140, 178, 181–182, 189, 205, 207–208, 210, 214, 220, 229–231, 237, 244, 247–249, 253, 281, 305, **310–367**, 390, 440, 500, 513, 546, 555–559, 569, 607–608, 610, 612, 644
see also abām, *abāmdān*, *tōzišn* and credit law
debt bondage 104, 106, 117, 334, 350, 351–353, 356, 358, 750–751
debtor 70, 85–87, 106, 118–119, 198–199, 207–209, 248, 252–253, 289, 303–305, 308–315, 317–319, 321–325, 328–331, 334–335, 337–347, 349–360, 362–366, 384, 527, 606–608, 610, 612, 617
see also hamāg-tōzišn and *xwāstag-tōzišn*
decree 99, 110, 248, 273, 275, 284, 443, 496, 503, 508, 510–511, 514–515, 517–518, 540–541, 583, 591, 593
see also abarmad and *framān*
defendant 8, 80, 101, 108, 116–117, 191, 196, 228, 268, 275, 287–290, 300, 331, 350, 361–363, 386–389, 408, 415–416, 430, 497–498, 500, 503, 506–508, 522–524, 533–544, 548, 555–559, 562–568, 586–587, 639–640, 668, 697, 717–722
see also pasēmāl
degrees of sins/offences 414, 439, 442, 449, 450, 457–458, 467, **468–486**, 687, 694, 697, 757, 783
see also pāyag
dehgān (landlord) 111, 129, 369–372, 516, 711–712, 727, 733, 762
see also dahigān
Dēl-Dēlān/Dēl ī Dēlān 321–322, 345–347, 370–371, 437, 507, 700–701, 703–704, 706, 709, 712–713, 715–723, 731, 733–734, 736
Dēlānfarrox 704, 707
Dēlāzād 437, 724
Dēlgušnasp 311, 315, 345–347, 711
Dēlgušnasp, son of Dērā 346, 347, 701, 703
deliberate injury, *see bōdōzed*
deliberate offence, *see bōdōwaršt*
delict 306–307, 311–312, 417, 463, 570
Dēlxwašīh 348, 371, 702, 712–713, 737
Dēlzād 370, 712
Dēnkard 2, 6, **24–27**, 35, 52, **60–61**, 65, 94, 96, 113, 116–117, 188, 203, 219, 257, 271, 273–274, 297, 316, 329, 332, 389,

400–401, 403–404, 408, 417, 421, 423, 425, 428, 435, 439, 441–442, 444–445, 464, 466, 471, 487, 493–494, 497–498, 507, 516, 520, 522, 545, 547–548, 552–554, 556–557, 559, 578, 664–665, 667, 669–675, 677, 679, 681–683, 685–687, 689, 738–739
Dēnohrmazd 721
Dēnyadān 536, 715–720
deposit 222, 270, 273, 285, 301–302, 312, 315, 317, 319, 323–326, 332, 334, 336, 340, 377–379, 501, 514, 564–566, 569, 619
depositum 316–317
deputy 539–541, 578
Dērā 209, 288–289, 322, 345–348, 371, 701–703, 705, 711, 714, 731, 733–734, 737
Dērwīndād 728
Dērzamān 709
descent groups (*paywand*, *tōhmag*) 94, 109, 121–122, **126–133**, 136, 138, 140, 149–151, 155–157, 162, 166, 170, 175, 183, 186, 187, 193, 202, 210 (fn. 110), 256, 410, 496, 626, 628, 633, 635–637, 638, 772, 784, 789, 793
  see also lineage
Dēwāstīč 42
Dēzā 723
dib (document) 270, 277, 284, 295, 500, 513–514, 537, 583, 742, 762
Dibīr (jurisconsult) 745
Digesta 57
dīnā (Syr. civil law) 615, 621
  see also ḥasīrūt dīnā and *yatīrūt dīnā*
Dīnawarī 54
disabled persons 32, 177–178, 233, 235, 409, 753–754, 792
disobedience 123, 138–139, 251, 491, 563, 739, 755
  see also atarsagāyīh
Dīv-tāgh 19
Divine Judge 8, 10, 551–552
divorce 34, 37, 39, 141, 273, 275, 280, 285, 383, 629, 631; certificate of (*hišt-nāmag*) 273, 285, 770
dīwān ī kardagān (archive of religious institutions) 270, 505–506, 509, 763
dīwāns according to al-Ḫwārezmī 99, 221, 228, 623, 624, 755, 760, 766, 772, 785–786
Do-āb 19
doctrine, legal 2, 6, 9–10, 65–67, 70–72, 79, 255–258, 342, 401, 403–404, 453, 466, 570–571, 616, 621–624, 627–628, 638, 669–670, 693–694
  see also čāštag
document of acquittal *see *bōxt-nāmag*
document of conveyance *see* conveyance
document of seal transfer *see muhr-dād*
documents 263–286
  see also abarmad, *ayādgār*, *čak*, *dib*, *mādayān*, *nāmag*, *nāmag/gittag*, *nāmag/gittag ī nēk*, *nibēg*, *nibištag*, *pădirāy*, *pādixšīr*, *pašn*, *pašt*, *paymān*, *paymān-nāmag*, *wizīr*
dominium 77, 194, 605, 639
  see also xwēšīh and ownership
donatio inter vivos see donation
donatio mortis causa see donation
donatio propter nuptias 140, 274, 771
  see also dower
donation (*dād*, *dāšn*) 78, 83–84, 114, 192–193, 211–212, 235–238, 239 (fn. 237), 245, 248, 264, 301, 363, 365, 376, **389–399**, 612, 624, 698, 759–761, 770, 782; formulae 627; in contemplation of death (*donatio mortis causa*) 70, 204, 235, 240, 305, 376, 390, 391, 396, 398, 399, 760, 773; in the donor's lifetime (*donatio inter vivos*) 236, 390, 391, 399, 760, 789; procedure 301–305
dos 141, 274, 784
  see also dowry
dower (*kābēn*) 139–142, 265, 274, 303, 305, 439, 771
dowry (*pēšīgān-wāspuhragān*) 139–141, 232–233, 274, 284, 515, 784
driyōšān jādag-gōw (ud dādwar) (title) **293–295**, 300, 501, 763, 771

drōš (penalty for theft) 108, 313, 382–383, 439–442, 444, 447, 449, 451, 485, 570, 584, 685–687, 763
  see also band and *band ud drōš*
dūdag-sālār/sālārīh (family guardian/ guardianship) 121–122, 125, 135, 170, 173–174, **178–179**, 182, 215, 217, 225, 231, 302, 360, 415–416, 539, 546, 614–615, 643, 645, 647–651, 653–656, 763–764, 786, 795
  see also sālār, sālārīh and *xwāstag-sālār/sālārīh*
duel (*ardīg tazišnīh*) 405–406, 425, 433, 754
Dunhuang 42
dusraw/dusrawīh (disrepute) 575, 584, 595, 764
duš-menišn (evil thought, malicious intent) 413, 432, 764, 770, 773
  see also kēn-menišn
duxt ī padīriftag (adopted daughter) 176, 764
  see also adoption
Duxtxwašīh 361, 534, 715–716, 728–730
duz(d) (thief) 25, 60, 312–313, 382, 388, 434–435, **439–451**, 519–520, 618, 685–689, 691–695, 764
  see also duz-menišnīh/menišnīgīh and thief
duzd ī +drozan 25, 60, 685
  duzd ī druz +tan 25, 60, 685
  duzd-sar-nizad/ōzad 25, 60, 685
duz(d)īh (theft) 67–68, 413–414, 421, **439–451**, 455–460, 462, 531, 565, 687–689, 693–695, 764, 768, 771, 783
  see also gād-duzīh; *tan-duzīh* and theft
duz-menišnīh/menišnīgīh (intent of the thief) 413–414, 422, 424, 445, 449, 451, 688, 764
Dvin 55

earnest money *see rabŭn/rabŭna*
earnings and revenue *see bandōzišn ud windišn*
East Christians (Nestorians) 1, 13, 66, 115, 120, 383, 588; canon law 46–49, 55, 74, 156–157, 163, 176, 232–233, 342, 375, 382–383, 435, 588–589, 602, **609–621**; jurisdiction 492, 494–496, 511, **526–532**, 572–573, 575, **577–581**; levirate 118–119, 620–621; martyrdom 49, 511, 527, 572; punishments 584–585; rights 208, 260, 342, 382–383, 488; temporary marriage 628, 630, 632
  see also Corpus Iuris of Īšōʿbōxt and Mār Abā
edict *see dib*
Egypt 15, 17, 58, 514
Egyptian 1, 15, 17, 58
Elam 347
Elamite 104
Elephantine 15, 389, 512
Ēmēd ī Ašawahištān 36
emergency, state of 75, 107, 231, 331, 446, 463–466, 468, 570
  see also adwadād
emphyteusis 209, 368
  see also lease and *tāg*
endogamy 94, 129, 133, 140, 148, **151–157**, 184, 186, 210, 219, 253, 462, 636, 758, 796
  see also xwēdōdah
endowments 16, 44, 56, 102, 107, 128–129, 177–178, 187, 191, 200, 216–217, 220–228, 254, 264, 270, 275–278, 284–285, 311, 502, 505, 623–626, 640
  see also charitable foundations and *ruwānagān*
ʿeqārā (Syr. ‘root’) 343–344, 617, 758
era Yazdegird 21, 35
ʿerabon see rabŭn/rabŭna
Ērānšahr 1, 10, 12, 99–103, 107, 112–113, 115, 117, 119, 121, 167, 169, 197, 227, 372, 410, 436, 486, 488–489, 493, 572, 578, 582, 588, 630, 774
Ēran-spāhbed 502
Ērān-Xwarrah-Šābuhr 294

Ērān-Xwarrah, fire of 277, 292–293, 742
Ērēǰ, son of Frēdōn 167
ergative (agential) construction 238–240, 396, 773
evidence and proof *see čim ud bōzišn*
ēwar (trustworthy, binding) 7, 69–70, 200, 269, 287, 291, 296, 299–301, 317–318, 323, 362, 486, 501, 504, 506–507, 510–511, 514, 518–520, 524, 545, 547, 550–552, 559, 566, 570, 593, 617, 620, 667–668, 676–677, 709, 727, 765
ēwarīh (trustworthiness) 69, 267, 272, 282, 288, 290, 298, 300–301, 320–322, 346–347, 398, 496–498, 503, 510–511, 545, 549, 551, 559–561, 567–568, 570, 620, 701, 703, 733, 737, 765
ēwēn (law) 4–5, 8, 88, 437, 446, 535, 668, 696–697, 702, 706–707, 715, 718–719, 723, 729, 732–733, 736, 765
ēwēn ī šahr (law of the state) 4, 446, 765
  see also dād ī šahr
ēw-kardag/kardagīh/kardagīhā (in one piece) 243, 250, 345, 347–348, 643, 684, 702
Exodus 411
ex lege (*pad čāštag*) 70, 71, 342, 571
  see also čāštag
exogamy 133, **148–151**, 157, 759, 796
  see also bayăspān
extension of justice *see mehdādestānīh* and *wehdādestānīh*
Ezra 600

false testimony 429, 549, 738, 740, 798
  see also zur-gugāyīh
family (*dūdag, nāf*), guardianship 177–183; *see also sālār(īh)*; inheritance 230–245; liabilities and claims 360–364; members 5, 120–124, 126, 175–177; offences against 460–462; property 78, 83, 187–188, 192–193, **202–230**; secondary succession *see ayōgēnīh* and *stŭrīh*; structure 93–95, 126–128, **128–133**, 151–157, 183–186
  see also descent group; lineage
family guardian/guardianship *see dūdag-sālār/sālārīh*
Farrbay (fire) 273, 284, 741
Farrbay (personal name) 292, 745
Farrbay-srōš ī Wahrāmān 21, 34–36, 38, 343
Farroxabzūd 507, 534, 536, 715–722, 728, 730
Farroxān 280, 705, 708, 732
Farroxbudān 717–718
Farroxdēl 732–734
Farroxgušnasp 252, 281, 311, 315, 345–347, 371, 437, 702–703, 705, 711–713, 723, 735–736
Farroxgyān ī Zarduxštān (*šahr dādwarān dādwar*) 277, 502, 742,745
Farroxmard ī Wahrāmān (compiler of the *Hazār dādestān*) 20–22, 741, 745
Farroxohrmazd 711–712, 729
Farrox-Xusrō/Xusroyān 321–322, 700–701, 704–705, 707–708
Farroxzād 34, 290, 346–347, 371, 703, 705, 713
Farroxzurwān (jurisconsult) 365, 745
Fārsnāmeh 54
Fasā 257, 670
Fāṭima 638
Fayyūm 17
fetters and mutilation (punishment for theft) *see band ud drōš*
feud 64, 256, 404–407, 409, 411, 489, 495, 676
fideicommissum 174–175, 177, 216
Fihrist 53
financial obligations *see* liabilities
fine *see tāwān* and *tōzišn*
Firdausi 54, 97, 167
fire, consecrated/sacred (*ādur, ātaxš*) 37, 75, 187, 200, 218, 220, 223–224, 276, 292, 421, 429, 463–464, 467, 481, 504, 623, 625, 743, 752, 755, 761;

ever-burning (*hamēšag-sōz*) 181, 219; guardianship (*sālārīh*) 82, 87, 94, 177–178, 180–181, 225, 250, 292, 761; loan from 745; partnership 249–250; property 222–223, 226–227, 506, 512, 586–587, 742, 794–796; register 99, 228, 270, 273, 741; trusteeship (*stŭrīh*) 205, 213, 216–219, 366, 761; tutorship (*dāštārīh*) 94, 254
see also ādurōg; fire foundations and Wahrām fire
fire foundations (*ādurān ātaxšān*) 99, 102, 105, 107, 109, 128–129, 163, 175 (fn. 270), 191, 213, **225–229**, 269–270, 273, 275–278, 285, 366–367, 504–505, 509, 512, 586, 601, 745, 752, 755, 776
see also anšahrīg ī ātaxš; *bandag(īh) ī ātaxš*; *nāmag-niyān*; *stŭrīh* and foundation deed with further references
Fire of Ērān-Xwarrah 277, 292, 742
Fīrūzābād 16, 224
foreclosure 328–329, 338
foreigners (*an-ēr, uzdehīg*) 34, 102–104, **113–117**, 118–119, 125, 262, 302, 333–334, 410, 451, 486, 548, 650, 677–678
formulaic expressions 80–81, 83, 309
see also certa verba and legal formulae
fornication 629, 690–691
foundation deed *see pādixšīr*; *mādayān* and *nāmag/gittag*
foundations 16, 56, 58 (fn. 179), 65, 87, 94, 98 (fn. 15), 99, 102, 129, 180, 187, 200, **220–229**, 242–243, 254, 264, 311, 391, 785, 795; non-profitable (*a-har*) 223–224; surplus producing (*barōmand*) 224–229; for the soul (*pad ruwān*, *ruwan ray*) 220–229; (Byzantine) *piae causae* 640; (Islamic) *waqf* 622–627
see also nihādag; *ruwānagān*; fire foundations and foundation deed with further references
fragard (division) 27–30, 236, 404, 653–654, 674
Frahang ī ōīm-ēk 30–31
framān (command, decree, instruction) 87, 216, 223, 250, 277, 281, 293, 295–296, 300, 369, 438, 495–496, 503, 508, 510–511, 515, 517–518, 524, 531–532, 545, 550–551, 580, 586–587, 591, 693; 704, 709, 711, 724–725, 732, 734, 736, 739–740, 742–743, 761–762, 765, 772, 775
see also kār-framān
framān (degree of sin) 468–473, 475–477, 481–482, 484, 765
frašgird (Restoration) 6–7, 184, 219, 401, 665–666
frayar (morning) 402, 537, 569, 765
Frāygušnasp 288
Frāyzarduxšt (*mowbed*) 295, 743, 745
Frāz-marā-āwar-xudāyā 226
Frēdōn saga 167
freeborn, noble *see āzād*
frēzwān (inspector) 288, 429–430, 497, 508, **518–519**, 521, 545, 574, 642, 765, 769, 788
fruit(s) *see bar*
full legal capacity *see tuwānīgīh*

gādār (adulterer, fornicator) 459; (husband in a consensus marriage) **78–79**, 122, 125, 132–133, **145–147**, 148–150, 157, 159–161, 176, 183, 185, 233–234, 631, 766, 794
see also xwasrāyēn/ūn and consensus marriage
gād-duzīh (theft of sexual intercourse) 414, 455–458, 460, 462, 531, 691, 766, 789
see also adultery and *tan-duzīh*
Gāh-nāmag (Book of rank) 110
gāhān (Gathas) 25
gāhānbār (festival) 481
Ǧāḥiẓ 97
Gaius 189, 306–307
gālīg (member of the household) 390
ganāḇā (Syr. 'thief') 382, 435, 450, 618

gaol 449, 798
see also zēndān
gaoler 500–501, 519–521, 545, 798
see also zēndānbān
garzišn (complaint) 252, 361, 437, 524–525, 533–535, 715–716, 719–720, 723, 728, 730, 736, 766
Gāthās 27, 698, 590
Gēlān 294
Gemara 50, 598
genetrix (natural mother) 133, 152
see also burdār
genitor (natural father) 127, 131, 144, 155, 166, 173
gētīy (corporal world) 6–7, 9–10, 401, 538, 552, 665–668, 696, 698
gift (*dād, dašn*) 44, 78, 89, 108, 140, 182, 192–193, 196, 205, 211–212, 220–221, 235–237, 239–240, 249, 263–264, 266, 269, 278, 301, 306, 340, 363–364, 376, **389–399**, 461, 507, 543, 596, 614, 624, 653
see also donation
gizīr (warden) 500–501, 767
ǧizya (poll tax) 99
glebae adscripti 107, 241, 328, 599
Gōdarz 99
Gōr 224, 227, 295–296, 348, 387, 703, 742–743
governor of a province *see ōstāndār*
graw/grawīh (pawn, pledge) 117, 249, 266, 301, 312, 317, **324–331**, 333, 335–339, 341, 344–345, 353, 564–566, 568, 612, 617, 750, 756, 767, 780, 795
grawagān/grawagānīh (mortgage of the fruits; *antichresis*) 87, 198, 209, 218, 266, 269, 301, 303, 311, 325–328, 330–331, 334–338, **343–349**, 617, 703, 708, 767, 778, 780, 795
see also antichresis
grawagāndār (mortgagee) 325–327, 330, 344–345, 349, 767
grawdār (pledgee) 324, 326, 331, 344–345, 767
grīw (measure) 281, **347–348**, 370–371, 379, 660, 704–707, 713, 735, 768, 771
guardian *see sālār*
guardianship *see sālārīh*
guardianship of family property *see xwāstag-sālārīh*
guardianship of the family *see dūdag-sālārīh*
gugāy (witness) 116, 282–283, 285, 298, 300, 386, 398, 499, 507–508, 534, 542, 545, 548–551, 559, 567–568, 697, 768
gugāyīh (testimony) 116, 298, 300, 427, 429, 508, 545–546, 549–551, 558, 583, 675, 688, 698–699, 733, 740, 743, 768
gugāy-muhr (witness-seal) **282–283**, 285, 298, 300, 550–551, 768
see also seals
guharēn (barter) 301, 372, 388, 768
see also barter
guharīg (substitute, compensation) 139, 169, 182, 249, 296, 329, 344–345, 387, 421, 442, 444–445, 447, 449, 451, 504–505, 520, 647–648, 680–681, 686–687, 768, 774
see also compensation; *tāwān* and *tōzišn*
guilds (*pēšag*) 517–518
Ġurar aḫbār mulūk al-furs wa siyarihim 54
Gurgān 294, 744
Gušnasp, King of Parišwar and Ṭabarestān 52, 711, 746
+Gušnasp-Ādur (secretary) 99
Gušnaspōy 732–734
Ǧuwānōy (scribe) 99
Gūzgān (Jūzǰān) 44

hādamānsᵃrīg (pertaining to the ritual) 25, 668
Hājjiābād 16, 111
Halīg 281, 321, 345, 437, 700–701, 736
Hamadān 294
hamāg-tōzišn (joint and several debtor) 118, 207, 209, 253, **308–310**, 319, 356, 360, 364–366, 764, 768–769, 773, 779, 795
see also debtor and *xwāstag-tōzišn*

hambarag (co-partner/shareholder of the fruits) 218, 244, 247, 250, 252, 768, 797
hambāy (partner, shareholder) 86, 129, 170, 179, 204–205, 208, 229, 234, **245–247**, 252, 267, 360, 364, 384, 445, 647–648, 768
see also brād ī hambāy
hambāyīh (partnership, shareholding) 129, 166, 230, 234, **245–247**, 249–252, 325, 351, 355, 769
hamēmāl (opponent; litigant), 3, 9–10, 39, 32, 62–63, 92, 191, 306, 400, 403, 406, 412, 421–422, 433, 440–442, 447, 449, 451–452, 454, 456–457, 459–460, 462, 467, 470, 481, 484, 486–489, 492–494, 506, 523, 526, 529–530, 537, 558–559, 565, 567, 569, 572, 615, 682, 686–687, 698–699, 769
see also wināh ī hamēmālān
Hammurabi 11, 544, 671
hamnāmīh (identification of the name) 288, 300, 500, 519–521, 769
hampaččēn (copy) 270, 283, 291–292, 301, 397, 416, 574, 741–742, 769, 774
see also paččēn
hampāyandān/hampāyandānīh (co-surety/co-suretyship) 247, 252–253, 364, 366, 509, 769
see also co-sureties, co-suretyship
hamtanīh (identification of the person) 288, 300, 500, 519, 521, 769
hamwindišn (joint earnings) 247, 251–252, 769
hamxwāstag(ān) (joint proprietor[s]), 86, 245–247, 249, 364, 252, 769
hamxwāstagīh (joint property) 245, 247, 249, 251, 770
Ḥamza al-Iṣfahānī 54, 226, 602
handarz (testament) **235–236**, 241, 245, 398–399, 405, 476–477, 481–483, 612, 642–643, 645, 651, 656, 669, 674, 731, 743, 770
see also testament
handarz-framān (degree of sin) **476–477**, 481–482, 765, 770
handōzišn ud windišn (acquisitions and revenue) 78, 192–193, 770
ḫarāǧ 99
Harwahišt 736
Harwān 226, 602
harzbed (*arzbed*) (title) 573
ḥasīrūt dīnā (Syr. 'decrease of justice'); opposite: *yaṯīrūt dīnā* 70, 73, 610, 783
*Haspin-raz *see* *Asp-gurd
al-Ḫaṣṣāf 623, 626
ḥāṭōpā (Syr. 'plunderer') 382, 435, 437, 450, 618–619
Hazār dādestān 20, 71, 741, 745
head of the household *see kadag-xwadāy*
head of the guild *see pēšag-sālār*
heir *see abarmānd-xwāstagdār* and *xwāstagdār*
hērbed 27, 33, 52, 94, 97, 99, 276, 454, 485, **506–507**, 509, 525, 534, 536, 602, 716, 720, 770
Hērbedestān 2, 26, **27**, 74, 119, 383, 400, 429, 435–436, 445, 447, **454–458**, 459, 469, 690–691, 693, 695
hereditary possession 205–206, 210–212, 750, 781, 796
see also xwāstagdārīh
heresy 60, 69, 113, 262, 291, 422, 490–494, 526, 572, 574, 580, 583–584, 595, 738
see also ahlomōyīh
heretic (*ahlomōγ*, *xwaddōšag*, **yō xᵛa-daēnā*) 54, 95, 112–113, 258, 493, 576, 579, 583–584, 670–673
Hilāl ar-Ra'y 623, 626
Hilāl b. Yaḥyā 623
History of Ałuank', 56
History of Łazar P'arpets'i 55
History of the Province of Siwnik' 56
homicide 62, 100, 105, 411, 423, **429–432**, 444, 488–489, 519, 572–574, 682, 778
homosexuality 452
Hormazyār Framarz 484
Hormizd 271–272, 322, 700, 711–712
horseman's document *see aswār-nibēg*

hostage 324, 326–327, 329, 332–335, 343, 350, 682
see also *nibāg/nabāg*
Hudād (legal authority) 292, 745
hudēnān-pēšōbāy (leader of the faithful) 33, 35
Huna, Rav 530
Hurām-Ardaxšēr 218, 273, 741
Huspārom nask 25, 27, 60–61, 653–654
Husraw (*čāšān*) 277, 293
Husraw I (Anōšag-ruwān/Anūšīrwān) (531–579 CE) 31, 46–47, 52, 54, 95, 99–100, 110–111, 155, 188, 217, 241, 256, 259, 271, 291–292, 294–295, 369, 442–443, 449, 490, 515, 573, 578–581, 742–743, 747
Husraw II (Parwēz) (590–628 CE) 17–18, 20–21, 704, 731
Husraw ī Kawādān ud rēdag-ē(w) 100
Husraw-Āduranāhīd (fire) 225
Husraw-Šābuhr (fire) 225
hutuxš (artisan) 95, 98, 372, 770
hutuxšbed (chief of the artisans) 373, 770
al-Ḫwārezmī 54, 98–99, 221, 228, 280, 623–624
hypothec 301, 323, 336, 340–341, 617, 752, 780, 795
see also āgraw
hypotheca 190, 208, 324, 326, 331, 340–341, 336
see also āgraw

Ibn al-Muqaffaʿ 52, 54
Ibn an-Nadīm 53
Ibn Balḫī 54
Ibn Isfandiyār 52
Ibn Miskawayh 53–54, 97
Ibn Qutaiba 54
ideal share (of the patrimony) *see a-baxt*
identification of a person/seal 288–289, 300, 521, 701, 703, 737
see also hamnāmīh; *hammuhrīh*; *hamtanīh*
illness, legal consequences of 70, 174, 244, 256, 405, 610, 643–645, 674–675
immovable property 190, 206, 209, 212, 639; as security 324, 326–327, 331–332, 339, 341, 343, 617; as *waqf* 624–625; lease of 367; sale of 376–377; transfer of 240–245
imprisonment 441, 449–450, 581
inability to maintain *see adwadād*
inalienable property 128, 199, 205, 207, 211, 214, 216, 229, 248, 254, 256, 625
incarceration 313
incest 129–131, 151–155, 186, 234, 253–254, 632, 636
see also endogamy and *xwēdōdah*
income 9–10, 74, 76, 78, 87, 108, 122–124, 139, 142, 160, 173, 182, 192–193, 195, **197–202**, 207–208, 210–211, 213, 218, 220, 222, 224–230, 244, 247–254, 278–279, 302, 305, 328, 343, 367–368, 371–372, 392–394, 402–403, 505, 516, 597–598, 603–606, 617, 624–627, 640, 648, 652, 661, 677, 712
see also abzōn; *bar*; *handōxt*; *handōzišn*; *mad ud rasēd*; *waxt*; *waxš* and *windišn*
income of the *pādixšāy*-wife *see abzōn* and *windišn*
indemnity 325, 355, 357–359, 608
see also suretyship
India 38, 41
Indian 147, 169
infanticide 452–453
inferior class/persons 106, 258, 464, 631
infidels 8,10, 34, 39, 69, 103, 112, 115, 117–119, 124–125, 302, 384, 436, 526–528, 532, 658–659, 662–664
see also agdēn and *juddēn*
inheritance 8, 229–230, 253–254, 340, 363; agnatic, cognatic, uterine systems of 127–128; claim to 70; components of the total patrimonial estate 202–206; direct and intermediary succession 74–75, 128–129, 138, 156, 163–168;

entitlement to 123, 137, 140, 256; fires and pious foundations as categories of 217–219, 220–229; intestacy 230–235; loss of entitlement to 111, 138; Mazdakite doctrine regarding 258; no entitlement to 144, 147; obligations of the heirs and legatees 87–88, 206–212; of a convert 436; regulations applying only to Zoroastrians 65, 69, 118–119, 124, 527–528; renunciation of 244–245, 612–613; shares and shareholding 77, 129, 153, 160, 187, 232–235, 245, 249, 252, 265; Shīʿite law of 589, 632–638; slaves bequeathed as part of 107; sources on 14, 19, 32, 36–39, 46, 48, 56, 59, 63, 134, 641–656, 664; substitute succession 153, 156, 168–174, 213–216, 505, 509, 620–621; terminology 79, 134, 203–206, 750, 757–759, 779, 784; testamentary dispositions 71, 235–245, 237–244, 376, 391, 398–399
see also abarmānd; *ayōgēnīh* and *stūrīh*
injury, physical 8, 307–308, 311–312, 332, 400, 405–407, 410–412, 415, 417–418, **423–433**, 444–445, 448, 454, 457, 465, 468–469, 471–476, 480–483, 488–489, 528, 533, 562, 570–572, 665–666, 675, 677–678, 682–684, 688, 695, 727
see also rēš; *zanišn* and *zaxm*
innate wisdom *see āsn-xrad*
inquisitorial system of adjudication 502, 569
instances *see* appellate courts
intent (*kām*, *menišn*, *menišnīgīh*) 7, 84, 238, 312, 315, 377, 383, 389, 391, 395, **412–422**, 424, 432, 445, 449, 451, 455–458, 466, 470, 472–473, 481–483, 562, 570, 588, 619, 666, 692–693
see also mens rea and following entries
intent of the robber *see appar-kām* and *appar-menišnīgīh*
intent of the thief *see duz-menišnīh*/*menišnīgīh*
intentional injury *see bōdōzed*
intentional offence *see bōdōwaršt*
intercessor 289–290, 295, 538–541, 557, 563
intercourse, illicit *see gād-duzīh* and *tan-duzīh*
interest *see waxš* and *waxt*
intermediary succession *see ayōgen*/*ayōgenīh*
intermediary successor *see ayōgēn* and *ayōgēn-stūr*
intestacy 210, 216, 231–232, 235, 376
irrigation 222–223, 321, 599
Isfahan 20, 226, 512, 602
Islam 10, 385, 408, 589–590, 621–622, 624, 629, 635
Īšōʿbōxt 48–49, 63–64, 70–71, 105, 109, 157, 176, 232–233, 245, 296–297, 329–331, 339–344, 374–375, 378–382, 435, 514, 550, 554, 589, 593, 602, 609–611, 613–621
Israel 530
ius 5
ius in personam 605
ius in re 605
ius in re aliena 341
ius talionis 410–411, 444

ǰādag (portion, share) 140, 345, 702, 706–707, 770–771
see also bahr
ǰādag-gōw (advocate, intercessor) 289, **537–541**, 543, 557, 563, 717, 719–721, 770–771
see also driyōšān ǰādag-gow and advocate
jamdar (pledgee) 326, 331–332, 771
ǰāmdārīh ([movable] pledge) 317, 324, 326, 334–335, 771
see also pledge
Jamšīd 97
Jaxartes 41

Jerusalem 50
Jesus (of Nazareth) 48, 581
Jewish law 1, 3, 13, 15, **39–40**, **49–51**, 74, 79, 143, 202, 356, 377, 495–496, 512, **526–532**, 588–589, **590–608**, 620–622
see also Babylonian Talmud
Jews 39, 46, 49, 51, 66, 107, 115, 118, 120, 208, 226, 260, 383, 488, 494, 496, **526–532**, 628, 630, 632
see also Jewish law
joint and several debtor *see hamāg-tōzišn*
joint income *see hamwindišn*
joint income with equal shares *see āgenēn hamwindišn*
joint ownership with equal shares *see āgenēn xwēš*
joint possession with equal shares *see āgenēn dārišn*
joint property *see hamxwāstagīh*
joint proprietors *see hamxwāstagān*
Judaeo-Persian legal texts **39–40**, 80, 759
Juddēwdād ī Mēdōmāh 29
judge *see dādwar*
Judge of the Defendant *see dādwar ī pasēmāl*
Judge of the Plaintiff *see dādwar ī pēšēmāl*
judicial dispute *see pahikār-radīh*
judiciary 1, 5, 9, 406, 422, 494–497, 499, 501, 503, 505–507, 509–511, 513, 515, 517, 519, 521–523, 525–527, 529–532, 537, 540–541, 549, 561–562, 568, 586, 744
see also dādestān
Junior Judge *see dādwar ī keh*
jurisdiction (*dādwarīh*) 3, 5, 16, 22, 34–35, 38, 51, 55, 59, 62, 65–66, 94, 120, 258, 263, 301, 387, 403, 410, 485–489, 494–497, 502–503, 505–506, 509, 515–518, 525–530, 532, 534–536, 540–541, 565, 578–580, 591, 615, 671, 731, 734, 744
see also dādestān
Justinian 57, 306–307, 317, 395, 640
justice *see dādestān*
Juwān-ǰam (jurisconsult) 746
Kaʿba-ye Zardušt 16, 41, 222, 225, 276, 514
kābēn (dower) 140, 274, 771
kabīz (measure) 347–348, 370–371, 379–380, 659–660, 702, 705–706, 712–713, 771
kadag (house, building) 240, 242, 244, 277–278, 376–377, 772; (household) 107; (lineage) 99, 128, 772, 793
see also bun-kadag; *xānag* and lineage
kadag-bānūg (mistress of the house) **122–124**, 128, 130, 132, **137**, 140, **142**, 181–182, 208, 232, 234–235, 323, 360–363, 509, 538–539, 546, 643, 645–646, 648–649, 757, 772
see also materfamilias
*kadag hamār *dibīrag* (register of the accounts of the [royal] house) 99, 772
kadag-xwadāy (master of the house) 5, 111, **120–122**, 128, 130, **132–133**, 137, **142**, 144, 174–176, 178, 180, 202, 205–206, 215, 229, 230–231, 233, 245, 254, 269, 323, 360, 362–363, 397, 546, 612, 615, 763–764, 772, 776, 781
see also paterfamilias
kādōzed (negligence) 412–413, **417–422**, 424, 444–445, 570–571, 688, 772–773, 788
Kałankatuats 56
kām (will, intent) 7, 380, 412–413, 422, 424, 570–571, 616, 659–660, 666–667, 688, 772
kāmag (will, intent) 211, 302–303, 305, 391, 396–397, 672, 772
Kanishka 43
kardag (legal practice) **66–72**, 79, 207, 214, 227, 243, 342, 345, 347–348, 386, 501, 504, 546, 549, 570–571, 583, 585–586, 616–617, 650–653, 670, 744, 759, 772, 780
see also sālār ī kardag and *stūr ī kardag*
kārdār (public official) 272, 497, 503, 509, 545, 772

Kārdār, son of Mihr-Narseh 226–227
Karēn 432
kār-framān 772; command (administrative seal) 270–271, 293, 295, 300, 515, 550–551, 580, 583, 595, 743, 775; decree 510–511; public official 270–271, 511, 709, 742, 744
see also muhr ī pad kār-framān dāštan
Kārnāmag (Kārnāmaǧ) 54, 120, 167, 359
Kawād I, son of Pērōz 95, 100, 256, 259, 293, 742
Kay-Ādurfarrbay 520
Kayanian 167
Kāzrōn 387
kēn-menišn (malicious intent) 413–414, 422, 472, 764, 770, 773
see also duš-menišn
Kērēn 158, 393–394
Kermān 1
Khwarezmian 13, 45, 74, 280
kinship 21, 47, 65, 93, **94–95**, 123, **126–133**, 157, 174–175, 186–187, 253–254, 259, 406, 631, 637
kirbag (virtuous deed) 7, 9, 62, 90, 220, 277, 384, 400, 403, 410, 441, 459, 469, 478–479, 493, 643, 645, 658–659, 666, 677, 682, 698, 773
Kirdīr 16, 104, 222, 227, 243, 275–278
Kirman 33
kirrōgbed (chief of the craftsmen) 373, 773
Kitāb al-aḫbār aṭ-ṭiwāl 54
Kitāb at-tanbīh wa'l-išrāf 54
Kitāb mā ʾamara Ardašīr bi-stiḫrāǧihi min ḫazāʾin al-kutub allatī wuḍuʿahā al-ḥukama fi-t-tadbīr 53
kitābat al-awqāf 98–99, 221, 624, 785
Kōfāhr 290
Kom 18
**kōybān* (keeper of a town/district?) 520–521, 773
kunmarz (anal intercourse) 34, 773
see also sodomy
Kurrag 281, 735
Kushan (empire, kings) 41, 43–44
lactation 453–454
land *see gil* and *zamīg*
land in one piece (not partitioned) *see ēw-kardag(īhā)*
landed estate *see dastgird*
landlord 281, 367, 372, 709, 737
see also dahigān and *dehgān*
law *see dād*; *dādestān* and *ēwēn*
law court *see dādestān*
law of the State *see dād ī šahr* and *ēwēn ī šahr*
Law-book, Sasanian *see Hazār dādestān*
Law-book of Īšōʿbōxt *see Corpus Iuris* of Īšōʿbōxt
lawsuits 5, 361, 415–416, 430, 496; barter 388–389; civil 79, 177, 200, 301, 319, 331, 334, 350, 354, 507, 509, 522, 525–526, **536–542**, 562–571, 585–587, 613, 616, 730, 756–757, 766, 768, 770, 772, 774, 778, 780, 786, 788, 793, 798; criminal 447; evidence in 89, 116, 287–289, 298–301, 323, **542–560**, 759; of religious minorities 531–532; Roman 196, 639–640; sale 385–387
see also dādestān; civil proceedings and criminal law
lawyer *see* advocate
layman/layperson 73, 135, 181, 226, 516, 538, 601
lease/leasehold 19, 44, 77, 192, 194, 198–199, 201–202, 209, 213, 281, 301, **367–372**, 563, 598, 628, 711, 713, 761, 788, 791
see also emphyteusis and *tāg*
legal doctrine/theory *see čāštag*
legal formulae 18, 22, 27–28, 40–41, 45, 56, 67, 70, 81–83, 158–159, 190, 216, 222, 237, 260, 265, 282, 303–306, 314, 318, 325, 334–335, 353–355, 390–391, 553, 570–571, 591, 624–625, 627
see also certa verba and formulaic expressions
legal personality 102–103, 115, 217

legal position in the social hierarchy: constituent elements 102–103, 110, 115, 124–126
legal practice *see kardag*
legal predecessor *see auctor* and *dastwar/dastwarīh*
legal proceedings *see dādestān* and lawsuits
legal rights, concept of 10, 53, **85–90**, 306; in *pādixšāy*-marriage 128–130, 132, **134–142**, 162, 782, 787, 798; in the social hierarchy 98, 100–103, **124–126**; infringement of 449, 462, 488; of children 175–177, 231; of citizens 113–117; of commoners 110–113; of creditors 320, 325, 350, 363, 784; of foreigners 113–117; of heirs 231–237; of infidels 118–120, 410; of men 120–122, 631, 778; of nobles 110–113; of slaves 104–110; of the sovereign 493; of women 122–124; of Zoroastrians 118–120; proprietary rights 193–197, 199–202, 205, 207, 212, 215, 217, 224, 228–230, 278, 301–302, 338–339, 391–392, 395, 398, 507, 534, 542, 597–598, 603, 605, 779
see also dastwarīh; *pādixšāy*; *tuwānīgīh* and animal rights
legal schools 2, 29, 32–33, 37, 59, 64, 80, 109, 179–180, 244, 289, 386, 454, 501, 526, 621–622, 624, 632, 634, 744–746
legal successor of a *paterfamilias see yōhē pasčaēta*
Leges Novellae 57
legis actio sacramento in rem 196, 386
legitimate brother *see dādestān-brād*
legitimate daughter *see dādestān-duxt*
legitimate sister *see dādestān-xwāh*
legitimate son *see dādestān-pus*
leniency in justice *see passand*
letter of attorney *see* mandate
levirate 143, 168, 184, 232, 620–621
liabilities *see abām*; *tōzišn* and obligations
liabilities of the parents/forefathers *see abām ī pidarān* and *tōzišn ī pidarān*
lineage 5, 47, 38, 183–186, 258–259, 321–322, 345, 673, 726, 732, 772, 784, 789, 793; change of 136–140, 148–151; children of a 175–177, 753; concept of **127–133**, 229; continuity of 133–134, 142, 157–162, 163–174, 187, 207, 214, 216, 253, 460–461, 620, 623, 626, 631–633, 636–637, 765, 776; guardianship *see sālārīh*; matrimony within the 153–157, 796; matrimony outside the 148–151, 758; privileges and property of a noble 9, 78–79, 94, 111–112, 118–119, 187, 193, 202, 205–230, 245, 253–255, 402, 750; status of the *paterfamilias* 121; women of a 123, 125–126, 136–140, 142–145, 163–174, 208, 234–235, 449, 756
see also kadag; *xānag*; descent group; endogamy and exogamy
litigant *see hamēmāl(ān)*
litigation 5, 88, 104, 108, 116–117, 125–126, 181–182, 189–191, 196, 286–291, 295, 301, 350, 360, 381, 404, 417, 451, 462, 495, 519, 524, 526, 530, 533, 536–538, 540–541, 543, 586, 592–593, 613, 639, 730
see also dādestān; civil proceedings and lawsuits
litigation costs 585–587
loan *see abām*; *abāmdān*; *tōzišn*; credit law and debt
loan contract *see paymān*; *paymān-nāmag*; *wizīr* and *wizīr ī abāmdān*
loan from (the property of) the fires *see abām az ādurān ud ātaxšān*

Machiavellian policy 493
mad ud rasēd (*bona adventitia*) 74, 78, 139, 190, **192–193**, 211, 392–393, 773–774, 785, 795
mādagwar 774; main claimant 355, 537–539, 541; original document,

template 270, 397, 769; principle organs/parts of the body 426, 683
mādayān (foundation deed) 227, 275–276, 278, 285, 679, 682, 685, 774
Mādayān ī gizastag Abālīš 35
Madayān ī hazār dādestān see Hazār dādestān
Mafātīhu'l-ʿulūm 54, 98, 221, 228
magian court 524, 530–532
magic 417–418, 422, 472, 754
Māhādur (*ōstāndār*) 288, 295
Māhādur-Frāy-Gušnasp (*mowbed*) 746
Māhādur-Frayzarduxšt (*ostīgān*) 743, 746
Māhanōš 705
Māhdād-Weh ī Māhānān 283, 298
Māhdād-Gušnasp ī Yazdān-afzūd 746
Māhgušnasp, son of Mihr-Narseh 226
Mahgušnasp 732
mahistag (Elder) 439, 714, 725
Māhōš 705
Māhōy 540–541, 705, 718
Mahoza 49, 630
Māhpērōz 283
mahr 140–141, 274, 628, 771
Māhweh (jurisconsult) 746
Māhwindād (jurisconsult) 746
Māhwindād ī Wuzurgbūdān (jurisconsult) 746
maidservant 142, 454–455, 457, 695
Maimonides 606
maintenance (*xwārišn ud dārišn*) 107, 123–124, 137–138, 141–142, 144, 147, 160, 173, 181–182, 199, 217, 224, 244, 252, 256, 258, 362, 372, 385, 464–467, 583, 587, 628, 644–645, 681
see also nourishment
Malalas 57
malevolence 417, 422, 738
malice, malicious intent 413–414, 422, 431, 472–473, 482–483, 570, 740
Mālikī 625
al-Ma'mun, Caliph 35
Mandaic 435, 514, 618
mandate 88, 264, 267, 269–270, 286, 290, 301, 375, 388, 538–539, 543, 563
Mani 257
Manichaean 24, 41, 221, 623
Manichaeism 65, 373, 584
manslaughter 62, 431–432
see also homicide
manumission 44, 104, 109–110, 125, 331, 599, 614
see also slavery
manus 78, 107, 121, 125, 136, 138, 145, 150, 179, 750, 786–787, 794
see also sālārīh
Manuščihr 33–34, 167, 379–380, 384–385, 453, 461, 663, 746
Mār Abā, Catholicos 47, 94, **155–157**, 232, 385, 492–493, 511, 527, 535, 572–573, **575–581**, 620
Mār Simeon, Catholicos 49
Mār Simon 573
Marakanda 41
Māraspand (*rad*) 742–743, 746
mard ī ahlaw (righteous man) 168, 217, 385, 464, 662, 774
mard ī šahr (citizen) 102–103, **114–117**, 120, 125, 207, 210, 245, 360, 434, 774
Mardag (jurisconsult) 565–566, 746
Mardag Pusānweh (jurisconsult) 746
Mardbūd (*mowbedān mowbed*) 277, 292, 746
margarzān (capital crime) 116, 172–173, 216, 236, 291, 340, 363–364, 410, 417, 429–431, 433–434, 436, 458, 462, 467, 469, 477–478, 480–483, 485, 489, 491, 519–520, 546–547, 549, 572, 574–575, 578, 580–583, 585–586, 595, 649–650, 652–653, 677, **738–740**, 753, 774–775, 786, 788, 790, 794, 797
Mark 581
marriage *see čagar*-marriage; consensus marriage, endogamy; exogamy; matrimony; *pādixšāy*-marriage and temporary marriage
martyrs 46, 49, 511, 572, 579–580, 584–585
martyrdom 46, 49
marzbān (title) 55

Māsabadān 294
master of the house *see kadag-xwadāy*
masturbation 453–454
Mas'ūdī 52, 54, 98, 373, 516
materfamilias 122–124, 129, 538, 546
see also kadag-bānūg
matrilineal descent 127–128, 258, 673
matrimony 47, 78–79, 87, 94–95, 122–123, 128–129, 131–135, 139–141, 143–148, 152–162, 183–186, 231–234, 254, 259, 305, 453, 566, 578, 628, 630–632, 637, 726, 729
see also čagar-marriage; consensus marriage; endogamy; exogamy; *pādixšāy*-marriage and temporary marriage
Matthew 581
mature person (*purnāy*) 76, 173, 182, 220, 303, 649–650
maturity (*purnayīh*) 122, 124, 147, 174, 180, 182–183, 215, 231, 234, 256, 303, 360–362, 396, 398, 458, 649, 729
Māzandarān 18–19, 437
Mazdaism 8, 10, 26, 60, 401, 454, 573
Mazdak/Mazdakism 95, 187, 256–257, 294
Mazdakite doctrine 11, 76, 93, 111–113, 188, 253, **256–259**, 262, 294, 464, 493, 578, 583, 669–673
Mazdean/Mazdeans 2–3, 6, 10–11, 24, 33, 46–48, 59, 65, 118–120, 130, 146, 152, 162, 181, 184, 219–220, 257, 263, 403, 409, 452–453, 495–496, 520, 525–529, 532, 552, 573, 575, 578–579, 591, 620, 665
see also māzdēsn/māzdēsnān
māzdēsn/māzdēsnān (Mazdean) 119, 260, 263, 520, 528, 665, 671–672
mediation of conflicts 369–370, 407–409, 488–489, 494–496, 498, 522, 529
Mēdōmāh (jurisconsult) 29, 32–33, 36, 64, 236, 386, 744, 746
mehdādestānīh (extension of justice) 72–73, 379, 384–385, 569, 571, 658
see also behdādestānīh and *wehdādestānīh*
memorandum 283–284, 291–292, 298, 574–575, 578–579, 741
see also ayādgār
Menōymardān (jurisconsult) 746
mens rea **412–413**, 424, 451, 457, 460, 570–571
menstruation 452–453, 446, 452–453, 457–458, 481, 570, 650, 695
mental element of an offence **412–414**, 416, 421–422, 424, 451, 457, 460, 570
see also mens rea
merchants 41–42, 97, 280, 310, 372–374, 376, 387, 662
Mesopotamia 40, 49, 590
Mihr (Mithra) 9, 260, 263–264, 278, 306, 401, 462, 538, 552, 731
mihr (contract) 7, 119, 260, 262–263, 462, 528, 666, 775
Mihr-Ādurfarrbay 520
Mihrān 99
Mihrbandag 283
Mihrēn 84, 106, 158, 223, 235, 266–267, 269, 273, 303–304, 327, 330, 335, 351–354, 374, 392–393, 396–397, 430–431, 612
Mihr-Narseh (*wuzurg framādār*) 16, 224, **226–227**, 255, 515, 601, 746
mihrōdruǰ (contract-breaker) 258, 262–263, 491, 574, 672–673, 775
mihrōdruǰīh (breach of contract) 68, 291, 313, 434, 595, 618, 775
Mihrōhrmazd 711
Mihrōy 282
Mihrpanāh 709
minor (*aburnāy*) 14, 75, 85–86, 103, 112, 121, 123, 135, 140, 177–180, 182, 225, 235, 239, 321, 410, 418, 420, 424–425, 457–458, 463–465, 477, 482–483, 528, 532, 535, 681
miscarriage 452–453
Mishna 50, 606–607
mistress of the house **122–124**, 129–130, 132, 137, 140, 142, 181, 208, 232,

234, 303, 361–362, 539, 556, 645–646, 649, 772
see also kadag-bānūg
Mithra 9, 260, 306–307, 317, 401, 462, 552
miϑōsāst (false teaching) 424–425, 427–429, 433, 466, 468, 681, 775
mortgage of the fruits *see antichresis* and *grawagān/grawagānīh*
mortgage of the substance *see āgraw/āgrawīh*; *hypotheca* and hypothec
Moses 40, 50
mosques 18, 626
movable property 190, 194, 206, 212, 316–317, 324, 326–328, 331–332, 334–335, 341, 343, 378, 617, 624–625, 639
Movsēs Kałankatuatsʻi 56
mowān handarzbed 502, **508–510**, 525, 546, 742–743, 745, 747, 775
mowbed 21, 34, 36, 55, 65, 86, 94, 97, 171, 180–181, 217, 227, 233, 241, 254, 257, 276, 278, 284, 288, 291–296, 303, 362, 398, 403, 408, 432, 463, 485, 491, 495–496, **503–504**, 505, 509, 512, 523–525, 530–532, 545–546, 574–575, 577, 587, 645, 741–747, 775
mowbedān mowbed 21, 34, 36, 65, 86, 94, 217, 241, 247, 278, 281, 291–294, 303, 362, 398, 462–463, 485, 491, 495, 503–504, **507–509**, 511, 523–525, 530–532, 545, 574–575, 577, 587, 645, 741–747, 775
Mugh documents 42–43, 280
Muḥammad, prophet of Islam 621
muhr see seals and following entries
muhr ī ēwar (reliable/binding seal) 296, 299–300, 547, 550–551, 593, 727, 775
muhr ī pad kār-framān dāštan (anonymous administrative seal) 271, 293, 295–296, 300, 511, 515, 550–551, 580, 583, 595, 743, 775
muhr ī wāwarīgān (valid seal) 51, 288–289, **296–298**, 300–301, **550–551**, 592, 593, 645, 775, 791
muhr ī wizurd (genuine seal) 296, 299, 300, 550–551, 547, 775, 793
muhraqē wāwarīgānē 592–594, 602
muhr-dād (document of seal transfer) 296, 300, 775
Muqaddimat al-ʾadab 45
Muslims 259, 383–384, 630, 640
Mustbahrnāmag 744
mustgarzīh (complaint of appeal) 524–525, 776
mutilation, penalty for theft 313, **439–447**, 444, 449, 451, 459, 584, 683, 686–687
see also band ud drōš and *drōš*
mutʿa (Shīʿite temporary marriage) 158–159, 162, **628–632**

nāmag (document, transcript, protocol) *see hišt-nāmag*; *paymān-nāmag*; *pursišn-nāmag*; *saxwan-nāmag*; *uzdād-nāmag*; *wizōst (wizōstan)-nāmag*; *xwēškārīh nāmag*; *yazišn-nāmag* and *zastbūd-nāmag*
nāmag-niyān (archive) 218, 227, 270, 273, 285, 741, 776
nāmag/gittag (foundation deed) 227, 272, **275–279**, 284, 293, 766, 776
nāmag/gittag ī nēk (valid document; transfer list) 275, **278–279**, 284, 766, 776
nāmagānīh (cult of the souls of the ancestors) 35, 121, 131, 140, 178, 218, 220, 231, 254, 258, 461, 647–648, 652–653, 670, 776
Nāmagīhā ī Manuščihr 33
nām-burdār/nām-burdārīh (name bearer/bearing) 120–121, 131, 138, 174, 765, 776
name-bearer *see nām-burdār*
nameless *see abē-nām*
nāmōsā 615
Naqš-e Rağab 16, 276
Naqš-e Rostam 16, 222, 276
Nariman Hoshang 38
nasā (dead matter) 28, 738, 739, 740

nasks ('bundles'; divisions of the Avesta) **24–28**, 32, 60–61, 66, 116, 203, 404, 423, 439–440, 443, 446, 467, 487, 516, 522, 653–654, 668, 674, 685
negligence 92, 183, **412–413**, 417–422, 424, 444–446, 463, 570–571, 688
see also kadōzēd
Nehardea 49
Nērangestān 27, 400, 403, 435, 469, 474, 537, 698
Nestorian law *see* East Christian law
Nestorians *see* East Christians
New Testament 615
Nēw-Gušnasp (jurisconsult) 746
next-of-kin marriage *see* endogamy and *xwēdōdah*
nexum 353
nibāg/nabāg (hostage) 117, 324, 326–327, 329, **332–335**, 682, 777
nibēg (template) 81, **270–272**, 285, 777
see also aswār-nibēg and *dast-nibēg*
nibištag (bill of indictment) 74, 79, 285, 429, 432, 510, 546, 549, 573–575, 578–579, 712, 742–743, 777
see also bill of indictment
Nīgādom (*nask*) 25, 60–61, 404, 674, 679, 682
nihādag (foundation) 221–222, 312, 315, 643, 777
nikāḥ 628–629
Nisā documents 513
nisāk see sāk
Nīšāpūr 141
Niyāyišn 30, 312, 435
nobility 93–95, 98, 100, 102, 110–111, 113, 157, 174, 186–188, 253–255, 259, 294, 311, 369, 372, 376, 492, 496, 516, 636
nobles 9, 11, 42, 47, 53, 94, 99–101, 103–104, 106, **110–113**, 119–120, 122, 124–126, 151, 162–163, 169, 172, 187, 254–256, 258, 311, 322, 360, 516, 573, 577, 582, 631
see also āzād and *āzādān*
Nokonzok 43
nomos 2
non-Iranian 116–117, 384, 528
see also an-ēr
notoriety 575, 584, 595
nourishment 74–75, 124, 138, 217, 463–464, 467–468, 645, 656
see also maintenance
Novellae 57
Noxzād 283
noxious creatures (*xrafstar*) *see* animals
Numerus Negidius (N.N.) 223, 430

oath 39, 72–73, 79, 196, 258, 272, 285, 359, 361–364, 430–431, 462, 497, 507, 518, 521, 523–524, 530–531, 534, 537, 539, 542, 545, **551–560**, 563, 584, 586–587, 594, 611, 673, 682, 696–699
see also passāxt and *war*
obedience (of wives, children, slaves) 34, 123–124, 142–144, 138, 477
see also tarsagāhīh
obligatio, concept 306–307
obligations 306–399; according to social status 124; arising from barter 388–389; arising from contract 260–263, **306–310**, 311–315, 320, 322, 324–326, 343, 346, 363, 374, 416, 434, 555–558, 618, 697, 700–701, 768, 778, 787, 789; arising from delict 308, 311–312, 789; arising from sale 374–380, 380–382; arising from suretyship 349–359, 607; in *auctor*-ship 80, 385–387; of the *čagar*-father 145; of foreigners and infidels 119; of the guardian 182, 362, 446, 570, 780, 792; of heirs 140, 207–208, 214–215, 230–231, 308, 323; of the *kadag-xwadāy* 34, 130–131, 138, 145, 229–230, 363, 781; of slaves 109; of spouses 34; of women 32, 79, 136, 142, 144, 159, 165, 171, 362, 765; release from 339, 364–367; religious 65, 75, 119–120, 133, 143, 155, 162, 175, 219, 637, 646;

terminology 87, 89, 318; towards animals 91
see also tōzišn; contract; credit law and suretyship
obstinacy 140–141, 490
obstruction of justice 236, 270, 289, 440, 499, 504, 509, 522, 537, 539–542, 559, **561–569**, 578, 581, 686
see also azišmānd and *waštagīh*
offences, Zoroastrian degrees of *see pāyag*
offences pertaining to the soul *see winā̆h ī ruwānīg*
offences regarding opponents/adversaries *see winā̆h ī hamēmālān*
Ohrmazd (Ahura Mazdā) 7–8, 119, 261, 133, 184, 261, 264, 311, 453, 464, 665, 671
Ohrmazd I (270/272–273 CE) 276, 704, 731, 743
Ohrmazd rūz (first day of the month) 353–354, 519
Ohrmazd-Ardaxšēr 295, 743, 745
opponent *see hamēmāl*
ordeal *see* oath; *passāxt* and *war*
order *see framān* and *kār-framān*
ōstān (province) 280, 283, 505, 511
ōstāndār (governor of a province) 272, 280–281, 283, 295, 511–513, 517, 778
overreaching (offence) 334, 388
owner/ownership of the fruits *see bar-xwēš/bar-xwēšīh*
owner/ownership of the substance *see bun-xwēš/bun-xwēšīh*
ownership (*xwēšīh*), category of property in the total patrimonial estate 178, 204–206, 207, **210–212**, 229–230, 237, 750, 791; claim to 80, 304, 385, 387, 795; concept of 77–78, **193–202**, 212, 639, 796; co-ownership 247–252, 281, 365, 752, 769, 779; distinguished from physical control 316; distinguished from possession, 74, **193–202**, 639, 759, 761; formulae and terminology 190, 238–239, 240, 390–395, 597–598, 782–783, 789; impeding a person's right to 756, 793; judgement of the Divine Judge on 7; lawsuits regarding 499, 506–507, 509, 513, 542–544, 556, 558, 561–568, 682; Mazdakite doctrine on 258, 670–671; of acquisitions 139, 192–193; of the compensation for theft 441–442, 447, 449, 457–458, 460, 687, 763, 769; of a fire 217–218, 222, 225; of the fruits (*bar*) distinguished from ownership of the substance (*bun*) **198–202**, 214–215, 254, 278, 603–606, 625–627, 758; of immovable property 264, 269, 528; of mortgaged property/pledge 324–325, 327–329, 331, 334–339, 343–344, 617–618; of *ruwān*-property 223–224; of slaves 105, 375–376; title to 89; transfer of 82, 242, 266–267, 269, 302–303, 376, **389–399**, 646, 652, 707–708, 729–730, 734, 760
see also bar-xwēšīh; *bun-xwēšīh* and *xwēšīh*
Oxus 41

Pābag 167, 226, 274
paččēn (copy) 709, 762
see also hampaččēn
pactum 263, 307, 462
padān ī dēn (religious authorities) 171, 181, 254, 651, 782
pādifrāh (punishment) 1, 178, 481, 595, 782
pādirāy (receipt) **281–283**, 298, 782
padīrišn (acceptance) 303–304, 391–392, 398–399, 522, 546, 653–654, 664, 782
pādixšāy (authorized, entitled) **85–89**, 108, 116, 223, 270, 329–330, 335, 337, 340, 344, 356, 368, 375, 384, 387, 436, 504, 538, 546–547, 549, 583, 612–614, 625, 642–645, 652,

662–663, 672, 676–677, 694, 731, 742, 762, 765, 772, 777, 782, 793
pādixšāy-bride 151
pādixšāy-children/offspring 138, 172, 233, 647–648
pādixšāy-daughter 252, 636, 654, 794
pādixšāy-father 172
pādixšāy heirs 237
pādixšāy-husband 34, 131, 137, 142–145, 147, 151, 161, 172, 184, 726, 787
pādixšāy-marriage 78–79, 106, 121–124, 126, 128–132, **134–142**, 143–144, 146–150, 154–155, 157, 159–163, 175–176, **183–185**, 231, 234, 251, 255–256, 267, 299, 631, 636, 756, 769, 772, 794
pādixšāy-son 179, 208, 232, 360, 794
pādixšāy-spouses 273, 770
pādixšāy-widow 154
pādixšāy-wife/wives 133, 137, 140, 142, 162, 166, 170, 175, 187, 191, 233, 245, 251–252, 269, 361, 397, 437, 449, 460, 465, 637, 646–651, 656, 724, 726, 745, 794, 798
pādixšāyīh(ā) (authorization, entitlement) 85, 112, 139, 292, 305, 408, 782
pādixšīr (foundation deed) 222, 225, 227, **275–276**, 278, 285, 782
pahikār-rad/radīh (person involved in a judicial dispute/judicial dispute); opposite: *a-pahikār-rad/radīh* **404–411**, 425, 495, 529, 674–678, 782–783
Pahlavi Archive 17–18, 200, 275, 278–281, 283, 298, 390, 511
Pahlavi papyri 15, 17, 58, 389, 511–512, 515
Pahlavi Riwāyat of *Ādurfarrbay and Farrbay-srōš* 34–35, 696–699
Paikūlī inscription 111, 332
Pandectae 57
paristār (maidservant) 172, 454, 457, 650, 694
Parišwār 52
Parišwārgar, King of 281, 345, 437, 701, 736
Parišwārgar rad 437, 505, 723, 725, 728, 730, 734
P'arpi 55
Pārsīs 38, 151, 168, 385
Partav 56
part-debtor *see xwāstag-tōzišn*
partnership 129, 140, 166, 234, 244, **245–253**, 308–309, 325, 351, 355, 360, 365, 431
see also hambāyīh
pasēmāl (defendant) 8, 108, 191, 275, 287, 290, 300, 388, 408, 497–498, 502–503, 506, 522–523, 533–535, 537, 539–541, 548, 555, 559, 563–565, 568, 587, 668, 697, 717–722, 783
pašn (contract) 117, 261, 264, 285, 333, 553, 672, 688, 783
passand (leniency in justice) 70–73, 334, 569, 571, 610–611, 616, 783
passandārīh (pawn) 317, 324, 326, 334–335, 783
passāxt (ordeal) 552–553, 558, 560, 698, 783
see also oath; *war*
pašt (contract) 82, 262, 264–267, 285, 297, 375, 380, 393, 659–660, 727, 783
see also contract
paterfamilias 5, 74, 77, 106–107, **120–122**, 123, 128–132, 137, 140, 143–144, 153–155, 159–160, 163, 166, 170, 175–176, 178–180, 182, 187, 202–203, 207, 213–214, 245, 254, 302, 340, 360–363, 465, 546, 555–556, 582, 586, 604, 612, 614–615, 637, 651
see also kadag-xwadāy
patit (penitential text) 30, 400, 403, 468–469; (redemption) 413, 756
Patit ī pašēmānīh II 738
patrilineal descent 105–106, 123, **127–129**, 133, 157, 162, 166, 171, 184–186, 210, 258, 452–453, 631–633, 636

patrimonial (residuary) estate *see abarmānd*
patrimonial (residuary) estate of a descent group *see abarmānd ī pidarān*
patrimonium 74, 130, 189, 639
see also abarmānd
pawn 117, 249, 302, 304, 312, 317, 323–324, **326–335**, 337, 339, 341, 357, 377–378, 390, 617, 619, 660, 682
see also graw and pledge
pāyag (degree of sin) 414, 439, 442, 449–450, 457–458, 467, **468–486**, 687, 694, 697, 757, 783; (social rank) 258, 670, 766, 783
see also degrees of sins/offences
pāyandān (surety) 325–326, 350, 354–357, 366, 783
see also hampāyandān and surety
pāyandānīh (suretyship) 326, **349–359**, 366, 783
see also hampāyandānīh and suretyship
paymān (contract) 235, 251, 265, **266–268**, 273–274, 286, 304–305, 327, 330, 335, 351, 368, 375, 439, 568, 657–658, 672, 683–684, 686, 707–709, 726, 729–730, 784
see also contract and suretyship
paymānag (contract) 22, 261, 408, 726
see also paymān and *paymān-nāmag*
Paymānag ī kadag-xwadāyīh 22
paymān-nāmag (written contract) **266–268**, 273, 285–286, 288–289, 320–321, 345, 701, 703, 736, 784
see also contract; *paymān* and *paymānag*
payment entitlement *see čak*
payment order *see framān*
Pāzand 22, 30, 96, 164–165, 418, 680
penal law 4, 30, 400–401, 403–405, 442, 468, 470–472, 474, 480, 485, 487, 744
penalties 4, 11, 29, 32, 34, 37, 68, 108, 307–308, 313, 361, 400, 403–404, 421, 427–429, 431, 440, 442, 444–445, 447, 449, 451, 458–460, 467–469, 477–479, **481–485**, 491, 493, 531, 562, 570, **584–585**, 677, 695
see also degrees of sins/offences
penitence 413
Penjikend 42
Pentateuch 50
penury 660
Pērōz (jurisconsult) 396, 746
Pērōz ī Weh-Ohrmazdān (jurisconsult) 746
Pērōz, son of Yazdegird II (459–484 CE) 226, 602, 746
Pērōz-Mihr 282
Pērōzohrmazd 735
Persarmenia 55
personae alieni iuris 124, 126, 398
personae sui iuris 120, 124–125
personal security *see pāyandānīh* and suretyship
pēšag (social estate, guild) 95, 98, 120, 138, 268, 372, 437, 448, 510–511, 517–518, 662–663, 723, 784
pēšag-framādār (head of the guild) 33
pēšag-sālār (head of the guild) 268, 372, 517–518, 784
Pēšagsīr (jurisconsult) 64, 244, 501, 744, 746
pēšēmāl (plaintiff) 8, 108, 191, 275, 289, 300, 408, 497–498, 502–503, 506–508, 524, 533–535, 537, 539–541, 548, 555, 565, 585, 668, 697, 717–722, 784
Peshawar 43
pēšīgān-wāspuhragān (dowry) 140–141, 232–233, 274, 515, 784
see also wāspuhragān
pēš-tōzišnīh (advance payment) 325–326, 339, 340, 363, 784
see also charge and pre-payment
Phoenician 377, 619, 660
physical element of an offence *see actus reus*
physical injury *see rēš*; *zanišn*; *zaxm*
piae causae 622–623, 640
Pidarōš (woman's name) 547, 731–734

Pilate, Pontius 581
pious foundations , 16, 56, 58, 65, 87, 94, 96, 98–99, 128–129, 135–136, 178, 180, 187, 200, 205, 210–211, 216–217, **220–230**, 237, 264, 266, 284–285, 311–312, 340, 363–364, 391, 400, 407–409, 418, 461–462, 505–506, 515, 550, 589, 597, 622–627, 638, 640, 653, 680
see also ādurān ātaxšān; fire foundations and *ruwānagān*
pious gifts *see ahlawdād*
pī'rā 344, 617
plaintiff 8, 104, 108, 116–117, 191, 196, 228, 268, 275, 287–290, 300, 331, 334, 350, 361, 363, 386–389, 408, 415, 430, 497, 500, 503, 506, 508, 524, 533–535, 537–544, 548, 555–557, 562–567, 586, 640, 668, 697, 717–722
see also pēšēmāl
Plato 2
plebeians 99, 104, 112–113, 582
see also commoners
pledge 77, 80, 106, 117, 138, 140, 249, 262, 266, 301–304, 312, 317, 323–324, **326–336**, 337, 339, 341, 343–345, 349–350, 353–354, 377–378, 390, 501, 504, 540–541, 563–566, 568–569, 598, 607, 612, 616–617, 619, 660, 682
see also graw; *ǰām*; *ǰāmag*; *nabāg/nibāg*; *passandārīh* and pawn
pledgee *see grawdār*
policeman (*frēzwan*) 288, 429, 497, 500, 518–519, 521, 574
polyandry 133, 137, 142, 157, 249, 299, 453, 631
polygyny 133, 142, 157, 185, 254, 256, 299, 453, 631
pōryōtkēšān (first authorities of the faith) 60
possessio 77, 194, 210, 639
see also dārišn
possession (*dārišn*) 761; claim to 80, 200, 304, 362, 540, 543–544, 562, 597, 718; distinguished from ownership, 74, 77–78, 139, **193–197**, 201–202, 205, 246, 271, 395, 566, 639, 671, 708, 759, 761; distinguished from mere physical control 316; hereditary 205–210, 229–230, 237, 340, 363, 750, 781, 796; for the soul 222–229; illegal 406, 436, 438, 446, 519, 598, 646, 775; in *stūrīh* 213–219, 734; interim possession 500–501; joint possession 247–253, 258, 670, 769–770, 779; obstruction of 562–563, 567–568, 756, 793; of economic resources 95; of a fire 277–278; of a grant 513; of a pledge 324–325, 327–331, 337, 339, 344, 767; proof of 386; transfer of 240–244, 302, 341, 344
see also dārišn
possessions, categories of 178, 192; illegally acquired 688; of families/noble lineages 112, 128, 187; terminology 191–192
see also abarmānd and property
post-mortem rites 222, 231, 254, 781, 785
post-Yazdgird era (PYE) 19, 21, 35, 715
potestas 121–122, 124–125, 177, 179
see also sālārīh
poverty 70, 380, 610, 624
praecipuum 204
praefectus Judaeae 581
praegustator 272
Praetor 210
pre-payment 325–326, 339, 363, 660–661
see also pēš-tōzišnīh
priesthood 9–11, 93–96, 100, 113, 126, 136, 157, 187–188, 254, 258–259, 295, 403, 454, 461, 496, 507–508, 511, 527, 672
primogeniture 129, 231, 256
principal, of a thing/property *see bun*
privileged marriage *see pādixšāy*-marriage
Procopius 57, 111
promiscuity 452–453

property, various categories *see xīr* and *xwāstag*
property for ceremonies, liturgies, rituals (*pad ruwān yazišn*) 121, 140, 178, 220, **222–223**, 254, 623, 625, 781, 785, 795, 797
property for pious purposes (*pad ahlawdād*) 135–136, 205, 208, 210–211, **220**, 222, 237, 254, 340, 364, 461, 623–624, 652–653, 753, 779, 781
property for substitute succession (*pad stūrīh*) 35, 84, 87–88, 145, 160–161, 163, 166, 170, 173–174, 178, 197, 200, 205–212, **213–219**, 229–232, 234, 254–256, 278, 367, 461, 547, 653, 728–734
property for the soul (*pad ruwān*) 35, 197, 200, 202, 205–213, 216, 219, **220–230**, 231, 234, 250, 254–255, 270, 277, 292, 312, 623–625
property in hereditary ownership (*pad xwēšīh ī xwēš*) 195, 795
property in hereditary possession (*pad xwāstagdārīh*) 205, **206–210**, 229–230
see also xwāstagdārīh
property in ownership (*pad xwēšīh*) **195**, 197, **210–212**, 215, 217, 229–230, 237, 246, 258, 392, 394, 398, 499, 513, 544, 564, 567, 625
property in ownership of the fire *see xwēšīh ī ātaxš*
property inherited from the forefathers *see abarmānd ī pidarān*
property of the fire(s) *see xīr ī ātaxš/ātaxšān*
property of the soul *see xwāstag ī ruwān*
property yielding revenue *see barōmand*
proprietas 77, 194, 639, 796
see also ownership and *xwēšīh*
prostitute (*ǰeh/ǰehi*) 452, 650, 771
see also whore
prostitution 159, 629
protocol *see saxwan-nāmag*; *pursišn-nāmag*; *uzdād-nāmag*; *wizōst-nāmag*; *yazišn-nāmag* and *zastbūd-nāmag*
proxy (*stūr*) 38, 76, 88, 118–119, 121, 131–134, 160, 162, **167–174**, 181, 184–185, 208, 213–216, 254, 273, 284, 383, 461–462, 465, 504–505, 509, 513, 528, 613, 648–653, 656
see also stūr
puberty 79, 146
Pumbedita 49
punishment for theft *see band ud drōš* and *drōš*
purgatory (**hamiyastagān*) 402
purnāy (mature) 76, 103, 120, 125, 238–239, 396, 647–649, 653–654, 679, 681, 729, 784
purnāyīh (maturity) 182, 238
pursišn-nāmag (*accusatio scripta*) 51, 74, 79, 272, 284–285, 291, 295, 463, 491, 505, 515, 529, 546, 557, **572–575**, 576, 579–581, 586, 594–595, 602, 743, 754–755, 763–764, 775–776, 784
pus ī padīriftag (adopted son) 170, 176, 179, 647, 650, 784, 786
see also frazand ī padīriftag; *duxt ī ī padīriftag* and adoption
Pusag 430
Pusānūz (jurisconsult) 746
Pusānweh (jurisconsult) 233, 242, 394, 746
Pusānweh ī Āzādmardān (jurisconsult) 506, 743, 746
Pusānweh ī Burzādurfarrbay(ān) (jurisconsult) 746

qāḍī 623
qafīz 348
qanāt 199, 250–251
qarāba 635, 638
Qiddušin 596–598
qinyan ha-gūf 603–606
Qom 18, 622
Qunyat al-Munya 45, 280
qurba 624, 626–627
Qurʾān 141, 633, 629
Qurʾānic heirs 633

Rabāṭak inscription 43
Rabba 607–608
rabŭn/rabŭna (earnest money) 379, 619, 660, 785
see also arra/arrabo/arrha and earnest money
rad (spiritual master, *ratu*) 33, 62–63, 65, 181, 227, 273, 284, 292, 328–329, 383, 400–401, 403–405, 407–409, 411, 425, 437–438, 485, 488–489, 495–496, 498, 503, **505–506**, 507, 509, 511–513, 522–526, 529–530, 532, 576–577, 583, 674–677, 681, 723–726, 728, 730, 734, 741–743, 746, 785
rad ī xwēš (one's own *rad*) **407–409**, 489, 495–496, 498, 529, 532, 785
rād (donor) 389, 396–397, 399, 785
Rādohrmazd (jurisconsult) 248, 376, 746
Rahāg 728–729
Rām (21st day of the month) 717, 719, 736
Ran 601
rank in the social hierarchy (*gāh*, *pāyag*) 8, 33, 94, 96–97, 100–103, 106, 110–112, 114–115, 120–121, 127, 130, 138, 209, 258, 260, 271, 369, 372, 516, 582, 638, 664, 670
see also gāh; *pāyag*
Rashbam 601
Rašn 9–10, 401–403, 552, 558, 646, 698, 704, 708–709, 717
Rašnu 9, 401, 552
Rašnweh 704
Rāstdād, son of Wištāsp 437, 724, 733–734
Rav 630
Rav Huna 530,
Rav Nahman 608, 630
Rav Yehuda 600
Rav Yosef 607–608
Rava 530, 600, 602
Ray 99, 294
Ra'y 623, 626
real security *see āgraw/āgrawīh*; *graw/grawīh* and *grawagān/grawagānīh*
rebellion *see xwadāy-dušmenīh*
receipt *see pădīrāy*
record of interrogation/investigation (criminal trial) *see pursišn-nāmag*
record of recitation (oath-taking) *see yazišn-nāmag*
record of statements (civil trial) *see saxwan-nāmag*
registers *see ātaš hamār *dibīrag*; *āxur hamār *dibīrag*; *dād *dibīrag*; *ganǧ hamār *dibīrag*; *kadag hamār *dibīrag*; *ruwānagān *dibīrag* and *šahr hamār *dibīrag*
see also archives
remuneration of the guardian (*sālār*) and the proxy (*stŭr*) *see srēnag/sēnag masāy ud bāzā masāy*
rent 192, 197, 209, 213, 281, 287, 297, 325, 338, 343, **367–372**, 402, 513, 563, 703, 712–713, 737
rental 592
request *see xwāhišn*
rēš (bodily harm) 7, 332, 383, 407, 411–412, 414–415, 423, **425–429**, 433, 442, 444–445, 448, 451, 456–458, 473–476, 480, 615, 665–666, 676–678, 682–684, 691–692, 694–695, 706–707, 727, 785
Rēšestān/rēšēstān (section on bodily harm) 423, 425, 679, 681–683, 785
Resh lakish 605–606
responsibility of officials *see xwēškārīh*
Restoration (*frašgird*) 6–7, 184, 219, 401–402, 665–666
retaliation (*abāz zaxm*) 406–407, 411, 488, 602, 678, 751
revenue 78, 139, 192, 197, 213, 216–217, 220, 222, 229, 402, 504
Rēw-Ardašīr 49
reward 263, 479, 624, 698
righteous (*ahlaw*; *weh*) 7, 65, 96, 139, 168, 217, 220, 260, 304, 385, 400, 435, 462, 464, 495, 498, 529, 658, 663, 666–667, 675, 728, 738, 765, 774
righteous gifts *see ahlawdād*
righteous man *see mard ī ahlaw*

rites 32–33, 61, 148, 187, 220, 222, 231, 254, 258, 403, 623, 625, 644, 646, 672, 695
see also yazišn
ritual 3, 8, 21, 23, 25, 27–28, 31–33, 36–37, 50, 58, 60–62, 64, 76, 91–93, 121, 140, 151, 178, 218–220, 222–223, 225, 254, 258–259, 359, 400–401, 403–404, 453, 481, 484, 487–488, 518, 528–529, 552–553, 644, 663, 668
see also yazišn
rituals for the soul of the deceased *see ruwān yazišn*
Riwāyat ī Ēmēd ī Ašawahištān 36
Riwāyats, New Persian 30, **38–39**, 59, 131, 134–135, 141, 143, 145, 164, 168, 232–233, 477, 480, 484, 486, 553
Riwāyats, Pahlavi 31–37
Rōb (Rūī), northern Hindukush 43
robber 7, 37, 312–314, 373, 382, 413–414, 422, 424, **434–439**, 442–445, 449–451, 455–457, 565, 584, 618, 677, 681, 689–692
see also appar/apparag and robbery
robbery 400, 421, **434–439**, 450, 489, 533, 572, 738–739, 754; categorization as offence regarding opponents 62, 492–493; definition as stealing openly 67–68; distinguished from theft 313–314, 434–439; intent of 413–415, 422, 424; penalty for 443–447, 492–494; lawsuits 565, 570; transposition to other fields (credit law; breach of contract; overreaching; sexual offences) 312–314, 382, 414, 434, 442, 447–449, 455–456, 458–459, 589, 618–619, 690–695
see also apparīh and robber
Roman (Byzantine) law 109, 188–189, 212, 263, 395, 588, 621, 638–639; classical sources 57–58; concepts and institutions 87, 115, 125, 127, 136, 174–175, 177, 179, 204, 216, 261, 305–308, 311, 316–317, 319, 340–341, 368, 381, 411, 462, 565, 604–605, 618, 626–627; (lack of) juridical equality 11; legal proceedings 89, 196–198, 304, 385–386, 542–543, 581, 596; terminology 5, 77–78, 80, 139–141, 188–189, 192, 194–195, 209–210, 223, 235, 264, 274, 323–324, 353, 368, 377–378, 390, 392, 430, 618–619, 660
Rome 55, 57–58, 128, 585, 638
Rosh, commentator of the Talmud 601
royal property *see šāhīgān*
rōzīg (daily ration, ration) 224, 252–253, 583, 785
rōzpīg (prostitute) 650
Rūī (Rōb), northern Hindukush 43
ruwān (soul) 7, 35, 197, 200–202, 205–213, 216, 219, **220–230**, 231, 234, 250, 254–255, 270, 277, 292, 312, 401–402, 413, 461, 479–480, 623–627, 660, 666, 698, 785
see also ruwān yazišn; *ruwānagān* and property for the soul
ruwān yazišn (rituals for the soul of the deceased) 121, 140, 178, 785
ruwānagān (pious foundations) 77, 98–99, 218, **220–229**, 254, 270, 623–625, 627, 640, 785
ruwānīg see wināh ī ruwānīg

šābestān (eunuch) 650
Šābuhr I (239/240–270/272 CE), fire foundations 222, 225–227, 515; inscriptions 4, 16, 99, 111–112, 271–272, 275–276
Šābuhr II (309–379 CE) 41, 600; persecution of Christians 46, 49, 572, 578, 580
sacrifice 27–28, 76, 91–92, 220, 577
see also animals
ṣadaqa 624
Saddar Bundahiš 484
Sagādom nask 26, 60
šāhān šāh bandag (subject of the King of Kings) **102–103**, 105, 109, 114–115, 120, 124–125, 169, 647, 649, 757, 785
see also bandag

šāhīgān (royal property) 209, 228, 270–271, 506, 512–513, 517, 583, 785
Šāhnāma of Firdausi 54, 97, 167
šahr (country, land, empire, state) *see dād ī šahr*; *ēwēn ī šahr*; *mard ī šahr*; *šahr dādwarān dādwar* and Ērānšahr
šahr dādwarān dādwar (Chief Judge of the State) 277, **502–503,** 508, 524–525, 742, 745, 786
see also dādwarān dādwar
šahrab (title) 515
aš-Šahrastānī 257
šahrdawer 502
šahrīg(ān) (title) 515–517, 786
šahryār(ān) 111, 786
šāk/nisāk (taxes) 227, 504–505, 512, 786
sālār (guardian) 177–183, 456, 549, 655–656, 750, 780, 782, 786; empowerment by 88, 116; of a fire 226, 601; of a pious foundation 254, 625–626, 627; public official 545, 796; remuneration of 76–77, 173–174, 182, 224, 787; rights 465; son as 147; supervisor of an estate 244; three types 179–181
see also a-sālār; *dūdag-sālār* and *xwāstag-sālār*
sālār ī būdag (natural guardian) 176, **179–180**, 182, 360–361, 786
sālār ī gumārdag (nominated guardian) **180–181**, 182, 203, 361, 504, 509, 786, 792
sālār ī kardag (appointed guardian) **180**, 302, 361, 504, 786
sālārīh (guardianship) 34–36, 83, 87, **177–183,** 231, 613, 642–645, 647–648, 655–656, 662, 692–693, 729, 738, 761, 781, 786–787; animals under 90; illegal 463; in *čagar*-marriage 144, 147; in *pādixšāy*-marriage 136, 138, 140, 142, 144, 154; in *xwasrāyēn/gādār*-marriage 147, 160; persons under 126, 235, 244, 385, 398; of a fire 94, 250, 277–278, 515; of pious foundations 187, 223, 625; release from 273; transfer of 88; women under 121–122, 124–125, 129, 166, 304, 458
see also dūdag-sālār(īh) and *xwāstag-sālār(īh)*
sale (*frōxš*; *frōxt*) 15, 20, 40, 43, 88, 141, 211–212, 264, 287, 301, **372–387,** 390, 414, 434, 596, 599, 657–663; breach of contract 313, 381–382, 434–435, 442, 449, 467, 618; contract 265–267, 285, 304, 320, **374–377**; earnest money **377–380,** 619; jurisdiction pertaining to 505, 507, 512; lawsuits 89, 116, 196, 297, **385–387,** 542–544; in public and private 380–382; of family members 104, 107; of immovable property 240, 376–377; of mortgaged property 340, 363; prohibited sales 382–385
Samarkand 41–42
Samuel, Jewish authority 527–528
sanctuary of a fire (*dādgāh*) 217–218, 225, 277, 761
Sar Mašhad 16, 276
Sāsān 167
Savādkūh 19
saxwan (statement in court) 7–8, 191, 478, 500–501, 504, 524, 553, 567–568, 668, 675, 683, 698, 727, 733, 781, 785–787
see also abēsaxwan; *saxwan-nāmag* and *waštag saxwanīh*
saxwan-nāmag (protocol/record/transcript of statements in a civil trial) 74, 79, 272, 279, 284–285, 289–290, 295, 301, **533–535**, 537, 541, 552, 557, 562, 572, 586, 595, 772, 776, 786
aš-Šaybānī 623
Šāyist nē šāyist 29, 32, 62, 400, 403
Sazā (woman's name) 437, 439, 723–724, 726–727
sazāgīh (suitability as *sālār* or *stūr*) 179, 647, 649, 653–654, 787

sazāgtar (most suitable as *sālār* or *stŭr*) 169–171, 180, 254, 647, 649, 652–655, 732, 787
see also wehsazāgtar
Saŋhauuācī 738
scales of justice (*tarāzūg*) 8–10, 402, 665, 789
scribes (*dibīr*) **96–100**, 124–125, 228, 252, 271–272, 274, 281, 285, 289, 311, 315, 345–347, 369–371, 373, 437, 497, 500–501, 508, 517–518, 702–703, 709, 711–712, 717–719, 721–723, 726, 735–736
seals (*muhr*) 16, 20, 268–270, **286–301**; administrative 271, 276–278, 287, **293–296**, 581, 583, 595, 709, 743, 763, 771; evaluation of 270, **296–301**, 550–551, 592, 620, 791; identification of 500, 519, 703, 769, 789; of legal authorities 267–268, 271, 280, 283–284, 287, **290–293**, 362, 504, 506, 509, 511–513, 515, 518, 521, 577, 580, 709, 741–742, 750, 758; of private individuals 286, **287–290**, 296, 303, 319, 346, 562, 710, 712, 714, 734; of witnesses 282–283, 304, 347; sealed contracts/documents/foundation deeds 273, 276–278; 285–286, 320–323, 326–327, 346, 365, 370–371, 375, 377, 380, 397–399, 501, 505, 531, 542, 550–551, 593–594, 614, 701, 726, 729, 737, 755, 762, 765, 793
see also gugāy-muhr; *muhr ī ēwar*; *muhr ī pad kar-framān dāštan*; *muhr ī wāwarīgān*; *muhr ī wizurd* and *muhr-dad*
security for a loan *see āgraw/āgrawīh*; *graw/grawīh*; *grawagān/grawagānīh*; *pāyandānīh* and suretyship
Šedreš (proper name) 721
Seleucia/Ctesiphon 49–50
Semitic 272, 275, 377, 521–522, 609, 619, 660
Serkhel, Mount in Savādkūh 19
servant of the fire *see ātaxš-bandag*; *ādurān-bandag* and *bandag ī ātaxš*
sexual offences 27, 62, 153, 159, 161, 313, 414, 424, 448–449, **452–460**, 462, 528, 562, 631, 673, 690–695, 749, 750, 766, 789
see also gād-duzīh; *tan-duzīh*
share (of property/inheritance) *see bahr*
share of the daughter (*bahr ī duxt/duxtīh*) 140, 153, 232, 757
share of the son (*bahr ī pus/pusīh*) 140, 232, 757
share of the wife (*bahr ī kadag-bānūg*, *bahr ī zanīh*) 123–124, 140, 153, 232, 757
shareholders 86, 108–109, 118–119, 200–201, 204–205, 207–210, 218, 229–230, 234, 242, 244, **245–253**, 256, 303, 345, 347, 360, 396, 445, 644, 702, 750, 758, 774, 797
see also brad ī hambay; *hambaragān* and *hambāy*
shareholding 129, 170, 209, 230, 234–235, **245–253**, 255, 259, 648
see also hambāyīh and *hamwindišn(īh)*
sheep 40, 76, 248, 262, 278–279, 329, 343, 378, 384–385, 440, 442, 617, 662–663
sheepdog 75, 464, 467
Shīʿite (Jaʿfarite) law 1, 15, 39, 127, 129, 133, 588, 621; law of succession 163, 589, **632–638**; *mutʿa* 158–159, 161–162, 589, **628–632**; *waqf* 622–627
Shīrāz 20, 218
siblings, marriage between 129–130, 152, 154–155, 458, 636; relationship of 175
ṣīge 158–159, 162, 628, 630–631
Šilag (scribe) *271–272*
sins, Zoroastrian degrees of *see pāyag*
sins pertaining to the soul *see wināh ī ruwānīg*
sins regarding opponents/adversaries *see wināh ī hamēmālān*

Sīrat Anušīrwān 54
Sīr-daryā 41
Sīrgān 33, 745
Sīrōze 30
Šīrzād (scribe) 721
Sīstān 167
Siwnik‘, 56
Siyāwaxš (jurisconsult) 746
slaves 40, 43–44, 92, 102–103, **104–110**, 112–113, 123–124, 168–169, 190, 221, 386, 563, 624–625, 650, 682; areas of occupation 107–108, 187, 592, 599–602, 753; as security/pledge 266, 324–325, 327–328, 330–332, 337–338, 343–344, 349, 375–376, 566, 617, 767, 790; causes of enslavement 104–107, 465; guardianship of 177, 182, 586–587, 646, 755, 789; legal status 125–126, 172, 200, 202, 212–213, 223, 226, 240–241, 243, 263, 302; legal status in litigation 108, 116–117, 125, 545–548, 565; manumission 108–110, 125–126, 331, 614, 619; offences committed by 432; sale of 377, 382–383; transfer of 304, 315, 388
see also anšahrīg; *bandag*
slavery 102, **104–110**, 168, 465, 600, 619
societas 246–247, 249–250, 252, 752, 768
see also hambāyīh
socius (*mērag*) 246, 252, 774
sodomy (*kunmarz*) 34, 452
sōgand (sulphurous water oath) 363, 539, **556**, 558, 560, 696, 698, 790
Sōgand nāma 39, 553
Sogdiana 41–42, 45
solvency 89, 351, 752, 790
solvent 355, 384, 566, 658, 663, 790
sorcerer (*ǰādūg*) 425, 433, 583–584, 681, 767
sorcery (*ǰādūgīh)* 422, 489–490, 493–494, 572, 583–584, 738–740, 759, 764, 771
see also witchcraft
Sōšāns (jurisconsult) 28, 64, 105
Spandarmad (12th month) 712, 718, 721–722
Sraoša 9, 401
see also Srōš
srēnag/sēnag masāy ud bazā masāy (remuneration of *sālār* and *stūr*) 76, **173–174**, 182, 203, 214, 643, 645, 648–649, 787
Srōš 9, 226, 401, 602, 696–697, 699
see also Sraoša
srōšōčaranām (degree of sin) 468–469, 471–473, 475, **476–477**, 482–484, 787
stahmag (oppressor) **435–436**, 450, 788
Staxr 294, 510, 546, 743
stēr (stater) 169, 262, 458, 647–648, 652
stipulatio 264, 305, 319
stipulation 72, 80–81, 84, 146, 170, 263–266, 285–286, 305, 390–399, 607
stōr (large cattle) 92, 168, 241, 262, 329, 440, 599
see also animals
stŭr (proxy, substitute successor) 38, 79, 134, 146, **168–174**, 178, 185, 273, 284, 366, 465, 632, 788; in *čagar*-marriage 160, 162; obligation to act as 123–124, 131, 137, 142, 144–145, 175, 636; prohibited to non-Zoroastrians 118, 528; nomination of 504–505, 509, 642–644, 646, 652, 655–656, 782; remuneration of 76, 173, 214, 464, 775, 787; replacement of 516; unsuitability as 172
see also tan-stŭr; *zīndag-stŭr* and following entries
stŭr ī būdag (natural proxy) 167, **170**, 171, 207–208, 504, 651, 756, 788
stŭr ī gumārdag (nominated proxy) **170–171**, 254, 651, 788
stŭr ī kardag (appointed proxy) **170**, 172, 176–177, 179–180, 214, 217, 461, 504, 647–651, 788
stŭrīh (substitute succession) 34–36, 77, 83–84, 87–88, 103, 111, 118, 121,

123–124, 133, 154, 156, 163–164,167, **168–174,** 179, 184, 229, 232, 236, 256, 367, 647–649, 728–734, 784, 788; children born in 175–176, 753; claim to 517, 547, 731–734; obligation to establish 174; practiced by Christians 620–621; property reserved for 153, 161, 166, 173, 178, 197, 200, 205–207, 209–211, **213–219,** 230–231, 234, 255, 750, 757, 781; sin of destroying 173, 258, 461–462, 653, 670, 738–740; suitability for 650, 787, 792; transfer of 509; trusteeship of a fire 217–219, 228, 278, 761
see also inheritance and preceding entries
substance *see bun*
substitute succession *see stŭrīh*
substitute successor (proxy) *see stŭr*
succession law *see abarmānd*; *ayōgēnīh*; *stŭrīh* and inheritance
suitability (for *sālārīh* and *stŭrīh*) *see sazāgīh*
sulphurous water oath (*sōgand*) 363, 556–558, 560, 790
summons (to court/hearing/presence of the king) 80, 189, 196, 369, 386, 438, 490, 493, 501, 507, 521–523, 533, 535–536, 540–542, 563, 576, 587, 715, 719, 724, 730
Sunnite 39, 159, 162–163, 621–622, 628–629, 632–633, 635, 638
Sūr saxwan 502
Sura 49, 629–630, 635
surety 309, 324–326, **349–359,** 366, 377, 606–608, 750–751, 764, 773, 780, 783, 785
see also hampāyandān; *pāyandān*
suretyship 51, 106, 247, 266, 324, 326, 329, **349–359,** 365–366, 509, 606–608, 783–784
see also hampāyandānīh and *pāyandānīh*
Surkh Kotal 43
*šus*ᵃ*r* (semen) 426, 433, 670, 683
Syriac, legal sources **46–49,** 58, 120, 155, 245, 492, 524, 526, 529, 535, 572, **575–580,** 584, 589; Iranian concepts **615–621**; terminology 70–73, 275, 297, 342, 347, 373, 378, 382, 435, 437, 450, 500, 502, 514–516, 531, 554, 573, 576, 593, 602, **609–615,** 660, 754, 757–758, 764
see also Corpus Iuris of Īšōʿbōxt

Tabarestān, legal documents from 5, **18–20,** 40, 56, 80, 129, 139, 182, 190, 196, 199–200, 209–210, 251–253, 255, 266–267, 272, 275, 280–281, 288, 290–291, 298, 311, 320–321, 336, 338, 343, 345, 361, 367, 369–372, 373, 385, 387, 437, 500, 505, 507, 514, 516, 523–524, 533–535, 537–538, 540–543, 547, 557, 587, 596, 621, 632, 660, 668; documents in the appendix 700–720; 722–737; Tansar-letter from 52–53
see also Tansar-letter
Ṭabarī 54, 97–99, 226, 512
tāg (lease) 209, 281, 301, **367–372,** 703, 712–713, 722, 737, 788
Taǧārib al-ʾumam 53–54
Tagōy (personal name) 711
tāiiu- (thief) 312–313, 382, 434–435, 450, 618
Tajikestān 41–42
tan (person, body) 7, 25, 60, 91, 158, 171, 386, 401–402, 410, 441, 665–666, 676–677, 683, 685–687, 712, 723–724, **788,** 794; person pledged as security 106, 117, 334, **351–354,** 357–359, 607, 773, 781, 788; personnel (of the court) 507–508, 788; pool members 707; process of identifying a person 288, 500, 519, 769; woman as her own guardian (*xwēš-tan/tan ī xwēš salār*) 88, 116, 546, 549, 750
tan-drustīh (good health) 237, 641, 644, 778, 789

tan-duzīh (body-theft) 414, 448, **455–460**, 462, 692–695, 789
tan-stūr (physical proxy) 171–172, 185, 789
see also zīndag-stūr
tanāpuhr (degree of sin) 308, 463, 467–469, **477–485**, 789
Tang-e Bolāghī 20
Tang-e Borāq 16, 20
tanīgzād (natural child) 175–176, 180
Tannaim 50, 606
Tansar letter 52–53; social estates 96–98, 100, 110–112, 255–256, 271, 372, 376; adultery 443, 449; criminal offences 490, 492–493, 572, 576, 579, 582; punishments 584; theft and robbery 442–445, 449, 459
Tansar/Tōsar 52, 274–275, 284, 443
Ta'rīḫ ar-rusul wa'l-mulūk 54
Tārīḫ-i Bal'amī 54
Tārīḫ-i Ṭabarestān 52
Ta'rīḫ sanī mulūk al-arḍ wa-'l-anbiyā' 54
tarsagāhīh (obedience); opposite: *a-tarsagāhīh* 123–124, 138, 142, 789
tāwān (fine) 92, 108, 182, 266–267, 308–309, 321–322, 389, 458–460, 466–467, 513, 517, 565, 701, 736, 766, 789
see also guharīg; *tōzišn* and compensation
taxes 46, 99, 209, 224, 227, 271, 367, 369, 504–505, 512–514, 517, 528, 591, 599–600, 602, 770, 779, 786
see also sāk/nisāk and taxation
taxation 51, 99, 279, 504, 509, 592, 603
see also taxes
Taxlīh 347–348, 702
template (*nibēg*; *aswār-nibēg*; *dast-nibēg*) 271–272, 285, 762, 777
temporary marriage 123, 127, 132, 136, 147, 154–155, **157–162**, 166, **183–186**, 210, 589, 622, **628–632**, 630, 636
testament (*handarz*) 20–21, 23, 70, 82–84, 170, 211–212, 214, 220, 231, **235–245**, 250, 275, 287, 301, 360, 363, 376, 398–399, 477, 482, 509, 514, 645, 648, 743, 770
Testament of Ardašīr 52–53
testamentary contract (*paymān*) **235**, 238–240, 264–265, 267, 277–278, 285–286, 376, 391, 773, 783–784
theft 328–329, 400, 415, **434–451**, 489, 519–520, 528, 533, 570, 572, 685–689, 768, 771–772, 783; categorization as offence regarding opponents 62, 493–494; definition as stealing secretly 67–68, 434, 764; distinguished from robbery 313–314, 434–437; intent of 413, 421, 424, 449; penalty for 4, 92, 108, 382–383, 439–447, 451, 485, 584, 757, 763, 769, 790, 795; testimony on 549; transposition to other fields (credit law; breach of contract; overreaching; sexual offences) 312–314, 382–383, 388, 414, 434, 447–449, 455–460, 531, 589, 618–619, 691–695
see also duz(d)īh and thief
Theodosian Code 57
Theophylact Simocatta 57
thief 4, 7, 25, 37, 68, 108, 312–315, 382–383, 388, 413–414, 422, 424, **434–451**, 455–457, 459, 485, 519–520, 618, 668, 685–695, 749, 763–764, 769, 777
see also duz(d) and theft
Tigris 49, 630
time-limited marriage *see* temporary marriage
Timotheos, Nestorian patriarch 48, 609
title deed (*wizīr*) 241–242, 245, 266–267, 269, 270, 286, 376–377, 397, 439, 550–551, 793
Torah 50, 526
torture 429, 442, 472, 584–585
Tōsar 52, 274–275, 284, 443
see also Tansar/Tōsar

total estate (of a *paterfamilias* or lineage) *see abarmānd*
tōzišn (liability, obligation) 3, 9, 88, 92, 118, 121, 140, 207–209, 253, **307–310**, 316, 318–319, 338, 356, 360–362, 364–367, 427–428, 440, 473–474, 476, 480, 484, 527, 555, 612, 642, 644, 680–681, 691, 696, 742, 764, 773–774, 778, 781, 789
see also abām and following entries
tōzišn ī pidarān (liabilities of the forefathers) 121, 140, 308, 318–319, 360, 362, 555, 789
see also abām ī pidarān
tōzišn-xwēš (creditor) 308, 790
tōzišnōmand(īh) (debtor/debt) 308, 310, 409, 697, 790
transcript of legal proceedings *see pursišn-nāmag; saxwan-nāmag; uzdād-nāmag; wizōst-nāmag; yazišn-nāmag* and *zastbūd-nāmag*
transfer of property *see* acquisition of property
transfer deed (*nāmag/gittag ī nēk*) 275, 278–279, 284, 767, 776
transgressions, Zoroastrian degrees *see pāyag*
see also windruh ī hamēmālān and *winah ī ruwānīg*
treason (*xwadāy-dušmenīh*) 422, 490–494, 526, 572, 574, 576, 578, 595
treasurer (*āmārgar; ganjwar*) 228, 321–322, 573, 701, 753, 766
triad of divinities 9, 401
trial *see* civil proceedings and criminal proceedings
tribunal 492, 572, 582
trusteeship (*dāštārīh; stūrīh*) 168, 219, 223, 278, 366
Turfan 43
tutor dativus 180
tutor legitimus 179
tutor testamentarius 180
tutorship 94, 187
tuwānīgīh (legal capacity; solvency) 89, 103, 120, 124–125, 351, 790
Twelver Shiʿite law 162, 622, 628, 630, 632–635

ʿulamā 490, 493, 629–630
Umayyad caliphate 14
unconscious act/offence *see a-bōyīh*
underage children (*aburnāy/aburnāyīg*) 103, 124, 126, 171, 178, 183, 234, 238–239, 244, 269, 302–303, 396, 398, 446, 465, 546, 644, 648–650, 654, 656, 677, 679, 682, 688, 751, 784
unilateral descent/succession 128, 267, 286, 314–315, 320
unilineal descent/succession 128
unintentional offence/injury 156, **412–415**, 422–424, 570–571, 751, 788, 792
see also a-bōyīh
usufruct **198–202**, 214, 216, 218, 247, 250, 258, 330, 337–338, 343–345, 349, 598, 604–605, 618, 626, 703, 708, 757
see also bar-xward
usufructarius 198, 214
usufructuary/usufructuaries 87, 251, 598, 757
ʿUyūn al-aḫbār 54
uzdād-nāmag (transcript of proceedings) **272**, 285, 553, 560, 586, 776, 790
uzdehīg (foreigner) 102, **114–115**, 548, 752, 790

validation of documents 289, 286, 295, 301, 550–551, 593–594
vendetta 404, 406
Vendidad 28
see also Widēwdād
via administrationis (*pad kardag*) 70–71, 342, 571, 617, 759, 772, 780
see also kardag
vineyard (*dastgird raz*) 15, 107, 128, 199–200, 209, 212–213, 221, 223, 325, 330, 343, 367, 369–370, 504, 624, 711–712

Vita of Mar Abā 47, 49, 157, 573, 575, 579–581
Vohu Manah 90
see also Wahman

wad-axw (evil-mind) 417, 422, 571, 785, 790
see also wad-xwāh/xwāhīh
Wādayyār (jurisconsult) 743, 746
wad-xwāh/xwāhīh (evil intent, malevolence); opposite: *rāst-xwāh* 415–417, 422, 432, 570–571, 738, 785, 790
see also wad-axw
wahāg (value) 173–174, 252, 267, 335, 344–345, 378, 393, 512, 659, 662, 790
Wahištwar 732
Wahman 90, 112, 236, 282, 353–354, 519, 717, 722, 730, 741
see also Vohu Manah
Wahmandād 706
Wahmanpanāh 209, 706
Wahrām (jurisconsult) 35, 375–376, 743, 746
Wahrām (20th day) 725
Wahrām I (273–276 CE) 105, 276
Wahrām II (276–293 CE) 105, 276
Wahrām V (421–439 CE) 746
Wahrām fire 181, 213, **217–219**, 225, 228, 250, 276–278, 502–503, 738, 740
Wahrāmšād (jurisconsult) 746
Wālaxšfarr 294
Wanandpanāh 704, 709–710
Wangird (scribe) 289, 346–347, 703, 707
waqf 221, 228, 589, **622–627**, 640
war (oath, ordeal) 72, 79, 258, **362–364**, 507, 518, 523–524, 534, 537, 539, 542, 545, **551–560**, 611, 672–673, 681–682, 696–699, 762, 777, 781–783, 789–790, 797
see also oath and following entries
war ī dēnīg (or: *dēnīg war*) 363, **555**, 558, 560, 762, 790
war ī pāy-nišān 363, **556**, 558, 560, 790
war ī pad sōgand 363, **556**, 558, 560, 698, 790
war ī pad nāmag-passāz 557, 560, 790
war-sālār (supervisor of the oath) 497, 508, 521, 553, 560, 791
Warangohrmazd (jurisconsult) 277, 292–293, 742, 746
warrantor *see* surety
warranty *see* suretyship
wasasəyāna 380, 659, 661
wāspuhragān (hereditary property) 258, 515, 670, 791
see also pēšīgān-wāspuhragān
wāspuhragān (noble families, princes) 99, 111, 791
waštag saxwanīh (distortion of statement) 499, **561–562**, 568, 791
see also waštagīh
waštagīh (distortion of a statement) 415, 499, 559, **561–562**, 567–568, 791
see also waštag saxwanīh
Wastān 501
wāstaryōšān (cultivators; 4th estate) 95, 98, 372
water canals (*kahas*) rules regarding **240–242**, 249, 377, 749, 772
water channels (*jōy-kahas*), rules regarding 250, 767, 771
waxš (interest) 78, 192, 197, 266, 319, 321, 340, 466, 791
waxt (interest) 78, 192, 197, 368, 791
Wayayyār (jurisconsult) 387, 396–397, 747
Wazurgnimād 370–371, 712–713
Wazurgummēd 732–734
weapons (*sneh*) causing bodily harm 414, 425, **426–428**, 433, 470–474, 482, 681, 684, 787
Weh-Ardaxšēr (administrative district) 294
wehdādestān(īh) (extension of justice) 48, **70–73**, 362, 379–380, 384–385, 554, 569, 571, 610–611, 774, 791–792
see also mehdādestānīh

wehdādestāntar (who fulfils justice best) 70, 72–73, 362, 364, 542, **554–555**, 560, 611, 697, 781, 791–792
Wehohrmazd (jurisconsult) 365, 747
Wehpanāh (jurisconsult) 742, 747
Wehšābuhr (*mowbedān mowbed*) 217, 241, 278, 284, 291, 741–743, 747
weh-sazāgtar (most suitable as *sālār* or *stŭr*) 732, 792
see also sazāgtar
whore (*ǰeh/ǰehi*) 452–453, 771
see also prostitute
Wīdēwdād **28–30**, 32, 61, 236, 262, 308, 312, 400, 404, 435, 440, 469, 474, 477–478, 482–483
widow 79, 122, 125, 131–132, 143, 146–147, 154, 160, 168, 182, 234, 323, 360–361, 620
wife *see čagar*-wife; *pādixšāy*-wife and *xwasrāyēn/ūn*
wināh ī hamēmālān (offences/sins regarding adversaries) 3, 9–10, 32, **62–63**, 92, 306, 400, 403, 406, 412, 421–422, 433, 441, 452, 454, 456–457, 459–460, 462, 467, 470, 481, 484, 486–488, **492–494**, 526, 529–530, 569, 572, 615, 682, 792
wināh ī ruwānīg (offences/sins pertaining to the soul) 3, 7, 9–10, 28, 32, **62–63**, 90–92, 306, 400, 403, 408, 412, 414, 421, 433–434, 452, 454, 456–458, 460, 462, 467, 470, 481, 484, 486–488, 493, 529–530, 615, 792
Windād-Burzmihr 279
Windād-Ohrmazd 371, 704, 708–710, 713, 731–734
Windād-Xwaršēd (*rad* of Parišwārgar) 437, 505, 723, 725, 728, 731, 734
Windād Yazd 709 710
Windāspagān 347–348, 702–703
windišn (income) 78, 86–87, 108, 122, 124, 139, 142, 192–193, 197, 251, 305, 386, 446, 661, 688, 793
witchcraft (*ǰādūgīh*) 738–739, 771
see also sorcery
witness-seals *see gugāy-muhr*
Wizīdagīhā ī Zādspram 61, 402
Wizīrkard ī dēnīg 36
wizōst-nāmag/wizōstan-nāmag (protocol of investigation) 272, 285, 727, 776, 793
women 122–124, 183–185; as heirs 208, 244–245, 636–637, 696; as intermediary successors 163–168 (*see also ayōgēn*); as proxies 168–174, 650, 656, 728–729, 731–734, 789 (*see also stŭr*); as servants of the fire 224; as *xwāstag-sālār* 178, 224–225; committing theft 446, 570, 688; commoners 111, 255; conflicts between 425, 681; co-owners 248–249; excluded from jurisdiction 383; legal status of 103, 116, 123, 398; litigation concerning 200, 299–301, 563, 565–566, 569; in *čagar*-marriage 142–145 (*see also čagar*-wife); in consensus-marriage 78, 125, 145–147; in endogamy 151–157; in exogamy 148–151; in litigation 182, 360–362, 510, 534, 546–547, 677, 715–716, 743; in Mazdakite doctrine 258, 669–670; in *pādixšāy*-marriage 134–142 (*see also pādixšāy*-wife); in the *ruwānīg* system 10; in temporary marriage 133, 157–162, 628–632; infidel 436; insubordination of 138, 251, 744, 755; of noble descent 256; property of 37, 245; pursuing religious studies 27, 448, 454–458; self-guardianship of 124, 146, 750; sexual offences against 452–460, 481, 531, 690–691, 695, 762; slaves 106, 263; rights and duties of 122–124, 303; under guardianship 92, 108, 122, 126, 177–183, 304, 465, 570; unmarried 122, 125, 131, 166, 177, 208, 231–232, 455, 458; violence against 448, 724, 731; with a physical defect 383

wuzurg/wuzurgān (Grandees) 99, 103, 111–112, 322, 793
wuzurg-framadār (title) 515
Wuzurgummēd 733

Xabr 218, 273, 741
xānag (house, building) 240, 242–243, 249, 376–377, 705–707, 723, 728; (lineage) 121, 128, 149–150, 321, 345, 700–701, 703, 736, 772, 793
  see also bun-xānag; *kadag* and lineage
xīr/xīrīh (thing, property) 189, **191–193**, 273, 366, 461, 513, 568, 587, 643, 645, 648–649, 652, 703, 708, 711, 716, 720, 724–727, 730, 741–742, 794–795
  see also xīr ī ātaxš/ātaxšān
xīr ī ātaxš/ātaxšān (property of the fire[s]), 220–222, **225–227**, 366, 505–506, 509, 587, 742, 794
Xorāsān-spāhbed 321, 345, 700
Xorde Awesta 30, 400, 738
Xradzād 437–438, 723, 725
xrafstar (noxious creature) 90
  see also animals
Xūnābagān 296, 515, 745
Xwad patit 468–469
Xwadāybūd ī Dibīr (jurisconsult) 208, 747
xwadāy-dušmenīh (rebellion, treason) 291, 491–494, 526, 572, 574, 585, 595, 794
xwaddōšag/xwaddōšagīh (wilful/ wilfulness) 69, 408
xwāhišn (request) 161, 360, 386, 425, 433, 459–460, 680, 682–683, 794
xwar (degree of sin) 468–469, 473, **474–475**, 476, 482–485, 794
xwar ud dād ī šahr (penal code of the State) 4
xwārestān (place of the oath) 359, 518, 523, 534, 552, 559–560, 794; *see also war gāh*
Xwaršēd 348, 703
xwasrāyēn/ūn (wife in a consensus marriage) 78–79, 122, 125, 132–133, 137–138, **145–147**, 149–151, 157, 159–161, 164, 176, **183–185**, 233–234, 237, 631, 766, 794
  see also gādār and consensus-marriage
Xwāst-Delān 321–322, 370–371, 700–701, 712–713, 726
xwāstag (NKSY'; money) 87, **190**, 268–269, 276, 308, 317, 319, 322, 327, 338, 346, 354–357, 365, 513, 612–614. 696, 700, 700–703, 736, 773, 778–780, 793–794
*xwāstag (*hw'stk'; thing, property, *res*, object of dispute) 9, 83–84, 88–89, 104, 107, 112, 116, **189–193**, 195, 244–246, 265–267, 273, 276, 305, 340, 365, 367–368, 376, 392, 395–397, 399, 416–417, 461, 504, 512, 540, 544, 564, 567–568, 583, 585–586, 597, 641–645, 647–648, 651–656, 658–661, 669–670, 680–681, 688, 708, 718, 723–724, 726–727, 728–729, 734, 739, 754, 761–762, 778, 781–784, 794–795; acquired property 192–193, 204; correspondence with Roman *res* 57, 189–190, 638–639; division in *bun* and *bar* 197, 201–202, 604, 757–758; for the soul, 220–229, 312, 623, 625–627; in ownership 210–212, 248–249, 393–394, 506, 796; in pledge 328–330, 333, 335–339, 756; in *stūrīh* 213–219; inheritance 233, 241–242; mortgaged property 342, 343, 349, 767
  see also hamxwāstag(ān); *hamxwāstagīh* and the following entries
xwāstagdār (heir) 120–121, 132, 140, 163, 201, **205–210**, 229, 231, 237, 245, 271, 345, 347, 360, 598, 655–656, 696, 702, 704–707, 796
  see also abarmānd-xwāstagdār
xwāstagdārīh (hereditary possession) 202, 205–206, **206–210**, 211–212, 229–230, 237, 750, 796

xwāstag-sālār/sālārīh (guardian/ guardianship of property) 122, **178–179**, 217, 225, 360, 795
see also dūdag-sālārīh; sālār; sālārīh
xwāstag-tōzišn (part-debtor) 118, 208–209, 253, **308–310**, 356, 360, 364–365, 527, 768, 795
see also hamāg-tōzišn
Xwāstdēlān 712
Xwāstnām 726
xwēdōdah/xwēdōdād (next-of-kin marriage) 32–34, 36, 39, 123, 129, 133, 148, **151–157**, 158, 162, 166, 183–185, 219, 234, 455, 457–458, 461, 632, 636, 694–695, 758, 796
see also endogamy
xwēšīh (ownership) 74, 77, 139, 192, **193–202**, 204–207, 210–212, 214–215, 217, 222–223, 225–226, 229–230, 237, 246, 250, 254, 258, 269, 278, 302–303, 334–336, 338, 343, 365, 385, 392–394, 398, 499, 506, 513, 543–544, 561, 563–564, 566–568, 597–598, 604–605, 618, 625–626, 639, 643, 646, 652, 670–671, 681–682, 707–708, 729, 750, 756, 758–759, 761–762, 782, 791, 793, 795–796
see also bar-xwēš/xwēšīh; bun-xwēš/ xwēšīh and ownership
xwēškārīh (obligation, competence, duty) 87, 96, 267, 274, 508, 516, 520, 545, 646, 653–654, 700, 736, 744, 796
xwēškārīh nāmag (document/book on specific duties/competences) 270, 272, 285, 583, 742, 744, 762, 796
xwurdag (commoner, plebeian) 103, 112, 653

Yasna 61, 435, 672
Yašt 27, 119, 260, 306, 401
Yatīmat ad-dahr fī fatāwā ʾahl al-ʿaṣr 45
yaṯīrūt dīnā (Syr. extension of justice); opposite: *ḥasīrūt dīnā* 71, 73, 610, 792
Yazd (personal name) 361, 437, 534, 708, 715–720, 722–723
yazdān-dušmenīh (blasphemy) 291, 491–494, 526, 572, 574, 576–577, 580, 585, 595, 797
Yazdānfarrox 732–734
Yazdāngird 348, 703, 720
Yazdānpādār 280
Yazdānpanāh 732
Yazdānwindād 288–289
Yazdegird I (399–421 CE) 46, 292, 745–746
Yazdegird II (439–457 CE) 226, 292, 602,
Yazdegird III (633–651 CE) 18–19, 21, 35, 52–53, 110, 704–705, 715, 731
Yazdfarrox 252, 371, 704, 708–710, 713
Yazdōy 705, 733
Yazdpanāh 709
Yazdsar, son of Dēlāzād
Yazdweh 252
yazišn-nāmag (protocol of oathtaking) 79, 272, 285, 518, 521, 553, 557, 560, 586, 776, 797
Yōdmardān (scribe) 370–371, 712–713, 732–734
yōhē pasčaēta (successor) 23, 74, 123, 130, 137, 142, 144, 163, 165, 176, 207, 231, 637, 797

Zādānfarrox 704–705
Zādōy 279, 731–734
Zādspram 33, 61, 402, 410, 426
az-Zamaḫšarī 45
Žāmāsp (jurisconsult) 747
zamīg (land) 199, 209–210, 218, 240, **243–244**, 250, 327, 345, 369, 372, 376, 471, 599, 702–707, 711–713, 735, 739, 756, 762, 768, 797
Zanbūd 235
zand (exegesis) 1–2, 24, 26, 31, 35, 50, 58, 64–66, 73–74, 116, 236, 313, 435, 462, 478, 487, 581, 591, 711
Zand ī fragard ī ǰuddēwdād 30, 404
Zand ī Wahman Yasn 112
zandīk/zandīkīh (heretic/heresy) 490, 583, 798

zanišn/zanišnīh (assault) **405–407**, 409, 411–412, 415, 418, 421–425, 470, 475–476, 482–483, 674, 677, 753, 758, 760, 772, 777–778, 780, 784, 788, 798
see also assault
Zarādušt, son of Xurrag 257
Zarathustra 59–61, 260, 292, 295, 671–672
Zarduxšt (*mowbed* in Bīšābuhr) 747
Zarduxšt, son of Xrōsag 257, 670–671
zastbūd-nāmag (transcript of interrogation) 272, 285, 371–372, 714, 776, 798
zaxm (bodily abuse) 108, 407, 411–412, 415, 418, 423–428, 431, 433, 473, 562, 676, 678–679, 681, 683–684, 798
see also assault and retaliation
Zaxmestān (Section on bodily abuse) 423, 679, 681, 683, 798
*Zāzā (personal name) 731
zēndān (gaol) 520, 798
zēndānbān (gaoler) 500, 519–521, 545, 798
zīndag-stūr̆ (proxy for life) 171–172, 185, 798
see also tan-stūr̆
ziyānag (young woman) 103, 246, 547, 696, 774
Zoroaster 36–37, 61, 64, 292, 487, 671
Zoroastrian triad, 6, 413, 541, 615, 787
Zurwāndād 20; (jurisconsult) 288, 432, 546, 564, 747; (son of Mihr-Narseh) 226–227
**zūr-gird* (false document) 615, 798
zur-gugāyīh (false testimony) 429, 549, 738, 740, 798
zyān (damage) 97, 346–347, 703, 706–707